Regulation of Bank Financial Service Activities

SELECTED STATUTES AND REGULATIONS

Fourth Edition

■ ■ ■

Selected and Edited By

Lissa L. Broome
Wachovia Professor of Banking Law
Director, Center for Banking and Finance
University of North Carolina School of Law

and

Jerry W. Markham
Professor of Law
Florida International University College of Law

AMERICAN CASEBOOK SERIES®

WEST®
A Thomson Reuters business

Mat #41079410

American Casebook Series and West Group are trademarks registered in the U.S. Patent and Trademark Office.

© West, a Thomson business, 2001, 2005, 2008
© 2011 Thomson Reuters
 610 Opperman Drive
 St. Paul, MN 55123
 1–800–313–9378
Printed in the United States of America

ISBN: 978–0–314–26852–5

PREFACE

This statutory supplement contains much, but not all, of Title 12 on Banks and Banking. We have included the major chapters covering the National Bank Act, the Federal Reserve Act, the FDIC Act, the Bank Holding Company Act, the Home Mortgage Disclosure Act, the Federal Financial Institutions Examination Council, and Alternative Mortgage Transactions. We have also included relevant provisions of the Securities Exchange Act, the federal provisions relating to insurance, and the Gramm–Leach–Bliley Act's provisions relating to privacy. To provide an example of state statutory regulation of banking, excerpts from New York's banking statutes are also included.

In addition, selected regulatory provisions from the Comptroller of the Currency, the Federal Reserve System Board of Governors, and the Federal Deposit Insurance Corporation are included.

The supplement is current through September 10, 2010. The Dodd–Frank Wall Street Reform and Consumer Protection Act (Dodd–Frank Act) was signed by President Obama on July 21, 2010. The Dodd–Frank Act was not codified into the United States Code at the time of this writing. The entire Act and a codification table for Act may be found at <www.llsdc.org/attachments/files/234/ PL111–203.pdf>. At the beginning of the text of the Act included at that website there is an explanation about how to calculate the exact statute page of a particular provision, and at page 850 there is a codification table. We examined the codification table and determined that Titles III and VI of the Act contained the most amendments to the statutes included in our supplement, so we have included those Titles in this version. They have been inserted after all the federal statutory material. We have also included selected provisions of Title X of the Act that relate to preemption. Further, within the current U.S.C. statutes included in the supplement we have inserted after the title of the various provisions affected by the Act a reference to the provisions of the Act which amend the provision (i.e., DFA § 324). We hope this will be helpful as you navigate the existing statutes so that you can see whether they have been amended by Dodd–Frank. An additional aid is a summary prepared by one of our research assistants of each of the Act's titles. It is included just before the Dodd–Frank statutory provisions. There are also numerous memos prepared by law firms summarizing the Act's provisions in greater detail. Some of these are linked from a resources page maintained by the Center for Banking and Finance at the University of North Carolina, http://www. law.unc.edu/centers/banking/resources/.

We encourage you to read the Student's Guide to the supplement, which explains how to use the supplement, how to find material not included in the supplement, and contains charts to convert the original section numbers of the Federal Deposit Insurance Act of 1950, the Bank Holding Company Act of 1956, and the Gramm–Leach–Bliley Act of 1999 into their codified sections in the United States Code.

Other features include a detailed Table of Contents, the section number of the statute or regulation as part of the page running header, and flip tabs on the back cover to aid you in quickly locating a section in the supplement.

For their work on the first edition of this supplement, we again thank Bonita Summers and Allison Stelljes for production work and Adam Wheeler for a remarkable job in compiling, formatting, and proofreading. Our thanks to Frances Hughes and Steve Lee for exemplary production work on the second edition, to Jaime Mitrani for fully orchestrating the third edition, to Eunice Park of UNC School of Law for terrific work on this edition, and to Rigers Gjyshi, Senior Research Fellow at FIU College of Law for the Dodd–Frank summary.

We hope you find this supplement useful. Please let us know how you think it may be improved.

A Student's Guide to Using this Statutory and Regulatory Supplement and a Guide to Banking Statutes, Regulations and Web Resources

FEDERAL STATUTES

Most federal banking statutes are located in Title 12 of the United States Code. This Supplement contains selected Chapters from Title 12. Each chapter included is reprinted in its entirety. Should you have need to consult another Chapter from Title 12 or another Title of a federal statute, the Government Printing Office (GPO) has a free website that is very user friendly, <www.gpo.gov>. You may retrieve a United States Code Section by number or use the browse feature to find the appropriate code section.

Banking law practitioners sometimes talk in code, referring to a statute by its original section number when it was introduced in Congress rather than the section of the United States Code where the statute is now codified. Some of the cases in the casebook do this as well. This code can be broken, however. We've included some of the common references you'll need to know below.

The Preface explains how we have included the Dodd–Frank Act in this edition, and where you may find a codification table for the Act.

Bank Holding Company Act of 1956
70 Stat. 133

Original Section Number	Codified at 12 U.S.C.
1	1841 nt
2	1841
3	1842
4	1843
5	1844
6	1845 [replaced]
7	1846
8	1847
9	1848
10A	1848a
11	1841 nt, 1849
12	1841 nt

Gramm-Leach–Bliley Act of 1999
113 Stat. 1338

Original Section Number	Codified at
101(a)	12 U.S.C. 377 [replaced]
101(b)	78 [replaced]
102(a)	1843
102(b)(1)	1850
102(b)(2)	1864
103(a)	1843

Original Section Number	Codified at
103(b)	2903
103(c)(1)	1841
103(c)(2)	1843
104	15 U.S.C. 6701
105	12 U.S.C. 1842
106	1835a
121(a)(1)	25a
121(a)(2)	24a
121(b)	371c
121(c)	1971
121(d)(1)	1831w
121(d)(2)	335
201	15 U.S.C. 78c
203	78o–3
204	12 U.S.C. 1828
211(a)	15 U.S.C. 80a–17
301	6711
302	6712
401	12 U.S.C. 1467a
501	15 U.S.C. 6801
502	6802
601	12 U.S.C. 1421 nt
602(1)	1422
702	15 U.S.C. 1693b
711	12 U.S.C. 1831y
712	2908
725	6901

Federal Deposit Insurance Act of 1950
64 Stat. 873

Original Section Number	Codified at
1 [2(1) of the Act]	12 U.S.C. 1811
2 [2(2) of the Act]	1812
3	1813
4	1814
5	1815
6	1816
7	1817
8	1818
9	1819
10	1820
11	1821
11A	1821a
18	1828
24	1831a
29	1831f
38	1831o
44	1831u
46	1831w

Here's how you can break this code on your own. First, if you know the name of the statute that is being referred to you can go to the U.S.C.A. Popular Name Table volume and look up the statute by its popular name or you can consult the list of major banking legislation at <www.fdic.gov/regulations/laws/important/index.html>. Both sources provide the statutes at large citation for the law. For instance, for the Bank Holding Company Act of 1956, the statutes at large citation is 70 Stat. 133.

Once you have the 70 Stat. 133 citation you can turn to the U.S.C.A. Tables volumes (usually shelved at the beginning or the end of the U.S.C.A. statutory volumes). These volumes include a table organized by statutes at large, indicating for each statute the original bill's section numbers and where each section has now been codified in the United States Code.

STATE STATUTES

Each state has its own statutes covering banks chartered in that state. This supplement includes excerpts from the New York state banking laws as examples. By using the index of your state's statutory compilation you should be able to find the comparable provisions in your state's laws.

FEDERAL REGULATIONS

This supplement also includes selected regulations from the Code of Federal Regulations (C.F.R.) for the three major federal banking regulatory agencies—the Office of the Comptroller of the Currency (OCC), the Federal Reserve System Board of Governors (FRB), and the Federal Deposit Insurance Corporation (FDIC). All of the regulations issued by these three agencies are found in Title 12 of C.F.R. These administrative agencies are empowered by some of the banking statutes included in this supplement to implement regulations to provide further guidance on how to comply with the applicable banking law statutes. The C.F.R. volumes are issued annually.

After the statutes in this volume, there is a section for each of the three federal bank regulatory agencies listing a broad outline of their regulatory actions (by C.F.R. part) and then reprinting some selected sections from certain parts. Again, the GPO website <www.gpo.gov> has everything you will need if you are interested in looking at a regulation that is not included in this supplement. You may browse the C.F.R. on the GPO's website. Each regulation is available in either text form (which permits easy cutting and pasting into another document) or in pdf format (which shows you the regulation exactly as it appears on the page of the C.F.R. or in the Federal Register).

For those who have not yet taken administrative law, here is a brief and oversimplified introduction to the process for creating regulations. An administrative agency such as the OCC, publishes a Notice of Proposed Rulemaking in the Federal Register, a GPO publication available at <www.gpo.gov>. The Federal Register is published every federal workday. This Notice sets forth the proposed regulation, the reasons behind it, and invites the public to comment on it by a specific deadline. The agency then studies the comments it receives and revises the proposed regulation. The final rule is then published in the Federal Register.

The final rule publication also includes background and discussion in addition to the text of the regulation. The discussion summarizes the comments received by the agency and explains how the agency revised the proposed regulation in the light of the comments received.

The Federal Register discussions in the Proposed Rule and in the Final Rule issuance are invaluable sources for someone who truly wants to understand the ins and outs of a particular regulation. In the C.F.R. there is often a reference at the end of the regulation to its publication in the Federal Register (FR), so you can easily find the Federal Register discussion of the rule. A rule may become effective before the next annual publication of the C.F.R. so, to be sure that you are dealing with a current regulation, read not only the C.F.R. version of the rule, but also search the Federal Register under the regulation number to find any regulatory activity after the publication of the most recent C.F.R. volume.

REGULATORY AGENCY WEBSITES

This is a good place to remind you that the regulatory agencies also issue interpretations, rulings, letters, memos, advisories, alerts, reports and all other manner of output that is helpful in understanding how they interpret the banking law statutes that they are empowered by Congress to enforce. Many of the statutes and regulations are also available on agency websites, although they may not be in the same format as the GPO website. We prefer the GPO website for statutes and regulations. The agency websites are the best source for other agency pronouncements. Be sure to spend some time looking at the wealth of material available on each of these websites.

Office of the Comptroller of the Currency

<www.occ.treas.gov>

Federal Reserve System Board of Governors

<www.federalreserve.gov>

Federal Deposit Insurance Corporation

<www.fdic.gov>

Office of Thrift Supervision (until its functions are transferred pursuant to the Dodd–Frank Act.)

<www.ots.gov>

Happy sleuthing as you learn how to find banking law statutes and regulations of interest to you.

Summary of Contents

TABLE OF CONTENTS

REGULATION OF BANK FINANCIAL SERVICE ACTIVITIES

SELECTED STATUTES AND REGULATIONS

Fourth Edition

CHAPTER 1. THE COMPTROLLER OF THE CURRENCY
12 U.S.C.A. §§ 1–15

CHAPTER 2. NATIONAL BANKS
12 U.S.C.A. §§ 21–216d

TITLE 12. BANKS AND BANKING

CHAPTER 1. THE COMPTROLLER OF THE CURRENCY

§ 1. Office of Comptroller of the Currency—DFA § 314

There shall be in the Department of the Treasury a bureau charged with the execution of all laws passed by Congress relating to the issue and regulation of a national currency secured by United States bonds and, under the general supervision of the Board of Governors of the Federal Reserve System, of all Federal Reserve notes, except for the cancellation and destruction, and accounting with respect to such cancellation and destruction, of Federal Reserve notes unfit for circulation, the chief officer of which bureau shall be called the Comptroller of the Currency, and shall perform his duties under the general directions of the Secretary of the Treasury. The Comptroller of the Currency shall have the same authority over matters within the jurisdiction of the Comptroller as the Director of the Office of Thrift Supervision has over matters within the Director's jurisdiction under section 1462a(b)(3) of this title. The Secretary of the Treasury may not delay or prevent the issuance of any rule or the promulgation of any regulation by the Comptroller of the Currency.

§ 2. Comptroller of the Currency; appointment; term

The Comptroller of the Currency shall be appointed by the President, by and with the advice and consent of the Senate, and shall hold his office for a term of five years unless sooner removed by the President, upon reasons to be communicated by him to the Senate.

§ 3. Oath of Comptroller

The Comptroller of the Currency shall, within fifteen days from the time of notice of his appointment, take and subscribe the oath of office.

§ 4. Deputy Comptrollers

The Secretary of the Treasury shall appoint no more than four Deputy Comptrollers of the Currency, one of whom shall be designated First Deputy Comptroller of the Currency, and shall fix their salaries. Each Deputy Comptroller shall take the oath of office and shall perform such duties as the Comptroller shall direct. During a vacancy in the office or during the absence or disability of the Comptroller, each Deputy Comptroller shall possess the power and perform the duties attached by law to the office of the Comptroller under such order of succession following the First Deputy Comptroller as the Comptroller shall direct.

§ 4a. Delegation of authority by Comptroller

The Comptroller of the Currency may delegate to any duly authorized employee, representative, or agent any power vested in the office by law.

§§ 5, 6. Repealed. Pub.L. 86–251, § 1(b), (c) (1), Sept. 9, 1959, 73 Stat. 487, 488

§ 7. Chief of examining division

The Comptroller of the Currency may designate a national bank examiner to act as chief of the examining division in his office.

§ 8. Clerks

The Comptroller of the Currency shall employ, from time to time, the necessary clerks, to be appointed and classified by the Secretary of the Treasury, to discharge such duties as the comptroller shall direct.

§ 9. Additional examiners, clerks, and other employees

The Comptroller of the Currency is authorized to employ such additional examiners, clerks, and other employees as he deems necessary to carry out the provisions of sections 4, 6, 9, 10, 1151 to 1318, and 1322 of this title and to assign to duty in the office of his bureau in Washington such examiners and assistant examiners as he shall deem necessary to assist in the performance of the work of that bureau.

§ 9a. Repealed. Pub.L. 89–554, § 8(a), Sept. 6, 1966, 80 Stat. 645

§ 10. Salaries of Deputy Comptrollers, examiners, and other employees as part of bank examination expenses

The salaries of the Deputy Comptrollers and of all national bank examiners and assistant examiners assigned to duty in the office of the bureau in Washington in connection with the supervision of national banks shall be considered part of the expenses of the examinations provided for by subchapter XV of chapter 3 of this title.

§ 11. Interest in national banks—DFA § 314

It shall not be lawful for the Comptroller or the Deputy Comptroller of the Currency, either directly or indirectly, to hold an interest in any national bank.

§ 12. Seal of Comptroller

The seal devised by the Comptroller of the Currency for his office, and approved by the Secretary of the Treasury, shall continue to be the seal of office of the comptroller, and may be renewed when necessary. A description of the seal, with an impression thereof, and a certificate of approval by the Secretary of the Treasury, shall be filed in the office of the Secretary of State.

§ 13. Rooms for Currency Bureau

There shall be assigned, from time to time, to the Comptroller of the Currency, by the Secretary of the Treasury, suitable rooms in the Treasury Building for conducting the business of the Currency Bureau, containing safe and secure fireproof vaults, in which the Comptroller shall deposit and safely keep all the plates not necessarily in the possession of engravers or printers, and other valuable things belonging to his department; and the Comptroller shall from time to time furnish the necessary furniture, stationery, fuel, lights, and other proper conveniences for the transaction of the business of his office.

§ 14. Report of Comptroller

The Comptroller of the Currency shall make an annual report to Congress. The report required under this section shall include the report required under section 57a (f)(7) of Title 15.

§ 15. Repealed. Aug. 7, 1946, c. 770, § 1 (40, 50), 60 Stat. 869, 870

CHAPTER 2. NATIONAL BANKS

§ 21. Formation of national banking associations; incorporators; articles of association

Associations for carrying on the business of banking under this chapter may be formed by any number of natural persons, not less in any case than five. They shall enter into articles of association, which shall specify in general terms the object for which the association is formed, and may contain any other provisions, not inconsistent with law, which the association may see fit to adopt for the regulation of its business and the conduct of its affairs. These articles shall be signed by the persons uniting to form the association, and a copy of them shall be forwarded to the Comptroller of the Currency, to be filed and preserved in his office.

§ 21a. Amendment of articles of association

Except as otherwise specifically provided by law, or by the articles of association of the particular national banking association, the articles of association of a national banking association may be amended with respect to any lawful matter, and any action requiring the approval of the stockholders of such association may be had by the approving vote of the holders of a majority of the voting shares of the stock of the association obtained at a meeting of the stockholders called and held pursuant to notice given by mail at least ten days prior to the meeting or pursuant to a waiver of such notice given by all stockholders entitled to receive notice of such meeting. A certified copy of every amendment to the articles of association adopted by the shareholders of a national banking association shall be forwarded to the Comptroller of the Currency, to be filed and preserved in his office.

§ 22. Organization certificate

The persons uniting to form such an association shall, under their hands, make an organization certificate, which shall specifically state:

First. The name assumed by such association; which name shall include the word "national".

Second. The place where its operations of discount and deposit are to be carried on, designating the State, Territory, or District, and the particular county and city, town, or village.

Third. The amount of capital stock and the number of shares into which the same is to be divided.

Fourth. The names and places of residence of the shareholders and the number of shares held by each of them.

Fifth. The fact that the certificate is made to enable such persons to avail themselves of the advantages of this chapter.

§ 23. Acknowledgment and filing of certificate

The organization certificate shall be acknowledged before a judge of some court of record, or notary public; and shall be, together with the acknowledgment thereof, authenticated by the seal of such court, or notary, transmitted to the Comptroller of the Currency, who shall record and carefully preserve the same in his office.

§ 24. Corporate powers of associations

Upon duly making and filing articles of association and an organization certificate a national banking association shall become, as from the date of the execution of its organization certificate, a body corporate, and as such, and in the name designated in the organization certificate, it shall have power—

First. To adopt and use a corporate seal.

Second. To have succession from February 25, 1927, or from the date of its organization if organized after February 25, 1927, until such time as it be dissolved by the act of its shareholders owning two-thirds of its stock, or until its franchise becomes forfeited by reason of violation of law, or until terminated by either a general or a special Act of Congress or until its affairs be placed in the hands of a receiver and finally wound up by him.

Third. To make contracts.

Fourth. To sue and be sued, complain and defend, in any court of law and equity, as fully as natural persons.

Fifth. To elect or appoint directors, and by its board of directors to appoint a president, vice president, cashier, and other officers, define their duties, require bonds of them and fix the penalty thereof, dismiss such officers or any of them at pleasure, and appoint others to fill their places.

Sixth. To prescribe, by its board of directors, bylaws not inconsistent with law, regulating the manner in which its stock shall be transferred, its directors elected or appointed, its officers appointed, its property transferred, its general business conducted, and the privileges granted to it by law exercised and enjoyed.

Seventh. To exercise by its board of directors or duly authorized officers or agents, subject to law, all such incidental powers as shall be necessary to carry on the business of banking; by discounting and negotiating promissory notes, drafts, bills of exchange, and other evidences of debt; by receiving deposits; by buying and selling exchange, coin, and bullion; by loaning money on personal security; and by obtaining, issuing, and circulating notes according to the provisions of title 62 of the Revised Statutes. The business of dealing in securities and stock by the association shall be limited to purchasing and selling such securities and stock without recourse, solely upon the order, and for the account of, customers, and in no case for its own account, and the association shall not underwrite any issue of securities or stock: *Provided*, That the association may purchase for its own account investment securities under such limitations and restrictions as the Comptroller of the Currency may by regulation prescribe. In no event shall the total amount of the investment securities of any one obligor or maker, held by the association for its own account, exceed at any time 10 per centum of its capital stock actually paid in and unimpaired and 10 per centum of its unimpaired surplus fund, except that this limitation shall not require any association to dispose of any securities lawfully held by it on August 23, 1935. As used in this section the term "investment securities" shall mean marketable obligations, evidencing indebtedness of any person, copartnership, association, or corporation in the form of bonds, notes and/or debentures commonly known as investment securities under such further definition of the term "investment securities" as may by regulation be prescribed by the Comptroller of the Currency. Except as herein after provided or otherwise permitted by law, nothing herein contained shall authorize the purchase by the association for its own account of any shares of stock of any corporation. The limitations and restrictions herein contained as to dealing in, underwriting and purchasing for its own account, investment securities shall not apply to obligations of the United States, or general obligations of any State or of any political subdivision thereof, or obligations of the Washington Metropolitan Area Transit Authority which are guaranteed by the Secretary of Transportation under section 9 of the National Capital Transportation Act of 1969 [D.C.Code § 1–2458], or obligations issued under authority of the Federal Farm Loan Act, as amended, or issued by the thirteen banks for the cooperatives of any of them or the Federal Home Loan Banks, or obligations which are insured by the Secretary of Housing and Urban Development under title XI of the National Housing Act [12 U.S.C.A. § 1749aaa et seq.] or obligations which are insured by the Secretary of Housing and Urban Development (hereafter in this sentence referred to as the "Secretary") pursuant to section 207 of the National Housing Act [12 U.S.C.A. § 1713], if the debentures to be issued in payment of such insured obligations are guaranteed as to principal and interest by the United States, or obligations, participations, or other instruments of or issued by the Federal National Mortgage Association or the Government National Mortgage Association, or mortgages, obligations, or other securities which are or ever have been sold by the Federal Home Loan Mortgage Corporation pursuant to Section 305 or Section 306 of the Federal Home Loan Mortgage Corporation Act [12 U.S.C.A. §§ 1434 or 1455], or obligations of the Federal Financing Bank or obligations of the Environmental Financing Authority, or obligations or other instruments or securities of the Student Loan Marketing Association, or such obligations of any local public agency (as defined in section 110(h) of the Housing Act of 1949 [42 U.S.C.A. § 1460(h)]) as are secured by an agreement between the local public agency and the Secretary in which the local public agency agrees to borrow from said Secretary, and said Secretary agrees to lend to said local public agency, monies in an aggregate amount which (together with any other monies irrevocably committed to the payment of interest or such obligations) will suffice to pay, when due, the interest on and all installments (including the final installment) of the principal of such obligations, which monies under the terms of said agreement are required to be used for such payments, or such obligations of a public housing agency (as defined in the United States Housing Act of 1937, as amended [42 U.S.C.A. § 1437 et seq.]) as are secured (1) by an agreement between the public housing agency and the Secretary in which the public housing agency agrees to borrow from the Secretary, and the Secretary agrees to lend to the public housing agency, prior to the maturity of such obligations, monies in an amount which (together with any other monies irrevocably committed to the payment of interest on such obligations) will suffice to pay the principal of such obligations with interest to maturity thereon, which monies under the terms of said agreement are required to be used for the purpose of paying the principal of and the interest on such obligations at their maturity, (2) by a pledge of annual contributions under an annual contributions contract between such public housing agency and the Secretary if such contract shall contain the covenant by the Secretary which is authorized by subsection (g) of section 6 of the United States Housing Act of 1937, as amended [42 U.S.C.A. § 1437a(g)], and if the maximum sum and the maximum period specified in such contract pursuant to said subsection 6(g) [42 U.S.C.A. § 1437d(g)] shall not be less than the annual amount and the period for payment which are requisite to provide for the payment when due of all installments of principal and interest on such obligations, or (3) by a pledge of both annual contributions under an annual contributions contract containing the covenant by the Secretary which is authorized by section 6(g) of the United States Housing Act of 1937 [42 U.S.C.A. § 1437d(g)], and a loan under an agreement between the local public housing agency and the Secretary in which the public housing agency agrees to borrow from the Secretary, and the Secretary agrees to lend to the public housing agency, prior to the maturity of the obligations involved, moneys in an amount which (together with any other moneys irrevocably committed under the annual contributions contract to the payment of principal and interest on such obligations) will suffice to provide for the payment when due of all installments of principal and interest on such obligations, which moneys under the terms of the agreement are required to be used for the purpose of paying the principal and interest on such obligations at their maturity: *Provided,* That in carrying on the business commonly known as the safe-deposit business the association shall not invest in the capital stock of a corporation organized under the law of any State to conduct a safe-deposit business in an amount in excess of 15 per centum of the capital stock of the association actually paid in and unimpaired and 15 per centum of its unimpaired surplus. The limitations and restrictions herein, contained as to dealing in and underwriting investment securities shall not apply to obligations issued by the International Bank for Reconstruction and Development, the European Bank for Reconstruction and Development, the Inter-American Development Bank Bank for Economic Cooperation and Development in the Middle East and North Africa the North American Development Bank, the Asian Development Bank, the African Development Bank, the Inter–American Investment Corporation, or the International Finance Corporation, or obligations issued by any State or political subdivision or any agency of a State or political subdivision for housing, university, or dormitory purposes, which are at the time eligible for purchase by a national bank for its own account, nor to bonds, notes and other obligations issued by the Tennessee Valley Authority or by the United States Postal Service: *Provided,* That no association shall hold obligations, issued by any of said organizations as a result of underwriting, dealing, or purchasing for its own account (and for this purpose obligations as to which it is under commitment shall be deemed to be held by it) in a total amount exceeding at any one time 10 per centum of its capital stock actually paid in and unimpaired and 10 per centum of its unimpaired surplus fund. Notwithstanding any other provision in this paragraph, the association may purchase for its own account shares of stock issued by a corporation authorized to be created pursuant to Title IX of the Housing and Urban Development Act of 1968 [42 U.S.C.A. § 3931 et seq.], and may make investments in a partnership, limited partnership, or joint venture formed pursuant to section 907(a) or 907(c) of that Act [42 U.S.C.A. § 3937(a) or 3937(c)]. Notwithstanding any other provision of this paragraph, the association may purchase for its own account shares of stock issued by any State housing corporation incorporated in the State in which the association is located and may make investments in loans and commitments for loans to any such corporation: *Provided,* That in no event shall the total amount of such stock held for its own account and such investments in loans and commitments made by the association exceed at any time 5 per centum of its capital stock actually paid in an unimpaired plus 5 per centum of its unimpaired surplus fund. Notwithstanding any other provision in this paragraph, the association may purchase for its own account shares of stock issued by a corporation organized solely for the purpose of making loans to farmers and ranchers for agricultural purposes, including the breeding, raising, fattening, or marketing of livestock. However, unless the association owns at least 80 per centum of the stock of such agricultural credit corporation the amount invested by the association at any one time in the stock of such corporation shall not exceed 20 per centum of the unimpaired capital and surplus of the association: *Provided further,* That, notwithstanding any other provision of this paragraph, the association may purchase for its own account shares of stock of a bank insured by the Federal Deposit Insurance Corporation or a holding company which owns or controls such an insured bank if the stock of such bank or company is owned exclusively (except to the extent directors' qualifying shares are required by law) by depository institutions or depository institution holding companies (as defined in section 1813 of this title) and such bank or company and all subsidiaries thereof are engaged exclusively in providing services to or for other depository institutions, their holding companies, and the officers, directors, and employees of such institutions and companies, and in providing correspondent banking services at the request of other depository institutions or their holding companies (also referred to as a "banker's bank"), but in no event shall the total amount of such stock held by the association in any bank or holding company exceed at any time 10 per centum of the association's capital stock and paid in and unimpaired surplus and in no event shall the purchase of such stock result in an association's acquiring more than 5 per centum of any class of voting securities of such bank or company. The limitations and restrictions contained in this paragraph as to an association purchasing for its own account investment securities shall not apply to securities that (A) are offered and sold pursuant to section 4(5) of the Securities Act of 1933 (15 U.S.C. 77d(5)); (B) are small business related securities (as defined in section 3(a)(53) of the Securities Exchange Act of 1934 [15 U.S.C.A. § 78c(a)(53)]); or (C) are mortgage related securities (as that term is defined in section 3(a)(41) of the Securities Exchange Act of 1934 (15 U.S.C. 78c(a)(41))). The exception provided for the securities described in subparagraphs (A), (B), and (C) shall be subject to such regulations as the Comptroller of the Currency may prescribe, including regulations prescribing minimum size of the issue (at the time of initial distribution) or minimum aggregate sales prices, or both.

A national banking association may deal in, underwrite, and purchase for such association's own account qualified Canadian government obligations to the same extent that such association may deal in, underwrite, and purchase for such association's own account obligations of the United States or general obligations of any State or of any political subdivision thereof. For purposes of this paragraph—

(1) the term "qualified Canadian government obligations" means any debt obligation which is backed by Canada, any Province of Canada, or any political subdivision of any such Province to a degree which is comparable to the liability of the United States, any State, or any political subdivision thereof for any obligation which is backed by the full faith and credit of the United States, such State, or such political subdivision, and such term includes any debt obligation of any agent of Canada or any such Province or any political subdivision of such Province if—

(A) the obligation of the agent is assumed in such agent's capacity as agent for Canada or such Province or such political subdivision; and

(B) Canada, such Province, or such political subdivision on whose behalf such agent is acting with respect to such obligation is ultimately and unconditionally liable for such obligation; and

(2) the term "Province of Canada" means a Province of Canada and includes the Yukon Territory and the Northwest Territories and their successors.

In addition to the provisions in this paragraph for dealing in, underwriting, or purchasing securities, the limitations and restrictions contained in this paragraph as to dealing in, underwriting, and purchasing investment securities for the national bank's own account shall not apply to obligations (including limited obligation bonds, revenue bonds, and obligations that satisfy the requirements of section 142(b)(1) of Title 26) issued by or on behalf of any State or political subdivision of a State, including any municipal corporate instrumentality of 1 or more States, or any public agency or authority of any State or political subdivision of a State, if the national bank is well capitalized (as defined in section 1831o of this title).

Eighth. To contribute to community funds, or to charitable, philanthropic, or benevolent instrumentalities conducive to public welfare, such sums as its board of directors may deem expedient and in the interests of the association, if it is located in a State the laws of which do not expressly prohibit State banking institutions from contributing to such funds or instrumentalities.

Ninth. To issue and sell securities which are guaranteed pursuant to section 1721(g) of this title.

Tenth. To invest in tangible personal property, including without limitation, vehicles, manufactured homes, machinery, equipment, or furniture, for lease financing transactions on a net lease basis, but such investment may not exceed 10 percent of the assets of the association.

Eleventh. To make investments directly or indirectly, each of which promotes the public welfare by benefiting primarily low- and moderate-income communities or families (such as by providing housing, services, or jobs). An association shall not make any such investment if the investment would expose the association to unlimited liability. The Comptroller of the Currency shall limit an association's investments in any 1 project and an association's aggregate investments under this paragraph. An association's aggregate investments under this paragraph shall not exceed an amount equal to the sum of 5 percent of the association's capital stock actually paid in and unimpaired and 5 percent of the association's unimpaired surplus fund, unless the Comptroller determines by order that the higher amount will pose no significant risk to the affected deposit insurance fund, and the association is adequately capitalized. In no case shall an association's aggregate investments under this paragraph exceed an amount equal to the sum of 15 percent of the association's capital stock actually paid in and unimpaired and 15 percent of the association's unimpaired surplus fund. The foregoing standards and limitations apply to investments under this paragraph made by a national bank directly and by its subsidiaries.

§ 24a. Financial subsidiaries of national banks—DFA § 939

(a) Authorization to conduct in subsidiaries certain activities that are financial in nature

(1) In general

Subject to paragraph (2), a national bank may control a financial subsidiary, or hold an interest in a financial subsidiary.

(2) Conditions and requirements

A national bank may control a financial subsidiary, or hold an interest in a financial subsidiary, only if—

(A) the financial subsidiary engages only in—

(i) activities that are financial in nature or incidental to a financial activity pursuant to subsection (b); and

(ii) activities that are permitted for national banks to engage in directly (subject to the same terms and conditions that govern the conduct of the activities by a national bank);

(B) the activities engaged in by the financial subsidiary as a principal do not include—

(i) insuring, guaranteeing, or indemnifying against loss, harm, damage, illness, disability, or death (except to the extent permitted under section 6712 or 6713(c) of Title 15) or providing or issuing annuities the income of which is subject to tax treatment under section 72 of Title 26;

(ii) real estate development or real estate investment activities, unless otherwise expressly authorized by law; or

(iii) any activity permitted in subparagraph (H) or (I) of section 1843(k)(4) of this title, except activities described in section 1843(k)(4)(H) of this title that may be permitted in accordance with section 122 of the Gramm–Leach–Bliley Act [12 U.S.C.A. 1843 note];

(C) the national bank and each depository institution affiliate of the national bank are well capitalized and well managed;

(D) the aggregate consolidated total assets of all financial subsidiaries of the national bank do not exceed the lesser of—

(i) 45 percent of the consolidated total assets of the parent bank; or

(ii) $50,000,000,000;

(E) except as provided in paragraph (4), the national bank meets any applicable rating or other requirement set forth in paragraph (3); and

(F) the national bank has received the approval of the Comptroller of the Currency for the financial subsidiary to engage in such activities, which approval shall be based solely upon the factors set forth in this section.

(3) Rating or comparable requirement

(A) In general

A national bank meets the requirements of this paragraph if—

(i) the bank is 1 of the 50 largest insured banks and has not fewer than 1 issue of outstanding eligible debt that is currently rated within the 3 highest investment grade rating categories by a nationally recognized statistical rating organization; or

(ii) the bank is 1 of the second 50 largest insured banks and meets the criteria set forth in clause (i) or such other criteria as the Secretary of the Treasury and the Board of Governors of the Federal Reserve System may jointly establish by regulation and determine to be comparable to and consistent with the purposes of the rating required in clause (i).

(B) Consolidated total assets

For purposes of this paragraph, the size of an insured bank shall be determined on the basis of the consolidated total assets of the bank as of the end of each calendar year.

(4) Financial agency subsidiary

The requirement in paragraph (2)(E) shall not apply with respect to the ownership or control of a financial subsidiary that engages in activities described in subsection (b)(1) solely as agent and not directly or indirectly as principal.

(5) Regulations required

Before the end of the 270–day period beginning on November 12, 1999, the Comptroller of the Currency shall, by regulation, prescribe procedures to implement this section.

(6) Indexed asset limit

The dollar amount contained in paragraph (2)(D) shall be adjusted according to an indexing mechanism jointly established by regulation by the Secretary of the Treasury and the Board of Governors of the Federal Reserve System.

(7) Coordination with section 1843(l)(2) of this title   *CRA ≥ Satisfactory 427*

Section 1843(l)(2) of this title applies to a national bank that controls a financial subsidiary in the manner provided in that section.

(b) Activities that are financial in nature

(1) Financial activities

(A) In general

An activity shall be financial in nature or incidental to such financial activity only if—

(i) such activity has been defined to be financial in nature or incidental to a financial activity for bank holding companies pursuant to section 1843(k)(4) of this title; or

(ii) the Secretary of the Treasury determines the activity is financial in nature or incidental to a financial activity in accordance with subparagraph (B).

(B) Coordination between the Board and the Secretary of the Treasury

(i) Proposals raised before the Secretary of the Treasury

(I) Consultation

The Secretary of the Treasury shall notify the Board of, and consult with the Board concerning, any request, proposal, or application under this section for a determination of whether an activity is financial in nature or incidental to a financial activity.

(II) Board view

The Secretary of the Treasury shall not determine that any activity is financial in nature or incidental to a financial activity under this section if the Board notifies the Secretary in writing, not later than 30 days after the date of receipt of the notice described in subclause (I) (or such longer period as the Secretary determines to be appropriate under the circumstances) that the Board believes that the activity is not financial in nature or incidental to a financial activity or is not otherwise permissible under this section.

(ii) Proposals raised by the Board

(I) Board recommendation

The Board may, at any time, recommend in writing that the Secretary of the Treasury find an activity to be financial in nature or incidental to a financial activity for purposes of this section.

(II) Time period for secretarial action

Not later than 30 days after the date of receipt of a written recommendation from the Board under subclause (I) (or such longer period as the Secretary of the Treasury

and the Board determine to be appropriate under the circumstances), the Secretary shall determine whether to initiate a public rulemaking proposing that the subject recommended activity be found to be financial in nature or incidental to a financial activity under this section, and shall notify the Board in writing of the determination of the Secretary and, in the event that the Secretary determines not to seek public comment on the proposal, the reasons for that determination.

(2) Factors to be considered

In determining whether an activity is financial in nature or incidental to a financial activity, the Secretary shall take into account—

(A) the purposes of this Act and the Gramm–Leach–Bliley Act;

(B) changes or reasonably expected changes in the marketplace in which banks compete;

(C) changes or reasonably expected changes in the technology for delivering financial services; and

(D) whether such activity is necessary or appropriate to allow a bank and the subsidiaries of a bank to—

(i) compete effectively with any company seeking to provide financial services in the United States;

(ii) efficiently deliver information and services that are financial in nature through the use of technological means, including any application necessary to protect the security or efficacy of systems for the transmission of data or financial transactions; and

(iii) offer customers any available or emerging technological means for using financial services or for the document imaging of data.

(3) Authorization of new financial activities

The Secretary of the Treasury shall, by regulation or order and in accordance with paragraph (1)(B), define, consistent with the purposes of this Act and the Gramm–Leach–Bliley Act, the following activities as, and the extent to which such activities are, financial in nature or incidental to a financial activity:

(A) Lending, exchanging, transferring, investing for others, or safeguarding financial assets other than money or securities.

(B) Providing any device or other instrumentality for transferring money or other financial assets.

(C) Arranging, effecting, or facilitating financial transactions for the account of third parties.

(c) Capital deduction

(1) Capital deduction required

In determining compliance with applicable capital standards—

(A) the aggregate amount of the outstanding equity investment, including retained earnings, of a national bank in all financial subsidiaries shall be deducted from the assets and tangible equity of the national bank; and

(B) the assets and liabilities of the financial subsidiaries shall not be consolidated with those of the national bank.

(2) Financial statement disclosure of capital deduction

Any published financial statement of a national bank that controls a financial subsidiary shall, in addition to providing information prepared in accordance with generally accepted accounting principles, separately present financial information for the bank in the manner provided in paragraph (1).

(d) Safeguards for the bank

A national bank that establishes or maintains a financial subsidiary shall assure that—

(1) the procedures of the national bank for identifying and managing financial and operational risks within the national bank and the financial subsidiary adequately protect the national bank from such risks;

(2) the national bank has, for the protection of the bank, reasonable policies and procedures to preserve the separate corporate identity and limited liability of the national bank and the financial subsidiaries of the national bank; and

(3) the national bank is in compliance with this section.

(e) Provisions applicable to national banks that fail to continue to meet certain requirements

(1) In general

If a national bank or insured depository institution affiliate does not continue to meet the requirements of subsection (a)(2)(C) or subsec-

tion (d), the Comptroller of the Currency shall promptly give notice to the national bank to that effect describing the conditions giving rise to the notice.

(2) Agreement to correct conditions

Not later than 45 days after the date of receipt by a national bank of a notice given under paragraph (1) (or such additional period as the Comptroller of the Currency may permit), the national bank shall execute an agreement with the Comptroller of the Currency and any relevant insured depository institution affiliate shall execute an agreement with its appropriate Federal banking agency to comply with the requirements of subsection (a)(2)(C) and subsection (d).

(3) Imposition of conditions

Until the conditions described in a notice under paragraph (1) are corrected—

(A) the Comptroller of the Currency may impose such limitations on the conduct or activities of the national bank or any subsidiary of the national bank as the Comptroller of the Currency determines to be appropriate under the circumstances and consistent with the purposes of this section; and

(B) the appropriate Federal banking agency may impose such limitations on the conduct or activities of any relevant insured depository institution affiliate or any subsidiary of the institution as such agency determines to be appropriate under the circumstances and consistent with the purposes of this section.

(4) Failure to correct

If the conditions described in a notice to a national bank under paragraph (1) are not corrected within 180 days after the date of receipt by the national bank of the notice, the Comptroller of the Currency may require the national bank, under such terms and conditions as may be imposed by the Comptroller and subject to such extension of time as may be granted in the discretion of the Comptroller, to divest control of any financial subsidiary.

(5) Consultation

In taking any action under this subsection, the Comptroller shall consult with all relevant Federal and State regulatory agencies and authorities.

(f) Failure to maintain public rating or meet applicable criteria

(1) In general

A national bank that does not continue to meet any applicable rating or other requirement of subsection (a)(2)(E) after acquiring or establishing a financial subsidiary shall not, directly or through a subsidiary, purchase or acquire any additional equity capital of any financial subsidiary until the bank meets such requirements.

(2) Equity capital

For purposes of this subsection, the term "equity capital" includes, in addition to any equity instrument, any debt instrument issued by a financial subsidiary, if the instrument qualifies as capital of the subsidiary under any Federal or State law, regulation, or interpretation applicable to the subsidiary.

(g) Definitions

For purposes of this section, the following definitions shall apply:

(1) Affiliate, company, control, and subsidiary

The terms "affiliate", "company", "control", and "subsidiary" have the meanings given those terms in section 1841 of this title.

(2) Appropriate Federal banking agency, depository institution, insured bank, and insured depository institution

The terms "appropriate Federal banking agency", "depository institution", "insured bank", and "insured depository institution" have the meanings given those terms in section 1813 of this title.

(3) Financial subsidiary

The term "financial subsidiary" means any company that is controlled by 1 or more insured depository institutions other than a subsidiary that—

(A) engages solely in activities that national banks are permitted to engage in directly and are conducted subject to the same terms and conditions that govern the conduct of such activities by national banks; or

(B) a national bank is specifically authorized by the express terms of a Federal statute (other than this section), and not by implication or interpretation, to control, such as by section 25 or 25A of the Federal Reserve Act

[12 U.S.C.A. §§ 601 to 604 or 611 to 631] or the Bank Service Company Act [12 U.S.C.A. § 1861 et seq.].

(4) Eligible debt

The term "eligible debt" means unsecured long-term debt that—

(A) is not supported by any form of credit enhancement, including a guarantee or standby letter of credit; and

(B) is not held in whole or in any significant part by any affiliate, officer, director, principal shareholder, or employee of the bank or any other person acting on behalf of or with funds from the bank or an affiliate of the bank.

(5) Well capitalized

The term "well capitalized" has the meaning given the term in section 1831o of this title.

(6) Well managed

The term "well managed" means—

(A) in the case of a depository institution that has been examined, unless otherwise determined in writing by the appropriate Federal banking agency—

(i) the achievement of a composite rating of 1 or 2 under the Uniform Financial Institutions Rating System (or an equivalent rating under an equivalent rating system) in connection with the most recent examination or subsequent review of the depository institution; and

(ii) at least a rating of 2 for management, if such rating is given; or

(B) in the case of any depository institution that has not been examined, the existence and use of managerial resources that the appropriate Federal banking agency determines are satisfactory.

§ 25. Omitted

§ 25a. Participation by national banks in lotteries and related activities

(a) Prohibited activities

A national bank may not—

(1) deal in lottery tickets;

(2) deal in bets used as a means or substitute for participation in a lottery;

(3) announce, advertise, or publicize the existence of any lottery;

(4) announce, advertise, or publicize the existence or identity of any participant or winner, as such, in a lottery.

(b) Use of banking premises prohibited

A national bank may not permit—

(1) the use of any part of any of its banking offices by any person for any purpose forbidden to the bank under subsection (a) of this section, or

(2) direct access by the public from any of its banking offices to any premises used by any person for any purpose forbidden to the bank under subsection (a) of this section.

(c) Definitions

As used in this section—

(1) The term "deal in" includes making, taking, buying, selling, redeeming, or collecting.

(2) The term "lottery" includes any arrangement whereby three or more persons (the "participants") advance money or credit to another in exchange for the possibility or expectation that one or more but not all of the participants (the "winners") will receive by reason of their advances more than the amounts they have advanced, the identity of the winners being determined by any means which includes—

(A) a random selection;

(B) a game, race, or contest; or

(C) any record or tabulation of the result of one or more events in which any participant has no interest except for its bearing upon the possibility that he may become a winner.

(3) The term "lottery ticket" includes any right, privilege, or possibility (and any ticket, receipt, record, or other evidence of any such right, privilege, or possibility) of becoming a winner in a lottery.

(d) Lawful banking services connected with operation of lotteries

Nothing contained in this section prohibits a national bank from accepting deposits or cashing or otherwise handling checks or other negotiable instruments, or performing other lawful banking services for a State operating a lottery, or for an officer or employee of that State who is charged with the administration of the lottery.

(e) Regulations; enforcement

The Comptroller of the Currency shall issue such regulations as may be necessary to the strict enforcement of this section and the prevention of evasions thereof.

§ 26. Comptroller to determine if association can commence business

Whenever a certificate is transmitted to the Comptroller of the Currency, as provided in this chapter, and the association transmitting the same notifies the Comptroller that all of its capital stock has been duly paid in, and that such association has complied with all the provisions of this chapter required to be complied with before an association shall be authorized to commence the business of banking, the Comptroller shall examine into the condition of such association, ascertain especially the amount of money paid in on account of its capital, the name and place of residence of each of its directors, and the amount of the capital stock of which each is the owner in good faith, and generally whether such association has complied with all the provisions of this chapter required to entitle it to engage in the business of banking; and shall cause to be made and attested by the oaths of a majority of the directors, and by the president or cashier of the association, a statement of all the facts necessary to enable the Comptroller to determine whether the association is lawfully entitled to commence the business of banking.

§ 27. Certificate of authority to commence banking

(a) If, upon a careful examination of the facts so reported, and of any other facts which may come to the knowledge of the Comptroller, whether by means of a special commission appointed by him for the purpose of inquiring into the condition of such association, or otherwise, it appears that such association is lawfully entitled to commence the business of banking, the Comptroller shall give to such association a certificate, under his hand and official seal, that such association has complied with all the provisions required to be complied with before commencing the business of banking, and that such association is authorized to commence such business. But the Comptroller may withhold from an association his certificate authorizing the commencement of business, whenever he has reason to suppose that the shareholders have formed the same for any other than the legitimate objects contemplated by this chapter. A National Bank Association, to which the Comptroller of the Currency has heretofore issued or hereafter issues such certificate, is not illegally constituted solely because its operations are or have been required by the Comptroller of the Currency to be limited to those of a trust company and activities related thereto.

(b) (1) The Comptroller of the Currency may also issue a certificate of authority to commence the business of banking pursuant to this section to a national banking association which is owned exclusively (except to the extent directors' qualifying shares are required by law) by other depository institutions or depository institution holding companies and is organized to engage exclusively in providing services to or for other depository institutions, their holding companies, and the officers, directors, and employees of such institutions and companies, and in providing correspondent banking services at the request of other depository institutions or their holding companies (also referred to as a "banker's bank").

(2) Any national banking association chartered pursuant to paragraph (1) shall be subject to such rules, regulations, and orders as the Comptroller deems appropriate, and, except as otherwise specifically provided in such rules, regulations, or orders, shall be vested with or subject to the same rights, privileges, duties, restrictions, penalties, liabilities, conditions, and limitations that would apply under the national banking laws to a national bank.

§ 28. Repealed. Pub.L. 103–325, Title VI, § 602(e)(1), Sept. 23, 1994, 108 Stat. 2291

§ 29. Power to hold real property

A national banking association may purchase, hold, and convey real estate for the following purposes, and for no others:

First. Such as shall be necessary for its accommodation in the transaction of its business.

Second. Such as shall be mortgaged to it in good faith by way of security for debts previously contracted.

Third. Such as shall be conveyed to it in satisfaction of debts previously contracted in the course of its dealings.

Fourth. Such as it shall purchase at sales under judgments, decrees, or mortgages held by the association, or shall purchase to secure debts due to it.

But no such association shall hold the possession of any real estate under mortgage, or the title and possession of any real estate purchased to secure any debts due to it, for a longer period than five years except as otherwise provided in this section.

For real estate in the possession of a national banking association upon application by the association, the Comptroller of the Currency may approve the possession of any such real estate by such association for a period longer than five years, but not to exceed an additional five years, if (1) the association has made a good faith attempt to dispose of the real estate within the five-year period, or (2) disposal within the five-year period would be detrimental to the association. Upon notification by the association to the Comptroller of the Currency that such conditions exist that require the expenditure of funds for the development and improvement of such real estate, and subject to such conditions and limitations as the Comptroller of the Currency shall prescribe, the association may expend such funds as are needed to enable such association to recover its total investment.

Notwithstanding the five-year holding limitation of this section or any other provision of this chapter, any national banking association which on October 15, 1982, held, directly or indirectly, real estate, including any subsurface rights or interests therein, that since December 31, 1979, had not been valued on the books of such association for more than a nominal amount, may continue to hold such real estate, rights, or interests for such longer period of time as would be permitted a State chartered bank by the law of the State in which the association is located if the aggregate amount of earnings from such real estate, rights, or interests is separately disclosed in the annual financial statements of the association.

§ 30. Change of name or location

(a) Name change

Any national banking association, upon written notice to the Comptroller of the Currency, may change its name, except that such new name shall include the word "National".

(b) Location change

Any national banking association, upon written notice to the Comptroller of the Currency, may change the location of its main office to any authorized branch location within the limits of the city, town, or village in which it is situated, or, with a vote of shareholders owning two-thirds of the stock of such association for a relocation outside such limits and upon receipt of a certificate of approval from the Comptroller of the Currency, to any other location within or outside the limits of the city, town, or village in which it is located, but not more than thirty miles beyond such limits.

(c) Coordination with section 36 of this title

In the case of a national bank which relocates the main office of such bank from 1 State to another State after May 31, 1997, the bank may retain and operate branches within the State from which the bank relocated such office only to the extent authorized in section 36(e)(2) of this title.

(d) Retention of "Federal" in name of converted Federal Savings Association

(1) In general

Notwithstanding subsection (a) or any other provision of law, any depository institution, the charter of which is converted from that of a Federal savings association to a national bank or a State bank after November 12, 1999, may retain the term "Federal" in the name of such institution if such institution remains an insured depository institution.

(2) Definitions

For purposes of this subsection, the terms "depository institution", "insured depository institution", "national bank", and "State bank" have the meanings given those terms in section 1813 of this title.

§ 31. Rights and liabilities as affected by change of name

All debts, liabilities, rights, provisions, and powers of the association under its old name shall devolve upon and inure to the association under its new name.

§ 32. Liabilities and suits as affected by change of name or location

Nothing contained in sections 30 and 31 of this title shall be so construed as in any manner to release any national banking association under its old name or at its old location from any liability, or affect any action or proceeding in law in which said association may be or become a party or interested.

§§ 33 to 34c. Transferred

§ 35. Organization of State banks as national banking associations—DFA § 612

Any bank incorporated by special law of any State or of the United States or organized under the general laws of any State or of the United States and having an unimpaired capital sufficient to entitle it to become a national banking association under the provisions of the existing laws may, by the vote of the shareholders owning not less than fifty-one per centum of the capital stock of such bank or banking association, with the approval of the Comptroller of the Currency be converted into a national banking association, with a name that contains the word "national": *Provided, however,* That said conversion shall not be in contravention of the State law. In such case the articles of association and organization certificate may be executed by a majority of the directors of the bank or banking institution, and the certificate shall declare that the owners of fifty-one per centum of the capital stock have authorized the directors to make such certificate and to change or convert the bank or banking institution into a national association. A majority of the directors, after executing the articles of association and the organization certificate, shall have power to execute all other papers and to do whatever may be required to make its organization perfect and complete as a national association. The shares of any such bank may continue to be for the same amount each as they were before the conversion, and the directors may continue to be directors of the association until others are elected or appointed in accordance with the provisions of the statutes of the United States. When the Comptroller has given to such bank or banking association a certificate that the provisions of this Act have been complied with, such bank or banking association, and all its stockholders, officers, and employees shall have the same powers and privileges, and shall be subject to the same duties, liabilities, and regulations, in all respects, as shall have been prescribed by the Federal Reserve Act [12 U.S.C.A. § 221 et seq.] and the National Banking Act for associations originally organized as national banking associations.

The Comptroller of the Currency may, in his discretion and subject to such conditions as he may prescribe, permit such converting bank to retain and carry at a value determined by the Comptroller such of the assets of such converting bank as do not conform to the legal requirements relative to assets acquired and held by national banking associations.

§ 36. Branch banks—DFA § 613

The conditions upon which a national banking association may retain or establish and operate a branch or branches are the following:

(a) Lawful and continuous operation

A national banking association may retain and operate such branch or branches as it may have had in lawful operation on February 25, 1927, and any national banking association which continuously maintained and operated not more than one branch for a period of more than twenty-five years immediately preceding February 25, 1927, may continue to maintain and operate such branch.

(b) Converted State banks

(1) A national bank resulting from the conversion of a State bank may retain and operate as a branch any office which was a branch of the State bank immediately prior to conversion if such office—

(A) might be established under subsection (c) of this section as a new branch of the resulting national bank, and is approved by the Comptroller of the Currency for continued operation as a branch of the resulting national bank;

(B) was a branch of any bank on February 25, 1927; or

(C) is approved by the Comptroller of the Currency for continued operation as a branch of the resulting national bank.

The Comptroller of the Currency may not grant approval under clause (C) of this paragraph if a State bank (in a situation identical to that of the national bank) resulting from the conversion of a national bank would be prohibited by the law of such State from retaining and operating as a branch an identically situat-

ed office which was a branch of the national bank immediately prior to conversion.

(2) A national bank (referred to in this paragraph as the "resulting bank"), resulting from the consolidation of a national bank (referred to in this paragraph as the "national bank") under whose charter the consolidation is effected with another bank or banks, may retain and operate as a branch any office which, immediately prior to such consolidation, was in operation as—

(A) a main office or branch office of any bank (other than the national bank) participating in the consolidation if, under subsection (c) of this section, it might be established as a new branch of the resulting bank, and if the Comptroller of the Currency approves of its continued operation after the consolidation;

(B) a branch of any bank participating in the consolidation, and which, on February 25, 1927, was in operation as a branch of any bank; or

(C) a branch of the national bank and which, on February 25, 1927, was not in operation as a branch of any bank, if the Comptroller of the Currency approves of its continued operation after the consolidation.

The Comptroller of the Currency may not grant approval under clause (C) of this paragraph if a State bank (in a situation identical to that of the resulting national bank) resulting from the consolidation into a State bank of another bank or banks would be prohibited by the law of such State from retaining and operating as a branch an identically situated office which was a branch of the State bank immediately prior to consolidation.

(3) As used in this subsection, the term "consolidation" includes a merger.

(c) New branches

A national banking association may, with the approval of the Comptroller of the Currency, establish and operate new branches: (1) Within the limits of the city, town or village in which said association is situated, if such establishment and operation are at the time expressly authorized to State banks by the law of the State in question; and (2) at any point within the State in which said association is situated, if such establishment and operation are at the time authorized to State banks by the statute law of the State in question by language specifically granting such authority affirmatively and not merely by implication or recognition, and subject to the restrictions as to location imposed by the law of the State on State banks. In any State in which State banks are permitted by statute law to maintain branches within county or greater limits, if no bank is located and doing business in the place where the proposed agency is to be located, any national banking association situated in such State may, with the approval of the Comptroller of the Currency, establish and operate, without regard to the capital requirements of this section, a seasonal agency in any resort community within the limits of the county in which the main office of such association is located, for the purpose of receiving and paying out deposits, issuing and cashing checks and drafts, and doing business incident thereto: *Provided,* That any permit issued under this sentence shall be revoked upon the opening of a State or national bank in such community. Except as provided in the immediately preceding sentence, no such association shall establish a branch outside of the city, town, or village in which it is situated unless it has a combined capital stock and surplus equal to the combined amount of capital stock and surplus, if any, required by the law of the State in which such association is situated for the establishment of such branches by State banks, or, if the law of such State requires only a minimum capital stock for the establishment of such branches by State banks, unless such association has not less than an equal amount of capital stock.

(d) Branches resulting from interstate merger transactions

A national bank resulting from an interstate merger transaction (as defined in section 1831u(f)(6) of this title) may maintain and operate a branch in a State other than the home State (as defined in subsection (g)(3)(B) of this section) of such bank in accordance with section 1831u of this title.

(e) Exclusive authority for additional branches

(1) In general

Effective June 1, 1997, a national bank may not acquire, establish, or operate a branch in any State other than the bank's home State (as defined in subsection (g)(3)(B) of this section) or a State in which the bank already has a branch unless the acquisition, establishment, or operation of such branch in such State by such national bank is authorized under this section or section 1823(f), 1823(k), or 1831u of this title.

(2) Retention of branches

In the case of a national bank which relocates the main office of such bank from 1 State to another State after May 31, 1997, the bank may retain and operate branches within the State which was the bank's home State (as defined in subsection (g)(3)(B) of this section) before the relocation of such office only to the extent the bank would be authorized, under this section or any other provision of law referred to in paragraph (1), to acquire, establish, or commence to operate a branch in such State if—

(A) the bank had no branches in such State; or

(B) the branch resulted from—

(i) an interstate merger transaction approved pursuant to section 1831u of this title; or

(ii) a transaction after May 31, 1997, pursuant to which the bank received assistance from the Federal Deposit Insurance Corporation under section 1823(c) of this title.

(f) Law applicable to interstate branching operations

(1) Law applicable to national bank branches

(A) In general

The laws of the host State regarding community reinvestment, consumer protection, fair lending, and establishment of intrastate branches shall apply to any branch in the host State of an out-of-State national bank to the same extent as such State laws apply to a branch of a bank chartered by that State, except—

(i) when Federal law preempts the application of such State laws to a national bank; or

(ii) when the Comptroller of the Currency determines that the application of such State laws would have a discriminatory effect on the branch in comparison with the effect the application of such State laws would have with respect to branches of a bank chartered by the host State.

(B) Enforcement of applicable State laws

The provisions of any State law to which a branch of a national bank is subject under this paragraph shall be enforced, with respect to such branch, by the Comptroller of the Currency.

(C) Review and report on actions by Comptroller

The Comptroller of the Currency shall conduct an annual review of the actions it has taken with regard to the applicability of State law to national banks (or their branches) during the preceding year, and shall include in its annual report required under section 333 of the Revised Statutes (12 U.S.C. 14) the results of the review and the reasons for each such action. The first such review and report after July 3, 1997 shall encompass all such actions taken on or after January 1, 1992.

(2) Treatment of branch as bank

All laws of a host State, other than the laws regarding community reinvestment, consumer protection, fair lending, establishment of intrastate branches, and the application or administration of any tax or method of taxation, shall apply to a branch (in such State) of an out-of-State national bank to the same extent as such laws would apply if the branch were a national bank the main office of which is in such State.

(3) Rule of construction

No provision of this subsection may be construed as affecting the legal standards for preemption of the application of State law to national banks.

(g) State "opt-in" election to permit interstate branching through de novo branches

(1) In general

Subject to paragraph (2), the Comptroller of the Currency may approve an application by a national bank to establish and operate a de novo branch in a State (other than the bank's home State) in which the bank does not maintain a branch if—

(A) there is in effect in the host State a law that—

(i) applies equally to all banks; and

(ii) expressly permits all out-of-State banks to establish de novo branches in such State; and

(B) the conditions established in, or made applicable to this paragraph by, paragraph (2) are met.

(2) Conditions on establishment and operation of interstate branch

(A) Establishment

An application by a national bank to establish and operate a de novo branch in a host State shall be subject to the same requirements and conditions to which an application for an interstate merger transaction is subject under paragraphs (1), (3), and (4) of section 1831u(b) of this title.

(B) Operation

Subsections (c) and (d)(2) of section 1831u of this title shall apply with respect to each branch of a national bank which is established and operated pursuant to an application approved under this subsection in the same manner and to the same extent such provisions of such section 1831u of this title apply to a branch of a national bank which resulted from an interstate merger transaction approved pursuant to such section 1831u of this title.

(3) Definitions

The following definitions shall apply for purposes of this section:

(A) De novo branch

The term "de novo branch" means a branch of a national bank which—

(i) is originally established by the national bank as a branch; and

(ii) does not become a branch of such bank as a result of—

(I) the acquisition by the bank of an insured depository institution or a branch of an insured depository institution; or

(II) the conversion, merger, or consolidation of any such institution or branch.

(B) Home State

The term "home State" means the State in which the main office of a national bank is located.

(C) Host State

The term "host State" means, with respect to a bank, a State, other than the home State of the bank, in which the bank maintains, or seeks to establish and maintain, a branch.

(h) Repealed. Pub.L. 104–208, Div. A, Title II, § 2204, Sept. 30, 1996, 110 Stat. 3009–405

(i) Prior approval of branch locations

No branch of any national banking association shall be established or moved from one location to another without first obtaining the consent and approval of the Comptroller of the Currency.

(j) Branch defined

The term "branch" as used in this section shall be held to include any branch bank, branch office, branch agency, additional office, or any branch place of business located in any State or Territory of the United States or in the District of Columbia at which deposits are received, or checks paid, or money lent. The term "branch", as used in this section, does not include an automated teller machine or a remote service unit.

(k) Branches in foreign countries, dependencies, or insular possessions

This section shall not be construed to amend or repeal section 25 of the Federal Reserve Act, as amended [12 U.S.C.A. § 601 et seq.], authorizing the establishment by national banking associations of branches in foreign countries, or dependencies, or insular possessions of the United States.

(l) "State bank" and "bank" defined

The words "State bank," "State banks," "bank," or "banks," as used in this section, shall be held to include trust companies, savings banks, or other such corporations or institutions carrying on the banking business under the authority of State laws.

§ 37. Associations governed by chapter

The provisions of this chapter, which are expressed without restrictive words, as applying to "national banking associations," or to "associations," apply to all associations organized to carry on the business of banking under any Act of Congress.

§ 38. The National Bank Act

The Act entitled "An Act to provide a national currency secured by a pledge of United States bonds, and to provide for the circulation and redemption thereof," approved June 3, 1864, shall be known as "The National Bank Act."

§ 39. Reservation of rights of associations organized under Act of 1863

Nothing in this chapter shall affect any appointments made, acts done, or proceedings had or commenced prior to the 3d day of June 1864, in or toward the organization of any national banking association under the Act of February 25, 1863; but all associations which, on the 3d day of June 1864, were organized or commenced to be organized under that Act, shall enjoy all the rights and privileges granted, and be subject to all the duties, liabilities, and restrictions imposed by this chapter, notwithstanding all the steps prescribed by this chapter for the organization of associations were not pursued, if such associations were duly organized under that Act.

§ 40. Virgin Islands; extension of National Bank Act

The National Bank Act [12 U.S.C.A. § 21 et seq.], and all other Acts of Congress relating to national banks, shall, in so far as not locally inapplicable on and after July 19, 1932, apply to the Virgin Islands of the United States.

§ 41. Guam; extension of National Bank Act

The National Bank Act [12 U.S.C.A. § 21 et seq.], and all other Acts of Congress relating to national banks, shall, insofar as not locally inapplicable on and after August 1, 1956, apply to Guam.

§ 42. Territorial application

The provisions of all Acts of Congress relating to national banks shall apply in the several States, the District of Columbia, the several Territories and possessions of the United States, and the Commonwealth of Puerto Rico.

§ 43. Interpretations concerning preemption of certain State laws

(a) Notice and opportunity for comment required

Before issuing any opinion letter or interpretive rule, in response to a request or upon the agency's own motion, that concludes that Federal law preempts the application to a national bank of any State law regarding community reinvestment, consumer protection, fair lending, or the establishment of intrastate branches, or before making a determination under section 36(f)(1)(A)(ii) of this title the appropriate Federal banking agency (as defined in section 1813 of this title) shall—

(1) publish in the Federal Register notice of the preemption or discrimination issue that the agency is considering (including a description of each State law at issue);

(2) give interested parties not less than 30 days in which to submit written comments; and

(3) in developing the final opinion letter or interpretive rule issued by the agency, or making any determination under section 36(f)(1)(A)(ii) of this title, consider any comments received.

(b) Publication required

The appropriate Federal banking agency shall publish in the Federal Register—

(1) any final opinion letter or interpretive rule concluding that Federal law preempts the application of any State law regarding community reinvestment, consumer protection, fair lending, or establishment of intrastate branches to a national bank; and

(2) any determination under section 36(f)(1)(A)(ii) of this title.

(c) Exceptions

(1) No new issue or significant basis

This section shall not apply with respect to any opinion letter or interpretive rule that—

(A) raises issues of Federal preemption of State law that are essentially identical to those previously resolved by the courts or on which the agency has previously issued an opinion letter or interpretive rule; or

(B) responds to a request that contains no significant legal basis on which to make a preemption determination.

(2) Judicial, legislative, or intragovernmental materials

This section shall not apply with respect to materials prepared for use in judicial proceedings or submission to Congress or a Member of Congress, or for intragovernmental use.

(3) Emergency

The appropriate Federal banking agency may make exceptions to subsection (a) of this section if—

(A) the agency determines in writing that the exception is necessary to avoid a serious and imminent threat to the safety and soundness of any national bank; or

(B) the opinion letter or interpretive rule is issued in connection with—

(i) an acquisition of 1 or more banks in default or in danger of default (as such terms are defined in section 1813 of this title); or

(ii) an acquisition with respect to which the Federal Deposit Insurance Corporation provides assistance under section 1823(c) of this title.

§ 51. Repealed. Pub.L. 106–569, Title XII, § 1233(a), Dec. 27, 2000, 114 Stat. 3037

§ 51a. Preferred stock; issuance authorized

Notwithstanding any other provision of law, any national banking association may, with the approval of the Comptroller of the Currency and by vote of shareholders owning a majority of the stock of such association, upon not less than five days' notice, given by registered mail or by certified mail pursuant to action taken by its board of directors, issue preferred stock of one or more classes, in such amount and with such par value as shall be approved by said Comptroller, and make such amendments to its articles of association as may be necessary for this purpose; but, in the case of any newly organized national banking association which has not yet issued common stock, the requirement of notice to and vote of shareholders shall not apply. No issue of preferred stock shall be valid until the par value of all stock so issued shall be paid in and notice thereof, duly acknowledged before a notary public by the president, vice president, or cashier of said association, has been transmitted to the Comptroller of the Currency and his certificate obtained specifying the amount of such issue of preferred stock and his approval thereof and that the amount has been duly paid in as a part of the capital of such association; which certificate shall be deemed to be conclusive evidence that such preferred stock has been duly and validly issued.

§ 51b. Dividends, voting, and retirement of preferred stock; individual liability

(a) Notwithstanding any other provision of law, whether relating to restriction upon the payment of dividends upon capital stock or otherwise, the holders of such preferred stock shall be entitled to receive such cumulative dividends and shall have such voting and conversion rights and such control of management, and such stock shall be subject to retirement in such manner and upon such conditions, as may be provided in the articles of association with the approval of the Comptroller of the Currency. The holders of such preferred stock shall not be held individually responsible as such holders for any debts, contracts, or engagements of such association, and shall not be liable for assessments to restore impairments in the capital of such association as now provided by law with reference to holders of common stock.

(b) No dividends shall be declared or paid on common stock until the cumulative dividends on the preferred stock shall have been paid in full; and, if the association is placed in voluntary liquidation or a conservator or a receiver is appointed therefor, no payments shall be made to the holders of the common stock until the holders of the preferred stock shall have been paid in full the par value of such stock plus all accumulated dividends.

§ 51b–1. Consideration of preferred stock in determining impairment of capital; dividends; retirement

If any part of the capital of a national bank, State member bank, or bank applying for membership in the Federal Reserve System consists of preferred stock, the determination of whether or not the capital of such bank is impaired and the amount of such impairment shall be based upon the par value of its stock even though the amount which the holders of such preferred stock shall be entitled to receive in the event of retirement or liquidation shall be in excess of the par value of such preferred stock. If any such bank or trust company shall have outstanding any capital notes or debentures of the type which the reconstruction finance corporation is authorized to purchase pursuant to the provisions of section 51d of this title, the capital of such bank may be deemed to be unimpaired if the sound value of its assets is not less than its total liabilities, including capital stock, but excluding such capital notes or debentures and any obligations of the bank expressly subordinated thereto. Notwithstanding any other provision of law, the holders of preferred stock issued by a national banking association pursuant to the provisions of the Emergency Banking and Bank Conservation Act, approved March 9, 1933, as amended, shall be entitled to receive such cumulative dividends on the purchase price received by the association for such stock and, in the event of the retirement of such stock, to receive such retirement price, not in excess of such purchase price plus all accumulated dividends, as may be provided in the articles of association with the approval of the Comptroller of the Currency. If the association is placed in voluntary liquidation, or if a conservator or a receiver is appointed therefor, no payment shall be made to the holders of common stock until the holders of preferred stock shall have been paid in full such amount as may be provided in the articles of association with the approval of the Comptroller of the Currency, not in excess of such purchase price of such preferred stock plus all accumulated dividends.

§ 51c. "Common stock," "capital," and "capital stock" defined

The term "common stock" as used in sections 51a, 51b, 51c, and 51d of this title means stock of national banking associations other than preferred stock issued under the provisions of said sections. The term "capital" as used in provisions of law relating to the capital of national banking associations shall mean the amount of unimpaired common stock plus the amount of preferred stock outstanding and unimpaired; and the term "capital stock", as used in sections 101, 177, and 178 of this title, shall mean only the amount of common stock outstanding.

§§ 51d to 51f. Repealed. June 30, 1947, c. 166, Title II, § 206(b), (o), 61 Stat. 208

§ 52. Par value and incidents of stock; transfer of shares

The capital stock of each association shall be divided into shares of $100 each, or into shares of such less amount as may be provided in the articles of association, and be deemed personal property, and transferable on the books of the association in such manner as may be prescribed in the by-laws or articles of association. Every person becoming a shareholder by such transfer shall, in proportion to his shares, succeed to all rights and liabilities of the prior holder of such shares; and no change shall be made in the articles of association by which the rights, remedies, or security of the existing creditors of the association shall be impaired.

Certificates issued after August 23, 1935, representing shares of stock of the association shall state (1) the name and location of the association, (2) the name of the holder of record of the stock represented thereby, (3) the number and class of shares which the certificate represents, and (4) if the association shall issue stock of more than one class, the respective rights, preferences, privileges, voting rights, powers, restrictions, limitations, and qualifications of each class of stock issued shall be stated in full or in summary upon the front or back of the certificates or shall be incorporated by a reference to the articles of association set forth on the front of the certificates. Every certificate shall be signed by the president and the cashier of the association, or by such other officers as the bylaws of the association shall provide, and shall be sealed with the seal of the association.

After August 23, 1935, no certificate evidencing the stock of any such association shall bear any statement purporting to represent the stock of any other corporation, except a member bank or a corporation engaged on June 16, 1934, in holding the bank premises of such association, nor shall the ownership, sale, or transfer of any certificate representing the stock of any such association be conditioned in any manner whatsoever upon the ownership, sale, or transfer of a certificate representing the stock of any other corporation, except a member bank or a corporation engaged on June 16, 1934 in holding the bank premises of such association: *Provided,* That this section shall not operate to prevent the ownership, sale, or transfer of stock of any other corporation being conditioned upon the ownership, sale, or transfer of a certificate representing stock of a national banking association.

§ 53. When capital stock paid in

All of the capital stock of every national banking association shall be paid in before it shall be authorized to commence business.

§ 54. Repealed. Pub.L. 86–230, § 5, Sept. 8, 1959, 73 Stat. 457

§ 55. Enforcing payment of deficiency in capital stock; assessments; liquidation; receivership

Every association which shall have failed to pay up its capital stock, as required by law, and every association whose capital stock shall have become impaired by losses or otherwise, shall, within three months after receiving notice thereof from the Comptroller of the Currency, pay the deficiency in the capital stock, by assessment upon the shareholders pro rata for the amount of capital stock held by each; and the Treasurer of the United States shall withhold the interest upon all bonds held by him in trust for any such association, upon notification from the Comptroller of the Currency, until otherwise notified by him. If any such association shall fail to pay up its capital stock, and shall refuse to go into liquidation, as provided by law, for three months after receiving notice from the comptroller, a receiver may be appointed to close up the business of the association, according to the provisions of section 192 of this title. And *Provided,* That if any shareholder or shareholders of such bank shall neglect or refuse, after three months' notice, to pay the assessment, as provided in this section, it shall be the duty of the board of directors to cause a sufficient amount of the capital stock of such shareholder or shareholders to be sold at public auction (after thirty days' notice shall be given by posting such notice of sale in the office of the bank, and by publishing such notice in a newspaper of the city or town in which the bank is located, or in a newspaper published nearest thereto), to make good the deficiency, and the balance, if any, shall be returned to such delinquent shareholder or shareholders.

§ 56. Prohibition on withdrawal of capital; unearned dividends

No association, or any member thereof, shall, during the time it shall continue its banking operations, withdraw, or permit to be withdrawn, either in the form of dividends or otherwise, any portion of its capital. If losses have at any time been sustained by any such association, equal to or exceeding its undivided profits then on hand, no dividend shall be made; and no dividend shall ever be made by any association, while it continues its banking operations, to an amount greater than its undivided profits, subject to other applicable provisions of law. But nothing in this section shall prevent the reduction of the capital stock of the association under section 59 of this title.

§ 57. Increase of capital by provision in articles of association

Any national banking association may, with the approval of the Comptroller of the Currency, and by a vote of shareholders owning two-thirds of the stock of such associations, increase its capital stock to any sum approved by the said comptroller, but no increase in capital shall be valid until the whole amount of such increase is paid in and notice thereof, duly acknowledged before a notary public by the president, vice president, or cashier of said association, has been transmitted to the Comptroller of the Currency and his certificate obtained specifying the amount of such increase in capital stock and his approval thereof, and that it has been duly paid in as part of the capital of such association: *Provided, however,* That a national banking association may, with the approval of the Comptroller of the Currency, and by the vote of shareholders owning two-thirds of the stock of such association, increase its capital stock by the declaration of a stock dividend, provided that the surplus of said association, after the approval of the increase, shall be at least equal to 20 per centum of the capital stock as increased. Such increase shall not be effective until a certificate certifying to such declaration of dividend, signed by the president, vice president, or cashier of said association and duly acknowledged before a notary public, shall have been forwarded to the Comptroller of the Currency and his certificate obtained specifying the amount of such increase of capital stock by stock dividend, and his approval thereof.

§ 58. Repealed. Pub.L. 86–230, § 6, Sept. 8, 1959, 73 Stat. 457

§ 59. Reduction of capital

(a) In general

Subject to the approval of the Comptroller of the Currency, a national banking association may, by a vote of shareholders owning, in the aggregate, two-thirds of its capital stock, reduce its capital.

(b) Shareholder distributions authorized

As part of its capital reduction plan approved in accordance with subsection (a) of this section, and with the affirmative vote of shareholders owning at least two thirds of the shares of each class of its stock outstanding (each voting as a class), a national banking association may distribute cash or other assets to its shareholders.

§ 60. National Bank Dividends

(a) In general

Subject to subsection (b) of this section, the directors of any National bank may declare a dividend of so much of the undivided profits of the bank as the directors judge to be expedient.

(b) Approval required under certain circumstances

A national bank may not declare and pay dividends in any year in excess of an amount equal to the sum of the total of the net income of the bank for that year and the retained net income of the bank for the preceding 2 years, minus the sum of any transfers required by the Comptroller of the Currency and any transfers required to be made to a fund for the retirement of any preferred stock, unless the Comptroller of the Currency approves the declaration and payment of dividends in excess of such amount.

§ 61. Shareholders' voting rights; cumulative and distributive voting; preferred stock; trust shares; proxies, liability restrictions; percentage requirement exclusion of trust shares

In all elections of directors, each shareholder shall have the right to vote the number of shares owned by him for as many persons as there are directors to be elected, or, if so provided by the articles of association of the national bank, to cumulate such shares and give one candidate as many votes as the number of directors multiplied by the number of his shares shall equal, or to distribute them on the same principle among as many candidates as he shall think fit; and in deciding all other questions at meetings of shareholders, each shareholder shall be entitled to one vote on each share of stock held by him; except that (1) this shall not be construed as limiting the voting rights of holders of preferred stock under the terms and provisions of articles of association, or amendments thereto, adopted pursuant to the provisions of section 51b of this title; (2) in the election of directors, shares of its own stock held by a national bank as sole trustee, whether registered in its own name as such trustee or in the name of its nominee, shall not be voted by the registered owner unless under the terms of the trust the manner in which such shares shall be voted may be determined by a donor or beneficiary of the trust and unless such donor or beneficiary actually directs how such shares shall be voted; and (3) shares of its own stock held by a national bank and one or more persons as trustees may be voted by such other person or persons, as trustees, in the same manner as if he or they were the sole trustee. Shareholders may vote by proxies duly authorized in writing; but no officer, clerk, teller, or bookkeeper of such bank shall act as proxy; and no shareholder whose liability is past due and unpaid shall be allowed to vote. Whenever shares of stock cannot be voted by reason of being held by the bank as sole trustee such shares shall be excluded in determining whether matters voted upon by the shareholders were adopted by the requisite percentage of shares.

§ 62.   List of shareholders

The president and cashier of every national banking association shall cause to be kept at all times a full and correct list of the names and residences of all the shareholders in the association, and the number of shares held by each, in the office where its business is transacted. Such list shall be subject to the inspection of all the shareholders and creditors of the association, and the officers authorized to assess taxes under State authority, during business hours of each day in which business may be legally transacted. A copy of such list, verified by the oath of such president or cashier, shall be transmitted to the Comptroller of the Currency within ten days of any demand therefor made by him.

§§ 63, 64.   Repealed. Pub.L. 86–230, § 7, Sept. 8, 1959, 73 Stat. 457

§ 64a.   Individual liability of shareholders; limitation on liability

The additional liability imposed upon shareholders in national banking associations by the provisions of sections 63 and 64 of this title shall not apply with respect to shares in any such association issued after June 16, 1933. Such additional liability shall cease on July 1, 1937, with respect to all shares issued by any association

which shall be transacting the business of banking on July 1, 1937: *Provided,* That not less than six months prior to such date, such association shall have caused notice of such prospective termination of liability to be published in a newspaper published in the city, town, or county in which such association is located, and if no newspaper is published in such city, town, or county, then in a newspaper of general circulation therein. If the association fail to give such notice as and when above provided, a termination of such additional liability may thereafter be accomplished as of the date six month subsequent to publication, in the manner above provided. In the case of each association which has not caused notice of such prospective termination of liability to be published prior to May 18, 1953, the Comptroller of the Currency shall cause such notice to be published in the manner provided in this section, and on the date six months subsequent to such publication by the Comptroller of the Currency such additional liability shall cease.

§ 65.   Repealed. Pub.L. 86–230, § 8, Sept. 8, 1959, 73 Stat. 457

§ 66.   Personal liability of representatives of stockholders

Persons holding stock as executors, administrators, guardians, or trustees, shall not be personally subject to any liabilities as stockholders; but the estates and funds in their hands shall be liable in like manner and to the same extent as the testator, intestate, ward, or person interested in such trust funds would be, if living and competent to act and hold the stock in his own name.

§ 67.   Individual liability of shareholders; compromises; authority of receiver

Any receiver of a national banking association is authorized, with the approval of the Comptroller of the Currency and upon the order of a court of record of competent jurisdiction, to compromise, either before or after judgment, the individual liability of any shareholder of such association.

§ 71.   Election

The affairs of each association shall be managed by not less than five directors, who shall be elected by the shareholders at a meeting to be held at any time before the association is authorized by the Comptroller of the Currency to commence the business of banking; and afterward at meetings to be held on such day of each year as is specified therefor in the bylaws. The directors shall hold office for a period of not more than 3 years and until their successors are elected and have qualified. In accordance with regulations issued by the Comptroller of the currency, a national bank may adopt by laws that provide for staggering the terms of its directors.

§ 71a. Number of directors; penalties

After one year from June 16, 1933, notwithstanding any other provision of law, the board of directors, board of trustees, or other similar governing body of every national banking association and of every State bank or trust company which is a member of the Federal Reserve System shall consist of not less than five nor more than twenty-five members, except that the Comptroller of the Currency may, by regulation or order, exempt a national bank from the 25–member limit established by this section. If any national banking association violates the provisions of this section and continues such violation after thirty days' notice from the Comptroller of the Currency, the said Comptroller may appoint a receiver or conservator therefor, in accordance with the provisions of existing law. If any State bank or trust company which is a member of the Federal Reserve System violates the provisions of this section and continues such violation after thirty days' notice from the Board of Governors of the Federal Reserve System, it shall be subject to the forfeiture of its membership in the Federal Reserve System in accordance with the provisions of section 327 of this title.

§ 72. Qualifications

Every director must, during his whole term of service, be a citizen of the United States, and at least a majority of the directors must have resided in the State, Territory, or District in which the association is located, or within one hundred miles of the location of the office of the association, for at least one year immediately preceding their election, and must be residents of such State or within a one-hundred-mile territory of the location of the association during their continuance in office, except that the Comptroller may, in the discretion of the Comptroller, waive the requirement of residency, and waive the requirement of citizenship in the case of not more than a minority of the total number of directors.

Every director must own in his or her own right either shares of the capital stock of the association of which he or she is a director the aggregate par value of which is not less than $1,000, or an equivalent interest, as determined by the Comptroller of the Currency, in any company which has control over such association within the meaning of section 1841 of this title. If the capital of the bank does not exceed $25,000, every director must own in his or her own right either shares of such capital stock the aggregate par value of which is not less than $500, or an equivalent interest, as determined by the Comptroller of the Currency, in any company which has control over such association within the meaning of section 1841 of this title. Any director who ceases to be the owner of the required number of shares of the stock, or who becomes in any other manner disqualified, shall thereby vacate his place.

§ 73. Oath

Each director, when appointed or elected, shall take an oath that he will, so far as the duty devolves on him, diligently and honestly administer the affairs of such association, and will not knowingly violate or willingly permit to be violated any of the provisions of this chapter, and that he is the owner in good faith, and in his own right, of the number of shares of stock required by this chapter, subscribed by him, or standing in his name on the books of the association, and that the same is not hypothecated, or in any way pledged, as security for any loan or debt. The oath shall be taken before a notary public, properly authorized and commissioned by the State in which he resides, or before any other officer having an official seal and authorized by the State to administer oaths, except that the oath shall not be taken before any such notary public or other officer who is an officer of the director's bank. The oath, subscribed by the director making it, and certified by the notary public or other officer before whom it is taken, shall be immediately transmitted to the Comptroller of the Currency and shall be filed and preserved in his office for a period of ten years.

§ 74. Vacancies

Any vacancy in the board shall be filled by appointment by the remaining directors, and any director so appointed shall hold his place until the next election.

§ 75. Legal holiday, annual meeting on; proceedings where no election held on proper day

When the day fixed in the bylaws for the regular annual meeting of the shareholders falls on a legal holiday in the State in which the bank is located, the shareholders meeting shall be held, and the directors elected, on the next following banking day. If, from any cause, an election of directors is not made on the day fixed, or in the event of a legal holiday, on the next following banking day, an election may be held on any subsequent day within sixty days of the day fixed, to be designated by the board of directors, or, if the directors fail to fix the day, by shareholders representing two-thirds of the shares, at least ten days' notice thereof in all cases having been given by first-class mail to the shareholders.

§ 76. President of bank as member of board; chairman of board

The president of the bank shall be a member of the board and shall be the chairman thereof, but the board may designate a director in lieu of the president to be chairman of the board, who shall perform such duties as may be designated by the board.

§ 77. Repealed. Pub.L. 89–695, Title II, § 207, Oct. 16, 1966, 80 Stat. 1055

§ 78. Repealed. Pub.L. 106–102, Title I, § 101(b), Nov. 12, 1999, 113 Stat. 1341

§ 81. Place of business

The general business of each national banking association shall be transacted in the place specified in its organization certificate and in the branch or branches, if any, established or maintained by it in accordance with the provisions of section 36 of this title.

§ 82. Repealed. Pub.L. 97–320, Title IV, § 402, Oct. 15, 1982, 96 Stat. 1510

§ 83. Loans by bank on its own stock

(a) General Prohibition

No national bank shall make any loan or discount on the security of the shares of its own capital stock.

(b) Exclusion

For purposes of this section, a national bank shall not be deemed to be making a loan or discount on the security of shares of its own capital stock if it acquires the stock to prevent loss upon a debt previously contracted for in good faith.

§ 84. Lending limits—DFA § 610

(a) Total loans and extensions of credit

(1) The total loans and extensions of credit by a national banking association to a person outstanding at one time and not fully secured, as determined in a manner consistent with paragraph (2) of this subsection, by collateral having a market value at least equal to the amount of the loan or extension of credit shall not exceed 15 per centum of the unimpaired capital and unimpaired surplus of the association.

(2) The total loans and extensions of credit by a national banking association to a person outstanding at one time and fully secured by readily marketable collateral having a market value, as determined by reliable and continuously available price quotations, at least equal to the amount of the funds outstanding shall not exceed 10 per centum of the unimpaired capital and unimpaired surplus of the association. This limitation shall be separate from and in addition to the limitation contained in paragraph (1) of this subsection.

(b) Definitions

For the purposes of this section—

(1) the term "loans and extensions of credit" shall include all direct or indirect advances of funds to a person made on the basis of any obligation of that person to repay the funds or repayable from specific property pledged by or on behalf of the person and, to the extent specified by the Comptroller of the Currency, such term shall also include any liability of a national banking association to advance funds to or on behalf of a person pursuant to a contractual commitment; and

(2) the term "person" shall include an individual, sole proprietorship, partnership, joint venture, association, trust, estate, business trust, corporation, sovereign government or agency, instrumentality, or political subdivision thereof, or any similar entity or organization.

(c) Exceptions

The limitations contained in subsection (a) of this section shall be subject to the following exceptions:

(1) Loans or extensions of credit arising from the discount of commercial or business paper evidencing an obligation to the person negotiating it with recourse shall not be subject to any limitation based on capital and surplus.

(2) The purchase of bankers' acceptances of the kind described in section 372 of this title and issued by other banks shall not be subject to any limitation based on capital and surplus.

(3) Loans and extensions of credit secured by bills of lading, warehouse receipts, or similar documents transferring or securing title to readily marketable staples shall be subject to a limitation of 35 per centum of capital and surplus in addition to the general limitations if the market value of the staples securing each additional loan or extension of credit at all times equals or exceeds 115 per centum of the outstanding amount of such loan or extension of credit. The staples shall be fully covered by insurance whenever it is customary to insure such staples.

(4) Loans or extensions of credit secured by bonds, notes, certificates of indebtedness, or Treasury bills of the United States or by other such obligations fully guaranteed as to principal and interest by the United States shall not be subject to any limitation based on capital and surplus.

(5) Loans or extensions of credit to or secured by unconditional takeout commitments or guarantees of any department, agency, bureau, board, commission, or establishment of the United States or any corporation wholly owned directly or indirectly by the United States shall not be subject to any limitation based on capital and surplus.

(6) Loans or extensions of credit secured by a segregated deposit account in the lending bank shall not be subject to any limitation based on capital and surplus.

(7) Loans or extensions of credit to any financial institution or to any receiver, conservator, superintendent of banks, or other agent in charge of the business and property of such financial institution, when such loans or extensions of credit are approved by the Comptroller of the Currency, shall not be subject to any limitation based on capital and surplus.

(8) (A) Loans and extensions of credit arising from the discount of negotiable or nonnegotiable installment consumer paper which carries a full recourse endorsement or unconditional guarantee by the person transferring the paper shall be subject under this section to a maximum limitation equal to 25 per centum of such capital and surplus, notwithstanding the collateral requirements set forth in subsection (a)(2) of this section.

(B) If the bank's files or the knowledge of its officers of the financial condition of each maker of such consumer paper is reasonably adequate, and an officer of the bank designated for that purpose by the board of directors of the bank certifies in writing that the bank is relying primarily upon the responsibility of each maker for payment of such loans or extensions of credit and not upon any full or partial recourse endorsement or guarantee by the transferor, the limitations of this section as to the loans or extensions of credit of each such maker shall be the sole applicable loan limitations.

(9) (A) Loans and extensions of credit secured by shipping documents or instruments transferring or securing title covering livestock or giving a lien on livestock when the market value of the livestock securing the obligation is not at any time less than 115 per centum of the face amount of the note covered, shall be subject under this section, notwithstanding the collateral requirements set forth in subsection (a)(2) of this section, to a maximum limitation equal to 25 per centum of such capital and surplus.

(B) Loans and extensions of credit which arise from the discount by dealers in dairy cattle of paper given in payment for dairy cattle, which paper carries a full recourse endorsement or unconditional guarantee of the seller, and which are secured by the cattle being sold, shall be subject under this section, notwithstanding the collateral requirements set forth in subsection (a)(2) of this section, to a limitation of 25 per centum of such capital and surplus.

(10) Loans or extensions of credit to the Student Loan Marketing Association shall not be

subject to any limitation based on capital and surplus.

(d) Authority of Comptroller of the Currency

(1) The Comptroller of the Currency may prescribe rules and regulations to administer and carry out the purposes of this section including rules or regulations to define or further define terms used in this section and to establish limits or requirements other than those specified in this section for particular classes or categories of loans or extensions of credit.

(2) The Comptroller of the Currency also shall have authority to determine when a loan putatively made to a person shall for purposes of this section be attributed to another person.

§ 85. Rate of interest on loans, discounts and purchases

Any association may take, receive, reserve, and charge on any loan or discount made, or upon any notes, bills of exchange, or other evidence of debt, interest at the rate allowed by the laws of the State, Territory, or District where the bank is located, or at a rate of 1 per centum in excess of the discount rate on ninety-day commercial paper in effect at the Federal reserve bank in the Federal reserve district where the bank is located, whichever may be the greater, and no more, except that where by the laws of any State a different rate is limited for banks organized under state laws, the rate so limited shall be allowed for associations organized or existing in any such State under this chapter. When no rate is fixed by the laws of the State, or Territory, or District, the bank may take, receive, reserve, or charge a rate not exceeding 7 per centum, or 1 per centum in excess of the discount rate on ninety-day commercial paper in effect at the Federal reserve bank in the Federal reserve district where the bank is located, whichever may be the greater, and such interest may be taken in advance, reckoning the days for which the note, bill, or other evidence of debt has to run. The maximum amount of interest or discount to be charged at a branch of an association located outside of the States of the United States and the District of Columbia shall be at the rate allowed by the laws of the country, territory, dependency, province, dominion, insular possession, or other political subdivision where the branch is located. And the purchase, discount, or sale of a bona fide bill of exchange, payable at another place than

the place of such purchase, discount, or sale, at not more than the current rate of exchange for sight drafts in addition to the interest, shall not be considered as taking or receiving a greater rate of interest.

§ 86. Usurious interest; penalty for taking; limitations

The taking, receiving, reserving, or charging a rate of interest greater than is allowed by section 85 of this title, when knowingly done, shall be deemed a forfeiture of the entire interest which the note, bill, or other evidence of debt carries with it, or which has been agreed to be paid thereon. In case the greater rate of interest has been paid, the person by whom it has been paid, or his legal representatives, may recover back, in an action in the nature of an action of debt, twice the amount of the interest thus paid from the association taking or receiving the same: *Provided,* That such action is commenced within two years from the time the usurious transaction occurred.

§ 86a.   Omitted

§ 87–89.   Repealed. Pub.L. 103–325, Title VI, § 602(e)(4), Sept. 23, 1994, 108 Stat. 2291

§ 90.   Depositaries of public moneys and financial agents of Government

All national banking associations, designated for that purpose by the Secretary of the Treasury, shall be depositaries of public money, under such regulations as may be prescribed by the Secretary; and they may also be employed as financial agents of the Government; and they shall perform all such reasonable duties, as depositaries of public money and financial agents of the Government, as may be required of them. The Secretary of the Treasury shall require the associations thus designated to give satisfactory security, by the deposit of United States bonds and otherwise, for the safe-keeping and prompt payment of the public money deposited with them, and for the faithful performance of their duties as financial agents of the Government: *Provided,* That the Secretary shall, on or before the 1st of January of each year, make a public statement of the securities required during that year for such deposits. And every association so designated as receiver or depositary of the public money shall take and receive at par all of the national currency bills, by whatever association issued, which have been paid into the Government for internal revenue, or for loans or stocks: *Provided,* That the Secretary of the Treasury shall distribute the deposits herein provided for, as far as practicable, equitably between the different States and sections.

Any national banking association may, upon the deposit with it of any funds by any State or political subdivision thereof or any agency or other governmental instrumentality of one or more States or political subdivisions thereof, including any officer, employee, or agent thereof in his official capacity, give security for the safekeeping and prompt payment of the funds so deposited to the same extent and of the same kind as is authorized by the law of the State in which such association is located in the case of other banking institutions in the State.

Any national banking association may, upon the deposit with it of any funds by any federally recognized Indian tribe, or any officer, employee, or agent thereof in his or her official capacity, give security for the safekeeping and prompt payment of the funds so deposited by the deposit of United States bonds and otherwise as may be prescribed by the Secretary of the Treasury for public funds under the first paragraph of this section.

Notwithstanding the Federal Property and Administrative Services Act of 1949, as amended, the Secretary may select associations as financial agents in accordance with any process the Secretary deems appropriate and their reasonable duties may include the provision of electronic benefit transfer services (including State-administered benefits with the consent of the States), as defined by the Secretary.

§ 91. Transfers by bank and other acts in contemplation of insolvency

All transfers of the notes, bonds, bills of exchange, or other evidences of debt owing to any national banking association, or of deposits to its credit; all assignments of mortgages, sureties on real estate, or of judgments or decrees in its favor; all deposits of money, bullion, or other valuable thing for its use, or for the use of any of its shareholders or creditors; and all payments of money to either, made after the commission of an act of insolvency, or in contemplation thereof, made with a view to prevent the application of its assets in the manner prescribed by this chapter, or with a view to the preference of one creditor to another, except in payment of its circulating notes, shall be utterly null and void; and no attachment, injunction, or execution, shall be issued against such association or its property before final judgment in any suit, action, or proceeding, in any State, county, or municipal court.

§ 92. Acting as insurance agent or broker

In addition to the powers now vested by law in national banking associations organized under the laws of the United States any such association located and doing business in any place the population of which does not exceed five thousand inhabitants, as shown by the last preceding decennial census, may, under such rules and regulations as may be prescribed by the Comptroller of the Currency, act as the agent for any fire, life, or other insurance company authorized by the authorities of the State in which said bank is located to do business in said State, by soliciting and selling insurance and collecting premiums on policies issued by such company; and may receive for services so rendered such fees or commissions as may be agreed upon between the said association and the insurance company for which it may act as agent: *Provided, however,* That no such bank shall in any case assume or guarantee the payment of any premium on insurance policies issued through its agency by its principal: *And provided further,* That the bank shall not guarantee the truth of any statement made by an assured in filing his application for insurance.

§ 92a. Trust powers

(a) Authority of Comptroller of the Currency

The Comptroller of the Currency shall be authorized and empowered to grant by special permit to national banks applying therefor, when not in contravention of State or local law, the right to act as trustee, executor, administrator, registrar of stocks and bonds, guardian of estates, assignee, receiver, committee of estates of lunatics, or in any other fiduciary capacity in which State banks, trust companies, or other corporations which come into competition with national banks are permitted to act under the laws of the State in which the national bank is located.

(b) Grant and exercise of powers deemed not in contravention of State or local law

Whenever the laws of such State authorize or permit the exercise of any or all of the foregoing powers by State banks, trust companies, or other corporations which compete with national banks, the granting to and the exercise of such powers by national banks shall not be deemed to be in contravention of State or local law within the meaning of this section.

(c) Segregation of fiduciary and general assets; separate books and records; access of State banking authorities to reports of examinations, books, records, and assets

National banks exercising any or all of the powers enumerated in this section shall segregate all assets held in any fiduciary capacity from the general assets of the bank and shall keep a separate set of books and records showing in proper detail all transactions engaged in under authority of this section. The State banking authorities may have access to reports of examination made by the Comptroller of the Currency insofar as such reports relate to the trust department of such bank, but nothing in this section shall be construed as authorizing the State banking authorities to examine the books, records, and assets of such bank.

(d) Prohibited operations; separate investment account; collateral for certain funds used in conduct of business

No national bank shall receive in its trust department deposits of current funds subject to check or the deposit of checks, drafts, bills of exchange, or other items for collection or exchange purposes. Funds deposited or held in trust by the bank awaiting investment shall be carried in a separate account and shall not be used by the bank in the conduct of its business unless it shall first set aside in the trust department United States bonds or other securities approved by the Comptroller of the Currency.

(e) Lien and claim upon bank failure

In the event of the failure of such bank the owners of the funds held in trust for investment shall have a lien on the bonds or other securities so set apart in addition to their claim against the estate of the bank.

(f) Deposits of securities for protection of private or court trusts; execution of and exemption from bond

Whenever the laws of a State require corporations acting in a fiduciary capacity to deposit securities with the State authorities for the protection of private or court trusts, national banks so acting shall be required to make similar deposits and securities so deposited shall be held for the protection of private or court trusts, as provided by the State law. National banks in such cases shall not be required to execute the bond usually required of individuals if State corporations under similar circumstances are exempt from this requirement. National banks shall have power to execute such bond when so required by the laws of the State.

(g) Officials' oath or affidavit

In any case in which the laws of a State require that a corporation acting as trustee, executor, administrator, or in any capacity specified in this section, shall take an oath or make an affidavit, the president, vice president, cashier, or trust officer of such national bank may take the necessary oath or execute the necessary affidavit.

(h) Loans of trust funds to officers and employees prohibited; penalties

It shall be unlawful for any national banking association to lend any officer, director, or employee any funds held in trust under the powers conferred by this section. Any officer, director, or employee making such loan, or to whom such loan is made, may be fined not more than $5,000, or imprisoned not more than five years, or may be both fined and imprisoned, in the discretion of the court.

(i) Considerations determinative of grant or denial of applications; minimum capital and surplus for issuance of permit

In passing upon applications for permission to exercise the powers enumerated in this section, the Comptroller of the Currency may take into consideration the amount of capital and surplus of the applying bank, whether or not such capital and surplus is sufficient under the circumstances of the case, the needs of the community to be served, and any other facts and circumstances that seem to him proper, and may grant or refuse the application accordingly: *Provided,* That no permit shall be issued to any national banking association having a capital and surplus less than the capital and surplus required by State law of State banks, trust companies, and corporations exercising such powers.

(j) Surrender of authorization; board resolution; Comptroller certification; activities affected; regulations

Any national banking association desiring to surrender its right to exercise the powers granted under this section, in order to relieve itself of the necessity of complying with the requirements of this section, or to have returned to it any securities which it may have deposited with the State authorities for the protection of private or court trusts, or for any other purpose, may file with the Comptroller of the Currency a certified copy of a resolution of its board of directors signifying such desire. Upon receipt of such resolution, the Comptroller of the Currency, after satisfying himself that such bank has been relieved in accordance with State law of all duties as trustee, executor, administrator, registrar of stocks and bonds, guardian of estates, assignee, receiver, committee of estates of lunatics or other fiduciary, under court, private, or other appointments previously accepted under authority of this section, may, in his discretion, issue to such bank a certificate certifying that such bank is no longer authorized to exercise the powers granted by this section. Upon the issuance of such a certificate by the Comptroller of the Currency, such bank (1) shall no longer be subject to the provisions of this section or the regulations of the Comptroller of the Currency made pursuant thereto, (2) shall be entitled to have returned to it any securities which it may have deposited with the State authorities for the protection of private or court trusts, and (3) shall not exercise thereafter any of the powers granted by this section without first applying for and obtaining a new permit to exercise such powers pursuant to the provisions of this section. The Comptroller of the Currency is authorized and empowered to promulgate such regulations as he may deem necessary to enforce compliance with the provisions of this section and the proper exercise of the powers granted therein.

(k) Revocation; procedures applicable

(1) In addition to the authority conferred by other law, if, in the opinion of the Comptroller of the Currency, a national banking association is unlawfully or unsoundly exercising, or has unlawfully or unsoundly exercised, or has failed for a period of five consecutive years to exercise, the powers granted by this section or otherwise fails or has failed to comply with the requirements of this section, the Comptroller may issue and serve upon the association a notice of intent to revoke the authority of the association to exercise the powers granted by this section. The notice shall contain a statement of the facts constituting the alleged unlawful or unsound exercise of powers, or failure to exercise powers, or failure to comply, and shall fix a time and place at which a hearing will be held to determine whether an order revoking authority to exercise such powers should issue against the association.

(2) Such hearing shall be conducted in accordance with the provisions of section 1818(h) of this title, and subject to judicial review as provided in such section, and shall be fixed for a date not earlier than thirty days nor later than sixty days after service of such notice unless an earlier or later date is set by the Comptroller at the request of any association so served.

(3) Unless the association so served shall appear at the hearing by a duly authorized representative, it shall be deemed to have consented to the issuance of the revocation order. In the event of such consent, or if upon the record made at any such hearing, the Comptroller shall find that any allegation specified in the notice of charges has been established, the comptroller may issue and serve upon the association an order prohibiting it from accepting any new or additional trust accounts and revoking authority to exercise any and all powers granted by this section, except that such order shall permit the association to continue to service all previously accepted trust accounts pending their expeditious divestiture or termination.

(4) A revocation order shall become effective not earlier than the expiration of thirty days after service of such order upon the association so served (except in the case of a revocation order issued upon consent, which shall become effective at the time specified therein), and shall remain effective and enforceable, except to such extent as it is stayed, modified, terminated, or set aside by action of the Comptroller or a reviewing court.

§ 93. Violations of provisions of chapter

(a) Forfeiture of franchise; personal liability of directors

If the directors of any national banking association shall knowingly violate, or knowingly permit any of the officers, agents, or servants of the association to violate any of the provisions of title 62 of the Revised Statutes, all the rights, privileges, and franchises of the association shall be thereby forfeited. Such violation shall, however, be determined and adjudged by a proper district or Territorial court of the United States in a suit brought for that purpose by the Comptroller of the Currency, in his own name, before the association shall be declared dissolved. And in cases of such violation, every director who participated in or assented to the same shall be held liable in his personal and individual capacity for all damages which the association, its shareholders, or any other person, shall have sustained in consequence of such violation.

(b) Civil money penalty

(1) First tier

Any national banking association which, and any institution-affiliated party (within the meaning of section 1813(u) of this title) with respect to such association who, violates any provision of this chapter or any of the provisions of section 92a of this title, or any regulation issued pursuant thereto, shall forfeit and pay a civil penalty of not more than $5,000 for each day during which such violation continues.

(2) Second tier

Notwithstanding paragraph (1), any national banking association which, and any institution-affiliated party (within the meaning of section 1813(u) of this title) with respect to such association who, commits any violation described in paragraph (1) which—

(A)(i) commits any violation described in any paragraph (1);

(ii) recklessly engages in an unsafe or unsound practice in conducting the affairs of such association; or

(iii) breaches any fiduciary duty;

(B) which violation, practice, or breach—

(i) is part of a pattern of misconduct;

(ii) causes or is likely to cause more than a minimal loss to such association; or

(iii) results in pecuniary gain or other benefit to such party,

shall forfeit and pay a civil penalty of not more than $25,000 for each day during which such violation, practice, or breach continues.

(3) Third tier

Notwithstanding paragraphs (1) and (2), any national banking association which, and any institution-affiliated party (within the meaning of section 1813(u) of this title) with respect to such association who—

(A) knowingly—

(i) commits any violation described in paragraph (1);

(ii) engages in any unsafe or unsound practice in conducting the affairs of such association; or

(iii) breaches any fiduciary duty; and

(B) knowingly or recklessly causes a substantial loss to such association or a substantial pecuniary gain or other benefit to such party by reason of such violation, practice, or breach,

shall forfeit and pay a civil penalty in an amount not to exceed the applicable maximum amount determined under paragraph (4) for each day during which such violation, practice, or breach continues.

(4) Maximum amounts of penalties for any violation described in paragraph (3)

The maximum daily amount of any civil penalty which may be assessed pursuant to paragraph (3) for any violation, practice, or breach described in such paragraph is—

(A) in the case of any person other than a national banking association, an amount to not exceed $1,000,000; and

(B) in the case of a national banking association, an amount not to exceed the lesser of—

(i) $1,000,000; or

(ii) 1 percent of the total assets of such association.

(5) Assessment; etc.

Any penalty imposed under paragraph (1), (2), or (3) shall be assessed and collected by the Comptroller of the Currency in the manner provided in subparagraphs (E), (F), (G), and (I) of section 1818(i)(2) of this title for penalties imposed (under such section) and any such assessment shall be subject to the provisions of such section.

(6) Hearing

The association or other person against whom any penalty is assessed under this subsection shall be afforded an agency hearing if such association or person submits a request for such hearing within 20 days after the issuance of the notice of assessment. Section 1818(h) of this title shall apply to any proceeding under this subsection.

(7) Disbursement

All penalties collected under authority of this subsection shall be deposited into the Treasury.

(8) Violate defined

For purposes of this section, the term "violate" includes any action (alone or with another or others) for or toward causing, bringing about, participating in, counseling, or aiding or abetting a violation.

(12) Regulations

The Comptroller shall prescribe regulations establishing such procedures as may be necessary to carry out this subsection.

(c) Notice under this section after separation from service

The resignation, termination of employment or participation, or separation of an institution-affiliated party (within the meaning of section 1813(u) of this title) with respect to such an association (including a separation caused by the closing of such an association) shall not affect the jurisdiction and authority of the Comptroller of the Currency to issue any notice and proceed under this section against any such party, if such notice is served before the end of the 6–year period beginning on the date such party ceased to be such a party with respect to such association (whether such date occurs before, on, or after August 9, 1989).

(d) Forfeiture of franchise for money laundering or cash transaction reporting offenses

(1) In general

(A) Conviction of Title 18 offenses

(i) Duty to notify

If a national bank, a Federal branch, or Federal agency has been convicted of any criminal offense under section 1956 or 1957 of Title 18, the Attorney General shall provide to the Comptroller of the Currency a written notification of the conviction and shall include a certified copy of the order of conviction from the court rendering the decision.

(ii) Notice of termination; pretermination hearing

After receiving written notification from the Attorney General of such a conviction, the Comptroller of the Currency shall issue to the national bank, Federal branch, or Federal agency a notice of the Comptroller's intention to terminate all rights, privileges, and franchises of the bank, Federal branch, or Federal agency and schedule a pretermination hearing.

(B) Conviction of Title 31 offenses

If a national bank, a Federal branch, or a Federal agency is convicted of any criminal offense under section 5322 or 5324 of Title 31, after receiving written notification from the Attorney General, the Comptroller of the Currency may issue to the national bank, Federal branch, or Federal agency a notice of the Comptroller's intention to terminate all rights, privileges, and franchises of the bank, Federal branch, or Federal agency and schedule a pretermination hearing.

(C) Judicial review

Section 1818(h) of this title shall apply to any proceeding under this subsection.

(2) Factors to be considered

In determining whether a franchise shall be forfeited under paragraph (1), the Comptroller of the Currency shall take into account the following factors:

(A) The extent to which directors or senior executive officers of the national bank, Federal branch, or Federal agency knew of, or were involved in,the commission of the money laundering offense of which the bank, Federal branch, or Federal agency was found guilty.

(B) The extent to which the offense occurred despite the existence of policies and procedures within the national bank, Federal branch, or Federal agency which were designed to prevent the occurrence of any such offense.

(C) The extent to which the national bank, Federal branch, or Federal agency has fully cooperated with law enforcement authorities with respect to the investigation of the money laundering offense of which the bank, Federal branch, or Federal agency was found guilty.

(D) The extent to which the national bank, Federal branch, or Federal agency has implemented additional internal controls (since the commission of the offense of which the bank, Federal branch, or Federal agency was found guilty) to prevent the occurrence of any other money laundering offense.

(E) The extent to which the interest of the local community in having adequate deposit and credit services available would be threatened by the forfeiture of the franchise.

(3) Successor liability

This subsection shall not apply to a successor to the interests of, or a person who acquires, a bank, a Federal branch, or a Federal agency that violated a provision of law described in paragraph (1), if the successor succeeds to the interests of the violator, or the acquisition is made, in good faith and not for purposes of evading this subsection or regulations prescribed under this subsection.

(4) Definition

The term "senior executive officer" has the same meaning as in regulations prescribed under section 1831i(f) of this title.

(d) Authority

The Comptroller of the Currency may act in the Comptroller's own name and through the Comptroller's own attorneys in enforcing any provision of title 62 of the Revised Statutes, regulations thereunder, or any other law or regulation, or in any action, suit, or proceeding to which the Comptroller of the Currency is a party.

§ 93a. Authority to prescribe rules and regulations

Except to the extent that authority to issue such rules and regulations has been expressly and exclusively granted to another regulatory agency, the Comptroller of the Currency is authorized to prescribe rules and regulations to carry out the responsibilities of the office, except that the authority conferred by this section does not apply to section 36 of this title or to securities activities of National Banks under the Act commonly known as the "Glass–Steagall Act".

§ 94. Venue of suits

Any action or proceeding against a national banking association for which the Federal Deposit Insurance Corporation has been appointed receiver, or against the Federal Deposit Insurance Corporation as receiver of such association, shall be brought in the district or territorial court of the United States held within the district in which that association's principal place of business is located, or, in the event any State, county, or municipal court has jurisdiction over such an action or proceeding, in such court in the county or city in which that association's principal place of business is located.

§ 94a. Repealed. June 25, 1948, c. 646, § 39, 62 Stat. 992, eff. Sept. 1, 1948

§ 95. Emergency limitations and restrictions on business of members of Federal reserve system; designation of legal holiday for national banking associations; exceptions; "State" defined

(a) In order to provide for the safer and more effective operation of the National Banking System and the Federal Reserve System, to preserve for the people the full benefits of the currency provided for by the Congress through the National Banking System and the Federal Reserve System, and to relieve interstate commerce of the burdens and obstructions resulting from the receipt on an unsound or unsafe basis of deposits subject to withdrawal by check, during such emergency period as the President of the United States by proclamation may prescribe, no member bank of the Federal Reserve System shall transact any banking business except to such extent and subject to such regulations, limitations and restrictions as may be prescribed by the Secretary of the Treasury, with the approval of the President. Any individual, partnership, corporation, or association, or any director, officer or employee thereof, violating any of the provisions of this section shall be deemed guilty of a misdemeanor and, upon conviction thereof, shall be fined not more than $10,000 or, if a natural person, may, in addition to such fine, be imprisoned for a term not exceeding ten years. Each day that any such violation continues shall be deemed a separate offense.

(b) (1) In the event of natural calamity, riot, insurrection, war, or other emergency conditions occurring in any State whether caused by acts of nature or of man, the Comptroller of the Currency may designate by proclamation any day a legal holiday for the national banking associations located in that State. In the event that the emergency conditions affect only part of a State, the Comptroller of the Currency may designate the part so affected and may proclaim a legal holiday for the national banking associations located in that affected part. In the event that a State or a State official authorized by law designates any day as a legal holiday for ceremonial or emergency reasons, for the State or any part thereof, that same day shall be a legal holiday for all national banking associations or their offices located in that State or the part so affected. A national banking association or its affected offices may close or remain open on such a State-designated holiday unless the Comptroller of the Currency by written order directs otherwise.

(2) For the purpose of this subsection, the term "State" means any of the several States, the District of Columbia, the Commonwealth of Puerto Rico, the Northern Mariana Islands, Guam, the Virgin Islands, American Samoa, the Trust Territory of the Pacific Islands, or any other territory or possession of the United States.

§ 95a. Regulation of transactions in foreign exchange of gold and silver; property transfers; vested interests, enforcement and penalties

(1) During the time of war, the President may, through any agency that he may designate, and under such rules and regulations as he may prescribe, by means of instructions, licenses, or otherwise—

(A) investigate, regulate, or prohibit, any transactions in foreign exchange, transfers of credit or payments between, by, through, or to any banking institution, and the importing, exporting, hoarding, melting, or earmarking of gold or silver coin or bullion, currency or securities, and

(B) investigate, regulate, direct and compel, nullify, void, prevent or prohibit, any acquisition holding, withholding, use, transfer, withdrawal, transportation, importation or exportation of, or dealing in, or exercising any right, power, or privilege with respect to, or transactions involving, any property in which any foreign country or a national thereof has any interest, by any person, or with respect to any property, subject to the jurisdiction of the United States; and any property or interest of any foreign country or national thereof shall vest, when, as, and upon the terms, directed by the President, in such agency or person as may be designated from time to time by the President, and upon such terms and conditions as the President may prescribe such interest or property shall be held, used, administered, liquidated, sold, or otherwise dealt with in the interest of and for the benefit of the United States, and such designated agency or person may perform any and all acts incident to the accomplishment or furtherance of these purposes; and the President shall, in the manner hereinabove provided, require any person to keep a full record of, and to furnish under oath, in the form of reports or otherwise, complete information relative to any act or transaction referred to in this subdivision either before, during, or after the completion thereof, or relative to any interest in foreign property, or relative to any property in which any foreign country or any national thereof has or has had any interest, or as may be otherwise necessary to enforce the provisions of this subdivision, and in any case in which a report could be required, the President may, in the manner hereinabove provided, require the production, or if necessary to the national security or defense, the seizure, of any books of account, records, contracts, letters, memoranda, or other papers, in the custody or control of such person.

(2) Any payment, conveyance, transfer, assignment, or delivery of property or interest therein, made to or for the account of the United States, or as otherwise directed, pursuant to this section or any rule, regulation, instruction, or direction issued hereunder shall to the extent thereof be a full acquittance and discharge for all purposes of the obligation of the person making the same; and no person shall be held liable in any court for or in respect to anything done or omitted in good faith in connection with the administration

of, or in pursuance of and in reliance on, this section, or any rule, regulation, instruction, or direction issued hereunder.

(3) As used in this section the term "United States" means the United States and any place subject to the jurisdiction thereof; *Provided, however,* That the foregoing shall not be construed as a limitation upon the power of the President, which is hereby conferred, to prescribe from time to time, definitions, not inconsistent with the purposes of this section, for any or all of the terms used in this section. As used in this section the term "person" means an individual, partnership, association, or corporation.

(4) The authority granted to the President by this section does not include the authority to regulate or prohibit, directly or indirectly, the importation from any country, or the exportation to any country, whether commercial or otherwise, regardless of format or medium of transmission, of any information or informational materials, including but not limited to, publications, films, posters, phonograph records, photographs, microfilms, microfiche, tapes, compact disks, CD ROMs, artworks, and news wire feeds. The exports exempted from regulation or prohibition by this paragraph do not include those which are otherwise controlled for export under section 2404 of the Appendix to Title 50, or under section 2405 of the Appendix to Title 50 to the extent that such controls promote the nonproliferation or antiterrorism policies of the United States, or with respect to which acts are prohibited by chapter 37 of Title 18. ·

§ 95b. Ratification of acts of President and Secretary of Treasury under section 95a

The actions, regulations, rules, licenses, orders and proclamations heretofore or hereafter taken, promulgated, made, or issued by the President of the United States or the Secretary of the Treasury since March 4, 1933, pursuant to the authority conferred by section 95a of this title, are approved and confirmed.

§§ 101, 101a, 102–110, 121. Repealed. Pub.L. 103–325, Title VI, § 602(e)-(g), Sept. 23, 1994, 108 Stat. 2292–2294

§ 121a. Redemption of notes unidentifiable as to bank of issue

Whenever any Federal Reserve bank notes or Federal Reserve notes are presented to the Trea-

surer of the United States for redemption and such notes cannot be identified as to the bank of issue or the bank through which issued, the Treasurer of the United States may redeem such notes under such rules and regulations as the Secretary of the Treasury may prescribe.

§ 122. Repealed. Pub.L. 97–258, § 5(b), Sept. 13, 1982, 96 Stat. 1069

§ 122a. Redeemed notes of unidentifiable issue; funds charged against

Federal Reserve bank notes redeemed by the Treasurer of the United States under section 121a of this title shall be charged against the balance of deposits for the retirement of Federal Reserve bank notes under the provisions of sections 122 and 445 of this title; and charges for Federal Reserve notes redeemed by the Treasurer of the United States under section 121a of this title shall be apportioned among the twelve Federal Reserve banks as determined by the Board of Governors of the Federal Reserve System.

§§ 123–126. Repealed. Pub.L. 103–325, Title VI, § 602(e)-(f), Sept. 23, 1994, 108 Stat. 2292–2293

§ 127. Repealed. Pub.L. 89–554, § 8(a), Sept. 6, 1966, 80 Stat. 633

§§ 131–138. Repealed. Pub.L. 103–325, Title VI, § 602(e), Sept. 23, 1994, 108 Stat. 2292

§ 141. Central reserve and reserve cities; designation

The cities of New York and Chicago are designated as central reserve cities, and the following cities are designated as reserve cities:

Boston, Louisville, St. Louis, Albany Memphis, Lincoln, Brooklyn and Bronx, Nashville, Omaha, Buffalo, Cincinnati, Kansas City, Kans., Philadelphia, Cleveland, Topeka, Pittsburgh, Columbus, Wichita, Baltimore, Toledo, Helena, Washington, Indianapolis, Denver, Richmond, Chicago , Pueblo, Atlanta, Peoria, Muskogee, Jacksonville, Detroit, Oklahoma City, Birmingham, Grand Rapids, Tulsa, New Orleans, Milwaukee, Savannah, Dallas, Minneapolis, Seattle, El Paso, St. Paul, Spokane, Fort Worth, Cedar Rapids, Portland, Galveston, Des Moines, Los Angeles, Houston, Dubuque, Oakland, San Antonio, Sioux City, San

Francisco, Waco, Kansas City, Mo. Ogden, Little Rock, St. Joseph, Salt Lake City.

The Board of Governors of the Federal Reserve System may at any time reclassify cities so designated as reserve and central reserve cities, may add to the number so classified, or terminate the designation of any cities as such.

§ 142. Banks in reserve cities; reserves

National banking associations located in reserve cities or central reserve cities shall maintain reserves provided for in section 462 of this title for banks so located.

§ 143. Banks in Alaska and insular possessions; lawful money reserves

Every national banking association located in Alaska or in a dependency or insular possession or any part of the United States outside of the continental United States, and not a member of the Federal Reserve System, shall at all times have on hand in lawful money of the United States an amount equal to at least 15 percent of the aggregate amount of its deposits in all respects. Whenever the lawful money of any such association shall fall below 15 percent of its deposits such association shall not increase its liabilities by making any new loans or discounts other than by discounting or purchasing bills of exchange payable at sight nor make any dividends of its profits until the required proportion between the aggregate amount of its deposits and its lawful money of the United States has been restored. And the Comptroller of the Currency shall notify any such association whose lawful money reserve shall be below the amount required to be kept on hand to make good such reserve, and if such association shall fail for thirty days thereafter so to make good its lawful money the Comptroller may, with the concurrence of the Secretary of the Treasury, appoint a receiver to wind up the business of the association as provided in section 192 of this title.

§ 144. Certain balances counted toward reserves in dependencies and insular possessions

Four-fifths of the reserve of 15 per centum which a national bank located in a dependency or insular possession or any part of the United States outside of the continental United States, and not a member of the Federal Reserve System, is required to keep, may consist of balances due such bank from associations approved by the Comptroller of the Currency and located in any one of the reserve cities as now or hereafter defined by law or designated by the Board of Governors of the Federal Reserve System.

§§ 145, 146. Repealed. Pub.L. 97–258, § 5(b), Sept. 13, 1982, 96 Stat. 1069

§ 151–153. Repealed. Pub.L. 103–325, Title VI, § 602(e)(f), Sept. 23, 1994, 108 Stat. 2292–2293

§ 161. Reports to Comptroller of the Currency

(a) Reports of condition; forms; contents; date of making; publication

Every association shall make reports of condition to the Comptroller of the Currency in accordance with the Federal Deposit Insurance Act [12 U.S.C.A. § 1811 et seq.]. The Comptroller of the Currency may call for additional reports of condition, in such form and containing such information as he may prescribe, on dates to be fixed by him, and may call for special reports from any particular association whenever in his judgment the same are necessary for his use in the performance of his supervisory duties. Each report of condition shall contain a declaration by the president, a vice president, the cashier, or by any other officer designated by the board of directors of the bank to make such declaration, that the report is true and correct to the best of his knowledge and belief. The correctness of the report of condition shall be attested by the signatures of at least three of the directors of the bank other than the officer making such declaration, with the declaration that the report has been examined by them and to the best of their knowledge and belief is true and correct. Each report shall exhibit in detail and under appropriate heads the resources and liabilities of the association at the close of business on any past day specified by the Comptroller, and shall be transmitted to the Comptroller within the period of time specified by the Comptroller. Special reports called for by the Comptroller need contain only such information as is specified by the Comptroller in his request therefor, and publication of such reports need be made only if directed by the Comptroller.

(b) Payment of dividends

Every association shall make to the Comptroller reports of the payment of dividends, including advance reports of dividends proposed to be declared or paid in such cases and under such conditions as the Comptroller deems necessary to carry out the purposes of the laws relating to national banking associations in such form and at such times as he may require.

(c) Reports of affiliates; form; contents; date of making; publication; penalties

Each national banking association shall obtain from each of its affiliates other than member banks and furnish to the Comptroller of the Currency not less than four reports during each year, in such form as the Comptroller may prescribe, verified by the oath or affirmation of the president or such other officer as may be designated by the board of directors of such affiliate to verify such reports, disclosing the information hereinafter provided for as of dates identical with those for which the Comptroller shall during such year require the reports of the condition of the association. Each such report of an affiliate shall be transmitted to the Comptroller at the same time as the corresponding report of the association, except that the Comptroller may, in his discretion, extend such time for good cause shown. Each such report shall contain such information as in the judgment of the Comptroller of the Currency shall be necessary to disclose fully the relations between such affiliate and such bank and to enable the Comptroller to inform himself as to the effect of such relations upon the affairs of such bank. The Comptroller shall also have power to call for additional reports with respect to any such affiliate whenever in his judgment the same are necessary in order to obtain a full and complete knowledge of the conditions of the association with which it is affiliated. Such additional reports shall be transmitted to the Comptroller of the Currency in such form as he may prescribe.

§ 162. Repealed. Pub.L. 86–671, § 6, July 14, 1960, 74 Stat. 552

§ 163. Repealed. Pub.L. 86–230, § 22(a), Sept. 8, 1959, 73 Stat. 466

§ 164. Penalty for failure to make reports.

(a) First tier

Any association which—

(1) maintains procedures reasonably adapted to avoid any inadvertent error and, unintentionally and as a result of such an error—

(A) fails to make, obtain, transmit, or publish any report or information required by the Comptroller of the Currency under section 161 of this title, within the period of time specified by the Comptroller; or

(B) submits or publishes any false or misleading report or information; or

(2) inadvertently transmits or publishes any report which is minimally late,

shall be subject to a penalty of not more than $2,000 for each day during which such failure continues or such false or misleading information is not corrected. The association shall have the burden of proving that an error was inadvertent and that a report was inadvertently transmitted or published late.

(b) Second tier

Any association which—

(1) fails to make, obtain, transmit, or publish any report or information required by the Comptroller of the Currency under section 161 of this title, within the period of time specified by the Comptroller; or

(2) submits or publishes any false or misleading report or information,

in a manner not described in subsection (a) of this section shall be subject to a penalty of not more than $20,000 for each day during which such failure continues or such false or misleading information is not corrected.

(c) Third tier

Notwithstanding subsections (a) and (b) of this section, if any association knowingly or with reckless disregard for the accuracy of any information or report described in subsection (b) of this section submits or publishes any false or misleading report or information, the Comptroller may assess a penalty of not more than $1,000,000 or 1 percent of total assets of the association, whichever is less, per day for each day during which such failure continues or such false or misleading information is not corrected.

(d) Assessment; etc.

Any penalty imposed under subsection (a), (b), or (c) of this section shall be assessed and collected by the Comptroller of the Currency in the manner provided in subparagraphs (E), (F), (G), and (I) of section 1818(i)(2) of this title (for penalties imposed under such section) and any such assessment (including the determination of the amount of the penalty) shall be subject to the provisions of such section.

(e) Hearing

Any association against which any penalty is assessed under this subsection shall be afforded an agency hearing if such association submits a request for such hearing within 20 days after the issuance of the notice of assessment. Section 1818(h) of this title shall apply to any proceeding under this section.

§ 165. Omitted

§ 168–177. Repealed. Pub.L. 103–325, Title VI, § 602(e)-(f), Sept. 23, 1994, 108 Stat. 2292–2293

§ 177a. Funds available for cost of transporting and redeeming national and Federal Reserve bank notes

The cost of transporting and redeeming outstanding national bank notes and Federal Reserve bank notes as may be presented to the Treasurer of the United States for redemption shall be paid from the regular annual appropriation for the Department of the Treasury.

§ 178. Repealed. Pub.L. 103–325, Title VI, § 602(f)(5)(B), Sept. 23, 1994, 108 Stat. 2293

§ 181. Voluntary dissolution; appointment and removal of liquidating agent or committee; examination

Any association may go into liquidation and be closed by the vote of its shareholders owning two-thirds of its stock. If the liquidation is to be effected in whole or in part through the sale of any of its assets to and the assumption of its deposit liabilities by another bank, the purchase and sale agreement must also be approved by its shareholders owning two-thirds of its stock unless an emergency exists and the Comptroller of the Currency specifically waives such requirement for shareholder approval.

The shareholders shall designate one or more persons to act as liquidating agent or committee, who shall conduct the liquidation in accordance with law and under the supervision of the board

of directors, who shall require a suitable bond to be given by said agent or committee. The liquidating agent or committee shall render annual reports to the Comptroller of the Currency on the 31st day of December of each year showing the progress of said liquidation until the same is completed. The liquidating agent or committee shall also make an annual report to a meeting of the shareholders to be held on the date fixed in the articles of association for the annual meeting, at which meeting the shareholders may, if they see fit, by a vote representing a majority of the entire stock of the bank, remove the liquidating agent or committee and appoint one or more others in place thereof. A special meeting of the shareholders may be called at any time in the same manner as if the bank continued an active bank and at said meeting the shareholders may, by vote of the majority of the stock, remove the liquidating agent or committee. The Comptroller of the Currency is authorized to have an examination made at any time into the affairs of the liquidating bank until the claims of all creditors have been satisfied, and the expense of making such examinations shall be assessed against such bank in the same manner as in the case of examinations made pursuant to subchapter XV of chapter 3 of this title.

§ 182. Notice of intent to dissolve

Whenever a vote is taken to go into liquidation it shall be the duty of the board of directors to cause notice of this fact to be certified, under the seal of the association, by its president or cashier, to the Comptroller of the Currency, and publication thereof to be made for a period of two months in every issue of a newspaper published in the city or town in which the association is located, or if no newspaper is there published, then in the newspaper published nearest thereto, that the association is closing up its affairs, and notifying its creditors to present their claims against the association for payment.

§ 183–186. Repealed. Pub.L. 103–325, Title VI, § 602(e), Sept. 23, 1994, 108 Stat. 2292

§ 191. Appointment of receiver for a National bank

(a) In general

The Comptroller of the Currency may, without prior notice or hearings, appoint a receiver for any national bank (and such receiver shall be the Federal Deposit Insurance Corporation if the national bank is an insured bank (as defined in section 1813(h) of this title)) if the Comptroller determines, in the Comptroller's discretion, that—

(1) 1 or more of the grounds specified in section 1821(c)(5) of this title exist; or

(2) the association's board of directors consists of fewer than 5 members.

(b) Judicial review

If the Comptroller of the Currency appoints a receiver under subsection (a) of this section, the national bank may, within 30 days thereafter, bring an action in the United States district court for the judicial district in which the home office of such bank is located, or in the United States District Court for the District of Columbia, for an order requiring the Comptroller of the Currency to remove the receiver, and the court shall, upon the merits, dismiss such action or direct the Comptroller of the Currency to remove the receiver.

§ 192. Default in payment of circulating notes

On becoming satisfied, as specified in sections 131 and 132 of this title, that any association is in default, the Comptroller of the Currency may forthwith appoint a receiver, and require of him such bond and security as he deems proper. Such receiver, under the direction of the Comptroller, shall take possession of the books, records, and assets of every description of such association, collect all debts, dues, and claims belonging to it, and, upon the order of a court of record of competent jurisdiction, may sell or compound all bad or doubtful debts, and, on a like order, may sell all the real and personal property of such association, on such terms as the court shall direct. Such receiver shall pay over all money so made to the Treasurer of the United States, subject to the order of the Comptroller, and also make report to the Comptroller of all his acts and proceedings. *Provided,* That the Comptroller may, if he deems proper, deposit any of the money so made in any regular Government depositary, or in any State or national bank either of the city or town in which the insolvent bank was located, or of a city or town as adjacent thereto as practicable; if such deposit is made he shall require the depositary to deposit United States bonds or other satisfactory securities with the Treasurer of the United States for the safekeeping and prompt payment of the money so deposited: *Provided,* That no security in the form of deposit of United States bonds, or otherwise, shall be required in the case of such parts of the deposits as are insured under section 12B of the Federal Reserve Act, as amended. Such depositary shall pay upon such money interest at such rate as the Comptroller may prescribe, not less, however, than 2 per centum per annum upon the average monthly amount of such deposits.

§ 193. Notice to present claims

The Comptroller shall, upon appointing a receiver, cause notice to be given, by advertisement in such newspapers as he may direct, for three consecutive months, calling on all persons who may have claims against such association to present the same, and to make legal proof thereof.

§ 194. Dividends on adjusted claims; distribution of assets

From time to time, the comptroller shall make a ratable dividend of the money so paid over to him by such receiver on all such claims as may have been proved to his satisfaction or adjudicated in a court of competent jurisdiction, and, as the proceeds of the assets of such association are paid over to him, shall make further dividends on all claims previously proved or adjudicated; and the remainder of the proceeds, if any, shall be paid over to the shareholders of such association, or their legal representatives, in proportion to the stock by them respectively held.

§ 195. Repealed. Pub.L. 103–325, Title VI, § 602(e)(36), Sept. 23, 1994, 108 Stat. 2292

§ 196. Expenses

All expenses of any preliminary or other examinations into the condition of any association shall be paid by such association. All expenses of any receivership shall be paid out of the assets of such association before distribution of the proceeds thereof.

§ 197. Shareholders' meeting; continuance of receivership; appointment of agent; winding up business; distribution of assets

(a) Whenever any national banking association shall have been or shall be placed in the hands of a receiver, as provided in section fifty-two hundred and thirty-four [12 U.S.C.A. § 192] and other sections of the Revised Statutes of the United States and section 1821(c) of this title, and when, as provided in section 194 of this title, there has been paid to each and every creditor of such association whose claim or claims as such creditor shall have been proved or allowed as therein prescribed, the full amount of such claims, and all expenses of the receivership, the Comptroller of the Currency or the Federal Deposit Insurance Corporation, where that Corporation has been appointed receiver of the bank, shall call a meeting of the shareholders of the association by giving notice thereof for thirty days in a newspaper published in the town, city, or county where the business of the association was carried on, or if no newspaper is there published, in the newspaper published nearest thereto. At such meeting the shareholders shall determine whether the receiver shall be continued and shall wind up the affairs of the association, or whether an agent shall be elected for that purpose, and in so determining the shareholders shall vote by ballot, in person or by proxy, each share of stock entitling the holder to one vote, and the majority of the stock in number of shares shall be necessary to determine whether the receiver shall be continued, or whether an agent shall be elected. In case such majority shall determine that the receiver shall be continued, the receiver shall thereupon proceed with the execution of the trust, and shall sell, dispose of, or otherwise collect the assets of the association, and shall possess all the powers and authority, and be subject to all the duties and liabilities originally conferred or imposed upon such receiver so far as they remain applicable. In case such meeting shall, by the vote of a majority of the stock in number of shares, determine that an agent shall be elected, the meeting shall thereupon proceed to elect an agent, voting by ballot, in person or by proxy, each share of stock entitling the holder to one vote, and the person who shall receive votes representing at least a majority of stock in number of shares shall be declared the agent for the purposes hereinafter provided; and when such agent shall have executed a bond to the shareholders conditioned for the payment and discharge in full or, to the extent possible from the remaining assets of the association, of each and every claim that may thereafter be proved and allowed by and before a competent court and for the faithful performance of his duties, in the penalty fixed by the shareholders at such meeting, with a surety or sureties to be approved by the district court of the United States for the district where the business of the association was carried on, and shall have filed such bond in the office of the clerk of such court, the Comptroller and the receiver, or the Federal Deposit Insurance Corporation, where that Corporation has been appointed receiver of the bank, shall thereupon transfer and deliver to such agent all the uncollected or other assets of the association then remaining in the hands or subject to the order and control of the Comptroller and such receiver, or either of them, or the Federal Deposit Insurance Corporation; and for this purpose the Comptroller and such receiver, or the Federal Deposit Insurance Corporation, as the case may be, are severally empowered and directed to execute any deed, assignment, transfer, or other instrument in writing that may be necessary and proper; and upon the execution and delivery of such instrument to such agent the Comptroller and such receiver or the Federal Deposit Insurance Corporation shall by virtue of this Act be discharged from any and all liabilities to the association and to each and all the creditors and shareholders thereof.

(b) Upon receiving such deed, assignment, transfer, or other instrument the person elected such agent shall hold, control, and dispose of the assets and property of the association which he may receive under the terms hereof for the benefit of the shareholders of the association, and he may in his own name, or in the name of the association, sue and be sued and do all other lawful acts and things necessary to finally settle and distribute the assets and property in his hands, and may sell, compromise, or compound the debts due to the association, with the consent and approval of the district court of the United States for the district where the business of the association was carried on, and shall at the conclusion of his trust render to such district court a full account of all his proceedings, receipts, and expenditures as such agent, which court shall, upon due notice, settle and adjust such accounts and discharge such agent and sureties upon such bond. In case any such agent so elected shall die, resign, or be removed, any shareholder may call a meeting of the shareholders of the association in the town, city, or village where the business of the association was carried on, by giving notice thereof for thirty days in a newspaper published in such town, city, or village, or if no newspaper is there published, in the newspaper published nearest thereto, at which meeting the shareholders shall elect an agent, voting by ballot, in person or by proxy, each share of stock entitling the holder to one vote, and when such agent shall have received votes representing at least a majority of the stock in number of shares, and shall have executed a bond to the shareholders conditioned for the payment and discharge in full or, to the extent possible from the remaining assets of the association, of each and every claim that may thereafter be proved and allowed by and before a competent court and for the faithful performance of his duties, in the penalty fixed by the shareholders at such meeting, with a surety or sureties, to be approved by such court, and file such bond in the office of the clerk of that court, he shall have all the rights, powers, and duties of the agent first elected as hereinbefore provided. At any meeting held as hereinbefore provided administrators or executors of deceased shareholders may act and sign as the decedent might have done if living, and guardians of minors and trustees of other persons may so act and sign for their ward or wards or cestui que trust. The proceeds of the assets or property of any such association which may be undistributed at the time of such meeting or may be subsequently received shall be distributed as follows:

First. To pay the expenses of the execution of the trust to the date of such payment.

Second. To repay any amount or amounts which have been paid in by any shareholder or shareholders of the association upon and by reason of any and all assessments made upon the stock of the association by order of the Comptroller of the Currency in accordance with the provisions of the statutes of the United States.

Third. To pay the balance ratably among such stockholders, in proportion to the number of shares held and owned by each. Such distribution shall be made from time to time as the proceeds shall be received and as shall be deemed advisable by the Comptroller of the Currency, or the Federal Deposit Insurance Corporation if continued as receiver of the bank under subsection (a) of this section, or such agent, as the case may be.

§ 197a. Resumption of business by closed bank on consent of depositors

In any case in which, in the opinion of the Comptroller of the Currency, it would be to the advantage of the depositors and unsecured creditors of any national banking association whose business has been closed, for such association to resume business upon the retention by the association, for a reasonable period to be prescribed by the Comptroller, of all or any part of its deposits, the Comptroller is authorized, in his discretion, to permit the association to resume business if depositors and unsecured creditors of the association representing at least 75 per centum of its total deposit and unsecured credit liabilities consent in writing to such retention of deposits. Nothing in this section shall be construed to affect in any manner any powers of the Comptroller under the provisions of law in force on June 16, 1933, with respect to the reorganization of national banking associations.

§ 198. Purchase by receiver of property of bank; request to Comptroller

Whenever the receiver of any national bank duly appointed by the Comptroller of the Currency, and who shall have duly qualified and entered upon the discharge of his trust, shall find it in his opinion necessary, in order to fully protect and benefit his said trust, to the extent of any and all equities that such trust may have in any property, real or personal, by reason of any bond, mortgage, assignment, or other proper legal claim attaching thereto, and which said property is to be sold under any execution, decree of foreclosure, or proper order of any court of jurisdiction, he may certify the facts in the case, together with his opinion as to the value of the property to be sold, and the value of the equity his said trust may have in the same, to the Comptroller of the Currency, together with a request for the right and authority to use and employ so much of the money of said trust as may be necessary to purchase such property at such sale.

§ 199. Approval of request

Such request, if approved by the Comptroller of the Currency, shall be, together with the certificate of facts in the case, and his recommendation as to the amount of money which, in his judgment, should be so used and employed, submitted to the Secretary of the Treasury, and if the same shall likewise be approved by him, the request shall be by the Comptroller of the Currency allowed, and notice thereof, with copies of the request, certificate of facts, and indorsement of approvals, shall be filed with the Treasurer of the United States.

§ 200. Payment

Whenever any such request shall be allowed as hereinbefore provided, the said Comptroller of the Currency shall be, and is, empowered to draw upon and from such funds of any such trust as may be deposited with the Treasurer of the United States for the benefit of the bank in interest, to the amount as may be recommended and allowed and for the purpose for which such allowance was made: *Provided, however,* That all payments to be made for or on account of the purchase of any such property and under any such allowance shall be made by the Comptroller of the Currency direct, with the approval of the Secretary of the Treasury, for such purpose only and in such manner as he may determine and order.

§ 201. Short title

This subchapter may be cited as the "Bank Conservation Act."

§ 202. Definitions

As used in this subchapter, the term "bank" means any national banking association or any other financial institution chartered or licensed under Federal law and subject to the supervision of the Comptroller of the Currency; the term "voluntary dissolution and liquidation" means a transaction pursuant to section 181 of this title that involves the assumption of the bank's insured deposit liabilities and the sale of the bank, or of control of the bank, as a going concern; and the term "State" means any State, Territory, or possession of the United States, and the Canal Zone.

§ 203. Appointment of conservator

(a) Appointment

The Comptroller of the Currency may, without prior notice or hearings, appoint a conservator (which may be the Federal Deposit Insurance Corporation) to the possession and control of a bank whenever the Comptroller of the Currency determines that 1 or more of the grounds specified in section 11(c)(5) of the Federal Deposit Insurance Act [12 U.S.C.A. § 1821(c)(5)] exist.

(b) Judicial review

(1) In general

Not later than 20 days after the initial appointment of a conservator pursuant to this section, the bank may bring an action in the United States district court for the judicial district in which the home office of such bank is located, or in the United States District Court for the District of Columbia, for an order requiring the Comptroller to terminate the appointment of the conservator, and the court, upon the merits, shall dismiss such action or shall direct the Comptroller to terminate the appointment of such conservator. The Comptroller's decision to appoint a conservator pursuant to this section shall be set aside only if the court finds that such decision was arbitrary, capricious, an abuse of discretion, or otherwise not in accordance with law.

(2) Stay

The conservator may request that any judicial action or proceeding to which the conservator or the bank is or may become a party be stayed for a period of up to 45 days after the appointment of the conservator. Upon petition, the court shall grant such stay as to all parties.

(3) Actions and orders

Except as otherwise provided in this subsection, no court may take any action regarding the removal of a conservator, or restrain, or affect the exercise of powers or functions of a conservator. A court, upon application by the Comptroller, shall have jurisdiction to enforce an order of the Comptroller relating to—

   (A) the conservatorship and the bank in conservatorship, or

   (B) restraining or affecting the exercise of powers or functions of a conservator.

(c) Additional grounds for appointment

In addition to the foregoing provisions, the Comptroller may appoint a conservator for a bank if—

   (1) the bank, by an affirmative vote of a majority of its board of directors or by an affirmative vote of a majority of its shareholders, consents to such appointment, or

   (2) the Federal Deposit Insurance Corporation terminates the bank's status as an insured bank.

The appointment of a conservator pursuant to this subsection shall not be subject to review.

(d) Exclusive authority

The Comptroller shall have exclusive power and jurisdiction to appoint a conservator for a bank. Whenever the Comptroller appoints a conservator for any bank, the Comptroller may appoint the Federal Deposit Insurance Corporation conservator for such bank. The Federal Deposit Insurance Corporation, as such conservator, shall have all the powers granted under the Federal Deposit Insurance Act [12 U.S.C.A. § 1811 et seq.], and (when not inconsistent therewith) any other rights, powers, and privileges possessed by conservators of banks under this Act and any other provision of law. The Comptroller may also appoint another person as conservator, who shall be subject to the provisions of this Act.

(e) Replacement of conservator

The Comptroller may, without notice or hearing, replace a conservator with another conservator. Such replacement shall not affect the bank's right under subsection (b) of this section to obtain judicial review of the Comptroller's original decision to appoint a conservator.

§ 204. Examinations

The Comptroller of the Currency (in consultation with the Board of Directors of the Federal Deposit Insurance Corporation when the Corporation is appointed conservator) is authorized to examine and supervise the bank in conservatorship as long as the bank continues to operate as a going concern. The Comptroller may use reports and other information provided by the Federal Deposit Insurance Corporation for this purpose.

§ 205. Termination of conservatorship

(a) General rule

At any time the Comptroller becomes satisfied that it may safely be done and that it would be in the public interest, the Comptroller (with the agreement of the Board of Directors of the Federal Deposit Insurance Corporation when the Corporation has been appointed conservator) may—

(1) terminate the conservatorship and permit the involved bank to resume the transaction of its business subject to such terms, conditions, and limitations as the Comptroller may prescribe; or

(2) terminate the conservatorship upon a sale, merger, consolidation, purchase and assumption, change in control, or voluntary dissolution and liquidation of the involved bank.

(b) Other grounds for termination

The Comptroller also may terminate the conservatorship upon the appointment of a receiver pursuant to section 191 of this title.

(c) Enforcement under Federal Deposit Insurance Act

Such terms, conditions, and limitations as may be prescribed under subsection (a)(1) of this section shall be enforceable under the provisions of section 8(i) of the Federal Deposit Insurance Act [12 U.S.C.A. § 1818(i)], to the same extent as an order issued pursuant to section 8(b) of the Federal Deposit Insurance Act [12 U.S.C.A. § 1818(b)] which has become final. The bank may bring an action in the United States district court for the judicial district in which the home office of such bank is located or in the United States District Court for the District of Columbia for an order requiring the Comptroller to terminate the order. An action for judicial review of the terms, conditions, and limitations may not be commenced later than 20 days from the date of the termination of the conservatorship or the imposition of the order, whichever is later.

(d) Action upon termination

(1) In general

Upon termination of the conservatorship under subsection (a)(2) of this section, the Federal Deposit Insurance Corporation, as conservator, or when another person is appointed conservator, such other person, shall conclude the affairs of the conservatorship in accordance with paragraph (2).

(2) Deposit and distribution of proceeds

(A) Within 180 days of the sale, merger, consolidation, purchase and assumption, change in control, or voluntary dissolution and liquidation, the conservator shall deposit all net proceeds received from the transaction, less any outstanding expenses of the conservatorship, with the United States district court for the judicial district in which the home office of such bank is located and shall cause notice to be published for three consecutive months and notify by mail all known and remaining creditors and shareholders. Within 60 days thereafter, any depositor, creditor, or other claimant of the bank, or any shareholder of the bank may bring an action in interpleader in that court for distribution of the proceeds. The district court shall distribute such funds equitably. If no such action is instituted within one year after the date the funds are deposited with the district court, title to such net proceeds shall revert to the United States and the district court shall remit the funds to the Treasury of the United States.

(B) The conservator shall be deemed to have discharged all responsibility of the conservatorship upon the deposit of the proceeds with the district court and giving the required notifications.

§ 206. Conservator; powers and duties

(a) General powers

A conservator shall have all the powers of the shareholders, directors, and officers of the bank and may operate the bank in its own name unless the Comptroller in the order of appointment limits the conservator's authority.

(b) Subject to rules of Comptroller

The conservator shall be subject to such rules, regulations, and orders as the Comptroller from time to time deems appropriate; and, except as otherwise specifically provided in such rules, regulations, or orders or in section 209 of this title, shall have the same rights and privileges and be subject to the same duties, restrictions, penalties, conditions, and limitations as apply to directors, officers, or employees of a national bank.

(c) Payment of depositors and creditors

The Comptroller may require the conservator to set aside and make available for withdrawal by depositors and payment to other creditors such amounts as in the opinion of the Comptroller may safely be used for that purpose. All depositors and creditors who are similarly situated shall be treated in the same manner.

(d) Compensation of conservator and employees

The conservator and professional employees appointed to represent or assist the conservator shall not be paid amounts greater than are payable to employees of the Federal Government for similar services, except that the Comptroller of the Currency may authorize payment at higher rates (but not in excess of rates prevailing in the private sector), if the Comptroller determines that paying such higher rates is necessary in order to recruit and retain competent personnel.

(e) Expenses

All expenses of any such conservatorship shall be paid by the bank and shall be a lien upon the bank which shall be prior to any other lien.

§§ 207–208. Repealed. Pub.L. 101–73, Title VIII, § 808, Aug. 9, 1989, 103 Stat. 446

§ 209. Liability protection

(a) Federal agency and employees

In any case in which the conservator is a Federal agency or an employee of the Government, the provisions of chapters 161 and 171 of Title 28 shall apply with respect to such conservator's liability for acts or omissions performed pursuant to and in the course of the duties and responsibilities of the conservatorship.

(b) Other conservators

In any case where the conservator is not a conservator described in subsection (a) of this section, the conservator shall not be liable for damages in tort or otherwise for acts or omissions performed pursuant to and in the course of the duties and responsibilities of the conservatorship, unless such acts or omissions constitute gross negligence, including any similar conduct or any form of intentional tortious conduct, as determined by a court.

(c) Indemnification

The Comptroller shall have authority to indemnify the conservator on such terms as the Comptroller deems proper.

§ 210. Governmental powers unimpaired

Nothing in this subchapter shall be construed to impair in any manner any powers of the President, the Secretary of the Treasury, the Comptroller of the Currency, or the Board of Governors of the Federal Reserve System.

§ 211. Rules and regulations

(a) In general

The Comptroller of the Currency may prescribe such rules and regulations as the Comptroller may deem necessary to carry out the provisions of this Act.

(b) F.D.I.C. as conservator

In any case in which the Federal Deposit Insurance Corporation is the conservator, any rules or regulations prescribed by the Comptroller shall be consistent with any rules and regulations prescribed by the Federal Deposit Insurance Corporation pursuant to the Federal Deposit Insurance Act [12 U.S.C.A. § 1811 et seq.].

§ 212. Right to amend; separability of provisions

The right to alter, amend, or repeal this Act is expressly reserved. If any provision of this Act, or the application thereof to any person or circumstances, is held invalid, the remainder of the Act, and the application of such provision to other persons or circumstances, shall not be affected thereby.

§ 213. Transferred

§ 214. Definitions

(a) As used in this subchapter and section 321 of this title the term "State bank" means any bank, banking association, trust company, savings bank (other than a mutual savings bank), or other banking institution which is engaged in the business of receiving deposits and which is incorporated under the laws of any State, any Territory of the United States, Puerto Rico, or the Virgin Islands, or which is operating under the Code of Law for the District of Columbia.

(b) For purposes of merger or consolidation under this subchapter and section 321 of this title the term "national banking association" means one or more national banking associations, and the term "State bank" means one or more State banks.

§ 214a. Procedure for conversion, merger, or consolidation; vote of stockholders

A national banking association may, by vote of the holders of at least two-thirds of each class of its capital stock, convert into, or merge or consolidate with, a State bank in the same State in which the national banking association is located, under a State charter, in the following manner:

(a) Approval of board of directors; publication of notice of stockholders' meeting; waiver of publication; notice by registered or certified mail

The plan of conversion, merger, or consolidation must be approved by a majority of the entire board of directors of the national banking association. The bank shall publish notice of the time, place, and object of the shareholders' meeting to act upon the plan, in some newspaper with general circulation in the place where the principal office of the national banking association is located, at least once a week for four consecutive weeks: *Provided,* That newspaper publication may be dispensed with entirely if waived by all the shareholders and in the case of a merger or consolidation one publication at least ten days before the meeting shall be sufficient if publication for four weeks is waived by holders of at least two-thirds of each class of capital stock and prior written consent of the Comptroller of the Currency is obtained. The national banking association shall send such notice to each shareholder of record by registered mail or by certified mail at least ten days prior to the meeting, which notice may be waived specifically by any shareholder.

(b) Rights of dissenting stockholders

A shareholder of a national banking association who votes against the conversion, merger, or consolidation, or who has given notice in writing to the bank at or prior to such meeting that he dissents from the plan, shall be entitled to receive in cash the value of the shares held by him, if and when the conversion, merger, or consolidation is consummated, upon written request made to the resulting State bank at any time before thirty days after the date of consummation of such conversation, merger, or consolidation, accompanied by the surrender of his stock certificates. The value of such shares shall be determined as of the date on which the shareholders' meeting was held authorizing the conversion, merger, or consolidation, by a committee of three persons, one to be selected by majority vote of the dissenting shareholders entitled to receive the value of their shares, one by the directors of the resulting State bank, and the third by the two so chosen. The valuation agreed upon by any two of three appraisers thus chosen shall govern; but, if the value so fixed shall not be satisfactory to any dissenting shareholder who has requested payment as provided herein, such shareholder may within five days after being notified of the appraised value of his shares appeal to the Comptroller of the Currency, who shall cause a reappraisal to be made, which shall be final and binding as to the value of the shares of the appellant. If, within ninety days from the date of consummation of the conversion, merger, or consolidation, for any reason one or more of the appraisers is not selected as herein provided, or the appraisers fail to determine the value of such shares, the Comptroller shall upon written request of any interested party, cause an appraisal to be made, which shall be final and binding on all parties. The expenses of the Comptroller in making the reappraisal, or the appraisal as the case may be, shall be paid by the resulting State bank. The plan of conversion, merger, or consolidation shall provide the manner of disposing of the shares of the resulting State bank not taken by the dissenting shareholders of the national banking association.

§ 214b. Continuation of business and corporate entity

The franchise of a national banking association as a national banking association shall automatically terminate when its conversion into or its merger or consolidation with a State bank under a State charter is consummated and the resulting State bank shall be considered the same business and corporate entity as the national banking association, although as to rights, powers, and duties the resulting bank is a State bank. Any reference to such national banking association in any contract, will, or document shall be considered a reference to the State bank if not inconsistent with the provisions of the contract, will, or document or applicable law.

§ 214c. Conversions in contravention of State law

No conversion of a national banking association into a State bank or its merger or consolidation with a State bank shall take place under this subchapter and section 321 of this title in contravention of the law of the State in which the national banking association is located; and no such conversion, merger, or consolidation shall take place under said sections unless under the law of the State in which such national banking association is located. State banks may without approval by any State authority convert into and merge or consolidate with national banking associations under limitations or conditions no more restrictive than those contained in section 214a of this title with respect to the conversion of a national bank into, or merger or consolidation of a national bank with, a State bank under State charter.

§ 215. Consolidation of banks within the same State

(a) In general

Any national bank or any bank incorporated under the laws of any State may, with the approval of the Comptroller, be consolidated with one or more national banking associations located in the same State under the charter of a national banking association on such terms and conditions as may be lawfully agreed upon by a majority of the board of directors of each association or bank proposing to consolidate, and be ratified and confirmed by the affirmative vote of the shareholders of each such association or bank owning at least two-thirds of its capital stock outstanding, or by a greater proportion of such capital stock in the case of such State bank if the laws of the State where it is organized so require, at a meeting to be held on the call of the directors after publishing notice of the time, place, and object of the meeting for four consecutive weeks in a newspaper of general circulation published in the place where the association or bank is located, or, if there is no such newspaper, then in the paper of general circulation published nearest thereto, and after sending such notice to each shareholder of record by certified or registered mail at least ten days prior to the meeting, except to those shareholders who specifically waive notice, but any additional notice shall be given to the shareholders of such State bank which may be required by the laws of the State where it is organized. Publication of notice may be waived, in cases where the Comptroller determines that an emergency exists justifying such waiver, by unanimous action of the shareholders of the association or State bank.

(b) Liability of consolidated association; capital stock; dissenting shareholders

The consolidated association shall be liable for all liabilities of the respective consolidating banks or associations. The capital stock of such consolidated association shall not be less than that required under existing law for the organization of a national bank in the place in which it is located: *Provided,* That if such consolidation shall be voted for at such meetings by the necessary majorities of the shareholders of each association and State bank proposing to consolidate, and thereafter the consolidation shall be approved by the Comptroller, any shareholder of any of the associations or State banks so consolidated who has voted against such consolidation at the meeting of the association or bank of which he is a stockholder, or who has given notice in writing at or prior to such meeting to the presiding officer that he dissents from the plan of consolidation, shall be entitled to receive the value of the shares so held by him when such consolidation is approved by the Comptroller upon written request made to the consolidated association at any time before thirty days after the date of consummation of the consolidation, accompanied by the surrender of his stock certificates.

(c) Valuation of shares

The value of the shares of any dissenting shareholder shall be ascertained, as of the effective date of the consolidation, by an appraisal made by a committee of three persons, composed of (1) one selected by the vote of the holders of the majority of the stock, the owners of which are entitled to payment in cash; (2) one selected by the directors of the consolidated banking association; and (3) one selected by the two so selected. The valuation agreed upon by any two of the three appraisers shall govern. If the value so fixed shall not be satisfactory to any dissenting shareholder who has requested payment, that shareholder may, within five days after being notified of the appraised value of his shares, appeal to the Comptroller, who shall cause a reappraisal to be made which shall be final and binding as to the value of the shares of the appellant.

(d) Appraisal by Comptroller; expenses of consolidated association; sale and resale of shares; State appraisal and consolidation law

If, within ninety days from the date of consummation of the consolidation, for any reason one or more of the appraisers is not selected as herein provided, or the appraisers fail to determine the value of such shares, the Comptroller shall upon written request of any interested party cause an appraisal to be made which shall be final and binding on all parties. The expenses of the Comptroller in making the reappraisal or the appraisal, as the case may be, shall be paid by the consolidated banking association. The value of the shares ascertained shall be promptly paid to the dissenting shareholders by the consolidated banking association. Within thirty days after payment has been made to all dissenting shareholders as provided for in this section the shares of stock of the consolidated banking association

which would have been delivered to such dissenting shareholders had they not requested payment shall be sold by the consolidated banking association at an advertised public auction, unless some other method of sale is approved by the Comptroller, and the consolidated banking association shall have the right to purchase any of such shares at such public auction, if it is the highest bidder therefor, for the purpose of reselling such shares within thirty days thereafter to such person or persons and at such price not less than par as its board of directors by resolution may determine. If the shares are sold at public auction at a price greater than the amount paid to the dissenting shareholders the excess in such sale price shall be paid to such shareholders. The appraisal of such shares of stock in any State bank shall be determined in the manner prescribed by the law of the State in such cases, rather than as provided in this section, if such provision is made in the State law; and no such consolidation shall be in contravention of the law of the State under which such bank is incorporated.

(e) Status of consolidated association; property rights and interests vested and held as fiduciary

The corporate existence of each of the consolidating banks or banking associations participating in such consolidation shall be merged into and continued in the consolidated national banking association and such consolidated national banking association shall be deemed to be the same corporation as each bank or banking association participating in the consolidation. All rights, franchises, and interests of the individual consolidating banks or banking associations in and to every type of property (real, personal, and mixed) and choses in action shall be transferred to and vested in the consolidated national banking association by virtue of such consolidation without any deed or other transfer. The consolidated national banking association, upon the consolidation and without any order or other action on the part of any court or otherwise, shall hold and enjoy all rights of property, franchises, and interests, including appointments, designations, and nominations, and all other rights and interests as trustee, executor, administrator, registrar of stocks and bonds, guardian of estates, assignee, receiver, and committee of estates of lunatics, and in every other fiduciary capacity, in the same manner and to the same extent as such rights, franchises, and interests were held or enjoyed by any one of the consolidating banks or banking associations at the time of consolidation, subject to the conditions hereinafter provided.

(f) Removal as fiduciary; discrimination

Where any consolidating bank or banking association, at the time of the consolidation, was acting under appointment of any court as trustee, executor, administrator, registrar of stocks and bonds, guardian of estates, assignee, receiver, or committee of estates of lunatics, or in any other fiduciary capacity, the consolidated national banking association shall be subject to removal by a court of competent jurisdiction in the same manner and to the same extent as was such consolidating bank or banking association prior to the consolidation. Nothing contained in this section shall be considered to impair in any manner the right of any court to remove the consolidated national banking association and to appoint in lieu thereof a substitute trustee, executor, or other fiduciary, except that such right shall not be exercised in such a manner as to discriminate against national banking associations, nor shall any consolidated national banking association be removed solely because of the fact that it is a national banking association.

(g) Issuance of stock by consolidated association; preemptive rights

Stock of the consolidated national banking association may be issued as provided by the terms of the consolidation agreement, free from any preemptive rights of the shareholders of the respective consolidating banks.

§ 215a. Merger of national banks or State banks into national banks

(a) Approval of Comptroller, board and shareholders; merger agreement; notice; capital stock; liability of receiving association

One or more national banking associations or one or more State banks, with the approval of the Comptroller, under an agreement not inconsistent with this subchapter, may merge into a national banking association located within the same State, under the charter of the receiving association. The merger agreement shall—

(1) be agreed upon in writing by a majority of the board of directors of each association or State bank participating in the plan of merger;

(2) be ratified and confirmed by the affirmative vote of the shareholders of each such association or State bank owning at least two-thirds of its capital stock outstanding, or by a greater proportion of such capital stock in the case of a State bank if the laws of the State where it is organized so require, at a meeting to be held on the call of the directors, after publishing notice of the time, place, and object of the meeting for four consecutive weeks in a newspaper of general circulation published in the place where the association or State bank is located, or, if there is no such newspaper, then in the newspaper of general circulation published nearest thereto, and after sending such notice to each shareholder of record by certified or registered mail at least ten days prior to the meeting, except to those shareholders who specifically waive notice, but any additional notice shall be given to the shareholders of such State bank which may be required by the laws of the State where it is organized. Publication of notice may be waived, in cases where the Comptroller determines that an emergency exists justifying such waiver, by unanimous action of the shareholders of the association or State banks;

(3) specify the amount of the capital stock of the receiving association, which shall not be less than that required under existing law for the organization of a national bank in the place in which it is located and which will be outstanding upon completion of the merger, the amount of stock (if any) to be allocated, and cash (if any) to be paid, to the shareholders of the association or State bank being merged into the receiving association; and

(4) provide that the receiving association shall be liable for all liabilities of the association or State bank being merged into the receiving association.

(b) Dissenting shareholders

If a merger shall be voted for at the called meetings by the necessary majorities of the shareholders of each association or State bank participating in the plan of merger, and thereafter the merger shall be approved by the Comptroller, any shareholder of any association or State bank to be merged into the receiving association who has voted against such merger at the meeting of the association or bank of which he is a stockholder, or has given notice in writing at or prior to such meeting to the presiding officer that he dissents from the plan of merger, shall be entitled to receive the value of the shares so held by him when such merger shall be approved by the Comptroller upon written request made to the receiving association at any time before thirty days after the date of consummation of the merger, accompanied by the surrender of his stock certificates.

(c) Valuation of shares

The value of the shares of any dissenting shareholder shall be ascertained, as of the effective date of the merger, by an appraisal made by a committee of three persons, composed of (1) one selected by the vote of the holders of the majority of the stock, the owners of which are entitled to payment in cash; (2) one selected by the directors of the receiving association; and (3) one selected by the two so selected. The valuation agreed upon by any two of the three appraisers shall govern. If the value so fixed shall not be satisfactory to any dissenting shareholder who has requested payment, that shareholder may, within five days after being notified of the appraised value of his shares, appeal to the Comptroller, who shall cause a reappraisal to be made which shall be final and binding as to the value of the shares of the appellant.

(d) Application to shareholders of merging associations: appraisal by Comptroller; expenses of receiving association; sale and resale of shares; State appraisal and merger law

If, within ninety days from the date of consummation of the merger, for any reason one or more of the appraisers is not selected as herein provided, or the appraisers fail to determine the value of such shares, the Comptroller shall upon written request of any interested party cause an appraisal to be made which shall be final and binding on all parties. The expenses of the Comptroller in making the reappraisal or the appraisal, as the case may be, shall be paid by the receiving association. The value of the shares ascertained shall be promptly paid to the dissenting shareholders by the receiving association. The shares of stock of the receiving association which would have been delivered to such dissenting shareholders had they not requested payment shall be sold by the receiving association at an advertised public auction, and the receiving association shall have the right to purchase any of such shares at such public auction, if it is the

highest bidder therefor, for the purpose of reselling such shares within thirty days thereafter to such person or persons and at such price not less than par as its board of directors by resolution may determine. If the shares are sold at public auction at a price greater than the amount paid to the dissenting shareholders, the excess in such sale price shall be paid to such dissenting shareholders. The appraisal of such shares of stock in any State bank shall be determined in the manner prescribed by the law of the State in such cases, rather than as provided in this section, if such provision is made in the State law; and no such merger shall be in contravention of the law of the State under which such bank is incorporated. The provisions of this subsection shall apply only to shareholders of (and stock owned by them in) a bank or association being merged into the receiving association.

(e) Status of receiving association; property rights and interests vested and held as fiduciary

The corporate existence of each of the merging banks or banking associations participating in such merger shall be merged into and continued in the receiving association and such receiving association shall be deemed to be the same corporation as each bank or banking association participating in the merger. All rights, franchises, and interests of the individual merging banks or banking associations in and to every type of property (real, personal, and mixed) and choses in action shall be transferred to and vested in the receiving association by virtue of such merger without any deed or other transfer. The receiving association, upon the merger and without any order or other action on the part of any court or otherwise, shall hold and enjoy all rights of property, franchises, and interests, including appointments, designations, and nominations, and all other rights and interests as trustee, executor, administrator, registrar of stocks and bonds, guardian of estates, assignee, receiver, and committee of estates of lunatics, and in every other fiduciary capacity, in the same manner and to the same extent as such rights, franchises, and interests were held or enjoyed by any one of the merging banks or banking associations at the time of the merger, subject to the conditions hereinafter provided.

(f) Removal as fiduciary; discrimination

Where any merging bank or banking association, at the time of the merger, was acting under appointment of any court as trustee, executor, administrator, registrar of stocks and bonds, guardian of estates, assignee, receiver, or committee of estates of lunatics, or in any other fiduciary capacity, the receiving association shall be subject to removal by a court of competent jurisdiction in the same manner and to the same extent as was such merging bank or banking association prior to the merger. Nothing contained in this section shall be considered to impair in any manner the right of any court to remove the receiving association and to appoint in lieu thereof a substitute trustee, executor, or other fiduciary, except that such right shall not be exercised in such a manner as to discriminate against national banking associations, nor shall any receiving association be removed solely because of the fact that it is a national banking association.

(g) Issuance of stock by receiving association; preemptive rights

Stock of the receiving association may be issued as provided by the terms of the merger agreement, free from any preemptive rights of the shareholders of the respective merging banks.

§ 215a–1. Interstate consolidations and mergers

(a) In general

A national bank may engage in a consolidation or merger under this subchapter with an out-of-State bank if the consolidation or merger is approved pursuant to section 1831u of this title.

(b) Scope of application

Subsection (a) of this section shall not apply with respect to any consolidation or merger before June 1, 1997, unless the home State of each bank involved in the transaction has in effect a law described in section 1831u(a)(3) of this title.

(c) Definitions

The terms "home State" and "out-of-State bank" have the same meaning as in section 1831u(f) of this title.

§ 215a–2. Expedited procedures for certain reorganizations

(a) In general

A national bank may, with the approval of the Comptroller, pursuant to rules and regulations promulgated by the Comptroller, and upon the affirmative vote of the shareholders of such bank owning at least two-thirds of its capital stock outstanding, reorganize so as to become a subsidiary of a bank holding company or of a company that will, upon consumption of such reorganization, become a bank holding company.

(b) Reorganization plan

A reorganization authorized under subsection (a) shall be carried out in accordance with a reorganization plan that—

(1) specifies the manner in which the reorganization shall be carried out;

(2) is approved be a majority of the entire board of the national bank;.

(3) specifies—

(A) the amount of cash or securities of the bank holding company, or both, or other consideration to be paid to the shareholders of the reorganizing bank in exchange for their shares of stock of the bank;

(B) the date as of which the rights of each shareholder to participate in such exchange will be determined; and

(C) the manner in which the exchange will be carried out; and

(4) is submitted to the shareholders of the reorganizing bank at a meeting to be held on the call of the directors in accordance with the procedures prescribed in connection with a merger of a national bank under section 215a of this title.

(c) Rights of dissenting shareholders

If, pursuant to this section, a reorganization plan has been approved by the shareholders and the Comptroller, any shareholder of the bank who has voted against the reorganization at the meeting referred to in subsection (b)(4), or has given notice in writing at or prior to that meeting to the presiding officer that the shareholder dissents from the reorganization plan, shall be entitled to receive the value of his or her shares, as provided by section 215a of this title for the merger of a national bank.

(d) Effect of the reorganization

The corporate existence of a national bank that reorganizes in accordance with this section shall not be deemed to have been affected in any way by reason of such reorganization.

(e) Approval under the Bank Holding Company Act

This section does not affect in any way the applicability of the Bank Holding Act of 1956 [12 U.S.C.A. § 1841 et seq.] to a transaction described in subsection (a). (Nov. 7, 1918, c. § 5, as added Dec. 27, 2000, Pub.L. 106–569, Title XII, § 1204 (2), 114 Stat. 3033.)

§ 215a–3. Mergers and consolidations with subsidiaries and nonbank affiliates

(a) In general

Upon the approval of the Comptroller, a national bank may merge with one or more of its nonbank subsidiaries or affiliates.

(b) Scope

Nothing in this section shall be construed—

(1) to affect the applicability of section 1828 of this title; or

(2) to grant a national bank any power or authority that is not permissible for a national bank under other applicable provisions of law.

§ 215b. Definitions

As used in this subchapter, the term—

(1) "State bank" means any bank, banking association, trust company, savings bank (other than a mutual savings bank), or other banking institution which is engaged in the business of receiving deposits and which is incorporated under the laws of any State, or which is operating under the Code of Law for the District of Columbia;

(2) "State" means the several States and Territories, the Commonwealth of Puerto Rico, the Virgin Islands, and the District of Columbia;

(3) "Comptroller" means the Comptroller of the Currency; and

(4) "Receiving association" means the national banking association into which one or more national banking associations or one or more State banks, located within the same State, merge.

§ 215c. Mergers, consolidations, and other acquisitions authorized

(a) In general

Subject to sections 1815(d)(3) and 1828(c) of this title and all other applicable laws, any national bank may acquire or be acquired by any insured depository institution.

(b) Expedited approval of acquisitions

(1) In general

Any application by a national bank to acquire or be acquired by another insured depository institution which is required to be filed with the Comptroller of the Currency under any applicable law or regulation shall be approved or disapproved in writing by the agency before the end of the 60–day period beginning on the date such application is filed with the agency.

(2) Extensions of period

The period for approval or disapproval referred to in paragraph (1) may be extended for an additional 30–day period if the Comptroller of the Currency determines that—

(A) an applicant has not furnished all of the information required to be submitted; or

(B) in the Comptroller's judgment, any material information submitted is substantially inaccurate or incomplete.

(c) Rule of construction

No provision of this section shall be construed as authorizing a national bank or a subsidiary of a national bank to engage in any activity not otherwise authorized under this chapter or any other law governing the powers of national banks.

(d) Acquire defined

For purposes of this section, the term "acquire" means to acquire, directly or indirectly, ownership or control through a merger or consolidation or an acquisition of assets or assumption of liabilities, provided that following such merger, consolidation, or acquisition, an acquiring insured depository institution may not own the shares of the acquired insured depository institution.

§ 216. Purpose

The purpose of this subchapter is to dispose of unclaimed property in the possession, custody, or control of the Comptroller of the Currency by—

(1) providing final notice of the availability of unclaimed property from closed national banks;

(2) barring rights of claimants to obtain such property from the Comptroller after a reasonable period of time following such notice; and

(3) authorizing the Comptroller to dispose of such property for which no claims have been filed and validated under this subchapter.

§ 216a. Definitions

For purposes of this subchapter—

(1) the term "Comptroller" means the Comptroller of the Currency;

(2) the term "unclaimed property" means any articles, items, assets, other property, or the proceeds thereof from safe deposit boxes or other safekeeping arrangements with closed national banks, which are in the possession, custody, or control of the Comptroller in its capacity as successor to receivers of those banks; and

(3) the term "claimant" means any person or entity, including a State under applicable statutory law, asserting a demonstrable legal interest in title to, or custody or possession of, unclaimed property.

§ 216b. Disposition of unclaimed property

(a) Limitations for filing claims, publication of notice in Federal Register; contents of notice; disclosure of descriptive information; inspection of specific property

(1) Within twelve months following October 15, 1982, the Comptroller shall publish formal notice in the Federal Register that all claims to rights of any claimant to obtain title to, or custody or possession of, any unclaimed property in the possession, custody, or control of the Comptroller must be filed within twelve months following the last date of publication of such formal notice in the Federal Register or shall thereafter be barred.

(2) Such notice shall contain the names of last known owners, if any, names and locations of affected closed banks, and a general description of the types of unclaimed property held by the Comptroller. The Comptroller may provide additional notice in local communities as it deems appropriate.

(3) (A) The Comptroller shall not disclose, by publication, inspection or otherwise, information relating to the ownership or description of any specific unclaimed property prior to publication of formal notice under this section.

(B) Thereafter, the Comptroller shall disclose descriptive information of specific unclaimed property only to a claimant thereof. The Comptroller may recoup expenses associated with any publication or other provision of notice from any sale of property authorized by this subchapter. Reasonable opportunity for inspection of specific property by a claimant thereof shall be provided in Washington, District of Columbia.

(b) Delivery of property to claimant upon proof of entitlement; determination of validity of claims; recoupment of expenses; liability for losses; insurance requirements

(1) The Comptroller shall deliver such property to any claimant or his or her legally authorized representative upon receiving proof deemed adequate by the Comptroller that such claimant is entitled to the property, but only if the claimant files for the property within twelve months following the last date formal notice is published in the Federal Register.

(2) (A) The Comptroller shall have authority to determine the validity of all claims filed. The Comptroller may recoup expenses associated with the handling and processing of claims from any sale of property authorized by this subchapter.

(B) All expenses associated with the delivery of any property shall be borne by the claimant. The Comptroller shall not be responsible for any loss in connection with the handling, storage, or delivery of any property to the claimant. The Comptroller may require the claimant to purchase insurance to cover the risk of any loss.

(c) Vesting of rights, title and interest in unclaimed property in United States; sale, use, destruction or disposition of property; proceeds of sale as miscellaneous receipts

(1) If, after twelve months from the date formal notice is published in the Federal Register, any such property remains in the possession, custody, or control of the Comptroller for which no valid claim has been filed, all rights, title, and interest in such property shall immediately be vested in the United States.

(2) The Comptroller shall thereupon, in his discretion, sell, use, destroy, or otherwise dispose of any such unclaimed property. Such disposition may include donations to the Smithsonian Institution for addition to the national collection.

(3) The proceeds of any sale authorized by this section, after recoupment by the Comptroller of any expenses incurred hereunder, shall be covered into the Treasury as miscellaneous receipts.

(d) Liability for determination of validity of claims; liability for delivery, sale, etc., of property

The United States, the Comptroller, or any officer, employee, or agent thereof shall not be subject to personal or legal liability for any determination as to the validity of any claim or claims filed under this subchapter or for any delivery, sale, destruction, or other disposition of unclaimed property.

(e) Court action for determination of ownership, etc., in State or Federal court of competent jurisdiction; de novo nature of action; parties

(1) A court action to determine legal ownership, entitlement, or right to possession may be filed in any State or Federal court of competent jurisdiction other than against the United States, the Comptroller, or any officer, agent, or employee thereof.

(2) Such actions shall be determined de novo without regard to any agency determination or any disposition or delivery by the Comptroller of any particular property to any person.

(3) The United States, the Comptroller, or any officer, employee, or agent thereof shall neither be a party to any such judicial proceeding nor be bound by any decision, decree, or order resulting therefrom.

(f) Jurisdiction of United States Court of Federal Claims of actions against United States, Comptroller, officer, etc.; scope of review of actions of Comptroller; limitations; claims against Comptroller, officer, etc., as claim against United States

(1) The United States Court of Federal Claims shall have exclusive jurisdiction to hear and determine any suit brought against the United States, the Comptroller, or any officer, employee, or agent thereof with regard to any determination of a claim or the disposition of any unclaimed property.

(2) The United States Court of Federal Claims may set aside actions of the Comptroller only if such actions are found to be arbitrary, capricious, an abuse of discretion, or otherwise not in accordance with law.

(3) All claims for which the United States Court of Federal Claims has jurisdiction under this subsection shall be barred unless suit is filed within two years from the date of expiration of the twelve-month notice period provided by this subchapter.

(4) For purposes of section 1491 of Title 28, any Claim against the Comptroller, the United States, or any officer, employee, or agent thereof shall be considered a claim against the United States.

§ 216c. Rules and regulations

The Comptroller may issue rules and regulations necessary or appropriate to carry out this subchapter.

§ 216d. Severability

If any provision of this subchapter or the application of such provision to any person or circumstance is held invalid, the remainder of this subchapter and the application of such provision to other persons or circumstances shall not be affected thereby.

CHAPTER 3. FEDERAL RESERVE SYSTEM
12 U.S.C.A. §§ 221–522

CHAPTER 3. FEDERAL RESERVE SYSTEM

§ 221.　Definitions

Wherever the word "bank" is used in this chapter, the word shall be held to include State bank, banking association, and trust company, except where national banks or Federal reserve banks are specifically referred to. For purposes of this chapter, a State bank includes any bank which is operating under the Code of Law for the District of Columbia.

The terms "national bank" and "national banking association" used in this chapter shall be held to be synonymous and interchangeable. The term "member bank" shall be held to mean any national bank, State bank, or bank or trust company which has become a member of one of the Federal reserve banks. The term "board" shall be held to mean Board of Governors of the Federal Reserve System; the term "district" shall be held to mean Federal reserve district; the term "reserve bank" shall be held to mean Federal reserve bank; the term "the continental United States" means the States of the United States and the District of Columbia.

The terms "bonds and notes of the United States", "bonds and notes of the Government of the United States", and "bonds or notes of the United States" used in this chapter shall be held to include certificates of indebtedness and Treasury bills issued under section 3104 of Title 31.

§ 221a.　Additional definitions

As used in this chapter—

(a) The terms "banks", "national bank", "national banking association", "member bank", "board", "district", and "reserve bank" shall have the meanings assigned to them in section 221 of this title.

(b) Except where otherwise specifically provided, the term "affiliate" shall include any corporation, business trust, association, or other similar organization—

(1) Of which a member bank, directly or indirectly, owns or controls either a majority of the voting shares or more than 50 per centum of the number of shares voted for the election of its directors, trustees, or other persons exercising similar functions at the preceding election, or controls in any manner the election of a majority of its directors, trustees, or other persons exercising similar functions; or

(2) Of which control is held, directly or indirectly, through stock ownership or in any other manner, by the shareholders of a member bank who own or control either a majority of the shares of such bank or more than 50 per centum of the number of shares voted for the election of directors of such bank at the preceding election, or by trustees for the benefit of the shareholders of any such bank; or

(3) Of which a majority of its directors, trustees, or other persons exercising similar functions are directors of any one member bank; or

(4) Which owns or controls, directly or indirectly, either a majority of the shares of capital stock of a member bank or more than 50 per centum of the number of shares voted for the election of directors of a member bank at the preceding election, or controls in any manner the election of a majority of the directors of a member bank, or for the benefit of whose shareholders or members all or substantially all the capital stock of a member bank is held by trustees.

§ 222.　Federal reserve districts; membership of national banks

The continental United States, excluding Alaska, shall be divided into not less than eight nor more than twelve districts. Such districts may be readjusted and new districts may from time to time be created by the Board of Governors of the Federal Reserve System, not to exceed twelve in all: Provided, That the districts shall be apportioned with due regard to the convenience and customary course of business and shall not necessarily be coterminous with any State or States. Such districts shall be known as Federal Reserve districts and may be designated by number. When the State of Alaska or Hawaii is hereafter admitted to the Union the Federal Reserve districts shall be readjusted by the Board of Governors of the Federal Reserve System in such manner as to include such State. Every national bank in any State shall, upon commencing business or within ninety days after admission into the Union of the State in which it is located, become a member bank of the Federal Reserve System by subscribing and paying for stock in the Federal Reserve bank of its district in accordance with the provisions of this chapter and shall thereupon be an insured bank under the Federal Deposit Insurance Act [12 U.S.C.A. § 1811 et seq.], and failure to do so shall subject such bank to the penalty provided by section 501a of this title.

§ 223. Number of Federal reserve cities in district

A Federal reserve district shall contain only one Federal reserve city.

§ 224. Status of reserve cities under former statutes

The organization of reserve districts and Federal reserve cities shall not be construed as changing the present status of reserve cities except insofar as this chapter changes the amount of reserves that may be carried with approved reserve agents located therein.

§ 225. Federal reserve banks; title

A Federal reserve bank shall include in its title the name of the city in which it is situated, as "Federal Reserve Bank of Chicago."

§ 225a. Maintenance of long run growth of monetary and credit aggregates

The Board of Governors of the Federal Reserve System and the Federal Open Market Committee shall maintain long run growth of the monetary and credit aggregates commensurate with the economy's long run potential to increase production, so as to promote effectively the goals of maximum employment, stable prices, and moderate long-term interest rates.

§ 225b. Appearances before and reports to the Congress—DFA § 1103

(a) Appearances before the Congress

(1) In general

The Chairman of the Board shall appear before the Congress at semi-annual hearings, as specified in paragraph (2), regarding—

(A) the efforts, activities, objectives and plans of the Board and the Federal Open Market Committee with respect to the conduct of monetary policy; and

(B) economic developments and prospects for the future described in the report required in subsection (b) of this section.

(2) Schedule

The Chairman of the Board shall appear—

(A) before the Committee on Banking and Financial Services of the House of Representatives on or about February 20 of even numbered calendar years and on or about July 20 of odd numbered calendar years; and

(B) before the Committee on Banking, Housing, and Urban Affairs of the Senate on or about July 20 of even numbered calendar years and on or about February 20 of odd numbered calendar years; and

(C) before either Committee referred to in subparagraph (A) or (B), upon request, following the scheduled appearance of the Chairman before the other Committee under subparagraph (A) or (B).

(b) Congressional report

The Board shall, concurrent with each semi-annual hearing required by this section, submit a written report to the Committee on Banking, Housing, and Urban Affairs of the Senate and the Committee on Banking and Financial Services of the House of Representatives, containing a discussion of the conduct of monetary policy and economic developments and prospects for the future, taking into account past and prospective developments in employment, unemployment, production, investment, real income, productivity, exchange rates, international trade and payments, and prices.

§ 226. "Federal Reserve Act"

The short title of the Act of December 23, 1913, ch. 6, 38 Stat. 251, shall be the "Federal Reserve Act."

§ 227. "Banking Act of 1933"

The short title of the Act of June 16, 1933, ch. 89, 48 Stat. 162, shall be the "Banking Act of 1933."

§ 228. "Banking Act of 1935"

The act of August 23, 1935, ch. 614, 49 Stat. 684, may be cited as the "Banking Act of 1935."

§ 241. Creation; membership; compensation and expenses

The Board of Governors of the Federal Reserve System (hereinafter referred to as the "Board") shall be composed of seven members, to be appointed by the President, by and with the advice and consent of the Senate, after August 23, 1935, for terms of fourteen years except as hereinafter provided, but each appointive member of the Federal Reserve Board in office on such date shall continue to serve as a member of the Board until February 1, 1936, and the Secretary of the Treasury and the Comptroller of the Currency shall continue to serve as members of the Board until February 1, 1936. In selecting the members of the Board, not more than one of whom shall be selected from any one Federal Reserve district, the President shall have due regard to a fair representation of the financial, agricultural, industrial, and commercial interests, and geographical divisions of the country. The members of the Board shall devote their entire time to the business of the Board and shall each receive basic compensation at the rate of $16,000 per annum, payable monthly, together with actual necessary traveling expenses.

§ 242. Ineligibility to hold office in member banks; qualifications and terms of office of members; chairman and vice chairman; oath of office—DFA § 1108

The members of the Board shall be ineligible during the time they are in office and for two years thereafter to hold any office, position, or employment in any member bank, except that this restriction shall not apply to a member who has served the full term for which he was appointed. Upon the expiration of the term of any appointive member of the Federal Reserve Board in office on August 23, 1935, the President shall fix the term of the successor to such member at not to exceed fourteen years, as designated by the President at the time of nomination, but in such manner as to provide for the expiration of the term of not more than one member in any two-year period, and thereafter each member shall hold office for a term of fourteen years from the expiration of the term of his predecessor, unless sooner removed for cause by the President. Of the persons thus appointed, one shall be designated by the President, by and with the advice and consent of the Senate, to serve as Chairman of the Board for a term of four years, and one shall be designated by the President, by and with the consent of the Senate, to serve as Vice Chairman of the Board for a term of four years. The Chairman of the Board, subject to its supervision, shall be its active executive officer.

Each member of the Board shall within fifteen days after notice of appointment make and subscribe to the oath of office. Upon the expiration of their terms of office, members of the Board shall continue to serve until their successors are appointed and have qualified. Any person appointed as a member of the Board after August 23, 1935, shall not be eligible for reappointment as such member after he shall have served a full term of fourteen years.

§ 243. Assessments upon Federal reserve banks to pay expenses

The Board of Governors of the Federal Reserve System shall have power to levy semiannually upon the Federal reserve banks, in proportion to their capital stock and surplus, an assessment sufficient to pay its estimated expenses and the salaries of its members and employees for the half year succeeding the levying of such assessment, together with any deficit carried forward from the preceding half year, and such assessments may include amounts sufficient to provide for the acquisition by the Board in its own name of such site or building in the District of Columbia as in its judgment alone shall be necessary for the purpose of providing suitable and adequate quarters for the performance of its functions. After approving such plans, estimates, and specifications as it shall have caused to be prepared, the Board may, notwithstanding any other provision of law, cause to be constructed on the site so acquired by it a building suitable and adequate in its judgment for its purposes and proceed to take all such steps as it may deem necessary or appropriate in connection with the construction, equipment, and furnishing of such building. The Board may maintain, enlarge, or remodel any building so acquired or constructed and shall have sole control of such building and space therein.

§ 244. Principal offices of Board; chairman of Board; obligations and expenses; qualifications of members; vacancies

The principal offices of the Board shall be in the District of Columbia. At meetings of the Board the chairman shall preside, and, in his absence, the vice chairman shall preside. In the absence of the chairman and the vice chairman, the Board shall elect a member to act as chairman pro tempore. The Board shall determine and prescribe the manner in which its obligations shall be incurred and its disbursements and expenses allowed and paid, and may leave on deposit in the Federal Reserve banks the proceeds of assessments levied upon them to defray its estimated expenses and the salaries of its members and employees, whose employment, compensation, leave, and expenses shall be governed solely by the provisions of this chapter and rules and regulations of the Board not inconsistent therewith; and funds derived from such assessments shall not be construed to be Government funds or appropriated moneys. No member of the Board of Governors of the Federal Reserve System shall be an officer or director of any bank, banking institution, trust company, or Federal Reserve bank or hold stock in any bank, banking institution, or trust company; and before entering upon his duties as a member of the Board of Governors of the Federal Reserve System he shall certify under oath that he has complied with this requirement, and such certification shall be filed with the secretary of the Board. Whenever a vacancy shall occur, other than by expiration of term, among the seven members of the Board of Governors of the Federal Reserve System appointed by the President as above provided, a successor shall be appointed by the President, by and with the advice and consent of the Senate, to fill such vacancy, and when appointed he shall hold office for the unexpired term of his predecessor.

§ 245. Vacancies during recess of Senate

The President shall have power to fill all vacancies that may happen on the Board of Governors of the Federal Reserve System during the recess of the Senate by granting commissions which shall expire with the next session of the Senate.

§ 246. Powers of Secretary of Treasury as affected by chapter

Nothing in this chapter contained shall be construed as taking away any powers heretofore vested by law in the Secretary of the Treasury which relate to the supervision, management, and control of the Treasury Department and bureaus under such department, and wherever any power vested by this chapter in the Board of Governors of the Federal Reserve System or the Federal reserve agent appears to conflict with the powers of the Secretary of the Treasury, such powers shall be exercised subject to the supervision and control of the Secretary.

§ 247. Reports to Congress

The Board of Governors of the Federal Reserve System shall annually make a full report of its operations to the Speaker of the House of Representatives, who shall cause the same to be printed for the information of the Congress. The report required under this paragraph shall include the reports required under section 1691f of title 15, section 57a(f)(7) of title 15, section 1613 of title 15, and section 247a of this title.

§ 247a. Records of action on policy relating to open-market operation and policies determined generally; inclusion in report to Congress

The Board of Governors of the Federal Reserve System shall keep a complete record of the action taken by the Board and by the Federal Open Market Committee upon all questions of policy relating to open-market operations and shall record therein the votes taken in connection with the determination of open-market policies and the reasons underlying the action of the Board and the Committee in each instance. The Board shall keep a similar record with respect to all questions of policy determined by the Board, and shall include in its annual report to the Congress a full account of the action so taken during the preceding year with respect to open-market policies and operations and with respect to the policies determined by it and shall include in such report a copy of the records required to be kept under the provisions of this section.

§ 248. Enumerated powers—DFA §§ 318, 1103, 1108

The Board of Governors of the Federal Reserve System shall be authorized and empowered:

(a) Examination of accounts and affairs of banks; publication of weekly statements; reports of liabilities and assets of depository institutions; covered institutions

(1) To examine at its discretion the accounts, books, and affairs of each Federal reserve bank and of each member bank and to require such statements and reports as it may deem necessary. The said board shall publish once each week a statement showing the condition of each Federal reserve bank and a consolidated

statement for all Federal reserve banks. Such statements shall show in detail the assets and liabilities of the Federal reserve banks, single and combined, and shall furnish full information regarding the character of the money held as reserve and the amount, nature, and maturities of the paper and other investments owned or held by Federal reserve banks.

(2) To require any depository institution specified in this paragraph to make, at such intervals as the Board may prescribe, such reports of its liabilities and assets as the Board may determine to be necessary or desirable to enable the Board to discharge its responsibility to monitor and control monetary and credit aggregates. Such reports shall be made (A) directly to the Board in the case of member banks and in the case of other depository institutions whose reserve requirements under sections 461, 463, 464, 465, and 466 of this title exceed zero, and (B) for all other reports to the Board through the (i) Federal Deposit Insurance Corporation in the case of insured State nonmember banks, savings banks, and mutual savings banks, (ii) National Credit Union Administration Board in the case of insured credit unions, (iii) the Director of the Office of Thrift Supervision in the case of any savings association which is an insured depository institution (as defined in section 1813 of this title) or which is a member as defined in section 1422 of this title, and (iv) such State officer or agency as the Board may designate in the case of any other type of bank, savings and loan association, or credit union. The Board shall endeavor to avoid the imposition of unnecessary burdens on reporting institutions and the duplication of other reporting requirements. Except as otherwise required by law, any data provided to any department, agency, or instrumentality of the United States pursuant to other reporting requirements shall be made available to the Board. The Board may classify depository institutions for the purposes of this paragraph and may impose different requirements on each such class.

(b) Permitting or requiring rediscounting of paper at specified rate

To permit, or, on the affirmative vote of at least five members of the Board of Governors, to require Federal reserve banks to rediscount the discounted paper of other Federal reserve banks at rates of interest to be fixed by the Board.

(c) Suspending reserve requirements

To suspend for a period not exceeding thirty days, and from time to time to renew such suspension for periods not exceeding fifteen days, any reserve requirements specified in this chapter.

(d) Supervising and regulating issue and retirement of notes

To supervise and regulate through the Secretary of the Treasury the issue and retirement of Federal Reserve notes, except for the cancellation and destruction, and accounting with respect to such cancellation and destruction, of notes unfit for circulation, and to prescribe rules and regulations under which such notes may be delivered by the Secretary of the Treasury to the Federal Reserve agents applying therefor.

(e) Adding to or reclassifying reserve cities

To add to the number of cities classified as reserve cities under existing law in which national banking associations are subject to the reserve requirements set forth in section 20 of this Act, or to reclassify existing reserve cities or to terminate their designation as such.

(f) Suspending or removing officers or directors of reserve banks

To suspend or remove any officer or director of any Federal reserve bank, the cause of such removal to be forthwith communicated in writing by the Board of Governors of the Federal Reserve System to the removed officer or director and to said bank.

(g) Requiring writing off of doubtful or worthless assets of banks

To require the writing off of doubtful or worthless assets upon the books and balance sheets of Federal reserve banks.

(h) Suspending operations of or liquidating or reorganizing banks

To suspend, for the violation of any of the provisions of this chapter, the operations of any Federal reserve bank, to take possession thereof, administer the same during the period of suspension, and, when deemed advisable, to liquidate or reorganize such bank.

(i) Requiring bonds of agents; safeguarding property in hands of agents

To require bonds of Federal reserve agents, to make regulations for the safeguarding of all collateral, bonds, Federal reserve notes, money, or property of any kind deposited in the hands of such agents, and said board shall perform the duties, functions, or services specified in this chapter, and make all rules and regulations necessary to enable said board effectively to perform the same.

(j) Exercising supervision over reserve banks

To exercise general supervision over said Federal reserve banks.

(k) Delegation of certain functions; power to delegate; review of delegated activities

To delegate, by published order or rule and subject to subchapter II of chapter 5, and chapter 7, of Title 5, any of its functions, other than those relating to rulemaking or pertaining principally to monetary and credit policies, to one or more administrative law judges, members or employees of the Board, or Federal Reserve banks. The assignment of responsibility for the performance of any function that the Board determines to delegate shall be a function of the Chairman. The Board shall, upon the vote of one member, review action taken at a delegated level within such time and in such manner as the Board shall by rule prescribe.

(*l*) Employing attorneys, experts, assistants, and clerks; salaries and fees

To employ such attorneys, experts, assistants, clerks, or other employees as may be deemed necessary to conduct the business of the board. All salaries and fees shall be fixed in advance by said board and shall be paid in the same manner as the salaries of the members of said board.

(m) Repealed. Pub.L. 106–102, Title VII, § 735, Nov. 12, 1999, 113 Stat. 1479

(n) Board's authority to examine depository institutions and affiliates

To examine, at the Board's discretion, any depository institution, and any affiliate of such depository institution, in connection with any advance to, any discount of any instrument for, or any request for any such advance or discount by, such depository institution under this chapter.

(o) Authority to appoint conservator or receiver

The Board may appoint the Federal Deposit Insurance Corporation as conservator or receiver for a State member bank under section 1821(c)(9) of this title.

(p) Authority

The Board may act in its own name and through its own attorneys in enforcing any provision of this title, regulations promulgated hereunder, or any other law or regulation, or in any action, suit, or proceeding to which the Board is a party and which involves the Board's regulation or supervision of any bank, bank holding company (as defined in section 1841 of this title), or other entity, or the administration of its operations.

(q) Uniform protection authority for Federal reserve facilities

(1) Notwithstanding any other provision of law, to authorize personnel to act as law enforcement officers to protect and safeguard the premises, grounds, property, personnel, including members of the Board, of the Board, or any Federal reserve bank, and operations conducted by or on behalf of the Board or a reserve bank.

(2) The Board may, subject to the regulations prescribed under paragraph (5), delegate authority to a Federal reserve bank to authorize personnel to act as law enforcement officers to protect and safeguard the bank's premises, grounds, property, personnel, and operations conducted by or on behalf of the bank.

(3) Law enforcement officers designated or authorized by the Board or a reserve bank under paragraph (1) or (2) are authorized while on duty to carry firearms and make arrests without warrants for any offense against the United States committed in their presence, or for any felony cognizable under the laws of the United States committed or being committed within the buildings and grounds of the Board or a reserve bank if they have reasonable grounds to believe that the person to be arrested has committed or is committing such a felony. Such officers shall have access to law enforcement information that may be necessary for the protection of the property or personnel of the Board or a reserve bank.

(4) For purposes of this subsection, the term "law enforcement officers" means personnel who have successfully completed law enforcement training and are authorized to carry firearms and make arrests pursuant to this subsection.

(5) The law enforcement authorities provided for in this subsection may be exercised only pursuant to regulations prescribed by the Board and approved by the Attorney General.

(r) (1) Any action that this chapter provides may be taken only upon the affirmative vote of 5 members of the Board may be taken upon the unanimous vote of all members then in office if there are fewer than 5 members in office at the time of the action.

(2)(A) Any action that the board is otherwise authorized to take under the second paragraph of section 343 of this title may be taken upon the unanimous vote of all available members then in office, if

(i) at least 2 members are available and all available members participate in the action;

(ii) the available members unanimously determine that—

(I) unusual and exigent circumstances exist and the borrower is unable to secure adequate credit accommodations from other sources;

(II) action on the matter is necessary to prevent, correct, or mitigate serious harm to the economy or the stability of the financial system of the United States;

(III) despite the use of all means available (including all available telephonic, telegraphic, and other electronic means), the other members of the Board have not been able to be contacted on the matter; and

(IV) action on matter is required before the number of Board members otherwise required to vote on the matter can be contacted through any available means (including all available telephonic, telegraphic, and other electronic means); and

(iii) any credit extended by a Federal reserve bank pursuant to such action is payable upon demand of the Board.

(B) The available members of the Board shall document in writing the determinations required by subparagraph (A)(ii), and such written findings shall be included in the record of the action and in the official minutes of the Board, and copies of such record shall be provided as soon as practicable to the members of the Board who were not available to participate in the action and to the Chairman of the Committee on Banking, Housing, and Urban Affairs of the Senate and to the Chairman of the Committee on Financial Services of the House of Representatives.

§ 248–1. Rules and regulations for transfer of funds and charges therefor among banks; clearing houses

The Board of Governors of the Federal Reserve System shall make and promulgate from time to time regulations governing the transfer of funds and charges therefor among Federal reserve banks and their branches, and may at its discretion exercise the functions of a clearing house for such Federal reserve banks, or may designate a Federal reserve bank to exercise such functions, and may also require each such bank to exercise the functions of a clearing house for depository institutions.

§ 248a. Pricing of services

(a) Publication of pricing principles and proposed schedule of fees; effective date of schedule of fees

Not later than the first day of the sixth month after March 31, 1980, the Board shall publish for public comment a set of pricing principles in accordance with this section and a proposed schedule of fees based upon those principles for Federal Reserve bank services to depository institutions, and not later than the first day of the eighteenth month after March 31, 1980, the Board shall begin to put into effect a schedule of fees for such services which is based on those principles.

(b) Covered services

The services which shall be covered by the schedule of fees under subsection (a) of this section are—

(1) currency and coin services;

(2) check clearing and collection services;

(3) wire transfer services;

(4) automated clearinghouse services;

(5) settlement services;

(6) securities safekeeping services;

(7) Federal Reserve float; and

(8) any new services which the Federal Reserve System offers, including but not limited to payment services to effectuate the electronic transfer of funds.

(c) Criteria applicable

The schedule of fees prescribed pursuant to this section shall be based on the following principles:

(1) All Federal Reserve bank services covered by the fee schedule shall be priced explicitly.

(2) All Federal Reserve bank services covered by the fee schedule shall be available to non-member depository institutions and such services shall be priced at the same fee schedule applicable to member banks, except that non-members shall be subject to any other terms, including a requirement of balances sufficient for clearing purposes, that the Board may determine are applicable to member banks.

(3) Over the long run, fees shall be established on the basis of all direct and indirect costs actually incurred in providing the Federal Reserve services priced, including interest on items credited prior to actual collection, overhead, and an allocation of imputed costs which takes into account the taxes that would have been paid and the return on capital that would have been provided had the services been furnished by a private business firm, except that the pricing principles shall give due regard to competitive factors and the provision of an adequate level of such services nationwide.

(4) Interest on items credited prior to collection shall be charged at the current rate applicable in the market for Federal funds.

(d) Budgetary consequences of decline in volume of services

The Board shall require reductions in the operating budgets of the Federal Reserve banks commensurate with any actual or projected decline in the volume of services to be provided by such banks. The full amount of any savings so realized shall be paid into the United States Treasury.

(e) Parity in clearing

All depository institutions, as defined in section 461(b)(1) of this title, may receive for deposit and as deposits any evidences of transaction accounts, as defined by section 461(b)(1) from other depository institutions, as defined in section 461(b)(1) of this title or from any office of any Federal Reserve bank without regard to any Federal or State law restricting the number or the physical location or locations of such depository institutions.

§ 248b. Annual independent audits of Federal reserve banks and Board

The Board shall order an annual independent audit of the financial statements of each Federal reserve bank and the Board.

§ 249. Repealed. Pub.L. 94–412, Title V, § 501(c), Sept. 14, 1976, 90 Stat. 1258

§ 250. Independence of financial regulatory agencies

No officer or agency of the United States shall have any authority to require the Securities and Exchange Commission, the Board of Governors of the Federal Reserve System, the Federal Deposit Insurance Corporation, the Comptroller of the Currency, the Director of the Office of Thrift Supervision, the Federal Housing Finance Board, or the National Credit Union Administration to submit legislative recommendations, or testimony, or comments on legislation, to any officer or agency of the United States for approval, comments, or review, prior to the submission of such recommendations, testimony, or comments to the Congress if such recommendations, testimony, or comments to the Congress include a statement indicating that the views expressed therein are those of the agency submitting them and do not necessarily represent the views of the President.

§ 251. Repealed. Pub.L. 104–208, Div. A, Title II, § 2224(a), Sept. 30, 1996, 110 Stat. 3009–415

§ 252. Credit availability assessment

(a) Study

(1) In general

Not later than 12 months after September 30, 1996, and once every 60 months thereafter, the Board, in consultation with the Director of the Office of Thrift Supervision, the Comptroller of the Currency, the Board of Directors of the Corporation, the Administrator of the National Credit Union Administration, the Administrator of the Small Business Administration, and the Secretary of Commerce, shall conduct a study and submit a report to the Congress detailing the extent of small business lending by all creditors.

(2) Contents of study

The study required under paragraph (1) shall identify, to the extent practicable, those factors which provide policymakers with insights into the small business credit market, including—

(A) the demand for small business credit, including consideration of the impact of economic cycles on the levels of such demand;

(B) the availability of credit to small businesses;

(C) the range of credit options available to small businesses, such as those available from insured depository institutions and other providers of credit;

(D) the types of credit products used to finance small business operations, including the use of traditional loans, leases, lines of credit, home equity loans, credit cards, and other sources of financing;

(E) the credit needs of small businesses, including, if appropriate, the extent to which such needs differ, based upon product type, size of business, cash flow requirements, characteristics of ownership or investors, or other aspects of such business;

(F) the types of risks to creditors in providing credit to small businesses; and

(G) such other factors as the Board deems appropriate.

(b) Use of existing data

The studies required by this section shall not increase the regulatory or paperwork burden on regulated financial institutions, other sources of small business credit, or small businesses.

§ 261. Creation; membership; compensation; meetings; officers; procedure; quorum; vacancies

There is created a Federal Advisory Council, which shall consist of as many members as there are Federal reserve districts. Each Federal reserve bank by its board of directors shall annually select from its own Federal reserve district one member of said council, who shall receive such compensation and allowances as may be fixed by his board of directors subject to the approval of the Board of Governors of the Federal Reserve System. The meetings of said advisory council shall be held at Washington, District of Columbia, at least four times each year, and oftener if called by the Board of Governors of the Federal Reserve System. The council may in addition to the meetings above provided for hold such other meetings in Washington, District of Columbia, or elsewhere, as it may deem necessary, may select its own officers and adopt its own methods of procedure, and a majority of its members shall constitute a quorum for the transaction of business. Vacancies in the council shall be filled by

the respective reserve banks, and members selected to fill vacancies shall serve for the unexpired term.

§ 262. Powers

The Federal Advisory Council shall have power, by itself or through its officers, (1) to confer directly with the Board of Governors of the Federal Reserve System on general business conditions; (2) to make oral or written representations concerning matters within the jurisdiction of said board; (3) to call for information and to make recommendations in regard to discount rates, rediscount business, note issues, reserve conditions in the various districts, the purchase and sale of gold or securities by reserve banks, open-market operations by said banks, and the general affairs of the reserve banking system.

§ 263. Federal Open Market Committee; creation; membership; regulations governing open-market transactions

(a) There is hereby created a Federal Open Market Committee (hereinafter referred to as the "Committee"), which shall consist of the members of the Board of Governors of the Federal Reserve System and five representatives of the Federal Reserve banks to be selected as hereinafter provided. Such representatives shall be presidents or first vice presidents of Federal Reserve banks and, beginning with the election for the term commencing March 1, 1943, shall be elected annually as follows: One by the board of directors of the Federal Reserve Bank of New York, one by the boards of directors of the Federal Reserve Banks of Boston, Philadelphia, and Richmond, one by the boards of directors of the Federal Reserve Banks of Cleveland and Chicago, one by the boards of directors of the Federal Reserve Banks of Atlanta, Dallas, and St. Louis, and one by the boards of directors of the Federal Reserve Banks of Minneapolis, Kansas City, and San Francisco. In such elections each board of directors shall have one vote; and the details of such elections may be governed by regulations prescribed by the committee, which may be amended from time to time. An alternate to serve in the absence of each such representative shall likewise be a president or first vice president of a Federal Reserve bank and shall be elected annually in the same manner. The meetings of said Committee shall be held at Washington, District of Columbia, at least four times each year upon the call of the chairman of the Board of Governors of the Federal Reserve System or at the request of any three members of the Committee.

(b) No Federal Reserve bank shall engage or decline to engage in open-market operations under sections 348a and 353 to 359 of this title except in accordance with the direction of and regulations adopted by the Committee. The Committee shall consider, adopt, and transmit to the several Federal Reserve banks, regulations relating to the open-market transactions of such banks.

(c) The time, character, and volume of all purchases and sales of paper described in sections 348a and 353 to 359 of this title as eligible for open-market operations shall be governed with a view to accommodating commerce and business and with regard to their bearing upon the general credit situation of the country.

§ 264. Transferred

§ 265. Insured banks as depositaries of public money; duties; security; discrimination between banks prohibited; repeal of inconsistent laws

All insured banks designated for that purpose by the Secretary of the Treasury shall be depositories of public money of the United States (including, without being limited to, revenues and funds of the United States, and any funds the deposit of which is subject to the control or regulation of the United States or any of its officers, agents, or employees, and Postal Savings funds), and the Secretary is authorized to deposit public money in such depositaries, under such regulations as may be prescribed by the Secretary; and they may also be employed as financial agents of the Government; and they shall perform all such reasonable duties, as depositaries of public money and financial agents of the Government as may be required of them. The Secretary of the Treasury shall require of the insured banks thus designated satisfactory security by the deposit of United States bonds or otherwise, for the safekeeping and prompt payment of public money deposited with them and for the faithful performance of their duties as financial agents of the Government: Provided, That no such security shall be required for the safekeeping and prompt payment of such parts of the deposits of the public money in such banks as are insured deposits and each officer, employee, or

agent of the United States having official custody of public funds and lawfully depositing the same in an insured bank shall, for the purpose of determining the amount of the insured deposits, be deemed a depositor in such custodial capacity separate and distinct from any other officer, employee, or agent of the United States having official custody of public funds and lawfully depositing the same in the same insured bank in custodial capacity. Notwithstanding any other provision of law, no department, board, agency, instrumentality, officer, employee, or agent of the United States shall issue or permit to continue in effect any regulations, rulings, or instructions or enter into or approve any contracts or perform any other acts having to do with the deposit, disbursement, or expenditure of public funds, or the deposit, custody, or advance of funds subject to the control of the United States as trustee or otherwise which shall discriminate against or prefer national banking associations, State banks members of the Federal Reserve System, or insured banks not members of the Federal Reserve System, by class, or which shall require those enjoying the benefits, directly or indirectly, of disbursed public funds so to discriminate. All Acts or parts thereof in conflict herewith are repealed. The terms "insured bank" and "insured deposit" as used in this section shall be construed according to the definitions of such terms in section 1813 of this title.

§ 266. State-chartered banks and other institutions as depositaries of public money; fiscal agents; duties

Banks, savings banks, and savings and loan, building and loan, homestead associations (including cooperative banks), and credit unions created under the laws of any State and the deposits or accounts of which are insured by a State or agency thereof or corporation chartered pursuant to the laws of any State may be depositories of public money and may be employed as fiscal agents of the United States. The Secretary of the Treasury is authorized to deposit public money in any such institution, and shall prescribe such regulations as may be necessary to enable such institutions to become depositories of public money and fiscal agents of the United States. Each such institution shall perform all such reasonable duties as depositary of public money and fiscal agent of the United States as may be required of it including services in connection with the collection of taxes and other obligations owed the United States.

§ 281. Capital

No Federal reserve bank shall commence business with a subscribed capital less than $4,000,000.

§ 282. Subscription to capital stock by national banking association

Every national banking association within each Federal reserve district shall be required to subscribe to the capital stock of the Federal reserve bank for that district in a sum equal to 6 per centum of the paid-up capital stock and surplus of such bank, one-sixth of the subscription to be payable on call of the Board of Governors of the Federal Reserve System, one-sixth within three months and one-sixth within six months thereafter, and the remainder of the subscription, or any part thereof, shall be subject to call when deemed necessary by the Board, said payments to be in gold or gold certificates.

§ 283. Public subscription to capital stock

No individual, copartnership, or corporation other than a member bank of its district shall be permitted to subscribe for or to hold at any time more than $25,000 par value of stock in any Federal reserve bank. Such stock shall be known as public stock and may be transferred on the books of the Federal reserve bank by the chairman of the board of directors of such bank.

§ 284. Omitted

§ 285. Nonvoting stock

Stock not held by member banks shall not be entitled to voting power.

§ 286. Transfers of stock; rules and regulations

The Board of Governors of the Federal Reserve System is empowered to adopt and promulgate rules and regulations governing the transfers of said stock.

§ 287. Value of shares of stock; increase and decrease of stock; member banks as shareholders; surrender of shares

The capital stock of each Federal reserve bank shall be divided into shares of $100 each. The outstanding capital stock shall be increased from time to time as member banks increase their capital stock and surplus or as additional banks become members, and may be decreased as member banks reduce their capital stock or surplus or cease to be members. Shares of the capital stock of Federal reserve banks owned by member banks shall not be transferred or hypothecated. When a member bank increases its capital stock or surplus, it shall thereupon subscribe for an additional amount of capital stock of the Federal reserve bank of its district equal to 6 per centum of the said increase, one-half of said subscription to be paid in the manner hereinbefore provided for original subscription, and one-half subject to call of the Board of Governors of the Federal Reserve System. A bank applying for stock in a Federal reserve bank at any time after the organization thereof must subscribe for an amount of the capital stock of the Federal reserve bank equal to 6 per centum of the paid-up capital stock and surplus of said applicant bank, paying therefor its par value plus one-half of 1 per centum a month from the period of the last dividend. When a member bank reduces its capital stock or surplus it shall surrender a proportionate amount of its holdings in the capital stock of said Federal Reserve bank. Any member bank which holds capital stock of a Federal Reserve bank in excess of the amount required on the basis of 6 per centum of its paid-up capital stock and surplus shall surrender such excess stock. When a member bank voluntarily liquidates it shall surrender all of its holdings of the capital stock of said Federal Reserve bank and be released from its stock subscription not previously called. In any such case the shares surrendered shall be canceled and the member bank shall receive in payment therefor, under regulations to be prescribed by the Board of Governors of the Federal Reserve System, a sum equal to its cash-paid subscriptions on the shares surrendered and one-half of 1 per centum a month from the period of the last dividend, not to exceed the book value thereof, less any liability of such member bank to the Federal Reserve bank.

§ 288. Cancellation of stock held by member bank on insolvency or discontinuance of banking operations for sixty days; repayment of cash-paid subscriptions

If any member bank shall be declared insolvent and a receiver appointed therefor, the stock held by it in said Federal reserve bank shall be canceled, without impairment of its liability, and all cash-paid subscriptions on said stock, with one-half of 1 per centum per month from the period of last dividend, if earned, not to exceed the book value thereof, shall be first applied to all debts of the insolvent member bank to the Federal reserve bank, and the balance, if any, shall be paid to the receiver of the insolvent bank.

If any national bank which has not gone into liquidation as provided in section 181 of this title, and for which a receiver has not already been appointed for other lawful cause, shall discontinue its banking operations for a period of sixty days the Comptroller of the Currency may, if he deems it advisable, appoint a receiver for such bank. The stock held by the said national bank in the Federal reserve bank of its district shall thereupon be canceled and said national bank shall receive in payment therefor, under regulations to be prescribed by the Board of Governors of the Federal Reserve System, a sum equal to its cash-paid subscriptions on the shares canceled and one-half of 1 per centum a month from the period of the last dividend, if earned, not to exceed the book value thereof, less any liability of such national bank to the Federal reserve bank.

§ 289. Dividends and surplus funds of reserve banks; transfer for fiscal year 2000

(a) Dividends and surplus funds of reserve banks

(1) Stockholder dividends

(A) In general

After all necessary expenses of a Federal reserve bank have been paid or provided for, the stockholders of the bank shall be entitled to receive an annual dividend of 6 percent on paid-in capital stock.

(B) Dividend cumulative

The entitlement to dividends under subparagraph (A) shall be cumulative.

(2) Deposit of net earnings in surplus fund

That portion of net earnings of each Federal reserve bank which remains after dividend claims under paragraph (1)(A) have been fully met shall be deposited in the surplus fund of the bank.

(b) Transfer for fiscal year 2000

(1) In general

The Federal reserve banks shall transfer from the surplus funds of such banks to the Board of Governors of the Federal Reserve System for transfer to the Secretary of the Treasury for deposit in the general fund of the Treasury, a total amount of $3,752,000,000 in fiscal year 2000.

(2) Allocated by Fed

Of the total amount required to be paid by the Federal reserve banks under paragraph (1) for fiscal year 2000, the Board shall determine the amount each such bank shall pay in such fiscal year.

(3) Replenishment of surplus fund prohibited

During fiscal year 2000, no Federal reserve bank may replenish such bank's surplus fund by the amount of any transfer by such bank under paragraph (1).

§ 290. Use of earnings transferred to the Treasury

The net earnings derived by the United States from Federal reserve banks shall, in the discretion of the Secretary, be used to supplement the gold reserve held against outstanding United States notes, or shall be applied to the reduction of the outstanding bonded indebtedness of the United States under regulations to be prescribed by the Secretary of the Treasury. Should a Federal reserve bank be dissolved or go into liquidation, any surplus remaining, after the payment of all debts, dividend requirements as hereinbefore provided, and the par value of the stock, shall be paid to and become the property of the United States and shall be similarly applied.

§ 301. Powers and duties of board of directors; suspension of member bank for undue use of bank credit

Every Federal reserve bank shall be conducted under the supervision and control of a board of directors.

The board of directors shall perform the duties usually appertaining to the office of directors of banking associations and all such duties as are prescribed by law.

Said board of directors shall administer the affairs of said bank fairly and impartially and without discrimination in favor of or against any member bank or banks and may, subject to the provisions of law and the orders of the Board of

Governors of the Federal Reserve System, extend to each member bank such discounts, advancements, and accommodations as may be safely and reasonably made with due regard for the claims and demands of other member banks, the maintenance of sound credit conditions, and the accommodation of commerce, industry, and agriculture. The Board of Governors of the Federal Reserve System may prescribe regulations further defining within the limitations of this chapter the conditions under which discounts, advancements, and the accommodations may be extended to member banks. Each Federal reserve bank shall keep itself informed of the general character and amount of the loans and investments of its member banks with a view to ascertaining whether undue use is being made of bank credit for the speculative carrying of or trading in securities, real estate, or commodities, or for any other purpose inconsistent with the maintenance of sound credit conditions; and, in determining whether to grant or refuse advances, rediscounts, or other credit accommodations, the Federal reserve bank shall give consideration to such information. The chairman of the Federal reserve bank shall report to the Board of Governors of the Federal Reserve System any such undue use of bank credit by any member bank, together with his recommendation. Whenever, in the judgment of the Board of Governors of the Federal Reserve System, any member bank is making such undue use of bank credit, the Board may, in its discretion, after reasonable notice and an opportunity for a hearing, suspend such bank from the use of the credit facilities of the Federal Reserve System and may terminate such suspension or may renew it from time to time.

§ 302.   Number of members; classes

Such board of directors shall be selected as hereinafter specified and shall consist of nine members, holding office for three years, and divided into three classes, designated as classes A, B, and C.

Class A shall consist of three members, without discrimination on the basis of race, creed, color, sex, or national origin, who shall be chosen by and be representative of the stockholding banks.

Class B shall consist of three members, who shall represent the public and shall be elected without discrimination on the basis of race, creed, color, sex, or national origin, and with due

but not exclusive consideration to the interests of agriculture, commerce, industry, services, labor, and consumers.

Class C shall consist of three members who shall be designated by the Board of Governors of the Federal Reserve System. They shall be elected to represent the public, without discrimination on the basis of race, creed, color, sex, or national origin, and with due but not exclusive consideration to the interests of agriculture, commerce, industry, services, labor, and consumers.

§ 303.   Qualifications and disabilities

No Senator or Representative in Congress shall be a member of the Board of Governors of the Federal Reserve System or an officer or a director of a Federal reserve bank.

No director of class B shall be an officer, director, or employee of any bank.

No director of class C shall be an officer, director, employee, or stockholder of any bank.

§ 304.   Class A and class B directors; selection

Directors of class A and class B shall be chosen in the following manner: The Board of Governors of the Federal Reserve System shall classify the member banks of the district into three general groups or divisions designating each group by number. Each group shall consist as nearly as may be of banks of similar capitalization. Each member bank shall be permitted to nominate to the chairman of the board of directors of the Federal reserve bank of the district one candidate for director of class A and one candidate for director of class B. The candidates so nominated shall be listed by the chairman, indicating by whom nominated, and a copy of said list shall, within fifteen days after its completion, be furnished by the chairman to each member bank. Each member bank by a resolution of the board or by an amendment to its bylaws shall authorize its president, cashier, or some other officer to cast the vote of the member bank in the elections of class A and class B directors: Provided, That whenever any member banks within the same Federal Reserve district are subsidiaries of the same bank holding company within the meaning of the Bank Holding Company Act of 1956 [12 U.S.C.A. § 1841 et seq.], participation in any such nomination or election by such member banks, including such bank holding company if it is also a member bank, shall be confined to one of such banks, which may be designated for the purpose by such holding company.

Within fifteen days after receipt of the list of candidates the duly authorized officer of a member bank shall certify to the chairman his first, second, and other choices for director of class A and class B, respectively, upon a preferential ballot upon a form furnished by the chairman of the board of directors of the Federal reserve bank of the district. Each such officer shall make a cross opposite the name of the first, second, and other choices for a director of class A and for a director of class B, but shall not vote more than one choice for any one candidate. No officer or director of a member bank shall be eligible to serve as a class A director unless nominated and elected by banks which are members of the same group as the member bank of which he is an officer or director.

Any person who is an officer or director of more than one member bank shall not be eligible for nomination as a class A director except by banks in the same group as the bank having the largest aggregate resources of any of those of which such person is an officer or director.

Any candidate having a majority of all votes cast in the column of first choice shall be declared elected. If no candidate have a majority of all the votes in the first column, then there shall be added together the votes cast by the electors for such candidates in the second column and the votes cast for the several candidates in the first column. The candidate then having a majority of the electors voting and the highest number of combined votes shall be declared elected. If no candidate have a majority of electors voting and the highest number of votes when the first and second choices shall have been added, then the votes cast in the third column for other choices shall be added together in like manner, and the candidate then having the highest number of votes shall be declared elected. An immediate report of election shall be declared.

§ 305. Class C directors; selection; "Federal reserve agent"

Class C directors shall be appointed by the Board of Governors of the Federal Reserve System. They shall have been for at least two years residents of the district for which they are appointed, one of whom shall be designated by said

board as chairman of the board of directors of the Federal reserve bank and as "Federal reserve agent." He shall be a person of tested banking experience and in addition to his duties as chairman of the board of directors of the Federal reserve bank he shall be required to maintain, under regulations to be established by the Board of Governors of the Federal Reserve System, a local office of said board on the premises of the Federal reserve bank. He shall make regular reports to the Board of Governors of the Federal Reserve System and shall act as its official representative for the performance of the functions conferred upon it by this chapter. He shall receive an annual compensation to be fixed by the Board of Governors of the Federal Reserve System and paid monthly by the Federal reserve bank to which he is designated. One of the directors of class C shall be appointed by the Board of Governors of the Federal Reserve System as deputy chairman to exercise the powers of the chairman of the board when necessary. In case of the absence of the chairman and deputy chairman, the third class C director shall preside at meetings of the board.

§ 306. Assistants to Federal reserve agent

Subject to the approval of the Board of Governors of the Federal Reserve System, the Federal reserve agent shall appoint one or more assistants. Such assistants, who shall be persons of tested banking experience, shall assist the Federal reserve agent in the performance of his duties and shall also have power to act in his name and stead during his absence or disability. The Board of Governors of the Federal Reserve System shall require such bonds of the assistant Federal reserve agents as it may deem necessary for the protection of the United States. Assistants to the Federal reserve agent shall receive an annual compensation, to be fixed and paid in the same manner as that of the Federal reserve agent.

§ 307. Compensation of directors

Directors of Federal reserve banks shall receive, in addition to any compensation otherwise provided, a reasonable allowance for necessary expenses in attending meetings of their respective boards, which amount shall be paid by the respective Federal reserve banks. Any compensation that may be provided by boards of directors of Federal reserve banks for directors, officers or employees shall be subject to the approval of the Board of Governors of the Federal Reserve System.

§ 308. Terms of directors; vacancies

At the first meeting of the full board of directors of each Federal reserve bank, it shall be the duty of the directors of classes A, B, and C, respectively, to designate one of the members of each class whose term of office shall expire in one year from the 1st of January nearest to date of such meeting, one whose term of office shall expire at the end of two years from said date, and one whose term of office shall expire at the end of three years from said date. Thereafter every director of a Federal reserve bank chosen as hereinbefore provided shall hold office for a term of three years. Vacancies that may occur in the several classes of directors of Federal reserve banks may be filled in the manner provided for the original selection of such directors, such appointees to hold office for the unexpired terms of their predecessors.

§ 321. Application for membership

Any bank incorporated by special law of any State, or organized under the general laws of any State or of the United States, including Morris Plan banks and other incorporated banking institutions engaged in similar business, desiring to become a member of the Federal Reserve System, may make application to the Board of Governors of the Federal Reserve System, under such rules and regulations as it may prescribe, for the right to subscribe to the stock of the Federal Reserve bank organized within the district in which the applying bank is located. Such application shall be for the same amount of stock that the applying bank would be required to subscribe to as a national bank. For the purposes of membership of any such bank the terms "capital" and "capital stock" shall include the amount of outstanding capital notes and debentures legally issued by the applying bank and purchased by the Reconstruction Finance Corporation. The Board of Governors of the Federal Reserve System, subject to the provisions of this title and to such conditions as it may prescribe pursuant thereto may permit the applying bank to become a stockholder of such Federal Reserve bank.

Upon the conversion of a national bank into a State bank, or the merger or consolidation of a national bank with a State bank which is not a member of the Federal Reserve System, the resulting or continuing State bank may be admitted to membership in the Federal Reserve System by the Board of Governors of the Federal Reserve System in accordance with the provisions of this section, but, otherwise, the Federal Reserve bank stock owned by the national bank shall be canceled and paid for as provided in section 287 of this title. Upon the merger or consolidation of a national bank with a State member bank under a State charter, the membership of the State bank in the Federal Reserve System shall continue.

Any such State bank which on February 25, 1927, has established and is operating a branch or branches in conformity with the State law, may retain and operate the same while remaining or upon becoming a stockholder of such Federal Reserve bank; but no such State bank may retain or acquire stock in a Federal Reserve bank except upon relinquishment of any branch or branches established after February 25, 1927, beyond the limits of the city, town, or village in which the parent bank is situated: Provided, however, That nothing herein contained shall prevent any State member bank from establishing and operating branches in the United States or any dependency or insular possession thereof or in any foreign country, on the same terms and conditions and subject to the same limitations and restrictions as are applicable to the establishment of branches by national banks except that the approval of the Board of Governors of the Federal Reserve System, instead of the Comptroller of the Currency, shall be obtained before any State member bank may hereafter establish any branch and before any State bank hereafter admitted to membership may retain any branch established after February 25, 1927, beyond the limits of the city, town, or village in which the parent bank is situated. The approval of the Board shall likewise be obtained before any State member bank may establish any new branch within the limits of any such city, town, or village.

§ 322. Determination on application

In acting upon such application the Board of Governors of the Federal Reserve System shall consider the financial condition of the applying bank, the general character of its management, and whether or not the corporate powers exercised are consistent with the purposes of this chapter.

§ 323. Stock in Federal reserve banks; method of payment

Whenever the Board of Governors of the Federal Reserve System shall permit the applying bank to become a stockholder in the Federal reserve bank of the district its stock subscription shall be payable on call of the Board of Governors of the Federal Reserve System, and stock issued to it shall be held subject to the provisions of this chapter.

§ 324. Laws applicable on becoming members

All banks admitted to membership under authority of this section shall be required to comply with the reserve and capital requirements of this chapter, to conform to those provisions of law imposed on national banks which prohibit such banks from lending on or purchasing their own stock and which relate to the withdrawal or impairment of their capital stock, and to conform to the provisions of sections 56 and 60(b) of this title with respect to the payment of dividends; except that any reference in any such provision to the Comptroller of the Currency shall be deemed for the purposes of this sentence to be a reference to the Board of Governors of the Federal Reserve System. Such banks and the officers, agents, and employees thereof shall also be subject to the provisions of and to the penalties prescribed by sections 334, 656, and 1005 of Title 18, and shall be required to make reports of condition and of the payment of dividends to the Federal Reserve bank of which they become a member. Not less than three of such reports shall be made annually on call of the Federal Reserve bank on dates to be fixed by the Board of Governors of the Federal Reserve System. Any bank which (A) maintains procedures reasonably adapted to avoid any inadvertent error and, unintentionally and as a result of such an error, fails to make or publish any report required under this paragraph, within the period of time specified by the Board, or submits or publishes any false or misleading report or information, or (B) inadvertently transmits or publishes any report which is minimally late, shall be subject to a penalty of not more than $2,000 for each day during which such failure continues or such false or misleading information is not corrected. The bank shall have the burden of proving that an error was inadvertent and that a report was inadvertently transmitted or published late. Any bank which fails to make or publish such reports within the period of time specified by the Board, or submits or publishes any false or misleading report or information, in a manner not described in the 2nd preceding sentence shall be subject to a penalty of not more than $20,000 for each day during which such failure continues or such false or misleading information is not corrected. Notwithstanding the preceding sentence, if any bank knowingly or with reckless disregard for the accuracy of any information or report described in such sentence submits or publishes any false or misleading report or information, the Board may assess a penalty of not more than $1,000,000 or 1 percent of total assets of such bank, whichever is less, per day for each day during which such failure continues or such false or misleading information is not corrected. Any penalty imposed under any of the 4 preceding sentences shall be assessed and collected by the Board in the manner provided in subparagraphs (E), (F), (G), and (I) of section 1818(i)(2) of this title (for penalties imposed under such section) and any such assessment (including the determination of the amount of the penalty) shall be subject to the provisions of such section. Any bank against which any penalty is assessed under this subsection shall be afforded an agency hearing if such bank submits a request for such hearing within 20 days after the issuance of the notice of assessment. Section 1818(h) of this title shall apply to any proceeding under this paragraph. Such reports of condition shall be in such form and shall contain such information as the Board of Governors of the Federal Reserve System may require.

§ 325. Examinations

As a condition of membership such banks shall likewise be subject to examinations made by direction of the Board of Governors of the Federal Reserve System or of the Federal reserve bank by examiners selected or approved by the Board of Governors of the Federal Reserve System.

§ 326. Acceptance of examinations and reports by State authorities; special examinations

Whenever the directors of the Federal reserve bank shall approve the examinations made by the State authorities, such examinations and the reports thereof may be accepted in lieu of examinations made by examiners selected or approved by the Board of Governors of the Federal Reserve System: Provided, however, That when it deems it necessary the board may order special examinations by examiners of its own selection and shall in all cases approve the form of the report. The expenses of all examinations, other than those made by State authorities, may, in the discretion of the Board of Governors of the Federal Reserve System, be assessed against the banks examined and, when so assessed, shall be paid by the banks examined. The Board of Governors of the Federal Reserve System, at its discretion, may furnish any report of examination or other confidential supervisory information concerning any State member bank or other entity examined under any other authority of the Board, to any Federal or State agency or authority with supervisory or regulatory authority over the examined entity, to any officer, director, or receiver of the examined entity, and to any other person that the Board determines to be proper.

§ 327. Surrender of stock and cancellation of memberships

If at any time it shall appear to the Board of Governors of the Federal Reserve System that a member bank has failed to comply with the provisions of this subchapter, or the regulations of the Board of Governors of the Federal Reserve System made pursuant thereto, or has ceased to exercise banking functions without a receiver or liquidating agent having been appointed therefor, it shall be within the power of the board after hearing to require such bank to surrender its stock in the Federal reserve bank and to forfeit all rights and privileges of membership. The Board of Governors of the Federal Reserve System may restore membership upon due proof of compliance with the conditions imposed by this subchapter.

§ 328. Withdrawals from membership

Any State bank or trust company desiring to withdraw from membership in a Federal Reserve bank may do so, after six months' written notice shall have been filed with the Board of Governors of the Federal Reserve System, upon the surrender and cancellation of all of its holdings of capital stock in the Federal reserve bank: Provided, That the Board of Governors of the Federal Reserve System, in its discretion and subject to

such conditions as it may prescribe, may waive such six months' notice in individual cases and may permit any such State bank or trust company to withdraw from membership in a Federal reserve bank prior to the expiration of six months from the date of the written notice of its intention to withdraw: Provided, however, That no Federal reserve bank shall, except under express authority of the Board of Governors of the Federal Reserve System, cancel within the same calendar year more than 25 per centum of its capital stock for the purpose of effecting voluntary withdrawals during that year. All such applications shall be dealt with in the order in which they are filed with the board. Whenever a member bank shall surrender its stock holdings in a Federal reserve bank, or shall be ordered to do so by the Board of Governors of the Federal Reserve System, under authority of law, all of its rights and privileges as a member bank shall thereupon cease and determine, and after due provision has been made for any indebtedness due or to become due to the Federal reserve bank it shall be entitled to a refund of its cash-paid subscription with interest at the rate of one-half of 1 per centum per month from date of last dividend, if earned, the amount refunded in no event to exceed the book value of the stock at that time, and shall likewise be entitled to repayment of deposits and of any other balance due from the Federal reserve bank.

§ 329. Capital stock required as condition precedent to membership

No applying bank shall be admitted to membership unless it possesses capital stock and surplus which, in the judgment of the Board of Governors of the Federal Reserve System, are adequate in relation to the character and condition of its assets and to its existing and prospective deposit liabilities and other corporate responsibilities: Provided, That no bank engaged in the business of receiving deposits other than trust funds, which does not possess capital stock and surplus in an amount equal to that which would be required for the establishment of a national banking association in the place in which it is located, shall be admitted to membership unless it is, or has been, approved for deposit insurance under the Federal Deposit Insurance Act [12 U.S.C.A. § 1811 et seq.]. The capital stock of a State member bank shall not be reduced except with the prior consent of the Board.

§ 329a. Omitted

§ 330. Laws applicable on becoming members; discounts for State banks

Banks becoming members of the Federal reserve system under authority of this subchapter shall be subject to the provisions of said sections and to those of this chapter which relate specifically to member banks, but shall not be subject to examination under the provisions of sections 481 and 482 of this title. Subject to the provisions of this chapter and to the regulations of the board made pursuant thereto, any bank becoming a member of the Federal reserve system shall retain its full charter and statutory rights as a State bank or trust company, and may continue to exercise all corporate powers granted it by the State in which it was created, and shall be entitled to all privileges of member banks, except that the Board of Governors of the Federal Reserve System may limit the activities of State member banks and subsidiaries of State member banks in a manner consistent with section 1831a of this title. No Federal reserve bank shall be permitted to discount for any State bank or trust company notes, drafts, or bills of exchange of any one borrower who is liable for borrowed money to such State bank or trust company in an amount greater than that which could be borrowed lawfully from such State bank or trust company were it a national banking association. The Federal reserve bank, as a condition of the discount of notes, drafts, and bills of exchange for such State bank or trust company, shall require a certificate or guaranty to the effect that the borrower is not liable to such bank in excess of the amount provided by this subchapter, and will not be permitted to become liable in excess of this amount while such notes, drafts, or bills of exchange are under discount with the Federal reserve bank.

§ 331. Certifying checks on State banks admitted as members

It shall be unlawful for any officer, clerk, or agent of any bank admitted to membership under authority of this subchapter, to certify any check drawn upon such bank unless the person or company drawing the check has on deposit therewith at the time such check is certified an amount of money equal to the amount specified in such check. Any check so certified by duly authorized officers shall be a good and valid obligation against such bank, but the act of any such officer, clerk, or agent in violation of this subchapter, may subject such bank to a forfeiture of its membership in the Federal reserve system upon hearing by the Board of Governors of the Federal Reserve System.

§ 332. Depositaries of public money; financial agents; security required

All banks or trust companies incorporated by special law or organized under the general laws of any State, which are members of the Federal reserve system, when designated for that purpose by the Secretary of the Treasury, shall be depositaries of public money, under such regulations as may be prescribed by the Secretary; and they may also be employed as financial agents of the Government; and they shall perform all such reasonable duties, as depositaries of public money and financial agents of the Government, as may be required of them. The Secretary of the Treasury shall require of the banks and trust companies thus designated satisfactory security, by the deposit of United States bonds or otherwise, for the safe keeping and prompt payment of the public money deposited with them and for the faithful performance of their duties as financial agents of the Government.

§ 333. Mutual savings banks; application and admission to membership in Federal Reserve System

Any mutual savings bank having no capital stock (including any other banking institution the capital of which consists of weekly or other time deposits which are segregated from all other deposits and are regarded as capital stock for the purposes of taxation and the declaration of dividends), but having surplus and undivided profits not less than the amount of capital required for the organization of a national bank in the same place, may apply for and be admitted to membership in the Federal Reserve System in the same manner and subject to the same provisions of law as State banks and trust companies, except that any such savings bank shall subscribe for capital stock of the Federal reserve bank in an amount equal to six-tenths of 1 per centum of its total deposit liabilities as shown by the most recent report of examination of such savings bank preceding its admission to membership. Thereafter such subscription shall be adjusted semiannually on the same percentage basis in accordance with rules and regulations prescribed by the Board of Governors of the Federal Reserve System. If any such mutual savings bank applying for membership is not permitted by the laws under which it was organized to purchase stock in a Federal reserve bank, it shall, upon admission to the system, deposit with the Federal reserve bank an amount equal to the amount which it would have been required to pay in on account of a subscription to capital stock. Thereafter such deposit shall be adjusted semiannually in the same manner as subscriptions for stock. Such deposits shall be subject to the same conditions with respect to repayment as amounts paid upon subscriptions to capital stock by other member banks and the Federal reserve bank shall pay interest thereon at the same rate as dividends are actually paid on outstanding shares of stock of such Federal reserve bank. If the laws under which any such savings bank was organized be amended so as to authorize mutual savings banks to subscribe for Federal reserve bank stock, such savings bank shall thereupon subscribe for the appropriate amount of stock in the Federal reserve bank, and the deposit hereinbefore provided for in lieu of payment upon capital stock shall be applied upon such subscription. If the laws under which any such savings bank was organized be not amended at the next session of the legislature following the admission of such savings bank to membership so as to authorize mutual savings banks to purchase Federal reserve bank stock, or if such laws be so amended and such bank fail within six months thereafter to purchase such stock, all of its rights and privileges as a member bank shall be forfeited and its membership in the Federal Reserve System shall be terminated in the manner prescribed in this subchapter with respect to State member banks and trust companies. Each such mutual savings bank shall comply with all the provisions of law applicable to State member banks and trust companies, with the regulations of the Board of Governors of the Federal Reserve System and with the conditions of membership prescribed for such savings bank at the time of admission to membership, except as otherwise hereinbefore provided with respect to capital stock.

§ 334. Reports from affiliates; penalty for failure to furnish

Each bank admitted to membership under this subchapter shall obtain from each of its affiliates other than member banks and furnish to the Federal reserve bank of its district and to the Board of Governors of the Federal Reserve System not less than three reports during each year. Such reports shall be in such form as the Board of Governors of the Federal Reserve System may prescribe, shall be verified by the oath or affirmation of the president or such other officer as may be designated by the board of directors of such affiliate to verify such reports, and shall disclose the information hereinafter provided for as of dates identical with those fixed by the Board of Governors of the Federal Reserve System for reports of the condition of the affiliated member bank. Each such report of an affiliate shall be transmitted as herein provided at the same time as the corresponding report of the affiliated member bank, except that the Board of Governors of the Federal Reserve System may, in its discretion, extend such time for good cause shown. Each such report shall contain such information as in the judgment of the Board of Governors of the Federal Reserve System shall be necessary to disclose fully the relations between such affiliate and such bank and to enable the board to inform itself as to the effect of such relations upon the affairs of such bank. The reports of such affiliates shall be published by the bank under the same conditions as govern its own condition reports.

Any such affiliated member bank may be required to obtain from any such affiliate such additional reports as in the opinion of its Federal reserve bank or the Board of Governors of the Federal Reserve System may be necessary in order to obtain a full and complete knowledge of the condition of the affiliated member bank. Such additional reports shall be transmitted to the Federal reserve bank and the Board of Governors of the Federal Reserve System and shall be in such form as the Board of Governors of the Federal Reserve System may prescribe.

Any such affiliated member bank which fails to obtain from any of its affiliates and furnish any report provided for by the two preceding paragraphs of this section shall be subject to a penalty of $100 for each day during which such failure continues, which, by direction of the Board of Governors of the Federal Reserve System, may be collected, by suit or otherwise, by the Federal reserve bank of the district in which such member bank is located.

§ 335. Dealing in investment securities; limitations and conditions

State member banks shall be subject to the same limitations and conditions with respect to the purchasing, selling, underwriting, and holding of investment securities and stock as are applicable in the case of national banks under paragraph "Seventh" of section 24 of this title. This paragraph shall not apply to any interest held by a State member bank in accordance with section 24a of this title and subject to the same conditions and limitations provided in such section.

§ 336. Certificates of stock; representation of stock of other corporations

After August 23, 1935, no certificate evidencing the stock of any State member bank shall bear any statement purporting to represent the stock of any other corporation, except a member bank or a corporation engaged on June 16, 1934, in holding the bank premises of such member bank, nor shall the ownership, sale, or transfer of any certificate representing the stock of any State member bank be conditioned in any manner whatsoever upon the ownership, sale, or transfer of a certificate representing the stock of any other corporation, except a member bank or a corporation engaged on June 16, 1934 in holding the bank premises of such member bank: Provided, That this subchapter shall not operate to prevent the ownership, sale, or transfer of stock of any other corporation being conditioned upon the ownership, sale, or transfer of a certificate representing stock of a State member bank.

§ 337. Repealed. Pub. L. 89–485, § 13(g), July 1, 1966, 80 Stat. 243

§ 338. Examination of affiliates; forfeiture of membership on refusal of affiliate to give information or pay expense

In connection with examinations of State member banks, examiners selected or approved by the Board of Governors of the Federal Reserve System shall make such examinations of the affairs of all affiliates of such banks as shall be necessary to disclose fully the relations between such banks and their affiliates and the effect of such relations upon the affairs of such banks. The expense of examination of affiliates of any State member bank may, in the discretion of the Board of Governors of the Federal Reserve System, be assessed against such bank and, when so assessed, shall be paid by such bank. In the event of the refusal to give any information requested in the course of the examination of any such affiliate, or in the event of the refusal to permit such examination, or in the event of the refusal to pay any expenses so assessed, the Board of Governors of the Federal Reserve System may, in its discretion, require any or all State member banks affiliated with such affiliate to surrender their stock in the Federal Reserve bank and to forfeit all rights and privileges of membership in the Federal Reserve System, as provided in this subchapter.

§ 338a. Investments to promote public welfare and community development; limitation on investments

A State member bank may make investments directly or indirectly, each of which promotes the public welfare by benefiting primarily low- and moderate-income communities or families (such as by providing housing, services, or jobs), to the extent permissible under State law. A State member bank shall not make any such investment if the investment would expose the State member bank to unlimited liability. The Board shall limit a State member bank's investment in any 1 project and a State member bank's aggregate investments under this paragraph. The aggregate amount of investments of any State member bank under this paragraph may not exceed an amount equal to the sum of 5 percent of the State member bank's capital stock actually paid in and unimpaired and 5 percent of the State member bank's unimpaired surplus, unless the Board determines, by order, that a higher amount will pose no significant risk to the affected deposit insurance fund; and the State member bank is adequately capitalized. In no case shall the aggregate amount of investments of any State member bank under this paragraph exceed an amount equal to the sum of 15 percent of the State member bank's capital stock actually paid in and unimpaired and 15 percent of the State member bank's unimpaired surplus. The foregoing standards and limitations apply to investments under this paragraph made by a State member bank directly and by its subsidiaries.

§ 339. Participation by State member banks in lotteries and related activities

(a) Prohibited activities

A State member bank may not—

(1) deal in lottery tickets;

(2) deal in bets used as a means or substitute for participation in a lottery;

(3) announce, advertise, or publicize the existence of any lottery;

(4) announce, advertise, or publicize the existence or identity of any participant or winner, as such, in a lottery.

(b) Use of banking premises prohibited

A State member bank may not permit—

(1) the use of any part of any of its banking offices by any person for any purpose forbidden to the bank under subsection (a) of this section, or

(2) direct access by the public from any of its banking offices to any premises used by any person for any purpose forbidden to the bank under subsection (a) of this section.

(c) Definitions

As used in this section—

(1) The term "deal in" includes making, taking, buying, selling, redeeming, or collecting.

(2) The term "lottery" includes any arrangement whereby three or more persons (the "participants") advance money or credit to another in exchange for the possibility or expectation that one or more but not all of the participants (the "winners") will receive by reason of their advances more than the amounts they have advanced, the identity of the winners being determined by any means which includes—

(A) a random selection;

(B) a game, race, or contest; or

(C) any record or tabulation of the result of one or more events in which any participant has no interest except for its bearing upon the possibility that he may become a winner.

(3) The term "lottery ticket" includes any right, privilege, or possibility (and any ticket, receipt, record, or other evidence of any such right, privilege, or possibility) of becoming a winner in a lottery.

(d) Lawful banking services connected with operation of lottery

Nothing contained in this section prohibits a State member bank from accepting deposits or cashing or otherwise handling checks or other negotiable instruments, or performing other lawful banking services for a State operating a lottery, or for an officer or employee of that State who is charged with the administration of the lottery.

(e) Regulations; enforcement

The Board of Governors of the Federal Reserve System shall issue such regulations as may be necessary to the strict enforcement of this section and the prevention of evasions thereof.

§ 339a.   Resolution of clearing banks

(a) Conservatorship or receivership

(1) Appointment

The Board may appoint a conservator or receiver to take possession and control of any uninsured State member bank which operates, or operates as, a multilateral clearing organization pursuant to section 4422 of this title to the same extent and in the same manner as the Comptroller of the Currency may appoint a conservator or receiver for a national bank.

(2) Powers

The conservator or receiver for an uninsured State member bank referred to in paragraph (1) shall exercise the same powers, functions, and duties, subject to the same limitations, as a conservator or receiver for a national bank.

(b) Board authority

The Board shall have the same authority with respect to any conservator or receiver appointed under subsection (a) of this section, and the uninsured State member bank for which the conservator or receiver has been appointed, as the Comptroller of the Currency has with respect to a conservator or receiver for a national bank and the national bank for which the conservator or receiver has been appointed.

(c) Bankruptcy proceedings

The Board (in the case of an uninsured State member bank which operates, or operates as, such a multilateral clearing organization) may direct a conservator or receiver appointed for the bank to file a petition pursuant to Title 11, in which case, Title 11 shall apply to the bank in lieu of otherwise applicable Federal or State insolvency law.

§ 341. General enumeration of powers— DFA § 1107

Upon the filing of the organization certificate with the Comptroller of the Currency a Federal Reserve bank shall become a body corporate and as such, and in the name designated in such organization certificate, shall have power—

First. To adopt and use a corporate seal.

Second. To have succession after February 25, 1927, until dissolved by Act of Congress or until forfeiture of franchise for violation of law.

Third. To make contracts.

Fourth. To sue and be sued, complain and defend, in any court of law or equity.

Fifth. To appoint by its board of directors a president, vice presidents, and such officers and employees as are not otherwise provided for in this chapter, to define their duties, require bonds for them and fix the penalty thereof, and to dismiss at pleasure such officers or employees. The president shall be the chief executive officer of the bank and shall be appointed by the board of directors, with the approval of the Board of Governors of the Federal Reserve System, for a term of five years; and all other executive officers and all employees of the bank shall be directly responsible to him. The first vice president of the bank shall be appointed in the same manner and for the same term as the president, and shall, in the absence or disability of the president or during a vacancy in the office of president, serve as chief executive officer of the bank. Whenever a vacancy shall occur in the office of the president or the first vice president, it shall be filled in the manner provided for original appointments; and the person so appointed shall hold office until the expiration of the term of his predecessor.

Sixth. To prescribe by its board of directors, bylaws not inconsistent with law, regulating the manner in which its general business may be conducted, and the privileges granted to it by law may be exercised and enjoyed.

Seventh. To exercise by its board of directors, or duly authorized officers or agents, all powers specifically granted by the provisions of this chapter and such incidental powers as shall be necessary to carry on the business of banking within the limitations prescribed by this chapter.

Eighth. Upon deposit with the Treasurer of the United States of any bonds of the United States in the manner provided by existing law relating to national banks, to receive from the Secretary of the Treasury circulating notes in blank, registered and countersigned as provided by law, equal in amount to the par value of the bonds so deposited, such notes to be issued under the same conditions and provisions of law as relate to the issue of circulating notes of national banks secured by bonds of the United States bearing the circulating privilege, except that the issue of such notes shall not be limited to the capital stock of such Federal Reserve bank.

But no Federal Reserve bank shall transact any business except such as is incidental and necessarily preliminary to its organization until it has been authorized by the Comptroller of the Currency to commence business under the provisions of this chapter.

§ 342. Deposits; exchange and collection; member and nonmember banks or other depository institutions; charges

Any Federal reserve bank may receive from any of its member banks, or other depository institutions, and from the United States, deposits of current funds in lawful money, national-bank notes, Federal reserve notes, or checks, and drafts, payable upon presentation or other items, and also, for collection, maturing notes and bills; or, solely for purposes of exchange or of collection, may receive from other Federal reserve banks deposits of current funds in lawful money, national-bank notes, or checks upon other Federal reserve banks, and checks and drafts, payable upon presentation within its district or other items, and maturing notes and bills payable within its district; or, solely for the purposes of exchange or of collection, may receive from any nonmember bank or trust company or other depository institution deposits of current funds in lawful money, national-bank notes, Federal reserve notes, checks and drafts payable upon presentation or other items, or maturing notes and bills: Provided, Such nonmember bank or trust company or other depository institution maintains with the Federal reserve bank of its district a balance in such amount as the Board determines taking into account items in transit, services provided by the Federal Reserve Bank, and other factors as the Board may deem appropriate: Provided further, That nothing in this or any other section of this chapter shall be construed as prohibiting a member or nonmember bank or other depository institution from making reasonable charges, to be determined and regulated by the Board of Governors of the Federal Reserve System, but in no case to exceed 10 cents per $100 or fraction thereof, based on the total of checks and drafts presented at any one time, for collection or payment of checks and drafts and remission therefor by exchange or otherwise; but no such charges shall be made against the Federal reserve banks.

§ 343. Discount of obligations arising out of actual commercial transactions— DFA § 1101

Upon the indorsement of any of its member banks, which shall be deemed a waiver of demand, notice and protest by such bank as to its own indorsement exclusively, any Federal reserve bank may discount notes, drafts, and bills of exchange arising out of actual commercial transactions; that is, notes, drafts, and bills of exchange issued or drawn for agricultural, industrial, or commercial purposes, or the proceeds of which have been used, or are to be used, for such purposes, the Board of Governors of the Federal Reserve System to have the right to determine or define the character of the paper thus eligible for discount, within the meaning of this chapter. Nothing in this chapter contained shall be construed to prohibit such notes, drafts, and bills of exchange, secured by staple agricultural products, or other goods, wares, or merchandise from being eligible for such discount, and the notes, drafts, and bills of exchange of factors issued as such making advances exclusively to producers of staple agricultural products in their raw state shall be eligible for such discount; but such definition shall not include notes, drafts, or bills covering merely investments or issued or drawn for the purpose of carrying or trading in stocks, bonds, or other investment securities, except bonds and notes of the Government of the United States. Notes, drafts, and bills admitted to discount under the terms of this paragraph must have a maturity at the time of discount of not more than ninety days, exclusive of grace.

In unusual and exigent circumstances, the Board of Governors of the Federal Reserve System, by the affirmative vote of not less than five members, may authorize any Federal reserve bank, during such periods as the said board may determine, at rates established in accordance with the provisions of section 357 of this title, to discount for any individual, partnership, or cor-poration, notes, drafts, and bills of exchange when such notes, drafts, and bills of exchange are indorsed or otherwise secured to the satisfaction of the Federal reserve bank: Provided, That before discounting any such note, draft, or bill of exchange for an individual or a partnership or corporation the Federal reserve bank shall obtain evidence that such individual, partnership, or corporation is unable to secure adequate credit accommodations from other banking institutions. All such discounts for individuals, partnerships, or corporations shall be subject to such limitations, restrictions, and regulations as the Board of Governors of the Federal Reserve System may prescribe.

§ 344. Discount or purchase of bills to finance agricultural shipments

Upon the indorsement of any of its member banks, which shall be deemed a waiver of demand, notice, and protest by such bank as to its own indorsement exclusively, and subject to regulations and limitations to be prescribed by the Board of Governors of the Federal Reserve System, any Federal reserve bank may discount or purchase bills of exchange payable at sight or on demand which grow out of the domestic shipment or the exportation of nonperishable, readily marketable agricultural and other staples and are secured by bills of lading or other shipping documents conveying or securing title to such staples: Provided, That all such bills of exchange shall be forwarded promptly for collection, and demand for payment shall be made with reasonable promptness after the arrival of such staples at their destination: Provided further, That no such bill shall in any event be held by or for the account of a Federal reserve bank for a period in excess of ninety days. In discounting such bills Federal reserve banks may compute the interest to be deducted on the basis of the estimated life of each bill and adjust the discount after payment of such bills to conform to the actual life thereof.

§ 345. Rediscount of notes, drafts, and bills for member banks; limitation of amount

The aggregate of notes, drafts, and bills upon which any person, copartnership, association, or corporation is liable as maker, acceptor, indorser, drawer, or guarantor, rediscounted for any member bank, shall at no time exceed the amount for which such person, copartnership, association, or corporation may lawfully become liable to a national banking association under the terms of section 84 of this title: Provided, however, That nothing in this section shall be construed to change the character or class of paper now eligible for rediscount by Federal reserve banks.

§ 346. Discount of acceptances

Any Federal reserve bank may discount acceptances of the kinds hereinafter described, which have a maturity at the time of discount of not more than ninety days' sight, exclusive of days of grace, and which are indorsed by at least one member bank: *Provided*, That such acceptances if drawn for an agricultural purpose and secured at the time of acceptance by warehouse receipts or other such documents conveying or securing title covering readily marketable staples may be discounted with a maturity at the time of discount of not more than six months' sight exclusive of days of grace.

§ 347. Advances to member banks on their notes

Any Federal reserve bank may make advances for periods not exceeding fifteen days to its member banks on their promissory notes secured by the deposit or pledge of bonds, notes, certificates of indebtedness, or Treasury bills of the United States, or by the deposit or pledge of debentures or other such obligations of Federal intermediate credit banks which are eligible for purchase by Federal reserve banks under section 350 of this title, or by the deposit or pledge of bonds issued under the provisions of subsection (c) of section 1463 of this title; and any Federal reserve bank may make advances for periods not exceeding ninety days to its member banks on their promissory notes secured by such notes, drafts, bills of exchange, or bankers' acceptances as are eligible for rediscount or for purchase by Federal reserve banks under the provisions of this chapter, or secured by such obligations as are eligible for purchase under section 355 of this title. All such advances shall be made at rates to be established by such Federal reserve banks, such rates to be subject to the review and determination of the Board of Governors of the Federal Reserve System. If any member bank to which any such advance has been made shall, during the life or continuance of such advance, and despite an official warning of the reserve bank of the district or

of the Board of Governors of the Federal Reserve System to the contrary, increase its outstanding loans secured by collateral in the form of stocks, bonds, debentures, or other such obligations, or loans made to members of any organized stock exchange, investment house, or dealer in securities, upon any obligation, note, or bill, secured or unsecured, for the purpose of purchasing and/or carrying stocks, bonds, or other investment securities (except obligations of the United States) such advance shall be deemed immediately due and payable, and such member bank shall be ineligible as a borrower at the reserve bank of the district under the provisions of this section for such period as the Board of Governors of the Federal Reserve System shall determine: Provided, That no temporary carrying or clearance loans made solely for the purpose of facilitating the purchase or delivery of securities offered for public subscription shall be included in the loans referred to in this section.

§ 347a. Advances to member bank groups; inadequate amounts of eligible and acceptable assets; liability of individual banks in group; distribution of loans among banks of group; rate of interest; notes accepted for advances as collateral security for Federal reserve notes; foreign obligations as security for advances

Upon receiving the consent of not less than five members of the Board of Governors of the Federal Reserve System, any Federal reserve bank may make advances, in such amount as the board of directors of such Federal reserve bank may determine, to groups of five or more member banks within its district, a majority of them independently owned and controlled, upon their time or demand promissory notes, provided the bank or banks which receive the proceeds of such advances as herein provided have no adequate amounts of eligible and acceptable assets available to enable such bank or banks to obtain sufficient credit accommodations from the Federal reserve bank through rediscounts or advances other than as provided in section 347b of this title. The liability of the individual banks in each group must be limited to such proportion of the total amount advanced to such group as the deposit liability of the respective banks bears to the aggregate deposit liability of all banks in such group, but such advances may be made to a lesser number of such member banks if the aggregate amount of their deposit liability constitutes at least 10 per centum of the entire deposit liability of the member banks within such district. Such banks shall be authorized to distribute the proceeds of such loans to such of their number and in such amount as they may agree upon, but before so doing they shall require such recipient banks to deposit with a suitable trustee, representing the entire group, their individual notes made in favor of the group protected by such collateral security as may be agreed upon. Any Federal reserve bank making such advance shall charge interest or discount thereon at a rate not less than 1 per centum above its discount rate in effect at the time of making such advance. No such note upon which advances are made by a Federal reserve bank under this section shall be eligible under section 412 of this title as collateral security for Federal reserve notes.

No obligations of any foreign government, individual, partnership, association, or corporation organized under the laws thereof shall be eligible as collateral security for advances under this section.

Member banks are authorized to obligate themselves in accordance with the provisions of this section.

§ 347b. Advances to individual member banks on time or demand notes; maturities; time notes secured by mortgages loans covering one-to-four family residences

(a) In general

Any Federal Reserve bank, under rules and regulations prescribed by the Board of Governors of the Federal Reserve System, may make advances to any member bank on its time or demand notes having maturities of not more than four months and which are secured to the satisfaction of such Federal Reserve bank.

Notwithstanding the foregoing, any Federal Reserve bank, under rules and regulations prescribed by the Board of Governors of the Federal Reserve System, may make advances to any member bank on its time notes having such maturities as the Board may prescribe and which are secured by mortgage loans covering a one-to-four family residence. Such advances shall bear interest at a rate equal to the lowest discount

rate in effect at such Federal Reserve bank on the date of such note.

(b) Limitations on advances

(1) Limitation on extended periods

Except as provided in paragraph (2), no advances to any undercapitalized depository institution by any Federal Reserve bank under this section may be outstanding for more than 60 days in any 120–day period.

(2) Viability exception

(A) In general

If—

(i) the head of the appropriate Federal banking agency certifies in advance in writing to the Federal Reserve bank that any depository institution is viable; or

(ii) the Board conducts an examination of any depository institution and the Chairman of the Board certifies in writing to the Federal Reserve bank that the institution is viable,

the limitation contained in paragraph (1) shall not apply during the 60–day period beginning on the date such certification is received.

(B) Extensions of period

The 60–day period may be extended for additional 60–day periods upon receipt by the Federal Reserve bank of additional written certifications under subparagraph (A) with respect to each such additional period.

(C) Authority to issue a certificate of viability may not be delegated

The authority of the head of any agency to issue a written certification of viability under this paragraph may not be delegated to any other person.

(D) Extended advances subject to paragraph (3)

Notwithstanding paragraph (1), an undercapitalized depository institution which does not have a certificate of viability in effect under this paragraph may have advances outstanding for more than 60 days in any 120–day period if the Board elects to treat—

(i) such institution as critically undercapitalized under paragraph (3); and

(ii) any such advance as an advance described in subparagraph (A)(i) of paragraph (3).

(3) Advances to critically undercapitalized depository institutions

(A) Liability for increased loss

Notwithstanding any other provision of this section, if—

(i) in the case of any critically undercapitalized depository institution—

(I) any advance under this section to such institution is outstanding without payment having been demanded as of the end of the 5–day period beginning on the date the institution becomes a critically undercapitalized depository institution; or

(II) any new advance is made to such institution under this section after the end of such period; and

(ii) after the end of that 5–day period, any deposit insurance fund in the Federal Deposit Insurance Corporation incurs a loss exceeding the loss that the Corporation would have incurred if it had liquidated that institution as of the end of that period,

the Board shall, subject to the limitations in subparagraph (B), be liable to the Federal Deposit Insurance Corporation for the excess loss, without regard to the terms of the advance or any collateral pledged to secure the advance.

(B) Limitation on excess loss

The liability of the Board under subparagraph (A) shall not exceed the lesser of the following:

(i) The amount of the loss the Board or any Federal Reserve bank would have incurred on the increases in the amount of advances made after the 5–day period referred to in subparagraph (A) if those increased advances had been unsecured.

(ii) The interest received on the increases in the amount of advances made after the 5–day period referred to in subparagraph (A).

(C) Federal Reserve to pay obligation

The Board shall pay the Federal Deposit Insurance Corporation the amount of any liability of the Board under subparagraph (A).

(D) Report

The Board shall report to the Congress on any excess loss liability it incurs under subparagraph (A), as limited by subparagraph (B)(i), and the reasons therefore, not later than 6 months after incurring the liability.

(4) No obligation to make advances

A Federal Reserve bank shall have no obligation to make, increase, renew, or extend any advance or discount under this chapter to any depository institution.

(5) Definitions

(A) Appropriate Federal banking agency

The term "appropriate Federal banking agency" has the same meaning as in section 1813 of this title.

(B) Critically undercapitalized

The term "critically undercapitalized" has the same meaning as in section 1831o of this title.

(C) Depository institution

The term "depository institution" has the same meaning as in section 1813 of this title.

(D) Undercapitalized depository institution

The term "undercapitalized depository institution" means any depository institution which—

(i) is undercapitalized, as defined in section 1831o of this title; or

(ii) has a composite CAMEL rating of 5 under the Uniform Financial Institutions Rating System (or an equivalent rating by any such agency under a comparable rating system) as of the most recent examination of such institution.

(E) Viable

A depository institution is "viable" if the Board or the appropriate Federal banking agency determines, giving due regard to the economic conditions and circumstances in the market in which the institution operates, that the institution—

(i) is not critically undercapitalized;

(ii) is not expected to become critically undercapitalized; and

(iii) is not expected to be placed in conservatorship or receivership.

§ 347c. Advances to individuals, partnerships, and corporations; security; interest rate

Subject to such limitations, restrictions and regulations as the Board of Governors of the Federal Reserve System may prescribe, any Federal reserve bank may make advances to any individual, partnership or corporation on the promissory notes of such individual, partnership or corporation secured by direct obligations of the United States or by any obligation which is a direct obligation of, or fully guaranteed as to principal and interest by, any agency of the United States. Such advances shall be made for periods not exceeding 90 days and shall bear interest at rates fixed from time to time by the Federal reserve bank, subject to the review and determination of the Board of Governors of the Federal Reserve System.

§ 347d. Transactions between Federal Reserve banks and branch or agency of foreign bank; matters considered

Subject to such restrictions, limitations, and regulations as may be imposed by the Board of Governors of the Federal Reserve System, each Federal Reserve bank may receive deposits from, discount paper endorsed by, and make advances to any branch or agency of a foreign bank in the same manner and to the same extent that it may exercise such powers with respect to a member bank if such branch or agency is maintaining reserves with such Reserve bank pursuant to section 3105 of this title. In exercising any such powers with respect to any such branch or agency, each Federal Reserve bank shall give due regard to account balances being maintained by such branch or agency with such Reserve bank and the proportion of the assets of such branch or agency being held as reserves under section 3105 of this title. For the purposes of this paragraph, the terms "branch", "agency", and "foreign bank" shall have the same meanings assigned to them in section 3101 of this title.

§ 348. Discount of obligations given for agricultural purposes or based upon livestock; collateral security for Federal reserve notes

Upon the indorsement of any of its member banks, which shall be deemed a waiver of demand, notice, and protest by such bank as to its own indorsement exclusively, any Federal reserve bank may, subject to regulations and limitations to be prescribed by the Board of Governors of the Federal Reserve System, discount notes, drafts, and bills of exchange issued or drawn for an agricultural purpose, or based upon livestock, and having a maturity, at the time of discount, exclusive of days of grace, not exceeding nine months, and such notes, drafts, and bills of exchange may be offered as collateral security for the issuance of Federal reserve notes under the provisions of section 16 of this Act: *Provided*, That notes, drafts, and bills of exchange with maturities in excess of six months shall not be eligible as a basis for the issuance of Federal reserve notes unless secured by warehouse receipts or other such negotiable documents conveying or securing title to readily marketable staple agricultural products or by chattel mortgage upon livestock which is being fattened for market.

§ 348a. Transactions with foreign banks; supervision of Board of Governors of the Federal Reserve System

The Board of Governors of the Federal Reserve System shall exercise special supervision over all relationships and transactions of any kind entered into by any Federal reserve bank with any foreign bank or banker, or with any group of foreign banks or bankers, and all such relationships and transactions shall be subject to such regulations, conditions, and limitations as the Board may prescribe. No officer or other representative of any Federal reserve bank shall conduct negotiations of any kind with the officers or representatives of any foreign bank or banker without first obtaining the permission of the Board of Governors of the Federal Reserve System. The Board of Governors of the Federal Reserve System shall have the right, in its discretion, to be represented in any conference or negotiations by such representative or representatives as the Board may designate. A full report of all conferences or negotiations, and all understandings or agreements arrived at or transactions agreed upon, and all other material facts appertaining to such conferences or negotiations, shall be filed with the Board of Governors of the Federal Reserve System in writing by a duly authorized officer of each Federal reserve bank which shall have participated in such conferences or negotiations.

§ 349. Rediscount for intermediate credit banks of obligations given for agricultural purposes; discount of notes made pursuant to section 1031

Any Federal reserve bank may, subject to regulations and limitations to be prescribed by the Board of Governors of the Federal Reserve System, rediscount such notes, drafts, and bills mentioned in section 348 of this title for any Federal intermediate credit bank, except that no Federal reserve bank shall rediscount for a Federal intermediate credit bank any such note or obligation which bears the indorsement of a nonmember State bank or trust company which is eligible for membership in the Federal reserve system, in accordance with subchapter VIII of this chapter. Any Federal reserve bank may also, subject to regulations and limitations to be prescribed by the Board of Governors of the Federal Reserve System, discount notes payable to and bearing the indorsement of any Federal intermediate credit bank, covering loans or advances made by such bank pursuant to the provisions of section 1031 of this title, which have maturities at the time of discount of not more than nine months, exclusive of days of grace, and which are secured by notes, drafts, or bills of exchange eligible for rediscount by Federal Reserve banks.

§ 350. Purchase and sale of debentures and like obligations of intermediate credit banks and agricultural credit corporations

Any Federal reserve bank may also buy and sell debentures and other such obligations issued by a Federal intermediate credit bank or by a national agricultural credit corporation, but only to the same extent as and subject to the same limitations as those upon which it may buy and sell bonds issued under Title I of the Federal Farm Loan Act.

§ 351. Obligations of cooperative marketing association as issued or drawn for agricultural purposes

Notes, drafts, bills of exchange or acceptances issued or drawn by cooperative marketing associations composed of producers of agricultural products shall be deemed to have been issued or drawn for an agricultural purpose, within the meaning of sections 348 and 349 to 352 of this title, if the proceeds thereof have been or are to be advanced by such association to any members thereof for an agricultural purpose, or have been or are to be used by such association in making payments to any members thereof on account of agricultural products delivered by such members to the association, or if such proceeds have been or are to be used by such association to meet expenditures incurred or to be incurred by the association in connection with the grading, processing, packing, preparation for market, or marketing of any agricultural product handled by such association for any of its members: Provided, That the express enumeration in this section of certain classes of paper of cooperative marketing associations as eligible for rediscount shall not be construed as rendering ineligible any other class of paper of such associations which is now eligible for rediscount.

§ 352. Limitation on amount of obligations of certain maturities which may be discounted and rediscounted

The Board of Governors of the Federal Reserve System may, by regulation, limit to a percentage of the assets of a Federal reserve bank the amount of notes, drafts, acceptances, or bills having a maturity in excess of three months, but not exceeding six months, exclusive of days of grace, which may be discounted by such bank, and the amount of notes, drafts, bills, or acceptances having a maturity in excess of six months, but not exceeding nine months, which may be rediscounted by such bank.

§ 352a. Repealed. Pub. L. 85–699, Title VI, § 601, Aug. 21, 1958, 72 Stat. 697

§ 353. Purchase and sale of cable transfers, acceptances and bills

Any Federal reserve bank may, under rules and regulations prescribed by the Board of Governors of the Federal Reserve System, purchase and sell in the open market, at home or abroad, either from or to domestic or foreign banks, firms, corporations, or individuals, cable transfers and bankers' acceptances and bills of exchange of the kinds and maturities by this chapter made eligible for rediscount, with or without the indorsement of a member bank.

§ 354. Transactions involving gold coin, bullion, and certificates

Every Federal reserve bank shall have power to deal in gold coin and bullion at home or abroad, to make loans thereon, exchange Federal reserve notes for gold, gold coin, or gold certificates, and to contract for loans of gold coin or bullion, giving therefor, when necessary, acceptable security, including the hypothecation of United States bonds or other securities which Federal reserve banks are authorized to hold.

§ 355. Purchase and sale of obligations of National, State, and municipal governments; open market operations; purchases and sales from or to United States; maximum aggregate amount of obligations acquired directly from or loaned directly to United States

Every Federal Reserve bank shall have power:

(1) To buy and sell, at home or abroad, bonds and notes of the United States, bonds issued under the provisions of subsection (c) of section 1463 of this title and having maturities from date of purchase of not exceeding six months, and bills, notes, revenue bonds, and warrants with a maturity from date of purchase of not exceeding six months, issued in anticipation of the collection of taxes or in anticipation of the receipt of assured revenues by any State, county, district, political subdivision, or municipality in the continental United States, including irrigation, drainage and reclamation districts, and obligations of, or fully guaranteed as to principal and interest by, a foreign government or agency thereof, such purchases to be made in accordance with rules and regulations prescribed by the Board of Governors of the Federal Reserve System. Notwithstanding any other provision of this chapter, any bonds, notes, or other obligations which are direct obligations of the United States or which are fully guaranteed by the United States as to principal and interest may be bought and sold without regard to maturities but only in the open market.

(2) To buy and sell in the open market, under the direction and regulations of the Federal Open Market Committee, any obligation which is a direct obligation of, or fully guaranteed as to principal and interest by, any agency of the United States.

§ 356. Purchase of commercial paper from member banks and sale of same

Every Federal reserve bank shall have power to purchase from member banks and to sell, with or without its indorsement, bills of exchange arising out of commercial transactions, as hereinbefore defined.

§ 357. Establishment of rates of discount

Every Federal reserve bank shall have power to establish from time to time, subject to review and determination of the Board of Governors of the Federal Reserve System, rates of discount to be charged by the Federal reserve bank for each class of paper, which shall be fixed with a view of accommodating commerce and business, but each such bank shall establish such rates every fourteen days, or oftener if deemed necessary by the Board.

§ 358. Establishment of accounts for purposes of open-market operations; correspondents and agencies

Every Federal reserve bank shall have power to establish accounts with other Federal reserve banks for exchange purposes and, with the consent or upon the order and direction of the Board of Governors of the Federal Reserve System and under regulations to be prescribed by said Board, to open and maintain accounts in foreign countries, appoint correspondents, and establish agencies in such countries wheresoever it may be deemed best for the purpose of purchasing, selling, and collecting bills of exchange, and to buy and sell, with or without its indorsement, through such correspondents or agencies, bills of exchange (or acceptances) arising out of actual commercial transactions which have not more than ninety days to run, exclusive of days of grace, and which bear the signature of two or more responsible parties, and, with the consent of the Board of Governors of the Federal Reserve System, to open and maintain banking accounts for such foreign correspondents or agencies, or for foreign banks or bankers, or for foreign states as defined in section 632 of this title. Whenever any such account has been opened or agency or correspondent has been appointed by a Federal reserve bank, with the consent of or under the order and direction of the Board of Governors of the Federal Reserve System, any other Federal reserve bank may, with the consent and approval of the Board of Governors of the Federal Reserve System, be permitted to carry on or conduct, through the Federal reserve bank opening such account or appointing such agency or correspondent, any transaction authorized by this section under rules and regulations to be prescribed by the board.

§ 359. Purchase and sale of acceptances of intermediate credit banks and agricultural credit corporations

Every Federal reserve bank shall have power to purchase and sell in the open market, either from or to domestic banks, firms, corporations, or individuals, acceptances of Federal Intermediate Credit Banks and of National Agricultural Credit Corporations, whenever the Board of Governors of the Federal Reserve System shall declare that the public interest so requires.

§ 359a. Omitted

§ 360. Receiving checks and drafts on deposit at par; charges for collections, exchange, and clearances

Every Federal reserve bank shall receive on deposit at par from depository institutions or from Federal reserve banks checks and other items, including negotiable orders of withdrawal and share drafts and drafts drawn upon any of its depositors, and when remitted by a Federal reserve bank, checks and other items, including negotiable orders of withdrawal and share drafts and drafts drawn by any depositor in any other Federal reserve bank or depository institution upon funds to the credit of said depositor in said reserve bank or depository institution. Nothing herein contained shall be construed as prohibiting a depository institution from charging its actual expense incurred in collecting and remitting funds, or for exchange sold to its patrons. The Board of Governors of the Federal Reserve System shall, by rule, fix the charges to be collected by the depository institutions from its patrons whose checks and other items, including negotiable orders of withdrawal and share drafts are cleared through the Federal reserve bank and the charge which may be imposed for the service of clearing or collection rendered by the Federal reserve bank.

§ 361. Bills receivable, bills of exchange, acceptances; regulations by Board of Governors

The discount and rediscount and the purchase and sale by any Federal reserve bank of any bills receivable and of domestic and foreign bills of exchange, and of acceptances authorized by this chapter, shall be subject to such restrictions, limitations, and regulations as may be imposed by the Board of Governors of the Federal Reserve System.

§§ 362 to 364. Omitted

§ 371. Real estate loans

(a) Authorization to make real estate loans; orders, rules, and regulations of Comptroller of the Currency

Any national banking association may make, arrange, purchase or sell loans or extensions of credit secured by liens on interests in real estate, subject to section 1828(o) of this title and such restrictions and requirements as the Comptroller of the Currency may prescribe by regulation or order.

(b) Eligibility for discount as commercial paper of notes representing loans financing construction of residential or farm buildings; prerequisites

Notes representing loans made under this section to finance the construction of residential or farm buildings and having maturities not to exceed nine months shall be eligible for discount as commercial paper within the terms of the first paragraph of section 343 of this title if accompanied by a valid and binding agreement to advance the full amount of the loan upon the completion of the building entered into by an individual, partnership, association, or corporation acceptable to the discounting bank.

§ 371a. Payment of interest on demand deposits—DFA § 627

No member bank shall, directly or indirectly, by any device whatsoever, pay any interest on any deposit which is payable on demand: *Provided*, That nothing herein contained shall be construed as prohibiting the payment of interest in accordance with the terms of any certificate of deposit or other contract entered into in good faith which is in force on the date on which the bank becomes subject to the provisions of this section; but no such certificate of deposit or other contract shall be renewed or extended unless it shall be modified to conform to this section, and every member bank shall take such action as may be necessary to conform to this section as soon as possible consistently with its contractual obligations: *Provided further*, That this section shall not apply to any deposit of such bank which is payable only at an office thereof located outside of the States of the United States and the District of Columbia: *Provided further*, That until the expiration of two years after August 23, 1935, this section shall not apply (1) to any deposit made by a savings bank as defined in section 12B of this Act, as amended, or by a mutual savings bank, or (2) to any deposit of public funds made by or on behalf of any State, county, school district, or other subdivision or municipality, or to any deposit of trust funds if the payment of interest with respect to such deposit of public funds or of trust funds is required by State law. So much of existing law as requires the payment of interest with respect to any funds deposited by the United States, by any Territory, District, or possession thereof, or by any public instrumentality, agency, or officer of the foregoing, as is inconsistent with the provisions of this section is repealed. Notwithstanding any other provision of this section, a member bank may permit withdrawals to be made automatically from a savings deposit that consists only of funds in which the entire beneficial interest is held by one or more individuals through payment to the bank itself or through transfer of credit to a demand deposit or other account pursuant to written authorization from the depositor to make such payments or transfers in connection with checks or drafts drawn upon the bank, pursuant to terms and conditions prescribed by the Board.

§ 371b.   Rate of interest on time and savings deposits

The Board may from time to time, after consulting with the Board of Directors of the Federal Deposit Insurance Corporation and the Federal Home Loan Bank Board, prescribe rules governing the advertisement of interest on deposits by member banks on time and savings deposits. The provisions of this section shall not apply to any deposit which is payable only at an office of a member bank located outside of the States of the United States and the District of Columbia. During the period commencing on October 15, 1962, and ending on October 15, 1968, the provisions of this paragraph shall not apply to the rate of interest which may be paid by member banks on time deposits of foreign governments, monetary and financial authorities of foreign governments

when acting as such, or international financial institutions of which the United States is a member.

§ 371b–1.   Repealed. Pub. L. 96–221, Title V, § 529, Mar. 31, 1980, 94 Stat. 168

§ 371b–2.   Interbank liabilities

(a) Purpose

The purpose of this section is to limit the risks that the failure of a large depository institution (whether or not that institution is an insured depository institution) would pose to insured depository institutions.

(b) Aggregate limits on insured depository institutions' exposure to other depository institutions

The Board shall, by regulation or order, prescribe standards that have the effect of limiting the risks posed by an insured depository institution's exposure to any other depository institution.

(c) "Exposure" defined

(1) In general

For purposes of subsection (b) of this section, an insured depository institution's "exposure" to another depository institution means—

(A) all extensions of credit to the other depository institution, regardless of name or description, including—

(i) all deposits at the other depository institution;

(ii) all purchases of securities or other assets from the other depository institution subject to an agreement to repurchase; and

(iii) all guarantees, acceptances, or letters of credit (including endorsements or standby letters of credit) on behalf of the other depository institution;

(B) all purchases of or investments in securities issued by the other depository institution;

(C) all securities issued by the other depository institution accepted as collateral for an extension of credit to any person; and

(D) all similar transactions that the Board by regulation determines to be exposure for purposes of this section.

(2) Exemptions

The Board may, at its discretion, by regulation or order, exempt transactions from the definition of "exposure" if it finds the exemptions to be in the public interest and consistent with the purpose of this section.

(3) Attribution rule

For purposes of this section, any transaction by an insured depository institution with any person is a transaction with another depository institution to the extent that the proceeds of the transaction are used for the benefit of, or transferred to, that other depository institution.

(d) Insured depository institution

For purposes of this section, the term "insured depository institution" has the same meaning as in section 1813 of this title.

(e) Rulemaking authority; enforcement

The Board may issue such regulations and orders, including definitions consistent with this section, as may be necessary to administer and carry out the purpose of this section. The appropriate Federal banking agency shall enforce compliance with those regulations under section 1818 of this title.

§ 371c. Banking affiliates—DFA §§ 608, 609

(a) Restrictions on transactions with affiliates

(1) A member bank and its subsidiaries may engage in a covered transaction with an affiliate only if—

(A) in the case of any affiliate, the aggregate amount of covered transactions of the member bank and its subsidiaries will not exceed 10 per centum of the capital stock and surplus of the member bank; and

(B) in the case of all affiliates, the aggregate amount of covered transactions of the member bank and its subsidiaries will not exceed 20 per centum of the capital stock and surplus of the member bank.

(2) For the purpose of this section, any transaction by a member bank with any person shall be deemed to be a transaction with an affiliate to the extent that the proceeds of the transaction are used for the benefit of, or transferred to, that affiliate.

(3) A member bank and its subsidiaries may not purchase a low-quality asset from an affiliate unless the bank or such subsidiary, pursuant to an independent credit evaluation, committed itself to purchase such asset prior to the time such asset was acquired by the affiliate.

(4) Any covered transactions and any transactions exempt under subsection (d) of this section between a member bank and an affiliate shall be on terms and conditions that are consistent with safe and sound banking practices.

(b) Definitions

For the purpose of this section—

(1) the term "affiliate" with respect to a member bank means—

(A) any company that controls the member bank and any other company that is controlled by the company that controls the member bank;

(B) a bank subsidiary of the member bank;

(C) any company—

(i) that is controlled directly or indirectly, by a trust or otherwise, by or for the benefit of shareholders who beneficially or otherwise control, directly or indirectly, by trust or otherwise, the member bank or any company that controls the member bank; or

(ii) in which a majority of its directors or trustees constitute a majority of the persons holding any such office with the member bank or any company that controls the member bank;

(D)(i) any company, including a real estate investment trust, that is sponsored and advised on a contractual basis by the member bank or any subsidiary or affiliate of the member bank; or

(ii) any investment company with respect to which a member bank or any affiliate thereof is an investment advisor as defined in section 80a-2(a)(20) of Title 15; and

(E) any company that the board determines by regulation or order to have a relationship with the member bank or any subsidiary or affiliate of the member bank, such that covered transactions by the member bank or its subsidiary with that company may be affected by the relationship to the detriment of the member bank or its subsidiary; and

(2) the following shall not be considered to be an affiliate:

(A) any company, other than a bank, that is a subsidiary of a member bank, unless a determination is made under paragraph (1)(E) not to exclude such subsidiary company from the definition of affiliate;

(B) any company engaged solely in holding the premises of the member bank;

(C) any company engaged solely in conducting a safe deposit business;

(D) any company engaged solely in holding obligations of the United States or its agencies or obligations fully guaranteed by the United States or its agencies as to principal and interest; and

(E) any company where control results from the exercise of rights arising out of a bona fide debt previously contracted, but only for the period of time specifically authorized under applicable State or Federal law or regulation or, in the absence of such law or regulation, for a period of two years from the date of the exercise of such rights or the effective date of this Act, whichever date is later, subject, upon application, to authorization by the Board for good cause shown of extensions of time for not more than one year at a time, but such extensions in the aggregate shall not exceed three years;

(3) (A) a company or shareholder shall be deemed to have control over another company if—

(i) such company or shareholder, directly or indirectly, or acting through one or more other persons owns, controls, or has power to vote 25 per centum or more of any class of voting securities of the other company;

(ii) such company or shareholder controls in any manner the election of a majority of the directors or trustees of the other company; or

(iii) the Board determines, after notice and opportunity for hearing, that such company or shareholder, directly or indirectly, exercises a controlling influence over the management or policies of the other company; and

(B) notwithstanding any other provision of this section, no company shall be deemed to own or control another company by virtue of its ownership or control of shares in a fiduciary capacity, except as provided in paragraph (1)(C) of this subsection or if the com-

pany owning or controlling such shares is a business trust;

(4) the term "subsidiary" with respect to a specified company means a company that is controlled by such specified company;

(5) the term "bank" includes a State bank, national bank, banking association, and trust company;

(6) the term "company" means a corporation, partnership, business trust, association, or similar organization and, unless specifically excluded, the term "company" includes a "member bank" and a "bank";

(7) the term "covered transaction" means with respect to an affiliate of a member bank—

(A) a loan or extension of credit to the affiliate;

(B) a purchase of or an investment in securities issued by the affiliate;

(C) a purchase of assets, including assets subject to an agreement to repurchase, from the affiliate, except such purchase of real and personal property as may be specifically exempted by the Board by order or regulation;

(D) the acceptance of securities issued by the affiliate as collateral security for a loan or extension of credit to any person or company; or

(E) the issuance of a guarantee, acceptance, or letter of credit, including an endorsement or standby letter of credit, on behalf of an affiliate;

(8) the term "aggregate amount of covered transactions" means the amount of the covered transactions about to be engaged in added to the current amount of all outstanding covered transactions;

(9) the term "securities" means stocks, bonds, debentures, notes, or other similar obligations; and

(10) the term "low-quality asset" means an asset that falls in any one or more of the following categories:

(A) an asset classified as "substandard", "doubtful", or "loss" or treated as "other loans especially mentioned" in the most recent report of examination or inspection of an affiliate prepared by either a Federal or State supervisory agency;

(B) an asset in a nonaccrual status;

(C) an asset on which principal or interest payments are more than thirty days past due; or

(D) an asset whose terms have been renegotiated or compromised due to the deteriorating financial condition of the obligor.

(11) Rebuttable presumption of control of portfolio companies

In addition to paragraph (3), a company or shareholder shall be presumed to control any other company if the company or shareholder, directly or indirectly, or acting through 1 or more other persons, owns or controls 15 percent or more of the equity capital of the other company pursuant to subparagraph (H) or (I) of section 1843(k)(4) of this title or rules adopted under section 122 of the Gramm–Leach–Bliley Act, if any, unless the company or shareholder provides information acceptable to the Board to rebut this presumption of control.

(c) Collateral for certain transactions with affiliates

(1) Each loan or extension of credit to, or guarantee, acceptance, or letter of credit issued on behalf of, an affiliate by a member bank or its subsidiary shall be secured at the time of the transaction by collateral having a market value equal to—

(A) 100 per centum of the amount of such loan or extension of credit, guarantee, acceptance, or letter of credit, if the collateral is composed of—

(i) obligations of the United states or its agencies;

(ii) obligations fully guaranteed by the United States or its agencies as to principal and interest;

(iii) notes, drafts, bills of exchange or bankers' acceptances that are eligible for rediscount or purchase by a Federal Reserve Bank; or

(iv) a segregated, earmarked deposit account with the member bank;

(B) 110 per centum of the amount of such loan or extension of credit, guarantee, acceptance, or letter of credit if the collateral is composed of obligations of any State or political subdivision of any State;

(C) 120 per centum of the amount of such loan or extension of credit, guarantee, acceptance, or letter of credit if the collateral is composed of other debt instruments, including receivables; or

(D) 130 per centum of the amount of such loan or extension of credit, guarantee, acceptance, or letter of credit if the collateral is composed of stock, leases, or other real or personal property.

(2) Any such collateral that is subsequently retired or amortized shall be replaced by additional eligible collateral where needed to keep the percentage of the collateral value relative to the amount of the outstanding loan or extension of credit, guarantee, acceptance, or letter of credit equal to the minimum percentage required at the inception of the transaction.

(3) A low-quality asset shall not be acceptable as collateral for a loan or extension of credit to, or guarantee, acceptance, or letter of credit issued on behalf of, an affiliate.

(4) The securities issued by an affiliate of the member bank shall not be acceptable as collateral for a loan or extension of credit to, or guarantee, acceptance, or letter of credit issued on behalf of, that affiliate or any other affiliate of the member bank.

(5) The collateral requirements of this paragraph shall not be applicable to an acceptance that is already fully secured either by attached documents or by other property having an ascertainable market value that is involved in the transaction.

(d) Exemptions

The provisions of this section, except paragraph (a)(4) of this section, shall not be applicable to—

(1) any transaction, subject to the prohibition contained in subsection (a)(3) of this section, with a bank—

(A) which controls 80 per centum or more of the voting shares of the member bank;

(B) in which the member bank controls 80 per centum or more of the voting shares; or

(C) in which 80 per centum or more of the voting shares are controlled by the company that controls 80 per centum or more of the voting shares of the member bank;

(2) making deposits in an affiliated bank or affiliated foreign bank in the ordinary course of correspondent business, subject to any restrictions that the Board may prescribe by regulation or order;

(3) giving immediate credit to an affiliate for uncollected items received in the ordinary course of business;

(4) making a loan or extension of credit to, or issuing a guarantee, acceptance, or letter of credit on behalf of, an affiliate that is fully secured by—

(A) obligations of the United States or its agencies;

(B) obligations fully guaranteed by the United States or its agencies as to principal and interest; or

(C) a segregated, earmarked deposit account with the member bank;

(5) purchasing securities issued by any company of the kinds described in section 1843(c)(1) of this title;

(6) purchasing assets having a readily identifiable and publicly available market quotation and purchased at that market quotation or, subject to the prohibition contained in subsection (a)(3) of this section, purchasing loans on a nonrecourse basis from affiliated banks; and

(7) purchasing from an affiliate a loan or extension of credit that was originated by the member bank and sold to the affiliate subject to a repurchase agreement or with recourse.

(e) Rules relating to banks with financial subsidiaries

(1) Financial subsidiary defined

For purposes of this section and section 371c–1 of this title, the term "financial subsidiary" means any company that is a subsidiary of a bank that would be a financial subsidiary of a national bank under section 24a of this title.

(2) Financial subsidiary treated as an affiliate

For purposes of applying this section and section 371c–1 of this title, and notwithstanding subsection (b)(2) of this section or section 371c–1(d)(1) of this title, a financial subsidiary of a bank—

(A) shall be deemed to be an affiliate of the bank; and

(B) shall not be deemed to be a subsidiary of the bank.

(3) Exceptions for transactions with financial subsidiaries

(A) Exception from limit on covered transactions with any individual financial subsidiary

Notwithstanding paragraph (2), the restriction contained in subsection (a)(1)(A) shall not apply with respect to covered transactions between a bank and any individual financial subsidiary of the bank.

(B) Exception for earnings retained by financial subsidiaries

Notwithstanding paragraph (2) or subsection (b)(7), a bank's investment in a financial subsidiary of the bank shall not include retained earnings of the financial subsidiary.

(4) Anti-evasion provision

For purposes of this section and section 371c–1 of this title—

(A) any purchase of, or investment in, the securities of a financial subsidiary of a bank by an affiliate of the bank shall be considered to be a purchase of or investment in such securities by the bank; and

(B) any extension of credit by an affiliate of a bank to a financial subsidiary of the bank shall be considered to be an extension of credit by the bank to the financial subsidiary if the Board determines that such treatment is necessary or appropriate to prevent evasions of this chapter and the Gramm–Leach–Bliley Act.

(f) Rulemaking and additional exemptions

(1) The Board may issue such further regulations and orders, including definitions consistent with this section, as may be necessary to administer and carry out the purposes of this section and to prevent evasions thereof.

(2) The board may, at its discretion, by regulation or order exempt transactions or relationships from the requirements of this section if it finds such exemptions to be in the public interest and consistent with the purposes of this section.

(3) Rulemaking required concerning derivative transactions and intraday credit

(A) In general

Not later than 18 months after November 12, 1999, the Board shall adopt final rules under this section to address as covered transactions credit exposure arising out of derivative transactions between member banks and their affiliates and intraday extensions of credit by member banks to their affiliates.

(B) Effective date

The effective date of any final rule adopted by the Board pursuant to subparagraph (A) shall be delayed for such period as the Board deems necessary or appropriate to permit banks to conform their activities to the requirements of the final rule without undue hardship.

§ 371c–1. Restrictions on transactions with affiliates

(a) In general

(1) Terms

A member bank and its subsidiaries may engage in any of the transactions described in paragraph (2) only—

(A) on terms and under circumstances, including credit standards, that are substantially the same, or at least as favorable to such bank or its subsidiary, as those prevailing at the time for comparable transactions with or involving other nonaffiliated companies, or

(B) in the absence of comparable transactions, on terms and under circumstances, including credit standards, that in good faith would be offered to, or would apply to, nonaffiliated companies.

(2) Transactions covered

Paragraph (1) applies to the following:

(A) Any covered transaction with an affiliate.

(B) The sale of securities or other assets to an affiliate, including assets subject to an agreement to repurchase.

(C) The payment of money or the furnishing of services to an affiliate under contract, lease, or otherwise.

(D) Any transaction in which an affiliate acts as an agent or broker or receives a fee

for its services to the bank or to any other person.

(E) Any transaction or series of transactions with a third party—

(i) if an affiliate has a financial interest in the third party, or

(ii) if an affiliate is a participant in such transaction or series of transactions.

(3) Transactions that benefit an affiliate

For the purpose of this subsection, any transaction by a member bank or its subsidiary with any person shall be deemed to be a transaction with an affiliate of such bank if any of the proceeds of the transaction are used for the benefit of, or transferred to, such affiliate.

(b) Prohibited transactions

(1) In general

A member bank or its subsidiary—

(A) shall not purchase as fiduciary any securities or other assets from any affiliate unless such purchase is permitted—

(i) under the instrument creating the fiduciary relationship,

(ii) by court order, or

(iii) by law of the jurisdiction governing the fiduciary relationship; and

(B) whether acting as principal or fiduciary, shall not knowingly purchase or otherwise acquire, during the existence of any underwriting or selling syndicate, any security if a principal underwriter of that security is an affiliate of such bank.

(2) Exception

Subparagraph (B) of paragraph (1) shall not apply if the purchase or acquisition of such securities has been approved, before such securities are initially offered for sale to the public, by a majority of the directors of the bank based on a determination that the purchase is a sound investment for the bank irrespective of the fact that an affiliate of the bank is a principal underwriter of the securities.

(3) Definitions

For the purpose of this subsection—

(A) the term "security" has the meaning given to such term in section 78c(a)(10) of Title 15; and

(B) the term "principal underwriter" means any underwriter who, in connection with a primary distribution of securities—

(i) is in privity of contract with the issuer or an affiliated person of the issuer;

(ii) acting alone or in concert with one or more other persons, initiates or directs the formation of an underwriting syndicate; or

(iii) is allowed a rate of gross commission, spread, or other profit greater than the rate allowed another underwriter participating in the distribution.

(c) Advertising restriction

A member bank or any subsidiary or affiliate of a member bank shall not publish any advertisement or enter into any agreement stating or suggesting that the bank shall in any way be responsible for the obligations of its affiliates.

(d) Definitions

For the purpose of this section—

(1) the term "affiliate" has the meaning given to such term in section 371c of this title (but does not include any company described in section(b)(2) of such section or any bank);

(2) the terms "bank", "subsidiary", "person", and "security" (other than security as used in subsection (b) of this section) have the meanings given to such terms in section 371c of this title; and

(3) the term "covered transaction" has the meaning given to such term in section 371c of this title (but does not include any transaction which is exempt from such definition under subsection (d) of such section).

(e) Regulations

The Board may prescribe regulations to administer and carry out the purposes of this section, including—

(1) regulations to further define terms used in this section; and

(2) regulations to—

(A) exempt transactions or relationships from the requirements of this section; and

(B) exclude any subsidiary of a bank holding company from the definition of affiliate for purposes of this section,

if the Board finds such exemptions or exclusions are in the public interest and are consistent with the purposes of this section.

§ 371d. Investment in bank premises or stock of corporation holding premises

(a) Conditions of investment

No national bank or State member bank shall invest in bank premises, or in the stock, bonds, debentures, or other such obligations of any corporation holding the premises of such bank, or make loans to or upon the security of any such corporation—

(1) unless the bank receives the prior approval of the Comptroller of the Currency (with respect to a national bank) or the Board (with respect to a State member bank);

(2) unless the aggregate of all such investments and loans, together with the amount of any indebtedness incurred by any such corporation that is an affiliate of the bank, is less than or equal to the amount of the capital stock of such bank; or

(3) unless—

(A) the aggregate of all such investments and loans, together with the amount of any indebtedness incurred by any such corporation that is an affiliate of the bank, is less than or equal to 150 percent of the capital and surplus of the bank; and

(B) the bank—

(i) has a CAMEL composite rating of 1 or 2 under the Uniform Financial Institutions Rating System (or an equivalent rating under a comparable rating system) as of the most recent examination of such bank;

(ii) is well capitalized and will continue to be well capitalized after the investment or loan; and

(iii) provides notification to the Comptroller of the Currency (with respect to a national bank) or to the Board (with respect to a State member bank) not later than 30 days after making the investment or loan.

(b) Definitions

For purposes of this section—

(1) the term "affiliate" has the same meaning as in section 2 of the Banking Act of 1933; and

(2) the term "well capitalized" has the same meaning as in section 1831o(b) of this title.

§ 372. Bankers' acceptances

(a) Institutions; drafts and bills of exchange; types

Any member bank and any Federal or State branch or agency of a foreign bank subject to reserve requirements under section 3105 of this title (hereinafter in this section referred to as "institutions"), may accept drafts or bills of exchange drawn upon it having not more than six months' sight to run, exclusive of days of grace—

(i) which grow out of transactions involving the importation or exportation of goods;

(ii) which grow out of transactions involving the domestic shipment of goods; or

(iii) which are secured at the time of acceptance by a warehouse receipt or other such document conveying or securing title covering readily marketable staples.

(b) Ratio limit of bills to unimpaired capital stock and surplus

Except as provided in subsection (c) of this section, no institution shall accept such bills, or be obligated for a participation share in such bills, in an amount equal at any time in the aggregate to more than 150 per centum of its paid up and unimpaired capital stock and surplus or, in the case of a United States branch or agency of a foreign bank, its dollar equivalent as determined by the Board under subsection (h) of this section.

(c) Authorization for special ratio limit; foreign banks

The Board, under such conditions as it may prescribe, may authorize, by regulation or order, any institution to accept such bills, or be obligated for a participation share in such bills, in an amount not exceeding at any time in the aggregate 200 per centum of its paid up and unimpaired capital stock and surplus or, in the case of a United States branch or agency of a foreign bank, its dollar equivalent as determined by the Board under subsection (h) of this section.

(d) Ratio limit for domestic transactions

Notwithstanding subsections (b) and (c) of this section, with respect to any institution, the aggregate acceptances, including obligations for a participation share in such acceptances, growing out of domestic transactions shall not exceed 50 per centum of the aggregate of all acceptances, including obligations for a participation share in such acceptances, authorized for such institution under this section.

(e) Ratio limit for single entity; foreign banks; security

No institution shall accept bills, or be obligated for a participation share in such bills, whether in a foreign or domestic transaction, for any one person, partnership, corporation, association or other entity in an amount equal at any time in the aggregate to more than 10 per centum of its paid up and unimpaired capital stock and surplus, or, in the case of a United States branch or agency of a foreign bank, its dollar equivalent as determined by the Board under subsection (h) of this section, unless the institution is secured either by attached documents or by some other actual security growing out of the same transaction as the acceptance.

(f) Exception for participation agreements

With respect to an institution which issues an acceptance, the limitations contained in this section shall not apply to that portion of an acceptance which is issued by such institution and which is covered by a participation agreement sold to another institution.

(g) Definitions by Board

In order to carry out the purposes of this section, the Board may define any of the terms used in this section, and, with respect to institutions which do not have capital or capital stock, the Board shall define an equivalent measure to which the limitations contained in this section shall apply.

(h) Dollar equivalent of foreign bank paid-up capital stock and surplus

Any limitation or restriction in this section based on paid-up and unimpaired capital stock and surplus of an institution shall be deemed to refer, with respect to a United States branch or agency of a foreign bank, to the dollar equivalent of the paid-up capital stock and surplus of the foreign bank, as determined by the Board, and if the foreign bank has more than one United States branch or agency, the business transacted by all such branches and agencies shall be aggregated in determining compliance with the limitation or restriction.

§ 373. Acceptance of drafts or bills drawn by banks in foreign countries or dependencies of United States for purpose of dollar exchange

Any member bank may accept drafts or bills of exchange drawn upon it having not more than three months' sight to run, exclusive of days of grace, drawn under regulations to be prescribed by the Board of Governors of the Federal Reserve System by banks or bankers in foreign countries or dependencies or insular possessions of the United States for the purpose of furnishing dollar exchange as required by the usages of trade in the respective countries, dependencies, or insular possessions. Such drafts or bills may be acquired by Federal reserve banks in such amounts and subject to such regulations, restrictions, and limitations as may be prescribed by the Board of Governors of the Federal Reserve System: Provided, however, That no member bank shall accept such drafts or bills of exchange referred to this paragraph for any one bank to an amount exceeding in the aggregate ten per centum of the paid-up and unimpaired capital and surplus of the accepting bank unless the draft or bill of exchange is accompanied by documents conveying or securing title or by some other adequate security: Provided further, That no member bank shall accept such drafts or bills in an amount exceeding at any time the aggregate of one-half of its paid-up and unimpaired capital and surplus.

§ 374. Acting as agent for nonmember bank in getting discounts from reserve bank

No member bank shall act as the medium or agent of a nonmember bank in applying for or receiving discounts from a Federal reserve bank under the provisions of this chapter, except by permission of the Board of Governors of the Federal Reserve System.

§ 374a. Acting as agent for nonbanking borrower in making loans on securities to dealers in stocks, bonds, etc.; penalties

No member bank shall act as the medium or agent of any nonbanking corporation, partnership, association, business trust, or individual in making loans on the security of stocks, bonds, and other investment securities to brokers or dealers in stocks, bonds, and other investment securities. Every violation of this provision by any member bank shall be punishable by a fine of not more than $100 per day during the continuance of such violation; and such fine may be collected, by suit or otherwise, by the Federal reserve bank of the district in which such member bank is located.

§ 375. Purchases from directors; sales to directors—DFA § 615

Any member bank may contract for, or purchase from, any of its directors or from any firm of which any of its directors is a member, any securities or other property, when (and not otherwise) such purchase is made in the regular course of business upon terms not less favorable to the bank than those offered to others, or when such purchase is authorized by a majority of the board of directors not interested in the sale of such securities or property, such authority to be evidenced by the affirmative vote or written assent of such directors: Provided, however, That when any director, or firm of which any director is a member, acting for or on behalf of others, sells securities or other property to a member bank, the Board of Governors of the Federal Reserve System by regulation may, in any or all cases, require a full disclosure to be made, on forms to be prescribed by it, of all commissions or other considerations received, and whenever such director or firm, acting in his or its own behalf, sells securities or other property to the bank the Board of Governors of the Federal Reserve System, by regulation, may require a full disclosure of all profit realized from such sale.

Any member bank may sell securities or other property to any of its directors, or to a firm of which any of its directors is a member, in the regular course of business on terms not more favorable to such director or firm than those offered to others, or when such sale is authorized by a majority of the board of directors of a member bank to be evidenced by their affirmative vote or written assent: Provided, however, That nothing in this section contained shall be construed as authorizing member banks to purchase or sell securities or other property which such banks are not otherwise authorized by law to purchase or sell.

§ 375a. Loans to executive officers of banks

(1) General prohibition; authorization for extension of credit; conditions for credit

Except as authorized under this section, no member bank may extend credit in any manner to any of its own executive officers. No executive officer of any member bank may become indebted to that member bank except by means of an extension of credit which the bank is authorized to make under this section. Any extension of credit under this section shall be promptly reported to the board of directors of the bank, and may be made only if—

(A) the bank would be authorized to make it to borrowers other than its officers;

(B) it is on terms not more favorable than those afforded other borrowers;

(C) the officer has submitted a detailed current financial statement; and

(D) it is on condition that it shall become due and payable on demand of the bank at any time when the officer is indebted to any other bank or banks on account of extensions of credit of any one of the three categories respectively referred to in paragraphs (2), (3), and (4) in an aggregate amount greater than the amount of credit of the same category that could be extended to him by the bank of which he is an officer.

(2) Mortgage loans

A member bank may make a loan to any executive officer of the bank if, at the time the loan is made—

(A) it is secured by a first lien on a dwelling which is expected, after the making of the loan, to be owned by the officer and used by him as his residence, and

(B) no other loan by the bank to the officer under authority of this paragraph is outstanding.

(3) Educational loans

A member bank may make extensions of credit to any executive officer of the bank to finance the education of the children of the officer.

(4) General limitation on amount of credit

A member bank may make extensions of credit not otherwise specifically authorized under this section to any executive officer of the bank, in an amount prescribed in a regulation of the member bank's appropriate Federal banking agency.

(5) Partnership loans

Except to the extent permitted under paragraph (4), a member bank may not extend credit to a partnership in which one or more of its executive officers are partners having either individually or together a majority interest. For the purposes of paragraph (4), the full amount of any credit so extended shall be considered to have been extended to each officer of the bank who is a member of the partnership.

(6) Endorsement or guarantee of loans or assets; protective indebtedness

This section does not prohibit any executive officer of a member bank from endorsing or guaranteeing for the protection of the bank any loan or other asset previously acquired by the bank in good faith or from incurring any indebtedness to the bank for the purpose of protecting the bank against loss or giving financial assistance to it.

(7) Continuation of violation

Each day that any extension of credit in violation of this section exists is a continuation of the violation for the purposes of section 1818 of this title.

(8) Rules and regulations; definitions

The Board of Governors of the Federal Reserve System may prescribe such rules and regulations, including definitions of terms, as it deems necessary to effectuate the purposes and to prevent evasions of this section.

(9) Repealed. Pub.L. 109–351, Title VI, § 601(a)(1), Oct. 13, 2006, 120 Stat. 1978

§ 375b. Extensions of credit to executive officers, directors, and principal shareholders of member banks—DFA § 614

(1) In general

No member bank may extend credit to any of its executive officers, directors, or principal shareholders, or to any related interest of such a person, except to the extent permitted under paragraphs (2), (3), (4), (5), and (6).

(2) Preferential terms prohibited

(A) In general

A member bank may extend credit to its executive officers, directors, or principal shareholders, or to any related interest of such a person, only if the extension of credit—

(i) is made on substantially the same terms, including interest rates and collateral, as those prevailing at the time for comparable transactions by the bank with persons who are not executive officers, directors, principal shareholders, or employees of the bank;

(ii) does not involve more than the normal risk of repayment or present other unfavorable features; and

(iii) the bank follows credit underwriting procedures that are not less stringent than those applicable to comparable transactions by the bank with persons who are not executive officers, directors, principal shareholders, or employees of the bank.

(B) Exception

Nothing in this paragraph shall prohibit any extension of credit made pursuant to a benefit or compensation program—

(i) that is widely available to employees of the member bank; and

(ii) that does not give preference to any officer, director, or principal shareholder of the member bank, or to any related interest of such person, over other employees of the member bank.

(3) Prior approval required

A member bank may extend credit to a person described in paragraph (1) in an amount that, when aggregated with the amount of all other outstanding extensions of credit by that bank to each such person and that person's related interests, would exceed an amount prescribed by regulation of the appropriate Federal banking agency (as defined in section 1813 of this title) only if—

(A) the extension of credit has been approved in advance by a majority vote of that bank's entire board of directors; and

(B) the interested party has abstained from participating, directly or indirectly, in the deliberations or voting on the extension of credit.

(4) Aggregate limit on extensions of credit to any executive officer, director, or principal shareholder

A member bank may extend credit to any executive officer, director, or principal shareholder, or to any related interest of such a person, only if the extension of credit is in an amount that, when aggregated with the amount of all outstanding extensions of credit by that bank to that

person and that person's related interests, would not exceed the limits on loans to a single borrower established by section 84 of this title. For purposes of this paragraph, section 84 of this title shall be deemed to apply to a State member bank as if the State member bank were a national banking association.

(5) Aggregate limit on extensions of credit to all executive officers, directors, and principal shareholders

(A) In general

A member bank may extend credit to any executive officer, director, or principal shareholder, or to any related interest of such a person, if the extension of credit is in an amount that, when aggregated with the amount of all outstanding extensions of credit by that bank to its executive officers, directors, principal shareholders, and those persons' related interests would not exceed the bank's unimpaired capital and unimpaired surplus.

(B) More stringent limit authorized

The Board may, by regulation, prescribe a limit that is more stringent than that contained in subparagraph (A).

(C) Board may make exceptions for certain banks

The Board may, by regulation, make exceptions to subparagraph (A) for member banks with less than $100,000,000 in deposits if the Board determines that the exceptions are important to avoid constricting the availability of credit in small communities or to attract directors to such banks. In no case may the aggregate amount of all outstanding extensions of credit to a bank's executive officers, directors, principal shareholders, and those persons' related interests be more than 2 times the bank's unimpaired capital and unimpaired surplus.

(6) Overdrafts by executive officers and directors prohibited

(A) In general

If any executive officer or director has an account at the member bank, the bank may not pay on behalf of that person an amount exceeding the funds on deposit in the account.

(B) Exceptions

Subparagraph (A) does not prohibit a member bank from paying funds in accordance with—

(i) a written preauthorized, interest-bearing extension of credit specifying a method of repayment; or

(ii) a written preauthorized transfer of funds from another account of the executive officer or director at that bank.

(7) Prohibition on knowingly receiving unauthorized extension of credit

No executive officer, director, or principal shareholder shall knowingly receive (or knowingly permit any of that person's related interests to receive) from a member bank, directly or indirectly, any extension of credit not authorized under this section.

(8) Executive officer, director, or principal shareholder of certain affiliates treated as executive officer, director, or principal shareholder of member bank

(A) In general

For purposes of this section, any executive officer, director, or principal shareholder (as the case may be) of any company of which the member bank is a subsidiary, or of any other subsidiary of that company, shall be deemed to be an executive officer, director, or principal shareholder (as the case may be) of the member bank.

(B) Exception

The Board may, by regulation, make exceptions to subparagraph (A) for any executive officer or director of a subsidiary of a company that controls the member bank if—

(i) the executive officer or director does not have authority to participate, and does not participate, in major policymaking functions of the member bank; and

(ii) the assets of such subsidiary do not exceed 10 percent of the consolidated assets of a company that controls the member bank and such subsidiary (and is not controlled by any other company).

(9) Definitions

For purposes of this section:

(A) Company

(i) In general

Except as provided in clause (ii), the term "company" means any corporation, partnership, business or other trust, association, joint venture, pool syndicate, sole proprietor-

ship, unincorporated organization, or other business entity.

(ii) Exceptions

The term "company" does not include—

(I) an insured depository institution (as defined in section 1813 of this title); or

(II) a corporation the majority of the shares of which are owned by the United States or by any State.

(B) Control

A person controls a company or bank if that person, directly or indirectly, or acting through or in concert with 1 or more persons-

(i) owns, controls, or has the power to vote 25 percent or more of any class of the company's voting securities;

(ii) controls in any manner the election of a majority of the company's directors; or

(iii) has the power to exercise a controlling influence over the company's management or policies.

(C) Executive officer

A person is an "executive officer" of a company or bank if that person participates or has authority to participate (other than as a director) in major policymaking functions of the company or bank.

(D) Extension of credit

(i) In general

A member bank extends credit by making or renewing any loan, granting a line of credit, or entering into any similar transaction as a result of which a person becomes obligated (directly or indirectly, or by any means whatsoever) to pay money or its equivalent to the bank.

(ii) Exceptions

The Board may, by regulation, make exceptions to clause (i) for transactions that the Board determines pose minimal risk.

(E) Member bank

The term "member bank" includes any subsidiary of a member bank.

(F) Principal shareholder

The term "principal shareholder"—

(i) means any person that directly or indirectly, or acting through or in concert with one or more persons, owns, controls, or has the power to vote more than 10 percent of any class of voting securities of a member bank or company; and

(ii) does not include a company of which a member bank is a subsidiary.

(G) Related interest

A "related interest" of a person is—

(i) any company controlled by that person; and

(ii) any political or campaign committee that is controlled by that person or the funds or services of which will benefit that person.

(H) Subsidiary

The term "subsidiary" has the same meaning as in section 1841 of this title.

(10) Board's rulemaking authority

The Board of Governors of the Federal Reserve System may prescribe such regulations, including definitions of terms, as it determines to be necessary to effectuate the purposes and prevent evasions of this section.

§ 376. Rate of interest paid to directors, etc.

No member bank shall pay to any director, officer, attorney, or employee a greater rate of interest on the deposits of such director, officer, attorney, or employee than that paid to other depositors on similar deposits with such member bank.

§ 377. Repealed. Pub.L. 106–102, Title I, § 101(a), Nov. 12, 1999, 113 Stat. 1341

§ 378. Dealers in securities engaging in banking business; individuals or associations engaging in banking business; examinations and reports; penalties

(a) After the expiration of one year after June 16, 1933, it shall be unlawful—

(1) For any person, firm, corporation, association, business trust, or other similar organization, engaged in the business of issuing, underwriting, selling, or distributing, at wholesale or retail, or through syndicate participation, stocks, bonds, debentures, notes, or other securities, to engage at the same time to any extent whatever in the business of receiving deposits subject to check or to repayment upon presen-

tation of a passbook, certificate of deposit, or other evidence of debt, or upon request of the depositor: Provided, That the provisions of this paragraph shall not prohibit national banks or State banks or trust companies (whether or not members of the Federal Reserve System) or other financial institutions or private bankers from dealing in, underwriting, purchasing, and selling investment securities, or issuing securities, to the extent permitted to national banking associations by the provisions of section 24 of this title: Provided further, That nothing in this paragraph shall be construed as affecting in any way such right as any bank, banking association, savings bank, trust company, or other banking institution, may otherwise possess to sell, without recourse or agreement to repurchase, obligations evidencing loans on real estate; or

(2) For any person, firm, corporation, association, business trust, or other similar organization to engage, to any extent whatever with others than his or its officers, agents or employees, in the business of receiving deposits subject to check or to repayment upon presentation of a pass book, certificate of deposit, or other evidence of debt, or upon request of the depositor, unless such person, firm, corporation, association, business trust, or other similar organization (A) shall be incorporated under, and authorized to engage in such business by, the laws of the United States or of any State, Territory, or District, and subjected, by the laws of the United States, or of the State, Territory, or District wherein located, to examination and regulation, or (B) shall be permitted by the United States, any State, territory, or district to engage in such business and shall be subjected by the laws of the United States, or such State, territory, or district to examination and regulations or, (C) shall submit to periodic examination by the banking authority of the State, Territory, or District where such business is carried on and shall make and publish periodic reports of its condition, exhibiting in detail its resources and liabilities, such examination and reports to be made and published at the same times and in the same manner and under the same conditions as required by the law of such State, Territory, or District in the case of incorporated banking institutions engaged in such business in the same locality.

(b) Whoever shall willfully violate any of the provisions of this section shall upon conviction be fined not more than $5,000 or imprisoned not more than five years, or both, and any officer, director, employee, or agent of any person, firm, corporation, association, business trust, or other similar organization who knowingly participates in any such violation shall be punished by a like fine or imprisonment or both.

§ 391.　Federal reserve banks as Government depositaries and fiscal agents

The moneys held in the general fund of the Treasury, except the 5 per centum fund for the redemption of outstanding national-bank notes may, upon the direction of the Secretary of the Treasury, be deposited in Federal reserve banks, which banks, when required by the Secretary of the Treasury, shall act as fiscal agents of the United States; and the revenues of the Government or any part thereof may be deposited in such banks, and disbursements may be made by checks drawn against such deposits.

§ 391a.　Reimbursement of Federal Reserve Banks

For necessary expenses of the Financial Management Service, $202,490,000, of which not to exceed $13,235,000 shall remain available until September 30, 2000 for information systems modernization initiatives: Provided, That beginning in fiscal year 1998 and thereafter, there are appropriated such sums as may be necessary to reimburse Federal Reserve Banks in their capacity as depositaries and fiscal agents for the United States for all services required or directed by the Secretary of the Treasury to be performed by such banks on behalf of the Treasury or other Federal agencies.

§ 392.　Depositaries of Government funds as confined to banks in Federal reserve system; member banks as depositories

No public funds of the postal savings, or any Government funds, shall be deposited in the continental United States in any bank not belonging to the system established by this chapter: *Provided, however,* That nothing in this chapter shall be construed to deny the right of the Secretary of the Treasury to use member banks as depositories.

§ 393.　Federal reserve banks as depositaries for Farm Credit System

The Federal Reserve banks are authorized to act as depositaries for and fiscal agents of any Federal land bank, Federal intermediate credit bank, bank for cooperatives, or other institutions of the Farm Credit System.

§ 394.　Federal reserve banks as depositaries for and fiscal agents of Home Owners' Loan Corporation

The Federal Reserve banks are authorized, with the approval of the Secretary of the Treasury, to act as depositaries, custodians, and fiscal agents for the Home Owners' Loan Corporation.

§ 395.　Federal reserve banks as depositaries, custodians and fiscal agents for Commodity Credit Corporation

The Federal Reserve banks are authorized to act as depositaries, custodians, and fiscal agents for the Commodity Credit Corporation.

§ 411.　Issuance to reserve banks; nature of obligation; redemption

Federal reserve notes, to be issued at the discretion of the Board of Governors of the Federal Reserve System for the purpose of making advances to Federal reserve banks through the Federal reserve agents as hereinafter set forth and for no other purpose, are authorized. The said notes shall be obligations of the United States and shall be receivable by all national and member banks and Federal reserve banks and for all taxes, customs, and other public dues. They shall be redeemed in lawful money on demand at the Treasury Department of the United States, in the city of Washington, District of Columbia, or at any Federal Reserve bank.

§ 412.　Application for notes; collateral required

Any Federal Reserve bank may make application to the local Federal Reserve agent for such amount of the Federal Reserve notes hereinbefore provided for as it may require. Such application shall be accompanied with a tender to the local Federal Reserve agent of collateral in amount equal to the sum of the Federal Reserve notes thus applied for and issued pursuant to such application. The collateral security thus offered shall be notes, drafts, bills of exchange, or acceptances acquired under section 92, 342 to 348, 349 to 352, 361, 372, or 373 of this title, or bills of exchange endorsed by a member bank of any Federal Reserve district and purchased under the provisions of sections 348a and 353 to 359 of this title, or bankers' acceptance purchased under the provisions of said sections 348a and 353 to 359 of this title, or gold certificates, or Special Drawing Right certificates, or any obligations which are direct obligations of, or are fully guaranteed as to principal and interest by, the United States or any agency thereof, or assets that Federal Reserve banks may purchase or hold under sections 348a and 353 to 359 of this title or any other asset of a Federal reserve bank. In no event shall such collateral security be less than the amount of Federal Reserve notes applied for. The Federal Reserve agent shall each day notify the Board of Governors of the Federal Reserve System of all issues and withdrawals of Federal Reserve notes to and by the Federal Reserve bank to which he is accredited. The said Board of Governors of the Federal Reserve System may at any time call upon a Federal Reserve bank for additional security to protect the Federal Reserve notes issued to it. Collateral shall not be required for Federal Reserve notes which are held in the vaults of, or are otherwise held by or on behalf of, Federal Reserve banks.

§ 413. Distinctive letter and serial number of notes; cancellation of notes unfit for circulation; accounting; apportionment of credit among Federal Reserve banks

Federal Reserve notes shall bear upon their faces a distinctive letter and serial number which shall be assigned by the Board of Governors of the Federal Reserve System to each Federal Reserve bank. Federal Reserve notes unfit for circulation shall be canceled, destroyed, and accounted for under procedures prescribed and at locations designated by the Secretary of the Treasury. Upon destruction of such notes, credit with respect thereto shall be apportioned among the twelve Federal Reserve banks as determined by the Board of Governors of the Federal Reserve System.

§ 414. Authority of Board of Governors respecting issuance of notes; interest; lien

The Board of Governors of the Federal Reserve System shall have the right, acting through the Federal Reserve agent, to grant in whole or in part, or to reject entirely the application of any Federal Reserve bank for Federal Reserve notes; but to the extent that such application may be granted the Board of Governors of the Federal Reserve System shall, through its local Federal Reserve agent, supply Federal Reserve notes to the banks so applying, and such bank shall be charged with the amount of the notes issued to it and shall pay such rate of interest as may be established by the Board of Governors of the Federal Reserve System on only that amount of such notes which equals the total amount of its outstanding Federal Reserve notes less the amount of gold certificates held by the Federal Reserve agent as collateral security. Federal Reserve notes issued to any such bank shall, upon delivery, together with such notes of such Federal Reserve bank as may be issued under subchapter XIII of this chapter upon security of United States 2 per centum Government bonds, become a first and paramount lien on all the assets of such bank.

§ 415. Reduction of liability for outstanding notes by depositing notes and collateral and payment of notes of series prior to 1928; reissue of deposited notes

Any Federal Reserve bank may at any time reduce its liability for outstanding Federal Reserve notes by depositing with the Federal Reserve agent its Federal Reserve notes, gold certificates, Special Drawing Right certificates, or lawful money of the United States. Federal Reserve notes so deposited shall not be reissued, except upon compliance with the conditions of an original issue. The liability of a Federal Reserve bank with respect to its outstanding Federal Reserve notes shall be reduced by any amount paid by such bank to the Secretary of the Treasury under section 4 of the Old Series Currency Adjustment Act.

§ 416. Withdrawal of collateral deposited to protect notes and substitution of other collateral; retirement of notes; payment of notes of series prior to 1928; recovery of collateral; reissue of deposited notes

Any Federal Reserve bank may at its discretion withdraw collateral deposited with the local Federal Reserve agent for the protection of its Federal Reserve notes issued to it, and shall at the same time substitute therefor other collateral of equal amount with the approval of the Federal Reserve agent under regulations to be prescribed by the Board of Governors of the Federal Reserve System. Any Federal Reserve bank may retire any of its Federal Reserve notes by depositing them with the Federal Reserve agent or with the Treasurer of the United States, and such Federal Reserve bank shall thereupon be entitled to receive back the collateral deposited with the Federal Reserve agent for the security of such notes. Any Federal Reserve bank shall further be entitled to receive back the collateral deposited with the Federal Reserve agent for the security of any notes with respect to which such bank has made payment to the Secretary of the Treasury under section 4 of the Old Series Currency Adjustment Act. Federal Reserve notes so deposited shall not be reissued except upon compliance with the conditions of an original issue.

§ 417. Custody and safe-keeping of notes issued to and collateral deposited with reserve agent

All Federal Reserve notes and all gold certificates, Special Drawing Right certificates, and lawful money issued to or deposited with any Federal Reserve agent under the provisions of this chapter shall be held for such agent, under such rules and regulations as the Board of Governors of the Federal Reserve System may prescribe, in the joint custody of himself and the Federal Reserve bank to which he is accredited. Such agent and such Federal Reserve bank shall be jointly liable for the safe-keeping of such Federal Reserve notes, gold certificates, Special Drawing Right certificates, and lawful money. Nothing herein contained, however, shall be construed to prohibit a Federal Reserve agent from depositing gold certificates and Special Drawing Right certificates with the Board of Governors of the Federal Reserve System, to be held by such Board subject to his order, or with the Treasurer of the United States, for the purposes authorized by law.

§ 418. Printing of notes; denomination and form

In order to furnish suitable notes for circulation as Federal reserve notes, the Secretary of the Treasury shall cause plates and dies to be engraved in the best manner to guard against counterfeits and fraudulent alterations, and shall have printed therefrom and numbered such quantities of such notes of the denominations of $1, $2, $5, $10, $20, $50, $100, $500, $1,000, $5,000, $10,000 as may be required to supply the Federal Reserve banks. Such notes shall be in form and tenor as directed by the Secretary of the Treasury under the provisions of this chapter and shall bear the distinctive numbers of the several Federal reserve banks through which they are issued.

§ 419. Delivery of notes prior to delivery to banks

When such notes have been prepared, the notes shall be delivered to the Board of Governors of the Federal Reserve System subject to the order of the Secretary of the Treasury for the delivery of such notes in accordance with this chapter.

§ 420. Control and direction of plates and dies; expense of issue and retirement of notes paid by banks

The plates and dies to be procured by the Secretary of the Treasury for the printing of such circulating notes shall remain under his control and direction, and the expenses necessarily incurred in executing the laws relating to the procuring of such notes, and all other expenses incidental to their issue and retirement, shall be paid by the Federal reserve banks, and the Board of Governors of the Federal Reserve System shall include in its estimate of expenses levied against the Federal reserve banks a sufficient amount to cover the expenses herein provided for.

§ 421. Examination of plates and dies

The Secretary of the Treasury may examine the plates, dies, bed pieces, and other material used in the printing of Federal Reserve notes and issue regulations relating to such examinations.

§ 422. Repealed. June 26, 1934, c. 756, § 1, 48 Stat. 1225

§§ 441 to 448. Omitted

§ 461. Reserve requirements

(a) Establishment of applicable definitions, payment of interest, obligations as deposits, and regulations

The Board is authorized for the purposes of this section to define the terms used in this section to determine what shall be deemed a payment of interest, to determine what types of obligations, whether issued directly by a member bank or indirectly by an affiliate of a member bank or by other means, and, regardless of the use of the proceeds, shall be deemed a deposit, and to prescribe such regulations as it may deem necessary to effectuate the purposes of this section and to prevent evasions thereof.

(b) Additional definitions; required amounts of reserves maintained against transaction accounts; waiver of ratio limits in extraordinary circumstances; supplemental reserves; reserves related to foreign obligations or assets; exemption for certain deposits; discount and borrowing; transitional adjustments; additional exemptions and waivers

(1) The following definitions and rules apply to this subsection, subsection (c) of this section, and sections 248–1, 248a, 342, 360, and 412 of this title.

(A) The term "depository institution" means—

(i) any insured bank as defined in section 3 of the Federal Deposit Insurance Act [12 U.S.C.A. § 1813] or any bank which is eligible to make application to become an insured bank under section 5 of such Act [12 U.S.C.A. § 1815];

(ii) any mutual savings bank as defined in section 3 of the Federal Deposit Insurance Act [12 U.S.C.A. § 1813] or any bank which is eligible to make application to become an insured bank under section 5 of such Act [12 U.S.C.A. § 1815];

(iii) any savings bank as defined in section 3 of the Federal Deposit Insurance Act [12 U.S.C.A. § 1813] or any bank which is eligible to make application to become an insured bank under section 5 of such Act [12 U.S.C.A. § 1815];

(iv) any insured credit union as defined in section 101 of the Federal Credit Union Act [12 U.S.C.A. § 1752] or any credit union which is eligible to make application to become an insured credit union pursuant to section 201 of such Act [12 U.S.C.A. § 1781];

(v) any member as defined in section 2 of the Federal Home Loan Bank Act [12 U.S.C.A. § 1422];

(vi) any savings association (as defined in section 3 of the Federal Deposit Insurance Act) [12 U.S.C.A. § 1813] which is an insured depository institution (as defined in such Act) [12 U.S.C.A. § 1811 et seq.] or is eligible to apply to become an insured depository institution under the Federal Deposit Insurance Act [12 U.S.C.A. § 1811 et seq.]; and

(vii) for the purpose of sections 248–1, 342 to 347, 347c, 347d, and 372 of this title, any association or entity which is wholly owned by or which consists only of institutions referred to in clauses (i) through (vi).

(B) The term "bank" means any insured or noninsured bank, as defined in section 3 of the Federal Deposit Insurance Act [12 U.S.C.A. § 1813], other than a mutual savings bank or a savings bank as defined in such section.

(C) The term "transaction account" means a deposit or account on which the depositor or account holder is permitted to make withdrawals by negotiable or transferable instrument, payment orders of withdrawal, telephone transfers, or other similar items for the purpose of making payments or transfers to third persons or others. Such term includes demand deposits, negotiable order of withdrawal accounts, savings deposits subject to automatic transfers, and share draft accounts.

(D) The term "nonpersonal time deposits" means a transferable time deposit or account or a time deposit or account representing funds deposited to the credit of, or in which any beneficial interest is held by, a depositor who is not a natural person.

(E) The term "reservable liabilities" means transaction accounts, nonpersonal time deposits, and all net balances, loans, assets, and obligations which are, or may be, subject to reserve requirements under paragraph (5).

(F) In order to prevent evasions of the reserve requirements imposed by this subsection, after consultation with the Board of Directors of the Federal Deposit Insurance

Corporation, the Director of the Office of Thrift Supervision, and the National Credit Union Administration Board, the Board of Governors of the Federal Reserve System is authorized to determine, by regulation or order, that an account or deposit is a transaction account if such account or deposit may be used to provide funds directly or indirectly for the purpose of making payments or transfers to third persons or others.

(2) (A) Each depository institution shall maintain reserves against its transaction accounts as the Board may prescribe by regulation solely for the purpose of implementing monetary policy—

(i) in a ratio of not greater than 3 percent (and which may be zero) for that portion of its total transaction accounts of $25,000,000 or less, subject to subparagraph (C); and

(ii) in the ratio of 12 per centum, or in such other ratio as the Board may prescribe not greater than 14 per centum (and which may be zero), for that portion of its total transaction accounts in excess of $25,000,000, subject to subparagraph (C).

(B) Each depository institution shall maintain reserves against its nonpersonal time deposits in the ratio of 3 per centum, or in such other ratio not greater than 9 per centum and not less than zero per centum as the Board may prescribe by regulation solely for the purpose of implementing monetary policy.

(C) Beginning in 1981, not later than December 31 of each year the Board shall issue a regulation increasing for the next succeeding calendar year the dollar amount which is contained in subparagraph (A) or which was last determined pursuant to this subparagraph for the purpose of such subparagraph, by an amount obtained by multiplying such dollar amount by 80 per centum of the percentage increase in the total transaction accounts of all depository institutions. The increase in such transaction accounts shall be determined by subtracting the amount of such accounts on June 30 of the preceding calendar year from the amount of such accounts on June 30 of the calendar year involved. In the case of any such 12-month

period in which there has been a decrease in the total transaction accounts of all depository institutions, the Board shall issue such a regulation decreasing for the next succeeding calendar year such dollar amount by an amount obtained by multiplying such dollar amount by 80 per centum of the percentage decrease in the total transaction accounts of all depository institutions. The decrease in such transaction accounts shall be determined by subtracting the amount of such accounts on June 30 of the calendar year involved from the amount of such accounts on June 30 of the previous calendar year.

(D) Any reserve requirement imposed under this subsection shall be uniformly applied to all transaction accounts at all depository institutions. Reserve requirements imposed under this subsection shall be uniformly applied to nonpersonal time deposits at all depository institutions, except that such requirements may vary by the maturity of such deposits.

(3) Upon a finding by at least 5 members of the Board that extraordinary circumstances require such action, the Board, after consultation with the appropriate committees of the Congress, may impose, with respect to any liability of depository institutions, reserve requirements outside the limitations as to ratios and as to types of liabilities otherwise prescribed by paragraph (2) for a period not exceeding 180 days, and for further periods not exceeding 180 days each by affirmative action by at least 5 members of the Board in each instance. The Board shall promptly transmit to the Congress a report of any exercise of its authority under this paragraph and the reasons for such exercise of authority.

(4) (A) The Board may, upon the affirmative vote of not less than 5 members, impose a supplemental reserve requirement on every depository institution of not more than 4 per centum of its total transaction accounts. Such supplemental reserve requirement may be imposed only if-

(i) the sole purpose of such requirement is to increase the amount of reserves maintained to a level essential for the conduct of monetary policy;

(ii) such requirement is not imposed for the purpose of reducing the cost burdens resulting from the imposition of the reserve requirements pursuant to paragraph (2);

(iii) such requirement is not imposed for the purpose of increasing the amount of balances needed for clearing purposes; and

(iv) on the date on which the supplemental reserve requirement is imposed, except as provided in paragraph (11), the total amount of reserves required pursuant to paragraph (2) is not less than the amount of reserves that would be required if the initial ratios specified in paragraph (2) were in effect.

(B) The Board may require the supplemental reserve authorized under subparagraph (A) only after consultation with the Board of Directors of the Federal Deposit Insurance Corporation, the Director of the Office of Thrift Supervision, and the National Credit Union Administration Board. The Board shall promptly transmit to the Congress a report with respect to any exercise of its authority to require supplemental reserves under subparagraph (A) and such report shall state the basis for the determination to exercise such authority.

(C) If a supplemental reserve under subparagraph (A) has been required of depository institutions for a period of one year or more, the Board shall review and determine the need for continued maintenance of supplemental reserves and shall transmit annual reports to the Congress regarding the need, if any, for continuing the supplemental reserve.

(D) Any supplemental reserve imposed under subparagraph (A) shall terminate at the close of the first 90-day period after such requirement is imposed during which the average amount of serves required under paragraph (2) are less than the amount of reserves which would be required during such period if the initial ratios specified in paragraph (2) were in effect.

(E) Redesignated (D)

(5) Foreign branches, subsidiaries, and international banking facilities of nonmember depository institutions shall maintain reserves to the same extent required by the Board of foreign branches, subsidiaries, and international banking facilities of member banks. In addition to any reserves otherwise required to be maintained pursuant to this subsection, any depository institution shall maintain reserves in such ratios as the Board may prescribe against—

(A) net balances owed by domestic offices of such depository institution in the United States to its directly related foreign offices and to foreign offices of nonrelated depository institutions;

(B) loans to United States residents made by overseas offices of such depository institution if such depository institution has one or more offices in the United States; and

(C) assets (including participations) held by foreign offices of a depository institution in the United States which were acquired from its domestic offices.

(6) The requirements imposed under paragraph (2) shall not apply to deposits payable only outside the States of the United States and the District of Columbia, except that nothing in this subsection limits the authority of the Board to impose conditions and requirements on member banks under section 25 of this Act [12 U.S.C.A. § 601 et seq.] or the authority of the Board under section 3105 of this title.

(7) Any depository institution in which transaction accounts or nonpersonal time deposits are held shall be entitled to the same discount and borrowing privileges as member banks. In the administration of discount and borrowing privileges, the Board and the Federal Reserve banks shall take into consideration the special needs of savings and other depository institutions for access to discount and borrowing facilities consistent with their long-term asset portfolios and the sensitivity of such institutions to trends in the national money markets.

(8) (A) Any depository institution required to maintain reserves under this subsection which was engaged in business on July 1, 1979, but was not a member of the Federal Reserve System on or after that date, shall maintain reserves against its deposits during the first twelve-month period following the effective date of this paragraph in amounts equal to one-eighth of those otherwise required by this subsection, during the second such twelve-month period in amounts equal to one-fourth of those otherwise required, during the third such twelve-month period in amounts equal to

three-eighths of those otherwise required, during the fourth twelve-month period in amounts equal to one-half of those otherwise required, and during the fifth twelve-month period in amounts equal to five-eighths of those otherwise required, during the sixth twelve-month period in amounts equal to three-fourths of those otherwise required, and during the seventh twelve-month period in amounts equal to seven-eighths of those otherwise required. This subparagraph does not apply to any category of deposits or accounts which are first authorized pursuant to Federal law in any State after April 1, 1980.

(B) With respect to any bank which was a member of the Federal Reserve System during the entire period beginning on July 1, 1979, and ending on the effective date of the Monetary Control Act of 1980, the amount of required reserves imposed pursuant to this subsection on and after the effective date of such Act that exceeds the amount of reserves which would have been required of such bank if the reserve ratios in effect during the reserve computation period immediately preceding such effective date were applied may, at the discretion of the Board and in accordance with such rules and regulations as it may adopt, be reduced by 75 per centum during the first year which begins after such effective date, 50 per centum during the second year, and 25 per centum during the third year.

(C)(i) With respect to any bank which is a member of the Federal Reserve System on the effective date of the Monetary Control Act of 1980, the amount of reserves which would have been required of such bank if the reserve ratios in effect during the reserve computation period immediately preceding such effective date were applied that exceeds the amount of required reserves imposed pursuant to this subsection shall, in accordance with such rules and regulations as the Board may adopt, be reduced by 25 per centum during the first year which begins after such effective date, 50 per centum during the second year, and 75 per centum during the third year.

(ii) If a bank becomes a member bank during the four-year period beginning on the effective date of the Monetary Control Act of 1980, and if the amount of reserves which would have been required of such bank, determined as if the reserve ratios in effect during the reserve computation period immediately preceding such effective date were applied, and as if such bank had been a member during such period, exceeds the amount of reserves required pursuant to this subsection, the amount of reserves required to be maintained by such bank beginning on the date on which such bank becomes a member of the Federal Reserve System shall be the amount of reserves which would have been required of such bank if it had been a member on the day before such effective date, except that the amount of such excess shall, in accordance with such rules and regulations as the Board may adopt, be reduced by 25 per centum during the first year which begins after such effective date, 50 per centum during the second year, and 75 per centum during the third year.

(D)(i) Any bank which was a member bank on July 1, 1979, and which withdrew from membership in the Federal Reserve System during the period beginning July 1, 1979, and ending on March 31, 1980, shall maintain reserves during the first twelve-month period beginning on the date of enactment of this clause in amounts equal to one-half of those otherwise required by this subsection, during the second such twelve-month period in amounts equal to two-thirds of those otherwise required, and during the third such twelve-month period in amounts equal to five-sixths of those otherwise required.

(ii) Any bank which withdraws from membership in the Federal Reserve System after March 31, 1980, shall maintain reserves in the same amount as member banks are required to maintain under this subsection, pursuant to subparagraphs (B) and (C)(i).

(E) This subparagraph applies to any depository institution that, on August 1, 1978, (i) was engaged in business as a depository institution in a State outside the continental limits of the United States, and (ii) was not a member of the Federal Reserve System at any time on or after such date. Such a depository institution shall not be required to maintain reserves against its deposits held or maintained at its offices located in a State outside the continental limits of the United

States until the first day of the sixth calendar year which begins after the effective date of the Monetary Control Act of 1980. Such a depository institution shall maintain reserves against such deposits during the sixth calendar year which begins after such effective date in an amount equal to one-eighth of that otherwise required by paragraph (2), during the seventh such year in an amount equal to one-fourth of that otherwise required, during the eighth such year in an amount equal to three-eighths of that otherwise required, during the ninth such year in an amount equal to one-half of that otherwise required, during the tenth such year in an amount equal to five-eighths of that otherwise required, during the eleventh such year in an amount equal to three-fourths of that otherwise required, and during the twelfth such year in an amount equal to seven-eighths of that otherwise required.

(9) This subsection shall not apply with respect to any financial institution which—

(A) is organized solely to do business with other financial institutions;

(B) is owned primarily by the financial institutions with which it does business; and

(C) does not do business with the general public.

(10) In individual cases, where a Federal supervisory authority waives a liquidity requirement, or waives the penalty for failing to satisfy a liquidity requirement, the Board shall waive the reserve requirement, or waive the penalty for failing to satisfy a reserve requirement, imposed pursuant to this subsection for the depository institution involved when requested by the Federal supervisory authority involved.

(11)(A)(i) Notwithstanding the reserve requirement ratios established under paragraphs (2) and (5) of this subsection, a reserve ratio of zero per centum shall apply to any combination of reservable liabilities, which do not exceed $2,000,000 (as adjusted under subparagraph (B)), of each depository institution.

(ii) Each depository institution may designate, in accordance with such rules and regulations as the Board shall prescribe, the types and amounts of reservable liabilities to which the reserve ratio of zero per centum shall apply, except that transaction accounts which are designated to be subject to a reserve ratio of zero per centum shall be accounts which would otherwise be subject to a reserve ratio of 3 per centum under paragraph (2).

(iii) The Board shall minimize the reporting necessary to determine whether depository institutions have total reservable liabilities of less than $2,000,000 (as adjusted under subparagraph (B)). Consistent with the Board's responsibility to monitor and control monetary and credit aggregates, depository institutions which have reserve requirements under this subsection equal to zero per centum shall be subject to less overall reporting requirements than depository institutions which have a reserve requirement under this subsection that exceeds zero per centum.

(B)(i) Beginning in 1982, not later than December 31 of each year, the Board shall issue a regulation increasing for the next succeeding calendar year the dollar amount specified in subparagraph (A), as previously adjusted under this subparagraph, by an amount obtained by multiplying such dollar amount by 80 per centum of the percentage increase in the total reservable liabilities of all depository institutions.

(ii) The increase in total reservable liabilities shall be determined by subtracting the amount of total reservable liabilities on June 30 of the preceding calendar year from the amount of total reservable liabilities on June 30 of the calendar year involved. In the case of any such twelve-month period in which there has been a decrease in the total reservable liabilities of all depository institutions, no adjustment shall be made. A decrease in total reservable liabilities shall be determined by subtracting the amount of total reservable liabilities on June 30 of the calendar year involved from the amount of total reservable liabilities on June 30 of the previous calendar year.

(c) Promulgation of rules and regulations respecting maintenance of balances

(1) Reserves held by a depository institution to meet the requirements imposed pursuant to subsection (b) of this section shall, subject to such rules and regulations as the Board shall prescribe, be in the form of—

(A) balances maintained for such purposes by such depository institution in the Federal Reserve bank of which it is a member or at which it maintains an account, except that (i) the Board may, by regulation or order, permit depository institutions to maintain all or a portion of their required reserves in the form of vault cash, except that any portion so permitted shall be identical for all depository institutions, and (ii) vault cash may be used to satisfy any supplemental reserve requirement imposed pursuant to subsection (b)(4) of this section, except that all such vault cash shall be excluded from any computation of earnings pursuant to subsection (b)(4)(C) of this section; and

(B) balances maintained by a depository institution which is not a member bank in a depository institution which maintains required reserve balances at a Federal Reserve bank, in a Federal Home Loan Bank, or in the National Credit Union Administration Central Liquidity Facility, if such depository institution, Federal Home Loan Bank, or National Credit Union Administration Central Liquidity Facility maintains such funds in the form of balances in a Federal Reserve bank of which it is a member or at which it maintains an account. Balances received by a depository institution from a second depository institution and used to satisfy the reserve requirement imposed on such second depository institution by this section shall not be subject to the reserve requirements of this section imposed on such first depository institution, and shall not be subject to assessments or reserves imposed on such first depository institution pursuant to section 7 of the Federal Deposit Insurance Act (12 U.S.C. 1817), section 404 of the National Housing Act (12 U.S.C. 1727), or section 202 of the Federal Credit Union Act (12 U.S.C. 1782).

(2) The balances maintained to meet the reserve requirements of subsection (b) of this section by a depository institution in a Federal Reserve bank or passed through a Federal Home Loan Bank or the National Credit Union Administration Central Liquidity Facility or another depository institution to a Federal Reserve bank may be used to satisfy liquidity requirements which may be imposed under other provisions of Federal or State law.

(12) Earnings on balances

(A) In general

Balances maintained at a Federal Reserve bank by or on behalf of a depository institution may receive earnings to be paid by the Federal Reserve bank at least once each calendar quarter, at a rate or rates not to exceed the general level of short-term interest rates.

(B) Regulations relating to payments and distributions

The Board may prescribe regulations concerning—

(i) the payment of earnings in accordance with this paragraph;

(ii) the distribution of such earnings to the depository institutions which maintain balances at such banks, or on whose behalf such balances are maintained; and

(iii) the responsibilities of depository institutions, Federal Home Loan Banks, and the National Credit Union Administration Central Liquidity Facility with respect to the crediting and distribution of earnings attributable to balances maintained, in accordance with subsection (c)(1)(A) of this section, in a Federal Reserve bank by any such entity on behalf of depository institutions.

(C) Depository institutions defined

For purposes of this paragraph, the term "depository institution", in addition to the institutions described in paragraph (1)(A), includes any trust company, corporation organized under section 25A or having an agreement with the Board under section 25, or nay branch or agency of a foreign bank (as defined in section 3101 of this title.)

§ 462. Omitted

§ 462a. Repealed. Pub.L. 97–258, § 5(b), Sept. 13, 1982, 96 Stat. 1068

§ 462a–1. Repealed.   Pub.L.   89–597, § 2(d), Sept. 21, 1966, 80 Stat. 824

§§ 462b, 462c. Omitted

§ 463. Limitation on amount of balance with any depository institution without access to Federal Reserve advances

No member bank shall keep on deposit with any depository institution which is not authorized to have access to Federal Reserve advances under section 347b of this title a sum in excess of 10 per centum of its own paid-up capital and surplus.

§ 464. Checking against and withdrawal of reserve balance

The required balance carried by a member bank with a Federal Reserve bank may, under the regulations and subject to such penalties as may be prescribed by the Board of Governors of the Federal Reserve System, be checked against and withdrawn by such member bank for the purpose of meeting existing liabilities.

§ 465. Basis for ascertaining deposits against which required balance is determined

In estimating the reserve balances required by this chapter, member banks may deduct from the amount of their gross demand deposits the amounts of balances due from other banks (except Federal Reserve banks and foreign banks) and cash items in process of collection payable immediately upon presentation in the United States, within the meaning of these terms as defined by the Board of Governors of the Federal Reserve System.

§ 466. Reserves of banks in dependencies or insular possessions

National banks, or banks organized under local laws, located in a dependency or insular possession or any part of the United States outside the continental United States, may remain nonmember banks, and shall in that event maintain reserves and comply with all the conditions now provided by law regulating them; or said banks may with the consent of the Board of Governors of the Federal Reserve System, become member banks of any one of the reserve districts, and shall in that event take stock, maintain reserves, and be subject to all the other provisions of this chapter.

§ 467. Deposits of gold coin, gold certificates, and Special Drawing Right certificates with United States Treasurer

The Secretary of the Treasury is authorized and directed to receive deposits of gold or of gold certificates or of Special Drawing Right certificates with the Treasurer or any designated de-

positary of the United States when tendered by any Federal Reserve bank or Federal Reserve agent for credit to its or his account with the Board of Governors of the Federal Reserve System. The Secretary shall prescribe by regulation the form of receipt to be issued by the Treasurer or designated depositary to the Federal Reserve bank or Federal Reserve agent making the deposit, and a duplicate of such receipt shall be delivered to the Board of Governors of the Federal Reserve System by the Treasury at Washington upon proper advice from any designated depositary that such deposit has been made. Deposits so made shall be held subject to the orders of the Board of Governors of the Federal Reserve System and deposits of gold or gold certificates shall be payable in gold certificates, and deposits of Special Drawing Right certificates shall be payable in Special Drawing Right certificates, on the order of the Board of Governors of the Federal Reserve System to any Federal Reserve bank or Federal Reserve agent at the Treasury or at the subtreasury of the United States nearest the place of business of such Federal Reserve bank or such Federal Reserve agent. The order used by the Board of Governors of the Federal Reserve System in making such payments shall be signed by the chairman or vice chairman, or such other officers or members as the Board may by regulation prescribe. The form of such order shall be approved by the Secretary of the Treasury.

The expenses necessarily incurred in carrying out these provisions, including the cost of the certificates or receipts issued for deposits received, and all expenses incident to the handling of such deposits shall be paid by the Board of Governors of the Federal Reserve System and included in its assessments against the several Federal Reserve banks.

Nothing in this section shall be construed as amending section 6 of Act March 14, 1900 as amended by Acts March 4, 1907, Mar. 2, 1911, June 12, 1916, nor shall the provisions of this section be construed to apply to the deposits made or to the receipts or certificates issued under that section.

§ 481. Appointment of examiners; examination of member banks, State banks, and trust companies; reports—DFA § 318

The Comptroller of the Currency, with the approval of the Secretary of the Treasury, shall appoint examiners who shall examine every national bank as often as the Comptroller of the

Currency shall deem necessary. The examiner making the examination of any national bank shall have power to make a thorough examination of all the affairs of the bank and in doing so he shall have power to administer oaths and to examine any of the officers and agents thereof under oath and shall make a full and detailed report of the condition of said bank to the Comptroller of the Currency: Provided, That in making the examination of any national bank the examiners shall include such an examination of the affairs of all its affiliates other than member banks as shall be necessary to disclose fully the relations between such bank and such affiliates and the effect of such relations upon the affairs of such bank; and in the event of the refusal to give any information required in the course of the examination of any such affiliate, or in the event of the refusal to permit such examination, all the rights, privileges, and franchises of the bank shall be subject to forfeiture in accordance with sections 141, 222 to 225, 281 to 283, 285, 286, 501a and 502 of this title. The Comptroller of the Currency shall have power, and he is authorized, to publish the report of his examination of any national banking association or affiliate which shall not within one hundred and twenty days after notification of the recommendations or suggestions of the Comptroller, based on said examination, have complied with the same to his satisfaction. Ninety days' notice prior to such publicity shall be given to the bank or affiliate.

The examiner making the examination of any affiliate of a national bank shall have power to make a thorough examination of all the affairs of the affiliate, and in doing so he shall have power to administer oaths and to examine any of the officers, directors, employees, and agents thereof under oath and to make a report of his findings to the Comptroller of the Currency. If any affiliate of a national bank refuses to pay any assessments, fees, or other charges imposed by the Comptroller of the Currency pursuant to this section or fails to make such payment not later than 60 days after the date on which they are imposed, the Comptroller of the Currency may impose such assessments, fees, or charges against the affiliated national bank, and such assessments, fees, or charges shall be paid by such national bank. If the affiliation is with 2 or more national banks, such assessments, fees, or charges may be imposed on, and collected from, any or all of such national banks in such proportions as the Comptroller of the Currency may

prescribe. The examiners and assistant examiners making the examinations of national banking associations and affiliates thereof herein provided for and the chief examiners, reviewing examiners and other persons whose services may be required in connection with such examinations or the reports thereof, shall be employed by the Comptroller of the Currency with the approval of the Secretary of the Treasury; the employment and compensation of examiners, chief examiners, reviewing examiners, assistant examiners, and of the other employees of the office of the Comptroller of the Currency whose compensation is and shall be paid from assessments on banks or affiliates thereof or from other fees or charges imposed pursuant to this section shall be without regard to the provisions of other laws applicable to officers or employees of the United States. The funds derived from such assessments , fees, or charges may be deposited by the Comptroller of the Currency in accordance with the provisions of section 192 of this title and shall not be construed to the Government funds or appropriated monies; and the Comptroller of the Currency is authorized and empowered to prescribe regulations governing the computation and assessment of the expenses of examinations herein provided for and the collection of such assessments from the banks and/or affiliates examined or of other fees or charges imposed pursuant to this section. Such funds shall not be subject to apportionment for the purpose of chapter 15 of Title 31, or under any other authority. If any affiliate of a national bank shall refuse to permit an examiner to make an examination of the affiliate or shall refuse to give any information required in the course of any such examination, the national bank with which it is affiliated shall be subject to a penalty of not more than $5,000 for each day that any such refusal shall continue. Such penalty may be assessed by the Comptroller of the Currency and collected in the same manner as expenses of examinations. The Comptroller of the Currency, upon the request of the Board of Governors of the Federal Reserve System, is authorized to assign examiners appointed under this section to examine foreign operations of State banks which are members of the Federal Reserve System.

§ 482. Employees of Office of Comptroller of the Currency; appointment; compensation and benefits—DFA § 318

Notwithstanding any of the provisions of section 481 of this title or section 301(f)(1) of Title

31 to the contrary, the Comptroller of the Currency shall fix the compensation and number of, and appoint and direct, all employees of the Office of the Comptroller of the Currency. Rates of basic pay for all employees of the Office may be set and adjusted by the Comptroller without regard to the provisions of chapter 51 or subchapter III of chapter 53 of Title 5. The Comptroller may provide additional compensation and benefits to employees of the Office if the same type of compensation or benefits are then being provided by any other Federal bank regulatory agency or, if not then being provided, could be provided by such an agency under applicable provisions of law, rule, or regulation. In setting and adjusting the total amount of compensation and benefits for employees of the Office, the Comptroller shall consult with, and seek to maintain comparability with, other Federal banking agencies.

The Comptroller of the Currency may impose and collect assessments, fees, or other charges as necessary or appropriate to carry out the responsibilities of the office of the Comptroller. Such assessments, fees, and other charges shall be set to meet the Comptroller's expenses in carrying out authorized activities.

§ 483. Special examination of member banks; information of condition furnished to Board of Governors of the Federal Reserve System

In addition to the examinations made and conducted by the Comptroller of the Currency, every Federal reserve bank may, with the approval of the Federal reserve agent or the Board of Governors of the Federal Reserve System, provide for special examination of member banks within its district. The expense of such examinations may, in the discretion of the Board of Governors of the Federal Reserve System, be assessed against the banks examined, and, when so assessed, shall be paid by the banks examined. Such examinations shall be so conducted as to inform the Federal reserve bank of the condition of its member banks and of the lines of credit which are being extended by them. Every Federal reserve bank shall at all times furnish to the Board of Governors of the Federal Reserve System such information as may be demanded concerning the condition of any member bank within the district of the said Federal reserve bank.

§ 484. Limitation on visitorial powers

(a) No national bank shall be subject to any visitorial powers except as authorized by Federal law, vested in the courts of justice or such as shall be, or have been exercised or directed by Congress or by either House thereof or by any committee of Congress or of either House duly authorized.

(b) Notwithstanding subsection (a) of this section, lawfully authorized State auditors and examiners may, at reasonable times and upon reasonable notice to a bank, review its records solely to ensure compliance with applicable State unclaimed property or escheat laws upon reasonable cause to believe that the bank has failed to comply with such laws.

§ 485. Examination of Federal reserve banks

The Board of Governors of the Federal Reserve System shall, at least once each year, order an examination of each Federal reserve bank, and upon joint application of ten member banks the Board of Governors of the Federal Reserve System shall order a special examination and report of the condition of any Federal reserve bank.

§ 486. Waiver of requirements as to reports from or examinations of affiliates

Whenever member banks are required to obtain reports from affiliates, or whenever affiliates of member banks are required to submit to examination, the Board of Governors of the Federal Reserve System or the Comptroller of the Currency, as the case may be, may waive such requirements with respect to any such report or examination of any affiliate if in the judgment of the said Board or Comptroller, respectively, such report or examination is not necessary to disclose fully the relations between such affiliate and such bank and the effect thereof upon the affairs of such bank.

§ 501. Liability of Federal reserve or member bank for certifying check when amount of deposit was inadequate

It shall be unlawful for any officer, director, agent, or employee of any Federal reserve bank, or any member bank as defined in this chapter 196, to certify any check drawn upon such Federal reserve bank or member bank unless the person, firm, or corporation drawing the check has on deposit with such Federal reserve bank or member bank, at the time such check is certified, an amount of money not less than the amount specified in such check. Any check so certified by a duly authorized officer, director, agent, or employee shall be a good and valid obligation against such Federal reserve bank or member bank; but the act of any officer, director, agent, or employee of any such Federal reserve bank or member bank in violation of this section shall, in the discretion of the Board of Governors of the Federal Reserve System, subject such Federal reserve bank to the penalties imposed by subsection (h) of section 248 of this title, and shall subject such member bank, if a national bank, to the liabilities and proceedings on the part of the Comptroller of the Currency provided for in section 192 of this title, and shall, in the discretion of the Board of Governors of the Federal Reserve System, subject any other member bank to the penalties imposed by subchapter VIII of chapter 3 of this title for the violation of any of the provisions of this chapter.

§ 501a. Forfeiture of franchise of national banks for failure to comply with provisions of this chapter

Should any national banking association in the United States now organized fail within one year after December 23, 1913, to become a member bank or fail to comply with any of the provisions of this chapter applicable thereto, all of the rights, privileges, and franchises of such association granted to it under the National Bank

Act [12 U.S.C.A. § 21 et seq.], or under the provisions of this chapter, shall be thereby forfeited. Any noncompliance with or violation of this chapter shall, however, be determined and adjudged by any court of the United States of competent jurisdiction in a suit brought for that purpose in the district or territory in which such bank is located, under direction of the Board of Governors of the Federal Reserve System by the Comptroller of the Currency in his own name before the association shall be declared dissolved. In cases of such noncompliance or violation, other than the failure to become a member bank under the provisions of this chapter, every director who participated in or assented to the same shall be held liable in his personal or individual capacity for all damages which said bank, its shareholders, or any other person shall have sustained in consequence of such violation.

Such dissolution shall not take away or impair any remedy against such corporation, its stockholders or officers, for any liability or penalty which shall have been previously incurred.

§ 502. Liability of shareholders of reserve banks on contracts, etc.

The shareholders of every Federal reserve bank shall be held individually responsible, equally and ratably, and not one for another, for all contracts, debts, and engagements of such bank to the extent of the amount of their subscriptions to such stock at the par value thereof in addition to the amount subscribed, whether such subscriptions have been paid up in whole or in part under the provisions of this chapter.

§ 503. Liability of directors and officers of member banks

If the directors or officers of any member bank shall knowingly violate or permit any of the agents, officers, or directors of any member bank to violate any of the provisions of sections 375, 375a, 375b, and 376 of this title or regulations of the board made under authority thereof, or any of the provisions of sections 212, 213, 214, 215, 655, 1005, 1014, 1906, or 1909 of Title 18, every director and officer participating in or assenting to such violation shall be held liable in his personal and individual capacity for all damages which the member bank, its shareholders, or any other persons shall have sustained in consequence of such violation.

§ 504. Civil money penalty

(a) First tier

Any member bank which, and any institution-affiliated party (within the meaning of section 1813(u) of this title) with respect to such member bank who, violates any provision of section 371c, 371c–1, 375, 375a, 375b, 376 or 503 of this title, or any regulation issued pursuant thereto, shall forfeit and pay a civil penalty of not more than $5,000 for each day during which such violation continues.

(b) Second tier

Notwithstanding subsection (a) of this section, any member bank which, and any institution-affiliated party (within the meaning of section 1813(u) of this title) with respect to such member bank who

(1)(A) commits any violation described in subsection (a) of this section;

(B) recklessly engages in an unsafe or unsound practice in conducting the affairs of such member bank; or

(C) breaches any fiduciary duty;

(2) which violation, practice, or breach—

(A) is part of a pattern of misconduct;

(B) causes or is likely to cause more than a minimal loss to such member bank; or

(C) results in pecuniary gain or other benefit to such party,

shall forfeit and pay a civil penalty of not more than $25,000 for each day during which such violation, practice, or breach continues.

(c) Third tier

Notwithstanding subsections (a) and (b) of this section, any member bank which, and any institution-affiliated party (within the meaning of section 1813(u) of this title) with respect to such member bank who—

(1) knowingly—

(A) commits any violation described in subsection (a) of this section;

(B) engages in any unsafe or unsound practice in conducting the affairs of such credit union; or

(C) breaches any fiduciary duty; and

(2) knowingly or recklessly causes a substantial loss to such credit union or a substantial pecuniary gain or other benefit to such party by reason of such violation, practice, or breach,

shall forfeit and pay a civil penalty in an amount not to exceed the applicable maximum amount determined under subsection (d) of this section for each day during which such violation, practice, or breach continues.

(d) Maximum amounts of penalties for any violation described in subsection (c)

The maximum daily amount of any civil penalty which may be assessed pursuant to subsection (c) of this section for any violation, practice, or breach described in such subsection is—

(1) in the case of any person other than a member bank, an amount to not exceed $1,000,000; and

(2) in the case of a member bank, an amount not to exceed the lesser of—

(A) $1,000,000; or

(B) 1 percent of the total assets of such member bank.

(e) Assessment; etc.

Any penalty imposed under subsection (a), (b), or (c) of this section shall be assessed and collected by

(1) in the case of a national bank, by the Comptroller of the Currency; and

(2) in the case of a State member bank, by the Board, in the manner provided in subparagraphs (E), (F), (G), and (I) of section 1818(i)(2) of this title for penalties imposed (under such section) and any such assessment shall be subject to the provisions of such section.

(f) Hearing

The member bank or other person against whom any penalty is assessed under this section shall be afforded an agency hearing if such member bank or person submits a request for such hearing within 20 days after the issuance of the notice of assessment. Section 1818(h) of this title shall apply to any proceeding under this section.

(g) Disbursement

All penalties collected under authority of this paragraph shall be deposited into the Treasury.

(h) "Violate" defined

For purposes of this section, the term "violate" includes any action (alone or with another or others) for or toward causing, bringing about, participating in, counseling, or aiding or abetting a violation.

(i) Regulations

The Comptroller of the Currency and the Board shall prescribe regulations establishing such procedures as may be necessary to carry out this section.

(m) Notice under this section after separation from service

The resignation, termination of employment or participation, or separation of an institution-affiliated party (within the meaning of section 1813(u) of this title) with respect to a member bank (including a separation caused by the closing of such a bank) shall not affect the jurisdiction and authority of the appropriate Federal banking agency to issue any notice and proceed under this section against any such party, if such notice is served before the end of the 6–year period beginning on the date such party ceased to be such a party with respect to such bank (whether such date occurs before, on, or after August 9, 1989).

§ 505. Civil money penalty

(1) First tier

Any member bank which, and any institution-affiliated party (within the meaning of section 1813(u) of this title) with respect to such member bank who, violates any provision of this section, or any regulation issued pursuant thereto, shall forfeit and pay a civil penalty of not more than $5,000 for each day during which such violation continues.

(2) Second tier

Notwithstanding paragraph (1), any member bank which, and any institution-affiliated party (within the meaning of section 1813(u) of this title) with respect to such member bank who—

(A) (i) commits any violation described in paragraph (1);

(ii) recklessly engages in an unsafe or unsound practice in conducting the affairs of such member bank; or

(iii) breaches any fiduciary duty;

(B) which violation, practice, or breach—

(i) is part of a pattern of misconduct;

(ii) causes or is likely to cause more than a minimal loss to such member bank; or

(iii) results in pecuniary gain or other benefit to such party,

shall forfeit and pay a civil penalty of not more than $25,000 for each day during which such violation, practice, or breach continues.

(3) Third tier

Notwithstanding paragraphs (1) and (2), any member bank which, and any institution-affiliated party (within the meaning of section 1813(u) of this title) with respect to such member bank who—

(A) knowingly—

(i) commits any violation described in paragraph (1);

(ii) engages in any unsafe or unsound practice in conducting the affairs of such member bank; or

(iii) breaches any fiduciary duty; and

(B) knowingly or recklessly causes a substantial loss to such member bank or a substantial pecuniary gain or other benefit to such party by reason of such violation, practice, or breach,

shall forfeit and pay a civil penalty in an amount not to exceed the applicable maximum amount determined under paragraph (4) for each day during which such violation, practice, or breach continues.

(4) Maximum amounts of penalties for any violation described in paragraph (3)

The maximum daily amount of any civil penalty which may be assessed pursuant to paragraph (3) for any violation, practice, or breach described in such paragraph is—

(A) in the case of any person other than a member bank, an amount not to exceed $1,000,000; and

(B) in the case of a member bank, an amount not to exceed the lesser of—

(i) $1,000,000; or

(ii) 1 percent of the total assets of such member bank.

(5) Assessment; etc.

Any penalty imposed under paragraph (1), (2), or (3) may be assessed and collected by the Board in the manner provided in subparagraphs (E), (F), (G), and (I) of section 1818(i)(2) of this title for penalties imposed (under such section) and any such assessment shall be subject to the provisions of such section.

(6) Hearing

The member bank or other person against whom any penalty is assessed under this subsection shall be afforded an agency hearing if such member bank or person submits a request for such hearing within 20 days after the issuance of the notice of assessment. Section 1818(h) of this title shall apply to any proceeding under this subsection.

(7) Disbursement

All penalties collected under authority of this subsection shall be deposited into the Treasury.

(8) "Violate" defined

For purposes of this section, the term "violate" includes any action (alone or with another or others) for or toward causing, bringing about, participating in, counseling, or aiding or abetting a violation.

(9) Regulations

The Board shall prescribe regulations establishing such procedures as may be necessary to carry out this subsection.

§ 506. Notice under this section after separation from service

The resignation, termination of employment or participation, or separation of an institution-affiliated party (within the meaning of section 1813(u) of this title) with respect to a member bank (including a separation caused by the closing of such a bank) shall not affect the jurisdiction and authority of the Board to issue any notice and proceed under this section against any such party, if such notice is served before the end of the 6–year period beginning on the date such party ceased to be such a party with respect to such bank (whether such date occurs before, on, or after August 9, 1989).

§ 521. Reserve-bank branches; establishment; directors; discontinuance of branches; approval for erection of branch bank building

The Board of Governors of the Federal Reserve System may permit or require any Federal reserve bank to establish branch banks within the Federal reserve district in which it is located or within the district of any Federal reserve bank which may have been suspended. Such branches, subject to such rules and regulations as the Board of Governors of the Federal Reserve System may prescribe, shall be operated under the supervision of a board of directors to consist of not more than seven nor less than three directors, of whom a majority of one shall be appointed by the Federal reserve bank of the district, and the remaining directors by the Board of Governors of the Federal Reserve System. Directors of branch banks shall hold office during the pleasure of the Board of Governors of the Federal Reserve System.

The Board of Governors of the Federal Reserve System may at any time require any Federal reserve bank to discontinue any branch of such Federal reserve bank established under this section. The Federal reserve bank shall thereupon proceed to wind up the business of such branch bank, subject to such rules and regulations as the Board of Governors of the Federal Reserve System may prescribe.

No Federal Reserve bank shall have authority hereafter to enter into any contract or contracts for the erection of any branch bank building of any kind or character or to authorize the erection of any such building, except with the approval of the Board of Governors of the Federal Reserve System.

§ 522. Federal Reserve branch bank buildings

No Federal Reserve bank may authorize the acquisition or construction of any branch building, or enter into any contract or other obligation for the acquisition or construction of any branch building, without the approval of the Board.

CHAPTER 12. SAVINGS ASSOCIATIONS
12 U.S.C.A. §§ 1461–1470

CHAPTER 12. SAVINGS ASSOCIATIONS

§ 1461. Short title

This chapter may be cited as the "Home Owners' Loan Act".

§ 1462. Definitions—DFA § 604

For purposes of this chapter—

(1) Director

The term "Director" means the Director of the Office of Thrift Supervision.

(2) Corporation

The term "Corporation" means the Federal Deposit Insurance Corporation.

(3) Office

The term "Office" means the Office of Thrift Supervision.

(4) Savings association

The term "savings association" means a savings association, as defined in section 3 of the Federal Deposit Insurance Act [12 U.S.C.A. § 1813], the deposits of which are insured by the Corporation.

(5) Federal savings association

The term "Federal savings association" means a Federal savings association or a Federal savings bank chartered under section 1464 of this title.

(6) National bank

The term "national bank" has the same meaning as in section 1813 of this title.

(7) Federal banking agencies

The term "Federal banking agencies" means the Office of the Comptroller of the Currency, the Board of Governors of the Federal Reserve System, and the Federal Deposit Insurance Corporation.

(8) State

The term "State" has the same meaning as in section 3 of the Federal Deposit Insurance Act [12 U.S.C.A. § 1813].

(9) Affiliate

The term "affiliate" means any person that controls, is controlled by, or is under common control with, a savings association, except as provided in section 1467a of this title.

§ 1462a. Director of the Office of Thrift Supervision

(a) Establishment of Office

There is established the Office of Thrift Supervision, which shall be an office in the Department of the Treasury.

(b) Establishment of position of Director

(1) In general

There is established the position of the Director of the Office of Thrift Supervision, who shall be the head of the Office of Thrift Supervision and shall be subject to the general oversight of the Secretary of the Treasury.

(2) Authority to prescribe regulations

The Director may prescribe such regulations and issue such orders as the Director may determine to be necessary for carrying out this chapter and all other laws within the Director's jurisdiction.

(3) Autonomy of Director

The Secretary of the Treasury may not intervene in any matter or proceeding before the Director (including agency enforcement actions) unless otherwise specifically provided by law.

(4) Banking agency rulemaking

The Secretary of the Treasury may not delay or prevent the issuance of any rule or the promulgation of any regulation by the Director.

(c) Appointment; term

(1) Appointment

The Director shall be appointed by the President, by and with the advice and consent of the Senate, from among individuals who are citizens of the United States.

(2) Term

The Director shall be appointed for a term of 5 years.

(3) Vacancy

(A) In general

A vacancy in the position of Director which occurs before the expiration of the term for which a Director was appointed shall be filled in the manner established in paragraph (1) and the Director appointed to fill such vacancy shall be appointed only for the remainder of such term.

(B) Acting director

(i) In general

In the event of a vacancy in the position of Director or during the absence or disability of the Director, the Deputy Director shall serve as Acting Director.

(ii) Succession in case of 2 or more deputy directors

If there are 2 or more Deputy Directors serving at the time a vacancy in the position of Director occurs or the absence or disability of the Director commences, the First Deputy Director shall serve as Acting Director under clause (i) followed by such other Deputy Directors under any order of succession the Director may establish.

(iii) Authority of acting director

Any Deputy Director, while serving as Acting Director under this subparagraph, shall be vested with all authority, duties, and privileges of the Director under this Act and any other provision of Federal law.

(4) Service after end of term

An individual may serve as Director after the expiration of the term for which appointed until a successor Director has been appointed.

(5) Deputy director

(A) In general

The Secretary of the Treasury shall appoint a Deputy Director, and may appoint not more than 3 additional Deputy Directors of the Office.

(B) First deputy director

If the Secretary of the Treasury appoints more than 1 Deputy Director of the Office, the Secretary shall designate one such appointee as the First Deputy Director.

(C) Duties

Each Deputy Director appointed under this paragraph shall take an oath of office and perform such duties as the Director shall direct.

(D) Compensation and benefits

The Director shall fix the compensation and benefits for each Deputy Director in accordance with this chapter.

(d) Prohibition on financial interests

The Director shall not have a direct or indirect financial interest in any insured depository institution, as defined in section 3 of the Federal Deposit Insurance Act [12 U.S.C.A. § 1813].

(e) Powers of the Director

The Director shall have all powers which—

(1) were vested in the Federal Home Loan Bank Board (in the Board's capacity as such) or the Chairman of such Board on the day before the date of the enactment of the Financial Institutions Reform, Recovery, and Enforcement Act of 1989[Aug. 9, 1989]; and

(2) were not—

(A) transferred to the Federal Deposit Insurance Corporation, the Federal Housing Finance Board, the Resolution Trust Corporation, or the Federal Home Loan Mortgage Corporation pursuant to any amendment made by such Act; or

(B) established under any provision of law repealed by such Act.

(f) State homestead provisions

No provision of this chapter or any other provision of law administered by the Director shall be construed as superseding any homestead provision of any State constitution, including any implementing State statute, in effect on September 29, 1994, or any subsequent amendment to such a State constitutional or statutory provision in effect on September 29, 1994, that exempts the homestead of any person from foreclosure, or forced sale, for the payment of all debts, other than a purchase money obligation relating to the homestead, taxes due on the homestead, or an obligation arising from work and material used in constructing improvements on the homestead.

(g) Annual report required

The Director shall make an annual report to the Congress. Such report shall include—

(1) a description of any changes the Director has made or is considering making in the district offices of the Office, including a description of the geographic allocation of the Office's resources and personnel used to carry out examination and supervision functions; and

(2) a description of actions taken to carry out section 308 of the Financial Institutions Reform, Recovery, and Enforcement Act of 1989.

(h) Staff

(1) Appointment and compensation

The Director shall fix the compensation and number of, and appoint and direct, all employees of the Office of Thrift Supervision notwithstanding section 301(f)(1) of Title 31. Such compensation shall be paid without regard to the provisions of other laws applicable to officers or employees of the United States.

(2) Rates of basic pay

Rates of basic pay for employees of the Office may be set and adjusted by the Director without regard to the provisions of chapter 51 or subchapter III of chapter 53 of Title 5.

(3) Additional compensation and benefits

The Director may provide additional compensation and benefits to employees of the Office if the same type of compensation or benefits are then being provided by any Federal banking agency or, if not then being provided, could be provided by such an agency under applicable provisions of law, rule, or regulation. In setting and adjusting the total amount of compensation and benefits for employees of the Office, the Director shall consult, and seek to maintain comparability with, the Federal banking agencies.

(4) Delegation authority

(A) In general

The Director may—

(i) designate who shall act as Director in the Director's absence; and

(ii) delegate to any employee, representative, or agent any power of the Director.

(B) Limitations

Notwithstanding subparagraph (A)(ii), the Director shall not, directly or indirectly—

(i) after October 10, 1989, delegate to any Federal home loan bank or to any officer, director, or employee of a Federal home loan bank, any power involving examining, supervising, taking enforcement action with respect to, or otherwise regulating any savings association, savings and loan holding company, or other person subject to regulation by the Director; or

(ii) delegate the Director's authority to serve as a member of the Corporation's Board of Directors.

(i) Funding through assessments

The compensation of the Director and other employees of the Office and all other expenses thereof may be paid from assessments levied under this chapter.

(j) GAO audit

The Director shall make available to the Comptroller General of the United States all books and records necessary to audit all of the activities of the Office of Thrift Supervision.

§ 1463. Supervision of savings associations

(a) Federal savings associations

(1) In general

The Director shall provide for the examination, safe and sound operation, and regulation of savings associations.

(2) Regulations

The Director may issue such regulations as the Director determines to be appropriate to carry out the responsibilities of the Director or the Office.

(3) Safe and sound housing credit to be encouraged

The Director shall exercise all powers granted to the Director under this Act so as to encourage savings associations to provide credit for housing safely and soundly.

(b) Accounting and disclosure

(1) In general

The Director shall, by regulation, prescribe uniform accounting and disclosure standards for savings associations, to be used in determining savings associations' compliance with all applicable regulations.

(2) Specific requirements for accounting standards

Subject to section 1464(t) of this title, the uniform accounting standards prescribed under paragraph (1) shall—

(A) incorporate generally accepted accounting principles to the same degree that such principles are used to determine compliance with regulations prescribed by the Federal banking agencies;

(B) allow for no deviation from full compliance with such standards as are in effect after December 31, 1993; and

(C) prior to January 1, 1994, require full compliance by savings associations with accounting standards in effect at any time before such date not later than provided under the schedule in section 563.23–3 of title 12, Code of Federal Regulations (as in effect on May 1, 1989).

(3) Authority to prescribe more stringent accounting standards

The Director may at any time prescribe accounting standards more stringent than required under paragraph (2) if the Director determines that the more stringent standards are necessary to ensure the safe and sound operation of savings associations.

(c) Stringency of standards

All regulations and policies of the Director governing the safe and sound operation of savings associations, including regulations and policies governing asset classification and appraisals, shall be no less stringent than those established by the Comptroller of the Currency for national banks.

(d) Investment of certain funds in accounts of savings associations

The savings accounts and share accounts of savings associations insured by the Corporation shall be lawful investments and may be accepted as security for all public funds of the United States, fiduciary and trust funds under the authority or control of the United States or any officer thereof, and for the funds of all corporations organized under the laws of the United States (subject to any regulatory authority otherwise applicable), regardless of any limitation of law upon the investment of any such funds or upon the acceptance of security for the investment or deposit of any of such funds.

(e) Participation by savings associations in lotteries and related activities

(1) Participation prohibited

No savings association may—

(A) deal in lottery tickets;

(B) deal in bets used as a means or substitute for participation in a lottery;

(C) announce, advertise, or publicize the existence of any lottery; or

(D) announce, advertise, or publicize the existence or identity of any participant or winner, as such, in a lottery.

(2) Use of facilities prohibited

No savings association may permit—

(A) the use of any part of any of its own offices by any person for any purpose forbidden to the institution under paragraph (1); or

(B) direct access by the public from any of its own offices to any premises used by any person for any purpose forbidden to the institution under paragraph (1).

(3) Definitions

For purposes of this subsection—

(A) Deal in

The term "deal in" includes making, taking, buying, selling, redeeming, or collecting.

(B) Lottery

The term "lottery" includes any arrangement under which—

(i) 3 or more persons (hereafter in this subparagraph referred to as the "participants") advance money or credit to another in exchange for the possibility or expectation that 1 or more but not all of the participants (hereafter in this paragraph referred to as the "winners") will receive by reason of those participants' advances more than the amounts those participants have advanced; and

(ii) the identity of the winners is determined by any means which includes—

(I) a random selection;

(II) a game, race, or contest; or

(III) any record or tabulation of the result of 1 or more events in which any participant has no interest except for the bearing that event has on the possibility that the participant may become a winner.

(C) Lottery ticket

The term "lottery ticket" includes any right, privilege, or possibility (and any ticket, receipt, record, or other evidence of any such right, privilege, or possibility) of becoming a winner in a lottery.

(4) Exception for State lotteries

Paragraphs (1) and (2) shall not apply with respect to any savings association accepting funds from, or performing any lawful services for, any State operating a lottery, or any officer or employee of such a State who is charged with administering the lottery.

(5) Regulations

The Director shall prescribe such regulations as may be necessary to provide for enforcement of this subsection and to prevent any evasion of any provision of this subsection.

(f) Federally related mortgage loan disclosures

A savings association may not make a federally related mortgage loan to an agent, trustee, nominee, or other person acting in a fiduciary capacity without requiring that the identity of the person receiving the beneficial interest of such loan shall at all times be revealed to the savings association. At the request of the Director, the savings association shall report to the Director the identity of such person and the nature and amount of the loan.

(g) Preemption of State usury laws

(1) Notwithstanding any State law, a savings association may charge interest on any extension of credit at a rate of not more than 1 percent in excess of the discount rate on 90–day commercial paper in effect at the Federal Reserve bank in the Federal Reserve district in which such savings association is located or at the rate allowed by the laws of the State in which such savings association is located, whichever is greater.

(2) If the rate prescribed in paragraph (1) exceeds the rate such savings association would be permitted to charge in the absence of this subsection, the receiving or charging a greater rate of interest than that prescribed by paragraph (1), when knowingly done, shall be deemed a forfeiture of the entire interest which the extension of credit carries with it, or which has been agreed to be paid thereon. If such greater rate of interest has been paid, the person who paid it may recover, in a civil action commenced in a court of appropriate jurisdiction not later than 2 years after the date of such payment, an amount equal to

twice the amount of the interest paid from the savings association taking or receiving such interest.

(h) Form and maturity of securities

No savings association shall—

(1) issue securities which guarantee a definite maturity except with the specific approval of the Director, or

(2) issue any securities the form of which has not been approved by the Director.

§ 1463a. Omitted

§ 1463b. Repealed. May 28, 1935, c. 150, § 17(b), 49 Stat. 297

§ 1464. Federal savings associations— DFA §§ 610, 612, 627

(a) In general

In order to provide thrift institutions for the deposit of funds and for the extension of credit for homes and other goods and services, the Director is authorized, under such regulations as the Director may prescribe—

(1) to provide for the organization, incorporation, examination, operation, and regulation of associations to be known as Federal savings associations (including Federal savings banks), and

(2) to issue charters therefor,

giving primary consideration of the best practices of thrift institutions in the United States. The lending and investment powers conferred by this section are intended to encourage such institutions to provide credit for housing safely and soundly.

(b) Deposits and related powers

(1) Deposit accounts

(A) Subject to the terms of its charter and regulations of the Director, a Federal savings association may—

(i) raise funds through such deposit, share, or other accounts, including demand deposit accounts (hereafter in this section referred to as "accounts"); and

(ii) issue passbooks, certificates, or other evidence of accounts.

(B) A Federal savings association may not—

(i) pay interest on a demand account; or

(ii) permit any overdraft (including an intra-day overdraft) on behalf of an affiliate, or incur any such overdraft in such savings association's account at a Federal reserve bank or Federal home loan bank on behalf of an affiliate.

All savings accounts and demand accounts shall have the same priority upon liquidation. Holders of accounts and obligors of a Federal savings association shall, to such extent as may be provided by its charter or by regulations of the Director, be members of the savings association, and shall have such voting rights and such other rights as are thereby provided.

(C) A Federal savings association may require not less than 14 days notice prior to payment of savings accounts if the charter of the savings association or the regulations of the Director so provide.

(D) If a Federal savings association does not pay all withdrawals in full (subject to the right of the association, where applicable, to require notice), the payment of withdrawals from accounts shall be subject to such rules and procedures as may be prescribed by the savings association's charter or by regulation of the Director. Except as authorized in writing by the Director, any Federal savings association that fails to make full payment of any withdrawal when due shall be deemed to be in an unsafe or unsound condition.

(E) Accounts may be subject to check or to withdrawal or transfer on negotiable or transferable or other order or authorization to the Federal savings association, as the Director may by regulation provide.

(F) A Federal savings association may establish remote service units for the purpose of crediting savings or demand accounts, debiting such accounts, crediting payments on loans, and the disposition of related financial transactions, as provided in regulations prescribed by the Director.

(2) Other liabilities

To such extent as the Director may authorize in writing, a Federal savings association may borrow, may give security, may be surety as defined by the Director and may issue such notes, bonds, debentures, or other obligations, or other securities, including capital stock.

(3) Loans from State housing finance agencies

(A) In general

Subject to regulation by the Director but without regard to any other provision of this subsection, any Federal savings association that is in compliance with the capital standards in effect under subsection (t) of this section may borrow funds from a State mortgage finance agency of the State in which the head office of such savings association is situated to the same extent as State law authorizes a savings association organized under the laws of such State to borrow from the State mortgage finance agency.

(B) Interest rate

A Federal savings association may not make any loan of funds borrowed under subparagraph (A) at an interest rate which exceeds by more than 1 3/4 percent per annum the interest rate paid to the State mortgage finance agency on the obligations issued to obtain the funds so borrowed.

(4) Mutual capital certificates

In accordance with regulations issued by the Director, mutual capital certificates may be issued and sold directly to subscribers or through underwriters. Such certificates may be included in calculating capital for the purpose of subsection (t) of this section to the extent permitted by the Director. The issuance of certificates under this paragraph does not constitute a change of control or ownership under this chapter or any other law unless there is in fact a change in control or reorganization. Regulations relating to the issuance and sale of mutual capital certificates shall provide that such certificates—

(A) are subordinate to all savings accounts, savings certificates, and debt obligations;

(B) constitute a claim in liquidation on the general reserves, surplus, and undivided profits of the Federal savings association remaining after the payment in full of all savings accounts, savings certificates, and debt obligations;

(C) are entitled to the payment of dividends; and

(D) may have a fixed or variable dividend rate.

(c) Loans and investments

To the extent specified in regulations of the Director, a Federal savings association may invest in, sell, or otherwise deal in the following loans and other investments:

(1) Loans or investments without percentage of assets limitation

Without limitation as a percentage of assets, the following are permitted:

(A) Account loans

Loans on the security of its savings accounts and loans specifically related to transaction accounts.

(B) Residential real property loans

Loans on the security of liens upon residential real property.

(C) United States government securities

Investments in obligations of, or fully guaranteed as to principal and interest by, the United States.

(D) Federal home loan bank and Federal National Mortgage Association securities

Investments in the stock or bonds of a Federal home loan bank or in the stock of the Federal National Mortgage Association.

(E) Federal Home Loan Mortgage Corporation instruments

Investments in mortgages, obligations, or other securities which are or have been sold by the Federal Home Loan Mortgage Corporation pursuant to section 305 or 306 of the Federal Home Loan Mortgage Corporation Act [12 U.S.C.A. § 1454 or 1455].

(F) Other Government securities

Investments in obligations, participations, securities, or other instruments issued by, or fully guaranteed as to principal and interest by, the Federal National Mortgage Association, the Student Loan Marketing Association, the Government National Mortgage Association, or any agency of the United States. A savings association may issue and sell securities which are guaranteed pursuant to section 306(g) of the National Housing Act [12 U.S.C.A. § 1721(g)].

(G) Deposits

Investments in accounts of any insured depository institution, as defined in section 3 of the Federal Deposit Insurance Act [12 U.S.C.A. § 1813].

(H) State securities

Investments in obligations issued by any State or political subdivision thereof (including any agency, corporation, or instrumentality of a State or political subdivision). A Federal savings association may not invest more than 10 percent of its capital in obligations of any one issuer, exclusive of investments in general obligations of any issuer.

(I) Purchase of insured loans

Purchase of loans secured by liens on improved real estate which are insured or guaranteed under the National Housing Act [12 U.S.C.A. § 1701 et seq.], the Servicemen's Readjustment Act of 1944, or chapter 37 of Title 38.

(J) Home improvement and manufactured home loans

Loans made to repair, equip, alter, or improve any residential real property, and loans made for manufactured home financing.

(K) Insured loans to finance the purchase of fee simple

Loans insured under section 240 of the National Housing Act [12 U.S.C.A. § 1715z–5].

(L) Loans to financial institutions, brokers, and dealers

Loans to—

(i) financial institutions with respect to which the United States or an agency or instrumentality thereof has any function of examination or supervision, or

(ii) any broker or dealer registered with the Securities and Exchange Commission,

which are secured by loans, obligations, or investments in which the Federal savings association has the statutory authority to invest directly.

(M) Liquidity investments

Investments (other than equity investments), identified by the Director, for liquidity purposes, including cash, funds on deposit at a Federal reserve bank or a Federal home loan bank, or bankers' acceptances.

(N) Investment in the National Housing Partnership Corporation, partnerships, and joint ventures

Investments in shares of stock issued by a corporation authorized to be created pursuant to title IX of the Housing and Urban Development Act of 1968 [42 U.S.C.A. § 3931 et seq.], and investments in any partnership, limited partnership, or joint venture formed pursuant to section 907(a) or 907(c) of such Act [42 U.S.C.A. § 3937(a) or (c)] .

(O) Certain HUD insured or guaranteed investments

Loans that are secured by mortgages—

(i) insured under title X of the National Housing Act [12 U.S.C.A. § 1749aa et seq.], or

(ii) guaranteed under title IV of the Housing and Urban Development Act of 1968, under part B of the National Urban Policy and New Community Development Act of 1970 [42 U.S.C.A. § 4511 et seq.], or under section 802 of the Housing and Community Development Act of 1974 [42 U.S.C.A. § 1440].

(P) State housing corporation investments

Obligations of and loans to any State housing corporation, if—

(i) such obligations or loans are secured directly, or indirectly through an agent or fiduciary, by a first lien on improved real estate which is insured under the provisions of the National Housing Act [12 U.S.C.A. § 1701 et seq.], and

(ii) in the event of default, the holder of the obligations or loans has the right directly, or indirectly through an agent or fiduciary, to cause to be subject to the satisfaction of such obligations or loans the real estate described in the first lien or the insurance proceeds under the National Housing Act.

(Q) Investment companies

A Federal savings association may invest in, redeem, or hold shares or certificates issued by any open-end management investment company which—

(i) is registered with the Securities and Exchange Commission under the Investment Company Act of 1940 [15 U.S.C.A. § 80a–1 et seq.], and

(ii) the portfolio of which is restricted by such management company's investment policy (changeable only if authorized by shareholder vote) solely to investments that a Federal savings association by law or regulation may, without limitation as to percentage of assets, invest in, sell, redeem, hold, or otherwise deal in.

(R) Mortgage-backed securities

Investments in securities that—

(i) are offered and sold pursuant to section 4(5) of the Securities Act of 1933 [15 U.S.C.A. § 77d(5)]; or

(ii) are mortgage related securities (as defined in section 3(a)(41) of Securities Exchange Act of 1934) [15 U.S.C.A. § 78c(a)(41)],

subject to such regulations as the Director may prescribe, including regulations prescribing minimum size of the issue (at the time of initial distribution) or minimum aggregate sales price, or both.

(S) Small business related securities

Investments in small business related securities (as defined in section 78c(a)(53) of Title 15), subject to such regulations as the Director may prescribe, including regulations concerning the minimum size of the issue (at the time of the initial distribution), the minimum aggregate sales price, or both.

(T) Credit card loans

Loans made through credit cards or credit card accounts.

(U) Educational loans

Loans made for the payment of educational expenses.

(2) Loans or investments limited to a percentage of assets or capital

The following loans or investments are permitted, but only to the extent specified:

(A) Commercial and other loans

Secured or unsecured loans for commercial, corporate, business, or agricultural purposes. The aggregate amount of loans made under this subparagraph may not exceed 20 percent of the total assets of the Federal savings association, and amounts in excess of 10 percent of such total assets may be used under this subparagraph only for small business loans, as that term is defined by the Director.

(B) Nonresidential real property loans

(i) In general

Loans on the security of liens upon nonresidential real property. Except as provided in clause (ii), the aggregate amount of such loans shall not exceed 400 percent of the Federal savings association's capital, as determined under subsection (t) of this section.

(ii) Exception

The Director may permit a savings association to exceed the limitation set forth in clause (i) if the Director determines that the increased authority—

(I) poses no significant risk to the safe and sound operation of the association, and

(II) is consistent with prudent operating practices.

(iii) Monitoring

If the Director permits any increased authority pursuant to clause (ii), the Director shall closely monitor the Federal savings association's condition and lending activities to ensure that the savings association carries out all authority under this paragraph in a safe and sound manner and complies with this subparagraph and all relevant laws and regulations.

(C) Investments in personal property

Investments in tangible personal property, including vehicles, manufactured homes, machinery, equipment, or furniture, for rental or sale. Investments under this subparagraph may not exceed 10 percent of the assets of the Federal savings association.

(D) Consumer loans and certain securities

A Federal savings association may make loans for personal, family, or household purposes, including loans reasonably incident to providing such credit, and may invest in, sell, or hold commercial paper and corporate debt securities, as defined and approved by the Director. Loans and other investments under this subparagraph may not exceed 35 percent of the assets of the Federal savings association, except that amounts in excess of 30 percent of the assets may be invested only in loans which are made by the association

directly to the original obligor and with respect to which the association does not pay any finder, referral, or other fee, directly or indirectly, to any third party.

(3) Loans or investments limited to 5 percent of assets

The following loans or investments are permitted, but not to exceed 5 percent of assets of a Federal savings association for each subparagraph:

(A) Community development investments

Investments in real property and obligations secured by liens on real property located within a geographic area or neighborhood receiving concentrated development assistance by a local government under title I of the Housing and Community Development Act of 1974 [42 U.S.C.A. § 5301 et seq.]. No investment under this subparagraph in such real property may exceed an aggregate of 2 percent of the assets of the Federal savings association.

(B) Nonconforming loans

Loans upon the security of or respecting real property or interests therein used for primarily residential or farm purposes that do not comply with the limitations of this subsection.

(C) Construction loans without security

Loans—

(i) the principal purpose of which is to provide financing with respect to what is or is expected to become primarily residential real estate; and

(ii) with respect to which the association-

(I) relies substantially on the borrower's general credit standing and projected future income for repayment, without other security; or

(II) relies on other assurances for repayment, including a guarantee or similar obligation of a third party.

The aggregate amount of such investments shall not exceed the greater of the Federal savings association's capital or 5 percent of its assets.

(4) Other loans and investments

The following additional loans and other investments to the extent authorized below:

(A) Business development credit corporations

A Federal savings association that is in compliance with the capital standards prescribed under subsection (t) of this section may invest in, lend to, or to commit itself to lend to, any business development credit corporation incorporated in the State in which the home office of the association is located in the same manner and to the same extent as savings associations chartered by such State are authorized. The aggregate amount of such investments, loans, and commitments of any such Federal savings association shall not exceed one-half of 1 percent of the association's total outstanding loans or $250,000, whichever is less.

(B) Service corporations

Investments in the capital stock, obligations, or other securities of any corporation organized under the laws of the State in which the Federal savings association's home office is located, if such corporation's entire capital stock is available for purchase only by savings associations of such State and by Federal associations having their home offices in such State. No Federal savings association may make any investment under this subparagraph if the association's aggregate outstanding investment under this subparagraph would exceed 3 percent of the association's assets. Not less than one-half of the investment permitted under this subparagraph which exceeds 1 percent of the association's assets shall be used primarily for community, inner-city, and community development purposes.

(C) Foreign assistance investments

Investments in housing project loans having the benefit of any guaranty under section 221 of the Foreign Assistance Act of 1961 [22 U.S.C.A. § 2181] or loans having the benefit of any guarantee under section 224 of such Act [22 U.S.C.A. § 2184], or any commitment or agreement with respect to such loans made pursuant to either of such sections and in the share capital and capital reserve of the Inter–American Savings and Loan Bank. This authority extends to the acquisition, holding, and disposition of loans guaranteed under section 221 or 222 of such Act [22 U.S.C.A. § 2181 or 2182]. Invest-

ments under this subparagraph shall not exceed 1 percent of the Federal savings association's assets.

(D) Small business investment companies

A Federal savings association may invest in stock, obligations, or other securities of any small business investment company formed pursuant to section 301(d) of the Small Business Investment Act of 1958 [15 U.S.C.A. § 681(d)] for the purpose of aiding members of a Federal home loan bank. A Federal savings association may not make any investment under this subparagraph if its aggregate outstanding investment under this subparagraph would exceed 1 percent of the assets of such savings association.

(E) Bankers' banks

A Federal savings association may purchase for its own account shares of stock of a bankers' bank, described in Paragraph Seventh of section 24 of this title or in section 27(b) of this title, on the same terms and conditions as a national bank may purchase such shares.

(F) New markets venture capital companies

A Federal savings association may invest in stock, obligations, or other securities of any New Markets Venture Capital company as defined in section 689 of Title 15, except that a Federal savings association may not make any investment under this subparagraph if its aggregate outstanding investment under this subparagraph would exceed 5 percent of the capital and surplus of such savings association.

(5) Transition rule for savings associations acquiring banks

(A) In general

If, under section 5(d)(3) of the Federal Deposit Insurance Act [12 U.S.C.A. § 1815(d)(3)], a savings association acquires all or substantially all of the assets of a bank, the Director may permit the savings association to retain any such asset during the 2–year period beginning on the date of the acquisition.

(B) Extension

The Director may extend the 2–year period described in subparagraph (A) for not more than 1 year at a time and not more than 2 years in the aggregate, if the Director determines that the extension is consistent with the purposes of this chapter.

(6) Definitions

For purposes of this subsection, the following definitions shall apply:

(A) Residential property

The terms "residential real property" or "residential real estate" mean leaseholds, homes (including condominiums and cooperatives, except that in connection with loans on individual cooperative units, such loans shall be adequately secured as defined by the Director) and, combinations of homes or dwelling units and business property, involving only minor or incidental business use, or property to be improved by construction of such structures.

(B) Loans

The term "loans" includes obligations and extensions or advances of credit; and any reference to a loan or investment includes an interest in such a loan or investment.

(d) Regulatory authority

(1) In general

(A) Enforcement

The Director shall have power to enforce this section, section 8 of the Federal Deposit Insurance Act [12 U.S.C.A. § 1818], and regulations prescribed hereunder. In enforcing any provision of this section, regulations prescribed under this section, or any other law or regulation, or in any other action, suit, or proceeding to which the Director is a party or in which the Director is interested, and in the administration of conservatorships and receiverships, the Director may act in the Director's own name and through the Director's own attorneys. Except as otherwise provided, the Director shall be subject to suit (other than suits on claims for money damages) by any Federal savings association or director or officer thereof with respect to any matter under this section or any other applicable law, or regulation thereunder, in the United States district court for the judicial district in which the savings association's home office is located, or in the United States District Court for the District of Columbia, and the Director may be served with process in the manner prescribed by the Federal Rules of Civil Procedure.

(B) Ancillary provisions

(i) In making examinations of savings associations, examiners appointed by the Director shall have power to make such examinations of the affairs of all affiliates of such savings associations as shall be necessary to disclose fully the relations between such savings associations and their affiliates and the effect of such relations upon such savings associations. For purposes of this subsection, the term "affiliate" has the same meaning as in section 2(b) of the Banking Act of 1933 [12 U.S.C.A. § 221a(b)], except that the term "member bank" in section 2(b) shall be deemed to refer to a savings association.

(ii) In the course of any examination of any savings association, upon request by the Director, prompt and complete access shall be given to all savings association officers, directors, employees, and agents, and to all relevant books, records, or documents of any type.

(iii) Upon request made in the course of supervision or oversight of any savings association, for the purpose of acting on any application or determining the condition of any savings association, including whether operations are being conducted safely, soundly, or in compliance with charters, laws, regulations, directives, written agreements, or conditions imposed in writing in connection with the granting of an application or other request, the Director shall be given prompt and complete access to all savings association officers, directors, employees, and agents, and to all relevant books, records, or documents of any type.

(iv) If prompt and complete access upon request is not given as required in this subsection, the Director may apply to the United States district court for the judicial district (or the United States court in any territory) in which the principal office of the institution is located, or in which the person denying such access resides or carries on business, for an order requiring that such information be promptly provided.

(v) In connection with examinations of savings associations and affiliates thereof, the Director may—

(I) administer oaths and affirmations and examine and to take and preserve testimony under oath as to any matter in respect of the affairs or ownership of any such savings association or affiliate, and

(II) issue subpoenas and, for the enforcement thereof, apply to the United States district court for the judicial district (or the United States court in any territory) in which the principal office of the savings association or affiliate is located, or in which the witness resides or carries on business.

Such courts shall have jurisdiction and power to order and require compliance with any such subpoena.

(vi) In any proceeding under this section, the Director may administer oaths and affirmations, take depositions, and issue subpoenas. The Director may prescribe regulations with respect to any such proceedings. The attendance of witnesses and the production of documents provided for in this subsection may be required from any place in any State or in any territory at any designated place where such proceeding is being conducted.

(vii) Any party to a proceeding under this section may apply to the United States District Court for the District of Columbia, or the United States district court for the judicial district (or the United States court in any territory) in which such proceeding is being conducted, or where the witness resides or carries on business, for enforcement of any subpoena issued pursuant to this subsection or section 10 (c) of the Federal Deposit Insurance Act [12 USCA § 1820(c)], and such courts shall have jurisdiction and power to order and require compliance therewith. Witnesses subpoenaed under this section shall be paid the same fees and mileage that are paid witnesses in the district courts of the United States. All expenses of the Director in connection with this section shall be considered as nonadministrative expenses. Any court having jurisdiction of any proceeding instituted under this section by a savings association, or a director or officer thereof, may allow to any such party reasonable expenses and attorneys' fees. Such expenses and fees shall be paid by the savings association.

(2) Conservatorships and receiverships

(A) Grounds for appointing conservator or receiver for insured savings association

The Director of the Office of Thrift Supervision may appoint a conservator or receiver for any insured savings association if the Director determines, in the Director's discretion, that 1 or more of the grounds specified in section 11(c)(5) of the Federal Deposit Insurance Act [12 U.S.C.A. § 1821(c)(5)] exists.

(B) Power of appointment; judicial review

The Director shall have exclusive power and jurisdiction to appoint a conservator or receiver for a Federal savings association. If, in the opinion of the Director, a ground for the appointment of a conservator or receiver for a savings association exists, the Director is authorized to appoint ex parte and without notice a conservator or receiver for the savings association. In the event of such appointment, the association may, within 30 days thereafter, bring an action in the United States district court for the judicial district in which the home office of such association is located, or in the United States District Court for the District of Columbia, for an order requiring the Director to remove such conservator or receiver, and the court shall upon the merits dismiss such action or direct the Director to remove such conservator or receiver. Upon the commencement of such an action, the court having jurisdiction of any other action or proceeding authorized under this subsection to which the association is a party shall stay such action or proceeding during the pendency of the action for removal of the conservator or receiver.

(C) Replacement

The Director may, without any prior notice, hearing, or other action, replace a conservator with another conservator or with a receiver, but such replacement shall not affect any right which the association may have to obtain judicial review of the original appointment, except that any removal under this subparagraph shall be removal of the conservator or receiver in office at the time of such removal.

(D) Court action

Except as otherwise provided in this subsection, no court may take any action for or toward the removal of any conservator or receiver or, except at the request of the Director, to restrain or affect the exercise of powers or functions of a conservator or receiver.

(E) Powers

(i) In general

A conservator shall have all the powers of the members, the stockholders, the directors, and the officers of the association and shall be authorized to operate the association in its own name or to conserve its assets in the manner and to the extent authorized by the Director.

(ii) FDIC or RTC as conservator or receiver

Except as provided in section 21A of the Federal Home Loan Bank Act [12 U.S.C.A. § 1441a], the Director, at the Director's discretion, may appoint the Federal Deposit Insurance Corporation or the Resolution Trust Corporation, as appropriate, as conservator for a savings association. The Director shall appoint only the Federal Deposit Insurance Corporation or the Resolution Trust Corporation, as appropriate, as receiver for a savings association for the purpose of liquidation or winding up the affairs of such savings association. The conservator or receiver so appointed shall, as such, have power to buy at its own sale. The Federal Deposit Insurance Corporation, as such conservator or receiver, shall have all the powers of a conservator or receiver, as appropriate, granted under the Federal Deposit Insurance Act [12 U.S.C.A. § 1811 et seq.], and (when not inconsistent therewith) any other rights, powers, and privileges possessed by conservators or receivers, as appropriate, of savings associations under this chapter and any other provisions of law.

(F) Disclosure requirement for those acting on behalf of conservator

A conservator shall require that any independent contractor, consultant, or counsel employed by the conservator in connection with the conservatorship of a savings association pursuant to this section shall fully disclose to all parties with which such contractor, consultant, or counsel is negotiating, any limitation on the authority of such contractor, consultant, or counsel to make legally binding representations on behalf of the conservator.

(3) Regulations

(A) In general

The Director may prescribe regulations for the reorganization, consolidation, liquidation, and dissolution of savings associations, for the merger of insured savings associations with insured savings associations, for savings associations in conservatorship and receivership, and for the conduct of conservatorships and receiverships. The Director may, by regulation or otherwise, provide for the exercise of functions by members, stockholders, directors, or officers of a savings association during conservatorship and receivership.

(B) FDIC or RTC as conservator or receiver

In any case where the Federal Deposit Insurance Corporation or the Resolution Trust Corporation is the conservator or receiver, any regulations prescribed by the Director shall be consistent with any regulations prescribed by the Federal Deposit Insurance Corporation pursuant to the Federal Deposit Insurance Act [12 U.S.C.A. § 1811 et seq.].

(4) Refusal to comply with demand

Whenever a conservator or receiver appointed by the Director demands possession of the property, business, and assets of any savings association, or of any part thereof, the refusal by any director, officer, employee, or agent of such association to comply with the demand shall be punishable by a fine of not more than $5,000 or imprisonment for not more than one year, or both.

(5) Definitions

As used in this subsection, the term "savings association" includes any savings association or former savings association that retains deposits insured by the Corporation, notwithstanding termination of its status as an institution insured by the Corporation.

(6) Compliance with monetary transaction recordkeeping and report requirements

(A) Compliance procedures required

The Director shall prescribe regulations requiring savings associations to establish and maintain procedures reasonably designed to assure and monitor the compliance of such associations with the requirements of subchapter II of chapter 53 of Title 31.

(B) Examinations of savings associations to include review of compliance procedures

(i) In general

Each examination of a savings association by the Director shall include a review of the procedures required to be established and maintained under subparagraph (A).

(ii) Exam report requirement

The report of examination shall describe any problem with the procedures maintained by the association.

(C) Order to comply with requirements

If the Director determines that a savings association—

(i) has failed to establish and maintain the procedures described in subparagraph (A); or

(ii) has failed to correct any problem with the procedures maintained by such association which was previously reported to the association by the Director,

the Director shall issue an order under section 8 of the Federal Deposit Insurance Act [12 U.S.C.A. § 1818] requiring such association to cease and desist from its violation of this paragraph or regulations prescribed under this paragraph.

(7) Regulation and examination of savings association service companies, subsidiaries, and service providers

(A) General examination and regulatory authority

A service company or subsidiary that is owned in whole or in part by a savings association shall be subject to examination and regulation by the Director to the same extent as that savings association.

(B) Examination by other banking agencies

The Director may authorize any other Federal banking agency that supervises any other owner of part of the service company or subsidiary to perform an examination described in subparagraph (A).

(C) Applicability of section 8 of the Federal Deposit Insurance Act

A service company or subsidiary that is owned in whole or in part by a saving association shall be subject to the provisions of section 8 of the Federal Deposit Insurance Act [12 U.S.C.A. § 1818] as if the service company or subsidiary were an insured depository institution. In any such case, the Director shall be deemed to be the appropriate Federal banking agency, pursuant to section 3(q) of the Federal Deposit Insurance Act [12 U.S.C.A. § 1813(q)].

(D) Service performed by contract or otherwise

Notwithstanding subparagraph (A), if a savings association, a subsidiary thereof, or any savings and loan affiliate or entity, as identified by section 8(b)(9) of the Federal Deposit Insurance Act [12 U.S.C.A. § 1818(b)(9)], that is regularly examined or subject to examination by the Director, causes to be performed for itself, by contract or otherwise, any service authorized under this chapter or, in the case of a State savings association, any applicable State law, whether on or off its premises—

(i) such performance shall be subject to regulation and examination by the Director to the same extent as if such services were being performed by the savings association on its own premises; and

(ii) the savings association shall notify the Director of the existence of the service relationship not later than 30 days after the earlier of—

(I) the date on which the contract is entered into; or

(II) the date on which the performance of the service is initiated.

(E) Administration by the director

The Director may issue such regulations and orders, including those issued pursuant to section 8 of the Federal Deposit Insurance Act [12 U.S.C.A. § 1818], as may be necessary to enable the Director to administer and carry out this paragraph and to prevent evasion of this paragraph.

(8) Definitions

For purposes of this section—

(A) the term "service company" means

(i) any corporation—

(I) that is organized to perform services authorized by this chapter or, in the case of a corporation owned in part by a State savings association, authorized by applicable State law; and

(II) all of the capital stock of which is owned by 1 or more insured savings associations; and

(ii) any limited liability company—

(I) that is organized to perform services authorized by this chapter or, in the case of a company, 1 of the members of which is a State savings association, authorized by applicable State law; and

(II) all of the members of which are 1 or more insured savings associations;

(B) the term "limited liability company" means any company, partnership, trust, or similar business entity organized under the law of a State (as defined in section 3 of the Federal Deposit Insurance Act [12 U.S.C.A. § 1813]) that provides that a member or manager of such company is not personally liable for a debt, obligation, or liability of the company solely by reason of being, or acting as, a member or manager of such company; and

(C) the terms "State savings association" and "subsidiary" have the same meanings as in section 3 of the Federal Deposit Insurance Act.

(e) Character and responsibility

A charter may be granted only—

(1) to persons of good character and responsibility,

(2) if in the judgment of the Director a necessity exists for such an institution in the community to be served,

(3) if there is a reasonable probability of its usefulness and success, and

(4) if the association can be established without undue injury to properly conducted existing local thrift and home financing institutions.

(f) Federal Home Loan Bank membership

After the end of the 6–month period beginning on November 12, 1999, a Federal savings association may become a member of the Federal Home Loan Bank System, and shall qualify for such membership in the manner provided by the Federal Home Loan Bank Act [12 U.S.C.A. § 1421 et seq.].

(g) Repealed. Pub.L. 101–73, Title III, § 301, Aug. 9, 1989, 103 Stat. 282

(h) Discriminatory State and local taxation prohibited

No State, county, municipal, or local taxing authority may impose any tax on Federal savings associations or their franchise, capital, reserves, surplus, loans, or income greater than that imposed by such authority on other similar local mutual or cooperative thrift and home financing institutions.

(i) Conversions

(1) In general

Any savings association which is, or is eligible to become, a member of a Federal home loan bank may convert into a Federal savings association (and in so doing may change directly from the mutual form to the stock form, or from the stock form to the mutual form). Such conversion shall be subject to such regulations as the Director shall prescribe. Thereafter such Federal savings association shall be entitled to all the benefits of this section and shall be subject to examination and regulation to the same extent as other associations incorporated pursuant to this chapter.

(2) Authority of Director

(A) No savings association may convert from the mutual to the stock form, or from the stock form to the mutual form, except in accordance with the regulations of the Director.

(B) Any aggrieved person may obtain review of a final action of the Director which approves or disapproves a plan of conversion pursuant to this subsection only by complying with the provisions of section 1467a(j) of this title within the time limit and in the manner therein prescribed, which provisions shall apply in all respects as if such final action were an order the review of which is therein provided for, except that such time limit shall commence upon publication of notice of such final action in the Federal Register or upon the giving of such general notice of such final action as is required by or approved under regulations of the Director, whichever is later.

(C) Any Federal savings association may change its designation from a Federal savings association to a Federal savings bank, or the reverse.

(3) Conversion to State association

(A) Any Federal savings association may convert itself into a savings association or savings bank organized pursuant to the laws of the State in which the principal office of such Federal savings association is located if—

(i) the State permits the conversion of any savings association or savings bank of such State into a Federal savings association;

(ii) such conversion of a Federal savings association into such a State savings association is determined—

(I) upon the vote in favor of such conversion cast in person or by proxy at a special meeting of members or stockholders called to consider such action, specified by the law of the State in which the home office of the Federal savings association is located, as required by such law for a State-chartered institution to convert itself into a Federal savings association, but in no event upon a vote of less than 51 percent of all the votes cast at such meeting, and

(II) upon compliance with other requirements reciprocally equivalent to the requirements of such State law for the conversion of a State-chartered institution into a Federal savings association;

(iii) notice of the meeting to vote on conversion shall be given as herein provided and no other notice thereof shall be necessary; the notice shall expressly state that such meeting is called to vote thereon, as well as the time and place thereof; and such notice shall be mailed, postage prepaid, at least 30 and not more than 60 days prior to the date of the meeting, to the Director and to each member or stockholder of record of the Federal savings association at the member's or

stockholder's last address as shown on the books of the Federal savings association;

(iv) when a mutual savings association is dissolved after conversion, the members or shareholders of the savings association will share on a mutual basis in the assets of the association in exact proportion to their relative share or account credits;

(v) when a stock savings association is dissolved after conversion, the stockholders will share on an equitable basis in the assets of the association; and

(vi) such conversion shall be effective upon the date that all the provisions of this chapter shall have been fully complied with and upon the issuance of a new charter by the State wherein the savings association is located.

(B)(i) The act of conversion constitutes consent by the institution to be bound by all the requirements that the Director may impose under this chapter.

(ii) The savings association shall upon conversion and thereafter be authorized to issue securities in any form currently approved at the time of issue by the Director for issuance by similar savings associations in such State.

(iii) If the insurance of accounts is terminated in connection with such conversion, the notice and other action shall be taken as provided by law and regulations for the termination of insurance of accounts.

(4) Savings bank activities

(A) To the extent authorized by the Director, but subject to section 18(m)(3) of the Federal Deposit Insurance Act [12 U.S.C.A. § 1828(m)(3)]—

(i) any Federal savings bank chartered as such prior to October 15, 1982, may continue to make any investment or engage in any activity not otherwise authorized under this section, to the degree it was permitted to do so as a Federal savings bank prior to October 15, 1982; and

(ii) any Federal savings bank in existence on August 9, 1989, and formerly organized as a mutual savings bank under State law may continue to make any investment or engage in any activity not otherwise authorized under this section, to the degree it was authorized to do so as a mutual savings bank under State law.

(B) The authority conferred by this paragraph may be utilized by any Federal savings association that acquires, by merger or consolidation, a Federal savings bank enjoying grandfather rights hereunder.

(5) Conversion to national or State bank

(A) In general

Any Federal savings association chartered and in operation before November 12, 1999, with branches in operation before such date in 1 or more States, may convert, at its option, with the approval of the Comptroller of the Currency for each national bank, and with the approval of the appropriate State bank supervisor and the appropriate Federal banking agency for each State bank, into 1 or more national or State banks, each of which may encompass 1 or more of the branches of the Federal savings association in operation before such date of enactment in 1 or more States subject to subparagraph (B).

(B) Conditions of conversion

The authority in subparagraph (A) shall apply only if each resulting national or State bank—

(i) will meet all financial, management, and capital requirements applicable to the resulting national or State bank; and

(ii) if more than 1 national or State bank results from a conversion under this subparagraph, has received approval from the Federal Deposit Insurance Corporation under section 1815(a) of this title.

(C) No merger application under FDIA required

No application under section 1828(c) of this title shall be required for a conversion under this paragraph.

(D) Definitions

For purposes of this paragraph, the terms "State bank" and "State bank supervisor" have the same meanings as in section 1813 of this title.

(j) Repealed. Pub.L. 101–73, Title III, Aug. 9, 1989, 1989, 103 Stat. 282

(k) Depository of public money

When designated for that purpose by the Secretary of the Treasury, a savings association the deposits of which are insured by the Corporation shall be a depository of public money and may be employed as fiscal agent of the Government under such regulations as may be prescribed by the Secretary and shall perform all such reasonable duties as fiscal agent of the Government as may be required of it. A savings association the deposits of which are insured by the Corporation may act as agent for any other instrumentality of the United States when designated for that purpose by such instrumentality, including services in connection with the collection of taxes and other obligations owed the United States, and the Secretary of the Treasury may deposit public money in any such savings association, and shall prescribe such regulations as may be necessary to carry out the purposes of this subsection.

(*l*) Retirement accounts

A Federal savings association is authorized to act as trustee of any trust created or organized in the United States and forming part of a stock bonus, pension, or profit-sharing plan which qualifies or qualified for specific tax treatment under section 401(d) of the Internal Revenue Code of 1986 [26 U.S.C.A. § 401(d)]and to act as trustee or custodian of an individual retirement account within the meaning of section 408 of such Code [26 U.S.C.A. § 408] if the funds of such trust or account are invested only in savings accounts or deposits in such Federal savings association or in obligations or securities issued by such Federal savings association. All funds held in such fiduciary capacity by any Federal savings association may be commingled for appropriate purposes of investment, but individual records shall be kept by the fiduciary for each participant and shall show in proper detail all transactions engaged in under this paragraph.

(m) Branching

(1) In general

(A) No savings association incorporated under the laws of the District of Columbia or organized in the District or doing business in the District shall establish any branch or move its principal office or any branch without the Director's prior written approval.

(B) No savings association shall establish any branch in the District of Columbia or move its principal office or any branch in the

District without the Director's prior written approval.

(2) Definition

For purposes of this subsection the term "branch" means any office, place of business, or facility, other than the principal office as defined by the Director, of a savings association at which accounts are opened or payments are received or withdrawals are made, or any other office, place of business, or facility of a savings association defined by the Director as a branch within the meaning of such sentence.

(n) Trusts

(1) Permits

The Director may grant by special permit to a Federal savings association applying therefor the right to act as trustee, executor, administrator, guardian, or in any other fiduciary capacity in which State banks, trust companies, or other corporations which compete with Federal savings associations are permitted to act under the laws of the State in which the Federal savings association is located. Subject to the regulations of the Director, service corporations may invest in State or federally chartered corporations which are located in the State in which the home office of the Federal savings association is located and which are engaged in trust activities.

(2) Segregation of assets

A Federal savings association exercising any or all of the powers enumerated in this section shall segregate all assets held in any fiduciary capacity from the general assets of the association and shall keep a separate set of books and records showing in proper detail all transactions engaged in under this subsection. The State banking authority involved may have access to reports of examination made by the Director insofar as such reports relate to the trust department of such association but nothing in this subsection shall be construed as authorizing such State banking authority to examine the books, records, and assets of such associations.

(3) Prohibitions

No Federal savings association shall receive in its trust department deposits of current funds subject to check or the deposit of checks, drafts, bills of exchange, or other items for collection or exchange purposes. Funds depos-

ited or held in trust by the association awaiting investment shall be carried in a separate account and shall not be used by the association in the conduct of its business unless it shall first set aside in the trust department United States bonds or other securities approved by the Director.

(4) Separate lien

In the event of the failure of a Federal savings association, the owners of the funds held in trust for investment shall have a lien on the bonds or other securities so set apart in addition to their claim against the estate of the association.

(5) Deposits

Whenever the laws of a State require corporations acting in a fiduciary capacity to deposit securities with the State authorities for the protection of private or court trusts, Federal savings associations so acting shall be required to make similar deposits. Securities so deposited shall be held for the protection of private or court trusts, as provided by the State law. Federal savings associations in such cases shall not be required to execute the bond usually required of individuals if State corporations under similar circumstances are exempt from this requirement. Federal savings associations shall have power to execute such bond when so required by the laws of the State involved.

(6) Oaths and affidavits

In any case in which the laws of a State require that a corporation acting as trustee, executor, administrator, or in any capacity specified in this section, shall take an oath or make an affidavit, the president, vice president, cashier, or trust officer of such association may take the necessary oath or execute the necessary affidavit.

(7) Certain loans prohibited

It shall be unlawful for any Federal savings association to lend any officer, director, or employee any funds held in trust under the powers conferred by this section. Any officer, director, or employee making such loan, or to whom such loan is made, may be fined not more than $50,000 or twice the amount of that person's gain from the loan, whichever is greater, or may be imprisoned not more than 5 years, or may be both fined and imprisoned, in the discretion of the court.

(8) Factors to be considered

In reviewing applications for permission to exercise the powers enumerated in this section, the Director may consider—

(A) the amount of capital of the applying Federal savings association,

(B) whether or not such capital is sufficient under the circumstances of the case,

(C) the needs of the community to be served, and

(D) any other facts and circumstances that seem to it proper.

The Director may grant or refuse the application accordingly, except that no permit shall be issued to any association having capital less than the capital required by State law of State banks, trust companies, and corporations exercising such powers.

(9) Surrender of charter

(A) Any Federal savings association may surrender its right to exercise the powers granted under this subsection, and have returned to it any securities which it may have deposited with the State authorities, by filing with the Director a certified copy of a resolution of its board of directors indicating its intention to surrender its right.

(B) Upon receipt of such resolution, the Director, if satisfied that such Federal savings association has been relieved in accordance with State law of all duties as trustee, executor, administrator, guardian or other fiduciary, may in the Director's discretion, issue to such association a certificate that such association is no longer authorized to exercise the powers granted by this subsection.

(C) Upon the issuance of such a certificate by the Director, such Federal savings association (i) shall no longer be subject to the provisions of this section or the regulations of the Director made pursuant thereto, (ii) shall be entitled to have returned to it any securities which it may have deposited with State authorities, and (iii) shall not exercise thereafter any of the powers granted by this section without first applying for and obtaining a new permit to exercise such powers pursuant to the provisions of this section.

(D) The Director may prescribe regulations necessary to enforce compliance with the provisions of this subsection.

(10) Revocation

(A) In addition to the authority conferred by other law, if, in the opinion of the Director, a Federal savings association is unlawfully or unsoundly exercising, or has unlawfully or unsoundly exercised, or has failed for a period of 5 consecutive years to exercise, the powers granted by this subsection or otherwise fails or has failed to comply with the requirements of this subsection, the Director may issue and serve upon the association a notice of intent to revoke the authority of the association to exercise the powers granted by this subsection. The notice shall contain a statement of the facts constituting the alleged unlawful or unsound exercise of powers, or failure to exercise powers, or failure to comply, and shall fix a time and place at which a hearing will be held to determine whether an order revoking authority to exercise such powers should issue against the association.

(B) Such hearing shall be conducted in accordance with the provisions of subsection (d)(1)(B) of this section, and subject to judicial review as therein provided, and shall be fixed for a date not earlier than 30 days and not later than 60 days after service of such notice unless the Director sets an earlier or later date at the request of any Federal savings association so served.

(C) Unless the Federal savings association so served shall appear at the hearing by a duly authorized representative, it shall be deemed to have consented to the issuance of the revocation order. In the event of such consent, or if upon the record made at any such hearing, the Director shall find that any allegation specified in the notice of charges has been established, the Director may issue and serve upon the association an order prohibiting it from accepting any new or additional trust accounts and revoking authority to exercise any and all powers granted by this subsection, except that such order shall permit the association to continue to service all previously accepted trust accounts pending their expeditious divestiture or termination.

(D) A revocation order shall become effective not earlier than the expiration of 30 days after service of such order upon the association so served (except in the case of a revocation order issued upon consent, which shall become effective at the time specified therein), and shall remain effective and enforceable, except to such extent as it is stayed, modified, terminated, or set aside by action of the Director or a reviewing court.

(o) Conversion of State savings banks

(1) Subject to the provisions of this subsection and under regulations of the Director, the Director may authorize the conversion of a State-chartered savings bank that is a Bank Insurance Fund member into a Federal savings bank, if such conversion is not in contravention of State law, and provide for the organization, incorporation, operation, examination, and regulation of such institution.

(2)(A) Any Federal savings bank chartered pursuant to this subsection shall continue to be insured by the Deposit Insurance Fund.

(B) The Director shall notify the Corporation of any application under this chapter for conversion to a Federal charter by an institution insured by the Corporation, shall consult with the Corporation before disposing of the application, and shall notify the Corporation of the Director's determination with respect to such application.

(C) Notwithstanding any other provision of law, if the Corporation determines that conversion into a Federal stock savings bank or the chartering of a Federal stock savings bank is necessary to prevent the default of a savings bank it insures or to reopen a savings bank in default that it insured, or if the Corporation determines, with the concurrence of the Director, that severe financial conditions exist that threaten the stability of a savings bank insured by the Corporation and that such a conversion or charter is likely to improve the financial condition of such savings bank, the Corporation shall provide the Director with a certificate of such determination, the reasons therefor in conformance with the requirements of this chapter, and the bank shall be converted or chartered by the Director, pursuant to the regulations thereof, from the time the Corporation issues the certificate.

(D) A bank may be converted under subparagraph (C) only if the board of trustees of the bank—

(i) has specified in writing that the bank is in danger of closing or is closed, or that severe financial conditions exist that threaten the stability of the bank and a conversion is likely to improve the financial condition of the bank; and

(ii) has requested in writing that the Corporation use the authority of subparagraph (C).

(E)(i) Before making a determination under subparagraph (D), the Corporation shall consult the State bank supervisor of the State in which the bank in danger of closing is chartered. The State bank supervisor shall be given a reasonable opportunity, and in no event less than 48 hours, to object to the use of the provisions of subparagraph (D).

(ii) If the State supervisor objects during such period, the Corporation may use the authority of subparagraph (D) only by an affirmative vote of three-fourths of the Board of Directors. The Board of Directors shall provide the State supervisor, as soon as practicable, with a written certification of its determination.

(3) A Federal savings bank chartered under this subsection shall have the same authority with respect to investments, operations, and activities, and shall be subject to the same restrictions, including those applicable to branching and discrimination, as would apply to it if it were chartered as a Federal savings bank under any other provision of this chapter.

(p) Conversions

(1) Notwithstanding any other provision of law, and consistent with the purposes of this chapter, the Director may authorize (or in the case of a Federal savings association, require) the conversion of any mutual savings association or Federal mutual savings bank that is insured by the Corporation into a Federal stock savings association or Federal stock savings bank, or charter a Federal stock savings association or Federal stock savings bank to acquire the assets of, or merge with such a mutual institution under the regulations of the Director.

(2) Authorizations under this subsection may be made only—

(A) if the Director has determined that severe financial conditions exist which threaten the stability of an association and that such authorization is likely to improve the financial condition of the association,

(B) when the Corporation has contracted to provide assistance to such association under section 13 of the Federal Deposit Insurance Act [12 U.S.C.A. § 1823], or

(C) to assist an institution in receivership.

(3) A Federal savings bank chartered under this subsection shall have the same authority with respect to investments, operations and activities, and shall be subject to the same restrictions, including those applicable to branching and discrimination, as would apply to it if it were chartered as a Federal savings bank under any other provision of this chapter, and may engage in any investment, activity, or operation that the institution it acquired was engaged in if that institution was a Federal savings bank, or would have been authorized to engage in had that institution converted to a Federal charter.

(q) Tying arrangements

(1) A savings association may not in any manner extend credit, lease, or sell property of any kind, or furnish any service, or fix or vary the consideration for any of the foregoing, on the condition or requirement—

(A) that the customer shall obtain additional credit, property, or service from such savings association, or from any service corporation or affiliate of such association, other than a loan, discount, deposit, or trust service;

(B) that the customer provide additional credit, property, or service to such association, or to any service corporation or affiliate of such association, other than those related to and usually provided in connection with a similar loan, discount, deposit, or trust service; and

(C) that the customer shall not obtain some other credit, property, or service from a competitor of such association, or from a competitor of any service corporation or affiliate of such association, other than a condition or requirement that such association shall reasonably impose in connection with credit transactions to assure the soundness of credit.

(2) (A) Any person may sue for and have injunctive relief, in any court of the United States having jurisdiction over the parties, against threatened loss or damage by reason of a violation of paragraph (1), under the same conditions and principles as injunctive relief against threatened conduct that will cause loss or damage is granted by courts of equity and under the rules governing such proceedings.

(B) Upon the execution of proper bond against damages for an injunction improvidently granted and a showing that the danger of irreparable loss or damage is immediate, a preliminary injunction may issue.

(3) Any person injured by a violation of paragraph (1) may bring an action in any district court of the United States in which the defendant resides or is found or has an agent, without regard to the amount in controversy, or in any other court of competent jurisdiction, and shall be entitled to recover three times the amount of the damages sustained, and the cost of suit, including a reasonable attorney's fee. Any such action shall be brought within 4 years from the date of the occurrence of the violation.

(4) Nothing contained in this subsection affects in any manner the right of the United States or any other party to bring an action under any other law of the United States or of any State, including any right which may exist in addition to specific statutory authority, challenging the legality of any act or practice which may be proscribed by this subsection. No regulation or order issued by the Director under this subsection shall in any manner constitute a defense to such action.

(5) For purposes of this subsection, the term "loan" includes obligations and extensions or advances of credit.

(6) Exceptions

The Director may, by regulation or order, permit such exceptions to the prohibitions of this subsection as the Director considers will not be contrary to the purposes of this subsection and which conform to exceptions granted by the Board of Governors of the Federal Reserve System pursuant to section 1972 of this title.

(r) Out-of-State branches

(1) No Federal savings association may establish, retain, or operate a branch outside the State in which the Federal savings association has its home office, unless the association qualifies as a domestic building and loan association under section 7701(a)(19) of the Internal Revenue Code of 1986 [26 U.S.C.A. § 7701(a)(19)] or meets the asset composition test imposed by subparagraph (C) of that section on institutions seeking so to qualify, or qualifies as a qualified thrift lender, as determined under section 1467a(m) of this title. No out-of-State branch so established shall be retained or operated unless the total assets of the Federal savings association attributable to all branches of the Federal savings association in that State would qualify the branches as a whole, were they otherwise eligible, for treatment as a domestic building and loan association under section 7701(a)(19) or as a qualified thrift lender, as determined under section 1467a(m) of this title, as applicable.

(2) The limitations of paragraph (1) shall not apply if—

(A) the branch results from a transaction authorized under section 13(k) of the Federal Deposit Insurance Act [12 U.S.C.A. § 1823(k)];

(B) the branch was authorized for the Federal savings association prior to October 15, 1982;

(C) the law of the State where the branch is located, or is to be located, would permit establishment of the branch if the association was a savings association or savings bank chartered by the State in which its home office is located; or

(D) the branch was operated lawfully as a branch under State law prior to the association's conversion to a Federal charter.

(3) The Director, for good cause shown, may allow Federal savings associations up to 2 years to comply with the requirements of this subsection.

(s) Minimum capital requirements

(1) In general

Consistent with the purposes of section 908 of the International Lending Supervision Act of 1983 [12 U.S.C.A. § 3907] and the capital requirement established pursuant to such section by the appropriate Federal banking agencies (as defined in section 903(1) of such Act [12 U.S.C.A. § 3902(1)]), the Director shall require all savings associations to achieve and maintain adequate capital by—

(A) establishing minimum levels of capital for savings associations; and

(B) using such other methods as the Director determines to be appropriate.

(2) Minimum capital levels may be determined by Director case-by-case

The Director may, consistent with subsection (t) of this section, establish the minimum level of capital for a savings association at such amount or at such ratio of capital-to-assets as the Director determines to be necessary or appropriate for such association in light of the particular circumstances of the association.

(3) Unsafe or unsound practice

In the Director's discretion, the Director may treat the failure of any savings association to maintain capital at or above the minimum level required by the Director under this subsection or subsection (t) of this section as an unsafe or unsound practice.

(4) Directive to increase capital

(A) Plan may be required

In addition to any other action authorized by law, including paragraph (3), the Director may issue a directive requiring any savings association which fails to maintain capital at or above the minimum level required by the Director to submit and adhere to a plan for increasing capital which is acceptable to the Director.

(B) Enforcement of plan

Any directive issued and plan approved under subparagraph (A) shall be enforceable under section 8 of the Federal Deposit Insurance Act [12 U.S.C.A. § 1818] to the same extent and in the same manner as an outstanding order which was issued under section 8 of the Federal Deposit Insurance Act and has become final.

(5) Plan taken into account in other proceedings

The Director may—

(A) consider a savings association's progress in adhering to any plan required under paragraph (4) whenever such association or any affiliate of such association (including any company which controls such association) seeks the Director's approval for any proposal which would have the effect of diverting earnings, diminishing capital, or otherwise impeding such association's progress in meeting the minimum level of capital required by the Director; and

(B) disapprove any proposal referred to in subparagraph (A) if the Director determines that the proposal would adversely affect the ability of the association to comply with such plan.

(t) Capital standards

(1) In general

(A) Requirement for standards to be prescribed

The Director shall, by regulation, prescribe and maintain uniformly applicable capital standards for savings associations. Those standards shall include—

(i) a leverage limit;

(ii) a tangible capital requirement; and

(iii) a risk-based capital requirement.

(B) Compliance

A savings association is not in compliance with capital standards for purposes of this subsection unless it complies with all capital standards prescribed under this paragraph.

(C) Stringency

The standards prescribed under this paragraph shall be no less stringent than the capital standards applicable to national banks.

(D) Deadline for regulations

The Director shall promulgate final regulations under this paragraph not later than 90 days after August 9, 1989, and those regulations shall become effective not later than 120 days after August 9, 1989.

(2) Content of standards

(A) Leverage limit

The leverage limit prescribed under paragraph (1) shall require a savings association to maintain core capital in an amount not less than 3 percent of the savings association's total assets.

(B) Tangible capital requirement

The tangible capital requirement prescribed under paragraph (1) shall require a savings association to maintain tangible capital in an amount not less than 1.5 percent of the savings association's total assets.

(C) Risk-based capital requirement

Notwithstanding paragraph (1)(C), the risk-based capital requirement prescribed under paragraph (1) may deviate from the risk-based capital standards applicable to national banks to reflect interest-rate risk or other risks, but such deviations shall not, in the aggregate, result in materially lower levels of capital being required of savings associations under the risk-based capital requirement than would be required under the risk-based capital standards applicable to national banks.

(3) Transition rule

(A) Certain qualifying supervisory goodwill included in calculating core capital

Notwithstanding paragraph (9)(A), an eligible savings association may include qualifying supervisory goodwill in calculating core capital. The amount of qualifying supervisory goodwill that may be included may not exceed the applicable percentage of total assets set forth in the following table:

For the following period:	The applicable percentage is:
Prior to January 1, 1992	1.500 percent
January 1, 1992–December 31, 1992	1.000 percent
January 1, 1993–December 31, 1993	0.750 percent
January 1, 1994–December 31, 1994	0.375 percent
Thereafter	0 percent

(B) Eligible savings associations

For purposes of subparagraph (A), a savings association is an eligible savings association so long as the Director determines that—

(i) the savings association's management is competent;

(ii) the savings association is in substantial compliance with all applicable statutes, regulations, orders, and supervisory agreements and directives; and

(iii) the savings association's management has not engaged in insider dealing, speculative practices, or any other activities that have jeopardized the association's safety and soundness or contributed to impairing the association's capital.

(4) Repealed. Pub.L. 109–351, Title IV, § 402(1), Oct. 13, 2006, 120 Stat. 1974

(5) Separate capitalization required for certain subsidiaries

(A) In general

In determining compliance with capital standards prescribed under paragraph (1), all of a savings association's investments in and extensions of credit to any subsidiary engaged in activities not permissible for a national bank shall be deducted from the savings association's capital.

(B) Exception for agency activities

Subparagraph (A) shall not apply with respect to a subsidiary engaged, solely as agent for its customers, in activities not permissible for a national bank unless the Corporation, in its sole discretion, determines that, in the interests of safety and soundness, this subparagraph should cease to apply to that subsidiary.

(C) Other exceptions

Subparagraph (A) shall not apply with respect to any of the following:

(i) Mortgage banking subsidiaries

A savings association's investments in and extensions of credit to a subsidiary engaged solely in mortgage-banking activities.

(ii) Subsidiary insured depository institutions

A savings association's investments in and extensions of credit to a subsidiary—

(I) that is itself an insured depository institution or a company the sole investment of which is an insured depository institution, and

(II) that was acquired by the parent insured depository institution prior to May 1, 1989.

(iii) Certain Federal savings banks

Any Federal savings association existing as a Federal savings association on August 9, 1989—

(I) that was chartered prior to October 15, 1982, as a savings bank or a cooperative bank under State law; or

(II) that acquired its principal assets from an association that was chartered prior to October 15, 1982, as a savings bank or a cooperative bank under State law.

(D) Transition rule

(i) Inclusion in capital

Notwithstanding subparagraph (A), if a savings association's subsidiary was, as of April 12, 1989, engaged in activities not permissible for a national bank, the savings association may include in calculating capital the applicable percentage (set forth in clause (ii)) of the lesser of—

(I) the savings association's investments in and extensions of credit to the subsidiary on April 12, 1989; or

(II) the savings association's investments in and extensions of credit to the subsidiary on the date as of which the savings association's capital is being determined.

(ii) Applicable percentage

For purposes of clause (i), the applicable percentage is as follows:

For the following period:	The applicable percentage is:
Prior to July 1, 1990	100 percent
July 1, 1990–June 30, 1991	90 percent
July 1, 1991–October 31, 1992	75 percent
November 1, 1992–June 30, 1993	60 percent
July 1, 1993–June 30, 1994	40 percent
Thereafter	0 percent

(iii) Agency discretion to prescribe greater percentage

Subject to clauses (iv), (v), and (vi), the Director may prescribe by order, with respect to a particular qualified savings association, an applicable percentage greater than that provided in clause (ii) if the Director determines, in the Director's sole discretion, that the use of the greater percentage, under the circumstances—

(I) would not constitute an unsafe or unsound practice;

(II) would not increase the risk to the affected deposit insurance fund; and

(III) would not be likely to result in the association's being in an unsafe or unsound condition.

(iv) Substantial compliance with approved capital plan

In the case of a savings association which is subject to a plan submitted under paragraph (7)(D) of this subsection or an order issued under this subsection, a directive issued or plan approved under subsection (s) of this section, or a capital restoration plan approved or order issued under section 38 or 39 of the Federal Deposit Insurance Act [12 U.S.C.A. § 1831o, 1831p–1], an order issued under clause (iii) with respect to the association shall be effective only so long as the association is in substantial compliance with such plan, directive, or order.

(v) Limitation on investments taken into account

In prescribing the amount by which an applicable percentage under clause (iii) may exceed the applicable percentage under clause (ii) with respect to a particular qualified savings association, the Director may take into account only the sum of—

(I) the association's investments in, and extensions of credit to, the subsidiary that were made on or before April 12, 1989; and

(II) the association's investments in, and extensions of credit to, the subsidiary that were made after April 12, 1989, and were necessary to complete projects initiated before April 12, 1989.

(vi) Limit

The applicable percentage limit allowed by the Director in an order under clause (iii) shall not exceed the following limits:

For the following period:	The limit is:
Prior to July 1, 1994	75 percent
July 1, 1994 through June 30, 1995	60 percent
July 1, 1995 through June 30, 1996	40 percent

(vii) Critically undercapitalized institution

In the case of a savings association that becomes critically undercapitalized (as defined in section 38 of the Federal Deposit Insurance Act [12 U.S.C.A. § 1831o]) as determined under this subparagraph without applying clause (iii), clauses (iii) through (v) shall be applied by substituting "Corporation" for "Director" each place such term appears.

(viii) Qualified savings association defined

For purposes of clause (iii), the term "qualified savings association" means an eligible savings association (as defined in paragraph (3)(B)) which is subject to this paragraph solely because of the real estate investments or other real estate activities of the association's subsidiary, and—

(I) is adequately capitalized (as defined in section 38 of the Federal Deposit Insurance Act [12 U.S.C.A. § 1831o]); or

(II) is in compliance with an approved capital restoration plan meeting the requirements of section 38 of the Federal Deposit Insurance Act [12 U.S.C.A. § 1831o], and is not critically undercapitalized (as defined in such section).

(ix) FDIC's discretion to prescribe lesser percentage

The Corporation may prescribe by order, with respect to a particular savings association, an applicable percentage less than that provided in clause (ii) or prescribed under clause (iii) if the Corporation determines, in its sole discretion, that the use of a greater percentage would, under the circumstances, constitute an unsafe or unsound practice or be likely to result in the association's being in an unsafe or unsound condition.

(E) Consolidation of subsidiaries not separately capitalized

In determining compliance with capital standards prescribed under paragraph (1), the assets and liabilities of each of a savings association's subsidiaries (other than any subsidiary described in subparagraph (C)(ii)) shall be consolidated with the savings association's assets and liabilities, unless all of the savings association's investments in and extensions of credit to the subsidiary are deducted from the savings association's capital pursuant to subparagraph (A).

(6) Consequences of failing to comply with capital standards

(A) Prior to January 1, 1991

Prior to January 1, 1991, the Director—

(i) may restrict the asset growth of any savings association not in compliance with capital standards; and

(ii) shall, beginning 60 days following the promulgation of final regulations under this subsection, require any savings association not in compliance with capital standards to submit a plan under subsection (s)(4)(A) of this section that—

(I) addresses the savings association's need for increased capital;

(II) describes the manner in which the savings association will increase its capital so as to achieve compliance with capital standards;

(III) specifies the types and levels of activities in which the savings association will engage;

(IV) requires any increase in assets to be accompanied by an increase in tangible capital not less in percentage amount than the leverage limit then applicable;

(V) requires any increase in assets to be accompanied by an increase in capital not less in percentage amount than required under the risk-based capital standard then applicable; and

(VI) is acceptable to the Director.

(B) On or after January 1, 1991

On or after January 1, 1991, the Director—

(i) shall prohibit any asset growth by any savings association not in compliance with capital standards, except as provided in subparagraph (C); and

(ii) shall require any savings association not in compliance with capital standards to comply with a capital directive issued by the Director (which may include such restrictions, including restrictions on the payment of dividends and on compensation, as the Director determines to be appropriate).

(C) Limited growth exception

The Director may permit any savings association that is subject to subparagraph (B) to increase its assets in an amount not exceeding the amount of net interest credited to the savings association's deposit liabilities if—

(i) the savings association obtains the Director's prior approval;

(ii) any increase in assets is accompanied by an increase in tangible capital in an amount not less than 6 percent of the increase in assets (or, in the Director's discretion if the leverage limit then applicable is less than 6 percent, in an amount equal to the increase in assets multiplied by the percentage amount of the leverage limit);

(iii) any increase in assets is accompanied by an increase in capital not less in percentage amount than required under the risk-based capital standard then applicable;

(iv) any increase in assets is invested in low-risk assets, such as first mortgage loans secured by 1– to 4–family residences and fully secured consumer loans; and

(v) the savings association's ratio of core capital to total assets is not less than the ratio existing on January 1, 1991.

(D) Additional restrictions in case of excessive risks or rates

The Director may restrict the asset growth of any savings association that the Director determines is taking excessive risks or paying excessive rates for deposits.

(E) Failure to comply with plan, regulation, or order

The Director shall treat as an unsafe and unsound practice any material failure by a savings association to comply with any plan, regulation, or order under this paragraph.

(F) Effect on other regulatory authority

This paragraph does not limit any authority of the Director under other provisions of law.

(7) Exemption from certain sanctions

(A) Application for exemption

Any savings association not in compliance with the capital standards prescribed under paragraph (1) may apply to the Director for an exemption from any applicable sanction or penalty for noncompliance which the Director may impose under this chapter.

(B) Effect of grant of exemption

If the Director approves any savings association's application under subparagraph (A), the only sanction or penalty to be imposed by the Director under this chapter for the savings association's failure to comply with the capital standards prescribed under paragraph (1) is the growth limitation contained in paragraph (6)(B) or paragraph (6)(C), whichever is applicable.

(C) Standards for approval or disapproval

(i) Approval

The Director may approve an application for an exemption if the Director determines that—

(I) such exemption would pose no significant risk to the affected deposit insurance fund;

(II) the savings association's management is competent;

(III) the savings association is in substantial compliance with all applicable statutes, regulations, orders, and supervisory agreements and directives; and

(IV) the savings association's management has not engaged in insider dealing, speculative practices, or any other activities that have jeopardized the association's safety and soundness or contributed to impairing the association's capital.

(ii) Denial or revocation of approval

The Director shall deny any application submitted under clause (i) and revoke any prior approval granted with respect to any such application if the Director determines that the association's failure to meet any capital standards prescribed under paragraph (1) is accompanied by—

(I) a pattern of consistent losses;

(II) substantial dissipation of assets;

(III) evidence of imprudent management or business behavior;

(IV) a material violation of any Federal law, any law of any State to which such association is subject, or any applicable regulation; or

(V) any other unsafe or unsound condition or activity, other than the failure to meet such capital standards.

(D) Submission of plan required

Any application submitted under subparagraph (A) shall be accompanied by a plan which—

(i) meets the requirements of paragraph (6)(A)(ii); and

(ii) is acceptable to the Director.

(E) Failure to comply with plan

The Director shall treat as an unsafe and unsound practice any material failure by any savings association which has been granted an exemption under this paragraph to comply with the provisions of any plan submitted by such association under subparagraph (D).

(F) Exemption not available with respect to unsafe or unsound practices

This paragraph does not limit any authority of the Director under any other provision of law, including section 8 of the Federal Deposit Insurance Act [12 U.S.C.A. § 1818], to take any appropriate action with respect to any unsafe or unsound practice or condition of any savings association, other than the failure of such savings association to comply with the capital standards prescribed under paragraph (1).

(8) Temporary authority to make exceptions for eligible savings associations

(A) In general

Notwithstanding paragraph (1)(C), the Director may, by order, make exceptions to the capital standards prescribed under paragraph (1) for eligible savings associations. No exception under this paragraph shall be effective after January 1, 1991.

(B) Standards for approval or disapproval

In determining whether to grant an exception under subparagraph (A), the Director shall apply the same standards as apply to determinations under paragraph (7)(C).

(9) Definitions

For purposes of this subsection—

(A) Core capital

Unless the Director prescribes a more stringent definition, the term "core capital" means core capital as defined by the Comptroller of the Currency for national banks, less any unidentifiable intangible assets.

(B) Qualifying supervisory goodwill

The term "qualifying supervisory goodwill" means supervisory goodwill existing on April 12, 1989, amortized on a straight line basis over the shorter of—

(i) 20 years, or

(ii) the remaining period for amortization in effect on April 12, 1989.

(C) Tangible capital

The term "tangible capital" means core capital minus any intangible assets (as intangible assets are defined by the Comptroller of the Currency for national banks).

(D) Total assets

The term "total assets" means total assets (as total assets are defined by the Comptroller of the Currency for national banks) adjusted in the same manner as total assets would be adjusted in determining compliance with the leverage limit applicable to national banks if the savings association were a national bank.

(10) Use of comptroller's definitions

(A) In general

The standards prescribed under paragraph (1) shall include all relevant substantive definitions established by the Comptroller of the Currency for national banks.

(B) Special rule

If the Comptroller of the Currency has not made effective regulations defining core capital or establishing a risk-based capital standard, the Director shall use the definition and standard contained in the Comptroller's most recently published final regulations.

(u) Limits on loans to one borrower

(1) In general

Section 5200 of the Revised Statutes [12 U.S.C.A. § 84] shall apply to savings associations in the same manner and to the same extent as it applies to national banks.

(2) Special rules

(A) Notwithstanding paragraph (1), a savings association may make loans to one borrower under one of the following clauses:

(i) for any purpose, not to exceed $500,000; or

(ii) to develop domestic residential housing units, not to exceed the lesser of $30,000,000 or 30 percent of the savings association's unimpaired capital and unimpaired surplus, if—

(I) the savings association is and continues to be in compliance with the fully phased-in capital standards prescribed under subsection (t) of this section;

(II) the Director, by order, permits the savings association to avail itself of the higher limit provided by this clause;

(III) loans made under this clause to all borrowers do not, in aggregate, exceed 150 percent of the savings association's unimpaired capital and unimpaired surplus; and

(IV) such loans comply with all applicable loan-to-value requirements.

(B) A savings association's loans to one borrower to finance the sale of real property acquired in satisfaction of debts previously contracted in good faith shall not exceed 50 percent of the savings association's unimpaired capital and unimpaired surplus.

(3) Authority to impose more stringent restrictions

The Director may impose more stringent restrictions on a savings association's loans to one borrower if the Director determines that such restrictions are necessary to protect the safety and soundness of the savings association.

(v) Reports of condition

(1) In general

Each association shall make reports of conditions to the Director which shall be in a form prescribed by the Director and shall contain—

(A) information sufficient to allow the identification of potential interest rate and credit risk;

(B) a description of any assistance being received by the association, including the type and monetary value of such assistance;

(C) the identity of all subsidiaries and affiliates of the association;

(D) the identity, value, type, and sector of investment of all equity investments of the associations and subsidiaries; and

(E) other information that the Director may prescribe.

(2) Public disclosure

(A) Reports required under paragraph (1) and all information contained therein shall be available to the public upon request, unless the Director determines—

(i) that a particular item or classification of information should not be made public in order to protect the safety or soundness of the institution concerned or institutions concerned, or the Deposit Insurance Fund; or

(ii) that public disclosure would not otherwise be in the public interest.

(B) Any determination made by the Director under subparagraph (A) not to permit the public disclosure of information shall be made in writing, and if the Director restricts any item of information for savings institutions generally, the Director shall disclose the reason in detail in the Federal Register.

(C) The Director's determinations under subparagraph (A) shall not be subject to judicial review.

(3) Access by certain parties

(A) Notwithstanding paragraph (2), the persons described in subparagraph (B) shall not be denied access to any information contained in a report of condition, subject to reasonable requirements of confidentiality. Those requirements shall not prevent such information from being transmitted to the Comptroller General of the United States for analysis.

(B) The following persons are described in this subparagraph for purposes of subparagraph (A):

(i) the Chairman and ranking minority member of the Committee on Banking, Housing, and Urban Affairs of the Senate and their designees; and

(ii) the Chairman and ranking minority member of the Committee on Banking, Finance and Urban Affairs of the House of Representatives and their designees.

(4) First tier penalties

Any savings association which—

(A) maintains procedures reasonably adapted to avoid any inadvertent and unintentional error and, as a result of such an error—

(i) fails to submit or publish any report or information required by the Director under paragraph (1) or (2), within the period of time specified by the Director; or

(ii) submits or publishes any false or misleading report or information; or

(B) inadvertently transmits or publishes any report which is minimally late, shall be subject to a penalty of not more than $2,000 for each day during which such failure continues or such false or misleading information is not corrected. The savings association shall have the burden of proving by a preponderance of the evidence that an error was inadvertent and unintentional and that a report was inadvertently transmitted or published late.

(5) Second tier penalties

Any savings association which—

(A) fails to submit or publish any report or information required by the Director under paragraph (1) or (2), within the period of time specified by the Director; or

(B) submits or publishes any false or misleading report or information,

in a manner not described in paragraph (4) shall be subject to a penalty of not more than $20,000 for each day during which such failure continues or such false or misleading information is not corrected.

(6) Third tier penalties

If any savings association knowingly or with reckless disregard for the accuracy of any information or report described in paragraph (5) submits or publishes any false or misleading report or information, the Director may assess a penalty of not more than $1,000,000 or 1 percent of total assets, whichever is less, per day for each day during which such failure continues or such false or misleading information is not corrected.

(7) Assessment

Any penalty imposed under paragraph (4), (5), or (6) shall be assessed and collected by the Director in the manner provided in subparagraphs (E), (F), (G), and (I) of section 8(i)(2) of the Federal Deposit Insurance Act [12 U.S.C.A. § 1818(i)(2)(E), (F), (G), (I)](for penalties imposed under such section), and any such assessment (including the determination of the amount of the penalty) shall be subject to the provisions of such subsection.

(8) Hearing

Any savings association against which any penalty is assessed under this subsection shall be afforded a hearing if such savings association submits a request for such hearing within 20 days after the issuance of the notice of assessment. Section 8(h) of the Federal Deposit Insurance Act [12 U.S.C.A. § 1818(h)] shall apply to any proceeding under this subsection.

(w) Forfeiture of franchise for money laundering or cash transaction reporting offenses

(1) In general

(A) Conviction of Title 18 offense

(i) Duty to notify

If a Federal savings association has been convicted of any criminal offense under section 1956 or 1957 of Title 18, the Attorney General shall provide to the Director a written notification of the conviction and shall include a certified copy of the order of conviction from the court rendering the decision.

(ii) Notice of termination; pretermination hearing

After receiving written notification from the Attorney General of such a conviction, the Director shall issue to the savings association a notice of the Director's intention to terminate all rights, privileges, and franchises of the savings association and schedule a pretermination hearing.

(B) Conviction of Title 31 offenses

If a Federal savings association is convicted of any criminal offense under section 5322 or 5324 of Title 31, after receiving written notification from the Attorney General, the Director may issue to the savings association a notice of the Director's intention to terminate all rights, privileges, and franchises of

the savings association and schedule a pretermination hearing.

(C) Judicial review

Subsection (d)(1)(B)(vii) of this section shall apply to any proceeding under this subsection.

(2) Factors to be considered

In determining whether a franchise shall be forfeited under paragraph (1), the Director shall take into account the following factors:

(A) The extent to which directors or senior executive officers of the savings association knew of, were involved in, the commission of the money laundering offense of which the association was found guilty.

(B) The extent to which the offense occurred despite the existence of policies and procedures within the savings association which were designed to prevent the occurrence of any such offense.

(C) The extent to which the savings association has fully cooperated with law enforcement authorities with respect to the investigation of the money laundering offense of which the association was found guilty.

(D) The extent to which the savings association has implemented additional internal controls (since the commission of the offense of which the savings association was found guilty) to prevent the occurrence of any other money laundering offense.

(E) The extent to which the interest of the local community in having adequate deposit and credit services available would be threatened by the forfeiture of the franchise.

(3) Successor liability

This subsection shall not apply to a successor to the interests of, or a person who acquires, a savings association that violated a provision of law described in paragraph (1), if the successor succeeds to the interests of the violator, or the acquisition is made, in good faith and not for purposes of evading this subsection or regulations prescribed under this subsection.

(4) Definition

The term "senior executive officer" has the same meaning as in regulations prescribed under section 32(f) of Federal Deposit Insurance Act [12 U.S.C.A. § 1831i(f)].

(x) Home State citizenship

In determining whether a Federal court has diversity jurisdiction over a case in which a Federal savings association is a party, the Federal savings association shall be considered to be a citizen only of the State in which such savings association has its home office.

§ 1465. Repealed. Pub.L. 106–569, Title XII, § 1021(a), Dec. 27, 2000, 114 Stat. 3032—DFA §§ 1046, 1047

§ 1466. Applicability

The provisions of this chapter shall apply to the United States and to Puerto Rico, Guam, and the Virgin Islands.

§ 1466a. District associations

(a) In general

The Director shall, with respect to all incorporated or unincorporated building, building or loan, building and loan, or homestead associations, and similar institutions, of or transacting or doing business in the District of Columbia, or maintaining any office in the District of Columbia (other than Federal savings associations), have the same powers and functions as to examination, operation, and regulation as the Director has with respect to Federal savings associations.

(b) Additional powers

Any such association or institution incorporated under the laws of, or organized in, the District of Columbia shall have in addition to any existing statutory authority such statutory authority as is vested in Federal savings associations.

(c) Charter amendments

Charters, certificates of incorporation, articles of incorporation, constitutions, bylaws, or other organic documents of associations or institutions referred to in subsection (b) of this section may, without regard to anything contained therein or otherwise, be amended in such manner and to such extent and upon such votes if any as the Director may by regulation or otherwise provide.

(d) Limitation

Nothing in this section shall cause, or permit the Director to cause, District of Columbia associations to be or become Federal savings associations, or require the Director to impose on District of Columbia associations the same regulations as are imposed on Federal savings associations.

§ 1467. Examination fees

(a) Examination of savings associations

The cost of conducting examinations of savings associations pursuant to section 1464(d) of this title shall be assessed by the Director against each such savings association as the Director deems necessary or appropriate.

(b) Examination of affiliates

The cost of conducting examinations of affiliates of savings associations pursuant to this chapter may be assessed by the Director against each affiliate that is examined as the Director deems necessary or appropriate.

(c) Assessment against association in case of affiliate's refusal to pay

(1) In general

Subject to paragraph (2), if any affiliate of any savings association—

(A) refuses to pay any assessment under subsection (b) of this section; or

(B) fails to pay any such assessment before the end of the 60–day period beginning on the date of the assessment,

the Director may assess such cost against, and collect such cost from, such savings association.

(2) Affiliate of more than 1 savings association

If any affiliate referred to in paragraph (1) is an affiliate of more than 1 savings association, the assessment with respect to the affiliate against, and collected from, any affiliated savings association in such proportions as the Director may prescribe.

(d) Civil money penalty for affiliate's refusal to cooperate

(1) Penalty imposed

If any affiliate of any savings association—

(A) refuses to permit any examiner appointed by the Director to make an examination; or

(B) refuses to provide any information required to be disclosed in the course of any examination, the savings association shall forfeit and pay a civil penalty of not more than $5,000 for each day that any such refusal continues.

(2) Assessment and collection

Any penalty imposed under paragraph (1) shall be assessed and collected by the Director, in the manner provided in section 8(i)(2) of the Federal Deposit Insurance Act [12 U.S.C.A. § 1818(i)(2)].

(e) Regulations

Only the Director may prescribe regulations with respect to—

(1) the computation of, and the assessment for, the cost of conducting examinations pursuant to this section; and

(2) the collection and use of such assessments and any fees under this section.

Such regulations may establish formulas to determine a fee or schedule of fees to cover the costs of examinations and also to cover the cost of processing applications, filings, notices, and requests for approvals by the Director or the Director's designee.

(f) Collection through FDIC or Federal home loan banks

The Corporation or the Federal home loan banks shall, upon request of and by agreement with the Director, collect fees and assessments on behalf of the Director and be reimbursed for the actual cost of collection.

(g) Costs of other examinations

(1) Examination of fiduciary activities

In addition to any assessment imposed pursuant to subsection (a) of this section, the cost of conducting examinations of fiduciary activities of savings associations which exercise fiduciary powers (including savings associations or similar institutions in the District of Columbia) shall be assessed by the Director against such savings associations (or similar institutions).

(2) Examinations in excess of 2 per calendar year

If any savings association or affiliate of a savings association is examined by the Director, or the Corporation, as the case may be, more than 2 times in any calendar year, the cost of conducting such additional examinations shall be assessed, in addition to any assessment imposed pursuant to subsection (a) of this sec-

tion, by the Director or the Corporation, as the case may be, against such savings association or affiliate.

(h) Additional information

Any savings association and any affiliate of any savings association shall provide the Director with access to any information or report with respect to any examination made by any public regulatory authority and furnish any additional information with respect thereto as the Director may require.

(i) Treatment of examination assessments

(1) Deposits

Amounts received by the Director from assessments under this section (other than an assessment under subsection (d)(2) of this section) or section 1467a(b)(4) of this title may be deposited in the manner provided in section 5234 of the Revised Statutes [12 U.S.C.A. § 192] with respect to assessments by the Comptroller of the Currency.

(2) Assessments are not government funds

The amounts received by the Director from any assessment under this section shall not be construed to be Government or public funds or appropriated money.

(3) Assessments are not subject to apportionment of funds

Notwithstanding any other provision of law, the amounts received by the Director from any assessment under this section shall not be subject to apportionment for the purpose of chapter 15 of Title 31 or under any other authority.

(j) Processing fee

The Director may, in the Director's sole discretion, assess against any person that submits to the Director an application, filing, notice, or request a fee to cover the cost of processing such submission.

(k) Fees for examinations and supervisory activities

The Director may assess against institutions for which the Director is the appropriate Federal banking agency, as defined in section 3 of the Federal Deposit Insurance Act [12 U.S.C.A. § 1813], fees to fund the direct and indirect expenses of the Office as the Director deems necessary or appropriate. The fees may be imposed more frequently than annually at the discretion of the Director.

(*l*) Working capital

The Director is authorized to impose fees and assessments pursuant to subsections (a), (b), (e), and (k) of this section, in excess of actual expenses for any given year, to permit the Director to maintain a working capital fund. The Director shall remit to the payors of such fees and assessments any funds collected in excess of what he deems necessary to maintain such working capital fund.

(m) Use of funds

The Director is authorized to use the combined resources retained through fees and assessments imposed pursuant to this section to pay all direct and indirect salary and administrative expenses of the Office, including contracts and purchases of property and services, and the direct and indirect expenses of the examinations and supervisory activities of the Office.

§ 1467a. Regulations of holding companies—DFA §§ 604, 606, 616, 623, 625

(a) Definitions

(1) In general

As used in this section, unless the context otherwise requires—

(A) Savings association

The term "savings association" includes a savings bank or cooperative bank which is deemed by the Director to be a savings association under subsection (*l*) of this section.

(B) Uninsured institution

The term "uninsured institution" means any depository institution the deposits of which are not insured by the Federal Deposit Insurance Corporation.

(C) Company

The term "company" means any corporation, partnership, trust, joint-stock company, or similar organization, but does not include the Federal Deposit Insurance Corporation, the Resolution Trust Corporation, any Federal home loan bank, or any company the majority of the shares of which is owned by the United States or any State, or by an instrumentality of the United States or any State.

(D) Savings and loan holding company

(i) In general

Except as provided in clause (ii), the term "savings and loan holding company" means any company that directly or indirectly controls a savings association or that controls any other company that is a savings and loan holding company.

(ii) Exclusion

The term "savings and loan holding company" does not include a bank holding company that is registered under, and subject to, the Bank Holding Company Act of 1956 [12 U.S.C.A. § 1841 et seq.], or to any company directly or indirectly controlled by such company (other than a savings association).

(E) Multiple savings and loan holding company

The term "multiple savings and loan holding company" means any savings and loan holding company which directly or indirectly controls 2 or more savings associations.

(F) Diversified savings and loan holding company

The term "diversified savings and loan holding company" means any savings and loan holding company whose subsidiary savings association and related activities as permitted under paragraph (2) of subsection (c) of this section represented, on either an actual or a pro forma basis, less than 50 percent of its consolidated net worth at the close of its preceding fiscal year and of its consolidated net earnings for such fiscal year, as determined in accordance with regulations issued by the Director.

(G) Subsidiary

The term "subsidiary" has the same meaning as in section 3 of the Federal Deposit Insurance Act [12 U.S.C.A. § 1813].

(H) Affiliate

The term "affiliate" of a savings association means any person which controls, is controlled by, or is under common control with, such savings association.

(I) Bank holding company

The terms "bank holding company" and "bank" have the meanings given to such terms in section 2 of the Banking Holding Company Act of 1956 [12 U.S.C.A. § 1841].

(J) Acquire

The term "acquire" has the meaning given to such term in section 3(f)(8) of the Federal Deposit Insurance Act [12 U.S.C.A. § 1823(f)(8)].

(2) Control

For purposes of this section, a person shall be deemed to have control of—

(A) a savings association if the person directly or indirectly or acting in concert with one or more other persons, or through one or more subsidiaries, owns, controls, or holds with power to vote, or holds proxies representing, more than 25 percent of the voting shares of such savings association, or controls in any manner the election of a majority of the directors of such association;

(B) any other company if the person directly or indirectly or acting in concert with one or more other persons, or through one or more subsidiaries, owns, controls, or holds with power to vote, or holds proxies representing, more than 25 percent of the voting shares or rights of such other company, or controls in any manner the election or appointment of a majority of the directors or trustees of such other company, or is a general partner in or has contributed more than 25 percent of the capital of such other company;

(C) a trust if the person is a trustee thereof; or

(D) a savings association or any other company if the Director determines, a§ fter reasonable notice and opportunity for hearing, that such person directly or indirectly exercises a controlling influence over the management or policies of such association or other company.

(3) Exclusions

Notwithstanding any other provision of this subsection, the term "savings and loan holding company" does not include—

(A) any company by virtue of its ownership or control of voting shares of a savings association or a savings and loan holding company acquired in connection with the underwriting of securities if such shares are held only for such period of time (not exceeding 120 days unless extended by the Director) as will permit the sale thereof on a reasonable basis; and

(B) any trust (other than a pension, profit-sharing, shareholders', voting, or business trust) which controls a savings association or a savings and loan holding company if such trust by its terms must terminate within 25 years or not later than 21 years and 10 months after the death of individuals living on the effective date of the trust, and is (i) in existence on June 26, 1967, or (ii) a testamentary trust created on or after June 26, 1967.

(4) Special rule relating to qualified stock issuance

No savings and loan holding company shall be deemed to control a savings association solely by reason of the purchase by such savings and loan holding company of shares issued by such savings association, or issued by any savings and loan holding company (other than a bank holding company) which controls such savings association, in connection with a qualified stock issuance if such purchase is approved by the Director under subsection (q)(1)(D) of this section, unless the acquiring savings and loan holding company, directly or indirectly, or acting in concert with 1 or more other persons, or through 1 or more subsidiaries, owns, controls, or holds with power to vote, or holds proxies representing, more than 15 percent of the voting shares of such savings association or holding company.

(b) Registration and examination

(1) In general

Within 90 days after becoming a savings and loan holding company, each savings and loan holding company shall register with the Director on forms prescribed by the Director, which shall include such information, under oath or otherwise, with respect to the financial condition, ownership, operations, management, and intercompany relationships of such holding company and its subsidiaries, and related matters, as the Director may deem necessary or appropriate to carry out the purposes of this section. Upon application, the Director may extend the time within which a savings and loan holding company shall register and file the requisite information.

(2) Reports

Each savings and loan holding company and each subsidiary thereof, other than a savings association, shall file with the Director, and the regional office of the Director of the district in which its principal office is located, such reports as may be required by the Director. Such reports shall be made under oath or otherwise, and shall be in such form and for such periods, as the Director may prescribe. Each report shall contain such information concerning the operations of such savings and loan holding company and its subsidiaries as the Director may require.

(3) Books and records

Each savings and loan holding company shall maintain such books and records as may be prescribed by the Director.

(4) Examinations

Each savings and loan holding company and each subsidiary thereof (other than a bank) shall be subject to such examinations as the Director may prescribe. The cost of such examinations shall be assessed against and paid by such holding company. Examination and other reports may be furnished by the Director to the appropriate State supervisory authority. The Director shall, to the extent deemed feasible, use for the purposes of this subsection reports filed with or examinations made by other Federal agencies or the appropriate State supervisory authority.

(5) Agent for service of process

The Director may require any savings and loan holding company, or persons connected therewith if it is not a corporation, to execute and file a prescribed form of irrevocable appointment of agent for service of process.

(6) Release from registration

The Director may at any time, upon the Director's own motion or upon application, release a registered savings and loan holding company from any registration theretofore made by such company, if the Director determines that such company no longer has control of any savings association.

(c) Holding company activities

(1) Prohibited activities

Except as otherwise provided in this subsection, no savings and loan holding company and no subsidiary which is not a savings association shall—

(A) engage in any activity or render any service for or on behalf of a savings association subsidiary for the purpose or with the effect of evading any law or regulation applicable to such savings association;

(B) commence any business activity, other than the activities described in paragraph (2); or

(C) continue any business activity, other than the activities described in paragraph (2), after the end of the 2–year period beginning on the date on which such company received approval under subsection (e) of this section to become a savings and loan holding company subject to the limitations contained in this subparagraph.

(2) Exempt activities

The prohibitions of subparagraphs (B) and (C) of paragraph (1) shall not apply to the following business activities of any savings and loan holding company or any subsidiary (of such company) which is not a savings association:

(A) Furnishing or performing management services for a savings association subsidiary of such company.

(B) Conducting an insurance agency or escrow business.

(C) Holding, managing, or liquidating assets owned or acquired from a savings association subsidiary of such company.

(D) Holding or managing properties used or occupied by a savings association subsidiary of such company.

(E) Acting as trustee under deed of trust.

(F) Any other activity—

(i) which the Board of Governors of the Federal Reserve System, by regulation, has determined to be permissible for bank holding companies under section 4(c) of the Bank Holding Company Act of 1956 [12 U.S.C.A. § 1843(c)] unless the Director, by regulation, prohibits or limits any such activity for savings and loan holding companies; or

(ii) in which multiple savings and loan holding companies were authorized (by regulation) to directly engage on March 5, 1987.

(G) In the case of a savings and loan holding company, purchasing, holding, or disposing of stock acquired in connection with a qualified stock issuance if the purchase of such stock by such savings and loan holding company is approved by the Director pursuant to subsection (q)(1)(D) of this section.

(3) Certain limitations on activities not applicable to certain holding companies

Notwithstanding paragraphs (4) and (6) of this subsection, the limitations contained in subparagraphs (B) and (C) of paragraph (1) shall not apply to any savings and loan holding company (or any subsidiary of such company) which controls—

(A) only 1 savings association, if the savings association subsidiary of such company is a qualified thrift lender (as determined under subsection (m) of this section); or

(B) more than 1 savings association, if—

(i) all, or all but 1, of the savings association subsidiaries of such company were initially acquired by the company or by an individual who would be deemed to control such company if such individual were a company—

(I) pursuant to an acquisition under section 13(c) or 13(k) of the Federal Deposit Insurance Act [12 U.S.C.A. § 1823(c) or (k)] or section 408(m) of the National Housing Act [12 U.S.C.A. § 1730(a)(m)]; or

(II) pursuant to an acquisition in which assistance was continued to a savings association under section 13(i) of the Federal Deposit Insurance Act; and

(ii) all of the savings association subsidiaries of such company are qualified thrift lenders (as determined under subsection (m) of this section).

(4) Prior approval of certain new activities required

(A) In general

No savings and loan holding company and no subsidiary which is not a savings association shall commence, either de novo or by an acquisition (in whole or in part) of a going concern, any activity described in paragraph (2)(F)(i) of this subsection without the prior approval of the Director.

(B) Factors to be considered by Director

In considering any application under subparagraph (A) by any savings and loan holding company or any subsidiary of any such company which is not a savings association, the Director shall consider—

(i) whether the performance of the activity described in such application by the company or the subsidiary can reasonably be expected to produce benefits to the public (such as greater convenience, increased competition, or gains in efficiency) that outweigh possible adverse effects of such activity (such as undue concentration of resources, decreased or unfair competition, conflicts of interest, or unsound financial practices);

(ii) the managerial resources of the companies involved; and

(iii) the adequacy of the financial resources, including capital, of the companies involved.

(C) Director may differentiate between new and ongoing activities

In prescribing any regulation or considering any application under this paragraph, the Director may differentiate between activities commenced de novo and activities commenced by the acquisition, in whole or in part, of a going concern.

(D) Approval or disapproval by order

The approval or disapproval of any application under this paragraph by the Director shall be made in an order issued by the Director containing the reasons for such approval or disapproval.

(5) Grace period to achieve compliance

If any savings association referred to in paragraph (3) fails to maintain the status of such association as a qualified thrift lender, the Director may allow, for good cause shown, any company that controls such association (or any subsidiary of such company which is not a savings association) up to 3 years to comply with the limitations contained in paragraph (1)(C).

(6) Special provisions relating to certain companies affected by 1987 amendments

(A) Exception to 2–year grace period for achieving compliance

Notwithstanding paragraph (1)(C), any company which received approval under subsection (e) of this section to acquire control of a savings association between March 5, 1987, and August 10, 1987, shall not continue any business activity other than an activity described in paragraph (2) after August 10, 1987.

(B) Exemption for activities lawfully engaged in before March 5, 1987

Notwithstanding paragraph (1)(C) and subject to subparagraphs (C) and (D), any savings and loan holding company which received approval, before March 5, 1987, under subsection (e) of this section to acquire control of a savings association may engage, directly or through any subsidiary (other than a savings association subsidiary of such company), in any activity in which such company or such subsidiary was lawfully engaged on such date.

(C) Termination of subparagraph (B) exemption

The exemption provided under subparagraph (B) for activities engaged in by any savings and loan holding company or a subsidiary of such company (which is not a savings association) which would otherwise be prohibited under paragraph (1)(C) shall terminate with respect to such activities of such company or subsidiary upon the occurrence (after August 10, 1987) of any of the following:

(i) The savings and loan holding company acquires control of a bank or an additional savings association (other than a savings association acquired pursuant to section 13(c) or 13(k) of the Federal Deposit Insurance Act [12 U.S.C.A. § 1823(c) or (k)] or section 406(f) or 408 (m) of the National Housing Act [12 U.S.C.A. § 1729(f) or 1730(a)(m)]).

(ii) Any savings association subsidiary of the savings and loan holding company fails to qualify as a domestic building and loan association under section 7701(a)(19) of the Internal Revenue Code of 1986 [26 U.S.C.A. § 7701(a)(19)].

(iii) The savings and loan holding company engages in any business activity—

(I) which is not described in paragraph (2); and

(II) in which it was not engaged on March 5, 1987.

(iv) Any savings association subsidiary of the savings and loan holding company increases the number of locations from which such savings association conducts business after March 5, 1987 (other than an increase which occurs in connection with a transaction under section 13(c) or (k) of the Federal Deposit Insurance Act or section 408(m) of the National Housing Act).

(v) Any savings association subsidiary of the savings and loan holding company permits any overdraft (including an intraday overdraft), or incurs any such overdraft in its account at a Federal Reserve bank, on behalf of an affiliate, unless such overdraft is the result of an inadvertent computer or accounting error that is beyond the control of both the savings association subsidiary and the affiliate.

(D) Order by Director to terminate subparagraph (B) activity

Any activity described in subparagraph (B) may also be terminated by the Director, after opportunity for hearing, if the Director determines, having due regard for the purposes of this chapter that such action is necessary to prevent conflicts of interest or unsound practices or is in the public interest.

(7) Foreign savings and loan holding company

Notwithstanding any other provision of this section, any savings and loan holding company organized under the laws of a foreign country as of June 1, 1984 (including any subsidiary thereof which is not a savings association), which controls a single savings association on August 10, 1987, shall not be subject to this subsection with respect to any activities of such holding company which are conducted exclusively in a foreign country.

(8) Exemption for bank holding companies

Except for paragraph (1)(A), this subsection shall not apply to any company that is treated as a bank holding company for purposes of section 4 of the Bank Holding Company Act of 1956 [12 U.S.C.A. § 1843], or any of its subsidiaries.

(9) Prevention of new affiliations between S & L holding companies and commercial firms

(A) In general

Notwithstanding paragraph (3), no company may directly or indirectly, including through any merger, consolidation, or other type of business combination, acquire control of a savings association after May 4, 1999, unless the company is engaged, directly or indirectly (including through a subsidiary other than a savings association), only in activities that are permitted—

(i) under paragraph (1)(C) or (2) of this subsection; or

(ii) for financial holding companies under section 4(k) of the Bank Holding Company Act of 1956 [12 U.S.C.A. § 1843(k)].

(B) Prevention of new commercial affiliations

Notwithstanding paragraph (3), no savings and loan holding company may engage directly or indirectly (including through a subsidiary other than a savings association) in any activity other than as described in clauses (i) and (ii) of subparagraph (A).

(C) Preservation of authority of existing unitary S & L holding companies

Subparagraphs (A) and (B) do not apply with respect to any company that was a savings and loan holding company on May 4, 1999, or that becomes a savings and loan holding company pursuant to an application pending before the Office on or before that date, and that—

(i) meets and continues to meet the requirements of paragraph (3); and

(ii) continues to control not fewer than 1 savings association that it controlled on May 4, 1999, or that it acquired pursuant to an application pending before the Office on or before that date, or the successor to such savings association.

(D) Corporate reorganizations permitted

This paragraph does not prevent a transaction that—

(i) involves solely a company under common control with a savings and loan holding company from acquiring, directly or indirectly, control of the savings and loan holding company or any savings association that is already a subsidiary of the savings and loan holding company; or

(ii) involves solely a merger, consolidation, or other type of business combination as a result of which a company under common control with the savings and loan holding company acquires, directly or indirectly, control of the savings and loan holding company or any savings association that is already a subsidiary of the savings and loan holding company.

(E) Authority to prevent evasions

The Director may issue interpretations, regulations, or orders that the Director determines necessary to administer and carry out the purpose and prevent evasions of this paragraph, including a determination that, notwithstanding the form of a transaction, the transaction would in substance result in a company acquiring control of a savings association.

(F) Preservation of authority for family trusts

Subparagraphs (A) and (B) do not apply with respect to any trust that becomes a savings and loan holding company with respect to a savings association, if—

(i) not less than 85 percent of the beneficial ownership interests in the trust are continuously owned, directly or indirectly, by or for the benefit of members of the same family, or their spouses, who are lineal descendants of common ancestors who controlled, directly or indirectly, such savings association on May 4, 1999, or a subsequent date, pursuant to an application pending before the Office on or before May 4, 1999; and

(ii) at the time at which such trust becomes a savings and loan holding company, such ancestors or lineal descendants, or spouses of such descendants, have directly or indirectly controlled the savings association continuously since May 4, 1999, or a subsequent date, pursuant to an application pending before the Office on or before May 4, 1999.

(d) Transactions with affiliates

Transactions between any subsidiary savings association of a savings and loan holding company and any affiliate (of such savings association subsidiary) shall be subject to the limitations and prohibitions specified in section 1468 of this title.

(e) Acquisitions

(1) In general

It shall be unlawful for—

(A) any savings and loan holding company directly or indirectly, or through one or more subsidiaries or through one or more transactions—

(i) to acquire, except with the prior written approval of the Director, the control of a savings association or a savings and loan holding company, or to retain the control of such an association or holding company acquired or retained in violation of this section as heretofore or hereafter in effect;

(ii) to acquire, except with the prior written approval of the Director, by the process of merger, consolidation, or purchase of assets, another savings association or a savings and loan holding company, or all or substantially all of the assets of any such association or holding company;

(iii) to acquire, by purchase or otherwise, or to retain, except with the prior written approval of the Director, more than 5 percent of the voting shares of a savings association not a subsidiary, or of a savings and loan holding company not a subsidiary, or in the case of a multiple savings and loan holding company (other than a company described in subsection (c)(8) of this section), to acquire or retain, and the Director may not authorize acquisition or retention of, more than 5 percent of the voting shares of any company not a subsidiary which is engaged in any business activity other than the activities specified in subsection (c)(2) of this section. This clause shall not apply to shares of a savings association or of a savings and loan holding company—

(I) held as a bona fide fiduciary (whether with or without the sole discretion to vote such shares);

(II) held temporarily pursuant to an underwriting commitment in the normal course of an underwriting business;

(III) held in an account solely for trading purposes;

(IV) over which no control is held other than control of voting rights acquired in the normal course of a proxy solicitation;

(V) acquired in securing or collecting a debt previously contracted in good faith, during the 2–year period beginning on the date of such acquisition or for such additional time (not exceeding 3 years) as the Director may permit if the Director determines that such an extension will not be detrimental to the public interest;

(VI) acquired under section 408(m) of the National Housing Act [12 U.S.C.A. § 1730a(m)] or section 13(k) of the Federal Deposit Insurance Act [12 U.S.C.A. § 1823(k)];

(VII) held by any insurance company, as defined in section 2(a)(17) of the Investment Company Act of 1940 [15 U.S.C.A. § 80a–2(a)(17)], except as provided in paragraph (6); or

(VIII) acquired pursuant to a qualified stock issuance if such purchase is approved by the Director under subsection (q)(1)(D) of this section;

except that the aggregate amount of shares held under this clause (other than under subclauses (I), (II), (III), (IV), and (VI)) may not exceed 15 percent of all outstanding shares or of the voting power of a savings association or savings and loan holding company; or

(iv) to acquire the control of an uninsured institution, or to retain for more than one year after February 14, 1968, or from the date on which such control was acquired, whichever is later, except that the Director may upon application by such company extend such one-year period from year to year, for an additional period not exceeding 3 years, if the Director finds such extension is warranted and is not detrimental to the public interest; and

(B) any other company, without the prior written approval of the Director, directly or indirectly, or through one or more subsidiaries or through one or more transactions, to acquire the control of one or more savings associations, except that such approval shall not be required in connection with the control of a savings association, (i) acquired by devise under the terms of a will creating a trust which is excluded from the definition of "savings and loan holding company" under subsection (a) of this section, (ii) acquired in connection with a reorganization in which a person or group of persons, having had control of a savings association for more than 3 years, vests control of that association in a newly formed holding company subject to the control of the same person or group of persons, or (iii) acquired by a bank holding company that is registered under, and subject to, the Bank Holding Company Act of 1956 [12 U.S.C.A. § 1841 et seq.], or any company controlled by such bank holding company. The Director shall approve an acquisition of a savings association under this subparagraph unless the Director finds the financial and managerial resources and future prospects of the company and association involved to be such that the acquisition would be detrimental to the association or the insurance risk of the Savings Association Insurance Fund or Bank Insurance Fund, and shall render a decision within 90 days after submission to the Director of the complete record on the application.

Consideration of the managerial resources of a company or savings association under subparagraph (B) shall include consideration of the competence, experience, and integrity of the officers, directors, and principal shareholders of the company or association.

(2) Factors to be considered

The Director shall not approve any acquisition under subparagraph (A)(i) or (A)(ii), or of more than one savings association under subparagraph (B) of paragraph (1) of this subsection, any acquisition of stock in connection with a qualified stock issuance, any acquisition under paragraph (4)(A), or any transaction under section 13(k) of Federal Deposit Insurance Act [12 U.S.C.A. § 1823(k)], except in accordance with this paragraph. In every case, the Director shall take into consideration the financial and managerial resources and future prospects of the company and association involved, the effect of the acquisition on the association, the insurance risk to the Savings Association Insurance Fund or the Bank Insurance Fund, and the convenience and needs of the community to be served, and shall render a decision within 90 days after submission to the Director of the complete record on the application. Consideration of the managerial resources of a company or savings association shall include consideration of the competence, experience,

and integrity of the officers, directors, and principal shareholders of the company or association. Before approving any such acquisition, except a transaction under section 13(k) of the Federal Deposit Insurance Act, the Director shall request from the Attorney General and consider any report rendered within 30 days on the competitive factors involved. The Director shall not approve any proposed acquisition—

(A) which would result in a monopoly, or which would be in furtherance of any combination or conspiracy to monopolize or to attempt to monopolize the savings and loan business in any part of the United States,

(B) the effect of which in any section of the country may be substantially to lessen competition, or tend to create a monopoly, or which in any other manner would be in restraint of trade, unless it finds that the anticompetitive effects of the proposed acquisition are clearly outweighed in the public interest by the probable effect of the acquisition in meeting the convenience and needs of the community to be served,

(C) if the company fails to provide adequate assurances to the Director that the company will make available to the Director such information on the operations or activities of the company, and any affiliate of the company, as the Director determines to be appropriate to determine and enforce compliance with this chapter, or

(D) in the case of an application involving a foreign bank, if the foreign bank is not subject to comprehensive supervision or regulation on a consolidated basis by the appropriate authorities in the bank's home country.

(3) Interstate acquisitions

No acquisition shall be approved by the Director under this subsection which will result in the formation by any company, through one or more subsidiaries or through one or more transactions, of a multiple savings and loan holding company controlling savings associations in more than one State, unless—

(A) such company, or a savings association subsidiary of such company, is authorized to acquire control of a savings association subsidiary, or to operate a home or branch office, in the additional State or States pursuant to section 13(k) of the Federal Deposit Insurance Act [12 U.S.C.A. § 1823(k)];

(B) such company controls a savings association subsidiary which operated a home or branch office in the additional State or States as of March 5, 1987; or

(C) the statutes of the State in which the savings association to be acquired is located permit a savings association chartered by such State to be acquired by a savings association chartered by the State where the acquiring savings association or savings and loan holding company is located or by a holding company that controls such a State chartered savings association, and such statutes specifically authorize such an acquisition by language to that effect and not merely by implication.

(4) Acquisitions by certain individuals

(A) In general

Notwithstanding subsection (h)(2) of this section, any director or officer of a savings and loan holding company, or any individual who owns, controls, or holds with power to vote (or holds proxies representing) more than 25 percent of the voting shares of such holding company, may acquire control of any savings association not a subsidiary of such savings and loan holding company with the prior written approval of the Director.

(B) Treatment of certain holding companies

If any individual referred to in subparagraph (A) controls more than 1 savings and loan holding company or more than 1 savings association, any savings and loan holding company controlled by such individual shall be subject to the activities limitations contained in subsection (c) of this section to the same extent such limitations apply to multiple savings and loan holding companies, unless all or all but 1 of the savings associations (including any institution deemed to be a savings association under subsection (*l*) of this section) controlled directly or indirectly by such individual was acquired pursuant to an acquisition described in subclause (I) or (II) of subsection (c)(3)(B)(i) of this section.

(5) Acquisitions pursuant to certain security interests

This subsection and subsection (c)(2) of this section do not apply to any savings and loan

holding company which acquired the control of a savings association or of a savings and loan holding company pursuant to a pledge or hypothecation to secure a loan, or in connection with the liquidation of a loan, made in the ordinary course of business. It shall be unlawful for any such company to retain such control for more than one year after February 14, 1968, or from the date on which such control was acquired, whichever is later, except that the Director may upon application by such company extend such one-year period from year to year, for an additional period not exceeding 3 years, if the Director finds such extension is warranted and would not be detrimental to the public interest.

(6) Shares held by insurance affiliates

Shares described in clause (iii)(VII) of paragraph (1)(A) shall not be excluded for purposes of clause (iii) of such paragraph if—

(A) all shares held under such clause (iii)(VII) by all insurance company affiliates of such savings association or savings and loan holding company in the aggregate exceed 5 percent of all outstanding shares or of the voting power of the savings association or savings and loan holding company; or

(B) such shares are acquired or retained with a view to acquiring, exercising, or transferring control of the savings association or savings and loan holding company.

(f) Declaration of dividend

Every subsidiary savings association of a savings and loan holding company shall give the Director not less than 30 days' advance notice of the proposed declaration by its directors of any dividend on its guaranty, permanent, or other nonwithdrawable stock. Such notice period shall commence to run from the date of receipt of such notice by the Director. Any such dividend declared within such period, or without the giving of such notice to the Director, shall be invalid and shall confer no rights or benefits upon the holder of any such stock.

(g) Administration and enforcement

(1) In general

The Director is authorized to issue such regulations and orders as the Director deems necessary or appropriate to enable the Director to administer and carry out the purposes of this section, and to require compliance therewith and prevent evasions thereof.

(2) Investigations

The Director may make such investigations as the Director deems necessary or appropriate to determine whether the provisions of this section, and regulations and orders thereunder, are being and have been complied with by savings and loan holding companies and subsidiaries and affiliates thereof. For the purpose of any investigation under this section, the Director may administer oaths and affirmations, issue subpenas, take evidence, and require the production of any books, papers, correspondence, memorandums, or other records which may be relevant or material to the inquiry. The attendance of witnesses and the production of any such records may be required from any place in any State. The Director may apply to the United States district court for the judicial district (or the United States court in any territory) in which any witness or company subpenaed resides or carries on business, for enforcement of any subpena issued pursuant to this paragraph, and such courts shall have jurisdiction and power to order and require compliance.

(3) Proceedings

(A) In any proceeding under subsection (a)(2)(D) of this section or under paragraph (5) of this section, the Director may administer oaths and affirmations, take or cause to be taken depositions, and issue subpoenas. The Director may make regulations with respect to any such proceedings. The attendance of witnesses and the production of documents provided for in this paragraph may be required from any place in any State or in any territory at any designated place where such proceeding is being conducted. Any party to such proceedings may apply to the United States District Court for the District of Columbia, or the United States district court for the judicial district or the United States court in any territory in which such proceeding is being conducted, or where the witness resides or carries on business, for enforcement of any subpoena issued pursuant to this paragraph, and such courts shall have jurisdiction and power to order and require compliance therewith. Witnesses subpoenaed under this section shall be paid

the same fees and mileage that are paid witnesses in the district courts of the United States.

(B) Any hearing provided for in subsection (a)(2)(D) of this section or under paragraph (5) of this section shall be held in the Federal judicial district or in the territory in which the principal office of the association or other company is located unless the party afforded the hearing consents to another place, and shall be conducted in accordance with the provisions of chapter 5 of Title 5.

(4) Injunctions

Whenever it appears to the Director that any person is engaged or has engaged or is about to engage in any acts or practices which constitute or will constitute a violation of the provisions of this section or of any regulation or order thereunder, the Director may bring an action in the proper United States district court, or the United States court of any territory or other place subject to the jurisdiction of the United States, to enjoin such acts or practices, to enforce compliance with this section or any regulation or order, or to require the divestiture of any acquisition in violation of this section, or for any combination of the foregoing, and such courts shall have jurisdiction of such actions. Upon a proper showing an injunction, decree, restraining order, order of divestiture, or other appropriate order shall be granted without bond.

(5) Cease and desist orders

(A) Notwithstanding any other provision of this section, the Director may, whenever the Director has reasonable cause to believe that the continuation by a savings and loan holding company of any activity or of ownership or control of any of its noninsured subsidiaries constitutes a serious risk to the financial safety, soundness, or stability of a savings and loan holding company's subsidiary savings association and is inconsistent with the sound operation of a savings association or with the purposes of this section or section 8 of the Federal Deposit Insurance Act [12 U.S.C.A. § 1818], order the savings and loan holding company or any of its subsidiaries, after due notice and opportunity for hearing, to terminate such activities or to terminate (within 120 days or such longer period as the Director directs in unusual circumstances) its ownership or control of any such noninsured subsidiary either by sale or by distribution of the shares of the subsidiary to the shareholders of the savings and loan holding company. Such distribution shall be pro rata with respect to all of the shareholders of the distributing savings and loan holding company, and the holding company shall not make any charge to its shareholders arising out of such a distribution.

(B) The Director may in the Director's discretion apply to the United States district court within the jurisdiction of which the principal office of the company is located, for the enforcement of any effective and outstanding order issued under this section, and such court shall have jurisdiction and power to order and require compliance therewith. Except as provided in subsection (j) of this section, no court shall have jurisdiction to affect by injunction or otherwise the issuance or enforcement of any notice or order under this section, or to review, modify, suspend, terminate, or set aside any such notice or order.

(h) Prohibited acts

It shall be unlawful for—

(1) any savings and loan holding company or subsidiary thereof, or any director, officer, employee, or person owning, controlling, or holding with power to vote, or holding proxies representing, more than 25 percent of the voting shares, of such holding company or subsidiary, to hold, solicit, or exercise any proxies in respect of any voting rights in a savings association which is a mutual association;

(2) any director or officer of a savings and loan holding company, or any individual who owns, controls, or holds with power to vote (or holds proxies representing) more than 25 percent of the voting shares of such holding company, to acquire control of any savings association not a subsidiary of such savings and loan holding company, unless such acquisition is approved by the Director pursuant to subsection (e)(4) of this section; or

(3) any individual, except with the prior approval of the Director, to serve or act as a director, officer, or trustee of, or become a partner in, any savings and loan holding company after having been convicted of any criminal offense involving dishonesty or breach of trust.

(i) Penalties

(1) Criminal penalty

(A) Whoever knowingly violates any provision of this section or being a company, violates any regulation or order issued by the Director under this section, shall be imprisoned not more than 1 year, fined not more than $100,000 per day for each day during which the violation continues, or both.

(B) Whoever, with the intent to deceive, defraud, or profit significantly, knowingly violates any provision of this section shall be fined not more than $1,000,000 per day for each day during which the violation continues, imprisoned not more than 5 years, or both.

(2) Civil money penalty

(A) Penalty

Any company which violates, and any person who participates in a violation of, any provision of this section, or any regulation or order issued pursuant thereto, shall forfeit and pay a civil penalty of not more than $25,000 for each day during which such violation continues.

(B) Assessment

Any penalty imposed under subparagraph (A) may be assessed and collected by the Director in the manner provided in subparagraphs (E), (F), (G), and (I) of section 8(i)(2) of Federal Deposit Insurance Act [12 U.S.C.A. § 1818(i)(2)(E), (F), (G), (I)] for penalties imposed (under such section) and any such assessment shall be subject to the provisions of such section.

(C) Hearing

The company or other person against whom any civil penalty is assessed under this paragraph shall be afforded a hearing if such company or person submits a request for such hearing within 20 days after the issuance of the notice of assessment. Section 8(h) of the Federal Deposit Insurance Act shall apply to any proceeding under this paragraph.

(D) Disbursement

All penalties collected under authority of this paragraph shall be deposited into the Treasury.

(E) Violate defined

For purposes of this section, the term "violate" includes any action (alone or with another or others) for or toward causing, bringing about, participating in, counseling, or aiding or abetting a violation.

(F) Regulations

The Director shall prescribe regulations establishing such procedures as may be necessary to carry out this paragraph.

(3) Civil money penalty

(A) Penalty

Any company which violates, and any person who participates in a violation of, any provision of this section, or any regulation or order issued pursuant thereto, shall forfeit and pay a civil penalty of not more than $25,000 for each day during which such violation continues.

(B) Assessment; etc.

Any penalty imposed under subparagraph (A) may be assessed and collected by the Director in the manner provided in subparagraphs (E), (F), (G), and (I) of section 8(i)(2) of the Federal Deposit Insurance Act [12 U.S.C.A. § 1818(i)(2)(E), (F), (G), (I)] for penalties imposed (under such section) and any such assessment shall be subject to the provisions of such section.

(C) Hearing

The company or other person against whom any penalty is assessed under this paragraph shall be afforded an agency hearing if such company or person submits a request for such hearing within 20 days after the issuance of the notice of assessment. Section 8(h) of the Federal Deposit Insurance Act shall apply to any proceeding under this paragraph.

(D) Disbursement

All penalties collected under authority of this paragraph shall be deposited into the Treasury.

(E) Violate defined

For purposes of this section, the term "violate" includes any action (alone or with another or others) for or toward causing, bringing about, participating in, counseling, or aiding or abetting a violation.

(F) Regulations

The Director shall prescribe regulations establishing such procedures as may be necessary to carry out this paragraph.

(4) Notice under this section after separation from service

The resignation, termination of employment or participation, or separation of an institution-affiliated party (within the meaning of section 3(u) of the Federal Deposit Insurance Act [12 U.S.C.A. § 1813(u)]) with respect to a savings and loan holding company or subsidiary thereof (including a separation caused by the deregistration of such a company or such a subsidiary) shall not affect the jurisdiction and authority of the Director to issue any notice and proceed under this section against any such party, if such notice is served before the end of the 6–year period beginning on the date such party ceased to be such a party with respect to such holding company or its subsidiary (whether such date occurs before, on, or after August 9, 1989).

(5) Redesignated (4).

(j) Judicial review

Any party aggrieved by an order of the Director under this section may obtain a review of such order by filing in the court of appeals of the United States for the circuit in which the principal office of such party is located, or in the United States Court of Appeals for the District of Columbia Circuit, within 30 days after the date of service of such order, a written petition praying that the order of the Director be modified, terminated, or set aside. A copy of the petition shall be forthwith transmitted by the clerk of the court to the Director, and thereupon the Director shall file in the court the record in the proceeding, as provided in section 2112 of Title 28. Upon the filing of such petition, such court shall have jurisdiction, which upon the filing of the record shall be exclusive, to affirm, modify, terminate, or set aside, in whole or in part, the order of the Director. Review of such proceedings shall be had as provided in chapter 7 of Title 5. The judgment and decree of the court shall be final, except that the same shall be subject to review by the Supreme Court upon certiorari as provided in section 1254 of Title 28.

(k) Savings clause

construction of 1– to 4–family residential real estate—

(I) which is located within the Commonwealth of Puerto Rico; and

(II) the value of which (at the time of acquisition or upon completion of the development and construction) is below the median value of newly constructed 1– to 4–family residences in the Commonwealth of Puerto Rico, which may be taken into account in determining the amount of the qualified thrift investments and of such savings association shall be doubled.

(B) Virgin Islands savings associations

With respect to any savings association headquartered and operating primarily in the Virgin Islands—

(i) the term "qualified thrift investments" includes, in addition to the items specified in paragraph (4)—

(I) the aggregate amount of loans for personal, family, educational, or household purposes made to persons residing or domiciled in the Virgin Islands; and

(II) the aggregate amount of loans for the acquisition or improvement of churches, schools, or nursing homes, and of loans to small businesses, located within the Virgin Islands; and

(ii) the aggregate amount of loans related to the purchase, acquisition, development and construction of 1–to 4–family residential real estate—

(I) which is located within the Virgin Islands; and

(II) the value of which (at the time of acquisition or upon completion of the development and construction) is below the median value of newly constructed 1– to 4–family residences in the Virgin Islands, which may be taken into account in determining the amount of the qualified thrift investments and of such savings association shall be doubled.

(7) Transitional rule for certain savings associations

(A) In general

If any Federal savings association in existence as a Federal savings association on August 9, 1989—

(i) that was chartered as a savings bank or a cooperative bank under State law before October 15, 1982; or

(ii) that acquired its principal assets from an association that was chartered before October 15, 1982, as a savings bank or a cooperative bank under State law,

meets the requirements of subparagraph (B), such savings association shall be treated as a qualified thrift lender during the period ending on September 30, 1995.

(B) Subparagraph (B) requirements

A savings association meets the requirements of this subparagraph if, in the determination of the Director—

(i) the actual thrift investment percentage of such association does not, after August 9, 1989, decrease below the actual thrift investment percentage of such association on July 15, 1989; and

(ii) the amount by which—

(I) the actual thrift investment percentage of such association at the end of each period described in the following table, exceeds

(II) the actual thrift investment percentage of such association on July 15, 1989,

is equal to or greater than the applicable percentage (as determined under the following table) of the amount by which 70 percent exceeds the actual thrift investment percentage of such association on August 9, 1989:

For the following period:	The applicable percentage is:
July 1, 1991–September 30, 1992	25 percent
October 1, 1992–March 31, 1994	50 percent
April 1, 1994–September 30, 1995	75 percent
Thereafter	100 percent

(C) For purposes of this paragraph, the actual thrift investment percentage of an association on July 15, 1989, shall be determined by applying the definition of "actual thrift investment percentage" that takes effect on July 1, 1991.

(n) Tying restrictions

A savings and loan holding company and any of its affiliates shall be subject to section 1464(q) of this title and regulations prescribed under such section, in connection with transactions involving the products or services of such company or affiliate and those of an affiliated savings association as if such company or affiliate were a savings association.

(*o*) Mutual holding companies

(1) In general

A savings association operating in mutual form may reorganize so as to become a holding company by—

(A) chartering an interim savings association, the stock of which is to be wholly owned, except as otherwise provided in this section, by the mutual association; and

(B) transferring the substantial part of its assets and liabilities, including all of its insured liabilities, to the interim savings association.

(2) Directors and certain account holders' approval of plan required

A reorganization is not authorized under this subsection unless—

(A) a plan providing for such reorganization has been approved by a majority of the board of directors of the mutual savings association; and

(B) in the case of an association in which holders of accounts and obligors exercise voting rights, such plan has been submitted to and approved by a majority of such individuals at a meeting held at the call of the directors in accordance with the procedures prescribed by the association's charter and bylaws.

(3) Notice to the Director; disapproval period

(A) Notice required

At least 60 days prior to taking any action described in paragraph (1), a savings association seeking to establish a mutual holding company shall provide written notice to the Director. The notice shall contain such relevant information as the Director shall require by regulation or by specific request in connection with any particular notice.

(B) Transaction allowed if not disapproved

Unless the Director within such 60–day notice period disapproves the proposed holding company formation, or extends for another 30 days the period during which such disapproval may be issued, the savings association providing such notice may proceed with the transaction, if the requirements of paragraph (2) have been met.

(C) Grounds for disapproval

The Director may disapprove any proposed holding company formation only if—

(i) such disapproval is necessary to prevent unsafe or unsound practices;

(ii) the financial or management resources of the savings association involved warrant disapproval;

(iii) the savings association fails to furnish the information required under subparagraph (A); or

(iv) the savings association fails to comply with the requirement of paragraph (2).

(D) Retention of capital assets

In connection with the transaction described in paragraph (1), a savings association may, subject to the approval of the Director, retain capital assets at the holding company level to the extent that such capital exceeds the association's capital requirement established by the Director pursuant to sections 1464(s) and (t) of this title.

(4) Ownership

(A) In general

Persons having ownership rights in the mutual association pursuant to section 1464(b)(1)(B) of this title or State law shall have the same ownership rights with respect to the mutual holding company.

(B) Holders of certain accounts

Holders of savings, demand or other accounts of—

(i) a savings association chartered as part of a transaction described in paragraph (1); or

(ii) a mutual savings association acquired pursuant to paragraph (5)(B),

shall have the same ownership rights with respect to the mutual holding company as persons described in subparagraph (A) of this paragraph.

(5) Permitted activities

A mutual holding company may engage only in the following activities:

(A) Investing in the stock of a savings association.

(B) Acquiring a mutual association through the merger of such association into a savings association subsidiary of such holding company or an interim savings association subsidiary of such holding company.

(C) Subject to paragraph (6), merging with or acquiring another holding company, one of whose subsidiaries is a savings association.

(D) Investing in a corporation the capital stock of which is available for purchase by a savings association under Federal law or under the law of any State where the subsidiary savings association or associations have their home offices.

(E) Engaging in the activities described in subsection (c)(2) or (c)(9)(A)(ii) of this section.

(6) Limitations on certain activities of acquired holding companies

(A) New activities

If a mutual holding company acquires or merges with another holding company under paragraph (5)(C), the holding company acquired or the holding company resulting from such merger or acquisition may only invest in assets and engage in activities which are authorized under paragraph (5).

(B) Grace period for divesting prohibited assets or discontinuing prohibited activities

Not later than 2 years following a merger or acquisition described in paragraph (5)(C), the acquired holding company or the holding company resulting from such merger or acquisition shall—

(i) dispose of any asset which is an asset in which a mutual holding company may not invest under paragraph (5); and

(ii) cease any activity which is an activity in which a mutual holding company may not engage under paragraph (5).

(7) Regulation

A mutual holding company shall be chartered by the Director and shall be subject to such regulations as the Director may prescribe. Unless the context otherwise requires, a mutual holding company shall be subject to the other requirements of this section regarding regulation of holding companies.

(8) Capital improvement

(A) Pledge of stock of savings association subsidiary

This section shall not prohibit a mutual holding company from pledging all or a portion of the stock of a savings association chartered as part of a transaction described in paragraph (1) to raise capital for such savings association.

(B) Issuance of nonvoting shares

This section shall not prohibit a savings association chartered as part of a transaction described in paragraph (1) from issuing any nonvoting shares or less than 50 percent of the voting shares of such association to any person other than the mutual holding company.

(9) Insolvency and liquidation

(A) In general

Notwithstanding any provision of law, upon—

(i) the default of any savings association—

(I) the stock of which is owned by any mutual holding company; and

(II) which was chartered in a transaction described in paragraph (1);

(ii) the default of a mutual holding company; or

(iii) a foreclosure on a pledge by a mutual holding company described in paragraph (8)(A),

a trustee shall be appointed receiver of such mutual holding company and such trustee shall have the authority to liquidate the assets of, and satisfy the liabilities of, such mutual holding company pursuant to Title 11.

(B) Distribution of net proceeds

Except as provided in subparagraph (C), the net proceeds of any liquidation of any mutual holding company pursuant to subparagraph (A) shall be transferred to persons who hold ownership interests in such mutual holding company.

(C) Recovery by Corporation

If the Corporation incurs a loss as a result of the default of any savings association subsidiary of a mutual holding company which is liquidated pursuant to subparagraph (A), the Corporation shall succeed to the ownership interests of the depositors of such savings association in the mutual holding company, to the extent of the Corporation's loss.

(10) Definitions

For purposes of this subsection—

(A) Mutual holding company

The term "mutual holding company" means a corporation organized as a holding company under this subsection.

(B) Mutual association

The term "mutual association" means a savings association which is operating in mutual form.

(C) Default

The term "default" means an adjudication or other official determination of a court of competent jurisdiction or other public authority pursuant to which a conservator, receiver, or other legal custodian is appointed.

(p) Holding company activities constituting serious risk to subsidiary savings association

(1) Determination and imposition of restrictions

If the Director determines that there is reasonable cause to believe that the continuation by a savings and loan holding company of any activity constitutes a serious risk to the financial safety, soundness, or stability of a savings and loan holding company's subsidiary savings association, the Director may impose such restrictions as the Director determines to be necessary to address such risk. Such restrictions shall be issued in the form of a directive to the holding company and any of its subsidiaries, limiting—

(A) the payment of dividends by the savings association;

(B) transactions between the savings association, the holding company, and the subsidiaries or affiliates of either; and

(C) any activities of the savings association that might create a serious risk that the liabilities of the holding company and its

other affiliates may be imposed on the savings association.

Such directive shall be effective as a cease and desist order that has become final.

(2) Review of directive

(A) Administrative review

After a directive referred to in paragraph (1) is issued, the savings and loan holding company, or any subsidiary of such holding company subject to the directive, may object and present in writing its reasons why the directive should be modified or rescinded. Unless within 10 days after receipt of such response the Director affirms, modifies, or rescinds the directive, such directive shall automatically lapse.

(B) Judicial review

If the Director affirms or modifies a directive pursuant to subparagraph (A), any affected party may immediately thereafter petition the United States district court for the district in which the savings and loan holding company has its main office or in the United States District Court for the District of Columbia to stay, modify, terminate or set aside the directive. Upon a showing of extraordinary cause, the savings and loan holding company, or any subsidiary of such holding company subject to a directive, may petition a United States district court for relief without first pursuing or exhausting the administrative remedies set forth in this paragraph.

(q) Qualified stock issuance by undercapitalized savings associations or holding companies

(1) In general

For purposes of this section, any issue of shares of stock shall be treated as a qualified stock issuance if the following conditions are met:

(A) The shares of stock are issued by—

(i) an undercapitalized savings association; or

(ii) a savings and loan holding company which is not a bank holding company but which controls an undercapitalized savings association if, at the time of issuance, the savings and loan holding company is legally obligated to contribute the net proceeds from the issuance of such stock to the capital of an undercapitalized savings association subsidiary of such holding company.

(B) All shares of stock issued consist of previously unissued stock or treasury shares.

(C) All shares of stock issued are purchased by a savings and loan holding company that is registered, as of the date of purchase, with the Director in accordance with the provisions of subsection (b)(1) of this section.

(D) Subject to paragraph (2), the Director approved the purchase of the shares of stock by the acquiring savings and loan holding company.

(E) The entire consideration for the stock issued is paid in cash by the acquiring savings and loan holding company.

(F) At the time of the stock issuance, each savings association subsidiary of the acquiring savings and loan holding company (other than an association acquired in a transaction pursuant to subsection (c) or (k) of section 13 of the Federal Deposit Insurance Act [12 U.S.C.A. § 1823(c) or (k)] or section 408(m) of the National Housing Act [12 U.S.C.A. § 1730(a)(m)]) has capital (after deducting any subordinated debt, intangible assets, and deferred, unamortized gains or losses) of not less than 6 1/2 percent of the total assets of such savings association.

(G) Immediately after the stock issuance, the acquiring savings and loan holding company holds not more than 15 percent of the outstanding voting stock of the issuing undercapitalized savings association or savings and loan holding company.

(H) Not more than one of the directors of the issuing association or company is an officer, director, employee, or other representative of the acquiring company or any of its affiliates.

(I) Transactions between the savings association or savings and loan holding company that issues the shares pursuant to this section and the acquiring company and any of its affiliates shall be subject to the provisions of section 1468 of this title.

(2) Approval of acquisitions

(A) Additional capital commitments not required

The Director shall not disapprove any application for the purchase of stock in connection with a qualified stock issuance on the grounds that the acquiring savings and loan holding company has failed to undertake to make subsequent additional capital contributions to maintain the capital of the undercapitalized savings association at or above the minimum level required by the Director or any other Federal agency having jurisdiction.

(B) Other conditions

Notwithstanding subsection (a)(4) of this section, the Director may impose such conditions on any approval of an application for the purchase of stock in connection with a qualified stock issuance as the Director determines to be appropriate, including—

(i) a requirement that any savings association subsidiary of the acquiring savings and loan holding company limit dividends paid to such holding company for such period of time as the Director may require; and

(ii) such other conditions as the Director deems necessary or appropriate to prevent evasions of this section.

(C) Application deemed approved if not disapproved within 90 days

An application for approval of a purchase of stock in connection with a qualified stock issuance shall be deemed to have been approved by the Director if such application has not been disapproved by the Director before the end of the 90–day period beginning on the date such application has been deemed sufficient under regulations issued by the Director.

(3) No limitation on class of stock issued

The shares of stock issued in connection with a qualified stock issuance may be shares of any class.

(4) Undercapitalized savings association defined

For purposes of this subsection, the term "undercapitalized savings association" means any savings association—

(A) the assets of which exceed the liabilities of such association; and

(B) which does not comply with one or more of the capital standards in effect under section 1464(t) of this title.

(r) Penalty for failure to provide timely and accurate reports

(1) First tier

Any savings and loan holding company, and any subsidiary of such holding company, which—

(A) maintains procedures reasonably adapted to avoid any inadvertent and unintentional error and, as a result of such an error—

(i) fails to submit or publish any report or information required under this section or regulations prescribed by the Director, within the period of time specified by the Director; or

(ii) submits or publishes any false or misleading report or information; or

(B) inadvertently transmits or publishes any report which is minimally late,

shall be subject to a penalty of not more than $2,000 for each day during which such failure continues or such false or misleading information is not corrected. Such holding company or subsidiary shall have the burden of proving by a preponder[a]nce of the evidence that an error was inadvertent and unintentional and that a report was inadvertently transmitted or published late.

(2) Second tier

Any savings and loan holding company, and any subsidiary of such holding company, which—

(A) fails to submit or publish any report or information required under this section or under regulations prescribed by the Director, within the period of time specified by the Director; or

(B) submits or publishes any false or misleading report or information,

in a manner not described in paragraph (1) shall be subject to a penalty of not more than $20,000 for each day during which such failure continues or such false or misleading information is not corrected.

(3) Third tier

If any savings and loan holding company or any subsidiary of such a holding company knowingly or with reckless disregard for the accuracy of any information or report described in paragraph (2) submits or publishes

any false or misleading report or information, the Director may assess a penalty of not more than $1,000,000 or 1 percent of total assets of such company or subsidiary, whichever is less, per day for each day during which such failure continues or such false or misleading information is not corrected.

(4) Assessment

Any penalty imposed under paragraph (1), (2), or (3) shall be assessed and collected by the Director in the manner provided in subparagraphs (E), (F), (G), and (I) of section 8(i)(2) of the Federal Deposit Insurance Act [12 U.S.C.A. § 1818(i)(2)(E), (F), (G), (I)] (for penalties imposed under such section) and any such assessment (including the determination of the amount of the penalty) shall be subject to the provisions of such subsection.

(5) Hearing

Any savings and loan holding company or any subsidiary of such a holding company against which any penalty is assessed under this subsection shall be afforded a hearing if such savings and loan holding company or such subsidiary, as the case may be, submits a request for such hearing within 20 days after the issuance of the notice of assessment. Section 8(h) of the Federal Deposit Insurance Act [12 U.S.C.A. § 1818(h)] shall apply to any proceeding under this subsection.

(s) Mergers, consolidations, and other acquisitions authorized

(1) In general

Subject to sections 5(d)(3) and 18(c) of the Federal Deposit Insurance Act [12 U.S.C.A. §§ 1815(d)(3), 1828(c)] and all other applicable laws, any Federal savings association may acquire or be acquired by any insured depository institution.

(2) Expedited approval of acquisitions

(A) In general

Any application by a savings association to acquire or be acquired by another insured depository institution which is required to be filed with the Director under any applicable law or regulation shall be approved or disapproved in writing by the Director before the end of the 60–day period beginning on the date such application is filed with the agency.

(B) Extension of period

The period for approval or disapproval referred to in subparagraph (A) may be extended for an additional 30–day period if the Director determines that—

(i) an applicant has not furnished all of the information required to be submitted; or

(ii) in the Director's judgment, any material information submitted is substantially inaccurate or incomplete.

(3) Acquire defined

For purposes of this subsection, the term "acquire" means to acquire, directly or indirectly, ownership or control through a merger or consolidation or an acquisition of assets or assumption of liabilities, provided that following such merger, consolidation, or acquisition, an acquiring insured depository institution may not own the shares of the acquired insured depository institution.

(4) Regulations

(A) Required

The Director shall prescribe such regulations as may be necessary to carry out paragraph (1).

(B) Effective date

The regulations required under subparagraph (A) shall—

(i) be prescribed in final form before the end of the 90–day period beginning on December 19, 1991; and

(ii) take effect before the end of the 120–day period beginning on December 19, 1991.

(5) Limitation

No provision of this section shall be construed to authorize a national bank or any subsidiary thereof to engage in any activity not otherwise authorized under the National Bank Act [12 U.S.C.A. § 21 et seq.] or any other law governing the powers of a national bank.

(t) Exemption for bank holding companies

This section shall not apply to a bank holding company that is subject to the Bank Holding Company Act of 1956 [12 U.S.C.A. § 1841 et seq.], or any company controlled by such bank holding company.

§ 1468. Transactions with affiliates; extensions of credit to executive officers, directors, and principal shareholders— DFA § 608

(a) Affiliate transactions

(1) In general

Sections 23A and 23B of the Federal Reserve Act [12 U.S.C.A. § § 371c and 371c–1] shall apply to every savings association in the same manner and to the same extent as if the savings association were a member bank (as defined in such Act), except that—

(A) no loan or other extension of credit may be made to any affiliate unless that affiliate is engaged only in activities described in section 1467a(c)(2)(F)(i) of this title; and

(B) no savings association may enter into any transaction described in section 23A(b)(7)(B) of the Federal Reserve Act [12 U.S.C.A. § § 371c(b)(7)(B)] with any affiliate other than with respect to shares of a subsidiary.

(2) Sister bank exemption made available to savings associations

(A) Savings associations controlled by bank holding companies

Every savings association more than 80 percent of the voting stock of which is owned by a company described in section 1467a(c)(8) of this title shall be treated as a bank for purposes of section 23A(d)(1) and section 23B of the Federal Reserve Act [12 U.S.C.A. § 371c(d)(1) and 371c–1], if every savings association and bank controlled by such company complies with all applicable capital requirements on a fully phased-in basis and without reliance on goodwill.

(B) Savings associations generally

Effective on and after January 1, 1995, every savings association shall be treated as a bank for purposes of section 23A(d)(1) and section 23B of the Federal Reserve Act [12 U.S.C.A. § § 371c(d)(1) and 371c–1].

(3) Affiliates described

Any company that would be an affiliate (as defined in sections 23A and 23B of the Federal Reserve Act [12 U.S.C.A. § § 371c and 371c–1]) of any savings association if such savings association were a member bank (as such term is defined in such Act) shall be deemed to be an affiliate of such savings association for purposes of paragraph (1).

(4) Additional restrictions authorized

The Director may impose such additional restrictions on any transaction between any savings association and any affiliate of such savings association as the Director determines to be necessary to protect the safety and soundness of the savings association.

(b) Extensions of credit to executive officers, directors, and principal shareholders

(1) In general

Subsections (g) and (h) of section 22 of the Federal Reserve Act [12 U.S.C.A. § § 375a and 375b] shall apply to every savings association in the same manner and to the same extent as if the savings association were a member bank (as defined in such Act).

(2) Additional restrictions authorized

The Director may impose such additional restrictions on loans or extensions of credit to any director or executive officer of any savings association, or any person who directly or indirectly owns, controls, or has the power to vote more than 10 percent of any class of voting securities of a savings association, as the Director determines to be necessary to protect the safety and soundness of the savings association.

(c) Administrative enforcement

The Director may take enforcement action with respect to violations of this section pursuant to section 8 or 18(j) of the Federal Deposit Insurance Act [12 U.S.C.A. § 1818 or 1828(j)], as appropriate.

§ 1468a. Advertising

No savings association shall carry on any sale, plan, or practices, or any advertising, in violation of regulations promulgated by the Director.

§ 1468b. Powers of examiners

For the purposes of this chapter, examiners appointed by the Director shall—

(1) be subject to the same requirements, responsibilities, and penalties as are applicable to examiners under the Federal Reserve Act [12 U.S.C.A. § 221 et seq.] and title LXII of the Revised Statutes; and

(2) have, in the exercise of functions under this chapter, the same powers and privileges as are vested in such examiners by law.

§ 1468c. Separability

If any provision of this chapter, or the application thereof to any person or circumstances, is held invalid, the remainder of the chapter, and the application of such provision to other persons or circumstances, shall not be affected thereby.

§ 1469. Authority to invest in State housing corporations

The Congress finds that Federal savings and loan associations and national banks should have the authority to assist in financing the organization and operation of any State housing corporation established under the laws of the State in which the corporation will carry on its operations. It is the purpose of this section to provide a means whereby private financial institutions can assist in providing housing, particularly for families of low-or moderate-income, by purchasing stock of and investing in loans to any such State housing corporation situated in the particular State in which the Federal savings and loan association or national bank involved is located.

§ 1470. Federal supervision of insured institutions, State member and nonmember banks; access to information; definitions

(a) (1) The Federal Savings and Loan Insurance Corporation with respect to insured institutions, the Board of Governors of the Federal Reserve System with respect to State member insured banks, and the Federal Deposit Insurance Corporation with respect to State nonmember insured banks shall by appropriate rule, regulation, order, or otherwise regulate investment in State housing corporations.

(2) A State housing corporation in which financial institutions invest under the authority of this section shall make available to the appropriate Federal supervisory agency referred to in paragraph (1) such information as may be necessary to insure that investments are properly made in accordance with this section.

(b) For the purposes of this section and any Act amended by this section—

(1) The term "insured institution" has the same meaning as in section 401(a) of the National Housing Act [12 U.S.C.A. § 1724(a)].

(2) The terms "State member insured banks" and "State nonmember insured banks" have the same meaning as when used in the Federal Deposit Insurance Act [12 U.S.C.A. § 1811 et seq.].

(3) The term "State housing corporation" means a corporation established by a State for the limited purpose of providing housing and incidental services, particularly for families of low or moderate income.

(4) The term "State" means any State, the District of Columbia, Guam, the Commonwealth of Puerto Rico, and the Virgin Islands.

CHAPTER 16. FEDERAL DEPOSIT INSURANCE CORPORATION
12 U.S.C.A. §§ 1811–1835a

12 U.S.C.A. § **Page**

CHAPTER 16. FEDERAL DEPOSIT INSURANCE CORPORATION

§ 1811. Federal Deposit Insurance Corporation—DFA § 601

(a) Establishment of Corporation

There is hereby established a Federal Deposit Insurance Corporation (hereinafter referred to as the "Corporation") which shall insure, as hereinafter provided, the deposits of all banks and savings associations which are entitled to the benefits of insurance under this chapter, and which shall have the powers hereinafter granted.

(b) Asset disposition division

(1) Establishment

The Corporation shall have a separate division of asset disposition.

(2) Management

The division of asset disposition shall have an administrator who shall be appointed by the Board of Directors.

(3) Responsibilities of division

The division of asset disposition shall carry out all of the responsibilities of the Corporation under this chapter relating to the liquidation of insured depository institutions and the disposition of assets of such institutions.

§ 1812. Management—DFA § 336

(a) Board of Directors

(1) In general

The management of the Corporation shall be vested in a Board of Directors consisting of 5 members—

(A) 1 of whom shall be the Comptroller of the Currency;

(B) 1 of whom shall be the Director of the Office of Thrift Supervision; and

(C) 3 of whom shall be appointed by the President, by and with the advice and consent of the Senate, from among individuals who are citizens of the United States, 1 of whom shall have State bank supervisory experience.

(2) Political affiliation

After February 28, 1993, not more than 3 of the members of the Board of Directors may be members of the same political party.

(b) Chairperson and Vice Chairperson

(1) Chairperson

1 of the appointed members shall be designated by the President, by and with the advice and consent of the Senate, to serve as Chairperson of the Board of Directors for a term of 5 years.

(2) Vice Chairperson

1 of the appointed members shall be designated by the President, by and with the advice and consent of the Senate, to serve as Vice Chairperson of the Board of Directors.

(3) Acting Chairperson

In the event of a vacancy in the position of Chairperson of the Board of Directors or during the absence or disability of the Chairperson, the Vice Chairperson shall act as Chairperson.

(c) Terms

(1) Appointed members

Each appointed member shall be appointed for a term of 6 years.

(2) Interim appointments

Any member appointed to fill a vacancy occurring before the expiration of the term for which such member's predecessor was appointed shall be appointed only for the remainder of such term.

(3) Continuation of service

The Chairperson, Vice Chairperson, and each appointed member may continue to serve after the expiration of the term of office to which such member was appointed until a successor has been appointed and qualified.

(d) Vacancy

(1) In general

Any vacancy on the Board of Directors shall be filled in the manner in which the original appointment was made.

(2) Acting officials may serve

In the event of a vacancy in the office of the Comptroller of the Currency or the office of Director of the Office of Thrift Supervision and pending the appointment of a successor, or during the absence or disability of the Comptroller or such Director, the acting Comptroller of the Currency or the acting Director of the Office of Thrift Supervision, as the case may be, shall be a member of the Board of Directors in the place of the Comptroller or Director.

(e) Ineligibility for other offices

(1) Postservice restriction

(A) In general

No member of the Board of Directors may hold any office, position, or employment in any insured depository institution or any depository institution holding company during—

(i) the time such member is in office; and

(ii) the 2–year period beginning on the date such member ceases to serve on the Board of Directors.

(B) Exception for members who serve full term

The limitation contained in subparagraph (A)(ii) shall not apply to any member who has ceased to serve on the Board of Directors after serving the full term for which such member was appointed.

(2) Restriction during service

No member of the Board of Directors may—

(A) be an officer or director of any insured depository institution, depository institution holding company, Federal Reserve bank, or Federal home loan bank; or

(B) hold stock in any insured depository institution or depository institution holding company.

(3) Certification

Upon taking office, each member of the Board of Directors shall certify under oath that such member has complied with this subsection and such certification shall be filed with the secretary of the Board of Directors.

(f) Status of employees

(1) In general

A director, member, officer, or employee of the Corporation has no liability under the Securities Act of 1933 [15 U.S.C.A. § 77a et seq.] with respect to any claim arising out of or resulting from any act or omission by such person within the scope of such person's employment in connection with any transaction involving the disposition of assets (or any interests in any assets or any obligations backed by any assets) by the Corporation. This subsection shall not be construed to limit personal liability for criminal acts or omissions, willful or malicious misconduct, acts or omissions for private gain, or any other acts or omissions outside the scope of such person's employment.

(2) Definition

For purposes of this subsection, the term "employee of the Corporation" includes any employee of the Office of the Comptroller of the Currency or of the Office of Thrift Supervision who serves as a deputy or assistant to a member of the Board of Directors of the Corporation in connection with activities of the Corporation.

(3) Effect on other law

This subsection does not affect—

(A) any other immunities and protections that may be available to such person under applicable law with respect to such transactions, or

(B) any other right or remedy against the Corporation, against the United States under applicable law, or against any person other than a person described in paragraph (1) participating in such transactions.

This subsection shall not be construed to limit or alter in any way the immunities that are available under applicable law for Federal officials and employees not described in this subsection.

§ 1813. Definitions—DFA §§ 312, 334

As used in this chapter—

(a) Definitions of bank and related terms

(1) Bank

The term "bank"—

(A) means any national bank and State bank, and any Federal branch and insured branch;

(B) includes any former savings association.

(2) State bank

The term "State bank" means any bank, banking association, trust company, savings bank, industrial bank (or similar depository institution which the Board of Directors finds to be operating substantially in the same manner as an industrial bank), or other banking institution which—

(A) is engaged in the business of receiving deposits, other than trust funds (as defined in this section); and

(B) is incorporated under the laws of any State or which is operating under the Code of Law for the District of Columbia,

including any cooperative bank or other unincorporated bank the deposits of which were insured by the Corporation on the day before August 9, 1989.

(3) State

The term "State" means any State of the United States, the District of Columbia, any territory of the United States, Puerto Rico, Guam, American Samoa, the Trust Territory of the Pacific Islands, the Virgin Islands, and the Northern Mariana Islands.

(4) Repealed. Pub.L. 108–386, § 8(a)(1)(B), Oct. 30, 2004, 118 Stat. 2231

(b) Definition of savings associations and related terms

(1) Savings association

The term "savings association" means—

(A) any Federal savings association;

(B) any State savings association; and

(C) any corporation (other than a bank) that the Board of Directors and the Director of the Office of Thrift Supervision jointly determine to be operating in substantially the same manner as a savings association.

(2) Federal savings association

The term "Federal savings association" means any Federal savings association or Federal savings bank which is chartered under section 1464 of this title.

(3) State savings association

The term "State savings association" means—

(A) any building and loan association, savings and loan association, or homestead association; or

(B) any cooperative bank (other than a cooperative bank which is a State bank as defined in subsection (a)(2) of this section),

which is organized and operating according to the laws of the State (as defined in subsection (a)(3) of this section) in which it is chartered or organized.

(c) Definitions relating to depository institutions

(1) Depository institution

The term "depository institution" means any bank or savings association.

(2) Insured depository institution

The term "insured depository institution" means any bank or savings association the deposits of which are insured by the Corporation pursuant to this chapter.

(3) Institutions included for certain purposes

The term "insured depository institution" includes any uninsured branch or agency of a foreign bank or a commercial lending company owned or controlled by a foreign bank for purposes of section 1818 of this title.

(4) Federal depository institution

The term "Federal depository institution" means any national bank, any Federal savings association, and any Federal branch.

(5) State depository institution

The term "State depository institution" means any State bank, any State savings association, and any insured branch which is not a Federal branch.

(d) Definitions relating to member banks

(1) National member bank

The term "national member bank" means any national bank which is a member of the Federal Reserve System.

(2) State member bank

The term "State member bank" means any State bank which is a member of the Federal Reserve System.

(e) Definitions relating to nonmember banks

(1) National nonmember bank

The term "national nonmember bank" means any national bank which—

(A) is located in any territory of the United States, Puerto Rico, Guam, American Samoa, the Virgin Islands, or the Northern Mariana Islands; and

(B) is not a member of the Federal Reserve System.

(2) State nonmember bank

The term "State nonmember bank" means any State bank which is not a member of the Federal Reserve System.

(f) Mutual savings bank

The term "mutual savings bank" means a bank without capital stock transacting a savings bank business, the net earnings of which inure wholly to the benefit of its depositors after payment of obligations for any advances by its organizers.

(g) Savings bank

The term "savings bank" means a bank (including a mutual savings bank) which transacts its ordinary banking business strictly as a savings bank under State laws imposing special requirements on such banks governing the manner of investing their funds and of conducting their business.

(h) Insured bank

The term "insured bank" means any bank (including a foreign bank having an insured branch) the deposits of which are insured in accordance with the provisions of this chapter; and the term "noninsured bank" means any bank the deposits of which are not so insured.

(i) New depository institution and bridge depository institution defined

(1) New depository institution

The term "new depository institution" means a new national bank or Federal savings association, other than a bridge depository institution, organized by the Corporation in accordance with section 1821(m) of this title.

(2) Bridge depository institution

The term "bridge depository institution" means a new national bank or Federal savings association organized by the Corporation in accordance with section 1821(n) of this title.

(j) Receiver

The term "receiver" includes a receiver, liquidating agent, conservator, commission, person, or other agency charged by law with the duty of winding up the affairs of a bank or savings association or of a branch of a foreign bank.

(k) Board of Directors

The term "Board of Directors" means the Board of Directors of the Corporation.

(l) Deposit

The term "deposit" means—

(1) the unpaid balance of money or its equivalent received or held by a bank or savings association in the usual course of business and for which it has given or is obligated to give credit, either conditionally or unconditionally, to a commercial, checking, savings, time, or thrift account, or which is evidenced by its certificate of deposit, thrift certificate, investment certificate, certificate of indebtedness, or other similar name, or a check or draft drawn against a deposit account and certified by the bank or savings association, or a letter of credit or a traveler's check on which the bank or savings association is primarily liable: *Provided*, That, without limiting the generality of the term "money or its equivalent", any such account or instrument must be regarded as evidencing the receipt of the equivalent of money when credited or issued in exchange for checks or drafts or for a promissory note upon which the person obtaining any such credit or instrument is primarily or secondarily liable, or for a charge against a deposit account, or in settlement of checks, drafts, or other instruments forwarded to such bank or savings association for collection.

(2) trust funds as defined in this chapter received or held by such bank or savings association, whether held in the trust department or held or deposited in any other department of such bank or savings association.

(3) money received or held by a bank or savings association, or the credit given for money or its equivalent received or held by a bank or savings association, in the usual course of business for a special or specific purpose, regardless of the legal relationship thereby established, including without being limited to, escrow funds, funds held as security for an obligation due to the bank or savings association or others (including funds held as dealers reserves) or for securities loaned by the bank or savings association, funds deposited by a debtor to meet maturing obligations, funds deposited as advance payment on subscriptions to United States Government securities, funds held for distribution or purchase of securities, funds held to meet its acceptances or letters of credit, and withheld taxes: *Provided*, That there shall not be included funds which are received by the bank or savings association for immediate application to the reduction of an

indebtedness to the receiving bank or savings association, or under condition that the receipt thereof immediately reduces or extinguishes such an indebtedness.

(4) outstanding draft (including advice or authorization to charge a bank's or a savings association's balance in another bank or savings association), cashier's check, money order, or other officer's check issued in the usual course of business for any purpose, including without being limited to those issued in payment for services, dividends, or purchases, and

(5) such other obligations of a bank or savings association as the Board of Directors, after consultation with the Comptroller of the Currency, Director of the Office of Thrift Supervision, and the Board of Governors of the Federal Reserve System, shall find and prescribe by regulation to be deposit liabilities by general usage, except that the following shall not be a deposit for any of the purposes of this chapter or be included as part of the total deposits or of an insured deposit:

(A) any obligation of a depository institution which is carried on the books and records of an office of such bank or savings association located outside of any State, unless—

(i) such obligation would be a deposit if it were carried on the books and records of the depository institution, and would be payable at, an office located in any State; and

(ii) the contract evidencing the obligation provides by express terms, and not by implication, for payment at an office of the depository institution located in any State;

(B) any international banking facility deposit, including an international banking facility time deposit, as such term is from time to time defined by the Board of Governors of the Federal Reserve System in regulation D or any successor regulation issued by the Board of Governors of the Federal Reserve System; and

(C) any liability of an insured depository institution that arises under an annuity contract, the income of which is tax deferred under section 72 of Title 26.

(m) Insured deposit

(1) In general

Subject to paragraph (2), the term "insured deposit" means the net amount due to any depositor for deposits in an insured depository institution as determined under sections 1817(i) and 1821(a) of this title.

(2) In the case of any deposit in a branch of a foreign bank, the term "insured deposit" means an insured deposit as defined in paragraph (1) of this subsection which—

(A) is payable in the United States to—

(i) an individual who is a citizen or resident of the United States,

(ii) a partnership, corporation, trust, or other legally cognizable entity created under the laws of the United States or any State and having its principal place of business within the United States or any State, or

(iii) an individual, partnership, corporation, trust, or other legally cognizable entity which is determined by the Board of Directors in accordance with its regulations to have such business or financial relationships in the United States as to make the insurance of such deposit consistent with the purposes of this chapter; and

(B) meets any other criteria prescribed by the Board of Directors by regulation as necessary or appropriate in its judgment to carry out the purposes of this chapter or to facilitate the administration thereof.

(3) Uninsured deposits

The term "uninsured deposit" means the amount of any deposit of any depositor at any insured depository institution in excess of the amount of the insured deposits of such depositor (if any) at such depository institution.

(4) Preferred deposits

The term "preferred deposits" means deposits of any public unit (as defined in paragraph (1)) at any insured depository institution which are secured or collateralized as required under State law.

(n) Transferred deposit

The term "transferred deposit" means a deposit in a new bank or other insured depository institution made available to a depositor by the Corporation as payment of the insured deposit of such depositor in a closed bank, and assumed by such new bank or other insured depository institution.

(o) Domestic branch

The term "domestic branch" includes any branch bank, branch office, branch agency, additional office, or any branch place of business located in any State of the United States or in any Territory of the United States, Puerto Rico, Guam, American Samoa, the Trust Territory of the Pacific Islands, or the Virgin Islands at which deposits are received or checks paid or money lent. The term "domestic branch" does not include an automated teller machine or a remote service unit. The term "foreign branch" means any office or place of business located outside the United States, its territories, Puerto Rico, Guam, American Samoa, the Trust Territory of the Pacific Islands, or the Virgin Islands, at which banking operations are conducted.

(p) Trust funds

The term "trust funds" means funds held by an insured depository institution in a fiduciary capacity and includes, without being limited to, funds held as trustee, executor, administrator, guardian, or agent.

(q) Appropriate Federal banking agency

The term "appropriate Federal banking agency" means—

(1) the Comptroller of the Currency, in the case of any national banking association, any District bank, or any Federal branch or agency of a foreign bank;

(2) the Board of Governors of the Federal Reserve System, in the case of—

(A) any State member insured bank,

(B) any branch or agency of a foreign bank with respect to any provision of the Federal Reserve Act [12 U.S.C.A. § 221 et seq.] which is made applicable under the International Banking Act of 1978 [12 U.S.C.A. § 3101 et seq.],

(C) any foreign bank which does not operate an insured branch,

(D) any agency or commercial lending company other than a Federal agency,

(E) supervisory or regulatory proceedings arising from the authority given to the Board of Governors under section 7(c)(1) of the International Banking Act of 1978 [12 U.S.C.A. § 3105(c)(1)], including such proceedings under the Financial Institutions Supervisory Act of 1966, and

(F) any bank holding company and any subsidiary of a bank holding company (other than a bank);

(3) the Federal Deposit Insurance Corporation in the case of a State nonmember insured bank, or a foreign bank having an insured branch; and

(4) the Director of the Office of Thrift Supervision in the case of any savings association or any savings and loan holding company.

Under the rule set forth in this subsection, more than one agency may be an appropriate Federal banking agency with respect to any given institution.

(r) State bank supervisor

(1) In general

The term "State bank supervisor" means any officer, agency, or other entity of any State which has primary regulatory authority over State banks or State savings associations in such State.

(2) Interstate application

The State bank supervisors of more than 1 State may be the appropriate State bank supervisor for any insured depository institution.

(s) Definitions relating to foreign banks and branches

(1) Foreign bank

The term "foreign bank" has the meaning given to such term by section 1(b)(7) of the International Banking Act of 1978 [12 U.S.C.A. § 3101(7)].

(2) Federal branch

The term "Federal branch" has the meaning given to such term by section 1(b)(6) of the International Banking Act of 1978 [12 U.S.C.A. § 3101(6)].

(3) Insured branch

The term "insured branch" means any branch (as defined in section 1(b)(3) of the International Banking Act of 1978 [12 U.S.C.A. § 3101(3)]) of a foreign bank any deposits in which are insured pursuant to this chapter.

(t) Includes, including

(1) In general

The terms "includes" and "including" shall not be construed more restrictively than the ordinary usage of such terms so as to exclude any other thing not referred to or described.

(2) Rule of construction

Paragraph (1) shall not be construed as creating any inference that the term "includes" or "including" in any other provision of Federal law may be deemed to exclude any other thing not referred to or described.

(u) Institution-affiliated party

The term "institution-affiliated party" means—

(1) any director, officer, employee, or controlling stockholder (other than a bank holding company) of, or agent for, an insured depository institution;

(2) any other person who has filed or is required to file a change-in-control notice with the appropriate Federal banking agency under section 1817(j) of this title;

(3) any shareholder (other than a bank holding company), consultant, joint venture partner, and any other person as determined by the appropriate Federal banking agency (by regulation or case-by-case) who participates in the conduct of the affairs of an insured depository institution; and

(4) any independent contractor (including any attorney, appraiser, or accountant) who knowingly or recklessly participates in—

(A) any violation of any law or regulation;

(B) any breach of fiduciary duty; or

(C) any unsafe or unsound practice,

which caused or is likely to cause more than a minimal financial loss to, or a significant adverse effect on, the insured depository institution.

(v) Violation

The term "violation" includes any action (alone or with another or others) for or toward causing, bringing about, participating in, counseling, or aiding or abetting a violation.

(w) Definitions relating to affiliates of depository institutions

(1) Depository institution holding company

The term "depository institution holding company" means a bank holding company or a savings and loan holding company.

(2) Bank holding company

The term "bank holding company" has the meaning given to such term in section 1841 of this title.

(3) Savings and loan holding company

The term "savings and loan holding company" has the meaning given to such term in section 1467a of this title.

(4) Subsidiary

The term "subsidiary"—

(A) means any company which is owned or controlled directly or indirectly by another company; and

(B) includes any service corporation owned in whole or in part by an insured depository institution or any subsidiary of such a service corporation.

(5) Control

The term "control" has the meaning given to such term in section 1841 of this title.

(6) Affiliate

The term "affiliate" has the meaning given to such term in section 1841(k) of this title.

(7) Company

The term "company" has the same meaning as in section 1841(b) of this title.

(x) Definitions relating to default

(1) Default

The term "default" means, with respect to an insured depository institution, any adjudication or other official determination by any court of competent jurisdiction, the appropriate Federal banking agency, or other public authority pursuant to which a conservator, receiver, or other legal custodian is appointed for an insured depository institution or, in the case of a foreign bank having an insured branch, for such branch.

(2) In danger of default

The term "in danger of default" means an insured depository institution with respect to which (or in the case of a foreign bank having an insured branch, with respect to such insured branch) the appropriate Federal banking agency or State chartering authority has advised the Corporation (or, if the appropriate Federal banking agency is the Corporation, the Corporation has determined) that—

(A) in the opinion of such agency or authority—

(i) the depository institution or insured branch is not likely to be able to meet the demands of the institution's or branch's depositors or pay the institution's or branch's obligations in the normal course of business; and

(ii) there is no reasonable prospect that the depository institution or insured branch will be able to meet such demands or pay such obligations without Federal assistance; or

(B) in the opinion of such agency or authority—

(i) the depository institution or insured branch has incurred or is likely to incur losses that will deplete all or substantially all of its capital; and

(ii) there is no reasonable prospect that the capital of the depository institution or insured branch will be replenished without Federal assistance.

(y) Definitions relating to Deposit Insurance Fund

(1) Deposit Insurance Fund

The term "Deposit Insurance Fund" means the Deposit Insurance Fund established under section 1821(a)(4) of this title.

(2) Designated reserve ratio

The term "designated reserve ratio" means the reserve ratio designated by the Board of Directors in accordance with section 1817(b)(3) of this title.

(3) Reserve ratio

The term "reserve ratio", when used with regard to the Deposit Insurance Fund other than in connection with a reference to the designated reserve ratio, means the ratio of the net worth of the Deposit Insurance Fund to the value of the aggregate estimated insured deposits.

(z) Federal banking agency

The term "Federal banking agency" means the Comptroller of the Currency, the Director of the Office of Thrift Supervision, the Board of Governors of the Federal Reserve System, or the Federal Deposit Insurance Corporation.

§ 1814. Insured depository institutions

(a) Continuation of insurance

(1) Banks

Each bank, which is an insured depository institution on September 21, 1950, shall be and continue to be, without application or approval, an insured depository institution and shall be subject to the provisions of this chapter.

(2) Savings associations

Each savings association the accounts of which were insured by the Federal Savings and Loan Insurance Corporation on the day before August 9,1989, shall be, without application or approval, an insured depository institution.

(b) Continuation of insurance upon becoming a member bank

In the case of an insured bank which is admitted to membership in the Federal Reserve System or an insured State bank which is converted into a national member bank, the bank shall continue as an insured bank.

(c) Continuation of insurance after conversion

Subject to section 1815(d) of this title and section 1464(i)(5) of this title

(1) any State depository institution which results from the conversion of any insured Federal depository institution; and

(2) any Federal depository institution which results from the conversion of any insured State or Federal depository institution,

shall continue as an insured depository institution.

(d) Continuation of insurance after merger or consolidation

Any State depository institution or any Federal depository institution which results from the merger or consolidation of insured depository institutions, or from the merger or consolidation of a noninsured depository institution with an insured depository institution, shall continue as an insured depository institution.

§ 1815. Deposit insurance—DFA §§ 602, 603

(a) Application to Corporation required

(1) In general

Except as provided in paragraphs (2) and (3), any depository institution which is engaged in the business of receiving deposits other than trust funds (as defined in section 1813(p) of this title), upon application to and examination by the Corporation and approval by the Board of Directors, may become an insured depository institution.

(2) Interim depository institutions

In the case of any interim Federal depository institution that is chartered by the appropriate Federal banking agency and will not open for business, the depository institution shall be an insured depository institution upon the issuance of the institution's charter by the agency.

(3) Application and approval not required in cases of continued insurance

Paragraph (1) shall not apply in the case of any depository institution whose insured status is continued pursuant to section 1814 of this title.

(4) Review requirements

In reviewing any application under this subsection, the Board of Directors shall consider the factors described in section 1816 of this title in determining whether to approve the application for insurance.

(5) Notice of denial of application for insurance

If the Board of Directors votes to deny any application for insurance by any depository institution, the Board of Directors shall promptly notify the appropriate Federal banking agency and, in the case of any State depository institution, the appropriate State banking supervisor of the denial of such application, giving specific reasons in writing for the Board of Directors' determination with reference to the factors described in section 1816 of this title.

(6) Nondelegation requirement

The authority of the Board of Directors to make any determination to deny any application under this subsection may not be delegated by the Board of Directors.

(b) Foreign branch nonmember banks; matters considered

Subject to the provisions of this chapter and to such terms and conditions as the Board of Directors may impose, any branch of a foreign bank, upon application by the bank to the Corporation, and examination by the Corporation of

the branch, and approval by the Board of Directors, may become an insured branch. Before approving any such application, the Board of Directors shall give consideration to—

(1) the financial history and condition of the bank,

(2) the adequacy of its capital structure,

(3) its future earnings prospects,

(4) the general character and fitness of its management, including but not limited to the management of the branch proposed to be insured,

(5) the risk presented to the Deposit Insurance Fund,

(6) the convenience and needs of the community to be served by the branch,

(7) whether or not its corporate powers, insofar as they will be exercised through the proposed insured branch, are consistent with the purposes of this chapter, and

(8) the probable adequacy and reliability of information supplied and to be supplied by the bank to the Corporation to enable it to carry out its functions under this chapter.

(c) Protection to deposit insurance fund; surety bond, pledge of assets, etc.; injunction

(1) Before any branch of a foreign bank becomes an insured branch, the bank shall deliver to the Corporation or as the Corporation may direct a surety bond, a pledge of assets, or both, in such amounts and of such types as the Corporation may require or approve, for the purpose set forth in paragraph (4) of this subsection.

(2) After any branch of a foreign bank becomes an insured branch, the bank shall maintain on deposit with the Corporation, or as the Corporation may direct, surety bonds or assets or both, in such amounts and of such types as shall be determined from time to time in accordance with such regulations as the Board of Directors may prescribe. Such regulations may impose differing requirements on the basis of any factors which in the judgment of the Board of Directors are reasonably related to the purpose set forth in paragraph (4).

(3) The Corporation may require of any given bank larger deposits of bonds and assets than required under paragraph (2) of this subsection if, in the judgment of the Corporation, the

situation of that bank or any branch thereof is or becomes such that the deposits of bonds and assets otherwise required under this section would not adequately fulfill the purpose set forth in paragraph (4). The imposition of any such additional requirements may be without notice or opportunity for hearing, but the Corporation shall afford an opportunity to any such bank to apply for a reduction or removal of any such additional requirements so imposed.

(4) The purpose of the surety bonds and pledges of assets required under this subsection is to provide protection to the deposit insurance fund against the risks entailed in insuring the domestic deposits of a foreign bank whose activities, assets, and personnel are in large part outside the jurisdiction of the United States. In the implementation of its authority under this subsection, however, the Corporation shall endeavor to avoid imposing requirements on such banks which would unnecessarily place them at a competitive disadvantage in relation to domestically incorporated banks.

(5) In the case of any failure or threatened failure of a foreign bank to comply with any requirement imposed under this subsection (c), the Corporation, in addition to all other administrative and judicial remedies, may apply to any United States district court, or United States court of any territory, within the jurisdiction of which any branch of the bank is located, for an injunction to compel such bank and any officer, employee, or agent thereof, or any other person having custody or control of any of its assets, to deliver to the Corporation such assets as may be necessary to meet such requirement, and to take any other action necessary to vest the Corporation with control of assets so delivered. If the court shall determine that there has been any such failure or threatened failure to comply with any such requirement, it shall be the duty of the court to issue such injunction. The propriety of the requirement may be litigated only as provided in chapter 7 of Title 5, and may not be made an issue in an action for an injunction under this paragraph.

(d) Insurance fees

(1) In general

Any institution that becomes insured by the Corporation, and any noninsured branch that becomes insured by the Corporation, shall pay the Corporation any fee which the Corporation may by regulation prescribe, after giving due consideration to the need to establish and maintain the reserve ratio of the Deposit Insurance Fund.

(2) Fee credited to the Deposit Insurance Fund

The fee paid by the depository institution under paragraph (1) shall be credited to the Deposit Insurance Fund.

(3) Exception for certain depository institutions

Any depository institution that becomes an insured depository institution by operation of section 1814(a) of this title shall not pay any fee.

(e) Liability of commonly controlled depository institutions

(1) In general

(A) Liability established

Any insured depository institution shall be liable for any loss incurred by the Corporation, or any loss which the Corporation reasonably anticipates incurring, after August 9, 1989 in connection with—

(i) the default of a commonly controlled insured depository institution; or

(ii) any assistance provided by the Corporation to any commonly controlled insured depository institution in danger of default.

(B) Payment upon notice

An insured depository institution shall pay the amount of any liability to the Corporation under subparagraph (A) upon receipt of written notice by the Corporation in accordance with this subsection.

(C) Notice required to be provided within 2 years of loss

No insured depository institution shall be liable to the Corporation under subparagraph (A) if written notice with respect to such liability is not received by such institution before the end of the 2–year period beginning on the date the Corporation incurred the loss.

(2) Amount of compensation; procedures

(A) Use of estimates

When an insured depository institution is in default or requires assistance to prevent default, the Corporation shall—

(i) in good faith, estimate the amount of the loss the Corporation will incur from such default or assistance;

(ii) if, with respect to such insured depository institution, there is more than 1 commonly controlled insured depository institution, estimate the amount of each such commonly controlled depository institution's share of such liability; and

(iii) advise each commonly controlled depository institution of the Corporation's estimate of the amount of such institution's liability for such losses.

(B) Procedures; immediate payment

The Corporation, after consultation with the appropriate Federal banking agency and the appropriate State chartering agency, shall—

(i) on a case-by-case basis, establish the procedures and schedule under which any insured depository institution shall reimburse the Corporation for such institution's liability under paragraph (1) in connection with any commonly controlled insured depository institution; or

(ii) require any insured depository institution to make immediate payment of the amount of such institution's liability under paragraph (1) in connection with any commonly controlled insured depository institution.

(C) Priority

The liability of any insured depository institution under this subsection shall have priority with respect to other obligations and liabilities as follows:

(i) Superiority

The liability shall be superior to the following obligations and liabilities of the depository institution:

(I) Any obligation to shareholders arising as a result of their status as shareholders (including any depository institution holding company or any shareholder or creditor of such company).

(II) Any obligation or liability owed to any affiliate of the depository institution (including any other insured depository institution) other than any secured obligation which was secured as of May 1, 1989.

(ii) Subordination

The liability shall be subordinate in right and payment to the following obligations and liabilities of the depository institution:

(I) Any deposit liability (which is not a liability described in clause (i)(II)).

(II) Any secured obligation, other than any obligation owed to any affiliate of the depository institution (including any other insured depository institution) which was secured after May 1, 1989.

(III) Any other general or senior liability (which is not a liability described in clause (i)).

(IV) Any obligation subordinated to depositors or other general creditors (which is not an obligation described in clause (i)).

(D) Adjustment of estimated payment

(i) Overpayment

If the amount of compensation estimated by and paid to the Corporation by 1 or more such commonly controlled depository institutions is greater than the actual loss incurred by the Corporation, the Corporation shall reimburse each such commonly controlled depository institution its pro rata share of any overpayment.

(ii) Underpayment

If the amount of compensation estimated by and paid to the Corporation by 1 or more such commonly controlled depository institutions is less than the actual loss incurred by the Corporation, the Corporation shall redetermine in its discretion the liability of each such commonly controlled depository institution to the Corporation and shall require each such commonly controlled depository institution to make payment of any additional liability to the Corporation.

(3) Review

(A) Judicial

Actions of the Corporation shall be reviewable pursuant to chapter 7 of Title 5.

(B) Administrative

The Corporation shall prescribe regulations and establish administrative procedures which provide for a hearing on the record for the review of—

(i) the amount of any loss incurred by the Corporation in connection with any insured depository institution;

(ii) the liability of individual commonly controlled depository institutions for the amount of such loss; and

(iii) the schedule of payments to be made by such commonly controlled depository institutions.

(4) Limitation on rights of private parties

To the extent the exercise of any right or power of any person would impair the ability of any insured depository institution to perform such institution's obligations under this subsection—

(A) the obligations of such insured depository institution shall supersede such right or power; and

(B) no court may give effect to such right or power with respect to such insured depository institution.

(5) Waiver authority

(A) In general

The Corporation, in its discretion, may exempt any insured depository institution from the provisions of this subsection if the Corporation determines that such exemption is in the best interests of the Deposit Insurance Fund.

(B) Condition

During the period any exemption granted to any insured depository institution under subparagraph (A) or (C) is in effect, such insured depository institution and all other insured depository institution affiliates of such depository institution shall comply fully with the restrictions of sections 371c and 371c–1 of this title without regard to section 371c(d)(1) of this title.

(C) Limited partnerships

(i) In general

The Corporation may, in its discretion, exempt any limited partnership and any affiliate of any limited partnership (other than any insured depository institution which is a majority owned subsidiary of such partnership) from the provisions of this subsection if such limited partnership or affiliate has filed a registration statement with the Securities and Exchange Commission on or before April 10, 1989, indicating that as of the date of such filing such partnership intended to acquire 1 or more insured depository institutions.

(ii) Review and notice

Within 10 business days after the date of submission of any request for an exemption under this subparagraph together with such information as shall be reasonably requested by the Corporation, the Corporation shall make a determination on the request and shall so advise the applicant.

(6) Exclusion for institutions acquired in debt collections

Any depository institution shall not be treated as commonly controlled, for purposes of this subsection, during the 5–year period beginning on the date of an acquisition described in subparagraph (A) or such longer period as the Corporation may determine after written application by the acquirer, if—

(A) 1 depository institution controls another by virtue of ownership of voting shares acquired in securing or collecting a debt previously contracted in good faith; and

(B) during the period beginning on August 9, 1989, and ending upon the expiration of the exclusion, the controlling bank and all other insured depository institution affiliates of such controlling bank comply fully with the restrictions of sections 371c and 371c–1 of this title, without regard to section 371c(d)(1) of this title, in transactions with the acquired insured depository institution.

(7) Exception for certain FSLIC assisted institutions

No depository institution shall have any liability to the Corporation under this subsection as the result of the default of, or assistance provided with respect to, an insured depository institution which is an affiliate of such depository institution if—

(A) such affiliate was receiving cash payments from the Federal Savings and Loan Insurance Corporation under an assistance agreement or note entered into before August 9, 1989;

(B) the Federal Savings and Loan Insurance Corporation, or such other entity which has succeeded to the payment obligations of such Corporation with respect to such assistance agreement or note, is unable to continue such payments; and

(C) such affiliate—

(i) is in default or in need of assistance solely as a result of the failure to meet the payment obligations referred to in subparagraph (B); and

(ii) is not otherwise in breach of the terms of any assistance agreement or note which would authorize the Federal Savings and Loan Insurance Corporation or such other successor entity, pursuant to the terms of such assistance agreement or note, to refuse to make such payments.

(8) Commonly controlled defined

For purposes of this subsection, depository institutions are commonly controlled if—

(A) such institutions are controlled by the same company; or

(B) 1 depository institution is controlled by another depository institution.

(9) Redesignated (8)

§ 1816. Factors to be considered

The factors that are required, under section 1814 of this title, to be considered in connection with, and enumerated in, any certificate issued pursuant to section 1814 of this title and that are required, under section 1815 of this title, to be considered by the Board of Directors in connection with any determination by such Board pursuant to section 1815 of this title are the following:

(1) The financial history and condition of the depository institution.

(2) The adequacy of the depository institution's capital structure.

(3) The future earnings prospects of the depository institution.

(4) The general character and fitness of the management of the depository institution.

(5) The risk presented by such depository institution to the Deposit Insurance Fund.

(6) The convenience and needs of the community to be served by such depository institution.

(7) Whether the depository institution's corporate powers are consistent with the purposes of this chapter.

§ 1817. Assessments—DFA §§ 331, 332, 334, 939

(a) Reports of condition; access to reports

(1) Each insured State nonmember bank and each foreign bank having an insured branch which is not a Federal branch shall make to the Corporation reports of condition which shall be in such form and shall contain such information as the Board of Directors may require. Such reports shall be made to the Corporation on the dates selected as provided in paragraph (3) of this subsection and the deposit liabilities shall be reported therein in accordance with and pursuant to paragraphs (4) and (5) of this subsection. The Board of Directors may call for additional reports of condition on dates to be fixed by it and may call for such other reports as the Board may from time to time require. Any such bank which (A) maintains procedures reasonably adapted to avoid any inadvertent error and, unintentionally and as a result of such an error, fails to make or publish any report required under this paragraph, within the period of time specified by the Corporation, or submits or publishes any false or misleading report or information, or (B) inadvertently transmits or publishes any report which is minimally late, shall be subject to a penalty of not more than $2,000 for each day during which such failure continues or such false or misleading information is not corrected. Such bank shall have the burden of proving that an error was inadvertent and that a report was inadvertently transmitted or published late. Any such bank which fails to make or publish any report required under this paragraph, within the period of time specified by the Corporation, or submits or publishes any false or misleading report or information, in a manner not described in the 2nd preceding sentence shall be subject to a penalty of not more than $20,000 for each day during which such failure continues or such false or misleading information is not corrected. Notwithstanding the preceding sentence, if any such bank knowingly

or with reckless disregard for the accuracy of any information or report described in such sentence submits or publishes any false or misleading report or information, the Corporation may assess a penalty of not more than $1,000,000 or 1 percent of total assets of such bank, whichever is less, per day for each day during which such failure continues or such false or misleading information is not corrected. Any penalty imposed under any of the 4 preceding sentences shall be assessed and collected by the Corporation in the manner provided in subparagraphs (E), (F), (G), and (I) of section 1818(i)(2) of this title (for penalties imposed under such section) and any such assessment (including the determination of the amount of the penalty) shall be subject to the provisions of such section. Any such bank against which any penalty is assessed under this subsection shall be afforded an agency hearing if such bank submits a request for such hearing within 20 days after the issuance of the notice of assessment. Section 1818(h) of this title shall apply to any proceeding under this paragraph.

(2) (A) The Corporation and, with respect to any State depository institution, any appropriate State bank supervisor for such institution, shall have access to reports of examination made by, and reports of condition made to, the Comptroller of the Currency, the Director of the Office of Thrift Supervision, the Federal Housing Finance Board, any Federal home loan bank, or any Federal Reserve bank and to all revisions of reports of condition made to any of them, and they shall promptly advise the Corporation of any revisions or changes in respect to deposit liabilities made or required to be made in any report of condition. The Corporation may accept any report made by or to any commission, board, or authority having supervision of a depository institution, and may furnish to the Comptroller of the Currency, the Director of the Office of Thrift Supervision, the Federal Housing Finance Board, any Federal home loan bank, to any Federal Reserve bank, and to any such commission, board, or authority, reports of examinations made on behalf of, and reports of condition made to, the Corporation.

(B) Additional reports

The Board of Directors may from time to time require any insured depository institution to file such additional reports as the Corporation, after agreement with the Comptroller of the Currency, the Board of Governors of the Federal Reserve System, and the Director of the Office of Thrift Supervision, as appropriate, may deem advisable for insurance purposes.

(C) Data sharing with other agencies and persons

In addition to reports of examination, reports of condition, and other reports required to be regularly provided to the Corporation (with respect to all insured depository institutions, including a depository institution for which the Corporation has been appointed conservator or receiver) or an appropriate State bank supervisor (with respect to a State depository institution) under subparagraph (A) or (B), a Federal banking agency may, in the discretion of the agency, furnish any report of examination or other confidential supervisory information concerning any depository institution or other entity examined by such agency under authority of any Federal law, to—

(i) any other Federal or State agency or authority with supervisory or regulatory authority over the depository institution or other entity;

(ii) any officer, director, or receiver of such depository institution or entity; and

(iii) any other person that the Federal banking agency determines to be appropriate.

(3) Each insured depository institution shall make to the appropriate Federal banking agency 4 reports of condition annually upon dates which shall be selected by the Chairman of the Board of Directors, the Comptroller of the Currency, the Chairman of the Board of Governors of the Federal Reserve System, and the Director of the Office of Thrift Supervision. The dates selected shall be the same for all insured depository institutions, except that when any of said reporting dates is a nonbusiness day for any depository institution, the preceding business day shall be its reporting date. Such reports of condition shall be the basis for the certified statements to be filed pursuant to subsection (c) of this section. The deposit liabilities shall be reported in said reports of

condition in accordance with and pursuant to paragraphs (4) and (5) of this subsection, and such other information shall be reported therein as may be required by the respective agencies. Each said report of condition shall contain a declaration by the president, a vice president, the cashier or the treasurer, or by any other officer designated by the board of directors or trustees of the reporting depository institution to make such declaration, that the report is true and correct to the best of his knowledge and belief. The correctness of said report of conditions shall be attested by the signatures of at least two directors or trustees of the reporting depository institution other than the officer making such declaration, with a declaration that the report has been examined by them and to the best of their knowledge and belief is true and correct. At the time of making said reports of condition each insured depository institution shall furnish to the Corporation a copy thereof containing such signed declaration and attestations. Nothing herein shall preclude any of the foregoing agencies from requiring the banks or savings associations under its jurisdiction to make additional reports of condition at any time.

(4) In the reports of condition required to be made by paragraph (3) of this subsection, each insured depository institution shall report the total amount of the liability of the depository institution for deposits in the main office and in any branch located in any State of the United States, the District of Columbia, any Territory of the United States, Puerto Rico, Guam, American Samoa, the Trust Territory of the Pacific Islands, or the Virgin Islands, according to the definition of the term "deposit" in and pursuant to subsection (*l*) of section 1813 of this title without any deduction for indebtedness of depositors or creditors or any deduction for cash items in the process of collection drawn on others than the reporting depository institution: *Provided,* That the depository institution in reporting such deposits may (i) subtract from the deposit balance due to any depository institution the deposit balance due from the same depository institution (other than trust funds deposited by either depository institution) and any cash items in the process of collection due from or due to such depository institutions shall be included in determining such net balance, except that balances of time deposits of any depository

institution and any balances standing to the credit of private depository institutions, of depository institutions in foreign countries, of foreign branches of other American depository institutions, and of American branches of foreign banks shall be reported gross without any such subtraction, and (ii) exclude any deposits received in any office of the depository institution for deposit in any other office of the depository institution: *And provided further,* That outstanding drafts (including advices and authorizations to charge depository institution's balance in another depository institution) drawn in the regular course of business by the reporting depository institution on depository institutions need not be reported as deposit liabilities. The amount of trust funds held in the depository institution's own trust department, which the reporting depository institution keeps segregated and apart from its general assets and does not use in the conduct of its business, shall not be included in the total deposits in such reports, but shall be separately stated in such reports. Deposits which are accumulated for the payment of personal loans and are assigned or pledged to assure payment of loans at maturity shall not be included in the total deposits in such reports, but shall be deducted from the loans for which such deposits are assigned or pledged to assure repayment.

(5) The deposits to be reported on such reports of condition shall be segregated between (i) time and savings deposits and (ii) demand deposits. For this purpose, the time and savings deposits shall consist of time certificates of deposit, time deposits-open account, and savings deposits; and demand deposits shall consist of all deposits other than time and savings deposits.

(6) Lifeline account deposits

In the reports of condition required to be reported under this subsection, the deposits in lifeline accounts (as defined in section 1834(a)(3)(C) of this title) shall be reported separately.

(7) The Board of Directors, after consultation with the Comptroller of the Currency, the Director of the Office of Thrift Supervision, and the Board of Governors of the Federal Reserve System, may by regulation define the terms "cash items" and "process of collection", and

shall classify deposits as "time", "savings", and "demand" deposits, for the purposes of this section.

(8) In respect of any report required or authorized to be supplied or published pursuant to this subsection or any other provision of law, the Board of Directors or the Comptroller of the Currency, as the case may be, may differentiate between domestic banks and foreign banks to such extent as, in their judgment, may be reasonably required to avoid hardship and can be done without substantial compromise of insurance risk or supervisory and regulatory effectiveness.

(9) Data collections

In addition to or in connection with any other report required under this subsection, the Corporation shall take such action as may be necessary to ensure that—

(A) each insured depository institution maintains; and

(B) the Corporation receives on a regular basis from such institution,

information on the total amount of all insured deposits, preferred deposits, and uninsured deposits at the institution. In prescribing reporting and other requirements for the collection of actual and accurate information pursuant to this paragraph, the Corporation shall minimize the regulatory burden imposed upon insured depository institutions that are well capitalized (as defined in section 1831o of this title) while taking into account the benefit of the information to the Corporation, including the use of the information to enable the Corporation to more accurately determine the total amount of insured deposits in each insured depository institution for purposes of compliance with this chapter.

(10) A Federal banking agency may not, by regulation or otherwise, designate, or require an insured institution or an affiliate to designate, a corporation as highly leveraged or a transaction with a corporation as a highly leveraged transaction solely because such corporation is or has been a debtor or bankrupt under Title 11, if, after confirmation of a plan of reorganization, such corporation would not otherwise be highly leveraged.

(11) Streamlining reports of condition

(A) Review of information and schedules

Before the end of the 1–year period beginning on October 13, 2006 and before the end of each 5–year period thereafter, each Federal banking agency shall, in conjunction with the other relevant Federal banking agencies, review the information and schedules that are required to be filed by an insured depository institution in a report of condition required under paragraph (3).

(B) Reduction or elimination of information found to be unnecessary

After completing the review required by subparagraph (A), a Federal banking agency, in conjunction with the other relevant Federal banking agencies, shall reduce or eliminate any requirement to file information or schedules under paragraph (3) (other than information or schedules that are otherwise required by law) if the agency determines that the continued collection of such information or schedules is no longer necessary or appropriate.

(b) Assessments

(1) Risk-based assessment system

(A) Risk-based assessment system required

The Board of Directors shall, by regulation, establish a risk-based assessment system for insured depository institutions.

(B) Private reinsurance authorized

In carrying out this paragraph, the Corporation may—

(i) obtain private reinsurance covering not more than 10 percent of any loss the Corporation incurs with respect to an insured depository institution; and

(ii) base that institution's assessment (in whole or in part) on the cost of the reinsurance.

(C) "Risk-based assessment system" defined

For purposes of this paragraph, the term "risk-based assessment system" means a system for calculating a depository institution's assessment based on—

(i) the probability that the Deposit Insurance Fund will incur a loss with respect to the institution, taking into consideration the risks attributable to—

(I) different categories and concentrations of assets;

(II) different categories and concentrations of liabilities, both insured and uninsured, contingent and noncontingent; and

(III) any other factors the Corporation determines are relevant to assessing such probability;

(ii) the likely amount of any such loss; and

(iii) the revenue needs of the Deposit Insurance Fund.

(D) Separate assessment systems

The Board of Directors may establish separate risk-based assessment systems for large and small members of the Deposit Insurance Fund.

(E) Information concerning risk of loss and economic conditions

(i) Sources of information

For purposes of determining risk of losses at insured depository institutions and economic conditions generally affecting depository institutions, the Corporation shall collect information, as appropriate, from all sources the Board of Directors considers appropriate, such as reports of condition, inspection reports, and other information from all Federal banking agencies, any information available from State bank supervisors, State insurance and securities regulators, the Securities and Exchange Commission (including information described in section 1831*l* of this title), the Secretary of the Treasury, the Commodity Futures Trading Commission, the Farm Credit Administration, the Federal Trade Commission, any Federal reserve bank or Federal home loan bank, and other regulators of financial institutions, and any information available from credit rating entities, and other private economic or business analysts.

(ii) Consultation with Federal banking agencies

(I) In general

Except as provided in subclause (II), in assessing the risk of loss to the Deposit Insurance Fund with respect to any insured depository institution, the Corporation shall consult with the appropriate Federal banking agency of such institution.

(II) Treatment on aggregate basis

In the case of insured depository institutions that are well capitalized (as defined in section 1831*o* of this title) and, in the most recent examination, were found to be well managed, the consultation under subclause (I) concerning the assessment of the risk of loss posed by such institutions may be made on an aggregate basis.

(iii) Rule of construction

No provision of this paragraph shall be construed as providing any new authority for the Corporation to require submission of information by insured depository institutions to the Corporation.

(F) Modifications to the risk-based assessment system allowed only after notice and comment

In revising or modifying the risk-based assessment system at any time after February 8, 2006, the Board of Directors may implement such revisions or modification in final form only after notice and opportunity for comment.

(2) Setting assessments

(A) In general

The Board of Directors shall set assessments for insured depository institutions in such amounts as the Board of Directors may determine to be necessary or appropriate, subject to subparagraph (D).

(B) Factors to be considered

In setting assessments under subparagraph (A), the Board of Directors shall consider the following factors:

(i) The estimated operating expenses of the Deposit Insurance Fund.

(ii) The estimated case resolution expenses and income of the Deposit Insurance Fund.

(iii) The projected effects of the payment of assessments on the capital and earnings of insured depository institutions.

(iv) The risk factors and other factors taken into account pursuant to paragraph (1) under the risk-based assessment system, including the requirement under such paragraph to maintain a risk-based system.

(v) Any other factors the Board of Directors may determine to be appropriate.

(C) Notice of assessments

The Corporation shall notify each insured depository institution of that institution's assessment.

(D) No discrimination based on size

No insured depository institution shall be barred from the lowest-risk category solely because of size.

(E) Bank Enterprise Act requirement

The Corporation shall design the risk-based assessment system so that, insofar as the system bases assessments, directly or indirectly, on deposits, the portion of the deposits of any insured depository institution which are attributable to lifeline accounts established in accordance with the Bank Enterprise Act of 1991 shall be subject to assessment at a rate determined in accordance with such Act.

(F), (G) Repealed. Pub.L. 109–173, § 3(a)(3)(A), Feb. 15, 2006, 119 Stat. 3605

(H) Redesignated (E)

(3) Designated reserve ratio

(A) Establishment

(i) In general

Before the beginning of each calendar year, the Board of Directors shall designate the reserve ratio applicable with respect to the Deposit Insurance Fund and publish the reserve ratio so designated.

(ii) Rulemaking requirement

Any change to the designated reserve ratio shall be made by the Board of Directors by regulation after notice and opportunity for comment.

(B) Range

The reserve ratio designated by the Board of Directors for any year—

(i) may not exceed 1.5 percent of estimated insured deposits; and

(ii) may not be less than 1.15 percent of estimated insured deposits.

(C) Factors

In designating a reserve ratio for any year, the Board of Directors shall—

(i) take into account the risk of losses to the Deposit Insurance Fund in such year and future years, including historic experience

and potential and estimated losses from insured depository institutions;

(ii) take into account economic conditions generally affecting insured depository institutions so as to allow the designated reserve ratio to increase during more favorable economic conditions and to decrease during less favorable economic conditions, notwithstanding the increased risks of loss that may exist during such less favorable conditions, as determined to be appropriate by the Board of Directors;

(iii) seek to prevent sharp swings in the assessment rates for insured depository institutions; and

(iv) take into account such other factors as the Board of Directors may determine to be appropriate, consistent with the requirements of this subparagraph.

(D) Publication of proposed change in ratio

In soliciting comment on any proposed change in the designated reserve ratio in accordance with subparagraph (A), the Board of Directors shall include in the published proposal a thorough analysis of the data and projections on which the proposal is based.

(E) DIF restoration plans

(i) In general

Whenever—

(I) the Corporation projects that the reserve ratio of the Deposit Insurance Fund will, within 6 months of such determination, fall below the minimum amount specified in subparagraph (B)(ii) for the designated reserve ratio; or

(II) the reserve ratio of the Deposit Insurance Fund actually falls below the minimum amount specified in subparagraph (B)(ii) for the designated reserve ratio without any determination under subclause (I) having been made,

the Corporation shall establish and implement a Deposit Insurance Fund restoration plan within 90 days that meets the requirements of clause (ii) and such other conditions as the Corporation determines to be appropriate.

(ii) Requirements of restoration plan

A Deposit Insurance Fund restoration plan meets the requirements of this clause if the plan provides that the reserve ratio of the Fund will meet or exceed the minimum amount specified in subparagraph (B)(ii) for the designated reserve ratio before the end of the 5–year period beginning upon the implementation of the plan (or such longer period as the Corporation may determine to be necessary due to extraordinary circumstances).

(iii) Restriction on assessment credits

As part of any restoration plan under this subparagraph, the Corporation may elect to restrict the application of assessment credits provided under subsection (e)(3) of this section for any period that the plan is in effect.

(iv) Limitation on restriction

Notwithstanding clause (iii), while any restoration plan under this subparagraph is in effect, the Corporation shall apply credits provided to an insured depository institution under subsection (e)(3) of this section against any assessment imposed on the institution for any assessment period in an amount equal to the lesser of—

(I) the amount of the assessment; or

(II) the amount equal to 3 basis points of the institution's assessment base.

(v) Transparency

Not more than 30 days after the Corporation establishes and implements a restoration plan under clause (i), the Corporation shall publish in the Federal Register a detailed analysis of the factors considered and the basis for the actions taken with regard to the plan.

(4) Depository institution required to maintain assessment-related records

Each insured depository institution shall maintain all records that the Corporation may require for verifying the correctness of any assessment on the insured depository institution under this subsection until the later of—

(A) the end of the 3–year period beginning on the due date of the assessment; or

(B) in the case of a dispute between the insured depository institution and the Corporation with respect to such assessment, the date of a final determination of any such dispute.

(5) Emergency special assessments

In addition to the other assessments imposed on insured depository institutions under this subsection, the Corporation may impose 1 or more special assessments on insured depository institutions in an amount determined by the Corporation if the amount of any such assessment is necessary—

(A) to provide sufficient assessment income to repay amounts borrowed from the Secretary of the Treasury under section 1824(a) of this title in accordance with the repayment schedule in effect under section 1824(c) of this title during the period with respect to which such assessment is imposed;

(B) to provide sufficient assessment income to repay obligations issued to and other amounts borrowed from insured depository institutions under section 1824(d) of this title; or

(C) for any other purpose that the Corporation may deem necessary.

(6) Community enterprise credits

The Corporation shall allow a credit against any semiannual assessment to any insured depository institution which satisfies the requirements of the Community Enterprise Assessment Credit Board under section 233(a)(1) of the Bank Enterprise Act of 1991 [12 U.S.C.A. § 1834a(a)(1)] in the amount determined by such Board by regulation.

(7) Redesignated (6)

(c) Certified statements; payments

(1) Certified statements required

(A) In general

Each insured depository institution shall file with the Corporation a certified statement containing such information as the Corporation may require for determining the institution's assessment.

(B) Form of certification

The certified statement required under subparagraph (A) shall—

(i) be in such form and set forth such supporting information as the Board of Directors shall prescribe; and

(ii) be certified by the president of the depository institution or any other officer designated by its board of directors or trustees that to the best of his or her knowledge and belief, the statement is true, correct and complete, and in accordance with this chapter and regulations issued hereunder.

(2) Payments required

(A) In general

Each insured depository institution shall pay to the Corporation the assessment imposed under subsection (b) of this section.

(B) Form of payment

The payments required under subparagraph (A) shall be made in such manner and at such time or times as the Board of Directors shall prescribe by regulation.

(3) Newly insured institutions

To facilitate the administration of this section, the Board of Directors may waive the requirements of paragraphs (1) and (2) for the initial assessment period in which a depository institution becomes insured.

(4) Penalty for failure to make accurate certified statement

(A) First tier

Any insured depository institution which—

(i) maintains procedures reasonably adapted to avoid any inadvertent error and, unintentionally and as a result of such an error, fails to submit the certified statement under paragraph (1) within the period of time required under paragraph (1) or submits a false or misleading certified statement; or

(ii) submits the statement at a time which is minimally after the time required in such paragraph,

shall be subject to a penalty of not more than $2,000 for each day during which such failure continues or such false and misleading information is not corrected. The institution shall have the burden of proving that an error was inadvertent or that a statement was inadvertently submitted late.

(B) Second tier

Any insured depository institution which fails to submit the certified statement under paragraph (1) within the period of time required under paragraph (1) or submits a

false or misleading certified statement in a manner not described in subparagraph (A) shall be subject to a penalty of not more than $20,000 for each day during which such failure continues or such false and misleading information is not corrected.

(C) Third tier

Notwithstanding subparagraphs (A) and (B), if any insured depository institution knowingly or with reckless disregard for the accuracy of any certified statement described in paragraph (1) submits a false or misleading certified statement under paragraph (1), the Corporation may assess a penalty of not more than $1,000,000 or not more than 1 percent of the total assets of the institution, whichever is less, per day for each day during which the failure continues or the false or misleading information in such statement is not corrected.

(D) Assessment procedure

Any penalty imposed under this paragraph shall be assessed and collected by the Corporation in the manner provided in subparagraphs (E), (F), (G), and (I) of section 1818(i)(2) of this title (for penalties imposed under such section) and any such assessment (including the determination of the amount of the penalty) shall be subject to the provisions of such section.

(E) Hearing

Any insured depository institution against which any penalty is assessed under this paragraph shall be afforded an agency hearing if the institution submits a request for such hearing within 20 days after the issuance of the notice of the assessment. Section 1818(h) of this title shall apply to any proceeding under this subparagraph.

(d) Corporation exempt from apportionment

Notwithstanding any other provision of law, amounts received pursuant to any assessment under this section and any other amounts received by the Corporation shall not be subject to apportionment for the purposes of chapter 15 of Title 31 or under any other authority.

(e) Refunds, dividends, and credits

(1) Refunds of overpayments

In the case of any payment of an assessment by an insured depository institution in excess of the amount due to the Corporation, the Corporation may—

(A) refund the amount of the excess payment to the insured depository institution; or

(B) credit such excess amount toward the payment of subsequent assessments until such credit is exhausted.

(2) Dividends from excess amounts in Deposit Insurance Fund

(A) Reserve ratio in excess of 1.5 percent of estimated insured deposits

If, at the end of a calendar year, the reserve ratio of the Deposit Insurance Fund exceeds 1.5 percent of estimated insured deposits, the Corporation shall declare the amount in the Fund in excess of the amount required to maintain the reserve ratio at 1.5 percent of estimated insured deposits, as dividends to be paid to insured depository institutions.

(B) Reserve ratio equal to or in excess of 1.35 percent of estimated insured deposits and not more than 1.5 percent

If, at the end of a calendar year, the reserve ratio of the Deposit Insurance Fund equals or exceeds 1.35 percent of estimated insured deposits and is not more than 1.5 percent of such deposits, the Corporation shall declare the amount in the Fund that is equal to 50 percent of the amount in excess of the amount required to maintain the reserve ratio at 1.35 percent of the estimated insured deposits as dividends to be paid to insured depository institutions.

(C) Basis for distribution of dividends

(i) In general

Solely for the purposes of dividend distribution under this paragraph, the Corporation shall determine each insured depository institution's relative contribution to the Deposit Insurance Fund (or any predecessor deposit insurance fund) for calculating such institution's share of any dividend declared under this paragraph, taking into account the factors described in clause (ii).

(ii) Factors for distribution

In implementing this paragraph in accordance with regulations, the Corporation shall take into account the following factors:

(I) The ratio of the assessment base of an insured depository institution (including any predecessor) on December 31, 1996, to the assessment base of all eligible insured depository institutions on that date.

(II) The total amount of assessments paid on or after January 1, 1997, by an insured depository institution (including any predecessor) to the Deposit Insurance Fund (and any predecessor deposit insurance fund).

(III) That portion of assessments paid by an insured depository institution (including any predecessor) that reflects higher levels of risk assumed by such institution.

(IV) Such other factors as the Corporation may determine to be appropriate.

(D) Notice and opportunity for comment

The Corporation shall prescribe by regulation, after notice and opportunity for comment, the method for the calculation, declaration, and payment of dividends under this paragraph.

(E) Limitation

The Board of Directors may suspend or limit dividends paid under subparagraph (B), if the Board determines in writing that—

(i) a significant risk of losses to the Deposit Insurance Fund exists over the next 1–year period; and

(ii) it is likely that such losses will be sufficiently high as to justify a finding by the Board that the reserve ratio should temporarily be allowed—

(I) to grow without requiring dividends under subparagraph (B); or

(II) to exceed the maximum amount established under subsection (b)(3)(B)(i) of this section.

(F) Considerations

In making a determination under subparagraph (E), the Board shall consider—

(i) national and regional conditions and their impact on insured depository institutions;

(ii) potential problems affecting insured depository institutions or a specific group or type of depository institution;

(iii) the degree to which the contingent liability of the Corporation for anticipated failures of insured institutions adequately addresses concerns over funding levels in the Deposit Insurance Fund; and

(iv) any other factors that the Board determines are appropriate.

(G) Review of determination

(i) Annual review

A determination to suspend or limit dividends under subparagraph (E) shall be reviewed by the Board of Directors annually.

(ii) Action by Board

Based on each annual review under clause (i), the Board of Directors shall either renew or remove a determination to suspend or limit dividends under subparagraph (E), or shall make a new determination in accordance with this paragraph. Unless justified under the terms of the renewal or new determination, the Corporation shall be required to provide cash dividends under subparagraph (A) or (B), as appropriate.

(3) One-time credit based on total assessment base at year-end 1996

(A) In general

Before the end of the 270–day period beginning on February 8, 2006, the Board of Directors shall, by regulation after notice and opportunity for comment, provide for a credit to each eligible insured depository institution (or a successor insured depository institution), based on the assessment base of the institution on December 31, 1996, as compared to the combined aggregate assessment base of all eligible insured depository institutions, taking into account such factors as the Board of Directors may determine to be appropriate.

(B) Credit limit

The aggregate amount of credits available under subparagraph (A) to all eligible insured depository institutions shall equal the amount that the Corporation could collect if the Corporation imposed an assessment of 10.5 basis points on the combined assessment base of the Bank Insurance Fund and the Savings Association Insurance Fund as of December 31, 2001.

(C) Eligible insured depository institution defined

For purposes of this paragraph, the term "eligible insured depository institution" means any insured depository institution that—

(i) was in existence on December 31, 1996, and paid a deposit insurance assessment prior to that date; or

(ii) is a successor to any insured depository institution described in clause (i).

(D) Application of credits

(i) In general

Subject to clause (ii), the amount of a credit to any eligible insured depository institution under this paragraph shall be applied by the Corporation, subject to subsection (b)(3)(E) of this section, to the assessments imposed on such institution under subsection (b) of this section that become due for assessment periods beginning after the effective date of regulations prescribed under subparagraph (A).

(ii) Temporary restriction on use of credits

The amount of a credit to any eligible insured depository institution under this paragraph may not be applied to more than 90 percent of the assessments imposed on such institution under subsection (b) of this section that become due for assessment periods beginning in fiscal years 2008, 2009, and 2010.

(iii) Regulations

The regulations prescribed under subparagraph (A) shall establish the qualifications and procedures governing the application of assessment credits pursuant to clause (i).

(E) Limitation on amount of credit for certain depository institutions

In the case of an insured depository institution that exhibits financial, operational, or compliance weaknesses ranging from moderately severe to unsatisfactory, or is not adequately capitalized (as defined in section 1831o of this title) at the beginning of an assessment period, the amount of any credit allowed under this paragraph against the assessment on that depository institution for such period may not exceed the amount calculated by applying to that depository institution the average assessment rate on all insured depository institutions for such assessment period.

(F) Successor defined

The Corporation shall define the term "successor" for purposes of this paragraph, by regulation, and may consider any factors as the Board may deem appropriate.

(4) Administrative review

(A) In general

The regulations prescribed under paragraphs (2)(D) and (3) shall include provisions allowing an insured depository institution a reasonable opportunity to challenge administratively the amount of the credit or dividend determined under paragraph (2) or (3) for such institution.

(B) Administrative review

Any review under subparagraph (A) of any determination of the Corporation under paragraph (2) or (3) shall be final and not subject to judicial review.

(f) Action against depository institutions failing to file certified statements

Any insured depository institution which fails to make any report of condition under subsection (a) of this section or to file any certified statement required to be filed by it in connection with determining the amount of any assessment payable by the depository institution to the Corporation may be compelled to make such report or file such statement by mandatory injunction or other appropriate remedy in a suit brought for such purpose by the Corporation against the depository institution and any officer or officers thereof in any court of the United States of competent jurisdiction in the District or Territory in which such depository institution is located.

(g) Assessment actions

(1) In general

The Corporation, in any court of competent jurisdiction, shall be entitled to recover from any insured depository institution the amount of any unpaid assessment lawfully payable by such insured depository institution.

(2) Statute of limitations

The following provisions shall apply to actions relating to assessments, notwithstanding any other provision in Federal law, or the law of any State:

(A) Any action by an insured depository institution to recover from the Corporation the overpaid amount of any assessment shall be brought within 3 years after the date the assessment payment was due, subject to the exception in subparagraph (E).

(B) Any action by the Corporation to recover from an insured depository institution the underpaid amount of any assessment shall be brought within 3 years after the date the assessment payment was due, subject to the exceptions in subparagraphs (C) and (E).

(C) If an insured depository institution has made a false or fraudulent statement with intent to evade any or all of its assessment, the Corporation shall have until 3 years after the date of discovery of the false or fraudulent statement in which to bring an action to recover the underpaid amount.

(D) Except as provided in subparagraph (C), assessment deposit information contained in records no longer required to be maintained pursuant to subsection (b)(4) shall be considered conclusive and not subject to change.

(E) Any action for the underpaid or overpaid amount of any assessment that became due before the amendment to this subsection under the Federal Deposit Insurance Reform Act of 2005 took effect shall be subject to the statute of limitations for assessments in effect at the time the assessment became due.

(h) Forfeiture of rights for failure to comply with law

Should any national member bank or any insured national nonmember bank fail to make any report of condition under subsection (a) of this section or to file any certified statement required to be filed by such bank under any provision of this section, or fail to pay any assessment required to be paid by such bank under any provision of this chapter, and should the bank not correct such failure within thirty days after written notice has been given by the Corporation to an officer of the bank, citing this subsection, and stating that the bank has failed to make any report of condition under subsection (a) of this section or to file or pay as required by law, all the rights, privileges, and franchises of the bank granted to it under the National Bank Act, as amended [12 U.S.C.A. § 21 et seq.], the Federal Reserve Act, as amended [12 U.S.C.A. § 221 et seq.], or this chapter, shall be thereby forfeited. Whether or not the penalty provided in this subsection has been incurred shall be determined and adjudged in the manner provided in the sixth paragraph of section 2 of the Federal Reserve Act, as amended [12 U.S.C.A. § 501a]. The remedies provided in this subsection and in subsections (f) and (g) of this section shall not be construed as limiting any other remedies against any insured depository institution, but shall be in addition thereto.

(i) Insurance of trust funds

(1) In general

Trust funds held on deposit by an insured depository institution in a fiduciary capacity as trustee pursuant to any irrevocable trust established pursuant to any statute or written trust agreement shall be insured in an amount not to exceed the standard maximum deposit insurance amount (as determined under section 1821(a)(1) of this title) for each trust estate.

(2) Interbank deposits

Trust funds described in paragraph (1) which are deposited by the fiduciary depository institution in another insured depository institution shall be similarly insured to the fiduciary depository institution according to the trust estates represented.

(3) Bank deposit financial assistance program

Notwithstanding paragraph (1), funds deposited by an insured depository institution pursuant to the Bank Deposit Financial Assistance Program of the Department of Energy shall be separately insured in an amount not to exceed the standard maximum deposit insurance amount (as determined under section 1821(a)(1) of this title) for each insured depository institution depositing such funds.

(4) Regulations

The Board of Directors may prescribe such regulations as may be necessary to clarify the insurance coverage under this subsection and to prescribe the manner of reporting and depositing such trust funds.

(j) Change in control of insured depository institutions

(1) No person, acting directly or indirectly or through or in concert with one or more other persons, shall acquire control of any insured depository institution through a purchase, assignment, transfer, pledge, or other disposition of voting stock of such insured depository institution unless the appropriate Federal banking agency has been given sixty days' prior written notice of such proposed acquisition and within that time period the agency has not issued a notice disapproving the proposed acquisition or, in the discretion of the agency, extending for an additional 30 days the period during which such a disapproval may issue. The period for disapproval under the preceding sentence may be extended not to exceed 2 additional times for not more than 45 days each time if—

(A) the agency determines that any acquiring party has not furnished all the information required under paragraph (6);

(B) in the agency's judgment, any material information submitted is substantially inaccurate;

(C) the agency has been unable to complete the investigation of an acquiring party under paragraph (2)(B) because of any delay caused by, or the inadequate cooperation of, such acquiring party; or

(D) the agency determines that additional time is needed—

(i) to investigate and determine that no acquiring party has a record of failing to comply with the requirements of subchapter II of chapter 53 of Title 31, or

(ii) to analyze the safety and soundness of any plans or proposals described in paragraph (6)(E) or the future prospects of the institution.

An acquisition may be made prior to expiration of the disapproval period if the agency issues written notice of its intent not to disapprove the action.

(2)(A) Notice to State agency

Upon receiving any notice under this subsection, the appropriate Federal banking agency shall forward a copy thereof to the appropriate State depository institution supervisory agency if the depository institution the voting shares of which are sought to be acquired is a State depository institution, and shall allow thirty days within which the views and recommendations of such State depository institution supervisory agency may be submitted. The appropriate Federal banking agency shall give due consideration to the views and recommendations of such State agency in determining whether to disapprove any proposed acquisition. Notwithstanding the provisions of this paragraph, if the appropriate Federal banking agency determines that it must act immediately upon any notice of a proposed acquisition in order to prevent the probable default of the depository institution involved in the proposed acquisition, such Federal banking agency may dispense with the requirements of this paragraph or, if a copy of the notice is forwarded to the State depository institution supervisory agency, such Federal banking agency may request that the views and recommendations of such State depository institution supervisory agency be submitted immediately in any form or by any means acceptable to such Federal banking agency.

(B) Investigation of principals required

Upon receiving any notice under this subsection, the appropriate Federal banking agency shall—

(i) conduct an investigation of the competence, experience, integrity, and financial ability of each person named in a notice of a proposed acquisition as a person by whom or for whom such acquisition is to be made; and

(ii) make an independent determination of the accuracy and completeness of any information described in paragraph (6) with respect to such person.

(C) Report

The appropriate Federal banking agency shall prepare a written report of any investigation under subparagraph (B) which shall contain, at a minimum, a summary of the results of such investigation. The agency shall retain such written report as a record of the agency.

(D) Public comment

Upon receiving notice of a proposed acquisition, the appropriate Federal banking agency shall, unless such agency determines that an emergency exists, within a reasonable period of time—

(i) publish the name of the insured depository institution proposed to be acquired and the name of each person identified in such notice as a person by whom or for whom such acquisition is to be made; and

(ii) solicit public comment on such proposed acquisition, particularly from persons in the geographic area where the bank proposed to be acquired is located, before final consideration of such notice by the agency,

unless the agency determines in writing that such disclosure or solicitation would seriously threaten the safety or soundness of such bank.

(3) Within three days after its decision to disapprove any proposed acquisition, the appropriate Federal banking agency shall notify the acquiring party in writing of the disapproval. Such notice shall provide a statement of the basis for the disapproval.

(4) Within ten days of receipt of such notice of disapproval, the acquiring party may request an agency hearing on the proposed acquisition. In such hearing all issues shall be determined on the record pursuant to section 554 of Title 5. The length of the hearing shall be determined by the appropriate Federal banking agency. At the conclusion thereof, the appropriate Federal banking agency shall by order approve or disapprove the proposed acquisition on the basis of the record made at such hearing.

(5) Any person whose proposed acquisition is disapproved after agency hearings under this subsection may obtain review by the United States court of appeals for the circuit in which the home office of the bank to be acquired is located, or the United States Court of Appeals for the District of Columbia Circuit, by filing a notice of appeal in such court within ten days from the date of such order, and simultaneously sending a copy of such notice by registered or certified mail to the appropriate Federal banking agency. The appropriate Federal banking agency shall promptly certify and file in such court the record upon which the disapproval was based. The findings of the appropriate Federal banking agency shall be set aside if found to be arbitrary or capricious or if found to violate procedures established by this subsection.

(6) Except as otherwise provided by regulation of the appropriate Federal banking agency, a notice filed pursuant to this subsection shall contain the following information:

(A) The identity, personal history, business background and experience of each person by whom or on whose behalf the acquisition is to be made, including his material business activities and affiliations during the past five years, and a description of any material pending legal or administrative proceedings in which he is a party and any criminal indictment or conviction of such person by a State or Federal court.

(B) A statement of the assets and liabilities of each person by whom or on whose behalf the acquisition is to be made, as of the end of the fiscal year for each of the five fiscal years immediately preceding the date of the notice, together with related statements of income and source and application of funds for each of the fiscal years then concluded, all prepared in accordance with generally accepted accounting principles consistently applied, and an interim statement of the assets and liabilities for each such person, together with related statements of income and source and application of funds, as of a date not more than ninety days prior to the date of the filing of the notice.

(C) The terms and conditions of the proposed acquisition and the manner in which the acquisition is to be made.

(D) The identity, source and amount of the funds or other consideration used or to be used in making the acquisition, and if any part of these funds or other consideration has been or is to be borrowed or otherwise obtained for the purpose of making the acquisition, a description of the transaction, the names of the parties, and any arrangements, agreements, or understandings with such persons.

(E) Any plans or proposals which any acquiring party making the acquisition may have to liquidate the [depository institution], to sell its assets or merge it with any company or to make any other major change in its business or corporate structure or management.

(F) The identification of any person employed, retained, or to be compensated by the acquiring party, or by any person on his behalf, to make solicitations or recommendations to stockholders for the purpose of assisting in the acquisition, and a brief description of the terms of such employment, retainer, or arrangement for compensation.

(G) Copies of all invitations or tenders or advertisements making a tender offer to stockholders for purchase of their stock to be used in connection with the proposed acquisition.

(H) Any additional relevant information in such form as the appropriate Federal banking agency may require by regulation or by specific request in connection with any particular notice.

(7) The appropriate Federal banking agency may disapprove any proposed acquisition if—

(A) the proposed acquisition of control would result in a monopoly or would be in furtherance of any combination or conspiracy to monopolize or to attempt to monopolize the business of banking in any part of the United States;

(B) the effect of the proposed acquisition of control in any section of the country may be substantially to lessen competition or to tend to create a monopoly or the proposed acquisition of control would in any other manner be in restraint of trade, and the anticompetitive effects of the proposed acquisition of control are not clearly outweighed in the public interest by the probable effect of the transaction in meeting the convenience and needs of the community to be served;

(C) either the financial condition of any acquiring person or the future prospects of the institution is such as might jeopardize the financial stability of the bank or prejudice the interests of the depositors of the [depository institution];

(D) the competence, experience, or integrity of any acquiring person or of any of the proposed management personnel indicates that it would not be in the interest of the depositors of the bank, or in the interest of the public to permit such person to control the [depository institution];

(E) any acquiring person neglects, fails, or refuses to furnish the appropriate Federal banking agency all the information required by the appropriate Federal banking agency; or

(F) the appropriate Federal banking agency determines that the proposed transaction would result in an adverse effect on the Deposit Insurance Fund.

(8) For the purposes of this subsection, the term—

(A) "person" means an individual or a corporation, partnership, trust, association, joint venture, pool, syndicate, sole proprietorship, unincorporated organization, or any other form of entity not specifically listed herein; and

(B) "control" means the power, directly or indirectly, to direct the management or policies of an insured depository institution or to vote 25 per centum or more of any class of voting securities of an insured depository institution.

(9) Reporting of stock loans

(A) Report required

Any foreign bank, or any affiliate thereof, that has credit outstanding to any person or group of persons which is secured, directly or indirectly, by shares of an insured depository institution shall file a consolidated report with the appropriate Federal banking agency for such insured depository institution if the extensions of credit by the foreign bank or any affiliate thereof, in the aggregate, are secured, directly or indirectly, by 25 percent or more of any class of shares of the same insured depository institution.

(B) Definitions

For purposes of this paragraph, the following definitions shall apply:

(i) Foreign bank

The terms "foreign bank" and "affiliate" have the same meanings as in section 3101 of this title.

(ii) Credit outstanding

The term "credit outstanding" includes—

(I) any loan or extension of credit,

(II) the issuance of a guarantee, acceptance, or letter of credit, including an endorsement or standby letter of credit, and

(III) any other type of transaction that extends credit or financing to the person or group of persons.

(iii) Group of persons

The term "group of persons" includes any number of persons that the foreign bank or any affiliate thereof reasonably believes—

(I) are acting together, in concert, or with one another to acquire or control shares of the same insured depository institution, including an acquisition of shares of the same insured depository institution at approximately the same time under substantially the same terms; or

(II) have made, or propose to make, a joint filing under section 78m of Title 15 regarding ownership of the shares of the same insured depository institution.

(C) Inclusion of shares held by the financial institution

Any shares of the insured depository institution held by the foreign bank or any affiliate thereof as principal shall be included in the calculation of the number of shares in which the foreign bank or any affiliate thereof has a security interest for purposes of subparagraph (A).

(D) Report requirements

(i) Timing of report

The report required under this paragraph shall be a consolidated report on behalf of the foreign bank and all affiliates thereof, and shall be filed in writing within 30 days of the date on which the foreign bank or affiliate thereof first believes that the security for any outstanding credit consists of 25 percent or more of any class of shares of an insured depository institution.

(ii) Content of report

The report under this paragraph shall indicate the number and percentage of shares securing each applicable extension of credit, the identity of the borrower, and the number of shares held as principal by the foreign bank and any affiliate thereof.

(iii) Copy to other agencies

A copy of any report under this paragraph shall be filed with the appropriate Federal banking agency for the foreign bank or any affiliate thereof (if other than the agency receiving the report under this paragraph).

(iv) Other information

Each appropriate Federal banking agency may require any additional information necessary to carry out the agency's supervisory responsibilities.

(E) Exceptions

(i) Exception where information provided by borrower

Notwithstanding subparagraph (A), a foreign bank or any affiliate thereof shall not be required to report a transaction under this paragraph if the person or group of persons referred to in such subparagraph has disclosed the amount borrowed from such foreign bank or any affiliate thereof and the security interest of the foreign bank or any affiliate thereof to the appropriate Federal banking agency for the insured depository institution in connection with a notice filed under this subsection, an application filed under the Bank Holding Company Act of 1956 [12 U.S.C.A. § 1841 et seq.], section 1467a of this title, or any other application filed with the appropriate Federal banking agency for the insured depository institution as a substitute for a notice under this subsection, such as an application for deposit insurance, membership in the Federal Reserve System, or a national bank charter.

(ii) Exception for shares owned for more than 1 year

Notwithstanding subparagraph (A), a foreign bank and any affiliate thereof shall not be required to report a transaction involving—

(I) a person or group of persons that has been the owner or owners of record of the stock for a period of 1 year or more; or

(II) stock issued by a newly chartered bank before the bank's opening.

(10) The reports required by paragraph (9) of this subsection shall contain such of the information referred to in paragraph (6) of this subsection, and such other relevant information, as the appropriate Federal banking agency may require by regulation or by specific request in connection with any particular report.

(11) The Federal banking agency receiving a notice or report filed pursuant to paragraph (1) or (9) shall immediately furnish to the other Federal banking agencies a copy of such notice or report.

(12) Whenever such a change in control occurs, each insured depository institution shall report promptly to the appropriate Federal banking agency any changes or replacement of its chief executive officer or of any director occurring in the next twelve-month period, including in its report a statement of the past and current business and professional affiliations of the new chief executive officer or directors.

(13) The appropriate Federal banking agencies are authorized to issue rules and regulations to carry out this subsection.

(14) Within two years after the effective date of the Change in Bank Control Act of 1978, and each year thereafter in each appropriate Federal banking agency's annual report to the Congress, the appropriate Federal banking agency shall report to the Congress the results of the administration of this subsection, and make any recommendations as to changes in the law which in the opinion of the appropriate Federal banking agency would be desirable.

(15) Investigative and enforcement authority

(A) Investigations

The appropriate Federal banking agency may exercise any authority vested in such agency under section 1818(n) of this title in the course of conducting any investigation under paragraph (2)(B) or any other investigation which the agency, in its discretion, determines is necessary to determine whether any person has filed inaccurate, incomplete, or misleading information under this subsection or otherwise is violating, has violated, or is about to violate any provision of this subsection or any regulation prescribed under this subsection.

(B) Enforcement

Whenever it appears to the appropriate Federal banking agency that any person is violating, has violated, or is about to violate any provision of this subsection or any regulation prescribed under this subsection, the agency may, in its discretion, apply to the appropriate district court of the United States or the United States court of any territory for—

(i) a temporary or permanent injunction or restraining order enjoining such person from violating this subsection or any regulation prescribed under this subsection; or

(ii) such other equitable relief as may be necessary to prevent any such violation (including divestiture).

(C) Jurisdiction

(i) The district courts of the United States and the United States courts in any territory shall have the same jurisdiction and power in connection with any exercise of any authority by the appropriate Federal banking agency under subparagraph (A) as such courts have under section 1818(n) of this title.

(ii) The district courts of the United States and the United States courts of any territory shall have jurisdiction and power to issue any injunction or restraining order or grant any equitable relief described in subparagraph (B). When appropriate, any injunction, order, or other equitable relief granted under this paragraph shall be granted without requiring the posting of any bond.

The resignation, termination of employment or participation, divestiture of control, or separation of or by an institution-affiliated party (including a separation caused by the closing of a depository institution) shall not affect the jurisdiction and authority of the appropriate Federal banking agency to issue any notice and proceed under this subsection against any such party, if such notice is served before the end of the 6–year period beginning on the date such party ceased to be such a party with respect to such depository institution (whether such date occurs before, on, or after August 9, 1989).

(16) Civil money penalty

(A) First tier

Any person who violates any provision of this subsection, or any regulation or order issued by the appropriate Federal banking agency under this subsection, shall forfeit and pay a civil penalty of not more than $5,000 for each day during which such violation continues.

(B) Second tier

Notwithstanding subparagraph (A), any person who—

(i)(I) commits any violation described in any clause of subparagraph (A);

(II) recklessly engages in an unsafe or unsound practice in conducting the affairs of a depository institution; or

(III) breaches any fiduciary duty;

(ii) which violation, practice, or breach—

(I) is part of a pattern of misconduct;

(II) causes or is likely to cause more than a minimal loss to such institution; or

(III) results in pecuniary gain or other benefit to such person,

shall forfeit and pay a civil penalty of not more than $25,000 for each day during which such violation, practice, or breach continues.

(C) Third Tier

Notwithstanding subparagraphs (A) and (B), any person who—

(i) knowingly—

(I) commits any violation described in any clause of subparagraph (A);

(II) engages in any unsafe or unsound practice in conducting the affairs of a depository institution; or

(III) breaches any fiduciary duty; and

(ii) knowingly or recklessly causes a substantial loss to such institution or a substantial pecuniary gain or other benefit to such person by reason of such violation, practice, or breach,

shall forfeit and pay a civil penalty in an amount not to exceed the applicable maximum amount determined under subparagraph (D) for each day during which such violation, practice, or breach continues.

(D) Maximum amounts of penalties for any violation described in subparagraph (C)

The maximum daily amount of any civil penalty which may be assessed pursuant to subparagraph (C) for any violation, practice, or breach described in such subparagraph is—

(i) in the case of any person other than a depository institution, an amount to not exceed $1,000,000; and

(ii) in the case of a depository institution, an amount not to exceed the lesser of—

(I) $1,000,000; or

(II) 1 percent of the total assets of such institution.

(E) Assessment; etc.

Any penalty imposed under subparagraph (A), (B), or (C) shall be assessed and collected by the appropriate Federal banking agency in the manner provided in subparagraphs (E), (F), (G), and (I) of section 1818(i)(2) of this title for penalties imposed (under such section) and any such assessment shall be subject to the provisions of such section.

(F) Hearing

The depository institution or other person against whom any penalty is assessed under this paragraph shall be afforded an agency hearing if such institution or other person submits a request for such hearing within 20 days after the issuance of the notice of assessment. Section 1818(h) of this title shall apply to any proceeding under this paragraph.

(G) Disbursement

All penalties collected under authority of this paragraph shall be deposited into the Treasury.

(17) Exceptions

This subsection shall not apply with respect to a transaction which is subject to—

(A) section 1842 of this title;

(B) section 1828(c) of this title; or

(C) section 1467a of this title.

(18) Applicability of change in control provisions to other institutions

For purposes of this subsection, the term "insured depository institution" includes—

(A) any depository institution holding company; and

(B) any other company which controls an insured depository institution and is not a depository institution holding company.

(k) Federal banking agency rules and regulations for reports and public disclosure by banks of extension of credit to executive officers or principal shareholders or the related interests of such persons

The appropriate Federal banking agencies are authorized to issue rules and regulations, including definitions of terms, to require the reporting and public disclosure of information by a bank or any executive officer or principal shareholder thereof concerning extensions of credit by the bank to any of its executive officers or principal shareholders, or the related interests of such persons.

(l) Designation of fund membership for newly insured depository institutions; definitions

For purposes of this section:

(1) Bank insurance fund

Any institution which—

(A) becomes an insured depository institution; and

(B) does not become a Savings Association Insurance Fund member pursuant to paragraph (2),

shall be a Bank Insurance Fund member.

(2) Savings association insurance fund

Any savings association, other than any Federal savings bank chartered pursuant to section 1464(o) of this title, which becomes an insured depository institution shall be a Savings Association Insurance Fund member.

(3) Transition provision

(A) Bank insurance fund

Any depository institution the deposits of which were insured by the Federal Deposit Insurance Corporation on the day before August 9, 1989, including—

(i) any Federal savings bank chartered pursuant to section 1464(o) of this title; and

(ii) any cooperative bank,

shall be a Bank Insurance Fund member as of August 9, 1989.

(B) Savings Association Insurance Fund

Any savings association which is an insured depository institution by operation of section 1814(a)(2) of this title shall be a Savings Association Insurance Fund member as of August 9, 1989.

(4) Bank Insurance Fund member

The term "Bank Insurance Fund member" means any depository institution the deposits of which are insured by the Bank Insurance Fund.

(5) Savings Association Insurance Fund member

The term "Savings Association Insurance Fund member" means any depository institution the deposits of which are insured by the Savings Association Insurance Fund.

(6) Bank Insurance Fund reserve ratio

The term "Bank Insurance Fund reserve ratio" means the ratio of the net worth of the Bank Insurance Fund to the value of the aggregate estimated insured deposits held in all Bank Insurance Fund members.

(7) Savings Association Insurance Fund reserve ratio

The term "Savings Association Insurance Fund reserve ratio" means the ratio of the net worth of the Savings Association Insurance Fund to the value of the aggregate estimated insured deposits held in all Savings Association Insurance Fund members.

(m) Secondary reserve offsets against premiums

(1) Offsets in calendar years beginning before 1993

Subject to the maximum amount limitation contained in paragraph (2) and notwithstanding any other provision of law, any insured savings association may offset such association's pro rata share of the statutorily prescribed amount against any premium assessed against such association under subsection (b) of this section for any calendar year beginning before 1993.

(2) Annual maximum amount limitation

The amount of any offset allowed for any savings association under paragraph (1) for any calendar year beginning before 1993 shall not exceed an amount which is equal to 20 percent of such association's pro rata share of the statutorily prescribed amount (as computed for such calendar year).

(3) Offsets in calendar years beginning after 1992

Notwithstanding any other provision of law, a savings association may offset such association's pro rata share of the statutorily prescribed amount against any premium assessed against such association under subsection (b) of this section for any calendar year beginning after 1992.

(4) Transferability

No right, title, or interest of any insured depository institution in or with respect to its pro rata share of the secondary reserve shall be assignable or transferable whether by operation of law or otherwise, except to the extent that the Corporation may provide for transfer of such pro rata share in cases of merger or consolidation, transfer of bulk assets or assumption of liabilities, and similar transactions, as defined by the Corporation for purposes of this paragraph.

(5) Pro rata distribution on termination of insured status

If—

(A) the status of any savings association as an insured depository institution is terminated pursuant to any provision of section 1818 of this title or the insurance of accounts of any such institution is otherwise terminated;

(B) a receiver or other legal custodian is appointed for the purpose of liquidation or winding up the affairs of any savings association; or

(C) the Corporation makes a determination that for the purposes of this subsection any savings association has otherwise gone into liquidation,

the Corporation shall pay in cash to such institution its pro rata share of the secondary reserve, in accordance with such terms and conditions as the Corporation may prescribe, or, at the option of the Corporation, the Corporation may apply the whole or any part of the amount which would otherwise be paid in cash toward the payment of any indebtedness or obligation, whether matured or not, of such institution to the Corporation, existing or arising before such payment in cash. Such payment or such application need not be made to the extent that the provisions of the exception in paragraph (4) are applicable.

(6) "Statutorily prescribed amount" defined

For purposes of this subsection, the term "statutorily prescribed amount" means, with respect to any calendar year which ends after August 9, 1989—

(A) $823,705,000, minus

(B) the sum of—

(i) the aggregate amount of offsets made before August 9, 1989, by all insured institutions under section 404(e)(2) of the National Housing Act [12 U.S.C.A. § 1727(e)(2)] (as in effect before August 9, 1989); and

(ii) the aggregate amount of offsets made by all savings associations under this subsection before the beginning of such calendar year.

(7) Savings association's pro rata amount

For purposes of this subsection, any savings association's pro rata share of the statutorily prescribed amount is the percentage which is equal to such association's share of the secondary reserve as determined under section 404(e) of the National Housing Act on the day before the date on which the Federal Savings and Loan Insurance Corporation ceased to recognize the secondary reserve (as such Act [12 U.S.C.A. § 1701 et seq.] was in effect on the day before such date).

(8) Year of enactment rule

With respect to the calendar year in which the Financial Institutions Reform, Recovery, and Enforcement Act of 1989 is enacted, the Corporation shall make such adjustments as may be necessary—

(A) in the computation of the statutorily prescribed amount which shall be applicable for the remainder of such calendar year after taking into account the aggregate amount of offsets by all insured institutions under section 404(e)(2) of the National Housing Act [12 U.S.C.A. § 1727(e)(2)] (as in effect before August 9, 1989) after the beginning of such calendar year and before August 9, 1989; and

(B) in the computation of the maximum amount of any savings association's offset for such calendar year under paragraph (1) after taking into account—

(i) the amount of any offset by such savings association under section 404(e)(2) of the National Housing Act (as in effect before August 9, 1989) after the beginning of such calendar year and before August 9, 1989; and

(ii) the change of such association's premium year from the 1–year period applicable under section 404(b) of the National Housing Act (as in effect before August 9, 1989) to a calendar year basis.

(n) Collections on behalf of Director of Office of Thrift Supervision

When requested by the Director of the Office of Thrift Supervision, the Corporation shall collect on behalf of the Director assessments on savings associations levied by the Director under section 1467 of this title. The Corporation shall be reimbursed for its actual costs for the collection of such assessments. Any such assessments by the Director shall be in addition to any amounts assessed by the Corporation, the Financing Corporation, and the Resolution Funding Corporation.

§ 1818.　Termination of status as insured depository institution—DFA §§ 172, 1090

(a) Termination of insurance

(1) Voluntary termination

Any insured depository institution which is not—

(A) a national member bank;

(B) a State member bank;

(C) a Federal branch;

(D) a Federal savings association; or

(E) an insured branch which is required to be insured under subsection (a) or (b) of section 3104 of this title,

may terminate such depository institution's status as an insured depository institution if such insured institution provides written notice to the Corporation of the institution's intent to terminate such status not less than 90 days before the effective date of such termination.

(2) Involuntary termination

(A) Notice to primary regulator

If the Board of Directors determines that—

(i) an insured depository institution or the directors or trustees of an insured depository institution have engaged or are engaging in unsafe or unsound practices in conducting the business of the depository institution;

(ii) an insured depository institution is in an unsafe or unsound condition to continue operations as an insured institution; or

(iii) an insured depository institution or the directors or trustees of the insured institution have violated any applicable law, regulation, order, condition imposed in writing by the Corporation in connection with the approval of any application or other request by the insured depository institution, or written agreement entered into between the insured depository institution and the Corporation,

the Board of Directors shall notify the appropriate Federal banking agency with respect to such institution (if other than the Corporation) or the State banking supervisor of such institution (if the Corporation is the appropriate Federal banking agency) of the Board's determination and the facts and circumstances on which such determination is based for the purpose of securing the correction of such practice, condition, or violation. Such notice shall be given to the appropriate Federal banking agency not less than 30 days before the notice required by subparagraph (B), except that this period for notice to the appropriate Federal banking agency may be reduced or eliminated with the agreement of such agency.

(B) Notice of intention to terminate insurance

If, after giving the notice required under subparagraph (A) with respect to an insured depository institution, the Board of Directors determines that any unsafe or unsound practice or condition or any violation specified in such notice requires the termination of the insured status of the insured depository institution, the Board shall—

(i) serve written notice to the insured depository institution of the Board's intention to terminate the insured status of the institution;

(ii) provide the insured depository institution with a statement of the charges on the basis of which the determination to terminate such institution's insured status was made (or a copy of the notice under subparagraph (A)); and

(iii) notify the insured depository institution of the date (not less than 30 days after notice

under this subparagraph) and place for a hearing before the Board of Directors (or any person designated by the Board) with respect to the termination of the institution's insured status.

(3) Hearing; termination

If, on the basis of the evidence presented at a hearing before the Board of Directors (or any person designated by the Board for such purpose), in which all issues shall be determined on the record pursuant to section 554 of Title 5 and the written findings of the Board of Directors (or such person) with respect to such evidence (which shall be conclusive), the Board of Directors finds that any unsafe or unsound practice or condition or any violation specified in the notice to an insured depository institution under paragraph (2)(B) or subsection (w) of this section has been established, the Board of Directors may issue an order terminating the insured status of such depository institution effective as of a date subsequent to such finding.

(4) Appearance; consent to termination

Unless the depository institution shall appear at the hearing by a duly authorized representative, it shall be deemed to have consented to the termination of its status as an insured depository institution and termination of such status thereupon may be ordered.

(5) Judicial review

Any insured depository institution whose insured status has been terminated by order of the Board of Directors under this subsection shall have the right of judicial review of such order only to the same extent as provided for the review of orders under subsection (h) of this section.

(6) Publication of notice of termination

The Corporation may publish notice of such termination and the depository institution shall give notice of such termination to each of its depositors at his last address of record on the books of the depository institution, in such manner and at such time as the Board of Directors may find to be necessary and may order for the protection of depositors.

(7) Temporary insurance of deposits insured as of termination

After the termination of the insured status of any depository institution under the provisions of this subsection, the insured deposits of each depositor in the depository institution on the date of such termination, less all subsequent withdrawals from any deposits of such depositor, shall continue for a period of at least 6 months or up to 2 years, within the discretion of the Board of Directors, to be insured, and the depository institution shall continue to pay to the Corporation assessments as in the case of an insured depository institution during such period. No additions to any such deposits and no new deposits in such depository institution made after the date of such termination shall be insured by the Corporation, and the depository institution shall not advertise or hold itself out as having insured deposits unless in the same connection it shall also state with equal prominence that such additions to deposits and new deposits made after such date are not so insured. Such depository institution shall, in all other respects, be subject to the duties and the period obligations of an insured depository institution for the period referred to in the 1st sentence from the date of such termination, and in the event that such depository institution shall be closed on account of inability to meet the demands of its depositors within such period, the Corporation shall have the same powers and rights with respect to such depository institution as in case of an insured depository institution.

(8) Temporary suspension of insurance

(A) In general

If the Board of Directors initiates a termination proceeding under paragraph (2), and the Board of Directors, after consultation with the appropriate Federal banking agency, finds that an insured depository institution (other than a savings association to which subparagraph (B) applies) has no tangible capital under the capital guidelines or regulations of the appropriate Federal banking agency, the Corporation may issue a temporary order suspending deposit insurance on all deposits received by the institution.

(B) Special rule for certain savings institutions

(i) Certain goodwill included in tangible capital

In determining the tangible capital of a savings association for purposes of this paragraph, the Board of Directors shall include goodwill to the extent it is considered a component of capital under section 1464(t) of this title. Any savings association which would be subject to a suspension order under subparagraph (A) but for the operation of this subparagraph, shall be considered by the Corporation to be a "special supervisory association."

(ii) Suspension order

The Corporation may issue a temporary order suspending deposit insurance on all deposits received by a special supervisory association whenever the Board of Directors determines that—

(I) the capital of such association, as computed utilizing applicable accounting standards, has suffered a material decline;

(II) that such association (or its directors or officers) is engaging in an unsafe or unsound practice in conducting the business of the association;

(III) that such association is in an unsafe or unsound condition to continue operating as an insured association; or

(IV) that such association (or its directors or officers) has violated any applicable law, rule, regulation, or order, or any condition imposed in writing by a Federal banking agency, or any written agreement including a capital improvement plan entered into with any Federal banking agency, or that the association has failed to enter into a capital improvement plan which is acceptable to the Corporation within the time period set forth in section 1464(t) of this title.

Nothing in this paragraph limits the right of the Corporation or the Director of the Office of Thrift Supervision to enforce a contractual provision which authorizes the Corporation or the Director of the Office of Thrift Supervision, as a successor to the Federal Savings and Loan Insurance Corporation or the Federal Home Loan Bank Board, to require a savings association to write down or amortize goodwill at a faster rate than otherwise required under this chapter or under applicable accounting standards.

(C) Effective period of temporary order

Any order issued under subparagraph (A) shall become effective not earlier than 10 days from the date of service upon the institution and, unless set aside, limited, or suspended by a court in proceedings authorized hereunder, such temporary order shall remain effective and enforceable until an order of the Board under paragraph (3) becomes final or until the Corporation dismisses the proceedings under paragraph (3).

(D) Judicial review

Before the close of the 10–day period beginning on the date any temporary order has been served upon an insured depository institution under subparagraph (A), such institution may apply to the United States District Court for the District of Columbia, or the United States district court for the judicial district in which the home office of the institution is located, for an injunction setting aside, limiting, or suspending the enforcement, operation, or effectiveness of such order, and such court shall have jurisdiction to issue such injunction.

(E) Continuation of insurance for prior deposits

The insured deposits of each depositor in such depository institution on the effective date of the order issued under this paragraph, minus all subsequent withdrawals from any deposits of such depositor, shall continue to be insured, subject to the administrative proceedings as provided in this chapter.

(F) Publication of order

The depository institution shall give notice of such order to each of its depositors in such manner and at such times as the Board of Directors may find to be necessary and may order for the protection of depositors.

(G) Notice by corporation

If the Corporation determines that the depository institution has not substantially complied with the notice to depositors required by the Board of Directors, the Corporation may provide such notice in such manner as the Board of Directors may find to be necessary and appropriate.

(H) Lack of notice

Notwithstanding subparagraph (A), any deposit made after the effective date of a suspension order issued under this paragraph shall remain insured to the extent that the depositor establishes that-

(i) such deposit consists of additions made by automatic deposit the depositor was unable to prevent; or

(ii) such depositor did not have actual knowledge of the suspension of insurance.

(9) Final decisions to terminate insurance

Any decision by the Board of Directors to—

(A) issue a temporary order terminating deposit insurance; or

(B) issue a final order terminating deposit insurance (other than under subsection (p) or (q) of this section);

shall be made by the Board of Directors and may not be delegated.

(10) Low-to moderate-income housing lender

In making any determination regarding the termination of insurance of a solvent savings association, the Corporation may consider the extent of the association's low-to moderate-income housing loans.

(b) Cease-and-desist proceedings

(1) If, in the opinion of the appropriate Federal banking agency, any insured depository institution, depository institution which has insured deposits, or any institution-affiliated party is engaging or has engaged, or the agency has reasonable cause to believe that the depository institution or any institution-affiliated party is about to engage, in an unsafe or unsound practice in conducting the business of such depository institution, or is violating or has violated, or the agency has reasonable cause to believe that the depository institution or any institution-affiliated party is about to violate, a law, rule, or regulation, or any condition imposed in writing by the agency in connection with the granting of any application or other request by the depository institution or any written agreement entered into with the agency, the agency may issue and serve upon the depository institution or such party a notice of charges in respect thereof. The notice shall contain a statement of the facts constituting the alleged violation or violations or the unsafe or unsound practice or practices, and

shall fix a time and place at which a hearing will be held to determine whether an order to cease and desist therefrom should issue against the depository institution or the institution-affiliated party. Such hearing shall be fixed for a date not earlier than thirty days nor later than sixty days after service of such notice unless an earlier or a later date is set by the agency at the request of any party so served. Unless the party or parties so served shall appear at the hearing personally or by a duly authorized representative, they shall be deemed to have consented to the issuance of the cease-and-desist order. In the event of such consent, or if upon the record made at any such hearing, the agency shall find that any violation or unsafe or unsound practice specified in the notice of charges has been established, the agency may issue and serve upon the depository institution or the institution-affiliated party an order to cease and desist from any such violation or practice. Such order may, by provisions which may be mandatory or otherwise, require the depository institution or its institution-affiliated parties to cease and desist from the same, and, further, to take affirmative action to correct the conditions resulting from any such violation or practice.

(2) A cease-and-desist order shall become effective at the expiration of thirty days after the service of such order upon the depository institution or other person concerned (except in the case of a cease-and-desist order issued upon consent, which shall become effective at the time specified therein), and shall remain effective and enforceable as provided therein, except to such extent as it is stayed, modified, terminated, or set aside by action of the agency or a reviewing court.

(3) This subsection and subsections (c) through (s) and subsection (u) of this section shall apply to any bank holding company, and to any subsidiary (other than a bank) of a bank holding company, as those terms are defined in the Bank Holding Company Act of 1956 [12 U.S.C.A. § 1841 et seq.], and to any organization organized and operated under section 25(a) of the Federal Reserve Act [12 U.S.C.A. § 611 et seq.] or operating under section 25 of the Federal Reserve Act [12 U.S.C.A. § 601 et seq.], in the same manner as they apply to a State member insured bank. Nothing in this subsection or in subsection (c) of this section

shall authorize any Federal banking agency, other than the Board of Governors of the Federal Reserve System, to issue a notice of charges or cease-and-desist order against a bank holding company or any subsidiary thereof (other than a bank or subsidiary of that bank).

(4) This subsection and subsections (c) through (s) and subsection (u) of this section, and section 1831aa of this title shall apply to any foreign bank or company to which subsection (a) of section 3106 of this title applies and to any subsidiary (other than a bank) of any such foreign bank or company in the same manner as they apply to a bank holding company and any subsidiary thereof (other than a bank) under paragraph (3) of this subsection. For the purposes of this paragraph, the term "subsidiary" shall have the meaning assigned it in section 2 of the Bank Holding Company Act of 1956 [12 U.S.C.A. § 1841].

(5) This section shall apply, in the same manner as it applies to any insured depository institution for which the appropriate Federal banking agency is the Comptroller of the Currency, to any national banking association chartered by the Comptroller of the Currency, including an uninsured association.

(6) Affirmative action to correct conditions resulting from violations or practices

The authority to issue an order under this subsection and subsection (c) of this section which requires an insured depository institution or any institution-affiliated party to take affirmative action to correct or remedy any conditions resulting from any violation or practice with respect to which such order is issued includes the authority to require such depository institution or such party to—

(A) make restitution or provide reimbursement, indemnification, or guarantee against loss if—

(i) such depository institution or such party was unjustly enriched in connection with such violation or practice; or

(ii) the violation or practice involved a reckless disregard for the law or any applicable regulations or prior order of the appropriate Federal banking agency;

(B) restrict the growth of the institution;

(C) dispose of any loan or asset involved;

(D) rescind agreements or contracts; and

(E) employ qualified officers or employees (who may be subject to approval by the appropriate Federal banking agency at the direction of such agency); and

(F) take such other action as the banking agency determines to be appropriate.

(7) Authority to limit activities

The authority to issue an order under this subsection or subsection (c) of this section includes the authority to place limitations on the activities or functions of an insured depository institution or any institution-affiliated party.

(8) Unsatisfactory asset quality, management, earnings, or liquidity as unsafe or unsound practice

If an insured depository institution receives, in its most recent report of examination, a less-than-satisfactory rating for asset quality, management, earnings, or liquidity, the appropriate Federal banking agency may (if the deficiency is not corrected) deem the institution to be engaging in an unsafe or unsound practice for purposes of this subsection.

(9) Expansion of authority to savings and loan affiliates and entities

Subsections (a) through (s) and subsection (u) of this section shall apply to any savings and loan holding company and to any subsidiary (other than a bank or subsidiary of that bank) of a savings and loan holding company, whether wholly or partly owned, in the same manner as such subsections apply to a savings association.

(10) Standard for certain orders

No authority under this subsection or subsection (c) of this section to prohibit any institution-affiliated party from withdrawing, transferring, removing, dissipating, or disposing of any funds, assets, or other property may be exercised unless the appropriate Federal banking agency meets the standards of Rule 65 of the Federal Rules of Civil Procedure, without regard to the requirement of such rule that the applicant show that the injury, loss, or damage is irreparable and immediate.

(c) Temporary cease-and-desist orders

(1) Whenever the appropriate Federal banking agency shall determine that the violation or threatened violation or the unsafe or unsound practice or practices, specified in the notice of charges served upon the depository institution or any institution-affiliated party pursuant to paragraph (1) of subsection (b) of this section, or the continuation thereof, is likely to cause insolvency or significant dissipation of assets or earnings of the depository institution, or is likely to weaken the condition of the depository institution or otherwise prejudice the interests of its depositors prior to the completion of the proceedings conducted pursuant to paragraph (1) of subsection (b) of this section, the agency may issue a temporary order requiring the depository institution or such party to cease and desist from any such violation or practice and to take affirmative action to prevent or remedy such insolvency, dissipation, condition, or prejudice pending completion of such proceedings. Such order may include any requirement authorized under subsection (b)(6) of this section. Such order shall become effective upon service upon the depository institution or such institution-affiliated party and, unless set aside, limited, or suspended by a court in proceedings authorized by paragraph (2) of this subsection, shall remain effective and enforceable pending the completion of the administrative proceedings pursuant to such notice and until such time as the agency shall dismiss the charges specified in such notice, or if a cease-and-desist order is issued against the depository institution or such party, until the effective date of such order.

(2) Within ten days after the depository institution concerned or any institution-affiliated party has been served with a temporary cease-and-desist order, the depository institution or such party may apply to the United States district court for the judicial district in which the home office of the depository institution is located, or the United States District Court for the District of Columbia, for an injunction setting aside, limiting, or suspending the enforcement, operation, or effectiveness of such order pending the completion of the administrative proceedings pursuant to the notice of charges served upon the depository institution or such party under paragraph (1) of subsection (b) of this section, and such court shall have jurisdiction to issue such injunction.

(3) Incomplete or inaccurate records

(A) Temporary order

If a notice of charges served under subsection (b)(1) of this section specifies, on the basis of particular facts and circumstances, that an insured depository institution's books and records are so incomplete or inaccurate that the appropriate Federal banking agency is unable, through the normal supervisory process, to determine the financial condition of that depository institution or the details or purpose of any transaction or transactions that may have a material effect on the financial condition of that depository institution, the agency may issue a temporary order requiring—

(i) the cessation of any activity or practice which gave rise, whether in whole or in part, to the incomplete or inaccurate state of the books or records; or

(ii) affirmative action to restore such books or records to a complete and accurate state, until the completion of the proceedings under subsection (b)(1) of this section.

(B) Effective period

Any temporary order issued under subparagraph (A)—

(i) shall become effective upon service; and

(ii) unless set aside, limited, or suspended by a court in proceedings under paragraph (2), shall remain in effect and enforceable until the earlier of—

(I) the completion of the proceeding initiated under subsection (b)(1) of this section in connection with the notice of charges; or

(II) the date the appropriate Federal banking agency determines, by examination or otherwise, that the insured depository institution's books and records are accurate and reflect the financial condition of the depository institution.

(4) False advertising or misuse of names to indicate insured status

(A) Temporary order

(i) In general

If a notice of charges served under subsection (b)(1) specifies on the basis of particular facts that any person engaged or is engaging in conduct described in section 1828 (a)(4) of this title, the Corporation or other appropriate Federal banking agency may issue a temporary order requiring—

(I) the immediate cessation of any activity or practice described, which gave rise to the notice of charges; and

(II) affirmative action to prevent any further, or to remedy any existing, violation.

(ii) Effect of order

Any temporary order issued under this subparagraph shall take effect upon service.

(B) Effective period of temporary order

A temporary order issued under subparagraph (A) shall remain effective and enforceable, pending the completion of an administrative proceeding pursuant to subsection (b)(1) in connection with the notice of charges—

(i) until such time as the Corporation or other appropriate Federal banking agency dismisses the charges specified in such notice; or

(ii) if a cease-and-desist order is issued against such person, until the effective date of such order.

(C) Civil money penalties

Any violation of section 1828(a)(4) of this title shall be subject to civil money penalties, as set forth in subsection (i), except that for any person other than an insured depository institution or an institution-affiliated party that is found to have violated this paragraph, the Corporation or other appropriate Federal banking agency shall not be required to demonstrate any loss to an insured depository institution.

(d) Temporary cease-and-desist orders; enforcement

In the case of violation or threatened violation of, or failure to obey, a temporary cease-and-desist order issued pursuant to paragraph (1) of subsection (c) of this section, the appropriate Federal banking agency may apply to the United States district court, or the United States court of any territory, within the jurisdiction of which the home office of the depository institution is located, for an injunction to enforce such order, and, if the court shall determine that there has been such violation or threatened violation or failure to obey, it shall be the duty of the court to issue such injunction.

(e) Removal and prohibition authority

(1) Authority to issue order

Whenever the appropriate Federal banking agency determines that—

(A) any institution-affiliated party has, directly or indirectly—

(i) violated—

(I) any law or regulation;

(II) any cease-and-desist order which has become final;

(III) any condition imposed in writing by a Federal banking agency in connection with any action on any application, notice, or request by such depository institution or institution-affiliated party; or

(IV) any written agreement between such depository institution and such agency;

(ii) engaged or participated in any unsafe or unsound practice in connection with any insured depository institution or business institution; or

(iii) committed or engaged in any act, omission, or practice which constitutes a breach of such party's fiduciary duty;

(B) by reason of the violation, practice, or breach described in any clause of subparagraph (A)—

(i) such insured depository institution or business institution has suffered or will probably suffer financial loss or other damage;

(ii) the interests of the insured depository institution's depositors have been or could be prejudiced; or

(iii) such party has received financial gain or other benefit by reason of such violation, practice, or breach; and

(C) such violation, practice, or breach—

(i) involves personal dishonesty on the part of such party; or

(ii) demonstrates willful or continuing disregard by such party for the safety or soundness of such insured depository institution or business institution,

the appropriate Federal banking agency for the depository institution may serve upon such party a written notice of the agency's intention to remove such party from office or to prohibit any further participation by such party, in any manner, in the conduct of the affairs of any insured depository institution.

(2) Specific violations

(A) In general

Whenever the appropriate Federal banking agency determines that—

(i) an institution-affiliated party has committed a violation of any provision of subchapter II of chapter 53 of Title 31 and such violation was not inadvertent or unintentional;

(ii) an officer or director of an insured depository institution has knowledge that an institution-affiliated party of the insured depository institution has violated any such provision or any provision of law referred to in subsection (g)(1)(A)(ii) of this section; or

(iii) an officer or director of an insured depository institution has committed any violation of the Depository Institution Management Interlocks Act [12 U.S.C.A. § 3201 et seq.]; or

(iv) an institution-affiliated party of a subsidiary (other than a bank) of a bank holding company or of a subsidiary (other than a savings association) of a savings and loan holding company has been convicted of any criminal offense involving dishonesty or a breach of trust or a criminal offense under section 1956, 1957, or 1960 of Title 18, or has agreed to enter into a pretrial diversion or similar program in connection with a prosecution for such an offense,

the agency may serve upon such party, officer, or director a written notice of the agency's intention to remove such party from office.

(B) Factors to be considered

In determining whether an officer or director should be removed as a result of the application of subparagraph (A)(ii), the agency shall consider whether the officer or director took appropriate action to stop, or to prevent the recurrence of, a violation described in such subparagraph.

(3) Suspension order

(A) Suspension or prohibition authorized

If the appropriate Federal banking agency serves written notice under paragraph (1) or

(2) to any institution-affiliated party of such agency's intention to issue an order under such paragraph, the appropriate Federal banking agency may suspend such party from office or prohibit such party from further participation in any manner in the conduct of the affairs of the depository institution, if the agency—

(i) determines that such action is necessary for the protection of the depository institution or the interests of the depository institution's depositors; and

(ii) serves such party with written notice of the suspension order.

(B) Effective period

Any suspension order issued under subparagraph (A)—

(i) shall become effective upon service; and

(ii) unless a court issues a stay of such order under subsection (f) of this section, shall remain in effect and enforceable until—

(I) the date the appropriate Federal banking agency dismisses the charges contained in the notice served under paragraph (1) or (2) with respect to such party; or

(II) the effective date of an order issued by the agency to such party under paragraph (1) or (2).

(C) Copy of order

If an appropriate Federal banking agency issues a suspension order under subparagraph (A) to any institution-affiliated party, the agency shall serve a copy of such order on any insured depository institution with which such party is associated at the time such order is issued.

(4) A notice of intention to remove an institution-affiliated party from office or to prohibit such party from participating in the conduct of the affairs of an insured depository institution, shall contain a statement of the facts constituting grounds therefor, and shall fix a time and place at which a hearing will be held thereon. Such hearing shall be fixed for a date not earlier than thirty days nor later than sixty days after the date of service of such notice, unless an earlier or a later date is set by the agency at the request of (A) such party, and for good cause shown, or (B) the Attorney General of the United States. Unless such party shall appear at the hearing in person or by a duly authorized representative, such party shall be deemed to have consented to the issuance of an order of such removal or prohibition. In the event of such consent, or if upon the record made at any such hearing the agency shall find that any of the grounds specified in such notice have been established, the agency may issue such orders of suspension or removal from office, or prohibition from participation in the conduct of the affairs of the depository institution, as it may deem appropriate. Any such order shall become effective at the expiration of thirty days after service upon such depository institution and such party concerned (except in the case of an order issued upon consent, which shall become effective at the time specified therein). Such order shall remain effective and enforceable except to such extent as it is stayed, modified, terminated, or set aside by action of the agency or a reviewing court.

(5) For the purpose of enforcing any law, rule, regulation, or cease-and-desist order in connection with an interlocking relationship, the term "officer" within the term "institution-affiliated party" as used in this subsection means an employee or officer with management functions, and the term "director" within the term "institution-affiliated party" as used in this subsection includes an advisory or honorary director, a trustee of a depository institution under the control of trustees, or any person who has a representative or nominee serving in any such capacity.

(6) Prohibition of certain specific activities

Any person subject to an order issued under this subsection shall not—

(A) participate in any manner in the conduct of the affairs of any institution or agency specified in paragraph (7)(A);

(B) solicit, procure, transfer, attempt to transfer, vote, or attempt to vote any proxy, consent, or authorization with respect to any voting rights in any institution described in subparagraph (A);

(C) violate any voting agreement previously approved by the appropriate Federal banking agency; or

(D) vote for a director, or serve or act as an institution-affiliated party.

(7) Industrywide prohibition

(A) In general

Except as provided in subparagraph (B), any person who, pursuant to an order issued under this subsection or subsection (g) of this section, has been removed or suspended from office in an insured depository institution or prohibited from participating in the conduct of the affairs of an insured depository institution may not, while such order is in effect, continue or commence to hold any office in, or participate in any manner in the conduct of the affairs of—

(i) any insured depository institution;

(ii) any institution treated as an insured bank under subsection (b)(3) or (b)(4) of this section, or as a savings association under subsection (b)(9) of this section;

(iii) any insured credit union under the Federal Credit Union Act [12 U.S.C.A. § 1781 et seq.];

(iv) any institution chartered under the Farm Credit Act of 1971 [12 U.S.C.A. § 2001 et seq.];

(v) any appropriate Federal depository institution regulatory agency;

(vi) the Federal Housing Finance Board and any Federal home loan bank; and

(vii) the Resolution Trust Corporation.

(B) Exception if agency provides written consent

If, on or after the date an order is issued under this subsection which removes or suspends from office any institution-affiliated party or prohibits such party from participating in the conduct of the affairs of an insured depository institution, such party receives the written consent of—

(i) the agency that issued such order; and

(ii) the appropriate Federal financial institutions regulatory agency of the institution described in any clause of subparagraph (A) with respect to which such party proposes to become an institution-affiliated party,

subparagraph (A) shall, to the extent of such consent, cease to apply to such party with respect to the institution described in each written consent. Any agency that grants such a written consent shall report such

action to the Corporation and publicly disclose such consent.

(C) Violation of paragraph treated as violation of order

Any violation of subparagraph (A) by any person who is subject to an order described in such subparagraph shall be treated as a violation of the order.

(D) Appropriate Federal financial institutions regulatory agency defined

For purposes of this paragraph and subsection (j) of this section, the term "appropriate Federal financial institutions regulatory agency" means—

(i) the appropriate Federal banking agency, in the case of an insured depository institution;

(ii) the Farm Credit Administration, in the case of an institution chartered under the Farm Credit Act of 1971 [12 U.S.C.A. § 2001 et seq.];

(iii) the National Credit Union Administration Board, in the case of an insured credit union (as defined in section 101(7) of the Federal Credit Union Act [12 U.S.C.A. § 1752(7)]);

(iv) the Secretary of the Treasury, in the case of the Federal Housing Finance Board and any Federal home loan bank; and

(v) the Thrift Depositor Protection Oversight Board, in the case of the Resolution Trust Corporation.

(E) Consultation between agencies

The agencies referred to in clauses (i) and (ii) of subparagraph (B) shall consult with each other before providing any written consent described in subparagraph (B).

(F) Applicability

This paragraph shall only apply to a person who is an individual, unless the appropriate Federal banking agency specifically finds that it should apply to a corporation, firm, or other business enterprise.

(f) Stay of suspension and/or prohibition of institution-affiliated party

Within ten days after any institution-affiliated party has been suspended from office and/or prohibited from participation in the conduct of the affairs of an insured depository institution under subsection (e)(3) of this section, such party may apply to the United States district court for the judicial district in which the home office of the depository institution is located, or the United States District Court for the District of Columbia, for a stay of such suspension and/or prohibition pending the completion of the administrative proceedings pursuant to the notice served upon such party under subsection (e)(1) or (e)(2) of this section, and such court shall have jurisdiction to stay such suspension and/or prohibition.

(g) Suspension, removal, and prohibition from participation orders in the case of certain criminal offenses

(1) Suspension or prohibition

(A) In general

Whenever any institution-affiliated party is the subject of any information, indictment, or complaint, involving the commission of or participation in—

(i) a crime involving dishonesty or breach of trust which is punishable by imprisonment for a term exceeding one year under State or Federal law, or

(ii) a criminal violation of section 1956, 1957, or 1960 of Title 18 or section 5322 or 5324 of Title 31,

the appropriate Federal banking agency may, if continued service or participation by such party posed, poses, or may pose a threat to the interests of the depositors of, or threatened, threatens, or may threaten to impair public confidence in, any relevant depository institution (as defined in subparagraph (E)), by written notice served upon such party, suspend such party from office or prohibit such party from further participation in any manner in the conduct of the affairs of any depository institution.

(B) Provisions applicable to notice

(i) Copy

A copy of any notice under subparagraph (A) shall also be served upon any depository institution that the subject of the notice is affiliated with at the time the notice is issued.

(ii) Effective period

A suspension or prohibition under subparagraph (A) shall remain in effect until the information, indictment, or complaint re-

ferred to in such subparagraph is finally disposed of or until terminated by the agency.

(C) Removal or prohibition

(i) In general

If a judgment of conviction or an agreement to enter a pretrial diversion or other similar program is entered against an institution-affiliated party in connection with a crime described in subparagraph (A)(i), at such time as such judgment is not subject to further appellate review, the appropriate Federal banking agency may, if continued service or participation by such party posed, poses, or may pose a threat to the interests of the depositors of, or threatened, threatens, or may threaten to impair public confidence in, any relevant depository institution (as defined in subparagraph (E)), issue and serve upon such party an order removing such party from office or prohibiting such party from further participation in any manner in the conduct of the affairs of any depository institution without the prior written consent of the appropriate agency.

(ii) Required for certain offenses

In the case of a judgment of conviction or agreement against an institution-affiliated party in connection with a violation described in subparagraph (A)(ii), the appropriate Federal banking agency shall issue and serve upon such party an order removing such party from office or prohibiting such party from further participation in any manner in the conduct of the affairs of any depository institution without the prior written consent of the appropriate agency.

(D) Provisions applicable to order

(i) Copy

A copy of any order under subparagraph (C) shall also be served upon any depository institution that the subject of the order is affiliated with at the time the order is issued, whereupon the institution-affiliated party who is subject to the order (if a director or an officer) shall cease to be a director or officer of such depository institution.

(ii) Effect of acquittal

A finding of not guilty or other disposition of the charge shall not preclude the agency from instituting proceedings after such finding or disposition to remove such party from office or to prohibit further participation in depository institution affairs, pursuant to paragraph (1), (2), or (3) of subsection (e) of this section.

(iii) Effective period

Any notice of suspension or order of removal issued under this paragraph shall remain effective and outstanding until the completion of any hearing or appeal authorized under paragraph (3) unless terminated by the agency.

(E) Relevant depository institution

For purposes of this subsection, the term "relevant depository institution" means any depository institution of which the party is or was an institution-affiliated party at the time at which—

(i) the information, indictment, or complaint described in subparagraph (A) was issued; or

(ii) the notice is issued under subparagraph (A) or the order is issued under subparagraph (C)(i).

(2) If at any time, because of the suspension of one or more directors pursuant to this section, there shall be on the board of directors of a national bank less than a quorum of directors not so suspended, all powers and functions vested in or exercisable by such board shall vest in and be exercisable by the director or directors on the board not so suspended, until such time as there shall be a quorum of the board of directors. In the event all of the directors of a national bank are suspended pursuant to this section, the Comptroller of the Currency shall appoint persons to serve temporarily as directors in their place and stead pending the termination of such suspensions, or until such time as those who have been suspended, cease to be directors of the bank and their respective successors take office.

(3) Within thirty days from service of any notice of suspension or order of removal issued pursuant to paragraph (1) of this subsection, the institution-affiliated party concerned may request in writing an opportunity to appear before the agency to show that the continued service to or participation in the conduct of the affairs of the depository institution by such party does not, or is not likely to, pose a threat to the interests of the [depository institution's] depositors or threaten to impair public confidence in the depository institution. Upon receipt of any such request, the appropriate Federal banking agency shall fix a time (not more than thirty days after receipt of such request, unless extended at the request of such party) and place at which such party may appear, personally or through counsel, before one or more members of the agency or designated employees of the agency to submit written materials (or, at the discretion of the agency, oral testimony) and oral argument. Within sixty days of such hearing, the agency shall notify such party whether the suspension or prohibition from participation in any manner in the conduct of the affairs of the depository institution will be continued, terminated, or otherwise modified, or whether the order removing such party from office or prohibiting such party from further participation in any manner in the conduct of the affairs of the depository institution will be rescinded or otherwise modified. Such notification shall contain a statement of the basis for the agency's decision, if adverse to such party. The Federal banking agencies are authorized to prescribe such rules as may be necessary to effectuate the purposes of this subsection.

(h) Hearings and judicial review

(1) Any hearing provided for in this section (other than the hearing provided for in subsection (g)(3) of this section) shall be held in the Federal judicial district or in the territory in which the home office of the depository institution is located unless the party afforded the hearing consents to another place, and shall be conducted in accordance with the provisions of chapter 5 of Title 5. After such hearing, and within ninety days after the appropriate Federal banking agency or Board of Governors of the Federal Reserve System has notified the parties that the case has been submitted to it for final decision, it shall render its decision (which shall include findings of fact upon which its decision is predicated) and shall issue and serve upon each party to the proceeding an order or orders consistent with the provisions of this section. Judicial review of any such order shall be exclusively as provided in this subsection (h) of this section. Unless a petition for review is timely filed in a court of appeals of the United States, as hereinafter provided in

paragraph (2) of this subsection, and thereafter until the record in the proceeding has been filed as so provided, the issuing agency may at any time, upon such notice and in such manner as it shall deem proper, modify, terminate, or set aside any such order. Upon such filing of the record, the agency may modify, terminate, or set aside any such order with permission of the court.

(2) Any party to any proceeding under paragraph (1) may obtain a review of any order served pursuant to paragraph (1) of this subsection (other than an order issued with the consent of the depository institution or the institution-affiliated party concerned, or an order issued under paragraph (1) of subsection (g) of this section) by the filing in the court of appeals of the United States for the circuit in which the home office of the depository institution is located, or in the United States Court of Appeals for the District of Columbia Circuit, within thirty days after the date of service of such order, a written petition praying that the order of the agency be modified, terminated, or set aside. A copy of such petition shall be forthwith transmitted by the clerk of the court to the agency, and thereupon the agency shall file in the court the record in the proceeding, as provided in section 2112 of Title 28. Upon the filing of such petition, such court shall have jurisdiction, which upon the filing of the record shall except as provided in the last sentence of said paragraph (1) be exclusive, to affirm, modify, terminate, or set aside, in whole or in part, the order of the agency. Review of such proceedings shall be had as provided in chapter 7 of Title 5. The judgment and decree of the court shall be final, except that the same shall be subject to review by the Supreme Court upon certiorari, as provided in section 1254 of Title 28.

(3) The commencement of proceedings for judicial review under paragraph (2) of this subsection shall not, unless specifically ordered by the court, operate as a stay of any order issued by the agency.

(i) Jurisdiction and enforcement; penalty

(1) The appropriate Federal banking agency may in its discretion apply to the United States district court, or the United States court of any territory, within the jurisdiction of which the home office of the depository institution is located, for the enforcement of any effective and outstanding notice or order issued under this section or under section 1831o or 1831p–1 of this title, and such courts shall have jurisdiction and power to order and require compliance herewith; but except as otherwise provided in this section or under section 1831o or 1831p–1 of this title no court shall have jurisdiction to affect by injunction or otherwise the issuance or enforcement of any notice or order under any such section, or to review, modify, suspend, terminate, or set aside any such notice or order.

(2) Civil money penalty

(A) First tier

Any insured depository institution which, and any institution-affiliated party who—

(i) violates any law or regulation;

(ii) violates any final order or temporary order issued pursuant to subsection (b), (c), (e), (g), or (s) of this section or any final order under section 1831o or 1831p–1 of this title;

(iii) violates any condition imposed in writing by a Federal banking agency in connection with any action on any application, notice, or other request by the depository institution or institution-affiliated party; or

(iv) violates any written agreement between such depository institution and such agency,

shall forfeit and pay a civil penalty of not more than $5,000 for each day during which such violation continues.

(B) Second tier

Notwithstanding subparagraph (A), any insured depository institution which, and any institution-affiliated party who—

(i)(I) commits any violation described in any clause of subparagraph (A);

(II) recklessly engages in an unsafe or unsound practice in conducting the affairs of such insured depository institution; or

(III) breaches any fiduciary duty;

(ii) which violation, practice, or breach—

(I) is part of a pattern of misconduct;

(II) causes or is likely to cause more than a minimal loss to such depository institution; or

(III) results in pecuniary gain or other benefit to such party,

shall forfeit and pay a civil penalty of not more than $25,000 for each day during which such violation, practice, or breach continues.

(C) Third tier

Notwithstanding subparagraphs (A) and (B), any insured depository institution which, and any institution-affiliated party who—

(i) knowingly—

(I) commits any violation described in any clause of subparagraph (A);

(II) engages in any unsafe or unsound practice in conducting the affairs of such depository institution; or

(III) breaches any fiduciary duty; and

(ii) knowingly or recklessly causes a substantial loss to such depository institution or a substantial pecuniary gain or other benefit to such party by reason of such violation, practice, or breach,

shall forfeit and pay a civil penalty in an amount not to exceed the applicable maximum amount determined under subparagraph (D) for each day during which such violation, practice, or breach continues.

(D) Maximum amounts of penalties for any violation described in subparagraph (c)

The maximum daily amount of any civil penalty which may be assessed pursuant to subparagraph (C) for any violation, practice, or breach described in such subparagraph is—

(i) in the case of any person other than an insured depository institution, an amount to not exceed $1,000,000; and

(ii) in the case of any insured depository institution, an amount not to exceed the lesser of—

(I) $1,000,000; or

(II) 1 percent of the total assets of such institution.

(E) Assessment

(i) Written notice

Any penalty imposed under subparagraph (A), (B), or (C) may be assessed and collected by the appropriate Federal banking agency by written notice.

(ii) Finality of assessment

If, with respect to any assessment under clause (i), a hearing is not requested pursuant to subparagraph (H) within the period of time allowed under such subparagraph, the assessment shall constitute a final and unappealable order.

(F) Authority to modify or remit penalty

Any appropriate Federal banking agency may compromise, modify, or remit any penalty which such agency may assess or had already assessed under subparagraph (A), (B), or (C).

(G) Mitigating factors

In determining the amount of any penalty imposed under subparagraph (A), (B), or (C), the appropriate agency shall take into account the appropriateness of the penalty with respect to—

(i) the size of financial resources and good faith of the insured depository institution or other person charged;

(ii) the gravity of the violation;

(iii) the history of previous violations; and

(iv) such other matters as justice may require.

(H) Hearing

The insured depository institution or other person against whom any penalty is assessed under this paragraph shall be afforded an agency hearing if such institution or person submits a request for such hearing within 20 days after the issuance of the notice of assessment.

(I) Collection

(i) Referral

If any insured depository institution or other person fails to pay an assessment after any penalty assessed under this paragraph has become final, the agency that imposed the penalty shall recover the amount assessed by action in the appropriate United States district court.

(ii) Appropriateness of penalty not reviewable

In any civil action under clause (i), the validity and appropriateness of the penalty shall not be subject to review.

(J) Disbursement

All penalties collected under authority of this paragraph shall be deposited into the Treasury.

(K) Regulations

Each appropriate Federal banking agency shall prescribe regulations establishing such procedures as may be necessary to carry out this paragraph.

(3) Notice under this section after separation from service

The resignation, termination of employment or participation, or separation of an institution-affiliated party (including a separation caused by the closing of an insured depository institution) shall not affect the jurisdiction and authority of the appropriate Federal banking agency to issue any notice and proceed under this section against any such party, if such notice is served before the end of the 6–year period beginning on the date such party ceased to be such a party with respect to such depository institution (whether such date occurs before, on, or after August 9, 1989).

(4) Prejudgment attachment

(A) In general

In any action brought by an appropriate Federal banking agency (excluding the Corporation when acting in a manner described in section 1821(d)(18) of this title) pursuant to this section, or in actions brought in aid of, or to enforce an order in, any administrative or other civil action for money damages, restitution, or civil money penalties brought by such agency, the court may, upon application of the agency, issue a restraining order that—

(i) prohibits any person subject to the proceeding from withdrawing, transferring, removing, dissipating, or disposing of any funds, assets or other property; and

(ii) appoints a temporary receiver to administer the restraining order.

(B) Standard

(i) Showing

Rule 65 of the Federal Rules of Civil Procedure shall apply with respect to any proceeding under subparagraph (A) without regard to the requirement of such rule that the applicant show that the injury, loss, or damage is irreparable and immediate.

(ii) State proceeding

If, in the case of any proceeding in a State court, the court determines that rules of civil procedure available under the laws of such State provide substantially similar protections to a party's right to due process as Rule 65 (as modified with respect to such proceeding by clause (i)), the relief sought under subparagraph (A) may be requested under the laws of such State.

(j) Criminal penalty

Whoever, being subject to an order in effect under subsection (e) or (g) of this section, without the prior written approval of the appropriate Federal financial institutions regulatory agency, knowingly participates, directly or indirectly, in any manner (including by engaging in an activity specifically prohibited in such an order or in subsection (e)(6) of this section) in the conduct of the affairs of—

(1) any insured depository institution;

(2) any institution treated as an insured bank under subsection (b)(3) or (b)(4) of this section, or as a savings association under subsection (b)(9) of this section;

(3) any insured credit union (as defined in section 1752(7) of this title);

(4) any institution chartered under the Farm Credit Act of [12 U.S.C.A. § 2001 et seq.]; or

(5) the Resolution Trust Corporation,

shall be fined not more than $1,000,000, imprisoned for not more than 5 years, or both.

(k) Repealed. Pub.L. 101–73, Title IX, § 920(c), Aug. 9, 1989, 103 Stat. 488

(*l*) Notice of service

Any service required or authorized to be made by the appropriate Federal banking agency under this section may be made by registered mail, or in such other manner reasonably calculated to give actual notice as the agency may by regulation or otherwise provide. Copies of any notice or order served by the agency upon any State depository institution or any institution-affiliated party, pursuant to the provisions of this section, shall also be sent to the appropriate State supervisory authority.

(m) Notice to State authorities

In connection with any proceeding under subsection (b), (c)(1), or (e) of this section involving an insured State bank or any institution-affiliated party, the appropriate Federal banking agency shall provide the appropriate State supervisory authority with notice of the agency's intent to institute such a proceeding and the grounds therefor. Unless within such time as the Federal banking agency deems appropriate in the light of the circumstances of the case (which time must be specified in the notice prescribed in the preceding sentence) satisfactory corrective action is effectuated by action of the State supervisory authority, the agency may proceed as provided in this section. No bank or other party who is the subject of any notice or order issued by the agency under this section shall have standing to raise the requirements of this subsection as ground for attacking the validity of any such notice or order.

(n) Ancillary provisions; subpena power, etc.

In the course of or in connection with any proceeding under this section, or in connection with any claim for insured deposits or any examination or investigation under section 1820(c) of this title, the agency conducting the proceeding, examination, or investigation or considering the claim for insured deposits, or any member or designated representative thereof, including any person designated to conduct any hearing under this section, shall have the power to administer oaths and affirmations, to take or cause to be taken depositions, and to issue, revoke, quash, or modify subpoenas and subpoenas duces tecum; and such agency is empowered to make rules and regulations with respect to any such proceedings, claims, examinations, or investigations. The attendance of witnesses and the production of documents provided for in this subsection may be required from any place in any State or in any territory or other place subject to the jurisdiction of the United States at any designated place where such proceeding is being conducted. Any such agency or any party to proceedings under this section may apply to the United States District Court for the District of Columbia, or the United States district court for the judicial district or the United States court in any territory in which such proceeding is being conducted, or where the witness resides or carries on business, for enforcement of any subpena or subpena duces tecum issued pursuant to this subsection, and such courts shall have jurisdiction and power to

order and require compliance therewith. Witnesses subpenaed under this subsection shall be paid the same fees and mileage that are paid witnesses in the district courts of the United States. Any court having jurisdiction of any proceeding instituted under this section by an insured depository institution or a director or officer thereof, may allow to any such party such reasonable expenses and attorneys' fees as it deems just and proper; and such expenses and fees shall be paid by the depository institution or from its assets. Any person who willfully shall fail or refuse to attend and testify or to answer any lawful inquiry or to produce books, papers, correspondence, memoranda, contracts, agreements, or other records, if in such person's power so to do, in obedience to the subpoena of the appropriate Federal banking agency, shall be guilty of a misdemeanor and, upon conviction, shall be subject to a fine of not more than $1,000 or to imprisonment for a term of not more than one year or both.

(o) Termination of membership of State bank in Federal Reserve System

Whenever the insured status of a State member bank shall be terminated by action of the Board of Directors, the Board of Governors of the Federal Reserve System shall terminate its membership in the Federal Reserve System in accordance with the provisions of subchapter VIII of chapter 3 of this title, and whenever the insured status of a national member bank shall be so terminated the Comptroller of the Currency shall appoint a receiver for the bank, which shall be the Corporation. Except as provided in subsection (c) or (d) of section 1814 of this title, whenever a member bank shall cease to be a member of the Federal Reserve System, its status as an insured depository institution shall, without notice or other action by the Board of Directors, terminate on the date the bank shall cease to be a member of the Federal Reserve System, with like effect as if its insured status had been terminated on said date by the Board of Directors after proceedings under subsection (a) of this section. Whenever the insured status of an insured Federal savings bank shall be terminated by action of the Board of Directors, the Director of the Office of Thrift Supervision shall appoint a receiver for the bank, which shall be the Corporation.

(p) Banks not receiving deposits

Notwithstanding any other provision of law, whenever the Board of Directors shall determine that an insured depository institution is not engaged in the business of receiving deposits, other than trust funds as herein defined, the Corporation shall notify the depository institution that its insured status will terminate at the expiration of the first full semiannual assessment period following such notice. A finding by the Board of Directors that a depository institution is not engaged in the business of receiving deposits, other than such trust funds, shall be conclusive. The Board of Directors shall prescribe the notice to be given by the depository institution of such termination and the Corporation may publish notice thereof. Upon the termination of the insured status of any such depository institution, its deposits shall thereupon cease to be insured and the depository institution shall thereafter be relieved of all future obligations to the Corporation, including the obligation to pay future assessments.

(q) Assumption of liabilities

Whenever the liabilities of an insured depository institution for deposits shall have been assumed by another insured depository institution or depository institutions, whether by way of merger, consolidation, or other statutory assumption, or pursuant to contract (1) the insured status of the depository institution whose liabilities are so assumed shall terminate on the date of receipt by the Corporation of satisfactory evidence of such assumption; (2) the separate insurance of all deposits so assumed shall terminate at the end of six months from the date such assumption takes effect or, in the case of any time deposit, the earliest maturity date after the six-month period. Where the deposits of an insured depository institution are assumed by a newly insured depository institution, the depository institution whose deposits are assumed shall not be required to pay any assessment with respect to the deposits which have been so assumed after the semiannual period in which the assumption takes effect.

(r) Action or proceeding against foreign bank; basis; removal of officer or other person; venue; service of process

(1) Except as otherwise specifically provided in this section, the provisions of this section shall be applied to foreign banks in accordance with this subsection.

(2) An act or practice outside the United States on the part of a foreign bank or any officer, director, employee, or agent thereof may not constitute the basis for any action by any officer or agency of the United States under this section, unless—

(A) such officer or agency alleges a belief that such act or practice has been, is, or is likely to be a cause of or carried on in connection with or in furtherance of an act or practice within any one or more States which, in and of itself, would constitute an appropriate basis for action by a Federal officer or agency under this section; or

(B) the alleged act or practice is one which, if proven, would, in the judgment of the Board of Directors, adversely affect the insurance risk assumed by the Corporation.

(3) In any case in which any action or proceeding is brought pursuant to an allegation under paragraph (2) of this subsection for the suspension or removal of any officer, director, or other person associated with a foreign bank, and such person fails to appear promptly as a party to such action or proceeding and to comply with any effective order or judgment therein, any failure by the foreign bank to secure his removal from any office he holds in such bank and from any further participation in its affairs shall, in and of itself, constitute grounds for termination of the insurance of the deposits in any branch of the bank.

(4) Where the venue of any judicial or administrative proceeding under this section is to be determined by reference to the location of the home office of a bank, the venue of such a proceeding with respect to a foreign bank having one or more branches or agencies in not more than one judicial district or other relevant jurisdiction shall be within such jurisdiction. Where such a bank has branches or agencies in more than one such jurisdiction, the venue shall be in the jurisdiction within which the branch or branches or agency or agencies involved in the proceeding are located, and if there is more than one such jurisdiction, the venue shall be proper in any such jurisdiction in which the proceeding is brought or to which it may appropriately be transferred.

(5) Any service required or authorized to be made on a foreign bank may be made on any branch or agency located within any State, but

if such service is in connection with an action or proceeding involving one or more branches or one or more agencies located in any State, service shall be made on at least one branch or agency so involved.

(s) Compliance with monetary transaction recordkeeping and report requirements

(1) Compliance procedures required

Each appropriate Federal banking agency shall prescribe regulations requiring insured depository institutions to establish and maintain procedures reasonably designed to assure and monitor the compliance of such depository institutions with the requirements of subchapter II of chapter 53 of Title 31.

(2) Examinations of bank to include review of compliance procedures

(A) In general

Each examination of an insured depository institution by the appropriate Federal banking agency shall include a review of the procedures required to be established and maintained under paragraph (1).

(B) Exam report requirement

The report of examination shall describe any problem with the procedures maintained by the insured depository institution.

(3) Order to comply with requirements

If the appropriate Federal banking agency determines that an insured depository institution—

(A) has failed to establish and maintain the procedures described in paragraph (1); or

(B) has failed to correct any problem with the procedures maintained by such depository institution which was previously reported to the depository institution by such agency,

the agency shall issue an order in the manner prescribed in subsection (b) or (c) of this section requiring such depository institution to cease and desist from its violation of this subsection or regulations prescribed under this subsection.

(t) Authority of FDIC to take enforcement action against insured depository institutions and institution-affiliated parties

(1) Recommending action by appropriate Federal banking agency

The Corporation, based on an examination of an insured depository institution by the Corporation or by the appropriate Federal banking agency or on other information, may recommend in writing to the appropriate Federal banking agency that the agency take any enforcement action authorized under section 1817(j) of this title, this section, or section 1828(j) of this title with respect to any insured depository institution or any institution-affiliated party. The recommendation shall be accompanied by a written explanation of the concerns giving rise to the recommendation.

(2) FDIC's authority to act if appropriate Federal banking agency fails to follow recommendation

If the appropriate Federal banking agency does not, before the end of the 60–day period beginning on the date on which the agency receives the recommendation under paragraph (1), take the enforcement action recommended by the Corporation or provide a plan acceptable to the Corporation for responding to the Corporation's concerns, the Corporation may take the recommended enforcement action if the Board of Directors determines, upon a vote of its members, that—

(A) the insured depository institution is in an unsafe or unsound condition;

(B) the institution or institution-affiliated party is engaging in unsafe or unsound practices, and the recommended enforcement action will prevent the institution or institution-affiliated party from continuing such practices; or

(C) the conduct or threatened conduct (including any acts or omissions) poses a risk to the deposit insurance fund, or may prejudice the interests of the institution's depositors.

(3) Effect of exigent circumstances

(A) Authority to act

The Corporation may, upon a vote of the Board of Directors, and after notice to the appropriate Federal banking agency, exercise its authority under paragraph (2) in exigent circumstances without regard to the time period set forth in paragraph (2).

(B) Agreement on exigent circumstances

The Corporation shall, by agreement with the appropriate Federal banking agency, set forth those exigent circumstances in which the Corporation may act under subparagraph (A).

(4) Corporation's powers; institution's duties

For purposes of this subsection—

(A) The Corporation shall have the same powers with respect to any insured depository institution and its affiliates as the appropriate Federal banking agency has with respect to the institution and its affiliates; and

(B) the institution and its affiliates shall have the same duties and obligations with respect to the Corporation as the institution and its affiliates have with respect to the appropriate Federal banking agency.

(5) Requests for formal actions and investigations

(A) Submission of requests

A regional office of an appropriate Federal banking agency (including a Federal Reserve bank) that requests a formal investigation of or civil enforcement action against an insured depository institution or institution-affiliated party shall submit the request concurrently to the chief officer of the appropriate Federal banking agency and to the Corporation.

(B) Agencies required to report on requests

Each appropriate Federal banking agency shall report semiannually to the Corporation on the status or disposition of all requests under subparagraph (A), including the reasons for any decision by the agency to approve or deny such requests.

(u) Public disclosures of final orders and agreements

(1) In general

The appropriate Federal banking agency shall publish and make available to the public on a monthly basis—

(A) any written agreement or other written statement for which a violation may be enforced by the appropriate Federal banking agency, unless the appropriate Federal banking agency, in its discretion, determines that publication would be contrary to the public interest;

(B) any final order issued with respect to any administrative enforcement proceeding

initiated by such agency under this section or any other law; and

(C) any modification to or termination of any order or agreement made public pursuant to this paragraph.

(2) Hearings

All hearings on the record with respect to any notice of charges issued by a Federal banking agency shall be open to the public, unless the agency, in its discretion, determines that holding an open hearing would be contrary to the public interest.

(3) Transcript of hearing

A transcript that includes all testimony and other documentary evidence shall be prepared for all hearings commenced pursuant to subsection (i) of this section. A transcript of public hearings shall be made available to the public pursuant to section 552 of Title 5.

(4) Delay of publication under exceptional circumstances

If the appropriate Federal banking agency makes a determination in writing that the publication of a final order pursuant to paragraph (1)(B) would seriously threaten the safety and soundness of an insured depository institution, the agency may delay the publication of the document for a reasonable time.

(5) Documents filed under seal in public enforcement hearings

The appropriate Federal banking agency may file any document or part of a document under seal in any administrative enforcement hearing commenced by the agency if disclosure of the document would be contrary to the public interest. A written report shall be made part of any determination to withhold any part of a document from the transcript of the hearing required by paragraph (2).

(6) Retention of documents

Each Federal banking agency shall keep and maintain a record, for a period of at least 6 years, of all documents described in paragraph (1) and all informal enforcement agreements and other supervisory actions and supporting documents issued with respect to or in connection with any administrative enforcement proceeding initiated by such agency under this section or any other laws.

(7) Disclosures to Congress

No provision of this subsection may be construed to authorize the withholding, or to prohibit the disclosure, of any information to the Congress or any committee or subcommittee of the Congress.

(v) Foreign investigations

(1) Requesting assistance from foreign banking authorities

In conducting any investigation, examination, or enforcement action under this chapter, the appropriate Federal banking agency may—

(A) request the assistance of any foreign banking authority; and

(B) maintain an office outside the United States.

(2) Providing assistance to foreign banking authorities

(A) In general

Any appropriate Federal banking agency may, at the request of any foreign banking authority, assist such authority if such authority states that the requesting authority is conducting an investigation to determine whether any person has violated, is violating, or is about to violate any law or regulation relating to banking matters or currency transactions administered or enforced by the requesting authority.

(B) Investigation by federal banking agency

Any appropriate Federal banking agency may, in such agency's discretion, investigate and collect information and evidence pertinent to a request for assistance under subparagraph (A). Any such investigation shall comply with the laws of the United States and the policies and procedures of the appropriate Federal banking agency.

(C) Factors to consider

In deciding whether to provide assistance under this paragraph, the appropriate Federal banking agency shall consider—

(i) whether the requesting authority has agreed to provide reciprocal assistance with respect to banking matters within the jurisdiction of any appropriate Federal banking agency; and

(ii) whether compliance with the request would prejudice the public interest of the United States.

(D) Treatment of foreign banking authority

For purposes of any Federal law or appropriate Federal banking agency regulation relating to the collection or transfer of information by any appropriate Federal banking agency, the foreign banking authority shall be treated as another appropriate Federal banking agency.

(3) Rule of construction

Paragraphs (1) and (2) shall not be construed to limit the authority of an appropriate Federal banking agency or any other Federal agency to provide or receive assistance or information to or from any foreign authority with respect to any matter.

(w) Termination of insurance for money laundering or cash transaction reporting offenses

(1) In general

(A) Conviction of Title 18 offenses

(i) Duty to notify

If an insured State depository institution has been convicted of any criminal offense under section 1956 or 1957 of Title 18, the Attorney General shall provide to the Corporation a written notification of the conviction and shall include a certified copy of the order of conviction from the court rendering the decision.

(ii) Notice of termination; pretermination hearing

After receipt of written notification from the Attorney General by the Corporation of such a conviction, the Board of Directors shall issue to the insured depository institution a notice of its intention to terminate the insured status of the insured depository institution and schedule a hearing on the matter, which shall be conducted in all respects as a termination hearing pursuant to paragraphs (3) through (5) of subsection (a) of this section.

(B) Conviction of Title 31 offenses

If an insured State depository institution is convicted of any criminal offense under section 5322 or 5324 of Title 31, after receipt of written notification from the Attorney General by the Corporation, the Board of Directors may initiate proceedings to terminate the insured status of the insured depository institution in the manner described in sub-paragraph (A).

(C) Notice to State supervisor

The Corporation shall simultaneously transmit a copy of any notice issued under this paragraph to the appropriate State financial institutions supervisor.

(2) Factors to be considered

In determining whether to terminate insurance under paragraph (1), the Board of Directors shall take into account the following factors:

(A) The extent to which directors or senior executive officers of the depository institution knew of, or were involved in, the commission of the money laundering offense of which the institution was found guilty.

(B) The extent to which the offense occurred despite the existence of policies and procedures within the depository institution which were designed to prevent the occurrence of any such offense.

(C) The extent to which the depository institution has fully cooperated with law enforcement authorities with respect to the investigation of the money laundering offense of which the institution was found guilty.

(D) The extent to which the depository institution has implemented additional internal controls (since the commission of the offense of which the depository institution was found guilty) to prevent the occurrence of any other money laundering offense.

(E) The extent to which the interest of the local community in having adequate deposit and credit services available would be threatened by the termination of insurance.

(3) Notice to State banking supervisor and public

When the order to terminate insured status initiated pursuant to this subsection is final, the Board of Directors shall—

(A) notify the State banking supervisor of any State depository institution described in paragraph (1) and the Office of Thrift Supervision, where appropriate, at least 10 days prior to the effective date of the order of termination of the insured status of such depository institution, including a State branch of a foreign bank; and

(B) publish notice of the termination of the insured status of the depository institution in the Federal Register.

(4) Temporary insurance of previously insured deposits

Upon termination of the insured status of any State depository institution pursuant to paragraph (1), the deposits of such depository institution shall be treated in accordance with subsection (a)(7) of this section.

(5) Successor liability

This subsection shall not apply to a successor to the interests of, or a person who acquires, an insured depository institution that violated a provision of law described in paragraph (1), if the successor succeeds to the interests of the violator, or the acquisition is made, in good faith and not for purposes of evading this subsection or regulations prescribed under this subsection.

(6) Definition

The term "senior executive officer" has the same meaning as in regulations prescribed under section 1831i(f) of this title.

§ 1819. Corporate powers

(a) In general

Upon June 16, 1933, the Corporation shall become a body corporate and as such shall have power—

First. To adopt and use a corporate seal.

Second. To have succession until dissolved by an Act of Congress.

Third. To make contracts.

Fourth. To sue and be sued, and complain and defend, by and through its own attorneys, in any court of law or equity, State or Federal.

Fifth. To appoint by its Board of Directors such officers and employees as are not otherwise provided for in this chapter, to define their duties, fix their compensation, require bonds of them and fix the penalty thereof, and to dismiss at pleasure such officers or employees. Nothing in this chapter or any other Act shall be construed to prevent the appointment and compensation as an officer or employee of the Corporation of any officer or employee of the United States in any board, commission, independent establishment, or executive department thereof.

Sixth. To prescribe, by its Board of Directors, bylaws not inconsistent with law, regulating the manner in which its general business may be conducted, and the privileges granted to it by law may be exercised and enjoyed.

Seventh. To exercise by its Board of Directors, or duly authorized officers or agents, all powers specifically granted by the provisions of this chapter, and such incidental powers as shall be necessary to carry out the powers so granted.

Eighth. To make examinations of and to require information and reports from depository institutions, as provided in this chapter.

Ninth. To act as receiver.

Tenth. To prescribe by its Board of Directors such rules and regulations as it may deem necessary to carry out the provisions of this chapter or of any other law which it has the responsibility of administering or enforcing (except to the extent that authority to issue such rules and regulations has been expressly and exclusively granted to any other regulatory agency).

(b) Agency Authority

(1) Status

The Corporation, in any capacity, shall be an agency of the United States for purposes of section 1345 of Title 28, without regard to whether the Corporation commenced the action.

(2) Federal court jurisdiction

   (A) In general

   Except as provided in subparagraph (D), all suits of a civil nature at common law or in equity to which the Corporation, in any capacity, is a party shall be deemed to arise under the laws of the United States.

   (B) Removal

   Except as provided in subparagraph (D), the Corporation may, without bond or security, remove any action, suit, or proceeding from a State court to the appropriate United States district court before the end of the 90–day period beginning on the date the action, suit, or proceeding is filed against the Corporation or the Corporation is substituted as a party.

   (C) Appeal of remand

   The Corporation may appeal any order of remand entered by any United States district court.

   (D) State actions

   Except as provided in subparagraph (E), any action—

   (i) to which the Corporation, in the Corporation's capacity as receiver of a State insured depository institution by the exclusive appointment by State authorities, is a party other than as a plaintiff;

   (ii) which involves only the preclosing rights against the State insured depository institution, or obligations owing to, depositors, creditors, or stockholders by the State insured depository institution; and

   (iii) in which only the interpretation of the law of such State is necessary,

   shall not be deemed to arise under the laws of the United States.

   (E) Rule of construction

   Subparagraph (D) shall not be construed as limiting the right of the Corporation to invoke the jurisdiction of any United States district court in any action described in such subparagraph if the institution of which the Corporation has been appointed receiver could have invoked the jurisdiction of such court.

(3) Service of process

The Board of Directors shall designate agents upon whom service of process may be made in any State, territory, or jurisdiction in which any insured depository institution is located.

(4) Bonds or fees

The Corporation shall not be required to post any bond to pursue any appeal and shall not be subject to payments of any filing fees in United States district courts or courts of appeal.

§ 1820. Administration of Corporation—DFA §§ 172, 318

(a) Board of Directors; use of mails; cooperation with other Federal agencies

The Board of Directors shall administer the affairs of the Corporation fairly and impartially and without discrimination. The Board of Directors of the Corporation shall determine and prescribe the manner in which its obligations shall be incurred and its expenses allowed and paid. The Corporation shall be entitled to the free use of the United States mails in the same manner as the executive departments of the Government. The Corporation with the consent of any Federal Reserve bank or of any board, commission, independent establishment, or executive department of the Government, including any field service thereof, may avail itself of the use of information, services, and facilities thereof in carrying out the provisions of this chapter.

(b) Examinations

(1) Appointment of examiners and claims agents

The Board of Directors shall appoint examiners and claims agents.

(2) Regular examinations

Any examiner appointed under paragraph (1) shall have power, on behalf of the Corporation, to examine—

(A) any insured State nonmember bank or insured State branch of any foreign bank;

(B) any depository institution which files an application with the Corporation to become an insured depository institution; and

(C) any insured depository institution in default,

whenever the Board of Directors determines an examination of any such depository institution is necessary.

(3) Special examination of any insured depository institution

In addition to the examinations authorized under paragraph (2), any examiner appointed under paragraph (1) shall have power, on behalf of the Corporation, to make any special examination of any insured depository institution whenever the Board of Directors determines a special examination of any such depository institution is necessary to determine the condition of such depository institution for insurance purposes.

(4) Examination of affiliates

(A) In general

In making any examination under paragraph (2) or (3), any examiner appointed under paragraph (1) shall have power, on behalf of the Corporation, to make such examinations of the affairs of any affiliate of any depository institution as may be necessary to disclose fully—

(i) the relationship between such depository institution and any such affiliate; and

(ii) the effect of such relationship on the depository institution.

(B) Commitment by foreign banks to allow examinations of affiliates

No branch or depository institution subsidiary of a foreign bank may become an insured depository institution unless such foreign bank submits a written binding commitment to the Board of Directors to permit any examination of any affiliate of such branch or depository institution subsidiary pursuant to subparagraph (A) to the extent determined by the Board of Directors to be necessary to carry out the purposes of this chapter.

(5) Examination of insured State branches

The Board of Directors shall—

(A) coordinate examinations of insured State branches of foreign banks with examinations conducted by the Board of Governors of the Federal Reserve System under section 3105(c)(1) of this title; and

(B) to the extent possible, participate in any simultaneous examination of the United States operations of a foreign bank requested by the Board under such section.

(6) Power and duty of examiners

Each examiner appointed under paragraph (1) shall—

(A) have power to make a thorough examination of any insured depository institution or affiliate under paragraph (2), (3), (4), or (5); and

(B) shall make a full and detailed report of condition of any insured depository institution or affiliate examined to the Corporation.

(7) Power of claim agents

Each claim agent appointed under paragraph (1) shall have power to investigate and examine all claims for insured deposits.

(c) Administration of oaths and affirmations; evidence; subpoena powers

In connection with examinations of insured depository institutions and any State nonmember bank, savings association, or other institution making application to become insured depository institutions and affiliates thereof, or with other types of investigations to determine compliance with applicable law and regulations, the appropriate Federal banking agency, or its designated representatives, are authorized to administer oaths and affirmations, and to examine and to take and preserve testimony under oath as to any matter in respect to the affairs or ownership of any such bank or institution or affiliate thereof, and to exercise such other powers as are set forth in section 1818(n) of this title.

(d) Annual on-site examinations of all insured depository institutions required

(1) In general

The appropriate Federal banking agency shall, not less than once during each 12–month period, conduct a full-scope, on-site examination of each insured depository institution.

(2) Examinations by corporation

Paragraph (1) shall not apply during any 12–month period in which the Corporation has conducted a full-scope, on-site examination of the insured depository institution.

(3) State examinations acceptable

The examinations required by paragraph (1) may be conducted in alternate 12–month periods, as appropriate, if the appropriate Federal banking agency determines that an examination of the insured depository institution conducted by the State during the intervening 12–month period carries out the purpose of this subsection.

(4) 18–month rule for certain small institutions

Paragraphs (1), (2), and (3) shall apply with "18–month" substituted for "12–month" if—

(A) the insured depository institution has total assets of less than $500,000,000;

(B) the institution is well capitalized, as defined in section 1831o of this title;

(C) when the institution was most recently examined, it was found to be well managed, and its composite condition—

(i) was found to be outstanding; or

(ii) was found to be outstanding or good, in the case of an insured depository institution that has total assets of not more than $100,000,000;

(D) the insured institution is not currently subject to a formal enforcement proceeding or order by the Corporation or the appropriate Federal banking agency; and

(E) no person acquired control of the institution during the 12–month period in which a full-scope, on-site examination would be required but for this paragraph.

(5) Certain government-controlled institutions exempted

Paragraph (1) does not apply to—

(A) any institution for which the Corporation or the Resolution Trust Corporation is conservator; or

(B) any bridge bank, none of the voting securities of which are owned by a person or agency other than the Corporation or the Resolution Trust Corporation.

(6) Coordinated examinations

To minimize the disruptive effects of examinations on the operations of insured depository institutions—

(A) each appropriate Federal banking agency shall, to the extent practicable and consistent with principles of safety and soundness and the public interest—

(i) coordinate examinations to be conducted by that agency at an insured depository institution and its affiliates;

(ii) coordinate with the other appropriate Federal banking agencies in the conduct of such examinations;

(iii) work to coordinate with the appropriate State bank supervisor—

(I) the conduct of all examinations made pursuant to this subsection; and

(II) the number, types, and frequency of reports required to be submitted to such agencies and supervisors by insured depository institutions, and the type and amount of information required to be included in such reports; and

(iv) use copies of reports of examinations of insured depository institutions made by any other Federal banking agency or appropriate State bank supervisor to eliminate duplicative requests for information; and

(B) not later than 2 years after September 23, 1994, the Federal banking agencies shall jointly establish and implement a system for determining which one of the Federal banking agencies or State bank supervisors shall be the lead agency responsible for managing a unified examination of each insured depository institution and its affiliates, as required by this subsection.

(7) Separate examinations permitted

Notwithstanding paragraph (6), each appropriate Federal banking agency may conduct a separate examination in an emergency or under other exigent circumstances, or when the agency believes that a violation of law may have occurred.

(8) Report

At the time the system provided for in paragraph (6) is established, the Federal banking agencies shall submit a joint report describing the system to the Committee on Banking, Housing, and Urban Affairs of the Senate and the Committee on Banking, Finance and Urban Affairs of the House of Representatives. Thereafter, the Federal banking agencies shall annually submit a joint report to the Committee on Banking, Housing, and Urban Affairs of the Senate and the Committee on Banking, Finance and Urban Affairs of the House of Representatives regarding the progress of the agencies in implementing the system and indicating areas in which enhancements to the system, including legislature improvements, would be appropriate.

(9) Standards for determining adequacy of State examinations

The Federal Financial Institutions Examination Council shall issue guidelines establishing standards to be used at the discretion of the appropriate Federal banking agency for purposes of making a determination under paragraph (3).

(10) Agencies authorized to increase maximum asset amount of institutions for certain purposes

At any time after the end of the 2–year period beginning on September 23, 1994, the appropriate Federal banking agency, in the agency's discretion, may increase the maximum amount limitation contained in paragraph (4)(C)(ii), by regulation, from $100,000,000 to an amount not to exceed $500,000,000 for purposes of such paragraph, if the agency determines that the greater amount would be consistent with the principles of safety and soundness for insured depository institutions.

(e) Examination fees

(1) Regular and special examinations of depository institutions

The cost of conducting any regular examination or special examination of any depository institution under subsection (b)(2), (b)(3), or (d) of this section may be assessed by the Corporation against the institution to meet the Corporation's expenses in carrying out such examinations.

(2) Examination of affiliates

The cost of conducting any examination of any affiliate of any insured depository institution under subsection (b)(4) of this section may be assessed by the Corporation against each affiliate which is examined to meet the Corporation's expenses in carrying out such examination.

(3) Assessment against depository institution in case of affiliate's refusal to pay

(A) In general

Subject to subparagraph (B), if any affiliate of any insured depository institution—

(i) refuses to pay any assessment under paragraph (2); or

(ii) fails to pay any such assessment before the end of the 60–day period beginning on the date the affiliate receives notice of the assessment,

the Corporation may assess such cost against, and collect such cost from, the depository institution.

(B) Affiliate of more than 1 depository institution

If any affiliate referred to in subparagraph (A) is an affiliate of more than 1 insured depository institution, the assessment under subparagraph (A) may be assessed against the depository institutions in such proportions as the Corporation determines to be appropriate.

(4) Civil money penalty for affiliate's refusal to cooperate

(A) Penalty imposed

If any affiliate of any insured depository institution—

(i) refuses to permit an examiner appointed by the Board of Directors under subsection (b)(1) of this section to conduct an examination; or

(ii) refuses to provide any information required to be disclosed in the course of any examination,

the depository institution shall forfeit and pay a penalty of not more than $5,000 for each day that any such refusal continues.

(B) Assessment and collection

Any penalty imposed under subparagraph (A) shall be assessed and collected by the Corporation in the manner provided in section 1818(i)(2) of this title.

(5) Deposits of examination assessment

Amounts received by the Corporation under this subsection (other than paragraph (4)) may be deposited in the manner provided in section 1823 of this title.

(f) Preservation of agency records

(1) In general

A Federal banking agency may cause any and all records, papers, or documents kept by the agency or in the possession or custody of the agency to be—

(A) photographed or microphotographed or otherwise reproduced upon film; or

(B) preserved in any electronic medium or format which is capable of—

(i) being read or scanned by computer; and

(ii) being reproduced from such electronic medium or format by printing any other form of reproduction of electronically stored data.

(2) Treatment as original records

Any photographs, microphotographs, or photographic film or copies thereof described in paragraph (1)(A) or reproduction of electronically stored data described in paragraph (1)(B) shall be deemed to be an original record for all purposes, including introduction in evidence in all State and Federal courts or administrative agencies, and shall be admissible to prove any act, transaction, occurrence, or event therein recorded.

(3) Authority of the Federal banking agencies

Any photographs, microphotographs, or photographic film or copies thereof described in paragraph (1)(A) or reproduction of electronically stored data described in paragraph (1)(B) shall be preserved in such manner as the Federal banking agency shall prescribe, and the original records, papers, or documents may be destroyed or otherwise disposed of as the Federal banking agency may direct.

(g) Authority to prescribe regulations and definitions

Except to the extent that authority under this chapter is conferred on any of the Federal banking agencies other than the Corporation, the Corporation may—

(1) prescribe regulations to carry out this chapter; and

(2) by regulation define terms as necessary to carry out this chapter.

(h) Coordination of examination authority

(1) State bank supervisors of home and host States

(A) Home State of bank

The appropriate State bank supervisor of the home State of an insured State bank has authority to examine and supervise the bank.

(B) Host State branches

The State bank supervisor of the home State of an insured State bank and any State bank supervisor of an appropriate host State shall exercise its respective authority to supervise and examine the branches of the bank in a host State in accordance with the terms of any applicable cooperative agreement between the home State bank supervisor and the State bank supervisor of the relevant host State.

(C) Supervisory fees

Except as expressly provided in a cooperative agreement between the State bank supervisors of the home State and any host State of an insured State bank, only the State bank supervisor of the home State of an insured State bank may levy or charge State supervisory fees on the bank.

(2) Host State examination

(A) In general

With respect to a branch operated in a host State by an out-of-State insured State bank that resulted from an interstate merger transaction approved under section 1831u of this title, or that was established in such State pursuant to section 5155(g) of the Revised Statutes of the United States, the third undesignated paragraph of section 9 of the Federal Reserve Act or section 1828(d)(4) of this title, the appropriate State bank supervisor of such host State may—

(i) with written notice to the State bank supervisor of the bank's home State and subject to the terms of any applicable cooperative agreement with the State bank supervisor of such home State, examine such branch for the purpose of determining compliance with host State laws that are applicable pursuant to section 1831a(j) of this title, including those that govern community reinvestment, fair lending, and consumer protection; and

(ii) if expressly permitted under and subject to the terms of a cooperative agreement with the State bank supervisor of the bank's home State or if such out-of-State insured State bank has been determined to be in a troubled condition by either the State bank supervisor of the bank's home State or the bank's appropriate Federal banking agency, participate in the examination of the bank by the State bank supervisor of the bank's home State to ascertain that the activities of the branch in such host State are not conducted in an unsafe or unsound manner.

(B) Notice of determination

(i) In general

The State bank supervisor of the home State of an insured State bank shall notify the State bank supervisor of each host State of the bank if there has been a final determination that the bank is in a troubled condition.

(ii) Timing of notice

The State bank supervisor of the home State of an insured State bank shall provide notice under clause (i) as soon as is reasonably possible, but in all cases not later than 15 business days after the date on which the State bank supervisor has made such final determination or has received written notification of such final determination.

(3) Host State enforcement

If the State bank supervisor of a host State determines that a branch of an out-of-State insured State bank is violating any law of the host State that is applicable to such branch pursuant to section 1831a(j) of this title, including a law that governs community reinvestment, fair lending, or consumer protection, the State bank supervisor of the host State or, to the extent authorized by the law of the host State, a host State law enforcement officer may, with written notice to the State bank supervisor of the bank's home State and subject to the terms of any applicable cooperative agreement with the State bank supervisor of the bank's home State, undertake such enforcement actions and proceedings as would be permitted under the law of the host State as if the branch were a bank chartered by that host State.

(4) Cooperative agreement

(A) In general

The State bank supervisors from 2 or more States may enter into cooperative agreements to facilitate State regulatory supervision of State banks, including cooperative agreements relating to the coordination of examinations and joint participation in examinations.

(B) Definition

For purposes of this subsection, the term "cooperative agreement" means a written agreement that is signed by the home State bank supervisor and the host State bank supervisor to facilitate State regulatory supervision of State banks, and includes nationwide or multi-State cooperative agreements and cooperative agreements solely between the home State and host State.

(C) Rule of construction

Except for State bank supervisors, no provision of this subsection relating to such cooperative agreements shall be construed as limiting in any way the authority of home State and host State law enforcement officers, regulatory supervisors, or other officials that have not signed such cooperative agreements to enforce host State laws that are applicable to a branch of an out-of-State insured State bank located in the host State pursuant to section 1831a(j) of this title.

(5) Federal regulatory authority

No provision of this subsection shall be construed as limiting in any way the authority of any Federal banking agency.

(6) State taxation authority not affected

No provision of this subsection shall be construed as affecting the authority of any State or political subdivision of any State to adopt, apply, or administer any tax or method of taxation to any bank, bank holding company, or foreign bank, or any affiliate of any bank, bank holding company, or foreign bank, to the extent that such tax or tax method is otherwise permissible by or under the Constitution of the United States or other Federal law.

(7) Definitions

For purpose of this section, the following definitions shall apply:

(A) Host state, home state, out-of-state bank

The terms "host State", "home State", and "out-of-State bank" have the same meanings as in section 1831u(g) of this title.

(B) State supervisory fees

The term "State supervisory fees" means assessments, examination fees, branch fees, license fees, and all other fees that are levied or charged by a State bank supervisor directly upon an insured State bank or upon branches of an insured State bank.

(C) Troubled condition

Solely for purposes of paragraph (2)(B), an insured State bank has been determined to be in "troubled condition" if the bank—

(i) has a composite rating, as determined in its most recent report of examination, of 4 or 5 under the Uniform Financial Institutions Ratings System;

(ii) is subject to a proceeding initiated by the Corporation for termination or suspension of deposit insurance; or

(iii) is subject to a proceeding initiated by the State bank supervisor of the bank's home State to vacate, revoke, or terminate the charter of the bank, or to liquidate the bank, or to appoint a receiver for the bank.

(D) Final determination

For purposes of paragraph (2)(B), the term "final determination" means the transmittal of a report of examination to the bank or transmittal of official notice of proceedings to the bank.

(i) Flood insurance compliance by insured depository institutions

(1) Examinations

The appropriate Federal banking agency shall, during each scheduled on-site examination required by this section, determine whether the insured depository institution is complying with the requirements of the national flood insurance program.

(2) Report

(A) Requirement

Not later than 1 year after September 23, 1994, and biennially thereafter for the next 4 years, each appropriate Federal banking agency shall submit a report to the Congress on compliance by insured depository institutions with the requirements of the national flood insurance program.

(B) Contents

Each report submitted under this paragraph shall include a description of the methods used to determine compliance, the number of institutions examined during the reporting year, a listing and total number of institutions found not to be in compliance, actions taken to correct incidents of noncompliance, and an analysis of compliance, including a discussion of any trends, patterns, and problems, and recommendations regarding reasonable actions to improve the efficiency of the examinations processes.

(j) Consultation among examiners

(1) In general

Each appropriate Federal banking agency shall take such action as may be necessary to ensure that examiners employed by the agency—

(A) consult on examination activities with respect to any depository institution; and

(B) achieve an agreement and resolve any inconsistencies in the recommendations to be given to such institution as a consequence of any examinations.

(2) Examiner-in-charge

Each appropriate Federal banking agency shall consider appointing an examiner-in-charge with respect to a depository institution to ensure consultation on examination activities among all of the examiners of that agency involved in examinations of the institution.

(k) One-year restrictions on Federal examiners of financial institutions

(1) In general

In addition to other applicable restrictions set forth in Title 18, the penalties set forth in paragraph (6) of this subsection shall apply to any person who—

(A) was an officer or employee (including any special Government employee) of a Federal banking agency or a Federal reserve bank;

(B) served 2 or more months during the final 12 months of his or her employment with such agency or entity as the senior examiner (or a functionally equivalent position) of a depository institution or depository institution holding company with continuing, broad responsibility for the examination (or inspection) of that depository institution or depository institution holding company on behalf of the relevant agency or Federal reserve bank; and

(C) within 1 year after the termination date of his or her service or employment with such agency or entity, knowingly accepts compensation as an employee, officer, director, or consultant from—

(i) such depository institution, any depository institution holding company that controls such depository institution, or any other company that controls such depository institution; or

(ii) such depository institution holding company or any depository institution that is controlled by such depository institution holding company.

(2) Definitions

For purposes of this subsection—

(A) the term "depository institution" includes an uninsured branch or agency of a foreign bank, if such branch or agency is located in any State; and

(B) the term "depository institution holding company" includes any foreign bank or company described in section 8(a) of the International Banking Act of 1978.

(3) Rules of construction

For purposes of this subsection, a foreign bank shall be deemed to control any branch or agency of the foreign bank, and a person shall be deemed to act as a consultant for a depository institution, depository institution holding company, or other company, only if such person directly works on matters for, or on behalf of, such depository institution, depository institution holding company, or other company.

(4) Regulations

(A) In general

Each Federal banking agency shall prescribe rules or regulations to administer and carry out this subsection, including rules, regulations, or guidelines to define the scope of persons referred to in paragraph (1)(B).

(B) Consultation required

The Federal banking agencies shall consult with each other for the purpose of assuring that the rules and regulations issued by the agencies under subparagraph (A) are, to the extent possible, consistent, comparable, and practicable, taking into account any differences in the supervisory programs utilized by the agencies for the supervision of depository institutions and depository institution holding companies.

(5) Waiver

(A) Agency authority

A Federal banking agency may grant a waiver, on a case by case basis, of the restriction imposed by this subsection to any officer or employee (including any special Government employee) of that agency, and the Board of Governors of the Federal Reserve System may grant a waiver of the restriction imposed by this subsection to any officer or employee of a Federal reserve bank, if the head of such agency certifies in writing that granting the waiver would not affect the integrity of the supervisory program of the relevant Federal banking agency.

(B) Definition

For purposes of this paragraph, the head of an agency is—

(i) the Comptroller of the Currency, in the case of the Office of the Comptroller of the Currency;

(ii) the Chairman of the Board of Governors of the Federal Reserve System, in the case of the Board of Governors of the Federal Reserve System;

(iii) the Chairperson of the Board of Directors, in the case of the Corporation; and

(iv) the Director of the Office of Thrift Supervision, in the case of the Office of Thrift Supervision.

(6) Penalties

(A) In general

In addition to any other administrative, civil, or criminal remedy or penalty that may otherwise apply, whenever a Federal banking agency determines that a person subject to paragraph (1) has become associated, in the manner described in paragraph (1)(C), with a depository institution, depository institution holding company, or other company for which such agency serves as the appropriate Federal banking agency, the agency shall impose upon such person one or more of the following penalties:

(i) Industry-wide prohibition order

The Federal banking agency shall serve a written notice or order in accordance with and subject to the provisions of section 1818(e)(4) of this title for written notices or orders under paragraph (1) or (2) of section 1818(e) of this title, upon such person of the intention of the agency—

(I) to remove such person from office or to prohibit such person from further participation in the conduct of the affairs of the depository institution, depository institution holding company, or other company for a period of up to 5 years; and

(II) to prohibit any further participation by such person, in any manner, in the conduct of the affairs of any insured depository institution for a period of up to 5 years.

(ii) Civil monetary penalty

The Federal banking agency may, in an administrative proceeding or civil action in an appropriate United States district court, impose on such person a civil monetary penalty of not more than $250,000. Any administrative proceeding under this clause shall be conducted in accordance with section 1818(i) of this title. In lieu of an action by the Federal banking agency under this clause, the Attorney General of the United States may bring a civil action under this clause in the appropriate United States district court.

(B) Scope of prohibition order

Any person subject to an order issued under subparagraph (A)(i) shall be subject to paragraphs (6) and (7) of section 1818(e) of this title in the same manner and to the same extent as a person subject to an order issued under such section.

(C) Definitions

Solely for purposes of this paragraph, the "appropriate Federal banking agency" for a company that is not a depository institution or depository institution holding company shall be the Federal banking agency on whose behalf the person described in paragraph (1) performed the functions described in paragraph (1)(B).

§ 1820a. Examination of investment companies

(a) Exclusive Commission authority

Except as provided in subsection (c), a Federal banking agency may not inspect or examine any registered investment company that is not a bank holding company or a savings and loan holding company.

(b) Examination results and other information

The Commission shall provide to any Federal banking agency, upon request, the results of any examination, reports, records, or other information with respect to any registered investment company to the extent necessary for the agency to carry out its statutory responsibilities.

(c) Certain examinations authorized

Nothing in this section shall prevent the Corporation, if the Corporation finds it necessary to determine the condition of an insured depository institution for insurance purposes, from examining an affiliate of any insured depository institution, pursuant to its authority under section 1820(b)(4) of this title, as may be necessary to disclose fully the relationship between the insured depository institution and the affiliate, and the effect of such relationship on the insured depository institution.

(d) Definitions

For purposes of this section, the following definitions shall apply:

(1) Bank holding company

The term "bank holding company" has the meaning given the term in section 1841 of this title.

(2) Commission

The term "Commission" means the Securities and Exchange Commission.

(3) Corporation

The term "Corporation" means the Federal Deposit Insurance Corporation.

(4) Federal banking agency

The term "Federal banking agency" has the meaning given the term in section 1813(z) of this title.

(5) Insured depository institution

The term "insured depository institution" has the meaning given the term in section 1813(c) of this title.

(6) Registered investment company

The term "registered investment company" means an investment company that is registered with the Commission under the Investment Company Act of 1940 [15 U.S.C.A. § 80a–1 et seq.].

(7) Savings and loan holding company

The term "savings and loan holding company" has the meaning given the term in section 1467a(a)(1)(D) of this title.

§ 1821.　Insurance funds—DFA § 335

(a) Deposit insurance

(1) Insured amounts payable

(A) In general

The Corporation shall insure the deposits of all insured depository institutions as provided in this chapter.

(B) Net amount of insured deposit

The net amount due to any depositor at an insured depository institution shall not exceed the standard maximum deposit insurance amount as determined in accordance with subparagraphs (C), (D), (E) and (F) and paragraph (3).

(C) Aggregation of deposits

For the purpose of determining the net amount due to any depositor under subparagraph (B), the Corporation shall aggregate the amounts of all deposits in the insured depository institution which are maintained by a depositor in the same capacity and the same right for the benefit of the depositor either in the name of the depositor or in the name of any other person, other than any amount in a trust fund described in paragraph (1) or (2) of section 1817(i) of this title or any funds described in section 1817(i)(3) of this title.

(D) Coverage for certain employee benefit plan deposits

(i) Pass-through insurance

The Corporation shall provide pass-through deposit insurance for the deposits of any employee benefit plan.

(ii) Prohibition on acceptance of benefit plan deposits

An insured depository institution that is not well capitalized or adequately capitalized may not accept employee benefit plan deposits.

(iii) Definitions

For purposes of this subparagraph, the following definitions shall apply:

(I) Capital standards

The terms "well capitalized" and "adequately capitalized" have the same meanings as in section 1831o of this title.

(II) Employee benefit plan

The term "employee benefit plan" has the same meaning as in paragraph (5)(B)(ii), and includes any eligible deferred compensation plan described in section 457 of title 26.

(III) Pass-through deposit insurance

The term "pass-through deposit insurance" means, with respect to an employee benefit plan, deposit insurance coverage based on the interest of each participant, in accordance with regulations issued by the Corporation.

(E) Standard maximum deposit insurance amount defined

For purposes of this chapter, the term "standard maximum deposit insurance amount" means $100,000, adjusted as provided under subparagraph (F) after March 31, 2010.

(F) Inflation adjustment

(i) In general

By April 1 of 2010, and the 1st day of each subsequent 5-year period, the Board of Directors and the National Credit Union Administration Board shall jointly consider the factors set forth under clause (v), and, upon determining that an inflation adjustment is appropriate, shall jointly prescribe the amount by which the standard maximum deposit insurance amount and the standard maximum share insurance amount (as defined in section 1787 (k) of this title) applicable to any depositor at an insured depository institution shall be increased by calculating the product of—

(I) $100,000; and

(II) the ratio of the published annual value of the Personal Consumption Expenditures Chain-Type Price Index (or any successor index thereto), published by the Department of Commerce, for the calendar year preceding the year in which the adjustment is calculated under this clause, to the published annual value of such index for the calendar year preceding April 1, 2006.

The values used in the calculation under subclause (II) shall be, as of the date of the calculation, the values most recently published by the Department of Commerce.

(ii) Rounding

If the amount determined under clause (ii) for any period is not a multiple of $10,000, the amount so determined shall be rounded down to the nearest $10,000.

(iii) Publication and report to the Congress

Not later than April 5 of any calendar year in which an adjustment is required to be calculated under clause (i) to the standard maximum deposit insurance amount and the

standard maximum share insurance amount under such clause, the Board of Directors and the National Credit Union Administration Board shall—

(I) publish in the Federal Register the standard maximum deposit insurance amount, the standard maximum share insurance amount, and the amount of coverage under paragraph (3)(A) and section 1787 (k)(3) of this title, as so calculated; and

(II) jointly submit a report to the Congress containing the amounts described in subclause (I).

(iv) 6-month implementation period

Unless an Act of Congress enacted before July 1 of the calendar year in which an adjustment is required to be calculated under clause (i) provides otherwise, the increase in the standard maximum deposit insurance amount and the standard maximum share insurance amount shall take effect on January 1 of the year immediately succeeding such calendar year.

(v) Inflation adjustment consideration

In making any determination under clause (i) to increase the standard maximum deposit insurance amount and the standard maximum share insurance amount, the Board of Directors and the National Credit Union Administration Board shall jointly consider—

(I) the overall state of the Deposit Insurance Fund and the economic conditions affecting insured depository institutions;

(II) potential problems affecting insured depository institutions; or

(III) whether the increase will cause the reserve ratio of the fund to fall below 1.15 percent of estimated insured deposits.

(2) Government depositors

(A) In general

Notwithstanding any limitation in this chapter or in any other provision of law relating to the amount of deposit insurance available to any 1 depositor—

(i) a government depositor shall, for the purpose of determining the amount of insured deposits under this subsection, be deemed to be a depositor separate and distinct from any other officer, employee, or agent of the United States or any public unit referred to in subparagraph (B); and

(ii) except as provided in subparagraph (C), the deposits of a government depositor shall be insured in an amount equal to the standard maximum deposit insurance amount (as determined under paragraph (1)).

(B) Government depositor

In this paragraph, the term "government depositor" means a depositor that is—

(i) an officer, employee, or agent of the United States having official custody of public funds and lawfully investing or depositing the same in time and savings deposits in an insured depository institution;

(ii) an officer, employee, or agent of any State of the United States, or of any county, municipality, or political subdivision thereof having official custody of public funds and lawfully investing or depositing the same in time and savings deposits in an insured depository institution in such State;

(iii) an officer, employee, or agent of the District of Columbia having official custody of public funds and lawfully investing or depositing the same in time and savings deposits in an insured depository institution in the District of Columbia;

(iv) an officer, employee, or agent of the Commonwealth of Puerto Rico, of the Virgin Islands, of American Samoa, of the Trust Territory of the Pacific Islands, or of Guam, or of any county, municipality, or political subdivision thereof having official custody of public funds and lawfully investing or depositing the same in time and savings deposits in an insured depository institution in the Commonwealth of Puerto Rico, the Virgin Islands, American Samoa, the Trust Territory of the Pacific Islands, or Guam, respectively; or

(v) an officer, employee, or agent of any Indian tribe (as defined in section 1452 (c) of title 25) or agency thereof having official custody of tribal funds and lawfully investing or depositing the same in time and savings deposits in an insured depository institution.

(C) Authority to limit deposits

The Corporation may limit the aggregate amount of funds that may be invested or deposited in deposits in any insured depository institution by any government depositor on the basis of the size of any such bank in terms of its assets: Provided, however, such limitation may be exceeded by the pledging of acceptable securities to the government depositor when and where required.

(3) Certain retirement accounts

(A) In general

Notwithstanding any limitation in this chapter relating to the amount of deposit insurance available for the account of any 1 depositor, deposits in an insured depository institution made in connection with—

(i) any individual retirement account described in section 408(a) of Title 26;

(ii) subject to the exception contained in paragraph (1)(D)(ii), any eligible deferred compensation plan described in section 457 of Title 26; and

(iii) any individual account plan defined in section 1002(34) of Title 29, and any plan described in section 401(d) of Title 26, to the extent that participants and beneficiaries under such plan have the right to direct the investment of assets held in individual accounts maintained on their behalf by the plan,

shall be aggregated and insured in an amount not to exceed $250,000 (which amount shall be subject to inflation adjustments as provided in paragraph (1)(F), except that $250,000 shall be substituted for $100,000 wherever such term appears in such paragraph) per participant per insured depository institution.

(B) Amounts taken into account

Purposes of subparagraph (A), the amount aggregated for insurance coverage under this paragraph shall consist of the present vested and ascertainable interest of each participant under the plan, excluding any remainder interest created by, or as a result of, the plan.

(4) Deposit Insurance Fund

(A) Establishment

There is established the Deposit Insurance Fund, which the Corporation shall—

(i) maintain and administer;

(ii) use to carry out its insurance purposes, in the manner provided by this subsection; and

(iii) invest in accordance with section 1823(a) of this title.

(B) Uses

The Deposit Insurance Fund shall be available to the Corporation for use with respect to insured depository institutions the deposits of which are insured by the Deposit Insurance Fund.

(C) Limitation on use

Notwithstanding any provision of law other than section 1823(c)(4)(G) of this title, the Deposit Insurance Fund shall not be used in any manner to benefit any shareholder or affiliate (other than an insured depository institution that receives assistance in accordance with the provisions of this chapter) of—

(i) any insured depository institution for which the Corporation has been appointed conservator or receiver, in connection with any type of resolution by the Corporation;

(ii) any other insured depository institution in default or in danger of default, in connection with any type of resolution by the Corporation; or

(iii) any insured depository institution, in connection with the provision of assistance under this section or section 1823 of this title with respect to such institution, except that this clause shall not prohibit any assistance to any insured depository institution that is not in default, or that is not in danger of default, that is acquiring (as defined in section 1823(f)(8)(B) of this title) another insured depository institution.

(D) Deposits

All amounts assessed against insured depository institutions by the Corporation shall be deposited into the Deposit Insurance Fund.

(5) Certain investment contracts not treated as insured deposits

(A) In general

A liability of an insured depository institution shall not be treated as an insured deposit if the liability arises under any insured depository institution investment contract between any insured depository institution and any employee benefit plan which expressly permits benefit-responsive withdrawals or transfers.

(B) Definitions

For purposes of subparagraph (A)—

(i) Benefit-responsive withdrawals or transfers

The term "benefit-responsive withdrawals or transfers" means any withdrawal or transfer of funds (consisting of any portion of the principal and any interest credited at a rate guaranteed by the insured depository institution investment contract) during the period in which any guaranteed rate is in effect, without substantial penalty or adjustment, to pay benefits provided by the employee benefit plan or to permit a plan participant or beneficiary to redirect the investment of his or her account balance.

(ii) Employee benefit plan

The term "employee benefit plan"—

(I) has the meaning given to such term in section 1002 (3) of title 29; and

(II) includes any plan described in section 401 (d) of title 26.

(6), (7) Repealed. Pub.L. 109-173, § 8(a)(11)(C), Feb. 15, 2006, 119 Stat. 3612

(8) Redesignated (5)

(b) Liquidation as closing of depository institution

For the purposes of this chapter an insured depository institution shall be deemed to have been closed on account of inability to meet the demands of its depositors in any case in which it has been closed for the purpose of liquidation without adequate provision being made for payment of its depositors.

(c) Appointment of Corporation as conservator or receiver

(1) In general

Notwithstanding any other provision of Federal law, the law of any State, or the constitution of any State, the Corporation may accept appointment and act as conservator or receiver for any insured depository institution upon appointment in the manner provided in paragraph (2) or (3).

(2) Federal depository institutions

(A) Appointment

(i) Conservator

The Corporation may, at the discretion of the supervisory authority, be appointed conservator of any insured Federal depository institution and the Corporation may accept such appointment.

(ii) Receiver

The Corporation shall be appointed receiver, and shall accept such appointment, whenever a receiver is appointed for the purpose of liquidation or winding up the affairs of an insured Federal depository institution by the appropriate Federal banking agency, notwithstanding any other provision of Federal law (other than section 1441a of this title).

(B) Additional powers

In addition to and not in derogation of the powers conferred and the duties imposed by this section on the Corporation as conservator or receiver, the Corporation, to the extent not inconsistent with such powers and duties, shall have any other power conferred on or any duty (which is related to the exercise of such power) imposed on a conservator or receiver for any Federal depository institution under any other provision of law.

(C) Corporation not subject to any other agency

When acting as conservator or receiver pursuant to an appointment described in subparagraph (A), the Corporation shall not be subject to the direction or supervision of any other agency or department of the United States or any State in the exercise of the Corporation's rights, powers, and privileges.

(D) Depository institution in conservatorship subject to banking agency supervision

Notwithstanding subparagraph (C), any Federal depository institution for which the Corporation has been appointed conservator shall remain subject to the supervision of the appropriate Federal banking agency.

(3) Insured State depository institutions

(A) Appointment by appropriate State supervisor

Whenever the authority having supervision of any insured State depository institution appoints a conservator or receiver for such institution and tenders appointment to the Corporation, the Corporation may accept such appointment.

(B) Additional powers

In addition to the powers conferred and the duties related to the exercise of such powers imposed by State law on any conservator or receiver appointed under the law of such State for an insured State depository institution, the Corporation, as conservator or receiver pursuant to an appointment described in subparagraph (A), shall have the powers conferred and the duties imposed by this section on the Corporation as conservator or receiver.

(C) Corporation not subject to any other agency

When acting as conservator or receiver pursuant to an appointment described in subparagraph (A), the Corporation shall not be subject to the direction or supervision of any other agency or department of the United States or any State in the exercise of its rights, powers, and privileges.

(D) Depository institution in conservatorship subject to banking agency supervision

Notwithstanding subparagraph (C), any insured State depository institution for which the Corporation has been appointed conservator shall remain subject to the supervision of the appropriate State bank or savings association supervisor.

(4) Appointment of Corporation by the Corporation

Except as otherwise provided in section 1441a of this title and notwithstanding any other provision of Federal law, the law of any State, or the constitution of any State, the Corporation may appoint itself as sole conservator or receiver of any insured State depository institution if—

(A) the Corporation determines—

(i) that—

(I) a conservator, receiver, or other legal custodian has been appointed for such institution;

(II) such institution has been subject to the appointment of any such conservator, receiver, or custodian for a period of at least 15 consecutive days; and

(III) 1 or more of the depositors in such institution is unable to withdraw any amount of any insured deposit; or

(ii) that such institution has been closed by or under the laws of any State; and

(B) the Corporation determines that 1 or more of the grounds specified in paragraph (5)—

(i) existed with respect to such institution at the time—

(I) the conservator, receiver, or other legal custodian was appointed; or

(II) such institution was closed; or

(ii) exist at any time—

(I) during the appointment of the conservator, receiver, or other legal custodian; or

(II) while such institution is closed.

(5) Grounds for appointing conservator or receiver

The grounds for appointing a conservator or receiver (which may be the Corporation) for any insured depository institution are as follows:

(A) Assets insufficient for obligations

The institution's assets are less than the institution's obligations to its creditors and others, including members of the institution.

(B) Substantial dissipation

Substantial dissipation of assets or earnings due to—

(i) any violation of any statute or regulation; or

(ii) any unsafe or unsound practice.

(C) Unsafe or unsound condition

An unsafe or unsound condition to transact business.

(D) Cease and desist orders

Any willful violation of a cease-and-desist order which has become final.

(E) Concealment

Any concealment of the institution's books, papers, records, or assets, or any refusal to submit the institution's books, papers, records, or affairs for inspection to any examin-

er or to any lawful agent of the appropriate Federal banking agency or State bank or savings association supervisor.

(F) Inability to meet obligations

The institution is likely to be unable to pay its obligations or meet its depositors' demands in the normal course of business.

(G) Losses

The institution has incurred or is likely to incur losses that will deplete all or substantially all of its capital, and there is no reasonable prospect for the institution to become adequately capitalized (as defined in section 1831o(b) of this title) without Federal assistance.

(H) Violations of law

Any violation of any law or regulation, or any unsafe or unsound practice or condition that is likely to—

(i) cause insolvency or substantial dissipation of assets or earnings;

(ii) weaken the institution's condition; or

(iii) otherwise seriously prejudice the interests of the institution's depositors or the deposit insurance fund.

(I) Consent

The institution, by resolution of its board of directors or its shareholders or members, consents to the appointment.

(J) Cessation of insured status

The institution ceases to be an insured institution.

(K) Undercapitalization

The institution is undercapitalized (as defined in section 1831o(b) of this title), and—

(i) has no reasonable prospect of becoming adequately capitalized (as defined in that section);

(ii) fails to become adequately capitalized when required to do so under section 1831o(f)(2)(A) of this title;

(iii) fails to submit a capital restoration plan acceptable to that agency within the time prescribed under section 1831o(e)(2)(D) of this title; or

(iv) materially fails to implement a capital restoration plan submitted and accepted under section 1831o(e)(2) of this title.

(L) The institution

(i) is critically undercapitalized, as defined in section 1831o(b) of this title; or

(ii) otherwise has substantially insufficient capital.

(M) Money laundering offense

The Attorney General notifies the appropriate Federal banking agency or the Corporation in writing that the insured depository institution has been found guilty of a criminal offense under section 1956 or 1957 of Title 18 or section 5322 or 5324 of Title 31.

(6) Appointment by Director of the Office of Thrift Supervision

(A) Conservator

The Corporation or the Resolution Trust Corporation may, at the discretion of the Director of the Office of Thrift Supervision, be appointed conservator and the Corporation may accept any such appointment.

(B) Receiver

Whenever the Director of the Office of Thrift Supervision appoints a receiver under the provisions of subparagraph (A) or (C) of section 1464(d)(2) of this title for the purpose of liquidation or winding up any savings association's affairs—

(i) before such date as is determined by the Chairperson of the Thrift Depositor Protection Oversight Board under section 1441a(b)(3)(A)(ii) of this title, the Resolution Trust Corporation shall be appointed;

(ii) on or after the date determined by the Chairperson of the Thrift Depositor Protection Oversight Board under section 1441a(b)(3)(A)(ii) of this title, the Resolution Trust Corporation shall be appointed if the Resolution Trust Corporation had been placed in control of the depository institution at any time before such date; and

(iii) on or after the date determined by the Chairperson of the Thrift Depositor Protection Oversight Board under section 1441a(b)(3)(A)(ii) of this title, the Corporation shall be appointed unless the Resolution Trust Corporation is required to be appointed under clause (ii).

(7) Judicial review

If the Corporation is appointed (including the appointment of the Corporation as receiver by the Board of Directors) as conservator or receiver of a depository institution under paragraph (4), (9), or (10), the depository institution may, not later than 30 days thereafter, bring an action in the United States district court for the judicial district in which the home office of such depository institution is located, or in the United States District Court for the District of Columbia, for an order requiring the Corporation to be removed as the conservator or receiver (regardless of how such appointment was made), and the court shall, upon the merits, dismiss such action or direct the Corporation to be removed as the conservator or receiver.

(8) Replacement of conservator of State depository institution—

(A) In general

In the case of any insured State depository institution for which the Corporation appointed itself as conservator pursuant to paragraph (4), the Corporation may, without any requirement of notice, hearing, or other action, replace itself as conservator with itself as receiver of such institution.

(B) Replacement treated as removal of incumbent

The replacement of a conservator with a receiver under subparagraph (A) shall be treated as the removal of the Corporation as conservator.

(C) Right of review of original appointment not affected

The replacement of a conservator with a receiver under subparagraph (A) shall not affect any right of the insured State depository institution to obtain review, pursuant to paragraph (7), of the original appointment of the conservator.

(9) Appropriate Federal banking agency may appoint Corporation as conservator or receiver for insured State depository institution to carry out section 1831o of this title.

(A) In general

The appropriate Federal banking agency may appoint the Corporation as sole receiver (or, subject to paragraph (11), sole conservator) of any insured State depository institution, after consultation with the appropriate State supervisor, if the appropriate Federal banking agency determines that—

(i) 1 or more of the grounds specified in subparagraphs (K) and (L) of paragraph (5) exist with respect to that institution; and

(ii) the appointment is necessary to carry out the purpose of section 1831o of this title.

(B) Nondelegation

The appropriate Federal banking agency shall not delegate any action under subparagraph (A).

(10) Corporation may appoint itself as conservator or receiver for insured depository institution to prevent loss to deposit insurance fund

The Board of Directors may appoint the Corporation as sole conservator or receiver of an insured depository institution, after consultation with the appropriate Federal banking agency and the appropriate State supervisor (if any), if the Board of Directors determines that—

(A) 1 or more of the grounds specified in any subparagraph of paragraph (5) exist with respect to the institution; and

(B) the appointment is necessary to reduce—

(i) the risk that the deposit insurance fund would incur a loss with respect to the insured depository institution, or

(ii) any loss that the deposit insurance fund is expected to incur with respect to that institution.

(11) Appropriate Federal banking agency shall not appoint conservator under certain provisions without giving Corporation opportunity to appoint receiver

The appropriate Federal banking agency shall not appoint a conservator for an insured depository institution under subparagraph (K) or (L) of paragraph (5) without the Corporation's consent unless the agency has given the Corporation 48 hours notice of the agency's intention to appoint the conservator and the grounds for the appointment.

(12) Directors not liable for acquiescing in appointment of conservator or receiver

The members of the board of directors of an insured depository institution shall not be liable to the institution's shareholders or creditors for acquiescing in or consenting in good faith to—

(A) the appointment of the Corporation or the Resolution Trust Corporation as conservator or receiver for that institution; or

(B) an acquisition or combination under section 1831o(f)(2)(A)(iii) of this title.

(13) Additional powers

In any case in which the Corporation is appointed conservator or receiver under paragraph (4), (6), (9), or (10) for any insured State depository institution—

(A) this section shall apply to the Corporation as conservator or receiver in the same manner and to the same extent as if that institution were a Federal depository institution for which the Corporation had been appointed conservator or receiver; and

(B) the Corporation as receiver of the institution may—

(i) liquidate the institution in an orderly manner; and

(ii) make any other disposition of any matter concerning the institution, as the Corporation determines is in the best interests of the institution, the depositors of the institution, and the Corporation.

(d) Powers and duties of Corporation as conservator or receiver

(1) Rulemaking authority of Corporation

The Corporation may prescribe such regulations as the Corporation determines to be appropriate regarding the conduct of conservatorships or receiverships.

(2) General powers

(A) Successor to institution

The Corporation shall, as conservator or receiver, and by operation of law, succeed to—

(i) all rights, titles, powers, and privileges of the insured depository institution, and of any stockholder, member, accountholder, depositor, officer, or director of such institution with respect to the institution and the assets of the institution; and

(ii) title to the books, records, and assets of any previous conservator or other legal custodian of such institution.

(B) Operate the institution

The Corporation may (subject to the provisions of section 1831q of this title), as conservator or receiver—

(i) take over the assets of and operate the insured depository institution with all the powers of the members or shareholders, the directors, and the officers of the institution and conduct all business of the institution;

(ii) collect all obligations and money due the institution;

(iii) perform all functions of the institution in the name of the institution which are consistent with the appointment as conservator or receiver; and

(iv) preserve and conserve the assets and property of such institution.

(C) Functions of institution's officers, directors, and shareholders

The Corporation may, by regulation or order, provide for the exercise of any function by any member or stockholder, director, or officer of any insured depository institution for which the Corporation has been appointed conservator or receiver.

(D) Powers as conservator

The Corporation may, as conservator, take such action as may be—

(i) necessary to put the insured depository institution in a sound and solvent condition; and

(ii) appropriate to carry on the business of the institution and preserve and conserve the assets and property of the institution.

(E) Additional powers as receiver

The Corporation may (subject to the provisions of section 1831q of this title), as receiver, place the insured depository institution in liquidation and proceed to realize upon the assets of the institution, having due regard to the conditions of credit in the locality.

(F) Organization of new institutions

The Corporation may, as receiver, with respect to any insured depository institution, organize a new depository institution under subsection (m) or a bridge depository institution under subsection (n).

(G) Merger; transfer of assets and liabilities

(i) In general

The Corporation may, as conservator or receiver—

(I) merge the insured depository institution with another insured depository institution; or

(II) subject to clause (ii), transfer any asset or liability of the institution in default (including assets and liabilities associated with any trust business) without any approval, assignment, or consent with respect to such transfer.

(ii) Approval by appropriate Federal banking agency

No transfer described in clause (i)(II) may be made to another depository institution (other than a new depository institution or a bridge depository institution established pursuant to subsection (m) or (n) of this section) without the approval of the appropriate Federal banking agency for such institution.

(H) Payment of valid obligations

The Corporation, as conservator or receiver, shall pay all valid obligations of the insured depository institution in accordance with the prescriptions and limitations of this chapter.

(I) Subpoena authority

(i) In general

The Corporation may, as conservator, receiver, or exclusive manager and for purposes of carrying out any power, authority, or duty with respect to an insured depository institution (including determining any claim against the institution and determining and realizing upon any asset of any person in the course of collecting money due the institution), exercise any power established under section 1818(n) of this title, and the provisions of such section shall apply with respect to the exercise of any such power under this subparagraph in the same manner as such provisions apply under such section.

(ii) Authority of board of directors

A subpoena or subpoena duces tecum may be issued under clause (i) only by, or with the written approval of, the Board of Directors or their designees (or, in the case of a subpoena or subpoena duces tecum issued by the Resolution Trust Corporation under this subparagraph and section 1441a(b)(4) of this title, only by, or with the written approval of, the Board of Directors of such Corporation or their designees).

(iii) Rule of construction

This subsection shall not be construed as limiting any rights that the Corporation, in any capacity, might otherwise have under section 1820(c) of this title.

(J) Incidental powers

The Corporation may, as conservator or receiver—

(i) exercise all powers and authorities specifically granted to conservators or receivers, respectively, under this chapter and such incidental powers as shall be necessary to carry out such powers; and

(ii) take any action authorized by this chapter, which the Corporation determines is in the best interests of the depository institution, its depositors, or the Corporation.

(K) Utilization of private sector

In carrying out its responsibilities in the management and disposition of assets from insured depository institutions, as conservator, receiver, or in its corporate capacity, the Corporation shall utilize the services of private persons, including real estate and loan portfolio asset management, property management, auction marketing, legal, and brokerage services, only if such services are available in the private sector and the Corporation determines utilization of such services is the most practicable, efficient, and cost effective.

(3) Authority of receiver to determine claims

(A) In general

The Corporation may, as receiver, determine claims in accordance with the requirements of this subsection and regulations prescribed under paragraph (4).

(B) Notice requirements

The receiver, in any case involving the liquidation or winding up of the affairs of a closed depository institution, shall—

(i) promptly publish a notice to the depository institution's creditors to present their claims, together with proof, to the receiver by a date specified in the notice which shall be not less than 90 days after the publication of such notice; and

(ii) republish such notice approximately 1 month and 2 months, respectively, after the publication under clause (i).

(C) Mailing required

The receiver shall mail a notice similar to the notice published under subparagraph (B)(i) at the time of such publication to any creditor shown on the institution's books—

(i) at the creditor's last address appearing in such books; or

(ii) upon discovery of the name and address of a claimant not appearing on the institution's books within 30 days after the discovery of such name and address.

(4) Rulemaking authority relating to determination of claims

(A) In general

The Corporation may prescribe regulations regarding the allowance or disallowance of claims by the receiver and providing for administrative determination of claims and review of such determination.

(B) Final settlement payment procedure

(i) In general

In the handling of receiverships of insured depository institutions, to maintain essential liquidity and to prevent financial disruption, the Corporation may, after the declaration of an institution's insolvency, settle all uninsured and unsecured claims on the receivership with a final settlement payment which shall constitute full payment and disposition of the Corporation's obligations to such claimants.

(ii) Final settlement payment

For purposes of clause (i), a final settlement payment shall be payment of an amount equal to the product of the final settlement payment rate and the amount of the uninsured and unsecured claim on the receivership; and

(iii) Final settlement payment rate

For purposes of clause (ii), the final settlement payment rate shall be a percentage rate reflecting an average of the Corporation's receivership recovery experience, determined by the Corporation in such a way that over such time period as the Corporation may deem appropriate, the Corporation in total will receive no more or less than it would have received in total as a general creditor standing in the place of insured depositors in each specific receivership.

(iv) Corporation authority

The Corporation may undertake such supervisory actions and promulgate such regulations as may be necessary to assure that the requirements of this section can be implemented with respect to each insured depository institution in the event of its insolvency.

(5) Procedures for determination of claims

(A) Determination period

(i) In general

Before the end of the 180–day period beginning on the date any claim against a depository institution is filed with the Corporation as receiver, the Corporation shall determine whether to allow or disallow the claim and shall notify the claimant of any determination with respect to such claim.

(ii) Extension of time

The period described in clause (i) may be extended by a written agreement between the claimant and the Corporation.

(iii) Mailing of notice sufficient

The requirements of clause (i) shall be deemed to be satisfied if the notice of any determination with respect to any claim is mailed to the last address of the claimant which appears—

(I) on the depository institution's books;

(II) in the claim filed by the claimant; or

(III) in documents submitted in proof of the claim.

(iv) Contents of notice of disallowance

If any claim filed under clause (i) is disallowed, the notice to the claimant shall contain—

(I) a statement of each reason for the disallowance; and

(II) the procedures available for obtaining agency review of the determination to disallow the claim or judicial determination of the claim.

(B) Allowance of proven claims

The receiver shall allow any claim received on or before the date specified in the notice published under paragraph (3)(B)(i) by the receiver from any claimant which is proved to the satisfaction of the receiver.

(C) Disallowance of claims filed after end of filing period

(i) In general

Except as provided in clause (ii), claims filed after the date specified in the notice published under paragraph (3)(B)(i) shall be disallowed and such disallowance shall be final.

(ii) Certain exceptions

Clause (i) shall not apply with respect to any claim filed by any claimant after the date specified in the notice published under paragraph (3)(B)(i) and such claim may be considered by the receiver if—

(I) the claimant did not receive notice of the appointment of the receiver in time to file such claim before such date; and

(II) such claim is filed in time to permit payment of such claim.

(D) Authority to disallow claims

(i) In general

The receiver may disallow any portion of any claim by a creditor or claim of security, preference, or priority which is not proved to the satisfaction of the receiver.

(ii) Payments to less than fully secured creditors

In the case of a claim of a creditor against an insured depository institution which is secured by any property or other asset of such institution, any receiver appointed for any insured depository institution—

(I) may treat the portion of such claim which exceeds an amount equal to the fair market value of such property or other asset as an unsecured claim against the institution; and

(II) may not make any payment with respect to such unsecured portion of the claim other than in connection with the disposition of all claims of unsecured creditors of the institution.

(iii) Exceptions

No provision of this paragraph shall apply with respect to—

(I) any extension of credit from any Federal home loan bank or Federal Reserve bank to any insured depository institution; or

(II) any security interest in the assets of the institution securing any such extension of credit.

(E) No judicial review of determination pursuant to subparagraph (d)

No court may review the Corporation's determination pursuant to subparagraph (D) to disallow a claim.

(F) Legal effect of filing

(i) Statute of limitation tolled

For purposes of any applicable statute of limitations, the filing of a claim with the receiver shall constitute a commencement of an action.

(ii) No prejudice to other actions

Subject to paragraph (12), the filing of a claim with the receiver shall not prejudice any right of the claimant to continue any action which was filed before the appointment of the receiver.

(6) Provision for agency review or judicial determination of claims

(A) In general

Before the end of the 60–day period beginning on the earlier of—

(i) the end of the period described in paragraph (5)(A)(i) with respect to any claim against a depository institution for which the Corporation is receiver; or

(ii) the date of any notice of disallowance of such claim pursuant to paragraph (5)(A)(i),

the claimant may request administrative review of the claim in accordance with subparagraph (A) or (B) of paragraph (7) or file suit

on such claim (or continue an action commenced before the appointment of the receiver) in the district or territorial court of the United States for the district within which the depository institution's principal place of business is located or the United States District Court for the District of Columbia (and such court shall have jurisdiction to hear such claim).

(B) Statute of limitations

If any claimant fails to—

(i) request administrative review of any claim in accordance with subparagraph (A) or (B) of paragraph (7); or

(ii) file suit on such claim (or continue an action commenced before the appointment of the receiver),

before the end of the 60–day period described in subparagraph (A), the claim shall be deemed to be disallowed (other than any portion of such claim which was allowed by the receiver) as of the end of such period, such disallowance shall be final, and the claimant shall have no further rights or remedies with respect to such claim.

(7) Review of claims

(A) Administrative hearing

If any claimant requests review under this subparagraph in lieu of filing or continuing any action under paragraph (6) and the Corporation agrees to such request, the Corporation shall consider the claim after opportunity for a hearing on the record. The final determination of the Corporation with respect to such claim shall be subject to judicial review under chapter 7 of Title 5.

(B) Other review procedures

(i) In general

The Corporation shall also establish such alternative dispute resolution processes as may be appropriate for the resolution of claims filed under paragraph (5)(A)(i).

(ii) Criteria

In establishing alternative dispute resolution processes, the Corporation shall strive for procedures which are expeditious, fair, independent, and low cost.

(iii) Voluntary binding or nonbinding procedures

The Corporation may establish both binding and nonbinding processes, which may be conducted by any government or private party, but all parties, including the claimant and the Corporation, must agree to the use of the process in a particular case.

(iv) Consideration of incentives

The Corporation shall seek to develop incentives for claimants to participate in the alternative dispute resolution process.

(8) Expedited determination of claims

(A) Establishment required

The Corporation shall establish a procedure for expedited relief outside of the routine claims process established under paragraph (5) for claimants who—

(i) allege the existence of legally valid and enforceable or perfected security interests in assets of any depository institution for which the Corporation has been appointed receiver; and

(ii) allege that irreparable injury will occur if the routine claims procedure is followed.

(B) Determination period

Before the end of the 90–day period beginning on the date any claim is filed in accordance with the procedures established pursuant to subparagraph (A), the Corporation shall—

(i) determine—

(I) whether to allow or disallow such claim; or

(II) whether such claim should be determined pursuant to the procedures established pursuant to paragraph (5); and

(ii) notify the claimant of the determination, and if the claim is disallowed, provide a statement of each reason for the disallowance and the procedure for obtaining agency review or judicial determination.

(C) Period for filing or renewing suit

Any claimant who files a request for expedited relief shall be permitted to file a suit, or to continue a suit filed before the appointment of the receiver, seeking a determination of the claimant's rights with respect to such security interest after the earlier of—

(i) the end of the 90–day period beginning on the date of the filing of a request for expedited relief; or

(ii) the date the Corporation denies the claim.

(D) Statute of limitations

If an action described in subparagraph (C) is not filed, or the motion to renew a previously filed suit is not made, before the end of the 30–day period beginning on the date on which such action or motion may be filed in accordance with subparagraph (B), the claim shall be deemed to be disallowed as of the end of such period (other than any portion of such claim which was allowed by the receiver), such disallowance shall be final, and the claimant shall have no further rights or remedies with respect to such claim.

(E) Legal effect of filing

(i) Statute of limitation tolled

For purposes of any applicable statute of limitations, the filing of a claim with the receiver shall constitute a commencement of an action.

(ii) No prejudice to other actions

Subject to paragraph (12), the filing of a claim with the receiver shall not prejudice any right of the claimant to continue any action which was filed before the appointment of the receiver.

(9) Agreement as basis of claim

(A) Requirements

Except as provided in subparagraph (B), any agreement which does not meet the requirements set forth in section 1823(e) of this title shall not form the basis of, or substantially comprise, a claim against the receiver or the Corporation.

(B) Exception to contemporaneous execution requirement

Notwithstanding section 1823(e)(2) of this title, any agreement relating to an extension of credit between a Federal home loan bank or Federal Reserve bank and any insured depository institution which was executed before the extension of credit by such bank to such institution shall be treated as having been executed contemporaneously with such extension of credit for purposes of subparagraph (A).

(10) Payment of claims

(A) In general

The receiver may, in the receiver's discretion and to the extent funds are available, pay creditor claims which are allowed by the receiver, approved by the Corporation pursuant to a final determination pursuant to paragraph (7) or (8), or determined by the final judgment of any court of competent jurisdiction in such manner and amounts as are authorized under this chapter.

(B) Payment of dividends on claims

The receiver may, in the receiver's sole discretion, pay dividends on proved claims at any time, and no liability shall attach to the Corporation (in such Corporation's corporate capacity or as receiver), by reason of any such payment, for failure to pay dividends to a claimant whose claim is not proved at the time of any such payment.

(C) Rulemaking authority of Corporation

The Corporation may prescribe such rules, including definitions of terms, as it deems appropriate to establish a single uniform interest rate for or to make payments of post insolvency interest to creditors holding proven claims against the receivership estates of insured Federal or State depository institutions following satisfaction by the receiver of the principal amount of all creditor claims.

(11) Depositor preference

(A) In general

Subject to section 1815(e)(2)(C) of this title, amounts realized from the liquidation or other resolution of any insured depository institution by any receiver appointed for such institution shall be distributed to pay claims (other than secured claims to the extent of any such security) in the following order of priority:

(i) Administrative expenses of the receiver.

(ii) Any deposit liability of the institution.

(iii) Any other general or senior liability of the institution (which is not a liability described in clause (iv) or (v)).

(iv) Any obligation subordinated to depositors or general creditors (which is not an obligation described in clause (v)).

(v) Any obligation to shareholders or members arising as a result of their status as shareholders or members (including any depository institution holding company or any shareholder or creditor of such company).

(B) Effect on State law

(i) In general

The provisions of subparagraph (A) shall not supersede the law of any State except to the extent such law is inconsistent with the provisions of such subparagraph, and then only to the extent of the inconsistency.

(ii) Procedure for determination of inconsistency

Upon the Corporation's own motion or upon the request of any person with a claim described in subparagraph (A) or any State which is submitted to the Corporation in accordance with procedures which the Corporation shall prescribe, the Corporation shall determine whether any provision of the law of any State is inconsistent with any provision of subparagraph (A) and the extent of any such inconsistency.

(iii) Judicial review

The final determination of the Corporation under clause (ii) shall be subject to judicial review under chapter 7 of Title 5.

(C) Accounting report

Any distribution by the Corporation in connection with any claim described in subparagraph (A)(v) shall be accompanied by the accounting report required under paragraph (15)(B).

(12) Suspension of legal actions

(A) In general

After the appointment of a conservator or receiver for an insured depository institution, the conservator or receiver may request a stay for a period not to exceed—

(i) 45 days, in the case of any conservator; and

(ii) 90 days, in the case of any receiver,

in any judicial action or proceeding to which such institution is or becomes a party.

(B) Grant of stay by all courts required

Upon receipt of a request by any conservator or receiver pursuant to subparagraph (A) for a stay of any judicial action or proceeding in any court with jurisdiction of such action or proceeding, the court shall grant such stay as to all parties.

(13) Additional rights and duties

(A) Prior final adjudication

The Corporation shall abide by any final unappealable judgment of any court of competent jurisdiction which was rendered before the appointment of the Corporation as conservator or receiver.

(B) Rights and remedies of conservator or receiver

In the event of any appealable judgment, the Corporation as conservator or receiver shall—

(i) have all the rights and remedies available to the insured depository institution (before the appointment of such conservator or receiver) and the Corporation in its corporate capacity, including removal to Federal court and all appellate rights; and

(ii) not be required to post any bond in order to pursue such remedies.

(C) No attachment or execution

No attachment or execution may issue by any court upon assets in the possession of the receiver.

(D) Limitation on judicial review

Except as otherwise provided in this subsection, no court shall have jurisdiction over—

(i) any claim or action for payment from, or any action seeking a determination of rights with respect to, the assets of any depository institution for which the Corporation has been appointed receiver, including assets which the Corporation may acquire from itself as such receiver; or

(ii) any claim relating to any act or omission of such institution or the Corporation as receiver.

(E) Disposition of assets

In exercising any right, power, privilege, or authority as conservator or receiver in connection with any sale or disposition of assets of any insured depository institution for which the Corporation has been appointed conservator or receiver, including any sale or disposition of assets acquired by the Corporation under section 1823(d)(1) of this title, the Corporation shall conduct its operations in a manner which—

(i) maximizes the net present value return from the sale or disposition of such assets;

(ii) minimizes the amount of any loss realized in the resolution of cases;

(iii) ensures adequate competition and fair and consistent treatment of offerors;

(iv) prohibits discrimination on the basis of race, sex, or ethnic groups in the solicitation and consideration of offers; and

(v) maximizes the preservation of the availability and affordability of residential real property for low-and moderate-income individuals.

(14) Statute of limitations for actions brought by conservator or receiver

(A) In general

Notwithstanding any provision of any contract, the applicable statute of limitations with regard to any action brought by the Corporation as conservator or receiver shall be—

(i) in the case of any contract claim, the longer of—

(I) the 6–year period beginning on the date the claim accrues; or

(II) the period applicable under State law; and

(ii) in the case of any tort claim (other than a claim which is subject to section 1441a(b)(14) of this title), the longer of—

(I) the 3–year period beginning on the date the claim accrues; or

(II) the period applicable under State law.

(B) Determination of the date on which a claim accrues

For purposes of subparagraph (A), the date on which the statute of limitations begins to run on any claim described in such subparagraph shall be the later of—

(i) the date of the appointment of the Corporation as conservator or receiver; or

(ii) the date on which the cause of action accrues.

(C) Revival of expired State causes of action

(i) In general

In the case of any tort claim described in clause (ii) for which the statute of limitation applicable under State law with respect to such claim has expired not more than 5 years before the appointment of the Corporation as conservator or receiver, the Corporation may bring an action as conservator or receiver on such claim without regard to the expiration of the statute of limitation applicable under State law.

(ii) Claims described

A tort claim referred to in clause (i) is a claim arising from fraud, intentional misconduct resulting in unjust enrichment, or intentional misconduct resulting in substantial loss to the institution.

(15) Accounting and recordkeeping requirements

(A) In general

The Corporation as conservator or receiver shall, consistent with the accounting and reporting practices and procedures established by the Corporation, maintain a full accounting of each conservatorship and receivership or other disposition of institutions in default.

(B) Annual accounting or report

With respect to each conservatorship or receivership to which the Corporation was appointed, the Corporation shall make an annual accounting or report, as appropriate, available to the Secretary of the Treasury, the Comptroller General of the United States, and the authority which appointed the Corporation as conservator or receiver.

(C) Availability of reports

Any report prepared pursuant to subparagraph (B) shall be made available by the Corporation upon request to any shareholder of the depository institution for which the Corporation was appointed conservator or receiver or any other member of the public.

(D) Recordkeeping requirement

(i) In general

Except as provided in clause (ii), after the end of the 6–year period beginning on the date the Corporation is appointed as receiver of an insured depository institution, the Corporation may destroy any records of such institution which the Corporation, in the Corporation's discretion, determines to be unnecessary unless directed not to do so by a court of competent jurisdiction or governmental agency, or prohibited by law.

(ii) Old records

Notwithstanding clause (i), the Corporation may destroy records of an insured depository institution which are at least 10 years old as of the date on which the Corporation is appointed as the receiver of such depository institution in accordance with clause (i) at any time after such appointment is final, without regard to the 6–year period of limitation contained in clause (i).

(16) Contracts with state housing finance authorities

(A) In general

The Corporation may enter into contracts with any State housing finance authority for the sale of mortgage-related assets (as such terms are defined in section 1441a–1 of this title) of any depository institution in default (including assets and liabilities associated with any trust business), such contracts to be effective in accordance with their terms without any further approval, assignment, or consent with respect thereto.

(B) Factors to consider

In evaluating the disposition of mortgage related assets to any State housing finance authority the Corporation shall consider—

(i) the State housing finance authority's ability to acquire and service current, delinquent, and defaulted mortgage related assets;

(ii) the State housing finance authority's ability to further national housing policies;

(iii) the State housing finance authority's sensitivity to the impact of the sale of mortgage related assets upon the State and local communities;

(iv) the costs to the Federal Government associated with alternative ownership or disposition of the mortgage related assets;

(v) the minimization of future guaranties which may be required of the Federal Government;

(vi) the maximization of mortgage related asset values; and

(vii) the utilization of institutions currently established in mortgage related asset market activities.

(17) Fraudulent transfers

(A) In general

The Corporation, as conservator or receiver for any insured depository institution, and any conservator appointed by the Comptroller of the Currency or the Director of the Office of Thrift Supervision may avoid a transfer of any interest of an institution-affiliated party, or any person who the Corporation or conservator determines is a debtor of the institution, in property, or any obligation incurred by such party or person, that was made within 5 years of the date on which the Corporation or conservator was appointed conservator or receiver if such party or person voluntarily or involuntarily made such transfer or incurred such liability with the intent to hinder, delay, or defraud the insured depository institution, the Corporation or other conservator, or any other appropriate Federal banking agency.

(B) Right of recovery

To the extent a transfer is avoided under subparagraph (A), the Corporation or any conservator described in such subparagraph may recover, for the benefit of the insured depository institution, the property transferred, or, if a court so orders, the value of such property (at the time of such transfer) from—

(i) the initial transferee of such transfer or the institution-affiliated party or person for whose benefit such transfer was made; or

(ii) any immediate or mediate transferee of any such initial transferee.

(C) Rights of transferee or obligee

The Corporation or any conservator described in subparagraph (A) may not recover under subparagraph (B) from—

(i) any transferee that takes for value, including satisfaction or securing of a present or antecedent debt, in good faith; or

(ii) any immediate or mediate good faith transferee of such transferee.

(D) Rights under this paragraph

The rights under this paragraph of the Corporation and any conservator described in subparagraph (A) shall be superior to any rights of a trustee or any other party (other than any party which is a Federal agency) under Title 11.

(18) Attachment of assets and other injunctive relief

Subject of paragraph (19), any court of competent jurisdiction may, at the request of—

(A) the Corporation (in the Corporation's capacity as conservator or receiver for any insured depository institution or in the Corporation's corporate capacity with respect to any asset acquired or liability assumed by the Corporation under section 1821, 1822, or 1823 of this title); or

(B) any conservator appointed by the Comptroller of the Currency or the Director of the Office of Thrift Supervision,

issue an order in accordance with Rule 65 of the Federal Rules of Civil Procedure, including an order placing the assets of any person designated by the Corporation or such conservator under the control of the court and appointing a trustee to hold such assets.

(19) Standards

(A) Showing

Rule 65 of the Federal Rules of Civil Procedure shall apply with respect to any proceeding under paragraph (18) without regard to the requirement of such rule that the applicant show that the injury, loss, or damage is irreparable and immediate.

(B) State proceeding

If, in the case of any proceeding in a State court, the court determines that rules of civil procedure available under the laws of such State provide substantially similar protections to such party's right to due process as Rule 65 (as modified with respect to such proceeding by subparagraph (A)), the relief sought by the Corporation or a conservator pursuant to paragraph (18) may be requested under the laws of such State.

(20) Treatment of claims arising from breach of contracts executed by the receiver or conservator

Notwithstanding any other provision of this subsection, any final and unappealable judgment for monetary damages entered against a receiver or conservator for an insured depository institution for the breach of an agreement executed or approved by such receiver or conservator after the date of its appointment shall be paid as an administrative expense of the receiver or conservator. Nothing in this paragraph shall be construed to limit the power of a receiver or conservator to exercise any rights under contract or law, including to terminate, breach, cancel, or otherwise discontinue such agreement.

(e) Provisions relating to contracts entered into before appointment of conservator or receiver

(1) Authority to repudiate contracts

In addition to any other rights a conservator or receiver may have, the conservator or receiver for any insured depository institution may disaffirm or repudiate any contract or lease—

(A) to which such institution is a party;

(B) the performance of which the conservator or receiver, in the conservator's or receiver's discretion, determines to be burdensome; and

(C) the disaffirmance or repudiation of which the conservator or receiver determines, in the conservator's or receiver's discretion, will promote the orderly administration of the institution's affairs.

(2) Timing of repudiation

The conservator or receiver appointed for any insured depository institution in accordance with subsection (c) of this section shall determine whether or not to exercise the rights of repudiation under this subsection within a reasonable period following such appointment.

(3) Claims for damages for repudiation

(A) In general

Except as otherwise provided in subparagraph (C) and paragraphs (4), (5), and (6), the liability of the conservator or receiver for the disaffirmance or repudiation of any contract pursuant to paragraph (1) shall be—

(i) limited to actual direct compensatory damages; and

(ii) determined as of—

(I) the date of the appointment of the conservator or receiver; or

(II) in the case of any contract or agreement referred to in paragraph (8), the date of the disaffirmance or repudiation of such contract or agreement.

(B) No liability for other damages

For purposes of subparagraph (A), the term "actual direct compensatory damages" does not include—

(i) punitive or exemplary damages;

(ii) damages for lost profits or opportunity; or

(iii) damages for pain and suffering.

(C) Measure of damages for repudiation of financial contracts

In the case of any qualified financial contract or agreement to which paragraph (8) applies, compensatory damages shall be—

(i) deemed to include normal and reasonable costs of cover or other reasonable measures of damages utilized in the industries for such contract and agreement claims; and

(ii) paid in accordance with this subsection and subsection (i) of this section except as otherwise specifically provided in this section.

(4) Leases under which the institution is the lessee

(A) In general

If the conservator or receiver disaffirms or repudiates a lease under which the insured depository institution was the lessee, the conservator or receiver shall not be liable for any damages (other than damages determined pursuant to subparagraph (B)) for the disaffirmance or repudiation of such lease.

(B) Payments of rent

Notwithstanding subparagraph (A), the lessor under a lease to which such subparagraph applies shall—

(i) be entitled to the contractual rent accruing before the later of the date—

(I) the notice of disaffirmance or repudiation is mailed; or

(II) the disaffirmance or repudiation becomes effective,

unless the lessor is in default or breach of the terms of the lease;

(ii) have no claim for damages under any acceleration clause or other penalty provision in the lease; and

(iii) have a claim for any unpaid rent, subject to all appropriate offsets and defenses, due as of the date of the appointment which shall be paid in accordance with this subsection and subsection (i) of this section.

(5) Leases under which the institution is the lessor

(A) In general

If the conservator or receiver repudiates an unexpired written lease of real property of the insured depository institution under which the institution is the lessor and the lessee is not, as of the date of such repudiation, in default, the lessee under such lease may either—

(i) treat the lease as terminated by such repudiation; or

(ii) remain in possession of the leasehold interest for the balance of the term of the lease unless the lessee defaults under the terms of the lease after the date of such repudiation.

(B) Provisions applicable to lessee remaining in possession

If any lessee under a lease described in subparagraph (A) remains in possession of a leasehold interest pursuant to clause (ii) of such subparagraph—

(i) the lessee—

(I) shall continue to pay the contractual rent pursuant to the terms of the lease after the date of the repudiation of such lease;

(II) may offset against any rent payment which accrues after the date of the repudiation of the lease, any damages which accrue after such date due to the nonperformance of any obligation of the insured depository institution under the lease after such date; and

(ii) the conservator or receiver shall not be liable to the lessee for any damages arising after such date as a result of the repudiation other than the amount of any offset allowed under clause (i)(II).

(6) Contracts for the sale of real property

(A) In general

If the conservator or receiver repudiates any contract (which meets the requirements of each paragraph of section 1823(e) of this title) for the sale of real property and the purchaser of such real property under such contract is in possession and is not, as of the date of such repudiation, in default, such purchaser may either—

(i) treat the contract as terminated by such repudiation; or

(ii) remain in possession of such real property.

(B) Provisions applicable to purchaser remaining in possession

If any purchaser of real property under any contract described in subparagraph (A) remains in possession of such property pursuant to clause (ii) of such subparagraph—

(i) the purchaser—

(I) shall continue to make all payments due under the contract after the date of the repudiation of the contract; and

(II) may offset against any such payments any damages which accrue after such date due to the nonperformance (after such date) of any obligation of the depository institution under the contract; and

(ii) the conservator or receiver shall—

(I) not be liable to the purchaser for any damages arising after such date as a result of the repudiation other than the amount of any offset allowed under clause (i)(II);

(II) deliver title to the purchaser in accordance with the provisions of the contract; and

(III) have no obligation under the contract other than the performance required under subclause (II).

(C) Assignment and sale allowed

(i) In general

No provision of this paragraph shall be construed as limiting the right of the conservator or receiver to assign the contract described in subparagraph (A) and sell the property subject to the contract and the provisions of this paragraph.

(ii) No liability after assignment and sale

If an assignment and sale described in clause (i) is consummated, the conservator or receiver shall have no further liability under the contract described in subparagraph (A) or with respect to the real property which was the subject of such contract.

(7) Provisions applicable to service contracts

(A) Services performed before appointment

In the case of any contract for services between any person and any insured depository institution for which the Corporation has been appointed conservator or receiver, any claim of such person for services performed before the appointment of the conservator or the receiver shall be—

(i) a claim to be paid in accordance with subsections (d) and (i) of this section; and

(ii) deemed to have arisen as of the date the conservator or receiver was appointed.

(B) Services performed after appointment and prior to repudiation

If, in the case of any contract for services described in subparagraph (A), the conservator or receiver accepts performance by the other person before the conservator or receiver makes any determination to exercise the right of repudiation of such contract under this section—

(i) the other party shall be paid under the terms of the contract for the services performed; and

(ii) the amount of such payment shall be treated as an administrative expense of the conservatorship or receivership.

(C) Acceptance of performance no bar to subsequent repudiation

The acceptance by any conservator or receiver of services referred to in subparagraph (B) in connection with a contract described in such subparagraph shall not affect the right of the conservator or receiver to repudiate such contract under this section at any time after such performance.

(8) Certain qualified financial contracts

(A) Rights of parties to contracts

Subject to paragraphs (9) and (10) of this subsection and notwithstanding any other provision of this chapter (other than subsection (d)(9) of this section and section 1823(e) of this title), any other Federal law, or the law of any State, no person shall be stayed or prohibited from exercising—

(i) any right such person has to cause the termination, liquidation, or acceleration of any qualified financial contract with an insured depository institution which arises upon the appointment of the Corporation as receiver for such institution at any time after such appointment;

(ii) any right under any security agreement or arrangement or other credit enhancement related to one or more qualified financial contracts described in clause (i);

(iii) any right to offset or net out any termination value, payment amount, or other transfer obligation arising under or in connection with 1 or more contracts and agreements described in clause (i), including any master agreement for such contracts or agreements.

(B) Applicability of other provisions

Subsection (d)(12) of this section shall apply in the case of any judicial action or proceeding brought against any receiver referred to in subparagraph (A), or the insured depository institution for which such receiver was appointed, by any party to a contract or agreement described in subparagraph (A)(i) with such institution.

(C) Certain transfers not avoidable

(i) In general

Notwithstanding paragraph (11), section 5242 of the Revised Statutes of the United States [12 U.S.C.A. § 91] or any other Federal or State law relating to the avoidance of preferential or fraudulent transfers, the Corporation, whether acting as such or as conservator or receiver of an insured depository institution, may not avoid any transfer of money or other property in connection with any qualified financial contract with an insured depository institution.

(ii) Exception for certain transfers

Clause (i) shall not apply to any transfer of money or other property in connection with any qualified financial contract with an insured depository institution if the Corporation determines that the transferee had actual intent to hinder, delay, or defraud such institution, the creditors of such institution, or any conservator or receiver appointed for such institution.

(D) Certain contracts and agreements defined

For purposes of this subsection, the following definitions shall apply:

(i) Qualified financial contract

The term "qualified financial contract" means any securities contract, commodity contract, forward contract, repurchase agreement, swap agreement, and any similar agreement that the Corporation determines by regulation, resolution, or order to be a qualified financial contract for purposes of this paragraph.

(ii) Securities contract

The term "securities contract"—

(I) means a contract for the purchase, sale, or loan of a security, a certificate of deposit, a mortgage loan, any interest in a mortgage loan, a group or index of securities, certificates of deposit, or mortgage loans or interests therein (including any interest therein or based on the value thereof) or any option on any of the foregoing, including any option to purchase or sell any such security, certificate of deposit, mortgage loan, interest, group or index, or option, and including any repurchase or reverse repurchase transaction on any such security, certificate of deposit, mortgage loan, interest, group or index, or option (whether or not such repurchase or reverse repurchase transaction is a "repurchase agreement", as defined in clause (v));

(II) does not include any purchase, sale, or repurchase obligation under a participation in a commercial mortgage loan unless the Corporation determines by regulation, resolution, or order to include any such agreement within the meaning of such term;

(III) means any option entered into on a national securities exchange relating to foreign currencies;

(IV) means the guarantee (including by novation) by or to any securities clearing

agency of any settlement of cash, securities, certificates of deposit, mortgage loans or interests therein, group or index of securities, certificates of deposit, or mortgage loans or interests therein (including any interest therein or based on the value thereof) or option on any of the foregoing, including any option to purchase or sell any such security, certificate of deposit, mortgage loan, interest, group or index, or option (whether or not such settlement is in connection with any agreement or transaction referred to in subclauses (I) through (XII) (other than subclause (II)));

(V) means any margin loan;

(VI) means any extension of credit for the clearance or settlement of securities transactions;

(VII) means any loan transaction coupled with a securities collar transaction, any prepaid securities forward transaction, or any total return swap transaction coupled with a securities sale transaction;

(VIII) means any other agreement or transaction that is similar to any agreement or transaction referred to in this clause;

(IX) means any combination of the agreements or transactions referred to in this clause;

(X) means any option to enter into any agreement or transaction referred to in this clause;

(XI) means a master agreement that provides for an agreement or transaction referred to in subclause (I), (III), (IV), (V), (VI), (VII), (VIII), (IX), or (X), together with all supplements to any such master agreement, without regard to whether the master agreement provides for an agreement or transaction that is not a securities contract under this clause, except that the master agreement shall be considered to be a securities contract under this clause only with respect to each agreement or transaction under the master agreement that is referred to in subclause (I), (III), (IV), (V), (VI), (VII), (VIII), (IX), or (X); and

(XII) means any security agreement or arrangement or other credit enhancement related to any agreement or transaction referred to in this clause, including any guarantee or reimbursement obligation in connection with any agreement or transaction referred to in this clause.

(iii) Commodity contract

The term "commodity contract" means—

(I) with respect to a futures commission merchant, a contract for the purchase or sale of a commodity for future delivery on, or subject to the rules of, a contract market or board of trade;

(II) with respect to a foreign futures commission merchant, a foreign future;

(III) with respect to a leverage transaction merchant, a leverage transaction;

(IV) with respect to a clearing organization, a contract for the purchase or sale of a commodity for future delivery on, or subject to the rules of, a contract market or board of trade that is cleared by such clearing organization, or commodity option traded on, or subject to the rules of, a contract market or board of trade that is cleared by such clearing organization;

(V) with respect to a commodity options dealer, a commodity option;

(VI) any other agreement or transaction that is similar to any agreement or transaction referred to in this clause;

(VII) any combination of the agreements or transactions referred to in this clause;

(VIII) any option to enter into any agreement or transaction referred to in this clause;

(IX) a master agreement that provides for an agreement or transaction referred to in subclause (I), (II), (III), (IV), (V), (VI), (VII), or (VIII), together with all supplements to any such master agreement, without regard to whether the master agreement provides for an agreement or transaction that is not a commodity contract under this clause, except that the master agreement shall be considered to be a commodity contract under this clause only with respect to each agreement or transaction under the master agreement that is referred to in subclause (I), (II), (III), (IV), (V), (VI), (VII), or (VIII); or

(X) any security agreement or arrangement or other credit enhancement related to any agreement or transaction referred to in this clause, including any guarantee or reimbursement obligation in connection with any agreement or transaction referred to in this clause.

(iv) Forward contract

The term "forward contract" means—

(I) a contract (other than a commodity contract) for the purchase, sale, or transfer of a commodity or any similar good, article, service, right, or interest which is presently or in the future becomes the subject of dealing in the forward contract trade, or product or byproduct thereof, with a maturity date more than 2 days after the date the contract is entered into, including, a repurchase or reverse repurchase transaction (whether or not such repurchase or reverse repurchase transaction is a "repurchase agreement", as defined in clause (v)), consignment, lease, swap, hedge transaction, deposit, loan, option, allocated transaction, unallocated transaction, or any other similar agreement;

(II) any combination of agreements or transactions referred to in subclauses (I) and (III);

(III) any option to enter into any agreement or transaction referred to in subclause (I) or (II);

(IV) a master agreement that provides for an agreement or transaction referred to in subclauses (I), (II), or (III), together with all supplements to any such master agreement, without regard to whether the master agreement provides for an agreement or transaction that is not a forward contract under this clause, except that the master agreement shall be considered to be a forward contract under this clause only with respect to each agreement or transaction under the master agreement that is referred to in subclause (I), (II), or (III); or

(V) any security agreement or arrangement or other credit enhancement related to any agreement or transaction referred to in subclause (I), (II), (III), or (IV), including any guarantee or reimbursement obligation in connection with any agreement or transaction referred to in any such subclause.

(v) Repurchase agreement

The term "repurchase agreement" (which definition also applies to a reverse repurchase agreement)—

(I) means an agreement, including related terms, which provides for the transfer of one or more certificates of deposit, mortgage-related securities (as such term is defined in the Securities Exchange Act of 1934), mortgage loans, interests in mortgage-related securities or mortgage loans, eligible bankers' acceptances, qualified foreign government securities or securities that are direct obligations of, or that are fully guaranteed by, the United States or any agency of the United States against the transfer of funds by the transferee of such certificates of deposit, eligible bankers' acceptances, securities, mortgage loans, or interests with a simultaneous agreement by such transferee to transfer to the transferor thereof certificates of deposit, eligible bankers' acceptances, securities, mortgage loans, or interests as described above, at a date certain not later than 1 year after such transfers or on demand, against the transfer of funds, or any other similar agreement;

(II) does not include any repurchase obligation under a participation in a commercial mortgage loan unless the Corporation determines by regulation, resolution, or order to include any such participation within the meaning of such term;

(III) means any combination of agreements or transactions referred to in subclauses (I) and (IV);

(IV) means any option to enter into any agreement or transaction referred to in subclause (I) or (III);

(V) means a master agreement that provides for an agreement or transaction referred to in subclause (I), (III), or (IV), together with all supplements to any such master agreement, without regard to whether the master agreement provides for an agreement or transaction that is not a repurchase agreement under this clause, except that the master agreement shall be considered to be a repurchase agreement under this subclause only with respect to each agreement or transaction under the master agreement that is referred to in subclause (I), (III), or (IV); and

(VI) means any security agreement or arrangement or other credit enhancement related to any agreement or transaction re-

ferred to in subclause (I), (III), (IV), or (V), including any guarantee or reimbursement obligation in connection with any agreement or transaction referred to in any such subclause.

For purposes of this clause, the term "qualified foreign government security" means a security that is a direct obligation of, or that is fully guaranteed by, the central government of a member of the Organization for Economic Cooperation and Development (as determined by regulation or order adopted by the appropriate Federal banking authority).

(vi) Swap agreement

The term "swap agreement" means—

(I) any agreement, including the terms and conditions incorporated by reference in any such agreement, which is an interest rate swap, option, future, or forward agreement, including a rate floor, rate cap, rate collar, cross-currency rate swap, and basis swap; a spot, same day-tomorrow, tomorrow-next, forward, or other foreign exchange, precious metals, or other commodity agreement; a currency swap, option, future, or forward agreement; an equity index or equity swap, option, future, or forward agreement; a debt index or debt swap, option, future, or forward agreement; a total return, credit spread or credit swap, option, future, or forward agreement; a commodity index or commodity swap, option, future, or forward agreement; weather swap, option, future, or forward agreement; an emissions swap, option, future, or forward agreement; or an inflation swap, option, future, or forward agreement;

(II) any agreement or transaction that is similar to any other agreement or transaction referred to in this clause and that is of a type that has been, is presently, or in the future becomes, the subject of recurrent dealings in the swap or other derivatives markets (including terms and conditions incorporated by reference in such agreement) and that is a forward, swap, future, option, or spot transaction on one or more rates, currencies, commodities, equity securities or other equity instruments, debt securities or other debt instruments, quantitative measures associated with an occurrence, extent of an occurrence, or contingency associated with a financial, commercial, or economic consequence, or economic or financial indices or measures of economic or financial risk or value;

(III) any combination of agreements or transactions referred to in this clause;

(IV) any option to enter into any agreement or transaction referred to in this clause;

(V) a master agreement that provides for an agreement or transaction referred to in subclause (I), (II), (III), or (IV), together with all supplements to any such master agreement, without regard to whether the master agreement contains an agreement or transaction that is not a swap agreement under this clause, except that the master agreement shall be considered to be a swap agreement under this clause only with respect to each agreement or transaction under the master agreement that is referred to in subclause (I), (II), (III), or (IV); and

(VI) any security agreement or arrangement or other credit enhancement related to any agreements or transactions referred to in subclause (I), (II), (III), (IV), or (V), including any guarantee or reimbursement obligation in connection with any agreement or transaction referred to in any such subclause.

Such term is applicable for purposes of this subsection only and shall not be construed or applied so as to challenge or affect the characterization, definition, or treatment of any swap agreement under any other statute, regulation, or rule, including the Gramm–Leach–Bliley Act, the Legal Certainty for Bank Products Act of 2000, the securities laws (as such term is defined in section 3(a)(47) of the Securities Exchange Act of 1934) and the Commodity Exchange Act.

(vii) Treatment of master agreement as one agreement

Any master agreement for any contract or agreement described in any preceding clause of this subparagraph (or any master agreement for such master agreement or agreements), together with all supplements to such master agreement, shall be treated as a single agreement and a single qualified financial contract. If a master agreement contains provisions relating to agreements or

transactions that are not themselves qualified financial contracts, the master agreement shall be deemed to be a qualified financial contract only with respect to those transactions that are themselves qualified financial contracts.

(viii) Transfer

The term "transfer" means every mode, direct or indirect, absolute or conditional, voluntary or involuntary, of disposing of or parting with property or with an interest in property, including retention of title as a security interest and foreclosure of the depository institution's equity of redemption.

(ix) Person

The term "person" includes any governmental entity in addition to any entity included in the definition of such term in section 1 of Title 1.

(E) Certain protections in event of appointment of conservator

Notwithstanding any other provision of this chapter (other than subsections (d)(9) and (e)(10) of this section, and section 1823(e) of this title), any other Federal law, or the law of any State, no person shall be stayed or prohibited from exercising—

(i) any right such person has to cause the termination, liquidation, or acceleration of any qualified financial contract with a depository institution in a conservatorship based upon a default under such financial contract which is enforceable under applicable noninsolvency law;

(ii) any right under any security agreement or arrangement or other credit enhancement related to one or more qualified financial contracts described in clause (i);

(iii) any right to offset or net out any termination values, payment amounts, or other transfer obligations arising under or in connection with such qualified financial contracts.

(F) Clarification

No provision of law shall be construed as limiting the right or power of the Corporation, or authorizing any court or agency to limit or delay, in any manner, the right or power of the Corporation to transfer any qualified financial contract in accordance with paragraphs (9) and (10) of this subsection or to disaffirm or repudiate any such contract in accordance with subsection (e)(1) of this section.

(G) Walkaway clauses not effective

(i) In general

Notwithstanding the provisions of subparagraphs (A) and (E), and sections 4403 and 4404 of this title, no walkaway clause shall be enforceable in a qualified financial contract of an insured depository institution in default.

(ii) Limited suspension of certain obligations

In the case of a qualified financial contract referred to in clause (i), any payment or delivery obligations otherwise due from a party pursuant to the qualified financial contract shall be suspended from the time the receiver is appointed until the earlier of—

(I) the time such party receives notice that such contract has been transferred pursuant to subparagraph (A); or

(II) 5:00 p.m. (eastern time) on the business day following the date of the appointment of the receiver.

(iii) Walkaway clause defined

For purposes of this subparagraph, the term "walkaway clause" means any provision in a qualified financial contract that suspends, conditions, or extinguishes a payment obligation of a party, in whole or in part, or does not create a payment obligation of a party that would otherwise exist, solely because of such party's status as a nondefaulting party in connection with the insolvency of an insured depository institution that is a party to the contract or the appointment of or the exercise of rights or powers by a conservator or receiver of such depository institution, and not as a result of a party's exercise of any right to offset, setoff, or net obligations that exist under the contract, any other contract between those parties, or applicable law.

(H) Recordkeeping requirements

The Corporation, in consultation with the appropriate Federal banking agencies, may prescribe regulations requiring more detailed recordkeeping by any insured depository institution with respect to qualified financial contracts (including market valuations) only if such insured depository institution is in a troubled condition (as such term is defined by the Corporation pursuant to section 1831i of this title).

(9) Transfer of qualified financial contracts

(A) In general

In making any transfer of assets or liabilities of a depository institution in default which includes any qualified financial contract, the conservator or receiver for such depository institution shall either—

(i) transfer to one financial institution, other than a financial institution for which a conservator, receiver, trustee in bankruptcy, or other legal custodian has been appointed or which is otherwise the subject of a bankruptcy or insolvency proceeding—

(I) all qualified financial contracts between any person or any affiliate of such person and the depository institution in default;

(II) all claims of such person or any affiliate of such person against such depository institution under any such contract (other than any claim which, under the terms of any such contract, is subordinated to the claims of general unsecured creditors of such institution);

(III) all claims of such depository institution against such person or any affiliate of such person under any such contract; and

(IV) all property securing or any other credit enhancement for any contract described in subclause (I) or any claim described in subclause (II) or (III) under any such contract; or

(ii) transfer none of the qualified financial contracts, claims, property or other credit enhancement referred to in clause (i) (with respect to such person and any affiliate of such person).

(B) Transfer to foreign bank, foreign financial institution, or branch or agency of a foreign bank or financial institution

In transferring any qualified financial contracts and related claims and property under subparagraph (A)(i), the conservator or receiver for the depository institution shall not make such transfer to a foreign bank, financial institution organized under the laws of a foreign country, or a branch or agency of a foreign bank or financial institution unless, under the law applicable to such bank, financial institution, branch or agency, to the qualified financial contracts, and to any netting contract, any security agreement or arrangement or other credit enhancement related to one or more qualified financial contracts, the contractual rights of the parties to such qualified financial contracts, netting contracts, security agreements or arrangements, or other credit enhancements are enforceable substantially to the same extent as permitted under this section.

(C) Transfer of contracts subject to the rules of a clearing organization

In the event that a conservator or receiver transfers any qualified financial contract and related claims, property, and credit enhancements pursuant to subparagraph (A)(i) and such contract is cleared by or subject to the rules of a clearing organization, the clearing organization shall not be required to accept the transferee as a member by virtue of the transfer.

(D) Definitions

For purposes of this paragraph, the term "financial institution" means a broker or dealer, a depository institution, a futures commission merchant, or any other institution, as determined by the Corporation by regulation to be a financial institution, and the term "clearing organization" has the same meaning as in section 4402 of this title.

(10) Notification of transfer

(A) In general

If—

(i) the conservator or receiver for an insured depository institution in default makes any transfer of the assets and liabilities of such institution; and

(ii) the transfer includes any qualified financial contract,

the conservator or receiver shall notify any person who is a party to any such contract of such transfer by 5:00 p.m. (eastern time) on the business day following the date of the appointment of the receiver in the case of a receivership, or the business day following

such transfer in the case of a conservatorship.

(B) Certain rights not enforceable

(i) Receivership

A person who is a party to a qualified financial contract with an insured depository institution may not exercise any right that such person has to terminate, liquidate, or net such contract under paragraph (8)(A) of this subsection or section 4403 or 4404 of this title, solely by reason of or incidental to the appointment of a receiver for the depository institution (or the insolvency or financial condition of the depository institution for which the receiver has been appointed)—

(I) until 5:00 p.m. (eastern time) on the business day following the date of the appointment of the receiver; or

(II) after the person has received notice that the contract has been transferred pursuant to paragraph (9)(A).

(ii) Conservatorship

A person who is a party to a qualified financial contract with an insured depository institution may not exercise any right that such person has to terminate, liquidate, or net such contract under paragraph (8)(E) of this subsection or section 4403 or 4404 of this title, solely by reason of or incidental to the appointment of a conservator for the depository institution (or the insolvency or financial condition of the depository institution for which the conservator has been appointed).

(iii) Notice

For purposes of this paragraph, the Corporation as receiver or conservator of an insured depository institution shall be deemed to have notified a person who is a party to a qualified financial contract with such depository institution if the Corporation has taken steps reasonably calculated to provide notice to such person by the time specified in subparagraph (A).

(C) Treatment of bridge depository institutions

The following institutions shall not be considered to be a financial institution for which a conservator, receiver, trustee in bankruptcy, or other legal custodian has been appointed or which is otherwise the subject of a bankruptcy or insolvency proceeding for purposes of paragraph (9):

(i) A bridge depository institution.

(ii) A depository institution organized by the Corporation, for which a conservator is appointed either—

(I) immediately upon the organization of the institution; or

(II) at the time of a purchase and assumption transaction between the depository institution and the Corporation as receiver for a depository institution in default.

(D) "Business day" defined

For purposes of this paragraph, the term "business day" means any day other than any Saturday, Sunday, or any day on which either the New York Stock Exchange or the Federal Reserve Bank of New York is closed.

(11) Disaffirmance or repudiation of qualified financial contracts

In exercising the rights of disaffirmance or repudiation of a conservator or receiver with respect to any qualified financial contract to which an insured depository institution is a party, the conservator or receiver for such institution shall either—

(A) disaffirm or repudiate all qualified financial contracts between—

(i) any person or any affiliate of such person; and

(ii) the depository institution in default; or

(B) disaffirm or repudiate none of the qualified financial contracts referred to in subparagraph (A) (with respect to such person or any affiliate of such person).

(12) Certain security interests not avoidable

No provision of this subsection shall be construed as permitting the avoidance of any legally enforceable or perfected security interest in any of the assets of any depository institution except where such an interest is taken in contemplation of the institution's insolvency or with the intent to hinder, delay, or defraud the institution or the creditors of such institution.

(13) Authority to enforce contracts

(A) In general

The conservator or receiver may enforce any contract, other than a director's or officer's liability insurance contract or a depository institution bond, entered into by the depository institution notwithstanding any provision of the contract providing for termination, default, acceleration, or exercise of rights upon, or solely by reason of, insolvency or the appointment of or the exercise of rights or powers by a conservator or receiver.

(B) Certain rights not affected

No provision of this paragraph may be construed as impairing or affecting any right of the conservator or receiver to enforce or recover under a director's or officer's liability insurance contract or depository institution bond under other applicable law.

(C) Consent requirement

(i) In general

Except as otherwise provided by this section or section 1825 of this title, no person may exercise any right or power to terminate, accelerate, or declare a default under any contract to which the depository institution is a party, or to obtain possession of or exercise control over any property of the institution or affect any contractual rights of the institution, without the consent of the conservator or receiver, as appropriate, during the 45–day period beginning on the date of the appointment of the conservator, or during the 90–day period beginning on the date of the appointment of the receiver, as applicable.

(ii) Certain exceptions

No provision of this subparagraph shall apply to a director or officer liability insurance contract or a depository institution bond, to the rights of parties to certain qualified financial contracts pursuant to paragraph (8), or to the rights of parties to netting contracts pursuant to subchapter I of chapter 45 of Tile 12 (12 U.S.C. 4401 et seq.), or shall be construed as permitting the conservator or receiver to fail to comply with otherwise enforceable provisions of such contract.

(iii) Rule of construction

Nothing in this subparagraph shall be construed to limit or otherwise affect the applicability of Title 11.

(14) Exception for federal reserve and federal home loan banks

No provision of this subsection shall apply with respect to—

(A) any extension of credit from any Federal home loan bank or Federal Reserve bank to any insured depository institution; or

(B) any security interest in the assets of the institution securing any such extension of credit.

(15) Selling credit card accounts receivable

(A) Notification required

An undercapitalized insured depository institution (as defined in section 1831o of this title) shall notify the Corporation in writing before entering into an agreement to sell credit card accounts receivable.

(B) Waiver by Corporation

The Corporation may at any time, in its sole discretion and upon such terms as it may prescribe, waive its right to repudiate an agreement to sell credit card accounts receivable if the Corporation—

(i) determines that the waiver is in the best interests of the Deposit Insurance Fund; and

(ii) provides a written waiver to the selling institution.

(C) Effect of waiver on successors

(i) In general

If, under subparagraph (B), the Corporation has waived its right to repudiate an agreement to sell credit card accounts receivable—

(I) any provision of the agreement that restricts solicitation of a credit card customer of the selling institution, or the use of a credit card customer list of the institution, shall bind any receiver or conservator of the institution; and

(II) the Corporation shall require any acquirer of the selling institution, or of substantially all of the selling institution's assets or liabilities, to agree to be bound by a provision described in subclause (I) as if the acquirer were the selling institution.

(ii) Exception

Clause (i)(II) does not—

(I) restrict the acquirer's authority to offer any product or service to any person identi-

fied without using a list of the selling institution's customers in violation of the agreement;

(II) require the acquirer to restrict any preexisting relationship between the acquirer and a customer; or

(III) apply to any transaction in which the acquirer acquires only insured deposits.

(D) Waiver not actionable

The Corporation shall not, in any capacity, be liable to any person for damages resulting from the waiver of or failure to waive the Corporation's right under this section to repudiate any contract or lease, including an agreement to sell credit card accounts receivable. No court shall issue any order affecting any such waiver or failure to waive.

(E) Other authority not affected

This paragraph does not limit any other authority of the Corporation to waive the Corporation's right to repudiate an agreement or lease under this section.

(16) Certain credit card customer lists protected

(A) In general

If any insured depository institution sells credit card accounts receivable under an agreement negotiated at arm's length that provides for the sale of the institution's credit card customer list, the Corporation shall prohibit any party to a transaction with respect to the institution under this section or section 1823 of this title from using the list, except as permitted under the agreement.

(B) Fraudulent transactions excluded

Subparagraph (A) does not limit the Corporation's authority to repudiate any agreement entered into with the intent to hinder, delay, or defraud the institution, the institution's creditors, or the Corporation.

(17) Savings clause

The meanings of terms used in this subsection are applicable for purposes of this subsection only, and shall not be construed or applied so as to challenge or affect the characterization, definition, or treatment of any similar terms under any other statute, regulation, or rule, including the Gramm–Leach–Bliley Act, the Legal Certainty for Bank Products Act of 2000, the securities laws (as that term is defined in section 3(a)(47) of the Securities Exchange Act of 1934), and the Commodity Exchange Act.

(f) Payment of insured deposits

(1) In general

In case of the liquidation of, or other closing or winding up of the affairs of, any insured depository institution, payment of the insured deposits in such institution shall be made by the Corporation as soon as possible, subject to the provisions of subsection (g) of this section, either by cash or by making available to each depositor a transferred deposit in a new insured depository institution in the same community or in another insured depository institution in an amount equal to the insured deposit of such depositor.

(2) Proof of claims

The Corporation, in its discretion, may require proof of claims to be filed and may approve or reject such claims for insured deposits.

(3) Resolution of disputes

A determination by the Corporation regarding any claim for insurance coverage shall be treated as a final determination for purposes of this section. In its discretion, the Corporation may promulgate regulations prescribing procedures for resolving any disputed claim relating to any insured deposit or any determination of insurance coverage with respect to any deposit.

(4) Review of corporation determination

A final determination made by the Corporation regarding any claim for insurance coverage shall be a final agency action reviewable in accordance with chapter 7 of Title 5, by the United States district court for the Federal judicial district where the principal place of business of the depository institution is located.

(5) Statute of limitations

Any request for review of a final determination by the Corporation regarding any claim for insurance coverage shall be filed with the appropriate United States district court not later than 60 days after the date on which such determination is issued.

(g) Subrogation of Corporation

(1) In general

Notwithstanding any other provision of Federal law, the law of any State, or the constitution of any State, the Corporation, upon the payment to any depositor as provided in subsection (f) of this section in connection with any insured depository institution or insured branch described in such subsection or the assumption of any deposit in such institution or branch by another insured depository institution pursuant to this section or section 1823 of this title, shall be subrogated to all rights of the depositor against such institution or branch to the extent of such payment or assumption.

(2) Dividends on subrogated amounts

The subrogation of the Corporation under paragraph (1) with respect to any insured depository institution shall include the right on the part of the Corporation to receive the same dividends from the proceeds of the assets of such institution and recoveries on account of stockholders' liability as would have been payable to the depositor on a claim for the insured deposit, but such depositor shall retain such claim for any uninsured or unassumed portion of the deposit.

(3) Waiver of certain claims

With respect to any bank which closes after May 25, 1938, the Corporation shall waive, in favor only of any person against whom stockholders' individual liability may be asserted, any claim on account of such liability in excess of the liability, if any, to the bank or its creditors, for the amount unpaid upon such stock in such bank; but any such waiver shall be effected in such manner and on such terms and conditions as will not increase recoveries or dividends on account of claims to which the Corporation is not subrogated.

(4) Applicability of State law

Subject to subsection (d)(11)of this section, if the Corporation is appointed pursuant to subsection (c)(3) of this section, or determines not to invoke the authority conferred in subsection (c)(4) of this section, the rights of depositors and other creditors of any State depository institution shall be determined in accordance with the applicable provisions of State law.

(h) Conditions applicable to resolution proceedings

(1) Consideration of local economic impact required

The Corporation shall fully consider the adverse economic impact on local communities, including businesses and farms, of actions to be taken by it during the administration and liquidation of loans of a depository institution in default.

(2) Actions to alleviate adverse economic impact to be considered

The actions which the Corporation shall consider include the release of proceeds from the sale of products and services for family living and business expenses and shortening the undue length of the decisionmaking process for the acceptance of offers of settlement contingent upon third party financing.

(3) Guidelines required

The Corporation shall adopt and publish procedures and guidelines to minimize adverse economic effects caused by its actions on individual debtors in the community.

(4) Financial services industry impact analysis

After the appointment of the Corporation as conservator or receiver for any insured depository institution and before taking any action under this section or section 1823 of this title in connection with the resolution of such institution, the Corporation shall—

(A) evaluate the likely impact of the means of resolution, and any action which the Corporation may take in connection with such resolution, on the viability of other insured depository institutions in the same community; and

(B) take such evaluation into account in determining the means for resolving the institution and establishing the terms and conditions for any such action.

(i) Valuation of claims in default

(1) In general

Notwithstanding any other provision of Federal law or the law of any State and regardless of the method which the Corporation determines to utilize with respect to an insured depository institution in default or in danger of default, including transactions authorized under subsection (n) of this section and section 1823(c) of this title, this subsection shall govern the

rights of the creditors (other than insured depositors) of such institution.

(2) Maximum liability

The maximum liability of the Corporation, acting as receiver or in any other capacity, to any person having a claim against the receiver or the insured depository institution for which such receiver is appointed shall equal the amount such claimant would have received if the Corporation had liquidated the assets and liabilities of such institution without exercising the Corporation's authority under subsection (n) of this section or section 1823 of this title.

(3) Additional payments authorized

(A) In general

The Corporation may, in its discretion and in the interests of minimizing its losses, use its own resources to make additional payments or credit additional amounts to or with respect to or for the account of any claimant or category of claimants. Notwithstanding any other provision of Federal or State law, or the constitution of any State, the Corporation shall not be obligated, as a result of having made any such payment or credited any such amount to or with respect to or for the account of any claimant or category of claimants, to make payments to any other claimant or category of claimants.

(B) Manner of payment

The Corporation may make the payments or credit the amounts specified in subparagraph (A) directly to the claimants or may make such payments or credit such amounts to an open insured depository institution to induce such institution to accept liability for such claims.

(j) Limitation on court action

Except as provided in this section, no court may take any action, except at the request of the Board of Directors by regulation or order, to restrain or affect the exercise of powers or functions of the Corporation as a conservator or a receiver.

(k) Liability of directors and officers

A director or officer of an insured depository institution may be held personally liable for monetary damages in any civil action by, on behalf of, or at the request or direction of the Corporation, which action is prosecuted wholly or partially for the benefit of the Corporation—

(1) acting as conservator or receiver of such institution,

(2) acting based upon a suit, claim, or cause of action purchased from, assigned by, or otherwise conveyed by such receiver or conservator, or

(3) acting based upon a suit, claim, or cause of action purchased from, assigned by, or otherwise conveyed in whole or in part by an insured depository institution or its affiliate in connection with assistance provided under section 1823 of this title,

for gross negligence, including any similar conduct or conduct that demonstrates a greater disregard of a duty of care (than gross negligence) including intentional tortious conduct, as such terms are defined and determined under applicable State law. Nothing in this paragraph shall impair or affect any right of the Corporation under other applicable law.

(*l*) Damages

In any proceeding related to any claim against an insured depository institution's director, officer, employee, agent, attorney, accountant, appraiser, or any other party employed by or providing services to an insured depository institution, recoverable damages determined to result from the improvident or otherwise improper use or investment of any insured depository institution's assets shall include principal losses and appropriate interest.

(m) New depository institutions

(1) Organization authorized

As soon as possible after the default of an insured depository institution, the Corporation, if it finds that it is advisable and in the interest of the depositors of the insured depository institution in default or the public shall organize a new national bank in the same community as the depository institution in default to assume the insured deposits of such depository institution in default and otherwise to perform temporarily the functions hereinafter provided for.

(2) Articles of association

The articles of association and the organization certificate of the new depository institution

shall be executed by representatives designated by the Corporation.

(3) Capital stock

No capital stock need be paid in by the Corporation.

(4) Executive officer

The new depository institution shall not have a board of directors, but shall be managed by an executive officer appointed by the Board of Directors of the Corporation who shall be subject to its directions.

(5) Subject to laws relating to national banks

In all other respects the new depository institution shall be organized in accordance with the then existing provisions of law relating to the organization of national banking associations.

(6) New deposits

The new depository institution may, with the approval of the Corporation, accept new deposits which shall be subject to withdrawal on demand and which, except where the new depository institution is the only depository institution in the community, shall not exceed an amount equal to the standard maximum deposit insurance amount from any depositor.

(7) Insured status

The new depository institution, without application to or approval by the Corporation, shall be an insured depository institution and shall maintain on deposit with the Federal Reserve bank of its district reserves in the amount required by law for member banks, but it shall not be required to subscribe for stock of the Federal Reserve bank.

(8) Investments

Funds of the new depository institution shall be kept on hand in cash, invested in obligations of the United States or obligations guaranteed as to principal and interest by the United States, or deposited with the Corporation, any Federal Reserve bank, or, to the extent of the insurance coverage on any such deposit, an insured depository institution.

(9) Conduct of business

The new depository institution, unless otherwise authorized by the Comptroller of the Currency or the Director of the Office of Thrift Supervision, as appropriate, shall transact business only as authorized by this chapter and as may be incidental to its organization.

(10) Exempt status

Notwithstanding any other provision of Federal or State law, the new depository institution, its franchise, property and income shall be exempt from all taxation now or hereafter imposed by the United States, by any territory, dependency, or possession thereof, or by any State, county, municipality, or local taxing authority.

(11) Transfer of deposits

(A) Upon the organization of a new depository institution, the Corporation shall promptly make available to it an amount equal to the estimated insured deposits of such depository institution in default plus the estimated amount of the expenses of operating the new depository institution, and shall determine as soon as possible the amount due each depositor for the depositor's insured deposit in the depository institution in default, and the total expenses of operation of the new depository institution.

(B) Upon such determination, the amounts so estimated and made available shall be adjusted to conform to the amounts so determined.

(12) Earnings

Earnings of the new depository institution shall be paid over or credited to the Corporation in such adjustment.

(13) Losses

If any new depository institution, during the period it continues its status as such, sustains any losses with respect to which it is not effectively protected except by reason of being an insured depository institution, the Corporation shall furnish to it additional funds in the amount of such losses.

(14) Payment of insured deposits

(A) The new depository institution shall assume as transferred deposits the payment of the insured deposits of such depository institution in default to each of its depositors.

(B) Of the amounts so made available, the Corporation shall transfer to the new depository institution, in cash, such sums as may be necessary to enable it to meet its expenses of operation and immediate cash demands on such transferred deposits, and the remainder of such amounts shall be subject to withdrawal by the new depository institution on demand.

(15) Issuance of stock

(A) Whenever in the judgment of the Board of Directors it is desirable to do so, the Corporation shall cause capital stock of the new depository institution to be offered for sale on such terms and conditions as the Board of Directors shall deem advisable in an amount sufficient, in the opinion of the Board of Directors, to make possible the conduct of the business of the new depository institution on a sound basis.

(B) The stockholders of the insured depository institution in default shall be given the first opportunity to purchase any shares of common stock so offered.

(16) Issuance of certificate

Upon proof that an adequate amount of capital stock in the new depository institution has been subscribed and paid for in cash, the Comptroller of the Currency or the Director of the Office of Thrift Supervision, as appropriate, shall require the articles of association and the organization certificate to be amended to conform to the requirements for the organization of a national bank or Federal savings association, and thereafter, when the requirements of law with respect to the organization of a national bank or Federal savings association have been complied with, the Comptroller of the Currency or the Director of the Office of Thrift Supervision, as appropriate, shall issue to the depository institution a certificate of authority to commence business, and thereupon the depository institution shall cease to have the status of a new depository institution, shall be managed by directors elected by its own shareholders, may exercise all the powers granted by law, and shall be subject to all provisions of law relating to national banks or Federal savings associations. Such depository institution shall thereafter be an insured national bank or Federal savings association, without certification to or approval by the Corporation.

(17) Transfer to other institution

If the capital stock of the new depository institution is not offered for sale, or if an adequate amount of capital for such new depository institution is not subscribed and paid for, the Board of Directors may offer to transfer its business to any insured depository institution in the same community which will take over its assets, assume its liabilities, and pay to the Corporation for such business such amount as the Board of Directors may deem adequate; or the Board of Directors in its discretion may change the location of the new depository institution to the office of the Corporation or to some other place or may at any time wind up its affairs as herein provided.

(18) Winding up

Unless the capital stock of the new depository institution is sold or its assets are taken over and its liabilities are assumed by an insured depository institution as above provided within 2 years after the date of its organization, the Corporation shall wind up the affairs of such depository institution, after giving such notice, if any, as the Comptroller of the Currency or the Director of the Office of Thrift Supervision, as appropriate, may require, and shall certify to the Comptroller of the Currency or the Director of the Office of Thrift Supervision, as appropriate, the termination of the new depository institution. Thereafter the Corporation shall be liable for the obligations of such depository institution and shall be the owner of its assets.

(19) Applicability of certain laws

The provisions of sections 181 and 182 of this title shall not apply to a new depository institution under this subsection.

(n) Bridge depository institutions

(1) Organization

(A) Purpose

When 1 or more insured depository institutions are in default, or when the Corporation anticipates that 1 or more insured depository institutions may become in default, the Corporation may, in its discretion, organize, and the Office of the Comptroller of the Currency shall charter, 1 or more national banks with respect thereto with the powers and attributes of national banking associations, subject to the provisions of this subsection, to be referred to as bridge depository institutions.

(B) Authorities

Upon the granting of a charter to a bridge depository institution, the bridge depository institution may—

(i) assume such deposits of such insured depository institution or institutions that is or are in default or in danger of default as the Corporation may, in its discretion, determine to be appropriate;

(ii) assume such other liabilities (including liabilities associated with any trust business) of such insured depository institution or institutions that is or are in default or in danger of default as the Corporation may, in its discretion, determine to be appropriate;

(iii) purchase such assets (including assets associated with any trust business) of such insured depository institution or institutions that is or are in default or in danger of default as the Corporation may, in its discretion, determine to be appropriate; and

(iv) perform any other temporary function which the Corporation may, in its discretion, prescribe in accordance with this chapter.

(C) Articles of association

The articles of association and organization certificate of a bridge bank as approved by the Corporation shall be executed by 3 representatives designated by the Corporation.

(D) Interim directors

A bridge depository institution shall have an interim board of directors consisting of not fewer than 5 nor more than 10 members appointed by the Corporation.

(E) National bank or Federal savings association

A bridge depository institution shall be organized as a national bank, in the case of 1 or more insured banks, and as a Federal savings association, in the case of 1 or more insured savings associations.

(2) Chartering

(A) Conditions

A national bank or Federal savings association may be chartered by the Comptroller of the Currency or the Director of the Office of Thrift Supervision as a bridge depository institution only if the Board of Directors determines that—

(i) the amount which is reasonably necessary to operate such bridge depository institution will not exceed the amount which is reasonably necessary to save the cost of liquidating, including paying the insured accounts of, 1 or more insured depository institutions in default or in danger of default with respect to which the bridge depository institution is chartered;

(ii) the continued operation of such insured depository institution or institutions in default or in danger of default with respect to which the bridge depository institution is chartered is essential to provide adequate banking services in the community where each such depository institution in default or in danger of default is located; or

(iii) the continued operation of such insured depository institution or institutions in default or in danger of default with respect to which the bridge depository institution is chartered is in the best interest of the depositors of such depository institution or institutions in default or in danger of default or the public.

(B) Insured national bank or Federal savings association

A bridge depository institution shall be an insured depository institution from the time it is chartered as a national bank or Federal savings association.

(C) Bridge bank treated as being in default for certain purposes

A bridge depository institution shall be treated as an insured depository institution in default at such times and for such purposes as the Corporation may, in its discretion, determine.

(D) Management

A bridge depository institution, upon the granting of its charter, shall be under the management of a board of directors consisting of not fewer than 5 nor more than 10 members appointed by the Corporation.

(E) Bylaws

The board of directors of a bridge depository institution shall adopt such bylaws as may be approved by the Corporation.

(3) Transfer of assets and liabilities

(A) In general

(i) Transfer upon grant of charter

Upon the granting of a charter to a bridge depository institution pursuant to this subsection, the Corporation, as receiver, or any other receiver appointed with respect to any insured depository institution in default with respect to which the bridge depository institution is chartered may transfer any assets and liabilities of such depository institution in default to the bridge depository institution in accordance with paragraph (1).

(ii) Subsequent transfers

At any time after a charter is granted to a bridge depository institution, the Corporation, as receiver, or any other receiver appointed with respect to an insured depository institution in default may transfer any assets and liabilities of such insured depository institution in default as the Corporation may, in its discretion, determine to be appropriate in accordance with paragraph (1).

(iii) Treatment of trust business

For purposes of this paragraph, the trust business, including fiduciary appointments, of any insured depository institution in default is included among its assets and liabilities.

(iv) Effective without approval

The transfer of any assets or liabilities, including those associated with any trust business, of an insured depository institution in default transferred to a bridge depository institution shall be effective without any further approval under Federal or State law, assignment, or consent with respect thereto.

(B) Intent of congress regarding continuing operations

It is the intent of the Congress that, in order to prevent unnecessary hardship or losses to the customers of any insured depository institution in default with respect to which a bridge depository institution is chartered, especially creditworthy farmers, small businesses, and households, the Corporation should—

(i) continue to honor commitments made by the depository institution in default to creditworthy customers, and

(ii) not interrupt or terminate adequately secured loans which are transferred under subparagraph (A) and are being repaid by the debtor in accordance with the terms of the loan instrument.

(4) Powers of bridge depository institutions

Each bridge depository institution chartered under this subsection shall have all corporate powers of, and be subject to the same provisions of law as, a national bank or Federal savings association, as appropriate, except that—

(A) the Corporation may—

(i) remove the interim directors and directors of a bridge depository institution;

(ii) fix the compensation of members of the interim board of directors and the board of directors and senior management, as determined by the Corporation in its discretion, of a bridge depository institution; and

(iii) waive any requirement established under section 71, 72, 73, 74, or 75 of this title (relating to directors of national banks) or section 71a of this title which would otherwise be applicable with respect to directors of a bridge depository institution by operation of paragraph (2)(B);

(B) the Corporation may indemnify the representatives for purposes of paragraph (1)(B) and the interim directors, directors, officers, employees, and agents of a bridge depository institution on such terms as the Corporation determines to be appropriate;

(C) no requirement under section 51 of this title or any other provision of law relating to the capital of a national bank shall apply with respect to a bridge depository institution;

(D) the Comptroller of the Currency and the Director of the Office of Thrift Supervision, as appropriate, may establish a limitation on the extent to which any person may become indebted to a bridge depository institution without regard to the amount of the bridge depository institution's capital or surplus;

(E)(i) the board of directors of a bridge depository institution shall elect a chairperson who may also serve in the position of chief executive officer, except that such person shall not serve either as chairperson or as chief executive officer without the prior approval of the Corporation; and

(ii) the board of directors of a bridge depository institution may appoint a chief executive officer who is not also the chairperson, except that such person shall not serve as chief executive officer without the prior approval of the Corporation;

(F) a bridge depository institution shall not be required to purchase stock of any Federal Reserve bank;

(G) the Comptroller of the Currency and the Director of the Office of Thrift Supervision, as appropriate, shall waive any requirement for a fidelity bond with respect to a bridge depository institution at the request of the Corporation;

(H) any judicial action to which a bridge depository institution becomes a party by virtue of its acquisition of any assets or assumption of any liabilities of a depository institution in default shall be stayed from further proceedings for a period of up to 45 days at the request of the bridge depository institution;

(I) no agreement which tends to diminish or defeat the right, title or interest of a bridge depository institution in any asset of an insured depository institution in default acquired by it shall be valid against the bridge depository institution unless such agreement—

(i) is in writing,

(ii) was executed by such insured depository institution in default and the person or persons claiming an adverse interest thereunder, including the obligor, contemporaneously with the acquisition of the asset by such insured depository institution in default,

(iii) was approved by the board of directors of such insured depository institution in default or its loan committee, which approval shall be reflected in the minutes of said board or committee, and

(iv) has been, continuously from the time of its execution, an official record of such insured depository institution in default;

(J) notwithstanding section 1823(e)(2) of this title, any agreement relating to an extension of credit between a Federal home loan bank or Federal Reserve bank and any insured depository institution which was executed before the extension of credit by such bank to such depository institution shall be treated as having been executed contemporaneously with such extension of credit for purposes of subparagraph (I); and

(K) except with the prior approval of the Corporation, a bridge depository institution may not, in any transaction or series of transactions, issue capital stock or be a party to any merger, consolidation, disposition of assets or liabilities, sale or exchange of capital stock, or similar transaction, or change its charter.

(5) Capital

(A) No capital required

The Corporation shall not be required to—

(i) issue any capital stock on behalf of a bridge depository institution chartered under this subsection; or

(ii) purchase any capital stock of a bridge depository institution, except that notwithstanding any other provision of Federal or State law, the Corporation may purchase and retain capital stock of a bridge depository institution in such amounts and on such terms as the Corporation, in its discretion, determines to be appropriate.

(B) Operating funds in lieu of capital

Upon the organization of a bridge depository institution, and thereafter, as the Board of Directors may, in its discretion, determine to be necessary or advisable, the Corporation may make available to the bridge depository institution, upon such terms and conditions and in such form and amounts as the Corporation may in its discretion determine, funds for the operation of the bridge depository institution in lieu of capital.

(C) Authority to issue capital stock

Whenever the Board of Directors determines it is advisable to do so, the Corporation shall cause capital stock of a bridge depository institution to be issued and offered for sale in such amounts and on such terms and conditions as the Corporation may, in its discretion, determine.

(D) Capital levels

A bridge depository institution shall not be considered an undercapitalized depository institution or a critically undercapitalized de-

pository institution for purposes of section 347b (b) of this title.

(6) No federal status

(A) Agency status

A bridge depository institution is not an agency, establishment, or instrumentality of the United States.

(B) Employee status

Representatives for purposes of paragraph (1)(B), interim directors, directors, officers, employees, or agents of a bridge depository institution are not, solely by virtue of service in any such capacity, officers or employees of the United States. Any employee of the Corporation or of any Federal instrumentality who serves at the request of the Corporation as a representative for purposes of paragraph (1)(B), interim director, director, officer, employee, or agent of a bridge depository institution shall not—

(i) solely by virtue of service in any such capacity lose any existing status as an officer or employee of the United States for purposes of Title 5 or any other provision of law, or

(ii) receive any salary or benefits for service in any such capacity with respect to a bridge depository institution in addition to such salary or benefits as are obtained through employment with the Corporation or such Federal instrumentality.

(7) Assistance authorized

The Corporation may, in its discretion, provide assistance under section 1823(c) of this title to facilitate any transaction described in clause (i), (ii), or (iii) of paragraph (10)(A) with respect to any bridge depository institution in the same manner and to the same extent as such assistance may be provided under such section with respect to an insured depository institution in default, or to facilitate a bridge depository institution's acquisition of any assets or the assumption of any liabilities of an insured depository institution in default.

(8) Acquisition

(A) In general

The responsible agency shall notify the Attorney General of any transaction involving the merger or sale of a bridge depository institution requiring approval under section

1828(c) of this title and if a report on competitive factors is requested within 10 days, such transaction may not be consummated before the 5th calendar day after the date of approval by the responsible agency with respect thereto. If the responsible agency has found that it must act immediately to prevent the probable failure of 1 of the depository institutions involved, the preceding sentence does not apply and the transaction may be consummated immediately upon approval by the agency.

(B) By out-of-State holding company

Any depository institution, including an out-of-State depository institution, or any out-of-State depository institution holding company may acquire and retain the capital stock or assets of, or otherwise acquire and retain a bridge depository institution if the bridge depository institution at any time had assets aggregating $500,000,000 or more, as determined by the Corporation on the basis of the bridge depository institution's reports of condition or on the basis of the last available reports of condition of any insured depository institution in default, which institution has been acquired, or whose assets have been acquired, by the bridge depository institution. The acquiring entity may acquire the bridge depository institution only in the same manner and to the same extent as such entity may acquire an insured depository institution in default under section 1823(f)(2) of this title.

(9) Duration of bridge depository institution

Subject to paragraphs (11) and (12), the status of a bridge depository institution as such shall terminate at the end of the 2–year period following the date it was granted a charter. The Board of Directors may, in its discretion, extend the status of the bridge depository institution as such for 3 additional 1–year periods.

(10) Termination of bridge depository institution status

The status of any bridge depository institution as such shall terminate upon the earliest of—

(A) the merger or consolidation of the bridge depository institution with a depository institution that is not a bridge depository institution;

(B) at the election of the Corporation, the sale of a majority of the capital stock of the bridge depository institution to an entity other than the Corporation and other than another bridge depository institution;

(C) the sale of 80 percent, or more, of the capital stock of the bridge depository institution to an entity other than the Corporation and other than another bridge depository institution;

(D) at the election of the Corporation, either the assumption of all or substantially all of the deposits and other liabilities of the bridge depository institution by a depository institution holding company or a depository institution that is not a bridge depository institution, or the acquisition of all or substantially all of the assets of the bridge depository institution by a depository institution holding company, a depository institution that is not a bridge depository institution, or other entity as permitted under applicable law; and

(E) the expiration of the period provided in paragraph (9), or the earlier dissolution of the bridge depository institution as provided in paragraph (12).

(11) Effect of termination events

(A) Merger or consolidation

A bridge depository institution that participates in a merger or consolidation as provided in paragraph (10)(A) shall be for all purposes a national bank or a Federal savings association as the case may be, with all the rights, powers, and privileges thereof, and such merger or consolidation shall be conducted in accordance with, and shall have the effect provided in, the provisions of applicable law.

(B) Charter conversion

Following the sale of a majority of the capital stock of the bridge depository institution as provided in paragraph (10)(B), the Corporation may amend the charter of the bridge depository institution to reflect the termination of the status of the bridge depository institution as such, whereupon the bank shall remain a national bank or a Federal savings association as the case may be, with all of the rights, powers, and privileges thereof, subject to all laws and regulations applicable thereto.

(C) Sale of stock

Following the sale of 80 percent or more of the capital stock of a bridge depository institution as provided in paragraph (10)(C), the depository institution shall remain a national bank, or a Federal savings association as the case may be, with all of the rights, powers, and privileges thereof, subject to all laws and regulations applicable thereto.

(D) Assumption of liabilities and sale of assets

Following the assumption of all or substantially all of the liabilities of the bridge depository institution, or the sale of all or substantially all of the assets of the bridge depository institution, as provided in paragraph (10)(D), at the election of the Corporation the bridge depository institution may retain its status as such for the period provided in paragraph (9).

(E) Effect on holding companies

A depository institution holding company acquiring a bridge depository institution under section 1823(f) of this title, paragraph (8)(B) (or any predecessor provision), or both provisions, shall not be impaired or adversely affected by the termination of the status of a bridge depository institution as a result of subparagraph (A), (B), (C), or (D) of paragraph (10), and shall be entitled to the rights and privileges provided in section 1823(f) of this title.

(F) Amendments to charter

Following the consummation of a transaction described in subparagraph (A), (B), (C), or (D) of paragraph (10), the charter of the resulting institution shall be amended to reflect the termination of bridge depository institution status, if appropriate.

(12) Dissolution of bridge depository institution

(A) In general

Notwithstanding any other provision of State or Federal law, if the bridge depository institution's status as such has not previously been terminated by the occurrence of an event specified in subparagraph (A), (B), (C), or (D) of paragraph (10)—

(i) the Board of Directors may, in its discretion, dissolve a bridge depository institution in accordance with this paragraph at any time; and

(ii) the Board of Directors shall promptly commence dissolution proceedings in accordance with this paragraph upon the expiration of the 2–year period following the date the bridge depository institution was chartered, or any extension thereof, as provided in paragraph (9).

(B) Procedures

The Comptroller of the Currency or the Director of the Office of Thrift Supervision, as appropriate, shall appoint the Corporation receiver for a bridge depository institution upon certification by the Board of Directors to the Comptroller of the Currency or the Director of the Office of Thrift Supervision, as appropriate, of its determination to dissolve the bridge depository institution. The Corporation as such receiver shall wind up the affairs of the bridge depository institution in conformity with the provisions of law relating to the liquidation of closed national banks or Federal savings associations, as appropriate. With respect to any such bridge depository institution, the Corporation as such receiver shall have all the rights, powers, and privileges and shall perform the duties related to the exercise of such rights, powers, or privileges granted by law to a receiver of any insured depository institution and notwithstanding any other provision of law in the exercise of such rights, powers, and privileges the Corporation shall not be subject to the direction or supervision of any State agency or other Federal agency.

(13) Multiple bridge depository institutions

Subject to paragraph (1)(B)(i), the Corporation may, in the Corporation's discretion, organize 2 or more bridge depository institutions under this subsection to assume any deposits of, assume any other liabilities of, and purchase any assets of a single depository institution in default.

(o) Supervisory records

In addition to the requirements of section 1817(a)(2) of this title to provide to the Corporation copies of reports of examination and reports of condition, whenever the Corporation has been appointed as receiver for an insured depository institution, the appropriate Federal banking agency shall make available all supervisory records to the receiver which may be used by the receiver in any manner the receiver determines to be appropriate.

(p) Certain sales of assets prohibited

(1) Persons who engaged in improper conduct with, or caused losses to, depository institutions

The Corporation shall prescribe regulations which, at a minimum, shall prohibit the sale of assets of a failed institution by the Corporation to—

(A) any person who—

(i) has defaulted, or was a member of a partnership or an officer or director of a corporation that has defaulted, on 1 or more obligations the aggregate amount of which exceed $1,000,000, to such failed institution;

(ii) has been found to have engaged in fraudulent activity in connection with any obligation referred to in clause (i); and

(iii) proposes to purchase any such asset in whole or in part through the use of the proceeds of a loan or advance of credit from the Corporation or from any institution for which the Corporation has been appointed as conservator or receiver;

(B) any person who participated, as an officer or director of such failed institution or of any affiliate of such institution, in a material way in transactions that resulted in a substantial loss to such failed institution;

(C) any person who has been removed from, or prohibited from participating in the affairs of, such failed institution pursuant to any final enforcement action by an appropriate Federal banking agency; or

(D) any person who has demonstrated a pattern or practice of defalcation regarding obligations to such failed institution.

(2) Convicted debtors

Except as provided in paragraph (3), any person who—

(A) has been convicted of an offense under section 215, 656, 657, 1005, 1006, 1007, 1008, 1014, 1032, 1341, 1343, or 1344 of Title 18 or of conspiring to commit such an offense, affecting any insured depository institution for which any conservator or receiver has been appointed; and

(B) is in default on any loan or other extension of credit from such insured depository institution which, if not paid, will cause substantial loss to the institution, any deposit insurance fund, the Corporation, the FSLIC Resolution Fund, or the Resolution Trust Corporation,

may not purchase any asset of such institution from the conservator or receiver.

(3) Settlement of claims

Paragraphs (1) and (2) shall not apply to the sale or transfer by the Corporation of any asset of any insured depository institution to any person if the sale or transfer of the asset resolves or settles, or is part of the resolution or settlement, of—

(A) 1 or more claims that have been, or could have been, asserted by the Corporation against the person; or

(B) obligations owed by the person to any insured depository institution, the FSLIC Resolution Fund, the Resolution Trust Corporation, or the Corporation.

(4) Definition of default

For purposes of this subsection, the term "default" means a failure to comply with the terms of a loan or other obligation to such an extent that the property securing the obligation is foreclosed upon.

(q) Expedited procedures for certain claims

(1) Time for filing notice of appeal

The notice of appeal of any order, whether interlocutory or final, entered in any case brought by the Corporation against an insured depository institution's director, officer, employee, agent, attorney, accountant, or appraiser or any other person employed by or providing services to an insured depository institution shall be filed not later than 30 days after the date of entry of the order. The hearing of the appeal shall be held not later than 120 days after the date of the notice of appeal. The appeal shall be decided not later than 180 days after the date of the notice of appeal.

(2) Scheduling

Consistent with section 1657 of Title 18, a court of the United States shall expedite the consideration of any case brought by the Corporation against an insured depository institution's director, officer, employee, agent, attorney, accountant, or appraiser or any other person employed by or providing services to an insured depository institution. As far as practicable the court shall give such case priority on its docket.

(3) Judicial discretion

The court may modify the schedule and limitations stated in paragraphs (1) and (2) in a particular case, based on a specific finding that the ends of justice that would be served by making such a modification would outweigh the best interest of the public in having the case resolved expeditiously.

(r) Foreign investigations

The Corporation and the Resolution Trust Corporation, as conservator or receiver of any insured depository institution and for purposes of carrying out any power, authority, or duty with respect to an insured depository institution—

(1) may request the assistance of any foreign banking authority and provide assistance to any foreign banking authority in accordance with section 1818(v) of this title; and

(2) may each maintain an office to coordinate foreign investigations or investigations on behalf of foreign banking authorities.

(s) Prohibition on entering secrecy agreements and protective orders

The Corporation may not enter into any agreement or approve any protective order which prohibits the Corporation from disclosing the terms of any settlement of an administrative or other action for damages or restitution brought by the Corporation in its capacity as conservator or receiver for an insured depository institution.

(t) Agencies may share information without waiving privilege

(1) In general

A covered agency shall not be deemed to have waived any privilege applicable to any information by transferring that information to or permitting that information to be used by—

(A) any other covered agency, in any capacity; or

(B) any other agency of the Federal Government (as defined in section 6 of Title 18).

(2) Definitions

For purposes of this subsection:

(A) Covered agency

The term "covered agency" means any of the following:

(i) Any Federal banking agency.

(ii) The Farm Credit Administration.

(iii) The Farm Credit System Insurance Corporation.

(iv) The National Credit Union Administration.

(v) The Government Accountability Office.

(B) Privilege

The term "privilege" includes any work-product, attorney-client, or other privilege recognized under Federal or State law.

(3) Rule of construction

Paragraph (1) shall not be construed as implying that any person waives any privilege applicable to any information because paragraph (1) does not apply to the transfer or use of that information.

(u) Purchase rights of tenants

(1) Notice

Except as provided in paragraph (3), the Corporation may make available for sale a 1–to 4–family residence (including a manufactured home) to which the Corporation acquires title only after the Corporation has provided the household residing in the property notice (in writing and mailed to the property) of the availability of such property and the preference afforded such household under paragraph (2).

(2) Preference

In selling such a property, the Corporation shall give preference to any bona fide offer made by the household residing in the property, if—

(A) such offer is substantially similar in amount to other offers made within such period (or expected by the Corporation to be made within such period);

(B) such offer is made during the period beginning upon the Corporation making such property available and of a reasonable duration, as determined by the Corporation based on the normal period for sale of such properties; and

(C) the household making the offer complies with any other requirements applicable to purchasers of such property, including any downpayment and credit requirements.

(3) Exceptions

Paragraphs (1) and (2) shall not apply to—

(A) any residence transferred in connection with the transfer of substantially all of the assets of an insured depository institution for which the Corporation has been appointed conservator or receiver;

(B) any eligible single family property (as such term is defined in section 1831q(p) of this title); or

(C) any residence for which the household occupying the residence was the mortgagor under a mortgage on such residence and to which the Corporation acquired title pursuant to default on such mortgage.

(v) Preference for sales for homeless families

Subject to subsection (u) of this section, in selling any real property (other than eligible residential property and eligible condominium property, as such terms are defined in section 1831q(p) of this title) to which the Corporation acquires title, the Corporation shall give preference among offers to purchase the property that will result in the same net present value proceeds, to any offer that would provide for the property to be used, during the remaining useful life of the property, to provide housing or shelter for homeless persons (as such term is defined in section 11302 of Title 42) or homeless families.

(w) Preferences for sales of certain commercial real properties

(1) Authority

In selling any eligible commercial real properties of the Corporation, the Corporation shall give preference, among offers to purchase the property that will result in the same net present value proceeds, to any offer—

(A) that is made by a public agency or nonprofit organization; and

(B) under which the purchaser agrees that the property shall be used, during the remaining useful life of the property, for offices and administrative purposes of the purchaser to carry out a program to acquire residential properties to provide (i) homeownership and rental housing opportunities for very-low, low-, and moderate-income families, or (ii) housing or shelter for home-

less persons (as such term is defined in section 11302 of Title 42) or homeless families.

(2) Definitions

For purposes of this subsection, the following definitions shall apply:

(A) Eligible commercial real property

The term "eligible commercial real property" means any property (i) to which the Corporation acquires title, and (ii) that the Corporation, in the discretion of the Corporation, determines is suitable for use for the location of offices or other administrative functions involved with carrying out a program referred to in paragraph (1)(B).

(B) Nonprofit organization and public agency

The terms "nonprofit organization" and "public agency" have the same meanings as in section 1831q(p) of this title.

§ 1821a.   FSLIC resolution fund

(a) Established

(1) In general

There is established a separate fund to be designated as the FSLIC Resolution Fund which shall be managed by the Corporation and separately maintained and not commingled.

(2) Transfer of FSLIC assets and liabilities

(A) In general

Except as provided in section 1441a of this title, all assets and liabilities of the Federal Savings and Loan Insurance Corporation on August 8, 1989, shall be transferred to the FSLIC Resolution Fund.

(B) Additional claims on assets

The FSLIC Resolution Fund shall pay to the Savings Association Insurance Fund such amounts as are needed for administrative and supervisory expenses from August 9, 1989, through September 30, 1992.

(3) Separate holding

Assets and liabilities transferred to the FSLIC Resolution Fund shall be the assets and liabilities of the Fund and not of the Corporation and shall not be consolidated with the assets and liabilities of the Deposit Insurance Fund, or the Corporation for accounting, reporting, or any other purpose.

(4) Rights, powers, and duties

Effective August 10, 1989, the Corporation shall have all rights, powers, and duties to carry out the Corporation's duties with respect to the assets and liabilities of the FSLIC Resolution Fund that the Corporation otherwise has under this chapter.

(5) Corporation as conservator or receiver

(A) In general

Effective August 10, 1989, the Corporation shall succeed the Federal Savings and Loan Insurance Corporation as conservator or receiver with respect to any depository institution—

(i) the accounts of which were insured before August 10, 1989 by the Federal Savings and Loan Insurance Corporation; and

(ii) for which a conservator or receiver was appointed before January 1, 1989.

(B) Rights, powers, and duties

When acting as conservator or receiver with respect to any depository institution described in subparagraph (A), the Corporation shall have all rights, powers, and duties that the Corporation otherwise has as conservator or receiver under this chapter.

(b) Source of funds

The FSLIC Resolution Fund shall be funded from the following sources to the extent funds are needed in the listed priority:

(1) Income earned on assets of the FSLIC Resolution Fund.

(2) Liquidating dividends and payments made on claims received by the FSLIC Resolution Fund from receiverships to the extent such funds are not required by the Resolution Funding Corporation pursuant to section 1441b of this title or the Financing Corporation pursuant to section 1441 of this title.

(3) Amounts borrowed by the Financing Corporation pursuant to section 1441 of this title.

(4) Repealed. Pub.L. 109-173, § 8(a)(16), Feb. 15, 2006, 199 Stat. 3612.

(c) Treasury backup

(1) In general

If the funds described in subsections (a) and (b) of this section are insufficient to satisfy the liabilities of the FSLIC Resolution Fund, the Secretary of the Treasury shall pay to the Fund such amounts as may be necessary, as determined by the Corporation and the Secretary, for FSLIC Resolution Fund purposes.

(2) Authorization of appropriations

There are authorized to be appropriated to the Secretary of the Treasury, without fiscal year limitation, such sums as may be necessary to carry out this section.

(d) Legal proceedings

Any judgment resulting from a proceeding to which the Federal Savings and Loan Insurance Corporation was a party prior to its dissolution or which is initiated against the Corporation with respect to the Federal Savings and Loan Insurance Corporation or with respect to the FSLIC Resolution Fund shall be limited to the assets of the FSLIC Resolution Fund.

(e) Transfer of net proceeds from sale of RTC assets

The FSLIC Resolution Fund shall transfer to the Resolution Funding Corporation any net proceeds from the sale of assets acquired from the Resolution Trust Corporation upon the termination of such Corporation pursuant to section 1441a of this title.

(f) Dissolution

The FSLIC Resolution Fund shall be dissolved upon satisfaction of all debts and liabilities and sale of all assets. Upon dissolution any remaining funds shall be paid into the Treasury. Any administrative facilities and supplies, including offices and office supplies, shall be transferred to the Corporation for use by and to be held as assets of the Deposit Insurance Fund.

§ 1822. Corporation as receiver

(a) Bond not required; agents; fee

The Corporation as receiver of an insured depository institution or branch of a foreign bank shall not be required to furnish bond and may appoint an agent or agents to assist it in its duties as such receiver. All fees, compensation, and expenses of liquidation and administration shall be fixed by the Corporation, and may be paid by it out of funds coming into its possession as such receiver.

(b) Payment of insured deposit as discharge from liability

Payment of an insured deposit to any person by the Corporation shall discharge the Corporation, and payment of a transferred deposit to any person by the new or by an insured depository institution in which a transferred deposit has been made available shall discharge the Corporation and such new or other insured depository institution, to the same extent that payment to such person by the depository institution in default would have discharged it from liability for the insured deposit.

(c) Recognition of claimant not on bank records

Except as otherwise prescribed by the Board of Directors, neither the Corporation nor such new or other insured depository institution shall be required to recognize as the owner of any portion of a deposit appearing on the records of the depository institution in default under a name other than that of the claimant, any person whose name or interest as such owner is not disclosed on the records of such depository institution in default as part owner of said deposit, if such recognition would increase the aggregate amount of the insured deposits in such depository institution in default.

(d) Withholding payments to meet liability to depository institution

The Corporation may withhold payment of such portion of the insured deposit of any depositor in a depository institution in default as may be required to provide for the payment of any liability of such depositor to the depository institution in default or its receiver, which is not offset against a claim due from such depository institution, pending the determination and payment of such liability by such depositor or any other person liable therefor.

(e) Disposition of unclaimed deposits

(1) Notices

(A) First notice

Within 30 days after the initiation of the payment of insured deposits under section 1821(f) of this title, the Corporation shall provide written notice to all insured depositors that they must claim their deposit from the Corporation, or if the deposit has been transferred to another institution, from the transferee institution.

(B) Second notice

A second notice containing this information shall be mailed by the Corporation to all insured depositors who have not responded to the first notice, 15 months after the Corporation initiates such payment of insured depositors.

(C) Address

The notices shall be mailed to the last known address of the depositor appearing on the records of the insured depository institution in default.

(2) Transfer to appropriate State

If an insured depositor fails to make a claim for his, her, or its insured or transferred deposit within 18 months after the Corporation initiates the payment of insured deposits under section 1821(f) of this title—

(A) any transferee institution shall refund the deposit to the Corporation, and all rights of the depositor against the transferee institution shall be barred; and

(B) with the exception of United States deposits, the Corporation shall deliver the deposit to the custody of the appropriate State as unclaimed property, unless the appropriate State declines to accept custody. Upon delivery to the appropriate State, all rights of the depositor against the Corporation with respect to the deposit shall be barred and the Corporation shall be deemed to have made payment to the depositor for purposes of section 1821(g)(1) of this title.

(3) Refusal of appropriate State to accept custody

If the appropriate State declines to accept custody of the deposit tendered pursuant to paragraph (2)(B), the deposit shall not be delivered to any State, and the insured depositor shall claim the deposit from the Corporation before the receivership is terminated, or all rights of the depositor with respect to such deposit shall be barred.

(4) Treatment of United States deposits

If the deposit is a United States deposit it shall be delivered to the Secretary of the Treasury for deposit in the general fund of the Treasury. Upon delivery to the Secretary of the Treasury, all rights of the depositor against the Corporation with respect to the deposit shall be barred and the Corporation shall be deemed to have made payment to the depositor for purposes of section 1821(g)(1) of this title.

(5) Reversion

If a depositor does not claim the deposit delivered to the custody of the appropriate State pursuant to paragraph (2)(B) within 10 years of the date of delivery, the deposit shall be immediately refunded to the Corporation and become its property. All rights of the depositor against the appropriate State with respect to such deposit shall be barred as of the date of the refund to the Corporation.

(6) Definitions

For purposes of this subsection—

(A) the term "transferee institution" means the insured depository institution in which the Corporation has made available a transferred deposit pursuant to section 1821(f)(1) of this title;

(B) the term "appropriate State" means the State to which notice was mailed under paragraph (1)(C), except that if the notice was not mailed to an address that is within a State it shall mean the State in which the depository institution in default has its main office; and

(C) the term "United States deposit" means an insured or transferred deposit for which the deposit records of the depository institution in default disclose that title to the deposit is held by the United States, any department, agency, or instrumentality of the Federal Government, or any officer or employee thereof in such person's official capacity.

(f) Conflict of interest

(1) Applicability of other provisions

(A) Clarification of status of Corporation

The Corporation is, and has been since its creation, an agency for purposes of Title 18.

(B) Treatment of contractors

Any individual who, pursuant to a contract or any other arrangement, performs functions or activities of the Corporation, under the direct supervision of an officer or employee of the Corporation, shall be deemed to be an employee of the Corporation for purposes of Title 18 and this chapter. Any individual who, pursuant to a contract or any other agreement, acts for or on behalf of the Corporation, and who is not otherwise treated as an officer or employee of the United States for purposes of Title 18, shall be deemed to be a public official for purposes of section 201 of Title 18.

(2) Regulations concerning employee conduct

The officers and employees of the Corporation and those individuals under contract to the Corporation who are deemed, under paragraph (1)(B), to be employees of the Corporation for purposes of Title 18, shall be subject to the ethics and conflict of interest rules and regulations issued by the Office of Government Ethics, including those concerning employee conduct, financial disclosure, and post-employment activities. The Board of Directors may prescribe regulations that supplement such rules and regulations only with the concurrence of that Office.

(3) Regulations concerning independent contractors

The Board of Directors shall prescribe regulations applicable to those independent contractors who are not deemed, under paragraph (1)(B), to be employees of the Corporation for purposes of Title 18, governing conflicts of interest, ethical responsibilities, and the use of confidential information consistent with the goals and purposes of Titles 18 and 41. Any such regulations shall be in addition to, and not in lieu of, any other statute or regulation which may apply to the conduct of such independent contractors.

(4) Disapproval of contractors

(A) In general

The Board of Directors shall prescribe regulations establishing procedures for ensuring that any individual who is performing, directly or indirectly, any function or service on behalf of the Corporation meets minimum standards of competence, experience, integrity, and fitness.

(B) Prohibition from service on behalf of Corporation

The procedures established under subparagraph (A) shall provide that the Corporation shall prohibit any person who does not meet the minimum standards of competence, experience, integrity, and fitness from—

(i) entering into any contract with the Corporation; or

(ii) becoming employed by the Corporation or otherwise performing any service for or on behalf of the Corporation.

(C) Information required to be submitted

The procedures established under subparagraph (A) shall require that any offer submitted to the Corporation by any person under this section and any employment application submitted to the Corporation by any person shall include—

(i) a list and description of any instance during the 5 years preceding the submission of such application in which the person or a company under such person's control defaulted on a material obligation to an insured depository institution; and

(ii) such other information as the Board may prescribe by regulation.

(D) Subsequent submissions

(i) In general

No offer submitted to the Corporation may be accepted unless the offeror agrees that no person will be employed, directly or indirectly, by the offeror under any contract with the Corporation unless-

(I) all applicable information described in subparagraph (C) with respect to any such person is submitted to the Corporation; and

(II) the Corporation does not disapprove of the direct or indirect employment of such person.

(ii) Finality of determination

Any determination made by the Corporation pursuant to this paragraph shall be in the Corporation's sole discretion and shall not be subject to review.

(E) Prohibition required in certain cases

The standards established under subparagraph (A) shall require the Corporation to prohibit any person who has—

(i) been convicted of any felony;

(ii) been removed from, or prohibited from participating in the affairs of, any insured depository institution pursuant to any final enforcement action by any appropriate Federal banking agency;

(iii) demonstrated a pattern or practice of defalcation regarding obligations to insured depository institutions; or

(iv) caused a substantial loss to the Deposit Insurance Fund (or any predecessor deposit insurance fund); from performing any service on behalf of the Corporation.

(5) Abrogation of contracts

The Corporation may rescind any contract with a person who—

(A) fails to disclose a material fact to the Corporation;

(B) would be prohibited under paragraph (6) from providing services to, receiving fees from, or contracting with the Corporation; or

(C) has been subject to a final enforcement action by any Federal banking agency.

(6) Priority of FDIC rules

To the extent that the regulations under this subsection conflict with rules of other agencies or Government corporations, officers, directors, employees, and independent contractors of the Corporation who are also subject to the conflict of interest or ethical rules of another agency or Government corporation, shall be governed by the regulations prescribed by the Board of Directors under this subsection when acting for or on behalf of the Corporation. Notwithstanding the preceding sentence, the rules of the Corporation shall not take priority over the ethics and conflict of interest rules and regulations promulgated by the Office of Government Ethics unless specifically authorized by that Office.

§ 1823. Corporation monies—DFA § 1106

(a) Investment of Corporation's funds

(1) Authority

Funds held in the Deposit Insurance Fund or the FSLIC Resolution Fund, that are not otherwise employed shall be invested in obligations of the United States or in obligations guaranteed as to principal and interest by the United States.

(2) Limitation

The Corporation shall not sell or purchase any obligations described in paragraph (1) for its own account, at any one time aggregating in excess of $100,000, without the approval of the Secretary of the Treasury. The Secretary may approve a transaction or class of transactions subject to the provisions of this paragraph under such conditions as the Secretary may determine.

(b) Depository accounts

The depository accounts of the Corporation shall be kept with the Treasurer of the United States, or, with the approval of the Secretary of the Treasury, with a Federal Reserve bank, or with a depository institution designated as a depository or fiscal agent of the United States: *Provided*, That the Secretary of the Treasury may waive the requirements of this subsection under such conditions as he may determine: *And provided further*, That this subsection shall not apply to the establishment and maintenance in any depository institution for temporary purposes of depository accounts not in excess of $50,000 in any one depository institution, or to the establishment and maintenance in any depository institution of any depository accounts to facilitate the payment of insured deposits, or the making of loans to, or the purchase of assets of, insured depository institutions. When designated for that purpose by the Secretary of the Treasury, the Corporation shall be a depository of public moneys, except receipts from customs, under such regulations as may be prescribed by the said Secretary, and may also be employed as a financial agent of the Government. It shall perform all such reasonable duties as depository of public moneys and financial agent of the Government as may be required of it.

(c) Assistance to insured depository institutions

(1) The Corporation is authorized, in its sole discretion and upon such terms and conditions as the Board of Directors may prescribe, to make loans to, to make deposits in, to purchase the assets or securities of, to assume the liabilities of, or to make contributions to, any insured depository institution—

(A) if such action is taken to prevent the default of such insured depository institution;

(B) if, with respect to an insured bank in default, such action is taken to restore such insured bank to normal operation; or

(C) if, when severe financial conditions exist which threaten the stability of a significant

number of insured depository institutions or of insured depository institutions possessing significant financial resources, such action is taken in order to lessen the risk to the Corporation posed by such insured depository institution under such threat of instability.

(2) (A) In order to facilitate a merger or consolidation of another insured depository institution described in subparagraph (B) with another insured depository institution or the sale of any or all of the assets of such insured depository institution or the assumption of any or all of such insured depository institution's liabilities by another insured depository institution, or the acquisition of the stock of such insured depository institution, the Corporation is authorized, in its sole discretion and upon such terms and conditions as the Board of Directors may prescribe—

(i) to purchase any such assets or assume any such liabilities;

(ii) to make loans or contributions to, or deposits in, or purchase the securities of, such other insured depository institution or the company which controls or will acquire control of such other insured depository institution;

(iii) to guarantee such other insured depository institution or the company which controls or will acquire control of such other insured depository institution against loss by reason of such insured institution's merging or consolidating with or assuming the liabilities and purchasing the assets of such insured depository institution or by reason of such company acquiring control of such insured depository institution; or

(iv) to take any combination of the actions referred to in subparagraphs (i) through (iii).

(B) For the purpose of subparagraph (A), the insured depository institution must be an insured depository institution—

(i) which is in default;

(ii) which, in the judgment of the Board of Directors, is in danger of default; or

(iii) which, when severe financial conditions exist which threaten the stability of a significant number of insured depository institutions or of insured depository institutions possessing significant financial resources, is determined by the Corporation, in its sole discretion, to require assistance under subparagraph (A) in order to lessen the risk to the Corporation posed by such insured depository institution under such threat of instability.

(C) Any action to which the Corporation is or becomes a party by acquiring any asset or exercising any other authority set forth in this section shall be stayed for a period of 60 days at the request of the Corporation.

(3) The Corporation may provide any person acquiring control of, merging with, consolidating with or acquiring the assets of an insured depository institution under subsection (f) or (k) of this section with such financial assistance as it could provide an insured institution under this subsection.

(4) Least-cost resolution required

(A) In general

Notwithstanding any other provision of this chapter, the Corporation may not exercise any authority under this subsection or subsection (d), (f), (h), (i), or (k) of this section with respect to any insured depository institution unless—

(i) the Corporation determines that the exercise of such authority is necessary to meet the obligation of the Corporation to provide insurance coverage for the insured deposits in such institution; and

(ii) the total amount of the expenditures by the Corporation and obligations incurred by the Corporation (including any immediate and long-term obligation of the Corporation and any direct or contingent liability for future payment by the Corporation) in connection with the exercise of any such authority with respect to such institution is the least costly to the deposit insurance fund of all possible methods for meeting the Corporation's obligation under this section.

(B) Determining least costly approach

In determining how to satisfy the Corporation's obligations to an institution's insured depositors at the least possible cost to the deposit insurance fund, the Corporation shall comply with the following provisions:

(i) Present-value analysis; documentation required

The Corporation shall—

(I) evaluate alternatives on a present-value basis, using a realistic discount rate;

(II) document that evaluation and the assumptions on which the evaluation is based, including any assumptions with regard to interest rates, asset recovery rates, asset holding costs, and payment of contingent liabilities; and

(III) retain the documentation for not less than 5 years.

(ii) Foregone tax revenues

Federal tax revenues that the Government would forego as the result of a proposed transaction, to the extent reasonably ascertainable, shall be treated as if they were revenues foregone by the deposit insurance fund.

(C) Time of determination

(i) General rule

For purposes of this subsection, the determination of the costs of providing any assistance under paragraph (1) or (2) or any other provision of this section with respect to any depository institution shall be made as of the date on which the Corporation makes the determination to provide such assistance to the institution under this section.

(ii) Rule for liquidations

For purposes of this subsection, the determination of the costs of liquidation of any depository institution shall be made as of the earliest of—

(I) the date on which a conservator is appointed for such institution;

(II) the date on which a receiver is appointed for such institution; or

(III) the date on which the Corporation makes any determination to provide any assistance under this section with respect to such institution.

(D) Liquidation costs

In determining the cost of liquidating any depository institution for the purpose of comparing the costs under subparagraph (A) (with respect to such institution), the amount of such cost may not exceed the amount which is equal to the sum of the insured deposits of such institution as of the earliest of the dates described in subparagraph (C), minus the present value of the total net amount the Corporation reasonably expects to receive from the disposition of the assets of such institution in connection with such liquidation.

(E) Deposit insurance funds available for intended purpose only

(i) In general

After December 31, 1994, or at such earlier time as the Corporation determines to be appropriate, the Corporation may not take any action, directly or indirectly, with respect to any insured depository institution that would have the effect of increasing losses to the Deposit Insurance Fund by protecting—

(I) depositors for more than the insured portion of deposits (determined without regard to whether such institution is liquidated); or

(II) creditors other than depositors.

(ii) Deadline for regulations

The Corporation shall prescribe regulations to implement clause (i) not later than January 1, 1994, and the regulations shall take effect not later than January 1, 1995.

(iii) Purchase and assumption transactions

No provision of this subparagraph shall be construed as prohibiting the Corporation from allowing any person who acquires any assets or assumes any liabilities of any insured depository institution for which the Corporation has been appointed conservator or receiver to acquire uninsured deposit liabilities of such institution so long as the insurance fund does not incur any loss with respect to such deposit liabilities in an amount greater than the loss which would have been incurred with respect to such liabilities if the institution had been liquidated.

(F) Discretionary determinations

Any determination which the Corporation may make under this paragraph shall be made in the sole discretion of the Corporation.

(G) Systemic risk

(i) Emergency determination by Secretary of the Treasury

Notwithstanding subparagraphs (A) and (E), if, upon the written recommendation of the Board of Directors (upon a vote of not less than two-thirds of the members of the Board of Directors) and the Board of Governors of the Federal Reserve System (upon a vote of not less than two-thirds of the members of such Board), the Secretary of the Treasury (in consultation with the President) determines that—

(I) the Corporation's compliance with subparagraphs (A) and (E) with respect to an insured depository institution would have serious adverse effects on economic conditions or financial stability; and

(II) any action or assistance under this subparagraph would avoid or mitigate such adverse effects,

the Corporation may take other action or provide assistance under this section as necessary to avoid or mitigate such effects.

(ii) Repayment of loss

(I) In general

The Corporation shall recover the loss to the Deposit Insurance Fund arising from any action taken or assistance provided with respect to an insured depository institution under clause (i) from 1 or more special assessments on insured depository institutions, depository institution holding companies (with the concurrence of the Secretary of the Treasury with respect to holding companies), or both, as the Corporation determines to be appropriate.

(II) Treatment of depository institution holding companies

For purposes of this clause, sections 1817 (c)(2) and 1828 (h) of this title shall apply to depository institution holding companies as if they were insured depository institutions.

(III) Regulations

The Corporation shall prescribe such regulations as it deems necessary to implement this clause. In prescribing such regulations, defining terms, and setting the appropriate assessment rate or rates, the Corporation shall establish rates sufficient to cover the losses incurred as a result of the actions of the Corporation under clause (i) and shall consider: the types of entities that benefit from any action taken or assistance provided under this subparagraph; economic conditions, the effects on the industry, and such other factors as the Corporation deems appropriate and relevant to the action taken or the assistance provided. Any funds so collected that exceed actual losses shall be placed in the Deposit Insurance Fund.

(iii) Documentation required

The Secretary of the Treasury shall—

(I) document any determination under clause (i); and

(II) retain the documentation for review under clause (iv).

(iv) GAO review

The Comptroller General of the United States shall review and report to the Congress on any determination under clause (i), including—

(I) the basis for the determination;

(II) the purpose for which any action was taken pursuant to such clause; and

(III) the likely effect of the determination and such action on the incentives and conduct of insured depository institutions and uninsured depositors.

(v) Notice

(I) In general

The Secretary of the Treasury shall provide written notice of any determination under clause (i) to the Committee on Banking, Housing, and Urban Affairs of the Senate and the Committee on Banking, Finance and Urban Affairs of the House of Representatives.

(II) Description of basis of determination

The notice under subclause (I) shall include a description of the basis for any determination under clause (i).

(H) Rule of construction

No provision of law shall be construed as permitting the Corporation to take any action prohibited by paragraph (4) unless such provision expressly provides, by direct reference to this paragraph, that this paragraph shall not apply with respect to such action.

(5) The Corporation may not use its authority under this subsection to purchase the voting or common stock of an insured depository institution. Nothing in the preceding sentence shall be construed to limit the ability of the Corporation to enter into and enforce covenants and agreements that it determines to be necessary to protect its financial interest.

(6) (A) During any period in which an insured depository institution has received assistance under this subsection and such assistance is still outstanding, such insured depository institution may defer the payment of any State or local tax which is determined on the basis of the deposits held by such insured depository institution or of the interest or dividends paid on such deposits.

(B) When such insured depository institution no longer has any outstanding assistance, such insured depository institution shall pay all taxes which were deferred under subparagraph (A). Such payments shall be made in accordance with a payment plan established by the Corporation, after consultation with the applicable State and local taxing authorities.

(7) The transfer of any assets or liabilities associated with any trust business of an insured depository institution in default under subparagraph (2)(A) shall be effective without any State or Federal approval, assignment, or consent with respect thereto.

(8) Assistance before appointment of conservator or receiver

(A) In general

Subject to the least-cost provisions of paragraph (4), the Corporation shall consider providing direct financial assistance under this section for depository institutions before the appointment of a conservator or receiver for such institution only under the following circumstances:

(i) Troubled condition criteria

The Corporation determines—

(I) grounds for the appointment of a conservator or receiver exist or likely will exist in the future unless the depository institution's capital levels are increased; and

(II) it is unlikely that the institution can meet all currently applicable capital standards without assistance.

(ii) Other criteria

The depository institution meets the following criteria:

(I) The appropriate Federal banking agency and the Corporation have determined that, during such period of time preceding the date of such determination as the agency or the Corporation considers to be relevant, the institution's management has been competent and has complied with applicable laws, rules, and supervisory directives and orders.

(II) The institution's management did not engage in any insider dealing, speculative practice, or other abusive activity.

(B) Public disclosure

Any determination under this paragraph to provide assistance under this section shall be made in writing and published in the Federal Register.

(9) Any assistance provided under this subsection may be in subordination to the rights of depositors and other creditors.

(10) In its annual report to the Congress, the Corporation shall report the total amount it has saved, or estimates it has saved, by exercising the authority provided in this subsection.

(11) Unenforceability of certain agreements

No provision contained in any existing or future standstill, confidentiality, or other agreement that, directly or indirectly—

(A) affects, restricts, or limits the ability of any person to offer to acquire or acquire,

(B) prohibits any person from offering to acquire or acquiring, or

(C) prohibits any person from using any previously disclosed information in connection with any such offer to acquire or acquisition of,

all or part of any insured depository institution, including any liabilities, assets, or interest therein, in connection with any transaction in which the Corporation exercises its authority under section 1821 of this title or this section, shall be enforceable against or impose any liability on such person, as such

enforcement or liability shall be contrary to public policy.

(d) Sale of assets to Corporation

(1) In general

Any conservator, receiver, or liquidator appointed for any insured depository institution in default, including the Corporation acting in such capacity, shall be entitled to offer the assets of such depository institutions for sale to the Corporation or as security for loans from the Corporation.

(2) Proceeds

The proceeds of every sale or loan of assets to the Corporation shall be utilized for the same purposes and in the same manner as other funds realized from the liquidation of the assets of such depository institutions.

(3) Rights and powers of Corporation

(A) In general

With respect to any asset acquired or liability assumed pursuant to this section, the Corporation shall have all of the rights, powers, privileges, and authorities of the Corporation as receiver under sections 1821 and 1825(b) of this title.

(B) Rule of construction

Such rights, powers, privileges, and authorities shall be in addition to and not in derogation of any rights, powers, privileges, and authorities otherwise applicable to the Corporation.

(C) Fiduciary responsibility

In exercising any right, power, privilege, or authority described in subparagraph (A), the Corporation shall continue to be subject to the fiduciary duties and obligations of the Corporation as receiver to claimants against the insured depository institution in receivership.

(D) Disposition of assets

In exercising any right, power, privilege, or authority described in subparagraph (A) regarding the sale or disposition of assets sold to the Corporation pursuant to paragraph (1), the Corporation shall conduct its operations in a manner which—

(i) maximizes the net present value return from the sale or disposition of such assets;

(ii) minimizes the amount of any loss realized in the resolution of cases;

(iii) ensures adequate competition and fair and consistent treatment of offerors;

(iv) prohibits discrimination on the basis of race, sex, or ethnic groups in the solicitation and consideration of offers; and

(v) maximizes the preservation of the availability and affordability of residential real property for low-and moderate-income individuals.

(4) Loans

The Corporation, in its discretion, may make loans on the security of or may purchase and liquidate or sell any part of the assets of an insured depository institution which is now or may hereafter be in default.

(e) Agreements against interests of Corporation

(1) In general

No agreement which tends to diminish or defeat the interest of the Corporation in any asset acquired by it under this section or section 1821 of this title, either as security for a loan or by purchase or as receiver of any insured depository institution, shall be valid against the Corporation unless such agreement—

(A) is in writing,

(B) was executed by the depository institution and any person claiming an adverse interest thereunder, including the obligor, contemporaneously with the acquisition of the asset by the depository institution,

(C) was approved by the board of directors of the depository institution or its loan committee, which approval shall be reflected in the minutes of said board or committee, and

(D) has been, continuously, from the time of its execution, an official record of the depository institution.

(2) Exemptions from contemporaneous execution requirement

An agreement to provide for the lawful collateralization of—

(A) deposits of, or other credit extension by, a Federal, State, or local governmental entity, or of any depositor referred to in section 1821(a)(2) of this title, including an agreement to provide collateral in lieu of a surety bond;

(B) bankruptcy estate funds pursuant to section 345(b)(2) of Title 11;

(C) extensions of credit, including any overdraft, from a Federal reserve bank or Federal home loan bank; or

(D) one or more qualified financial contracts, as defined in section 1821(e)(8)(D) of this title,

shall not be deemed invalid pursuant to paragraph (1)(B) solely because such agreement was not executed contemporaneously with the acquisition of the collateral or because of pledges, delivery, or substitution of the collateral made in accordance with such agreement.

(f) Assisted emergency interstate acquisitions

(1) This subsection shall apply only to an acquisition of an insured bank or a holding company by an out-of-State bank savings association or out-of-State holding company for which the Corporation provides assistance under subsection (c) of this section.

(2) (A) Whenever an insured bank with total assets of $500,000,000 or more (as determined from its most recent report of condition) is in default, the Corporation, as receiver, may, in its discretion and upon such terms and conditions as the Corporation may determine, arrange the sale of assets of the bank in default and the assumption of the liabilities of the bank in default, including the sale of such assets to and the assumption of such liabilities by an insured depository institution located in the State where the bank in default was chartered but established by an out-of-State bank or holding company. Where otherwise lawfully required, a transaction under this subsection must be approved by the primary Federal or State supervisor of all parties thereto.

(B)(i) Before making a determination to take any action under subparagraph (A), the Corporation shall consult the State bank supervisor of the State in which the insured bank in default was chartered.

(ii) The State bank supervisor shall be given a reasonable opportunity, and in no event less than forty-eight hours, to object to the use of the provisions of this paragraph. Such notice may be provided by the Corporation prior to its appointment as receiver, but in anticipation of an impending appointment.

(iii) If the State supervisor objects during such period, the Corporation may use the authority of this paragraph only by a vote of 75 percent of the Board of Directors. The Board of Directors shall provide to the State supervisor, as soon as practicable, a written certification of its determination.

(3) Emergency interstate acquisitions of insured banks in danger of default

(A) Acquisition of insured banks in danger of default

One or more out-of-State banks or out-of-State holding companies may acquire and retain all or part of the shares or assets of, or otherwise acquire and retain—

(i) an insured bank in danger of default which has total assets of $500,000,000 or more; or

(ii) 2 or more affiliated insured banks in danger of closing which have aggregate total assets of $500,000,000 or more, if the aggregate total assets of such banks is equal to or greater than 33 percent of the aggregate total assets of all affiliated insured banks.

(B) Acquisition of a holding company or other bank affiliate

If one or more out-of-State banks or out-of-State holding companies acquire 1 or more affiliated insured banks under subparagraph (A) the aggregate total assets of which is equal to or greater than 33 percent of the aggregate total assets of all affiliated insured banks, any such out-of-State bank or out-of-State holding company may also, as part of the same transaction, acquire and retain the shares or assets of, or otherwise acquire and retain—

(i) the holding company which controls the affiliated insured banks so acquired; or

(ii) any other affiliated insured bank.

(C) Request for assistance by corporate board of directors

The Corporation may assist an acquisition or merger authorized under subparagraph (A) only if the board of directors or trustees of each insured bank in danger of default which is being acquired has requested in writing that the Corporation assist the acquisition or merger.

(D) Certain acquisitions authorized after assistance is provided

Notwithstanding paragraph (1), if—

(i) at any time after August 10, 1987, the Corporation provides any assistance under subsection (c) of this section to an insured bank; and

(ii) at the time such assistance is granted, the insured bank, the holding company which controls the insured bank (if any), or any affiliated insured bank is eligible to be acquired by an out-of-State bank or out-of-State holding company under this paragraph,

the insured bank, the holding company, and such other affiliated insured bank shall remain eligible, subject to such terms and conditions as the Corporation (in the Corporation's discretion) may impose, to be acquired by an out-of-State bank or out-of-State holding company under this paragraph as long as any portion of such assistance remains outstanding.

(E) State bank supervisor approval

The Corporation may take no final action in connection with any acquisition under this paragraph unless the State bank supervisor of the State in which the bank in danger of default is located approves the acquisition.

(F) Other requirements not affected

This paragraph does not affect any other requirement under Federal or State law for regulatory approval of an acquisition under this paragraph.

(G) Acquisition may be conditioned on receipt of consideration for Corporation's assistance

Any acquisition described in subparagraph (D) may be conditioned on the receipt of such consideration for the Corporation's assistance as the Board of Directors deems appropriate.

(4) (A) Acquisitions not subject to certain other laws

Section 1842(d) of this title, any provision of State law, and section 1730a(e)(3) of this title shall not apply to prohibit any acquisition under paragraph (2) or (3), except that an out-of-State bank may make such an acquisition only if such ownership is otherwise specifically authorized.

(B) Any subsidiary created by operation of this subsection may retain and operate any existing branch or branches of the institution merged with or acquired under paragraph (2) or (3), but otherwise shall be subject to the conditions upon which a national bank may establish and operate branches in the State in which such insured institution is located.

(C) No insured institution acquired under this subsection shall after it is acquired move its principal office or any branch office which it would be prohibited from moving if the institution were a national bank.

(D) Subsequent nonemergency interstate acquisitions subject to State law

(i) In general

Any out-of-State bank holding company which acquires control of an insured bank in any State under paragraph (2) or (3) may acquire any other insured bank and establish branches in such State to the same extent as a bank holding company whose insured bank subsidiaries' operations are principally conducted in such State may acquire any other insured bank or establish branches.

(ii) Delayed date of applicability

Clause (i) shall not apply with respect to any out-of-State bank holding company referred to in such clause before the earlier of—

(I) the end of the 2–year period beginning on the date the acquisition referred to in such clause with respect to such company is consummated; or

(II) the end of any period established under State law during which such out-of-State bank holding company may not be treated as a bank holding company whose insured bank subsidiaries' operations are principally conducted in such State for purposes of acquiring other insured banks or establishing bank branches.

(iii) Determination of principally conducted

For purposes of this subparagraph, the State in which the operations of a holding company's insured bank subsidiaries are principally conducted is the State determined under section 1842(d) of this title with respect to such holding company.

(E) Certain State interstate banking laws inapplicable

Any holding company which acquires control of any insured bank or holding company under paragraph (2) or (3) or subparagraph (D) of this paragraph shall not, by reason of such acquisition, be required under the law of any State to divest any other insured bank or be prevented from acquiring any other bank or holding company.

(5) In determining whether to arrange a sale of assets and assumption of liabilities or an acquisition or a merger under the authority of paragraph (2) or (3), the Corporation may solicit such offers or proposals as are practicable from any prospective purchasers or merger partners it determines, in its sole discretion, are both qualified and capable of acquiring the assets and liabilities of the bank in default or the bank in danger of default.

(6) (A) If, after receiving offers, the offer presenting the lowest expense to the Corporation, that is in a form and with conditions acceptable to the Corporation (hereinafter referred to as the "lowest acceptable offer"), is from an offeror that is not an existing in-State bank of the same type as the bank that is in default or is in danger of default (or, where the bank is an insured bank other than a mutual savings bank, the lowest acceptable offer is not from an in-State holding company), the Corporation shall permit the offeror which made the initial lowest acceptable offer and each offeror who made an offer the estimated cost of which to the Corporation was within 15 per centum or $15,000,000, whichever is less, of the initial lowest acceptable offer to submit a new offer.

(B) In considering authorizations under this subsection, the Corporation shall give consideration to the need to minimize the cost of financial assistance and to the maintenance of specialized depository institutions. The Corporation shall authorize transactions under this subsection considering the following priorities:

(i) First, between depository institutions of the same type within the same State.

(ii) Second, between depository institutions of the same type—

(I) in different States which by statute specifically authorize such acquisitions; or

(II) in the absence of such statutes, in different States which are contiguous.

(iii) Third, between depository institutions of the same type in different States other than the States described in clause (ii).

(iv) Fourth, between depository institutions of different types in the same State.

(v) Fifth, between depository institutions of different types—

(I) in different States which by statute specifically authorize such acquisitions; or

(II) in the absence of such statutes, in different States which are contiguous.

(vi) Sixth, between depository institutions of different types in different States other than the States described in clause (v).

(C) Minority bank priority

In the case of a minority-controlled bank, the Corporation shall seek an offer from other minority-controlled banks before proceeding with the bidding priorities set forth in subparagraph (B).

(D) In determining the cost of offers and reoffers, the Corporation's calculations and estimations shall be determinative. The Corporation may set reasonable time limits on offers and reoffers.

(7) No sale may be made under the provisions of paragraph (2) or (3)—

(A) which would result in a monopoly, or which would be in furtherance of any combination or conspiracy to monopolize or to attempt to monopolize the business of banking in any part of the United States;

(B) whose effect in any section of the country may be substantially to lessen competition, or to tend to create a monopoly, or which in any other manner would be in restraint of trade, unless the Corporation finds that the anticompetitive effects of the proposed transactions are clearly outweighed in the public interest by the probable effect of the transaction in meeting the conven-

ience and needs of the community to be served; or

(C) if in the opinion of the Corporation the acquisition threatens the safety and soundness of the acquirer or does not result in the future viability of the resulting depository institution.

(8) As used in this subsection—

(A) the term "in-State depository institution or in-State holding company" means an existing insured depository institution currently operating in the State in which the bank in default or the bank in danger of default is chartered or a company that is operating an insured depository institution subsidiary in the State in which the bank in default or the bank in danger of default is chartered;

(B) the term "acquire" means to acquire, directly or indirectly, ownership or control through—

(i) an acquisition of shares;

(ii) an acquisition of assets or assumption of liabilities;

(iii) a merger or consolidation; or

(iv) any similar transaction;

(C) the term "affiliated insured bank" means—

(i) when used in connection with a reference to a holding company, an insured bank which is a subsidiary of such holding company; and

(ii) when used in connection with a reference to 2 or more insured banks, insured banks which are subsidiaries of the same holding company; and

(D) the term "subsidiary" has the meaning given to such term in section 1841(d) of this title.

(9) No assistance authorized for certain subsidiaries of holding companies

(A) In general

The Corporation shall not provide any assistance to a subsidiary, other than a subsidiary that is an insured depository institution, of a holding company in connection with any acquisition under this subsection.

(B) Intermediate holding company permitted

This paragraph does not prohibit an intermediate holding company or an affiliate of an insured depository institution from being a conduit for assistance ultimately intended for an insured bank.

(10) Annual report

(A) Required

In its annual report to Congress the Corporation shall include a report on the acquisitions under this subsection during the preceding year.

(B) Contents

The report required under subparagraph (A) shall contain the following information:

(i) The number of acquisitions under this subsection.

(ii) A brief description of each such acquisition and the circumstances under which such acquisition occurred.

(11) Determination of total assets

For purposes of this subsection, the total assets of any insured bank shall be determined on the basis of the most recent report of condition of such bank which is available at the time of such determination.

(12) Acquisition of minority bank by minority bank holding company without regard to asset size

(A) In general

For the purpose of ensuring continued minority control of a minority-controlled bank, paragraphs (2) and (3) shall apply with respect to the acquisition of a minority-controlled bank by an out-of-State minority-controlled depository institution or depository institution holding company without regard to the fact that the total assets of such minority-controlled bank are less than $500,000,000.

(B) Definitions

For purposes of this paragraph:

(i) Minority bank

The term "minority bank" means any depository institution described in clause (i), (ii), or (iii) of section 461(b)(1)(A) of this title—

(I) more than 50 percent of the ownership or control of which is held by one or more minority individuals; and

(II) more than 50 percent of the net profit or loss of which accrues to minority individuals.

(ii) Minority

The term "minority" means any Black American, Native American, Hispanic American, or Asian American.

(g) Payment of interest on stock subscriptions

Prior to July 1, 1951, the Corporation shall pay out of its capital account to the Secretary of the Treasury an amount equal to 2 per centum simple interest per annum on amounts advanced to the Corporation on stock subscriptions by the Secretary of the Treasury and the Federal Reserve banks, from the time of such advances until the amounts thereof were repaid. The amount payable hereunder shall be paid in two equal installments, the first installment to be paid prior to December 31, 1950.

(h) Reopening or aversion of closing of insured branch of foreign bank

The powers conferred on the Board of Directors and the Corporation by this section to take action to reopen an insured depository institution in default or to avert the default of an insured depository institution may be used with respect to an insured branch of a foreign bank if, in the judgment of the Board of Directors, the public interest in avoiding the default of such branch substantially outweighs any additional risk of loss to the Bank Insurance Fund which the exercise of such powers would entail.

(i) Repealed. Pub.L. 97–320, § 206, Oct. 15, 1982, 96 Stat. 1496

(j) Loan loss amortization for certain banks

(1) Eligibility

The appropriate Federal banking agency shall permit an agricultural bank to take the actions referred to in paragraph (2) if it finds that—

(A) there is no evidence that fraud or criminal abuse on the part of the bank led to the losses referred to in paragraph (2); and

(B) the agricultural bank has a plan to restore its capital, not later than the close of the amortization period established under paragraph (2), to a level prescribed by the appropriate Federal banking agency.

(2) Seven-year loss amortization

(A) Any loss on any qualified agricultural loan that an agricultural bank would otherwise be required to show on its annual financial statement for any year between December 31, 1983, and January 1, 1992, may be amortized on its financial statements over a period of not to exceed 7 years, as provided in regulations issued by the appropriate Federal banking agency.

(B) An agricultural bank may reappraise any real estate or other property, real or personal, that it acquired coincident to the making of a qualified agricultural loan and that it owned on January 1, 1983, and any such additional property that it acquires prior to January 1, 1992. Any loss that such bank would otherwise be required to show on its annual financial statements as the result of any such reappraisal may be amortized on its financial statements over a period of not to exceed 7 years, as provided in regulations issued by the appropriate Federal banking agency.

(3) Regulations

Not later than 90 days after August 10, 1987, the appropriate Federal banking agency shall issue regulations implementing this subsection with respect to banks that it supervises, including regulations implementing the capital restoration requirement of paragraph (1)(B).

(4) Definitions

As used in this subsection—

(A) the term "agricultural bank" means a bank—

(i) the deposits of which are insured by the Federal Deposit Insurance Corporation;

(ii) which is located in an area the economy of which is dependent on agriculture;

(iii) which has assets of $100,000,000 or less; and

(iv) which has—

(I) at least 25 percent of its total loans in qualified agricultural loans; or

(II) fewer than 25 percent of its total loans in qualified agricultural loans but which the appropriate Federal banking agency or State bank commissioner recommends to the Corporation for eligibility under this section, or which the Corporation, on its motion, deems eligible; and

(B) the term "qualified agricultural loan" means a loan made to finance the production of agricultural products or livestock in the United States, a loan secured by farmland or farm machinery, or such other category of loans as the appropriate Federal banking agency may deem eligible.

(5) Maintenance of portfolio

As a condition of eligibility under this subsection, the agricultural bank must agree to maintain in its loan portfolio a percentage of agricultural loans which is not lower than the percentage of such loans in its loan portfolio on January 1, 1986.

(k) Emergency acquisitions

(1) In general

(A) Acquisitions authorized

(i) Transactions described

Notwithstanding any provision of State law, upon determining that severe financial conditions threaten the stability of a significant number of savings associations, or of savings associations possessing significant financial resources, the Corporation, in its discretion and if it determines such authorization would lessen the risk to the Corporation, may authorize—

(I) a savings association that is eligible for assistance pursuant to subsection (c) of this section to merge or consolidate with, or to transfer its assets and liabilities to, any other savings association or any insured bank,

(II) any other savings association to acquire control of such savings association, or

(III) any company to acquire control of such savings association or to acquire the assets or assume the liabilities thereof.

The Corporation may not authorize any transaction under this subsection unless the Corporation determines that the authorization will not present a substantial risk to the safety or soundness of the savings association to be acquired or any acquiring entity.

(ii) Terms of transactions

Mergers, consolidations, transfers, and acquisitions under this subsection shall be on such terms as the Corporation shall provide.

(iii) Approval by appropriate agency

Where otherwise required by law, transactions under this subsection must be approved by the appropriate Federal banking agency of every party thereto.

(iv) Acquisitions by savings associations

Any Federal savings association that acquires another savings association pursuant to clause (i) may, with the concurrence of the Director of the Office of Thrift Supervision, hold that savings association as a subsidiary notwithstanding the percentage limitations of section 1464(c)(4)(B) of this title.

(v) Dual service

Dual service by a management official that would otherwise be prohibited under the Depository Institution Management Interlocks Act [12 U.S.C.A. § 3201 et seq.] may, with the approval of the Corporation, continue for up to 10 years.

(vi) Continued applicability of certain state restrictions

Nothing in this subsection overrides or supersedes State laws restricting or limiting the activities of a savings association on behalf of another entity.

(B) Consultation with State official

(i) Consultation required

Before making a determination to take any action under subparagraph (A), the Corporation shall consult the State official having jurisdiction of the acquired institution.

(ii) Period for State response

The official shall be given a reasonable opportunity, and in no event less than 48 hours, to object to the use of the provisions of this paragraph. Such notice may be provided by the Corporation prior to its appointment as receiver, but in anticipation of an impending appointment.

(iii) Approval over objection of State official

If the official objects during such period, the Corporation may use the authority of this paragraph only by a vote of 75 percent or more of the voting members of the Board of Directors. The Corporation shall provide to the official, as soon as practicable, a written certification of its determination.

(2) Solicitation of offers

(A) In general

In considering authorizations under this subsection, the Corporation may solicit such offers or proposals as are practicable from any prospective purchasers or merger partners it determines, in its sole discretion, are both qualified and capable of acquiring the assets and liabilities of the savings association.

(B) Minority-controlled institutions

In the case of a minority-controlled depository institution, the Corporation shall seek an offer from other minority-controlled depository institutions before seeking an offer from other persons or entities.

(3) Determination of costs

In determining the cost of offers under this subsection, the Corporation's calculations and estimations shall be determinative. The Corporation may set reasonable time limits on offers.

(4) Branching provisions

(A) In general

If a merger, consolidation, transfer, or acquisition under this subsection involves a savings association eligible for assistance and a bank or bank holding company, a savings association may retain and operate any existing branch or branches or any other existing facilities. If the savings association continues to exist as a separate entity, it may establish and operate new branches to the same extent as any savings association that is not affiliated with a bank holding company and the home office of which is located in the same State.

(B) Restrictions

(i) In general

Notwithstanding subparagraph (A), if—

(I) a savings association described in such subparagraph does not have its home office in the State of the bank holding company bank subsidiary, and

(II) such association does not qualify as a domestic building and loan association under section 7701(a)(19) of Title 26, or does not meet the asset composition test imposed by subparagraph (C) of that section on institutions seeking so to qualify,

such savings association shall be subject to the conditions upon which a bank may retain, operate, and establish branches in the State in which the savings association is located.

(ii) Transition period

The Corporation, for good cause shown, may allow a savings association up to 2 years to comply with the requirements of clause (i).

(5) Assistance before appointment of conservator or receiver

(A) Assistance proposals

The Corporation shall consider proposals by savings associations for assistance pursuant to subsection (c) of this section before grounds exist for appointment of a conservator or receiver for such member under the following circumstances:

(i) Troubled condition criteria

The Corporation determines—

(I) that grounds for appointment of a conservator or receiver exist or likely will exist in the future unless the member's tangible capital is increased;

(II) that it is unlikely that the member can achieve positive tangible capital without assistance; and

(III) that providing assistance pursuant to the member's proposal would be likely to lessen the risk to the Corporation.

(ii) Other criteria

The member meets the following criteria:

(I) Before August 9, 1989, the member was solvent under applicable regulatory accounting principles but had negative tangible capital.

(II) The member's negative tangible capital position is substantially attributable to its participation in acquisition and merger transactions that were instituted by the Federal Home Loan Bank Board or the Federal Savings and Loan Insurance Corporation for supervisory reasons.

(III) The member is a qualified thrift lender (as defined in section 1467a(m) of this title) or would be a qualified thrift lender if commercial real estate owned and nonperforming commercial loans acquired in acquisition and merger transactions that were instituted by the Federal Home Loan Bank Board or the Federal Savings and Loan Insurance

Corporation for supervisory reasons were excluded from the member's total assets.

(IV) The appropriate Federal banking agency has determined that the member's management is competent and has complied with applicable laws, rules, and supervisory directives and orders.

(V) The member's management did not engage in insider dealing or speculative practices or other activities that jeopardized the member's safety and soundness or contributed to its impaired capital position.

(VI) The member's offices are located in an economically depressed region.

(B) Corporation consideration of assistance proposal

If a member meets the requirements of clauses (i) and (ii) of subparagraph (A), the Corporation shall consider providing direct financial assistance.

(C) Economically depressed region defined

For purposes of this paragraph, the term "economically depressed region" means any geographical region which the Corporation determines by regulation to be a region within which real estate values have suffered serious decline due to severe economic conditions, such as a decline in energy or agricultural values or prices.

§ 1824. Borrowing authority

(a) Borrowing from Treasury

(1) In general

The Corporation is authorized to borrow from the Treasury, and the Secretary of the Treasury is authorized and directed to loan to the Corporation on such terms as may be fixed by the Corporation and the Secretary, such funds as in the judgment of the Board of Directors of the Corporation are from time to time required for insurance purposes, not exceeding in the aggregate $100,000,000,000 outstanding at any one time, subject to the approval of the Secretary of the Treasury: Provided, That the rate of interest to be charged in connection with any loan made pursuant to this subsection shall not be less than an amount determined by the Secretary of the Treasury, taking into consideration current market yields on outstanding marketable obligations of the United

States of comparable maturities. For such purpose the Secretary of the Treasury is authorized to use as a public-debt transaction the proceeds of the sale of any securities hereafter issued under chapter 31 of title 31, and the purposes for which securities may be issued under chapter 31 of title 31 are extended to include such loans. Any such loan shall be used by the Corporation solely in carrying out its functions with respect to such insurance. All loans and repayments under this subsection shall be treated as public-debt transactions of the United States. The Corporation may employ any funds obtained under this section for purposes of the Deposit Insurance Fund and the borrowing shall become a liability of the Deposit Insurance Fund to the extent funds are employed therefor.

(2) Funding

There are hereby appropriated to the Secretary, for fiscal year 1989 and each fiscal year thereafter, such sums as may be necessary to carry out this subsection.

(3) Temporary increases authorized

(A) Recommendations for increase

During the period beginning on May 20, 2009, and ending on December 31, 2010, if, upon the written recommendation of the Board of Directors (upon a vote of not less than two-thirds of the members of the Board of Directors) and the Board of Governors of the Federal Reserve System (upon a vote of not less than two-thirds of the members of such Board), the Secretary of the Treasury (in consultation with the President) determines that additional amounts above the $100,000,000,000 amount specified in paragraph (1) are necessary, such amount shall be increased to the amount so determined to be necessary, not to exceed $500,000,000,000.

(B) Report required

If the borrowing authority of the Corporation is increased above $100,000,000,000 pursuant to subparagraph (A), the Corporation shall promptly submit a report to the Committee on Banking, Housing, and Urban Affairs of the Senate and the Committee on Financial Services of the House of Representatives describing the reasons and need for the additional borrowing authority and its intended uses.

(C) Restriction on usage

The Corporation may not borrow pursuant to subparagraph (A) to fund obligations of the Corporation incurred as a part of a program established by the Secretary of the Treasury pursuant to the Emergency Economic Stabilization Act of 2008 to purchase or guarantee assets.

(b) Borrowing from Federal Financing Bank

The Corporation is authorized to issue and sell the Corporation's obligations, on behalf of the Deposit Insurance Fund, to the Federal Financing Bank established by the Federal Financing Bank Act of 1973 [12 U.S.C.A. § 2281 et seq.]. The Federal Financing Bank is authorized to purchase and sell the Corporation's obligations on terms and conditions determined by the Federal Financing Bank. Any such borrowings shall be obligations subject to the obligation limitation of section 1825(c) of this title. This subsection does not affect the eligibility of any other entity to borrow from the Federal Financing Bank.

(c) Repayment schedules required for any borrowing

(1) In general

No amount may be provided by the Secretary of the Treasury to the Corporation under subsection (a) of this section unless an agreement is in effect between the Secretary and the Corporation which—

(A) provides a schedule for the repayment of the outstanding amount of any borrowing under such subsection; and

(B) demonstrates that income to the Corporation from assessments under this chapter will be sufficient to amortize the outstanding balance within the period established in the repayment schedule and pay the interest accruing on such balance.

(2) Consultation with and report to Congress

The Secretary of the Treasury and the Corporation shall—

(A) consult with the Committee on Banking, Finance and Urban Affairs of the House of Representatives and the Committee on Banking, Housing, and Urban Affairs of the Senate on the terms of any repayment schedule agreement described in paragraph (1) relating to repayment, including terms relating to any emergency special assessment under section 1817(b)(7) of this title; and

(B) submit a copy of each repayment schedule agreement entered into under paragraph (1) to the Committee on Banking, Finance and Urban Affairs of the House of Representatives and the Committee on Banking, Housing, and Urban Affairs of the Senate before the end of the 30–day period beginning on the date any amount is provided by the Secretary of the Treasury to the Corporation under subsection (a) of this section.

(3) Repealed. Pub.L. 109-173, § 8(a)(22), Feb. 15, 2006, 119 Stat. 3613

(d) Borrowing for the Deposit Insurance Fund from insured depository institutions

(1) Borrowing authority

The Corporation may issue obligations to insured depository institutions, and may borrow from insured depository institutions and give security for any amount borrowed, and may pay interest on (and any redemption premium with respect to) any such obligation or amount to the extent—

(A) the proceeds of any such obligation or amount are used by the Corporation solely for purposes of carrying out the Corporation's functions with respect to the Deposit Insurance Fund; and

(B) the terms of the obligation or instrument limit the liability of the Corporation or the Deposit Insurance Fund for the payment of interest and the repayment of principal to the amount which is equal to the amount of assessment income received by the Fund from assessments under section 1817 of this title.

(2) Limitations on borrowing

(A) Applicability of public debt limit

For purposes of the public debt limit established in section 3101(b) of Title 31, any obligation issued, or amount borrowed, by the Corporation under paragraph (1) shall be considered to be an obligation to which such limit applies.

(B) Applicability of FDIC borrowing limit

For purposes of the dollar amount limitation established in subsection (a) of this section, any obligation issued, or amount borrowed, by the Corporation under paragraph (1) shall be considered to be an amount borrowed from the Treasury under such section.

(C) Interest rate limit

The rate of interest payable in connection with any obligation issued, or amount borrowed, by the Corporation under paragraph (1) shall not exceed an amount determined by the Secretary of the Treasury, taking into consideration current market yields on outstanding marketable obligations of the United States of comparable maturities.

(D) Obligations to be held only by BIF members

The terms of any obligation issued by the Corporation under paragraph (1) shall provide that the obligation will be valid only if held by a insured depository institution.

(3) Liability of the Deposit Insurance Fund

Any obligation issued or amount borrowed under paragraph (1) shall be a liability of the Deposit Insurance Fund.

(4) Terms and conditions

Subject to paragraphs (1) and (2), the Corporation shall establish the terms and conditions for obligations issued or amounts borrowed under paragraph (1), including interest rates and terms to maturity.

(5) Investment by insured depository institutions

(A) Authority to invest

Subject to subparagraph (B) and notwithstanding any other provision of Federal law or the law of any State, any insured depository institution may purchase and hold for investment any obligation issued by the Corporation under paragraph (1) without limitation, other than any limitation the appropriate Federal banking agency may impose specifically with respect to such obligations.

(B) Investment only from capital and retained earnings

Any insured depository institution may purchase obligations or make loans to the Corporation under paragraph (1) only to the extent the purchase money or the money loaned is derived from the member's capital or retained earnings.

(6) Accounting treatment

In accounting for any investment in an obligation purchased from, or any loan made to, the Corporation for purposes of determining compliance with any capital standard and preparing any report required pursuant to section 1817(a) of this title, the amount of such investment or loan shall be treated as an asset.

(e) Borrowing for the Deposit Insurance Fund from Federal home loan banks

(1) In general

The Corporation may borrow from the Federal home loan banks, with the concurrence of the Federal Housing Finance Board, such funds as the Corporation considers necessary for the use of the Deposit Insurance Fund.

(2) Terms and conditions

Any loan from any Federal home loan bank under paragraph (1) to the Deposit Insurance Fund shall—

(A) bear a rate of interest of not less than the current marginal cost of funds to that bank, taking into account the maturities involved;

(B) be adequately secured, as determined by the Federal Housing Finance Board;

(C) be a direct liability of the Deposit Insurance Fund; and

(D) be subject to the limitations of section 1825 (c) of this title.

§ 1825. Issuance of notes, debentures, bonds, and other obligations; exemption from taxation

(a) General rule

All notes, debentures, bonds, or other such obligations issued by the Corporation shall be exempt, both as to principal and interest, from all taxation (except estate and inheritance taxes) now or hereafter imposed by the United States, by any Territory, dependency, or possession thereof, or by any State, county, municipality, or local taxing authority: *Provided*, That interest upon or any income from any such obligations and gain from the sale or other disposition of such obligations shall not have any exemption, as such, and loss from the sale or other disposition of such obligations shall not have any special treatment, as such, under the Internal Revenue Code, or laws amendatory or supplementary thereto. The Corporation, including its franchise, its capital, reserves, and surplus, and its income, shall be exempt from all taxation now or hereaf-

ter imposed by the United States, by any Territory, dependency, or possession thereof, or by any State, county, municipality, or local taxing authority, except that any real property of the Corporation shall be subject to State, Territorial, county, municipal, or local taxation to the same extent according to its value as other real property is taxed.

(b) Other exemptions

When acting as a receiver, the following provisions shall apply with respect to the Corporation:

(1) The Corporation including its franchise, its capital, reserves, and surplus, and its income, shall be exempt from all taxation imposed by any State, county, municipality, or local taxing authority, except that any real property of the Corporation shall be subject to State, territorial, county, municipal, or local taxation to the same extent according to its value as other real property is taxed, except that, notwithstanding the failure of any person to challenge an assessment under State law of such property's value, such value, and the tax thereon, shall be determined as of the period for which such tax is imposed.

(2) No property of the Corporation shall be subject to levy, attachment, garnishment, foreclosure, or sale without the consent of the Corporation, nor shall any involuntary lien attach to the property of the Corporation.

(3) The Corporation shall not be liable for any amounts in the nature of penalties or fines, including those arising from the failure of any person to pay any real property, personal property, probate, or recording tax or any recording or filing fees when due.

(4) Exemption from criminal prosecution

The Corporation shall be exempt from all prosecution by the United States or any State, county, municipality, or local authority for any criminal offense arising under Federal, State, county, municipal, or local law, which was allegedly committed by the institution, or persons acting on behalf of the institution, prior to the appointment of the Corporation as receiver.

This subsection shall not apply with respect to any tax imposed (or other amount arising) under Title 26.

(c) Limitation on borrowing

(1) Cost estimate for outstanding obligations, guarantees, and liabilities

As soon as practicable after August 9, 1989, the Corporation shall estimate the aggregate cost to the Corporation for all outstanding obligations and guarantees of the Corporation which were issued, and all outstanding liabilities which were incurred, by the Corporation before such date.

(2) Estimate of notes and other obligations required

Before issuing an obligation or making a guarantee, the Corporation shall estimate the cost of such obligations or guarantees.

(3) Inclusion of estimates in financial statements

The Corporation shall—

(A) reflect in its financial statements the estimates made by the Corporation under paragraphs (1) and (2) of the aggregate amount of the costs to the Corporation for outstanding obligations and other liabilities, and

(B) make such adjustments as are appropriate in the estimate of such aggregate amount not less frequently than quarterly.

(4) Estimate of other assets required

The Corporation shall—

(A) estimate the market value of assets held by it as a result of case resolution activities, with a reduction for expenses expected to be incurred by the Corporation in connection with the management and sale of such assets;

(B) reflect the amounts so estimated in its financial statements; and

(C) make such adjustments as are appropriate of such market value not less than quarterly.

(5) Maximum amount limitation on outstanding obligations

Notwithstanding any other provisions of this chapter, the Corporation may not issue or incur any obligation, if, after issuing or incurring the obligation, the aggregate amount of obligations of the Deposit Insurance Fund outstanding would exceed the sum of—

(A) the amount of cash or the equivalent of cash held by the Deposit Insurance Fund;

(B) the amount which is equal to 90 percent of the Corporation's estimate of the fair market value of assets held by the Deposit Insurance Fund, other than assets described in subparagraph (A); and

(C) the total of the amounts authorized to be borrowed from the Secretary of the Treasury pursuant to section 1824(a) of this title.

(6) Obligation defined

(A) In general

For purposes of paragraph (5), the term "obligation" includes—

(i) any guarantee issued by the Corporation, other than deposit guarantees;

(ii) any amount borrowed pursuant to section 1824 of this title; and

(iii) any other obligation for which the Corporation has a direct or contingent liability to pay any amount.

(B) Valuation of contingent liabilities

The Corporation shall value any contingent liability at its expected cost to the Corporation.

(d) Full faith and credit

The full faith and credit of the United States is pledged to the payment of any obligation issued after August 9, 1989 by the Corporation, with respect to both principal and interest, if—

(1) the principal amount of such obligation is stated in the obligation; and

(2) the term to maturity or the date of maturity of such obligation is stated in the obligation.

§ 1826. Forms of obligations; preparation by Secretary of the Treasury

In order that the Corporation may be supplied with such forms of notes, debentures, bonds, or other such obligations as it may need for issuance under this chapter, the Secretary of the Treasury is authorized to prepare such forms as shall be suitable and approved by the Corporation, to be held in the Treasury subject to delivery, upon order of the Corporation. The engraved plates, dies, bed pieces, and other material executed in connection therewith shall remain in the custody of the Secretary of the Treasury. The Corporation shall reimburse the Secretary of the Treasury for any expenses incurred in the preparation, custody, and delivery of such notes, debentures, bonds, or other such obligations.

§ 1827. Reports by Corporation; audit of financial transactions; report on audits; employment of certified public accountants for audits

(a) Annual reports on the Deposit Insurance Fund and the FSLIC Resolution Fund

(1) In general

The Corporation shall annually submit a full report of its operations, activities, budget, receipts, and expenditures for the preceding 12-month period. The report shall include, with respect to the Deposit Insurance Fund and the FSLIC Resolution Fund, an analysis by the Corporation of—

(A) the current financial condition of each such fund;

(B) the purpose, effect, and estimated cost of each resolution action taken for an insured depository institution during the preceding year;

(C) the extent to which the actual costs of assistance provided to, or for the benefit of, an insured depository institution during the preceding year exceeded the estimated costs of such assistance reported in a previous year under paragraph (A);

(D) the exposure of the Deposit Insurance Fund to changes in those economic factors most likely to affect the condition of that fund;

(E) a current estimate of the resources needed for the Deposit Insurance Fund or the FSLIC Resolution Fund to achieve the purposes of this chapter; and

(F) any findings, conclusions, and recommendations for legislative and administrative actions considered appropriate to future resolution activities by the Corporation.

(2) Manner of submission

Such report shall be submitted to the President of the Senate and the Speaker of the House of Representatives, who shall cause the same to be printed for the information of Congress, and the President as soon as practicable after the first day of January each year.

(3) Coordination with other report requirements

The report required under this subsection shall include the report required under section 57a(f)(7) of Title 15.

(b) Quarterly reports to treasury

(1) Financial operating plans and forecasts

Before the beginning of each fiscal quarter, the Corporation shall provide to the Secretary of the Treasury a copy of the Corporation's financial operating plans and forecasts.

(2) Financial condition and reports of operations

As soon as practicable after the end of each fiscal quarter, the Corporation shall submit to the Secretary of the Treasury a copy of the report of the Corporation's financial condition as of the end of such fiscal quarter and the results of the Corporation's operations during such fiscal quarter.

(3) Items to be included

The plans, forecasts, and reports required under this subsection shall reflect the estimates required to be made under section 1825(b) of this title of the liabilities and obligations of the Corporation described in such section.

(4) Rule of construction

The requirement to provide plans, forecasts, and reports to the Secretary of the Treasury under this subsection may not be construed as implying any obligation on the part of the Corporation to obtain the consent or approval of such Secretary with respect to such plans, forecasts, and reports.

(c) Reports to OMB

(1) Financial information

The Corporation shall continue to provide to the Director of the Office of Management and Budget financial information consistent with that contained in the reports that were being provided to the Director immediately prior to August 9, 1989.

(2) Financial operating plans and forecasts

The Corporation shall also provide to the Director copies of the Corporation's financial operating plans and forecasts as prepared by the Corporation in the ordinary course of its operations, and copies of the quarterly reports of the Corporation's financial condition and results of operations as prepared by the Corporation in the ordinary course of its operations.

(3) Rule of construction

This subsection may not be construed as implying any obligation on the part of the Corporation to consult with or obtain the consent or approval of the Director with respect to any reports, plans, forecasts, or other information referred to in paragraph (1) or (2) or any jurisdiction or oversight over the affairs or operations of the Corporation.

(d) Audit

(1) Audit required

The Comptroller General shall audit annually the financial transactions of the Corporation, the Deposit Insurance Fund, and the FSLIC Resolution Fund in accordance with generally accepted government auditing standards.

(2) Access to books and records

All books, records, accounts, reports, files, and property belonging to or used by the Corporation, the Deposit Insurance Fund and the FSLIC Resolution Fund, or by an independent certified public accountant retained to audit the Fund's financial statements, shall be made available to the Comptroller General.

(e) Audit of Corporation

The financial transactions of the Corporation shall be audited by the Government Accountability Office in accordance with the principles and procedures applicable to commercial corporate transactions and under such rules and regulations as may be prescribed by the Comptroller General of the United States. The audit shall be conducted at the place or places where accounts of the Corporation are normally kept. The representatives of the Government Accountability Office shall have access to all books, accounts, records, reports, files, and all other papers, things, or property belonging to or in use by the Corporation pertaining to its financial transactions and necessary to facilitate the audit, and they shall be afforded full facilities for verifying transactions with the balances or securities held by depositaries, fiscal agents, and custodians. All such books, accounts, records, reports, files, papers, and property of the Corporation shall remain in possession and custody of the Corporation. The audit shall begin with financial transactions occurring on and after August 31, 1948. The Corporation shall be audited at least once in every three years.

(f) Report of audit

A report of each audit conducted under subsection (b) of this section shall be made by the Comptroller General to the Congress not later than six and one-half months following the close of the last year covered by such audit. The report to the Congress shall set forth the scope of the audit and shall include a statement of assets and liabilities and surplus or deficit; a statement of surplus or deficit analysis; a statement of income and expenses; a statement of sources and application of funds and such comments and information as may be deemed necessary to inform Congress of the financial operations and condition of the Corporation, together with such recommendations with respect thereto as the Comptroller General may deem advisable. The report shall also show specifically any program, expenditure, or other financial transaction or undertaking observed in the course of the audit, which, in the opinion of the Comptroller General, has been carried on or made without authority of law. A copy of each report shall be furnished to the President, to the Secretary of the Treasury, and to the Corporation at the time submitted to the Congress.

(g) Assistance in audit; costs

For the purpose of conducting such audit the Comptroller General is authorized in his discretion to employ by contract, without regard to section 5 of Title 41, professional services of firms and organizations of certified public accountants, with the concurrence of the Corporation, for temporary periods or for special purposes. The Corporation shall reimburse the Government Accountability Office for the cost of any such audit as billed therefor by the Comptroller General, and the Government Accountability Office shall deposit the sums so reimbursed into the Treasury as miscellaneous receipts.

§ 1828. Regulations governing insured depository institutions—DFA §§ 604, 611, 613, 615, 623, 627

(a) Representations of deposit insurance

(1) Insured depository institutions

(A) In general

Each insured depository institution shall display at each place of business maintained by that institution a sign or signs relating to the insurance of the deposits of the institution, in accordance with regulations to be prescribed by the Corporation.

(B) Statement to be included

Each sign required under subparagraph (A) shall include a statement that insured deposits are backed by the full faith and credit of the United States Government.

(2) Regulations

The Corporation shall prescribe regulations to carry out this subsection, including regulations governing the substance of signs required by paragraph (1) and the manner of display or use of such signs.

(3) Penalties

For each day that an insured depository institution continues to violate paragraph (1) or any regulation issued under paragraph (2), it shall be subject to a penalty of not more than $100, which the Corporation may recover for its use.

(4) False advertising, misuse of FDIC names, and misrepresentation to indicate insured status

(A) Prohibition on false advertising and misuse of FDIC names

No person may represent or imply that any deposit liability, obligation, certificate,or share is insured or guaranteed by the Corporation, if such deposit liability, obligation, certificate, or share is not insured or guaranteed by the Corporation—

(i) by using the terms "Federal Deposit", "Federal Deposit Insurance", "Federal Deposit Insurance Corporation", any combination of such terms, or the abbreviation "FDIC" as part of the business name or firm name of any person, including any corporation, partnership, business trust, association, or other business entity; or

(ii) by using such terms or any other terms, sign, or symbol as part of an advertisement, solicitation, or other document.

(B) Prohibition on misrepresentations of insured status

No person may knowingly misrepresent—

(i) that any deposit liability, obligation, certificate, or share is insured, under this chapter, if such deposit liability, obligation, certificate, or share is not so insured; or

(ii) the extent to which or the manner in which any deposit liability, obligation, certificate, or share is insured under this chapter, if such deposit liability, obligation, certificate, or share is not so insured, to the extent or in the manner represented.

(C) Authority of the appropriate Federal banking agency

The appropriate Federal banking agency shall have enforcement authority in the case of a violation of this paragraph by any person for which the agency is the appropriate Federal banking agency, or any institution-affiliated party thereof.

(D) Corporation authority if the appropriate Federal banking agency fails to follow recommendation

(i) Recommendation

The Corporation may recommend in writing to the appropriate Federal banking agency that the agency take any enforcement action authorized under section 1818 of this title for purposes of enforcement of this paragraph with respect to any person for which the agency is the appropriate Federal banking agency or any institution-affiliated party thereof.

(ii) Agency response

If the appropriate Federal banking agency does not, within 30 days of the date of receipt of a recommendation under clause (i), take the enforcement action with respect to this paragraph recommended by the Corporation or provide a plan acceptable to the Corporation for responding to the situation presented, the Corporation may take the recommended enforcement action against such person or institution-affiliated party.

(E) Additional authority

In addition to its authority under subparagraphs (C) and (D), for purposes of this paragraph, the Corporation shall have, in the same manner and to the same extent as with respect to a State nonmember insured bank—

(i) jurisdiction over—

(I) any person other than a person for which another agency is the appropriate Federal banking agency or any institution-affiliated party thereof; and

(II) any person that aids or abets a violation of this paragraph by a person described in subclause (I); and

(ii) for purposes of enforcing the requirements of this paragraph, the authority of the Corporation under—

(I) section 1820 (c) of this title to conduct investigations; and

(II) subsections (b), (c), (d) and (i) of section 1818 of this title to conduct enforcement actions.

(F) Other actions preserved

No provision of this paragraph shall be construed as barring any action otherwise available, under the laws of the United States or any State, to any Federal or State agency or individual.

(b) Payment of dividends by defaulting depository institutions

No insured depository institution shall pay any dividends on its capital stock or interest on its capital notes or debentures (if such interest is required to be paid only out of net profits) or distribute any of its capital assets while it remains in default in the payment of any assessment due to the Corporation; and any director or officer of any insured depository institution who participates in the declaration or payment of any such dividend or interest or in any such distribution shall, upon conviction, be fined not more than $1,000 or imprisoned not more than one year, or both: Provided, That, if such default is due to a dispute between the insured depository institution and the Corporation over the amount of such assessment, this subsection shall not apply, if the insured depository institution deposits security satisfactory to the Corporation for payment upon final determination of the issue.

(c) Merger transactions; consent of banking agencies; emergency approval; notice; uniform standards; antitrust actions; review de novo; limitations; report to Congress; applicability

(1) Except with the prior written approval of the responsible agency, which shall in every case referred to in this paragraph be the Cor-

poration, no insured depository institution shall—

(A) merge or consolidate with any noninsured bank or institution;

(B) assume liability to pay any deposits (including liabilities which would be "deposits" except for the proviso in section 1813(l)(5) of this title) made in, or similar liabilities of, any noninsured bank or institution; or

(C) transfer assets to any noninsured bank or institution in consideration of the assumption of liabilities for any portion of the deposits made in such insured depository institution.

(2) No insured depository institution shall merge or consolidate with any other insured depository institution or, either directly or indirectly, acquire the assets of, or assume liability to pay any deposits made in, any other insured depository institution except with the prior written approval of the responsible agency, which shall be—

(A) the Comptroller of the Currency if the acquiring, assuming, or resulting bank is to be a national bank;

(B) the Board of Governors of the Federal Reserve System if the acquiring, assuming, or resulting bank is to be a State member bank;

(C) the Corporation if the acquiring, assuming, or resulting bank is to be a State nonmember insured bank (except a savings bank supervised by the Director of the Office of Thrift Supervision); and

(D) the Director of the Office of Thrift Supervision if the acquiring, assuming, or resulting institution is to be a savings association.

(3) Notice of any proposed transaction for which approval is required under paragraph (1) or (2) (referred to hereafter in this subsection as a "merger transaction") shall, unless the responsible agency finds that it must act immediately in order to prevent the probable default of one of the banks or savings associations involved, be published—

(A) prior to the granting of approval of such transaction,

(B) in a form approved by the responsible agency,

(C) at appropriate intervals during a period at least as long as the period allowed for furnishing reports under paragraph (4) of this subsection, and

(D) in a newspaper of general circulation in the community or communities where the main offices of the banks or savings associations involved are located, or, if there is no such newspaper in any such community, then in the newspaper of general circulation published nearest thereto.

(4) Reports on competitive factors

(A) Request for report

In the interests of uniform standards and subject to subparagraph (B), before acting on any application for approval of a merger transaction, the responsible agency shall—

(i) request a report on the competitive factors involved from the Attorney General of the United States; and

(ii) provide a copy of the request to the Corporation (when the Corporation is not the responsible agency).

(B) Furnishing of report

The report requested under subparagraph (A) shall be furnished by the Attorney General to the responsible agency—

(i) not later than 30 calendar days after the date on which the Attorney General received the request; or

(ii) not later than 10 calendar days after such date, if the requesting agency advises the Attorney General that an emergency exists requiring expeditious action.

(C) Exceptions

A responsible agency may not be required to request a report under subparagraph (A) if—

(i) the responsible agency finds that it must act immediately in order to prevent the probable failure of 1 of the insured depository institutions involved in the merger transaction; or

(ii) the merger transaction involves solely an insured depository institution and 1 or more of the affiliates of such depository institution.

(5) The responsible agency shall not approve—

(A) any proposed merger transaction which would result in a monopoly, or which would be in furtherance of any combination or conspiracy to monopolize or to attempt to monopolize the business of banking in any part of the United States, or

(B) any other proposed merger transaction whose effect in any section of the country may be substantially to lessen competition, or to tend to create a monopoly, or which in any other manner would be in restraint of trade, unless it finds that the anticompetitive effects of the proposed transaction are clearly outweighed in the public interest by the probable effect of the transaction in meeting the convenience and needs of the community to be served.

In every case, the responsible agency shall take into consideration the financial and managerial resources and future prospects of the existing and proposed institutions, and the convenience and needs of the community to be served.

(6) The responsible agency shall immediately notify the Attorney General of any approval by it pursuant to this subsection of a proposed merger transaction. If the agency has found that it must act immediately to prevent the probable failure of one of the insured depository institutions involved, or if the proposed merger transaction is solely between an insured depository institution and 1 or more of its affiliates, and the report on the competitive factors has been dispensed with, the transaction may be consummated immediately upon approval by the agency. If the agency has advised the Attorney General under paragraph (4)(B)(ii) of the existence of an emergency requiring expeditious action and has requested a report on the competitive factors within 10 days, the transaction may not be consummated before the fifth calendar day after the date of approval by the agency. In all other cases, the transaction may not be consummated before the thirtieth calendar day after the date of approval by the agency or, if the agency has not received any adverse comment from the Attorney General of the United States relating to competitive factors, such shorter period of time as may be prescribed by the agency with the concurrence of the Attorney General, but in no event less than 15 calendar days after the date of approval.

(7) (A) Any action brought under the antitrust laws arising out of a merger transaction shall be commenced prior to the earliest time under paragraph (6) at which a merger transaction approved under paragraph (5) might be consummated. The commencement of such an action shall stay the effectiveness of the agency's approval unless the court shall otherwise specifically order. In any such action, the court shall review de novo the issues presented.

(B) In any judicial proceeding attacking a merger transaction approved under paragraph (5) on the ground that the merger transaction alone and of itself constituted a violation of any antitrust laws other than section 2 of Title 15, the standards applied by the court shall be identical with those that the banking agencies are directed to apply under paragraph (5).

(C) Upon the consummation of a merger transaction in compliance with this subsection and after the termination of any antitrust litigation commenced within the period prescribed in this paragraph, or upon the termination of such period if no such litigation is commenced therein, the transaction may not thereafter be attacked in any judicial proceeding on the ground that it alone and of itself constituted a violation of any antitrust laws other than section 2 of Title 15, but nothing in this subsection shall exempt any bank or savings association resulting from a merger transaction from complying with the antitrust laws after the consummation of such transaction.

(D) In any action brought under the antitrust laws arising out of a merger transaction approved by a Federal supervisory agency pursuant to this subsection, such agency, and any State banking supervisory agency having jurisdiction within the State involved, may appear as a party of its own motion and as of right, and be represented by its counsel.

(8) For the purposes of this subsection, the term "antitrust laws" means the Act of July 2, 1890 (the Sherman Antitrust Act), the Act of October 15, 1914 (the Clayton Act), and any other Acts in pari materia.

(9) Each of the responsible agencies shall include in its annual report to the Congress a description of each merger transaction approved by it during the period covered by the report, along with—

(A) the name and total resources of each bank or savings association involved;

(B) whether a report was submitted by the Attorney General under paragraph (4), and, if so, a summary by the Attorney General of the substance of such report; and

(C) a statement by the responsible agency of the basis for its approval.

(10) Until June 30, 1976, the responsible agency shall not grant any approval required by law which has the practical effect of permitting a conversion from the mutual to the stock form of organization, including approval of any application pending on the date of enactment of this subsection, except that this sentence shall not be deemed to limit now or hereafter the authority of the responsible agency to grant approvals in cases where the responsible agency finds that it must act in order to maintain the safety, soundness, and stability of an insured depository institution. The responsible agency may by rule, regulation, or otherwise and under such civil penalties (which shall be cumulative to any other remedies) as it may prescribe take whatever action it deems necessary or appropriate to implement or enforce this subsection.

(11) Money Laundering

In every case, the responsible agency, shall take into consideration the effectiveness of any insured depository institution involved in the proposed merger transaction in combatting money laundering activities, including in overseas branches.

(12) The provisions of this subsection do not apply to any merger transaction involving a foreign bank if no party to the transaction is principally engaged in business in the United States.

(d) Branch banks

(1) No State nonmember insured bank shall establish and operate any new domestic branch unless it shall have the prior written consent of the Corporation, and no State nonmember insured bank shall move its main office or any such branch from one location to another with-

out such consent. No foreign bank may move any insured branch from one location to another without such consent. The factors to be considered in granting or withholding the consent of the Corporation under this subsection shall be those enumerated in section 1816 of this title.

(2) No State nonmember insured bank shall establish or operate any foreign branch, except with the prior written consent of the Corporation and upon such conditions and pursuant to such regulations as the Corporation may prescribe from time to time.

(3) Exclusive authority for additional branches

(A) In general

Effective June 1, 1997, a State nonmember bank may not acquire, establish, or operate a branch in any State other than the bank's home State (as defined in section 1831u(f)(4) of this title) or a State in which the bank already has a branch unless the acquisition, establishment, or operation of a branch in such State by a State nonmember bank is authorized under this subsection or section 1823(f), 1823(k), or 1831u of this title.

(B) Retention of branches

In the case of a State nonmember bank which relocates the main office of such bank from 1 State to another State after May 31, 1997, the bank may retain and operate branches within the State which was the bank's home State (as defined in section 1831u(f)(4) of this title) before the relocation of such office only to the extent the bank would be authorized, under this section or any other provision of law referred to in subparagraph (A), to acquire, establish, or commence to operate a branch in such State if—

(i) the bank had no branches in such State; or

(ii) the branch resulted from—

(I) an interstate merger transaction approved pursuant to section 1831u of this title; or

(II) a transaction after May 31, 1997, pursuant to which the bank received assistance from the Corporation under section 1823(c)of this title.

(4) State "opt-in" election to permit interstate branching through de novo branches

(A) In general

Subject to subparagraph (B), the Corporation may approve an application by an insured State nonmember bank to establish and operate a de novo branch in a State (other than the bank's home State) in which the bank does not maintain a branch if—

(i) there is in effect in the host State a law that—

(I) applies equally to all banks; and

(II) expressly permits all out-of-State banks to establish de novo branches in such State; and

(ii) the conditions established in, or made applicable to this paragraph by, subparagraph (B) are met.

(B) Conditions on establishment and operation of interstate branch

(i) Establishment

An application by an insured State nonmember bank to establish and operate a de novo branch in a host State shall be subject to the same requirements and conditions to which an application for a merger transaction is subject under paragraphs (1), (3), and (4) of section 1831u(b) of this title.

(ii) Operation

Subsections (c) and (d)(2) of section 1831u of this title shall apply with respect to each branch of an insured State nonmember bank which is established and operated pursuant to an application approved under this paragraph in the same manner and to the same extent such provisions of such section apply to a branch of a State bank which resulted from a merger transaction under such section 1831u of this title.

(C) De novo branch defined

For purposes of this paragraph, the term "de novo branch" means a branch of a State bank which—

(i) is originally established by the State bank as a branch; and

(ii) does not become a branch of such bank as a result of—

(I) the acquisition by the bank of an insured depository institution or a branch of an insured depository institution; or

(II) the conversion, merger, or consolidation of any such institution or branch.

(D) Home State defined

The term "home State" means the State by which a State bank is chartered.

(E) Host State defined

The term "host State" means, with respect to a bank, a State, other than the home State of the bank, in which the bank maintains, or seeks to establish and maintain, a branch.

(e) Indemnity insurance

The Corporation may require any insured depository institution to provide protection and indemnity against burglary, defalcation, and other similar insurable losses. Whenever any insured depository institution refuses to comply with any such requirement the Corporation may contract for such protection and indemnity and add the cost thereof to the assessment otherwise payable by such bank.

(f) Publication of reports

Whenever any insured depository institution (except a national bank), after written notice of the recommendations of the Corporation based on a report of examination of such insured depository institution by an examiner of the Corporation, shall fail to comply with such recommendations within one hundred and twenty days after such notice, the Corporation shall have the power, and is authorized, to publish only such part of such report of examination as relates to any recommendation not complied with: *Provided*, That notice of intention to make such publication shall be given to the insured depository institution at least ninety days before such publication is made.

(g) Interest or dividend on demand deposits; definitions; regulation of interest rates

(1) The Board of Directors shall by regulation prohibit the payment of interest or dividends on demand deposits in insured nonmember banks and in insured branches of foreign banks and for such purpose it may define the term "demand deposits"; but such exceptions from this prohibition shall be made as are now or may hereafter be prescribed with respect to deposits payable on demand in member banks by section 19 of the Federal Reserve Act, as amended, or by regulation of the Board of Governors of the Federal Reserve System. The Board of Directors may from time to time, after consulting with the Board of Governors of the Federal Reserve System and the Director of the Office of Thrift Supervision, prescribe rules governing the advertisement of interest or dividends on deposits by insured nonmember banks (including insured mutual savings banks) on time and savings deposits. The Board of Directors is authorized for the purposes of this subsection to define the terms "time deposits" and "savings deposits", to determine what shall be deemed a payment of interest, and to prescribe such regulations as it may deem necessary to effectuate the purposes of this subsection and to prevent evasions thereof. The provisions of this subsection and of regulations issued thereunder shall also apply, in the discretion of the Board of Directors, to obligations other than deposits that are undertaken by insured nonmember banks or their affiliates. As used in this subsection, the term "affiliate" has the same meaning as when used in section 221a(b) of this title, except that the term "member bank", as used in such section 221a(b), shall be deemed to refer to an insured nonmember bank. During the period commencing on October 15, 1962, and ending on October 15, 1968, the provisions of this subsection shall not apply to the rate of interest which may be paid by insured nonmember banks on time deposits of foreign governments, monetary and financial authorities of foreign governments when acting as such, or international financial institutions of which the United States is a member. The authority conferred by this subsection shall also apply to noninsured banks in any State if the total amount of time and savings deposits held in all such banks in the State, plus the total amount of deposits, shares, and withdrawable accounts held in all building and loan, savings and loan, and homestead associations (including cooperative banks) in the State which are not members of a Federal home loan bank, is more than 20 per centum of the total amount of such deposits, shares, and withdrawable accounts held in all banks, and building and loan, savings and loan, and homestead associations (including cooperative banks) in the State. Such authority shall only be exercised by the Board of Directors with respect to such noninsured

banks prior to July 31, 1970, to limit the rates of interest or dividends which such banks may pay on time and savings deposits to maximum rates not lower than 5 1/2 per centum per annum. Whenever it shall appear to the Board of Directors that any noninsured bank or any affiliate thereof is engaged or has engaged or is about to engage in any acts or practices which constitute or will constitute a violation of the provisions of this subsection or of any regulations thereunder, the Board of Directors may, in its discretion, bring an action in the United States district court for the judicial district in which the principal office of the noninsured bank or affiliate thereof is located to enjoin such acts or practices, to enforce compliance with this subsection or any regulations thereunder, or for a combination of the foregoing, and such courts shall have jurisdiction of such actions, and, upon a proper showing, an injunction, restraining order, or other appropriate order may be granted without bond.

(2) Notwithstanding the provisions of paragraph (1), an insured nonmember bank may permit withdrawals to be made automatically from a savings deposit that consists only of funds in which the entire beneficial interest is held by one or more individuals through payment to the bank itself or through transfer of credit to a demand deposit or other account pursuant to written authorization from the depositor to make such payments or transfers in connection with checks or drafts drawn upon the bank, pursuant to terms and conditions prescribed by the Board of Directors.

(h) Penalty for failure to timely pay assessments

(1) In general

Subject to paragraph (3), any insured depository institution which fails or refuses to pay any assessment shall be subject to a penalty in an amount of not more than 1 percent of the amount of the assessment due for each day that such violation continues.

(2) Exception in case of dispute

Paragraph (1) shall not apply if—

(A) the failure to pay an assessment is due to a dispute between the insured depository institution and the Corporation over the amount of such assessment; and

(B) the insured depository institution deposits security satisfactory to the Corporation

for payment upon final determination of the issue.

(3) Special rule for small assessment amounts

If the amount of the assessment which an insured depository institution fails or refuses to pay is less than $10,000 at the time of such failure or refusal, the amount of any penalty to which such institution is subject under paragraph (1) shall not exceed $100 for each day that such violation continues.

(4) Authority to modify or remit penalty

The Corporation, in the sole discretion of the Corporation, may compromise, modify or remit any penalty which the Corporation may assess or has already assessed under paragraph (1) upon a finding that good cause prevented the timely payment of an assessment.

(i) Reduction or retirement of capital stock, notes, or debentures; conversion of insured Federal depository institutions to insured State depository institutions or noninsured institutions; consent of banking agencies; applicability

(1) No insured State nonmember bank shall, without the prior consent of the Corporation, reduce the amount or retire any part of its common or preferred capital stock, or retire any part of its capital notes or debentures.

(2) No insured Federal depository institution shall convert into an insured State depository institution if its capital stock or its surplus will be less than the capital stock or surplus, respectively, of the converting bank at the time of the shareholder's meeting approving such conversion, without the prior written consent of—

(A) the Board of Governors of the Federal Reserve System if the resulting bank is to be a State member bank;

(B) the Corporation if the resulting bank is to be a State nonmember insured bank; and

(C) the Director of the Office of Thrift Supervision if the resulting institution is to be an insured State savings association.

(D) Redesignated (C).

(3) Without the prior written consent of the Corporation, no insured depository institution shall convert into a noninsured bank or institution.

(4) In granting or withholding consent under this subsection, the responsible agency shall consider—

(A) the financial history and condition of the bank,

(B) the adequacy of its capital structure,

(C) its future earnings prospects,

(D) the general character and fitness of its management,

(E) the convenience and needs of the community to be served, and

(F) whether or not its corporate powers are consistent with the purposes of this chapter.

(j) Restrictions on transactions with affiliates and insiders

(1) Transactions with affiliates

(A) In general

Sections 371c and 371c–1 of this title shall apply with respect to every nonmember insured bank in the same manner and to the same extent as if the nonmember insured bank were a member bank.

(B) Affiliate defined

For the purpose of subparagraph (A), any company that would be an affiliate (as defined in sections 371c and 371c–1 of this title) of a nonmember insured bank if the nonmember insured bank were a member bank shall be deemed to be an affiliate of that nonmember insured bank.

(2) Extensions of credit to officers, directors, and principal shareholders

Sections 375a and 375b of this title shall apply with respect to every nonmember insured bank in the same manner and to the same extent as if the nonmember insured bank were a member bank.

(3) Avoiding extraterritorial application to foreign banks

(A) Transactions with affiliates

Paragraph (1) shall not apply with respect to a foreign bank solely because the foreign bank has an insured branch.

(B) Extensions of credit to officers, directors, and principal shareholders

Paragraph (2) shall not apply with respect to a foreign bank solely because the foreign

bank has an insured branch, but shall apply with respect to the insured branch.

(C) Foreign bank defined

For purposes of this paragraph, the term "foreign bank" has the same meaning as in section 3101(7) of this title.

(k) Authority to regulate or prohibit certain forms of benefits to institution-affiliated parties

(1) Golden parachutes and indemnification payments

The Corporation may prohibit or limit, by regulation or order, any golden parachute payment or indemnification payment.

(2) Factors to be taken into account

The Corporation shall prescribe, by regulation, the factors to be considered by the Corporation in taking any action pursuant to paragraph (1) which may include such factors as the following:

(A) Whether there is a reasonable basis to believe that the institution-affiliated party has committed any fraudulent act or omission, breach of trust or fiduciary duty, or insider abuse with regard to the depository institution or depository institution holding company that has had a material affect on the financial condition of the institution.

(B) Whether there is a reasonable basis to believe that the institution-affiliated party is substantially responsible for—

(i) the insolvency of the depository institution or covered company;

(ii) the appointment of a conservator or receiver for the depository institution; or

(iii) the troubled condition of the depository institution (as defined in the regulations prescribed pursuant to section 1831i(f) of this title).

(C) Whether there is a reasonable basis to believe that the institution-affiliated party has materially violated any applicable Federal or State banking law or regulation that has had a material affect on the financial condition of the institution.

(D) Whether there is a reasonable basis to believe that the institution-affiliated party has violated or conspired to violate—

(i) section 215, 656, 657, 1005, 1006, 1007, 1014, 1032, or 1344 of Title 18; or

(ii) section 1341 or 1343 of such title affecting a federally insured financial institution.

(E) Whether the institution-affiliated party was in a position of managerial or fiduciary responsibility.

(F) The length of time the party was affiliated with the insured depository institution or covered company, and the degree to which—

(i) the payment reasonably reflects compensation earned over the period of employment; and

(ii) the compensation involved represents a reasonable payment for services rendered.

(3) Certain payments prohibited

No insured depository institution or depository institution holding company may prepay the salary or any liability or legal expense of any institution-affiliated party if such payment is made—

(A) in contemplation of the insolvency of such institution or covered company or after the commission of an act of insolvency; and

(B) with a view to, or has the result of—

(i) preventing the proper application of the assets of the institution to creditors; or

(ii) preferring one creditor over another.

(4) Golden parachute payment defined

For purposes of this subsection—

(A) In general

The term "golden parachute payment" means any payment (or any agreement to make any payment) in the nature of compensation by any insured depository institution or covered company for the benefit of any institution-affiliated party pursuant to an obligation of such institution or covered company that—

(i) is contingent on the termination of such party's affiliation with the institution or covered company; and—

(ii) is received on or after the date on which—

(I) the insured depository institution or covered company, or any insured depository institution subsidiary of such covered company, is insolvent;

(II) any conservator or receiver is appointed for such institution;

(III) the institution's appropriate Federal banking agency determines that the insured depository institution is in a troubled condition (as defined in the regulations prescribed pursuant to section 1831i(f) of this title);

(IV) the insured depository institution has been assigned a composite rating by the appropriate Federal banking agency or the Corporation of 4 or 5 under the Uniform Financial Institutions Rating System; or

(V) the insured depository institution is subject to a proceeding initiated by the Corporation to terminate or suspend deposit insurance for such institution.

(B) Certain payments in contemplation of an event

Any payment which would be a golden parachute payment but for the fact that such payment was made before the date referred to in subparagraph (A)(ii) shall be treated as a golden parachute payment if the payment was made in contemplation of the occurrence of an event described in any subclause of such subparagraph.

(C) Certain payments not included

The term "golden parachute payment" shall not include—

(i) any payment made pursuant to a retirement plan which is qualified (or is intended to be qualified) under section 401 of Title 26 or other nondiscriminatory benefit plan;

(ii) any payment made pursuant to a bona fide deferred compensation plan or arrangement which the Board determines, by regulation or order, to be permissible; or

(iii) any payment made by reason of the death or disability of an institution-affiliated party.

(5) Other definitions

For purposes of this subsection—

(A) Indemnification payment

Subject to paragraph (6), the term "indemnification payment" means any payment (or any agreement to make any payment) by any insured depository institution or covered company for the benefit of any person who is or was an institution-affiliated party, to pay or reimburse such person for any liability or legal expense with regard to any administrative proceeding or civil action instituted by the appropriate Federal banking agency which results in a final order under which such person—

(i) is assessed a civil money penalty;

(ii) is removed or prohibited from participating in conduct of the affairs of the insured depository institution; or

(iii) is required to take any affirmative action described in section 1818(b)(6) of this title with respect to such institution.

(B) Liability or legal expense

The term "liability or legal expense" means—

(i) any legal or other professional expense incurred in connection with any claim, proceeding, or action;

(ii) the amount of, and any cost incurred in connection with, any settlement of any claim, proceeding, or action; and

(iii) the amount of, and any cost incurred in connection with, any judgment or penalty imposed with respect to any claim, proceeding, or action.

(C) Payment

The term "payment" includes—

(i) any direct or indirect transfer of any funds or any asset; and

(ii) any segregation of any funds or assets for the purpose of making, or pursuant to an agreement to make, any payment after the date on which such funds or assets are segregated, without regard to whether the obligation to make such payment is contingent on—

(I) the determination, after such date, of the liability for the payment of such amount; or

(II) the liquidation, after such date, of the amount of such payment.

(D) Covered company

The term "covered company" means any depository institution holding company (including any company required to file a report under section 1843(f)(6) of this title), or any other company that controls an insured depository institution.

(6) Certain commercial insurance coverage not treated as covered benefit payment

No provision of this subsection shall be construed as prohibiting any insured depository institution or covered company, from purchasing any commercial insurance policy or fidelity bond, except that, subject to any requirement described in paragraph (5)(A)(iii), such insurance policy or bond shall not cover any legal or liability expense of the institution or covered company which is described in paragraph (5)(A).

(*l*) Acquisition of foreign banks or entities

When authorized by State law, a State nonmember insured bank may, but only with the prior written consent of the Corporation and upon such conditions and under such regulations as the Corporation may prescribe from time to time, acquire and hold, directly or indirectly, stock or other evidences of ownership in one or more banks or other entities organized under the law of a foreign country or a dependency or insular possession of the United States and not engaged, directly or indirectly, in any activity in the United States except as, in the judgment of the Board of Directors, shall be incidental to the international or foreign business of such foreign bank or entity; and, notwithstanding the provisions of subsection (j) of this section, such State nonmember insured bank may, as to such foreign bank or entity, engage in transactions that would otherwise be covered thereby, but only in the manner and within the limit prescribed by the Corporation by general or specific regulation or ruling.

(m) Activities of savings associations and their subsidiaries

(1) Procedures

When an insured savings association establishes or acquires a subsidiary or when an insured savings association elects to conduct any new activity through a subsidiary that the insured savings association controls, the insured savings association—

(A) shall notify the Corporation and the Director of the Office of Thrift Supervision not less than 30 days prior to the establishment, or acquisition, of any such subsidiary, and not less than 30 days prior to the commencement of any such activity, and in either case shall provide at that time such information as each such agency may, by regulation, require; and

(B) shall conduct the activities of the subsidiary in accordance with regulations and orders of the Director of the Office of Thrift Supervision.

(2) Enforcement powers

With respect to any subsidiary of an insured savings association:

(A) the Corporation and the Director of the Office of Thrift Supervision shall each have, with respect to such subsidiary, the respective powers that each has with respect to the insured savings association pursuant to this section or section 1818 of this title; and

(B) the Director of the Office of Thrift Supervision may determine, after notice and opportunity for hearing, that the continuation by the insured savings association of its ownership or control of, or its relationship to, the subsidiary—

(i) constitutes a serious risk to the safety, soundness, or stability of the insured savings association, or

(ii) is inconsistent with sound banking principles or with the purposes of this chapter.

Upon making any such determination, the Corporation or the Director of the Office of Thrift Supervision shall have authority to order the insured savings association to divest itself of control of the subsidiary. The Director of the Office of Thrift Supervision may take any other corrective measures with respect to the subsidiary, including the authority to require the subsidiary to terminate the activities or operations posing such risks, as the Director may deem appropriate.

(3) Activities incompatible with deposit insurance

(A) In general

The Corporation may determine by regulation or order that any specific activity poses a serious threat to the Deposit Insurance Fund. Prior to adopting any such regulation, the Corporation shall consult with the Director of the Office of Thrift Supervision and shall provide appropriate State supervisors the opportunity to comment thereon, and the Corporation shall specifically take such comments into consideration. Any such regu-

lation shall be issued in accordance with section 553 of title 5. If the Board of Directors makes such a determination with respect to an activity, the Corporation shall have authority to order that no savings association may engage in the activity directly.

(B) Authority of director

This section does not limit the authority of the Office of Thrift Supervision to issue regulations to promote safety and soundness or to enforce compliance with other applicable laws.

(C) Additional authority of FDIC to prevent serious risks to insurance fund

Notwithstanding subparagraph (A), the Corporation may prescribe and enforce such regulations and issue such orders as the Corporation determines to be necessary to prevent actions or practices of savings associations that pose a serious threat to the Deposit Insurance Fund.

(4) "Subsidiary" defined

As used in this subsection, the term "subsidiary" does not include an insured depository institution.

(5) Applicability to certain savings banks

Subparagraphs (A) and (B) of paragraph (1) of this subsection do not apply to—

(A) any Federal savings bank that was chartered prior to October 15, 1982, as a savings bank under State law, or

(B) a savings association that acquired its principal assets from an institution that was chartered prior to October 15, 1982, as a savings bank under State law.

(n) Calculation of Capital

No appropriate Federal banking agency shall allow any insured depository institution to include an unidentifiable intangible asset in its calculation of compliance with the appropriate capital standard, if such unidentifiable intangible asset was acquired after April 12, 1989, except to the extent permitted under section 1464(t) of this title.

(o) Real estate lending

(1) Uniform regulations

Not more than 9 months after December 19, 1991, each appropriate Federal banking agency shall adopt uniform regulations prescribing standards for extensions of credit that are—

(A) secured by liens on interests in real estate; or

(B) made for the purpose of financing the construction of a building or other improvements to real estate.

(2) Standards

(A) Criteria

In prescribing standards under paragraph (1), the agencies shall consider—

(i) the risk posed to the deposit insurance funds by such extensions of credit;

(ii) the need for safe and sound operation of insured depository institutions; and

(iii) the availability of credit.

(B) Variations permitted

In prescribing standards under paragraph (1), the appropriate Federal banking agencies may differentiate among types of loans—

(i) as may be required by Federal statute;

(ii) as may be warranted, based on the risk to the deposit insurance fund; or

(iii) as may be warranted, based on the safety and soundness of the institutions.

(3) Loan evaluation standard

No appropriate Federal banking agency shall adversely evaluate an investment or a loan made by an insured depository institution, or consider such a loan to be nonperforming, solely because the loan is made to or the investment is in commercial, residential, or industrial property, unless such investment or loan may affect the institution's safety and soundness.

(4) Effective date

The regulations adopted under paragraph (1) shall become effective not later than 15 months after December 19, 1991. Such regulations shall continue in effect except as uniformly amended by the appropriate Federal banking agencies, acting in concert.

(p) Periodic review of capital standards

Each appropriate Federal banking agency shall, in consultation with the other Federal banking agencies, biennially review its capital standards

for insured depository institutions to determine whether those standards require sufficient capital to facilitate prompt corrective action to prevent or minimize loss to the deposit insurance funds, consistent with section 1831o of this title.

(q) Sovereign risk

Section 633 of this title shall apply to every nonmember insured bank in the same manner and to the same extent as if the nonmember insured bank were a member bank.

(r) Subsidiary depository institutions as agents for certain affiliates

(1) In general

Any bank subsidiary of a bank holding company may receive deposits, renew time deposits, close loans, service loans, and receive payments on loans and other obligations as an agent for a depository institution affiliate.

(2) Bank acting as agent is not a branch

Notwithstanding any other provision of law, a bank acting as an agent in accordance with paragraph (1) for a depository institution affiliate shall not be considered to be a branch of the affiliate.

(3) Prohibitions on activities

A depository institution may not—

(A) conduct any activity as an agent under paragraph (1) or (6) which such institution is prohibited from conducting as a principal under any applicable Federal or State law; or

(B) as a principal, have an agent conduct any activity under paragraph (1) or (6) which the institution is prohibited from conducting under any applicable Federal or State law.

(4) Existing authority not affected

No provision of this subsection shall be construed as affecting—

(A) the authority of any depository institution to act as an agent on behalf of any other depository institution under any other provision of law; or

(B) whether a depository institution which conducts any activity as an agent on behalf of any other depository institution under any other provision of law shall be considered to be a branch of such other institution.

(5) Agency relationship required to be consistent with safe and sound banking practices

An agency relationship between depository institutions under paragraph (1) or (6) shall be on terms that are consistent with safe and sound banking practices and all applicable regulations of any appropriate Federal banking agency.

(6) Affiliated insured savings associations

An insured savings association which was an affiliate of a bank on July 1, 1994, may conduct activities as an agent on behalf of such bank in the same manner as an insured bank affiliate of such bank may act as agent for such bank under this subsection to the extent such activities are conducted only in—

(A) any State in which—

(i) the bank is not prohibited from operating a branch under any provision of Federal or State law; and

(ii) the savings association maintained an office or branch and conducted business as of July 1, 1994; or

(B) any State in which—

(i) the bank is not expressly prohibited from operating a branch under a State law described in section 1831u(a)(2) of this title; and

(ii) the savings association maintained a main office and conducted business as of July 1, 1994.

(s) Prohibition on certain affiliations

(1) In general

No depository institution may be an affiliate of, be sponsored by, or accept financial support, directly or indirectly, from any Government-sponsored enterprise.

(2) Exception for members of a Federal home loan bank

Paragraph (1) shall not apply with respect to the membership of a depository institution in a Federal home loan bank.

(3) Routine business financing

Paragraph (1) shall not apply with respect to advances or other forms of financial assistance provided by a Government-sponsored enterprise pursuant to the statutes governing such enterprise.

(4) Student loans

(A) In general

This subsection shall not apply to any arrangement between the Holding Company (or any subsidiary of the Holding Company other than the Student Loan Marketing Association) and a depository institution, if the Secretary approves the affiliation and determines that—

(i) the reorganization of such Association in accordance with section 1087–3 of Title 20, as amended, will not be adversely affected by the arrangement;

(ii) the dissolution of the Association pursuant to such reorganization will occur before the end of the 2–year period beginning on the date on which such arrangement is consummated or on such earlier date as the Secretary deems appropriate: *Provided*, That the Secretary may extend this period for not more than 1 year at a time if the Secretary determines that such extension is in the public interest and is appropriate to achieve an orderly reorganization of the Association or to prevent market disruptions in connection with such reorganization, but no such extensions shall in the aggregate exceed 2 years;

(iii) the Association will not purchase or extend credit to, or guarantee or provide credit enhancement to, any obligation of the depository institution;

(iv) the operations of the Association will be separate from the operations of the depository institution; and

(v) until the "dissolution date" (as that term is defined in section 1087–3 of Title 20, as amended) has occurred, such depository institution will not use the trade name or service mark "Sallie Mae" in connection with any product or service it offers if the appropriate Federal banking agency for such depository institution determines that—

(I) the depository institution is the only institution offering such product or service using the "Sallie Mae" name; and

(II) such use would result in the depository institution having an unfair competitive advantage over other depository institutions.

(B) Terms and conditions

In approving any arrangement referred to in subparagraph (A) the Secretary may impose any terms and conditions on such an arrangement that the Secretary considers appropriate, including:

(i) imposing additional restrictions on the issuance of debt obligations by the Association; or

(ii) restricting the use of proceeds from the issuance of such debt.

(C) Additional limitations

In the event that the Holding Company (or any subsidiary of the Holding Company) enters into such an arrangement, the value of the Association's "investment portfolio" shall not at any time exceed the lesser of—

(i) the value of such portfolio on October 21, 1998; or

(ii) the value of such portfolio on the date such an arrangement is consummated. The term "investment portfolio" shall mean all investments shown on the consolidated balance sheet of the Association other than—

(I) any instrument or assets described in section 1087–2(d) of title 20, as such section existed on the day before the date of the repeal of such section;

(II) any direct noncallable obligations of the United States or any agency thereof for which the full faith and credit of the United States is pledged; or

(III) cash or cash equivalents.

(D) Enforcement

The terms and conditions imposed under subparagraph (B) may be enforced by the Secretary in accordance with section 1087–3 of Title 20.

(E) Definitions

For purposes of this paragraph, the following definition shall apply—

(i) Association; holding company

Notwithstanding any provision in section 1813 of this title, the terms "Association" and "Holding Company" have the same meanings as in section 1087–3(i) of Title 20.

(ii) Secretary

The term "Secretary" means the Secretary of the Treasury.

(5) "Government-sponsored enterprise" defined

For purposes of this subsection, the term "Government-sponsored enterprise" has the meaning given to such term in section 1404(e)(1)(A) of the Financial Institutions Reform, Recovery, and Enforcement Act of 1989.

(t) Recordkeeping requirements

(1) Requirements

Each appropriate Federal banking agency, after consultation with and consideration of the views of the Commission, shall establish recordkeeping requirements for banks relying on exceptions contained in paragraphs (4) and (5) of section 78c(a) of Title 15. Such recordkeeping requirements shall be sufficient to demonstrate compliance with the terms of such exceptions and be designed to facilitate compliance with such exceptions.

(2) Availability to Commission; confidentiality

Each appropriate Federal banking agency shall make any information required under paragraph (1) available to the Commission upon request. Notwithstanding any other provision of law, the Commission shall not be compelled to disclose any such information. Nothing in this paragraph shall authorize the Commission to withhold information from Congress, or prevent the Commission from complying with a request for information from any other Federal department or agency or any self-regulatory organization requesting the information for purposes within the scope of its jurisdiction, or complying with an order of a court of the United States in an action brought by the United States or the Commission. For purposes of section 552 of Title 5, this paragraph shall be considered a statute described in subsection (b)(3)(B) of such section 552.

(3) Definition

As used in this subsection the term 'Commission' means the Securities and Exchange Commission.

(u) Limitation on claims

(1) In general

No person may bring a claim against any Federal banking agency (including in its capacity as conservator or receiver) for the return of assets of an affiliate or controlling shareholder of the insured depository institution transferred to, or for the benefit of, an insured depository institution by such affiliate or controlling shareholder of the insured depository institution, or a claim against such Federal banking agency for monetary damages or other legal or equitable relief in connection with such transfer, if at the time of the transfer—

(A) the insured depository institution is subject to any direction issued in writing by a Federal banking agency to increase its capital; and

(B) for that portion of the transfer that is made by an entity covered by section 1844(g) of this title or section 1831v of this title, the Federal banking agency has followed the procedure set forth in such section.

(C) Redesignated (B).

(2) Definition of claim

For purposes of paragraph (1), the term "claim"—

(A) means a cause of action based on Federal or State law that—

(i) provides for the avoidance of preferential or fraudulent transfers or conveyances; or

(ii) provides similar remedies for preferential or fraudulent transfers or conveyances; and

(B) does not include any claim based on actual intent to hinder, delay, or defraud pursuant to such a fraudulent transfer or conveyance law.

(v) Loans by insured institutions on their own stock

(1) General prohibition

No insured depository institution may make any loan or discount on the security of the shares of its own capital stock.

(2) Exclusion

For purposes of this subsection, an insured depository institution shall not be deemed to be making a loan or discount on the security of the shares of its own capital stock if it acquires the stock to prevent loss upon a debt previously contracted for in good faith.

(w) Written employment references may contain suspicions of involvement in illegal activity

(1) Authority to disclose information

Notwithstanding any other provision of law, any insured depository institution, and any director, officer, employee, or agent of such institution, may disclose in any written employment reference relating to a current or former institution-affiliated party of such institution which is provided to another insured depository institution in response to a request from such other institution, information concerning the possible involvement of such institution-affiliated party in potentially unlawful activity.

(2) Information not required

Nothing in paragraph (1) shall be construed, by itself, to create any affirmative duty to include any information described in paragraph (1) in any employment reference referred to in paragraph (1).

(3) Malicious intent

Notwithstanding any other provision of this subsection, voluntary disclosure made by an insured depository institution, and any director, officer, employee, or agent of such institution under this subsection concerning potentially unlawful activity that is made with malicious intent, shall not be shielded from liability from the person identified in the disclosure.

(4) Definition

For purposes of this subsection, the term "insured depository institution" includes any uninsured branch or agency of a foreign bank.

(x) Privileges not affected by disclosure to banking agency or supervisor

(1) In general

The submission by any person of any information to any Federal banking agency, State bank supervisor, or foreign banking authority for any purpose in the course of any supervisory or regulatory process of such agency, supervisor, or authority shall not be construed as waiving, destroying, or otherwise affecting any privilege such person may claim with respect to such information under Federal or State law as to any person or entity other than such agency, supervisor, or authority.

(2) Rule of construction

No provision of paragraph (1) may be construed as implying or establishing that—

(A) any person waives any privilege applicable to information that is submitted or transferred under any circumstance to which paragraph (1) does not apply; or

(B) any person would waive any privilege applicable to any information by submitting the information to any Federal banking agency, State bank supervisor, or foreign banking authority, but for this subsection.

§ 1828a. Prudential safeguards

(a) Comptroller of the Currency

(1) In general

The Comptroller of the Currency may, by regulation or order, impose restrictions or requirements on relationships or transactions between a national bank and a subsidiary of the national bank that the Comptroller finds are—

(A) consistent with the purposes of this Act, title LXII of the Revised Statutes of the United States, and other Federal law applicable to national banks; and

(B) appropriate to avoid any significant risk to the safety and soundness of insured depository institutions or any Federal deposit insurance fund or other adverse effects, such as undue concentration of resources, decreased or unfair competition, conflicts of interests, or unsound banking practices.

(2) Review

The Comptroller of the Currency shall regularly—

(A) review all restrictions or requirements established pursuant to paragraph (1) to determine whether there is a continuing need for any such restriction or requirement to carry out the purposes of the Act, including the avoidance of any adverse effect referred to in paragraph (1)(B); and

(B) modify or eliminate any such restriction or requirement the Comptroller finds is no longer required for such purposes.

(b) Board of Governors of the Federal Reserve System

(1) In general

The Board of Governors of the Federal Reserve System may, by regulation or order, impose restrictions or requirements on relationships or transactions—

(A) between a depository institution subsidiary of a bank holding company and any affiliate of such depository institution (other than a subsidiary of such institution); or

(B) between a State member bank and a subsidiary of such bank;

if the Board makes a finding described in paragraph (2) with respect to such restriction or requirement.

(2) Finding

The Board of Governors of the Federal Reserve System may exercise authority under paragraph (1) if the Board finds that the exercise of such authority is—

(A) consistent with the purposes of this Act, the Bank Holding Company Act of 1956 [12 U.S.C.A. § 1841 et seq.], the Federal Reserve Act [12 U.S.C.A. § 221 et seq.], and other Federal law applicable to depository institution subsidiaries of bank holding companies or State member banks, as the case may be; and

(B) appropriate to prevent an evasion of any provision of law referred to in subparagraph (A) or to avoid any significant risk to the safety and soundness of depository institutions or any Federal deposit insurance fund or other adverse effects, such as undue concentration of resources, decreased or unfair competition, conflicts of interests, or unsound banking practices.

(3) Review

The Board of Governors of the Federal Reserve System shall regularly—

(A) review all restrictions or requirements established pursuant to paragraph (1) or (4) to determine whether there is a continuing need for any such restriction or requirement to carry out the purposes of the Act, including the avoidance of any adverse effect referred to in paragraph (2)(B) or (4)(B); and

(B) modify or eliminate any such restriction or requirement the Board finds is no longer required for such purposes.

(4) Foreign banks

The Board may, by regulation or order, impose restrictions or requirements on relationships or transactions between a branch, agency, or commercial lending company of a foreign bank in the United States and any affiliate in the United States of such foreign bank that the Board finds are—

(A) consistent with the purposes of this Act, the Bank Holding Company Act of 1956 [12

U.S.C.A. § 1841 et seq.], the Federal Reserve Act [12 U.S.C.A. § 221 et seq.], and other Federal law applicable to foreign banks and their affiliates in the United States; and

(B) appropriate to prevent an evasion of any provision of law referred to in subparagraph (A) or to avoid any significant risk to the safety and soundness of depository institutions or any Federal deposit insurance fund or other adverse effects, such as undue concentration of resources, decreased or unfair competition, conflicts of interests, or unsound banking practices.

(c) Federal Deposit Insurance Corporation

(1) In general

The Federal Deposit Insurance Corporation may, by regulation or order, impose restrictions or requirements on relationships or transactions between a State nonmember bank (as defined in section 1813 of this title) and a subsidiary of the State nonmember bank that the Corporation finds are—

(A) consistent with the purposes of this Act, the Federal Deposit Insurance Act [12 U.S.C.A. § 1811 et seq.], or other Federal law applicable to State nonmember banks; and

(B) appropriate to avoid any significant risk to the safety and soundness of depository institutions or any Federal deposit insurance fund or other adverse effects, such as undue concentration of resources, decreased or unfair competition, conflicts of interests, or unsound banking practices.

(2) Review

The Federal Deposit Insurance Corporation shall regularly—

(A) review all restrictions or requirements established pursuant to paragraph (1) to determine whether there is a continuing need for any such restriction or requirement to carry out the purposes of the Act, including the avoidance of any adverse effect referred to in paragraph (1)(B); and

(B) modify or eliminate any such restriction or requirement the Corporation finds is no longer required for such purposes.

§ 1828b.   Interagency data sharing

(a) In general

To the extent not prohibited by other law, the Comptroller of the Currency, the Director of the Office of Thrift Supervision, the Federal Deposit Insurance Corporation, and the Board of Governors of the Federal Reserve System shall make available to the Attorney General and the Federal Trade Commission any data in the possession of any such banking agency that the antitrust agency deems necessary for antitrust review of any transaction requiring notice to any such antitrust agency or the approval of such agency under section 1842 or 1843 of this title, section 1828(c) of this title, the National Bank Consolidation and Merger Act [12 U.S.C.A. § 215 et seq.], section 1467a of this title, or the antitrust laws.

(b) Confidentiality requirements

(1) In general

Any information or material obtained by any agency pursuant to subsection (a) shall be treated as confidential.

(2) Procedures for disclosure

If any information or material obtained by any agency pursuant to subsection (a) is proposed to be disclosed to a third party, written notice of such disclosure shall first be provided to the agency from which such information or material was obtained and an opportunity shall be given to such agency to oppose or limit the proposed disclosure.

(3) Other privileges not waived by disclosure under this section

The provision by any Federal agency of any information or material pursuant to subsection (a) to another agency shall not constitute a waiver, or otherwise affect, any privilege any agency or person may claim with respect to such information under Federal or State law.

(4) Exception

No provision of this section shall be construed as preventing or limiting access to any information by any duly authorized committee of the Congress or the Comptroller General of the United States.

(c) Banking agency information sharing

The provisions of subsection (b) shall apply to—

(1) any information or material obtained by any Federal banking agency (as defined in section 1813(z) of this title) from any other Federal banking agency; and

(2) any report of examination or other confidential supervisory information obtained by any State agency or authority, or any other person, from a Federal banking agency.

§ 1829. Penalty for unauthorized participation by convicted individual

(a) Prohibition

(1) In general

Except with the prior written consent of the Corporation—

(A) any person who has been convicted of any criminal offense involving dishonesty or a breach of trust, or money laundering or has agreed to enter into a pretrial diversion or similar program in connection with a prosecution for such offense, may not—

(i) become, or continue as, an institution-affiliated party with respect to any insured depository institution;

(ii) own or control, directly or indirectly, any insured depository institution; or

(iii) otherwise participate, directly or indirectly, in the conduct of the affairs of any insured depository institution; and

(B) any insured depository institution may not permit any person referred to in subparagraph (A) to engage in any conduct or continue any relationship prohibited under such subparagraph.

(2) Minimum 10–year prohibition period for certain offenses

(A) In general

If the offense referred to in paragraph (1)(A) in connection with any person referred to in such paragraph is—

(i) an offense under—

(I) section 215, 656, 657, 1005, 1006, 1007, 1008, 1014, 1032, 1344, 1517, 1956, or 1957 of Title 18; or

(II) section 1341 or 1343 of such title which affects any financial institution (as defined in section 20 of such title); or

(ii) the offense of conspiring to commit any such offense,

the Corporation may not consent to any exception to the application of paragraph (1) to such person during the 10–year period beginning on the date the conviction or the agreement of the person becomes final.

(B) Exception by order of sentencing court

(i) In general

On motion of the Corporation, the court in which the conviction or the agreement of a person referred to in subparagraph (A) has been entered may grant an exception to the application of paragraph (1) to such person if granting the exception is in the interest of justice.

(ii) Period for filing

A motion may be filed under clause (i) at any time during the 10–year period described in subparagraph (A) with regard to the person on whose behalf such motion is made.

(b) Penalty

Whoever knowingly violates subsection (a) shall be fined not more than $1,000,000 for each day such prohibition is violated or imprisoned for not more than 5 years, or both.

(c) [eds. None in original.]

(d) Bank holding companies

(1) In general

Subsections (a) and (b) of this section shall apply to any company (other than a foreign bank) that is a bank holding company and any organization organized and operated under section 25A of the Federal Reserve Act or operating under section 25 of the Federal Reserve Act, as if such bank holding company or organization were an insured depository institution, except that such subsections shall be applied for purposes of this subsection by substituting "Board of Governors of the Federal Reserve System" for "Corporation" each place that term appears in such subsections.

(2) Authority of board

The Board of Governors of the Federal Reserve System may provide exemptions, by regulation or order, from the application of paragraph (1) if the exemption is consistent with the purposes of this subsection.

(e) Savings and loan holding companies

(1) In general

Subsections (a) and (b) of this section shall apply to any savings and loan holding company as if such savings and loan holding company were an insured depository institution, except that such subsections shall be applied for purposes of this subsection by substituting "Director of the Office of Thrift Supervision" for "Corporation" each place that term appears in such subsections.

(2) Authority of director

The Director of the Office of Thrift Supervision may provide exemptions, by regulation or order, from the application of paragraph (1) if the exemption is consistent with the purposes of this subsection.

§ 1829a. Participation by State nonmember insured banks in lotteries and related activities

(a) Prohibited activities

A State nonmember insured bank may not—

(1) deal in lottery tickets;

(2) deal in bets used as a means or substitute for participation in a lottery;

(3) announce, advertise, or publicize the existence of any lottery; or

(4) announce, advertise, or publicize the existence or identity of any participant or winner, as such, in a lottery.

(b) Use of banking premises prohibited

A State nonmember insured bank may not permit-

(1) the use of any part of any of its banking offices by any person for any purpose forbidden to the bank under subsection (a) of this section, or

(2) direct access by the public from any of its banking offices to any premises used by any person for any purpose forbidden to the bank under subsection (a) of this section.

(c) Definitions

As used in this section—

(1) The term "deal in" includes making, taking, buying, selling, redeeming, or collecting.

(2) The term "lottery" includes any arrangement whereby three or more persons (the "participants") advance money or credit to another in exchange for the possibility or expectation that one or more but not all of the participants (the "winners") will receive by reason of their advances more than the

amounts they have advanced, the identity of the winners being determined by any means which includes-

(A) a random selection;

(B) a game, race, or contest; or

(C) any record or tabulation of the result of one or more events in which any participant has no interest except for its bearing upon the possibility that he may become a winner.

(3) The term "lottery ticket" includes any right, privilege, or possibility (and any ticket, receipt, record, or other evidence of any such right, privilege, or possibility), of becoming a winner in a lottery.

(d) Lawful banking services connected with operation of lottery

Nothing contained in this section prohibits a State nonmember insured bank from accepting deposits or cashing or otherwise handling checks or other negotiable instruments, or performing other lawful banking services for a State operating a lottery, or for an officer or employee of that State who is charged with the administration of the lottery.

(e) Regulations; enforcement

The Board of Directors shall prescribe such regulations as may be necessary to the strict enforcement of this section and the prevention of evasions thereof.

§ 1829b. Retention of records by insured depository institutions

(a) Congressional findings and declaration of purpose

(1) Findings

Congress finds that—

(A) adequate records maintained by insured depository institutions have a high degree of usefulness in criminal, tax, and regulatory investigations and proceedings, and that, given the threat posed to the security of the Nation on and after the terrorist attacks against the United States on September 11, 2001, such records may also have a high degree of usefulness in the conduct of intelligence or counterintelligence activities, including analysis, to protect against domestic and international terrorism; and

(B) microfilm or other reproductions and other records made by insured depository institutions of checks, as well as records kept by such institutions, of the identity of persons maintaining or authorized to act with respect to accounts therein, have been of particular value in proceedings described in subparagraph (A).

(2) Purpose

It is the purpose of this section to require the maintenance of appropriate types of records by insured depository institutions in the United States where such records have a high degree of usefulness in criminal, tax, or regulatory investigations or proceedings, recognizes that, given the threat posed to the security of the Nation on and after the terrorist attacks against the United States on September 11, 2001, such records may also have a high degree of usefulness in the conduct of intelligence or counterintelligence activities, including analysis, to protect against international terrorism.

(b) Recordkeeping regulations

(1) In general

Where the Secretary of the Treasury (referred to in this section as the "Secretary") determines that the maintenance of appropriate types of records and other evidence by insured depository institutions has a high degree of usefulness in criminal, tax, or regulatory investigations or proceedings, he shall prescribe regulations to carry out the purposes of this section.

(2) Domestic funds transfers

Whenever the Secretary and the Board of Governors of the Federal Reserve System (hereafter in this section referred to as the "Board") determine that the maintenance of records, by insured depository institutions, of payment orders which direct transfers of funds over wholesale funds transfer systems has a high degree of usefulness in criminal, tax, or regulatory investigations or proceedings, the Secretary and the Board shall jointly prescribe regulations to carry out the purposes of this section with respect to the maintenance of such records.

(3) International funds transfers

(A) In general

The Secretary and the Board shall jointly prescribe, after consultation with State banking supervisors, final regulations requiring that insured depository institutions, businesses that provide check cashing services, money transmitting businesses, and businesses that issue or redeem money orders, travelers' checks or other similar instruments maintain such records of payment orders which—

(i) involve international transactions; and

(ii) direct transfers of funds over wholesale funds transfer systems or on the books of any insured depository institution, or on the books of any business that provides check cashing services, any money transmitting business, and any business that issues or redeems money orders, travelers' checks or similar instruments,

that will have a high degree of usefulness in criminal, tax, or regulatory investigations or proceedings.

(B) Factors for consideration

In prescribing the regulations required under subparagraph (A), the Secretary and the Board shall consider—

(i) the usefulness in criminal, tax, or regulatory investigations or proceedings of any record required to be maintained pursuant to the proposed regulations; and

(ii) the effect the recordkeeping required pursuant to such proposed regulations will have on the cost and efficiency of the payment system.

(C) Availability of records

Any records required to be maintained pursuant to the regulations prescribed under subparagraph (A) shall be submitted or made available to the Secretary or the Board upon request.

(c) Identity of persons having accounts and persons authorized to act with respect to such accounts; exemptions

Subject to the requirements of any regulations prescribed jointly by the Secretary and the Board under paragraph (2) or (3) of subsection (b) of this section, each insured depository institution shall maintain such records and other evidence, in such form as the Secretary shall require, of the identity of each person having an account in the United States with the insured depository institution and of each individual authorized to sign checks, make withdrawals, or otherwise act with respect to any such account. The Secretary may make such exemptions from any requirement otherwise imposed under this subsection as are consistent with the purposes of this section.

(d) Reproduction of checks, drafts, and other instruments; record of transactions; identity of party

Each insured depository institution shall make, to the extent that the regulations of the Secretary so require—

(1) a microfilm or other reproduction of each check, draft, or similar instrument drawn on it and presented to it for payment; and

(2) a record of each check, draft, or similar instrument received by it for deposit or collection, together with an identification of the party for whose account it is to be deposited or collected, unless the insured depository institution has already made a record of the party's identity pursuant to subsection (c) of this section.

(e) Identity of persons making reportable currency and foreign transactions

Subject to the requirements of any regulations prescribed jointly by the Secretary and the Board under paragraph (2) or (3) of subsection (b) of this section whenever any individual engages (whether as principal, agent, or bailee) in any transaction with an insured depository institution which is required to be reported or recorded under subchapter II of chapter 53 of Title 31, the insured depository institution shall require and retain such evidence of the identity of that individual as the Secretary may prescribe as appropriate under the circumstances.

(f) Additions to or substitutes for required records

Subject to the requirements of any regulations prescribed jointly by the Secretary and the Board under paragraph (2) or (3) of subsection (b) of this section and in addition to or in lieu of the records and evidence otherwise referred to in this section, each insured depository institution shall maintain such records and evidence as the Secretary may prescribe to carry out the purposes of this section.

(g) Retention period

Any type of record or evidence required under this section shall be retained for such period as the Secretary may prescribe for the type in question. Any period so prescribed shall not exceed six years unless the Secretary determines, having regard for the purposes of this section, that a longer period is necessary in the case of a particular type of record or evidence.

(h) Report to Congress by Secretary of the Treasury

The Secretary shall include in his annual report to the Congress information on his implementation of the authority conferred by this section and any similar authority with respect to recordkeeping or reporting requirements conferred by other provisions of law.

(i) Application of provisions to foreign banks

The provisions of this section shall not apply to any foreign bank except with respect to the transactions and records of any insured branch of such a bank.

(j) Civil penalties

(1) Penalty imposed

Any insured depository institution and any director, officer, or employee of an insured depository institution who willfully or through gross negligence violates, or any person who willfully causes such a violation, any regulation prescribed under subsection (b) of this section shall be liable to the United States for a civil penalty of not more than $10,000.

(2) Treatment of continuing violation

A separate violation of any regulation prescribed under subsection (b) of this section occurs for each day the violation continues and at each office, branch, or place of business at which such violation occurs.

(3) Assessment

Any penalty imposed under paragraph (1) shall be assessed, mitigated, and collected in the manner provided in subsections (b) and (c) of section 5321 of Title 31.

§ 1830. Nondiscrimination

It is not the purpose of this chapter to discriminate in any manner against State nonmember banks or State savings associations and in favor of national or member banks or Federal savings associations, respectively. It is the purpose of this chapter to provide all banks and savings associations with the same opportunity to obtain and enjoy the benefits of this chapter.

§ 1831. Separability of certain provisions of this chapter

The provisions of this chapter limiting the insurance of the deposits of any depositor to a maximum less than the full amount shall be independent and separable from each and all of the provisions of this chapter.

§ 1831a. Activities of insured State banks

(a) Permissible activities

  (1) In general

  After the end of the 1–year period beginning on December 19, 1991, an insured State bank may not engage as principal in any type of activity that is not permissible for a national bank unless—

    (A) the Corporation has determined that the activity would pose no significant risk to the appropriate deposit insurance fund; and

    (B) the State bank is, and continues to be, in compliance with applicable capital standards prescribed by the appropriate Federal banking agency.

  (2) Processing period

    (A) In general

    The Corporation shall make a determination under paragraph (1)(A) not later than 60 days after receipt of a completed application that may be required under this subsection.

    (B) Extension of time period

    The Corporation may extend the 60–day period referred to in subparagraph (A) for not more than 30 additional days, and shall notify the applicant of any such extension.

(b) Insurance underwriting

  (1) In general

  Notwithstanding subsection (a) of this section, an insured State bank may not engage in insurance underwriting except to the extent that activity is permissible for national banks.

  (2) Exception for certain Federally reinsured crop insurance

  Notwithstanding any other provision of law, an insured State bank or any of its subsidiaries that provided insurance on or before September 30, 1991, which was reinsured in whole or in part by the Federal Crop Insurance Corporation may continue to provide such insurance.

(c) Equity Investments by insured State banks

  (1) In general

  An insured State bank may not, directly or indirectly, acquire or retain any equity investment of a type that is not permissible for a national bank.

  (2) Exception for certain subsidiaries

  Paragraph (1) shall not prohibit an insured State bank from acquiring or retaining an equity investment in a subsidiary of which the insured State bank is a majority owner.

  (3) Exception for qualified housing projects

    (A) Exception

    Notwithstanding any other provision of this subsection, an insured State bank may invest as a limited partner in a partnership, the sole purpose of which is direct or indirect investment in the acquisition, rehabilitation, or new construction of a qualified housing project.

    (B) Limitation

    The aggregate of the investments of any insured State bank pursuant to this paragraph shall not exceed 2 percent of the total assets of the bank.

    (C) Qualified housing project defined

    As used in this paragraph—

    (i) Qualified housing project

    The term "qualified housing project" means residential real estate that is intended to primarily benefit lower income people throughout the period of the investment.

    (ii) Lower income

    The term "lower income" means income that is less than or equal to the median income based on statistics from State or Federal sources.

  (4) Transition rule

    (A) In general

    The Corporation shall require any insured State bank to divest any equity investment the retention of which is not permissible under this subsection as quickly as can be prudently done, and in any event before the end of the 5–year period beginning on December 19, 1991.

(B) Treatment of noncompliance during divestment

With respect to any equity investment held by any insured State bank on December 19, 1991 which was lawfully acquired before such date, the bank shall be deemed not to be in violation of the prohibition in this subsection on retaining such investment so long as the bank complies with the applicable requirements established by the Corporation for divesting such investments.

(d) Subsidiaries of insured State banks

(1) In general

After the end of the 1–year period beginning on December 19, 1991, a subsidiary of an insured State bank may not engage as principal in any type of activity that is not permissible for a subsidiary of a national bank unless—

(A) the Corporation has determined that the activity poses no significant risk to the appropriate deposit insurance fund; and

(B) the bank is, and continues to be, in compliance with applicable capital standards prescribed by the appropriate Federal banking agency.

(2) Insurance underwriting prohibited

(A) Prohibition

Notwithstanding paragraph (1), no subsidiary of an insured State bank may engage in insurance underwriting except to the extent such activities are permissible for national banks.

(B) Continuation of existing activities

Notwithstanding subparagraph (A), a well-capitalized insured State bank or any of its subsidiaries that was lawfully providing insurance as principal in a State on November 21, 1991, may continue to provide, as principal, insurance of the same type to residents of the State (including companies or partnerships incorporated in, organized under the laws of, licensed to do business in, or having an office in the State, but only on behalf of their employees resident in or property located in the State), individuals employed in the State, and any other person to whom the bank or subsidiary has provided insurance as

principal, without interruption, since such person resided in or was employed in such State.

(C) Exception

Subparagraph (A) does not apply to a subsidiary of an insured State bank if—

(i) the insured State bank was required, before June 1, 1991, to provide title insurance as a condition of the bank's initial chartering under State law; and

(ii) control of the insured State bank has not changed since that date.

(3) Processing period

(A) In general

The Corporation shall make a determination under paragraph (1)(A) not later than 60 days after receipt of a completed application that may be required under this subsection.

(B) Extension of time period

The Corporation may extend the 60–day period referred to in subparagraph (A) for not more than 30 additional days, and shall notify the applicant of any such extension.

(e) Savings bank life insurance

(1) In general

No provision of this chapter shall be construed as prohibiting or impairing the sale or underwriting of savings bank life insurance, or the ownership of stock in a savings bank life insurance company, by any insured bank which—

(A) is located in the Commonwealth of Massachusetts or the State of New York or Connecticut; and

(B) meets applicable consumer disclosure requirements with respect to such insurance.

(2) FDIC finding and action regarding risk

(A) Finding

Before the end of the 1–year period beginning on December 19, 1991, the Corporation shall make a finding whether savings bank life insurance activities of insured banks pose or may pose any significant risk to the insurance fund of which such banks are members.

(B) Actions

(i) In general

The Corporation shall, pursuant to any finding made under subparagraph (A), take appropriate actions to address any risk that exists or may subsequently develop with respect to insured banks described in paragraph (1)(A).

(ii) Authorized actions

Actions the Corporation may take under this subparagraph include requiring the modification, suspension, or termination of insurance activities conducted by any insured bank if the Corporation finds that the activities pose a significant risk to any insured bank described in paragraph (1)(A) or to the insurance fund of which such bank is a member.

(f) Common and preferred stock investment

(1) In general

An insured State bank shall not acquire or retain, directly or indirectly, any equity investment of a type or in an amount that is not permissible for a national bank or is not otherwise permitted under this section.

(2) Exception for banks in certain states

Notwithstanding paragraph (1), an insured State bank may, to the extent permitted by the Corporation, acquire and retain ownership of securities described in paragraph (1) to the extent the aggregate amount of such investment does not exceed an amount equal to 100 percent of the bank's capital if such bank—

(A) is located in a State that permitted, as of September 30, 1991, investment in common or preferred stock listed on a national securities exchange or shares of an investment company registered under the Investment Company Act of 1940 [15 U.S.C.A. § 80a–1 et seq.]; and

(B) made or maintained an investment in such securities during the period beginning on September 30, 1990, and ending on November 26, 1991.

(3) Exception for certain types of institutions

Notwithstanding paragraph (1), an insured State bank may—

(A) acquire not more than 10 percent of a corporation that only—

(i) provides directors', trustees', and officers' liability insurance coverage or bankers' blanket bond group insurance coverage for insured depository institutions; or

(ii) reinsures such policies; and

(B) acquire or retain shares of a depository institution if—

(i) the institution engages only in activities permissible for national banks;

(ii) the institution is subject to examination and regulation by a State bank supervisor;

(iii) 20 or more depository institutions own shares of the institution and none of those institutions owns more than 15 percent of the institution's shares; and

(iv) the institution's shares (other than directors' qualifying shares or shares held under or initially acquired through a plan established for the benefit of the institution's officers and employees) are owned only by the institution.

(4) Transition period for common and preferred stock investments

(A) In general

During each year in the 3–year period beginning on December 19, 1991, each insured State bank shall reduce by not less than 1/3 of its shares (as of December 19, 1991) the bank's ownership of securities in excess of the amount equal to 100 percent of the capital of such bank.

(B) Compliance at end of period

By the end of the 3–year period referred to in subparagraph (A), each insured State bank and each subsidiary of a State bank shall be in compliance with the maximum amount limitations on investments referred to in paragraph (1).

(5) Loss of exception upon acquisition

Any exception applicable under paragraph (2) with respect to any insured State bank shall cease to apply with respect to such bank upon any change in control of such bank or any conversion of the charter of such bank.

(6) Notice and approval

An insured State bank may only engage in any investment pursuant to paragraph (2) if—

(A) the bank has filed a 1–time notice of the bank's intention to acquire and retain investments described in paragraph (1); and

(B) the Corporation has determined, within 60 days of receiving such notice, that acquiring or retaining such investments does not pose a significant risk to the insurance fund of which such bank is a member.

(7) Divestiture

(A) In general

The Corporation may require divestiture by an insured State bank of any investment permitted under this subsection if the Corporation determines that such investment will have an adverse effect on the safety and soundness of the bank.

(B) Reasonable standard

The Corporation shall not require divestiture by any bank pursuant to subparagraph (A) without reason to believe that such investment will have an adverse effect on the safety and soundness of the bank.

(g) Determinations

The Corporation shall make determinations under this section by regulation or order.

(h) "Activity" defined

For purposes of this section, the term "activity" includes acquiring or retaining any investment.

(i) Other authority not affected

This section shall not be construed as limiting the authority of any appropriate Federal banking agency or any State supervisory authority to impose more stringent restrictions.

(j) Activities of branches of out-of-state banks

(1) Application of host state law

The laws of a host State, including laws regarding community reinvestment, consumer protection, fair lending, and establishment of intrastate branches, shall apply to any branch in the host State of an out-of-State State bank to the same extent as such State laws apply to a branch in the host State of an out-of-State national bank. To the extent host State law is inapplicable to a branch of an out-of-State State bank in such host State pursuant to the preceding sentence, home State law shall apply to such branch.

(2) Activities of branches

An insured State bank that establishes a branch in a host State may conduct any activity at such branch that is permissible under the laws of the home State of such bank, to the extent such activity is permissible either for a bank chartered by the host State (subject to the restrictions in this section) or for a branch in the host State of an out-of-State national bank.

(3) Savings provision

No provision of this subsection shall be construed as affecting the applicability of—

(A) any State law of any home State under subsection (b), (c), or (d) of section 1831u of this title; or

(B) Federal law to State banks and State bank branches in the home State or the host State.

(4) Definitions

The terms "host State", "home State", and "out-of-State bank" have the same meanings as in section 1831u(f) of this title.

§ 1831b. Disclosures with respect to certain federally related mortgage loans

(a) Identity of beneficiary interest as condition for a loan; report to Corporation

No insured depository institution, insured branch of a foreign bank, or mutual savings or cooperative bank which is not an insured depository institution, shall make any federally related mortgage loan to any agent, trustee, nominee, or other person acting in a fiduciary capacity without the prior condition that the identity of the person receiving the beneficial interest of such loan shall at all times be revealed to the insured depository institution, insured branch, or bank. At the request of the Corporation, the insured depository institution, insured branch, or bank shall report to the Corporation on the identity of such person and the nature and amount of the loan, discount, or other extension of credit.

(b) Enforcement; bank status

In addition to other available remedies, this section may be enforced with respect to mutual savings and cooperative banks which are not insured depository institutions in accordance with section 1818 of this title, and for such purpose such mutual savings and cooperative banks shall be held and considered to be State nonmember insured banks and the appropriate Federal agency with respect to such mutual savings and cooperative banks shall be the Federal Deposit Insurance Corporation.

§ 1831c. Repealed. Pub.L. 103–325, Title VI, § 602(f)(1), Sept. 23, 1994, 108 Stat. 2292—DFA § 605

§ 1831d. State-chartered insured depository institutions and insured branches of foreign banks

(a) Interest rates

In order to prevent discrimination against State-chartered insured depository institutions, including insured savings banks, or insured branches of foreign banks with respect to interest rates, if the applicable rate prescribed in this subsection exceeds the rate such State bank or insured branch of a foreign bank would be permitted to charge in the absence of this subsection, such State bank or such insured branch of a foreign bank may, notwithstanding any State constitution or statute which is hereby preempted for the purposes of this section, take, receive, reserve, and charge on any loan or discount made, or upon any note, bill of exchange, or other evidence of debt, interest at a rate of not more than 1 per centum in excess of the discount rate on ninety-day commercial paper in effect at the Federal Reserve bank in the Federal Reserve district where such State bank or such insured branch of a foreign bank is located or at the rate allowed by the laws of the State, territory, or district where the bank is located, whichever may be greater.

(b) Interest overcharge; forfeiture; interest payment recovery

If the rate prescribed in subsection (a) of this section exceeds the rate such State bank or such insured branch of a foreign bank would be permitted to charge in the absence of this section, and such State fixed rate is thereby preempted by the rate described in subsection (a) of this section, the taking, receiving, reserving, or charging a greater rate of interest than is allowed by subsection (a) of this section, when knowingly done, shall be deemed a forfeiture of the entire interest which the note, bill, or other evidence of debt carries with it, or which has been agreed to be paid thereon. If such greater rate of interest has been paid, the person who paid it may recover in a civil action commenced in a court of appropriate jurisdiction not later than two years after the date of such payment, an amount equal to twice the amount of the interest paid from

such State bank or such insured branch of a foreign bank taking, receiving, reserving, or charging such interest.

§ 1831e. Activities of savings associations—DFA § 939

(a) In general

On and after January 1, 1990, a savings association chartered under State law may not engage as principal in any type of activity, or in any activity in an amount, that is not permissible for a Federal savings association unless—

(1) the Corporation has determined that the activity would pose no significant risk to the affected deposit insurance fund; and

(2) the savings association is and continues to be in compliance with the fully phased-in capital standards prescribed under section 1464(t) of this title.

(b) Differences of magnitude between state and federal powers

Notwithstanding subsection (a)(1) of this section, if an activity (other than an activity described in section 1464(c)(2)(B) of this title) is permissible for a Federal savings association, a savings association chartered under State law may engage as principal in that activity in an amount greater than the amount permissible for a Federal savings association if—

(1) the Corporation has not determined that engaging in that amount of the activity poses any significant risk to the affected deposit insurance fund; and

(2) the savings association chartered under State law is and continues to be in compliance with the fully phased-in capital standards prescribed under section 1464(t) of this title.

(c) Equity investments by state savings associations

(1) In general

Notwithstanding subsections (a) and (b) of this section, a savings association chartered under State law may not directly acquire or retain any equity investment of a type or in an amount that is not permissible for a Federal savings association.

(2) Exception for service corporations

Paragraph (1) does not prohibit a savings association from acquiring or retaining shares of one or more service corporations if—

(A) the Corporation has determined that no significant risk to the affected deposit insurance fund is posed by—

(i) the amount that the association proposes to acquire or retain; or

(ii) the activities in which the service corporation engages; and

(B) the savings association is and continues to be in compliance with the fully phased-in capital standards prescribed under section 1464(t) of this title.

(3) Transition rule

(A) In general

The Corporation shall require any savings association to divest any equity investment the retention of which is not permissible under paragraph (1) or (2) as quickly as can be prudently done, and in any event not later than July 1, 1994.

(B) Treatment of noncompliance during divestment

With respect to any equity investment held by any savings association on May 1, 1989, the savings association shall be deemed not to be in violation of the prohibition in paragraph (1) or (2) on retaining such investment so long as the savings association complies with any applicable requirement established by the Corporation pursuant to subparagraph (A) for divesting such investments.

(d) Corporate debt securities not of investment grade

(1) In general

No savings association may, directly or through a subsidiary, acquire or retain any corporate debt security not of investment grade.

(2) Exception for securities held by qualified affiliate

Paragraph (1) shall not apply with respect to any corporate debt security not of investment grade which is acquired and retained by any qualified affiliate of a savings association.

(3) Transition rule

(A) In general

The Corporation shall require any savings association or any subsidiary of any savings association to divest any corporate debt security not of investment grade the retention of which is not permissible under paragraph (1) as quickly as can be prudently done, and in any event not later than July 1, 1994.

(B) Treatment of noncompliance during divestment

With respect to any corporate debt security not of investment grade held by any savings association or subsidiary on August 9, 1989, the savings association or subsidiary shall be deemed not to be in violation of the prohibition in paragraph (1) on retaining such investment so long as the association or subsidiary complies with any applicable requirement established by the Corporation pursuant to subparagraph (A) for divesting such securities.

(4) Definitions

For purposes of this section—

(A) Investment grade

Any corporate debt security is not of "investment grade" unless that security, when acquired by the savings association or subsidiary, was rated in one of the 4 highest rating categories by at least one nationally recognized statistical rating organization.

(B) Qualified affiliate

The term "qualified affiliate" means—

(i) in the case of a stock savings association, an affiliate other than a subsidiary or an insured depository institution; and

(ii) in the case of a mutual savings association, a subsidiary other than an insured depository institution, so long as all of the savings association's investments in and extensions of credit to the subsidiary are deducted from the savings association's capital.

(C) Certain securities not included

The term "corporate debt security not of investment grade" does not include any obligation issued or guaranteed by a corporation that may be held by a Federal savings association without limitation as to percentage of assets under subparagraph (D), (E), or (F) of section 1464(c)(1) of this title.

(e) Transfer of corporate debt security not of investment grade in exchange for a qualified note

(1) Acquisition of note

Notwithstanding subsections (a), (b), and (c) of section 1464 of this title and any other provision of Federal or State law governing extensions of credit by savings associations, any insured savings association, and any subsidiary of any insured savings association, that, on August 9, 1989, holds any corporate debt security not of investment grade may acquire a qualified note in exchange for the transfer of such security to—

(A) any holding company which controls 80 percent or more of the shares of such insured savings association; or

(B) any company other than an insured savings association, or any subsidiary of any insured savings association, 80 percent or more of the shares of which are controlled by such holding company,

if the conditions of paragraph (2) are met.

(2) Conditions for exchange of security for qualified note

The conditions of this paragraph are met if—

(A) the insured savings association was in compliance with applicable capital requirements on December 31, 1988, and the insured savings association after such date—

(i) remains in compliance with applicable capital requirements; or

(ii) adopts and complies with a capital plan acceptable to the Director of the Office of Thrift Supervision;

(B) the company to which the corporate debt security not of investment grade is transferred is not a bank holding company, an insured savings association, or a direct or indirect subsidiary of such holding company or insured savings association;

(C) before the end of the 90-day period beginning on August 9, 1989, the insured savings association notifies the Director of the Office of Thrift Supervision of such association's intention to transfer the corporate debt security not of investment grade to the savings and loan holding company or the subsidiary of such holding company;

(D) the transfer of the corporate debt security not of investment grade is completed—

(i) before the end of the 1-year period beginning on August 9, 1989, in the case of an insured savings association that, as of such date, is controlled by a savings and loan holding company; or

(ii) before the end of the 2-year period beginning on such date, in the case of a savings association that is not, as of such date, a subsidiary of a savings and loan holding company;

(E) the insured savings association receives in exchange for the corporate debt security not of investment grade the fair market value of such security;

(F) the Director of the Office of Thrift Supervision has—

(i) approved the transaction; and

(ii) determined that the transfer represents a complete and effective divestiture of the corporate debt security not of investment grade and is in compliance with the provisions of this subsection; and

(G) any gain on the sale of the corporate debt security not of investment grade is recognized, and included for applicable regulatory capital requirements, by the insured savings association only at such time and to the extent that the insured savings association receives payment of principal on the note in cash in excess of the fair market value of the transferred corporate debt security not of investment grade as carried on the accounts of the insured savings association immediately prior to the transfer.

(3) "Qualified note" defined

The term "qualified note" means any note that—

(A) is at all times fully secured by the corporate debt security not of investment grade transferred in exchange for the note, or by other collateral of at least equivalent value that is acceptable to the Director of the Office of Thrift Supervision;

(B) contains provisions acceptable to the Director of the Office of Thrift Supervision that would—

(i) prevent any action to encumber or impair the value of the collateral referred to in subparagraph (A); and

(ii) allow the sale of the corporate debt security not of investment grade if the proceeds of the sale are reinvested in assets of equivalent value;

(C) is on market terms, including interest rate, which must in all cases be above the insured savings association's borrowing rate for similar term funds;

(D) is fully repayable over a period of time not to exceed 5 years from the date of transfer;

(E) is repaid with annual principal payments at least as large as would be necessary to repay the note within 5 years if it were on a level payment amortization schedule and the interest rate for the first year of repayment were fixed throughout the amortization period;

(F) is fully guaranteed by each holding company of the insured savings association that acquires such note; and

(G) is repaid in full in cash in accordance with its terms and this subsection.

(4) Failure to repay on schedule

The exemption provided by this subsection from subsections (a), (b), and (c) of section 1468 of this title and any other applicable provision of Federal or State law shall terminate immediately if the insured savings association or any affiliate of such association fails to comply with the terms of the qualified note or this subsection.

(f) Determinations

The Corporation shall make determinations under this section by regulation or order.

(g) "Activity" defined

For purposes of subsections (a) and (b) of this section—

(1) In general

The term "activity" includes acquiring or retaining any investment.

(2) Divestiture of certain assets

Notwithstanding paragraph (1), subsections (a) and (b) of this section shall not be construed to require a savings association to divest itself of any assets acquired before August 9, 1989.

(h) Other authority not affected

This section may not be construed as limiting—

(1) any other authority of the Corporation; or

(2) any authority of the Director of the Office of Thrift Supervision or of a State to impose more stringent restrictions.

§ 1831f.   Brokered deposits

(a) In general

An insured depository institution that is not well capitalized may not accept funds obtained, directly or indirectly, by or through any deposit broker for deposit into 1 or more deposit accounts.

(b) Renewals and rollovers treated as acceptance of funds

Any renewal of an account in any troubled institution and any rollover of any amount on deposit in any such account shall be treated as an acceptance of funds by such troubled institution for purposes of subsection (a) of this section.

(c) Waiver authority

The Corporation may, on a case-by-case basis and upon application by an insured depository institution which is adequately capitalized (but not well capitalized), waive the applicability of subsection (a) of this section upon a finding that the acceptance of such deposits does not constitute an unsafe or unsound practice with respect to such institution.

(d) Limited exception for certain conservatorships

In the case of any insured depository institution for which the Corporation has been appointed as conservator, subsection (a) of this section shall not apply to the acceptance of deposits (described in such subsection) by such institution if the Corporation determines that the acceptance of such deposits—

(1) is not an unsafe or unsound practice;

(2) is necessary to enable the institution to meet the demands of its depositors or pay its obligations in the ordinary course of business; and

(3) is consistent with the conservator's fiduciary duty to minimize the institution's losses.

Effective 90 days after the date on which the institution was placed in conservatorship, the institution may not accept such deposits.

(e) Restriction on interest rate paid

Any insured depository institution which, under subsection (c) or (d) of this section, accepts funds obtained, directly or indirectly, by or through a deposit broker, may not pay a rate of interest on such funds which, at the time that such funds are accepted, significantly exceeds—

(1) the rate paid on deposits of similar maturity in such institution's normal market area for deposits accepted in the institution's normal market area; or

(2) the national rate paid on deposits of comparable maturity, as established by the Corporation, for deposits accepted outside the institution's normal market area.

(f) Additional restrictions

The Corporation may impose, by regulation or order, such additional restrictions on the acceptance of brokered deposits by any institution as the Corporation may determine to be appropriate.

(g) Definitions relating to deposit broker

(1) Deposit broker

The term "deposit broker" means—

(A) any person engaged in the business of placing deposits, or facilitating the placement of deposits, of third parties with insured depository institutions or the business of placing deposits with insured depository institutions for the purpose of selling interests in those deposits to third parties; and

(B) an agent or trustee who establishes a deposit account to facilitate a business arrangement with an insured depository institution to use the proceeds of the account to fund a prearranged loan.

(2) Exclusions

The term "deposit broker" does not include—

(A) an insured depository institution, with respect to funds placed with that depository institution;

(B) an employee of an insured depository institution, with respect to funds placed with the employing depository institution;

(C) a trust department of an insured depository institution, if the trust in question has not been established for the primary purpose of placing funds with insured depository institutions;

(D) the trustee of a pension or other employee benefit plan, with respect to funds of the plan;

(E) a person acting as a plan administrator or an investment adviser in connection with a pension plan or other employee benefit plan provided that that person is performing managerial functions with respect to the plan;

(F) the trustee of a testamentary account;

(G) the trustee of an irrevocable trust (other than one described in paragraph (1)(B)), as long as the trust in question has not been established for the primary purpose of placing funds with insured depository institutions;

(H) a trustee or custodian of a pension or profitsharing plan qualified under section 401(d) or 403(a) of Title 26; or

(I) an agent or nominee whose primary purpose is not the placement of funds with depository institutions.

(3) Inclusion of depository institutions engaging in certain activities

Notwithstanding paragraph (2), the term "deposit broker" includes any insured depository institution that is not well capitalized (as defined in section 1831o of this title), and any employee of such institution, which engages, directly or indirectly, in the solicitation of deposits by offering rates of interest which are significantly higher than the prevailing rates of interest on deposits offered by other insured depository institutions in such depository institution's normal market area.

(4) Employee

For purposes of this subsection, the term "employee" means any employee—

(A) who is employed exclusively by the insured depository institution;

(B) whose compensation is primarily in the form of a salary;

(C) who does not share such employee's compensation with a deposit broker; and

(D) whose office space or place of business is used exclusively for the benefit of the insured depository institution which employs such individual.

(h) Deposit solicitation restricted

An insured depository institution that is undercapitalized, as defined in section 1831o of this title, shall not solicit deposits by offering rates of interest that are significantly higher than the prevailing rates of interest on insured deposits—

(1) in such institution's normal market areas; or

(2) in the market area in which such deposits would otherwise be accepted.

§ 1831f–1. Repealed. Pub.L. 106–569, Title XII, § 1203, Dec. 27, 2000, 114 Stat. 3032

§ 1831g. Contracts between depository institutions and persons providing goods, products, or services

(a) In general

An insured depository institution may not enter into a written or oral contract with any person to provide goods, products, or services to or for the benefit of such depository institution if the performance of such contract would adversely affect the safety or soundness of the institution.

(b) Rulemaking

The Corporation shall prescribe such regulations and issue such orders, including definitions consistent with this section, as may be necessary to administer and carry out the purposes of, and prevent evasions of, this section.

(c) Enforcement

Any action taken by any appropriate Federal banking agency under section 1818 of this title to enforce compliance on the part of any insured depository institution with the requirements of this section may include a requirement that such institution properly reflect the transaction on its books and records.

(d) No private right of action

This section may not be construed as creating any private right of action.

(e) Study

(1) In general

The Attorney General and the Comptroller General of the United States shall jointly conduct a study on the extent to which—

(A) insured depository institutions are entering into contracts with vendors under which the vendors agree to purchase stock or assets from insured depository institutions or to invest capital in or make deposits in such institutions; and

(B) if such practices occur, the extent to which such practices are having an anticompetitive effect and should be prohibited.

(2) Report to Congress

Before the end of the 1–year period beginning on August 9, 1989, the Attorney General and the Comptroller General shall submit a report to the Congress on the results of the study conducted pursuant to paragraph (1).

§ 1831h. Savings association insurance fund industry advisory committee

(a) Establishment

There is hereby established the Savings Association Insurance Fund Industry Advisory Committee (hereinafter referred to in this section as the "Committee").

(b) Membership

The Committee shall consist of 18 members, appointed as follows:

(1) 1 member elected from each Federal home loan bank district (by the members of the board of directors of each such bank who were elected by the members of such bank) from among individuals residing therein who are officers of insured depository institutions that are Savings Association Insurance Fund members.

(2) 6 members appointed by the Corporation from among individuals who shall represent the public interest.

(c) Vacancies

Any vacancy on the Committee shall be filled in the same manner in which the original appointment was made.

(d) Pay and expenses

Members of the Committee shall serve without pay, but each member shall be reimbursed, in such manner as the Corporation shall prescribe by regulation, for expenses incurred in connection with attendance of such members at meetings of the Committee.

(e) Terms

Members shall be appointed or elected for terms of 1 year.

(f) Authority of the Committee

The Committee may select its Chairperson, Vice Chairperson, and Secretary, and adopt methods of procedure, and shall have power—

(1) to confer with the Board of Directors on general and special business conditions and regulatory and other matters affecting insured financial institutions that are members of the Savings Association Insurance Fund; and

(2) to request information, and to make recommendations, with respect to matters within the jurisdiction of the Corporation.

(g) Meetings

The Committee shall meet 4 times each year, and more frequently if requested by the Corporation.

(h) Reports

The Committee shall submit a semiannual written report to the Committee on Banking, Finance and Urban Affairs of the House and to the Committee on Banking, Housing, and Urban Affairs of the Senate. Such report shall describe the activities of the Committee for such semiannual period and contain such recommendations as the Committee considers appropriate.

(i) Provision of staff and other resources

The Corporation shall provide the Committee with the use of such resources, including staff, as the Committee reasonably shall require to carry out its duties, including the preparation and submission of reports to Congress, under this section.

(j) Federal Advisory Committee Act does not apply

The Federal Advisory Committee Act shall not apply to the Committee.

(k) Sunset

The Committee shall cease to exist 10 years after August 9, 1989.

§ 1831i. Agency disapproval of directors and senior executive officers of insured depository institutions or depository institution holding companies

(a) Prior notice required

An insured depository institution or depository institution holding company shall notify the appropriate Federal banking agency of the proposed addition of any individual to the board of directors or the employment of any individual as a senior executive officer of such institution or holding company at least 30 days (or such other period, as determined by the appropriate Federal banking agency) before such addition or employment becomes effective, if—

(1) the insured depository institution or depository institution holding company is not in compliance with the minimum capital requirement applicable to such institution or is otherwise in a troubled condition, as determined by such agency on the basis of such institution's or holding company's most recent report of condition or report of examination or inspection; or

(2) the agency determines, in connection with the review by the agency of the plan required under section 1831o of this title or otherwise, that such prior notice is appropriate.

(b) Disapproval by agency

An insured depository institution or depository institution holding company may not add any individual to the board of directors or employ any individual as a senior executive officer if the appropriate Federal banking agency issues a notice of disapproval of such addition or employment before the end of the notice period, not to exceed 90 days, beginning on the date the agency receives notice of the proposed action pursuant to subsection (a) of this section.

(c) Exception in extraordinary circumstances

(1) In general

Each appropriate Federal banking agency may prescribe by regulation conditions under which the prior notice requirement of subsection (a) of this section may be waived in the event of extraordinary circumstances.

(2) No effect on disapproval authority of agency

Such waivers shall not affect the authority of each agency to issue notices of disapproval of such additions or employment of such individuals within 30 days after each such waiver.

(d) Additional information

Any notice submitted to an appropriate Federal banking agency with respect to an individual by any insured depository institution or depository institution holding company pursuant to subsection (a) of this section shall include—

    (1) the information described in section 1817(j)(6)(A) of this title about the individual; and

    (2) such other information as the agency may prescribe by regulation.

(e) Standard for disapproval

The appropriate Federal banking agency shall issue a notice of disapproval with respect to a notice submitted pursuant to subsection (a) of this section if the competence, experience, character, or integrity of the individual with respect to whom such notice is submitted indicates that it would not be in the best interests of the depositors of the depository institution or in the best interests of the public to permit the individual to be employed by, or associated with, the depository institution or depository institution holding company.

(f) Definition regulations

Each appropriate Federal banking agency shall prescribe by regulation a definition for the terms "troubled condition" and "senior executive officer" for purposes of subsection (a) of this section.

§ 1831j. Depository institution employee protection remedy

(a) In general

    (1) Employees of depository institutions

    No insured depository institution may discharge or otherwise discriminate against any employee with respect to compensation, terms, conditions, or privileges of employment because the employee (or any person acting pursuant to the request of the employee) provided information to any Federal Banking agency or to the Attorney General regarding—

        (A) a possible violation of any law or regulation; or

        (B) gross mismanagement, a gross waste of funds, an abuse of authority, or a substantial and specific danger to public health or safety;

    by the depository institution or any director, officer, or employee of the institution.

    (2) Employees of banking agencies

    No Federal banking agency, Federal home loan bank, Federal reserve bank, or any person who is performing, directly or indirectly, any function or service on behalf of the Corporation may discharge or otherwise discriminate against any employee with respect to compensation, terms, conditions, or privileges of employment because the employee (or any person acting pursuant to the request of the employee) provided information to any such agency or bank or to the Attorney General regarding any possible violation of any law or regulation, gross mismanagement, a gross waste of funds, an abuse of authority, or a substantial and specific danger to public health or safety by—

        (A) any depository institution or any such bank or agency;

        (B) any director, officer, or employee of any depository institution or any such bank;

        (C) any officer or employee of the agency which employs such employee; or

        (D) the person, or any officer or employee of the person, who employs such employee.

(b) Enforcement

Any employee or former employee who believes he has been discharged or discriminated against in violation of subsection (a) of this section may file a civil action in the appropriate United States district court before the close of the 2–year period beginning on the date of such discharge or discrimination. The complainant shall also file a copy of the complaint initiating such action with the appropriate Federal banking agency.

(c) Remedies

If the district court determines that a violation of subsection (a) of this section has occurred, it may order the depository institution, Federal home loan bank, Federal Reserve bank, or Federal banking agency which committed the violation—

    (1) to reinstate the employee to his former position;

    (2) to pay compensatory damages; or

    (3) take other appropriate actions to remedy any past discrimination.

(d) Limitation

The protections of this section shall not apply to any employee who—

    (1) deliberately causes or participates in the alleged violation of law or regulation; or

(2) knowingly or recklessly provides substantially false information to such an agency or the Attorney General.

(e) "Federal banking agency" defined

For purposes of subsections (a) and (c) of this section, the term "Federal banking agency" means the Corporation, the Board of Governors of the Federal Reserve System, the Federal Housing Finance Board, the Comptroller of the Currency, and the Director of the Office of Thrift Supervision.

(f) Burdens of proof

The legal burdens of proof that prevail under subchapter III of chapter 12 of Title 5 shall govern adjudication of protected activities under this section.

§ 1831k. Reward for information leading to recoveries or civil penalties

(a) In general

An appropriate Federal banking agency, with the concurrence of the Attorney General, may pay a reward to a person who provides original information which leads to—

(1) recovery of a criminal fine, restitution, or civil penalty—

(A) under—

(i) the Federal Deposit Insurance Act [12 U.S.C.A. § 1811 et seq.];

(ii) the Federal Credit Union Act [12 U.S.C.A. § 1751 et seq.];

(iii) section 93(b), 164 or 481 to 485 of this title;

(iv) the Federal Reserve Act;

(v) the Bank Holding Company Act Amendments of 1970;

(vi) the Bank Holding Company Act of 1956 [12 U.S.C.A. § 1841 et seq.];

(vii) the Home Owners' Loan Act [12 U.S.C.A. § 1461 et seq.]; or

(viii) section 3663 of Title 18 pursuant to a conviction for an offense referred to in subparagraph (B) of this paragraph;

(B) pursuant to a conviction for an offense under section 215, 656, 657, 1005, 1006, 1007, 1014, 1341, 1343, or 1344 of Title 18 affecting a depository institution insured by the Federal Deposit Insurance Corporation,

or for a conspiracy to commit such an offense; or

(C) under section 1833a of this title; or

(2) a forfeiture under section 981 or 982 of Title 18, that arises in connection with a depository institution insured by the Federal Deposit Insurance Corporation.

(b) Percentage limitation

An appropriate Federal banking agency may not pay a reward under subsection (a) of this section of more than 25 percent of the amount of the fine, penalty, restitution, or forfeiture or $100,000, whichever is less.

(c) Officials and persons ineligible

An appropriate Federal banking agency may not pay a reward under subsection (a) of this section to—

(1) an officer or employee of the United States or of a State or local government who provides information described in subsection (a) of this section, obtained in the performance of official duties; or

(2) a person who—

(A) deliberately causes or participates in the alleged violation of law or regulation, or

(B) knowingly or recklessly provides substantially false information to such an agency or the Attorney General.

(d) Nonreviewability

Any agency decision under this section is final and not reviewable by any court.

§ 1831l. Coordination of risk analysis between SEC and Federal banking agencies

Any appropriate Federal banking agency shall notify the Securities and Exchange Commission of any concerns of the agency regarding significant financial or operational risks to any registered broker or dealer, or any registered municipal securities dealer, government securities broker, or government securities dealer for which the Commission is the appropriate regulatory agency (as defined in section 78c of Title 15), resulting from the activities of any insured depository institution, any depository institution holding company, or any affiliate of any such institution or company if such broker, dealer, municipal securities dealer, government securities broker, or government securities dealer is an affiliate of any such institution, company, or affiliate.

§ 1831m. Early identification of needed improvements in financial management

(a) Annual report on financial condition and management

(1) Report required

Each insured depository institution shall submit an annual report to the Corporation, the appropriate Federal banking agency, and any appropriate State bank supervisor (including any State bank supervisor of a host State).

(2) Contents of report

Any annual report required under paragraph (1) shall contain—

(A) the information required to be provided by—

(i) the institution's management under subsection (b) of this section; and

(ii) an independent public accountant under subsections (c) and (d) of this section; and

(B) such other information as the Corporation and the appropriate Federal banking agency may determine to be necessary to assess the financial condition and management of the institution.

(3) Public availability

Any annual report required under paragraph (1) shall be available for public inspection. Notwithstanding the preceding sentence, the Corporation and the appropriate Federal banking agencies may designate certain information as privileged and confidential and not available to the public.

(b) Management responsibility for financial statements and internal controls

Each insured depository institution shall prepare—

(1) annual financial statements in accordance with generally accepted accounting principles and such other disclosure requirements as the Corporation and the appropriate Federal banking agency may prescribe; and

(2) a report signed by the chief executive officer and the chief accounting or financial officer of the institution which contains—

(A) a statement of the management's responsibilities for—

(i) preparing financial statements;

(ii) establishing and maintaining an adequate internal control structure and procedures for financial reporting; and

(iii) complying with the laws and regulations relating to safety and soundness which are designated by the Corporation and the appropriate Federal banking agency; and

(B) an assessment, as of the end of the institution's most recent fiscal year, of—

(i) the effectiveness of such internal control structure and procedures; and

(ii) the institution's compliance with the laws and regulations relating to safety and soundness which are designated by the Corporation and the appropriate Federal banking agency.

(c) Internal control evaluation and reporting requirements for independent public accountants

(1) In general

With respect to any internal control report required by subsection (b)(2) of this section of any institution, the institution's independent public accountant shall attest to, and report separately on, the assertions of the institution's management contained in such report.

(2) Attestation requirements

Any attestation pursuant to paragraph (1) shall be made in accordance with generally accepted standards for attestation engagements.

(d) Annual independent audits of financial statements

(1) Audits required

The Corporation, in consultation with the appropriate Federal banking agencies, shall prescribe regulations requiring that each insured depository institution shall have an annual independent audit made of the institution's financial statements by an independent public accountant in accordance with generally accepted auditing standards and section 1831n of this title.

(2) Scope of audit

In connection with any audit under this subsection, the independent public accountant shall determine and report whether the financial statements of the institution—

(A) are presented fairly in accordance with generally accepted accounting principles; and

(B) comply with such other disclosure requirements as the Corporation and the appropriate Federal banking agency may prescribe.

(3) Requirements for insured subsidiaries of holding companies

The requirements for an independent audit under this subsection may be satisfied for insured depository institutions that are subsidiaries of a holding company by an independent audit of the holding company.

(e) Repealed. Pub.L. 104–208, Div. A, Title II, § 2301(a), Sept. 30, 1996, 110 Stat. 3009–419

(f) Form and content of reports and auditing standards

(1) In general

The scope of each report by an independent public accountant pursuant to this section, and the procedures followed in preparing such report, shall meet or exceed the scope and procedures required by generally accepted auditing standards and other applicable standards recognized by the Corporation.

(2) Consultation

The Corporation shall consult with the other appropriate Federal banking agencies in implementing this subsection.

(g) Improved accountability

(1) Independent audit committee

(A) Establishment

Each insured depository institution (to which this section applies) shall have an independent audit committee entirely made up of outside directors who are independent of management of the institution, except as provided in subparagraph (D), and who satisfy any specific requirements the Corporation may establish.

(B) Duties

An independent audit committee's duties shall include reviewing with management and the independent public accountant the

basis for the reports issued under subsections (b)(2), (c), and (d) of this section.

(C) Criteria applicable to committees of large insured depository institutions

In the case of each insured depository institution which the Corporation determines to be a large institution, the audit committee required by subparagraph (A) shall—

(i) include members with banking or related financial management expertise;

(ii) have access to the committee's own outside counsel; and

(iii) not include any large customers of the institution.

(D) Exemption authority

(i) In general

An appropriate Federal banking agency may, by order or regulation, permit the independent audit committee of an insured depository institution to be made up of less than all, but no fewer than a majority of, outside directors, if the agency determines that the institution has encountered hardships in retaining and recruiting a sufficient number of competent outside directors to serve on the internal audit committee of the institution.

(ii) Factors to be considered

In determining whether an insured depository institution has encountered hardships referred to in clause (i), the appropriate Federal banking agency shall consider factors such as the size of the institution, and whether the institution has made a good faith effort to elect or name additional competent outside directors to the board of directors of the institution who may serve on the internal audit committee.

(2) Review of quarterly reports of large insured depository institutions

(A) In general

In the case of any insured depository institution which the Corporation has determined to be a large institution, the Corporation may require the independent public accountant retained by such institution to perform reviews of the institution's quarterly financial reports in accordance with procedures agreed upon by the Corporation.

(B) Report to audit committee

The independent public accountant referred to in subparagraph (A) shall provide the audit committee of the insured depository institution with reports on the reviews under such subparagraph and the audit committee shall provide such reports to the Corporation, any appropriate Federal banking agency, and any appropriate State bank supervisor.

(C) Limitation on notice

Reports provided under subparagraph (B) shall be only for the information and use of the insured depository institution, the Corporation, any appropriate Federal banking agency, and any State bank supervisor that received the report.

(D) Notice to institution

The Corporation shall promptly notify an insured depository institution, in writing, of a determination pursuant to subparagraph (A) to require a review of such institution's quarterly financial reports.

(3) Qualifications of independent public accountants

(A) In general

All audit services required by this section shall be performed only by an independent public accountant who—

(i) has agreed to provide related working papers, policies, and procedures to the Corporation, any appropriate Federal banking agency, and any State bank supervisor, if requested; and

(ii) has received a peer review that meets guidelines acceptable to the Corporation.

(B) Reports on peer reviews

Reports on peer reviews shall be filed with the Corporation and made available for public inspection.

(4) Enforcement actions

(A) In general

In addition to any authority contained in section 1818 of this title, the Corporation or an appropriate Federal banking agency may remove, suspend, or bar an independent public accountant, upon a showing of good cause, from performing audit services required by this section.

(B) Joint rulemaking

The appropriate Federal banking agencies shall jointly issue rules of practice to implement this paragraph.

(5) Notice by accountant of termination of services

Any independent public accountant performing an audit under this section who subsequently ceases to be the accountant for the institution shall promptly notify the Corporation and each appropriate Federal banking agency pursuant to such rules as the Corporation and each appropriate Federal banking agency shall prescribe.

(h) Exchange of reports and information

(1) Report to the independent auditor

(A) In general

Each insured depository institution which has engaged the services of an independent auditor to audit such institution shall transmit to the auditor a copy of the most recent report of condition made by the institution (pursuant to this chapter or any other provision of law) and a copy of the most recent report of examination received by the institution.

(B) Additional information

In addition to the copies of the reports required to be provided under subparagraph (A), each insured depository institution shall provide the auditor with—

(i) a copy of any supervisory memorandum of understanding with such institution and any written agreement between such institution and any appropriate Federal banking agency or any appropriate State bank supervisor which is in effect during the period covered by the audit; and

(ii) a report of—

(I) any action initiated or taken by the appropriate Federal banking agency or the Corporation during such period under subsection (a), (b), (c), (e), (g), (i), (s), or (t) of section 1818 of this title;

(II) any action taken by any appropriate State bank supervisor under State law which is similar to any action referred to in subclause (I); or

(III) any assessment of any civil money penalty under any other provision of law with respect to the institution or any institution-affiliated party.

(2) Reports to banking agencies

(A) Independent auditor reports

Each insured depository institution shall provide to the Corporation, any appropriate Federal banking agency, and any appropriate State bank supervisor, a copy of each audit report and any qualification to such report, any management letter, and any other report within 15 days of receipt of any such report, qualification, or letter from the institution's independent auditors.

(B) Notice of change of auditor

Each insured depository institution shall provide written notification to the Corporation, the appropriate Federal banking agency, and any appropriate State bank supervisor of the resignation or dismissal of the institution's independent auditor or the engagement of a new independent auditor by the institution, including a statement of the reasons for such change within 15 calendar days of the occurrence of the event.

(i) Requirements for insured subsidiaries of holding companies

(1) In general

Except with respect to any audit requirements established under or pursuant to subsection (d) of this section, the requirements of this section may be satisfied for insured depository institutions that are subsidiaries of a holding company, if—

(A) services and functions comparable to those required under this section are provided at the holding company level; and

(B) the institution—

(i) has total assets, as of the beginning of such fiscal year, of less than $5,000,000,000; or

(ii) has—

(I) total assets, as of the beginning of such fiscal year, of $5,000,000,000, or more; and

(II) a CAMEL composite rating of 1 or 2 under the Uniform Financial Institutions Rating System (or an equivalent rating by any such agency under a comparable rating system) as of the most recent examination of

such institution by the Corporation or the appropriate Federal banking agency.

(2) Large institutions

For purposes of this subsection, in the case of an insured depository institution described in paragraph (1)(B)(ii) that the Corporation determines to be a large institution, the audit committee of the holding company of such an institution shall not include any large customers of the institution.

(3) Applicability based on risk to fund

The appropriate Federal banking agency may require an institution with total assets in excess of $9,000,000,000 to comply with this section, notwithstanding the exemption provided by this subsection, if it determines that such exemption would create a significant risk to the affected deposit insurance fund if applied to that institution.

(j) Exemption for small depository institutions

This section shall not apply with respect to any fiscal year of any insured depository institution the total assets of which, as of the beginning of such fiscal year, are less than the greater of—

(1) $150,000,000; or

(2) such amount (in excess of $150,000,000) as the Corporation may prescribe by regulation.

§ 1831m–1. Reports of information regarding safety and soundness of depository institutions

(a) Reports to appropriate Federal banking agencies

(1) In general

The Attorney General, the Secretary of the Treasury, and the head of any other agency or instrumentality of the United States shall, unless otherwise prohibited by law, disclose to the appropriate Federal banking agency any information that the Attorney General, the Secretary of the Treasury, or such agency head believes raises significant concerns regarding the safety or soundness of any depository institution doing business in the United States.

(2) Exceptions

(A) Intelligence information

(i) In general

The Director of Central Intelligence shall disclose to the Attorney General or the Secretary of the Treasury any intelligence information that would otherwise be reported to an appropriate Federal banking agency pursuant to paragraph (1). After consultation with the Director of Central Intelligence, the Attorney General or the Secretary of the Treasury, shall disclose the intelligence information to the appropriate Federal banking agency.

(ii) Procedures for receipt of intelligence information

Each appropriate Federal banking agency, in consultation with the Director of Central Intelligence, shall establish procedures for receipt of intelligence information that are adequate to protect the intelligence information.

(B) Criminal investigations, safety of government investigators, informants, and witnesses

If the Attorney General, the Secretary of the Treasury or their respective designees determines that the disclosure of information pursuant to paragraph (1) may jeopardize a pending civil investigation or litigation, or a pending criminal investigation or prosecution, may result in serious bodily injury or death to Government employees, informants, witnesses or their respective families, or may disclose sensitive investigative techniques and methods, the Attorney General or the Secretary of the Treasury shall—

(i) provide the appropriate Federal banking agency a description of the information that is as specific as possible without jeopardizing the investigation, litigation, or prosecution, threatening serious bodily injury or death to Government employees, informants, or witnesses or their respective families, or disclosing sensitive investigation techniques and methods; and

(ii) permit a full review of the information by the Federal banking agency at a location and under procedures that the Attorney General determines will ensure the effective protection of the information while permitting the Federal banking agency to ensure the safety and soundness of any depository institution.

(C) Grand jury investigations; criminal procedure

Paragraph (1) shall not—

(i) apply to the receipt of information by an agency or instrumentality in connection with a pending grand jury investigation; or

(ii) be construed to require disclosure of information prohibited by rule 6 of the Federal Rules of Criminal Procedure.

(b) Procedures for receipt of disclosure reports

(1) In general

Within 90 days after October 28, 1992, each appropriate Federal banking agency shall establish procedures for receipt of a disclosure report by an agency or instrumentality made in accordance with subsection (a)(1) of this section. The procedures established in accordance with this subsection shall ensure adequate protection of information disclosed, including access control and information accountability.

(2) Procedures related to each disclosure report

Upon receipt of a report in accordance with subsection (a)(1) of this section, the appropriate Federal banking agency shall—

(A) consult with the agency or instrumentality that made the disclosure regarding the adequacy of the procedures established pursuant to paragraph (1), and

(B) adjust the procedures to ensure adequate protection of the information disclosed.

(c) Effect on agencies

This section does not impose an affirmative duty on the Attorney General, the Secretary of the Treasury, or the head of any agency or instrumentality of the United States to collect new or to review existing information.

(d) Definitions

For purposes of this section, the terms "appropriate Federal banking agency" and "depository institution" have the same meanings as in section 1818 of this title.

§ 1831n. Accounting objectives, standards, and requirements

(a) In general

(1) Objectives

Accounting principles applicable to reports or statements required to be filed with Federal banking agencies by insured depository institutions should—

(A) result in financial statements and reports of condition that accurately reflect the capital of such institutions;

(B) facilitate effective supervision of the institutions; and

(C) facilitate prompt corrective action to resolve the institutions at the least cost to the insurance funds.

(2) Standards

(A) Uniform accounting principles consistent with GAAP

Subject to the requirements of this chapter and any other provision of Federal law, the accounting principles applicable to reports or statements required to be filed with Federal banking agencies by all insured depository institutions shall be uniform and consistent with generally accepted accounting principles.

(B) Stringency

If the appropriate Federal banking agency or the Corporation determines that the application of any generally accepted accounting principle to any insured depository institution is inconsistent with the objectives described in paragraph (1), the agency or the Corporation may, with respect to reports or statements required to be filed with such agency or Corporation, prescribe an accounting principle which is applicable to such institutions which is no less stringent than generally accepted accounting principles.

(3) Review and implementation of accounting principles required

Before the end of the 1–year period beginning on December 19, 1991, each appropriate Federal banking agency shall take the following actions:

(A) Review of accounting principles

Review—

(i) all accounting principles used by depository institutions with respect to reports or statements required to be filed with a Federal banking agency;

(ii) all requirements established by the agency with respect to such accounting procedures; and

(iii) the procedures and format for reports to the agency, including reports of condition.

(B) Modification of noncomplying measures

Modify or eliminate any accounting principle or reporting requirement of such Federal agency which the agency determines fails to comply with the objectives and standards established under paragraphs (1) and (2).

(C) Inclusion of "off balance sheet" items

Develop and prescribe regulations which require that all assets and liabilities, including contingent assets and liabilities, of insured depository institutions be reported in, or otherwise taken into account in the preparation of any balance sheet, financial statement, report of condition, or other report of such institution, required to be filed with a Federal banking agency.

(b) Uniform accounting of capital standards

(1) In general

Each appropriate Federal banking agency shall maintain uniform accounting standards to be used for determining compliance with statutory or regulatory requirements of depository institutions.

(2) Transition provision

Any standards in effect on December 19, 1991, under section 1833d of this title shall continue in effect after December 19, 1991, until amended by the appropriate Federal banking agency under paragraph (1).

(c) Reports to banking committees

(1) Annual reports required

The Federal banking agencies shall jointly submit an annual report to the Committee on Banking, Finance and Urban Affairs of the House of Representatives and the Committee on Banking, Housing, and Urban Affairs of the Senate containing a description of any difference between any accounting or capital standard used by any such agency and any accounting or capital standard used by any other agency.

(2) Explanation of reasons for discrepancy

Each report submitted under paragraph (1) shall contain an explanation of the reasons for any discrepancy between any accounting or capital standard used by any such agency and any accounting or capital standard used by any other agency.

(3) Publication

Each report under this subsection shall be published in the Federal Register.

§ 1831*o*.   Prompt corrective action—DFA § 616

(a) Resolving problems to protect deposit insurance funds

(1) Purpose

The purpose of this section is to resolve the problems of insured depository institutions at the least possible long-term loss to the deposit insurance fund.

(2) Prompt corrective action required

Each appropriate Federal banking agency and the Corporation (acting in the Corporation's capacity as the insurer of depository institutions under this chapter) shall carry out the purpose of this section by taking prompt corrective action to resolve the problems of insured depository institutions.

(b) Definitions

For purposes of this section:

(1) Capital categories

(A) Well capitalized

An insured depository institution is "well capitalized" if it significantly exceeds the required minimum level for each relevant capital measure.

(B) Adequately capitalized

An insured depository institution is "adequately capitalized" if it meets the required minimum level for each relevant capital measure.

(C) Undercapitalized

An insured depository institution is "undercapitalized" if it fails to meet the required minimum level for any relevant capital measure.

(D) Significantly undercapitalized

An insured depository institution is "significantly undercapitalized" if it is significantly

below the required minimum level for any relevant capital measure.

(E) Critically undercapitalized

An insured depository institution is "critically undercapitalized" if it fails to meet any level specified under subsection (c)(3)(A) of this section.

(2) Other definitions

(A) Average

(i) In general

The "average" of an accounting item (such as total assets or tangible equity) during a given period means the sum of that item at the close of business on each business day during that period divided by the total number of business days in that period.

(ii) Agency may permit weekly averaging for certain institutions

In the case of insured depository institutions that have total assets of less than $300,000,000 and normally file reports of condition reflecting weekly (rather than daily) averages of accounting items, the appropriate Federal banking agency may provide that the "average" of an accounting item during a given period means the sum of that item at the close of business on the relevant business day each week during that period divided by the total number of weeks in that period.

(B) Capital distribution

The term "capital distribution" means—

(i) a distribution of cash or other property by any insured depository institution or company to its owners made on account of that ownership, but not including—

(I) any dividend consisting only of shares of the institution or company or rights to purchase such shares; or

(II) any amount paid on the deposits of a mutual or cooperative institution that the appropriate Federal banking agency determines is not a distribution for purposes of this section;

(ii) a payment by an insured depository institution or company to repurchase, redeem, retire, or otherwise acquire any of its shares or other ownership interests, including any extension of credit to finance an affiliated company's acquisition of those shares or interests; or

(iii) a transaction that the appropriate Federal banking agency or the Corporation determines, by order or regulation, to be in substance a distribution of capital to the owners of the insured depository institution or company.

(C) Capital restoration plan

The term "capital restoration plan" means a plan submitted under subsection (e)(2) of this section.

(D) Company

The term "company" has the same meaning as in section 1841 of this title.

(E) Compensation

The term "compensation" includes any payment of money or provision of any other thing of value in consideration of employment.

(F) Relevant capital measure

The term "relevant capital measure" means the measures described in subsection (c) of this section.

(G) Required minimum level

The term "required minimum level" means, with respect to each relevant capital measure, the minimum acceptable capital level specified by the appropriate Federal banking agency by regulation.

(H) Senior executive officer

The term "senior executive officer" has the same meaning as the term "executive officer" in section 375b of this title.

(I) Subordinated debt

The term "subordinated debt" means debt subordinated to the claims of general creditors.

(c) Capital standards

(1) Relevant capital measures

(A) In general

Except as provided in subparagraph (B)(ii), the capital standards prescribed by each appropriate Federal banking agency shall include—

(i) a leverage limit; and

(ii) a risk-based capital requirement.

(B) Other capital measures

An appropriate Federal banking agency may, by regulation—

(i) establish any additional relevant capital measures to carry out the purpose of this section; or

(ii) rescind any relevant capital measure required under subparagraph (A) upon determining (with the concurrence of the other Federal banking agencies) that the measure is no longer an appropriate means for carrying out the purpose of this section.

(2) Capital categories generally

Each appropriate Federal banking agency shall, by regulation, specify for each relevant capital measure the levels at which an insured depository institution is well capitalized, adequately capitalized, undercapitalized, and significantly undercapitalized.

(3) Critical capital

(A) Agency to specify level

(i) Leverage limit

Each appropriate Federal banking agency shall, by regulation, in consultation with the Corporation, specify the ratio of tangible equity to total assets at which an insured depository institution is critically undercapitalized.

(ii) Other relevant capital measures

The agency may, by regulation, specify for 1 or more other relevant capital measures, the level at which an insured depository institution is critically undercapitalized.

(B) Leverage limit range

The level specified under subparagraph (A)(i) shall require tangible equity in an amount—

(i) not less than 2 percent of total assets; and

(ii) except as provided in clause (i), not more than 65 percent of the required minimum level of capital under the leverage limit.

(C) FDIC's concurrence required

The appropriate Federal banking agency shall not, without the concurrence of the Corporation, specify a level under subparagraph (A)(i) lower than that specified by the

Corporation for State nonmember insured banks.

(d) Provisions applicable to all institutions

(1) Capital distributions restricted

(A) In general

An insured depository institution shall make no capital distribution if, after making the distribution, the institution would be undercapitalized.

(B) Exception

Notwithstanding subparagraph (A), the appropriate Federal banking agency may permit, after consultation with the Corporation, an insured depository institution to repurchase, redeem, retire, or otherwise acquire shares or ownership interests if the repurchase, redemption, retirement, or other acquisition—

(i) is made in connection with the issuance of additional shares or obligations of the institution in at least an equivalent amount; and

(ii) will reduce the institution's financial obligations or otherwise improve the institution's financial condition.

(2) Management fees restricted

An insured depository institution shall pay no management fee to any person having control of that institution if, after making the payment, the institution would be undercapitalized.

(e) Provisions applicable to undercapitalized institutions

(1) Monitoring required

Each appropriate Federal banking agency shall—

(A) closely monitor the condition of any undercapitalized insured depository institution;

(B) closely monitor compliance with capital restoration plans, restrictions, and requirements imposed under this section; and

(C) periodically review the plan, restrictions, and requirements applicable to any undercapitalized insured depository institution to determine whether the plan, restrictions, and requirements are achieving the purpose of this section.

(2) Capital restoration plan required

(A) In general

Any undercapitalized insured depository institution shall submit an acceptable capital restoration plan to the appropriate Federal banking agency within the time allowed by the agency under subparagraph (D).

(B) Contents of plan

The capital restoration plan shall—

(i) specify—

(I) the steps the insured depository institution will take to become adequately capitalized;

(II) the levels of capital to be attained during each year in which the plan will be in effect;

(III) how the institution will comply with the restrictions or requirements then in effect under this section; and

(IV) the types and levels of activities in which the institution will engage; and

(ii) contain such other information as the appropriate Federal banking agency may require.

(C) Criteria for accepting plan

The appropriate Federal banking agency shall not accept a capital restoration plan unless the agency determines that—

(i) the plan—

(I) complies with subparagraph (B);

(II) is based on realistic assumptions, and is likely to succeed in restoring the institution's capital; and

(III) would not appreciably increase the risk (including credit risk, interest-rate risk, and other types of risk) to which the institution is exposed; and

(ii) if the insured depository institution is undercapitalized, each company having control of the institution has—

(I) guaranteed that the institution will comply with the plan until the institution has been adequately capitalized on average during each of 4 consecutive calendar quarters; and

(II) provided appropriate assurances of performance.

(D) Deadlines for submission and review of plans

The appropriate Federal banking agency shall by regulation establish deadlines that—

(i) provide insured depository institutions with reasonable time to submit capital restoration plans, and generally require an institution to submit a plan not later than 45 days after the institution becomes undercapitalized;

(ii) require the agency to act on capital restoration plans expeditiously, and generally not later than 60 days after the plan is submitted; and

(iii) require the agency to submit a copy of any plan approved by the agency to the Corporation before the end of the 45–day period beginning on the date such approval is granted.

(E) Guarantee liability limited

(i) In general

The aggregate liability under subparagraph (C)(ii) of all companies having control of an insured depository institution shall be the lesser of—

(I) an amount equal to 5 percent of the institution's total assets at the time the institution became undercapitalized; or

(II) the amount which is necessary (or would have been necessary) to bring the institution into compliance with all capital standards applicable with respect to such institution as of the time the institution fails to comply with a plan under this subsection.

(ii) Certain affiliates not affected

This paragraph may not be construed as—

(I) requiring any company not having control of an undercapitalized insured depository institution to guarantee, or otherwise be liable on, a capital restoration plan;

(II) requiring any person other than an insured depository institution to submit a capital restoration plan; or

(III) affecting compliance by brokers, dealers, government securities brokers, and government securities dealers with the financial responsibility requirements of the Securities Exchange Act of 1934 [15 U.S.C.A. § 78a et seq.] and regulations and orders thereunder.

(3) Asset growth restricted

An undercapitalized insured depository institution shall not permit its average total assets during any calendar quarter to exceed its average total assets during the preceding calendar quarter unless—

(A) the appropriate Federal banking agency has accepted the institution's capital restoration plan;

(B) any increase in total assets is consistent with the plan; and

(C) the institution's ratio of tangible equity to assets increases during the calendar quarter at a rate sufficient to enable the institution to become adequately capitalized within a reasonable time.

(4) Prior approval required for acquisitions, branching, and new lines of business

An undercapitalized insured depository institution shall not, directly or indirectly, acquire any interest in any company or insured depository institution, establish or acquire any additional branch office, or engage in any new line of business unless—

(A) the appropriate Federal banking agency has accepted the insured depository institution's capital restoration plan, the institution is implementing the plan, and the agency determines that the proposed action is consistent with and will further the achievement of the plan; or

(B) the Board of Directors determines that the proposed action will further the purpose of this section.

(5) Discretionary safeguards

The appropriate Federal banking agency may, with respect to any undercapitalized insured depository institution, take actions described in any subparagraph of subsection (f)(2) of this section if the agency determines that those actions are necessary to carry out the purpose of this section.

(f) Provisions applicable to significantly undercapitalized institutions and undercapitalized institutions that fail to submit and implement capital restoration plans

(1) In general

This subsection shall apply with respect to any insured depository institution that—

(A) is significantly undercapitalized; or

(B) is undercapitalized and—

(i) fails to submit an acceptable capital restoration plan within the time allowed by the appropriate Federal banking agency under subsection (e)(2)(D) of this section; or

(ii) fails in any material respect to implement a plan accepted by the agency.

(2) Specific actions authorized

The appropriate Federal banking agency shall carry out this section by taking 1 or more of the following actions:

(A) Requiring recapitalization

Doing 1 or more of the following:

(i) Requiring the institution to sell enough shares or obligations of the institution so that the institution will be adequately capitalized after the sale.

(ii) Further requiring that instruments sold under clause (i) be voting shares.

(iii) Requiring the institution to be acquired by a depository institution holding company, or to combine with another insured depository institution, if 1 or more grounds exist for appointing a conservator or receiver for the institution.

(B) Restricting transactions with affiliates

(i) Requiring the institution to comply with section 371c of this title as if subsection (d)(1) of that section (exempting transactions with certain affiliated institutions) did not apply.

(ii) Further restricting the institution's transactions with affiliates.

(C) Restricting interest rates paid

(i) In general

Restricting the interest rates that the institution pays on deposits to the prevailing rates of interest on deposits of comparable amounts and maturities in the region where the institution is located, as determined by the agency.

(ii) Retroactive restrictions prohibited

This subparagraph does not authorize the agency to restrict interest rates paid on time deposits made before (and not renewed or renegotiated after) the agency acted under this subparagraph.

(D) Restricting asset growth

Restricting the institution's asset growth more stringently than subsection (e)(3) of this section, or requiring the institution to reduce its total assets.

(E) Restricting activities

Requiring the institution or any of its subsidiaries to alter, reduce, or terminate any activity that the agency determines poses excessive risk to the institution.

(F) Improving management

Doing 1 or more of the following:

(i) New election of directors

Ordering a new election for the institution's board of directors.

(ii) Dismissing directors or senior executive officers

Requiring the institution to dismiss from office any director or senior executive officer who had held office for more than 180 days immediately before the institution became undercapitalized. Dismissal under this clause shall not be construed to be a removal under section 1818 of this title.

(iii) Employing qualified senior executive officers

Requiring the institution to employ qualified senior executive officers (who, if the agency so specifies, shall be subject to approval by the agency).

(G) Prohibiting deposits from correspondent banks

Prohibiting the acceptance by the institution of deposits from correspondent depository institutions, including renewals and rollovers of prior deposits.

(H) Requiring prior approval for capital distributions by bank holding company

Prohibiting any bank holding company having control of the insured depository institution from making any capital distribution without the prior approval of the Board of Governors of the Federal Reserve System.

(I) Requiring divestiture

Doing one or more of the following:

(i) Divestiture by the institution

Requiring the institution to divest itself of or liquidate any subsidiary if the agency determines that the subsidiary is in danger of becoming insolvent and poses a significant risk to the institution, or is likely to cause a significant dissipation of the institution's assets or earnings.

(ii) Divestiture by parent company of nondepository affiliate

Requiring any company having control of the institution to divest itself of or liquidate any affiliate other than an insured depository institution if the appropriate Federal banking agency for that company determines that the affiliate is in danger of becoming insolvent and poses a significant risk to the institution, or is likely to cause a significant dissipation of the institution's assets or earnings.

(iii) Divestiture of institution

Requiring any company having control of the institution to divest itself of the institution if the appropriate Federal banking agency for that company determines that divestiture would improve the institution's financial condition and future prospects.

(J) Requiring other action

Requiring the institution to take any other action that the agency determines will better carry out the purpose of this section than any of the actions described in this paragraph.

(3) Presumption in favor of certain actions

In complying with paragraph (2), the agency shall take the following actions, unless the agency determines that the actions would not further the purpose of this section:

(A) The action described in clause (i) or (iii) of paragraph (2)(A) (relating to requiring the sale of shares or obligations, or requiring the institution to be acquired by or combine with another institution).

(B) The action described in paragraph (2)(B)(i) (relating to restricting transactions with affiliates).

(C) The action described in paragraph (2)(C) (relating to restricting interest rates).

(4) Senior executive officers' compensation restricted

(A) In general

The insured depository institution shall not do any of the following without the prior written approval of the appropriate Federal banking agency:

(i) Pay any bonus to any senior executive officer.

(ii) Provide compensation to any senior executive officer at a rate exceeding that officer's average rate of compensation (excluding bonuses, stock options, and profit-sharing) during the 12 calendar months preceding the calendar month in which the institution became undercapitalized.

(B) Failing to submit plan

The appropriate Federal banking agency shall not grant any approval under subparagraph (A) with respect to an institution that has failed to submit an acceptable capital restoration plan.

(5) Discretion to impose certain additional restrictions

The agency may impose 1 or more of the restrictions prescribed by regulation under subsection (i) of this section if the agency determines that those restrictions are necessary to carry out the purpose of this section.

(6) Consultation with other regulators

Before the agency or Corporation makes a determination under paragraph (2)(I) with respect to an affiliate that is a broker, dealer, government securities broker, government securities dealer, investment company, or investment adviser, the agency or Corporation shall consult with the Securities and Exchange Commission and, in the case of any other affiliate which is subject to any financial responsibility or capital requirement, any other appropriate regulator of such affiliate with respect to the proposed determination of the agency or the Corporation and actions pursuant to such determination.

(g) More stringent treatment based on other supervisory criteria

(1) In general

If the appropriate Federal banking agency determines (after notice and an opportunity for hearing) that an insured depository institution is in an unsafe or unsound condition or, pursuant to section 1818(b)(8) of this title, deems the institution to be engaging in an unsafe or unsound practice, the agency may—

(A) if the institution is well capitalized, reclassify the institution as adequately capitalized;

(B) if the institution is adequately capitalized (but not well capitalized), require the institution to comply with 1 or more provisions of subsections (d) and (e) of this section, as if the institution were undercapitalized; or

(C) if the institution is undercapitalized, take any 1 or more actions authorized under subsection (f)(2) of this section as if the institution were significantly undercapitalized.

(2) Contents of plan

Any plan required under paragraph (1) shall specify the steps that the insured depository institution will take to correct the unsafe or unsound condition or practice. Capital restoration plans shall not be required under paragraph (1)(B).

(h) Provisions applicable to critically undercapitalized institutions

(1) Activities restricted

Any critically undercapitalized insured depository institution shall comply with restrictions prescribed by the Corporation under subsection (i) of this section.

(2) Payments on subordinated debt prohibited

(A) In general

A critically undercapitalized insured depository institution shall not, beginning 60 days after becoming critically undercapitalized, make any payment of principal or interest on the institution's subordinated debt.

(B) Exceptions

The Corporation may make exceptions to subparagraph (A) if—

(i) the appropriate Federal banking agency has taken action with respect to the insured depository institution under paragraph (3)(A)(ii); and

(ii) the Corporation determines that the exception would further the purpose of this section.

(C) Limited exemption for certain subordinated debt

Until July 15, 1996, subparagraph (A) shall not apply with respect to any subordinated debt outstanding on July 15, 1991, and not extended or otherwise renegotiated after July 15, 1991.

(D) Accrual of interest

Subparagraph (A) does not prevent unpaid interest from accruing on subordinated debt under the terms of that debt, to the extent otherwise permitted by law.

(3) Conservatorship, receivership, or other action required

(A) In general

The appropriate Federal banking agency shall, not later than 90 days after an insured depository institution becomes critically undercapitalized—

(i) appoint a receiver (or, with the concurrence of the Corporation, a conservator) for the institution; or

(ii) take such other action as the agency determines, with the concurrence of the Corporation, would better achieve the purpose of this section, after documenting why the action would better achieve that purpose.

(B) Periodic redeterminations required

Any determination by an appropriate Federal banking agency under subparagraph (A)(ii) to take any action with respect to an insured depository institution in lieu of appointing a conservator or receiver shall cease to be effective not later than the end of the 90–day period beginning on the date that the determination is made and a conservator or receiver shall be appointed for that institution under subparagraph (A)(i) unless the agency makes a new determination under subparagraph (A)(ii) at the end of the effective period of the prior determination.

(C) Appointment of receiver required if other action fails to restore capital

(i) In general

Notwithstanding subparagraphs (A) and (B), the appropriate Federal banking agency shall appoint a receiver for the insured depository institution if the institution is critically undercapitalized on average during the calendar quarter beginning 270 days after the date on which the institution became critically undercapitalized.

(ii) Exception

Notwithstanding clause (i), the appropriate Federal banking agency may continue to take such other action as the agency determines to be appropriate in lieu of such appointment if—

(I) the agency determines, with the concurrence of the Corporation, that (aa) the insured depository institution has positive net worth, (bb) the insured depository institution has been in substantial compliance with an approved capital restoration plan which requires consistent improvement in the institution's capital since the date of the approval of the plan, (cc) the insured depository institution is profitable or has an upward trend in earnings the agency projects as sustainable, and (dd) the insured depository institution is reducing the ratio of nonperforming loans to total loans; and

(II) the head of the appropriate Federal banking agency and the Chairperson of the Board of Directors both certify that the institution is viable and not expected to fail.

(i) Restricting activities of critically undercapitalized institutions

To carry out the purpose of this section, the Corporation shall, by regulation or order—

(1) restrict the activities of any critically undercapitalized insured depository institution; and

(2) at a minimum, prohibit any such institution from doing any of the following without the Corporation's prior written approval:

(A) Entering into any material transaction other than in the usual course of business, including any investment, expansion, acquisition, sale of assets, or other similar action with respect to which the depository institution is required to provide notice to the appropriate Federal banking agency.

(B) Extending credit for any highly leveraged transaction.

(C) Amending the institution's charter or bylaws, except to the extent necessary to carry out any other requirement of any law, regulation, or order.

(D) Making any material change in accounting methods.

(E) Engaging in any covered transaction (as defined in section 371c(b) of this title).

(F) Paying excessive compensation or bonuses.

(G) Paying interest on new or renewed liabilities at a rate that would increase the institution's weighted average cost of funds to a level significantly exceeding the prevailing rates of interest on insured deposits in the institution's normal market areas.

(j) Certain government-controlled institutions exempted

Subsections (e) through (i) of this section (other than paragraph (3) of subsection (e) of this section) shall not apply—

(1) to an insured depository institution for which the Corporation or the Resolution Trust Corporation is conservator; or

(2) to a bridge bank, none of the voting securities of which are owned by a person or agency other than the Corporation or the Resolution Trust Corporation.

(k) Review required when deposit insurance fund incurs material loss

(1) In general

If a deposit insurance fund incurs a material loss with respect to an insured depository institution on or after July 1, 1993, the inspector general of the appropriate Federal banking agency shall—

(A) make a written report to that agency reviewing the agency's supervision of the institution (including the agency's implementation of this section), which shall—

(i) ascertain why the institution's problems resulted in a material loss to the deposit insurance fund; and

(ii) make recommendations for preventing any such loss in the future; and

(B) provide a copy of the report to—

(i) the Comptroller General of the United States;

(ii) the Corporation (if the agency is not the Corporation);

(iii) in the case of a State depository institution, the appropriate State banking supervisor; and

(iv) upon request by any Member of Congress, to that Member.

(2) Material loss incurred

For purposes of this subsection:

(A) Loss incurred

A deposit insurance fund incurs a loss with respect to an insured depository institution—

(i) if the Corporation provides any assistance under section 1823(c) of this title with respect to that institution; and—

(I) it is not substantially certain that the assistance will be fully repaid not later than 24 months after the date on which the Corporation initiated the assistance; or

(II) the institution ceases to repay the assistance in accordance with its terms; or

(ii) if the Corporation is appointed receiver of the institution, and it is or becomes apparent that the present value of the deposit insurance fund's outlays with respect to that institution will exceed the present value of receivership dividends or other payments on the claims held by the Corporation.

(B) Material loss

A loss is material if it exceeds the greater of—

(i) $25,000,000; or

(ii) 2 percent of the institution's total assets at the time the Corporation initiated assistance under section 1823(c) of this title or was appointed receiver.

(3) Deadline for report

The inspector general of the appropriate Federal banking agency shall comply with paragraph (1) expeditiously, and in any event (except with respect to paragraph (1)(B)(iv)) as follows:

(A) If the institution is described in paragraph (2)(A)(i), during the 6–month period beginning on the earlier of—

(i) the date on which the institution ceases to repay assistance under section 1823(c) of this title in accordance with its terms, or

(ii) the date on which it becomes apparent that the assistance will not be fully repaid during the 24–month period described in paragraph (2)(A)(i).

(B) If the institution is described in paragraph (2)(A)(ii), during the 6–month period beginning on the date on which it becomes apparent that the present value of the deposit insurance fund's outlays with respect to that institution will exceed the present value of receivership dividends or other payments on the claims held by the Corporation.

(4) Public disclosure required

(A) In general

The appropriate Federal banking agency shall disclose the report upon request under section 552 of Title 5 without excising—

(i) any portion under section 552(b)(5) of that title; or

(ii) any information about the insured depository institution under paragraph (4) (other than trade secrets) or paragraph (8) of section 552(b) of that title.

(B) Exception

Subparagraph (A) does not require the agency to disclose the name of any customer of the insured depository institution (other than an institution-affiliated party), or information from which such a person's identity could reasonably be ascertained.

(5) GAO review

The Comptroller General of the United States shall, under such conditions as the Comptroller General determines to be appropriate, review reports made under paragraph (1) and recommend improvements in the supervision of insured depository institutions (including the implementation of this section).

(6) Transition rule

During the period beginning on July 1, 1993, and ending on June 30, 1997, a loss incurred by the Corporation with respect to an insured depository institution—

(A) with respect to which the Corporation initiates assistance under section 1823(c) of this title during the period in question, or

(B) for which the Corporation was appointed receiver during the period in question, is material for purposes of this subsection only if that loss exceeds the greater of $25,000,000 or the applicable percentage of the institution's total assets at that time, set forth in the following table:

For the following period:	The applicable percentage is:
July 1, 1993–June 30, 1994	7 percent
July 1, 1994–June 30, 1995	5 percent
July 1, 1995–June 30, 1996	4 percent
July 1, 1996–June 30, 1997	3 percent

(*l*) Implementation

(1) Regulations and other actions

Each appropriate Federal banking agency shall prescribe such regulations (in consultation with the other Federal banking agencies), issue such orders, and take such other actions as are necessary to carry out this section.

(2) Written determination and concurrence required

Any determination or concurrence by an appropriate Federal banking agency or the Corporation required under this section shall be written.

(m) Other authority not affected

This section does not limit any authority of an appropriate Federal banking agency, the Corporation, or a State to take action in addition to (but not in derogation of) that required under this section.

(n) Administrative review of dismissal orders

(1) Timely petition required

A director or senior executive officer dismissed pursuant to an order under subsection (f)(2)(F)(ii) of this section may obtain review of that order by filing a written petition for reinstatement with the appropriate Federal banking agency not later than 10 days after receiving notice of the dismissal.

(2) Procedure

(A) Hearing required

The agency shall give the petitioner an opportunity to—

(i) submit written materials in support of the petition; and

(ii) appear, personally or through counsel, before 1 or more members of the agency or designated employees of the agency.

(B) Deadline for hearing

The agency shall—

(i) schedule the hearing referred to in subparagraph (A)(ii) promptly after the petition is filed; and

(ii) hold the hearing not later than 30 days after the petition is filed, unless the petitioner requests that the hearing be held at a later time.

(C) Deadline for decision

Not later than 60 days after the date of the hearing, the agency shall—

(i) by order, grant or deny the petition;

(ii) if the order is adverse to the petitioner, set forth the basis for the order; and

(iii) notify the petitioner of the order.

(3) Standard for review of dismissal orders

The petitioner shall bear the burden of proving that the petitioner's continued employment would materially strengthen the insured depository institution's ability—

(A) to become adequately capitalized, to the extent that the order is based on the institution's capital level or failure to submit or implement a capital restoration plan; and

(B) to correct the unsafe or unsound condition or unsafe or unsound practice, to the extent that the order is based on subsection (g)(1) of this section.

(*o*) Transition rules for savings associations

Subsections (e)(2), (f), and (h) of this section shall not apply before July 1, 1994, to any insured savings association if—

(1) before December 19, 1991—

(A) the savings association had submitted a plan meeting the requirements of section 1464 (t)(6)(A)(ii) of this title; and

(B) the Director of the Office of Thrift Supervision had accepted the plan;

(2) the plan remains in effect; and

(3) the savings association remains in compliance with the plan or is operating under a written agreement with the appropriate Federal banking agency.

§ 1831p. Transferred

§ 1831p–1. Standards for safety and soundness

(a) Operational and managerial standards

Each appropriate Federal banking agency shall, for all insured depository institutions, prescribe—

(1) standards relating to—

(A) internal controls, information systems, and internal audit systems, in accordance with section 1831m of this title;

(B) loan documentation;

(C) credit underwriting;

(D) interest rate exposure;

(E) asset growth; and

(F) compensation, fees, and benefits, in accordance with subsection (c) of this section; and

(2) such other operational and managerial standards as the agency determines to be appropriate.

(b) Asset quality, earnings, and stock valuation standards

Each appropriate Federal banking agency shall prescribe standards, by regulation or guideline, for all insured depository institutions relating to asset quality, earnings, and stock valuation that the agency determines to be appropriate.

(c) Compensation standards

Each appropriate Federal banking agency shall, for all insured depository institutions, prescribe—

(1) standards prohibiting as an unsafe and unsound practice any employment contract, compensation or benefit agreement, fee arrangement, perquisite, stock option plan, postemployment benefit, or other compensatory arrangement that—

(A) would provide any executive officer, employee, director, or principal shareholder of the institution with excessive compensation, fees or benefits; or

(B) could lead to material financial loss to the institution;

(2) standards specifying when compensation, fees, or benefits referred to in paragraph (1) are excessive, which shall require the agency to determine whether the amounts are unreasonable or disproportionate to the services actually performed by the individual by considering—

(A) the combined value of all cash and noncash benefits provided to the individual;

(B) the compensation history of the individual and other individuals with comparable expertise at the institution;

(C) the financial condition of the institution;

(D) comparable compensation practices at comparable institutions, based upon such factors as asset size, geographic location, and the complexity of the loan portfolio or other assets;

(E) for postemployment benefits, the projected total cost and benefit to the institution;

(F) any connection between the individual and any fraudulent act or omission, breach of trust or fiduciary duty, or insider abuse with regard to the institution; and

(G) other factors that the agency determines to be relevant; and

(3) such other standards relating to compensation, fees, and benefits as the agency determines to be appropriate.

(d) Standards to be prescribed

(1) In general

Standards under subsections (a), (b), and (c) of this section shall be prescribed by regulation or guideline. Such regulations or guidelines may not prescribe standards that set a specific level or range of compensation for directors, officers, or employees of insured depository institutions.

(2) Applicability of other laws

Paragraph (1) shall not affect the authority of any appropriate Federal banking agency to restrict the level of compensation, including golden parachute payments (as defined in section 1828(k)(4) of this title), paid to any director, officer, or employee of an insured depository institution under any other provision of law.

(3) Senior executive officers at undercapitalized institutions

Paragraph (1) shall not affect the authority of any appropriate Federal banking agency to restrict compensation paid to any senior executive officer of an undercapitalized insured depository institution pursuant to section 1831o of this title.

(4) Safety and soundness or enforcement actions

Paragraph (1) shall not be construed as affecting the authority of any appropriate Federal banking agency under any provision of this chapter other than this section, or under any other provision of law, to prescribe a specific level or range of compensation for any director, officer, or employee of an insured depository institution—

(A) to preserve the safety and soundness of the institution; or

(B) in connection with any action under section 1818 of this title or any order issued by the agency, any agreement between the agency and the institution, or any condition imposed by the agency in connection with the agency's approval of an application or other request by the institution, which is enforceable under section 1818 of this title.

(e) Failure to meet standards

(1) Plan required

(A) In general

If the appropriate Federal banking agency determines that an insured depository institution fails to meet any standard prescribed under subsection (a) or (b) of this section—

(i) if such standard is prescribed by regulation of the agency, the agency shall require the institution to submit an acceptable plan to the agency within the time allowed by the agency under subparagraph (C); and

(ii) if such standard is prescribed by guideline, the agency may require the institution to submit a plan described in clause (i).

(B) Contents of plan

Any plan required under subparagraph (A) shall specify the steps that the institution will take to correct the deficiency. If the institution is undercapitalized, the plan may be part of a capital restoration plan.

(C) Deadlines for submission and review of plans

The appropriate Federal banking agency shall by regulation establish deadlines that—

(i) provide institutions with reasonable time to submit plans required under subparagraph (A), and generally require the institution to submit a plan not later than 30 days after the agency determines that the institution fails to meet any standard prescribed under subsection (a), (b), or (c) of this section; and

(ii) require the agency to act on plans expeditiously, and generally not later than 30 days after the plan is submitted.

(2) Order required if institution fails to submit or implement plan

If an insured depository institution fails to submit an acceptable plan within the time allowed under paragraph (1)(C), or fails in any material respect to implement a plan accepted by the appropriate Federal banking agency, the agency, by order—

(A) shall require the institution to correct the deficiency; and

(B) may do 1 or more of the following until the deficiency has been corrected:

(i) Prohibit the institution from permitting its average total assets during any calendar quarter to exceed its average total assets during the preceding calendar quarter, or restrict the rate at which the average total assets of the institution may increase from one calendar quarter to another.

(ii) Require the institution to increase its ratio of tangible equity to assets.

(iii) Take the action described in section 1831o(f)(2)(C) of this title.

(iv) Require the institution to take any other action that the agency determines will better carry out the purpose of section 1831o of this title than any of the actions described in this subparagraph.

(3) Restrictions mandatory for certain institutions

In complying with paragraph (2), the appropriate Federal banking agency shall take 1 or more of the actions described in clauses (i) through (iii) of paragraph (2)(B) if—

(A) the agency determines that the insured depository institution fails to meet any standard prescribed under subsection (a)(1) or (b)(1) of this section;

(B) the institution has not corrected the deficiency; and

(C) either—

(i) during the 24–month period before the date on which the institution first failed to meet the standard—

(I) the institution commenced operations; or

(II) 1 or more persons acquired control of the institution; or

(ii) during the 18–month period before the date on which the institution first failed to meet the standard, the institution underwent extraordinary growth, as defined by the agency.

(f) Definitions

For purposes of this section, the terms "average" and "capital restoration plan" have the same meanings as in section 1831o of this title.

(g) Other authority not affected

The authority granted by this section is in addition to any other authority of the Federal banking agencies.

§ 1831q. FDIC affordable housing program

(a) Purpose

The purpose of this section is to provide homeownership and rental housing opportunities for very low-income, low-income, and moderate-income families.

(b) Funding and limitations of program

(1) Duration of program

The provisions of this section shall be effective, subject to the provisions of paragraph (2), only during the 3–year period beginning upon the commencement of the first fiscal year for which amounts are provided pursuant to paragraph (2)(A).

(2) Annual fiscal limitations

(A) In general

In each fiscal year during the 3–year period referred to in paragraph (1), the provisions of this section shall apply only-

(i) to such extent or in such amounts as are provided in appropriations Acts for any losses resulting during the fiscal year from the sale of properties under this section, except that such amounts for losses may not exceed $30,000,000 in any fiscal year; and

(ii) to the extent that amounts are provided in appropriations Acts pursuant to subparagraph (C) for any other costs relating to the program under this section.

(B) Definition of losses

For purposes of this paragraph, the amount of losses resulting from the sale of properties under this section during any fiscal year shall be the amount equal to the sum of any affordable housing discounts reasonably anticipated to accrue during the fiscal year.

(C) Authorization of appropriations

There are authorized to be appropriated, for each fiscal year during the 3–year period referred to in paragraph (1), such sums as may be necessary for any costs of the program under this section other than losses resulting from the sale of properties under this section.

(D) Other definitions

For purposes of this paragraph:

(i) Affordable housing discount

The term "affordable housing discount" means, with respect to any eligible residential or eligible condominium property transferred under this section by the Corporation, the difference (if any) between the realizable disposition value of the property and the actual sale price of the property under this section.

(ii) Realizable disposition value

The term "realizable disposition value" means the estimated sale price that the Corporation reasonably would be able to obtain upon the sale of a property by the Corporation under the provisions of this chapter, not including this section, and any other applicable laws. Not later than the expiration of the 120–day period beginning upon the commencement of the first fiscal year for which amounts are provided pursuant to paragraph (2)(A), the Corporation shall establish, and publish in the Federal Register, procedures for determining the realizable disposition value of a property transferred under this section, which shall take into consideration such factors as the Corporation considers appropriate, including the actual sale prices of properties disposed of by the Resolution Trust Corporation under section 1441a(c) of this title, the prices of other properties sold under similar programs, and the appraised value of the property transferred under this section. Until such procedures are established, the Corporation may consider the realizable disposition value of any eligible residential or condominium property to be equal to the appraised value of the property.

(3) Existing contracts

The provisions of this section shall not apply to any eligible residential property or any eligible condominium property that is subject to an agreement entered into by the Corporation before the commencement of the first fiscal year for which amounts are provided pursuant to paragraph (2)(A) that provides for any other disposition of the property.

(c) Rules governing disposition of eligible single family properties

(1) Notice to clearinghouses

Within a reasonable period of time after acquiring title to an eligible single family property, the Corporation shall provide written notice to clearinghouses. Such notice shall contain basic information about the property, including but not limited to location, condition, and information relating to the estimated fair market value of the property. Each clearinghouse shall make such information available, upon request, to other public agencies, other nonprofit organizations, and qualifying households. The Corporation shall allow public agencies, nonprofit organizations, and qualifying households reasonable access to eligible single family property for purposes of inspection.

(2) Offers to sell to nonprofit organizations, public agencies, and qualifying households

During the 180–day period beginning on the date on which the Corporation makes an eligible single family property available for sale, the Corporation shall offer to sell the property to—

(A) qualifying households (including qualifying households with members who are veterans); or

(B) public agencies or nonprofit organizations that agree to (i) make the property available for occupancy by and maintain it as affordable for low-income families (including low-income families with members who are veterans) for the remaining useful life of such property, or (ii) make the property available for purchase by any such family who, except as provided in paragraph (4), agrees to occupy the property as a principal residence for at least 12 months and certifies in writing that the family intends to occupy the property for at least 12 months.

The restrictions described in clause (i) of subparagraph (B) shall be contained in the deed or other recorded instrument. If, upon the expiration of such 180–day period, no qualifying household, public agency, or nonprofit organization has made a bona fide offer to purchase the property, the Corporation may offer to sell the property to any purchaser. The Corporation shall actively market eligible single family properties for sale to low-income families and to low-income families with members who are veterans.

(3) Recapture of profits from resale

Except as provided in paragraph (4), if any eligible single family property sold (A) to a qualifying household, or (B) to a low-income family pursuant to paragraph (2)(B)(ii), subsection (j)(3)(A) of this section, or subsection (k)(2) of this section, is resold by the qualifying household or low-income family during the 1–year period beginning upon initial acquisition by the household or low-income family, the Corporation shall recapture 75 percent of the amount of any proceeds from the resale that exceed the sum of (i) the original sale price for the acquisition of the property by the qualifying household or low-income family, (ii) the costs of any improvements to the property made after the date of the acquisition, and (iii) any closing costs in connection with the acquisition.

(4) Exceptions to recapture requirement

(A) Relocation

The Corporation may in its discretion waive the applicability (i) to any qualifying household of the requirement under paragraph (3) and the requirements relating to residency of a qualifying household under subparagraphs (B) and (C) of subsection (p)(12) of this section, and (ii) to any low-income family of the requirement under paragraph (3) and the residency requirements under paragraph (2)(B)(ii). The Corporation may grant any such waiver only for good cause shown, including any necessary relocation of the qualifying household or low-income family.

(B) Other recapture provisions

The requirement under paragraph (3) shall not apply to any eligible single family property for which, upon resale by the qualifying household or low-income family during the

1–year period beginning upon initial acquisition by the household or family, a portion of the sale proceeds or any subsidy provided in connection with the acquisition of the property by the household or family is required to be recaptured or repaid under any other Federal, State, or local law (including section 143(m) of Title 26) or regulation or under any sale agreement.

(5) Exception to avoid displacement of existing residents

Notwithstanding the first sentence of paragraph (2), during the 180–day period following the date on which the Corporation makes an eligible single family property available for sale, the Corporation may sell the property to the household residing in the property, but only if (A) such household was residing in the property at the time notice regarding the property was provided to clearinghouses under paragraph (1), (B) such sale is necessary to avoid the displacement of, and unnecessary hardship to, the resident household, (C) the resident household intends to occupy the property as a principal residence for at least 12 months, and (D) the resident household certifies in writing that the household intends to occupy the property for at least 12 months.

(d) Rules governing disposition of eligible multifamily housing properties

(1) Notice to clearinghouses

Within a reasonable period of time after acquiring title to an eligible multifamily housing property, the Corporation shall provide written notice to clearinghouses. Such notice shall contain basic information about the property, including but not limited to location, number of units (identified by number of bedrooms), and information relating to the estimated fair market value of the property. Each clearinghouse shall make such information available, upon request, to qualifying multifamily purchasers. The Corporation shall allow qualifying multifamily purchasers reasonable access to eligible multifamily housing properties for purposes of inspection.

(2) Expression of serious interest

Qualifying multifamily purchasers may give written notice of serious interest in a property during a period ending 90 days after the time the Corporation provides notice under paragraph (1). The notice of serious interest shall be in such form and include such information as the Corporation may prescribe.

(3) Notice of readiness for sale

Upon the expiration of the period referred to in paragraph (2) for a property, the Corporation shall provide written notice to any qualifying multifamily purchaser that has expressed serious interest in the property. Such notice shall specify the minimum terms and conditions for sale of the property.

(4) Offers by qualifying multifamily purchasers

A qualifying multifamily purchaser receiving notice in accordance with paragraph (3) shall have 45 days (from the date notice is received) to make a bona fide offer to purchase the property. The Corporation shall accept an offer that complies with the terms and conditions established by the Corporation. If, before the expiration of such 45–day period, any offer to purchase a property initially accepted by the Corporation is subsequently rejected or fails (for any reason), the Corporation shall accept another offer to purchase the property made during such period that complies with the terms and conditions established by the Corporation (if such another offer is made). The preceding sentence may not be construed to require a qualifying multifamily purchaser whose offer is accepted during the 45–day period to purchase the property before the expiration of the period.

(5) Extension of restricted offer periods

The Corporation may provide notice to clearinghouses regarding, and offer for sale under the provisions of paragraphs (1) through (4), any eligible multifamily housing property—

(A) in which no qualifying multifamily purchaser has expressed serious interest during the period referred to in paragraph (2), or

(B) for which no qualifying multifamily purchaser has made a bona fide offer before the expiration of the period referred to in paragraph (4),

except that the Corporation may, in the discretion of the Corporation, alter the duration of the periods referred to in paragraphs (2) and (4) in offering any property for sale under this paragraph.

(6) Sale of multifamily properties to other purchasers

(A) Timing

If, upon the expiration of the period referred to in paragraph (2), no qualifying multifamily purchaser has expressed serious interest in a property, the Corporation may offer to sell the property, individually or in combination with other properties, to any purchaser.

(B) Limitation on combination sales

The Corporation may not sell in combination with other properties any property for which a qualifying multifamily purchaser has expressed serious interest in purchasing individually.

(C) Expiration of offer period

If, upon the expiration of the period referred to in paragraph (4), no qualifying multifamily purchaser has made an offer to purchase a property, the Corporation may offer to sell the property, individually or in combination with other properties, to any purchaser.

(7) Low-income occupancy requirements

(A) Single property purchases

With respect to any purchase of a single eligible multifamily housing property by a qualifying multifamily purchaser under paragraph (4) or (5)—

(i) not less than 35 percent of all dwelling units purchased shall be made available for occupancy by and maintained as affordable for low-income and very low-income families during the remaining useful life of the property in which the units are located; provided that

(ii) not less than 20 percent of all dwelling units purchased shall be made available for occupancy by and maintained as affordable for very low-income families during the remaining useful life of the property in which the units are located.

(B) Aggregation requirements for multiproperty purchases

With respect to any purchase under paragraph (4) or (5) by a qualifying multifamily purchaser involving more than one eligible multifamily housing property as a part of the same negotiation, with respect to which the purchaser intends to aggregate the low-income occupancy required under this paragraph over the total number of units so purchased—

(i) not less than 40 percent of the aggregate number of all dwelling units purchased shall be made available for occupancy by and maintained as affordable for low-income and very low-income families during the remaining useful life of the building or structure in which the units are located; provided that

(ii) not less than 20 percent of the aggregate number of all dwelling units purchased shall be made available for occupancy by and maintained a affordable for very low-income families during the remaining useful life of the building or structure in which the units are located; and further provided that

(iii) not less than 10 percent of the dwelling units in each separate property purchased shall be made available for occupancy by and maintained as affordable for low-income families during the remaining useful life of the property in which the units are located.

The requirements of this paragraph shall be contained in the deed or other recorded instrument.

(8) Exemptions

(A) Continued occupancy of current residents

No purchaser of an eligible multifamily property may terminate the occupancy of any person residing in the property on the date of purchase for purposes of meeting the low-income occupancy requirement applicable to the property under paragraph (7). The purchaser shall be considered to be in compliance with this subsection if each newly vacant dwelling unit is reserved for low-income occupancy until the low-income occupancy requirement is met.

(B) Financial infeasibility

The Secretary or the State housing finance agency for the State in which an eligible multifamily housing property is located may temporarily reduce the low-income occupancy requirements under paragraph (7) applicable to the property, if the Secretary or such agency determines that an owner's compliance with such requirements is no longer financially feasible. The owner of the property shall make a good-faith effort to return low-income occupancy to the level required under paragraph (7), and the Secretary or the State housing finance agency, as appropriate, shall review the reduction annually to determine whether financial infeasibility continues to exist.

(e) Rent limitations

(1) In general

With respect to properties under paragraph (2), rents charged to tenants for units made available for occupancy by very low-income families shall not exceed 30 percent of the adjusted income of a family whose income equals 50 percent of the median income for the area, as determined by the Secretary, with adjustment for family size. Rents charged to tenants for units made available for occupancy by low-income families other than very low-income families shall not exceed 30 percent of the adjusted income of a family whose income equals 65 percent of the median income for the area, as determined by the Secretary, with adjustment for family size.

(2) Applicability

The rent limitations under this subsection shall apply to any eligible single family property sold pursuant to subsection (c)(2)(B)(i) of this section and to any eligible multifamily housing property sold pursuant to subsection (d) of this section.

(f) Preferences for sales

(1) In general

In selling any eligible multifamily housing property or combinations of eligible residential properties, the Corporation shall give preference, among substantially similar offers, to the offer that would reserve the highest percentage of dwelling units for occupancy or purchase by very low-income and low-income families and would retain such affordability for the longest term.

(2) Multiproperty purchases

The Corporation shall give preference, among substantially similar offers made under paragraph (4) or (5) of subsection (d) of this section to purchase more than one eligible multifamily housing property as a part of the same negotiation, to offers made by purchasers who agree to maintain low-income occupancy in each separate property purchased in compliance with the

levels required for properties under subsection (d)(7)(A).

(3) Definition of substantially similar offers

For purposes of this subsection, a given offer to purchase eligible multifamily housing property or combinations of such properties shall be considered to be substantially similar to another offer if the purchase price under such given offer is not less than 85 percent of the purchase price under the other offer.

(g) Financing sales

(1) Assistance by corporation

(A) Sale price

The Corporation shall establish a market value for each eligible multifamily housing property. The Corporation shall sell eligible multifamily housing property at the net realizable market value, except that the Corporation may agree to sell eligible multifamily housing property at a price below the net realizable market value to the extent necessary to facilitate an expedited sale of such property and enable a public agency or nonprofit organization to comply with the low-income occupancy requirements applicable to such property under subsection (d)(7) of this section. The Corporation may sell eligible single family property or eligible condominium property to qualifying households, nonprofit organizations, and public agencies without regard to any minimum sale price.

(B) Purchase loan

The Corporation may provide a loan at market interest rates to any purchaser of eligible residential property for all or a portion of the purchase price, which loan shall be secured by a first or second mortgage on the property. The Corporation may provide the loan at below market interest rates to the extent necessary to facilitate an expedited sale of eligible residential property and permit (i) a low-income family to purchase an eligible single family property under subsection (c) of this section, or (ii) a public agency or nonprofit organization to comply with the low-income occupancy requirements applicable to the purchase of an eligible residential property under subsection (c) or (d) of this section. The Corporation shall provide loans under this subparagraph in a form permitting sale or transfer of the loan to a subsequent holder. In providing financing for combinations of eligible multifamily housing properties under this section, the Corporation may hold a participating share, including a subordinate participation. The Corporation shall periodically provide, to a wide range of minority-and women-owned businesses engaged in providing affordable housing and to nonprofit organizations, more than 50 percent of the control of which is held by 1 or more minority individuals, that are engaged in providing affordable housing, information that is sufficient to inform such businesses and organizations of the availability and terms of financing under this subparagraph; such information may be provided directly, by notices published in periodicals and other publications that regularly provide information to such businesses or organizations, and through persons and organizations that regularly provide information or services to such businesses or organizations. For purposes of this subparagraph, the terms "women-owned business" and "minority-owned business" have the meanings given such terms in section 1441a(r) of this title, and the term "minority" has the meaning given such term in section 1204(c)(3) of the Financial Institutions Reform, Recovery, and Enforcement Act of 1989.

(2) Assistance by HUD

The Secretary shall take such action as may be necessary to expedite the processing of applications for assistance under section 202 of the Housing Act of 1959 [12 U.S.C.A. § 1701q], the United States Housing Act of 1937 [42 U.S.C.A. § 1437 et seq.], title IV of the McKinney–Vento Homeless Assistance Act [42 U.S.C.A. § 11361 et seq.], and the National Housing Act [12 U.S.C.A. § 1701 et seq.], to enable any organization or individual to purchase eligible residential property.

(3) Assistance by FMHA

The Secretary of Agriculture shall take such action as may be necessary to expedite the processing of applications for assistance under title V of the Housing Act of 1949 [42 U.S.C.A. § 1471 et seq.] to enable any organization or individual to purchase eligible residential property.

(4) Exception to disposition rules

Notwithstanding the requirements under paragraphs (1), (2), (3), (4), (6), and (8) of subsection (d), the Corporation may provide for the disposition of eligible multifamily housing properties as necessary to facilitate purchase of such properties for use in connection with section 202 of the Housing Act of 1959 [12 U.S.C.A. § 1701q].

(5) Bulk acquisitions under Home Investment Partnerships Act

(A) Purchase price

In providing for bulk acquisition of eligible single family properties by participating jurisdictions for inclusion in affordable housing activities under title II of the Cranston–Gonzalez National Affordable Housing Act [42 U.S.C.A. § 12721 et seq.], the Corporation shall agree to an amount to be paid for acquisition of such properties. The acquisition price shall include discounts for bulk purchase and for holding of the property such that the acquisition price for each property shall not exceed the fair market value of the property, as valued individually.

(B) Exemptions

To the extent necessary to facilitate sale of properties under this paragraph, the requirements of subsections (c) and (f) and of paragraph (1) of this subsection shall not apply to such transactions and properties involved in such transactions.

(C) Inventories

To facilitate acquisitions by such participating jurisdictions, the Corporation shall provide the participating jurisdictions with inventories of eligible single family properties not less than 4 times each year.

(h) Coordination with other programs

(1) Use of secondary market agencies

In the disposition of eligible residential properties, the Corporation (in consultation with the Secretary) shall explore opportunities to work with secondary market entities to provide housing for low-and moderate-income families.

(2) Credit enhancement

(A) In general

With respect to such properties, the Secretary may, consistent with statutory authorities, work through the Federal Housing Administration, the Government National Mortgage Association, the Federal National Mortgage Association, the Federal Home Loan Mortgage Corporation, and other secondary market entities to develop risk-sharing structures, mortgage insurance, and other credit enhancements to assist in the provision of property ownership, rental, and cooperative housing opportunities for low- and moderate-income families.

(B) Certain tax-exempt bonds

The Corporation may provide credit enhancements with respect to tax-exempt bonds issued on behalf of nonprofit organizations pursuant to section 103, and subpart A of part IV of subchapter A of chapter 1, of Title 26, with respect to the disposition of eligible residential properties for the purposes described in subparagraph (A).

(3) National Affordable Housing Act

The Corporation shall coordinate the disposition of eligible residential property under this section with appropriate programs and provisions of, and amendments made by, the Cranston–Gonzalez National Affordable Housing Act [42 U.S.C.A. § 12701 et seq.], including titles II and IV [42 U.S.C.A. § § 12721 et seq. and 12871 et seq.] of such Act.

(i) Exemption for certain transactions with insured depository institutions

The provisions of this section shall not apply with respect to any eligible residential property after the date the Corporation enters into a contract to sell such property to an insured depository institution (as defined in section 1813 of this title), including any sale in connection with a transfer of all or substantially all of the assets of a closed insured depository institution (including such property) to another insured depository institution.

(j) Transfer of certain eligible residential properties to state housing agencies for disposition

Notwithstanding subsections (c), (d), (f), and (g) of this section, the Corporation may transfer eligible residential properties to the State housing finance agency or any other State housing agency for the State in which the property is located, or to any local housing agency in whose jurisdiction the property is located. Transfers of eligible residential properties under this subsection may be conducted by direct sale, consign-

ment sale, or any other method the Corporation considers appropriate and shall be subject to the following requirements:

(1) Individual or bulk transfer

The Corporation may transfer such properties individually or in bulk, as agreed to by the Corporation and the State housing finance agency or State or local housing agency.

(2) Acquisition price

The acquisition price paid by the State housing finance agency or State or local housing agency to the Corporation for properties transferred under this subsection shall be an amount agreed to by the Corporation and the transferee agency.

(3) Low-income use

Any State housing finance agency or State or local housing agency acquiring properties under this subsection shall offer to sell or transfer the properties only as follows:

(A) Eligible single family properties

For eligible single family properties—

(i) to purchasers described under subparagraphs (A) and (B) of subsection (c)(2) of this section;

(ii) if the purchaser is a purchaser described under subsection (c)(2)(B)(i) of this section, subject to the rent limitations under subsection (e)(1) of this section;

(iii) subject to the requirement in the second sentence of subsection (c)(2) of this section; and

(iv) subject to recapture by the Corporation of excess proceeds from resale of the properties under paragraphs (3) and (4) of subsection (c) of this section.

(B) Eligible multifamily housing properties

For eligible multifamily housing properties—

(i) to qualifying multifamily purchasers;

(ii) subject to the low-income occupancy requirements under subsection (d)(7) of this section;

(iii) subject to the provisions of subsection (d)(8) of this section;

(iv) subject to a preference, among financially acceptable offers, to the offer that would reserve the highest percentage of dwelling units for occupancy or purchase by very low-

and low-income families and would retain such affordability for the longest term; and

(v) subject to the rent limitations under subsection (e)(1) of this section.

(4) Affordability

The State housing finance agency or State or local housing agency shall endeavor to make the properties transferred under this subsection more affordable to low-income families based upon the extent to which the acquisition price of a property under paragraph (2) is less than the market value of the property.

(k) Exception for sales to nonprofit organizations and public agencies

(1) Suspension of offer periods

With respect to any eligible residential property, the Corporation may (in the discretion of the Corporation) suspend any of the requirements of paragraphs (1) and (2) of subsection (c) of this section and paragraphs (1) through (4) of subsection (d) of this section, as applicable, but only to the extent that for the duration of the suspension the Corporation negotiates the sale of the property to a nonprofit organization or public agency. If the property is not sold pursuant to such negotiations, the requirements of any provisions suspended shall apply upon the termination of the suspension. Any time period referred to in such subsections shall toll for the duration of any suspension under this paragraph.

(2) Use restrictions

(A) Eligible single family property

Any eligible single family property sold under this subsection shall be (i) made available for occupancy by and maintained as affordable for low-income families for the remaining useful life of the property, or made available for purchase by such families, (ii) subject to the rent limitations under subsection (e)(1) of this section, (iii) subject to the requirements relating to residency of a qualifying household under subsection (p)(12) of this section and to residency of a low-income family under subsection (c)(2)(B) of this section, and (iv) subject to recapture by the Corporation of excess proceeds from resale of the property under paragraphs (3) and (4) of subsection (c) of this section.

(B) Eligible multifamily housing property

Any eligible multifamily housing property sold under this subsection shall comply with the low-income occupancy requirements under subsection (d)(7) of this section and shall be subject to the rent limitations under subsection (e)(1) of this section.

(*l*) Rules governing disposition of eligible condominium property

(1) Notice to clearinghouses

Within a reasonable period of time after acquiring title to an eligible condominium property, the Corporation shall provide written notice to clearinghouses. Such notice shall contain basic information about the property. Each clearinghouse shall make such information available, upon request, to purchasers described in subparagraphs (A) through (D) of paragraph (2). The Corporation shall allow such purchasers reasonable access to an eligible condominium property for purposes of inspection.

(2) Offers to sell

For the 180–day period following the date on which the Corporation makes an eligible condominium property available for sale, the Corporation may offer to sell the property, at the discretion of the Corporation, to 1 or more of the following purchasers:

(A) Qualifying households.

(B) Nonprofit organizations.

(C) Public agencies.

(D) For-profit entities.

(3) Low-income occupancy requirements

(A) In general

Except as provided in subparagraph (B), any nonprofit organization, public agency, or for-profit entity that purchases an eligible condominium property shall (i) make the property available for occupancy by and maintain it as affordable for low-income families for the remaining useful life of the property, or (ii) make the property available for purchase by any such family who, except as provided in paragraph (5), agrees to occupy the property as a principal residence for at least 12 months and certifies in writing that the family intends to occupy the property for at least 12 months. The restriction described in clause (i) of the preceding sentence shall be contained in the deed or other recorded instrument.

(B) Multiple-unit purchases

If any nonprofit organization, public agency, or for-profit entity purchases more than 1 eligible condominium property as a part of the same negotiation or purchase, the Corporation may (in the discretion of the Corporation) waive the requirement under subparagraph (A) and provide instead that not less than 35 percent of all eligible condominium properties purchased shall be (i) made available for occupancy by and maintained as affordable for low-income families for the remaining useful life of the property, or (ii) made available for purchase by any such family who, except as provided in paragraph (5), agrees to occupy the property as a principal residence for at least 12 months and certifies in writing that the family intends to occupy the property for at least 12 months. The restriction described in clause (i) of the preceding sentence shall be contained in the deed or other recorded instrument.

(C) Sale to other purchasers

If, upon the expiration of the 180–day period referred to in paragraph (2), no purchaser described in subparagraphs (A) through (D) of paragraph (2) has made a bona fide offer to purchase the property, the Corporation may offer to sell the property to any other purchaser.

(4) Recapture of profits from resale

Except as provided in paragraph (5), if any eligible condominium property sold (A) to a qualifying household, or (B) to a low-income family pursuant to paragraph (3)(A)(ii) or (3)(B)(ii), is resold by the qualifying household or low-income family during the 1–year period beginning upon initial acquisition by the household or family, the Corporation shall recapture 75 percent of the amount of any proceeds from the resale that exceed the sum of (i) the original sale price for the acquisition of the property by the qualifying household or low-income family, (ii) the costs of any improvements to the property made after the date of the acquisition, and (iii) any closing costs in connection with the acquisition.

(5) Exception to recapture requirement

The Corporation (or its successor) may in its discretion waive the applicability to any qualifying household or low-income family of the requirement under paragraph (4) and the requirements relating to residency of a qualifying household or low-income family (under subsection (p)(12) of this section and paragraph (3) of this subsection, respectively). The Corporation may grant any such a waiver only for good cause shown, including any necessary relocation of the qualifying household or low-income family.

(6) Limitations on multiple unit purchases

The Corporation may not sell or offer to sell as part of the same negotiation or purchase any eligible condominium properties that are not located in the same condominium project (as such term is defined in section 3603 of Title 15). The preceding sentence may not be construed to require all eligible condominium properties offered or sold as part of the same negotiation or purchase to be located in the same structure.

(7) Rent limitations

Rents charged to tenants of eligible condominium properties made available for occupancy by very low-income families shall not exceed 30 percent of the adjusted income of a family whose income equals 50 percent of the median income for the area, as determined by the Secretary, with adjustment for family size. Rents charged to tenants of eligible condominium properties made available for occupancy by low-income families other than very low-income families shall not exceed 30 percent of the adjusted income of a family whose income equals 65 percent of the median income for the area, as determined by the Secretary, with adjustment for family size.

(m) Liability provisions

(1) In general

The provisions of this section, or any failure by the Corporation to comply with such provisions, may not be used by any person to attack or defeat any title to property after it is conveyed by the Corporation.

(2) Low-income occupancy

The low-income occupancy requirements under subsections (c), (d), (j)(3), (k)(2), and (l)(3) of this section shall be judicially enforceable against purchasers of property under this section and their successors in interest by affected very low-and low-income families, State housing finance agencies, and any agency, corporation, or authority of the United States. The parties specified in the preceding sentence shall be entitled to reasonable attorney fees upon prevailing in any such judicial action.

(3) Clearinghouses

A clearinghouse shall not be subject to suit for its failure to comply with the requirements of this section.

(4) Corporation

The Corporation shall not be liable to any depositor, creditor, or shareholder of any insured depository institution for which the Corporation has been appointed receiver or conservator, or of any subsidiary corporation of a depository institution under receivership or conservatorship, or any claimant against such institution or subsidiary, because the disposition of assets of the institution or the subsidiary under this section affects the amount of return from the assets.

(n) Unified affordable housing programs

(1) In general

Not later than 4 months after December 17, 1993, the Corporation shall enter into an agreement, as described in paragraph (3), with the Resolution Trust Corporation that sets out a plan for the orderly unification of the Corporation's activities, authorities, and responsibilities under this section with the authorities, activities, and responsibilities of the Resolution Trust Corporation pursuant to section 1441a(c) of this title in a manner that best achieves an effective and comprehensive affordable housing program management structure. The agreement shall be entered into after consultation with the Affordable Housing Advisory Board under section 14(b) of the Resolution Trust Corporation Completion Act.

(2) Authority and implementation

The Corporation shall have the authority to carry out the provisions of the agreement entered into pursuant to paragraph (1) and shall implement such agreement as soon as practicable but in no event later than 8 months after December 17, 1993.

(3) Terms of agreement

The agreement required under paragraph (1) shall provide a plan for—

(A) a program unifying all activities and responsibilities of the Corporation and the Resolution Trust Corporation, and the design of the unified program shall take into consideration the substantial experience of the Resolution Trust Corporation regarding—

(i) seller financing;

(ii) technical assistance;

(iii) marketing skills and relationships with public and nonprofit entities; and

(iv) staff resources;

(B) the elimination of duplicative and unnecessary administrative costs and resources;

(C) the management structure of the unified program;

(D) a timetable for the unification; and

(E) a methodology to determine the extent to which the provisions of this section shall be effective, in accordance with the limitations under subsection (b)(2) of this section.

(4) Transfer to FDIC

Beginning not later than October 1, 1995, the Corporation shall carry out any remaining authority and responsibilities of the Resolution Trust Corporation, as set forth in section 1441a(c) of this title.

(o) Report

To the extent applicable, in the annual report submitted by the Secretary to the Congress under section 3536 of Title 42, the Secretary shall include a detailed description of any activities under this section, including recommendations for any additional authority the Secretary considers necessary to implement the provisions of this section.

(p) Definitions

For purposes of this section:

(1) Adjusted income and income

The terms "adjusted income" and "income" shall have the meaning given such terms in section 3(b) of the United States Housing Act of 1937 [42 U.S.C.A. § 1437a(b)].

(2) Clearinghouse

The term "clearinghouse" means—

(A) the State housing finance agency for the State in which an eligible residential property or eligible condominium property is located;

(B) the Office of Community Investment (or other comparable division) within the Federal Housing Finance Board; and

(C) any national nonprofit organizations (including any nonprofit entity established by the corporation established under title IX of the Housing and Community Development Act of 1968) that the Corporation determines has the capacity to act as a clearinghouse for information.

(3) Corporation

The term "Corporation" means the Federal Deposit Insurance Corporation acting in its corporate capacity or its capacity as receiver.

(4) Eligible condominium property

The term "eligible condominium property" means a condominium unit, as such term is defined in section 3603 of Title 15—

(A) to which such Corporation acquires title in its corporate capacity, its capacity as conservator, or its capacity as receiver (including in its capacity as the sole owner of a subsidiary corporation of a depository institution under conservatorship or receivership, which subsidiary has as its principal business the ownership of real property); and

(B) that has an appraised value that does not exceed the amount provided in section 1709(b)(2)(A) of this title except that such amount shall not exceed $101,250 in the case of a 1–family residence, $114,000 in the case of a 2–family residence, $138,000 in the case of a 3–family residence, and $160,000 in the case of a 4–family residence.

(5) Eligible multifamily housing property

The term "eligible multifamily housing property" means a property consisting of more than 4 dwelling units—

(A) to which the Corporation acquires title in its corporate capacity, its capacity as conservator, or its capacity as receiver (including in its capacity as the sole owner of a subsidiary corporation of a depository institution under conservatorship or receivership, which subsidiary has as its principal business the ownership of real property); and

(B) that has an appraised value that does not exceed the applicable dollar amount specified in section 221(d)(3)(ii) of the National Housing Act [12 U.S.C.A. § 1715l(d)(3)(ii)] for elevator-type structures, as such dollar amount is increased under such section for geographical areas or on a project-by-project basis (except that any such increase on a project-by-project basis shall be made pursuant to a determination by the Corporation that such increase is necessary).

(6) Eligible residential property

The term "eligible residential property" includes eligible single family properties and eligible multifamily housing properties.

(7) Eligible single family property

The term "eligible single family property" means a 1–to 4–family residence (including a manufactured home)—

(A) to which the Corporation acquires title in its corporate capacity, its capacity as conservator, or its capacity as receiver (including in its capacity as the sole owner of a subsidiary corporation of a depository institution under conservatorship or receivership, which subsidiary has as its principal business the ownership of real property); and

(B) that has an appraised value that does not exceed the amount provided in section 1709(b)(2)(A) of this title except that such amount shall not exceed $101,250 in the case of a 1–family residence, $114,000 in the case of a 2–family residence, $138,000 in the case of a 3–family residence, and $160,000 in the case of a 4–family residence.

(8) Low-income families

The term "low-income families" means families and individuals whose incomes do not exceed 80 percent of the median income of the area involved, as determined by the Secretary, with adjustment for family size.

(9) Net realizable market value

The term "net realizable market value" means a price below the market value that takes into account (A) any reductions in holding costs resulting from the expedited sale of a property, including foregone real estate taxes, insurance, maintenance costs, security costs, and loss of use of funds, and (B) the avoidance, if applicable, of fees paid to real estate brokers, auctioneers, or other individuals or organizations involved in the sale of property owned by the Corporation.

(10) Nonprofit organization

The term "nonprofit organization" means a private organization (including a limited equity cooperative)—

(A) no part of the earnings of which inures to the benefit of any member, shareholder, founder, contributor, or individual; and

(B) that is approved by the Corporation as to financial responsibility.

(11) Public agency

The term "public agency" means any Federal, State, local, or other governmental entity, and includes any public housing agency.

(12) Qualifying household

The term "qualifying household" means a household—

(A) who intends to occupy eligible single family property as a principal residence;

(B) who agrees to occupy the property as a principal residence for at least 12 months;

(C) who certifies in writing that the household intends to occupy the property as a principal residence for at least 12 months; and

(D) whose income does not exceed 115 percent of the median income for the area, as determined by the Secretary, with adjustment for family size.

(13) Qualifying multifamily purchaser

The term "qualifying multifamily purchaser" means—

(A) a public agency;

(B) a nonprofit organization; or

(C) a for-profit entity, which makes a commitment (for itself or any related entity) to comply with the low-income occupancy requirements under subsection (d)(7) of this section for any eligible multifamily housing property for which an offer to purchase is made during or after the periods specified under subsection (d) of this section.

(14) Secretary

The term "Secretary" means the Secretary of Housing and Urban Development.

(15) State housing finance agency

The term "State housing finance agency" means the public agency, authority, corporation, or other instrumentality of a State that has the authority to provide residential mortgage loan financing throughout the State.

(16) Very low-income families

The term "very low-income families" means families and individuals whose incomes do not exceed 50 percent of the median income of the area involved, as determined by the Secretary, with adjustment for family size.

(q) Notice to clearinghouses regarding ineligible properties

(1) In general

Within a reasonable period of time after acquiring title to an ineligible residential property, the Corporation shall, to the extent practicable, provide written notice to clearinghouses.

(2) Content

For ineligible single family properties, such notice shall contain the same information about such properties that the notice required under subsection (c)(1) of this section contains with respect to eligible single family properties. For ineligible multifamily housing properties, such notice shall contain the same information about such properties that the notice required under subsection (d)(1) of this section contains with respect to eligible multifamily housing properties. For ineligible condominium properties, such notice shall contain the same information about such properties that the notice required under subsection (l)(1) of this section contains with respect to eligible condominium properties.

(3) Availability

The clearinghouses shall make such information available, upon request, to other public agencies, other nonprofit organizations, qualifying households, qualifying multifamily purchasers, and other purchasers, as appropriate.

(4) Definitions

For purposes of this subsection, the following definitions shall apply:

(A) Ineligible condominium property

The term "ineligible condominium property" means any eligible condominium property to which the provisions of this section do not apply as a result of the limitations under subsection (b)(2)(A) of this section.

(B) Ineligible multifamily housing property

The term "ineligible multifamily housing property" means any eligible multifamily housing property to which the provisions of this section do not apply as a result of the limitations under subsection (b)(2)(A) of this section.

(C) Ineligible single family property

The term "ineligible single family property" means any eligible single family property to which the provisions of this section do not apply as a result of the limitations under subsection (b)(2)(A) of this section.

(D) Ineligible residential property

The term "ineligible residential property" includes ineligible single family properties, ineligible multifamily housing properties, and ineligible condominium properties.

§ 1831r. Payments on foreign deposits prohibited

(a) In general

Notwithstanding any other provision of law, the Corporation, the Board of Governors of the Federal Reserve System, the Resolution Trust Corporation, any other agency, department, and instrumentality of the United States, and any corporation owned or controlled by the United States may not, directly or indirectly, make any payment or provide any assistance, guarantee, or transfer under this chapter or any other provision of law in connection with any insured depository institution which would have the direct or indirect effect of satisfying, in whole or in part, any claim against the institution for obligations of the institution which would constitute deposits as defined in section 1813(*l*) of this title but for subparagraphs (A) and (B) of section 1813(*l*)(5) of this title.

(b) Exception

Subsection (a) of this section shall not apply to any payment, assistance, guarantee, or transfer made or provided by the Corporation if the Board of Directors determines in writing that such ac-

tion is not inconsistent with any requirement of section 1823(c) of this title.

(c) Discount window lending

No provision of this section shall be construed as prohibiting any Federal Reserve bank from making advances or otherwise extending credit pursuant to the Federal Reserve Act [12 U.S.C.A. § 221 et seq.] to any insured depository institution to the extent that such advance or extension of credit is consistent with the conditions and limitations imposed under section 10B of such Act [12 U.S.C.A. § 347b].

§ 1831r–1. Notice of branch closure

(a) Notice to appropriate Federal banking agency

(1) In general

An insured depository institution which proposes to close any branch shall submit a notice of the proposed closing to the appropriate Federal banking agency not later than the first day of the 90–day period ending on the date proposed for the closing.

(2) Contents of notice

A notice under paragraph (1) shall include—

(A) a detailed statement of the reasons for the decision to close the branch; and

(B) statistical or other information in support of such reasons.

(b) Notice to customers

(1) In general

An insured depository institution which proposes to close a branch shall provide notice of the proposed closing to its customers.

(2) Contents of notice

Notice under paragraph (1) shall consist of—

(A) posting of a notice in a conspicuous manner on the premises of the branch proposed to be closed during not less than the 30–day period ending on the date proposed for that closing; and

(B) inclusion of a notice in—

(i) at least one of any regular account statements mailed to customers of the branch proposed to be closed, or

(ii) in a separate mailing,

by not later than the beginning of the 90–day period ending on the date proposed for that closing.

(c) Adoption of policies

Each insured depository institution shall adopt policies for closings of branches of the institution.

(d) Branch closures in interstate banking or branching operations

(1) Notice requirements

In the case of an interstate bank which proposes to close any branch in a low-or moderate-income area, the notice required under subsection (b)(2) of this section shall contain the mailing address of the appropriate Federal banking agency and a statement that comments on the proposed closing of such branch may be mailed to such agency.

(2) Action required by appropriate Federal banking agency

If, in the case of a branch referred to in paragraph (1)—

(A) a person from the area in which such branch is located—

(i) submits a written request relating to the closing of such branch to the appropriate Federal banking agency; and

(ii) includes a statement of specific reasons for the request, including a discussion of the adverse effect of such closing on the availability of banking services in the area affected by the closing of the branch; and

(B) the agency concludes that the request is not frivolous,

the agency shall consult with community leaders in the affected area and convene a meeting of representatives of the agency and other interested depository institution regulatory agencies with community leaders in the affected area and such other individuals, organizations, and depository institutions (as defined in section 461(b)(1)(A) of this title) as the agency may determine, in the discretion of the agency, to be appropriate, to explore the feasibility of obtaining adequate alternative facilities and services for the affected area, including the establishment of a new branch by another depository institution, the chartering of a new depository institution, or the establishment of

a community development credit union, following the closing of the branch.

(3) No effect on closing

No action by the appropriate Federal banking agency under paragraph (2) shall affect the authority of an interstate bank to close a branch (including the timing of such closing) if the requirements of subsections (a) and (b) of this section have been met by such bank with respect to the branch being closed.

(4) Definitions

For purposes of this subsection, the following definitions shall apply:

(A) Interstate bank defined

The term "interstate bank" means a bank which maintains branches in more than 1 State.

(B) Low-or moderate-income area

The term "low-or moderate-income area" means a census tract for which the median family income is—

(i) less than 80 percent of the median family income for the metropolitan statistical area (as designated by the Director of the Office of Management and Budget) in which the census tract is located; or

(ii) in the case of a census tract which is not located in a metropolitan statistical area, less than 80 percent of the median family income for the State in which the census tract is located, as determined without taking into account family income in metropolitan statistical areas in such State.

(e) Scope of application

This section shall not apply with respect to—

(1) an automated teller machine;

(2) the relocation of a branch or consolidation of one or more branches into another branch, if the relocation or consolidation—

(A) occurs within the immediate neighborhood; and

(B) does not substantially affect the nature of the business or customers served; or

(3) a branch that is closed in connection with—

(A) an emergency acquisition under—

(i) section 1821(n) of this title; or

(ii) subsection (f) or (k) of section 1823 of this title; or

(B) any assistance provided by the Corporation under section 1823(c) of this title.

§ 1831s. Transferred

§ 1831t. Depository institutions lacking Federal deposit insurance—DFA § 1090

(a) Annual independent audit of private deposit insurers

(1) Audit required

Any private deposit insurer shall obtain an annual audit from an independent auditor using generally accepted auditing standards. The audit shall include a determination of whether the private deposit insurer follows generally accepted accounting principles and has set aside sufficient reserves for losses.

(2) Providing copies of audit report

(A) Private deposit insurer

The private deposit insurer shall provide a copy of the audit report—

(i) to each depository institution the deposits of which are insured by the private deposit insurer, not later than 14 days after the audit is completed; and

(ii) to the appropriate supervisory agency of each State in which such an institution receives deposits, not later than 7 days after the audit is completed.

(B) Depository institution

Any depository institution the deposits of which are insured by the private deposit insurer shall provide a copy of the audit report, upon request, to any current or prospective customer of the institution.

(3) Enforcement by appropriate State supervisor

Any appropriate State supervisor of a private deposit insurer, and any appropriate State supervisor of a depository institution which receives deposits that are insured by a private deposit insurer, may examine and enforce compliance with this subsection under the applicable regulatory authority of such supervisor.

(b) Disclosure required

Any depository institution lacking Federal deposit insurance shall, within the United States, do the following:

(1) Periodic statements; account records

Include conspicuously in all periodic statements of account, on each signature card, and on each passbook, certificate of deposit, or share certificate[,] a notice that the institution is not federally insured, and that if the institution fails, the Federal Government does not guarantee that depositors will get back their money.

(2) Advertising; premises

(A) In general

Include clearly and conspicuously in all advertising, except as provided in subparagraph (B); and at each station or window where deposits are normally received, its principal place of business and all its branches where it accepts deposits or opens accounts (excluding automated teller machines or point of sale terminals), and on its main Internet page, a notice that the institution is not federally insured.

(B) Exceptions

The following need not include a notice that the institution is not federally insured:

(i) Any sign, document, or other item that contains the name of the depository institution, its logo, or its contact information, but only if the sign, document, or item does not include any information about the institution's products or services or information otherwise promoting the institution.

(ii) Small utilitarian items that do not mention deposit products or insurance if inclusion of the notice would be impractical.

(3) Acknowledgement of disclosure

(A) New depositors obtained other than through a conversion or merger

With respect to any depositor who was not a depositor at the depository institution before the effective date of the Financial Services Regulatory Relief Act of 2006, and who is not a depositor as described in subparagraph (B), receive any deposit for the account of such depositor only if the depositor has signed a written acknowledgement that—

(i) the institution is not federally insured; and

(ii) if the institution fails, the Federal Government does not guarantee that the depositor will get back the depositor's money.

(B) New depositors obtained through a conversion or merger

With respect to a depositor at a federally insured depository institution that converts to, or merges into, a depository institution lacking federal insurance after the effective date of the Financial Services Regulatory Relief Act of 2006, receive any deposit for the account of such depositor only if—

(i) the depositor has signed a written acknowledgement described in subparagraph (A); or

(ii) the institution makes an attempt, as described in subparagraph (D) and sent by mail no later than 45 days after the effective date of the conversion or merger, to obtain the acknowledgment.

(C) Current depositors

Receive any deposit after the effective date of the Financial Services Regulatory Relief Act of 2006 for the account of any depositor who was a depositor on that date only if—

(i) the depositor has signed a written acknowledgement described in subparagraph (A); or

(ii) the institution has complied with the provisions of subparagraph (E) which are applicable as of the date of the deposit.

(D) Alternative provision of notice to new depositors obtained through a conversion or merger

(i) In general

Transmit to each depositor who has not signed a written acknowledgement described in subparagraph (A)—

(I) a conspicuous card containing the information described in clauses (i) and (ii) of subparagraph (A), and a line for the signature of the depositor; and

(II) accompanying materials requesting the depositor to sign the card, and return the signed card to the institution.

(E) Alternative provision of notice to current depositors

(i) In general

Transmit to each depositor who was a depositor before the effective date of the Financial Services Regulatory Relief Act of 2006, and has not signed a written acknowledgement described in subparagraph (A)—

(I) a conspicuous card containing the information described in clauses (i) and (ii) of subparagraph (A), and a line for the signature of the depositor; and

(II) accompanying materials requesting the depositor to sign the card, and return the signed card to the institution.

(ii) Manner and timing of notice

(I) First notice

Make the transmission described in clause (i) via mail not later than three months after the effective date of the Financial Services Regulatory Relief Act of 2006.

(II) Second notice

Make a second transmission described in clause (i) via mail not less than 30 days and not more than three months after a transmission to the depositor in accordance with subclause (I), if the institution has not, by the date of such mailing, received from the depositor a card referred to in clause (i) which has been signed by the depositor.

(c) Manner and content of disclosure

To ensure that current and prospective customers understand the risks involved in foregoing Federal deposit insurance, the Federal Trade Commission, by regulation or order, shall prescribe the manner and content of disclosure required under this section, which shall be presented in such format and in such type size and manner as to be simple and easy to understand.

(d) Exceptions for institutions not receiving retail deposits

The Federal Trade Commission may, by regulation or order, make exceptions to subsection (b) of this section for any depository institution that, within the United States, does not receive initial deposits of less than an amount equal to the standard maximum deposit insurance amount from individuals who are citizens or residents of the United States, other than money received in connection with any draft or similar instrument issued to transmit money.

(e) Definitions

For purposes of this section:

(1) Appropriate supervisor

The "appropriate supervisor" of a depository institution means the agency primarily responsible for supervising the institution.

(2) Depository institution

The term "depository institution" includes—

(A) any entity described in section 461(b)(1)(A)(iv) of this title; and

(B) any entity that, as determined by the Federal Trade Commission—

(i) is engaged in the business of receiving deposits; and

(ii) could reasonably be mistaken for a depository institution by the entity's current or prospective customers.

(3) Lacking Federal deposit insurance

A depository institution lacks Federal deposit insurance if the institution is not either—

(A) an insured depository institution; or

(B) an insured credit union, as defined in section 101 of the Federal Credit Union Act [12 U.S.C.A. § 1752].

(4) Private deposit insurer

The term "private deposit insurer" means any entity insuring the deposits of any depository institution lacking Federal deposit insurance.

(f) Enforcement

(1) Limited FTC enforcement authority

Compliance with the requirements of subsections (b), (c) and (e) of this section, and any regulation prescribed or order issued under any such subsection, shall be enforced under the Federal Trade Commission Act by the Federal Trade Commission.

(2) Broad State enforcement authority

(A) In general

Subject to subparagraph (C), an appropriate State supervisor of a depository institution lacking Federal deposit insurance may examine and enforce compliance with the requirements of this section, and any regulation prescribed under this section.

(B) State powers

For purposes of bringing any action to enforce compliance with this section, no provision of this section shall be construed as preventing an appropriate State supervisor of a depository institution lacking Federal deposit insurance from exercising any powers conferred on such official by the laws of such State.

(C) Limitation on State action while Federal action pending

If the Federal Trade Commission has instituted an enforcement action for a violation of this section, no appropriate State supervisor may, during the pendency of such action, bring an action under this section against any defendant named in the complaint of the Commission for any violation of this section that is alleged in that complaint.

§ 1831u. Interstate bank mergers—DFA § 607

(a) Approval of interstate merger transactions authorized

(1) In general

Beginning on June 1, 1997, the responsible agency may approve a merger transaction under section 1828(c) of this title between insured banks with different home States, without regard to whether such transaction is prohibited under the law of any State.

(2) State election to prohibit interstate merger transactions

(A) In general

Notwithstanding paragraph (1), a merger transaction may not be approved pursuant to paragraph (1) if the transaction involves a bank the home State of which has enacted a law after September 29, 1994, and before June 1, 1997, that—

(i) applies equally to all out-of-State banks; and

(ii) expressly prohibits merger transactions involving out-of-State banks.

(B) No effect on prior approvals of merger transactions

A law enacted by a State pursuant to subparagraph (A) shall have no effect on merger transactions that were approved before the effective date of such law.

(3) State election to permit early interstate merger transactions

(A) In general

A merger transaction may be approved pursuant to paragraph (1) before June 1, 1997, if the home State of each bank involved in the transaction has in effect, as of the date of the approval of such transaction, a law that—

(i) applies equally to all out-of-State banks; and

(ii) expressly permits interstate merger transactions with all out-of-State banks.

(B) Certain conditions allowed

A host State may impose conditions on a branch within such State of a bank resulting from an interstate merger transaction if—

(i) the conditions do not have the effect of discriminating against out-of-State banks, out-of-State bank holding companies, or any subsidiary of such bank or company (other than on the basis of a nationwide reciprocal treatment requirement);

(ii) the imposition of the conditions is not preempted by Federal law; and

(iii) the conditions do not apply or require performance after May 31, 1997.

(4) Interstate merger transactions involving acquisitions of branches

(A) In general

An interstate merger transaction may involve the acquisition of a branch of an insured bank without the acquisition of the bank only if the law of the State in which the branch is located permits out-of-State banks to acquire a branch of a bank in such State without acquiring the bank.

(B) Treatment of branch for purposes of this section

In the case of an interstate merger transaction which involves the acquisition of a branch of an insured bank without the acquisition of the bank, the branch shall be treated, for purposes of this section, as an insured bank the home State of which is the State in which the branch is located.

(5) Preservation of State age laws

(A) In general

The responsible agency may not approve an application pursuant to paragraph (1) that would have the effect of permitting an out-of-State bank or out-of-State bank holding company to acquire a bank in a host State that has not been in existence for the minimum period of time, if any, specified in the statutory law of the host State.

(B) Special rule for State age laws specifying a period of more than 5 years

Notwithstanding subparagraph (A), the responsible agency may approve a merger transaction pursuant to paragraph (1) involving the acquisition of a bank that has been in existence at least 5 years without regard to any longer minimum period of time specified in a statutory law of the host State.

(6) Shell banks

For purposes of this subsection, a bank that has been chartered solely for the purpose of, and does not open for business prior to, acquiring control of, or acquiring all or substantially all of the assets of, an existing bank or branch shall be deemed to have been in existence for the same period of time as the bank or branch to be acquired.

(b) Provisions relating to application and approval process

(1) Compliance with State filing requirements

(A) In general

Any bank which files an application for an interstate merger transaction shall—

(i) comply with the filing requirements of any host State of the bank which will result from such transaction to the extent that the requirement—

(I) does not have the effect of discriminating against out-of-State banks or out-of-State bank holding companies or subsidiaries of such banks or bank holding companies; and

(II) is similar in effect to any requirement imposed by the host State on a nonbanking corporation incorporated in another State that engages in business in the host State; and

(ii) submit a copy of the application to the State bank supervisor of the host State.

(B) Penalty for failure to comply

The responsible agency may not approve an application for an interstate merger transaction if the applicant materially fails to comply with subparagraph (A).

(2) Concentration limits

(A) Nationwide concentration limits

The responsible agency may not approve an application for an interstate merger transaction if the resulting bank (including all insured depository institutions which are affiliates of the resulting bank), upon consummation of the transaction, would control more than 10 percent of the total amount of deposits of insured depository institutions in the United States.

(B) Statewide concentration limits other than with respect to initial entries

The responsible agency may not approve an application for an interstate merger transaction if—

(i) any bank involved in the transaction (including all insured depository institutions which are affiliates of any such bank) has a branch in any State in which any other bank involved in the transaction has a branch; and

(ii) the resulting bank (including all insured depository institutions which would be affiliates of the resulting bank), upon consummation of the transaction, would control 30 percent or more of the total amount of deposits of insured depository institutions in any such State.

(C) Effectiveness of State deposit caps

No provision of this subsection shall be construed as affecting the authority of any State to limit, by statute, regulation, or order, the percentage of the total amount of deposits of insured depository institutions in the State which may be held or controlled by any bank or bank holding company (including all insured depository institutions which are affiliates of the bank or bank holding company) to the extent the application of such limitation does not discriminate against out-of-State banks, out-of-State bank holding companies, or subsidiaries of such banks or holding companies.

(D) Exceptions to subparagraph (B)

The responsible agency may approve an application for an interstate merger transaction pursuant to subsection (a) without regard to the applicability of subparagraph (B) with respect to any State if—

(i) there is a limitation described in subparagraph (C) in a State statute, regulation, or order which has the effect of permitting a bank or bank holding company (including all insured depository institutions which are affiliates of the bank or bank holding company) to control a greater percentage of total deposits of all insured depository institutions in the State than the percentage permitted under subparagraph (B); or

(ii) the transaction is approved by the appropriate State bank supervisor of such State and the standard on which such approval is based does not have the effect of discriminating against out-of-State banks, out-of-State bank holding companies, or subsidiaries of such banks or holding companies.

(E) Exception for certain banks

This paragraph shall not apply with respect to any interstate merger transaction involving only affiliated banks.

(3) Community reinvestment compliance

In determining whether to approve an application for an interstate merger transaction in which the resulting bank would have a branch or bank affiliate immediately following the transaction in any State in which the bank submitting the application (as the acquiring bank) had no branch or bank affiliate immediately before the transaction, the responsible agency shall-

(A) comply with the responsibilities of the agency regarding such application under section 2903 of this title;

(B) take into account the most recent written evaluation under section 2903 of this title of any bank which would be an affiliate of the resulting bank; and

(C) take into account the record of compliance of any applicant bank with applicable State community reinvestment laws.

(4) Adequacy of capital and management skills

The responsible agency may approve an application for an interstate merger transaction pursuant to subsection (a) of this section only if—

(A) each bank involved in the transaction is adequately capitalized as of the date the application is filed; and

(B) the responsible agency determines that the resulting bank will continue to be adequately capitalized and adequately managed upon the consummation of the transaction.

(5) Surrender of charter after merger transaction

The charters of all banks involved in an interstate merger transaction, other than the charter of the resulting bank, shall be surrendered, upon request, to the Federal banking agency or State bank supervisor which issued the charter.

(c) Applicability of certain laws to interstate banking operations

(1) State taxation authority not affected

(A) In general

No provision of this section shall be construed as affecting the authority of any State or political subdivision of any State to adopt, apply, or administer any tax or method of taxation to any bank, bank holding company, or foreign bank, or any affiliate of any bank, bank holding company, or foreign bank, to the extent such tax or tax method is otherwise permissible by or under the Constitution of the United States or other Federal law.

(B) Imposition of shares tax by host States

In the case of a branch of an out-of-State bank which results from an interstate merger transaction, a proportionate amount of the value of the shares of the out-of-State bank may be subject to any bank shares tax levied or imposed by the host State, or any political subdivision of such host State that imposes such tax based upon a method adopted by the host State, which may include allocation and apportionment.

(2) Applicability of antitrust laws

No provision of this section shall be construed as affecting—

(A) the applicability of the antitrust laws; or

(B) the applicability, if any, of any State law which is similar to the antitrust laws.

(3) Reservation of certain rights to States

No provision of this section shall be construed as limiting in any way the right of a State to—

(A) determine the authority of State banks chartered by that State to establish and maintain branches; or

(B) supervise, regulate, and examine State banks chartered by that State.

(4) State-imposed notice requirements

A host State may impose any notification or reporting requirement on a branch of an out-of-State bank if the requirement—

(A) does not discriminate against out-of-State banks or bank holding companies; and

(B) is not preempted by any Federal law regarding the same subject.

(d) Operations of the resulting bank

(1) Continued operations

A resulting bank may, subject to the approval of the appropriate Federal banking agency, retain and operate, as a main office or a branch, any office that any bank involved in an interstate merger transaction was operating as a main office or a branch immediately before the merger transaction.

(2) Additional branches

Following the consummation of any interstate merger transaction, the resulting bank may establish, acquire, or operate additional branches at any location where any bank involved in the transaction could have established, acquired, or operated a branch under applicable Federal or State law if such bank had not been a party to the merger transaction.

(3) Certain conditions and commitments continued

If, as a condition for the acquisition of a bank by an out-of-State bank holding company before September 29, 1994—

(A) the home State of the acquired bank imposed conditions on such acquisition by such out-of-State bank holding company; or

(B) the bank holding company made commitments to such State in connection with the acquisition,

the State may enforce such conditions and commitments with respect to such bank holding company or any affiliated successor company which controls a bank or branch in such State as a result of an interstate merger transaction to the same extent as the State could enforce such conditions or commitments against the bank holding company before the consummation of the merger transaction.

(e) Exception for banks in default or in danger of default

If an application under subsection (a)(1) of this section for approval of a merger transaction which involves 1 or more banks in default or in danger of default or with respect to which the Corporation provides assistance under section 1823(c) of this title, the responsible agency may approve such application without regard to subsection (b) of this section, or paragraph (2), (4), or (5) of subsection (a) of this section.

(f) Applicable rate and other charge limitations

(1) In general

In the case of any State that has a constitutional provision that sets a maximum lawful annual percentage rate of interest on any contract at not more than 5 percent above the discount rate for 90-day commercial paper in effect at the Federal reserve bank for the Federal reserve district in which such State is located, except as provided in paragraph (2), upon the establishment in such State of a branch of any out-of-State insured depository institution in such State under this section, the maximum interest rate or amount of interest, discount points, finance charges, or other similar charges that may be charged, taken, received, or reserved (or in the case of a governmental entity located in such State, paid) from time to time in any loan or discount made or upon any note, bill of exchange, financing transaction, or other evidence of debt by—

(A) any insured depository institution whose home State is such State shall be equal to not more than the greater of—

(i) the maximum interest rate or amount of interest, discount points, finance charges, or other similar charges that may be charged, taken, received, or reserved in a similar transaction under the constitution or any statute or other law of the home State of the out-of-State insured depository institution establishing any such branch, without reference to this section, as such maximum inter-

est rate or amount of interest may change from time to time; or

(ii) the maximum rate or amount of interest, discount points, finance charges, or other similar charges that may be charged, taken, received, or reserved in a similar transaction by a State insured depository institution chartered under the laws of such State or a national bank or Federal savings association whose main office is located in such State without reference to this section; and

(B) any governmental entity located in such State or any person that is not a depository institution described in subparagraph (A) doing business in such State, shall be equal to not more than the greater of the State's maximum lawful annual percentage rate or 17 percent—

(i) to facilitate the uniform implementation of federally mandated or federally established programs and financings related thereto, including—

(I) uniform accessibility of student loans, including the issuance of qualified student loan bonds as set forth in section 144 (b) of title 26;

(II) the uniform accessibility of mortgage loans, including the issuance of qualified mortgage bonds and qualified veterans' mortgage bonds as set forth in section 143 of such title;

(III) the uniform accessibility of safe and affordable housing programs administered or subject to review by the Department of Housing and Urban Development, including—

(aa) the issuance of exempt facility bonds for qualified residential rental property as set forth in section 142(d) of such title; and

(bb) the issuance of low income housing tax credits as set forth in section 42 of such title; and

(IV) the uniform accessibility of bonds and obligations issued under the American Recovery and Reinvestment Act of 2009;

(ii) to facilitate interstate commerce through the issuance of bonds and obligations under any provision of State law, including bonds and obligations for the purpose of economic development, education, and improvements to infrastructure; and

(iii) to facilitate interstate commerce generally, including consumer loans, in the case of any person or governmental entity (other than a depository institution subject to subparagraph (A) and paragraph (2)).

(2) Rule of construction

(A) In general

No provision of this subsection shall be construed as superseding or affecting—

(i) the authority of any insured depository institution to take, receive, reserve, and charge interest on any loan made in any State other than the State referred to in paragraph (1); or

(ii) the applicability of section 1735f-7a of this title, section 85 of this title, or section 1831d of this title.

(B) Applicability

This subsection shall be construed to apply to any loan or discount made, or note, bill of exchange, financing transaction, or other evidence of debt, originated by an insured depository institution, a governmental entity located in such State, or a person that is not a depository institution described in subparagraph (A) doing business in such State.

(g) Definitions

For purposes of this section, the following definitions shall apply:

(1) Adequately capitalized

The term "adequately capitalized" has the same meaning as in section 1831o of this title.

(2) Antitrust laws

The term "antitrust laws"—

(A) has the same meaning as in subsection (a) of section 12 of Title 15; and

(B) includes section 45 of Title 15 to the extent such section 45 relates to unfair methods of competition.

(3) Branch

The term "branch" means any domestic branch.

(4) Home State

The term "home State"—

(A) means—

(i) with respect to a national bank, the State in which the main office of the bank is located; and

(ii) with respect to a State bank, the State by which the bank is chartered; and

(B) with respect to a bank holding company, has the same meaning as in section 1841(o)(4) of this title.

(5) Host State

The term "host State" means, with respect to a bank, a State, other than the home State of the bank, in which the bank maintains, or seeks to establish and maintain, a branch.

(6) Interstate merger transaction

The term "interstate merger transaction" means any merger transaction approved pursuant to subsection (a)(1) of this section.

(7) Merger transaction

The term "merger transaction" has the meaning determined under section 1828(c)(3) of this title.

(8) Out-of-State bank

The term "out-of-State bank" means, with respect to any State, a bank whose home State is another State.

(9) Out-of-State bank holding company

The term "out-of-State bank holding company" means, with respect to any State, a bank holding company whose home State is another State.

(10) Responsible agency

The term "responsible agency" means the agency determined in accordance with section 1828(c)(2) of this title with respect to a merger transaction.

(11) Resulting bank

The term "resulting bank" means a bank that has resulted from an interstate merger transaction under this section.

§ 1831v. Authority of State insurance regulator and securities and exchange Commission

(a) In general

Notwithstanding any other provision of law, the provisions of—

(1) section 1844(c) of this title that limit the authority of the Board of Governors of the Federal Reserve System to require reports from, to make examinations of, or to impose capital requirements on holding companies and their functionally regulated subsidiaries or that require deference to other regulators;

(2) section 1844(g) of this title that limit the authority of the Board to require a functionally regulated subsidiary of a holding company to provide capital or other funds or assets to a depository institution subsidiary of the holding company and to take certain actions including requiring divestiture of the depository institution; and

(3) section 1848a of this title that limit whatever authority the Board might otherwise have to take direct or indirect action with respect to holding companies and their functionally regulated subsidiaries;

shall also limit whatever authority that a Federal banking agency might otherwise have under any statute or regulation to require reports, make examinations, impose capital requirements, or take any other direct or indirect action with respect to any functionally regulated affiliate of a depository institution, subject to the same standards and requirements as are applicable to the Board under those provisions

(b) Certain exemption authorized

No provision of this section shall be construed as preventing the Corporation, if the Corporation finds it necessary to determine the condition of a depository institution for insurance purposes, from examining an affiliate of any depository institution, pursuant to section 1820(b)(4) of this title, as may be necessary to disclose fully the relationship between the depository institution and the affiliate, and the effect of such relationship on the depository institution.

(c) Definitions

For purposes of this section, the following definitions shall apply:

(1) Functionally regulated subsidiary

The term "functionally regulated subsidiary" has the meaning given the term in section 1844(c)(5) of this title.

(2) Functionally regulated affiliate

The term "functionally regulated affiliate" means, with respect to any depository institu-

tion, any affiliate of such depository institution that is—

(A) not a depository institution holding company; and

(B) a company described in any clause of section 1844(c)(5)(B) of this title.

§ 1831w. Safety and soundness firewalls applicable to financial subsidiaries of banks

(a) In general

An insured State bank may control or hold an interest in a subsidiary that engages in activities as principal that would only be permissible for a national bank to conduct through a financial subsidiary if—

(1) the State bank and each insured depository institution affiliate of the State bank are well capitalized (after the capital deduction required by paragraph (2));

(2) the State bank complies with the capital deduction and financial statement disclosure requirements in section 24a(c) of this title;

(3) the State bank complies with the financial and operational safeguards required by section 24a(d) of this title; and

(4) the State bank complies with the amendments to sections 371c and 371c–1 of this title made by section 121(b) of the Gramm–Leach–Bliley Act.

(b) Preservation of existing subsidiaries

Notwithstanding subsection (a), an insured State bank may retain control of a subsidiary, or retain an interest in a subsidiary, that the State bank lawfully controlled or acquired before November 12, 1999, and conduct through such subsidiary any activities lawfully conducted in such subsidiary as of such date.

(c) Definitions

For purposes of this section, the following definitions shall apply:

(1) Subsidiary

The term "subsidiary" means any company that is a subsidiary (as defined in section 1813(w)(4) of this title) of 1 or more insured banks.

(2) Financial subsidiary

The term "financial subsidiary" has the meaning given the term in section 24a(g) of this title.

(d) Preservation of authority

(1) Federal Deposit Insurance Act

No provision of this section shall be construed as superseding the authority of the Federal Deposit Insurance Corporation to review subsidiary activities under section 1831a of this title.

(2) Federal Reserve Act

No provision of this section shall be construed as affecting the applicability of the 20th undesignated paragraph of section 9 Federal Reserve Act [12 U.S.C.A. § 321 et seq.].

§ 1831x. Insurance customer protections

(a) Regulations required

(1) In general

The Federal banking agencies shall prescribe and publish in final form, before the end of the 1–year period beginning on November 12, 1999, customer protection regulations (which the agencies jointly determine to be appropriate) that—

(A) apply to retail sales practices, solicitations, advertising, or offers of any insurance product by any depository institution or any person that is engaged in such activities at an office of the institution or on behalf of the institution; and

(B) are consistent with the requirements of this chapter and provide such additional protections for customers to whom such sales, solicitations, advertising, or offers are directed.

(2) Applicability to subsidiaries

The regulations prescribed pursuant to paragraph (1) shall extend such protections to any subsidiary of a depository institution, as deemed appropriate by the regulators referred to in paragraph(3), where such extension is determined to be necessary to ensure the consumer protections provided by this section.

(3) Consultation and joint regulations

The Federal banking agencies shall consult with each other and prescribe joint regulations pursuant to paragraph (1), after consultation with the State insurance regulators, as appropriate.

(b) Sales practices

The regulations prescribed pursuant to subsection (a) shall include antitying and anticoercion rules applicable to the sale of insurance products that prohibit a depository institution from engaging in any practice that would lead a customer to believe an extension of credit, in violation of section 1972 of this title, is conditional upon—

(1) the purchase of an insurance product from the institution or any of its affiliates; or

(2) an agreement by the consumer not to obtain, or a prohibition on the consumer from obtaining, an insurance product from an unaffiliated entity.

(c) Disclosures and advertising

The regulations prescribed pursuant to subsection (a) shall include the following provisions relating to disclosures and advertising in connection with the initial purchase of an insurance product:

(1) Disclosures

(A) In general

Requirements that the following disclosures be made orally and in writing before the completion of the initial sale and, in the case of clause (iii), at the time of application for an extension of credit:

(i) Uninsured status

As appropriate, the product is not insured by the Federal Deposit Insurance Corporation, the United States Government, or the depository institution.

(ii) Investment risk

In the case of a variable annuity or other insurance product which involves an investment risk, that there is an investment risk associated with the product, including possible loss of value.

(iii) Coercion

The approval of an extension of credit may not be conditioned on—

(I) the purchase of an insurance product from the institution in which the application for credit is pending or of any affiliate of the institution; or

(II) an agreement by the consumer not to obtain, or a prohibition on the consumer from obtaining, an insurance product from an unaffiliated entity.

(B) Making disclosure readily understandable

Regulations prescribed under subparagraph (A) shall encourage the use of disclosure that is conspicuous, simple, direct, and readily understandable, such as the following:

(i) "NOT FDIC–INSURED".

(ii) "NOT GUARANTEED BY THE BANK".

(iii) "MAY GO DOWN IN VALUE".

(iv) "NOT INSURED BY ANY GOVERNMENT AGENCY".

(C) Limitation

Nothing in this paragraph requires the inclusion of the foregoing disclosures in advertisements of a general nature describing or listing the services or products offered by an institution.

(D) Meaningful disclosures

Disclosures shall not be considered to be meaningfully provided under this paragraph if the institution or its representative states that disclosures required by this subsection were available to the customer in printed material available for distribution, where such printed material is not provided and such information is not orally disclosed to the customer.

(E) Adjustments for alternative methods of purchase

In prescribing the requirements under subparagraphs (A) and (F), necessary adjustments shall be made for purchase in person, by telephone, or by electronic media to provide for the most appropriate and complete form of disclosure and acknowledgments.

(F) Consumer acknowledgment

A requirement that a depository institution shall require any person selling an insurance product at any office of, or on behalf of, the institution to obtain, at the time a consumer receives the disclosures required under this paragraph or at the time of the initial purchase by the consumer of such product, an acknowledgment by such consumer of the receipt of the disclosure required under this subsection with respect to such product.

(2) Prohibition on misrepresentations

A prohibition on any practice, or any advertising, at any office of, or on behalf of, the depository institution, or any subsidiary, as appropriate, that could mislead any person or otherwise cause a reasonable person to reach an erroneous belief with respect to—

(A) the uninsured nature of any insurance product sold, or offered for sale, by the institution or any subsidiary of the institution;

(B) in the case of a variable annuity or insurance product that involves an investment risk, the investment risk associated with any such product; or

(C) in the case of an institution or subsidiary at which insurance products are sold or offered for sale, the fact that—

(i) the approval of an extension of credit to a customer by the institution or subsidiary may not be conditioned on the purchase of an insurance product by such customer from the institution or subsidiary; and

(ii) the customer is free to purchase the insurance product from another source.

(d) Separation of banking and nonbanking activities

(1) Regulations required

The regulations prescribed pursuant to subsection (a) shall include such provisions as the Federal banking agencies consider appropriate to ensure that the routine acceptance of deposits is kept, to the extent practicable, physically segregated from insurance product activity.

(2) Requirements

Regulations prescribed pursuant to paragraph (1) shall include the following requirements:

(A) Separate setting

A clear delineation of the setting in which, and the circumstances under which, transactions involving insurance products should be conducted in a location physically segregated from an area where retail deposits are routinely accepted.

(B) Referrals

Standards that permit any person accepting deposits from the public in an area where such transactions are routinely conducted in a depository institution to refer a customer who seeks to purchase any insurance product to a qualified person who sells such product, only if the person making the referral receives no more than a one-time nominal fee of a fixed dollar amount for each referral that does not depend on whether the referral results in a transaction.

(C) Qualification and licensing requirements

Standards prohibiting any depository institution from permitting any person to sell or offer for sale any insurance product in any part of any office of the institution, or on behalf of the institution, unless such person is appropriately qualified and licensed.

(e) Domestic violence discrimination prohibition

(1) In general

In the case of an applicant for, or an insured under, any insurance product described in paragraph (2), the status of the applicant or insured as a victim of domestic violence, or as a provider of services to victims of domestic violence, shall not be considered as a criterion in any decision with regard to insurance underwriting, pricing, renewal, or scope of coverage of insurance policies, or payment of insurance claims, except as required or expressly permitted under State law.

(2) Scope of application

The prohibition contained in paragraph (1) shall apply to any life or health insurance product which is sold or offered for sale, as principal, agent, or broker, by any depository institution or any person who is engaged in such activities at an office of the institution or on behalf of the institution.

(3) Domestic violence defined

For purposes of this subsection, the term "domestic violence" means the occurrence of one or more of the following acts by a current or former family member, household member, intimate partner, or caretaker:

(A) Attempting to cause or causing or threatening another person physical harm, severe emotional distress, psychological trauma, rape, or sexual assault.

(B) Engaging in a course of conduct or repeatedly committing acts toward another person, including following the person with-

out proper authority, under circumstances that place the person in reasonable fear of bodily injury or physical harm.

(C) Subjecting another person to false imprisonment.

(D) Attempting to cause or cause damage to property so as to intimidate or attempt to control the behavior of another person.

(f) Consumer grievance process

The Federal banking agencies shall jointly establish a consumer complaint mechanism, for receiving and expeditiously addressing consumer complaints alleging a violation of regulations issued under the section, which shall—

(1) establish a group within each regulatory agency to receive such complaints;

(2) develop procedures for investigating such complaints;

(3) develop procedures for informing consumers of rights they may have in connection with such complaints; and

(4) develop procedures for addressing concerns raised by such complaints, as appropriate, including procedures for the recovery of losses to the extent appropriate.

(g) Effect on other authority

(1) In general

No provision of this section shall be construed as granting, limiting, or otherwise affecting—

(A) any authority of the Securities and Exchange Commission, any self-regulatory organization, the Municipal Securities Rulemaking Board, or the Secretary of the Treasury under any Federal securities law; or

(B) except as provided in paragraph (2), any authority of any State insurance commission (or any agency or office performing like functions), or of any State securities commission (or any agency or office performing like functions), or other State authority under any State law.

(2) Coordination with State law

(A) In general

Except as provided in subparagraph (B), insurance customer protection regulations prescribed by a Federal banking agency under this section shall not apply to retail sales, solicitations, advertising, or offers of any insurance product by any depository institution or to any person who is engaged in such activities at an office of such institution or on behalf of the institution, in a State where the State has in effect statutes, regulations, orders, or interpretations, that are inconsistent with or contrary to the regulations prescribed by the Federal banking agencies.

(B) Preemption

(i) In general

If, with respect to any provision of the regulations prescribed under this section, the Board of Governors of the Federal Reserve System, the Comptroller of the Currency, and the Board of Directors of the Corporation determine jointly that the protection afforded by such provision for customers is greater than the protection provided by a comparable provision of the statutes, regulations, orders, or interpretations referred to in subparagraph (A) of any State, the appropriate State regulatory authority shall be notified of such determination in writing.

(ii) Considerations

Before making a final determination under clause (i), the Federal agencies referred to in clause (i) shall give appropriate consideration to comments submitted by the appropriate State regulatory authorities relating to the level of protection afforded to consumers under State law.

(iii) Federal preemption and ability of States to override Federal preemption

If the Federal agencies referred to in clause (i) jointly determine that any provision of the regulations prescribed under this section affords greater protections than a comparable State law, rule, regulation, order, or interpretation, those agencies shall send a written preemption notice to the appropriate State regulatory authority to notify the State that the Federal provision will preempt the State provision and will become applicable unless, not later than 3 years after the date of such notice, the State adopts legislation to override such preemption.

(h) Non-discrimination against non-affiliated agents

The Federal banking agencies shall ensure that the regulations prescribed pursuant to subsection (a) shall not have the effect of discriminating, either intentionally or unintentionally, against any person engaged in insurance sales or solicitations that is not affiliated with a depository institution.

§ 1831y.   CRA sunshine requirements

(a) Public disclosure of agreements

Any agreement (as defined in subsection (e)) entered into after November 12, 1999, by an insured depository institution or affiliate with a nongovernmental entity or person made pursuant to or in connection with the Community Reinvestment Act of 1977 [12 U.S.C.A. § 2901 et seq.] involving funds or other resources of such insured depository institution or affiliate—

(1) shall be in its entirety fully disclosed, and the full text thereof made available to the appropriate Federal banking agency with supervisory responsibility over the insured depository institution and to the public by each party to the agreement; and

(2) shall obligate each party to comply with this section.

(b) Annual report of activity by insured depository institution

Each insured depository institution or affiliate that is a party to an agreement described in subsection (a) shall report to the appropriate Federal banking agency with supervisory responsibility over the insured depository institution, not less frequently than once each year, such information as the Federal banking agency may by rule require relating to the following actions taken by the party pursuant to the agreement during the preceding 12–month period:

(1) Payments, fees, or loans made to any party to the agreement or received from any party to the agreement and the terms and conditions of the same.

(2) Aggregate data on loans, investments, and services provided by each party in its community or communities pursuant to the agreement.

(3) Such other pertinent matters as determined by regulation by the appropriate Federal banking agency with supervisory responsibility over the insured depository institution.

(c) Annual report of activity by nongovernmental entities

(1) In general

Each nongovernmental entity or person that is not an affiliate of an insured depository institution and that is a party to an agreement described in subsection (a) shall report to the appropriate Federal banking agency with supervisory responsibility over the insured depository institution that is a party to such agreement, not less frequently than once each year, an accounting of the use of funds received pursuant to each such agreement during the preceding 12–month period.

(2) Submission to insured depository institution

A nongovernmental entity or person referred to in paragraph (1) may comply with the reporting requirement in such paragraph by transmitting the report to the insured depository institution that is a party to the agreement, and such insured depository institution shall promptly transmit such report to the appropriate Federal banking agency with supervisory authority over the insured depository institution.

(3) Information to be included

The accounting referred to in paragraph (1) shall include a detailed, itemized list of the uses to which such funds have been made, including compensation, administrative expenses, travel, entertainment, consulting and professional fees paid, and such other categories, as determined by regulation by the appropriate Federal banking agency with supervisory responsibility over the insured depository institution.

(d) Applicability

Subsections (b) and (c) shall not apply with respect to any agreement entered into before the end of the 6–month period beginning on November 12, 1999.

(e) Definitions

(1) Agreement

For purposes of this section, the term "agreement"—

(A) means—

(i) any written contract, written arrangement, or other written understanding that provides for cash payments, grants, or other consideration with a value in excess of $10,000, or for loans the aggregate amount

of principal of which exceeds $50,000, annually (or the sum of all such agreements during a 12–month period with an aggregate value of cash payments, grants, or other consideration in excess of $10,000, or with an aggregate amount of loan principal in excess of $50,000); or

(ii) a group of substantively related contracts with an aggregate value of cash payments, grants, or other consideration in excess of $10,000, or with an aggregate amount of loan principal in excess of $50,000, annually;

made pursuant to, or in connection with, the fulfillment of the Community Reinvestment Act of 1977 [12 U.S.C.A. § 2901 et seq.], at least 1 party to which is an insured depository institution or affiliate thereof, whether organized on a profit or not-for-profit basis; and

(B) does not include—

(i) any individual mortgage loan;

(ii) any specific contract or commitment for a loan or extension of credit to individuals, businesses, farms, or other entities, if the funds are loaned at rates not substantially below market rates and if the purpose of the loan or extension of credit does not include any re-lending of the borrowed funds to other parties; or

(iii) any agreement entered into by an insured depository institution or affiliate with a nongovernmental entity or person who has not commented on, testified about, or discussed with the institution, or otherwise contacted the institution, concerning the Community Reinvestment Act of 1977 [12 U.S.C.A. § 2901 et seq.].

(2) Fulfillment of CRA

For purposes of subparagraph (A), the term "fulfillment" means a list of factors that the appropriate Federal banking agency determines have a material impact on the agency's decision—

(A) to approve or disapprove an application for a deposit facility (as defined in section 2902 of this title); or

(B) to assign a rating to an insured depository institution under section 2906 of this title.

(f) Violations

(1) Violations by persons other than insured depository institutions or their affiliates

(A) Material failure to comply

If the party to an agreement described in subsection (a) that is not an insured depository institution or affiliate willfully fails to comply with this section in a material way, as determined by the appropriate Federal banking agency, the agreement shall be unenforceable after the offending party has been given notice and a reasonable period of time to perform or comply.

(B) Diversion of funds or resources

If funds or resources received under an agreement described in subsection (a) have been diverted contrary to the purposes of the agreement for personal financial gain, the appropriate Federal banking agency with supervisory responsibility over the insured depository institution may impose either or both of the following penalties:

(i) Disgorgement by the offending individual of funds received under the agreement.

(ii) Prohibition of the offending individual from being a party to any agreement described in subsection (a) for a period of not to exceed 10 years.

(2) Designation of successor nongovernmental party

If an agreement described in subsection (a) is found to be unenforceable under this subsection, the appropriate Federal banking agency may assist the insured depository institution in identifying a successor nongovernmental party to assume the responsibilities of the agreement.

(3) Inadvertent or de minimis reporting errors

An error in a report filed under subsection (c) that is inadvertent or de minimis shall not subject the filing party to any penalty.

(g) Rule of construction

No provision of this section shall be construed as authorizing any appropriate Federal banking agency to enforce the provisions of any agreement described in subsection (a).

(h) Regulations

(1) In general

Each appropriate Federal banking agency shall prescribe regulations, in accordance with para-

graph (4), requiring procedures reasonably designed to ensure and monitor compliance with the requirements of this section.

(2) Protection of parties

In carrying out paragraph (1), each appropriate Federal banking agency shall—

(A) ensure that the regulations prescribed by the agency do not impose an undue burden on the parties and that proprietary and confidential information is protected; and

(B) establish procedures to allow any nongovernmental entity or person who is a party to a large number of agreements described in subsection (a) to make a single or consolidated filing of a report under subsection (c) to an insured depository institution or an appropriate Federal banking agency.

(3) Parties not subject to reporting requirements

The Board of Governors of the Federal Reserve System may prescribe regulations—

(A) to prevent evasions of subsection (e)(1)(B)(iii); and

(B) to provide further exemptions under such subsection, consistent with the purposes of this section.

(4) Coordination, consistency, and comparability

In carrying out paragraph (1), each appropriate Federal banking agency shall consult and coordinate with the other such agencies for the purposes of assuring, to the extent possible, that the regulations prescribed by each such agency are consistent and comparable with the regulations prescribed by the other such agencies.

§ 1831z. Bi-annual FDIC survey and report on increasing the deposit base by encouraging use of depository institutions by the unbanked

(a) Survey required

(1) In general

The Corporation shall conduct a bi-annual survey on efforts by insured depository institutions to bring those individuals and families who have rarely, if ever, held a checking account, a savings account or other type of transaction or check cashing account at an insured depository institution (hereafter in this section referred to as the "unbanked") into the conventional finance system.

(2) Factors and questions to consider

In conducting the survey, the Corporation shall take the following factors and questions into account:

(A) To what extent do insured depository institutions promote financial education and financial literacy outreach?

(B) Which financial education efforts appear to be the most effective in bringing "unbanked" individuals and families into the conventional finance system?

(C) What efforts are insured institutions making at converting "unbanked" money order, wire transfer, and international remittance customers into conventional account holders?

(D) What cultural, language and identification issues as well as transaction costs appear to most prevent "unbanked" individuals from establishing conventional accounts?

(E) What is a fair estimate of the size and worth of the "unbanked" market in the United States?

(b) Reports

The Chairperson of the Board of Directors shall submit a bi-annual report to the Committee on Financial Services of the House of Representatives and the Committee on Banking, Housing, and Urban Affairs of the Senate containing the Corporation's findings and conclusions with respect to the survey conducted pursuant to subsection (a) of this section, together with such recommendations for legislative or administrative action as the Chairperson may determine to be appropriate.

§ 1831aa. Enforcement of agreements

(a) In general

Notwithstanding clause (i) or (ii) of section 1818(b)(6)(A) of this title or section 1831o of this title, the appropriate Federal banking agency for a depository institution may enforce, under section 1818 of this title, the terms of—

(1) any condition imposed in writing by the agency on the depository institution or an institution-affiliated party in connection with any action on any application, notice, or other

request concerning the depository institution; or

(2) any written agreement entered into between the agency and the depository institution or an institution-affiliated party.

(b) Receiverships and conservatorships

After the appointment of the Corporation as the receiver or conservator for a depository institution, the Corporation may enforce any condition or agreement described in paragraph (1) or (2) of subsection (a) of this section imposed on or entered into with such institution or institution-affiliated party through an action brought in an appropriate United States district court.

§ 1832. Withdrawals by negotiable or transferable instruments for transfers to third parties

(a) Authority of depository institution; applicability

(1) Notwithstanding any other provision of law but subject to paragraph (2), a depository institution is authorized to permit the owner of a deposit or account on which interest or dividends are paid to make withdrawals by negotiable or transferable instruments for the purpose of making transfers to third parties.

(2) Paragraph (1) shall apply only with respect to deposits or accounts which consist solely of funds in which the entire beneficial interest is held by one or more individuals or by an organization which is operated primarily for religious, philanthropic, charitable, educational, political, or other similar purposes and which is not operated for profit, and with respect to deposits of public funds by an officer, employee, or agent of the United States, any State, county, municipality, or political subdivision thereof, the District of Columbia, the Commonwealth of Puerto Rico, American Samoa, Guam, any territory or possession of the United States, or any political subdivision thereof.

(b) Definition

For purposes of this section, the term "depository institution" means—

(1) any insured bank as defined in section 1813 of this title;

(2) any State bank as defined in section 1813 of this title;

(3) any mutual savings bank as defined in section 1813 of this title;

(4) any savings bank as defined in section 1813 of this title;

(5) any insured institution as defined in section 1724 of this title; and

(6) any building and loan association or savings and loan association organized and operated according to the laws of the State in which it is chartered or organized; and, for purposes of this paragraph, the term "State" means any State of the United States, the District of Columbia, any territory of the United States, Puerto Rico, Guam, American Samoa, or the Virgin Islands.

(c) Fine

Any depository institution which violates this section shall be fined $1,000 for each violation.

§ 1833. Repealed. Pub.L. 104–208, Div. A, Title II, § 2224(b), Sept. 30, 1996, 110 Stat. 3009–415

§ 1833a. Civil penalties

(a) In general

Whoever violates any provision of law to which this section is made applicable by subsection (c) of this section shall be subject to a civil penalty in an amount assessed by the court in a civil action under this section.

(b) Maximum amount of penalty

(1) Generally

The amount of the civil penalty shall not exceed $1,000,000.

(2) Special rule for continuing violations

In the case of a continuing violation, the amount of the civil penalty may exceed the amount described in paragraph (1) but may not exceed the lesser of $1,000,000 per day or $5,000,000.

(3) Special rule for violations creating gain or loss

(A) If any person derives pecuniary gain from the violation, or if the violation results in pecuniary loss to a person other than the violator, the amount of the civil penalty may exceed the amounts described in paragraphs (1) and (2) but may not exceed the amount of such gain or loss.

(B) As used in this paragraph, the term "person" includes the Bank Insurance Fund, the Savings Association Insurance Fund, and after the merger of such funds, the Deposit Insurance Fund, and the National Credit Union Share Insurance Fund.

(c) Violations to which penalty is applicable

This section applies to a violation of, or a conspiracy to violate—

(1) section 215, 656, 657, 1005, 1006, 1007, 1014, or 1344 of Title 18;

(2) section 287, 1001, 1032, 1341 or 1343 of Title 18 affecting a federally insured financial institution; or

(3) section 16(a) of the Small Business Act (15 U.S.C. 645(a)).

(d) Effective date

This section shall apply to violations occurring on or after August 10, 1984.

(e) Attorney general to bring action

A civil action to recover a civil penalty under this section shall be commenced by the Attorney General.

(f) Burden of proof

In a civil action to recover a civil penalty under this section, the Attorney General must establish the right to recovery by a preponderance of the evidence.

(g) Administrative subpoenas

(1) In general

For the purpose of conducting a civil investigation in contemplation of a civil proceeding under this section, the Attorney General may—

(A) administer oaths and affirmations;

(B) take evidence; and

(C) by subpoena, summon witnesses and require the production of any books, papers, correspondence, memoranda, or other records which the Attorney General deems relevant or material to the inquiry. Such subpoena may require the attendance of witnesses and the production of any such records from any place in the United States at any place in the United States designated by the Attorney General.

(2) Procedures applicable

The same procedures and limitations as are provided with respect to civil investigative demands in subsections (g), (h), and (j) of section 1968 of Title 18 apply with respect to a subpoena issued under this subsection. Process required by such subsections to be served upon the custodian shall be served on the Attorney General. Failure to comply with an order of the court to enforce such subpoena shall be punishable as contempt.

(3) Limitation

In the case of a subpoena for which the return date is less than 5 days after the date of service, no person shall be found in contempt for failure to comply by the return date if such person files a petition under paragraph (2) not later than 5 days after the date of service.

(h) Statute of limitations

A civil action under this section may not be commenced later than 10 years after the cause of action accrues.

§ 1833b. Comparability in compensation schedules—DFA § 152

(a) In general

The Federal Deposit Insurance Corporation, the Comptroller of the Currency, the National Credit Union Administration Board, the Federal Housing Finance Board, the Farm Credit Administration, and the Office of Thrift Supervision, in establishing and adjusting schedules of compensation and benefits which are to be determined solely by each agency under applicable provisions of law, shall inform the heads of the other agencies and the Congress of such compensation and benefits and shall seek to maintain comparability regarding compensation and benefits.

(b) Commodity futures trading Commission

In establishing and adjusting schedules of compensation and benefits for employees of the Commodity Futures Trading Commission under applicable provisions of law, the Commission shall—

(1) inform the heads of the agencies referred to in subsection (a) of this section and Congress of such compensation and benefits; and

(2) seek to maintain comparability with those agencies regarding compensation and benefits.

§ 1833c. Comptroller General audit and access to records

(a) Audit of agencies or other persons performing functions under banking laws

(1) In general

Except as provided in paragraph (2), all agencies, corporations, organizations, and other persons of any description which perform any function or activity under this Act, or any other Act which is amended by this Act, shall be subject to audit by the Comptroller General of the United States with respect to such function or activity.

(2) Exceptions

Paragraph (1) shall not apply to—

(A) any function or activity of the Board of Governors of the Federal Reserve System or the Federal Reserve banks that is described in any paragraph of section 714(b) of Title 31; and

(B) any function or activity of the Federal National Mortgage Association, except as provided in section 1723a(j) of this title.

(b) Audit of persons providing certain goods or services

All persons and organizations which, by contract, grant, or otherwise, provide goods or services to, or receive financial assistance from, any agency or other person performing functions or activities under this Act shall be subject to audit by the Comptroller General with respect to such provision of goods or services or receipt of financial assistance.

(c) Provisions applicable to audits under this section

(1) Nature and scope of audit

The Comptroller General shall determine the nature, scope, and terms and conditions of audits conducted under this section.

(2) Coordination with other provisions of law

The authority of the Comptroller General under this section shall be in addition to any audit authority available to the Comptroller General under other provisions of this Act or any other law.

(3) Rights of access, examination, and copying

The Comptroller General, and any duly authorized representative of the Comptroller

General, shall have access to, and the right to examine and copy, all records and other recorded information in any form, and to examine any property, within the possession or control of any agency or person which is subject to audit under this section which the Comptroller General deems relevant to an audit conducted under this section.

(4) Enforcement of right of access

The Comptroller General's right of access to information under this section shall be enforceable pursuant to section 716 of Title 31.

(5) Maintenance of confidential records

The provisions of section 716(e) of Title 31 shall apply to information obtained by the Comptroller General under this section.

§ 1833d. Repealed. Pub.L. 102–242, Title I, § 121(b), Dec. 19, 1991, 105 Stat. 2251

§ 1833e.   Equal opportunity

(a) In general

For purposes of this Act, Executive Order Numbered 11478, providing for equal employment opportunity in the Federal Government, shall apply to—

(1) the Comptroller of the Currency;

(2) the Director of the Office of Thrift Supervision;

(3) the Federal Housing Finance Agency;

(4) the Federal Deposit Insurance Corporation;

(5) the Thrift Depositor Protection Oversight Board of the Resolution Trust Corporation; and

(6) the Resolution Trust Corporation.

(b) Affirmative program for equal employment opportunity

For purposes of this Act, sections 1 and 2 of Executive Order Numbered 11478, providing for the adoption and implementation of equal employment opportunity, shall apply to the Federal National Mortgage Association and the Federal Home Loan Mortgage Corporation.

(c) Solicitation of contracts

The Federal Deposit Insurance Corporation, the Comptroller of the Currency, the Director of the Office of Thrift Supervision, the Federal Housing Finance Board, the Thrift Depositor Protection Oversight Board of the Resolution Trust Corpo-

ration, and the Resolution Trust Corporation shall each prescribe regulations to establish and oversee a minority outreach program within each such agency to ensure inclusion, to the maximum extent possible, of minorities and women, and entities owned by minorities and women, including financial institutions, investment banking firms, underwriters, accountants, and providers of legal services, in all contracts entered into by the agency with such persons or entities, public and private, in order to manage the institutions and their assets for which the agency is responsible or to perform such other functions authorized under any law applicable to such agency.

(d) Report to Congress

Before the end of the 180–day period beginning on August 9, 1989—

(1) the Federal Deposit Insurance Corporation;

(2) the Comptroller of the Currency;

(3) the Director of the Office of Thrift Supervision;

(4) the Federal Housing Finance Board;

(5) the Thrift Depositor Protection Oversight Board of the Resolution Trust Corporation;

(6) the Resolution Trust Corporation;

(7) the Federal Home Loan Mortgage Corporation; and

(8) the Federal National Mortgage Association,

shall each submit to the Congress a report containing a complete description of the actions taken by such agency pursuant to subsections (a) and (b) of this section and such recommendations for administrative and legislative action as each such agency may determine to be appropriate to carry out the purposes of such subsection.

§ 1834.   Reduced assessment rate for deposits attributable to lifeline accounts

(a) Qualification of lifeline accounts by Federal Reserve Board

(1) In general

The Board of Governors of the Federal Reserve System, and the Federal Deposit Insurance Corporation shall establish minimum requirements for accounts providing basic transaction services for consumers at insured depository institutions in order for such accounts to qualify as lifeline accounts for purposes of this section and section 1817(b)(2)(H) of this title.

(2) Factors to be considered

In determining the minimum requirements under paragraph (1) for lifeline accounts at insured depository institutions, the Board and the Corporation shall consider the following factors:

(A) Whether the account is available to provide basic transaction services for individuals who maintain a balance of less than $1,000 or such other amount which the Board may determine to be appropriate.

(B) Whether any service charges or fees to which the account is subject, if any, for routine transactions do not exceed a minimal amount.

(C) Whether any minimum balance or minimum opening requirement to which the account is subject, if any, is not more than a minimal amount.

(D) Whether checks, negotiable orders of withdrawal, or similar instruments for making payments or other transfers to third parties may be drawn on the account.

(E) Whether the depositor is permitted to make more than a minimal number of withdrawals from the account each month by any means described in subparagraph (D) or any other means.

(F) Whether a monthly statement itemizing all transactions for the monthly reporting period is made available to the depositor with respect to such account or a passbook is provided in which all transactions with respect to such account are recorded.

(G) Whether depositors are permitted access to tellers at the institution for conducting transactions with respect to such account.

(H) Whether other account relationships with the institution are required in order to open any such account.

(I) Whether individuals are required to meet any prerequisite which discriminates against low-income individuals in order to open such account.

(J) Such other factors as the Corporation may determine to be appropriate.

(3) Definitions

For purposes of this subsection—

(A) Corporation

The term "Corporation" means the Federal Deposit Insurance Corporation.

(B) Insured depository institution

The term "insured depository institution" has the meaning given to such term in section 1813(c)(2) of this title.

(C) Lifeline account

The term "lifeline account" means any transaction account (as defined in section 461(b)(1)(C) of this title) which meets the minimum requirements established by the Corporation under this subsection.

(b) Omitted

(c) Availability of funds

The provisions of this section shall not take effect until appropriations are specifically provided in advance. There are hereby authorized to be appropriated such sums as may be necessary to carry out the provisions of this section.

§ 1834a. Assessment credits for qualifying activities relating to distressed communities

(a) Determination of credits for increases in community enterprise activities

(1) In general

The Community Enterprise Assessment Credit Board established under subsection (d) of this section shall issue guidelines for insured depository institutions eligible under this subsection for any community enterprise assessment credit with respect to any semiannual period. Such guidelines shall—

(A) designate the eligibility requirements for any institution meeting applicable capital standards to receive an assessment credit under section 1817(b)(7) of this title; and

(B) determine the community enterprise assessment credit available to any eligible institution under paragraph (3).

(2) Qualifying activities

An insured depository institution may apply for for any community enterprise assessment credit for any semiannual period for—

(A) the amount, during such period, of new originations of qualified loans and other assistance provided for low-and moderate-income persons in distressed communities, or enterprises integrally involved with such neighborhoods, which the Board determines are qualified to be taken into account for purposes of this subsection;

(B) the amount, during such period, of deposits accepted from persons domiciled in the distressed community, at any office of the institution (including any branch) located in any qualified distressed community, and new originations of any loans and other financial assistance made within that community, except that in no case shall the credit for deposits at any institution or branch exceed the credit for loans and other financial assistance by the bank or branch in the distressed community; and

(C) any increase during the period in the amount of new equity investments in community development financial institutions.

(3) Amount of assessment credit

The amount of any community enterprise assessment credit available under section 1817(b)(7) of this title for any insured depository institution, or a qualified portion thereof, for any semiannual period shall be the amount which is equal to 5 percent, in the case of an institution which does not meet the community development organization requirements under section 1834b of this title, and 15 percent, in the case of an institution, or a qualified portion thereof, which meets such requirements (or any percentage designated under paragraph (5)) of the sum of—

(A) for the first full semiannual period in which community enterprise assessment credits are available, the sum of—

(i) the amounts of assets described in paragraph (2)(A); and

(ii) the amounts of deposits, loans, and other financial assistance described in paragraph (2)(B); and

(B) for any subsequent semiannual period, the sum of—

(i) any increase during such period in the amount of assets described in paragraph (2)(A) that has been deemed eligible for credit by the Board; and

(ii) any increase during such period in the amounts of deposits, loans, and other financial assistance described in paragraph (2)(B)

that has been deemed eligible for credit by the Board.

(4) Determination of qualified loans and other financial assistance

Except as provided in paragraph (6), the types of loans and other assistance which the Board may determine to be qualified to be taken into account under paragraph (2)(A) for purposes of the community enterprise assessment credit, may include the following:

(A) Loans insured or guaranteed by the Secretary of Housing and Urban Development, the Secretary of the Department of Veterans Affairs, the Administrator of the Small Business Administration, and the Secretary of Agriculture.

(B) Loans or financing provided in connection with activities assisted by the Administrator of the Small Business Administration or any small business investment company and investments in small business investment companies.

(C) Loans or financing provided in connection with any neighborhood housing service program assisted under the Neighborhood Reinvestment Corporation Act [42 U.S.C.A. § 8101 et seq.].

(D) Loans or financing provided in connection with any activities assisted under the community development block grant program under title I of the Housing and Community Development Act of 1974 [42 U.S.C.A. § 5301 et seq.].

(E) Loans or financing provided in connection with activities assisted under title II of the Cranston–Gonzalez National Affordable Housing Act [42 U.S.C.A. § 12721 et seq.].

(F) Loans or financing provided in connection with a homeownership program assisted under title III of the United States Housing Act of 1937 [42 U.S.C.A. § 1437aaa et seq.] or subtitle B or C of title IV of the Cranston-Gonzalez National Affordable Housing Act [42 U.S.C.A. § 12871 et seq. or 12891 et seq.].

(G) Financial assistance provided through community development corporations.

(H) Federal and State programs providing interest rate assistance for homeowners.

(I) Extensions of credit to nonprofit developers or purchasers of low-income housing and small business developments.

(J) In the case of members of any Federal home loan bank, participation in the community investment fund program established by the Federal home loan banks.

(K) Conventional mortgages targeted to low- or moderate-income persons.

(L) Loans made for the purpose of developing or supporting—

(i) commercial facilities that enhance revitalization, community stability, or job creation and retention efforts;

(ii) business creation and expansion efforts that—

(I) create or retain jobs for low-income people;

(II) enhance the availability of products and services to low-income people; or

(III) create or retain businesses owned by low-income people or residents of a targeted area;

(iii) community facilities that provide benefits to low-income people or enhance community stability;

(iv) home ownership opportunities that are affordable to low-income households;

(v) rental housing that is principally affordable to low-income households; and

(vi) other activities deemed appropriate by the Board.

(M) The provision of technical assistance to residents of qualified distressed communities in managing their personal finances through consumer education programs either sponsored or offered by insured depository institutions.

(N) The provision of technical assistance and consulting services to newly formed small businesses located in qualified distressed communities.

(O) The provision of technical assistance to, or servicing the loans of low- or moderate-income homeowners and homeowners located in qualified distressed communities.

(5) Adjustment of percentage

The Board may increase or decrease the percentage referred to in paragraph (3)(A) for determining the amount of any community enterprise assessment credit pursuant to such paragraph, except that the percentage established for insured depository institutions which meet the community development organization requirements under section 1834b of this title shall not be less than 3 times the amount of the percentage applicable for insured depository institutions which do not meet such requirements.

(6) Certain investments not eligible to be taken into account

Loans, financial assistance, and equity investments made by any insured depository institution that are not the result of originations by the institution shall not be taken into account for purposes of determining the amount of any credit pursuant to this subsection.

(7) Quantitative analysis of technical assistance

The Board may establish guidelines for analyzing the technical assistance described in subparagraphs (M), (N), and (O) of paragraph (4) for the purpose of quantifying the results of such assistance in determining the amount of any community assessment credit under this subsection.

(b) "Qualified distressed community" defined

(1) In general

For purposes of this section, the term "qualified distressed community" means any neighborhood or community which—

(A) meets the minimum area requirements under paragraph (3) and the eligibility requirements of paragraph (4); and

(B) is designated as a distressed community by any insured depository institution in accordance with paragraph (2) and such designation is not disapproved under such paragraph.

(2) Designation requirements

(A) Notice of designation

(i) Notice to agency

Upon designating an area as a qualified distressed community, an insured depository institution shall notify the appropriate Federal banking agency of the designation.

(ii) Public notice

Upon the effective date of any designation of an area as a qualified distressed community, an insured depository institution shall publish a notice of such designation in major newspapers and other community publications which serve such area.

(B) Agency duties relating to designations

(i) Providing information

At the request of any insured depository institution, the appropriate Federal banking agency shall provide to the institution appropriate information to assist the institution to identify and designate a qualified distressed community.

(ii) Period for disapproval

Any notice received by the appropriate Federal banking agency from any insured depository institution under subparagraph (A)(i) shall take effect at the end of the 90–day period beginning on the date such notice is received unless written notice of the approval or disapproval of the application by the agency is provided to the institution before the end of such period.

(3) Minimum area requirements

For purposes of this subsection, an area meets the requirements of this paragraph if—

(A) the area is within the jurisdiction of 1 unit of general local government;

(B) the boundary of the area is contiguous; and

(C) the area—

(i) has a population, as determined by the most recent census data available, of not less than—

(I) 4,000, if any portion of such area is located within a metropolitan statistical area (as designated by the Director of the Office of Management and Budget) with a population of 50,000 or more; or

(II) 1,000, in any other case; or

(ii) is entirely within an Indian reservation (as determined by the Secretary of the Interior).

(4) Eligibility requirements

For purposes of this subsection, an area meets the requirements of this paragraph if the following criteria are met:

(A) At least 30 percent of the residents residing in the area have incomes which are less than the national poverty level.

(B) The unemployment rate for the area is 1 1/2 times greater than the national average (as determined by the Bureau of Labor Statistics' most recent figures).

(C) Such additional eligibility requirements as the Board may, in its discretion, deem necessary to carry out the provisions of this subtitle.

(c) Omitted

(d) Community Enterprise Assessment Credit Board

(1) Establishment

There is hereby established the "Community Enterprise Assessment Credit Board".

(2) Number and appointment

The Board shall be composed of 5 members as follows:

(A) The Secretary of the Treasury or a designee of the Secretary.

(B) The Secretary of Housing and Urban Development or a designee of the Secretary.

(C) The Chairperson of the Federal Deposit Insurance Corporation or a designee of the Chairperson.

(D) 2 individuals appointed by the President from among individuals who represent community organizations.

(3) Terms

(A) Appointed members

Each appointed member shall be appointed for a term of 5 years.

(B) Interim appointment

Any member appointed to fill a vacancy occurring before the expiration of the term to which such member's predecessor was appointed shall be appointed only for the remainder of such term.

(C) Continuation of service

Each appointed member may continue to serve after the expiration of the period to which such member was appointed until a successor has been appointed.

(4) Chairperson

The Secretary of the Treasury shall serve as the Chairperson of the Board.

(5) No pay

No members of the Commission may receive any pay for service on the Board.

(6) Travel expenses

Each member shall receive travel expenses, including per diem in lieu of subsistence, in accordance with sections 5702 and 5703 of Title 5.

(7) Meetings

The Board shall meet at the call of the Chairperson or a majority of the Board's members.

(e) Duties of the Board

(1) Procedure for determining community enterprise assessment credits

The Board shall establish procedures for accepting and considering applications by insured depository institutions under subsection (a)(1) of this section for community enterprise assessment credits and making determinations with respect to such applications.

(2) Notice to FDIC

The Board shall notify the applicant and the Federal Deposit Insurance Corporation of any determination of the Board with respect to any application referred to in paragraph (1) in sufficient time for the Corporation to include the amount of such credit in the computation of the semiannual assessment to which such credit is applicable.

(f) Availability of funds

The provisions of this section shall not take effect until appropriations are specifically provided in advance. There are hereby authorized to be appropriated such sums as may be necessary to carry out the provisions of this section.

(g) Prohibition on double funding for same activities

No community development financial institution may receive a community enterprise assessment credit if such institution, either directly or through a community partnership—

(1) has received assistance within the preceding 12–month period, or has an application for

assistance pending, under section 4704 of this title; or

(2) has ever received assistance, under section 4707 of this title, for the same activity during the same semi-annual period for which the institution seeks a community enterprise assessment credit under this section.

(h) Priority of awards

(1) Qualifying loans and services

(A) In general

If the amount of funds appropriated for purposes of carrying out this section for any fiscal year are insufficient to award the amount of assessment credits for which insured depository institutions have applied and are eligible under this section, the Board shall, in awarding community enterprise assessment credits for qualifying activities under subparagraphs (A) and (B) of subsection (a)(2) of this section for any semiannual period for which such appropriation is available, determine which institutions shall receive an award.

(B) Priority for support of efforts of CDFI

The Board shall give priority to institutions that have supported the efforts of community development financial institutions in the qualified distressed community.

(C) Other factors

The Board may also consider the following factors:

(i) Degree of difficulty

The degree of difficulty in carrying out the activities that form the basis for the institution's application.

(ii) Community impact

The extent to which the activities that form the basis for the institution's application have benefitted the qualified distressed community.

(iii) Innovation

The degree to which the activities that form the basis for the institution's application have incorporated innovative methods for meeting community needs.

(iv) Leverage

The leverage ratio between the dollar amount of the activities that form the basis for the institution's application and the amount of the assessment credit calculated in accordance with this section for such activities.

(v) Size

The amount of total assets of the institution.

(vi) New entry

Whether the institution had provided financial services in the designated distressed community before such semiannual period.

(vii) Need for subsidy

The degree to which the qualified activity which forms the basis for the application needs enhancement through an assessment credit.

(viii) Extent of distress in community

The degree of poverty and unemployment in the designated distressed community, the proportion of the total population of the community which are low-income families and unrelated individuals, and the extent of other adverse economic conditions in such community.

(2) Qualifying investments

If the amount of funds appropriated for purposes of carrying out this section for any fiscal year are insufficient to award the amount of assessment credits for which insured depository institutions have applied and are eligible under this section, the Board shall, in awarding community enterprise assessment credits for qualifying activities under subsection (a)(2)(C) of this section for any semiannual period for which such appropriation is available, determine which institutions shall receive an award based on the leverage ratio between the dollar amount of the activities that form the basis for the institution's application and the amount of the assessment credit calculated in accordance with this section for such activities.

(i) Determination of amount of assessment credit

Notwithstanding any other provision of this section, the determination of the amount of any community enterprise assessment credit under subsection (a)(3) of this section for any insured depository institution for any semiannual period shall be made solely at the discretion of the Board. No insured depository institution shall be awarded community enterprise assessment cred-

its for any semiannual period in excess of an amount determined by the Board.

(j) Definitions

For purposes of this section—

(1) Appropriate Federal banking agency

The term "appropriate Federal banking agency" has the meaning given to such term in section 1813(q) of this title.

(2) Board

The term "Board" means the Community Enterprise Assessment Credit Board established under the amendment made by subsection (d) of this section.

(3) Insured depository institution

The term "insured depository institution" has the meaning given to such term in section 1813(c)(2) of this title.

(4) Community development financial institution

The term "community development financial institution" has the same meaning as in section 4702(5) of this title.

(5) Affiliate

The term "affiliate" has the same meaning as in section 1841 of this title.

§ 1834b. Community development organizations

(a) Community development organizations described

For purposes of this subtitle, any insured depository institution, or a qualified portion thereof, shall be treated as meeting the community development organization requirements of this section if—

(1) the institution—

(A) is a community development bank, or controls any community development bank, which meets the requirements of subsection (b) of this section;

(B) controls any community development corporation, or maintains any community development unit within the institution, which meets the requirements of subsection (c) of this section;

(C) invests in accounts in any community development credit union designated as a low-income credit union, subject to restrictions established for such credit unions by the National Credit Union Administration Board; or

(D) invests in a community development organization jointly controlled by two or more institutions;

(2) except in the case of an institution which is a community development bank, the amount of the capital invested, in the form of debt or equity, by the institution in the community development organization referred to in paragraph (1) (or, in the case of any community development unit, the amount which the institution irrevocably makes available to such unit for the purposes described in paragraph (3)) is not less than the greater of—

(A) 1/2 of 1 percent of the capital, as defined by generally accepted accounting principles, of the institution; or

(B) the sum of the amounts invested in such community development organization; and

(3) the community development organization provides loans for residential mortgages, home improvement, and community development and other financial services, other than financing for the purchase of automobiles or extension of credit under any open-end credit plan (as defined in section 1602(i) of Title 15), to low-and moderate-income persons, nonprofit organizations, and small businesses located in qualified distressed communities in a manner consistent with the intent of this subtitle.

(b) Community development bank requirements

A community development bank meets the requirements of this subsection if—

(1) the community development bank has a 15–member advisory board designated as the "Community Investment Board" and consisting entirely of community leaders who—

(A) shall be appointed initially by the board of directors of the community development bank and thereafter by the Community Investment Board from nominations received from the community; and

(B) are appointed for a single term of 2 years, except that, of the initial members appointed to the Community Investment Board, 1/3 shall be appointed for a term of 8

months, 1/3 shall be appointed for a term of 16 months, and 1/3 shall be appointed for a term of 24 months, as designated by the board of directors of the community development bank at the time of the appointment;

(2) 1/3 of the members of the community development bank's board of directors are appointed from among individuals nominated by the Community Investment Board; and

(3) the bylaws of the community development bank require that the board of directors of the bank meet with the Community Investment Board at least once every 3 months.

(c) Community development corporation requirements

Any community development corporation, or community development unit within any insured depository institution meets the requirements of this subsection if the corporation or unit provides the same or greater, as determined by the appropriate Federal banking agency, community participation in the activities of such corporation or unit as would be provided by a Community Investment Board under subsection (b) of this section if such corporation or unit were a community development bank.

(d) Adequate dispersal requirement

The appropriate Federal banking agency may approve the establishment of a community development organization under this subtitle only upon finding that the distressed community is not adequately served by an existing community development organization.

(e) Definitions

For purposes of this section—

(1) Community development bank

The term "community development bank" means any depository institution (as defined in section 1813(c)(1) of this title).

(2) Community development organization

The term "community development organization" means any community development bank, community development corporation, community development unit within any insured depository institution, or community development credit union.

(3) Low-and moderate-income persons

The term "low-and moderate-income persons" has the meaning given such term in section 5302(a)(20) of Title 42.

(4) Nonprofit organization; small business

The terms "nonprofit organization" and "small business" have the meanings given to such terms by regulations which the appropriate Federal banking agency shall prescribe for purposes of this section.

(5) Qualified distressed community

The term "qualified distressed community" has the meaning given to such term in section 1834a(b) of this title.

§ 1835. Insured depository institution capital requirements for transfers of small business obligations

(a) Accounting principles

The accounting principles applicable to the transfer of a small business loan or a lease of personal property with recourse contained in reports or statements required to be filed with Federal banking agencies by a qualified insured depository institution shall be consistent with generally accepted accounting principles.

(b) Capital and reserve requirements

With respect to the transfer of a small business loan or lease of personal property with recourse that is a sale under generally accepted accounting principles, each qualified insured depository institution shall—

(1) establish and maintain a reserve equal to an amount sufficient to meet the reasonable estimated liability of the institution under the recourse arrangement; and

(2) include, for purposes of applicable capital standards and other capital measures, only the amount of the retained recourse in the risk-weighted assets of the institution.

(c) Qualified institutions criteria

An insured depository institution is a qualified insured depository institution for purposes of this section if, without regard to the accounting principles or capital requirements referred to in subsections (a) and (b) of this section, the institution is—

(1) well capitalized; or

(2) with the approval, by regulation or order, of the appropriate Federal banking agency, adequately capitalized.

(d) Aggregate amount of recourse

The total outstanding amount of recourse retained by a qualified insured depository institution with respect to transfers of small business loans and leases of personal property under subsections (a) and (b) of this section shall not exceed—

(1) 15 percent of the risk-based capital of the institution; or

(2) such greater amount, as established by the appropriate Federal banking agency by regulation or order.

(e) Institutions that cease to be qualified or exceed aggregate limits

If an insured depository institution ceases to be a qualified insured depository institution or exceeds the limits under subsection (d) of this section, this section shall remain applicable to any transfers of small business loans or leases of personal property that occurred during the time that the institution was qualified and did not exceed such limit.

(f) Prompt corrective action not affected

The capital of an insured depository institution shall be computed without regard to this section in determining whether the institution is adequately capitalized, undercapitalized, significantly undercapitalized, or critically undercapitalized under section 1831o of this title.

(g) Regulations required

Not later than 180 days after September 23, 1994 each appropriate Federal banking agency shall promulgate final regulations implementing this section.

(h) Alternative system permitted

(1) In general

At the discretion of the appropriate Federal banking agency, this section shall not apply if the regulations of the agency provide that the aggregate amount of capital and reserves required with respect to the transfer of small business loans and leases of personal property with recourse does not exceed the aggregate amount of capital and reserves that would be required under subsection (b) of this section.

(2) Existing transactions not affected

Notwithstanding paragraph (1), this section shall remain in effect with respect to transfers of small business loans and leases of personal property with recourse by qualified insured depository institutions occurring before the effective date of regulations referred to in paragraph (1).

(i) Definitions

For purposes of this section—

(1) the term "adequately capitalized" has the same meaning as in section 1831o(b) of this title;

(2) the term "appropriate Federal banking agency" has the same meaning as in section 1813 of this title;

(3) the term "capital standards" has the same meaning as in section 1831o(c) of this title;

(4) the term "Federal banking agencies" has the same meaning as in section 1813 of this title;

(5) the term "insured depository institution" has the same meaning as in section 1813 of this title;

(6) the term "other capital measures" has the meaning as in section 1831o(c) of this title;

(7) the term "recourse" has the meaning given to such term under generally accepted accounting principles;

(8) the term "small business" means a business that meets the criteria for a small business concern established by the Small Business Administration under section 632(a) of Title 15; and

(9) the term "well capitalized" has the same meaning as in section 1831o(b) of this title.

§ 1835a. Prohibition against deposit production offices

(a) Regulations

The appropriate Federal banking agencies shall prescribe uniform regulations effective June 1, 1997, which prohibit any out-of-State bank from using any authority to engage in interstate branching pursuant to this title, or any amendment made by this title to any other provision of law, primarily for the purpose of deposit production.

(b) Guidelines for meeting credit needs

Regulations issued under subsection (a) of this section shall include guidelines to ensure that interstate branches operated by an out-of-State bank in a host State are reasonably helping to meet the credit needs of the communities which the branches serve.

(c) Limitation on out-of-State loans

(1) Limitation

Regulations issued under subsection (a) of this section shall require that, beginning no earlier than 1 year after establishment or acquisition of an interstate branch or branches in a host State by an out-of-State bank, if the appropriate Federal banking agency for the out-of-State bank determines that the bank's level of lending in the host State relative to the deposits from the host State (as reasonably determinable from available information including the agency's sampling of the bank's loan files during an examination or such data as is otherwise available) is less than half the average of total loans in the host State relative to total deposits from the host State (as determinable from relevant sources) for all banks the home State of which is such State—

(A) the appropriate Federal banking agency for the out-of-State bank shall review the loan portfolio of the bank and determine whether the bank is reasonably helping to meet the credit needs of the communities served by the bank in the host State; and

(B) if the agency determines that the out-of-State bank is not reasonably helping to meet those needs—

(i) the agency may order that an interstate branch or branches of such bank in the host State be closed unless the bank provides reasonable assurances to the satisfaction of the appropriate Federal banking agency that the bank has an acceptable plan that will reasonably help to meet the credit needs of the communities served by the bank in the host State, and

(ii) the out-of-State bank may not open a new interstate branch in the host State unless the bank provides reasonable assurances to the satisfaction of the appropriate Federal banking agency that the bank will reasonably help to meet the credit needs of the community that the new branch will serve.

(2) Considerations

In making a determination under paragraph (1)(A), the appropriate Federal banking agency shall consider—

(A) whether the interstate branch or branches of the out-of-State bank were formerly part of a failed or failing depository institution;

(B) whether the interstate branch was acquired under circumstances where there was a low loan-to-deposit ratio because of the nature of the acquired institution's business or loan portfolio;

(C) whether the interstate branch or branches of the out-of-State bank have a higher concentration of commercial or credit card lending, trust services, or other specialized activities;

(D) the ratings received by the out-of-State bank under the Community Reinvestment Act of 1977 [12 U.S.C.A. § 2901 et seq.];

(E) economic conditions, including the level of loan demand, within the communities served by the interstate branch or branches of the out-of-State bank; and

(F) the safe and sound operation and condition of the out-of-State bank.

(3) Branch closing procedure

(A) Notice required

Before exercising any authority under paragraph (1)(B)(i), the appropriate Federal banking agency shall issue to the bank a notice of the agency's intention to close an interstate branch or branches and shall schedule a hearing.

(B) Hearing

Section 1818(h) of this title shall apply to any proceeding brought under this paragraph.

(d) Application

This section shall apply with respect to any interstate branch established or acquired in a host State pursuant to this title or any amendment made by this title to any other provision of law.

(e) Definitions

For the purposes of this section, the following definitions shall apply:

(1) Appropriate Federal banking agency, bank, State, and State bank

The terms "appropriate Federal banking agency", "bank", "State", and "State bank" have the same meanings as in section 1813 of this title.

(2) Home State

The term "home State" means—

(A) in the case of a national bank, the State in which the main office of the bank is located; and

(B) in the case of a State bank, the State by which the bank is chartered.

(3) Host State

The term "host State" means a State in which a bank establishes a branch other than the home State of the bank.

(4) Interstate branch

The term "interstate branch" means a branch established pursuant to this title or any amendment made by this title to any other provision of law and any branch of a bank controlled by an out-of-State bank holding company (as defined in section 1841(o)(7) of this title).

(5) Out-of-State bank

The term "out-of-State bank" means, with respect to any State, a bank the home State of which is another State and, for purposes of this section, includes a foreign bank, the home State of which is another State.

CHAPTER 17. BANK HOLDING COMPANIES
12 U.S.C.A. §§ 1841–1850

CHAPTER 17. BANK HOLDING COMPANIES

§ 1841. Definitions—DFA §§ 623, 628

(a) (1) Except as provided in paragraph (5) of this subsection, "bank holding company" means any company which has control over any bank or over any company that is or becomes a bank holding company by virtue of this chapter.

(2) Any company has control over a bank or over any company if—

    (A) the company directly or indirectly or acting through one or more other persons owns, controls, or has power to vote 25 per centum or more of any class of voting securities of the bank or company;

    (B) the company controls in any manner the election of a majority of the directors or trustees of the bank or company; or

    (C) the Board determines, after notice and opportunity for hearing, that the company directly or indirectly exercises a controlling influence over the management or policies of the bank or company.

(3) For the purposes of any proceeding under paragraph (2)(C) of this subsection, there is a presumption that any company which directly or indirectly owns, controls, or has power to vote less than 5 per centum of any class of voting securities of a given bank or company does not have control over that bank or company.

(4) In any administrative or judicial proceeding under this chapter, other than a proceeding under paragraph (2)(C) of this subsection, a company may not be held to have had control over any given bank or company at any given time unless that company, at the time in question, directly or indirectly owned, controlled, or had power to vote 5 per centum or more of any class of voting securities of the bank or company, or had already been found to have control in a proceeding under paragraph (2)(C).

(5) Notwithstanding any other provision of this subsection—

    (A) No bank and no company owning or controlling voting shares of a bank is a bank holding company by virtue of its ownership or control of shares in a fiduciary capacity, except as provided in paragraphs (2) and (3) of subsection (g) of this section. For the purpose of the preceding sentence, bank shares shall not be deemed to have been acquired in a fiduciary capacity if the acquiring bank or company has sole discretionary authority to exercise voting rights with respect thereto; except that this limitation is applicable in the case of a bank or company acquiring such shares prior to December 31, 1970, only if the bank or company has the right consistent with its obligations under the instrument, agreement, or other arrangement establishing the fiduciary relationship to divest itself of such voting rights and fails to exercise that right to divest within a reasonable period not to exceed one year after December 31, 1970.

    (B) No company is a bank holding company by virtue of its ownership or control of shares acquired by it in connection with its underwriting of securities if such shares are held only for such period of time as will permit the sale thereof on a reasonable basis.

    (C) No company formed for the sole purpose of participating in a proxy solicitation is a bank holding company by virtue of its control of voting rights of shares acquired in the course of such solicitation.

    (D) No company is a bank holding company by virtue of its ownership or control of shares acquired in securing or collecting a debt previously contracted in good faith, until two years after the date of acquisition. The Board is authorized upon application by a company to extend, from time to time for not more than one year at a time, the two-year period referred to herein for disposing of any shares acquired by a company in the regular course of securing or collecting a debt previously contracted in good faith, if, in the Board's judgment, such an extension would not be detrimental to the public interest, but no such extension shall in the aggregate exceed three years.

    (E) No company is a bank holding company by virtue of its ownership or control of any State-chartered bank or trust company which—

(i) is wholly owned by 1 or more thrift institutions or savings banks; and

(ii) is restricted to accepting—

(I) deposits from thrift institutions or savings banks;

(II) deposits arising out of the corporate business of the thrift institutions or savings banks that own the bank or trust company; or

(III) deposits of public moneys.

(F) No trust company or mutual savings bank which is an insured bank under the Federal Deposit Insurance Act [12 U.S.C.A. § 1811 et seq.] is a bank holding company by virtue of its direct or indirect ownership or control of one bank located in the same State, if (i) such ownership or control existed on December 31, 1970, and is specifically authorized by applicable State law, and (ii) the trust company or mutual savings bank does not after that date acquire an interest in any company that, together with any other interest it holds in that company, will exceed 5 per centum of any class of the voting shares of that company, except that this limitation shall not be applicable to investments of the trust company or mutual savings bank, direct and indirect, which are otherwise in accordance with the limitations applicable to national banks under section 24 of this title.

(6) For the purposes of this chapter, any successor to a bank holding company shall be deemed to be a bank holding company from the date on which the predecessor company became a bank holding company.

(b) "Company" means any corporation, partnership, business trust, association, or similar organization, or any other trust unless by its terms it must terminate within twenty-five years or not later than twenty-one years and ten months after the death of individuals living on the effective date of the trust but shall not include any corporation the majority of the shares of which are owned by the United States or by any State, and shall not include a qualified family partnership. "Company covered in 1970" means a company which becomes a bank holding company as a result of the enactment of the Bank Holding Company Act Amendments of 1970 and which would have been a bank holding company on June 30, 1968, if those amendments had been enacted on that date.

(c) Bank defined

For purposes of this chapter—

(1) In general

Except as provided in paragraph (2), the term "bank" means any of the following:

(A) An insured bank as defined in section 1813(h) of this title.

(B) An institution organized under the laws of the United States, any State of the United States, the District of Columbia, any territory of the United States, Puerto Rico, Guam, American Samoa, or the Virgin Islands which both—

(i) accepts demand deposits or deposits that the depositor may withdraw by check or similar means for payment to third parties or others; and

(ii) is engaged in the business of making commercial loans.

(2) Exceptions

The term "bank" does not include any of the following:

(A) A foreign bank which would be a bank within the meaning of paragraph (1) solely because such bank has an insured or uninsured branch in the United States.

(B) An insured institution (as defined in subsection (j) of this section).

(C) An organization that does not do business in the United States except as an incident to its activities outside the United States.

(D) An institution that functions solely in a trust or fiduciary capacity, if—

(i) all or substantially all of the deposits of such institution are in trust funds and are received in a bona fide fiduciary capacity;

(ii) no deposits of such institution which are insured by the Federal Deposit Insurance Corporation are offered or marketed by or through an affiliate of such institution;

(iii) such institution does not accept demand deposits or deposits that the depositor may withdraw by check or similar means for payment to third parties or others or make commercial loans; and

(iv) such institution does not—

(I) obtain payment or payment related services from any Federal Reserve bank, including any service referred to in section 248a of this title; or

(II) exercise discount or borrowing privileges pursuant to section 461(b)(7) of this title.

(E) A credit union (as described in section 461(b)(1)(A)(iv) of this title).

(F) An institution, including an institution that accepts collateral for extensions of credit by holding deposits under $100,000, and by other means which—

(i) engages only in credit card operations;

(ii) does not accept demand deposits or deposits that the depositor may withdraw by check or similar means for payment to third parties or others;

(iii) does not accept any savings or time deposit of less than $100,000;

(iv) maintains only one office that accepts deposits; and

(v) does not engage in the business of making commercial loans.

(G) An organization operating under section 25 [12 U.S.C.A. § 601 et seq.] or section 25(a) [12 U.S.C.A. § 611 et seq.] of the Federal Reserve Act.

(H) An industrial loan company, industrial bank, or other similar institution which is—

(i) an institution organized under the laws of a State which, on March 5, 1987, had in effect or had under consideration in such State's legislature a statute which required or would require such institution to obtain insurance under the Federal Deposit Insurance Act [12 U.S.C.A. § 1811 et seq.]—

(I) which does not accept demand deposits that the depositor may withdraw by check or similar means for payment to third parties;

(II) which has total assets of less than $100,000,000; or

(III) the control of which is not acquired by any company after August 10, 1987; or

(ii) an institution which does not, directly, indirectly, or through an affiliate, engage in any activity in which it was not lawfully engaged as of March 5, 1987, except that this subparagraph shall cease to apply to any institution which permits any overdraft (including any intraday overdraft), or which incurs any such overdraft in such institu-

tion's account at a Federal Reserve bank, on behalf of an affiliate if such overdraft is not the result of an inadvertent computer or accounting error that is beyond the control of both the institution and the affiliate, or that is otherwise permissible for a bank controlled by a company described in section 1843(f)(1) of this title.

(I), (J) Repealed. Pub.L. 109–351, Title VII, § 727(a)(1), Oct. 13, 2006, 120 Stat. 2003

(3) Repealed. Pub.L. 108–386, § 8(c)(1), Oct. 30, 2004, 118 Stat. 2231

(d) "Subsidiary", with respect to a specified bank holding company, means (1) any company 25 per centum or more of whose voting shares (excluding shares owned by the United States or by any company wholly owned by the United States) is directly or indirectly owned or controlled by such bank holding company, or is held by it with power to vote; (2) any company the election of a majority of whose directors is controlled in any manner by such bank holding company; or (3) any company with respect to the management of policies of which such bank holding company has the power, directly or indirectly, to exercise a controlling influence, as determined by the Board, after notice and opportunity for hearing.

(e) The term "successor" shall include any company which acquires directly or indirectly from a bank holding company shares of any bank, when and if the relationship between such company and the bank holding company is such that the transaction effects no substantial change in the control of the bank or beneficial ownership of such shares of such bank. The Board may, by regulation, further define the term "successor" to the extent necessary to prevent evasion of the purposes of this chapter.

(f) "Board" means the Board of Governors of the Federal Reserve System.

(g) For the purposes of this chapter—

(1) shares owned or controlled by any subsidiary of a bank holding company shall be deemed to be indirectly owned or controlled by such bank holding company; and

(2) shares held or controlled directly or indirectly by trustees for the benefit of (A) a company, (B) the shareholders or members of a company, or (C) the employees (whether exclu-

sively or not) of a company, shall be deemed to be controlled by such company, unless the Board determines that such treatment is not appropriate in light of the facts and circumstances of the case and the purposes of this chapter.

(h) (1) Except as provided by paragraph (2), the application of this chapter and of section 371c of this title shall not be affected by the fact that a transaction takes place wholly or partly outside the United States or that a company is organized or operates outside the United States.

(2) Except as provided in paragraph (3), the prohibitions of section 1843 of this title shall not apply to shares of any company organized under the laws of a foreign country (or to shares held by such company in any company engaged in the same general line of business as the investor company or in a business related to the business of the investor company) that is principally engaged in business outside the United States if such shares are held or acquired by a bank holding company organized under the laws of a foreign country that is principally engaged in the banking business outside the United States. For the purpose of this subsection, the term "section 2(h)(2) company" means any company whose shares are held pursuant to this paragraph.

(3) Nothing in paragraph (2) authorizes a section 2(h)(2) company to engage in (or acquire or hold more than 5 percent of the outstanding shares of any class of voting securities of a company engaged in) any banking, securities, insurance, or other financial activities, as defined by the Board, in the United States. This paragraph does not prohibit a section 2(h)(2) company from holding shares that were lawfully acquired before August 10, 1987.

(4) No domestic office or subsidiary of a bank holding company or subsidiary thereof holding shares of a section 2(h)(2) company may extend credit to a domestic office or subsidiary of such section 2(h)(2) company on terms more favorable than those afforded similar borrowers in the United States.

(5) No domestic banking office or bank subsidiary of a bank holding company that controls a section 2(h)(2) company may offer or market products or services of such section 2(h)(2) company, or permit its products or services to be offered or marketed by or through such section 2(h)(2) company, unless such products or services were being so offered or marketed as of March 5, 1987, and then only in the same manner in which they were being offered or marketed as of that date.

(i) Thrift institution

For purposes of this chapter, the term "thrift institution" means—

(1) any domestic building and loan or savings and loan association;

(2) any cooperative bank without capital stock organized and operated for mutual purposes and without profit;

(3) any Federal savings bank; and

(4) any State-chartered savings bank the holding company of which is registered pursuant to section 1730a of this title.

(j) Definition of savings associations and related term

The term "savings association" or "insured institution" means—

(1) any Federal savings association or Federal savings bank;

(2) any building and loan association, savings and loan association, homestead association, or cooperative bank if such association or cooperative bank is a member of the Savings Association Insurance Fund; and

(3) any savings bank or cooperative bank which is deemed by the Director of the Office of Thrift Supervision to be a savings association under section 1467a(1) of this title.

(k) Affiliate

For purposes of this chapter, the term "affiliate" means any company that controls, is controlled by, or is under common control with another company.

(l) Savings bank holding company

For purposes of this chapter, the term "savings bank holding company" means any company which controls one or more qualified savings banks if the aggregate total assets of such savings banks constitute, upon formation of the holding company and at all times thereafter, at least 70 percent of the total assets of such company.

(m) Repealed. Pub.L. 109–351, Title VII, § 727(a)(2), Oct. 13, 2006, 120 Stat. 2003

(n) Incorporated definitions

For purposes of this chapter, the terms "depository institution", "insured depository institution", "appropriate Federal banking agency", "default", "in danger of default", and "State bank supervisor" have the same meanings as in section 1813 of this title.

(o) Other definitions

For purposes of this chapter, the following definitions shall apply:

(1) Capital terms

(A) Insured depository institutions

With respect to insured depository institutions, the terms "well capitalized", "adequately capitalized", and "undercapitalized" have the same meanings as in section 1831*o* of this title.

(B) Bank holding company

(i) Adequately capitalized

With respect to a bank holding company, the term "adequately capitalized" means a level of capitalization which meets or exceeds all applicable Federal regulatory capital standards.

(ii) Well capitalized

A bank holding company is "well capitalized" if it meets the required capital levels for well capitalized bank holding companies established by the Board.

(C) Other capital terms

The terms "Tier 1" and "risk-weighted assets" have the meanings given those terms in the capital guidelines or regulations established by the Board for bank holding companies.

(2) Antitrust laws

Except as provided in section 1849 of this title, the term "antitrust laws"—

(A) has the same meaning as in subsection (a) of section 12 of Title 15; and

(B) includes section 45 of Title 15 to the extent that such section 45 relates to unfair methods of competition.

(3) Branch

The term "branch" means a domestic branch (as defined in section 1813 of this title).

(4) Home State

The term "home State" means—

(A) with respect to a national bank, the State in which the main office of the bank is located;

(B) with respect to a State bank, the State by which the bank is chartered; and

(C) with respect to a bank holding company, the State in which the total deposits of all banking subsidiaries of such company are the largest on the later of—

(i) July 1, 1966; or

(ii) the date on which the company becomes a bank holding company under this chapter.

(5) Host State

The term "host State" means—

(A) with respect to a bank, a State, other than the home State of the bank, in which the bank maintains, or seeks to establish and maintain, a branch; and

(B) with respect to a bank holding company, a State, other than the home State of the company, in which the company controls, or seeks to control, a bank subsidiary.

(6) Out-of-State bank

The term "out-of-State bank" means, with respect to any State, a bank whose home State is another State.

(7) Out-of-State bank holding company

The term "out-of-State bank holding company" means, with respect to any State, a bank holding company whose home State is another State.

(8) Lead insured depository institutions

(A) In general

The term "lead insured depository institution" means the largest insured depository institution controlled by the subject bank holding company at any time, based on a comparison of the average total risk-weighted assets controlled by each insured depository institution during the previous 12–month period.

(B) Branch or agency

For purposes of this paragraph and section 1843(j)(4) of this title, the term "insured depository institution" includes any branch or agency operated in the United States by a foreign bank.

(9) Well managed

The term "well managed" means—

(A) in the case of any company or depository institution which receives examinations, the achievement of—

(i) a CAMEL composite rating of 1 or 2 (or an equivalent rating under an equivalent rating system) in connection with the most recent examination or subsequent review of such company or institution; and

(ii) at least a satisfactory rating for management, if such rating is given; or

(B) in the case of a company or depository institution that has not received an examination rating, the existence and use of managerial resources which the Board determines are satisfactory.

(10) Qualified family partnership

The term "qualified family partnership" means a general or limited partnership that the Board determines—

(A) does not directly control any bank, except through a registered bank holding company;

(B) does not control more than 1 registered bank holding company;

(C) does not engage in any business activity, except indirectly through ownership of other business entities;

(D) has no investments other than those permitted for a bank holding company pursuant to section 1843(c) of this title;

(E) is not obligated on any debt, either directly or as a guarantor;

(F) has partners, all of whom are either—

(i) individuals related to each other by blood, marriage (including former marriage), or adoption; or

(ii) trusts for the primary benefit of individuals related as described in clause (i); and

(G) has filed with the Board a statement that includes—

(i) the basis for the eligibility of the partnership under subparagraph (F);

(ii) a list of the existing activities and investments of the partnership;

(iii) a commitment to comply with this paragraph;

(iv) a commitment to comply with section 1817 of this title with respect to any acquisition of control of an insured depository institution occurring after September 30, 1996; and

(v) a commitment to be subject, to the same extent as if the qualified family partnership were a bank holding company—

(I) to examination by the Board to assure compliance with this paragraph; and

(II) to section 1818 of this title.

(p) Financial holding company

For purposes of this chapter, the term "financial holding company" means a bank holding company that meets the requirements of section 1843(*l*)(1) of this title.

(q) Insurance company

For purposes of sections 1843 and 1844 of this title, the term "insurance company" includes any person engaged in the business of insurance to the extent of such activities.

§ 1842. Acquisition of bank shares or assets—DFA §§ 604, 607

(a) Prior approval of Board as necessary; exceptions; disposition, time extension; subsequent approval or disposition upon disapproval

It shall be unlawful, except with the prior approval of the Board, (1) for any action to be taken that causes any company to become a bank holding company; (2) for any action to be taken that causes a bank to become a subsidiary of a bank holding company; (3) for any bank holding company to acquire direct or indirect ownership or control of any voting shares of any bank if, after such acquisition, such company will directly or indirectly own or control more than 5 per centum of the voting shares of such bank; (4) for any bank holding company or subsidiary thereof, other than a bank, to acquire all or substantially all of the assets of a bank; or (5) for any bank holding company to merge or consolidate with any other bank holding company. Notwithstanding the foregoing this prohibition shall not apply to (A) shares acquired by a bank, (i) in good faith in a fiduciary capacity, except where such shares are held under a trust that constitutes a company as defined in section 1841(b) of this title and except as provided in paragraphs (2) and (3) of section 1841(g) of this title, or (ii) in the regular course of securing or collecting a debt previously contracted in good faith, but any shares acquired after May 9, 1956, in securing or collecting any such previously contracted debt shall be disposed of within a period of two years from the date on which they were acquired; (B) additional shares acquired by a bank holding company in a bank in which such bank holding company owned or controlled a majority of the voting shares prior to such acquisition. The Board is authorized upon application by a bank to extend, from time to time for not more than one year at a time, the two-year period referred to above for disposing of any shares acquired by a bank in the regular course of securing or collecting a debt previously contracted in good faith, if, in the Board's judgment, such an extension would not be detrimental to the public interest, but no such extension shall in the aggregate exceed three years. For the purpose of the preceding sentence, bank shares acquired after December 31, 1970, shall not be deemed to have been acquired in good faith in a fiduciary capacity if the acquiring bank or company has sole discretionary authority to exercise voting rights with respect thereto, but in such instances acquisitions may be made without prior approval of the Board if the Board, upon application filed within ninety days after the shares are acquired, approves retention or, if retention is disapproved, the acquiring bank disposes of the shares or its sole discretionary voting rights within two years after issuance of the order of disapproval; or (C) the acquisition, by a company, of control of a bank in a reorganization in which a person or group of persons exchanges their shares of the bank for shares of a newly formed bank holding company and receives after the reorganization substantially the same proportional share interest in the holding company as they held in the bank except for changes in shareholders' interests resulting from the exercise of dissenting shareholders' rights under State or Federal law if—

   (i) immediately following the acquisition-

     (I) the bank holding company meets the capital and other financial standards prescribed by the Board by regulation for such a bank holding company; and

     (II) the bank is adequately capitalized (as defined in section 1831o of this title);

   (ii) the holding company does not engage in any activities other than those of managing and controlling banks as a result of the reorganization;

   (iii) the company provides 30 days prior notice to the Board and the Board does not object to such transaction during such 30–day period; and

   (iv) the holding company will not acquire control of any additional bank as a result of the reorganization . .

(b) Application for approval; notice to Comptroller of Currency or State authority; views and recommendations; disapproval; hearings; order of Board; nonaction deemed grant of application; procedure in emergencies or probable failures requiring immediate Board action and orders

(1) Notice and hearing requirements

Upon receiving from a company any application for approval under this section, the Board shall give notice to the Comptroller of the Currency, if the applicant company or any bank the voting shares or assets of which are sought to be required is a national banking association, or to the appropriate supervisory authority of the interested State, if the applicant company or any bank the voting shares or assets of which are sought to be acquired is a State bank, in order to provide for the submission of the views and recommendations of the Comptroller of the Currency or the State supervisory authority, as the case may be. The views and recommendations shall be submitted within thirty calendar days of the date on which notice is given, or within ten calendar days of such date if the Board advises the Comptroller of the Currency or the State supervisory authority that an emergency exists requiring expeditious action. If the thirty-day notice period applies and if the Comptroller of the Currency or the State supervisory authority so notified by the Board disapproves the application in writing within this period, the Board shall forthwith give written notice of that fact to the applicant. Within three days after giving such notice to the applicant, the

Board shall notify in writing the applicant and the disapproving authority of the date for commencement of a hearing by it on such application. Any such hearing shall be commenced not less than ten nor more than thirty days after the Board has given written notice to the applicant of the action of the disapproving authority. The length of any such hearing shall be determined by the Board, but it shall afford all interested parties a reasonable opportunity to testify at such hearing. At the conclusion thereof, the Board shall, by order, grant or deny the application on the basis of the record made at such hearing. In the event of the failure of the Board to act on any application for approval under this section within the ninety-one-day period which begins on the date of submission to the Board of the complete record on that application, the application shall be deemed to have been granted. Notwithstanding any other provision of this subsection, if the Board finds that it must act immediately on any application for approval under this section in order to prevent the probable failure of a bank or bank holding company involved in a proposed acquisition, merger, or consolidation transaction, the Board may dispense with the notice requirements of this subsection, and if notice is given, the Board may request that the views and recommendations of the Comptroller of the Currency or the State supervisory authority, as the case may be, be submitted immediately in any form or by any means acceptable to the Board. If the Board has found pursuant to this subsection either that an emergency exists requiring expeditious action or that it must act immediately to prevent probable failure, the Board may grant or deny any such application without a hearing notwithstanding any recommended disapproval by the appropriate supervisory authority.

(2) Waiver in case of bank in danger of closing

If the Board receives a certification described in section 1823(f)(8)(D) of this title from the appropriate Federal or State chartering authority that a bank is in danger of closing, the Board may dispense with the notice and hearing requirements of paragraph (1) with respect to any application received by the Board relating to the acquisition of such bank, the bank holding company which controls such bank, or any other affiliated bank.

(c) Factors for consideration by Board

(1) Competitive factors

The Board shall not approve—

(A) any acquisition or merger or consolidation under this section which would result in a monopoly, or which would be in furtherance of any combination or conspiracy to monopolize or to attempt to monopolize the business of banking in any part of the United States, or

(B) any other proposed acquisition or merger or consolidation under this section whose effect in any section of the country may be substantially to lessen competition, or to tend to create a monopoly, or which in any other manner would be in restraint or trade, unless it finds that the anticompetitive effects of the proposed transaction are clearly outweighed in the public interest by the probable effect of the transaction in meeting the convenience and needs of the community to be served.

(2) Banking and community factors

In every case, the Board shall take into consideration the financial and managerial resources and future prospects of the company or companies and the banks concerned, and the convenience and needs of the community to be served.

(3) Supervisory factors

The Board shall disapprove any application under this section by any company if—

(A) the company fails to provide the Board with adequate assurances that the company will make available to the Board such information on the operations or activities of the company, and any affiliate of the company, as the Board determines to be appropriate to determine and enforce compliance with this chapter; or

(B) in the case of an application involving a foreign bank, the foreign bank is not subject to comprehensive supervision or regulation on a consolidated basis by the appropriate authorities in the bank's home country.

(4) Treatment of certain bank stock loans

Notwithstanding any other provision of law, the Board shall not follow any practice or policy in the consideration of any application for the formation of a one-bank holding company if following such practice or policy would result in the rejection of such application solely because the transaction to form such one-bank holding company involves a bank stock loan which is for a period of not more than twenty-five years. The previous sentence shall not be construed to prohibit the Board from rejecting any application solely because the other financial arrangements are considered unsatisfactory. The Board shall consider transactions involving bank stock loans for the formation of a one-bank holding company having a maturity of twelve years or more on a case by case basis and no such transaction shall be approved if the Board believes the safety or soundness of the bank may be jeopardized.

(5) Managerial resources

Consideration of the managerial resources of a company or bank under paragraph (2) shall include consideration of the competence, experience, and integrity of the officers, directors, and principal shareholders of the company or bank.

(6) Money laundering

In every case, the Board shall take into consideration the effectiveness of the company of companies in combatting money laundering activities, including in overseas branches.

(d) Interstate banking

(1) Approvals authorized

(A) Acquisition of banks

The Board may approve an application under this section by a bank holding company that is adequately capitalized and adequately managed to acquire control of, or acquire all or substantially all of the assets of, a bank located in a State other than the home State of such bank holding company, without regard to whether such transaction is prohibited under the law of any State.

(B) Preservation of State age laws

(i) In general

Notwithstanding subparagraph (A), the Board may not approve an application pursuant to such subparagraph that would have the effect of permitting an out-of-State bank holding company to acquire a bank in a host State that has not been in existence for the minimum period of time, if any, specified in the statutory law of the host State.

(ii) Special rule for State age laws specifying a period of more than 5 years

Notwithstanding clause (i), the Board may approve, pursuant to subparagraph (A), the acquisition of a bank that has been in existence for at least 5 years without regard to any longer minimum period of time specified in a statutory law of the host State.

(C) Shell banks

For purposes of this subsection, a bank that has been chartered solely for the purpose of, and does not open for business prior to, acquiring control of, or acquiring all or substantially all of the assets of, an existing bank shall be deemed to have been in existence for the same period of time as the bank to be acquired.

(D) Effect on State contingency laws

No provision of this subsection shall be construed as affecting the applicability of a State law that makes an acquisition of a bank contingent upon a requirement to hold a portion of such bank's assets available for call by a State-sponsored housing entity established pursuant to State law, if—

(i) the State law does not have the effect of discriminating against out-of-State banks, out-of-State bank holding companies, or subsidiaries of such banks or bank holding companies;

(ii) that State law was in effect as of September 29, 1994;

(iii) the Federal Deposit Insurance Corporation has not determined that compliance with such State law would result in an unacceptable risk to the appropriate deposit insurance fund; and

(iv) the appropriate Federal banking agency for such bank has not found that compliance with such State law would place the bank in an unsafe or unsound condition.

(2) Concentration limits

(A) Nationwide concentration limits

The Board may not approve an application pursuant to paragraph (1)(A) if the applicant (including all insured depository institutions which are affiliates of the applicant) controls, or upon consummation of the acquisition for which such application is filed would control, more than 10 percent of the total amount of deposits of insured depository institutions in the United States.

(B) Statewide concentration limits other than with respect to initial entries

The Board may not approve an application pursuant to paragraph (1)(A) if—

(i) immediately before the consummation of the acquisition for which such application is filed, the applicant (including any insured depository institution affiliate of the applicant) controls any insured depository institution or any branch of an insured depository institution in the home State of any bank to be acquired or in any host State in which any such bank maintains a branch; and

(ii) the applicant (including all insured depository institutions which are affiliates of the applicant), upon consummation of the acquisition, would control 30 percent or more of the total amount of deposits of insured depository institutions in any such State.

(C) Effectiveness of State deposit caps

No provision of this subsection shall be construed as affecting the authority of any State to limit, by statute, regulation, or order, the percentage of the total amount of deposits of insured depository institutions in the State which may be held or controlled by any bank or bank holding company (including all insured depository institutions which are affiliates of the bank or bank holding company) to the extent the application of such limitation does not discriminate against out-of-State banks, out-of-State bank holding companies, or subsidiaries of such banks or holding companies.

(D) Exceptions to subparagraph (B)

The Board may approve an application pursuant to paragraph (1)(A) without regard to the applicability of subparagraph (B) with respect to any State if—

(i) there is a limitation described in subparagraph (C) in a State statute, regulation, or order which has the effect of permitting a bank or bank holding company (including all insured depository institutions which are affiliates of the bank or bank holding company) to control a greater percentage of total deposits of all insured depository institutions

in the State than the percentage permitted under subparagraph (B); or

(ii) the acquisition is approved by the appropriate State bank supervisor of such State and the standard on which such approval is based does not have the effect of discriminating against out-of-State banks, out-of-State bank holding companies, or subsidiaries of such banks or holding companies.

(E) "Deposit" defined

For purposes of this paragraph, the term "deposit" has the same meaning as in section 1813(*l*) of this title.

(3) Community reinvestment compliance

In determining whether to approve an application under paragraph (1)(A), the Board shall—

(A) comply with the responsibilities of the Board regarding such application under section 2903 of this title; and

(B) take into account the applicant's record of compliance with applicable State community reinvestment laws.

(4) Applicability of antitrust laws

No provision of this subsection shall be construed as affecting—

(A) the applicability of the antitrust laws; or

(B) the applicability, if any, of any State law which is similar to the antitrust laws.

(5) Exception for banks in default or in danger of default

The Board may approve an application pursuant to paragraph (1)(A) which involves—

(A) an acquisition of 1 or more banks in default or in danger of default; or

(B) an acquisition with respect to which assistance is provided under section 1823(c) of this title;

without regard to subparagraph (B) or (D) of paragraph (1) or paragraph (2) or (3).

(e) Insured depository institution

Every bank that is a holding company and every bank that is a subsidiary of such a company shall become and remain an insured depository institution as defined in section 1813 of this title.

(f) Repealed. Pub.L. 106–102, Title I, § 118, Nov. 12, 1999, 113 Stat. 1373

(g) Mutual bank holding company

(1) Establishment

Notwithstanding any provision of Federal law other than this chapter, a savings bank or cooperative bank operating in mutual form may reorganize so as to form a holding company.

(2) Regulations

A bank holding company organized as a mutual holding company shall be regulated on terms, and shall be subject to limitations, comparable to those applicable to any other bank holding company.

§ 1843. Interests in nonbanking organizations—DFA §§ 604, 606, 623

(a) Ownership or control of voting shares of any company not a bank; engagement in activities other than banking

Except as otherwise provided in this chapter, no bank holding company shall—

(1) after May 9, 1956, acquire direct or indirect ownership or control of any voting shares of any company which is not a bank, or

(2) after two years from the date as of which it becomes a bank holding company, or in the case of a company which has been continuously affiliated since May 15, 1955, with a company which was registered under the Investment Company Act of 1940 [15 U.S.C.A. § 80a–1 et seq.], prior to May 15, 1955, in such a manner as to constitute an affiliated company within the meaning of that Act, after December 31, 1978, or, in the case of any company which becomes, as a result of the enactment of the Bank Holding Company Act Amendments of 1970, a bank holding company on December 31, 1970, after December 31, 1980, retain direct or indirect ownership or control of any voting shares of any company which is not a bank or bank holding company or engage in any activities other than (A) those of banking or of managing or controlling banks and other subsidiaries authorized under this chapter or of furnishing services to or performing services for its subsidiaries, and (B) those permitted under paragraph (8) of subsection (c) of this section subject to all the conditions specified in such paragraph or in any order or regulation issued by the Board under such paragraph: *Provided,* That a company covered in 1970 may also engage in those activities in which directly

or through a subsidiary (i) it was lawfully engaged on June 30, 1968 (or on a date subsequent to June 30, 1968, in the case of activities carried on as the result of the acquisition by such company or subsidiary, pursuant to a binding written contract entered into on or before June 30, 1968, of another company engaged in such activities at the time of the acquisition), and (ii) it has been continuously engaged since June 30, 1968 (or such subsequent date). The Board by order, after opportunity for hearing, may terminate the authority conferred by the preceding proviso on any company to engage directly or through a subsidiary in any activity otherwise permitted by that proviso if it determines, having due regard to the purposes of this chapter, that such action is necessary to prevent undue concentration of resources, decreased or unfair competition, conflicts of interest, or unsound banking practices; and in the case of any such company controlling a bank having bank assets in excess of $60,000,000 on or after December 31, 1970, the Board shall determine, within two years after such date (or, if later, within two years after the date on which the bank assets first exceed $60,000,000), whether the authority conferred by the preceding proviso with respect to such company should be terminated as provided in this sentence. Nothing in this paragraph shall be construed to authorize any bank holding company referred to in the preceding proviso, or any subsidiary thereof, to engage in activities authorized by that proviso through the acquisition, pursuant to a contract entered into after June 30, 1968, of any interest in or the assets of a going concern engaged in such activities. Any company which is authorized to engage in any activity pursuant to the preceding proviso or subsection (d) of this section but, as a result of action of the Board, is required to terminate such activity may (notwithstanding any otherwise applicable time limit prescribed in this paragraph) retain the ownership or control of shares in any company carrying on such activity for a period of ten years from the date on which its authority was so terminated by the Board. Notwithstanding any other provision of this paragraph, if any company that became a bank holding company as a result of the enactment of the Competitive Equality Amendments of 1987 acquired, between March 5, 1987, and August 10, 1987, an institution that became a bank as a result of the enactment of such Amendments, that company shall, upon the enactment of such Amendments, immediately come into compliance with the requirements of this chapter.

The Board is authorized, upon application by a bank holding company, to extend the two year period referred to in paragraph (2) above from time to time as to such bank holding company for not more than one year at a time, if, in its judgment, such an extension would not be detrimental to the public interest, but no such extensions shall in the aggregate exceed three years. Notwithstanding any other provision of this chapter, the period ending December 31, 1980, referred to in paragraph (2) above, may be extended by the Board of Governors to December 31, 1984, but only for the divestiture by a bank holding company of real estate or interests in real estate lawfully acquired for investment or development. In making its decision whether to grant such extension, the Board shall consider whether the company has made a good faith effort to divest such interests and whether such extension is necessary to avert substantial loss to the company.

(b) Statement purporting to represent shares of any company except a bank or bank holding company

After two years from May 9, 1956, no certificate evidencing shares of any bank holding company shall bear any statement purporting to represent shares of any other company except a bank or a bank holding company, nor shall the ownership, sale, or transfer of shares of any bank holding company be conditioned in any manner whatsoever upon the ownership, sale, or transfer of shares of any other company except a bank or a bank holding company.

(c) Exemptions

The prohibitions in this section shall not apply to (i) any company that was on January 4, 1977, both a bank holding company and a labor, agricultural, or horticultural organization exempt from taxation under section 501 of Title 26, or to any labor, agricultural, or horticultural organization to which all or substantially all of the assets of such company are hereafter transferred, or (ii) a company covered in 1970 more than 85 per centum of the voting stock of which was collectively owned on June 30, 1968, and continuously thereafter, directly or indirectly, by or for members of the same family, or their spouses, who are

lineal descendants of common ancestors; and such prohibitions shall not, with respect to any other bank holding company, apply to—

(1) shares of any company engaged or to be engaged solely in one or more of the following activities: (A) holding or operating properties used wholly or substantially by any banking subsidiary of such bank holding company in the operations of such banking subsidiary or acquired for such future use; or (B) conducting a safe deposit business; or (C) furnishing services to or performing services for such bank holding company or its banking subsidiaries; or (D) liquidating assets acquired from such bank holding company or its banking subsidiaries or acquired from any other source prior to May 9, 1956, or the date on which such company became a bank holding company, whichever is later;

(2) shares acquired by a bank holding company or any of its subsidiaries in satisfaction of a debt previously contracted in good faith, but such shares shall be disposed of within a period of two years from the date on which they were acquired, except that the Board is authorized upon application by such bank holding company to extend such period of two years from time to time as to such holding company if, in its judgment, such an extension would not be detrimental to the public interest, and, in the case of a bank holding company which has not disposed of such shares within 5 years after the date on which such shares were acquired, the Board may, upon the application of such company, grant additional exemptions if, in the judgment of the Board, such extension would not be detrimental to the public interest and, either the bank holding company has made a good faith attempt to dispose of such shares during such 5-year period, or the disposal of such shares during such 5-year period would have been detrimental to the company, except that the aggregate duration of such extensions shall not extend beyond 10 years after the date on which such shares were acquired;

(3) shares acquired by such bank holding company from any of its subsidiaries which subsidiary has been requested to dispose of such shares by any Federal or State authority having statutory power to examine such subsidiary, but such bank holding company shall dispose of such shares within a period of two

years from the date on which they were acquired;

(4) shares held or acquired by a bank in good faith in a fiduciary capacity, except where such shares are held under a trust that constitutes a company as defined in section 1841(b) of this title and except as provided in paragraphs (2) and (3) of section 1841(g) of this title;

(5) shares which are of the kinds and amounts eligible for investment by national banking associations under the provisions of section 24 of this title;

(6) shares of any company which do not include more than 5 per centum of the outstanding voting shares of such company;

(7) shares of an investment company which is not a bank holding company and which is not engaged in any business other than investing in securities, which securities do not include more than5 per centum of the outstanding voting shares of any company;

(8) shares of any company the activities of which had been determined by the Board by regulation or order under this paragraph as of the day before November 12, 1999, to be so closely related to banking as to be a proper incident thereto (subject to such terms and conditions contained in such regulation or order, unless modified by the Board);

(9) shares held or activities conducted by any company organized under the laws of a foreign country the greater part of whose business is conducted outside the United States, if the Board by regulation or order determines that, under the circumstances and subject to the conditions set forth in the regulation or order, the exemption would not be substantially at variance with the purposes of this chapter and would be in the public interest;

(10) shares lawfully acquired and owned prior to May 9, 1956, by a bank which is a bank holding company, or by any of its wholly owned subsidiaries;

(11) shares owned directly or indirectly by a company covered in 1970 in a company which does not engage in any activities other than those in which the bank holding company, or its subsidiaries, may engage by virtue of this section, but nothing in this paragraph authorizes any bank holding company, or subsidiary thereof, to acquire any interest in or the assets

of any going concern (except pursuant to a binding written contract entered into before June 30, 1968, or pursuant to another provision of this chapter) other than one which was a subsidiary on June 30, 1968;

(12) shares retained or acquired, or activities engaged in, by any company which becomes, as a result of the enactment of the Bank Holding Company Act Amendments of 1970, a bank holding company on December 31, 1970, or by any subsidiary thereof, if such company—

(A) within the applicable time limits prescribed in subsection (a)(2) of this section (i) ceases to be a bank holding company, or (ii) ceases to retain direct or indirect ownership or control of those shares and to engage in those activities not authorized under this section; and

(B) complies with such other conditions as the Board may by regulation or order prescribe;

(13) shares of, or activities conducted by, any company which does no business in the United States except as an incident to its international or foreign business, if the Board by regulation or order determines that, under the circumstances and subject to the conditions set forth in the regulation or order, the exemption would not be substantially at variance with the purposes of this chapter and would be in the public interest; or

(14) shares of any company which is an export trading company whose acquisition (including each acquisition of shares) or formation by a bank holding company has not been disapproved by the Board pursuant to this paragraph, except that such investments, whether direct or indirect, in such shares shall not exceed 5 per centum of the bank holding company's consolidated capital and surplus.

(A)(i) No bank holding company shall invest in an export trading company under this paragraph unless the Board has been given sixty days' prior written notice of such proposed investment and within such period has not issued a notice disapproving the proposed investment or extending for up to another thirty days the period during which such disapproval may be issued.

(ii) The period for disapproval may be extended for such additional thirty-day period only if the Board determines that a bank holding company proposing to invest in an export trading company has not furnished all the information required to be submitted or that in the Board's judgment any material information submitted is substantially inaccurate.

(iii) The notice required to be filed by a bank holding company shall contain such relevant information as the Board shall require by regulation or by specific request in connection with any particular notice.

(iv) The Board may disapprove any proposed investment only if—

(I) such disapproval is necessary to prevent unsafe or unsound banking practices, undue concentration of resources, decreased or unfair competition, or conflicts of interest;

(II) the Board finds that such investment would affect the financial or managerial resources of a bank holding company to an extent which is likely to have a materially adverse effect on the safety and soundness of any subsidiary bank of such bank holding company, or

(III) the bank holding company fails to furnish the information required under clause (iii).

(v) Leverage

The Board may not disapprove any proposed investment solely on the basis of the anticipated or proposed asset-to-equity ratio of the export trading company with respect to which such investment is proposed, unless the anticipated or proposed annual average asset-to-equity ratio is greater than 20–to–1.

(vi) Within three days after a decision to disapprove an investment, the Board shall notify the bank holding company in writing of the disapproval and shall provide a written statement of the basis for the disapproval.

(vii) A proposed investment may be made prior to the expiration of the disapproval period if the Board issues written notice of its intent not to disapprove the investment.

(B)(i) The total amount of extensions of credit by a bank holding company which invests in an export trading company, when combined with all such extensions of credit by all

the subsidiaries of such bank holding company, to an export trading company shall not exceed at any one time 10 per centum of the bank holding company's consolidated capital and surplus. For purposes of the preceding sentence, an extension of credit shall not be deemed to include any amount invested by a bank holding company in the shares of an export trading company.

(ii) No provision of any other Federal law in effect on October 1, 1982, relating specifically to collateral requirements shall apply with respect to any such extension of credit.

(iii) No bank holding company or subsidiary of such company which invests in an export trading company may extend credit to such export trading company or to customers of such export trading company on terms more favorable than those afforded similar borrowers in similar circumstances, and such extension of credit shall not involve more than the normal risk of repayment or present other unfavorable features.

(C) For purposes of this paragraph, an export trading company—

(i) may engage in or hold shares of a company engaged in the business of underwriting, selling, or distributing securities in the United States only to the extent that any bank holding company which invests in such export trading company may do so under applicable Federal and State banking laws and regulations; and

(ii) may not engage in agricultural production activities or in manufacturing, except for such incidental product modification including repackaging, reassembling or extracting byproducts, as is necessary to enable United States goods or services to conform with requirements of a foreign country and to facilitate their sale in foreign countries.

(D) A bank holding company which invests in an export trading company may be required, by the Board, to terminate its investment or may be made subject to such limitations or conditions as may be imposed by the Board, if the Board determines that the export trading company has taken positions in commodities or commodity contracts, in securities, or in foreign exchange, other than as may be necessary in the course of the export trading company's business operations.

(E) Notwithstanding any other provision of law, an Edge Act corporation, organized under section 25(a) of the Federal Reserve Act (12 U.S.C. 611–631), which is a subsidiary of a bank holding company, or an agreement corporation, operating subject to section 25 of the Federal Reserve Act [12 U.S.C.A. § 601 et seq.], which is a subsidiary of a bank holding company, may invest directly and indirectly in the aggregate up to 5 per centum of its consolidated capital and surplus (25 per centum in the case of a corporation not engaged in banking) in the voting stock of other evidences of ownership in one or more export trading companies.

(F) For purposes of this paragraph—

(i) the term "export trading company" means a company which does business under the laws of the United States or any State, which is exclusively engaged in activities related to international trade, and which is organized and operated principally for purposes of exporting goods or services produced in the United States or for purposes of facilitating the exportation of goods or services produced in the United States by unaffiliated persons by providing one or more export trade services.

(ii) the term "export trade services" includes, but is not limited to, consulting, international market research, advertising, marketing, insurance (other than acting as principal, agent or broker in the sale of insurance on risks resident or located, or activities performed, in the United States, except for insurance covering the transportation of cargo from any point of origin in the United States to a point of final destination outside the United States), product research and design, legal assistance, transportation, including trade documentation and freight forwarding, communication and processing of foreign orders to and for exporters and foreign purchasers, warehousing, foreign exchange, financing, and taking title to goods, when provided in order to facilitate the export of goods or services produced in the United States;

(iii) the term "bank holding company" shall include a bank which (I) is organized solely to do business with other banks and their officers, directors, or employees; (II) is owned primarily by the banks with which it does business; and (III) does not do business with the general public. No such other bank, owning stock in a bank described in this clause that invests in an export trading company, shall extend credit to an export trading company in an amount exceeding at any one time 10 per centum of such other bank's capital and surplus; and

(iv) the term "extension of credit" shall have the same meaning given such term in the fourth paragraph of section 371c of this title.

(G) Determination of status as export trading company

(i) Time period requirements

For purposes of determining whether an export trading company is operated principally for the purposes described in subparagraph (F)(I)—

(I) the operations of such company during the 2–year period beginning on the date such company commences operations shall not be taken into account in making any such determination; and

(II) not less than 4 consecutive years of operations of such company (not including any portion of the period referred to in subclause (I)) shall be taken into account in making any such determination.

(ii) Export revenue requirements

A company shall not be treated as operated principally for the purposes described in subparagraph (F)(i) unless—

(I) the revenues of such company from the export, or facilitating the export, of goods or services produced in the United States exceed the revenues of such company from the import, or facilitating the import, into the United States of goods or services produced outside the United States; and

(II) at least 1/3 of such company's total revenues are revenues from the export, or facilitating the export, of goods or services produced in the United States by persons not affiliated with such company.

(H) Inventory

(i) No general limitation

The Board may not prescribe by regulation any maximum dollar amount limitation on the value of goods which an export trading company may maintain in inventory at any time.

(ii) Specific limitation by order

Notwithstanding clause (i), the Board may issue an order establishing a maximum dollar amount limitation on the value of goods which a particular export trading company may maintain in inventory at any time (after such company has been operating for a reasonable period of time) if the Board finds that, under the facts and circumstances, such limitation is necessary to prevent risks that would affect the financial or managerial resources of an investor bank holding company to an extent which would be likely to have a materially adverse effect on the safety and soundness of any subsidiary bank of such bank holding company.

The Board shall include in its annual report to the Congress a description and a statement of the reasons for approval of each activity approved by it by order or regulation under such paragraph during the period covered by the report.

(d) Exemption of company controlling one bank prior to July 1, 1968

To the extent that such action would not be substantially at variance with the purposes of this chapter and subject to such conditions as it considers necessary to protect the public interest, the Board by order, after opportunity for hearing, may grant exemptions from the provisions of this section to any bank holding company which controlled one bank prior to July 1, 1968, and has not thereafter acquired the control of any other bank in order (1) to avoid disrupting business relationships that have existed over a long period of years without adversely affecting the banks or communities involved, or (2) to avoid forced sales of small locally owned banks to purchasers not similarly representative of community interests, or (3) to allow retention of banks that are so small in relation to the holding company's total interests and so small in relation to the banking market to be served as to minimize the likelihood that the bank's powers to grant or deny credit may be influenced by a desire to further the holding company's other interests.

(e) Divestiture of nonexempt shares

With respect to shares which were not subject to the prohibitions of this section as originally enacted by reason of any exemption with respect thereto but which were made subject to such prohibitions by the subsequent repeal of such exemption, no bank holding company shall retain direct or indirect ownership or control of such shares after five years from the date of the repeal of such exemption, except as provided in paragraph (2) of subsection (a) of this section. Any bank holding company subject to such five-year limitation on the retention of nonbanking assets shall endeavor to divest itself of such shares promptly and such bank holding company shall report its progress in such divestiture to the Board two years after repeal of the exemption applicable to it and annually thereafter.

(f) Certain companies not treated as bank holding companies

(1) In general

Except as provided in paragraph (9), any company which—

(A) on March 5, 1987, controlled an institution which became a bank as a result of the enactment of the Competitive Equality Amendments of 1987; and

(B) was not a bank holding company on the day before August 10, 1987,

shall not be treated as a bank holding company for purposes of this chapter solely by virtue of such company's control of such institution.

(2) Loss of exemption

Subject to paragraph (3), a company described in paragraph (1) shall no longer qualify for the exemption provided under that paragraph if—

(A) such company directly or indirectly—

(i) acquires control of an additional bank or an insured institution (other than an insured institution described in paragraph (10) or (12) of this subsection) after March 5, 1987; or

(ii) acquires control of more than 5 percent of the shares or assets of an additional bank or a savings association other than—

(I) shares held as a bona fide fiduciary (whether with or without the sole discretion to vote such shares);

(II) shares held by any person as a bona fide fiduciary solely for the benefit of employees of either the company described in paragraph (1) or any subsidiary of that company and the beneficiaries of those employees;

(III) shares held temporarily pursuant to an underwriting commitment in the normal course of an underwriting business;

(IV) shares held in an account solely for trading purposes;

(V) shares over which no control is held other than control of voting rights acquired in the normal course of a proxy solicitation;

(VI) loans or other accounts receivable acquired in the normal course of business;

(VII) shares or assets acquired in securing or collecting a debt previously contracted in good faith, during the 2–year period beginning on the date of such acquisition or for such additional time (not exceeding 3 years) as the Board may permit if the Board determines that such an extension will not be detrimental to the public interest;

(VIII) shares or assets of a savings association described in paragraph (10) or (12) of this subsection;

(IX) shares of a savings association held by any insurance company, as defined in section 80a–2(a)(17) of Title 15, except as provided in paragraph (11);

(X) shares issued in a qualified stock issuance under section 1467a(q) of this title; and

(XI) assets that are derived from, or incidental to, activities in which institutions described in subparagraph (F) or (H) of section 1841(c)(2) of this title are permitted to engage;

except that the aggregate amount of shares held under this clause (other than under subclauses (I), (II), (III), (IV), (V), and (VIII)) may not exceed 15 percent of all outstanding shares or of the voting power of a savings association;

(B) any bank subsidiary of such company-

(i) accepts demand deposits or deposits that the depositor may withdraw by check or similar means for payment to third parties; and

(ii) engages in the business of making commercial loans (except that, for purposes of this clause, loans made in the ordinary course of a credit card operation shall not be treated as commercial loans); or

(C) after August 10, 1987, any bank subsidiary of such company permits any overdraft (including any intraday overdraft), or incurs any such overdraft in the account of the bank at a Federal reserve bank, on behalf of an affiliate, other than an overdraft described in paragraph (3).

(3) Permissible overdrafts described

For purposes of paragraph (2)(C), an overdraft is described in this paragraph if—

(A) such overdraft results from an inadvertent computer or accounting error that is beyond the control of both the bank and the affiliate;

(B) such overdraft—

(i) is permitted or incurred on behalf of an affiliate that is monitored by, reports to, and is recognized as a primary dealer by the Federal Reserve Bank of New York; and

(ii) is fully secured, as required by the Board, by bonds, notes, or other obligations that are direct obligations of the United States or on which the principal and interest are fully guaranteed by the United States or by securities and obligations eligible for settlement on the Federal Reserve book entry system; or

(C) such overdraft—

(i) is permitted or incurred by, or on behalf of, an affiliate in connection with an activity that is financial in nature or incidental to a financial activity; and

(ii) does not cause the bank to violate any provision of section 371c or 371c–1 of this title, either directly, in the case of a bank that is a member of the Federal Reserve System, or by virtue of section 1828(j) of this title, in the case of a bank that is not a member of the Federal Reserve System.

(4) Divestiture in case of loss of exemption

If any company described in paragraph (1) fails to qualify for the exemption provided under paragraph (1) by operation of paragraph (2), such exemption shall cease to apply to such company and such company shall divest control of each bank it controls before the end of the 180–day period beginning on the date on which the company receives notice from the Board that the company has failed to continue to qualify for such exemption, unless, before the end of such 180–day period, the company has—

(A) either—

(i) corrected the condition or ceased the activity that caused the company to fail to continue to qualify for the exemption; or

(ii) submitted a plan to the Board for approval to cease the activity or correct the condition in a timely manner (which shall not exceed 1 year); and

(B) implemented procedures that are reasonably adapted to avoid the reoccurrence of such condition or activity.

(5) Subsection ceases to apply under certain circumstances

This subsection shall cease to apply to any company described in paragraph (1) if such company—

(A) registers as a bank holding company under section 1844(a) of this title;

(B) immediately upon such registration, complies with all of the requirements of this chapter, and regulations prescribed by the Board pursuant to this chapter, including the nonbanking restrictions of this section; and

(C) does not, at the time of such registration, control banks in more than one State, the acquisition of which would be prohibited by section 1842(d) of this title if an application for such acquisition by such company were filed under section 1842(a) of this title.

(6) Information requirement

Each company described in paragraph (1) shall, within 60 days after August 10, 1987, provide the Board with the name and address of such company, the name and address of each bank such company controls, and a description of each such bank's activities.

(7) Examination

The Board may, from time to time, examine a company described in paragraph (1), or a bank controlled by such company, or require reports under oath from appropriate officers or directors of such company or bank solely for purposes of assuring compliance with the provisions of this subsection and enforcing such compliance.

(8) Enforcement

(A) In general

In addition to any other power of the Board, the Board may enforce compliance with the provisions of this chapter which are applicable to any company described in paragraph (1), and any bank controlled by such company, under section 1818 of this title and such company or bank shall be subject to such section (for such purposes) in the same manner and to the same extent as if such company or bank were a State member insured bank.

(B) Application of other Act

Any violation of this Act by any company described in paragraph (1), and any bank controlled by such company, may also be treated as a violation of the Federal Deposit Insurance Act [12 U.S.C.A. § 1811 et seq.] for purposes of subparagraph (A).

(C) No effect on other authority

No provision of this paragraph shall be construed as limiting any authority of the Comptroller of the Currency or the Federal Deposit Insurance Corporation.

(9) Tying provisions

A company described in paragraph (1) shall be—

(A) treated as a bank holding company for purposes of section 106 of the Bank Holding Company Act Amendments of 1970 [12 U.S.C.A. § 1971 et seq.] and section 22(h) of the Federal Reserve Act [12 U.S.C.A. § 375b] and any regulation prescribed under any such section; and

(B) subject to the restrictions of section 106 of the Bank Holding Company Act Amendments of 1970 [12 U.S.C.A. § 1971 et seq.], in connection with any transaction involving the products or services of such company or affiliate and those of a bank affiliate, as if such company or affiliate were a bank and such bank were a subsidiary of a bank holding company.

(10) Exemption unaffected by certain emergency acquisitions

For purposes of clauses (i) and (ii)(VIII) of paragraph (2)(A), an insured institution is described in this paragraph if—

(A) the insured institution was acquired (or any shares or assets of such institution were acquired) by a company described in paragraph (1) in an acquisition under section 1730a(m) or section 1823(k) of this title; and

(B) either—

(i) the insured institution is located in a State in which such company controlled a bank on March 5, 1987; or

(ii) the insured institution has total assets of $500,000,000 or more at the time of such acquisition.

(11) Shares held by insurance affiliates

Shares described in clause (ii)(IX) of paragraph (2)(A) shall not be excluded for purposes of clause (ii) of such paragraph if—

(A) all shares held under such clause (ii)(IX) by all insurance company affiliates of such savings association in the aggregate exceed 5 percent of all outstanding shares or of the voting power of the savings association; or

(B) such shares are acquired or retained with a view to acquiring, exercising, or transferring control of the savings association.

(12) Exemption unaffected by certain other acquisitions

For purposes of clauses (i) and (ii)(VIII) of paragraph (2)(A), an insured institution is described in this paragraph if the insured institution was acquired (or any shares or assets of such institution were acquired) by a company described in paragraph (1)—

(A) from the Resolution Trust Corporation, the Federal Deposit Insurance Corporation, or the Director of the Office of Thrift Supervision, in any capacity; or

(B) in an acquisition in which the insured institution has been found to be in danger of default (as defined in section 1813 of this title by the appropriate Federal or State authority).

(13) Special rule relating to shares acquired in a qualified stock issuance

A company described in paragraph (1) that holds shares issued in a qualified stock issu-

ance pursuant to section 1467a(q) of this title by any savings association or savings and loan holding company (neither of which is a subsidiary) shall not be deemed to control such savings association or savings and loan holding company solely because such company holds such shares unless—

(A) the company fails to comply with any requirement or condition imposed by paragraph (2)(A)(ii)(X) or section 1467a(q) of this title with respect to such shares; or

(B) the shares are acquired or retained with a view to acquiring, exercising, or transferring control of the savings association or savings and loan holding company.

(14) Foreign bank subsidiaries of limited purpose credit card banks

(A) In general

An institution described in section 1841(c)(2)(F) of this title may control a foreign bank if—

(i) the investment of the institution in the foreign bank meets the requirements of section 25 or 25A of the Federal Reserve Act [12 U.S.C.A. §§ 601 to 604 or 611 to 631] the foreign bank qualifies under such sections;

(ii) the foreign bank does not offer any products or services in the United States; and

(iii) the activities of the foreign bank are permissible under otherwise applicable law.

(B) Other limitations inapplicable

The limitations contained in any clause of section 1841(c)(2)(F) of this title shall not apply to a foreign bank described in subparagraph (A) that is controlled by an institution described in such section.

(g) Limitations on certain banks

(1) In general

Notwithstanding any other provision of this section (other than the last sentence of subsection (a)(2)), a bank holding company which controls an institution that became a bank as a result of the enactment of the Competitive Equality Amendments of 1987 may retain control of such institution if such institution does not—

(A) engage in any activity after August 10, 1987, which would have caused such institution to be a bank (as defined in section

1841(c) of this title, as in effect before such date) if such activities had been engaged in before such date; or

(B) increase the number of locations from which such institution conducts business after March 5, 1987.

(2) Limitations cease to apply under certain circumstances

The limitations contained in paragraph (1) shall cease to apply to a bank described in such paragraph at such time as the acquisition of such bank, by the bank holding company referred to in such paragraph, would not be prohibited under section 1842(d) of this title if—

(A) an application for such acquisition were filed under section 1842(a) of this title; and

(B) such bank were treated as an additional bank (under section 1842(d) of this title).

(h) Tying provisions

(1) Applicable to certain exempt institutions and parent companies

An institution described in subparagraph (D), (F), (G), (H), (I), or (J) of section 1841(c)(2) of this title shall be treated as a bank, and a company that controls such an institution shall be treated as a bank holding company, for purposes of section 106 of the Bank Holding Company Act Amendments of 1970 [12 U.S.C.A. § 1971 et seq.] and section 22(h) of the Federal Reserve Act [12 U.S.C.A. § 375b] and any regulation prescribed under any such section.

(2) Applicable with respect to certain transactions

A company that controls an institution described in subparagraph (D), (F), (G), (H), (I), or (J) of section 1841(c)(2) of this title and any of such company's other affiliates, shall be subject to the tying restrictions of section 106 of the Bank Holding Company Act Amendments of 1970 [12 U.S.C.A. § 1971 et seq.] in connection with any transaction involving the products or services of such company or affiliate and those of such institution, as if such company or affiliate were a bank and such institution were a subsidiary of a bank holding company.

(i) Acquisition of savings associations

(1) In general

The Board may approve an application by any bank holding company under subsection (c)(8) of this section to acquire any savings association in accordance with the requirements and limitations of this section.

(2) Prohibition on tandem restrictions

In approving an application by a bank holding company to acquire a savings association, the Board shall not impose any restriction on transactions between the savings association and its holding company affiliates, except as required under sections 371 and 371c–1 of this title or any other applicable law.

(3) Acquisition of insolvent savings associations

(A) In general

Notwithstanding any other provision of this chapter, any qualified savings association which became a federally chartered stock company in December of 1986 and which is acquired by any bank holding company without Federal financial assistance after June 1, 1991, and before March 1, 1992, and any subsidiary of any such association, may after such acquisition continue to engage within the home State of the qualified savings association in insurance agency activities in which any Federal savings association (or any subsidiary thereof) may engage in accordance with the Home Owners' Loan Act [12 U.S.C.A. § 1461 et seq.] and regulations pursuant to such Act if the qualified savings association or subsidiary thereof was continuously engaged in such activity from June 1, 1991, to the date of the acquisition.

(B) Definition of qualified savings association

For purposes of this paragraph, the term "qualified savings association" means any savings association that—

(i) was chartered or organized as a savings association before June 1, 1991;

(ii) had, immediately before the acquisition of such association by the bank holding company referred to in subparagraph (A), negative tangible capital and total insured deposits in excess of $3,000,000,000; and

(iii) will meet all applicable regulatory capital requirements as a result of such acquisition.

(4) Solicitation of views

(A) Notice to director

Upon receiving any application or notice by a bank holding company to acquire, directly or indirectly, a savings association under subsection (c)(8) of this section, the Board shall solicit comments and recommendations from the Director with respect to such acquisition.

(B) Comment period

The comments and recommendations of the Director under subparagraph (A) with respect to any acquisition subject to such subparagraph shall be transmitted to the Board not later than 30 days after the receipt by the Director of the notice relating to such acquisition (or such shorter period as the Board may specify if the Board advises the Director that an emergency exists that requires expeditious action).

(5) Examination

(A) Scope

The Board shall consult with the Director, as appropriate, in establishing the scope of an examination by the Board of a bank holding company that directly or indirectly controls a savings association.

(B) Access to inspection reports

Upon the request of the Director, the Board shall furnish the Director with a copy of any inspection report, additional examination materials, or supervisory information relating to any bank holding company that directly or indirectly controls a savings association.

(6) Coordination of enforcement efforts

The Board and the Director shall cooperate in any enforcement action against any bank holding company that controls a savings association, if the relevant conduct involves such association.

(7) Director defined

For purposes of this section, the term "Director" means the Director of the Office of Thrift Supervision.

(j) Notice procedures for nonbanking activities

(1) General notice procedure

(A) Notice requirement

Except as provided in paragraph (3), no bank holding company may engage in any nonbanking activity or acquire or retain ownership or control of the shares of a company engaged in activities based on subsection (c)(8) or (a)(2) of this section or in any complementary activity under subsection (k)(1)(B) of this section without providing the Board with written notice of the proposed transaction or activity at least 60 days before the transaction or activity is proposed to occur or commence.

(B) Contents of notice

The notice submitted to the Board shall contain such information as the Board shall prescribe by regulation or by specific request in connection with a particular notice.

(C) Procedure for agency action

(i) Notice of disapproval

Any notice filed under this subsection shall be deemed to be approved by the Board unless, before the end of the 60–day period beginning on the date the Board receives a complete notice under subparagraph (A), the Board issues an order disapproving the transaction or activity and setting forth the reasons for disapproval.

(ii) Extension of period

The Board may extend the 60–day period referred to in clause (i) for an additional 30 days. The Board may further extend the period with the agreement of the bank holding company submitting the notice pursuant to this subsection.

(iii) Determination of period in case of public hearing

In the event a hearing is requested or the Board determines that a hearing is warranted, the Board may extend the notice period provided in this subsection for such time as is reasonably necessary to conduct a hearing and to evaluate the hearing record. Such extension shall not exceed the 91–day period beginning on the date that the hearing record is complete.

(D) Approval before end of period

(i) In general

Any transaction or activity may commence before the expiration of any period for disapproval established under this paragraph if the Board issues a written notice of approval.

(ii) Shorter periods by regulation

The Board may prescribe regulations which provide for a shorter notice period with respect to particular activities or transactions.

(E) Extension of period

In the case of any notice to engage in, or to acquire or retain ownership or control of shares of any company engaged in, any activity pursuant to subsection (c)(8) or (a)(2) of this section or in any complementary activity under subsection (k)(1)(B) of this section that has not been previously approved by regulation, the Board may extend the notice period under this subsection for an additional 90 days. The Board may further extend the period with the agreement of the bank holding company submitting the notice pursuant to this subsection.

(2) General standards for review

(A) Criteria

In connection with a notice under this subsection, the Board shall consider whether performance of the activity by a bank holding company or a subsidiary of such company can reasonably be expected to produce benefits to the public, such as greater convenience, increased competition, or gains in efficiency, that outweigh possible adverse effects, such as undue concentration of resources, decreased or unfair competition, conflicts of interests, or unsound banking practices.

(B) Grounds for disapproval

The Board may deny any proposed transaction or activity for which notice has been submitted pursuant to this subsection if the bank holding company submitting such notice neglects, fails, or refuses to furnish the Board all the information required by the Board.

(C) Conditional action

Nothing in this subsection limits the authority of the Board to impose conditions in connection with an action under this section.

(3) No notice required for certain transactions

No notice under paragraph (1) of this subsection or under subsection (c)(8) or (a)(2)(B) of this section is required for a proposal by a bank holding company to engage in any activity, other than any complementary activity under subsection (k)(1)(B) of this section, or acquire the shares or assets of any company, other than an insured depository institution or a company engaged in any complementary activity under subsection (k)(1)(B) of this section, if the proposal qualifies under paragraph (4).

(4) Criteria for statutory approval

A proposal qualifies under this paragraph if all of the following criteria are met:

(A) Financial criteria

Both before and immediately after the proposed transaction—

(i) the acquiring bank holding company is well capitalized;

(ii) the lead insured depository institution of such holding company is well capitalized;

(iii) well capitalized insured depository institutions control at least 80 percent of the aggregate total risk-weighted assets of insured depository institutions controlled by such holding company; and

(iv) no insured depository institution controlled by such holding company is undercapitalized.

(B) Managerial criteria

(i) Well managed

At the time of the transaction, the acquiring bank holding company, its lead insured depository institution, and insured depository institutions that control at least 90 percent of the aggregate total risk-weighted assets of insured depository institutions controlled by such holding company are well managed.

(ii) Limitation on poorly managed institutions

Except as provided in paragraph (6), no insured depository institution controlled by the acquiring bank holding company has received 1 of the 2 lowest composite ratings at the later of the institution's most recent examination or subsequent review.

(C) Activities permissible

Following consummation of the proposal, the bank holding company engages directly or through a subsidiary solely in—

(i) activities that are permissible under subsection (c)(8) of this section, as determined by the Board by regulation or order thereunder, subject to all of the restrictions, terms, and conditions of such subsection and such regulation or order; and

(ii) such other activities as are otherwise permissible under this section, subject to the restrictions, terms and conditions, including any prior notice or approval requirements, provided in this section.

(D) Size of acquisition

(i) Asset size

The book value of the total assets to be acquired does not exceed 10 percent of the consolidated total risk-weighted assets of the acquiring bank holding company.

(ii) Consideration

The gross consideration to be paid for the securities or assets does not exceed 15 percent of the consolidated Tier 1 capital of the acquiring bank holding company.

(E) Notice not otherwise warranted

For proposals described in paragraph (5)(B), the Board has not, before the conclusion of the period provided in paragraph (5)(B), advised the bank holding company that a notice under paragraph (1) is required.

(F) Compliance criterion

During the 12–month period ending on the date on which the bank holding company proposes to commence an activity or acquisition, no administrative enforcement action has been commenced, and no cease and desist order has been issued pursuant to section 1818 of this title, against the bank holding company or any depository institution subsidiary of the holding company, and no such enforcement action, order, or other administrative enforcement proceeding is pending as of such date.

(5) Notification

(A) Commencement of activities approved by rule

A bank holding company that qualifies under paragraph (4) and that proposes to engage de novo, directly or through a subsidiary, in any activity that is permissible under subsection (c)(8) of this section, as determined by the

Board by regulation, may commence that activity without prior notice to the Board and must provide written notification to the Board not later than 10 business days after commencing the activity.

(B) Activities permitted by order and acquisitions

(i) In general

At least 12 business days before commencing any activity pursuant to paragraph (3) (other than an activity described in subparagraph (A) of this paragraph) or acquiring shares or assets of any company pursuant to paragraph (3), the bank holding company shall provide written notice of the proposal to the Board, unless the Board determines that no notice or a shorter notice period is appropriate.

(ii) Description of activities and terms

A notification under this subparagraph shall include a description of the proposed activities and the terms of any proposed acquisition.

(6) Recently acquired institutions

Any insured depository institution which has been acquired by a bank holding company during the 12–month period preceding the date on which the company proposes to commence an activity or acquisition pursuant to paragraph (3) may be excluded for purposes of paragraph (4)(B)(ii) if—

(A) the bank holding company has developed a plan for the institution to restore the capital and management of the institution which is acceptable to the appropriate Federal banking agency; and

(B) all such insured depository institutions represent, in the aggregate, less than 10 percent of the aggregate total risk-weighted assets of all insured depository institutions controlled by the bank holding company.

(7) Adjustment of percentages

The Board may, by regulation, adjust the percentages and the manner in which the percentages of insured depository institutions are calculated under paragraph (4)(B)(i), (4)(D), or (6)(B) if the Board determines that any such adjustment is consistent with safety and soundness and the purposes of this chapter.

(k) Engaging in activities that are financial in nature

(1) In general

Notwithstanding subsection (a), a financial holding company may engage in any activity, and may acquire and retain the shares of any company engaged in any activity, that the Board, in accordance with paragraph (2), determines (by regulation or order)—

(A) to be financial in nature or incidental to such financial activity; or

(B) is complementary to a financial activity and does not pose a substantial risk to the safety or soundness of depository institutions or the financial system generally.

(2) Coordination between the Board and the Secretary of the Treasury

(A) Proposals raised before the Board

(i) Consultation

The Board shall notify the Secretary of the Treasury of, and consult with the Secretary of the Treasury concerning, any request, proposal, or application under this subsection for a determination of whether an activity is financial in nature or incidental to a financial activity.

(ii) Treasury view

The Board shall not determine that any activity is financial in nature or incidental to a financial activity under this subsection if the Secretary of the Treasury notifies the Board in writing, not later than 30 days after the date of receipt of the notice described in clause (i) (or such longer period as the Board determines to be appropriate under the circumstances) that the Secretary of the Treasury believes that the activity is not financial in nature or incidental to a financial activity or is not otherwise permissible under this section.

(B) Proposals raised by the Treasury

(i) Treasury recommendation

The Secretary of the Treasury may, at any time, recommend in writing that the Board find an activity to be financial in nature or incidental to a financial activity.

(ii) Time period for Board action

Not later than 30 days after the date of receipt of a written recommendation from the Secretary of the Treasury under clause (i) (or such longer period as the Secretary of the Treasury and the Board determine to be appropriate under the circumstances), the Board shall determine whether to initiate a public rulemaking proposing that the recommended activity be found to be financial in nature or incidental to a financial activity under this subsection, and shall notify the Secretary of the Treasury in writing of the determination of the Board and, if the Board determines not to seek public comment on the proposal, the reasons for that determination.

(3) Factors to be considered

In determining whether an activity is financial in nature or incidental to a financial activity, the Board shall take into account—

(A) the purposes of this chapter and the Gramm–Leach–Bliley Act;

(B) changes or reasonably expected changes in the marketplace in which financial holding companies compete;

(C) changes or reasonably expected changes in the technology for delivering financial services; and

(D) whether such activity is necessary or appropriate to allow a financial holding company and the affiliates of a financial holding company to—

(i) compete effectively with any company seeking to provide financial services in the United States;

(ii) efficiently deliver information and services that are financial in nature through the use of technological means, including any application necessary to protect the security or efficacy of systems for the transmission of data or financial transactions; and

(iii) offer customers any available or emerging technological means for using financial services or for the document imaging of data.

(4) Activities that are financial in nature

For purposes of this subsection, the following activities shall be considered to be financial in nature:

(A) Lending, exchanging, transferring, investing for others, or safeguarding money or securities.

(B) Insuring, guaranteeing, or indemnifying against loss, harm, damage, illness, disability, or death, or providing and issuing annuities, and acting as principal, agent, or broker for purposes of the foregoing, in any State.

(C) Providing financial, investment, or economic advisory services, including advising an investment company (as defined in section 80a–3 of Title 15).

(D) Issuing or selling instruments representing interests in pools of assets permissible for a bank to hold directly.

(E) Underwriting, dealing in, or making a market in securities.

(F) Engaging in any activity that the Board has determined, by order or regulation that is in effect on November 12, 1999, to be so closely related to banking or managing or controlling banks as to be a proper incident thereto (subject to the same terms and conditions contained in such order or regulation, unless modified by the Board).

(G) Engaging, in the United States, in any activity that—

(i) a bank holding company may engage in outside of the United States; and

(ii) the Board has determined, under regulations prescribed or interpretations issued pursuant to subsection (c)(13) (as in effect on the day before November 12, 1999) to be usual in connection with the transaction of banking or other financial operations abroad.

(H) Directly or indirectly acquiring or controlling, whether as principal, on behalf of 1 or more entities (including entities, other than a depository institution or subsidiary of a depository institution, that the bank holding company controls), or otherwise, shares, assets, or ownership interests (including debt or equity securities, partnership interests, trust certificates, or other instruments representing ownership) of a company or other entity, whether or not constituting control of such company or entity, engaged in any activity not authorized pursuant to this section if—

(i) the shares, assets, or ownership interests are not acquired or held by a depository institution or subsidiary of a depository institution;

(ii) such shares, assets, or ownership interests are acquired and held by—

(I) a securities affiliate or an affiliate thereof; or

(II) an affiliate of an insurance company described in subparagraph (I)(ii) that provides investment advice to an insurance company and is registered pursuant to the Investment Advisers Act of 1940 [15 U.S.C.A. § 80b–1 et seq.], or an affiliate of such investment adviser;

as part of a bona fide underwriting or merchant or investment banking activity, including investment activities engaged in for the purpose of appreciation and ultimate resale or disposition of the investment;

(iii) such shares, assets, or ownership interests are held for a period of time to enable the sale or disposition thereof on a reasonable basis consistent with the financial viability of the activities described in clause (ii); and

(iv) during the period such shares, assets, or ownership interests are held, the bank holding company does not routinely manage or operate such company or entity except as may be necessary or required to obtain a reasonable return on investment upon resale or disposition.

(I) Directly or indirectly acquiring or controlling, whether as principal, on behalf of 1 or more entities (including entities, other than a depository institution or subsidiary of a depository institution, that the bank holding company controls) or otherwise, shares, assets, or ownership interests (including debt or equity securities, partnership interests, trust certificates or other instruments representing ownership) of a company or other entity, whether or not constituting control of such company or entity, engaged in any activity not authorized pursuant to this section if—

(i) the shares, assets, or ownership interests are not acquired or held by a depository institution or a subsidiary of a depository institution;

(ii) such shares, assets, or ownership interests are acquired and held by an insurance company that is predominantly engaged in underwriting life, accident and health, or property and casualty insurance (other than credit-related insurance) or providing and issuing annuities;

(iii) such shares, assets, or ownership interests represent an investment made in the ordinary course of business of such insurance company in accordance with relevant State law governing such investments; and

(iv) during the period such shares, assets, or ownership interests are held, the bank holding company does not routinely manage or operate such company except as may be necessary or required to obtain a reasonable return on investment.

(5) Actions required

(A) In general

The Board shall, by regulation or order, define, consistent with the purposes of this chapter, the activities described in subparagraph (B) as financial in nature, and the extent to which such activities are financial in nature or incidental to a financial activity.

(B) Activities

The activities described in this subparagraph are as follows:

(i) Lending, exchanging, transferring, investing for others, or safeguarding financial assets other than money or securities.

(ii) Providing any device or other instrumentality for transferring money or other financial assets.

(iii) Arranging, effecting, or facilitating financial transactions for the account of third parties.

(6) Required notification

(A) In general

A financial holding company that acquires any company or commences any activity pursuant to this subsection shall provide written notice to the Board describing the activity commenced or conducted by the company acquired not later than 30 calendar days after commencing the activity or consummating the acquisition, as the case may be.

(B) Approval not required for certain financial activities

Except as provided in subsection (j) with regard to the acquisition of a savings association, a financial holding company may com-

mence any activity, or acquire any company, pursuant to paragraph (4) or any regulation prescribed or order issued under paragraph (5), without prior approval of the Board.

(7) Merchant banking activities

(A) Joint regulations

The Board and the Secretary of the Treasury may issue such regulations implementing paragraph (4)(H), including limitations on transactions between depository institutions and companies controlled pursuant to such paragraph, as the Board and the Secretary jointly deem appropriate to assure compliance with the purposes and prevent evasions of this chapter and the Gramm–Leach–Bliley Act and to protect depository institutions.

(B) Sunset of restrictions on merchant banking activities of financial subsidiaries

The restrictions contained in paragraph (4)(H) on the ownership and control of shares, assets, or ownership interests by or on behalf of a subsidiary of a depository institution shall not apply to a financial subsidiary (as defined in section 24a of this title) of a bank, if the Board and the Secretary of the Treasury jointly authorize financial subsidiaries of banks to engage in merchant banking activities pursuant to section 122 of the Gramm–Leach–Bliley Act.

(*l*) Conditions for engaging in expanded financial activities

(1) In general

Notwithstanding subsection (k), (n), or (*o*), a bank holding company may not engage in any activity, or directly or indirectly acquire or retain shares of any company engaged in any activity, under subsection (k), (n), or (*o*), other than activities permissible for any bank holding company under subsection (c)(8), unless—

(A) all of the depository institution subsidiaries of the bank holding company are well capitalized;

(B) all of the depository institution subsidiaries of the bank holding company are well managed; and

(C) the bank holding company has filed with the Board—

(i) a declaration that the company elects to be a financial holding company to engage in activities or acquire and retain shares of a company that were not permissible for a bank holding company to engage in or acquire before the enactment of the Gramm–Leach–Bliley Act; and

(ii) a certification that the company meets the requirements of subparagraphs (A) and (B).

(2) CRA requirement

Notwithstanding subsection (k) or (n) of this section, section 24a of this title, or section 1831w(a) of this title, the appropriate Federal banking agency shall prohibit a financial holding company or any insured depository institution from—

(A) commencing any new activity under subsection (k) or (n) of this section, section 24a of this title, or section 1831w(a) of this title; or

(B) directly or indirectly acquiring control of a company engaged in any activity under subsection (k) or (n) of this section, section 24a of this title, or section 1831w(a) of this title (other than an investment made pursuant to subparagraph (H) or (I) of subsection (k)(4), or section 122 of the Gramm–Leach–Bliley Act, or under section 1831w(a) of this title by reason of such section 122, by an affiliate already engaged in activities under any such provision);

if any insured depository institution subsidiary of such financial holding company, or the insured depository institution or any of its insured depository institution affiliates, has received in its most recent examination under the Community Reinvestment Act of 1977, a rating of less than "satisfactory record of meeting community credit needs".

(3) Foreign banks

For purposes of paragraph (1), the Board shall apply comparable capital and management standards to a foreign bank that operates a branch or agency or owns or controls a commercial lending company in the United States, giving due regard to the principle of national treatment and equality of competitive opportunity.

(m) Provisions applicable to financial holding companies that fail to meet certain requirements

(1) In general

If the Board finds that—

(A) a financial holding company is engaged, directly or indirectly, in any activity under subsection (k), (n), or (o), other than activities that are permissible for a bank holding company under subsection (c)(8); and

(B) such financial holding company is not in compliance with the requirements of subsection (l)(1);

the Board shall give notice to the financial holding company to that effect, describing the conditions giving rise to the notice.

(2) Agreement to correct conditions required

Not later than 45 days after the date of receipt by a financial holding company of a notice given under paragraph (1) (or such additional period as the Board may permit), the financial holding company shall execute an agreement with the Board to comply with the requirements applicable to a financial holding company under subsection (l)(1).

(3) Board may impose limitations

Until the conditions described in a notice to a financial holding company under paragraph (1) are corrected, the Board may impose such limitations on the conduct or activities of that financial holding company or any affiliate of that company as the Board determines to be appropriate under the circumstances and consistent with the purposes of this chapter.

(4) Failure to correct

If the conditions described in a notice to a financial holding company under paragraph (1) are not corrected within 180 days after the date of receipt by the financial holding company of a notice under paragraph (1), the Board may require such financial holding company, under such terms and conditions as may be imposed by the Board and subject to such extension of time as may be granted in the discretion of the Board, either—

(A) to divest control of any subsidiary depository institution; or

(B) at the election of the financial holding company instead to cease to engage in any activity conducted by such financial holding company or its subsidiaries (other than a depository institution or a subsidiary of a depository institution) that is not an activity that is permissible for a bank holding company under subsection (c)(8).

(5) Consultation

In taking any action under this subsection, the Board shall consult with all relevant Federal and State regulatory agencies and authorities.

(n) Authority to retain limited nonfinancial activities and affiliations

(1) In general

Notwithstanding subsection (a) of this section, a company that is not a bank holding company or a foreign bank (as defined in section 3101(b)(7) of this title) and becomes a financial holding company after November 12, 1999, may continue to engage in any activity and retain direct or indirect ownership or control of shares of a company engaged in any activity if—

(A) the holding company lawfully was engaged in the activity or held the shares of such company on September 30, 1999;

(B) the holding company is predominantly engaged in financial activities as defined in paragraph (2); and

(C) the company engaged in such activity continues to engage only in the same activities that such company conducted on September 30, 1999, and other activities permissible under this chapter.

(2) Predominantly financial

For purposes of this subsection, a company is predominantly engaged in financial activities if the annual gross revenues derived by the holding company and all subsidiaries of the holding company (excluding revenues derived from subsidiary depository institutions), on a consolidated basis, from engaging in activities that are financial in nature or are incidental to a financial activity under subsection (k) represent at least 85percent of the consolidated annual gross revenues of the company.

(3) No expansion of grandfathered commercial activities through merger or consolidation

A financial holding company that engages in activities or holds shares pursuant to this subsection, or a subsidiary of such financial holding company, may not acquire, in any merger, consolidation, or other type of business combination, assets of any other company that is engaged in any activity that the Board has not determined to be financial in nature or incidental to a financial activity under subsection (k), except this paragraph shall not apply with respect to a company that owns a broadcasting station licensed under title III of the Communications Act of 1934 and the shares of which are under common control with an insurance company since January 1, 1998, unless such company is acquired by, or otherwise becomes an affiliate of, a bank holding company that, at the time such acquisition or affiliation is consummated, is 1 of the 5 largest domestic bank holding companies (as determined on the basis of the consolidated total assets of such companies).

(4) Continuing revenue limitation on grandfathered commercial activities

Notwithstanding any other provision of this subsection, a financial holding company may continue to engage in activities or hold shares in companies pursuant to this subsection only to the extent that the aggregate annual gross revenues derived from all such activities and all such companies does not exceed 15 percent of the consolidated annual gross revenues of the financial holding company (excluding revenues derived from subsidiary depository institutions).

(5) Cross marketing restrictions applicable to commercial activities

(A) In general

A depository institution controlled by a financial holding company shall not-

(i) offer or market, directly or through any arrangement, any product or service of a company whose activities are conducted or whose shares are owned or controlled by the financial holding company pursuant to this subsection or subparagraph (H) or (I) of subsection (k)(4); or

(ii) permit any of its products or services to be offered or marketed, directly or through any arrangement, by or through any company described in clause (i).

(B) Rule of construction

Subparagraph (A) shall not be construed as prohibiting an arrangement between a depository institution and a company owned or controlled pursuant to subparagraph (H) or (I) of subsection (k)(4) for the marketing of products or services through statement inserts or Internet websites if—

(i) such arrangement does not violate section 106 of the Bank Holding Company Act Amendments of 1970; and

(ii) the Board determines that the arrangement is in the public interest, does not undermine the separation of banking and commerce, and is consistent with the safety and soundness of depository institutions.

(6) Transactions with nonfinancial affiliates

A depository institution controlled by a financial holding company may not engage in a covered transaction (as defined in section 371c(b)(7) of this title) with any affiliate controlled by the company pursuant to this subsection.

(7) Sunset of grandfather

A financial holding company engaged in any activity, or retaining direct or indirect ownership or control of shares of a company, pursuant to this subsection, shall terminate such activity and divest ownership or control of the shares of such company before the end of the 10–year period beginning on November 12, 1999. The Board may, upon application by a financial holding company, extend such 10–year period by a period not to exceed an additional 5 years if such extension would not be detrimental to the public interest.

(o) Regulation of certain financial holding companies

Notwithstanding subsection (a) of this section, a company that is not a bank holding company or a foreign bank (as defined in section 3101(b)(7) of this title) and becomes a financial holding company after November 12, 1999, may continue to engage in, or directly or indirectly own or control shares of a company engaged in, activities related to the trading, sale, or investment in commodities and underlying physical properties that were not permissible for bank holding companies to conduct in the United States as of September 30, 1997, if—

(1) the holding company, or any subsidiary of the holding company, lawfully was engaged, directly or indirectly, in any of such activities as of September 30, 1997, in the United States;

(2) the attributed aggregate consolidated assets of the company held by the holding com-

pany pursuant to this subsection, and not otherwise permitted to be held by a financial holding company, are equal to not more than 5 percent of the total consolidated assets of the bank holding company, except that the Board may increase that percentage by such amounts and under such circumstances as the Board considers appropriate, consistent with the purposes of this chapter; and

(3) the holding company does not permit—

(A) any company, the shares of which it owns or controls pursuant to this subsection, to offer or market any product or service of an affiliated depository institution; or

(B) any affiliated depository institution to offer or market any product or service of any company, the shares of which are owned or controlled by such holding company pursuant to this subsection.

§ 1844. Administration—DFA §§ 604, 616

(a) Registration of bank holding company

Within one hundred and eighty days after May 9, 1956, or within one hundred and eighty days after becoming a bank holding company, whichever is later, each bank holding company shall register with the Board on forms prescribed by the Board, which shall include such information with respect to the financial condition and operations, management, and intercompany relationships of the bank holding company and its subsidiaries, and related matters, as the Board may deem necessary or appropriate to carry out the purposes of this chapter. The Board may, in its discretion, extend the time within which a bank holding company shall register and file the requisite information. A declaration filed in accordance with section 1843(l)(1)(C) of this title shall satisfy the requirements of this subsection with regard to the registration of a bank holding company but not any requirement to file an application to acquire a bank pursuant to section 1842 of this title.

(b) Regulations and orders

The Board is authorized to issue such regulations and orders as may be necessary to enable it to administer and carry out the purposes of this chapter and prevent evasions thereof.

(c) Reports and examinations

(1) Reports

(A) In general

The Board, from time to time, may require a bank holding company and any subsidiary of such company to submit reports under oath to keep the Board informed as to—

(i) its financial condition, systems for monitoring and controlling financial and operating risks, and transactions with depository institution subsidiaries of the bank holding company; and

(ii) compliance by the company or subsidiary with applicable provisions of this chapter or any other Federal law that the Board has specific jurisdiction to enforce against such company or subsidiary.

(B) Use of existing reports

(i) In general

For purposes of compliance with this paragraph, the Board shall, to the fullest extent possible, accept—

(I) reports that a bank holding company or any subsidiary of such company has provided or been required to provide to other Federal or State supervisors or to appropriate self-regulatory organizations;

(II) information that is otherwise required to be reported publicly; and

(III) externally audited financial statements.

(ii) Availability

A bank holding company or a subsidiary of such company shall provide to the Board, at the request of the Board, a report referred to in clause (i).

(iii) Reports filed with other agencies

(I) In general

In the event that the Board requires a report under this subsection from a functionally regulated subsidiary of a bank holding company of a kind that is not required by another Federal or State regulatory authority or an appropriate self-regulatory organization, the Board shall first request that the appropriate regulatory authority or self-regulatory organization obtain such report.

(II) Availability from other subsidiary

If the report is not made available to the Board, and the report is necessary to assess a material risk to the bank holding company or any of its depository institution subsidiaries or compliance with this chapter or any other Federal law that the Board has specific jurisdiction to enforce against such company or subsidiary or the systems described in paragraph (2)(A)(ii)(II), the Board may require such functionally regulated subsidiary to provide such a report to the Board.

(2) Examinations

(A) Examination authority for bank holding companies and subsidiaries

Subject to subparagraph (B), the Board may make examinations of each bank holding company and each subsidiary of such holding company in order—

(i) to inform the Board of the nature of the operations and financial condition of the holding company and such subsidiaries;

(ii) to inform the Board of—

(I) the financial and operational risks within the holding company system that may pose a threat to the safety and soundness of any depository institution subsidiary of such holding company; and

(II) the systems for monitoring and controlling such risks; and

(iii) to monitor compliance with the provisions of this chapter or any other Federal law that the Board has specific jurisdiction to enforce against such company or subsidiary and those governing transactions and relationships between any depository institution subsidiary and its affiliates.

(B) Functionally regulated subsidiaries

Notwithstanding subparagraph (A), the Board may make examinations of a functionally regulated subsidiary of a bank holding company only if—

(i) the Board has reasonable cause to believe that such subsidiary is engaged in activities that pose a material risk to an affiliated depository institution;

(ii) the Board reasonably determines, after reviewing relevant reports, that examination of the subsidiary is necessary to adequately inform the Board of the systems described in subparagraph (A)(ii)(II); or

(iii) based on reports and other available information, the Board has reasonable cause to believe that a subsidiary is not in compliance with this chapter or any other Federal law that the Board has specific jurisdiction to enforce against such subsidiary, including provisions relating to transactions with an affiliated depository institution, and the Board cannot make such determination through examination of the affiliated depository institution or the bank holding company.

(C) Restricted focus of examinations

The Board shall, to the fullest extent possible, limit the focus and scope of any examination of a bank holding company to—

(i) the bank holding company; and

(ii) any subsidiary of the bank holding company that could have a materially adverse effect on the safety and soundness of any depository institution subsidiary of the holding company due to-

(I) the size, condition, or activities of the subsidiary; or

(II) the nature or size of transactions between the subsidiary and any depository institution that is also a subsidiary of the bank holding company.

(D) Deference to bank examinations

The Board shall, to the fullest extent possible, for the purposes of this paragraph, use the reports of examinations of depository institutions made by the appropriate Federal and State depository institution supervisory authority.

(E) Deference to other examinations

The Board shall, to the fullest extent possible, forego an examination by the Board under this paragraph and instead review the reports of examination made of—

(i) any registered broker or dealer by or on behalf of the Securities and Exchange Commission;

(ii) any registered investment adviser properly registered by or on behalf of either the Securities and Exchange Commission or any State;

(iii) any licensed insurance company by or on behalf of any State regulatory authority responsible for the supervision of insurance companies; and

(iv) any other subsidiary that the Board finds to be comprehensively supervised by a Federal or State authority.

(3) Capital

(A) In general

The Board may not, by regulation, guideline, order, or otherwise, prescribe or impose any capital or capital adequacy rules, guidelines, standards, or requirements on any functionally regulated subsidiary of a bank holding company that—

(i) is not a depository institution; and

(ii) is—

(I) in compliance with the applicable capital requirements of its Federal regulatory authority (including the Securities and Exchange Commission) or State insurance authority;

(II) properly registered as an investment adviser under the Investment Advisers Act of 1940 [15 U.S.C.A. § 80b–1 et seq.], or with any State; or

(III) is licensed as an insurance agent with the appropriate State insurance authority.

(B) Rule of construction

Subparagraph (A) shall not be construed as preventing the Board from imposing capital or capital adequacy rules, guidelines, standards, or requirements with respect to—

(i) activities of a registered investment adviser other than with respect to investment advisory activities or activities incidental to investment advisory activities; or

(ii) activities of a licensed insurance agent other than insurance agency activities or activities incidental to insurance agency activities.

(C) Limitations on indirect action

In developing, establishing, or assessing bank holding company capital or capital adequacy rules, guidelines, standards, or requirements for purposes of this paragraph, the Board may not take into account the activities, operations, or investments of an affiliated investment company registered under the Investment Company Act of 1940 [15 U.S.C.A. § 80a–1 et seq.], unless the investment company is—

(i) a bank holding company; or

(ii) controlled by a bank holding company by reason of ownership by the bank holding company (including through all of its affiliates) of 25 percent or more of the shares of the investment company, and the shares owned by the bank holding company have a market value equal to more than $1,000,000.

(4) Functional regulation of securities and insurance activities

(A) Securities activities

Securities activities conducted in a functionally regulated subsidiary of a depository institution shall be subject to regulation by the Securities and Exchange Commission, and by relevant State securities authorities, as appropriate, subject to section 6701 of Title 15, to the same extent as if they were conducted in a nondepository institution subsidiary of a bank holding company.

(B) Insurance activities

Subject to section 6701 of Title 15, insurance agency and brokerage activities and activities as principal conducted in a functionally regulated subsidiary of a depository institution shall be subject to regulation by a State insurance authority to the same extent as if they were conducted in a nondepository institution subsidiary of a bank holding company.

(5) Definition

For purposes of this subsection, the term "functionally regulated subsidiary" means any company—

(A) that is not a bank holding company or a depository institution; and

(B) that is—

(i) a broker or dealer that is registered under the Securities Exchange Act of 1934 [15 U.S.C.A. § 78a et seq.];

(ii) a registered investment adviser, properly registered by or on behalf of either the Securities and Exchange Commission or any State, with respect to the investment advisory activities of such investment adviser and activities incidental to such investment advisory activities;

(iii) an investment company that is registered under the Investment Company Act of 1940 [15 U.S.C.A. § 80a–1 et seq.];

(iv) an insurance company, with respect to insurance activities of the insurance company and activities incidental to such insurance activities, that is subject to supervision by a State insurance regulator; or

(v) an entity that is subject to regulation by the Commodity Futures Trading Commission, with respect to the commodities activities of such entity and activities incidental to such commodities activities.

(d) Reports to the Congress; recommendations

Before the expiration of two years following May 9, 1956, and each year thereafter in the Board's annual report to the Congress, the Board shall report to the Congress the results of the administration of this chapter, stating what, if any, substantial difficulties have been encountered in carrying out the purposes of this chapter, and any recommendations as to changes in the law which in the opinion of the Board would be desirable.

(e) Termination of activities or ownership or control of nonbank subsidiaries constituting serious risk

(1) Notwithstanding any other provision of this chapter, the Board may, whenever it has reasonable cause to believe that the continuation by a bank holding company of any activity or of ownership or control of any of its nonbank subsidiaries, other than a nonbank subsidiary of a bank, constitutes a serious risk to the financial safety, soundness, or stability of a bank holding company subsidiary bank and is inconsistent with sound banking principles or with the purposes of this chapter or with the Financial Institutions Supervisory Act of 1966, at the election of the bank holding company—

(A) order the bank holding company or any such nonbank subsidiaries, after due notice and opportunity for hearing, and after considering the views of the bank's primary supervisor, which shall be the Comptroller of the Currency in the case of a national bank or the Federal Deposit Insurance Corporation and the appropriate State supervisory authority in the case of an insured nonmember bank, to terminate such activities or to terminate (within one hundred and twenty days or such longer period as the Board may direct in unusual circumstances) its ownership or control of any such subsidiary either by sale or by distribution of the shares of the subsidiary to the shareholders of the bank holding company; or

(B) order the bank holding company, after due notice and opportunity for hearing, and after consultation with the primary supervisor for the bank, which shall be the Comptroller of the Currency in the case of a national bank, and the Federal Deposit Insurance Corporation and the appropriate State supervisor in the case of an insured nonmember bank, to terminate (within 120 days or such longer period as the Board may direct) the ownership or control of any such bank by such company.

The distribution referred to in subparagraph (A) shall be pro rata with respect to all of the shareholders of the distributing bank holding company, and the holding company shall not make any charge to its shareholders arising out of such a distribution.

(2) The Board may in its discretion apply to the United States district court within the jurisdiction of which the principal office of the holding company is located, for the enforcement of any effective and outstanding order issued under this section, and such court shall have jurisdiction and power to order and require compliance therewith, but except as provided in section 1848 of this title, no court shall have jurisdiction to affect by injunction or otherwise the issuance or enforcement of any notice or order under this section, or to review, modify, suspend, terminate, or set aside any such notice or order.

(f) Powers of Board respecting applications, examinations, or other proceedings

In the course of or in connection with an application, examination, investigation or other proceeding under this chapter, the Board, or any member or designated representative thereof, including any person designated to conduct any hearing under this chapter, shall have the power to administer oaths and affirmations, to take or cause to be taken depositions, and to issue, revoke, quash, or modify subpenas and subpenas duces tecum; and the Board is empowered to make rules and regulations to effectuate the purposes of this subsection. The attendance of witnesses and the production of documents provided for in this subsection may be required from any place in any State or in any territory or other place subject to the jurisdiction of the United

States at any designated place where such proceeding is being conducted. Any party to proceedings under this chapter may apply to the United States District Court for the District of Columbia, or the United States district court for the judicial district or the United States court in any territory in which such proceeding is being conducted or where the witness resides or carries on business, for the enforcement of any subpena or subpoena duces tecum issued pursuant to this subsection, and such courts shall have jurisdiction and power to order and require compliance therewith. Witnesses subpenaed under this subsection shall be paid the same fees and mileage that are paid witnesses in the district courts of the United States. Any service required under this subsection may be made by registered mail, or in such other manner reasonably calculated to give actual notice as the Board may by regulation or otherwise provide. Any court having jurisdiction of any proceeding instituted under this subsection may allow to any such party such reasonable expenses and attorneys' fees as it deems just and proper. Any person who willfully shall fail or refuse to attend and testify or to answer any lawful inquiry or to produce books, papers, correspondence, memoranda, contracts, agreements, or other records, if in such person's power so to do, in obedience to the subpena of the Board, shall be guilty of a misdemeanor and, upon conviction, shall be subject to a fine of not more than $1,000 or to imprisonment for a term of not more than one year or both.

(g) Authority of State insurance regulator and the securities and exchange Commission

(1) In general

Notwithstanding any other provision of law, any regulation, order, or other action of the Board that requires a bank holding company to provide funds or other assets to a subsidiary depository institution shall not be effective nor enforceable with respect to an entity described in subparagraph (A) if—

(A) such funds or assets are to be provided by—

(i) a bank holding company that is an insurance company, a broker or dealer registered under the Securities Exchange Act of 1934 [15 U.S.C.A. § 78a et seq.], an investment company registered under the Investment Company Act of 1940 [15 U.S.C.A. § 80a–1 et seq.], or an investment adviser registered by or on behalf of either the Securities and Exchange Commission or any State; or

(ii) an affiliate of the depository institution that is an insurance company or a broker or dealer registered under the Securities Exchange Act of 1934 [15 U.S.C.A. § 78a et seq.], an investment company registered under the Investment Company Act of 1940 [15 U.S.C.A. § 80a–1 et seq.], or an investment adviser registered by or on behalf of either the Securities and Exchange Commission or any State; and

(B) the State insurance authority for the insurance company or the Securities and Exchange Commission for the registered broker, dealer, investment adviser (solely with respect to investment advisory activities or activities incidental thereto), or investment company, as the case may be, determines in writing sent to the holding company and the Board that the holding company shall not provide such funds or assets because such action would have a material adverse effect on the financial condition of the insurance company or the broker, dealer, investment company, or investment adviser, as the case may be.

(2) Notice to State insurance authority or SEC required

If the Board requires a bank holding company, or an affiliate of a bank holding company, that is an insurance company or a broker, dealer, investment company, or investment adviser described in paragraph (1)(A) to provide funds or assets to a depository institution subsidiary of the holding company pursuant to any regulation, order, or other action of the Board referred to in paragraph (1), the Board shall promptly notify the State insurance authority for the insurance company, the Securities and Exchange Commission, or State securities regulator, as the case may be, of such requirement.

(3) Divestiture in lieu of other action

If the Board receives a notice described in paragraph (1)(B) from a State insurance authority or the Securities and Exchange Commission with regard to a bank holding company or affiliate referred to in that paragraph, the Board may order the bank holding company to divest the depository institution not later than 180 days after receiving the notice, or

such longer period as the Board determines consistent with the safe and sound operation of the depository institution.

(4) Conditions before divestiture

During the period beginning on the date an order to divest is issued by the Board under paragraph (3) to a bank holding company and ending on the date the divestiture is completed, the Board may impose any conditions or restrictions on the holding company's ownership or operation of the depository institution, including restricting or prohibiting transactions between the depository institution and any affiliate of the institution, as are appropriate under the circumstances.

(5) Rule of construction

No provision of this subsection may be construed as limiting or otherwise affecting, except to the extent specifically provided in this subsection, the regulatory authority, including the scope of the authority, of any Federal agency or department with regard to any entity that is within the jurisdiction of such agency or department.

§ 1845. Repealed. Pub.L. 89–485, § 9, July 1, 1966, 80 Stat. 240

§ 1846. Reservation of rights to States

(a) In general

No provision of this chapter shall be construed as preventing any State from exercising such powers and jurisdiction which it now has or may hereafter have with respect to companies, banks, bank holding companies, and subsidiaries thereof.

(b) State taxation authority not affected

No provision of this chapter shall be construed as affecting the authority of any State or political subdivision of any State to adopt, apply, or administer any tax or method of taxation to any bank, bank holding company, or foreign bank, or any affiliate of any bank, bank holding company, or foreign bank, to the extent that such tax or tax method is otherwise permissible by or under the Constitution of the United States or other Federal law.

§ 1847. Penalties

(a) Criminal penalty

(1) Whoever knowingly violates any provision of this chapter or, being a company, violates any regulation or order issued by the Board under this chapter, shall be imprisoned not more than 1 year, fined not more than $100,000 per day for each day during which the violation continues, or both.

(2) Whoever, with the intent to deceive, defraud, or profit significantly, knowingly violates any provision of this chapter shall be imprisoned not more than 5 years, fined not more than $1,000,000 per day for each day during which the violation continues, or both.

Every officer, director, agent, and employee of a bank holding company shall be subject to the same penalties for false entries in any book, report, or statement of such bank holding company as are applicable to officers, directors, agents, and employees of member banks for false entries in any books, reports, or statements of member banks under section 1005 of Title 18.

(b) Civil money penalty

(1) Penalty

Any company which violates, and any individual who participates in a violation of, any provision of this chapter, or any regulation or order issued pursuant thereto, shall forfeit and pay a civil penalty of not more than $25,000 for each day during which such violation continues.

(2) Assessment; etc.

Any penalty imposed under paragraph (1) may be assessed and collected by the Board in the manner provided in subparagraphs (E), (F), (G), and (I) of section 1818(i)(2) of this title for penalties imposed (under such section) and any such assessment shall be subject to the provisions of such section.

(3) Hearing

The company or other person against whom any penalty is assessed under this subsection shall be afforded an agency hearing if such association or person submits a request for such hearing within 20 days after the issuance of the notice of assessment. Section 1818(h) of this title shall apply to any proceeding under this subsection.

(4) Disbursement

All penalties collected under authority of this subsection shall be deposited into the Treasury.

(5) Violate defined

For purposes of this section, the term "violate" includes any action (alone or with another or others) for or toward causing, bringing about, participating in, counseling, or aiding or abetting a violation.

(6) Regulations

The Board shall prescribe regulations establishing such procedures as may be necessary to carry out this subsection.

(c) Notice under this section after separation from service

The resignation, termination of employment or participation, or separation of an institution-affiliated party (within the meaning of section 1813(u) of this title) with respect to a bank holding company (including a separation caused by the deregistration of such a company) shall not affect the jurisdiction and authority of the Board to issue any notice and proceed under this section against any such party, if such notice is served before the end of the 6–year period beginning on the date such party ceased to be such a party with respect to such holding company (whether such date occurs before, on, or after August 9, 1989).

(d) Penalty for failure to make reports

(1) First tier

Any company which—

(A) maintains procedures reasonably adapted to avoid any inadvertent error and, unintentionally and as a result of such an error—

(i) fails to make, submit, or publish such reports or information as may be required under this chapter or under regulations prescribed by the Board pursuant to this chapter, within the period of time specified by the Board; or

(ii) submits or publishes any false or misleading report or information; or

(B) inadvertently transmits or publishes any report which is minimally late,

shall be subject to a penalty of not more than $2,000 for each day during which such failure continues or such false or misleading information is not corrected. The company shall have the burden of proving that an error was inadvertent and that a report was inadvertently transmitted or published late.

(2) Second tier

Any company which—

(A) fails to make, submit, or publish such reports or information as may be required under this chapter or under regulations prescribed by the Board pursuant to this chapter, within the period of time specified by the Board; or

(B) submits or publishes any false or misleading report or information,

in a manner not described in paragraph (1) shall be subject to a penalty of not more than $20,000 for each day during which such failure continues or such false or misleading information is not corrected.

(3) Third tier

Notwithstanding paragraph (2), if any company knowingly or with reckless disregard for the accuracy of any information or report described in paragraph (2) submits or publishes any false or misleading report or information, the Board may, in its discretion, assess a penalty of not more than $1,000,000 or 1 percent of total assets of such company, whichever is less, per day for each day during which such failure continues or such false or misleading information is not corrected.

(4) Assessment; etc.

Any penalty imposed under paragraph (1), (2), or (3) shall be assessed and collected by the Board in the manner provided in subsection (b) of this section (for penalties imposed under such subsection) and any such assessment (including the determination of the amount of the penalty) shall be subject to the provisions of such subsection.

(5) Hearing

Any company against which any penalty is assessed under this subsection shall be afforded an agency hearing if such company submits a request for such hearing within 20 days after the issuance of the notice of assessment. Section 1818(h) of this title shall apply to any proceeding under this subsection.

§ 1848. Judicial review

Any party aggrieved by an order of the Board under this chapter may obtain a review of such order in the United States Court of Appeals within any circuit wherein such party has its principal place of business, or in the Court of Appeals in the District of Columbia, by filing in the court, within thirty days after the entry of the Board's order, a petition praying that the order of the Board be set aside. A copy of such petition shall be forthwith transmitted to the Board by the clerk of the court, and thereupon the Board shall file in the court the record made before the Board, as provided in section 2112 of Title 28. Upon the filing of such petition the court shall have jurisdiction to affirm, set aside, or modify the order of the Board and to require the Board to take such action with regard to the matter under review as the court deems proper. The findings of the Board as to the facts, if supported by substantial evidence, shall be conclusive.

§ 1848a. Limitation on rulemaking, prudential, supervisory, and enforcement authority of the Board—DFA § 604

(a) Limitation on direct action

The Board may not prescribe regulations, issue or seek entry of orders, impose restraints, restrictions, guidelines, requirements, safeguards, or standards, or otherwise take any action under or pursuant to any provision of this chapter or section 1818 of this title against or with respect to a functionally regulated subsidiary of a bank holding company unless—

(1) the action is necessary to prevent or redress an unsafe or unsound practice or breach of fiduciary duty by such subsidiary that poses a material risk to—

(A) the financial safety, soundness, or stability of an affiliated depository institution; or

(B) the domestic or international payment system; and

(2) the Board finds that it is not reasonably possible to protect effectively against the material risk at issue through action directed at or against the affiliated depository institution or against depository institutions generally.

(b) Limitation on indirect action

The Board may not prescribe regulations, issue or seek entry of orders, impose restraints, restrictions, guidelines, requirements, safeguards, or standards, or otherwise take any action under or pursuant to any provision of this chapter or section 1818 of this title against or with respect to a bank holding company that requires the bank holding company to require a functionally regulated subsidiary of the holding company to engage, or to refrain from engaging, in any conduct or activities unless the Board could take such action directly against or with respect to the functionally regulated subsidiary in accordance with subsection (a).

(c) Actions specifically authorized

Notwithstanding subsection (a) or (b), the Board may take action under this chapter or section 1818 of this title to enforce compliance by a functionally regulated subsidiary of a bank holding company with any Federal law that the Board has specific jurisdiction to enforce against such subsidiary.

(d) Functionally regulated subsidiary defined

For purposes of this section, the term "functionally regulated subsidiary" has the meaning given the term in section 1844(c)(5) of this title.

§ 1849. Saving provision

(a) General rule

Nothing herein contained shall be interpreted or construed as approving any act, action, or conduct which is or has been or may be in violation of existing law, nor shall anything herein contained constitute a defense to any action, suit, or proceeding pending or hereafter instituted on account of any prohibited antitrust or monopolistic act, action, or conduct, except as specifically provided in this section.

(b) Antitrust review

(1) In general

The Board shall immediately notify the Attorney General of any approval by it pursuant to section 1842 of this title of a proposed acquisition, merger, or consolidation transaction and, if the transaction also involves an acquisition under section 1843 of this title, the Board shall also notify the Federal Trade Commission of such approval. If the Board has found that it must act immediately in order to prevent the probable failure of a bank or bank holding company involved in any such transaction, the transaction may be consummated immediately upon approval by the Board. If the Board has advised the Comptroller of the Currency or the State supervisory authority, as the case may be, of the existence of an emergency requiring expeditious action and has required the sub-

mission of views and recommendations within ten days, the transaction may not be consummated before the fifth calendar day after the date of approval by the Board. In all other cases, the transaction may not be consummated before the thirtieth calendar day after the date of approval by the Board or, if the Board has not received any adverse comment from the Attorney General of the United States relating to competitive factors, such shorter period of time as may be prescribed by the Board with the concurrence of the Attorney General, but in no event less than 15 calendar days after the date of approval. Any action brought under the antitrust laws arising out of an acquisition, merger, or consolidation transaction approved under section 1842 of this title shall be commenced prior to the earliest time under this subsection at which the transaction approval under section 1842 of this title might be consummated. The commencement of such an action shall stay the effectiveness of the Board's approval unless the court shall otherwise specifically order. In any such action, the court shall review de novo the issues presented. In any judicial proceeding attacking any acquisition, merger, or consolidation transaction approved pursuant to section 1842 of this title on the ground that such transaction alone and of itself constituted a violation of any antitrust laws other than section 2 of Title 15, the standards applied by the court shall be identical with those that the Board is directed to apply under section 1842 of this title. Upon the consummation of an acquisition, merger, or consolidation transaction approved under section 1842 of this title in compliance with this chapter and after the termination of any antitrust litigation commenced within the period prescribed in this section, or upon the termination of such period if no such litigation is commenced therein, the transaction may not thereafter be attacked in any judicial proceeding on the ground that it alone and of itself constituted a violation of any antitrust laws other than section 2 of Title 15, but nothing in this chapter shall exempt any bank holding company involved in such a transaction from complying with the antitrust laws after the consummation of such transaction.

(2) Section 1823(f) cases

(A) If—

(i) the Federal Deposit Insurance Corporation learns that a bank insured by such Corporation is in danger of closing; and

(ii) the Corporation is considering assisting the acquisition of such bank and its affiliated banks by another bank or holding company under section 1823(f) of this title and such acquisition is subject to the approval of the Board under section 1842 of this title,

the Corporation shall immediately notify the Board of such facts.

(B) Upon receipt of notice from the Federal Deposit Insurance Corporation under subparagraph (A) or at such earlier time as deemed appropriate by the Board, the Board shall immediately notify the Attorney General of the United States of the facts concerning the possible acquisition.

(C) Within 5 days of receiving notice under subparagraph (B), the Attorney General shall notify the Board in writing of the Attorney General's preliminary finding as to the consistency of the possible acquisition with the antitrust laws.

(D) The Board may reduce or eliminate the post-approval waiting period established under paragraph (1) for an acquisition to which this paragraph applies, except that such period may not be eliminated or reduced to less than 5 days without the concurrence of the Attorney General.

(c) Antitrust proceedings; Board and State banking agency as party; representation by counsel

In any action brought under the antitrust laws arising out of any acquisition, merger, or consolidation transaction approved by the Board under section 1842 of this title, the Board and any State banking supervisory agency having jurisdiction within the State involved, may appear as a party of its own motion and as of right, and be represented by its counsel.

(d) Treatment of merger transactions consummated prior or subsequent to May 9, 1956, and not in litigation prior to July 1, 1966

Any acquisition, merger, or consolidation of the kind described in section 1842(a) of this title which was consummated at any time prior or subsequent to May 9, 1956, and as to which no litigation was initiated by the Attorney General prior to July 1, 1966, shall be conclusively presumed not to have been in violation of any antitrust laws other than section 2 of Title 15.

(e) Antitrust litigation; substantive law applicable to proceedings pending on or after July 1, 1966, with respect to merger transactions

Any court having pending before it on or after July 1, 1966, any litigation initiated under the antitrust laws by the Attorney General with respect to any acquisition, merger, or consolidation of the kind described in section 1842(a) of this title shall apply the substantive rule of law set forth in section 1842 of this title.

(f) "Antitrust laws" defined

For the purposes of this section, the term "antitrust laws" means the Act of July 2, 1890 (the Sherman Antitrust Act), the Act of October 15, 1914 (the Clayton Act), and any other Acts in pari materia.

§ 1850. Acquisition of subsidiary, nonbanking activity or business, and tying arrangement: Federal Reserve Board proceedings; application for authorization; competitor as party in interest and person aggrieved; judicial review

With respect to any proceeding before the Federal Reserve Board wherein an applicant seeks authority to acquire a subsidiary which is a bank under section 1842 of this title or to engage in an activity otherwise prohibited under chapter 22 of this title [12 U.S.C.A. § 1971 et seq.], a party who would become a competitor of the applicant or subsidiary thereof by virtue of the applicant's or its subsidiary's acquisition, entry into the business involved, or activity, shall have the right to be a party in interest in the proceeding and, in the event of an adverse order of the Board, shall have the right as an aggrieved party to obtain judicial review thereof as provided in section 1848 of this title or as otherwise provided by law.

CHAPTER 22. TYING ARRANGEMENTS
12 U.S.C.A. §§ 1971–1978

12 U.S.C.A. §   **Page**

CHAPTER 22. TYING ARRANGEMENTS

§ 1971. Definitions

As used in this chapter, the terms "bank", "bank holding company", "subsidiary", and "Board" have the meaning ascribed to such terms in section 1841 of this title. For purposes of this chapter only, the term "company", as used in section 1841 of this title, means any person, estate, trust, partnership, corporation, association, or similar organization, but does not include any corporation the majority of the shares of which are owned by the United States or by any State. The term "trust service" means any service customarily performed by a bank trust department. For purposes of this chapter, a financial subsidiary of a national bank engaging in activities pursuant to section 24a(a) of this title shall be deemed to be a subsidiary of a bank holding company, and not a subsidiary of a bank.

§ 1972. Certain tying arrangements prohibited; correspondent accounts

(1) A bank shall not in any manner extend credit, lease or sell property of any kind, or furnish any service, or fix or vary the consideration for any of the foregoing, on the condition or requirement—

(A) that the customer shall obtain some additional credit, property, or service from such bank other than a loan, discount, deposit, or trust service;

(B) that the customer shall obtain some additional credit, property, or service from a bank holding company of such bank, or from any other subsidiary of such bank holding company;

(C) that the customer provide some additional credit, property, or service to such bank, other than those related to and usually provided in connection with a loan, discount, deposit, or trust service;

(D) that the customer provide some additional credit, property, or service to a bank holding company of such bank, or to any other subsidiary of such bank holding company; or

(E) that the customer shall not obtain some other credit, property, or service from a competitor of such bank, a bank holding company of such bank, or any subsidiary of such bank

holding company, other than a condition or requirement that such bank shall reasonably impose in a credit transaction to assure the soundness of the credit.

The Board may by regulation or order permit such exceptions to the foregoing prohibition and the prohibitions of section 1843(f)(9) and 1843(h)(2) of this title as it considers will not be contrary to the purposes of this chapter.

(2) (A) No bank which maintains a correspondent account in the name of another bank shall make an extension of credit to an executive officer or director of, or to any person who directly or indirectly or acting through or in concert with one or more persons owns, controls, or has the power to vote more than 10 per centum of any class of voting securities of, such other bank or to any related interest of such person unless such extension of credit is made on substantially the same terms, including interest rates and collateral as those prevailing at the time for comparable transactions with other persons and does not involve more than the normal risk of repayment or present other unfavorable features.

(B) No bank shall open a correspondent account at another bank while such bank has outstanding an extension of credit to an executive officer or director of, or other person who directly or indirectly or acting through or in concert with one or more persons owns, controls, or has the power to vote more than 10 per centum of any class of voting securities of, the bank desiring to open the account or to any related interest of such person, unless such extension of credit was made on substantially the same terms, including interest rates and collateral as those prevailing at the time for comparable transactions with other persons and does not involve more than the normal risk of repayment or present other unfavorable features.

(C) No bank which maintains a correspondent account at another bank shall make an extension of credit to an executive officer or director of, or to any person who directly or indirectly acting through or in concert with one or more persons owns, controls, or has the power to vote more than 10 per centum of any class of voting securities of, such other bank or to any related interest of such person, unless such extension of credit is made on substantially the same terms, including interest rates and collateral as those prevailing at the time for comparable transactions with other persons and does not involve more than the normal risk of repayment or present other unfavorable features.

(D) No bank which has outstanding an extension of credit to an executive officer or director of, or to any person who directly or indirectly or acting through or in concert with one or more persons owns, controls, or has the power to vote more than 10 per centum of any class of voting securities of, another bank or to any related interest of such person shall open a correspondent account at such other bank, unless such extension of credit was made on substantially the same terms, including interest rates and collateral as those prevailing at the time for comparable transactions with other persons and does not involve more than the normal risk of repayment or present other unfavorable features.

(E) For purposes of this paragraph, the term "extension of credit" shall have the meaning prescribed by the Board pursuant to section 375b of this title and the term "executive officer" shall have the same meaning given it under section 375a of this title.

(F) Civil money penalty

  (i) First tier

Any bank which, and any institution-affiliated party (within the meaning of section 1813(u) of this title) with respect to such bank who, violates any provision of this paragraph shall forfeit and pay a civil penalty of not more than $5,000 for each day during which such violation continues.

  (ii) Second tier

Notwithstanding clause (i), any bank which, any institution-affiliated party (within the meaning of section 1813(u) of this title) with respect to such bank who—

(I)(aa) commits any violation described in clause (i);

(bb) recklessly engages in an unsafe or unsound practice in conducting the affairs of such bank; or

(cc) breaches any fiduciary duty;

(II) which violation, practice or breach—

(aa) is part of a pattern of misconduct;

(bb) causes or is likely to cause more than a minimal loss to such bank; or

(cc) results in pecuniary gain or other benefit to such party,

shall forfeit and pay a civil penalty of not more than $25,000 for each day during which such violation, practice, or breach continues.

  (iii) Third tier

Notwithstanding clauses (i) and (ii), any bank which, and any institution-affiliated party (within the meaning of section 1813(u) of this title) with respect to such bank who—

(I) knowingly—

(aa) commits any violation described in clause (i);

(bb) engages in any unsafe or unsound practice in conducting the affairs of such bank; or

(cc) breaches any fiduciary duty; and

(II) knowingly or recklessly causes a substantial loss to such bank or a substantial pecuniary gain or other benefit to such party by reason of such violation, practice or breach,

shall forfeit and pay a civil penalty in an amount not to exceed the applicable maximum amount determined under clause (iv) for each day during which such violation, practice or breach continues.

  (iv) Maximum amounts of penalties for any violation described in clause (iii)

The maximum daily amount of any civil penalty which may be assessed pursuant to clause (iii) for any violation, practice or breach described in such clause is—

(I) in the case of any person other than a bank, an amount to not exceed $1,000,000; and

(II) in the case of a bank, an amount not to exceed the lesser of–

(aa) $1,000,000; or

(bb) 1 percent of the total assets of such bank.

  (v) Assessment; etc.

Any penalty imposed under clause (i), (ii), or (iii) may be assessed and collected—

(I) in the case of a national bank, by the Comptroller of the Currency;

(II) in the case of a State member bank, by the Board; and

(III) in the case of an insured nonmember State bank, by the Federal Deposit Insurance Corporation,

in the manner provided in subparagraphs (E), (F), (G), and (I) of section 1818(i)(2) of this title for penalties imposed (under such section) and any such assessment shall be subject to the provisions of such section.

(vi) Hearing

The bank or other person against whom any penalty is assessed under this subparagraph shall be afforded an agency hearing if such bank or person submits a request for such hearing within 20 days after the issuance of the notice of assessment. Section 1818(h) of this title shall apply to any proceeding under this subparagraph.

(vii) Disbursement

All penalties collected under authority of this subsection shall be deposited into the Treasury.

(viii) Violate defined

For purposes of this paragraph, the term 'violate' includes any action (alone or with another or others) for or toward causing, bringing about, participating in, counseling, or aiding or abetting a violation.

(ix) Regulations

The Comptroller of the Currency, the Board, and the Federal Deposit Insurance Corporation shall prescribe regulations establishing such procedures as may be necessary to carry out this subparagraph.

(G) For the purpose of this paragraph—

(i) the term "bank" includes a mutual savings bank, a savings bank, and a savings association (as those terms are defined in section 1813 of this title);

(ii) the term "related interests of such persons" includes any company controlled by such executive officer, director, or person, or any political or campaign committee the funds or services of which will benefit such executive officer, director, or person or which

is controlled by such executive officer, director, or person; and

(iii) the terms "control of a company" and "company" have the same meaning as under section 375b of this title.

(H) Notice under this section after separation from service

The resignation, termination of employment or participation, or separation of an institution-affiliated party (within the meaning of section 1813(u) of this title) with respect to such a bank (including a separation caused by the closing of such a bank) shall not affect the jurisdiction and authority of the appropriate Federal banking agency to issue any notice and proceed under this section against any such party, if such notice is served before the end of the 6–year period beginning on the date such party ceased to be such a party with respect to such bank (whether such date occurs before, on, or after August 9, 1989).

§ 1973. Jurisdiction of courts; duty of United States attorneys; equitable proceedings; petition; expedition of cases; temporary restraining orders; bringing in additional parties; subpoenas

The district courts of the United States have jurisdiction to prevent and restrain violations of section 1972 of this title and it is the duty of the United States attorneys, under the direction of the Attorney General, to institute proceedings in equity to prevent and restrain such violations. The proceedings may be by way of a petition setting forth the case and praying that the violation be enjoined or otherwise prohibited. When the parties complained of have been duly notified of the petition, the court shall proceed, as soon as possible, to the hearing and determination of the case. While the petition is pending, and before final decree, the court may at any time make such temporary restraining order or prohibition as it deems just. Whenever it appears to the court that the ends of justice require that other parties be brought before it, the court may cause them to be summoned whether or not they reside in the district in which the court is held, and subpenas to that end may be served in any district by the marshal thereof.

§ 1974. Actions by United States; subpoenas for witnesses

In any action brought by or on behalf of the United States under section 1972 of this title, subpoenas for witnesses may run into any district, but no writ of subpoena may issue for witnesses living out of the district in which the court is held at a greater distance than one hundred miles from the place of holding the same without the prior permission of the trial court upon proper application and cause shown.

§ 1975. Civil actions by persons injured; jurisdiction and venue; amount of recovery

Any person who is injured in his business or property by reason of anything forbidden in section 1972 of this title may sue therefor in any district court of the United States in which the defendant resides or is found or has an agent, without regard to the amount in controversy, and shall be entitled to recover three times the amount of the damages sustained by him, and the cost of suit, including a reasonable attorney's fee.

§ 1976. Injunctive relief for persons against threatened loss or damages; equitable proceedings; preliminary injunctions

Any person may sue for and have injunctive relief, in any court of the United States having jurisdiction over the parties, against threatened loss or damage by reason of a violation of section 1972 of this title, under the same conditions and principles as injunctive relief against threatened conduct that will cause loss or damage is granted by courts of equity and under the rules governing such proceedings. Upon the execution of proper bond against damages for an injunction improvidently granted and a showing that the danger of irreparable loss or damage is immediate, a preliminary injunction may issue.

§ 1977. Limitation of actions; suspension of limitations

(1) Subject to paragraph (2) of this section, any action to enforce any cause of action under this chapter shall be forever barred unless commenced within four years after the cause of action accrued.

(2) Whenever any enforcement action is instituted by or on behalf of the United States with respect to any matter which is or could be the subject of a private right of action under this chapter, the running of the statute of limitations in respect of every private right of action arising under this chapter and based in whole or in part on such matter shall be suspended during the pendency of the enforcement action so instituted and for one year thereafter: *Provided*, That whenever the running of the statute of limitations in respect of a cause of action arising under this chapter is suspended under this paragraph, any action to enforce such cause of action shall be forever barred unless commenced either within the period of suspension or within the four-year period referred to in paragraph (1) of this section.

§ 1978. Actions under other Federal or State laws unaffected; regulations or orders barred as defense

Nothing contained in this chapter shall be construed as affecting in any manner the right of the United States or any other party to bring an action under any other law of the United States or of any State, including any right which may exist in addition to specific statutory authority, challenging the legality of any act or practice which may be proscribed by this chapter. No regulation or order issued by the Board under this chapter shall in any manner constitute a defense to such action.

CHAPTER 29. HOME MORTGAGE DISCLOSURE
12 U.S.C.A. §§ 2801–2811

CHAPTER 29. HOME MORTGAGE DISCLOSURE

§ 2801. Congressional findings and declaration of purpose

(a) Findings of Congress

The Congress finds that some depository institutions have sometimes contributed to the decline of certain geographic areas by their failure pursuant to their chartering responsibilities to provide adequate home financing to qualified applicants on reasonable terms and conditions.

(b) Purpose of chapter

The purpose of this chapter is to provide the citizens and public officials of the United States with sufficient information to enable them to determine whether depository institutions are filling their obligations to serve the housing needs of the communities and neighborhoods in which they are located and to assist public officials in their determination of the distribution of public sector investments in a manner designed to improve the private investment environment.

(c) Construction of chapter

Nothing in this chapter is intended to, nor shall it be construed to, encourage unsound lending practices or the allocation of credit.

§ 2802. Definitions—DFA § 1094

For purposes of this chapter—

(1) the term "mortgage loan" means a loan which is secured by residential real property or a home improvement loan;

(2) the term "depository institution"—

(A) means—

(i) any bank (as defined in section 1813(a)(1) of this title);

(ii) any savings association (as defined in section 1813(b)(1) of this title); and

(iii) any credit union,

which makes federally related mortgage loans as determined by the Board; and

(B) includes any other lending institution (as defined in paragraph (4)) other than any institution described in subparagraph (A);

(3) the term "completed application" means an application in which the creditor has received the information that is regularly ob-

tained in evaluating applications for the amount and type of credit requested;

(4) the term "other lending institutions" means any person engaged for profit in the business of mortgage lending;

(5) the term "Board" means the Board of Governors of the Federal Reserve System; and

(6) the term "Secretary" means the Secretary of Housing and Urban Development.

§ 2803. Maintenance of records and public disclosure—DFA § 1094

(a) Duty of depository institutions; nature and content of information

(1) Each depository institution which has a home office or branch office located within a primary metropolitan statistical area, metropolitan statistical area, or consolidated metropolitan statistical area that is not comprised of designated primary metropolitan statistical areas, as defined by the Department of Commerce shall compile and make available, in accordance with regulations of the Board, to the public for inspection and copying at the home office, and at least one branch office within each primary metropolitan statistical area, metropolitan statistical area, or consolidated metropolitan statistical area that is not comprised of designated primary metropolitan statistical areas in which the depository institution has an office the number and total dollar amount of mortgage loans which were (A) originated (or for which the institution received completed applications), or (B) purchased by that institution during each fiscal year (beginning with the last full fiscal year of that institution which immediately preceded the effective date of this chapter).

(2) The information required to be maintained and made available under paragraph (1) shall also be itemized in order to clearly and conspicuously disclose the following:

(A) The number and dollar amount for each item referred to in paragraph (1), by census tracts for mortgage loans secured by property located within any county with a population of more than 30,000, within that primary metropolitan statistical area, metropolitan statistical area, or consolidated metropolitan statistical area that is not comprised of designated primary metropolitan statistical areas, otherwise, by county, for mortgage loans secured by property located within any other county within that primary metropolitan statistical area, metropolitan statistical area, or consolidated metropolitan statistical area that is not comprised of designated primary metropolitan statistical areas.

(B) The number and dollar amount for each item referred to in paragraph (1) for all such mortgage loans which are secured by property located outside that primary metropolitan statistical area, metropolitan statistical area, or consolidated metropolitan statistical area that is not comprised of designated primary metropolitan statistical areas.

For the purpose of this paragraph, a depository institution which maintains offices in more than one primary metropolitan statistical area, metropolitan statistical area, or consolidated metropolitan statistical area that is not comprised of designated primary metropolitan statistical areas shall be required to make the information required by this paragraph available at any such office only to the extent that such information relates to mortgage loans which were originated or purchased (or for which completed applications were received) by an office of that depository institution located in the primary metropolitan statistical area, metropolitan statistical area, or consolidated metropolitan statistical area that is not comprised of designated primary metropolitan statistical areas in which the office making such information available is located. For purposes of this paragraph, other lending institutions shall be deemed to have a home office or branch office within a primary metropolitan statistical area, metropolitan statistical area, or consolidated metropolitan statistical area that is not comprised of designated primary metropolitan statistical areas if such institutions have originated or purchased or received completed applications for at least 5 mortgage loans in such area in the preceding calendar year.

(b) Itemization of loan data

Any item of information relating to mortgage loans required to be maintained under subsection (a) of this section shall be further itemized in order to disclose for each such item—

(1) the number and dollar amount of mortgage loans which are insured under Title II of the National Housing Act [12 U.S.C.A. § 1707 et seq.] or under Title V of the Housing Act of 1949 [42 U.S.C.A. § 1471 et seq.] or which are guaranteed under chapter 37 of Title 38;

(2) the number and dollar amount of mortgage loans made to mortgagors who did not, at the time of execution of the mortgage, intend to reside in the property securing the mortgage loan;

(3) the number and dollar amount of home improvement loans; and

(4) the number and dollar amount of mortgage loans and completed applications involving mortgagors or mortgage applicants grouped according to census tract, income level, racial characteristics, and gender.

(c) Period of maintenance

Any information required to be compiled and made available under this section, other than loan application register information under subsection (j) of this section, shall be maintained and made available for a period of five years after the close of the first year during which such information is required to be maintained and made available.

(d) Duration of disclosure requirements

Notwithstanding the provisions of subsection (a)(1) of this section, data required to be disclosed under this section for 1980 and thereafter shall be disclosed for each calendar year. Any depository institution which is required to make disclosures under this section but which has been making disclosures on some basis other than a calendar year basis shall make available a separate disclosure statement containing data for any period prior to calendar year 1980 which is not covered by the last full year report prior to the 1980 calendar year report.

(e) Format for disclosures

Subject to subsection (h) of this section, the Board shall prescribe a standard format for the disclosures required under this section.

(f) Data disclosure system; operation, etc.

The Federal Financial Institutions Examination Council, in consultation with the Secretary, shall implement a system to facilitate access to data required to be disclosed under this section. Such system shall include arrangements for a central depository of data in each primary metropolitan statistical area, metropolitan statistical area, or consolidated metropolitan statistical area that is not comprised of designated primary metropolitan statistical areas. Disclosure statements shall be made available to the public for inspection and copying at such central depository of data for all depository institutions which are required to disclose information under this section (or which are exempted pursuant to section 2805(b) of this title) and which have a home office or branch office within such primary metropolitan statistical area, metropolitan statistical area, or consolidated metropolitan statistical area that is not comprised of designated primary metropolitan statistical areas.

(g) Exceptions

The requirements of subsections (a) and (b) of this section shall not apply with respect to mortgage loans that are—

(1) made (or for which completed applications are received) by any mortgage banking subsidiary of a bank holding company or savings and loan holding company or by any savings and loan service corporation that originates or purchases mortgage loans; and

(2) approved (or for which completed applications are received) by the Secretary for insurance under Title I or II of the National Housing Act [12 U.S.C.A. §§ 1702 et seq. and 1707 et seq.].

(h) Submission to agencies

The data required to be disclosed under subsection (b)(4) of this section shall be submitted to the appropriate agency for each institution reporting under this chapter. Notwithstanding the requirement of subsection (a)(2)(A) of this section for disclosure by census tract, the Board, in cooperation with other appropriate regulators, including—

(1) the Office of the Comptroller of the Currency for national banks and Federal branches and Federal agencies of foreign banks;

(2) the Director of the Office of Thrift Supervision for savings associations;

(3) the Federal Deposit Insurance Corporation for banks insured by the Federal Deposit Insurance Corporation (other than members of the Federal Reserve System), mutual savings banks, insured State branches of foreign banks, and any other depository institution

described in section 2802(2)(A) of this title which is not otherwise referred to in this paragraph;

(4) the National Credit Union Administration Board for credit unions; and

(5) the Secretary of Housing and Urban Development for other lending institutions not regulated by the agencies referred to in paragraphs (1) through (4),

shall develop regulations prescribing the format for such disclosures, the method for submission of the data to the appropriate regulatory agency, and the procedures for disclosing the information to the public. These regulations shall also require the collection of data required to be disclosed under subsection (b)(4) of this section with respect to loans sold by each institution reporting under this chapter, and, in addition, shall require disclosure of the class of the purchaser of such loans. Any reporting institution may submit in writing to the appropriate agency such additional data or explanations as it deems relevant to the decision to originate or purchase mortgage loans.

(i) Exemption from certain disclosure requirements

The requirements of subsection (b)(4) of this section shall not apply with respect to any depository institution described in section 2802(2)(A) of this title which has total assets, as of the most recent full fiscal year of such institution, of $30,000,000 or less.

(j) Loan application register information

(1) In general

In addition to the information required to be disclosed under subsections (a) and (b) of this section, any depository institution which is required to make disclosures under this section shall make available to the public, upon request, loan application register information (as defined by the Board by regulation) in the form required under regulations prescribed by the Board.

(2) Format of disclosure

(A) Unedited format

Subject to subparagraph (B), the loan application register information described in paragraph (1) may be disclosed by a depository institution without editing or compilation and in the format in which such information is maintained by the institution.

(B) Protection of applicant's privacy interest

The Board shall require, by regulation, such deletions as the Board may determine to be appropriate to protect—

(i) any privacy interest of any applicant, including the deletion of the applicant's name and identification number, the date of the application, and the date of any determination by the institution with respect to such application; and

(ii) a depository institution from liability under any Federal or State privacy law.

(C) Census tract format encouraged

It is the sense of the Congress that a depository institution should provide loan register information under this section in a format based on the census tract in which the property is located.

(3) Change of form not required

A depository institution meets the disclosure requirement of paragraph (1) if the institution provides the information required under such paragraph in the form in which the institution maintains such information.

(4) Reasonable charge for information

Any depository institution which provides information under this subsection may impose a reasonable fee for any cost incurred in reproducing such information.

(5) Time of disclosure

The disclosure of the loan application register information described in paragraph (1) for any year pursuant to a request under paragraph (1) shall be made—

(A) in the case of a request made on or before March 1 of the succeeding year, before April 1 of the succeeding year; and

(B) in the case of a request made after March 1 of the succeeding year, before the end of the 30–day period beginning on the date the request is made.

(6) Retention of information

Notwithstanding subsection (c) of this section, the loan application register information described in paragraph (1) for any year shall be maintained and made available, upon request,

for 3 years after the close of the 1st year during which such information is required to be maintained and made available.

(7) Minimizing compliance costs

In prescribing regulations under this subsection, the Board shall make every effort to minimize the costs incurred by a depository institution in complying with this subsection and such regulations.

(k) Disclosure of statements by depository institutions

(1) In general

In accordance with procedures established by the Board pursuant to this section, any depository institution required to make disclosures under this section—

(A) shall make a disclosure statement available, upon request, to the public no later than 3 business days after the institution receives the statement from the Federal Financial Institutions Examination Council; and

(B) may make such statement available on a floppy disc which may be used with a personal computer or in any other media which is not prohibited under regulations prescribed by the Board.

(2) Notice that data is subject to correction after final review

Any disclosure statement provided pursuant to paragraph (1) shall be accompanied by a clear and conspicuous notice that the statement is subject to final review and revision, if necessary.

(3) Reasonable charge for information

Any depository institution which provides a disclosure statement pursuant to paragraph (1) may impose a reasonable fee for any cost incurred in providing or reproducing such statement.

(l) Prompt disclosures

(1) In general

Any disclosure of information pursuant to this section or section 2809 of this title shall be made as promptly as possible.

(2) Maximum disclosure period

(A) 6– and 9–month maximum periods

Except as provided in subsections (j)(5) and (k)(1) of this section and regulations prescribed by the Board and subject to subparagraph (B), any information required to be disclosed for any year beginning after December 31, 1992, under—

(i) this section shall be made available to the public before September 1 of the succeeding year; and

(ii) section 2809 of this title shall be made available to the public before December 1 of the succeeding year.

(B) Shorter periods encouraged after 1994

With respect to disclosures of information under this section or section 2809 of this title for any year beginning after December 31, 1993, every effort shall be made—

(i) to make information disclosed under this section available to the public before July 1 of the succeeding year; and

(ii) to make information required to be disclosed under section 2809 of this title available to the public before September 1 of the succeeding year.

(3) Improved procedure

The Federal Financial Institutions Examination Council shall make such changes in the system established pursuant to subsection (f) of this section as may be necessary to carry out the requirements of this subsection.

(m) Opportunity to reduce compliance burden

(1) In general

(A) Satisfaction of public availability requirements

A depository institution shall be deemed to have satisfied the public availability requirements of subsection (a) of this section if the institution compiles the information required under that subsection at the home office of the institution and provides notice at the branch locations specified in subsection (a) of this section that such information is available from the home office of the institution upon written request.

(B) Provision of information upon request

Not later than 15 days after the receipt of a written request for any information required to be compiled under subsection (a) of this section, the home office of the depository institution receiving the request shall provide the information pertinent to the location of the branch in question to the person requesting the information.

(2) Form of information

In complying with paragraph (1), a depository institution shall, in the sole discretion of the institution, provide the person requesting the information with—

(A) a paper copy of the information requested; or

(B) if acceptable to the person, the information through a form of electronic medium, such as a computer disk.

§ 2804. Enforcement—DFA § 1094

(a) Regulations

The Board shall prescribe such regulations as may be necessary to carry out the purposes of this chapter. These regulations may contain such classifications, differentiations, or other provisions, and may provide for such adjustments and exceptions for any class of transactions, as in the judgment of the Board are necessary and proper to effectuate the purposes of this chapter, and prevent circumvention or evasion thereof, or to facilitate compliance therewith.

(b) Powers of certain other agencies

Compliance with the requirements imposed under this chapter shall be enforced under—

(1) section 1818 of this title, in the case of—

(A) national banks, and Federal branches and Federal agencies of foreign banks, by the Office of the Comptroller of the Currency;

(B) member banks of the Federal Reserve System (other than national banks), branches and agencies of foreign banks (other than Federal branches, Federal agencies, and insured State branches of foreign banks), commercial lending companies owned or controlled by foreign banks, and organizations operating under section 25 or 25(a) of the Federal Reserve Act [12 U.S.C.A. §§ 601 et seq., 611 et seq.], by the Board; and

(C) banks insured by the Federal Deposit Insurance Corporation (other than members of the Federal Reserve System), mutual savings banks as defined in section 1813(f) of this title, insured State branches of foreign banks, and any other depository institution not referred to in this paragraph or paragraph (2) or (3) of this subsection, by the Board of Directors of the Federal Deposit Insurance Corporation;

(2) section 1818 of this title, by the Director of the Office of Thrift Supervision, in the case of a savings association the deposits of which are insured by the Federal Deposit Insurance Corporation;

(3) the Federal Credit Union Act [12 U.S.C.A. § 1751 et seq.], by the Administrator of the National Credit Union Administration with respect to any credit union; and

(4) other lending institutions, by the Secretary of Housing and Urban Development.

The terms used in paragraph (1) that are not defined in this chapter or otherwise defined in section 1813(s) of this title shall have the meaning given to them in section 3101 of this title.

(c) Violations of this chapter deemed violations of certain other provisions

For the purpose of the exercise by any agency referred to in subsection (b) of this section of its powers under any Act referred to in that subsection, a violation of any requirement imposed under this chapter shall be deemed to be a violation of a requirement imposed under that Act. In addition to its powers under any provision of law specifically referred to in subsection (b) of this section, each of the agencies referred to in that subsection may exercise, for the purpose of enforcing compliance with any requirement imposed under this chapter, any other authority conferred on it by law.

§ 2805. Relation to State laws—DFA § 1094

(a) This chapter does not annul, alter, or affect, or exempt any State chartered depository institution subject to the provisions of this chapter from complying with the laws of any State or subdivision thereof with respect to public disclosure and recordkeeping by depositor institutions, except to the extent that those laws are inconsistent with any provision of this chapter, and then only to the extent of the inconsistency. The Board is authorized to determine whether such inconsistencies exist. The Board may not determine that any such law is inconsistent with any provision

of this chapter if the Board determines that such law requires the maintenance of records with greater geographic or other detail than is required under this chapter, or that such law otherwise provides greater disclosure than is required under this chapter.

(b) The Board may by regulation exempt from the requirements of this chapter any State chartered depository institution within any State or subdivision thereof if it determines that, under the law of such State or subdivision, that institution is subject to requirements substantially similar to those imposed under this chapter, and that such law contains adequate provisions for enforcement. Notwithstanding any other provision of this subsection, compliance with the requirements imposed under this subsection shall be enforced under—

(1) section 1818 of this title in the case of national banks, by the Comptroller of the Currency; and

(2) section 1818 of this title, by the Director of the Office of Thrift Supervision in the case of a savings association the deposits of which are insured by the Federal Deposit Insurance Corporation.

§ 2806. Research and improved methods; authorization of appropriations; recommendations to Congressional committees—DFA § 1094

(a)(1) The Director of the Office of Thrift Supervision, with the assistance of the Secretary, the Director of the Bureau of the Census, the Comptroller of the Currency, the Board of Governors of the Federal Reserve System, the Federal Deposit Insurance Corporation, and such other persons as the Director of the Office of Thrift Supervision deems appropriate, shall develop, or assist in the improvement of, methods of matching addresses and census tracts to facilitate compliance by depository institutions in as economical a manner as possible with the requirements of this chapter.

(2) There is authorized to be appropriated such sums as may be necessary to carry out this subsection.

(3) The Director of the Office of Thrift Supervision is authorized to utilize, contract with, act through, or compensate any person or agency in order to carry out this subsection.

(b) The Director of the Office of Thrift Supervision shall recommend to the Committee on Banking, Finance and Urban Affairs of the House of Representatives and the Committee on Banking, Housing, and Urban Affairs of the Senate such additional legislation as the Director of the Office of Thrift Supervision deems appropriate to carry out the purpose of this chapter.

§ 2807.   Report—DFA § 1094

The Board, in consultation with the Secretary of Housing and Urban Development, shall report annually to the Congress on the utility of the requirements of section 2803(b)(4) of this title.

§ 2808.   Effective date—DFA § 1094

(a) In general

This chapter shall take effect on the one hundred and eightieth day beginning after December 31, 1975. Any institution specified in section 2802(2)(A) of this title which has total assets as of its last full fiscal year of $10,000,000 or less is exempt from the provisions of this chapter. The Board, in consultation with the Secretary, may exempt institutions described in section 2802(2)(B) of this title that are comparable within their respective industries to institutions that are exempt under the preceding sentence (as determined without regard to the adjustment made by subsection (b) of this section).

(b) CPI adjustments

  (1) In general

  Subject to paragraph (2), the dollar amount applicable with respect to institutions described in section 2802(2)(A) of this title under the 2d sentence of subsection (a) of this section shall be adjusted annually after December 31, 1996, by the annual percentage increase in the Consumer Price Index for Urban Wage Earners and Clerical Workers published by the Bureau of Labor Statistics.

  (2) 1–time adjustment for prior inflation

  The first adjustment made under paragraph (1) after September 30, 1996, shall be the percentage by which—

    (A) the Consumer Price Index described in such paragraph for the calendar year 1996, exceeds

    (B) such Consumer Price Index for the calendar year 1975.

  (3) Rounding

  The dollar amount applicable under paragraph (1) for any calendar year shall be the amount determined in accordance with subparagraphs (A) and (B) of paragraph (2) and rounded to the nearest multiple of $1,000,000.

§ 2809.   Compilation of aggregate data—DFA § 1094

(a) Commencement; scope of data and tables

Beginning with data for calendar year 1980, the Federal Financial Institutions Examination Council shall compile each year, for each primary metropolitan statistical area, metropolitan statistical area, or consolidated metropolitan statistical area that is not comprised of designated primary metropolitan statistical areas, aggregate data by census tract for all depository institutions which are required to disclose data under section 2803 of this title or which are exempt pursuant to section 2805(b) of this title. The Council shall also produce tables indicating, for each primary metropolitan statistical area, metropolitan statistical area, or consolidated metropolitan statistical area that is not comprised of designated primary metropolitan statistical areas, aggregate lending patterns for various categories of census tracts grouped according to location, age of housing stock, income level, and racial characteristics.

(b) Staff and data processing resources

The Board shall provide staff and data processing resources to the Council to enable it to carry out the provisions of subsection (a) of this section.

(c) Availability to public

The data and tables required pursuant to subsection (a) of this section shall be made available to the public by no later than December 31 of the year following the calendar year on which the data is based.

§ 2810.   Disclosure by Secretary; commencement, scope, etc.

Beginning with data for calendar year 1980, the Secretary shall make publicly available data in the Secretary's possession for each mortgagee which is not otherwise subject to the requirements of this chapter and which is not exempt pursuant to section 2805(b) of this title (and for each mortgagee making mortgage loans exempted under section 2803(g) of this title), with respect to mortgage loans approved (or for which completed applications are received) by the Secretary for insurance under Title I or II of the National Housing Act [12 U.S.C.A. §§ 1702 et seq., 1707 et seq.]. Such data to be disclosed shall consist of data comparable to the data which would be disclosed if such mortgagee were subject to the requirements of section 2803 of this title. Disclosure statements containing data for each such mortgagee for a primary metropolitan statistical area, metropolitan statistical area, or consolidated metropolitan statistical area that is not comprised of designated primary metropolitan statistical areas shall, at a minimum, be publicly available at the central depository of data established pursuant to section 2803(f) of this title for such primary metropolitan statistical area, metropolitan statistical area, or consolidated metropolitan statistical area that is not comprised of designated primary metropolitan statistical areas. The Secretary shall also compile and make publicly available aggregate data for such mortgagees by census tract, and tables indicating aggregate lending patterns, in a manner comparable to the information required to be made publicly available in accordance with section 2809 of this title.

§ 2811. Repealed. Pub.L. 100–242, Title V, § 565(b), Feb. 5, 1988, 101 Stat. 1945

CHAPTER 30. COMMUNITY REINVESTMENT
12 U.S.C.A. §§ 2901–2908

CHAPTER 30. COMMUNITY REIN-VESTMENT

§ 2901. Congressional findings and statement of purpose

(a) The Congress finds that—

(1) regulated financial institutions are required by law to demonstrate that their deposit facilities serve the convenience and needs of the communities in which they are chartered to do business;

(2) the convenience and needs of communities include the need for credit services as well as deposit services; and

(3) regulated financial institutions have continuing and affirmative obligation to help meet the credit needs of the local communities in which they are chartered.

(b) It is the purpose of this chapter to require each appropriate Federal financial supervisory agency to use its authority when examining financial institutions, to encourage such institutions to help meet the credit needs of the local communities in which they are chartered consistent with the safe and sound operation of such institutions.

§ 2902. Definitions

For the purposes of this chapter—

(1) the term "appropriate Federal financial supervisory agency" means—

(A) the Comptroller of the Currency with respect to national banks;

(B) the Board of Governors of the Federal Reserve System with respect to State chartered banks which are members of the Federal Reserve System and bank holding companies;

(C) the Federal Deposit Insurance Corporation with respect to State chartered banks and savings banks which are not members of the Federal Reserve System and the deposits of which are insured by the Corporation; and

(D) section 1818 of this title, by the Director of the Office of Thrift Supervision, in the case of a savings association (the deposits of which are insured by the Federal Deposit Insurance Corporation) and a savings and loan holding company;

(2) the term "regulated financial institution" means an insured depository institution (as defined in section 1813 of this title); and

(3) the term "application for a deposit facility" means an application to the appropriate Federal financial supervisory agency otherwise required under Federal law or regulations thereunder for-

(A) a charter for a national bank or Federal savings and loan association;

(B) deposit insurance in connection with a newly chartered State bank, savings bank, savings and loan association or similar institution;

(C) the establishment of a domestic branch or other facility with the ability to accept deposits of a regulated financial institution;

(D) the relocation of the home office or a branch office of a regulated financial institution;

(E) the merger or consolidation with, or the acquisition of the assets, or the assumption of the liabilities of a regulated financial institution requiring approval under section 1828(c) of this title or under regulations issued under the authority of title IV of the National Housing Act [12 U.S.C.A. § 1724 et seq.]; or

(F) the acquisition of shares in, or the assets of, a regulated financial institution requiring approval under section 1842 of this title or section 408(e) of the National Housing Act [12 U.S.C.A. § 1730a(e)].

(4) A financial institution whose business predominately consists of serving the needs of military personnel who are not located within a defined geographic area may define its "entire community" to include its entire deposit customer base without regard to geographic proximity.

§ 2903. Financial institutions; evaluation

(a) In general

In connection with its examination of a financial institution, the appropriate Federal financial supervisory agency shall—

(1) assess the institution's record of meeting the credit needs of its entire community, including low-and moderate-income neighbor-

hoods, consistent with the safe and sound operation of such institution; and

(2) take such record into account in its evaluation of an application for a deposit facility by such institution.

(b) Majority-owned institutions

In assessing and taking into account, under subsection (a) of this section, the record of a non-minority-owned and nonwomen-owned financial institution, the appropriate Federal financial supervisory agency may consider as a factor capital investment, loan participation, and other ventures undertaken by the institution in cooperation with minority-and women-owned financial institutions and low-income credit unions provided that these activities help meet the credit needs of local communities in which such institutions and credit unions are chartered.

(c) Financial holding company requirement

(1) In general

An election by a bank holding company to become a financial holding company under section 1843 of this title shall not be effective if—

(A) the Board finds that, as of the date the declaration of such election and the certification is filed by such holding company under section 1843(l)(1)(C) of this title, not all of the subsidiary insured depository institutions of the bank holding company had achieved a rating of "satisfactory record of meeting community credit needs", or better, at the most recent examination of each such institution; and

(B) the Board notifies the company of such finding before the end of the 30–day period beginning on such date.

(2) Limited exclusions for newly acquired insured depository institutions

Any insured depository institution acquired by a bank holding company during the 12–month period preceding the date of the submission to the Board of the declaration and certification under section 1843(l)(1)(C) of this title may be excluded for purposes of paragraph (1) during the 12–month period beginning on the date of such acquisition if–

(A) the bank holding company has submitted an affirmative plan to the appropriate Federal financial supervisory agency to take such action as may be necessary in order for

such institution to achieve a rating of "satisfactory record of meeting community credit needs", or better, at the next examination of the institution; and

(B) the plan has been accepted by such agency.

(3) Definitions

For purposes of this subsection, the following definitions shall apply:

(A) Bank holding company; financial holding company

The terms "bank holding company" and "financial holding company" have the meanings given those terms in section 1841 of this title.

(B) Board

The term "Board" means the Board of Governors of the Federal Reserve System.

(C) Insured depository institution

The term "insured depository institution" has the meaning given the term in section 1813(c) of this title.

§ 2904. Report to Congress

Each appropriate Federal financial supervisory agency shall include in its annual report to the Congress a section outlining the actions it has taken to carry out its responsibilities under this chapter.

§ 2905. Regulations

Regulations to carry out the purposes of this chapter shall be published by each appropriate Federal financial supervisory agency, and shall take effect no later than 390 days after October 12, 1977.

§ 2906. Written evaluations

(a) Required

(1) In general

Upon the conclusion of each examination of an insured depository institution under section 2903 of this title, the appropriate Federal financial supervisory agency shall prepare a written evaluation of the institution's record of meeting the credit needs of its entire community, including low and moderate-income neighborhoods.

(2) Public and confidential sections

Each written evaluation required under paragraph (1) shall have a public section and a confidential section.

(b) Public section of report

(1) Findings and conclusions

(A) Contents of written evaluation

The public section of the written evaluation shall–

(i) state the appropriate Federal financial supervisory agency's conclusions for each assessment factor identified in the regulations prescribed by the Federal financial supervisory agencies to implement this chapter;

(ii) discuss the facts and data supporting such conclusions; and

(iii) contain the institution's rating and a statement describing the basis for the rating.

(B) Metropolitan area distinctions

The information required by clauses (i) and (ii) of subparagraph (A) shall be presented separately for each metropolitan area in which a regulated depository institution maintains one or more domestic branch offices.

(2) Assigned rating

The institution's rating referred to in paragraph (1)(C) shall be 1 of the following:

(A) "Outstanding record of meeting community credit needs".

(B) "Satisfactory record of meeting community credit needs".

(C) "Needs to improve record of meeting community credit needs".

(D) "Substantial noncompliance in meeting community credit needs".

Such ratings shall be disclosed to the public on and after July 1, 1990.

(c) Confidential section of report

(1) Privacy of named individuals

The confidential section of the written evaluation shall contain all references that identify any customer of the institution, any employee or officer of the institution, or any person or organization that has provided information in confidence to a Federal or State financial supervisory agency.

(2) Topics not suitable for disclosure

The confidential section shall also contain any statements obtained or made by the appropriate Federal financial supervisory agency in the course of an examination which, in the judgment of the agency, are too sensitive or speculative in nature to disclose to the institution or the public.

(3) Disclosure to depository institution

The confidential section may be disclosed, in whole or part, to the institution, if the appropriate Federal financial supervisory agency determines that such disclosure will promote the objectives of this chapter. However, disclosure under this paragraph shall not identify a person or organization that has provided information in confidence to a Federal or State financial supervisory agency.

(d) Institutions with interstate branches

(1) State-by-State evaluation

In the case of a regulated financial institution that maintains domestic branches in 2 or more States, the appropriate Federal financial supervisory agency shall prepare—

(A) a written evaluation of the entire institution's record of performance under this chapter, as required by subsections (a), (b), and (c) of this section; and

(B) for each State in which the institution maintains 1 or more domestic branches, a separate written evaluation of the institution's record of performance within such State under this chapter, as required by subsections (a), (b), and (c) of this section.

(2) Multistate metropolitan areas

In the case of a regulated financial institution that maintains domestic branches in 2 or more States within a multistate metropolitan area, the appropriate Federal financial supervisory agency shall prepare a separate written evaluation of the institution's record of performance within such metropolitan area under this chapter, as required by subsections (a), (b), and (c) of this section. If the agency prepares a written evaluation pursuant to this paragraph, the scope of the written evaluation required under paragraph (1)(B) shall be adjusted accordingly.

(3) Content of State level evaluation

A written evaluation prepared pursuant to paragraph (1)(B) shall—

(A) present the information required by subparagraphs (A) and (B) of subsection (b)(1) of this section separately for each metropolitan area in which the institution maintains 1 or more domestic branch offices and separately for the remainder of the nonmetropolitan area of the State if the institution maintains 1 or more domestic branch offices in such nonmetropolitan area; and

(B) describe how the Federal financial supervisory agency has performed the examination of the institution, including a list of the individual branches examined.

(e) Definitions

For purposes of this section the following definitions shall apply:

(1) Domestic branch

The term "domestic branch" means any branch office or other facility of a regulated financial institution that accepts deposits, located in any State.

(2) Metropolitan area

The term "metropolitan area" means any primary metropolitan statistical area, metropolitan statistical area, or consolidated metropolitan statistical area, as defined by the Director of the Office of Management and Budget, with a population of 250,000 or more, and any other area designated as such by the appropriate Federal financial supervisory agency.

(3) State

The term "State" has the same meaning as in section 1813 of this title.

§ 2907. Operation of branch facilities by minorities and women

(a) In general

In the case of any depository institution which donates, sells on favorable terms (as determined by the appropriate Federal financial supervisory agency), or makes available on a rent-free basis any branch of such institution which is located in any predominantly minority neighborhood to any minority depository institution or women's depository institution, the amount of the contribution or the amount of the loss incurred in connection with such activity may be a factor in determining whether the depository institution is

meeting the credit needs of the institution's community for purposes of this chapter.

(b) Definitions

For purposes of this section—

(1) Minority depository institution

The term "minority institution" means a depository institution (as defined in section 1813(c) of this title)—

(A) more than 50 percent of the ownership or control of which is held by 1 or more minority individuals; and

(B) more than 50 percent of the net profit or loss of which accrues to 1 or more minority individuals.

(2) Women's depository institution

The term "women's depository institution" means a depository institution (as defined in section 1813(c) of this title)—

(A) more than 50 percent of the ownership or control of which is held by 1 or more women;

(B) more than 50 percent of the net profit or loss of which accrues to 1 or more women; and

(C) a significant percentage of senior management positions of which are held by women.

(3) Minority

The term "minority" has the meaning given to such term by section 1204(c)(3) of the Financial Institutions Reform, Recovery and Enforcement Act of 1989.

§ 2908. Small bank regulatory relief

(a) In general

Except as provided in subsections (b) and (c), any regulated financial institution with aggregate assets of not more than $250,000,000 shall be subject to routine examination under this chapter—

(1) not more than once every 60 months for an institution that has achieved a rating of "outstanding record of meeting community credit needs" at its most recent examination under section 2903 of this title;

(2) not more than once every 48 months for an institution that has received a rating of "satis-

factory record of meeting community credit needs" at its most recent examination under section 2903 of this title; and

(3) as deemed necessary by the appropriate Federal financial supervisory agency, for an institution that has received a rating of less than "satisfactory record of meeting community credit needs" at its most recent examination under section 2903 of this title.

(b) No exception from CRA examinations in connection with applications for deposit facilities

A regulated financial institution described in subsection (a) shall remain subject to examination under this chapter in connection with an application for a deposit facility.

(c) Discretion

A regulated financial institution described in subsection (a) may be subject to more frequent or less frequent examinations for reasonable cause under such circumstances as may be determined by the appropriate Federal financial supervisory agency.

CHAPTER 33.   DEPOSITORY INSTITUTION MANAGEMENT INTERLOCKS
12 U.S.C.A. §§ 3201–3208

12 U.S.C.A. §   **Page**

CHAPTER 33. DEPOSITORY INSTITUTION MANAGEMENT INTERLOCKS

§ 3201. Definitions

As used in this chapter—

(1) the term "depository institution" means a commercial bank, a savings bank, a trust company, a savings and loan association, a building and loan association, a homestead association, a cooperative bank, an industrial bank, or a credit union;

(2) the term "depository holding company" means a bank holding company as defined in section 1841(a) of this title, a company which would be a bank holding company as defined in section 1841(a) of this title but for the exemption contained in subsection (a)(5)(F) thereof, or a savings and loan holding company as defined in section 1730a(a)(1)(D) of this title;

(3) the characterization of any corporation (including depository institutions and depository holding companies), as an "affiliate of," or as "affiliated" with any other corporation means that—

(A) one of the corporations is a depository holding company and the other is a subsidiary thereof, or both corporations are subsidiaries of the same depository holding company, as the term "subsidiary" is defined in either section 1841(d) of this title in the case of a bank holding company or section 1730a(a)(1)(H) of this title in the case of a savings and loan holding company; or

(B) more than 25 percent of the voting stock of one corporation is beneficially owned in the aggregate by one or more persons who also beneficially own in the aggregate more than 25 percent of the voting stock of the other corporation; or

(C) one of the corporations is a trust company all of the stock of which, except for directors qualifying shares, was owned by one or more mutual savings banks on November 10, 1978, and the other corporation is a mutual savings bank; or

(D) one of the corporations is a bank, insured by the Federal Deposit Insurance Corporation and chartered under State law, and is a bankers' bank, described in Paragraph Seventh of section 24 of this title; or

(E) one of the corporations is a bank, chartered under State law and insured by the Federal Deposit Insurance Corporation, the voting securities of which are held only by persons who are officers of other banks, as permitted by State law, and which bank is primarily engaged in providing banking services for other banks and not the public: *Provided, however,* That in no case shall the voting securities of such corporation be held by such officers of other banks in excess of 6 per centum of the paid-in capital and 6 per centum of the surplus of such a bank.

(4) the term "management official" means an employee or officer with management functions, a director (including an advisory or honorary director, except in the case of a depository institution with total assets of less than $100,000,000), a trustee of a business organization under the control of trustees, or any person who has a representative or nominee serving in any such capacity: *Provided,* That if a corporator, trustee, director, or other officer of a State-chartered savings bank or cooperative bank is specifically authorized under the laws of the State in which said institution is located to serve as a trustee, director, or other officer of a State-chartered trust company which does not make real estate mortgage loans and does not accept savings deposits from natural persons, then, for the purposes of this chapter, such corporator, trustee, director, or other officer shall not be deemed to be a management official of such trust company: *And provided further,* That if a management official of a State-chartered trust company which does not make real estate mortgage loans and does not accept savings deposits from natural persons is specifically authorized under the laws of the State in which said institution is located to serve as a corporator, trustee, director, or other officer of a State-chartered savings bank or cooperative bank, then, for the purposes of this chapter, such management official shall not be deemed to be a management official of any such savings bank or cooperative bank;

(5) the term "office" used with reference to a depository institution means either a principal office or a branch; and

(6) the term "appropriate Federal depository institutions regulatory agency" means, with respect to any depository institution or depository holding company, the agency referred to in sec-

tion 3207 of this title in connection with such institution or company.

§ 3202. Dual service of management official as management official of unaffiliated institution or holding company in same area, town, or village prohibited

A management official of a depository institution or a depository holding company may not serve as a management official of any other depository institution or depository holding company not affiliated therewith if an office of one of the institutions or any depository institution that is an affiliate of such institutions is located within either—

(1) the same primary metropolitan statistical area, the same metropolitan statistical area, or the same consolidated metropolitan statistical area that is not comprised of designated primary metropolitan statistical areas as defined by the Office of Management and Budget, except in the case of depository institutions with less than $50,000,000 in assets in which case the provision of paragraph (2) shall apply, as that in which an office of the other institution or any depository institution that is an affiliate of such other institution is located, or

(2) the same city, town, or village as that in which an office of the other institution or any depository institution that is an affiliate of such other institution is located, or in any city, town, or village contiguous or adjacent thereto.

§ 3203. Dual service of management official of $2,500,000,000 institution or holding company as management official of unaffiliated $1,500,000,000 institution or holding company prohibited

If a depository institution or a depository holding company has total assets exceeding $2,500,000,000 a management official of such institution or any affiliate thereof may not serve as a management official of any other nonaffiliated depository institution or depository holding company having total assets exceeding $1,500,000,000 or as a management official of any affiliate of such other institution. In order to allow for inflation or market changes, the appropriate Federal depository institutions regulatory agencies may, by regulation, adjust, as necessary, the amount of total assets required for depository

institutions or depository holding companies under this section.

§ 3204. Exceptions

The prohibitions contained in sections 3202 and 3203 of this title shall not apply in the case of any one or more of the following or subsidiary thereof:

(1) A depository institution or depository holding company which has been placed formally in liquidation, or which is in the hands of a receiver, conservator, or other official exercising a similar function.

(2) A corporation operating under section 25 or 25(a) of the Federal Reserve Act 12 U.S.C.A. § § 601 et seq., 611 et seq.

(3) A credit union being served by a management official of another credit union.

(4) A depository institution or depository holding company which does not do business within any State of the United States, the District of Columbia, any territory of the United States, Puerto Rico, Guam, American Samoa, or the Virgin Islands except as an incident to its activities outside the United States.

(5) A State-chartered savings and loan guaranty corporation.

(6) A Federal Home Loan Bank or any other bank organized specifically to serve depository institutions.

(7) A depository institution or a depository holding company which—

(A) is closed or is in danger of closing, as determined by the appropriate Federal depository institutions regulatory agency in accordance with regulations prescribed by such agency; and

(B) is acquired by another depository institution or depository holding company, during the 5–year period beginning on the date of the acquisition of the depository institution or depository holding company described in subparagraph (A).

(8) (A) A diversified savings and loan holding company (as defined in section 1730a(a)(1)(F) of this title) with respect to the service of a director of such company who is also a director of any nonaffiliated depository institution or depository holding

company (including a savings and loan holding company) if—

(i) notice of the proposed dual service is given by such diversified savings and loan holding company to—

(I) the appropriate Federal depository institutions regulatory agency for such company; and

(II) the appropriate Federal depository institutions regulatory agency for the nonaffiliated depository institution or depository holding company of which such person is also a director,

not less than 60 days before such dual service is proposed to begin; and

(ii) the proposed dual service is not disapproved by any such appropriate Federal depository institutions regulatory agency before the end of such 60–day period.

(B) Any appropriate Federal depository institutions regulatory agency may disapprove, under subparagraph (A)(ii), a notice of proposed dual service by any individual if such agency finds that—

(i) the dual service cannot be structured or limited so as to preclude the dual service's resulting in a monopoly or substantial lessening of competition in financial services in any part of the United States;

(ii) the dual service would lead to substantial conflicts of interest or unsafe or unsound practices; or

(iii) the diversified savings and loan holding company has neglected, failed, or refused to furnish all the information required by such agency.

(C) Any appropriate Federal depository institutions regulatory agency may, at any time after the end of the 60–day period referred to in subparagraph (A), require that any dual service by any individual which was not disapproved by such agency during such period be terminated if a change in circumstances occurs with respect to any depository institution or depository holding company of which such individual is a director that would have provided a basis for disapproval of the dual service during such period.

(9) Any savings association (as defined in section 10(a)(1)(A) of the Home Owners' Loan Act [12 U.S.C.A. § 1467a(a)(1)(A)] or any savings and loan holding company (as defined in section 10(a)(1)(D) of such Act)) [12 U.S.C.A. § 1467a(a)(1)(D)] which has issued stock in connection with a qualified stock issuance pursuant to section 10(q) of such Act [12 U.S.C.A. § 1467a(q)], except that this paragraph shall apply only with respect to service as a single management official of such savings association or holding company, or any subsidiary of such savings association or holding company, by a single management official of the savings and loan holding company which purchased the stock issued in connection with such qualified stock issuance, and shall apply only when the Director of the Office of Thrift Supervision has determined that such service is consistent with the purposes of this chapter and the Home Owners' Loan Act [12 U.S.C.A. § 1461 et seq.].

§ 3205. Management official in position prior to November 10, 1978

(a) Continuation of service

A person whose service in a position as a management official began prior to November 10, 1978, and who was not immediately prior to November 10, 1978, in violation of section 19 of Title 15 is not prohibited by section 3202 or section 3203 of this title from continuing to serve in that position. The appropriate Federal depository institutions regulatory agency may provide a reasonable period of time for compliance with this chapter, not exceeding fifteen months, after any change in circumstances which makes service described in the preceding sentence prohibited by this chapter, except that a merger, acquisition, increase in total assets, establishment of one or more offices, or change in management responsibilities shall not constitute changes in circumstances which would make such service prohibited by section 3202 or section 3203 of this title.

(b) Depository institution and diversified savings and loan holding company

Effective on November 10, 1978, a person who serves as a management official of a company which is not a depository institution or a depository holding company and as a management official of a depository institution or a depository holding company is not prohibited from continuing to serve as a management official of that depository institution or depository holding company as a result of that company which is not a depository institution or depository holding company becoming a diversified savings and loan holding company as that term is defined in section 1730a(a) of this title.

§ 3206. Administration and enforcement

This chapter shall be administered and enforced by—

(1) the Comptroller of the Currency with respect to national banks,

(2) the Board of Governors of the Federal Reserve System with respect to State banks which are members of the Federal Reserve System, and bank holding companies,

(3) the Board of Directors of the Federal Deposit Insurance Corporation with respect to State banks which are not members of the Federal Reserve System but the deposits of which are insured by the Federal Deposit Insurance Corporation,

(4) the Director of the Office of Thrift Supervision with respect to a savings association (the deposits of which are insured by the Federal Deposit Insurance Corporation) and savings and loan holding companies,

(5) the National Credit Union Administration with respect to credit unions the accounts of which are insured by the National Credit Union Administration, and

(6) upon referral by the agencies named in the foregoing paragraphs (1) through (5), the Attorney General shall have the authority to enforce compliance by any person with this chapter.

§ 3207. Rules and regulations

Regulations to carry out this chapter, including regulations that permit service by a management official that would otherwise be prohibited by section 3202 of this title or section 3203 of this title, if such service would not result in a monopoly or substantial lessening of competition, may be prescribed by—

(1) the Comptroller of the Currency with respect to national banks,

(2) the Board of Governors of the Federal Reserve System with respect to State banks which are members of the Federal Reserve System, and bank holding companies,

(3) the Board of Directors of the Federal Deposit Insurance Corporation with respect to State banks which are not members of the Federal Reserve System but the deposits of which are insured by the Federal Deposit Insurance Corporation,

(4) the Director of the Office of Thrift Supervision with respect to institutions the accounts of which are insured by the Federal Deposit Insurance Corporation, and savings and loan holding companies, and

(5) the National Credit Union Administration with respect to credit unions the accounts of which are insured by the National Credit Union Administration.

§ 3208. Powers available to Attorney General for enforcement

(a) For the purpose of the exercise by the Attorney General of his enforcement functions under section 3206(6) of this title, all of the functions and powers of the Attorney General under the Clayton Act [15 U.S.C.A. § 12 et seq.] are available to the Attorney General, irrespective of any jurisdictional tests in the Clayton Act, including the power to take enforcement actions in the same manner as if the violation had been a violation of the Clayton Act.

(b) All of the functions and powers of the Attorney General or the Assistant Attorney General in charge of the Antitrust Division of the Department of Justice are available to the Attorney General or to such Assistant Attorney General to investigate possible violations under section 3206(6) of the title in the same manner as if such possible violations were possible violations of the Clayton Act [15 U.S.C.A. § 12 et seq.].

CHAPTER 34. FEDERAL FINANCIAL INSTITUTIONS EXAMINATION COUNCIL
12 U.S.C.A. §§ 3301–3311

§ 3301.　Declaration of purpose

It is the purpose of this chapter to establish a Financial Institutions Examination Council which shall prescribe uniform principles and standards for the Federal examination of financial institutions by the Office of the Comptroller of the Currency, the Federal Deposit Insurance Corporation, the Board of Governors of the Federal Reserve System, the Federal Home Loan Bank Board, and the National Credit Union Administration and make recommendations to promote uniformity in the supervision of these financial institutions. The Council's actions shall be designed to promote consistency in such examination and to insure progressive and vigilant supervision.

§ 3302.　Definitions

As used in this chapter—

(1) the term "Federal financial institutions regulatory agencies" means the Office of the Comptroller of the Currency, the Board of Governors of the Federal Reserve System, the Federal Deposit Insurance Corporation, the Office of Thrift Supervision, and the National Credit Union Administration;

(2) the term "Council" means the Financial Institutions Examination Council; and

(3) the term "financial institution" means a commercial bank, a savings bank, a trust company, a savings association, a building and loan association, a homestead association, a cooperative bank, or a credit union[.]

§ 3303.　Financial Institutions Examination Council—DFA § 1091

(a) Establishment; composition

There is established the Financial Institutions Examination Council which shall consist of—

(1) the Comptroller of the Currency,

(2) the Chairman of the Board of Directors of the Federal Deposit Insurance Corporation,

(3) a Governor of the Board of Governors of the Federal Reserve System designated by the Chairman of the Board,

(4) the Director, Office of Thrift Supervision,

(5) the Chairman of the National Credit Union Administration Board, and

(6) the Chairman of the State Liaison Committee.

(b) Chairmanship

The members of the Council shall select the first chairman of the Council. Thereafter the chairmanship shall rotate among the members of the Council.

(c) Term of office

The term of the Chairman of the Council shall be two years.

(d) Designation of officers and employees

The members of the Council may, from time to time, designate other officers or employees of their respective agencies to carry out their duties on the Council.

(e) Compensation and expenses

Each member of the Council shall serve without additional compensation but shall be entitled to reasonable expenses incurred in carrying out his official duties as such a member.

§ 3304.　Costs and expenses of Council

One-fifth of the costs and expenses of the Council, including the salaries of its employees, shall be paid by each of the Federal financial institutions regulatory agencies. Annual assessments for such share shall be levied by the Council based upon its projected budget for the year, and additional assessments may be made during the year if necessary.

§ 3305.　Functions of Council

(a) Establishment of principles and standards

The Council shall establish uniform principles and standards and report forms for the examination of financial institutions which shall be applied by the Federal financial institutions regulatory agencies.

(b) Making recommendations regarding supervisory matters and adequacy of supervisory tools

(1) The Council shall make recommendations for uniformity in other supervisory matters, such as, but not limited to, classifying loans subject to country risk, identifying financial institutions in need of special supervisory attention, and evaluating the soundness of large loans that are shared by two or more financial institutions. In addition, the Council shall make recommendations regarding the adequa-

cy of supervisory tools for determining the impact of holding company operations on the financial institutions within the holding company and shall consider the ability of supervisory agencies to discover possible fraud or questionable and illegal payments and practices which might occur in the operation of financial institutions or their holding companies.

(2) When a recommendation of the Council is found unacceptable by one or more of the applicable Federal financial institutions regulatory agencies, the agency or agencies shall submit to the Council, within a time period specified by the Council, a written statement of the reasons the recommendation is unacceptable.

(c) Development of uniform reporting system

The Council shall develop uniform reporting systems for federally supervised financial institutions, their holding companies, and nonfinancial institution subsidiaries of such institutions or holding companies. The authority to develop uniform reporting systems shall not restrict or amend the requirements of section 78l(i) of Title 15.

(d) Conducting schools for examiners and assistant examiners

The Council shall conduct schools for examiners and assistant examiners employed by the Federal financial institutions regulatory agencies. Such schools shall be open to enrollment by employees of State financial institutions supervisory agencies and employees of the Federal Housing Finance Board under conditions specified by the Council.

(e) Affect on Federal regulatory agency research and development of new financial institutions supervisory agencies

Nothing in this chapter shall be construed to limit or discourage Federal regulatory agency research and development of new financial institutions supervisory methods and tools, nor to preclude the field testing of any innovation devised by any Federal regulatory agency.

(f) Annual report

Not later than April 1 of each year, the Council shall prepare an annual report covering its activities during the preceding year.

(g) Flood insurance

The Council shall consult with and assist the Federal entities for lending regulation, as such term is defined in section 4121(a) of Title 42, in developing and coordinating uniform standards and requirements for use by regulated lending institutions under the national flood insurance program.

§ 3306. State liaison

To encourage the application of uniform examination principles and standards by State and Federal supervisory agencies, the Council shall establish a liaison committee composed of five representatives of State agencies which supervise financial institutions which shall meet at least twice a year with the Council. Members of the liaison committee shall receive a reasonable allowance for necessary expenses incurred in attending meetings. Members of the Liaison Committee shall elect a chairperson from among the members serving on the committee.

§ 3307. Administration

(a) Authority of Chairman of Council

The Chairman of the Council is authorized to carry out and to delegate the authority to carry out the internal administration of the Council, including the appointment and supervision of employees and the distribution of business among members, employees, and administrative units.

(b) Use of personnel, services, and facilities of Federal financial institutions regulatory agencies, Federal Reserve banks, and Federal Home Loan Banks

[I]n addition to any other authority conferred upon it by this chapter, in carrying out its functions under this chapter, the Council may utilize, with their consent and to the extent practical, the personnel, services, and facilities of the Federal financial institutions regulatory agencies, Federal Reserve banks, and Federal Home Loan Banks, with or without reimbursement therefor.

(c) Compensation, authority, and duties of officers and employees; experts and consultants

In addition, the Council may—

(1) subject to the provisions of Title 5 relating to the competitive service, classification, and General Schedule pay rates, appoint and fix the compensation of such officers and employees as are necessary to carry out the provisions

of this chapter, and to prescribe the authority and duties of such officers and employees; and

(2) obtain the services of such experts and consultants as are necessary to carry out the provisions of this chapter.

§ 3308. Access to books, accounts, records, etc., by Council

For the purpose of carrying out this chapter, the Council shall have access to all books, accounts, records, reports, files, memorandums, papers, things, and property belonging to or in use by Federal financial institutions regulatory agencies, including reports of examination of financial institutions or their holding companies from whatever source, together with workpapers and correspondence files related to such reports, whether or not a part of the report, and all without any deletions.

§ 3309. Risk management training

(a) Seminars

The Council shall develop and administer training seminars in risk management for its employees and the employees of insured financial institutions.

(b) Study of risk management training program

Not later than end of the 1–year period beginning on August 9, 1989, the Council shall—

(1) conduct a study on the feasibility and appropriateness of establishing a formalized risk management training program designed to lead to the certification of Risk Management Analysts; and

(2) report to the Congress the results of such study.

§ 3310. Establishment of Appraisal Subcommittee

There shall be within the Council a subcommittee to be known as the "Appraisal Subcommittee", which shall consist of the designees of the heads of the Federal financial institutions regulatory agencies. Each such designee shall be a person who has demonstrated knowledge and competence concerning the appraisal profession.

§ 3311. Required review of regulations

(a) In general

Not less frequently than once every 10 years, the Council and each appropriate Federal banking agency represented on the Council shall conduct a review of all regulations prescribed by the Council or by any such appropriate Federal banking agency, respectively, in order to identify outdated or otherwise unnecessary regulatory requirements imposed on insured depository institutions.

(b) Process

In conducting the review under subsection (a) of this section, the Council or the appropriate Federal banking agency shall—

(1) categorize the regulations described in subsection (a) of this section by type (such as consumer regulations, safety and soundness regulations, or such other designations as determined by the Council, or the appropriate Federal banking agency); and

(2) at regular intervals, provide notice and solicit public comment on a particular category or categories of regulations, requesting commentators to identify areas of the regulations that are outdated, unnecessary, or unduly burdensome.

(c) Complete review

The Council or the appropriate Federal banking agency shall ensure that the notice and comment period described in subsection (b)(2) of this section is conducted with respect to all regulations described in subsection (a) of this section not less frequently than once every 10 years.

(d) Regulatory response

The Council or the appropriate Federal banking agency shall—

(1) publish in the Federal Register a summary of the comments received under this section, identifying significant issues raised and providing comment on such issues; and

(2) eliminate unnecessary regulations to the extent that such action is appropriate.

(e) Report to Congress

Not later than 30 days after carrying out subsection (d)(1) of this section, the Council shall submit to the Congress a report, which shall include—

(1) a summary of any significant issues raised by public comments received by the Council and the appropriate Federal banking agencies

under this section and the relative merits of such issues; and

(2) an analysis of whether the appropriate Federal banking agency involved is able to address the regulatory burdens associated with such issues by regulation, or whether such burdens must be addressed by legislative action.

CHAPTER 35.   RIGHT TO FINANCIAL PRIVACY
12 U.S.C.A. §§ 3401–3422

CHAPTER 35. RIGHT TO FINANCIAL PRIVACY

§ 3401. Definitions—DFA § 1099

For the purpose of this chapter, the term—

(1) "financial institution", except as provided in section 3414 of this title, means any office of a bank, savings bank, card issuer as defined in section 1602(n) of Title 15, industrial loan company, trust company, savings association, building and loan, or homestead association (including cooperative banks), credit union, or consumer finance institution, located in any State or territory of the United States, the District of Columbia, Puerto Rico, Guam, American Samoa, or the Virgin Islands;

(2) "financial record" means an original of, a copy of, or information known to have been derived from, any record held by a financial institution pertaining to a customer's relationship with the financial institution;

(3) "Government authority" means any agency or department of the United States, or any officer, employee, or agent thereof;

(4) "person" means an individual or a partnership of five or fewer individuals;

(5) "customer" means any person or authorized representative of that person who utilized or is utilizing any service of a financial institution, or for whom a financial institution is acting or has acted as a fiduciary, in relation to an account maintained in the person's name;

(6) "holding company" means—

(A) any bank holding company (as defined in section 1841 of this title);

(B) any company described in section 1843(f)(1) of this title; and

(C) any savings and loan holding company (as defined in the Home Owners' Loan Act [12 U.S.C.A. § 1461 et seq.]);

(7) "supervisory agency" means with respect to any particular financial institution, holding company, or any subsidiary of a financial institution or holding company, any of the following which has statutory authority to examine the financial condition, business operations, or records or transactions of that institution, holding company, or subsidiary—

(A) the Federal Deposit Insurance Corporation;

(B) Director, Office of Thrift Supervision;

(C) the National Credit Union Administration;

(D) the Board of Governors of the Federal Reserve System;

(E) the Comptroller of the Currency;

(F) the Securities and Exchange Commission;

(G) the Commodity Futures Trading Commission;

(H) the Secretary of the Treasury, with respect to the Bank Secrecy Act (Public Law 91–508, Title I [12 U.S.C.A. § 1951 et seq.]) and subchapter II of chapter 53 of Title 31; or

(I) any State banking or securities department or agency; and

(8) "law enforcement inquiry" means a lawful investigation or official proceeding inquiring into a violation of, or failure to comply with, any criminal or civil statute or any regulation, rule, or order issued pursuant thereto.

§ 3402. Access to financial records by Government authorities prohibited; exceptions

Except as provided by section 3403(c) or (d), 3413, or 3414 of this title, no Government authority may have access to or obtain copies of, or the information contained in the financial records of any customer from a financial institution unless the financial records are reasonably described and—

(1) such customer has authorized such disclosure in accordance with section 3404 of this title;

(2) such financial records are disclosed in response to an administrative subpena or summons which meets the requirements of section 3405 of this title;

(3) such financial records are disclosed in response to a search warrant which meets the requirements of section 3406 of this title;

(4) such financial records are disclosed in response to a judicial subpena which meets the requirements of section 3407 of this title; or

(5) such financial records are disclosed in response to a formal written request which meets the requirements of section 3408 of this title.

§ 3403. Confidentiality of financial records

(a) Release of records by financial institutions prohibited

No financial institution, or officer, employees, or agent of a financial institution, may provide to any Government authority access to or copies of, or the information contained in, the financial records of any customer except in accordance with the provisions of this chapter.

(b) Release of records upon certification of compliance with chapter

A financial institution shall not release the financial records of a customer until the Government authority seeking such records certifies in writing to the financial institution that it has complied with the applicable provisions of this chapter.

(c) Notification to Government authority of existence of relevant information in records

Nothing in this chapter shall preclude any financial institution, or any officer, employee, or agent of a financial institution, from notifying a Government authority that such institution, or officer, employee, or agent has information which may be relevant to a possible violation of any statute or regulation. Such information may include only the name or other identifying information concerning any individual, corporation, or account involved in and the nature of any suspected illegal activity. Such information may be disclosed notwithstanding any constitution, law, or regulation of any State or political subdivision thereof to the contrary. Any financial institution, or officer, employee, or agent thereof, making a disclosure of information pursuant to this subsection, shall not be liable to the customer under any law or regulation of the United States or any constitution, law, or regulation of any State or political subdivision thereof, for such disclosure or for any failure to notify the customer of such disclosure.

(d) Release of records as incident to perfection of security interest, proving a claim in bankruptcy, collecting a debt, or processing an application with regard to a Government loan, loan guarantee, etc.

(1) Nothing in this chapter shall preclude a financial institution, as an incident to perfecting a security interest, proving a claim in bankruptcy, or otherwise collecting on a debt owing either to the financial institution itself or in its role as a fiduciary, from providing copies of any financial record to any court or Government authority.

(2) Nothing in this chapter shall preclude a financial institution, as an incident to processing an application for assistance to a customer in the form of a Government loan, loan guaranty, or loan insurance agreement, or as an incident to processing a default on, or administering, a Government guaranteed or insured loan, from initiating contact with an appropriate Government authority for the purpose of providing any financial record necessary to permit such authority to carry out its responsibilities under a loan, loan guaranty, or loan insurance agreement.

§ 3404. Customer authorizations

(a) Statement furnished by customer to financial institution and Government authority; contents

A customer may authorize disclosure under section 3402(1) of this title if he furnishes to the financial institution and to the Government authority seeking to obtain such disclosure a signed and dated statement which—

(1) authorizes such disclosure for a period not in excess of three months;

(2) states that the customer may revoke such authorization at any time before the financial records are disclosed;

(3) identifies the financial records which are authorized to be disclosed;

(4) specifies the purposes for which, and the Government authority to which, such records may be disclosed; and

(5) states the customer's rights under this chapter.

(b) Authorization as condition of doing business prohibited

No such authorization shall be required as a condition of doing business with any financial institution.

(c) Right of customer to access to financial institution's record of disclosures

The customer has the right, unless the Government authority obtains a court order as provided in section 3409 of this title, to obtain a copy of the record which the financial institution shall keep of all instances in which the customer's record is disclosed to a Government authority pursuant to this section, including the identity of the Government authority to which such disclosure is made.

§ 3405. Administrative subpoena and summons

A Government authority may obtain financial records under section 3402(2) of this title pursuant to an administrative subpoena or summons otherwise authorized by law only if—

(1) there is reason to believe that the records sought are relevant to a legitimate law enforcement inquiry;

(2) a copy of the subpoena or summons has been served upon the customer or mailed to his last known address on or before the date on which the subpoena or summons was served on the financial institution together with the following notice which shall state with reasonable specificity the nature of the law enforcement inquiry:

"Records or information concerning your transactions held by the financial institution named in the attached subpena or summons are being sought by this (agency or department) in accordance with the Right to Financial Privacy Act of 1978 [12 U.S.C.A. § 3401 et seq.] for the following purpose: If you desire that such records or information not be made available, you must:

"1. Fill out the accompanying motion paper and sworn statement or write one of your own, stating that you are the customer whose records are being requested by the Government and either giving the reasons you believe that the records are not relevant to the legitimate law enforcement inquiry stated in this notice or any other legal basis for objecting to the release of the records.

"2. File the motion and statement by mailing or delivering them to the clerk of any one of the following United States district courts:

"3. Serve the Government authority requesting the records by mailing or delivering a copy of your motion and statement to .

"4. Be prepared to come to court and present your position in further detail.

"5. You do not need to have a lawyer, although you may wish to employ one to represent you and protect your rights.

If you do not follow the above procedures, upon the expiration of ten days from the date of service or fourteen days from the date of mailing of this notice, the records or information requested therein will be made available. These records may be transferred to other Government authorities for legitimate law enforcement inquiries, in which event you will be notified after the transfer."; and

(3) ten days have expired from the date of service of the notice or fourteen days have expired from the date of mailing the notice to the customer and within such time period the customer has not filed a sworn statement and motion to quash in an appropriate court, or the customer challenge provisions of section 3410 of this title have been complied with.

§ 3406.   Search warrants

(a) Applicability of Federal Rules of Criminal Procedure

A Government authority may obtain financial records under section 3402(3) of this title only if it obtains a search warrant pursuant to the Federal Rules of Criminal Procedure.

(b) Mailing of copy and notice to customer

No later than ninety days after the Government authority serves the search warrant, it shall mail to the customer's last known address a copy of the search warrant together with the following notice:

"Records or information concerning your transactions held by the financial institution named in the attached search warrant were obtained by this (agency or department) on (date) for the following purpose:_____. You may have rights under the Right to Financial Privacy Act of 1978 [12 U.S.C.A. § 3401 et seq.].".

(c) Court-ordered delays in mailing

Upon application of the Government authority, a court may grant a delay in the mailing of the notice required in subsection (b) of this section, which delay shall not exceed one hundred and eighty days following the service of the warrant, if the court makes the findings required in section 3409(a) of this title. If the court so finds, it shall enter an ex parte order granting the requested delay and an order prohibiting the financial institution from disclosing that records have been obtained or that a search warrant for such records has been executed. Additional delays of up to ninety days may be granted by the court upon application, but only in accordance with this subsection. Upon expiration of the period of delay of notification of the customer, the following notice shall be mailed to the customer along with a copy of the search warrant:

"Records or information concerning your transactions held by the financial institution named in the attached search warrant were obtained by this (agency or department) on (date). Notification was delayed beyond the statutory ninety-day delay period pursuant to a determination by the court that such notice would seriously jeopardize an investigation concerning:_____. You may have rights under the Right to Financial Privacy Act of 1978 [12 U.S.C.A. § 3401 et seq.].".

§ 3407. Judicial subpoena

A Government authority may obtain financial records under section 3402(4) of this title pursuant to judicial subpoena only if—

(1) such subpoena is authorized by law and there is reason to believe that the records sought are relevant to a legitimate law enforcement inquiry;

(2) a copy of the subpoena has been served upon the customer or mailed to his last known address on or before the date on which the subpoena was served on the financial institution together with the following notice which shall state with reasonable specificity the nature of the law enforcement inquiry:

"Records or information concerning your transactions which are held by the financial institution named in the attached subpena are being sought by this (agency or department or authority) in accordance with the Right to Financial Privacy Act of 1978 [12 U.S.C.A. § 3401 et seq.] for the following purpose: If you desire that such records or information not be made available, you must:

"1. Fill out the accompanying motion paper and sworn statement or write one of your own,

stating that you are the customer whose records are being requested by the Government and either giving the reasons you believe that the records are not relevant to the legitimate law enforcement inquiry stated in this notice or any other legal basis for objecting to the release of the records.

"2. File the motion and statement by mailing or delivering them to the clerk of the Court.

"3. Serve the Government authority requesting the records by mailing or delivering a copy of your motion and statement to:_____.

"4. Be prepared to come to court and present your position in further detail.

"5. You do not need to have a lawyer, although you may wish to employ one to represent you and protect your rights.

If you do not follow the above procedures, upon the expiration of ten days from the date of service or fourteen days from the date of mailing of this notice, the records or information requested therein will be made available. These records may be transferred to other government authorities for legitimate law enforcement inquiries, in which event you will be notified after the transfer;" and

(3) ten days have expired from the date of service or fourteen days from the date of mailing of the notice to the customer and within such time period the customer has not filed a sworn statement and motion to quash in an appropriate court, or the customer challenge provisions of section 3410 of this title have been complied with.

§ 3408. Formal written request

A Government authority may request financial records under section 3402(5) of this title pursuant to a formal written request only if—

(1) no administrative summons or subpena authority reasonably appears to be available to that Government authority to obtain financial records for the purpose for which such records are sought;

(2) the request is authorized by regulations promulgated by the head of the agency or department;

(3) there is reason to believe that the records sought are relevant to a legitimate law enforcement inquiry; and

(4) (A) a copy of the request has been served upon the customer or mailed to his last known address on or before the date on which the request was made to the financial institution together with the following notice which shall state with reasonable specificity the nature of the law enforcement inquiry:

"Records or information concerning your transactions held by the financial institution named in the attached request are being sought by this (agency or department) in accordance with the Right to Financial Privacy Act of 1978 [12 U.S.C.A. § 3401 et seq.] for the following purpose:

"If you desire that such records or information not be made available, you must:

"1. Fill out the accompanying motion paper and sworn statement or write one of your own, stating that you are the customer whose records are being requested by the Government and either giving the reasons you believe that the records are not relevant to the legitimate law enforcement inquiry stated in this notice or any other legal basis for objecting to the release of the records.

"2. File the motion and statement by mailing or delivering them to the clerk of any one of the following United States District Courts:

"3. Serve the Government authority requesting the records by mailing or delivering a copy of your motion and statement to:_____.

"4. Be prepared to come to court and present your position in further detail.

"5. You do not need to have a lawyer, although you may wish to employ one to represent you and protect your rights.

If you do not follow the above procedures, upon the expiration of ten days from the date of service or fourteen days from the date of mailing of this notice, the records or information requested therein may be made available. These records may be transferred to other Government authorities for legitimate law enforcement inquiries, in which event you will be notified after the transfer;" and

(B) ten days have expired from the date of service or fourteen days from the date of mailing of the notice by the customer and within such time period the customer has not filed a sworn statement and an application to enjoin the Government authority in an appropriate court, or the customer challenge provisions of section 3410 of this title have been complied with.

§ 3409. Delayed notice

(a) Application by Government authority; findings

Upon application of the Government authority, the customer notice required under section 3404(c), 3405(2), 3406(c), 3407(2), 3408(4), or 3412(b) of this title may be delayed by order of an appropriate court if the presiding judge or magistrate finds that—

(1) the investigation being conducted is within the lawful jurisdiction of the Government authority seeking the financial records;

(2) there is reason to believe that the records being sought are relevant to a legitimate law enforcement inquiry; and

(3) there is reason to believe that such notice will result in—

(A) endangering life or physical safety of any person;

(B) flight from prosecution;

(C) destruction of or tampering with evidence;

(D) intimidation of potential witnesses; or

(E) otherwise seriously jeopardizing an investigation or official proceeding or unduly delaying a trial or ongoing official proceeding to the same extent as the circumstances in the preceding subparagraphs.

An application for delay must be made with reasonable specificity.

(b) Grant of delay order; duration and specifications; extensions; copy of request and notice to customer

(1) If the court makes the findings required in paragraphs (1), (2), and (3) of subsection (a) of this section, it shall enter an ex parte order granting the requested delay for a period not to exceed ninety days and an order prohibiting the financial institution from disclosing that records have been obtained or that a request for records has been made, except that, if the records have been sought by a Government

authority exercising financial controls over foreign accounts in the United States under section 5(b) of the Trading With the Enemy Act [12 U.S.C.A. § 95a, 50 App. U.S.C.A. § 5(b)], the International Emergency Economic Powers Act (title II, Public Law 95–223) [50 U.S.C.A. § 1701 et seq.], or section 287c of Title 22, and the court finds that there is reason to believe that such notice may endanger the lives or physical safety of a customer or group of customers, or any person or group of persons associated with a customer, the court may specify that the delay be indefinite.

(2) Extensions of the delay of notice provided in paragraph (1) of up to ninety days each may be granted by the court upon application, but only in accordance with this subsection.

(3) Upon expiration of the period of delay of notification under paragraph (1) or (2), the customer shall be served with or mailed a copy of the process or request together with the following notice which shall state with reasonable specificity the nature of the law enforcement inquiry:

"Records or information concerning your transactions which are held by the financial institution named in the attached process or request were supplied to or requested by the Government authority named in the process or request on (date). Notification was withheld pursuant to a determination by the (title of court so ordering) under the Right to Financial Privacy Act of 1978 [12 U.S.C.A. § 3401 et seq.] that such notice might (state reason). The purpose of the investigation or official proceeding was:_____.".

(c) Notice requirement respecting emergency access to financial records

When access to financial records is obtained pursuant to section 3414(b) of this title (emergency access), the Government authority shall, unless a court has authorized delay of notice pursuant to subsections (a) and (b) of this section, as soon as practicable after such records are obtained serve upon the customer, or mail by registered or certified mail to his last known address, a copy of the request to the financial institution together with the following notice which shall state with reasonable specificity the nature of the law enforcement inquiry:

"Records concerning your transactions held by the financial institution named in the attached request were obtained by (agency or department) under the Right to Financial Privacy Act of 1978 [12 U.S.C.A. § 3401 et seq.] on (date) for the following purpose:_____ Emergency access to such records was obtained on the grounds that (state grounds).".

(d) Preservation of memorandums, affidavits, or other papers

Any memorandum, affidavit, or other paper filed in connection with a request for delay in notification shall be preserved by the court. Upon petition by the customer to whom such records pertain, the court may order disclosure of such papers to the petitioner unless the court makes the findings required in subsection (a) of this section.

§ 3410. Customer challenges

(a) Filing of motion to quash or application to enjoin; proper court; contents

Within ten days of service or within fourteen days of mailing of a subpoena, summons, or formal written request, a customer may file a motion to quash an administrative summons or judicial subpoena, or an application to enjoin a Government authority from obtaining financial records pursuant to a formal written request, with copies served upon the Government authority. A motion to quash a judicial subpoena shall be filed in the court which issued the subpoena. A motion to quash an administrative summons or an application to enjoin a Government authority from obtaining records pursuant to a formal written request shall be filed in the appropriate United States district court. Such motion or application shall contain an affidavit or sworn statement—

(1) stating that the applicant is a customer of the financial institution from which financial records pertaining to him have been sought; and

(2) stating the applicant's reasons for believing that the financial records sought are not relevant to the legitimate law enforcement inquiry stated by the Government authority in its notice, or that there has not been substantial compliance with the provisions of this chapter.

Service shall be made under this section upon a Government authority by delivering or mailing by registered or certified mail a copy of the papers to the person, office, or department specified in the notice which the customer has received pursuant to this chapter. For the purposes of this section, "delivery" has the meaning stated in rule 5(b) of the Federal Rules of Civil Procedure.

(b) Filing of response; additional proceedings

If the court finds that the customer has complied with subsection (a) of this section, it shall order the Government authority to file a sworn response, which may be filed in camera if the Government includes in its response the reasons which make in camera review appropriate. If the court is unable to determine the motion or application on the basis of the parties' initial allegations and response, the court may conduct such additional proceedings as it deems appropriate. All such proceedings shall be completed and the motion or application decided within seven calendar days of the filing of the Government's response.

(c) Decision of court

If the court finds that the applicant is not the customer to whom the financial records sought by the Government authority pertain, or that there is a demonstrable reason to believe that the law enforcement inquiry is legitimate and a reasonable belief that the records sought are relevant to that inquiry, it shall deny the motion or application, and, in the case of an administrative summons or court order other than a search warrant, order such process enforced. If the court finds that the applicant is the customer to whom the records sought by the Government authority pertain, and that there is not a demonstrable reason to believe that the law enforcement inquiry is legitimate and a reasonable belief that the records sought are relevant to that inquiry, or that there has not been substantial compliance with the provisions of this chapter, it shall order the process quashed or shall enjoin the Government authority's formal written request.

(d) Appeals

A court ruling denying a motion or application under this section shall not be deemed a final order and no interlocutory appeal may be taken therefrom by the customer. An appeal of a ruling denying a motion or application under this section may be taken by the customer (1) within such period of time as provided by law as part of any appeal from a final order in any legal proceeding initiated against him arising out of or based upon the financial records, or (2) within

thirty days after a notification that no legal proceeding is contemplated against him. The Government authority obtaining the financial records shall promptly notify a customer when a determination has been made that no legal proceeding against him is contemplated. After one hundred and eighty days from the denial of the motion or application, if the Government authority obtaining the records has not initiated such a proceeding, a supervisory official of the Government authority shall certify to the appropriate court that no such determination has been made. The court may require that such certifications be made, at reasonable intervals thereafter, until either notification to the customer has occurred or a legal proceeding is initiated as described in clause (A).

(e) Sole judicial remedy available to customer

The challenge procedures of this chapter constitute the sole judicial remedy available to a customer to oppose disclosure of financial records pursuant to this chapter.

(f) Affect on challenges by financial institutions

Nothing in this chapter shall enlarge or restrict any rights of a financial institution to challenge requests for records made by a Government authority under existing law. Nothing in this chapter shall entitle a customer to assert the rights of a financial institution.

§ 3411. Duty of financial institutions

Upon receipt of a request for financial records made by a Government authority under section 3405 or 3407 of this title, the financial institution shall, unless otherwise provided by law, proceed to assemble the records requested and must be prepared to deliver the records to the Government authority upon receipt of the certificate required under section 3403(b) of this title.

§ 3412. Use of information—DFA § 1099

(a) Transfer of financial records to other agencies or departments; certification

Financial records originally obtained pursuant to this chapter shall not be transferred to another agency or department unless the transferring agency or department certifies in writing that there is reason to believe that the records are relevant to a legitimate law enforcement inquiry, or intelligence or counterintelligence activity, investigation or analysis related to international terrorism within the jurisdiction of the receiving agency or department.

(b) Mailing of copy of certification and notice to customer

When financial records subject to this chapter are transferred pursuant to subsection (a) of this section, the transferring agency or department shall, within fourteen days, send to the customer a copy of the certification made pursuant to subsection (a) of this section and the following notice, which shall state the nature of the law enforcement inquiry with reasonable specificity: "Copies of, or information contained in, your financial records lawfully in possession of have been furnished to pursuant to the Right of Financial Privacy Act of 1978 [12 U.S.C.A. § 3401 et seq.] for the following purpose:_____. If you believe that this transfer has not been made to further a legitimate law enforcement inquiry, you may have legal rights under the Financial Privacy Act of 1978 or the Privacy Act of 1974 [5 U.S.C.A. § 552a]."

(c) Court-ordered delays in mailing

Notwithstanding subsection (b) of this section, notice to the customer may be delayed if the transferring agency or department has obtained a court order delaying notice pursuant to section 3409(a) and (b) of this title and that order is still in effect, or if the receiving agency or department obtains a court order authorizing a delay in notice pursuant to section 3409(a) and (b) of this title. Upon the expiration of any such period of delay, the transferring agency or department shall serve to the customer the notice specified in subsection (b) of this section and the agency or department that obtained the court order authorizing a delay in notice pursuant to section 3409(a) and (b) of this title shall serve to the customer the notice specified in section 3409(b) of this title.

(d) Exchanges of examination reports by supervisory agencies; transfer of financial records to defend customer action; withholding of information

Nothing in this chapter prohibits any supervisory agency from exchanging examination reports or other information with another supervisory agency. Nothing in this chapter prohibits the transfer of a customer's financial records needed by counsel for a Government authority to defend an action brought by the customer. Nothing in this chapter shall authorize the withholding of information by any officer or employee of a supervisory agency from a duly authorized committee or subcommittee of the Congress.

(e) Exchange of records, reports, or other information

Notwithstanding section 3401(6) of this title or any other provision of law, the exchange of financial records, examination reports or other information with respect to a financial institution, holding company, or any subsidiary of a depository institution or holding company, among and between the five member supervisory agencies of the Federal Financial Institutions Examination Council, the Securities and Exchange Commission, the Federal Trade Commission, and the Commodity Futures Trading Commission is permitted.

(f) Transfer to Attorney General or Secretary of the Treasury

(1) In general

Nothing in this chapter shall apply when financial records obtained by an agency or department of the United States are disclosed or transferred to the Attorney General or the Secretary of the Treasury upon the certification by a supervisory level official of the transferring agency or department that—

(A) there is reason to believe that the records may be relevant to a violation of Federal criminal law; and

(B) the records were obtained in the exercise of the agency's or department's supervisory or regulatory functions.

(2) Limitation on use

Records so transferred shall be used only for criminal investigative or prosecutive purposes, for civil actions under section 1833a of this title, or for forfeiture under sections 981 or 982 of Title 18 by the Department of Justice and only for criminal investigative purposes relating to money laundering and other financial crimes by the Department of the Treasury and shall, upon completion of the investigation or prosecution (including any appeal), be returned only to the transferring agency or department. No agency or department so transferring such records shall be deemed to have waived any privilege applicable to those records under law.

§ 3413.   Exceptions—DFA § 1099

(a) Disclosure of financial records not identified with particular customers

Nothing in this chapter prohibits the disclosure of any financial records or information which is not identified with or identifiable as being derived from the financial records of a particular customer.

(b) Disclosure to, or examination by, supervisory agency pursuant to exercise of supervisory, regulatory, or monetary functions with respect to financial institutions, holding companies, subsidiaries, institution-affiliated parties, or other persons

This chapter shall not apply to the examination by or disclosure to any supervisory agency of financial records or information in the exercise of its supervisory, regulatory, or monetary functions, including conservatorship or receivership functions, with respect to any financial institution, holding company, subsidiary of a financial institution or holding company, institution-affiliated party (within the meaning of section 1813(u) of this title) with respect to a financial institution, holding company, or subsidiary, or other person participating in the conduct of the affairs thereof.

(c) Disclosure pursuant to Title 26

Nothing in this chapter prohibits the disclosure of financial records in accordance with procedures authorized by Title 26.

(d) Disclosure pursuant to Federal statute or rule promulgated thereunder

Nothing in this chapter shall authorize the withholding of financial records or information required to be reported in accordance with any Federal statute or rule promulgated thereunder.

(e) Disclosure pursuant to Federal Rules of Criminal Procedure or comparable rules of other courts

Nothing in this chapter shall apply when financial records are sought by a Government authority under the Federal Rules of Civil or Criminal Procedure or comparable rules of other courts in connection with litigation to which the Government authority and the customer are parties.

(f) Disclosure pursuant to administrative subpoena issued by administrative law judge

Nothing in this chapter shall apply when financial records are sought by a Government authority pursuant to an administrative subpena issued by an administrative law judge in an adjudicatory proceeding subject to section 554 of Title 5 and to which the Government authority and the customer are parties.

(g) Disclosure pursuant to legitimate law enforcement inquiry respecting name, address, account number, and type of account of particular customers

The notice requirements of this chapter and sections 3410 and 3412 of this title shall not apply when a Government authority by a means described in section 3402 of this title and for a legitimate law enforcement inquiry is seeking only the name, address, account number, and type of account of any customer or ascertainable group of customers associated (1) with a financial transaction or class of financial transactions, or (2) with a foreign country or subdivision thereof in the case of a Government authority exercising financial controls over foreign accounts in the United States under section 5(b) of the Trading With the Enemy Act [12 U.S.C.A. § 95a, 50 App. U.S.C.A. § 5(b)]; the International Emergency Economic Powers Act (Title II, Public Law 95–223) [50 U.S.C.A. § 1701 et seq.]; or section 287c of Title 22.

(h) Disclosure pursuant to lawful proceeding, investigation, etc., directed at financial institution or legal entity or consideration or administration respecting Government loans, loan guarantees, etc.

(1) Nothing in this chapter (except sections 3403, 3417 and 3418 of this title) shall apply when financial records are sought by a Government authority—

(A) in connection with a lawful proceeding, investigation, examination, or inspection directed at a financial institution (whether or not such proceeding, investigation, examination, or inspection is also directed at a customer) or at a legal entity which is not a customer; or

(B) in connection with the authority's consideration or administration of assistance to the customer in the form of a Government loan, loan guaranty, or loan insurance program.

(2) When financial records are sought pursuant to this subsection, the Government authority shall submit to the financial institution the

certificate required by section 3403(b) of this title. For access pursuant to paragraph (1)(B), no further certification shall be required for subsequent access by the certifying Government authority during the term of the loan, loan guaranty, or loan insurance agreement.

(3) After the effective date of this chapter, whenever a customer applies for participation in a Government loan, loan guaranty, or loan insurance program, the Government authority administering such program shall give the customer written notice of the authority's access rights under this subsection. No further notification shall be required for subsequent access by that authority during the term of the loan, loan guaranty, or loan insurance agreement.

(4) Financial records obtained pursuant to this subsection may be used only for the purpose for which they were originally obtained, and may be transferred to another agency or department only when the transfer is to facilitate a lawful proceeding, investigation, examination, or inspection directed at a financial institution (whether or not such proceeding, investigation, examination, or inspection is also directed at a customer), or at a legal entity which is not a customer, except that—

(A) nothing in this paragraph prohibits the use or transfer of a customer's financial records needed by counsel representing a Government authority in a civil action arising from a Government loan, loan guaranty, or loan insurance agreement; and

(B) nothing in this paragraph prohibits a Government authority providing assistance to a customer in the form of a loan, loan guaranty, or loan insurance agreement from using or transferring financial records necessary to process, service or foreclose a loan, or to collect on an indebtedness to the Government resulting from a customer's default.

(5) Notification that financial records obtained pursuant to this subsection may relate to a potential civil, criminal, or regulatory violation by a customer may be given to an agency or department with jurisdiction over that violation, and such agency or department may then seek access to the records pursuant to the provisions of this chapter.

(6) Each financial institution shall keep a notation of each disclosure made pursuant to paragraph (1)(B) of this subsection, including

the date of such disclosure and the Government authority to which it was made. The customer shall be entitled to inspect this information.

(i) Disclosure pursuant to issuance of subpena or court order respecting grand jury proceeding

Nothing in this chapter (except sections 3415 and 3420 of this title) shall apply to any subpena or court order issued in connection with proceedings before a grand jury, except that a court shall have authority to order a financial institution, on which a grand jury subpoena for customer records has been served, not to notify the customer of the existence of the subpoena or information that has been furnished to the grand jury, under the circumstances and for the period specified and pursuant to the procedures established in section 3409 of this title.

(j) Disclosure pursuant to proceeding, investigation, etc., instituted by Government Accountability Office and directed at a government authority

This chapter shall not apply when financial records are sought by the Government Accountability Office pursuant to an authorized proceeding, investigation, examination or audit directed at a government authority.

(k) Disclosure necessary for proper administration of programs of withholding taxes on nonresident aliens, Federal Old–Age, Survivors, and Disability Insurance Benefits, and Railroad Retirement Act Benefits

(1) Nothing in this chapter shall apply to the disclosure by the financial institution of the name and address of any customer to the Department of the Treasury, the Social Security Administration, or the Railroad Retirement Board, where the disclosure of such information is necessary to, and such information is used solely for the purpose of, the proper administration of section 1441 of Title 26, title II of the Social Security Act [42 U.S.C.A. § 401 et seq.], or the Railroad Retirement Act of 1974 [45 U.S.C.A. § 231 et seq.].

(2) Notwithstanding any other provision of law, any request authorized by paragraph (1) (and the information contained therein) may be used by the financial institution or its agents solely for the purpose of providing the customer's name and address to the Department of the Treasury, the Social Security Ad-

ministration, or the Railroad Retirement Board and shall be barred from redisclosure by the financial institution or its agents.

(*l*) Crimes against financial institutions by insiders

Nothing in this chapter shall apply when any financial institution or supervisory agency provides any financial record of any officer, director, employee, or controlling shareholder (within the meaning of subparagraph (A) or (B) of section 1841(a)(2) of this title or subparagraph (A) or (B) of section 1730a(a)(2) of this title) of such institution, or of any major borrower from such institution who there is reason to believe may be acting in concert with any such officer, director, employee, or controlling shareholder, to the Attorney General of the United States, to a State law enforcement agency, or, in the case of a possible violation of subchapter II of chapter 53 of Title 31, to the Secretary of the Treasury if there is reason to believe that such record is relevant to a possible violation by such person of—

(1) any law relating to crimes against financial institutions or supervisory agencies by directors, officers, employees, or controlling shareholders of, or by borrowers from, financial institutions; or

(2) any provision of subchapter II of chapter 53 of Title 31 or of section 1956 or 1957 of Title 18.

No supervisory agency which transfers any such record under this subsection shall be deemed to have waived any privilege applicable to that record under law.

(m) Disclosure to, or examination by, employees or agents of Board of Governors of Federal Reserve System or Federal Reserve Bank

This chapter shall not apply to the examination by or disclosure to employees or agents of the Board of Governors of the Federal Reserve System or any Federal Reserve Bank of financial records or information in the exercise of the Federal Reserve System's authority to extend credit to the financial institutions or others.

(n) Disclosure to, or examination by, Resolution Trust Corporation or its employees or agents

This chapter shall not apply to the examination by or disclosure to the Resolution Trust Corporation or its employees or agents of financial records or information in the exercise of its conser-

vatorship, receivership, or liquidation functions with respect to a financial institution.

(o) Disclosure to, or examination by, Federal Housing Finance Board or Federal home loan banks

This chapter shall not apply to the examination by or disclosure to the Federal Housing Finance Board or any of the Federal home loan banks of financial records or information in the exercise of the Federal Housing Finance Board's authority to extend credit (either directly or through a Federal home loan bank) to financial institutions or others.

(p) Access to information necessary for administration of certain veteran benefits laws

(1) Nothing in this chapter shall apply to the disclosure by the financial institution of the name and address of any customer to the Department of Veterans Affairs where the disclosure of such information is necessary to, and such information is used solely for the purposes of, the proper administration of benefits programs under laws administered by the Secretary.

(2) Notwithstanding any other provision of law, any request authorized by paragraph (1) (and the information contained therein) may be used by the financial institution or its agents solely for the purpose of providing the customer's name and address to the Department of Veterans Affairs and shall be barred from redisclosure by the financial institution or its agents.

(q) Official Government travel

Nothing in this chapter shall apply to the disclosure of any financial record or information to a Government authority in conjunction with a Federal contractor-issued travel charge card issued for official Government travel.

§ 3414. Special procedures

(a)(1) Nothing in this chapter (except sections 3415, 3417, 3418, and 3421 of this title) shall apply to the production and disclosure of financial records pursuant to requests from—

(A) a Government authority authorized to conduct foreign counter-or foreign positive-intelligence activities for purposes of conducting such activities;

(B) the Secret Service for the purpose of conducting its protective functions (18 U.S.C. 3056; 3 U.S.C. 202, Public Law 90–331, as amended); or

(C) a Government authority authorized to conduct investigations of, or intelligence or counterintelligence analyses related to, international terrorism for the purpose of conducting such investigations or analyses.

(2) In the instances specified in paragraph (1), the Government authority shall submit to the financial institution the certificate required in section 3403(b) of this title signed by a supervisory official of a rank designated by the head of the Government authority.

(3) (A) If the Government authority described in paragraph (1) or the Secret Service, as the case may be, certifies that otherwise there may result a danger to the national security of the United States, interference with a criminal, counterterrorism, or counterintelligence investigation, interference with diplomatic relations, or danger to the life or physical safety of any person, no financial institution, or officer, employee, or agent of such institution, shall disclose to any person (other than those to whom such disclosure is necessary to comply with the request or an attorney to obtain legal advice or legal assistance with respect to the request) that the Government authority or the Secret Service has sought or obtained access to a customer's financial records.

(B) The request shall notify the person or entity to whom the request is directed of the nondisclosure requirement under subparagraph (A).

(C) Any recipient disclosing to those persons necessary to comply with the request or to an attorney to obtain legal advice or legal assistance with respect to the request shall inform such persons of any applicable nondisclosure requirement. Any person who receives a disclosure under this subsection shall be subject to the same prohibitions on disclosure under subparagraph (A).

(D) At the request of the authorized Government authority or the Secret Service, any person making or intending to make a disclosure under this section shall identify to the requesting official of the authorized Government authority or the Secret Service the

person to whom such disclosure will be made or to whom such disclosure was made prior to the request, except that nothing in this section shall require a person to inform the requesting official of the authorized Government authority or the Secret Service of the identity of an attorney to whom disclosure was made or will be made to obtain legal advice or legal assistance with respect to the request for financial records under this subsection.

(4) The Government authority specified in paragraph (1) shall compile an annual tabulation of the occasions in which this section was used.

(5) (A) Financial institutions, and officers, employees, and agents thereof, shall comply with a request for a customer's or entity's financial records made pursuant to this subsection by the Federal Bureau of Investigation when the Director of the Federal Bureau of Investigation (or the Director's designee in a position not lower than Deputy Assistant Director at Bureau headquarters or a Special Agent in Charge in a Bureau field office designated by the Director) certifies in writing to the financial institution that such records are sought for foreign counter intelligence purposes to protect against international terrorism or clandestine intelligence activities, provided that such an investigation of a United States person is not conducted solely upon the basis of activities protected by the first amendment to the Constitution of the United States.

(B) The Federal Bureau of Investigation may disseminate information obtained pursuant to this paragraph only as provided in guidelines approved by the Attorney General for foreign intelligence collection and foreign counterintelligence investigations conducted by the Federal Bureau of Investigation, and, with respect to dissemination to an agency of the United States, only if such information is clearly relevant to the authorized responsibilities of such agency.

(C) On the dates provided in section 415b of Title 50, the Attorney General shall fully inform the congressional intelligence committees (as defined in section 401a of Title

50) concerning all requests made pursuant to this paragraph.

(D) Prohibition of certain disclosure.—

(i) If the Director of the Federal Bureau of Investigation, or his designee in a position not lower than Deputy Assistant Director at Bureau headquarters or a Special Agent in Charge in a Bureau field office designated by the Director, certifies that otherwise there may result a danger to the national security of the United States, interference with a criminal, counterterrorism, or counterintelligence investigation, interference with diplomatic relations, or danger to the life or physical safety of any person, no financial institution, or officer, employee, or agent of such institution, shall disclose to any person (other than those to whom such disclosure is necessary to comply with the request or an attorney to obtain legal advice or legal assistance with respect to the request) that the Federal Bureau of Investigation has sought or obtained access to a customer's or entity's financial records under subparagraph (A).

(ii) The request shall notify the person or entity to whom the request is directed of the nondisclosure requirement under clause (i).

(iii) Any recipient disclosing to those persons necessary to comply with the request or to an attorney to obtain legal advice or legal assistance with respect to the request shall inform such persons of any applicable nondisclosure requirement. Any person who receives a disclosure under this subsection shall be subject to the same prohibitions on disclosure under clause (i).

(iv) At the request of the Director of the Federal Bureau of Investigation or the designee of the Director, any person making or intending to make a disclosure under this section shall identify to the Director or such designee the person to whom such disclosure will be made or to whom such disclosure was made prior to the request, except that nothing in this section shall require a person to inform the Director or such designee of the identity of an attorney to whom disclosure was made or will be made to obtain legal advice or legal assistance with respect to the request for financial records under subparagraph (A).

(b)(1) Nothing in this chapter shall prohibit a Government authority from obtaining financial records from a financial institution if the Government authority determines that delay in obtaining access to such records would create imminent danger of—

(A) physical injury to any person;

(B) serious property damage; or

(C) flight to avoid prosecution.

(2) In the instances specified in paragraph (1), the Government shall submit to the financial institution the certificate required in section 3403(b) of this title signed by a supervisory official of a rank designated by the head of the Government authority.

(3) Within five days of obtaining access to financial records under this subsection, the Government authority shall file with the appropriate court a signed, sworn statement of a supervisory official of a rank designated by the head of the Government authority setting forth the grounds for the emergency access. The Government authority shall thereafter comply with the notice provisions of section 3409(c) of this title.

(4) The Government authority specified in paragraph (1) shall compile an annual tabulation of the occasions in which this section was used.

(d) For purposes of this section, and sections 1115 and 1117 of this title insofar as they relate to the operation of this section, the term "financial institution" has the same meaning as in subsections (a)(2) and (c)(1) of section 5312 of Title 31, except that, for purposes of this section, such term shall include only such a financial institution any part of which is located inside any State or territory of the United States, the District of Columbia, Puerto Rico, Guam, American Samoa, the Commonwealth of the Northern Mariana Islands, or the United States Virgin Islands.

§ 3415. Cost reimbursement

Except for records obtained pursuant to section 3403(d) or 3413(a) through (h) of this title, or as otherwise provided by law, a Government authority shall pay to the financial institution assembling or providing financial records pertaining to a customer and in accordance with procedures established by this chapter a fee for reimbursement for such costs as are reasonably necessary and which have been directly incurred in searching for, reproducing, or transporting books, papers, records, or other data required or requested to be produced. The Board of Governors of the Federal Reserve System shall, by regulation, establish the rates and conditions under which such payment may be made.

§ 3416. Jurisdiction

An action to enforce any provision of this chapter may be brought in any appropriate United States district court without regard to the amount in controversy within three years from the date on which the violation occurs or the date of discovery of such violation, whichever is later.

§ 3417. Civil penalties

(a) Liability of agencies or departments of United States or financial institutions

Any agency or department of the United States or financial institution obtaining or disclosing financial records or information contained therein in violation of this chapter is liable to the customer to whom such records relate in an amount equal to the sum of—

(1) $100 without regard to the volume of records involved;

(2) any actual damages sustained by the customer as a result of the disclosure;

(3) such punitive damages as the court may allow, where the violation is found to have been willful or intentional; and

(4) in the case of any successful action to enforce liability under this section, the costs of the action together with reasonable attorney's fees as determined by the court.

(b) Disciplinary action for willful or intentional violation of chapter by agents or employees of department or agency

Whenever the court determines that any agency or department of the United States has violated any provision of this chapter and the court finds that the circumstances surrounding the violation raise questions of whether an officer or employee of the department or agency acted willfully or intentionally with respect to the violation, the Director of the Office of Personnel Management shall promptly initiate a proceeding to determine whether disciplinary action is warranted against the agent or employee who was primarily responsible for the violation. The Director after in-

vestigation and consideration of the evidence submitted, shall submit his findings and recommendations to the administrative authority of the agency concerned and shall send copies of the findings and recommendations to the officer or employee or his representative. The administrative authority shall take the corrective action that the Director recommends.

(c) Good faith defense

Any financial institution or agent or employee thereof making a disclosure of financial records pursuant to this chapter in good-faith reliance upon a certificate by any Government authority or pursuant to the provisions of section 3413(*l*) of this title shall not be liable to the customer for such disclosure under this chapter, the constitution of any State, or any law or regulation of any State or any political subdivision of any State.

(d) Exclusive judicial remedies and sanctions

The remedies and sanctions described in this chapter shall be the only authorized judicial remedies and sanctions for violations of this chapter.

§ 3418. Injunctive relief

In addition to any other remedy contained in this chapter, injunctive relief shall be available to require that the procedures of this chapter are complied with. In the event of any successful action, costs together with reasonable attorney's fees as determined by the court may be recovered.

§ 3419. Suspension of limitations

If any individual files a motion or application under this chapter which has the effect of delaying the access of a Government authority to financial records pertaining to such individual, any applicable statute of limitations shall be deemed to be tolled for the period extending from the date such motion or application was filed until the date upon which the motion or application is decided.

§ 3420. Grand jury information; notification of certain persons prohibited

(a) Financial records about a customer obtained from a financial institution pursuant to a subpoena issued under the authority of a Federal grand jury—

(1) shall be returned and actually presented to the grand jury unless the volume of such records makes such return and actual presentation impractical in which case the grand jury shall be provided with a description of the contents of the records.;

(2) shall be used only for the purpose of considering whether to issue an indictment or presentment by that grand jury, or of prosecuting a crime for which that indictment or presentment is issued, or for a purpose authorized by rule 6(e) of the Federal Rules of Criminal Procedure, or for a purpose authorized by section 1112(a);

(3) shall be destroyed or returned to the financial institution if not used for one of the purposes specified in paragraph (2); and

(4) shall not be maintained, or a description of the contents of such records shall not be maintained by any Government authority other than in the sealed records of the grand jury, unless such record has been used in the prosecution of a crime for which the grand jury issued an indictment or presentment or for a purpose authorized by rule 6(e) of the Federal Rules of Criminal Procedure.

(b)(1) No officer, director, partner, employee, or shareholder of, or agent or attorney for, a financial institution shall, directly or indirectly, notify any person named in a grand jury subpoena served on such institution in connection with an investigation relating to a possible—

(A) crime against any financial institution or supervisory agency or crime involving a violation of the Controlled Substance Act [21 U.S.C.A. § 801 et seq.], the Controlled Substances Import and Export Act [21 U.S.C.A. § 951 et seq.], section 1956 or 1957 of Title 18, sections 5313, 5316, and 5324 of Title 31, or section 6050I of Title 26; or

(B) conspiracy to commit such a crime,

about the existence or contents or such subpoena, or information that has been furnished to the grand jury in response to such subpoena.

(2) Section 1818 of this title and section 1786(k)(2) of this title shall apply to any violation of this subsection.

§ 3421. Repealed. Pub.L. 104–66, Title III, § 3001(d), Dec. 21, 1995, 109 Stat. 734

§ 3422. Applicability to Securities and Exchange Commission

Except as provided in the Securities Exchange Act of 1934 [15 U.S.C.A. § 78a et seq.], this chapter shall apply with respect to the Securities and Exchange Commission.

CHAPTER 39. ALTERNATIVE MORTGAGE TRANSACTIONS 12 U.S.C.A. §§ 3801–3806

12 U.S.C.A. §§ 3801–3806

CHAPTER 39. ALTERNATIVE MORT-GAGE TRANSACTIONS 12 U.S.C.A. §§ 3801–3806

§ 3801. Findings and purpose

(a) The Congress hereby finds that—

(1) increasingly volatile and dynamic changes in interest rates have seriously impa[i]red the ability of housing creditors to provide consumers with fixed-term, fixed-rate credit secured by interests in real property, cooperative housing, manufactured homes, and other dwellings;

(2) alternative mortgage transactions are essential to the provision of an adequate supply of credit secured by residential property necessary to meet the demand expected during the 1980's; and

(3) the Comptroller of the Currency, the National Credit Union Administration, and the Director of the Office of Thrift Supervision have recognized the importance of alternative mortgage transactions and have adopted regulations authorizing federally chartered depository institutions to engage in alternative mortgage financing.

(b) It is the purpose of this chapter to eliminate the discriminatory impact that those regulations have upon nonfederally chartered housing creditors and provide them with parity with federally chartered institutions by authorizing all housing creditors to make, purchase, and enforce alternative mortgage transactions so long as the transactions are in conformity with the regulations issued by the Federal agencies.

§ 3802. Definitions—DFA § 1083

As used in this chapter—

(1) the term "alternative mortgage transaction" means a loan or credit sale secured by an interest in residential real property, a dwelling, all stock allocated to a dwelling unit in a residential cooperative housing corporation, or a residential manufactured home (as that term is defined in section 5402(6) of Title 42)—

(A) in which the interest rate or finance charge may be adjusted or renegotiated;

(B) involving a fixed-rate, but which implicitly permits rate adjustments by having the debt mature at the end of an interval shorter than the term of the amortization schedule; or

(C) involving any similar type of rate, method of determining return, term, repayment, or other variation not common to traditional fixed-rate, fixed-term transactions, including without limitation, transactions that involve the sharing of equity or appreciation;

described and defined by applicable regulation; and

(2) the term "housing creditor" means—

(A) a depository institution, as defined in section 501(a)(2) of the Depository Institutions Deregulation and Monetary Control Act of 1980;

(B) a lender approved by the Secretary of Housing and Urban Development for participation in any mortgage insurance program under the National Housing Act [12 U.S.C.A. § 1701 et seq.];

(C) any person who regularly makes loans, credit sales, or advances secured by interests in properties referred to in paragraph (1); or

(D) any transferee of any of them.

A person is not a "housing creditor" with respect to a specific alternative mortgage transaction if, except for this chapter, in order to enter into that transaction, the person would be required to comply with licensing requirements imposed under State law, unless such person is licensed under applicable State law and such person remains, or becomes, subject to the applicable regulatory requirements and enforcement mechanisms provided by State law.

§ 3803. Alternative mortgage authority—DFA § 1083

(a) General authority; compliance by banks, credit unions and all other housing creditors with applicable regulations

In order to prevent discrimination against State-chartered depository institutions, and other non-federally chartered housing creditors, with respect to making, purchasing, and enforcing alternative mortgage transactions, housing creditors may make, purchase, and enforce alternative mortgage transactions, except that this section shall apply—

(1) with respect to banks, only to transactions made in accordance with regulations governing alternative mortgage transactions as issued by the Comptroller of the Currency for national banks, to the extent that such regulations are authorized by rulemaking authority granted to the Comptroller of the Currency with regard to national banks under laws other than this section;

(2) with respect to credit unions, only to transactions made in accordance with regulations governing alternative mortgage transactions as issued by the National Credit Union Administration Board for Federal credit unions, to the extent that such regulations are authorized by rulemaking authority granted to the National Credit Union Administration with regard to Federal credit unions under laws other than this section; and

(3) with respect to all other housing creditors, including without limitation, savings and loan associations, mutual savings banks, and savings banks, only to transactions made in accordance with regulations governing alternative mortgage transactions as issued by the Director of the Office of Thrift Supervision for federally chartered savings and loan associations, to the extent that such regulations are authorized by rulemaking authority granted to the Director of the Office of Thrift Supervision with regard to federally chartered savings and loan associations under laws other than this section.

(b) Transactions deemed in compliance with applicable regulations

For the purpose of determining the applicability of this section, an alternative mortgage transaction shall be deemed to be made in accordance with the applicable regulation notwithstanding the housing creditor's failure to comply with the regulation, if—

(1) the transaction is in substantial compliance with the regulation; and

(2) within sixty days of discovering any error, the housing creditor corrects such error, including making appropriate adjustments, if any, to the account.

(c) Preemption of State constitutions, laws or regulations

An alternative mortgage transaction may be made by a housing creditor in accordance with this section, notwithstanding any State constitution, law, or regulation.

§ 3804. Applicability of preemption provisions

(a) The provisions of section 3803 of this title shall not apply to any alternative mortgage transaction in any State made on or after the effective date (if such effective date occurs on or after October 15, 1982, and prior to a date three years after October 15, 1982) of a State law or a certification that the voters of such State have voted in favor of any provision, constitutional or otherwise, which states explicitly and by its terms that such State does not want the preemption provided in section 3803 of this title to apply with respect to alternative mortgage transactions (or to any class or type of alternative mortgage transaction) subject to the laws of such State, except that section 3803 of this title shall continue to apply to—

(1) any alternative mortgage transaction undertaken on or after such date pursuant to an agreement to undertake such alternative mortgage transaction which was entered into on or after October 15, 1982, and prior to such later date (the "preemption period"); and

(2) any renewal, extension, refinancing, or other modification of an alternative mortgage transaction that was entered into during the preemption period.

(b) An alternative mortgage transaction shall be deemed to have been undertaken during the preemption period to which this section applies if it—

(1) is funded or extended in whole or in part during the preemption period, regardless of whether pursuant to a commitment or other agreement therefor made prior to that period; or

(2) is a renewal, extension, refinancing, or other modification of an alternative mortgage transaction entered into before the preemption period and such renewal, extension, or other modification is made during such period with the written consent of any person obligated to repay such credit.

§ 3805. Applicability of consumer protection provisions

Section 501(c)(1) of the Depository Institutions Deregulation and Monetary Control Act of 1980 shall not apply to transactions which are subject to this chapter.

§ 3806. Adjustable rate mortgage caps

(a) In general

Any adjustable rate mortgage loan originated by a creditor shall include a limitation on the maximum interest rate that may apply during the term of the mortgage loan.

(b) Regulations

The Board of Governors of the Federal Reserve System shall prescribe regulations to carry out the purposes of this section.

(c) Enforcement

Any violation of this section shall be treated as a violation of the Truth in Lending Act [15 U.S.C.A. § 1601 et seq.] and shall be subject to administrative enforcement under section 108 [15 U.S.C.A. § 1607] or civil damages under sec-tion 130 of such Act [15 U.S.C.A. § 1640], or both.

(d) Definitions

For the purpose of this section—

(1) the term "creditor" means a person who regularly extends credit for personal, family, or household purposes; and

(2) the term "adjustable rate mortgage loan" means any consumer loan secured by a lien on a one-to four-family dwelling unit, including a condominium unit, cooperative housing unit, or mobile home, where the loan is made pursu-ant to an agreement under which the creditor may, from time to time, adjust the rate of interest.

(e) Effective date

This section shall take effect upon the expiration of 120 days after August 10, 1987.

TITLE 15, CHAPTER 2B. SECURITIES EXCHANGES
15 U.S.C.A. §§ 78a–78mm

SECURITIES EXCHANGE ACT OF 1934. REGISTRATION AND REGULATION OF BROKERS AND DEALERS

15 U.S.C. A. § 78c(a)(4)–(5)

(a) Definitions

When used in this chapter, unless the context otherwise requires—

* * *

(4) Broker

(A) In general

The term "broker" means any person engaged in the business of effecting transactions in securities for the account of others.

(B) Exception for certain bank activities

A bank shall not be considered to be a broker because the bank engages in any one or more of the following activities under the conditions described:

(i) Third party brokerage arrangements

The bank enters into a contractual or other written arrangement with a broker or dealer registered under this chapter under which the broker or dealer offers brokerage services on or off the premises of the bank if—

(I) such broker or dealer is clearly identified as the person performing the brokerage services;

(II) the broker or dealer performs brokerage services in an area that is clearly marked and, to the extent practicable, physically separate from the routine deposit-taking activities of the bank;

(III) any materials used by the bank to advertise or promote generally the availability of brokerage services under the arrangement clearly indicate that the brokerage services are being provided by the broker or dealer and not by the bank;

(IV) any materials used by the bank to advertise or promote generally the availability of brokerage services under the arrangement are in compliance with the Federal securities laws before distribution;

(V) bank employees (other than associated persons of a broker or dealer who are qualified pursuant to the rules of a self-regulatory organization) perform only clerical or ministerial functions in connection with brokerage transactions including scheduling appointments with the associated persons of a broker or dealer, except that bank employees may forward customer funds or securities and may describe in general terms the types of investment vehicles available from the bank and the broker or dealer under the arrangement;

(VI) bank employees do not receive incentive compensation for any brokerage transaction unless such employees are associated persons of a broker or dealer and are qualified pursuant to the rules of a self-regulatory organization, except that the bank employees may receive compensation for the referral of any customer if the compensation is a nominal one-time cash fee of a fixed dollar amount and the payment of the fee is not contingent on whether the referral results in a transaction;

(VII) such services are provided by the broker or dealer on a basis in which all customers that receive any services are fully disclosed to the broker or dealer;

(VIII) the bank does not carry a securities account of the customer except as permitted under clause (ii) or (viii) of this subparagraph; and

(IX) the bank, broker, or dealer informs each customer that the brokerage services are provided by the broker or dealer and not by the bank and that the securities are not deposits or other obligations of the bank, are not guaranteed by the bank, and are not insured by the Federal Deposit Insurance Corporation.

(ii) Trust activities

The bank effects transactions in a trustee capacity, or effects transactions in a fiduciary capacity in its trust department or other department that is regularly examined by bank examiners for compliance with fiduciary principles and standards, and—

(I) is chiefly compensated for such transactions, consistent with fiduciary principles and standards, on the basis of an administration or annual fee (payable on a monthly, quarterly, or other basis), a percentage of assets under management, or a flat or capped per order processing fee equal to not more than the cost incurred by the bank in connection with executing securities transactions for trustee and fiduciary customers, or any combination of such fees; and

(II) does not publicly solicit brokerage business, other than by advertising that it effects transactions in securities in conjunction with advertising its other trust activities.

(iii) Permissible securities transactions

The bank effects transactions in—

(I) commercial paper, bankers acceptances, or commercial bills;

(II) exempted securities;

(III) qualified Canadian government obligations as defined in section 24 of Title 12, in conformity with section 78o–5 of this title and the rules and regulations thereunder, or obligations of the North American Development Bank; or

(IV) any standardized, credit enhanced debt security issued by a foreign government pursuant to the March 1989 plan of then Secretary of the Treasury Brady, used by such foreign government to retire outstanding commercial bank loans.

(iv) Certain stock purchase plans

(I) Employee benefit plans

The bank effects transactions, as part of its transfer agency activities, in the securities of an issuer as part of any pension, retirement, profit-sharing, bonus, thrift, savings, incentive, or other similar benefit plan for the employees of that issuer or its affiliates (as defined in section 1841 of Title 12), if the bank does not solicit transactions or provide investment advice with respect to the purchase or sale of securities in connection with the plan.

(II) Dividend reinvestment plans

The bank effects transactions, as part of its transfer agency activities, in the securities of an issuer as part of that issuer's dividend reinvestment plan, if—

(aa) the bank does not solicit transactions or provide investment advice with respect to the purchase or sale of securities in connection with the plan; and

(bb) the bank does not net shareholders' buy and sell orders, other than for programs for odd-lot holders or plans registered with the Commission.

(III) Issuer plans

The bank effects transactions, as part of its transfer agency activities, in the securities of an issuer as part of a plan or program for the purchase or sale of that issuer's shares, if—

(aa) the bank does not solicit transactions or provide investment advice with respect to the purchase or sale of securities in connection with the plan or program; and

(bb) the bank does not net shareholders' buy and sell orders, other than for programs for odd-lot holders or plans registered with the Commission.

(IV) Permissible delivery of materials

The exception to being considered a broker for a bank engaged in activities described in subclauses (I), (II), and (III) will not be affected by delivery of written or electronic plan materials by a bank to employees of the issuer, shareholders of the issuer, or members of affinity groups of the issuer, so long as such materials are—

(aa) comparable in scope or nature to that permitted by the Commission as of November 12, 1999; or

(bb) otherwise permitted by the Commission.

(v) Sweep accounts

The bank effects transactions as part of a program for the investment or reinvestment of deposit funds into any no-load, open-end management investment company registered under the Investment Company Act of 1940 [15 U.S.C.A. § 80a–1 et seq.] that holds itself out as a money market fund.

(vi) Affiliate transactions

The bank effects transactions for the account of any affiliate of the bank (as defined in section 1841 of Title 12) other than—

(I) a registered broker or dealer; or

(II) an affiliate that is engaged in merchant banking, as described in section 1843(k)(4)(H) of Title 12.

(vii) Private securities offerings

The bank—

(I) effects sales as part of a primary offering of securities not involving a public offering, pursuant to section 77c(b), 77d(2), or 77d(6) of this title or the rules and regulations issued thereunder;

(II) at any time after the date that is 1 year after November 12, 1999, is not affiliated with a broker or dealer that has been registered for more than 1 year in accordance with this chapter, and engages in dealing, market making, or underwriting activities, other than with respect to exempted securities; and

(III) if the bank is not affiliated with a broker or dealer, does not effect any primary offering described in subclause (I) the aggregate amount of which exceeds 25 percent of the capital of the bank, except that the limitation of this subclause shall not apply with respect to any sale of government securities or municipal securities.

(viii) Safekeeping and custody activities

(I) In general

The bank, as part of customary banking activities—

(aa) provides safekeeping or custody services with respect to securities, including the exercise of warrants and other rights on behalf of customers;

(bb) facilitates the transfer of funds or securities, as a custodian or a clearing agency, in connection with the clearance and settlement of its customers' transactions in securities;

(cc) effects securities lending or borrowing transactions with or on behalf of customers as part of services provided to customers pursuant to division (aa) or (bb) or invests cash collateral pledged in connection with such transactions;

(dd) holds securities pledged by a customer to another person or securities subject to purchase or resale agreements involving a customer, or facilitates the pledging or transfer of such securities by book entry or as otherwise provided under applicable law, if the bank maintains records separately identifying the securities and the customer; or

(ee) serves as a custodian or provider of other related administrative services to any individual retirement account, pension, retirement, profit sharing, bonus, thrift savings, incentive, or other similar benefit plan.

(II) Exception for carrying broker activities

The exception to being considered a broker for a bank engaged in activities described in subclause (I) shall not apply if the bank, in connection with such activities, acts in the United States as a carrying broker (as such term, and different formulations thereof, are used in section 78o(c)(3) of this title and the rules and regulations thereunder) for any broker or dealer, unless such carrying broker activities are engaged in with respect to government securities (as defined in paragraph (42) of this subsection)

(ix) Identified banking products

The bank effects transactions in identified banking products as defined in section 206 of the Gramm–Leach–Bliley Act [15 U.S.C.A. § 78c note].

(x) Municipal securities

The bank effects transactions in municipal securities.

(xi) De minimis exception

The bank effects, other than in transactions referred to in clauses (i) through (x), not more than 500 transactions in securities in any calendar year, and such transactions are not effected by an employee of the bank who is also an employee of a broker or dealer.

(C) Execution by broker or dealer

The exception to being considered a broker for a bank engaged in activities described in clauses (ii), (iv), and (viii) of subparagraph (B) shall not apply if the activities described in such provisions result in the trade in the United States of any security that is a publicly traded security in the United States, unless—

(i) the bank directs such trade to a registered broker or dealer for execution;

(ii) the trade is a cross trade or other substantially similar trade of a security that—

(I) is made by the bank or between the bank and an affiliated fiduciary; and

(II) is not in contravention of fiduciary principles established under applicable Federal or State law; or

(iii) the trade is conducted in some other manner permitted under rules, regulations, or orders as the Commission may prescribe or issue.

(D) Fiduciary capacity

For purposes of subparagraph (B)(ii), the term 'fiduciary capacity' means–

(i) in the capacity as trustee, executor, administrator, registrar of stocks and bonds, transfer agent, guardian, assignee, receiver, or custodian under a uniform gift to minor act, or as an investment adviser if the bank receives a fee for its investment advice;

(ii) in any capacity in which the bank possesses investment discretion on behalf of another; or

(iii) in any other similar capacity.

(E) Exception for entities subject to section 78o(e) of this title

The term "broker" does not include a bank that—

(i) was, on the day before November 12, 1999, subject to section 78o(e) of this title; and

(ii) is subject to such restrictions and requirements as the Commission considers appropriate.

(5) Dealer

(A) In general

The term "dealer" means any person engaged in the business of buying and selling securities for such person's own account through a broker or otherwise.

(B) Exception for person not engaged in the business of dealing

The term "dealer" does not include a person that buys or sells securities for such person's own account, either individually or in a fiduciary capacity, but not as a part of a regular business.

(C) Exception for certain bank activities

A bank shall not be considered to be a dealer because the bank engages in any of the following activities under the conditions described:

(i) Permissible securities transactions

The bank buys or sells—

(I) commercial paper, bankers acceptances, or commercial bills;

(II) exempted securities;

(III) qualified Canadian government obligations as defined in section 24 of Title 12, in conformity with section 78o–5 of this title and the rules and regulations thereunder, or obligations of the North American Development Bank; or

(IV) any standardized, credit enhanced debt security issued by a foreign government pursuant to the March 1989 plan of then Secretary of the Treasury Brady, used by such foreign government to retire outstanding commercial bank loans.

(ii) Investment, trustee, and fiduciary transactions

The bank buys or sells securities for investment purposes—

(I) for the bank; or

(II) for accounts for which the bank acts as a trustee or fiduciary.

(iii) Asset-backed transactions

The bank engages in the issuance or sale to qualified investors, through a grantor trust or other separate entity, of securities backed by or representing an interest in notes, drafts, acceptances, loans, leases, receivables, other obligations (other than securities of which the bank is not the issuer), or pools of any such obligations predominantly originated by—

(I) the bank;

(II) an affiliate of any such bank other than a broker or dealer; or

(III) a syndicate of banks of which the bank is a member, if the obligations or pool of obligations consists of mortgage obligations or consumer-related receivables.

(iv) Identified banking products

The bank buys or sells identified banking products, as defined in section 206 of the Gramm–Leach–Bliley Act [15 U.S.C.A. § 78c note].

15 U.S.C.A § 78c note—DFA §§ 742, 762

Pub.L. 106–102, Title II, § 206, Nov. 12, 1999, 113 Stat. 1393, provided that:

(a) Definition of identified banking product.

For purposes of paragraphs (4) and (5) of section 3(a) of the Securities Exchange Act of 1934 (15 U.S.C. 78c(a)(4), (5)), the term 'identified banking product' means—

(1) a deposit account, savings account, certificate of deposit, or other deposit instrument issued by a bank;

(2) a banker's acceptance;

(3) a letter of credit issued or loan made by a bank;

(4) a debit account at a bank arising from a credit card or similar arrangement;

(5) a participation in a loan which the bank or an affiliate of the bank (other than a broker or dealer) funds, participates in, or owns that is sold—

(A) to qualified investors; or

(B) to other persons that—

(i) have the opportunity to review and assess any material information, including information regarding the borrower's credit worthiness; and

(ii) based on such factors as financial sophistication, net worth, and knowledge and experience in financial matters, have the capability to evaluate the information available, as determined under generally applicable banking standards or guidelines; or

(6) any swap agreement, including credit and equity swaps, except that an equity swap that is sold directly to any person other than a qualified investor (as defined in section 3(a)(54) of the Securities Act of 1934 [subsec. (a)(54) of this section]) shall not be treated as an identified banking product.

(b) Definition of swap agreement.

For purposes of subsection (a)(6), the term 'swap agreement' means any individually negotiated contract, agreement, warrant, note, or option that is based, in whole or in part, on the value of, any interest in, or any quantitative measure or the occurrence of any event relating to, one or more commodities, securities, currencies, interest or other rates, indices, or other assets, but does not include any other identified banking product, as defined in paragraphs (1) through (5) of subsection (a).

(c) Classification limited.

Classification of a particular product as an identified banking product pursuant to this section shall not be construed as finding or implying that such product is or is not a security for any purpose under the securities laws, or is or is not an account, agreement, contract, or transaction for any purpose under the Commodity Exchange Act [7 U.S.C.A.§ 1 et seq].

(d) Incorporated definitions.

For purposes of this section, the terms 'bank' and 'qualified investor' have the same meanings as given in section 3(a) of the Securities Exchange Act of 1934 [subsec. (a) of this section], as amended by this Act [the Gramm–Leach–Bliley Act, Pub.L. 106–102; see Tables for classification].

[Section 206 of Pub.L. 106–102 (set out as a note under this section) shall take effect at the end of 18 months after Nov. 12, 1999, see section 209 of Pub.L. 106–102, set out as a note under section 1828 of Title 12.]

15 U.S.C.A. § 78o(i)—DFA § 762

* * *

(i) Rulemaking to extend requirements to new hybrid products

(1) Consultation

Prior to commencing a rulemaking under this subsection, the Commission shall consult with and seek the concurrence of the Board concerning the imposition of broker or dealer registration requirements with respect to any new hybrid product. In developing and promulgating rules under this subsection, the Commission shall consider the views of the Board, including views with respect to the nature of the new hybrid product; the history, purpose, extent, and appropriateness of the regulation of the new product under the Federal banking laws; and the impact of the proposed rule on the banking industry.

(2) Limitation

The Commission shall not—

(A) require a bank to register as a broker or dealer under this section because the bank engages in any transaction in, or buys or sells, a new hybrid product; or

(B) bring an action against a bank for a failure to comply with a requirement described in subparagraph (A),

unless the Commission has imposed such requirement by rule or regulation issued in accordance with this section.

(3) Criteria for rulemaking

The Commission shall not impose a requirement under paragraph (2) of this subsection with respect to any new hybrid product unless the Commission determines that—

(A) the new hybrid product is a security; and

(B) imposing such requirement is necessary and appropriate in the public interest and for the protection of investors.

(4) Considerations

In making a determination under paragraph (3), the Commission shall consider—

(A) the nature of the new hybrid product; and

(B) the history, purpose, extent, and appropriateness of the regulation of the new hybrid product under the Federal securities laws and under the Federal banking laws.

(5) Objection to Commission regulation

(A) Filing of petition for review

The Board may obtain review of any final regulation described in paragraph (2) in the United States Court of Appeals for the District of Columbia Circuit by filing in such court, not later than 60 days after the date of publication of the final regulation, a written petition requesting that the regulation be set aside. Any proceeding to challenge any such rule shall be expedited by the Court of Appeals.

(B) Transmittal of petition and record

A copy of a petition described in subparagraph (A) shall be transmitted as soon as possible by the Clerk of the Court to an officer or employee of the Commission designated for that purpose. Upon receipt of the petition, the Commission shall file with the court the regulation under review and any documents referred to therein, and any other relevant materials prescribed by the court.

(C) Exclusive jurisdiction

On the date of the filing of the petition under subparagraph (A), the court has jurisdiction, which becomes exclusive on the filing of the materials set forth in subparagraph (B), to affirm and enforce or to set aside the regulation at issue.

(D) Standard of review

The court shall determine to affirm and enforce or set aside a regulation of the Commission under this subsection, based on the determination of the court as to whether—

(i) the subject product is a new hybrid product, as defined in this subsection;

(ii) the subject product is a security; and

(iii) imposing a requirement to register as a broker or dealer for banks engaging in transactions in such product is appropriate in light of the history, purpose, and extent of regulation under the Federal securities laws and under the Federal banking laws, giving deference neither to the views of the Commission nor the Board.

(E) Judicial stay

The filing of a petition by the Board pursuant to subparagraph (A) shall operate as a judicial stay, until the date on which the determination of the court is final (including any appeal of such determination).

(F) Other authority to challenge

Any aggrieved party may seek judicial review of the Commission's rulemaking under this subsection pursuant to section 78y of this title.

(6) Definitions

For purposes of this subsection:

(A) New hybrid product

The term "new hybrid product" means a product that—

(i) was not subjected to regulation by the Commission as a security prior to November 12, 1999;

(ii) is not an identified banking product as such term is defined in section 206 of such Act [15 U.S.C.A. § 78c note]; and

(iii) is not an equity swap within the meaning of section 206(a)(6) of such Act [15 U.S.C.A. § 78c note].

(B) Board

The term ''Board'' means the Board of Governors of the Federal Reserve System.

(i) Limitation

The authority of the Commission under this section with respect to security-based swap agreements (as defined in section 206B of the Gramm–Leach–Bliley Act) shall be subject to the restrictions and limitations of section 78c–1(b) of this title.

CHAPTER 93. INSURANCE
15 U.S.C.A. §§ 6701–6717; 6751–6766

15 U.S.C.A. § **Page**

§ 6701. Operation of State law

(a) State regulation of the business of insurance

The Act entitled "An Act to express the intent of Congress with reference to the regulation of the business of insurance" and approved March 9, 1945 (15 U.S.C. 1011 et seq.) (commonly referred to as the "McCarran–Ferguson Act") remains the law of the United States.

(b) Mandatory insurance licensing requirements

No person shall engage in the business of insurance in a State as principal or agent unless such person is licensed as required by the appropriate insurance regulator of such State in accordance with the relevant State insurance law, subject to subsections (c), (d), and (e).

(c) Affiliations

(1) In general

Except as provided in paragraph (2), no State may, by statute, regulation, order, interpretation, or other action, prevent or restrict a depository institution, or an affiliate thereof, from being affiliated directly or indirectly or associated with any person, as authorized or permitted by this Act or any other provision of Federal law.

(2) Insurance

With respect to affiliations between depository institutions, or any affiliate thereof, and any insurer, paragraph (1) does not prohibit—

(A) any State from—

(i) collecting, reviewing, and taking actions (including approval and disapproval) on applications and other documents or reports concerning any proposed acquisition of, or a change or continuation of control of, an insurer domiciled in that State; and

(ii) exercising authority granted under applicable State law to collect information concerning any proposed acquisition of, or a change or continuation of control of, an insurer engaged in the business of insurance in, and regulated as an insurer by, such State;

during the 60–day period preceding the effective date of the acquisition or change or continuation of control, so long as the collecting, reviewing, taking actions, or exercising authority by the State does not have the effect of discriminating, intentionally or un-

intentionally, against a depository institution or an affiliate thereof, or against any other person based upon an association of such person with a depository institution;

(B) any State from requiring any person that is acquiring control of an insurer domiciled in that State to maintain or restore the capital requirements of that insurer to the level required under the capital regulations of general applicability in that State to avoid the requirement of preparing and filing with the insurance regulatory authority of that State a plan to increase the capital of the insurer, except that any determination by the State insurance regulatory authority with respect to such requirement shall be made not later than 60 days after the date of notification under subparagraph (A); or

(C) any State from restricting a change in the ownership of stock in an insurer, or a company formed for the purpose of controlling such insurer, after the conversion of the insurer from mutual to stock form so long as such restriction does not have the effect of discriminating, intentionally or unintentionally, against a depository institution or an affiliate thereof, or against any other person based upon an association of such person with a depository institution.

(d) Activities

(1) In general

Except as provided in paragraph (3), and except with respect to insurance sales, solicitation, and cross marketing activities, which shall be governed by paragraph (2), no State may, by statute, regulation, order, interpretation, or other action, prevent or restrict a depository institution or an affiliate thereof from engaging directly or indirectly, either by itself or in conjunction with an affiliate, or any other person, in any activity authorized or permitted under this Act and the amendments made by this Act.

(2) Insurance sales

(A) In general

In accordance with the legal standards for preemption set forth in the decision of the Supreme Court of the United States in Barnett Bank of Marion County N.A. v. Nelson, 517 U.S. 25 (1996), no State may, by statute, regulation, order, interpretation, or other action, prevent or significantly interfere with the ability of a depository institution, or an affiliate thereof, to engage, directly or indirectly, either by itself or in conjunction with an affiliate or any other person, in any insurance sales, solicitation, or crossmarketing activity.

(B) Certain State laws preserved

Notwithstanding subparagraph (A), a State may impose any of the following restrictions, or restrictions that are substantially the same as but no more burdensome or restrictive than those in each of the following clauses:

(i) Restrictions prohibiting the rejection of an insurance policy by a depository institution or an affiliate of a depository institution, solely because the policy has been issued or underwritten by any person who is not associated with such depository institution or affiliate when the insurance is required in connection with a loan or extension of credit.

(ii) Restrictions prohibiting a requirement for any debtor, insurer, or insurance agent or broker to pay a separate charge in connection with the handling of insurance that is required in connection with a loan or other extension of credit or the provision of another traditional banking product by a depository institution, or any affiliate of a depository institution, unless such charge would be required when the depository institution or affiliate is the licensed insurance agent or broker providing the insurance.

(iii) Restrictions prohibiting the use of any advertisement or other insurance promotional material by a depository institution or any affiliate of a depository institution that would cause a reasonable person to believe mistakenly that—

(I) the Federal Government or a State is responsible for the insurance sales activities of, or stands behind the credit of, the institution or affiliate; or

(II) a State, or the Federal Government guarantees any returns on insurance products, or is a source of payment on any insurance obligation of or sold by the institution or affiliate;

(iv) Restrictions prohibiting the payment or receipt of any commission or brokerage fee or other valuable consideration for services as an insurance agent or broker to or by any person, unless such person holds a valid State license regarding the applicable class of insurance at the time at which the services are performed, except that, in this clause, the term "services as an insurance agent or broker" does not include a referral by an unlicensed person of a customer or potential customer to a licensed insurance agent or broker that does not include a discussion of specific insurance policy terms and conditions.

(v) Restrictions prohibiting any compensation paid to or received by any individual who is not licensed to sell insurance, for the referral of a customer that seeks to purchase, or seeks an opinion or advice on, any insurance product to a person that sells or provides opinions or advice on such product, based on the purchase of insurance by the customer.

(vi) Restrictions prohibiting the release of the insurance information of a customer (defined as information concerning the premiums, terms, and conditions of insurance coverage, including expiration dates and rates, and insurance claims of a customer contained in the records of the depository institution or an affiliate thereof) to any person other than an officer, director, employee, agent, or affiliate of a depository institution, for the purpose of soliciting or selling insurance, without the express consent of the customer, other than a provision that prohibits—

(I) a transfer of insurance information to an unaffiliated insurer in connection with transferring insurance in force on existing insureds of the depository institution or an affiliate thereof, or in connection with a merger with or acquisition of an unaffiliated insurer; or

(II) the release of information as otherwise authorized by State or Federal law.

(vii) Restrictions prohibiting the use of health information obtained from the insurance records of a customer for any purpose, other than for its activities as a licensed agent or broker, without the express consent of the customer.

(viii) Restrictions prohibiting the extension of credit or any product or service that is equivalent to an extension of credit, lease or sale of property of any kind, or furnishing of any services or fixing or varying the consideration for any of the foregoing, on the condition or requirement that the customer obtain insurance from a depository institution or an affiliate of a depository institution, or a particular insurer, agent, or broker, other than a prohibition that would prevent any such depository institution or affiliate—

(I) from engaging in any activity described in this clause that would not violate section 106 of the Bank Holding Company Act Amendments of 1970 [12 U.S.C.A. § 1971 et seq.], as interpreted by the Board of Governors of the Federal Reserve System; or

(II) from informing a customer or prospective customer that insurance is required in order to obtain a loan or credit, that loan or credit approval is contingent upon the procurement by the customer of acceptable insurance, or that insurance is available from the depository institution or an affiliate of the depository institution.

(ix) Restrictions requiring, when an application by a consumer for a loan or other extension of credit from a depository institution is pending, and insurance is offered or sold to the consumer or is required in connection with the loan or extension of credit by the depository institution or any affiliate thereof, that a written disclosure be provided to the consumer or prospective customer indicating that the customer's choice of an insurance provider will not affect the credit decision or credit terms in any way, except that the depository institution may impose reasonable requirements concerning the credit worthiness of the insurer and scope of coverage chosen.

(x) Restrictions requiring clear and conspicuous disclosure, in writing, where practicable, to the customer prior to the sale of any insurance policy that such policy–

(I) is not a deposit;

(II) is not insured by the Federal Deposit Insurance Corporation;

(III) is not guaranteed by any depository institution or, if appropriate, an affiliate of

any such institution or any person soliciting the purchase of or selling insurance on the premises thereof; and

(IV) where appropriate, involves investment risk, including potential loss of principal.

(xi) Restrictions requiring that, when a customer obtains insurance (other than credit insurance or flood insurance) and credit from a depository institution, or any affiliate of such institution, or any person soliciting the purchase of or selling insurance on the premises thereof, the credit and insurance transactions be completed through separate documents.

(xii) Restrictions prohibiting, when a customer obtains insurance (other than credit insurance or flood insurance) and credit from a depository institution or an affiliate of such institution, or any person soliciting the purchase of or selling insurance on the premises thereof, inclusion of the expense of insurance premiums in the primary credit transaction without the express written consent of the customer.

(xiii) Restrictions requiring maintenance of separate and distinct books and records relating to insurance transactions, including all files relating to and reflecting consumer complaints, and requiring that such insurance books and records be made available to the appropriate State insurance regulator for inspection upon reasonable notice.

(C) Limitations

(i) OCC deference

Section 6714(e) of this title does not apply with respect to any State statute, regulation, order, interpretation, or other action regarding insurance sales, solicitation, or cross marketing activities described in subparagraph (A) that was issued, adopted, or enacted before September 3, 1998, and that is not described in subparagraph (B).

(ii) Nondiscrimination

Subsection (e) does not apply with respect to any State statute, regulation, order, interpretation, or other action regarding insurance sales, solicitation, or cross marketing activities described in subparagraph (A) that was issued, adopted, or enacted before September 3, 1998, and that is not described in subparagraph (B).

(iii) Construction

Nothing in this paragraph shall be construed—

(I) to limit the applicability of the decision of the Supreme Court in Barnett Bank of Marion County N.A. v. Nelson, 517 U.S. 25 (1996) with respect to any State statute, regulation, order, interpretation, or other action that is not referred to or described in subparagraph (B); or

(II) to create any inference with respect to any State statute, regulation, order, interpretation, or other action that is not described in this paragraph.

(3) Insurance activities other than sales

State statutes, regulations, interpretations, orders, and other actions shall not be preempted under paragraph (1) to the extent that they—

(A) relate to, or are issued, adopted, or enacted for the purpose of regulating the business of insurance in accordance with the Act entitled "An Act to express the intent of Congress with reference to the regulation of the business of insurance" and approved March 9, 1945 (15 U.S.C. 1011 et seq.) (commonly referred to as the "McCarran–Ferguson Act");

(B) apply only to persons that are not depository institutions, but that are directly engaged in the business of insurance (except that they may apply to depository institutions engaged in providing savings bank life insurance as principal to the extent of regulating such insurance);

(C) do not relate to or directly or indirectly regulate insurance sales, solicitations, or cross marketing activities; and

(D) are not prohibited under subsection (e).

(4) Financial activities other than insurance

No State statute, regulation, order, interpretation, or other action shall be preempted under paragraph (1) to the extent that—

(A) it does not relate to, and is not issued and adopted, or enacted for the purpose of regulating, directly or indirectly, insurance sales, solicitations, or cross marketing activities covered under paragraph (2);

(B) it does not relate to, and is not issued and adopted, or enacted for the purpose of regulating, directly or indirectly, the business of insurance activities other than sales, solicitations, or cross marketing activities, covered under paragraph (3);

(C) it does not relate to securities investigations or enforcement actions referred to in subsection (f); and

(D) it—

(i) does not distinguish by its terms between depository institutions, and affiliates thereof, engaged in the activity at issue and other persons engaged in the same activity in a manner that is in any way adverse with respect to the conduct of the activity by any such depository institution or affiliate engaged in the activity at issue;

(ii) as interpreted or applied, does not have, and will not have, an impact on depository institutions, or affiliates thereof, engaged in the activity at issue, or any person who has an association with any such depository institution or affiliate, that is substantially more adverse than its impact on other persons engaged in the same activity that are not depository institutions or affiliates thereof, or persons who do not have an association with any such depository institution or affiliate;

(iii) does not effectively prevent a depository institution or affiliate thereof from engaging in activities authorized or permitted by this Act or any other provision of Federal law; and

(iv) does not conflict with the intent of this Act generally to permit affiliations that are authorized or permitted by Federal law.

(e) Nondiscrimination

Except as provided in any restrictions described in subsection (d)(2)(B), no State may, by statute, regulation, order, interpretation, or other action, regulate the insurance activities authorized or permitted under this Act or any other provision of Federal law of a depository institution, or affiliate thereof, to the extent that such statute, regulation, order, interpretation, or other action—

(1) distinguishes by its terms between depository institutions, or affiliates thereof, and other persons engaged in such activities, in a manner that is in any way adverse to any such depository institution, or affiliate thereof;

(2) as interpreted or applied, has or will have an impact on depository institutions, or affiliates thereof, that is substantially more adverse than its impact on other persons providing the same products or services or engaged in the same activities that are not depository institutions, or affiliates thereof, or persons or entities affiliated therewith;

(3) effectively prevents a depository institution, or affiliate thereof, from engaging in insurance activities authorized or permitted by this Act or any other provision of Federal law; or

(4) conflicts with the intent of this Act generally to permit affiliations that are authorized or permitted by Federal law between depository institutions, or affiliates thereof, and persons engaged in the business of insurance.

(f) Limitation

Subsections (c) and (d) shall not be construed to affect—

(1) the jurisdiction of the securities commission (or any agency or office performing like functions) of any State, under the laws of such State—

(A) to investigate and bring enforcement actions, consistent with section 77r(c) of this title, with respect to fraud or deceit or unlawful conduct by any person, in connection with securities or securities transactions; or

(B) to require the registration of securities or the licensure or registration of brokers, dealers, or investment advisers (consistent with section 80b–3a of this title), or the associated persons of a broker, dealer, or investment adviser (consistent with such section 80b–3a of this title); or

(2) State laws, regulations, orders, interpretations, or other actions of general applicability relating to the governance of corporations, partnerships, limited liability companies, or other business associations incorporated or formed under the laws of that State or domiciled in that State, or the applicability of the antitrust laws of any State or any State law that is similar to the antitrust laws if such laws, regulations, orders, interpretations, or other actions are not inconsistent with the purposes of this Act to authorize or permit certain affiliations and to remove barriers to such affiliations.

(g) Definitions

For purposes of this section, the following definitions shall apply:

(1) Affiliate

The term "affiliate" means any company that controls, is controlled by, or is under common control with another company.

(2) Antitrust laws

The term "antitrust laws" has the meaning given the term in subsection (a) of section 12 of this title, and includes section 45 of this title (to the extent that such section 45 of this title relates to unfair methods of competition).

(3) Depository institution

The term "depository institution"—

(A) has the meaning given the term in section 1813 of Title 12; and

(B) includes any foreign bank that maintains a branch, agency, or commercial lending company in the United States.

(4) Insurer

The term "insurer" means any person engaged in the business of insurance.

(5) State

The term "State" means any State of the United States, the District of Columbia, any territory of the United States, Puerto Rico, Guam, American Samoa, the Trust Territory of the Pacific Islands, the Virgin Islands, and the Northern Mariana Islands.

§ 6711. Functional regulation of insurance

The insurance activities of any person (including a national bank exercising its power to act as agent under section 92 of Title 12) shall be functionally regulated by the States, subject to section 6701 of this title.

§ 6712. Insurance underwriting in national banks

(a) In general

Except as provided in section 6713 of this title, a national bank and the subsidiaries of a national bank may not provide insurance in a State as principal except that this prohibition shall not apply to authorized products.

(b) Authorized products

For the purposes of this section, a product is authorized if—

(1) as of January 1, 1999, the Comptroller of the Currency had determined in writing that national banks may provide such product as principal, or national banks were in fact lawfully providing such product as principal;

(2) no court of relevant jurisdiction had, by final judgment, overturned a determination of the Comptroller of the Currency that national banks may provide such product as principal; and

(3) the product is not title insurance, or an annuity contract the income of which is subject to tax treatment under section 72 of Title 26.

(c) Definition

For purposes of this section, the term "insurance" means—

(1) any product regulated as insurance as of January 1, 1999, in accordance with the relevant State insurance law, in the State in which the product is provided;

(2) any product first offered after January 1, 1999, which—

(A) a State insurance regulator determines shall be regulated as insurance in the State in which the product is provided because the product insures, guarantees, or indemnifies against liability, loss of life, loss of health, or loss through damage to or destruction of property, including, but not limited to, surety bonds, life insurance, health insurance, title insurance, and property and casualty insurance (such as private passenger or commercial automobile, homeowners, mortgage, commercial multiperil, general liability, professional liability, workers' compensation, fire and allied lines, farm owners multiperil, aircraft, fidelity, surety, medical malpractice, ocean marine, inland marine, and boiler and machinery insurance); and

(B) is not a product or service of a bank that is–

(i) a deposit product;

(ii) a loan, discount, letter of credit, or other extension of credit;

(iii) a trust or other fiduciary service;

(iv) a qualified financial contract (as defined in or determined pursuant to section 1821(e)(8)(D)(i) of Title 12); or

(v) a financial guaranty, except that this subparagraph (B) shall not apply to a product that includes an insurance component such that if the product is offered or proposed to be offered by the bank as principal—

(I) it would be treated as a life insurance contract under section 7702 of Title 26; or

(II) in the event that the product is not a letter of credit or other similar extension of credit, a qualified financial contract, or a financial guaranty, it would qualify for treatment for losses incurred with respect to such product under section 832(b)(5) of Title 26, if the bank were subject to tax as an insurance company under section 831 of that title; or

(3) any annuity contract, the income on which is subject to tax treatment under section 72 of Title 26.

(d) Rule of construction

For purposes of this section, providing insurance (including reinsurance) outside the United States that insures, guarantees, or indemnifies insurance products provided in a State, or that indemnifies an insurance company with regard to insurance products provided in a State, shall be considered to be providing insurance as principal in that State.

§ 6713. Title insurance activities of national banks and their affiliates

(a) General prohibition

No national bank may engage in any activity involving the underwriting or sale of title insurance.

(b) Nondiscrimination parity exception

(1) In general

Notwithstanding any other provision of law (including section 6701 of this title), in the case of any State in which banks organized under the laws of such State are authorized to sell title insurance as agent, a national bank may sell title insurance as agent in such State, but only in the same manner, to the same extent, and under the same restrictions as such State banks are authorized to sell title insurance as agent in such State.

(2) Coordination with "wildcard" provision

A State law which authorizes State banks to engage in any activities in such State in which a national bank may engage shall not be treated as a statute which authorizes State banks to sell title insurance as agent, for purposes of paragraph (1).

(c) Grandfathering with consistent regulation

(1) In general

Except as provided in paragraphs (2) and (3) and notwithstanding subsections (a) and (b) of this section, a national bank, and a subsidiary of a national bank, may conduct title insurance activities which such national bank or subsidiary was actively and lawfully conducting before November 12, 1999.

(2) Insurance affiliate

In the case of a national bank which has an affiliate which provides insurance as principal and is not a subsidiary of the bank, the national bank and any subsidiary of the national bank may not engage in the underwriting of title insurance pursuant to paragraph (1).

(3) Insurance subsidiary

In the case of a national bank which has a subsidiary which provides insurance as principal and has no affiliate other than a subsidiary which provides insurance as principal, the national bank may not directly engage in any activity involving the underwriting of title insurance.

(d) "Affiliate" and "subsidiary" defined

For purposes of this section, the terms "affiliate" and "subsidiary" have the same meanings as in section 1841 of Title 12.

(e) Rule of construction

No provision of this Act or any other Federal law shall be construed as superseding or affecting a State law which was in effect before November 12, 1999, and which prohibits title insurance from being offered, provided, or sold in such State, or from being underwritten with respect to real property in such State, by any person whatsoever.

§ 6714. Expedited and equalized dispute resolution for Federal regulators

(a) Filing in Court of Appeals

In the case of a regulatory conflict between a State insurance regulator and a Federal regulator regarding insurance issues, including whether a State law, rule, regulation, order, or interpretation regarding any insurance sales or solicitation activity is properly treated as preempted under Federal law, the Federal or State regulator may seek expedited judicial review of such determination by the United States Court of Appeals for the circuit in which the State is located or in the United States Court of Appeals for the District of Columbia Circuit by filing a petition for review in such court.

(b) Expedited review

The United States Court of Appeals in which a petition for review is filed in accordance with subsection (a) of this section shall complete all action on such petition, including rendering a judgment, before the end of the 60-day period beginning on the date on which such petition is filed, unless all parties to such proceeding agree to any extension of such period.

(c) Supreme Court review

Any request for certiorari to the Supreme Court of the United States of any judgment of a United States Court of Appeals with respect to a petition for review under this section shall be filed with the Supreme Court of the United States as soon as practicable after such judgment is issued.

(d) Statute of limitation

No petition may be filed under this section challenging an order, ruling, determination, or other action of a Federal regulator or State insurance regulator after the later of—

(1) the end of the 12-month period beginning on the date on which the first public notice is made of such order, ruling, determination or other action in its final form; or

(2) the end of the 6-month period beginning on the date on which such order, ruling, determination, or other action takes effect.

(e) Standard of review

The court shall decide a petition filed under this section based on its review on the merits of all questions presented under State and Federal law, including the nature of the product or activity and the history and purpose of its regulation under State and Federal law, without unequal deference.

§ 6715. Certain State affiliation laws preempted for insurance companies and affiliates

Except as provided in section 6701(c)(2) of this title, no State may, by law, regulation, order, interpretation, or otherwise—

(1) prevent or significantly interfere with the ability of any insurer, or any affiliate of an insurer (whether such affiliate is organized as a stock company, mutual holding company, or otherwise), to become a financial holding company or to acquire control of a depository institution;

(2) limit the amount of an insurer's assets that may be invested in the voting securities of a depository institution (or any company which controls such institution), except that the laws of an insurer's State of domicile may limit the amount of such investment to an amount that is not less than 5 percent of the insurer's admitted assets; or

(3) prevent, significantly interfere with, or have the authority to review, approve, or disapprove a plan of reorganization by which an insurer proposes to reorganize from mutual form to become a stock insurer (whether as a director indirect subsidiary of a mutual holding company or otherwise) unless such State is the State of domicile of the insurer.

§ 6716. Interagency consultation

(a) Purpose

It is the intention of the Congress that the Board of Governors of the Federal Reserve System, as the umbrella supervisor for financial holding companies, and the State insurance regulators, as the functional regulators of companies engaged in insurance activities, coordinate efforts to supervise companies that control both a depository institution and a company engaged in insurance activities regulated under State law. In particular, Congress believes that the Board and the State insurance regulators should share, on a confidential basis, information relevant to the supervision of companies that control both a depository institution and a company engaged in insurance activities, including information regarding the financial health of the consolidated organization and information regarding transactions and relationships between insurance companies and affiliated depository institutions. The appropriate Federal banking agencies for deposi-

tory institutions should also share, on a confidential basis, information with the relevant State insurance regulators regarding transactions and relationships between depository institutions and affiliated companies engaged in insurance activities. The purpose of this section is to encourage this coordination and confidential sharing of information, and to thereby improve both the efficiency and the quality of the supervision of financial holding companies and their affiliated depository institutions and companies engaged in insurance activities.

(b) Examination results and other information

(1) Information of the Board

Upon the request of the appropriate insurance regulator of any State, the Board may provide any information of the Board regarding the financial condition, risk management policies, and operations of any financial holding company that controls a company that is engaged in insurance activities and is regulated by such State insurance regulator, and regarding any transaction or relationship between such an insurance company and any affiliated depository institution. The Board may provide any other information to the appropriate State insurance regulator that the Board believes is necessary or appropriate to permit the State insurance regulator to administer and enforce applicable State insurance laws.

(2) Banking agency information

Upon the request of the appropriate insurance regulator of any State, the appropriate Federal banking agency may provide any information of the agency regarding any transaction or relationship between a depository institution supervised by such Federal banking agency and any affiliated company that is engaged in insurance activities regulated by such State insurance regulator. The appropriate Federal banking agency may provide any other information to the appropriate State insurance regulator that the agency believes is necessary or appropriate to permit the State insurance regulator to administer and enforce applicable State insurance laws.

(3) State insurance regulator information

Upon the request of the Board or the appropriate Federal banking agency, a State insurance regulator may provide any examination or other reports, records, or other information to which such insurance regulator may have access with respect to a company which—

    (A) is engaged in insurance activities and regulated by such insurance regulator; and

    (B) is an affiliate of a depository institution or financial holding company.

(c) Consultation

Before making any determination relating to the initial affiliation of, or the continuing affiliation of, a depository institution or financial holding company with a company engaged in insurance activities, the appropriate Federal banking agency shall consult with the appropriate State insurance regulator of such company and take the views of such insurance regulator into account in making such determination.

(d) Effect on other authority

Nothing in this section shall limit in any respect the authority of the appropriate Federal banking agency with respect to a depository institution or bank holding company or any affiliate thereof under any provision of law.

(e) Confidentiality and privilege

    (1) Confidentiality

The appropriate Federal banking agency shall not provide any information or material that is entitled to confidential treatment under applicable Federal banking agency regulations, or other applicable law, to a State insurance regulator unless such regulator agrees to maintain the information or material in confidence and to take all reasonable steps to oppose any effort to secure disclosure of the information or material by the regulator. The appropriate Federal banking agency shall treat as confidential any information or material obtained from a State insurance regulator that is entitled to confidential treatment under applicable State regulations, or other applicable law, and take all reasonable steps to oppose any effort to secure disclosure of the information or material by the Federal banking agency.

    (2) Privilege

The provision pursuant to this section of information or material by a Federal banking agency or State insurance regulator shall not constitute a waiver of, or otherwise affect, any privilege to which the information or material is otherwise subject.

(f) Definitions

For purposes of this section, the following definitions shall apply:

    (1) Appropriate Federal banking agency; depository institution

The terms "appropriate Federal banking agency" and "depository institution" have the same meanings as in section 1813 of Title 12.

    (2) Board and financial holding company

The terms "Board" and "financial holding company" have the same meanings as in section 1841 of Title 12.

§ 6717. Definition of State

For purposes of this subchapter, the term "State" means any State of the United States, the District of Columbia, any territory of the United States, Puerto Rico, Guam, American Samoa, the Trust Territory of the Pacific Islands, the Virgin Islands, and the Northern Mariana Islands.

§ 6751. State flexibility in multistate licensing reforms

(a) In general

The provisions of this subchapter shall take effect unless, not later than 3 years after November 12, 1999, at least a majority of the States—

    (1) have enacted uniform laws and regulations governing the licensure of individuals and entities authorized to sell and solicit the purchase of insurance within the State; or

    (2) have enacted reciprocity laws and regulations governing the licensure of nonresident individuals and entities authorized to sell and solicit insurance within those States.

(b) Uniformity required

States shall be deemed to have established the uniformity necessary to satisfy subsection (a)(1) of this section if the States—

    (1) establish uniform criteria regarding the integrity, personal qualifications, education, training, and experience of licensed insurance producers, including the qualification and training of sales personnel in ascertaining the appropriateness of a particular insurance product for a prospective customer;

    (2) establish uniform continuing education requirements for licensed insurance producers;

(3) establish uniform ethics course requirements for licensed insurance producers in conjunction with the continuing education requirements under paragraph (2);

(4) establish uniform criteria to ensure that an insurance product, including any annuity contract, sold to a consumer is suitable and appropriate for the consumer based on financial information disclosed by the consumer; and

(5) do not impose any requirement upon any insurance producer to be licensed or otherwise qualified to do business as a nonresident that has the effect of limiting or conditioning that producer's activities because of its residence or place of operations, except that countersignature requirements imposed on nonresident producers shall not be deemed to have the effect of limiting or conditioning a producer's activities because of its residence or place of operations under this section.

(c) Reciprocity required

States shall be deemed to have established the reciprocity required to satisfy subsection (a)(2) of this section if the following conditions are met:

(1) Administrative licensing procedures

At least a majority of the States permit a producer that has a resident license for selling or soliciting the purchase of insurance in its home State to receive a license to sell or solicit the purchase of insurance in such majority of States as a nonresident to the same extent that such producer is permitted to sell or solicit the purchase of insurance in its State, if the producer's home State also awards such licenses on such a reciprocal basis, without satisfying any additional requirements other than submitting—

(A) a request for licensure;

(B) the application for licensure that the producer submitted to its home State;

(C) proof that the producer is licensed and in good standing in its home State; and

(D) the payment of any requisite fee to the appropriate authority.

(2) Continuing education requirements

A majority of the States accept an insurance producer's satisfaction of its home State's continuing education requirements for licensed insurance producers to satisfy the States' own continuing education requirements if the producer's home State also recognizes the satisfaction of continuing education requirements on such a reciprocal basis.

(3) No limiting nonresident requirements

A majority of the States do not impose any requirement upon any insurance producer to be licensed or otherwise qualified to do business as a nonresident that has the effect of limiting or conditioning that producer's activities because of its residence or place of operations, except that countersignature requirements imposed on nonresident producers shall not be deemed to have the effect of limiting or conditioning a producer's activities because of its residence or place of operations under this section.

(4) Reciprocal reciprocity

Each of the States that satisfies paragraphs (1), (2), and (3) grants reciprocity to residents of all of the other States that satisfy such paragraphs.

(d) Determination

(1) NAIC determination

At the end of the 3–year period beginning on November 12, 1999, the National Association of Insurance Commissioners (hereafter in this subchapter referred to as the "NAIC") shall determine, in consultation with the insurance commissioners or chief insurance regulatory officials of the States, whether the uniformity or reciprocity required by subsections (b) and (c) of this section has been achieved.

(2) Judicial review

The appropriate United States district court shall have exclusive jurisdiction over any challenge to the NAIC's determination under this section and such court shall apply the standards set forth in section 706 of Title 5, when reviewing any such challenge.

(e) Continued application

If, at any time, the uniformity or reciprocity required by subsections (b) and (c) of this section no longer exists, the provisions of this subchapter shall take effect 2 years after the date on which such uniformity or reciprocity ceases to exist, unless the uniformity or reciprocity required by those provisions is satisfied before the expiration of that 2–year period.

(f) Savings provision

No provision of this section shall be construed as requiring that any law, regulation, provision, or action of any State which purports to regulate insurance producers, including any such law, regulation, provision, or action which purports to regulate unfair trade practices or establish consumer protections, including countersignature laws, be altered or amended in order to satisfy the uniformity or reciprocity required by subsections(b) and (c) of this section, unless any such law, regulation, provision, or action is inconsistent with a specific requirement of any such subsection and then only to the extent of such inconsistency.

(g) Uniform licensing

Nothing in this section shall be construed to require any State to adopt new or additional licensing requirements to achieve the uniformity necessary to satisfy subsection (a)(1) of this section.

§ 6752. National association of registered agents and brokers

(a) Establishment

There is established the National Association of Registered Agents and Brokers (hereafter in this subchapter referred to as the "Association").

(b) Status

The Association shall—

(1) be a nonprofit corporation;

(2) have succession until dissolved by an Act of Congress;

(3) not be an agent or instrumentality of the United States Government; and

(4) except as otherwise provided in this Act, be subject to, and have all the powers conferred upon a nonprofit corporation by the District of Columbia Nonprofit Corporation Act (D.C. Code, sec. 29y–1001 et seq.).

§ 6753. Purpose

The purpose of the Association shall be to provide a mechanism through which uniform licensing, appointment, continuing education, and other insurance producer sales qualification requirements and conditions can be adopted and applied on a multistate basis, while preserving the right of States to license, supervise, and discipline insurance producers and to prescribe and enforce laws and regulations with regard to insurance-related consumer protection and unfair trade practices.

§ 6754. Relationship to the Federal Government

The Association shall be subject to the supervision and oversight of the NAIC.

§ 6755. Membership

(a) Eligibility

(1) In general

Any State-licensed insurance producer shall be eligible to become a member in the Association.

(2) Ineligibility for suspension or revocation of license

Notwithstanding paragraph (1), a State-licensed insurance producer shall not be eligible to become a member if a State insurance regulator has suspended or revoked such producer's license in that State during the 3–year period preceding the date on which such producer applies for membership.

(3) Resumption of eligibility

Paragraph (2) shall cease to apply to any insurance producer if—

(A) the State insurance regulator renews the license of such producer in the State in which the license was suspended or revoked; or

(B) the suspension or revocation is subsequently overturned.

(b) Authority to establish membership criteria

The Association shall have the authority to establish membership criteria that—

(1) bear a reasonable relationship to the purposes for which the Association was established; and

(2) do not unfairly limit the access of smaller agencies to the Association membership.

(c) Establishment of classes and categories

(1) Classes of membership

The Association may establish separate classes of membership, with separate criteria, if the Association reasonably determines that performance of different duties requires different levels of education, training, or experience.

(2) Categories

The Association may establish separate categories of membership for individuals and for other persons. The establishment of any such categories of membership shall be based either on the types of licensing categories that exist under State laws or on the aggregate amount of business handled by an insurance producer. No special categories of membership, and no distinct membership criteria, shall be established for members which are depository institutions or for their employees, agents, or affiliates.

(d) Membership criteria

(1) In general

The Association may establish criteria for membership which shall include standards for integrity, personal qualifications, education, training, and experience.

(2) Minimum standard

In establishing criteria under paragraph (1), the Association shall consider the highest levels of insurance producer qualifications established under the licensing laws of the States.

(e) Effect of membership

Membership in the Association shall entitle the member to licensure in each State for which the member pays the requisite fees, including licensing fees and, where applicable, bonding requirements, set by such State.

(f) Annual renewal

Membership in the Association shall be renewed on an annual basis.

(g) Continuing education

The Association shall establish, as a condition of membership, continuing education requirements which shall be comparable to or greater than the continuing education requirements under the licensing laws of a majority of the States.

(h) Suspension and revocation

The Association may–

(1) inspect and examine the records and offices of the members of the Association to determine compliance with the criteria for membership established by the Association; and

(2) suspend or revoke the membership of an insurance producer if—

(A) the producer fails to meet the applicable membership criteria of the Association; or

(B) the producer has been subject to disciplinary action pursuant to a final adjudicatory proceeding under the jurisdiction of a State insurance regulator, and the Association concludes that retention of membership in the Association would not be in the public interest.

(i) Office of consumer complaints

(1) In general

The Association shall establish an office of consumer complaints that shall—

(A) receive and investigate complaints from both consumers and State insurance regulators related to members of the Association; and

(B) recommend to the Association any disciplinary actions that the office considers appropriate, to the extent that any such recommendation is not inconsistent with State law.

(2) Records and referrals

The office of consumer complaints of the Association shall—

(A) maintain records of all complaints received in accordance with paragraph (1) and make such records available to the NAIC and to each State insurance regulator for the State of residence of the consumer who filed the complaint; and

(B) refer, when appropriate, any such complaint to any appropriate State insurance regulator.

(3) Telephone and other access

The office of consumer complaints shall maintain a toll-free telephone number for the purpose of this subsection and, as practicable, other alternative means of communication with consumers, such as an Internet home page.

§ 6756. Board of directors

(a) Establishment

There is established the board of directors of the Association (hereafter in this subchapter referred to as the "Board") for the purpose of governing and supervising the activities of the Association and the members of the Association.

(b) Powers

The Board shall have such powers and authority as may be specified in the bylaws of the Association.

(c) Composition

(1) Members

The Board shall be composed of 7 members appointed by the NAIC.

(2) Requirement

At least 4 of the members of the Board shall each have significant experience with the regulation of commercial lines of insurance in at least 1 of the 20 States in which the greatest total dollar amount of commercial-lines insurance is placed in the United States.

(3) Initial Board membership

(A) In general

If, by the end of the 2–year period beginning on November 12, 1999, the NAIC has not appointed the initial 7 members of the Board of the Association, the initial Board shall consist of the 7 State insurance regulators of the 7 States with the greatest total dollar amount of commercial-lines insurance in place as of the end of such period.

(B) Alternate composition

If any of the State insurance regulators described in subparagraph (A) declines to serve on the Board, the State insurance regulator with the next greatest total dollar amount of commercial-lines insurance in place, as determined by the NAIC as of the end of such period, shall serve as a member of the Board.

(C) Inoperability

If fewer than 7 State insurance regulators accept appointment to the Board, the Association shall be established without NAIC oversight pursuant to section 6762 of this title.

(d) Terms

The term of each director shall, after the initial appointment of the members of the Board, be for 3 years, with one-third of the directors to be appointed each year.

(e) Board vacancies

A vacancy on the Board shall be filled in the same manner as the original appointment of the initial Board for the remainder of the term of the vacating member.

(f) Meetings

The Board shall meet at the call of the chairperson, or as otherwise provided by the bylaws of the Association.

§ 6757. Officers

(a) In general

(1) Positions

The officers of the Association shall consist of a chairperson and a vice chairperson of the Board, a president, secretary, and treasurer of the Association, and such other officers and assistant officers as may be deemed necessary.

(2) Manner of selection

Each officer of the Board and the Association shall be elected or appointed at such time and in such manner and for such terms not exceeding 3 years as may be prescribed in the bylaws of the Association.

(b) Criteria for chairperson

Only individuals who are members of the NAIC shall be eligible to serve as the chairperson of the board of directors.

§ 6758. Bylaws, rules, and disciplinary action

(a) Adoption and amendment of bylaws

(1) Copy required to be filed with the NAIC

The board of directors of the Association shall file with the NAIC a copy of the proposed bylaws or any proposed amendment to the bylaws, accompanied by a concise general statement of the basis and purpose of such proposal.

(2) Effective date

Except as provided in paragraph (3), any proposed bylaw or proposed amendment shall take effect—

(A) 30 days after the date of the filing of a copy with the NAIC;

(B) upon such later date as the Association may designate; or

(C) upon such earlier date as the NAIC may determine.

(3) Disapproval by the NAIC

Notwithstanding paragraph (2), a proposed bylaw or amendment shall not take effect if, after public notice and opportunity to participate in a public hearing—

(A) the NAIC disapproves such proposal as being contrary to the public interest or contrary to the purposes of this subchapter and provides notice to the Association setting forth the reasons for such disapproval; or

(B) the NAIC finds that such proposal involves a matter of such significant public interest that public comment should be obtained, in which case it may, after notifying the Association in writing of such finding, require that the procedures set forth in subsection (b) be followed with respect to such proposal, in the same manner as if such proposed bylaw change were a proposed rule change within the meaning of such subsection.

(b) Adoption and amendment of rules

(1) Filing proposed regulations with the NAIC

(A) In general

The board of directors of the Association shall file with the NAIC a copy of any proposed rule or any proposed amendment to a rule of the Association which shall be accompanied by a concise general statement of the basis and purpose of such proposal.

(B) Other rules and amendments ineffective

No proposed rule or amendment shall take effect unless approved by the NAIC or otherwise permitted in accordance with this paragraph.

(2) Initial consideration by the NAIC

Not later than 35 days after the date of publication of notice of filing of a proposal, or before the end of such longer period not to exceed 90 days as the NAIC may designate after such date, if the NAIC finds such longer period to be appropriate and sets forth its reasons for so finding, or as to which the Association consents, the NAIC shall—

(A) by order approve such proposed rule or amendment; or

(B) institute proceedings to determine whether such proposed rule or amendment should be modified or disapproved.

(3) NAIC proceedings

(A) In general

Proceedings instituted by the NAIC with respect to a proposed rule or amendment pursuant to paragraph (2) shall—

(i) include notice of the grounds for disapproval under consideration;

(ii) provide opportunity for hearing; and

(iii) be concluded not later than 180 days after the date of the Association's filing of such proposed rule or amendment.

(B) Disposition of proposal

At the conclusion of any proceeding under subparagraph (A), the NAIC shall, by order, approve or disapprove the proposed rule or amendment.

(C) Extension of time for consideration

The NAIC may extend the time for concluding any proceeding under subparagraph (A) for—

(i) not more than 60 days if the NAIC finds good cause for such extension and sets forth its reasons for so finding; or

(ii) such longer period as to which the Association consents.

(4) Standards for review

(A) Grounds for approval

The NAIC shall approve a proposed rule or amendment if the NAIC finds that the rule or amendment is in the public interest and is consistent with the purposes of this Act.

(B) Approval before end of notice period

The NAIC shall not approve any proposed rule before the end of the 30-day period beginning on the date on which the Association files proposed rules or amendments in accordance with paragraph (1), unless the NAIC finds good cause for so doing and sets forth the reasons for so finding.

(5) Alternate procedure

(A) In general

Notwithstanding any provision of this subsection other than subparagraph (B), a proposed rule or amendment relating to the administration or organization of the Association shall take effect—

(i) upon the date of filing with the NAIC, if such proposed rule or amendment is designated by the Association as relating solely to matters which the NAIC, consistent with the public interest and the purposes of this subsection, determines by rule do not require the procedures set forth in this paragraph; or

(ii) upon such date as the NAIC shall for good cause determine.

(B) Abrogation by the NAIC

(i) In general

At any time within 60 days after the date of filing of any proposed rule or amendment under subparagraph (A)(i) or clause (ii) of this subparagraph, the NAIC may repeal such rule or amendment and require that the rule or amendment be refiled and reviewed in accordance with this paragraph, if the NAIC finds that such action is necessary or appropriate in the public interest, for the protection of insurance producers or policyholders, or otherwise in furtherance of the purposes of this subchapter.

(ii) Effect of reconsideration by the NAIC

Any action of the NAIC pursuant to clause (i) shall–

(I) not affect the validity or force of a rule change during the period such rule or amendment was in effect; and

(II) not be considered to be a final action.

(c) Action required by the NAIC

The NAIC may, in accordance with such rules as the NAIC determines to be necessary or appropriate to the public interest or to carry out the purposes of this subchapter, require the Association to adopt, amend, or repeal any bylaw, rule, or amendment of the Association, whenever adopted.

(d) Disciplinary action by the Association

(1) Specification of charges

In any proceeding to determine whether membership shall be denied, suspended, revoked, or not renewed (hereafter in this section referred to as a "disciplinary action"), the Association shall bring specific charges, notify such member of such charges, give the member an opportunity to defend against the charges, and keep a record.

(2) Supporting statement

A determination to take disciplinary action shall be supported by a statement setting forth—

(A) any act or practice in which such member has been found to have been engaged;

(B) the specific provision of this subchapter, the rules or regulations under this subchapter, or the rules of the Association which any such act or practice is deemed to violate; and

(C) the sanction imposed and the reason for such sanction.

(e) NAIC review of disciplinary action

(1) Notice to the NAIC

If the Association orders any disciplinary action, the Association shall promptly notify the NAIC of such action.

(2) Review by the NAIC

Any disciplinary action taken by the Association shall be subject to review by the NAIC—

(A) on the NAIC's own motion; or

(B) upon application by any person aggrieved by such action if such application is filed with the NAIC not more than 30 days after the later of—

(i) the date the notice was filed with the NAIC pursuant to paragraph (1); or

(ii) the date the notice of the disciplinary action was received by such aggrieved person.

(f) Effect of review

The filing of an application to the NAIC for review of a disciplinary action, or the institution of review by the NAIC on the NAIC's own motion, shall not operate as a stay of disciplinary action unless the NAIC otherwise orders.

(g) Scope of review

(1) In general

In any proceeding to review such action, after notice and the opportunity for hearing, the NAIC shall—

(A) determine whether the action should be taken;

(B) affirm, modify, or rescind the disciplinary sanction; or

(C) remand to the Association for further proceedings.

(2) Dismissal of review

The NAIC may dismiss a proceeding to review disciplinary action if the NAIC finds that—

(A) the specific grounds on which the action is based exist in fact;

(B) the action is in accordance with applicable rules and regulations; and

(C) such rules and regulations are, and were, applied in a manner consistent with the purposes of this subchapter.

§ 6759. Assessments

(a) Insurance producers subject to assessment

The Association may establish such application and membership fees as the Association finds necessary to cover the costs of its operations, including fees made reimbursable to the NAIC under subsection (b) of this section, except that, in setting such fees, the Association may not discriminate against smaller insurance producers.

(b) NAIC assessments

The NAIC may assess the Association for any costs that the NAIC incurs under this subchapter.

§ 6760. Functions of the NAIC

(a) Administrative procedure

Determinations of the NAIC, for purposes of making rules pursuant to section 6758 of this title, shall be made after appropriate notice and opportunity for a hearing and for submission of views of interested persons.

(b) Examinations and reports

(1) Examinations

The NAIC may make such examinations and inspections of the Association and require the Association to furnish to the NAIC such reports and records or copies thereof as the NAIC may consider necessary or appropriate in the public interest or to effectuate the purposes of this subchapter.

(2) Report by Association

As soon as practicable after the close of each fiscal year, the Association shall submit to the NAIC a written report regarding the conduct of its business, and the exercise of the other rights and powers granted by this subchapter, during such fiscal year. Such report shall include financial statements setting forth the financial position of the Association at the end of such fiscal year and the results of its operations (including the source and application of its funds) for such fiscal year. The NAIC shall transmit such report to the President and the Congress with such comment thereon as the NAIC determines to be appropriate.

§ 6761. Liability of the Association and the directors, officers, and employees of the Association

(a) In general

The Association shall not be deemed to be an insurer or insurance producer within the meaning of any State law, rule, regulation, or order regulating or taxing insurers, insurance producers, or other entities engaged in the business of insurance, including provisions imposing premium taxes, regulating insurer solvency or financial condition, establishing guaranty funds and levying assessments, or requiring claims settlement practices.

(b) Liability of the Association, its directors, officers, and employees

Neither the Association nor any of its directors, officers, or employees shall have any liability to any person for any action taken or omitted in good faith under or in connection with any matter subject to this subchapter.

§ 6762. Elimination of NAIC oversight

(a) In general

The Association shall be established without NAIC oversight and the provisions set forth in section 6754 of this title, subsections (a), (b), (c), and (e) of section 6758 of this title, and sections 6759(b) and 6760 of this title shall cease to be effective if, at the end of the 2–year period beginning on the date on which the provisions of this subchapter take effect pursuant to section 6751 of this title—

(1) at least a majority of the States representing at least 50 percent of the total United States commercial-lines insurance premiums have not satisfied the uniformity or reciprocity requirements of subsections (a), (b), and (c) of section 6751 of this title; and

(2) the NAIC has not approved the Association's bylaws as required by section 6758 of this title or is unable to operate or supervise

the Association, or the Association is not conducting its activities as required under this Act.

(b) Board appointments

If the repeals required by subsection (a) of this section are implemented, the following shall apply:

(1) General appointment power

The President, with the advice and consent of the Senate, shall appoint the members of the Association's Board established under section 6756 of this title from lists of candidates recommended to the President by the NAIC.

(2) Procedures for obtaining NAIC appointment recommendations

(A) Initial determination and recommendations

After the date on which the provisions of subsection (a) of this section take effect, the NAIC shall, not later than 60 days thereafter, provide a list of recommended candidates to the President. If the NAIC fails to provide a list by that date, or if any list that is provided does not include at least 14 recommended candidates or comply with the requirements of section 6756(c) of this title, the President shall, with the advice and consent of the Senate, make the requisite appointments without considering the views of the NAIC.

(B) Subsequent appointments

After the initial appointments, the NAIC shall provide a list of at least six recommended candidates for the Board to the President by January 15 of each subsequent year. If the NAIC fails to provide a list by that date, or if any list that is provided does not include at least six recommended candidates or comply with the requirements of section 6756(c) of this title, the President, with the advice and consent of the Senate, shall make the requisite appointments without considering the views of the NAIC.

(C) Presidential oversight

(i) Removal

If the President determines that the Association is not acting in the interests of the public, the President may remove the entire existing Board for the remainder of the term to which the members of the Board were

appointed and appoint, with the advice and consent of the Senate, new members to fill the vacancies on the Board for the remainder of such terms.

(ii) Suspension of rules or actions

The President, or a person designated by the President for such purpose, may suspend the effectiveness of any rule, or prohibit any action, of the Association which the President or the designee determines is contrary to the public interest.

(c) Annual report

As soon as practicable after the close of each fiscal year, the Association shall submit to the President and to the Congress a written report relative to the conduct of its business, and the exercise of the other rights and powers granted by this subchapter, during such fiscal year. Such report shall include financial statements setting forth the financial position of the Association at the end of such fiscal year and the results of its operations (including the source and application of its funds) for such fiscal year.

§ 6763. Relationship to State law

(a) Preemption of State laws

State laws, regulations, provisions, or other actions purporting to regulate insurance producers shall be preempted as provided in subsection (b) of this section.

(b) Prohibited actions

No State shall—

(1) impede the activities of, take any action against, or apply any provision of law or regulation to, any insurance producer because that insurance producer or any affiliate plans to become, has applied to become, or is a member of the Association;

(2) impose any requirement upon a member of the Association that it pay different fees to be licensed or otherwise qualified to do business in that State, including bonding requirements, based on its residency;

(3) impose any licensing, appointment, integrity, personal or corporate qualifications, education, training, experience, residency, or continuing education requirement upon a member of the Association that is different from the criteria for membership in the Association or

renewal of such membership, except that countersignature requirements imposed on nonresident producers shall not be deemed to have the effect of limiting or conditioning a producer's activities because of its residence or place of operations under this section; or

(4) implement the procedures of such State's system of licensing or renewing the licenses of insurance producers in a manner different from the authority of the Association under section 6755 of this title.

(c) Savings provision

Except as provided in subsections (a) and (b) of this section, no provision of this section shall be construed as altering or affecting the continuing effectiveness of any law, regulation, provision, or other action of any State which purports to regulate insurance producers, including any such law, regulation, provision, or action which purports to regulate unfair trade practices or establish consumer protections, including countersignature laws.

§ 6764. Coordination with other regulators

(a) Coordination with State insurance regulators

The Association shall have the authority to—

(1) issue uniform insurance producer applications and renewal applications that may be used to apply for the issuance or removal of State licenses, while preserving the ability of each State to impose such conditions on the issuance or renewal of a license as are consistent with section 6763 of this title;

(2) establish a central clearinghouse through which members of the Association may apply for the issuance or renewal of licenses in multiple States; and

(3) establish or utilize a national database for the collection of regulatory information concerning the activities of insurance producers.

(b) Coordination with the National Association of Securities Dealers

The Association shall coordinate with the National Association of Securities Dealers in order to ease any administrative burdens that fall on persons that are members of both associations, consistent with the purposes of this subchapter and the Federal securities laws.

§ 6765. Judicial review

(a) Jurisdiction

The appropriate United States district court shall have exclusive jurisdiction over litigation involving the Association, including disputes between the Association and its members that arise under this subchapter. Suits brought in State court involving the Association shall be deemed to have arisen under Federal law and therefore be subject to jurisdiction in the appropriate United States district court.

(b) Exhaustion of remedies

An aggrieved person shall be required to exhaust all available administrative remedies before the Association and the NAIC before it may seek judicial review of an Association decision.

(c) Standards of review

The standards set forth in section 553 of Title 5 shall be applied whenever a rule or bylaw of the Association is under judicial review, and the standards set forth in section 554 of Title 5 shall be applied whenever a disciplinary action of the Association is judicially reviewed.

§ 6766. Definitions

For purposes of this subchapter, the following definitions shall apply:

(1) Home State

The term "home State" means the State in which the insurance producer maintains its principal place of residence and is licensed to act as an insurance producer.

(2) Insurance

The term "insurance" means any product, other than title insurance, defined or regulated as insurance by the appropriate State insurance regulatory authority.

(3) Insurance producer

The term "insurance producer" means any insurance agent or broker, surplus lines broker, insurance consultant, limited insurance representative, and any other person that solicits, negotiates, effects, procures, delivers, renews, continues or binds policies of insurance or offers advice, counsel, opinions or services related to insurance.

(4) State

The term "State" includes any State, the District of Columbia, any territory of the United States, Puerto Rico, Guam, American Samoa, the Trust Territory of the Pacific Islands, the Virgin Islands, and the Northern Mariana Islands.

(5) State law

The term "State law" includes all laws, decisions, rules, regulations, or other State action having the effect of law, of any State. A law of the United States applicable only to the District of Columbia shall be treated as a State law rather than a law of the United States.

CHAPTER 94. PRIVACY
15 U.S.C.A. §§ 6801–6827

§ 6801. Protection of nonpublic personal information

(a) Privacy obligation policy

, v. broad

It is the policy of the Congress that each financial institution has an affirmative and continuing obligation to respect the privacy of its customers and to protect the security and confidentiality of those customers' nonpublic personal information.

(b) Financial institutions safeguards

In furtherance of the policy in subsection (a) of this section, each agency or authority described in section 6805(a) of this title shall establish appropriate standards for the financial institutions subject to their jurisdiction relating to administrative, technical, and physical safeguards—

(1) to insure the security and confidentiality of customer records and information;

(2) to protect against any anticipated threats or hazards to the security or integrity of such records; and

(3) to protect against unauthorized access to or use of such records or information which could result in substantial harm or inconvenience to any customer.

§ 6802. Obligations with respect to disclosures of personal information

(a) Notice requirements

Except as otherwise provided in this subchapter, a financial institution may not, directly or through any affiliate, disclose to a nonaffiliated third party any nonpublic personal information, unless such financial institution provides or has provided to the consumer a notice that complies with section 6803 of this title.

(b) Opt out

(1) In general

A financial institution may not disclose nonpublic personal information to a nonaffiliated third party unless—

(A) such financial institution clearly and conspicuously discloses to the consumer, in writing or in electronic form or other form permitted by the regulations prescribed under section 6804 of this title, that such information may be disclosed to such third party;

(B) the consumer is given the opportunity, before the time that such information is initially disclosed, to direct that such information not be disclosed to such third party; and

(C) the consumer is given an explanation of how the consumer can exercise that nondisclosure option.

(2) Exception

This subsection shall not prevent a financial institution from providing nonpublic personal information to a nonaffiliated third party to perform services for or functions on behalf of the financial institution, including marketing of the financial institution's own products or services, or financial products or services offered pursuant to joint agreements between two or more financial institutions that comply with the requirements imposed by the regulations prescribed under section 6804 of this title, if the financial institution fully discloses the providing of such information and enters into a contractual agreement with the third party that requires the third party to maintain the confidentiality of such information.

(c) Limits on reuse of information

Except as otherwise provided in this subchapter, a nonaffiliated third party that receives from a financial institution nonpublic personal information under this section shall not, directly or through an affiliate of such receiving third party, disclose such information to any other person that is a nonaffiliated third party of both the financial institution and such receiving third party, unless such disclosure would be lawful if made directly to such other person by the financial institution.

(d) Limitations on the sharing of account number information for marketing purposes

A financial institution shall not disclose, other than to a consumer reporting agency, an account number or similar form of access number or access code for a credit card account, deposit account, or transaction account of a consumer to any nonaffiliated third party for use in telemarketing, direct mail marketing, or other marketing through electronic mail to the consumer.

(e) General exceptions

Subsections (a) and (b) of this section shall not prohibit the disclosure of nonpublic personal information—

(1) as necessary to effect, administer, or enforce a transaction requested or authorized by the consumer, or in connection with—

(A) servicing or processing a financial product or service requested or authorized by the consumer;

(B) maintaining or servicing the consumer's account with the financial institution, or with another entity as part of a private label credit card program or other extension of credit on behalf of such entity; or

(C) a proposed or actual securitization, secondary market sale (including sales of servicing rights), or similar transaction related to a transaction of the consumer;

(2) with the consent or at the direction of the consumer;

(3) (A) to protect the confidentiality or security of the financial institution's records pertaining to the consumer, the service or product, or the transaction therein; (B) to protect against or prevent actual or potential fraud, unauthorized transactions, claims, or other liability; (C) for required institutional risk control, or for resolving customer disputes or inquiries; (D) to persons holding a legal or beneficial interest relating to the consumer; or (E) to persons acting in a fiduciary or representative capacity on behalf of the consumer;

(4) to provide information to insurance rate advisory organizations, guaranty funds or agencies, applicable rating agencies of the financial institution, persons assessing the institution's compliance with industry standards, and the institution's attorneys, accountants, and auditors;

(5) to the extent specifically permitted or required under other provisions of law and in accordance with the Right to Financial Privacy Act of 1978 [12 U.S.C.A. § 3401 et seq.], to law enforcement agencies (including a Federal functional regulator, the Secretary of the Treasury with respect to subchapter II of chapter 53 of Title 31, and chapter 2 of Title I of Public Law 91–508 (12 U.S.C. 1951–1959), a State insurance authority, or the Federal Trade Commission), self-regulatory organizations, or for an investigation on a matter related to public safety;

(6) (A) to a consumer reporting agency in accordance with the Fair Credit Reporting Act [15 U.S.C.A. § 1681 et seq.], or (B) from a consumer report reported by a consumer reporting agency;

(7) in connection with a proposed or actual sale, merger, transfer, or exchange of all or a portion of a business or operating unit if the disclosure of nonpublic personal information concerns solely consumers of such business or unit; or

(8) to comply with Federal, State, or local laws, rules, and other applicable legal requirements; to comply with a properly authorized civil, criminal, or regulatory investigation or subpoena or summons by Federal, State, or local authorities; or to respond to judicial process or government regulatory authorities having jurisdiction over the financial institution for examination, compliance, or other purposes as authorized by law.

§ 6803. Disclosure of institution privacy policy

(a) Disclosure required

At the time of establishing a customer relationship with a consumer and not less than annually during the continuation of such relationship, a financial institution shall provide a clear and conspicuous disclosure to such consumer, in writing or in electronic form or other form permitted by the regulations prescribed under section 6804 of this title, of such financial institution's policies and practices with respect to—

(1) disclosing nonpublic personal information to affiliates and nonaffiliated third parties, consistent with section 6802 of this title, including the categories of information that may be disclosed;

(2) disclosing nonpublic personal information of persons who have ceased to be customers of the financial institution; and

(3) protecting the nonpublic personal information of consumers.

(b) Regulations

Disclosures required by subsection (a) of this section shall be made in accordance with the regulations prescribed under section 6804 of this title.

(c) Information to be included

The disclosure required by subsection (a) of this section shall include–

(1) the policies and practices of the institution with respect to disclosing nonpublic personal information to nonaffiliated third parties, other than agents of the institution, consistent with section 6802 of this title, and including—

(A) the categories of persons to whom the information is or may be disclosed, other than the persons to whom the information may be provided pursuant to section 6802(e) of this title; and

(B) the policies and practices of the institution with respect to disclosing of nonpublic personal information of persons who have ceased to be customers of the financial institution;

(2) the categories of nonpublic personal information that are collected by the financial institution;

(3) the policies that the institution maintains to protect the confidentiality and security of nonpublic personal information in accordance with section 6801 of this title; and

(4) the disclosures required, if any, under section 1681a(d)(2)(A)(iii) of this title.

(d) Exemption for certified public accountants

(1) In general

The disclosure requirements of subsection (a) of this section do not apply to any person, to the extent that the person is—

(A) a certified public accountant;

(B) certified or licensed for such purpose by a State; and

(C) subject to any provision of law, rule, or regulation issued by a legislative or regulatory body of the State, including rules of professional conduct or ethics, that prohibits disclosure of nonpublic personal information without the knowing and expressed consent of the consumer.

(2) Limitation

Nothing in this subsection shall be construed to exempt or otherwise exclude any financial institution that is affiliated or becomes affiliated with a certified public accountant described in paragraph (1) from any provision of this section.

(3) Definitions

For purposes of this subsection, the term "State" means any State or territory of the United States, the District of Columbia, Puerto Rico, Guam, American Samoa, the Trust Territory of the Pacific Islands, the Virgin Islands, or the Northern Mariana Islands.

(e) Model forms

(1) In general

The agencies referred to in section 6804(a)(1) of this title shall jointly develop a model form which may be used, at the option of the financial institution, for the provision of disclosures under this section.

(2) Format

A model form developed under paragraph (1) shall—

(A) be comprehensible to consumers, with a clear format and design;

(B) provide for clear and conspicuous disclosures;

(C) enable consumers easily to identify the sharing practices of a financial institution and to compare privacy practices among financial institutions; and

(D) be succinct, and use an easily readable type font.

(3) Timing

A model form required to be developed by this subsection shall be issued in proposed form for public comment not later than 180 days after October 13, 2006.

(4) Safe harbor

Any financial institution that elects to provide the model form developed by the agencies under this subsection shall be deemed to be in compliance with the disclosures required under this section.

§ 6804. Rulemaking

(a) Regulatory authority

(1) Rulemaking

The Federal banking agencies, the National Credit Union Administration, the Secretary of the Treasury, the Securities and Exchange Commission, and the Federal Trade Commission shall each prescribe, after consultation as appropriate with representatives of State insurance authorities designated by the National Association of Insurance Commissioners, such regulations as may be necessary to carry out the purposes of this subchapter with respect to the financial institutions subject to their jurisdiction under section 6805 of this title.

(2) Coordination, consistency, and comparability

Each of the agencies and authorities required under paragraph (1) to prescribe regulations shall consult and coordinate with the other such agencies and authorities for the purposes of assuring, to the extent possible, that the regulations prescribed by each such agency and authority are consistent and comparable with the regulations prescribed by the other such agencies and authorities.

(3) Procedures and deadline

Such regulations shall be prescribed in accordance with applicable requirements of Title 5 and shall be issued in final form not later than 6 months after November 12, 1999.

(b) Authority to grant exceptions

The regulations prescribed under subsection (a) of this section may include such additional exceptions to subsections (a) through (d) of section 6802 of this title as are deemed consistent with the purposes of this subchapter.

§ 6805. Enforcement

(a) In general

This subchapter and the regulations prescribed thereunder shall be enforced by the Federal functional regulators, the State insurance authorities, and the Federal Trade Commission with respect to financial institutions and other persons subject to their jurisdiction under applicable law, as follows:

(1) Under section 1818 of Title 12, in the case of—

(A) national banks, Federal branches and Federal agencies of foreign banks, and any subsidiaries of such entities (except brokers, dealers, persons providing insurance, investment companies, and investment advisers), by the Office of the Comptroller of the Currency;

(B) member banks of the Federal Reserve System (other than national banks), branches and agencies of foreign banks (other than Federal branches, Federal agencies, and insured State branches of foreign banks),

commercial lending companies owned or controlled by foreign banks, organizations operating under section 25 or 25A of the Federal Reserve Act [12 U.S.C.A. § 601 et seq. or 611 et seq.], and bank holding companies and their nonbank subsidiaries or affiliates (except brokers, dealers, persons providing insurance, investment companies, and investment advisers), by the Board of Governors of the Federal Reserve System;

(C) banks insured by the Federal Deposit Insurance Corporation (other than members of the Federal Reserve System), insured State branches of foreign banks, and any subsidiaries of such entities (except brokers, dealers, persons providing insurance, investment companies, and investment advisers), by the Board of Directors of the Federal Deposit Insurance Corporation; and

(D) savings associations the deposits of which are insured by the Federal Deposit Insurance Corporation, and any subsidiaries of such savings associations (except brokers, dealers, persons providing insurance, investment companies, and investment advisers), by the Director of the Office of Thrift Supervision.

(2) Under the Federal Credit Union Act [12 U.S.C.A. § 1751 et seq.], by the Board of the National Credit Union Administration with respect to any federally insured credit union, and any subsidiaries of such an entity.

(3) Under the Securities Exchange Act of 1934 [15 U.S.C.A. § 78a et seq.], by the Securities and Exchange Commission with respect to any broker or dealer.

(4) Under the Investment Company Act of 1940 [15 U.S.C.A. § 80a–1 et seq.], by the Securities and Exchange Commission with respect to investment companies.

(5) Under the Investment Advisers Act of 1940 [15 U.S.C.A. § 80b–1 et seq.], by the Securities and Exchange Commission with respect to investment advisers registered with the Commission under such Act.

(6) Under State insurance law, in the case of any person engaged in providing insurance, by the applicable State insurance authority of the State in which the person is domiciled, subject to section 6701 of this title.

(7) Under the Federal Trade Commission Act [15 U.S.C.A. § 41 et seq.], by the Federal Trade Commission for any other financial institution or other person that is not subject to the jurisdiction of any agency or authority under paragraphs (1) through (6) of this subsection.

(b) Enforcement of section 6801 of this title

(1) In general

Except as provided in paragraph (2), the agencies and authorities described in subsection (a) of this section shall implement the standards prescribed under section 6801(b) of this title in the same manner, to the extent practicable, as standards prescribed pursuant to section 1831p–1(a) of Title 12 are implemented pursuant to such section.

(2) Exception

The agencies and authorities described in paragraphs (3), (4), (5), (6), and (7) of subsection (a) of this section shall implement the standards prescribed under section 6801(b) of this title by rule with respect to the financial institutions and other persons subject to their respective jurisdictions under subsection (a) of this section.

(c) Absence of State action

If a State insurance authority fails to adopt regulations to carry out this subchapter, such State shall not be eligible to override, pursuant to section 1831x(g)(2)(B)(iii) of Title 12, the insurance customer protection regulations prescribed by a Federal banking agency under section 1831x(a) of Title 12.

(d) Definitions

The terms used in subsection (a)(1) of this section that are not defined in this subchapter or otherwise defined in section 1813(s) of Title 12 shall have the same meaning as given in section 3101 of Title 12.

§ 6806. Relation to other provisions

Except for the amendments made of subsections (a) and (b), nothing in this chapter shall be construed to modify, limit, or supersede the operation of the Fair Credit Reporting Act [15 U.S.C.A. § 1681 et seq.], and no inference shall be drawn on the basis of the provisions of this chapter regarding whether information is trans-

action or experience information under section 603 of such Act [15 U.S.C.A. § 1681a].

§ 6807. Relation to State laws

(a) In general

This subchapter and the amendments made to this subchapter shall not be construed as superseding, altering, or affecting any statute, regulation, order, or interpretation in effect in any State, except to the extent that such statute, regulation, order, or interpretation is inconsistent with the provisions of this subchapter, and then only to the extent of the inconsistency.

(b) Greater protection under State law

For purposes of this section, a State statute, regulation, order, or interpretation is not inconsistent with the provisions of this subchapter if the protection such statute, regulation, order, or interpretation affords any person is greater than the protection provided under this subchapter and the amendments made by this subchapter, as determined by the Federal Trade Commission, after consultation with the agency or authority with jurisdiction under section 6805(a) of this title of either the person that initiated the complaint or that is the subject of the complaint, on its own motion or upon the petition of any interested party.

§ 6808. Study of information sharing among financial affiliates

(a) In general

The Secretary of the Treasury, in conjunction with the Federal functional regulators and the Federal Trade Commission, shall conduct a study of information sharing practices among financial institutions and their affiliates. Such study shall include—

(1) the purposes for the sharing of confidential customer information with affiliates or with nonaffiliated third parties;

(2) the extent and adequacy of security protections for such information;

(3) the potential risks for customer privacy of such sharing of information;

(4) the potential benefits for financial institutions and affiliates of such sharing of information;

(5) the potential benefits for customers of such sharing of information;

(6) the adequacy of existing laws to protect customer privacy;

(7) the adequacy of financial institution privacy policy and privacy rights disclosure under existing law;

(8) the feasibility of different approaches, including opt-out and opt-in, to permit customers to direct that confidential information not be shared with affiliates and nonaffiliated third parties; and

(9) the feasibility of restricting sharing of information for specific uses or of permitting customers to direct the uses for which information may be shared.

(b) Consultation

The Secretary shall consult with representatives of State insurance authorities designated by the National Association of Insurance Commissioners, and also with financial services industry, consumer organizations and privacy groups, and other representatives of the general public, in formulating and conducting the study required by subsection (a) of this section.

(c) Report

On or before January 1, 2002, the Secretary shall submit a report to the Congress containing the findings and conclusions of the study required under subsection (a) of this section, together with such recommendations for legislative or administrative action as may be appropriate.

§ 6809. Definitions

As used in this subchapter:

(1) Federal banking agency

The term "Federal banking agency" has the same meaning as given in section 1813 of Title 12.

(2) Federal functional regulator

The term "Federal functional regulator" means—

(A) the Board of Governors of the Federal Reserve System;

(B) the Office of the Comptroller of the Currency;

(C) the Board of Directors of the Federal Deposit Insurance Corporation;

(D) the Director of the Office of Thrift Supervision;

(E) the National Credit Union Administration Board; and

(F) the Securities and Exchange Commission.

(3) Financial institution

(A) In general

The term "financial institution" means any institution the business of which is engaging in financial activities as described in section 1843(k) of Title 12.

(B) Persons subject to CFTC regulation

Notwithstanding subparagraph (A), the term "financial institution" does not include any person or entity with respect to any financial activity that is subject to the jurisdiction of the Commodity Futures Trading Commission under the Commodity Exchange Act [7 U.S.C.A. § 1 et seq.].

(C) Farm credit institutions

Notwithstanding subparagraph (A), the term "financial institution" does not include the Federal Agricultural Mortgage Corporation or any entity chartered and operating under the Farm Credit Act of 1971 [12 U.S.C.A. § 2001 et seq.].

(D) Other secondary market institutions

Notwithstanding subparagraph (A), the term "financial institution" does not include institutions chartered by Congress specifically to engage in transactions described in section 6802(e)(1)(C) of this title, as long as such institutions do not sell or transfer nonpublic personal information to a nonaffiliated third party.

(4) Nonpublic personal information

(A) The term "nonpublic personal information" means personally identifiable financial information—

(i) provided by a consumer to a financial institution;

(ii) resulting from any transaction with the consumer or any service performed for the consumer; or

(iii) otherwise obtained by the financial institution.

(B) Such term does not include publicly available information, as such term is defined by the regulations prescribed under section 6804 of this title.

(C) Notwithstanding subparagraph (B), such term—

(i) shall include any list, description, or other grouping of consumers (and publicly available information pertaining to them) that is derived using any nonpublic personal information other than publicly available information; but

(ii) shall not include any list, description, or other grouping of consumers (and publicly available information pertaining to them) that is derived without using any nonpublic personal information.

(5) Nonaffiliated third party

The term "nonaffiliated third party" means any entity that is not an affiliate of, or related by common ownership or affiliated by corporate control with, the financial institution, but does not include a joint employee of such institution.

(6) Affiliate

The term "affiliate" means any company that controls, is controlled by, or is under common control with another company.

(7) Necessary to effect, administer, or enforce

The term "as necessary to effect, administer, or enforce the transaction" means—

(A) the disclosure is required, or is a usual, appropriate, or acceptable method, to carry out the transaction or the product or service business of which the transaction is a part, and record or service or maintain the consumer's account in the ordinary course of providing the financial service or financial product, or to administer or service benefits or claims relating to the transaction or the product or service business of which it is a part, and includes—

(i) providing the consumer or the consumer's agent or broker with a confirmation, statement, or other record of the transaction, or information on the status or value of the financial service or financial product; and

(ii) the accrual or recognition of incentives or bonuses associated with the transaction that are provided by the financial institution or any other party;

(B) the disclosure is required, or is one of the lawful or appropriate methods, to enforce the rights of the financial institution or of other persons engaged in carrying out the financial transaction, or providing the product or service;

(C) the disclosure is required, or is a usual, appropriate, or acceptable method, for insurance underwriting at the consumer's request or for reinsurance purposes, or for any of the following purposes as they relate to a consumer's insurance: Account administration, reporting, investigating, or preventing fraud or material misrepresentation, processing premium payments, processing insurance claims, administering insurance benefits (including utilization review activities), participating in research projects, or as otherwise required or specifically permitted by Federal or State law; or

(D) the disclosure is required, or is a usual, appropriate or acceptable method, in connection with—

(i) the authorization, settlement, billing, processing, clearing, transferring, reconciling, or collection of amounts charged, debited, or otherwise paid using a debit, credit or other payment card, check, or account number, or by other payment means;

(ii) the transfer of receivables, accounts or interests therein; or

(iii) the audit of debit, credit or other payment information.

(8) State insurance authority

The term "State insurance authority" means, in the case of any person engaged in providing insurance, the State insurance authority of the State in which the person is domiciled.

(9) Consumer

The term "consumer" means an individual who obtains, from a financial institution, financial products or services which are to be used primarily for personal, family, or household purposes, and also means the legal representative of such an individual.

(10) Joint agreement

The term "joint agreement" means a formal written contract pursuant to which two or more financial institutions jointly offer, endorse, or sponsor a financial product or service, and as may be further defined in the regulations prescribed under section 6804 of this title.

(11) Customer relationship

The term "time of establishing a customer relationship" shall be defined by the regulations prescribed under section 6804 of this title, and shall, in the case of a financial institution engaged in extending credit directly to consumers to finance purchases of goods or services, mean the time of establishing the credit relationship with the consumer.

§ 6821. Privacy protection for customer information of financial institutions

(a) Prohibition on obtaining customer information by false pretenses

It shall be a violation of this subchapter for any person to obtain or attempt to obtain, or cause to be disclosed or attempt to cause to be disclosed to any person, customer information of a financial institution relating to another person—

(1) by making a false, fictitious, or fraudulent statement or representation to an officer, employee, or agent of a financial institution;

(2) by making a false, fictitious, or fraudulent statement or representation to a customer of a financial institution; or

(3) by providing any document to an officer, employee, or agent of a financial institution, knowing that the document is forged, counterfeit, lost, or stolen, was fraudulently obtained, or contains a false, fictitious, or fraudulent statement or representation.

(b) Prohibition on solicitation of a person to obtain customer information from financial institution under false pretenses

It shall be a violation of this subchapter to request a person to obtain customer information of a financial institution, knowing that the person will obtain, or attempt to obtain, the information from the institution in any manner described in subsection (a) of this section.

(c) Nonapplicability to law enforcement agencies

No provision of this section shall be construed so as to prevent any action by a law enforcement agency, or any officer, employee, or agent of such agency, to obtain customer information of a financial institution in connection with the performance of the official duties of the agency.

(d) Nonapplicability to financial institutions in certain cases

No provision of this section shall be construed so as to prevent any financial institution, or any officer, employee, or agent of a financial institution, from obtaining customer information of such financial institution in the course of—

(1) testing the security procedures or systems of such institution for maintaining the confidentiality of customer information;

(2) investigating allegations of misconduct or negligence on the part of any officer, employee, or agent of the financial institution; or

(3) recovering customer information of the financial institution which was obtained or received by another person in any manner described in subsection (a) or (b) of this section.

(e) Nonapplicability to insurance institutions for investigation of insurance fraud

No provision of this section shall be construed so as to prevent any insurance institution, or any officer, employee, or agency of an insurance institution, from obtaining information as part of an insurance investigation into criminal activity, fraud, material misrepresentation, or material nondisclosure that is authorized for such institution under State law, regulation, interpretation, or order.

(f) Nonapplicability to certain types of customer information of financial institutions

No provision of this section shall be construed so as to prevent any person from obtaining customer information of a financial institution that otherwise is available as a public record filed pursuant to the securities laws (as defined in section 78c(a)(47) of this title).

(g) Nonapplicability to collection of child support judgments

No provision of this section shall be construed to prevent any State-licensed private investigator, or any officer, employee, or agent of such private investigator, from obtaining customer information of a financial institution, to the extent reasonably necessary to collect child support from a person adjudged to have been delinquent in his or her obligations by a Federal or State court, and to the extent that such action by a State-licensed private investigator is not unlawful under any other Federal or State law or regulation, and has been authorized by an order or judgment of a court of competent jurisdiction.

§ 6822. Administrative enforcement

(a) Enforcement by Federal Trade Commission

Except as provided in subsection (b) of this section, compliance with this subchapter shall be enforced by the Federal Trade Commission in the same manner and with the same power and authority as the Commission has under the Fair Debt Collection Practices Act [15 U.S.C.A § 1692 et seq.] to enforce compliance with such Act.

(b) Enforcement by other agencies in certain cases

(1) In general

Compliance with this subchapter shall be enforced under—

(A) section 8 of the Federal Deposit Insurance Act [12 U.S.C.A. § 1818], in the case of—

(i) national banks, and Federal branches and Federal agencies of foreign banks, by the Office of the Comptroller of the Currency;

(ii) member banks of the Federal Reserve System (other than national banks), branches and agencies of foreign banks (other than Federal branches, Federal agencies, and insured State branches of foreign banks), commercial lending companies owned or controlled by foreign banks, and organizations operating under section 25 or 25A of the Federal Reserve Act [12 U.S.C.A § 601 et seq. or 611 et seq.], by the Board;

(iii) banks insured by the Federal Deposit Insurance Corporation (other than members of the Federal Reserve System and national nonmember banks) and insured State branches of foreign banks, by the Board of Directors of the Federal Deposit Insurance Corporation; and

(iv) savings associations the deposits of which are insured by the Federal Deposit Insurance Corporation, by the Director of the Office of Thrift Supervision; and

(B) the Federal Credit Union Act [12 U.S.C.A § 1751 et seq.], by the Administrator of the National Credit Union Administration with respect to any Federal credit union.

(2) Violations of this subchapter treated as violations of other laws

For the purpose of the exercise by any agency referred to in paragraph (1) of its powers under any Act referred to in that paragraph, a violation of this subchapter shall be deemed to be a violation of a requirement imposed under that Act. In addition to its powers under any provision of law specifically referred to in paragraph (1), each of the agencies referred to in that paragraph may exercise, for the purpose of enforcing compliance with this subchapter, any other authority conferred on such agency by law.

§ 6823. Criminal penalty

(a) In general

Whoever knowingly and intentionally violates, or knowingly and intentionally attempts to violate, section 6821 of this title shall be fined in accordance with Title 18, or imprisoned for not more than 5 years, or both.

(b) Enhanced penalty for aggravated cases

Whoever violates, or attempts to violate, section 6821 of this title while violating another law of the United States or as part of a pattern of any illegal activity involving more than $100,000 in a 12–month period shall be fined twice the amount provided in subsection (b)(3) or (c)(3) (as the case may be) of section 3571 of Title 18, imprisoned for not more than 10 years, or both.

§ 6824. Relation to State laws

(a) In general

This subchapter shall not be construed as superseding, altering, or affecting the statutes, regulations, orders, or interpretations in effect in any State, except to the extent that such statutes, regulations, orders, or interpretations are inconsistent with the provisions of this subchapter, and then only to the extent of the inconsistency.

(b) Greater protection under State law

For purposes of this section, a State statute, regulation, order, or interpretation is not inconsistent with the provisions of this subchapter if the protection such statute, regulation, order, or interpretation affords any person is greater than the protection provided under this subchapter as determined by the Federal Trade Commission, after consultation with the agency or authority with jurisdiction under section 6822 of this title of either the person that initiated the complaint or that is the subject of the complaint, on its own motion or upon the petition of any interested party.

§ 6825. Agency guidance

In furtherance of the objectives of this subchapter, each Federal banking agency (as defined in section 1813(z) of Title 12), the National Credit Union Administration, and the Securities and Exchange Commission or self-regulatory organizations, as appropriate, shall review regulations and guidelines applicable to financial institutions under their respective jurisdictions and shall prescribe such revisions to such regulations and guidelines as may be necessary to ensure that such financial institutions have policies, procedures, and controls in place to prevent the unauthorized disclosure of customer financial information and to deter and detect activities proscribed under section 6821 of this title.

§ 6826. Reports

(a) Report to the Congress

Before the end of the 18–month period beginning on November 12, 1999, the Comptroller General, in consultation with the Federal Trade Commission, Federal banking agencies, the National Credit Union Administration, the Securities and Exchange Commission, appropriate Federal law enforcement agencies, and appropriate State insurance regulators, shall submit to the Congress a report on the following:

(1) The efficacy and adequacy of the remedies provided in this subchapter in addressing attempts to obtain financial information by fraudulent means or by false pretenses.

(2) Any recommendations for additional legislative or regulatory action to address threats to the privacy of financial information created by attempts to obtain information by fraudulent means or false pretenses.

(b) Annual report by administering agencies

The Federal Trade Commission and the Attorney General shall submit to Congress an annual report on number and disposition of all enforcement actions taken pursuant to this subchapter.

§ 6827. Definitions

For purposes of this subchapter, the following definitions shall apply:

(1) Customer

The term "customer" means, with respect to a financial institution, any person (or authorized representative of a person) to whom the financial institution provides a product or service, including that of acting as a fiduciary.

(2) Customer information of a financial institution

The term "customer information of a financial institution" means any information maintained by or for a financial institution which is derived from the relationship between the financial institution and a customer of the financial institution and is identified with the customer.

(3) Document

The term "document" means any information in any form.

(4) Financial institution

(A) In general

The term "financial institution" means any institution engaged in the business of providing financial services to customers who maintain a credit, deposit, trust, or other financial account or relationship with the institution.

(B) Certain financial institutions specifically included

The term "financial institution" includes any depository institution (as defined in section 461(b)(1)(A) of Title 12), any broker or dealer, any investment adviser or investment company, any insurance company, any loan or finance company, any credit card issuer or operator of a credit card system, and any consumer reporting agency that compiles and maintains files on consumers on a nationwide basis (as defined in section 1681a(p) of this title).

(C) Securities institutions

For purposes of subparagraph (B)—

(i) the terms "broker" and "dealer" have the same meanings as given in section 78c of this title;

(ii) the term "investment adviser" has the same meaning as given in section 202(a)(11) of the Investment Advisers Act of 1940 (15 U.S.C. 80b–2(a)); and

(iii) the term "investment company" has the same meaning as given in section 80a–3 of this title.

(D) Certain persons and entities specifically excluded

The term "financial institution" does not include any person or entity with respect to any financial activity that is subject to the jurisdiction of the Commodity Futures Trading Commission under the Commodity Exchange Act [7 U.S.C.A. § 1 et seq.] and does not include the Federal Agricultural Mortgage Corporation or any entity chartered and operating under the Farm Credit Act of 1971 [12 U.S.C.A. § 2001 et seq.].

(E) Further definition by regulation

The Federal Trade Commission, after consultation with Federal banking agencies and the Securities and Exchange Commission, may prescribe regulations clarifying or describing the types of institutions which shall be treated as financial institutions for purposes of this subchapter.

SUMMARY OF THE DODD–FRANK WALL STREET REFORM AND CONSUMER PROTECTION ACT

Rigers Gjyshi
Senior Research Fellow
FIU College of Law

TITLE I—FINANCIAL STABILITY

Title 1 may be cited as the "Financial Stability Act of 2010." It establishes a specific framework for ensuring financial stability, defines target entities such as nonbank financial entities as a company that is registered with a governmental or private regulatory entity, Sec. 102a(4)(B), and such companies that the Council determines undress Section113 should be supervised by the Board of Governors, Sec. 102a(4)(D). It consists of three subtitles. *Subtitle A* establishes a Financial Stability Oversight Council, Sec. 111a, and identifies its voting, Sec. 111b(1), and nonvoting members, Sec. 111b(2), sets forth serving terms for members, Sec. 111c(1), meeting times and rules, Sec. 111e(1), voting procedures, Sec. 111f , and compensation guidelines, Sec. 111i. It requires a Executive Schedule Level III pay grade, which, as of 2010, stood at $165,300. It charges the Council with monitoring and identifying potential threats to the financial system and responding with more stringent regulation of nonbank financial companies and financial activities that it determines, based on consideration of risk-related factors, pose risks to financial stability, and eliminates the expectation of governmental bailouts. Sec. 112a(1)(A), (B) and (C). The Council will also direct the Office of Financial research, monitor threats and proposed regulation, advise Congress, facilitate information sharing, identify monitor priorities, and may also recommend that the Board of Governors issue heightened prudential standards for certain financial instruments held by subject entities. Sec. 112a(2)(B)–(I). The Commission has the power to obtain information from governmental regulators, Sec. 112d(1), and, if the information is not available from them, may require a report target entities, Sec. 112d(3)(A)–(C). Importantly, Subtitle A allows the Council to vote to impose stricter rules on nonbank financial companies it determines to be under financial distress, Sec. 113a(1), but only after considering risk-related factors, Sec. 113a(2)(A)–(K) gives the Council the ability to establish an intermediate holding company to run the activities of a company is found to be attempting to evade these rules, Sec. 113c(3)(A) and (B), requires an annual 2/3 vote and annual reviews of risk determinations, Sec. 113d(1) and (2), and allows subject companies to challenge any of the above determination as arbitrary and capricious, Sec. 113i. In addition, the Council may recommend that the Board impose stricter standards on nonbank financial and interconnected bank holding companies based on risk-related factors, Sec. 115a(1)(A) and (B), may impose higher contingent capital requirements for certain companies after conducting a feasibility study, Sec. 115c(1)–(3), require distressed entities to have a rapid resolution/liquidation plan, Sec. 115d(1) and (2), and may require certified reports regarding their financial condition and risk management system by certain bank and nonbank financial companies that may be a threat, Sec. 116a and b. Lastly, it gives the Board authority to impose section 113 rules on bank holding companies that took TARP funds and cease to be bank holding companies, Sec. 117a and b, allows the Council to resolve jurisdictional disputes between members, Sec. 119a(1)–(3), allows the Council to ask a regulator to impose higher supervisory standards on practices that it determines may pose a risk to the financial stability, Sec. 120a, gives the Board the ability to limit the activities of certain companies that it determines pose a grave threat to U.S. financial stability, Sec. 121b–d.

Subtitle B establishes an Office of Financial Research within the Dept. of the Treasury, Sec. 152a, which supports the Council by collecting information, conducting research, analyzing data, and making them accessible to regulators, Sec. 153a(1)–(7). Within the OFR there is the Data Center, which collects and maintain information, 154b(1), and the Research and Analysis Center, which shall develop analytical and computing tools, monitor changes in risk metrics, evaluate stability measures, and investigate disruptions in the market and the effect of proposed policies, Sec. 154c(1)(A)–(H). *Subtitle C* provides a specific, more stringent supervisory framework for regulating large, interconnected bank holding companies, nonbank financial companies that the Council subjects to more stringent regulation, and activities and practices that the Council determines may pose systemic threats. Specifically, the Board may require reports from nonbank financial companies it supervises, disclosing their financial condition and risk monitoring system, among other things, Sec. 161a(1) and (2), as well as actually examine said companies to figure out their conditions and potential risk, Sec. 161b(1)(A)–(D), and allows the Board to treat these companies as if they were bank holding companies under Section 8 of FDIC Act (12 USC 1818), Sec. 162a. In addition, it treats a company that buys a bank as a bank holding company, Sec. 163a, and requires notice to the Board before a subject entity acquires a large company (assets greater than $10 billion) that is engaged in activities described in Section 4(k) of the Bank Holding Company Act, Sec. 163b(2). The Board may impose more stringent prudential standards, based on risk related factors, on nonbank financial companies and bank holding companies with more than $50 billion that it determines pose a risk to financial stability, Sec. 165a and b, it may limit risks that a single entity poses to others by requirement that the credit exposure be below 25% of capital stock and surplus, Sec. 165e(1) and (2), it may require the company to limit the amount of short-term debt, Sec. 165g(1), and to establish risk committees, Sec. 165h(2), may review the risk by conducting annual stress tests, Sec. 165i(1)(A) and (B), and impose debt/equity ratio requirements, Sec. 165j. Lastly, this subtitle requires that relevant banking regulators set a minimum leverage capital requirements and minimum risk-based capital requirements rules. Sec. 171b(1) and (2).

TITLE II—ORDERLY LIQUIDATION AUTHORITY

Title II establishes an orderly liquidation authority that may be used only if the Secretary of the Treasury (in consultation with the President), based on the written recommendation of two other federal regulators, Sec. 203a(1)(A)–(C), agrees that doing so is necessary to mitigate serious adverse effects on financial stability in the United States, Sec. 203b(1)–(7). If the Secretary determines that a company is in, or at risk of, default, it may, by acquiescence of the Board of Directors or by judicial order, appoint the FDIC as receiver to liquidate its assets, Sec. 202a(1)(A)(i)–(v), which must be liquidated within three years with the chance of two one year or litigation extension, Sec. 202d(1)–(3). The liquidation rules under this Title do not apply to "covered financial companies" that are insurance companies, and they must be liquidated under State law. Sec. 202e. The FDIC must liquidate

the company in a manner that mitigates significant risks to financial stability and minimizes moral hazard, with all costs of an orderly liquidation under this title borne first by shareholders and unsecured creditors. Sec. 204a(1)–(4); Sec. 206(1)–(6). If the companies in receivership are covered broker and dealers, the FDIC shall appoint the SIPC as trustee, Sec. 205a(1), which shall have all the powers provided by the SIPA of 1970, with certain restrictions, Sec. 205b(1) and (b). In addition, once a covered financial company enters into receivership all cases and proceedings over its assets shall be dismissed, Sec. 208a, and any assets that have vested on another entity shall revest on the subject entity, Sec. 208b. The FDIC shall succeed full rights and powers to run the company and any covered subsidiary entities, Sec. 210a(A)–(E), including the ability to terminate all rights and claims of shareholders and creditors, Sec. 210a(M), subject to notice and claim resolution requirements, Sec. 210a(3); Sec. 210b(1)(A)–(H), and subject to some agreements that go against the FDIC's interest but were in place before the receivership and was entered into as part of the entity's regular course of business, Sec. 210a(6), but the FDIC may avoid transfers made within 2 years of receivership that are found to have been made will ill-intent or under certain conditions, Sec. 210a(11)(A)(1)(i)–(iv). In addition, the FDIC, as a receiver, may repudiate any contract (including financial contracts) that makes its job more difficult, not matter when entered, and damages are only limited to direct compensatory amounts. Sec. 210c(1)(A)–(E). In addition, this Title defines common terms, makes walkway clauses infective, Sec. 210c(8)(F), directs the FDIC to use best efforts and meet obligations to clearing organizations and makes it liable to said organizations if it fails to do so, Sec. 210c(8)(G), limits the liability of the FDIC, if any, to any party at the rate that would have been due had the FDIC not been appointed as receiver and the company would have gone into liquidation under the Bankruptcy Code, Sec. 210d(1) and (2), unless the claimant was covered by the SIPA, Sec. 210d(3). The FDIC, in order to facilitate its functions, may establish a "bridge company" to assume liabilities, purchase assets and carry out any other functions, Sec. 210h(1), but it may not assume any obligations to shareholders, members or other type of ownership interest, Sec. 210h(3)(B). Establishes an Orderly Liquidation Fund within the Department of Treasury that will pay for, and receive the proceeds of, any liquidation carried by the FDIC, and said funds may be invested, Sec. 210n(1)–(3), and gives the FDIC the authority to sell, and the Secretary to buy, obligations from said fund, Sec. 210n(5) and (6). In addition, it allows the FDIC to charge a risk-based assessments to large financial companies if necessary to pay the expenses incurred under this title, Sec. 210o, prohibits the FDIC from selling assets to persons who were involved in causing the losses to the subject entity, Sec. 210r, allows the FDIC to recover compensation for the two years prior receivership from any directory or executive responsible for the failed condition, Sec. 210s. Taxpayers specifically are protected from losses associated with use of this authority. Sec. 214a–c. Lastly, this Title directs the Council and the Board to carry out three individual studies analyzing the impact on taxpayers of the rules regarding the treatment of secured creditors during liquidation, Sec. 215a(1)–(6), the resolution of financial companies under the Bankruptcy Code, Sec. 216a(1) and (2)(A)–(E), and the international coordination of bankruptcy of nonbank financial institution, Sec. 217aa(1) and (2)(A)–(D).

TITLE III—TRANSFER OF POWERS TO THE COMPTROLLER OF THE CURRENCY, THE FDIC, AND THE BOARD OF GOVERNORS

Title III, which may be cited as the "Enhancing Financial Institution Safety and Soundness Act of 2010", Sec. 300, addresses the operation of the banking system, preservation of the dual system of Federal/State chartered depository institutions, and the supervision of depository institutions and their holding companies, Sec. 301. It has three Subtitles. *Subtitle A*, within ONE year of passage of this Act, Sec. 311a, transfers from the Office of Thrift Supervision (OTS) to the Board the supervision of any state-chartered savings & loan holding company and related subsidiaries, Sec. 312b(1)(I) and (II), transfers from the OTS to the Office of the Comptroller of the Currency the supervision of federal savings/loan associations, Sec. 312b(2)(B), transfers from the OTS to the FDIC the supervision of all state-chartered savings & loan companies, Sec. 312b(2)(C), and eliminates the OTS, Sec. 313, but directs the new supervisory agencies to publish which laws and regulations from the OTS they are going to retain, Sec. 316c(1)–(3). It es-

tablishes within the Treasury the Office of the Comptroller of the Currency. Sec. 314a. Establishes funding for the office of the Comptroller of the Currency, Board and FDIC for these new roles, by giving them the ability to asses a fee on institutions under their jurisdiction. Sec. 318b–d.

Subtitle B provides rules aimed at facilitating the transition to the new supervisory system. It calls for the transferring of some employees from the OTS to the Office of the Comptroller of the Currency or the FDIC, Sec. 322a, transfers any property and funds held by the OTS to the other agencies, Sec. 323 and 324. The rest of Subtitle C deals with the coordination of the integration of the agencies, and reporting to the appropriate Congressional committees. *Subtitle C* provides new rules dealing with the FDIC. It revises the FDIC's assessment base for deposit insurance, Sec. 331b(1)–(2), it gives it the power to suspend dividends it pays to member institutions, Sec. 332(1), increases the FDIC's reserve ratio to 1.35%, Sec. 334a, permanently increases the insured amount to $250,000 and makes it retroactive to January 1, 2008, Sec. 335a(1) and (2), and changes membership to the FDIC board to reflect the changes in the agencies, Sec. 336a(1)–(3). *Subtitle D* contains other general matters. It allows a savings association that becomes a bank to continue operating branches that it operated immediately before it became a bank or open new ones within the State. Sec. 341(1) and (2). Directs each agency to establish an Office of Minority and Women Inclusion to provide assistance and include businesses owned by said groups, and promote diversity in the workforce. Sec. 342. Lastly, it extends insurance for noninterest bearing transaction accounts for an additional two years, Sec. 343a(1)–(3), and extends a similar program for authorized credit unions, Sec. 343b(1)–(3). *Subtitle E* provides technical assistance and sets forth conforming amendments. Makes technical amendments to the federal acts that Title III affects to be in conformance with changes made by the Title.

TITLE IV—REGULATION OF ADVISERS TO HEDGE FUNDS AND OTHERS

Title IV may be cited as the "Private Fund Investment Advisers Registration Act of 2010". Amends the Investment Advisers Act of 1940 (IAA) to provide for new definitions of terms like private fund and foreign private adviser. Sec.

402a. Amends the IAA by eliminating the private adviser exemption for private fund advisers and registers them with the SEC, Sec. 403(1), allowing the SEC to expand reporting requirements for private funds investment advisers for risk assessment and oversight purposes, make those reports available to the Council, set forth guidelines for data required in the reports, conduct periodic and special examinations of these advisers, Sec. 404(2). The new registration rules do not apply to advisers of venture capital funds (as will be defined by the SEC), Sec. 407, or to advisors who deal solely with private funds and manage assets in the U.S. that are less than $150 million (unless these funds may pose systemic risks), Sec. 408. It raises the federal regulatory threshold to 100 million, Sec. 410(2), and requires registration of investment advisers who are required to register with 15 or more State securities regulators, Sec. 410(1). Sets forth rules adjusting the net worth standards for accredited investors to $1 million, Sec. 413a, retains rules and requirements applicable under CFTC and CEA, Sec. 414, directs the Office of the Comptroller to conduct a study on criteria for accredited investors and on SROs for private funds, Sec. 415 and 416, and the SEC to conduct a study on short selling, Sec. 417. Finally, directs advisers to comply with the new provisions within one year, or earlier if the choose so, of enactment. Sec. 419.

TITLE V—INSURANCE

Title V has two subtitles. *Subtitle A* may be cited as the "Federal Insurance Office Act of 2010", and deals with the creation of the Federal Insurance Office (FIO). It establishes the FIO under the Treasury Department, Sec. 502a, to monitor , but not supervise or regulate, the insurance industry (except small insurance companies, health, long-term care and crop insurance), make recommendations to the Council, coordinate efforts on the development of Federal prudential insurance standards, advise the Secretary of the Treasury, gather information from subject entities, preempt state insurance measure to the extent that they give less favorable treatment to certain non-U.S. insurers (i.e. organized under U.S. law, but that do not have any business in the U.S.), and submit annual reports to Congress regarding insurance industry, global reinsurance market, regulation of insurance, Sec. 502a.

Subtitle B may be cited as the "Nonadmitted and *Reinsurance Reform Act of 2010,"* and it has three parts. *Part I* deals with reforms to the commercial insurance marketplace, nonadmitted insurance. Reserves to the home state the authority to impose on insured a premium tax on nonadmitted insurance or enter into a multistate compact regarding such insurance, Sec. 521a and b, gives the home state authority to regulate placement of nonadmitted insurance and issue licensing rules for said brokers, Sec. 522a and b, and encourages the development of uniform rules for nonadmitted insurance, Sec. 524. Lastly, it allows direct access to nonadmitted insurance markets for certain sophisticated commercial purchasers. Sec. 525. *Part II* deals with reforms to the Reinsurance and Reinsurance Agreements. States of domicile that are NAIC-accredited or have similar solvency rules will control credit reinsurance determinations, Sec. 531a, preempts the non-domiciliary states' laws and rules that conflict with this section, Sec. 531b, and allows domiciliary state to control reinsurance solvency regulation if they are NAIC-accredited or have similar requirements, Sec. 532a. *Part III* sets forth rules of construction.

TITLE VI—IMPROVEMENTS TO REGULATION OF BANK AND SAVINGS ASSOCIATION HOLDING COMPANIES AND DEPOSITORY INSTITUTIONS

Title VI may be cited as the "Bank and Savings Association Holding Company and Depository Institutions Regulatory Improvements Act of 2010". It defines a commercial firm as one that has less than 15% of its annual gross revenues from financial activities, including ownership of insured depository instructions. Sec. 602. Prohibits the FDIC from approving an application for deposit insurance, received after Nov. 23, 2009, for an industrial bank, credit card bank or trust bank that is controlled by a commercial firm, Sec. 603a(2), directs federal banking agency, for a three year period, to disapprove a change in control that would circumvent the preceding prohibition, unless they are in danger of default or a bona fide merger of two commercial firms, Sec. 603(3)(A) and (B). Also directs the GAO to conduct a study to determine whether to eliminate the exceptions under Section 2 of the Bank Holding Company Act and the sufficiency of other regulatory frameworks. Sec. 603b(1)–(3). Allows the FIDC to require bank holding companies to submit periodic reports to verify compliance with this act and other federal laws, Sec. 604a(1),

examine banking holding companies to determine their condition and risks/threats, Sec. 604b,
and determine the effect of acquisitions of banks
and nonbanks on the U.S. banking and financial
systems, Sec. 604d. Allows the FDIC to examine
any savings and loan holding company to determine its condition and risks/threats, Sec.
604h(4)(A)(i)(I)–(III), and allows the FDIC to examine a nondepository subsidiary of a depository
institution after coordinating with applicable
state banking association, Sec. 605a. Allows federal banking agencies to request an examination
or enforcement action by the FDIC on nondepository subsidiary and carry out such examination
or enforcement action if the FDIC does not act.
Sec. 605a. Amends current banking law to require that financial holding companies, in addition to their deposit institutions, be well capitalized and managed, Sec. 606a, and allows savings
and loan holding companies to engage in the
same activities as financial holding companies if
they meet certain conditions, Sec. 606b. It expands the definition of "transactions with bank
affiliates" to include investment funds of which
the member bank is an investment adviser, Sec.
608a(1)(A), and expands the types of transactions
that fall under the affiliate transactions restrictions, e.g. credit or derivative transactions, and
allows the FDIC to give exemptions if it finds
that they are in the public interest, Sec.
608a(1)(B), it eliminates some exemptions provided in the Federal Reserve Act regarding transactions with financial subsidiaries, Sec. 609a. Expands the definitions of "loan and extension of
credit" for banking purposes to include credit
exposures from derivative transactions, repur-
chase/reverse repurchase agreements etc., and
also defines the term derivative transaction. Sec.
610a(1)–(3). Prohibits a national banking association from converging to a State bank or savings
association if it is subject to a cease and desist
order and vice versa, Sec. 612a, as well as it
prohibits the conversion of a federal savings association that is subject to such an order (with
certain exceptions), Sec. 612a. Limits extension
of credit to insiders to include exposure to derivative transactions and others, Sec. 614a, and sets
conditions on purchases of assets from insiders,
Sec. 615a. Expands the power of the Board and
relevant banking regulators to regulate capital
requirements bank holding and savings/loan
companies and directs it to make those requirements countercyclical, Sec. 616a and b, and requires holding and other companies to serve as

sources of strength for their subsidiaries, Sec.
616d. Eliminates the rules allowing investment
bank holding companies to elect or withdraw
their supervision by the SEC. Sec. 617a. Allows
securities holding companies to register with the
Board in order for them to meet requirements of
foreign laws/regulators, Sec. 618b(1), and directs
the Board to make appropriate regulations/re-
quirements regarding the risk management of
such holding companies and makes them subject
to other banking acts, Sec. 618d(1). Amends the
Bank Holding Company Act of 1956 by prohibiting banking entities from engaging in proprietary trading or acquiring/retaining ownership interests on hedge or private equity funds, Sec.
619, imposes additional capital requirements on
Board supervised nonbank financial companies
that engage in proprietary trading or have ownership share in hedge or private equity funds,
Sec. 619, provides deadlines for carrying out
these requirements and sets forth certain permitted activities notwithstanding the preceding prohibitions, Sec. 619. Limits the ability of banking
entities to enter "covered transactions" with
hedge or private equity funds for which they are
serving as investment advisers, with certain exceptions. Sec. 619. Imposes a one year conflict of
interest trading restriction period on underwriters, promoters and the like, of asset-backed securities who were involved in initially placing that
security, with some exceptions relating to bona
fide underwriting and market making activities.
Sec. 621. Prohibits a large financial company ac-
quiring/merging with another company, if the
surviving company would hold 10% of the aggregate liabilities of all financial companies at the
end of the preceding calendar year, Sec. 622,
imposes the same limitation on interstate mergers of insured depository institution if it result in
one such institution holding more than 10% of
the aggregate bank deposits of U.S. insured depository institutions, Sec. 623a, and imposes the
same limitation in cases where a bank holding
company or thrift holding company attempts to
acquire an insured depository institution in another state and the acquisition violates the 10%
limit, Sec. 623b and c.

TITLE VII—WALL STREET TRANSPAREN-
CY AND ACCOUNTABILITY

Title VII may be cited as the "Wall Street
Transparency and Accountability Act". It has
three subtitles. *Subtitle A* has two parts. *Part I*

covers regulatory authority of federal agencies. It directs the CFTC and the SEC to coordinate with each other and other regulation regarding the regulation of swap and related instruments, Sec. 712a, while still maintaining the jurisdictional separation between the CFTC and SEC in regulation of swaps, Sec. 712b. It enhances record keeping requirements for security-based swaps by registered swap repositories, Sec. 712d(2)(B), allows a broker or dealer registered under SEA of 1934 and the CEA to hold cash and securities in portfolio margin accounts carried as a futures account, Sec. 713a, and a futures commission merchant to hold a futures contract or an option in a margin account subject to similar requirements, Sec. 713b. Gives authority to the CFTC and SEC to report/regulate what they determine to be abusive swaps, Sec. 714, and prohibit foreign entities they determine are engaged in dangerous swap agreements abroad from operating in the U.S., Sec. 715, and prohibits federal assistance to swap entities, Sec. 716a, (except for insured depository institutions if they are using swaps for hedging or traditional banking purposes, Sec. 716d). Requires a FDIC insured institution put into receivership because of participation in a swap agreement and significant financial institution deemed to be at risk under Section 113 of Title I, to liquidate or transfer the swap agreements. Sec. 716i(1)(A) and (B). Requires a bank holding entity to comply to minimum regulatory standards before it may become a swap entity, Sec. 716j, allows the Council to deny access to federal funds if it determines that current rules are not sufficient to mitigate systemic risks, Sec. 716l, and imposes the ban on proprietary trading in derivatives on insured depository institutions pursuant to Section 619, Sec. 716m. It gives the CFTC concurrent jurisdiction to put, call or other securities options, even if they are exempt from the SEC. Sec. 717a2. In the case of a novel derivative instrument, the person introducing it may notify and request a determination of whether it is a security or commodity (if it has aspects of both) and the CFTC and SEC shall coordinate with each other in making such determination or providing exemptions. Sec. 718. Directs the CFTC to conduct a study on the feasibility of position limits and the SEC to conduct a study on the feasibility of requiring companies to make an algorithmic description of financial derivatives, Sec. 719a and b, and conduct a study on whether stable value contracts fall within the meaning of

a swap, Sec. 719d. *Part II of* subtitle A regulates the swap market. Section 721 effectively rewrites/amends the definition section of the CEA, section 1a, to account for the new swap instruments, define which regulatory agencies cover particular institutions/persons engaged in swaps, provides an expansive definition of term swap but excludes certain instruments from it, defines different professional engaged in swap trading, treats forex swaps and forwards as swaps unless the Commission determines otherwise, provides regulatory parameters for mixed swaps, etc. Sec. 721. Makes statutory amendments to bring the new swap regulation within the different regulatory legislation, including section 2(a)(1) of the CEA, Sec. 722a(1), excludes swaps from definition of insurance with regard to State insurance regulatory jurisdiction, e.g. it limits the SEC's jurisdiction only to security based swaps and no other securities, Sec. 722a(1). It limits the preceding rules from applying to activities outside of the U.S., unless they have a direct impact in the U.S. Sec. 722d. However, Section 722h provides specific factors that the Treasury must consider before exempting foreign exchanged swaps. Protects the FERC's power to regulate tariff or rate schedule agreements that it has approved and which do not trade on a registered trading facility or in one owned by a regional transmission organization or independent system operator. Sec. 722e. Limits the ability to participate in a swap, other than eligible contract participants, unless it is regulated by the rules of a board of trade designated as a contract market, makes it unlawful to engage in a swap that has not been cleared by a derivatives clearing organization if it is required to be cleared (as determined by the CFTC in accordance to factors set forth therein). Sec. 723a. Bans agricultural swaps unless they are exempted under the public interest exemption of the CEA (section 6(c). Sec. 723c(3). Restricts the ability to hold margin accounts related to cleared swaps to registered commission merchants and imposes segregation requirements, Sec. 724a, provides bankruptcy rules for cleared swaps, Sec. 724b, and permits a counterparty to require segregation of funds in non-cleared swaps, Sec. 724c. Amends Section 7a–1 of the CEA, regulation of futures trading for derivatives clearing organizations, to include the term swap, Sec. 725a, and sets forth core principles for derivatives clearing organizations, like requirements on minimum capital, credit exposure periodic testing, enhanced public disclosure and compliance with the law, Sec. 725c. Excludes identified banking products from the reach of the CFTC or the SEC, unless that product is being treated as a swap and the applicable banking regulator provides an exemption against the preceding exclusion. Sec. 725g(2). Directs the CFTC to require public disclosures of cleared swaps but in accordance to confidentiality rules, Sec. 727, requires the registration of "swap data repositories" and sets forth operational requirements for these entities, Sec. 728, and requires the reporting of non-cleared swaps to "swap data repositories" or (if the former doesn't accept them) to the CFTC, Sec. 729. Amends the CEA by inserting section 4s to require registration with the CFTC of persons acting as swap dealers or major swap participants before they can engage in swap transactions, Sec. 730a, regardless of whether they are depository institution or registered with the SEC as a securities-based swap dealers, directs the CFTC, SEC and other applicable regulators to issue prudential standards related to capital and margin requirements for these entities, requires that these trading entities maintain daily trading records and disclose certain material risks to counterparties, imposes stricter rules and enhanced disclosure requires when swap dealers deal with special entities (e.g. federal/state government or employee pension plans), Sec. 730. Requires that swap registration facilities register with the CFTC as such or as a designated contract market, before executing any swaps, regardless of whether it is registered as such with the SEC, and once registered such facility must execute any swap (except for agricultural swaps, which shall be done pursuant to CFTC rule). Sec. 733. In addition, swap execution facilities that are trading facilities must impose position limits in compliance with position limits set by the CFTC to ensure orderly trading. Sec. 733. Repeals the exemptions under section 5a and section 5d of the CEA relating to derivatives execution facilities and exempt boards of trade, Sec. 734a, amends section 5 of the CEA relating to boards of trade acting as designated contract markets and sets forth similar position limit rules as for the previous section, Sec. 735. Amends section 8a(7)(c) of the CEA to allow the CFTC to regulate margin requirements of registered entities if done to protect the integrity of derivative clearing organizations, designed to manage risk and not set specific margin levels. Sec. 736. Amends section 4a(a) of the CEA to expand the CFTC's ability to impose position limits regarding excessive speculation on swap transactions, Sec. 737a, to define 'bona fide hedging transactions' that are exempt from the position limits under section 4a(c) of the CEA, Sec. 737c(2), to allow the CFTC to require the registration of foreign board that want to allow U.S. trader access to their electronic trading systems, provided that certain regulatory conditions are met, Sec. 738a. Provides safe harbors provisions which allow enforcement of swaps even if they do not comply with CFTC rules, and grandfathers long term swaps that may be affected (including their position limits) by the financial reform bill. Sec. 739. It repeals sections 4421 and 4422 of the FDIC improvement Act of 1991 relating to multilateral clearing organizations for over the counter derivative contracts. Sec. 740. Provides guidelines and separation of enforcement for preceding rules between regulators, with the CFTC having exclusive authority to enforce the rules under this subtitle, but with other prudential federal regulators having exclusive swap regulatory authority over institutions they supervise. Sec. 741. Amends section 2c of CEA to give the CFTC jurisdiction over retail commodity transactions, Sec. 742a, allows the CFTC the new ability to seek restitution and disgorgement as a remedy as civil penalties, Sec. 744, establishes a whistleblower fund to pay a percentage of any monetary recovery to whistleblowers, Sec. 748. It requires a study on the regulation of carbon markets, Sec. 750, amends section 6(c) of the CEA to imposes new manipulation and attempted manipulation prohibitions on swaps and contracts for the sale of a commodity, including rules on manipulation by false reporting, Sec. 753a, and provides for a private rights of actions on manipulation of swap agreements, Sec. 753c.

Subtitle B deals with the regulation of the security-based swap market, Most of the rules under this Subtitle mirror the ones set forth in Subtitle A regarding the CFTC. It amends the definition of the Securities Exchange Act of 1934 to account for the regulation of security-based swaps, e.g. defining terms like major security-based swaps participants and security-based swaps. Sec. 761a. It repeals the prohibition on regulation of security-based swaps imposed by the Gramm–Leach–Bliley Act. Sec. 762. Imposes rules that are nearly identical to the swap rules for the CFTC under section 721 of *Subtitle* A, e.g. clearing rules for security-based swaps are almost the same as the ones under the CEA, Sec. 763a, requires security-based swap execution facilities to register and set forth core principles, Sec. 763c, segregate funds, Sec. 763d, allows the SEC to set position limits regarding security-based swaps if necessary to prevent fraud or manipulation and to direct SROs to impose position limits on its members, Sec. 763h. The SEC may required large traders to report their positions in certain swap related instruments. Sec. 763h. Each security-based swap, whether cleared, must be reported to a registered public security-based swap data repository, Sec. 763i, and security-based swap data repositories must register, Sec. 763i. Requires the registration of major security-based swap participants and dealers regardless of whether they are registered with another regulator (SEC may not impose prudential requirements on persons/entities for which there already is a prudential regulator), the SEC may impose capital and margin requirements, and the SEC has primary enforcement authority for the rules in *Subtitle B,* with certain exceptions for prudential regulatory authority that is given to other prudential regulators. Sec. 764. It directs the SEC to issue conflict of interest rules covering clearing facilities, security-based swap execution facilities and other big institutions, Sec. 765, imposes reporting requirements for security-based swaps, Sec. 766, imposes limitations on recovery from private judgments to actual damages and preempts state gaming regulations, Sec. 767. Amends section 24b of SEA of 1934, to impose civil penalties of twice the amount allowed under on clearing agencies or major security-based swap participants and dealers that knowingly or recklessly participate in trying to evade these rules. Sec. 773.

TITLE VIII—PAYMENT, CLEARING, AND SETTLEMENT SUPERVISION

Title VIII may be cited as "Payment, Clearing, and Settlement Supervision Act of 2010". It establishes a specific framework for promoting uniform risk-management standards for systemically important financial market utilities (FMUs) and systemically important payment, clearing, and settlement (PCS) activities conducted by financial institutions. It defines important terms under this Title like, clearing agencies, financial institutions, financial market utility, and sets jurisdictional boundaries for federal regulators of financial market utilities. Sec. 802 and 803. Di-

rects the Council to designate those financial market utility, payment or other activities that it deems are likely to be of systemic importance. Sec. 804a. Allows the Board to prescribe risk management standards to regulate operation of payments, clearing and clearing of designated financial utility and designated financial institutions, Sec. 805a(1), and the CFTC/SEC may do the same for such entities/activities that fall under their jurisdictions, Sec. 805b(2)(A). Authorizes the Board to allow the Federal Reserve Bank to establish an account for a designated financial market utility, Sec. 806a, and give said entity discount and borrowing privileges only under exigent circumstances when the utility is unable to secure credit, without requiring it to convert into a bank or bank holding company, Sec. 806b, and may exempt it from reserve requirements, Sec. 806d. The supervisory agency shall examine a designated financial market utility annually to determine the nature of its financial operations and risks, its soundness and other factors, Sec. 807a(1)–(5), allows each supervisor to enforce these rules as if the subject entity was an insured depository institution under the Federal Deposit Insurance Act, Sec. 807c. The Council may vote to force a regulator to enforce a Board recommendation against its will, Sec. 807e, and the Board may, in cases of emergency and after a vote by the Council, enforce these rules on a financial market utility whose actions or conditions are a threat to other companies or the financial markets, Sec. 807f. Financial regulators may examine financial institutions that are engaged in a "designated activity", as defined in section 805, in order to determine its effects and the ability of the institution to handle any potential risks. Sec. 808a. The Board may request information from the FMU and financial institutions engaged in clearing, settlements etc, in order to determine whether they are systemically important. Sec. 809a(1) and (2). Directs the Board to develop, in coordination with the CFTC and SEC, to develop risk management programs for designated clearing entities. Sec. 813.

TITLE IX—INVESTOR PROTECTIONS AND IMPROVEMENTS TO THE REGULATION OF SECURITIES

This Title may be cited as "Investor Protection and Securities Reform Act of 2010". It has nine subtitles. *Subtitle A* attempts to increase investor protection. It amends the SEA of 1934 by establishing an Investor Advisory Committee that will advise the SEC in regulating securities and other instruments in such a way that will protect investors and promote confidence in the regulatory system, and its members shall be from different parts of the securities field and shall not be considered SEC employees. Sec. 911. Amends the SEC to conduct a study regarding the effectiveness of current rules/regulation of broker, dealers and investment advisers, Sec. 913, and amends section 15 of the SEA of 1934 to allow the SEC to impose the same fiduciary duties on broker dealers that investment advisors have to their customers, Sec. 913g. The SEC shall conduct a study on the need for further examination and enforcement recourse regarding investment advisers. Sec. 914a. Amends section 4 of the SEA of 1934 to establish the office of the Investor Advocate within the SEC, to aid retailer investors resolve issues with the SEC or SROs, recommend changes that would be beneficial to retail investors and identify problems that retail investors may have in dealing with financial firms. Sec. 915. The SEC will conduct a study on the financial literacy of retail investors and on the advertising guidelines for mutual funds. Sec. 917 and 918. The SEC may issue regulations regarding information that a broker or dealer shall provide to a retail customer before the purchase of a financial product, Sec. 9 19, and shall conduct a study on possible conflict of interest between investment banking and equity and fixed income security analysts within the same firm, Sec. 919A. The newly created Investor Advocate shall appoint an Ombudsman within its office who shall act as a liaison between the SEC and a retail investor. Sec. 919D.

Subtitle B strengthens the SEC's authority to conduct investigations, impose liability on control persons, and assess penalties for violations of the securities laws. Specifically, it allows the SEC to limit the use of pre-dispute arbitration in disputes arising under Federal securities laws, Sec. 921, provides protection and whistleblower incentives of up to 30% of recovery, Sec. 922, and establishes the SEC Investor Protection Fund to pay out these and other awards, Sec. 922. Enhances the SEC's ability to ban violators from all aspects of the securities industry, Sec. 925, bans persons who have been subject to state financial regulatory action or have been convicted of a felony or misdemeanor in connection to securities trading, from using Reg D offering exemptions, Sec. 926, and imposes equal treatment for

SRO rules, Sec. 929T. Increases the ability of the SEC to borrow from the Treasury from $1 billion to $2.5 billion, Sec. 929C, enhances the SEC's ability to serve a subpoena anywhere in the U.S. and exempts such subpoenas from the Federal Rules of Civil Procedure, Sec. 929E, reforms the SEC's hiring authority for market specialists and advisers, Sec. 929G. It increases SIPC protection from $100,000 to $250,000 and allows for its adjustment for inflation. Sec. 929H. Restricts the use of confidential information obtained by the SEC under this title, Sec. 929I, enhances audit disclosure information for foreign accounting firms that produce documents on which domestic firms and the SEC rely and brings them under the jurisdiction of U.S. courts, Sec. 929J. It enhances the SEC's antifraud authority under the SEA of 1934, Sec. 929L, amends the SA of 1933 and ICC of 1940 to provide for aiding and abetting liability any person who *knowingly OR recklessly* participated in the violation, Sec. 929M and 929N, allows the SEC to impose financial penalties in cease and desist proceedings and provides for 3–tier penalty system depending on the severity of the violation, Sec. 929Pa. Provides for extra-territorial jurisdiction for anti-fraud provisions, Sec. 929Pb, amends section 13 of the SEA of 1934 relating to the reporting of beneficial ownership and short-swing profits, Sec. 929R. It increases the annual dues for SIPC members from $150 to .02 percent of their gross annual revenues from securities trading and increases the amount that a SPIC member can be fined, Sec. 929V. Imposes a prohibition on manipulative short sales and allows customers to elect that their securities not be used in connection with a short sale. Sec. 929Xb and c.

Subtitle C reforms/improves the regulation of credit rating agencies. It gives broader powers to the SEC to regulate nationally recognized statistical rating organizations (Organizations). It directs the organizations to set up and implement internal control structures relating to the determination of credit rating, allows the SEC to sanction these organizations if it finds that they have not committed enough resources to carry out their functions properly, requires the organizations to separate their rating functions from their marketing efforts and prohibits the compensation of their officers from being linked to the financial performance of the organizations. Sec. 932a(2)–(4). Establishes the Office of Credit Ratings to examine rating organizations at least once a year, requires the SEC to establish transparency rules for companies to evaluate the soundness of the credit rating process, requires the SEC to establish rating guidelines to be used by rating organization in order to ensure accurate rating methods and account for material changes in credit conditions, imposes additional disclosure requirements on the rating agencies, requires that rating organizations have a board of directors with at least ½ being independent, and requires the issuer or underwriter of an asset-backed security to make public the due diligence report of a third party. Sec. 932a(8). Allows for private liability for statements made by rating agencies to the same extent that they apply to other professionals, like accountants, and the plaintiffs only need to plea that the rating organization whether knowledgeably or recklessly failed to investigate or verify the financial conditions. Sec. 933a and b. Requires the rating organization to report to the SEC potential violations of state or Federal law that it discovers during its rating process, Sec. 934, and removes the exemptions of ratings organizations from Regulation FD regarding fair disclosure, Sec. 939B.

Subtitle D improves the asset backed securitization process. It requires securitizers to retain an economic interest in a material portion of the credit risk, (depending on the type of the asset), for any asset-backed security (ABS), including those backed by residential mortgages, that they convey to a third party. Sec. 941b. The regulators shall determine how to distribute the risk between originators or underwriters, depending on the type of risk and assets involved, however, the risk retention program will not apply to qualified residential mortgages, which will be defined as a mortgage backed by ample proof of the mortgagor's ability to pay it back. Sec. 941b. Directs the SEC to require issuers to disclose the assets backing each tranche of asset-backed securities, Sec. 942b, and issue regulation regarding registration statements for issuers of ABS that require them to examine the assets underlying the securities, Sec. 945.

Subtitle E deals with executive compensation for publicly held companies, and regulates shareholder rights and executive compensation practices. Amends the SEA of 1934 to require companies to solicit proxies not less than every three years for a resolution approving the amount that company executives shall be paid, although the

shareholders may decide to vote every 1, 2, or 3 years, Sec. 951, and during the a merger/acquisition the issuer/acquirer shall disclose, during the proxy solicitation process, any proposed golden parachutes that the company may become liable for, Sec. 951. It requires that these companies create independent compensation committees to set the compensation rates, Sec. 952a, disclose to shareholders the relationship between the executive compensation and the company's performance, Sec. 953, allows the board to recover any compensation deemed erroneous by virtue of noncompliance with the financial disclosure requirements of federal laws, Sec. 954, and prohibits compensation structures that are deemed to encourage taking inappropriate risks/excessive, Sec. 955b. Lastly, it prohibits brokers from using the voting rights of their clients for compensation related purposes, unless they are the beneficial owners of the securities or have said owner's instruction. Sec. 957.

Subtitle F improves the management of the SEC. It requires the SEC to submit several reports that: certify the adequacy of internal controls and examination procedures, Sec. 961a, quality of personnel management, Sec. 962a, adequacy of control for financial reporting, Sec. 963a, oversight of national securities associations registered under section 15A of the SEA of 1934, Sec. 964a. Hire a high caliber consultant to conduct a thorough evaluation of the operational adequacy of the SEC as an organization and its regulations, and make recommendations. Sec. 967a. The GAO shall conduct a study on the "revolving door" policy, examining how much of the staff leaves the SEC and goes to work for private financial firms. Sec. 968a.

Subtitle G strengthens corporate governance by authorizing the SEC to write rules allowing shareholders to nominate candidates for an issuer's board of directors, and to have such candidates listed on the issuer's own proxy materials. Sec. 971a. Requires a company to disclose on its annual proxy why it has chosen the same person to serve on its board of directors or CEO. Sec. 972.

Subtitle H regulates municipal securities (munis). Amends <u>section 15B</u> of the SEA of 1934 to require the registration of municipal financial advisors before they may advise their customers about the purchase of financial products, Sec. 975a, and subjects them to rules promulgated by the Municipal Securities Rulemaking Board

TITLE III—TRANSFER OF POWERS TO THE COMPTROLLER OF THE CURRENCY, THE CORPORATION, AND THE BOARD OF GOVERNORS

§ 300.   Short Title

This title may be cited as the "Enhancing Financial Institution Safety and Soundness Act of 2010".

§ 301.   Purposes

The purposes of this title are—

(1) to provide for the safe and sound operation of the banking system of the United States;

(2) to preserve and protect the dual system of Federal and State-chartered depository institutions;

(3) to ensure the fair and appropriate supervision of each depository institution, regardless of the size or type of charter of the depository institution; and

(4) to streamline and rationalize the supervision of depository institutions and the holding companies of depository institutions.

§ 302.   Definition

In this title, the term "transferred employee" means, as the context requires, an employee transferred to the Office of the Comptroller of the Currency or the Corporation under section 322.

Subtitle A—Transfer of Powers and Duties

§ 311.   Transfer Date

(a) TRANSFER DATE

Except as provided in subsection (b), the term "transfer date" means the date that is 1 year after the date of enactment of this Act.

(b) EXTENSION PERMITTED

(1) NOTICE REQUIRED

The Secretary, in consultation with the Comptroller of the Currency, the Director of the Office of Thrift Supervision, the Chairman of the Board of Governors, and the Chairperson of the Corporation, may extend the period under subsection (a) and designate a transfer date that is not later than 18 months after the date of enactment of this Act, if the Secretary transmits to the Committee on Banking, Housing, and Urban Affairs of the Senate and the Committee on Financial Services of the House of Representatives—

(A) a written determination that commencement of the orderly process to implement this title is not feasible by the date that is 1 year after the date of enactment of this Act;

(B) an explanation of why an extension is necessary to commence the process of orderly implementation of this title;

(C) the transfer date designated under this subsection; and

(D) a description of the steps that will be taken to initiate the process of an orderly and timely implementation of this title within the extended time period.

(2) PUBLICATION OF NOTICE

Not later than 270 days after the date of enactment of this Act, the Secretary shall publish in the Federal Register notice of any transfer date designated under paragraph (1).

§ 312.   Powers and Duties Transferred

(a) EFFECTIVE DATE

This section, and the amendments made by this section, shall take effect on the transfer date.

(b) FUNCTIONS OF THE OFFICE OF THRIFT SUPERVISION

(1) SAVINGS AND LOAN HOLDING COMPANY FUNCTIONS TRANSFERRED

(A) TRANSFER OF FUNCTIONS

There are transferred to the Board of Governors all functions of the Office of Thrift Supervision and the Director of the Office of Thrift Supervision (including the authority to issue orders) relating to—

(i) the supervision of—

(I) any savings and loan holding company; and

(II) any subsidiary (other than a depository institution) of a savings and loan holding company; and

(ii) all rulemaking authority of the Office of Thrift Supervision and the Director of the Office of Thrift Supervision relating to savings and loan holding companies.

(B) POWERS, AUTHORITIES, RIGHTS, AND DUTIES

The Board of Governors shall succeed to all powers, authorities, rights, and duties that were vested in the Office of Thrift Supervision and the Director of the Office of Thrift Supervision on the day before the transfer date relating to the functions and authority transferred under subparagraph (A).

(2) ALL OTHER FUNCTIONS TRANSFERRED

(A) BOARD OF GOVERNORS

All rulemaking authority of the Office of Thrift Supervision and the Director of the Office of Thrift Supervision under section 11 of the Home Owners' Loan Act (12 U.S.C. 1468) relating to transactions with affiliates and extensions of credit to executive officers, directors, and principal shareholders and under section 5(q) of such Act relating to tying arrangements is transferred to the Board of Governors.

(B) COMPTROLLER OF THE CURRENCY

Except as provided in paragraph (1) and subparagraph (A)—

(i) there are transferred to the Office of the Comptroller of the Currency and the Comptroller of the Currency—

(I) all functions of the Office of Thrift Supervision and the Director of the Office of Thrift Supervision, respectively, relating to Federal savings associations; and

(II) all rulemaking authority of the Office of Thrift Supervision and the Director of the Office of Thrift Supervision, respectively, relating to savings associations; and

(ii) the Office of the Comptroller of the Currency and the Comptroller of the Currency shall succeed to all powers, authorities, rights, and duties that were vested in the Office of Thrift Supervision and the Director of the Office of Thrift Supervision, respectively, on the day before the transfer date relating to the functions and authority transferred under clause (i).

(C) CORPORATION

Except as provided in paragraph (1) and subparagraphs (A) and (B)—

(i) all functions of the Office of Thrift Supervision and the Director of the Office of Thrift Supervision relating to State savings associations are transferred to the Corporation; and

(ii) the Corporation shall succeed to all powers, authorities, rights, and duties that were vested in the Office of Thrift Supervision and the Director of the Office of Thrift Supervision on the day before the transfer date relating to the functions transferred under clause (i).

(c) CONFORMING AMENDMENTS

Section 3 of the Federal Deposit Insurance Act (12 U.S.C. 1813) is amended—

(1) in subsection (q), by striking paragraphs (1) through (4) and inserting the following:

"(1) the Office of the Comptroller of the Currency, in the case of—

"(A) any national banking association;

"(B) any Federal branch or agency of a foreign bank; and

"(C) any Federal savings association;

"(2) the Federal Deposit Insurance Corporation, in the case of—

"(A) any State nonmember insured bank;

"(B) any foreign bank having an insured branch; and

"(C) any State savings association;

"(3) the Board of Governors of the Federal Reserve System, in the case of—

"(A) any State member bank;

"(B) any branch or agency of a foreign bank with respect to any provision of the Federal Reserve Act which is made applicable under the International Banking Act of 1978;

"(C) any foreign bank which does not operate an insured branch;

"(D) any agency or commercial lending company other than a Federal agency;

"(E) supervisory or regulatory proceedings arising from the authority given to the Board of Governors under section 7(c)(1) of the International Banking Act of 1978, including such proceedings under the Financial Institutions Supervisory Act of 1966;

"(F) any bank holding company and any subsidiary (other than a depository institution) of a bank holding company; and

"(G) any savings and loan holding company and any subsidiary (other than a depository institution) of a savings and loan holding company."; and (2) in paragraphs (1) and (3) of subsection (u), by striking "(other than a bank holding company" and inserting "(other than a bank holding company or savings and loan holding company".

(d) CONSUMER PROTECTION

Nothing in this section may be construed to limit or otherwise affect the transfer of powers under title X.

§ 313. Abolishment

Effective 90 days after the transfer date, the Office of Thrift Supervision and the position of Director of the Office of Thrift Supervision are abolished.

§ 314. Amendments to the Revised Statutes

(a) AMENDMENT TO SECTION 324

Section 324 of the Revised Statutes of the United States (12 U.S.C. 1) is amended to read as follows:

> "SEC. 324. COMPTROLLER OF THE CURRENCY
>
> "(a) OFFICE OF THE COMPTROLLER OF THE CURRENCY ESTABLISHED
>
> There is established in the Department of the Treasury a bureau to be known as the 'Office of the Comptroller of the Currency' which is charged with assuring the safety and soundness of, and compliance with laws and regulations, fair access to financial services, and fair treatment of customers by, the institutions and other persons subject to its jurisdiction.
>
> "(b) COMPTROLLER OF THE CURRENCY
>
> "(1) IN GENERAL
>
> The chief officer of the Office of the Comptroller of the Currency shall be known as the Comptroller of the Currency. The Comptroller of the Currency shall perform the duties of the Comptroller of the Currency under the general direction of the Secretary of the Treasury. The Secretary of the Treasury may not delay or prevent the issuance of any rule or the promulgation of any regulation by the Comptroller of the Currency, and may not intervene in any matter or proceeding before the Comptroller of the Currency (including agency enforcement actions), unless otherwise specifically provided by law.
>
> "(2) ADDITIONAL AUTHORITY
>
> The Comptroller of the Currency shall have the same authority with respect to functions

transferred to the Comptroller of the Currency under the Enhancing Financial Institution Safety and Soundness Act of 2010 as was vested in the Director of the Office of Thrift Supervision on the transfer date, as defined in section 311 of that Act."

(b) SUPERVISION OF FEDERAL SAVINGS ASSOCIATIONS

Chapter 9 of title VII of the Revised Statutes of the United States (12 U.S.C. 1 et seq.) is amended by inserting after section 327A (12 U.S.C. 4a) the following:

> "SEC. 327B. DEPUTY COMPTROLLER FOR THE SUPERVISION AND EXAMINATION OF FEDERAL SAVINGS ASSOCIATIONS
>
> "The Comptroller of the Currency shall designate a Deputy Comptroller, who shall be responsible for the supervision and examination of Federal savings associations."

(c) AMENDMENT TO SECTION 329

Section 329 of the Revised Statutes of the United States (12 U.S.C. 11) is amended by inserting before the period at the end the following: "or any Federal savings association".

(d) EFFECTIVE DATE

This section, and the amendments made by this section, shall take effect on the transfer date.

§ 315. Federal Information Policy

Section 3502(5) of title 44, United States Code, is amended by inserting "Office of the Comptroller of the Currency," after "the Securities and Exchange Commission".

§ 316. Savings Provisions

(a) OFFICE OF THRIFT SUPERVISION

(1) EXISTING RIGHTS, DUTIES, AND OBLIGATIONS NOT AFFECTED

Sections 312(b) and 313 shall not affect the validity of any right, duty, or obligation of the United States, the Director of the Office of Thrift Supervision, the Office of Thrift Supervision, or any other person, that existed on the day before the transfer date.

(2) CONTINUATION OF SUITS

This title shall not abate any action or proceeding commenced by or against the Director of the Office of Thrift Supervision or the Office of

Thrift Supervision before the transfer date, except that—

(A) for any action or proceeding arising out of a function of the Office of Thrift Supervision or the Director of the Office of Thrift Supervision transferred to the Board of Governors by this title, the Board of Governors shall be substituted for the Office of Thrift Supervision or the Director of the Office of Thrift Supervision as a party to the action or proceeding on and after the transfer date;

(B) for any action or proceeding arising out of a function of the Office of Thrift Supervision or the Director of the Office of Thrift Supervision transferred to the Office of the Comptroller of the Currency or the Comptroller of the Currency by this title, the Office of the Comptroller of the Currency or the Comptroller of the Currency shall be substituted for the Office of Thrift Supervision or the Director of the Office of Thrift Supervision, as the case may be, as a party to the action or proceeding on and after the transfer date; and

(C) for any action or proceeding arising out of a function of the Office of Thrift Supervision or the Director of the Office of Thrift Supervision transferred to the Corporation by this title, the Corporation shall be substituted for the Office of Thrift Supervision or the Director of the Office of Thrift Supervision as a party to the action or proceeding on and after the transfer date.

(b) CONTINUATION OF EXISTING OTS ORDERS, RESOLUTIONS, DETERMINATIONS, AGREEMENTS, REGULATIONS, ETC.

All orders, resolutions, determinations, agreements, and regulations, interpretative rules, other interpretations, guidelines, procedures, and other advisory materials, that have been issued, made, prescribed, or allowed to become effective by the Office of Thrift Supervision or the Director of the Office of Thrift Supervision, or by a court of competent jurisdiction, in the performance of functions that are transferred by this title and that are in effect on the day before the transfer date, shall continue in effect according to the terms of such orders, resolutions, determinations, agreements, and regulations, interpretative rules, other interpretations, guidelines, procedures, and other advisory materials, and shall be enforceable by or against—

(1) the Board of Governors, in the case of a function of the Office of Thrift Supervision or the Director of the Office of Thrift Supervision transferred to the Board of Governors, until modified, terminated, set aside, or superseded in accordance with applicable law by the Board of Governors, by any court of competent jurisdiction, or by operation of law;

(2) the Office of the Comptroller of the Currency or the Comptroller of the Currency, in the case of a function of the Office of Thrift Supervision or the Director of the Office of Thrift Supervision transferred to the Office of the Comptroller of the Currency or the Comptroller of the Currency, respectively, until modified, terminated, set aside, or superseded in accordance with applicable law by the Office of the Comptroller of the Currency or the Comptroller of the Currency, by any court of competent jurisdiction, or by operation of law; and

(3) the Corporation, in the case of a function of the Office of Thrift Supervision or the Director of the Office of Thrift Supervision transferred to the Corporation, until modified, terminated, set aside, or superseded in accordance with applicable law by the Corporation, by any court of competent jurisdiction, or by operation of law.

(c) IDENTIFICATION OF REGULATIONS CONTINUED

(1) BY THE BOARD OF GOVERNORS

Not later than the transfer date, the Board of Governors shall—

(A) identify the regulations continued under subsection (b) that will be enforced by the Board of Governors; and

(B) publish a list of the regulations identified under subparagraph (A) in the Federal Register.

(2) BY OFFICE OF THE COMPTROLLER OF THE CURRENCY

Not later than the transfer date, the Office of the Comptroller of the Currency shall—

(A) after consultation with the Corporation, identify the regulations continued under subsection (b) that will be enforced by the Office of the Comptroller of the Currency; and

(B) publish a list of the regulations identified under subparagraph (A) in the Federal Register.

(3) BY THE CORPORATION

Not later than the transfer date, the Corporation shall—

(A) after consultation with the Office of the Comptroller of the Currency, identify the regulations continued under subsection (b) that will be enforced by the Corporation; and

(B) publish a list of the regulations identified under subparagraph (A) in the Federal Register.

(d) STATUS OF REGULATIONS PROPOSED OR NOT YET EFFECTIVE

(1) PROPOSED REGULATIONS

Any proposed regulation of the Office of Thrift Supervision, which the Office of Thrift Supervision in performing functions transferred by this title, has proposed before the transfer date but has not published as a final regulation before such date, shall be deemed to be a proposed regulation of the Office of the Comptroller of the Currency or the Board of Governors, as appropriate, according to the terms of the proposed regulation.

(2) REGULATIONS NOT YET EFFECTIVE

Any interim or final regulation of the Office of Thrift Supervision, which the Office of Thrift Supervision, in performing functions transferred by this title, has published before the transfer date but which has not become effective before that date, shall become effective as a regulation of the Office of the Comptroller of the Currency or the Board of Governors, as appropriate, according to the terms of the interim or final regulation, unless modified, terminated, set aside, or superseded in accordance with applicable law by the Office of the Comptroller of the Currency or the Board of Governors, as appropriate, by any court of competent jurisdiction, or by operation of law.

§ 317. References in Federal Law to Federal Banking Agencies

On and after the transfer date, any reference in Federal law to the Director of the Office of Thrift Supervision or the Office of Thrift Supervision, in connection with any function of the Director of the Office of Thrift Supervision or the Office of Thrift Supervision transferred under

section 312(b) or any other provision of this subtitle, shall be deemed to be a reference to the Comptroller of the Currency, the Office of the Comptroller of the Currency, the Chairperson of the Corporation, the Corporation, the Chairman of the Board of Governors, or the Board of Governors, as appropriate and consistent with the amendments made in subtitle E.

§ 318. Funding

(a) COMPENSATION OF EXAMINERS

Section 5240 of the Revised Statutes of the United States (12 U.S.C. 481 et seq.) is amended—

(1) in the second undesignated paragraph (12 U.S.C. 481), in the fourth sentence, by striking "without regard to the provisions of other laws applicable to officers or employees of the United States" and inserting the following: "set and adjusted subject to chapter 71 of title 5, United States Code, and without regard to the provisions of other laws applicable to officers or employees of the United States"; and

(2) in the third undesignated paragraph (12 U.S.C. 482), in the first sentence, by striking "shall fix" and inserting "shall, subject to chapter 71 of title 5, United States Code, fix".

(b) FUNDING OF OFFICE OF THE COMPTROLLER OF THE CURRENCY

Chapter 4 of title LXII of the Revised Statutes is amended by inserting after section 5240 (12 U.S.C. 481, 482) the following:

"SEC. 5240A. The Comptroller of the Currency may collect an assessment, fee, or other charge from any entity described in section 3(q)(1) of the Federal Deposit Insurance Act (12 U.S.C. 1813(q)(1)), as the Comptroller determines is necessary or appropriate to carry out the responsibilities of the Office of the Comptroller of the Currency. In establishing the amount of an assessment, fee, or charge collected from an entity under this section, the Comptroller of the Currency may take into account the nature and scope of the activities of the entity, the amount and type of assets that the entity holds, the financial and managerial condition of the entity, and any other factor, as the Comptroller of the Currency determines is appropriate. Funds derived from any assessment, fee, or charge collected or payment made pursuant to this section may be deposited by the Comptroller of the Currency in accordance with the provisions of section 5234. Such funds shall not be construed to be Government funds or appropriated monies, and shall not be subject to apportionment for purposes of chapter 15 of title 31, United States Code, or any other provision of law. The authority of the Comptroller of the Currency under this section shall be in addition to the authority under section 5240.

"The Comptroller of the Currency shall have sole authority to determine the manner in which the obligations of the Office of the Comptroller of the Currency shall be incurred and its disbursements and expenses allowed and paid, in accordance with this section, except as provided in chapter 71 of title 5, United States Code (with respect to compensation)."

(c) FUNDING OF BOARD OF GOVERNORS

Section 11 of the Federal Reserve Act (12 U.S.C. 248) is amended by adding at the end the following:

"(s) ASSESSMENTS, FEES, AND OTHER CHARGES FOR CERTAIN COMPANIES.—

"(1) IN GENERAL

The Board shall collect a total amount of assessments, fees, or other charges from the companies described in paragraph (2) that is equal to the total expenses the Board estimates are necessary or appropriate to carry out the supervisory and regulatory responsibilities of the Board with respect to such companies.

"(2) COMPANIES

The companies described in this paragraph are—

"(A) all bank holding companies having total consolidated assets of $50,000,000,000 or more;

"(B) all savings and loan holding companies having total consolidated assets of $50,000,000,000 or more; and

"(C) all nonbank financial companies supervised by the Board under section 113 of the Dodd–Frank Wall Street Reform and Consumer Protection Act."

(d) CORPORATION EXAMINATION FEES

Section 10(e) of the Federal Deposit Insurance Act (12 U.S.C. 1820(e)) is amended by striking paragraph (1) and inserting the following:

"(1) REGULAR AND SPECIAL EXAMINATIONS OF DEPOSITORY INSTITUTIONS

The cost of conducting any regular examination or special examination of any depository institution under subsection (b)(2), (b)(3), or (d) or of any entity described in section 3(q)(2) may be assessed by the Corporation against the institution or entity to meet the expenses of the Corporation in carrying out such examinations.".

(e) EFFECTIVE DATE

This section, and the amendments made by this section, shall take effect on the transfer date.

§ 319. Contracting and Leasing Authority

Notwithstanding the Federal Property and Administrative Services Act of 1949 (41 U.S.C. 251 et seq.) or any other provision of law (except the full and open competition requirements of the Competition in Contracting Act), the Office of the Comptroller of the Currency may—

(1) enter into and perform contracts, execute instruments, and acquire real property (or property interest) as the Comptroller deems necessary to carry out the duties and responsibilities of the Office of the Comptroller of the Currency; and

(2) hold, maintain, sell, lease, or otherwise dispose of the property (or property interest) acquired under paragraph (1).

Subtitle B—Transitional Provisions

§ 321. Interim Use of Funds, Personnel, and Property of the Office of Thrift Supervision

(a) IN GENERAL

Before the transfer date, the Office of the Comptroller of the Currency, the Corporation, and the Board of Governors shall—

(1) consult and cooperate with the Office of Thrift Supervision to facilitate the orderly transfer of functions to the Office of the Comptroller of the Currency, the Corporation, and the Board of Governors in accordance with this title;

(2) determine jointly, from time to time—

(A) the amount of funds necessary to pay any expenses associated with the transfer of functions (including expenses for personnel, property, and administrative services) during the period beginning on the date of enactment of this Act and ending on the transfer date;

(B) which personnel are appropriate to facilitate the orderly transfer of functions by this title; and

(C) what property and administrative services are necessary to support the Office of the Comptroller of the Currency, the Corporation, and the Board of Governors during the period beginning on the date of enactment of this Act and ending on the transfer date; and

(3) take such actions as may be necessary to provide for the orderly implementation of this title.

(b) AGENCY CONSULTATION

When requested jointly by the Office of the Comptroller of the Currency, the Corporation, and the Board of Governors to do so before the transfer date, the Office of Thrift Supervision shall—

(1) pay to the Office of the Comptroller of the Currency, the Corporation, or the Board of Governors, as applicable, from funds obtained by the Office of Thrift Supervision through assessments, fees, or other charges that the Office of Thrift Supervision is authorized by law to impose, such amounts as the Office of the Comptroller of the Currency, the Corporation, and the Board of Governors jointly determine to be necessary under subsection (a);

(2) detail to the Office of the Comptroller of the Currency, the Corporation, or the Board of Governors, as applicable, such personnel as the Office of the Comptroller of the Currency, the Corporation, and the Board of Governors jointly determine to be appropriate under subsection (a); and

(3) make available to the Office of the Comptroller of the Currency, the Corporation, or the Board of Governors, as applicable, such property and provide to the Office of the Comptroller of the Currency, the Corporation, or the Board of Governors, as applicable, such administrative services as the Office of the Comptroller of the Currency, the Corporation, and the Board of Governors jointly determine to be necessary under subsection (a).

(c) NOTICE REQUIRED

The Office of the Comptroller of the Currency, the Corporation, and the Board of Governors shall jointly give the Office of Thrift Supervision reasonable prior notice of any request that the Office of the Comptroller of the Currency, the Corporation, and the Board of Governors jointly intend to make under subsection (b).

§ 322. Transfer of Employees

(a) IN GENERAL

(1) OFFICE OF THRIFT SUPERVISION EMPLOYEES

(A) IN GENERAL

Except as provided in section 1064, all employees of the Office of Thrift Supervision shall be transferred to the Office of the Comptroller of the Currency or the Corporation for employment in accordance with this section.

(B) ALLOCATING EMPLOYEES FOR TRANSFER TO RECEIVING AGENCIES

The Director of the Office of Thrift Supervision, the Comptroller of the Currency, and the Chairperson of the Corporation shall—

(i) jointly determine the number of employees of the Office of Thrift Supervision necessary to perform or support the functions that are transferred to the Office of the Comptroller of the Currency or the Corporation by this title; and

(ii) consistent with the determination under clause (i), jointly identify employees of the Office of Thrift Supervision for transfer to the Office of the Comptroller of the Currency or the Corporation.

(2) EMPLOYEES TRANSFERRED; SERVICE PERIODS CREDITED

For purposes of this section, periods of service with a Federal home loan bank, a joint office of Federal home loan banks, or a Federal reserve bank shall be credited as periods of service with a Federal agency.

(3) APPOINTMENT AUTHORITY FOR EXCEPTED SERVICE TRANSFERRED

(A) IN GENERAL

Except as provided in subparagraph (B), any appointment authority of the Office of Thrift Supervision under Federal law that relates to the functions transferred under section 312, including the regulations of the Office of Personnel Management, for filling the positions of employees in the excepted service shall be transferred to the Comptroller of the

Currency or the Chairperson of the Corporation, as appropriate.

(B) DECLINING TRANSFERS ALLOWED

The Comptroller of the Currency or the Chairperson of the Corporation may decline to accept a transfer of authority under subparagraph (A) (and the employees appointed under that authority) to the extent that such authority relates to positions excepted from the competitive service because of their confidential, policy-making, policy-determining, or policy-advocating character.

(4) ADDITIONAL APPOINTMENT AUTHORITY

Notwithstanding any other provision of law, the Office of the Comptroller of the Currency and the Corporation may appoint transferred employees to positions in the Office of the Comptroller of the Currency or the Corporation, respectively.

(b) TIMING OF TRANSFERS AND POSITION ASSIGNMENTS

Each employee to be transferred under subsection (a)(1) shall—

(1) be transferred not later than 90 days after the transfer date; and

(2) receive notice of the position assignment of the employee not later than 120 days after the effective date of the transfer of the employee.

(c) TRANSFER OF FUNCTIONS

(1) IN GENERAL

Notwithstanding any other provision of law, the transfer of employees under this subtitle shall be deemed a transfer of functions for the purpose of section 3503 of title 5, United States Code.

(2) PRIORITY

If any provision of this subtitle conflicts with any protection provided to a transferred employee under section 3503 of title 5, United States Code, the provisions of this subtitle shall control.

(d) EMPLOYEE STATUS AND ELIGIBILITY

The transfer of functions and employees under this subtitle, and the abolishment of the Office of Thrift Supervision under section 313, shall not affect the status of the transferred employees as employees of an agency of the United States under any provision of law.

(e) EQUAL STATUS AND TENURE POSITIONS

(1) STATUS AND TENURE

Each transferred employee from the Office of Thrift Supervision shall be placed in a position at the Office of the Comptroller of the Currency or the Corporation with the same status and tenure as the transferred employee held on the day before the date on which the employee was transferred.

(2) FUNCTIONS

To the extent practicable, each transferred employee shall be placed in a position at the Office of the Comptroller of the Currency or the Corporation, as applicable, responsible for the same functions and duties as the transferred employee had on the day before the date on which the employee was transferred, in accordance with the expertise and preferences of the transferred employee.

(f) NO ADDITIONAL CERTIFICATION REQUIREMENTS

An examiner who is a transferred employee shall not be subject to any additional certification requirements before being placed in a comparable position at the Office of the Comptroller of the Currency or the Corporation, if the examiner carries out examinations of the same type of institutions as an employee of the Office of the Comptroller of the Currency or the Corporation as the employee was responsible for carrying out before the date on which the employee was transferred.

(g) PERSONNEL ACTIONS LIMITED

(1) PROTECTION

(A) IN GENERAL

Except as provided in paragraph (2), each affected employee shall not, during the 30–month period beginning on the transfer date, be involuntarily separated, or involuntarily reassigned outside his or her locality pay area.

(B) AFFECTED EMPLOYEES

For purposes of this paragraph, the term "affected employee" means—

(i) an employee transferred from the Office of Thrift Supervision holding a permanent position on the day before the transfer date; and

(ii) an employee of the Office of the Comptroller of the Currency or the Corporation holding a permanent position on the day before the transfer date.

(2) EXCEPTIONS

Paragraph (1) does not limit the right of the Office of the Comptroller of the Currency or the Corporation to—

(A) separate an employee for cause or for unacceptable performance;

(B) terminate an appointment to a position excepted from the competitive service because of its confidential policy-making, policy-determining, or policy-advocating character; or

(C) reassign an employee outside such employee's locality pay area when the Office of the Comptroller of the Currency or the Corporation determines that the reassignment is necessary for the efficient operation of the agency.

(h) PAY

(1) 30–MONTH PROTECTION

Except as provided in paragraph (2), during the 30–month period beginning on the date on which the employee was transferred under this subtitle, a transferred employee shall be paid at a rate that is not less than the basic rate of pay, including any geographic differential, that the transferred employee received during the pay period immediately preceding the date on which the employee was transferred. Notwithstanding the preceding sentence, if the employee was receiving a higher rate of basic pay on a temporary basis (because of a temporary assignment, temporary promotion, or other temporary action) immediately before the transfer, the Agency may reduce the rate of basic pay on the date the rate would have been reduced but for the transfer, and the protected rate for the remainder of the 30–month period will be the reduced rate that would have applied but for the transfer.

(2) EXCEPTIONS

The Comptroller of the Currency or the Corporation may reduce the rate of basic pay of a transferred employee—

(A) for cause, including for unacceptable performance; or

(B) with the consent of the transferred employee.

(3) PROTECTION ONLY WHILE EMPLOYED

This subsection shall apply to a transferred employee only during the period that the transferred employee remains employed by Office of the Comptroller of the Currency or the Corporation.

(4) PAY INCREASES PERMITTED

Nothing in this subsection shall limit the authority of the Comptroller of the Currency or the Chairperson of the Corporation to increase the pay of a transferred employee.

(i) BENEFITS

(1) RETIREMENT BENEFITS FOR TRANSFERRED EMPLOYEES

(A) IN GENERAL

(i) CONTINUATION OF EXISTING RETIREMENT PLAN

Each transferred employee shall remain enrolled in the retirement plan of the transferred employee, for as long as the transferred employee is employed by the Office of the Comptroller of the Currency or the Corporation.

(ii) EMPLOYER'S CONTRIBUTION

The Comptroller of the Currency or the Chairperson of the Corporation, as appropriate, shall pay any employer contributions to the existing retirement plan of each transferred employee, as required under each such existing retirement plan.

(B) DEFINITION

In this paragraph, the term "existing retirement plan" means, with respect to a transferred employee, the retirement plan (including the Financial Institutions Retirement Fund), and any associated thrift savings plan, of the agency from which the employee was transferred in which the employee was enrolled on the day before the date on which the employee was transferred.

(2) BENEFITS OTHER THAN RETIREMENT BENEFITS

(A) DURING FIRST YEAR

(i) EXISTING PLANS CONTINUE

During the 1–year period following the transfer date, each transferred employee may retain membership in any employee benefit program (other than a retirement benefit program) of the agency from which the employee was transferred under this title, including any dental, vision, long term care, or life insurance program to which the employee belonged on the day before the transfer date.

(ii) EMPLOYER'S CONTRIBUTION

The Office of the Comptroller of the Currency or the Corporation, as appropriate, shall pay any employer cost required to extend coverage in the benefit program to the transferred employee as required under that program or negotiated agreements.

(B) DENTAL, VISION, OR LIFE INSURANCE AFTER FIRST YEAR

If, after the 1–year period beginning on the transfer date, the Office of the Comptroller of the Currency or the Corporation determines that the Office of the Comptroller of the Currency or the Corporation, as the case may be, will not continue to participate in any dental, vision, or life insurance program of an agency from which an employee was transferred, a transferred employee who is a member of the program may, before the decision takes effect and without regard to any regularly scheduled open season, elect to enroll in—

(i) the enhanced dental benefits program established under chapter 89A of title 5, United States Code;

(ii) the enhanced vision benefits established under chapter 89B of title 5, United States Code; and

(iii) the Federal Employees' Group Life Insurance Program established under chapter 87 of title 5, United States Code, without regard to any requirement of insurability.

(C) LONG TERM CARE INSURANCE AFTER 1ST YEAR

If, after the 1–year period beginning on the transfer date, the Office of the Comptroller of the Currency or the Corporation determines that the Office of the Comptroller of the Currency or the Corporation, as appropriate, will not continue to participate in any long term care insurance program of an

agency from which an employee transferred, a transferred employee who is a member of such a program may, before the decision takes effect, elect to apply for coverage under the Federal Long Term Care Insurance Program established under chapter 90 of title 5, United States Code, under the underwriting requirements applicable to a new active workforce member, as described in part 875 of title 5, Code of Federal Regulations (or any successor thereto).

(D) CONTRIBUTION OF TRANSFERRED EMPLOYEE

(i) IN GENERAL

Subject to clause (ii), a transferred employee who is enrolled in a plan under the Federal Employees Health Benefits Program shall pay any employee contribution required under the plan.

(ii) COST DIFFERENTIAL

The Office of the Comptroller of the Currency or the Corporation, as applicable, shall pay any difference in cost between the employee contribution required under the plan provided to transferred employees by the agency from which the employee transferred on the date of enactment of this Act and the plan provided by the Office of the Comptroller of the Currency or the Corporation, as the case may be, under this section.

(iii) FUNDS TRANSFER

The Office of the Comptroller of the Currency or the Corporation, as the case may be, shall transfer to the Employees Health Benefits Fund established under section 8909 of title 5, United States Code, an amount determined by the Director of the Office of Personnel Management, after consultation with the Comptroller of the Currency or the Chairperson of the Corporation, as the case may be, and the Office of Management and Budget, to be necessary to reimburse the Fund for the cost to the Fund of providing any benefits under this subparagraph that are not otherwise paid for by a transferred employee under clause (i).

(E) SPECIAL PROVISIONS TO ENSURE CONTINUATION OF LIFE INSURANCE BENEFITS

(i) IN GENERAL

An annuitant, as defined in section 8901 of title 5, United States Code, who is enrolled in a life insurance plan administered by an agency from which employees are transferred under this title on the day before the transfer date shall be eligible for coverage by a life insurance plan under sections 8706(b), 8714a, 8714b, or 8714c of title 5, United States Code, or by a life insurance plan established by the Office of the Comptroller of the Currency or the Corporation, as applicable, without regard to any regularly scheduled open season or any requirement of insurability.

(ii) CONTRIBUTION OF TRANSFERRED EMPLOYEE

(I) IN GENERAL

Subject to subclause (II), a transferred employee enrolled in a life insurance plan under this subparagraph shall pay any employee contribution required by the plan.

(II) COST DIFFERENTIAL

The Office of the Comptroller of the Currency or the Corporation, as the case may be, shall pay any difference in cost between the benefits provided by the agency from which the employee transferred on the date of enactment of this Act and the benefits provided under this section.

(III) FUNDS TRANSFER

The Office of the Comptroller of the Currency or the Corporation, as the case may be, shall transfer to the Federal Employees' Group Life Insurance Fund established under section 8714 of title 5, United States Code, an amount determined by the Director of the Office of Personnel Management, after consultation with the Comptroller of the Currency or the Chairperson of the Corporation, as the case may be, and the Office of Management and Budget, to be necessary to reimburse the Federal Employees' Group Life Insurance Fund for the cost to the Federal Employees' Group Life Insurance Fund of providing benefits under this subparagraph not otherwise paid for by a transferred employee under subclause (I).

(IV) CREDIT FOR TIME ENROLLED IN OTHER PLANS

For any transferred employee, enrollment in a life insurance plan administered by the agency from which the employee transferred, immediately before enrollment in a life insurance plan under chapter 87 of title 5, United States Code, shall be considered as enrollment in a life insurance plan under that chapter for purposes of section 8706(b)(1)(A) of title 5, United States Code.

(j) INCORPORATION INTO AGENCY PAY SYSTEM

Not later than 30 months after the transfer date, the Comptroller of the Currency and the Chairperson of the Corporation shall place each transferred employee into the established pay system and structure of the appropriate employing agency.

(k) EQUITABLE TREATMENT

In administering the provisions of this section, the Comptroller of the Currency and the Chairperson of the Corporation—

(1) may not take any action that would unfairly disadvantage a transferred employee relative to any other employee of the Office of the Comptroller of the Currency or the Corporation on the basis of prior employment by the Office of Thrift Supervision;

(2) may take such action as is appropriate in an individual case to ensure that a transferred employee receives equitable treatment, with respect to the status, tenure, pay, benefits (other than benefits under programs administered by the Office of Personnel Management), and accrued leave or vacation time for prior periods of service with any Federal agency of the transferred employee;

(3) shall, jointly with the Director of the Office of Thrift Supervision, develop and adopt procedures and safeguards designed to ensure that the requirements of this subsection are met; and

(4) shall conduct a study detailing the position assignments of all employees transferred pursuant to subsection (a), describing the procedures and safeguards adopted pursuant to paragraph (3), and demonstrating that the requirements of this subsection have been met; and shall, not later than 365 days after the transfer date, submit a copy of such study to Congress.

(l) REORGANIZATION

(1) IN GENERAL

If the Comptroller of the Currency or the Chairperson of the Corporation determines, during the 2–year period beginning 1 year after the transfer date, that a reorganization of the staff of the Office of the Comptroller of the Currency or the Corporation, respectively, is required, the reorganization shall be deemed a "major reorganization" for purposes of affording affected employees retirement under section 8336(d)(2) or 8414(b)(1)(B) of title 5, United States Code.

(2) SERVICE CREDIT

For purposes of this subsection, periods of service with a Federal home loan bank or a joint office of Federal home loan banks shall be credited as periods of service with a Federal agency.

§ 323. Property Transferred

(a) PROPERTY DEFINED

For purposes of this section, the term "property" includes all real property (including leaseholds) and all personal property, including computers, furniture, fixtures, equipment, books, accounts, records, reports, files, memoranda, paper, reports of examination, work papers, and correspondence related to such reports, and any other information or materials.

(b) PROPERTY OF THE OFFICE OF THRIFT SUPERVISION

(1) IN GENERAL

No later than 90 days after the transfer date, all property of the Office of Thrift Supervision (other than property described under paragraph (b)(2)) that the Comptroller of the Currency and the Chairperson of the Corporation jointly determine is used, on the day before the transfer date, to perform or support the functions of the Office of Thrift Supervision transferred to the Office of the Comptroller of the Currency or the Corporation under this title, shall be transferred to the Office of the Comptroller of the Currency or the Corporation in a manner consistent with the transfer of employees under this subtitle.

(2) PERSONAL PROPERTY

All books, accounts, records, reports, files, memoranda, papers, documents, reports of examination, work papers, and correspondence of the Office of Thrift Supervision that the Comptroller of the Currency, the Chairperson of the

Corporation, and the Chairman of the Board of Governors jointly determine is used, on the day before the transfer date, to perform or support the functions of the Office of Thrift Supervision transferred to the Board of Governors under this title shall be transferred to the Board of Governors in a manner consistent with the purposes of this title.

(c) CONTRACTS RELATED TO PROPERTY TRANSFERRED

Each contract, agreement, lease, license, permit, and similar arrangement relating to property transferred to the Office of the Comptroller of the Currency or the Corporation by this section shall be transferred to the Office of the Comptroller of the Currency or the Corporation, as appropriate, together with the property to which it relates.

(d) PRESERVATION OF PROPERTY

Property identified for transfer under this section shall not be altered, destroyed, or deleted before transfer under this section.

§ 324. Funds Transferred

The funds that, on the day before the transfer date, the Director of the Office of Thrift Supervision (in consultation with the Comptroller of the Currency, the Chairperson of the Corporation, and the Chairman of the Board of Governors) determines are not necessary to dispose of the affairs of the Office of Thrift Supervision under section 325 and are available to the Office of Thrift Supervision to pay the expenses of the Office of Thrift Supervision—

(1) relating to the functions of the Office of Thrift Supervision transferred under section 312(b)(2)(B), shall be transferred to the Office of the Comptroller of the Currency on the transfer date;

(2) relating to the functions of the Office of Thrift Supervision transferred under section 312(b)(2)(C), shall be transferred to the Corporation on the transfer date; and

(3) relating to the functions of the Office of Thrift Supervision transferred under section 312(b)(1)(A), shall be transferred to the Board of Governors on the transfer date.

§ 325. Disposition of Affairs

(a) AUTHORITY OF DIRECTOR

During the 90–day period beginning on the transfer date, the Director of the Office of Thrift Supervision—

(1) shall, solely for the purpose of winding up the affairs of the Office of Thrift Supervision relating to any function transferred to the Office of the Comptroller of the Currency, the Corporation, or the Board of Governors under this title—

(A) manage the employees of the Office of Thrift Supervision who have not yet been transferred and provide for the payment of the compensation and benefits of the employees that accrue before the date on which the employees are transferred under this title; and

(B) manage any property of the Office of Thrift Supervision, until the date on which the property is transferred under section 323; and

(2) may take any other action necessary to wind up the affairs of the Office of Thrift Supervision.

(b) STATUS OF DIRECTOR

(1) IN GENERAL

Notwithstanding the transfer of functions under this subtitle, during the 90–day period beginning on the transfer date, the Director of the Office of Thrift Supervision shall retain and may exercise any authority vested in the Director of the Office of Thrift Supervision on the day before the transfer date, only to the extent necessary—

(A) to wind up the Office of Thrift Supervision; and

(B) to carry out the transfer under this subtitle during such 90–day period.

(2) OTHER PROVISIONS

For purposes of paragraph (1), the Director of the Office of Thrift Supervision shall, during the 90–day period beginning on the transfer date, continue to be—

(A) treated as an officer of the United States; and

(B) entitled to receive compensation at the same annual rate of basic pay that the Director of the Office of Thrift Supervision received on the day before the transfer date.

§ 326. Continuation of Services

Any agency, department, or other instrumentality of the United States, and any successor to any such agency, department, or instrumentality, that was, before the transfer date, providing support services to the Office of Thrift Supervision in connection with functions transferred to the Office of the Comptroller of the Currency, the Corporation or the Board of Governors under this title, shall—

(1) continue to provide such services, subject to reimbursement by the Office of the Comptroller of the Currency, the Corporation, or the Board of Governors, until the transfer of functions under this title is complete; and

(2) consult with the Comptroller of the Currency, the Chairperson of the Corporation, or the Chairman of the Board of Governors, as appropriate, to coordinate and facilitate a prompt and orderly transition.

§ 327. Implementation Plan and Reports

(a) PLAN SUBMISSION

Within 180 days of the enactment of the Dodd–Frank Wall Street Reform and Consumer Protection Act, the Board of Governors, the Corporation, the Office of the Comptroller of the Currency, and the Office of Thrift Supervision, shall jointly submit a plan to the Committee on Banking, Housing, and Urban Affairs of the Senate, the Committee on Financial Services of the House of Representatives, and the Inspectors General of the Department of the Treasury, the Corporation, and the Board of Governors detailing the steps the Board of Governors, the Corporation, the Office of the Comptroller of the Currency, and the Office of Thrift Supervision will take to implement the provisions of sections 301 through 326, and the provisions of the amendments made by such sections.

(b) INSPECTORS GENERAL REVIEW OF THE PLAN

Within 60 days of receiving the plan required under subsection (a), the Inspectors General of the Department of the Treasury, the Corporation, and the Board of Governors shall jointly provide a written report to the Board of Governors, the Corporation, the Office of the Comptroller of the Currency, and the Office of Thrift Supervision and shall submit a copy to the Committee on Banking, Housing, and Urban Affairs of the Senate and the Committee on Financial Services of the House of Representatives detailing whether the plan conforms with the provisions of sections 301 through 326, and the provisions of the amendments made by such sections, including—

(1) whether the plan sufficiently takes into consideration the orderly transfer of personnel;

(2) whether the plan describes procedures and safeguards to ensure that the Office of Thrift Supervision employees are not unfairly disadvantaged relative to employees of the Office of the Comptroller of the Currency and the Corporation;

(3) whether the plan sufficiently takes into consideration the orderly transfer of authority and responsibilities;

(4) whether the plan sufficiently takes into consideration the effective transfer of funds;

(5) whether the plan sufficiently takes in consideration the orderly transfer of property; and

(6) any additional recommendations for an orderly and effective process.

(c) IMPLEMENTATION REPORTS

Not later than 6 months after the date on which the Committee on Banking, Housing, and Urban Affairs of the Senate and the Committee on Financial Services of the House of Representatives receives the report required under subsection (b), and every 6 months thereafter until all aspects of the plan have been implemented, the Inspectors General of the Department of the Treasury, the Corporation, and the Board of Governors shall jointly provide a written report on the status of the implementation of the plan to the Board of Governors, the Corporation, the Office of the Comptroller of the Currency, and the Office of Thrift Supervision and shall submit a copy to the Committee on Banking, Housing, and Urban Affairs of the Senate and the Committee on Financial Services of the House of Representatives.

Subtitle C—Federal Deposit Insurance Corporation

§ 331. Deposit Insurance Reforms

(a) SIZE DISTINCTIONS

Section 7(b)(2) of the Federal Deposit Insurance Act (12 U.S.C. 1817(b)(2)) is amended—

(1) by striking subparagraph (D); and

(2) by redesignating subparagraph (C) as subparagraph (D).

(b) ASSESSMENT BASE

The Corporation shall amend the regulations issued by the Corporation under section 7(b)(2) of the Federal Deposit Insurance Act (12 U.S.C. 1817(b)(2)) to define the term "assessment base" with respect to an insured depository institution for purposes of that section 7(b)(2), as an amount equal to—

(1) the average consolidated total assets of the insured depository institution during the assessment period; minus

(2) the sum of—(A) the average tangible equity of the insured depository institution during the assessment period; and (B) in the case of an insured depository institution that is a custodial bank (as defined by the Corporation, based on factors including the percentage of total revenues generated by custodial businesses and the level of assets under custody) or a banker's bank (as that term is used in section 5136 of the Revised Statutes (12 U.S.C. 24)), an amount that the Corporation determines is necessary to establish assessments consistent with the definition under section 7(b)(1) of the Federal Deposit Insurance Act (12 U.S.C. 1817(b)(1)) for a custodial bank or a banker's bank.

§ 332. Elimination of Procyclical Assessments

Section 7(e) of the Federal Deposit Insurance Act is amended—(1) in paragraph (2)—

(A) by amending subparagraph (B) to read as follows:

"(B) LIMITATION

The Board of Directors may, in its sole discretion, suspend or limit the declaration of payment of dividends under subparagraph (A).";

(B) by amending subparagraph (C) to read as follows:

"(C) NOTICE AND OPPORTUNITY FOR COMMENT.—The Corporation shall prescribe, by regulation, after notice and opportunity for comment, the method for the declaration, calculation, distribution, and payment of dividends under this paragraph"; and

(C) by striking subparagraphs (D) through (G); and (2) in paragraph (4)(A) by striking "paragraphs (2)(D) and" and inserting "paragraphs (2) and".

§ 333. Enhanced Access to Information for Deposit Insurance Purposes

(a) Section 7(a)(2)(B) of the Federal Deposit Insurance Act is amended by striking "agreement" and inserting "consultation".

(b) Section 7(b)(1)(E) of the Federal Deposit Insurance Act is amended—

(1) in clause (i), by striking "such as" and inserting "including"; and

(2) in clause (iii), by striking "Corporation" and inserting "Corporation, except as provided in section 7(a)(2)(B)".

§ 334. Transition Reserve Ratio Requirements to Reflect New Assessment Base

(a) Section 7(b)(3)(B) of the Federal Deposit Insurance Act is amended to read as follows:

"(B) MINIMUM RESERVE RATIO.—The reserve ratio designated by the Board of Directors for any year may not be less than 1.35 percent of estimated insured deposits, or the comparable percentage of the assessment base set forth in paragraph (2)(C)."

(b) Section 3(y)(3) of the Federal Deposit Insurance Act is amended by inserting ", or such comparable percentage of the assessment base set forth in section 7(b)(2)(C)" before the period.

(c) For a period of not less than 5 years after the date of the enactment of this title, the Federal Deposit Insurance Corporation shall make available to the public the reserve ratio and the designated reserve ratio using both estimated insured deposits and the assessment base under section 7(b)(2)(C) of the Federal Deposit Insurance Act.

(d) RESERVE RATIO

Notwithstanding the timing requirements of section 7(b)(3)(E)(ii) of the Federal Deposit Insurance Act, the Corporation shall take such steps as may be necessary for the reserve ratio of the Deposit Insurance Fund to reach 1.35 percent of estimated insured deposits by September 30, 2020.

(e) OFFSET

In setting the assessments necessary to meet the requirements of subsection (d), the Corporation shall offset the effect of subsection (d) on insured depository institutions with total consolidated assets of less than $10,000,000,000.

§ 335. Permanent Increase in Deposit and Share Insurance

(a) PERMANENT INCREASE IN DEPOSIT INSURANCE

Section 11(a)(1)(E) of the Federal Deposit Insurance Act (12 U.S.C. 1821(a)(1)(E)) is amended—

(1) by striking "$100,000" and inserting "$250,000"; and

(2) by adding at the end the following new sentences: "Notwithstanding any other provision of law, the increase in the standard maximum deposit insurance amount to $250,000 shall apply to depositors in any institution for which the Corporation was appointed as receiver or conservator on or after January 1, 2008, and before October 3, 2008. The Corporation shall take such actions as are necessary to carry out the requirements of this section with respect to such depositors, without regard to any time limitations under this Act. In implementing this and the preceding 2 sentences, any payment on a deposit claim made by the Corporation as receiver or conservator to a depositor above the standard maximum deposit insurance amount in effect at the time of the appointment of the Corporation as receiver or conservator shall be deemed to be part of the net amount due to the depositor under subparagraph (B)."

(b) PERMANENT INCREASE IN SHARE INSURANCE

Section 207(k)(5) of the Federal Credit Union Act (12 U.S.C. 1787(k)(5)) is amended by striking "$100,000" and inserting "$250,000".

§ 336. Management of the Federal Deposit Insurance Corporation

(a) IN GENERAL

Section 2 of the Federal Deposit Insurance Act (12 U.S.C. 1812) is amended—

(1) in subsection (a)(1)(B), by striking "Director of the Office of Thrift Supervision" and

inserting "Director of the Consumer Financial Protection Bureau";

(2) by amending subsection (d)(2) to read as follows: "(2) ACTING OFFICIALS MAY SERVE.—In the event of a vacancy in the office of the Comptroller of the Currency or the office of Director of the Consumer Financial Protection Bureau and pending the appointment of a successor, or during the absence or disability of the Comptroller of the Currency or the Director of the Consumer Financial Protection Bureau, the acting Comptroller of the Currency or the acting Director of the Consumer Financial Protection Bureau, as the case may be, shall be a member of the Board of Directors in the place of the Comptroller or Director."; and

(3) in subsection (f)(2), by striking "Office of Thrift Supervision" and inserting "Consumer Financial Protection Bureau".

(b) EFFECTIVE DATE

This section, and the amendments made by this section, shall take effect on the transfer date.

Subtitle D—Other Matters

§ 341. Branching

Notwithstanding the Federal Deposit Insurance Act (12 U.S.C. 1811 et seq.), the Bank Holding Company Act of 1956 (12 U.S.C. 1841 et seq.), or any other provision of Federal or State law, a savings association that becomes a bank may—

(1) continue to operate any branch or agency that the savings association operated immediately before the savings association became a bank; and

(2) establish, acquire, and operate additional branches and agencies at any location within any State in which the savings association operated a branch immediately before the savings association became a bank, if the law of the State in which the branch is located, or is to be located, would permit establishment of the branch if the bank were a State bank chartered by such State.

§ 342. Office of Minority and Women Inclusion

(a) OFFICE OF MINORITY AND WOMEN INCLUSION

(1) ESTABLISHMENT

(A) IN GENERAL

Except as provided in subparagraph (B), not later than 6 months after the date of enactment of this Act, each agency shall establish an Office of Minority and Women Inclusion that shall be responsible for all matters of the agency relating to diversity in management, employment, and business activities.

(B) BUREAU

The Bureau shall establish an Office of Minority and Women Inclusion not later than 6 months after the designated transfer date established under section 1062.

(2) TRANSFER OF RESPONSIBILITIES

Each agency that, on the day before the date of enactment of this Act, assigned the responsibilities described in paragraph (1) (or comparable responsibilities) to another office of the agency shall ensure that such responsibilities are transferred to the Office.

(3) DUTIES WITH RESPECT TO CIVIL RIGHTS LAWS

The responsibilities described in paragraph (1) do not include enforcement of statutes, regulations, or executive orders pertaining to civil rights, except each Director shall coordinate with the agency administrator, or the designee of the agency administrator, regarding the design and implementation of any remedies resulting from violations of such statutes, regulations, or executive orders.

(b) DIRECTOR

(1) IN GENERAL

The Director of each Office shall be appointed by, and shall report to, the agency administrator. The position of Director shall be a career reserved position in the Senior Executive Service, as that position is defined in section 3132 of title 5, United States Code, or an equivalent designation.

(2) DUTIES

Each Director shall develop standards for—

(A) equal employment opportunity and the racial, ethnic, and gender diversity of the workforce and senior management of the agency;

(B) increased participation of minority-owned and women-owned businesses in the programs and contracts of the agency, including standards for coordinating technical assistance to such businesses; and

(C) assessing the diversity policies and practices of entities regulated by the agency.

(3) OTHER DUTIES

Each Director shall advise the agency administrator on the impact of the policies and regulations of the agency on minority-owned and women-owned businesses.

(4) RULE OF CONSTRUCTION

Nothing in paragraph (2)(C) may be construed to mandate any requirement on or otherwise affect the lending policies and practices of any regulated entity, or to require any specific action based on the findings of the assessment.

(c) INCLUSION IN ALL LEVELS OF BUSINESS ACTIVITIES

(1) IN GENERAL

The Director of each Office shall develop and implement standards and procedures to ensure, to the maximum extent possible, the fair inclusion and utilization of minorities, women, and minority-owned and women-owned businesses in all business and activities of the agency at all levels, including in procurement, insurance, and all types of contracts.

(2) CONTRACTS

The procedures established by each agency for review and evaluation of contract proposals and for hiring service providers shall include, to the extent consistent with applicable law, a component that gives consideration to the diversity of the applicant. Such procedure shall include a written statement, in a form and with such content as the Director shall prescribe, that a contractor shall ensure, to the maximum extent possible, the fair inclusion of women and minorities in the workforce of the contractor and, as applicable, subcontractors.

(3) TERMINATION

(A) DETERMINATION

The standards and procedures developed and implemented under this subsection shall include a procedure for the Director to make a determination whether an agency contractor, and, as applicable, a subcontractor has failed to make a good faith effort to include minorities and women in their workforce.

(B) EFFECT OF DETERMINATION

(i) RECOMMENDATION TO AGENCY ADMINISTRATOR

Upon a determination described in subparagraph (A), the Director shall make a recommendation to the agency administrator that the contract be terminated.

(ii) ACTION BY AGENCY ADMINISTRATOR

Upon receipt of a recommendation under clause (i), the agency administrator may—

(I) terminate the contract;

(II) make a referral to the Office of Federal Contract Compliance Programs of the Department of Labor; or

(III) take other appropriate action.

(d) APPLICABILITY

This section shall apply to all contracts of an agency for services of any kind, including the services of financial institutions, investment banking firms, mortgage banking firms, asset management firms, brokers, dealers, financial services entities, underwriters, accountants, investment consultants, and providers of legal services. The contracts referred to in this subsection include all contracts for all business and activities of an agency, at all levels, including contracts for the issuance or guarantee of any debt, equity, or security, the sale of assets, the management of the assets of the agency, the making of equity investments by the agency, and the implementation by the agency of programs to address economic recovery.

(e) REPORTS

Each Office shall submit to Congress an annual report regarding the actions taken by the agency and the Office pursuant to this section, which shall include—

(1) a statement of the total amounts paid by the agency to contractors since the previous report;

(2) the percentage of the amounts described in paragraph (1) that were paid to contractors described in subsection (c)(1);

(3) the successes achieved and challenges faced by the agency in operating minority and women outreach programs;

(4) the challenges the agency may face in hiring qualified minority and women employees and contracting with qualified minority-owned and women-owned businesses; and

(5) any other information, findings, conclusions, and recommendations for legislative or agency action, as the Director determines appropriate.

(f) DIVERSITY IN AGENCY WORKFORCE

Each agency shall take affirmative steps to seek diversity in the workforce of the agency at all levels of the agency in a manner consistent with applicable law. Such steps shall include—

(1) recruiting at historically black colleges and universities, Hispanic-serving institutions, women's colleges, and colleges that typically serve majority minority populations;

(2) sponsoring and recruiting at job fairs in urban communities;

(3) placing employment advertisements in newspapers and magazines oriented toward minorities and women;

(4) partnering with organizations that are focused on developing opportunities for minorities and women to place talented young minorities and women in industry internships, summer employment, and full-time positions;

(5) where feasible, partnering with inner-city high schools, girls' high schools, and high schools with majority minority populations to establish or enhance financial literacy programs and provide mentoring; and

(6) any other mass media communications that the Office determines necessary.

(g) DEFINITIONS

For purposes of this section, the following definitions shall apply:

(1) AGENCY

The term "agency" means—

(A) the Departmental Offices of the Department of the Treasury;

(B) the Corporation;

(C) the Federal Housing Finance Agency;

(D) each of the Federal reserve banks;

(E) the Board;

(F) the National Credit Union Administration;

(G) the Office of the Comptroller of the Currency;

(H) the Commission; and

(I) the Bureau.

(2) AGENCY ADMINISTRATOR

The term "agency administrator" means the head of an agency.

(3) MINORITY

The term "minority" has the same meaning as in section 1204(c) of the Financial Institutions Reform, Recovery, and Enforcement Act of 1989 (12 U.S.C. 1811 note).

(4) MINORITY–OWNED BUSINESS

The term "minority-owned business" has the same meaning as in section 21A(r)(4)(A) of the Federal Home Loan Bank Act (12 U.S.C. 1441a(r)(4)(A)), as in effect on the day before the transfer date.

(5) OFFICE

The term "Office" means the Office of Minority and Women Inclusion established by an agency under subsection (a).

(6) WOMEN–OWNED BUSINESS

The term "women-owned business" has the meaning given the term "women's business" in section 21A(r)(4)(B) of the Federal Home Loan Bank Act (12 U.S.C. 1441a(r)(4)(B)), as in effect on the day before the transfer date.

§ 343. Insurance of Transaction Accounts

(a) BANKS AND SAVINGS ASSOCIATIONS

(1) AMENDMENTS

Section 11(a)(1) of the Federal Deposit Insurance Act (12 U.S.C. 1821(a)(1)) is amended—

(A) in subparagraph (B)—

(i) by striking "The net amount" and inserting the following:

"(i) IN GENERAL

Subject to clause (ii), the net amount"; and

(ii) by adding at the end the following new clauses:

"(ii) INSURANCE FOR NONINTEREST-BEARING TRANSACTION ACCOUNTS

Notwithstanding clause (i), the Corporation shall fully insure the net amount that any depositor at an insured depository institution maintains in a noninterest-bearing transaction account. Such amount shall not be taken into account when computing the net amount due to such depositor under clause (i).

"(iii) NONINTEREST–BEARING TRANSACTION ACCOUNT DEFINED

For purposes of this subparagraph, the term 'noninterest-bearing transaction account' means a deposit or account maintained at an insured depository institution—

"(I) with respect to which interest is neither accrued nor paid;

"(II) on which the depositor or account holder is permitted to make withdrawals by negotiable or transferable instrument, payment orders of withdrawal, telephone or other electronic media transfers, or other similar items for the purpose of making payments or transfers to third parties or others; and

"(III) on which the insured depository institution does not reserve the right to require advance notice of an intended withdrawal."; and (B) in subparagraph (C), by striking "subparagraph (B)" and inserting "subparagraph (B)(i)".

(2) EFFECTIVE DATE

The amendments made by paragraph (1) shall take effect on December 31, 2010.

(3) PROSPECTIVE REPEAL

Effective January 1, 2013, section 11(a)(1) of the Federal Deposit Insurance Act (12 U.S.C. 1821(a)(1)), as amended by paragraph (1), is amended—(A) in subparagraph (B)—

(i) by striking "DEPOSIT.—" and all that follows through "clause (ii), the net amount" and insert "DEPOSIT.—The net amount"; and

(ii) by striking clauses (ii) and (iii); and (B) in subparagraph (C), by striking "subparagraph (B)(i)" and inserting "subparagraph (B)".

(b) CREDIT UNIONS

(1) AMENDMENTS

Section 207(k)(1) of the Federal Credit Union Act (12 U.S.C. 1787(k)(1)) is amended—(A) in subparagraph (A)—

(i) by striking "Subject to the provisions of paragraph (2), the net amount" and inserting the following:

"(i) NET AMOUNT OF INSURANCE PAYABLE.—Subject to clause (ii) and the provisions of paragraph (2), the net amount"; and

(ii) by adding at the end the following new clauses:

"(ii) INSURANCE FOR NONINTEREST–BEARING TRANSACTION ACCOUNTS.— Notwithstanding clause (i), the Board shall fully insure the net amount that any member or depositor at an insured credit union maintains in a noninterest-bearing transaction account. Such amount shall not be taken into account when computing the net amount due to such member or depositor under clause (i).

"(iii) NONINTEREST–BEARING TRANSACTION ACCOUNT DEFINED

For purposes of this subparagraph, the term 'noninterest-bearing transaction account' means an account or deposit maintained at an insured credit union—

"(I) with respect to which interest is neither accrued nor paid;

"(II) on which the account holder or depositor is permitted to make withdrawals by negotiable or transferable instrument, payment orders of withdrawal, telephone or other electronic media transfers, or other similar items for the purpose of making payments or transfers to third parties or others; and

"(III) on which the insured credit union does not reserve the right to require advance notice of an intended withdrawal."; and (B) in subparagraph (B), by striking "subparagraph (A)" and inserting "subparagraph (A)(i)".

(2) EFFECTIVE DATE

The amendments made by paragraph (1) shall take effect upon the date of the enactment of this Act

(3) PROSPECTIVE REPEAL

Effective January 1, 2013, section 207(k)(1) of the Federal Credit Union Act (12 U.S.C. 1787(k)(1)), as amended by paragraph (1), is amended—(A) in subparagraph (A)—

(i) by striking "(i) NET AMOUNT OF INSURANCE PAYABLE.—" and all that follows through "paragraph (2), the net amount" and inserting "Subject to the provisions of paragraph (2), the net amount"; and

(ii) by striking clauses (ii) and (iii); and (B) in subparagraph (B), by striking "subparagraph (A)(i)" and inserting "subparagraph (A)".

Subtitle E—Technical and Conforming Amendments

§ 351. Effective Date

Except as provided in section 364(a), the amendments made by this subtitle shall take effect on the transfer date.

§ 352. Balanced Budget and Emergency Deficit Control Act of 1985

Section 256(h) of the Balanced Budget and Emergency Deficit Control Act of 1985 (2 U.S.C. 906(h)) is amended—

(1) in paragraph (4), by striking subparagraphs (C) and (G); and

(2) by redesignating subparagraphs (D), (E), (F), and (H) as subparagraphs (C), (D), (E), and (F), respectively.

§ 353. Bank Enterprise Act of 1991

Section 232(a) of the Bank Enterprise Act of 1991 (12 U.S.C. 1834(a)) is amended—

(1) in the subsection heading, by striking "BY FEDERAL RESERVE BOARD";

(2) in paragraph (1)

(A) by striking "The Board of Governors of the Federal Reserve System," and inserting "The Comptroller of the Currency"; and

(B) by striking "section 7(b)(2)(H)" and inserting "section 7(b)(2)(E)";

(3) in paragraph (2)(A), by striking "Board" and inserting "Comptroller"; and

(4) in paragraph (3)

(A) by redesignating subparagraphs (A) through (C) as subparagraphs (B) through (D), respectively; and

(B) by inserting before subparagraph (B) the following: "(A) COMPTROLLER.—The term 'Comptroller' means the Comptroller of the Currency.".

§ 354. Bank Holding Company Act of 1956

The Bank Holding Company Act of 1956 (12 U.S.C. 1841 et seq.) is amended—

(1) in section 2(j)(3) (12 U.S.C. 1841(j)(3)), strike "Director of the Office of Thrift Supervision" and inserting "appropriate Federal banking agency";

(2) in section 4 (12 U.S.C. 1843) (A) in subsection (i)—

(i) in paragraph (4)—

(I) in subparagraph (A)—

(aa) in the subparagraph heading, by striking "TO DIRECTOR"; and

(bb) by striking "Board" and all that follows through the end of the subparagraph and inserting "Board shall solicit comments and recommendations from—"(i) the Comptroller of the Currency, with respect to the acquisition of a Federal savings association; and "(ii) the Federal Deposit Insurance Corporation, with respect to the acquisition of a State savings association.".

(II) in subparagraph (B), by striking "Director" each place that term appears and inserting "Comptroller of the Currency or the Federal Deposit Insurance Corporation, as applicable,";

(ii) in paragraph (5)—

(I) in subparagraph (B), by striking "Director with" and inserting "Comptroller of the Currency or the Federal Deposit Insurance Corporation, as applicable, with"; and

(II) by striking "Director" each place that term appears and inserting "Comptroller of the Currency or the Federal Deposit Insurance Corporation";

(iii) in paragraph (6), by striking "Director" and inserting "Comptroller of the Currency or the Federal Deposit Insurance Corporation, as applicable,"; and

(iv) by striking paragraph (7); and

(3) in section 5(f) (12 U.S.C. 1844(f))—

(A) by striking "subpena" each place that term appears and inserting "subpoena";

(B) by striking "subpenas" each place that term appears and inserting "subpoenas"; and

(C) by striking "subpenaed" and inserting "subpoenaed".

§ 355. Bank Holding Company Act Amendments of 1970

Section 106(b)(1) of the Bank Holding Company Act Amendments of 1970 (12 U.S.C. 1972(1)) is amended in the undesignated matter following subparagraph (E) by inserting "issue such regulations as are necessary to carry out this section, and, in consultation with the Comptroller of the Currency and the Federal Deposit Insurance Company, may" after "The Board may".

§ 356. Bank Protection Act of 1968

The Bank Protection Act of 1968 (12 U.S.C. 1881 et seq.) is amended—

(1) in section 2 (12 U.S.C. 1881), by striking "the term" and all that follows through the end of the section and inserting "the term 'Federal supervisory agency' means the appropriate Federal banking agency, as defined in section 3(q) of the Federal Deposit Insurance Act (12 U.S.C. 1813(q)).";

(2) in section 3 (12 U.S.C. 1882), by striking "and loan" each place that term appears; and

(3) in section 5 (12 U.S.C. 1884), by striking "and loan".

§ 357. Bank Service Company Act

The Bank Service Company Act (12 U.S.C. 1861 et seq.) is amended—

(1) in section 1(b)(4) (12 U.S.C. 1861(b)(4))—

(A) by inserting after "an insured bank," the following: "a savings association,";

(B) by striking "Director of the Office of Thrift Supervision" and inserting "appropriate Federal banking agency"; and

(C) by striking ", the Federal Savings and Loan Insurance Corporation,";

(2) in section1(b)(5), by striking "term 'insured depository institution' has the same meaning as in section 3(c)" and inserting "terms 'depository institution' and 'savings association' have the same meanings as in section 3"; and

(3) in section 7(c)(2) (12 U.S.C. 1867(c)(2)), by inserting "each" after "notify".

§ 358. Community Reinvestment Act of 1977

The Community Reinvestment Act of 1977 (12 U.S.C. 2901 et seq.) is amended—

(1) in section 803 (12 U.S.C. 2902)—

(A) in paragraph (1)—

(i) in subparagraph (A), by inserting "and Federal savings associations (the deposits of which are insured by the Federal Deposit Insurance Corporation)" after "banks";

(ii) in subparagraph (B), by striking "and bank holding companies" and inserting ", bank holding companies, and savings and loan holding companies"; and

(iii) in subparagraph (C), by striking "; and" and inserting ", and State savings associations (the deposits of which are insured by the Federal Deposit Insurance Corporation).."; and

(B) by striking paragraph (2) (relating to the Office of Thrift Supervision), as added by section 744(q) of the Financial Institutions Reform, Recovery, and Enforcement Act of 1989 (Public Law 101–73; 103 Stat. 440); and

(2) in section 806 (12 U.S.C. 2905), by inserting ", except that the Comptroller of the Currency shall prescribe regulations applicable to savings associations and the Board of Governors shall prescribe regulations applicable to insured State member banks, bank holding companies and savings and loan holding companies," after "supervisory agency".

§ 359. Crime Control Act of 1990

The Crime Control Act of 1990 is amended—

(1) in section 2539(c)(2) (28 U.S.C. 509 note)—

(A) by striking subparagraphs (C) and (D); and

(B) by redesignating subparagraphs (E) through (H) as subparagraphs (C) through (G), respectively; and

(2) in section 2554(b)(2) (Public Law 101–647; 104 Stat. 4890)—

(A) in subparagraph (A), by striking ", the Director of the Office of Thrift Supervision," and inserting "the Comptroller of the Currency"; and

(B) in subparagraph (B), by striking ", the Director" and all that follows through

"Trust Corporation" and inserting "or the Federal Deposit Insurance Corporation".

§ 360. Depository Institution Management Interlocks Act

The Depository Institution Management Interlocks Act (12 U.S.C. 3201 et seq.) is amended—

(1) in section 207 (12 U.S.C. 3206)—

(A) in paragraph (1), by inserting before the comma at the end the following: "and Federal savings associations (the deposits of which are insured by the Federal Deposit Insurance Corporation)";

(B) in paragraph (2), by striking ", and bank holding companies" and inserting ", bank holding companies, and savings and loan holding companies";

(C) in paragraph (3), by striking "Corporation," and inserting "Corporation and State savings associations (the deposits of which are insured by the Federal Deposit Insurance Corporation),";

(D) by striking paragraph (4);

(E) by redesignating paragraphs (5) and (6) as paragraphs (4) and (5), respectively; and

(F) in paragraph (5), as so redesignated, by striking "through (5)" and inserting "through (4)";

(2) in section 209 (12 U.S.C. 3207)—

(A) in paragraph (1), by inserting before the comma at the end the following: "and Federal savings associations (the deposits of which are insured by the Federal Deposit Insurance Corporation)";

(B) in paragraph (2), by striking ", and bank holding companies" and inserting ", bank holding companies, and savings and loan holding companies";

(C) in paragraph (3), by striking "Corporation," and inserting "Corporation and State savings associations (the deposits of which are insured by the Federal Deposit Insurance Corporation),";

(D) by striking paragraph (4); and

(E) by redesignating paragraph (5) as paragraph (4); and

(3) in section 210(a) (12 U.S.C. 3208(a))—

(A) by striking "his" and inserting "the"; and

(B) by inserting "of the Attorney General" after "enforcement functions".

§ 361. Emergency Homeowners' Relief Act

Section 110 of the Emergency Homeowners' Relief Act (12 U.S.C. 2709) is amended in the second sentence, by striking "Home Loan Bank Board, the Federal Savings and Loan Insurance Corporation" and inserting "Housing Finance Agency".

§ 362. Federal Credit Union Act

The Federal Credit Union Act (12 U.S.C. 1751 et seq.) is amended—

(1) in section 107(8) (12 U.S.C. 1757(8)), by striking "or the Federal Savings and Loan Insurance Corporation";

(2) in section 205 (12 U.S.C. 1785)—

(A) in subsection (b)(2)(G)(i), by striking "the Office of Thrift Supervision and"; and

(B) in subsection (i)(1), by striking "or the Federal Savings and Loan Insurance Corporation"; and

(3) in section 206(g)(7) (12 U.S.C. 1786(g)(7))—

(A) in subparagraph (A)—

(i) in clause (ii), by striking "(b)(8)" and inserting "(b)(9)";

(ii) in clause (v)—

(I) by striking "depository" and inserting "financial"; and

(II) by adding "and" at the end;

(iii) in clause (vi)—

(I) by striking "Board" and inserting "Agency"; and

(II) by striking "; and" and inserting a period; and

(iv) by striking clause (vii); and (B) in subparagraph (D)—(i) in clause (iii), by adding "and" at the end; (ii) in clause (iv)—

(I) by striking "Board" and inserting "Agency"; and

(II) by striking "and" at the end; and (iii) by striking clause (v).

§ 363. Federal Deposit Insurance Act

The Federal Deposit Insurance Act (12 U.S.C. 1811 et seq.) is amended—

(1) in section 3 (12 U.S.C. 1813)

    (A) in subsection (b)(1)(C), by striking "Director of the Office of Thrift Supervision" and inserting "Comptroller of the Currency";

    (B) in subsection (l)(5), in the matter preceding subparagraph (A), by striking "Director of the Office of Thrift Supervision,"; and

    (C) in subsection (z), by striking "the Director of the Office of Thrift Supervision,";

(2) in section 7 (12 U.S.C. 1817)

    (A) in subsection (a)—

    (i) in paragraph (2)—

    (I) in subparagraph (A)—

    (aa) in the first sentence, by striking "the Director of the Office of Thrift Supervision,";

    (bb) in the second sentence—(AA) by striking "the Director of the Office of Thrift Supervision," and inserting "to"; and

    (BB) by inserting "to" before "any Federal home"; and

    (cc) by striking "Finance Board" each place that term appears and inserting "Finance Agency"; and

    (II) in subparagraph (B), by striking "the Comptroller of the Currency, the Board of Governors of the Federal Reserve System, and the Director of the Office of Thrift Supervision," and inserting "the Comptroller of the Currency and the Board of Governors of the Federal Reserve System,";

    (ii) in paragraph (3), in the first sentence, by striking "Comptroller of the Currency, the Chairman of the Board of Governors of the Federal Reserve System, and the Director of the Office of Thrift Supervision." and inserting "Comptroller of the Currency, and the Chairman of the Board of Governors of the Federal Reserve System.";

    (iii) in paragraph (6), by striking "section 232(a)(3)(C)" and inserting "section 232(a)(3)(D)"; and

    (iv) in paragraph (7), by striking ", the Director of the Office of Thrift Supervision,"; and

    (B) in subsection (n)—

    (i) in the heading, by striking "DIRECTOR OF THE OFFICE OF THRIFT SUPERVISION" and inserting "COMPTROLLER OF THE CURRENCY";

    (ii) in the first sentence—

    (I) by striking "the Director of the Office of Thrift Supervision" and inserting "the Comptroller of the Currency"; and

    (II) by inserting "Federal" before "savings associations";

    (iii) in the third sentence, by striking ", the Financing Corporation, and the Resolution Funding Corporation"; and

    (iv) by striking "the Director" each place that term appears and inserting "the Comptroller";

(3) in section 8 (12 U.S.C. 1818)

    (A) in subsection (a)(8)(B)(ii), in the last sentence, by striking "Director of the Office of Thrift Supervision" each place that term appears and inserting "Comptroller of the Currency";

    (B) in subsection (b)(3)—

    (i) by inserting "any savings and loan holding company and any subsidiary (other than a depository institution) of a savings and loan holding company (as such terms are defined in section 10 of Home Owners' Loan Act), any noninsured State member bank" after "Bank Holding Company Act of 1956,"; and

    (ii) by inserting "or against a savings and loan holding company or any subsidiary thereof (other than a depository institution or a subsidiary of such depository institution)" before the period at the end;

    (C) by striking paragraph (9) of subsection (b) and inserting the following new paragraph: "(9) [Repealed]".

    (D) in subsection (e)(7)—

    (i) in subparagraph (A)—

    (I) in clause (v), by inserting "and" after the semicolon;

    (II) in clause (vi)—

(aa) by striking "Board" and inserting "Agency"; and

(bb) by striking "; and" and inserting a period; and

(III) by striking clause (vii); and

(ii) in subparagraph (D)—

(I) in clause (iii), by inserting "and" after the semicolon;

(II) in clause (iv)—

(aa) by striking "Board" and inserting "Agency"; and

(bb) by striking "; and" and inserting a period; and =

(III) by striking clause (v);

(E) in subsection (j)—

(i) in paragraph (2), by striking ", or as a savings association under subsection (b)(9) of this section";

(ii) in paragraph (3), by inserting "or" after the semicolon;

(iii) in paragraph (4), by striking "; or" and inserting a comma; and

(iv) by striking paragraph (5);

(F) in subsection (o), by striking "Director of the Office of Thrift Supervision" and inserting "Comptroller of the Currency"; and

(G) in subsection (w)(3)(A), by striking "and the Office of Thrift Supervision";

(4) in section 10 (12 U.S.C. 1820)

(A) in subsection (d)(5), by striking "or the Resolution Trust Corporation" each place that term appears; and

(B) in subsection (k)(5)(B)—

(i) in clause (ii), by inserting "and" after the semicolon;

(ii) in clause (iii), by striking "; and" and inserting a period; and

(iii) by striking clause (iv);

(5) in section 11 (12 U.S.C. 1821)

(A) in subsection (c)—

(i) in paragraph (2)(A)(ii), by striking "(other than section 21A of the Federal Home Loan Bank Act)";

(ii) in paragraph (4), by striking "Except as otherwise provided in section 21A of the

Federal Home Loan Bank Act and notwithstanding" and inserting "Notwithstanding";

(iii) in paragraph (6)—

(I) in the heading, by striking "DIRECTOR OF THE OFFICE OF THRIFT SUPERVISION" and inserting "COMPTROLLER OF THE CURRENCY";

(II) in subparagraph (A)—

(aa) by striking "or the Resolution Trust Corporation"; and

(bb) by striking "Director of the Office of Thrift Supervision" and inserting "Comptroller of the Currency"; and

(III) by amending subparagraph (B) to read as follows: "(B) RECEIVER.—The Corporation may, at the discretion of the Comptroller of the Currency, be appointed receiver and the Corporation may accept any such appointment.";

(iv) in paragraph (12)(A), by striking "or the Resolution Trust Corporation";

(B) in subsection (d)—

(i) in paragraph (17)(A), by striking "or the Director of the Office of Thrift Supervision"; and

(ii) in paragraph (18)(B), by striking "or the Director of the Office of Thrift Supervision";

(C) in subsection (m)—

(i) in paragraph (9), by striking "or the Director of the Office of Thrift Supervision, as appropriate";

(ii) in paragraph (16), by striking "or the Director of the Office of Thrift Supervision, as appropriate" each place that term appears; and

(iii) in paragraph (18), by striking "or the Director of the Office of Thrift Supervision, as appropriate" each place that term appears;

(D) in subsection (n)—

(i) in paragraph (1)(A)—

(I) by striking ", or the Director of the Office of Thrift Supervision, with respect to" and inserting "or"; and

(II) by striking "applicable,," and inserting "applicable,";

(ii) in paragraph (2)(A), by striking "or the Director of the Office of Thrift Supervision";

(iii) in paragraph (4)(D), by striking "and the Director of the Office of Thrift Supervision, as appropriate,";

(iv) in paragraph (4)(G), by striking "and the Director of the Office of Thrift Supervision, as appropriate,"; and

(v) in paragraph (12)(B)—

(I) by inserting "as" after "shall appoint the Corporation";

(II) by striking "or the Director of the Office of Thrift Supervision, as appropriate," each place such term appears;

(E) in subsection (p)—

(i) in paragraph (2)(B), by striking "the Corporation, the FSLIC Resolution Fund, or the Resolution Trust Corporation," and inserting "or the Corporation,"; and

(ii) in paragraph (3)(B), by striking ", the FSLIC Resolution Fund, the Resolution Trust Corporation,"; and

(F) in subsection (r), by striking "and the Resolution Trust Corporation";

(6) in section 13(k)(1)(A)(iv) (12 U.S.C. 1823(k)(1)(A)(iv)), by striking "Director of the Office of Thrift Supervision" and inserting "Comptroller of the Currency";

(7) in section 18 (12 U.S.C. 1828)

(A) in subsection (c)(2)—

(i) in subparagraph (A), by inserting "or a Federal savings association" before the semicolon;

(ii) in subparagraph (B), by adding "and" at the end;

(iii) in subparagraph (C), by striking "(except" and all that follows through "; and" and inserting "or a State savings association."; and

(iv) by striking subparagraph (D);

(B) in subsection (g)(1), by striking "the Director of the Office of Thrift Supervision"and inserting "the Comptroller of the Currency";

(C) in subsection (i)(2)(C), by striking "Director of the Office of Thrift Supervision" and inserting "Corporation"; and

(D) in subsection (m)—

(i) in paragraph (1)—

(I) in subparagraph (A), by striking "and the Director of the Office of Thrift Supervision" and inserting "or the Comptroller of the Currency, as appropriate,"; and

(II) in subparagraph (B), by striking "and orders of the Director of the Office of Thrift Supervision" and inserting "of the Comptroller of the Currency and orders of the Corporation and the Comptroller of the Currency";

(ii) in paragraph (2)—

(I) in subparagraph (A), by striking "Director of the Office of Thrift Supervision" and inserting "Comptroller of the Currency, as appropriate,"; and

(II) in subparagraph (B)—

(aa) in the matter before clause (i), by striking "Director of the Office of Thrift Supervision" and inserting "Corporation or the Comptroller of the Currency, as appropriate,"; and

(bb) in the matter following clause (ii)—

(AA) in the first sentence, by striking "Director of the Office of Thrift Supervision" and inserting "Office of the Comptroller of the Currency, as appropriate,"; and

(BB) by striking the second sentence and inserting the following: "The Corporation or the Comptroller of the Currency, as appropriate, may take any other corrective measures with respect to the subsidiary, including the authority to require the subsidiary to terminate the activities or operations posing such risks, as the Corporation or the Comptroller of the Currency, respectively, may deem appropriate."; and

(iii) in paragraph (3)—

(I) in subparagraph (A), in the second sentence—

(aa) by inserting ", in the case of a Federal savings association," before "consult with"; and

(bb) by striking "Director of the Office of Thrift Supervision" and inserting "Comptroller of the Currency"; and

(II) in subparagraph (B)—

(aa) in the subparagraph heading, by striking "DIRECTOR" and inserting "COMPTROLLER OF THE CURRENCY";

(bb) by striking "Office of Thrift Supervision" and inserting "Comptroller of the Currency";

(cc) by inserting a comma after "soundness"; and

(dd) by inserting "as to Federal savings associations" after "compliance";

(8) in section 19(e) (12 U.S.C. 1829(e))

(A) in paragraph (1), by striking "Director of the Office of Thrift Supervision" and inserting "Board of Governors of the Federal Reserve System"; and

(B) in paragraph (2), by striking "Director of the Office of Thrift Supervision" and inserting "Board of Governors of the Federal Reserve System";

(9) in section 28 (12 U.S.C. 1831e)

(A) in subsection (e)—

(i) in paragraph (2)—

(I) in subparagraph (A)(ii), by striking "Director of the Office of Thrift Supervision" and inserting "Comptroller of the Currency or the Corporation, as appropriate";

(II) in subparagraph (C), by striking "Director of the Office of Thrift Supervision" and inserting "Comptroller of the Currency or the Corporation, as appropriate,"; and

(III) in subparagraph (F), by striking "Director of the Office of Thrift Supervision" and inserting "Comptroller of the Currency or the Corporation, as appropriate"; and

(ii) in paragraph (3)—

(I) in subparagraph (A), by striking "Director of the Office of Thrift Supervision" and inserting "Comptroller of the Currency or the Corporation, as appropriate"; and

(II) in subparagraph (B), by striking "Director of the Office of Thrift Supervision" and inserting "Comptroller of the Currency or the Corporation, as appropriate,"; and

(B) in subsection (h)(2), by striking "Director of the Office of Thrift Supervision" and inserting "Comptroller of the Currency, of the Corporation,"; and

(10) in section 33(e) (12 U.S.C. 1831j(e)), by striking "Federal Housing Finance Board, the Comptroller of the Currency, and the Director of the Office of Thrift Supervision" and inserting "Federal Housing Finance Agency and the Comptroller of the Currency".

§ 364. Federal Home Loan Bank Act

(a) REPEAL OF SECTION 18(c)
Effective 90 days after the transfer date, section 18(c) of the Federal Home Loan Bank Act (12 U.S.C. 1438(c)) is repealed.

(b) REPEAL OF SECTION 21A
Section 21A of the Federal Home Loan Bank Act (12 U.S.C. 1441a) is repealed.

§ 365. Federal Housing Enterprises Financial Safety and Soundness Act of 1992

The Federal Housing Enterprises Financial Safety and Soundness Act of 1992 (12 U.S.C. 4501 et seq.) is amended—

(1) in section 1315(b) (12 U.S.C. 4515(b)), by striking "the Federal Deposit Insurance Corporation, and the Office of Thrift Supervision." and inserting "and the Federal Deposit Insurance Corporation."; and

(2) in section 1317(c) (12 U.S.C. 4517(c)), by striking "the Federal Deposit Insurance Corporation, or the Director of the Office of Thrift Supervision" and inserting "or the Federal Deposit Insurance Corporation".

§ 366. Federal Reserve Act

The Federal Reserve Act (12 U.S.C. 221 et seq.) is amended—

(1) in section 11(a)(2) (12 U.S.C. 248(a)(2))—

(A) by inserting "State savings associations that are insured depository institutions (as defined in section 3 of the Federal Deposit Insurance Act)," after "case of insured";

(B) by striking "Director of the Office of Thrift Supervision" and inserting "Comptroller of the Currency";

(C) by inserting "Federal" before "savings association which"; and

(D) by striking "savings and loan association" and inserting "savings association"; and

(2) in section 19(b) (12 U.S.C. 461(b))—

(A) in paragraph (1)(F), by striking "Director of the Office of Thrift Supervision" and inserting "Comptroller of the Currency"; and

(B) in paragraph (4)(B), by striking "Director of the Office of Thrift Supervision" and inserting "Comptroller of the Currency".

§ 367. Financial Institutions Reform, Recovery, and Enforcement Act of 1989

The Financial Institutions Reform, Recovery, and Enforcement Act of 1989 is amended—

(1) in section 203 (12 U.S.C. 1812 note), by striking subsection (b);

(2) in section 302(1) (12 U.S.C. 1467a note), by striking "Director of the Office of Thrift Supervision" and inserting "Comptroller of the Currency";

(3) in section 305(12 U.S.C. 1464 note), by striking subsection (b);

(4) in section 308 (12 U.S.C. 1463 note)

(A) in subsection (a), by striking "Director of the Office of Thrift Supervision" and inserting "Chairman of the Board of Governors of the Federal Reserve System, the Comptroller of the Currency, the Chairman of the National Credit Union Administration,"; and

(B) by adding at the end the following new subsection: "(c) REPORTS.—The Secretary of the Treasury, the Chairman of the Board of Governors of the Federal Reserve System, the Comptroller of the Currency, the Chairman of the National Credit Union Administration, and the Chairperson of Board of Directors of the Federal Deposit Insurance Corporation shall each submit an annual report to the Congress containing a description of actions taken to carry out this section.";

(5) in section 402 (12 U.S.C. 1437 note)

(A) in subsection (a), by striking "Director of the Office of Thrift Supervision" and inserting "Comptroller of the Currency";

(B) by striking subsection (b);

(C) in subsection (e)—

(i) in paragraph (1), by striking "Office of Thrift Supervision" and inserting "Comptroller of the Currency"; and

(ii) in each of paragraphs (2), (3), and (4), by striking "Director of the Office of Thrift Supervision" each place that term appears and inserting "Comptroller of the Currency"; and

(D) by striking "Federal Housing Finance Board" each place that term appears and inserting "Federal Housing Finance Agency";

(6) in section 1103(a) (12 U.S.C. 3332(a)), by striking "and the Resolution Trust Corporation";

(7) in section 1205(b) (12 U.S.C. 1818 note)

(A) in paragraph (1)—

(i) by striking subparagraph (B); and

(ii) by redesignating subparagraphs (C) through (F) as subparagraphs (B) through (E), respectively; and

(B) in paragraph (2), by striking "paragraph (1)(F)" and inserting "paragraph (1)(E)";

(8) in section 1206 (12 U.S.C. 1833b)

(A) by striking "Board, the Oversight Board of the Resolution Trust Corporation" and inserting "Agency, and"; and

(B) by striking ", and the Office of Thrift Supervision";

(9) in section 1216 (12 U.S.C. 1833e)

(A) in subsection (a)—

(i) in paragraph (3), by adding "and" at the end;

(ii) in paragraph (4), by striking the semicolon at the end and inserting a period;

(iii) by striking paragraphs (2), (5), and (6); and

(iv) by redesignating paragraphs (3) and (4), as paragraphs (2) and (3), respectively;

(B) in subsection (c)—

(i) by striking "the Director of the Office of Thrift Supervision," and inserting "and"; and

(ii) by striking "the Thrift Depositor Protection Oversight Board of the Resolution Trust Corporation, and the Resolution Trust Corporation"; and

(C) in subsection (d)—

(i) by striking paragraphs (3), (5), and (6); and

(ii) by redesignating paragraphs (4), (7), and (8) as paragraphs (3), (4), and (5), respectively.

§ 368.   Flood Disaster Protection Act of 1973

Section 3(a)(5) of the Flood Disaster Protection Act of 1973 (42 U.S.C. 4003(a)(5)) is amended by striking ", the Office of Thrift Supervision".

§ 369.   Home Owners' Loan Act

The Home Owners' Loan Act (12 U.S.C. 1461 et seq.) is amended—

(1) in section 1 (12 U.S.C. 1461), by striking the table of contents;

(2) in section 2 (12 U.S.C. 1462), as amended by this Act

(A) by striking paragraphs (1) and (3);

(B) by redesignating paragraph (2) as paragraph (1);

(C) by redesignating paragraphs (4) through (9) as paragraphs (2) through (7), respectively; and

(D) by adding at the end the following: "(8) BOARD.—The term 'Board', other than in the context of the Board of Directors of the Corporation, means the Board of Governors of the Federal Reserve System. "(9) COMPTROLLER.—The term 'Comptroller' means the Comptroller of the Currency.";

(3) in section 3 (12 U.S.C. 1462a)

(A) by striking the section heading and inserting the following: "SEC. 3. ADMINISTRATIVE PROVISIONS.";

(B) by striking subsections (a), (b), (c), (d), (g), (h), (i), and (j);

(C) by redesignating subsections (e) and (f) as subsections (a) and (b), respectively;

(D) in subsection (a), as so redesignated—

(i) in the heading by striking "OF THE DIRECTOR"; and

(ii) in the matter preceding paragraph (1), by striking "The Director" and inserting "In accordance with subtitle A of title III of the Dodd–Frank Wall Street Reform and Consumer Protection Act, the appropriate Federal banking agency"; and

(E) in subsection (b), as so redesignated, by striking "Director" and inserting "appropriate Federal banking agency";

(4) in section 4 (12 U.S.C. 1463)

(A) in subsection (a)—

(i) in the subsection heading, by striking "FEDERAL";

(ii) by striking paragraphs (1) and (2) and inserting the following:

"(1) EXAMINATION AND SAFE AND SOUND OPERATION.—

"(A) FEDERAL SAVINGS ASSOCIATIONS.—The Comptroller shall provide for the examination and safe and sound operation of Federal savings associations.

"(B) STATE SAVINGS ASSOCIATIONS.—The Corporation shall provide for the examination and safe and sound operation of State savings associations.

"(2) REGULATIONS FOR SAVINGS ASSOCIATIONS.—The Comptroller may prescribe regulations with respect to savings associations, as the Comptroller determines to be appropriate to carry out the purposes of this Act."; and

(iii) in paragraph (3), by striking "Director" each place that term appears and inserting "Comptroller and the Corporation";

(B) in subsection (b)—

(i) in paragraph (2)—

(I) in subparagraph (A), by adding "and" at the end;

(II) in subparagraph (B), by striking "; and" and inserting a period; and

(III) by striking subparagraph (C); and

(ii) by striking "Director" each place that term appears and inserting "Comptroller";

(C) in subsection (c)—

(i) by striking "All regulations and policies of the Director" and inserting "The regulations of the Comptroller and the policies of the Comptroller and the Corporation"; and

(ii) by striking "of the Currency";

(D) in subsection (e)(5), by striking "Director" and inserting "Comptroller";

(E) in subsection (f), by striking "Director" each place that term appears and inserting "appropriate Federal banking agency"; and

(F) in subsection (h), by striking "Director" each place that term appears and inserting "appropriate Federal banking agency";

(5) in section 5 (12 U.S.C. 1464)—

(A) in subsection (a), by striking "Director", each place such term appears and inserting "Comptroller of the Currency";

(B) in subsection (b), by striking "Director", each place such term appears and inserting "Comptroller of the Currency";

(C) in subsection (c)—

(i) in paragraph (5)—

(I) in subparagraph (A), by striking "Director" and inserting "appropriate Federal banking agency"; and

(II) in subparagraph (B)—

(aa) by striking "The Director" and inserting "The appropriate Federal banking agency"; and

(bb) by striking "the Director" and inserting "the appropriate Federal banking agency";

(D) in subsection (d)—

(i) in paragraph (1)—

(I) in subparagraph (A)—

(aa) in the first sentence, by striking "Director" and inserting "appropriate Federal banking agency";

(bb) in the second sentence—

(AA) by striking "Director's own name and through the Director's own attorneys" and inserting "name of the appropriate Federal banking agency and through the attorneys of the appropriate Federal banking agency"; and

(BB) by striking "Director" each place that term appears and inserting "appropriate Federal banking agency"; and

(cc) in the third sentence, by striking "Director" each place that term appears and inserting "Comptroller";

(II) in subparagraph (B)—

(aa) in clauses (i) through (iv), by striking "Director" each place that term appears and

inserting "appropriate Federal banking agency";

(III) in clause (v)—

(aa) in the matter preceding subclause (I), by striking "Director" and inserting "appropriate Federal banking agency";

(bb) in subclause (II), by striking "subpenas" and inserting "subpoenas"; and

(cc) in the matter following subclause (II), by striking "subpena" and inserting "subpoena";

(IV) in clause (vi)—

(aa) in the first sentence, by striking "Director" and inserting "appropriate Federal banking agency"; and

(bb) in the second sentence, by striking "Director" and inserting "Comptroller";

(V) in clause (vii)—

(aa) in the first sentence, by striking "subpena" and inserting "subpoena";

(bb) in the second sentence, by striking "subpenaed" and inserting "subpoenaed"; and

(cc) in the third sentence, by striking "Director" and inserting "appropriate Federal banking agency";

(ii) in paragraph (2)—

(I) in subparagraph (A)—

(aa) by striking "Director of the Office of Thrift Supervision" and inserting "appropriate Federal banking agency";

(bb) by striking "any insured savings association" and inserting "an insured savings association"; and

(cc) by striking "Director determines, in the Director's discretion" and inserting "appropriate Federal banking agency determines, in the discretion of the appropriate Federal banking agency";

(II) in subparagraph (B), by striking "Director" each place that term appears and inserting "appropriate Federal banking agency";

(III) in subparagraphs (C) and (D), by striking "Director" and inserting "appropriate Federal banking agency";

(IV) in subparagraph (E)—

(aa) in clause (ii)—

(AA) in the clause heading, by striking "OR RTC"; and

(BB) by striking "or the Resolution Trust Corporation, as appropriate," each place that term appears; and

(bb) by striking "Director" each place that term appears and inserting "appropriate Federal banking agency"; and

(iii) in paragraph (3)—

(I) in subparagraph (A), by striking "Director" each place that term appears and inserting "Comptroller"; and

(II) in subparagraph (B)—

(aa) in the subparagraph heading, by striking "OR RTC";

(bb) by striking "Corporation or the Resolution Trust"; and

(cc) by striking "Director" and inserting "Comptroller";

(iv) in paragraph (4), by striking "Director" and inserting "appropriate Federal banking agency";

(v) in paragraph (6)—

(I) in subparagraph (A), by striking "Director" and inserting "Comptroller"; and

(II) in subparagraphs (B) and (C), by striking "Director" each place that term appears and inserting "appropriate Federal banking agency";

(vi) in paragraph (7)—

(I) in subparagraphs (A), (B), and (D), by striking "Director" each place that term appears and inserting "appropriate Federal banking agency";

(II) in subparagraph (C), by striking "Director" and inserting "Federal Deposit Insurance Corporation or the Comptroller, as appropriate,"; and

(III) by striking subparagraph (E) and inserting the following: "(E) ADMINISTRATION BY THE COMPTROLLER AND THE CORPORATION.—The Comptroller may issue such regulations, and the appropriate Federal banking agency may issue such orders, including those issued pursuant to section 8 of the Federal Deposit Insurance Act, as may be necessary to administer and carry out this paragraph and to prevent evasion of this paragraph.";

(E) in subsection (e)(2), strike "Director" and insert "Comptroller";

(F) in subsection (i)—

(i) by striking "Director", each place such term appears, and inserting "Comptroller";

(ii) in paragraph (2), in the heading, by striking "DIRECTOR" and inserting "COMPTROLLER";

(iii) in paragraph (5)(A), by striking "of the Currency"; and

(iv) except as provided in clauses (i) through (iii), by striking "Director" each place such term appears and inserting "Comptroller";

(G) in subsection (o)—

(i) in paragraph (1), by striking "Director" and inserting "Comptroller"; and

(ii) in paragraph (2)(B), by striking "Director's determination" and inserting "determination of the Comptroller";

(H) in subsections (m), (n), (o), and (p), by striking "Director", each place such term appears, and inserting "Comptroller";

(I) in subsection (q)—

(i) in paragraph (6), by striking "of Governors of the Federal Reserve System";

(ii) by striking "Director" each place that term appears and inserting "Board"; and

(iii) by inserting "in consultation with the Comptroller and the Corporation," before "considers";

(J) in subsection (r)(3), by striking "Director" and inserting "Comptroller of the Currency";

(K) in subsection (s)—

(i) in paragraph (1), strike "Director" and insert "Comptroller of the Currency";

(ii) in paragraph (2), strike "Director" and insert "Comptroller of the Currency";

(iii) in paragraph (3), by striking "Director's discretion, the Director" and inserting "discretion of the appropriate Federal banking agency, the appropriate Federal banking agency,";

(iv) in paragraph (4), by striking "Director" each place that term appears and inserting "appropriate Federal banking agency"; and

(v) in paragraph (5)—

(I) by striking "Director", each place such term appears, and inserting "appropriate Federal banking agency"; and

(II) by striking "Director's approval" and inserting "approval of the appropriate Federal banking agency";

(L) in subsection (t)—

(i) in paragraph (1), by striking subparagraph (D);

(ii) by striking paragraph (3) and inserting the following: "(3) [Repealed].";

(iii) in paragraph (5)—

(I) in subparagraph (B), by striking "Corporation, in its sole discretion" and inserting "appropriate Federal banking agency, in the sole discretion of the appropriate Federal banking agency"; and

(II) by striking subparagraph (D);

(iv) in paragraph (6)—

(I) by striking subparagraph (A) and inserting the following: "(A) [Reserved].";

(II) in subparagraph (B), by striking "Director" each place that term appears and inserting "appropriate Federal banking agency";

(III) in subparagraph (C)—

(aa) in clause (i), by striking "Director's prior approval" and inserting "prior approval of the appropriate Federal banking agency";

(bb) in clause (ii), by striking "Director's discretion" and inserting "discretion of the appropriate Federal banking agency"; and

(cc) by striking "Director" each place that term appears and inserting "appropriate Federal banking agency";

(IV) in subparagraph (E), by striking "Director shall" and inserting "appropriate Federal banking agency may"; and

(V) in subparagraph (F), by striking "Director" and all that follows through the end of the subparagraph and inserting "appropriate Federal banking agency under this Act or any other provision of law.";

(v) in paragraph (7), by striking "Director" each place that term appears and inserting "appropriate Federal banking agency";

(vi) by striking paragraph (8) and inserting the following: "(8) [Repealed].";

(vii) in paragraph (9)—

(I) in subparagraph (A), by striking "Director" and inserting "Comptroller";

(II) in subparagraph (C), by striking "of the Currency"; and

(III) by striking subparagraph (B) and redesignating subparagraphs (C) and (D) as subparagraphs (B) and (C), respectively; and

(viii) except as provided in clauses (i) through (vii), by striking "Director" each place that term appears and inserting "appropriate Federal banking agency";

(M) in subsection (u), by striking "Director" each place that term appears and inserting "appropriate Federal banking agency";

(N) in subsection (v)—

(i) in paragraph (2), by striking "Director's determinations" and inserting "determinations of the appropriate Federal banking agency"; and

(ii) by striking "Director" each place that term appears and inserting "appropriate Federal banking agency";

(O) in subsection (w)(1)—

(i) in subparagraph (A)(II), by striking "Director's intention" and inserting "intention of the Comptroller"; and

(ii) in subparagraph (B), by striking "Director's intention" and inserting "intention of the Comptroller"; and

(P) except as provided in subparagraphs (A) through (J), by striking "Director" each place that term appears and inserting "Comptroller"; (6) in section 8 (12 U.S.C. 1466a), by striking "Director" each place that term appears and inserting "Comptroller"; (7) in section 9 (12 U.S.C. 1467)—

(A) in subsection (a), by striking "assessed by the Director" and all that follows through the end of the subsection and inserting the following: "assessed by—

"(1) the Comptroller, against each such Federal savings association, as the Comptroller deems necessary or appropriate; and "(2) the Corporation, against each such State savings association, as the Corporation deems necessary or appropriate.";

(B) in subsection (b), by striking "Director", each place such term appears, and inserting "Comptroller or Corporation, as appropriate";

(C) in subsection (e)—

(i) by striking "Only the Director" and inserting "The Comptroller"; and

(ii) by striking "Director's designee" and inserting "designee of the Comptroller";

(D) by striking subsection (f) and inserting the following: "(f) [Reserved].";

(E) in subsection (g)—

(i) in paragraph (1), by striking "Director" and inserting "appropriate Federal banking agency"; and

(ii) in paragraph (2), by striking "Director, or the Corporation, as the case may be," and inserting "appropriate Federal banking agency for the savings association";

(F) in subsection (i), by striking "Director" each place that term appears and inserting "appropriate Federal banking agency";

(G) in subsection (j), by striking "Director's sole discretion" and inserting "sole discretion of the appropriate Federal banking agency";

(H) in subsection (k), by striking "Director may assess against institutions for which the Director is the appropriate Federal banking agency, as defined in section 3 of the Federal Deposit Insurance Act," and inserting "appropriate Federal banking agency may assess against an institution"; and

(I) except as provided in subparagraphs (A) through (G), by striking "Director" each place that term appears and inserting "appropriate Federal banking agency"; (8) in section 10 (12 U.S.C. 1467a)—

(A) in subsection (a)(1), by striking "Director" each place that term appears and inserting "appropriate Federal banking agency";

(B) in subsection (b)—

(i) in paragraph (2), by striking "and the regional office of the Director of the district in which its principal office is located,"; and

(ii) in paragraph (6), by striking "Director's own motion or application" and inserting "motion or application of the Board";

(C) in subsection (c)—

(i) in paragraph (2)(F), by striking "of Governors of the Federal Reserve System";

(ii) in paragraph (4)(B), in the subparagraph heading, by striking "BY DIRECTOR";

(iii) in paragraph (6)(D), in the subparagraph heading, by striking "BY DIRECTOR"; and

(iv) in paragraph (9)(E), by inserting "(in consultation with the appropriate Federal banking agency)" after "including a determination";

(D) in subsection (g)(5)(B), by striking "the Director's discretion" and inserting "the discretion of the Board";

(E) in subsection (*l*), by striking "Director" each place that term appears and inserting "appropriate Federal banking agency";

(F) in subsection (m), by striking "Director" and inserting "appropriate Federal banking agency";

(G) in subsection (p)—

(i) in paragraph (1)—

(I) by striking "Director determines" the 1st place such term appears and inserting "Board or the appropriate Federal banking agency for the savings association determines";

(II) by striking "Director may" and inserting "Board may"; and

(III) by striking "Director determines" the 2nd place such term appears and inserting "Board, in consultation with the appropriate Federal banking agency for the savings association determines"; and

(ii) in paragraph (2), by striking "Director", each place such term appears, and inserting "Board";

(H) in subsection (q), by striking "Director", each place such term appears, and inserting "Board";

(I) in subsection (r), by striking "Director", each place such term appears, and inserting "Board or appropriate Federal banking agency";

(J) in subsection (s)—

(i) in paragraph (2)—

(I) in subparagraph (B)(ii), by striking "Director's judgment" and inserting "judgment of the appropriate Federal banking agency for the savings association"; and

(II) by striking "Director" each place that term appears and inserting "appropriate Federal banking agency for the savings association"; and (ii) in paragraph (4), by striking "Director" and inserting "Comptroller"; and

(K) except as provided in subparagraphs (A) through (J), by striking "Director" each place that term appears and inserting "Board"; (9) in section 11 (12 U.S.C. 1468), by striking "Director" each place that term appears and inserting "appropriate Federal banking agency"; (10) in section 12 (12 U.S.C. 1468a), by striking "the Director" and inserting "a Federal banking agency"; and (11) in section 13 (12 U.S.C. 1468a) is amended by striking "Director" and inserting "a Federal banking agency".

§ 370. Housing Act of 1948

Section 502(c) of the Housing Act of 1948 (12 U.S.C. 1701c(c)) is amended—

(1) in the matter preceding paragraph (1), by striking "and the Director of the Office of Thrift Supervision" and inserting ", the Comptroller of the Currency, and the Federal Deposit Insurance Corporation"; and

(2) in paragraph (3), by striking "Board" and inserting "Agency".

§ 371. Housing and Community Development Act of 1992

Section 543 of the Housing and Community Development Act of 1992 (Public Law 102–550; 106 Stat. 3798) is amended—

(1) in subsection (c)(1)—

(A) by striking subparagraphs (D) through (F); and

(B) by redesignating subparagraphs (G) and (H) as subparagraphs (D) and (E), respectively; and

(2) in subsection (f)—

(A) in paragraph (2), by striking "the Office of Thrift Supervision," each place that term appears; and

(B) in paragraph (3)—

(i) in the matter preceding subparagraph (A), by striking "the Office of Thrift Supervision,"; and

(ii) in subparagraph (D), by striking "Office of Thrift Supervision,".

§ 372. Housing and Urban–Rural Recovery Act of 1983

Section 469 of the Housing and Urban–Rural Recovery Act of 1983 (12 U.S.C. 1701p–1) is amended in the first sentence, by striking "Federal Home Loan Bank Board" and inserting "Federal Housing Finance Agency".

§ 373. National Housing Act

Section 202(f) of the National Housing Act (12 U.S.C. 1708(f)) is amended—

(1) by striking paragraph (5) and inserting the following: "(5) if the mortgagee is a national bank, a subsidiary or affiliate of such bank, a Federal savings association or a subsidiary or affiliate of a savings association, the Comptroller of the Currency;";

(2) in paragraph (6), by adding "and" at the end;

(3) in paragraph (7)—

(A) by inserting "or State savings association" after "State bank"; and

(B) by striking "; and" and inserting a period; and

(4) by striking paragraph (8).

§ 374. Neighborhood Reinvestment Corporation Act

Section 606(c)(3) of the Neighborhood Reinvestment Corporation Act (42 U.S.C. 8105(c)(3)) is amended by striking "Federal Home Loan Bank Board" and inserting "Federal Housing Finance Agency".

§ 375. Public Law 93–100

Section 5(d) of Public Law 93–100 (12 U.S.C. 1470(a)) is amended—

(1) in paragraph (1), by striking "Federal Savings and Loan Insurance Corporation with respect to insured institutions, the Board of Governors of the Federal Reserve System with respect to State member insured banks, and the Federal Deposit Insurance Corporation with respect to State nonmember insured banks" and inserting "appropriate Federal banking agency, with respect to the institutions subject to the jurisdiction of each such agency,"; and

(2) in paragraph (2), by striking "supervisory" and inserting "banking".

§ 376. Securities Exchange Act of 1934

The Securities Exchange Act of 1934 (15 U.S.C. 78a et seq.) is amended—

(1) in section 3(a)(34) (15 U.S.C. 78c(a)(34))—

(A) in subparagraph (A)—

(i) in clause (i), by striking "or a subsidiary or a department or division of any such bank" and inserting "a subsidiary or a department or division of any such bank, a Federal savings association (as defined in section 3(b)(2) of the Federal Deposit Insurance Act (12 U.S.C. 1813(b)(2))), the deposits of which are insured by the Federal Deposit Insurance Corporation, or a subsidiary or department or division of any such Federal savings association";

(ii) in clause (ii), by striking "or a subsidiary or a department or division of such subsidiary" and inserting "a subsidiary or a department or division of such subsidiary, or a savings and loan holding company";

(iii) in clause (iii), by striking "or a subsidiary or department or division thereof;" and inserting "a subsidiary or department or division of any such bank, a State savings association (as defined in section 3(b)(3) of the Federal Deposit Insurance Act (12 U.S.C. 1813(b)(3))), the deposits of which are insured by the Federal Deposit Insurance Corporation, or a subsidiary or a department or division of any such State savings association; and";

(iv) by striking clause (iv); and

(v) by redesignating clause (v) as clause (iv);

(B) in subparagraph (B)—

(i) in clause (i), by striking "or a subsidiary of any such bank" and inserting "a subsidiary of any such bank, a Federal savings association (as defined in section 3(b)(2) of the Federal Deposit Insurance Act (12 U.S.C. 1813(b)(2))), the deposits of which are insured by the Federal Deposit Insurance Corporation, or a subsidiary of any such Federal savings association";

(ii) in clause (ii), by striking "or a subsidiary of a bank holding company which is a bank other than a bank specified in clause (i), (iii), or (iv) of this subparagraph" and inserting "a subsidiary of a bank holding company that is a bank other than a bank specified in clause (i) or (iii) of this subparagraph, or a savings and loan holding company";

(iii) in clause (iii), by striking "or a subsidiary thereof;" and inserting "a subsidiary of any such bank, a State savings association (as defined in section 3(b)(3) of the Federal Deposit Insurance Act (12 U.S.C. 1813(b)(3))), the deposits of which are insured by the Federal Deposit Insurance Corporation, or a subsidiary of any such State savings association; and";

(iv) by striking clause (iv); and

(v) by redesignating clause (v) as clause (iv);

(C) in subparagraph (C)—

(i) in clause (i), by striking "bank" and inserting "bank or a Federal savings association (as defined in section 3(b)(2) of the Federal Deposit Insurance Act (12 U.S.C. 1813(b)(2))), the deposits of which are insured by the Federal Deposit Insurance Corporation";

(ii) in clause (ii), by striking "or a subsidiary of a bank holding company which is a bank other than a bank specified in clause (i), (iii), or (iv) of this subparagraph" and inserting "a subsidiary of a bank holding company that is a bank other than a bank specified in clause (i) or (iii) of this subparagraph, or a savings and loan holding company";

(iii) in clause (iii), by striking "System)" and inserting, "System) or a State savings association (as defined in section 3(b)(3) of the Federal Deposit Insurance Act (12 U.S.C.

1813(b)(3))), the deposits of which are insured by the Federal Deposit Insurance Corporation; and'';

(iv) by striking clause (iv); and

(v) by redesignating clause (v) as clause (iv);

(D) in subparagraph (D)—

(i) in clause (i), by inserting after "bank" the following: "or a Federal savings association (as defined in section 3(b)(2) of the Federal Deposit Insurance Act (12 U.S.C. 1813(b)(2))), the deposits of which are insured by the Federal Deposit Insurance Corporation'';

(ii) in clause (ii), by adding "and" at the end;

(iii) by striking clause (iii);

(iv) by redesignating clause (iv) as clause (iii); and

(v) in clause (iii), as so redesignated, by inserting after "bank" the following: "or a State savings association (as defined in section 3(b)(3) of the Federal Deposit Insurance Act (12 U.S.C. 1813(b)(3))), the deposits of which are insured by the Federal Deposit Insurance Corporation'';

(E) in subparagraph (F)—

(i) in clause (i), by inserting after "bank" the following: "or a Federal savings association (as defined in section 3(b)(2) of the Federal Deposit Insurance Act (12 U.S.C. 1813(b)(2))), the deposits of which are insured by the Federal Deposit Insurance Corporation'';

(ii) by striking clause (ii);

(iii) by redesignating clauses (iii), (iv), and (v) as clauses (ii), (iii), and (iv), respectively; and

(iv) in clause (iii), as so redesignated, by inserting before the semicolon the following: "or a State savings association (as defined in section 3(b)(3) of the Federal Deposit Insurance Act (12 U.S.C. 1813(b)(3))), the deposits of which are insured by the Federal Deposit Insurance Corporation'';

(F) in subparagraph (G)—

(i) in clause (i), by inserting after "national bank" the following: ", a Federal savings association (as defined in section 3(b)(2) of the Federal Deposit Insurance Act), the de-

posits of which are insured by the Federal Deposit Insurance Corporation,'';

(ii) in clause (iii)—

(I) by inserting after "bank)" the following: ", a State savings association (as defined in section 3(b)(3) of the Federal Deposit Insurance Act), the deposits of which are insured by the Federal Deposit Insurance Corporation,''; and

(II) by adding "and" at the end;

(iii) by striking clause (iv); and

(iv) by redesignating clause (v) as clause (iv); and

(G) in the undesignated matter following subparagraph

(H) , by striking ", and the term 'District of Columbia savings and loan association' means any association subject to examination and supervision by the Office of Thrift Supervision under section 8 of the Home Owners' Loan Act of 1933''; (2) in section 12

(i) (15 U.S.C. 78l(i))—

(A) in paragraph (1), by inserting after "national banks" the following: "and Federal savings associations, the accounts of which are insured by the Federal Deposit Insurance Corporation'';

(B) by striking "(3)" and all that follows through "vested in the Office of Thrift Supervision" and inserting "and (3) with respect to all other insured banks and State savings associations, the accounts of which are insured by the Federal Deposit Insurance Corporation, are vested in the Federal Deposit Insurance Corporation''; and

(C) in the second sentence, by striking "the Federal Deposit Insurance Corporation, and the Office of Thrift Supervision" and inserting "and the Federal Deposit Insurance Corporation''; (3) in section 15C(g)(1) (15 U.S.C. 78o–5(g)(1)), by striking "the Director of the Office of Thrift Supervision, the Federal Savings and Loan Insurance Corporation,''; and (4) in section 23(b)(1) (15 U.S.C.78w(b)(1)), by striking ", other than the Office of Thrift Supervision,''.

§ 377. Title 18, United States Code

Title 18, United States Code, is amended—

(1) in section 212(c)(2)—

(A) by striking subparagraph (C); and

(B) by redesignating subparagraphs (D) through (H) as subparagraphs (C) through (G), respectively;

(2) in section 657, by striking "Office of Thrift Supervision, the Resolution Trust Corporation,";

(3) in section 981(a)(1)(D)—

(A) by striking "Resolution Trust Corporation,"; and

(B) by striking "or the Office of Thrift Supervision";

(4) in section 982(a)(3)—

(A) by striking "Resolution Trust Corporation,"; and

(B) by striking "or the Office of Thrift Supervision";

(5) in section 1006—

(A) by striking "Office of Thrift Supervision,"; and

(B) by striking "the Resolution Trust Corporation,";

(6) in section 1014—

(A) by striking "the Office of Thrift Supervision"; and

(B) by striking "the Resolution Trust Corporation,"; and

(7) in section 1032(1)—

(A) by striking "the Resolution Trust Corporation,"; and

(B) by striking "or the Director of the Office of Thrift Supervision".

§ 378. Title 31, United States Code

Title 31, United States Code, is amended—

(1) in section 321—

(A) in subsection (c)—

(i) in paragraph (1), by adding "and" at the end;

(ii) in paragraph (2), by striking "; and" and inserting a period; and

(iii) by striking paragraph (3); and

(B) by striking subsection (e); and

(2) in section 714(a), by striking "the Office of the Comptroller of the Currency, and the Office of Thrift Supervision." and inserting "and the Office of the Comptroller of the Currency."

TITLE VI—IMPROVEMENTS TO THE REGULATION OF BANK AND SAVINGS ASSOCIATION HOLDING COMPANIES AND DEPOSITORY INSTITUTIONS

§ 601. Short Title

This title may be cited as the "Bank and Savings Association Holding Company and Depository Institution Regulatory Improvements Act of 2010".

§ 602. Definition

For purposes of this title, a company is a "commercial firm" if the annual gross revenues derived by the company and all of its affiliates from activities that are financial in nature (as defined in section 4(k) of the Bank Holding Company Act of 1956 (12 U.S.C. 1843(k))) and, if applicable, from the ownership or control of one or more insured depository institutions, represent less than 15 percent of the consolidated annual gross revenues of the company.

§ 603. Moratorium and Study on Treatment of Credit Card Banks, Industrial Loan Companies, and Certain Other Companies Under the Bank Holding Company Act of 1956

(a) MORATORIUM

(1) DEFINITIONS

In this subsection—

(A) the term "credit card bank" means an institution described in section 2(c)(2)(F) of the Bank Holding Company Act of 1956 (12 U.S.C. 1841(c)(2)(F));

(B) the term "industrial bank" means an institution described in section 2(c)(2)(H) of the Bank Holding Company Act of 1956 (12 U.S.C. 1841(c)(2)(H)); and

(C) the term "trust bank" means an institution described in section 2(c)(2)(D) of the Bank Holding Company Act of 1956 (12 U.S.C. 1841(c)(2)(D)).

(2) MORATORIUM ON PROVISION OF DEPOSIT INSURANCE

The Corporation may not approve an application for deposit insurance under section 5 of the Federal Deposit Insurance Act (12 U.S.C. 1815) that is received after November 23, 2009, for an industrial bank, a credit card bank, or a trust bank that is directly or indirectly owned or controlled by a commercial firm.

(3) CHANGE IN CONTROL

(A) IN GENERAL

Except as provided in subparagraph (B), the appropriate Federal banking agency shall disapprove a change in control, as provided in section 7(j) of the Federal Deposit Insurance Act (12 U.S.C. 1817(j)), of an industrial bank, a credit card bank, or a trust bank if the change in control would result in direct or indirect control of the industrial bank, credit card bank, or trust bank by a commercial firm.

(B) EXCEPTIONS

Subparagraph (A) shall not apply to a change in control of an industrial bank, credit card bank, or trust bank—

(i) that—

(I) is in danger of default, as determined by the appropriate Federal banking agency;

(II) results from the merger or whole acquisition of a commercial firm that directly or indirectly controls the industrial bank, credit card bank, or trust bank in a bona fide merger with or acquisition by another commercial firm, as determined by the appropriate Federal banking agency; or

(III) results from an acquisition of voting shares of a publicly traded company that controls an industrial bank, credit card bank, or trust bank, if, after the acquisition, the acquiring shareholder (or group of shareholders acting in concert) holds less than 25 percent of any class of the voting shares of the company; and

(ii) that has obtained all regulatory approvals otherwise required for such change of control under any applicable Federal or State law, including section 7(j) of the Federal Deposit Insurance Act (12 U.S.C. 1817(j)).

(4) SUNSET

This subsection shall cease to have effect 3 years after the date of enactment of this Act.

(b) GOVERNMENT ACCOUNTABILITY OFFICE STUDY OF EXCEPTIONS UNDER THE BANK HOLDING COMPANY ACT OF 1956

(1) STUDY REQUIRED

The Comptroller General of the United States shall carry out a study to determine whether it is necessary, in order to strengthen the safety and soundness of institutions or the stability of the financial system, to eliminate the exceptions under section 2 of the Bank Holding Company Act of 1956 (12 U.S.C. 1841) for institutions described in—

(A) section 2(a)(5)(E) of the Bank Holding Company Act of 1956 (12 U.S.C. 1841(a)(5)(E));

(B) section 2(a)(5)(F) of the Bank Holding Company Act of 1956 (12 U.S.C. 1841(a)(5)(F));

(C) section 2(c)(2)(D) of the Bank Holding Company Act of 1956 (12 U.S.C. 1841(c)(2)(D));

(D) section 2(c)(2)(F) of the Bank Holding Company Act of 1956 (12 U.S.C. 1841(c)(2)(F));

(E) section 2(c)(2)(H) of the Bank Holding Company Act of 1956 (12 U.S.C. 1841(c)(2)(H)); and

(F) section 2(c)(2)(B) of the Bank Holding Company Act of 1956 (12 U.S.C. 1841(c)(2)(B)).

(2) CONTENT OF STUDY

(A) IN GENERAL

The study required under paragraph (1), with respect to the institutions referenced in each of subparagraphs (A) through (E) of paragraph (1), shall, to the extent feasible be based on information provided to the Comptroller General by the appropriate Federal or State regulator, and shall—

(i) identify the types and number of institutions excepted from section 2 of the Bank Holding Company Act of 1956 (12 U.S.C. 1841) under each of the subparagraphs described in subparagraphs (A) through (E) of paragraph (1);

(ii) generally describe the size and geographic locations of the institutions described in clause (i);

(iii) determine the extent to which the institutions described in clause (i) are held by holding companies that are commercial firms;

(iv) determine whether the institutions described in clause (i) have any affiliates that are commercial firms;

(v) identify the Federal banking agency responsible for the supervision of the institu-

tions described in clause (i) on and after the transfer date;

(vi) determine the adequacy of the Federal bank regulatory framework applicable to each category of institution described in clause (i), including any restrictions (including limitations on affiliate transactions or cross-marketing) that apply to transactions between an institution, the holding company of the institution, and any other affiliate of the institution; and

(vii) evaluate the potential consequences of subjecting the institutions described in clause (i) to the requirements of the Bank Holding Company Act of 1956, including with respect to the availability and allocation of credit, the stability of the financial system and the economy, the safe and sound operation of each category of institution, and the impact on the types of activities in which such institutions, and the holding companies of such institutions, may engage.

(B) SAVINGS ASSOCIATIONS

With respect to institutions described in paragraph (1)(F), the study required under paragraph (1) shall—

(i) determine the adequacy of the Federal bank regulatory framework applicable to such institutions, including any restrictions (including limitations on affiliate transactions or cross-marketing) that apply to transactions between an institution, the holding company of the institution, and any other affiliate of the institution; and

(ii) evaluate the potential consequences of subjecting the institutions described in paragraph (1)(F) to the requirements of the Bank Holding Company Act of 1956, including with respect to the availability and allocation of credit, the stability of the financial system and the economy, the safe and sound operation of such institutions, and the impact on the types of activities in which such institutions, and the holding companies of such institutions, may engage.

(3) REPORT

Not later than 18 months after the date of enactment of this Act, the Comptroller General shall submit to the Committee on Banking, Housing, and Urban Affairs of the Senate and the Committee on Financial Services of the

House of Representatives a report on the study required under paragraph (1).

§ 604. Reports and Examinations of Holding companies; Regulation of Functionally Regulated Subsidiaries

(a) REPORTS BY BANK HOLDING COMPANIES

Sections 5(c)(1) of the Bank Holding Company Act of 1956 (12 U.S.C. 1844(c)(1)) is amended—

(1) by striking subclause (A)(ii) and inserting the following:

"(ii) compliance by the bank holding company or subsidiary with—

"(I) this Act;

"(II) Federal laws that the Board has specific jurisdiction to enforce against the company or subsidiary; and

"(III) other than in the case of an insured depository institution or functionally regulated subsidiary, any other applicable provision of Federal law.";

(2) by striking subparagraph (B) and inserting the following:

"(B) USE OF EXISTING REPORTS AND OTHER SUPERVISORY INFORMATION.—The Board shall, to the fullest extent possible, use—

"(i) reports and other supervisory information that the bank holding company or any subsidiary thereof has been required to provide to other Federal or State regulatory agencies;

"(ii) externally audited financial statements of the bank holding company or subsidiary;

"(iii) information otherwise available from Federal or State regulatory agencies; and

"(iv) information that is otherwise required to be reported publicly."; and

(3) by adding at the end the following: "(C) AVAILABILITY.—Upon the request of the Board, the bank holding company or a subsidiary of the bank holding company shall promptly provide to the Board any information described in clauses (i) through (iii) of subparagraph (B).".

(b) EXAMINATIONS OF BANK HOLDING COMPANIES

Section 5(c)(2) of the Bank Holding Company Act of 1956 (12 U.S.C. 1844(c)(2)) is amended to read as follows:

"(2) EXAMINATIONS.—

"(A) IN GENERAL

Subject to subtitle B of the Consumer Financial Protection Act of 2010, the Board may make examinations of a bank holding company and each subsidiary of a bank holding company in order to—

"(i) inform the Board of—

"(I) the nature of the operations and financial condition of the bank holding company and the subsidiary;

"(II) the financial, operational, and other risks within the bank holding company system that may pose a threat to—

"(aa) the safety and soundness of the bank holding company or of any depository institution subsidiary of the bank holding company; or

"(bb) the stability of the financial system of the United States; and

"(III) the systems of the bank holding company for monitoring and controlling the risks described in subclause (II); and

"(ii) monitor the compliance of the bank holding company and the subsidiary with—

"(I) this Act;

"(II) Federal laws that the Board has specific jurisdiction to enforce against the company or subsidiary; and

"(III) other than in the case of an insured depository institution or functionally regulated subsidiary, any other applicable provisions of Federal law.

"(B) USE OF REPORTS TO REDUCE EXAMINATIONS

For purposes of this paragraph, the Board shall, to the fullest extent possible, rely on—

"(i) examination reports made by other Federal or State regulatory agencies relating to a bank holding company and any subsidiary of a bank holding company; and

"(ii) the reports and other information required under paragraph (1).

"(C) COORDINATION WITH OTHER REGULATORS

The Board shall—

"(i) provide reasonable notice to, and consult with, the appropriate Federal banking agency, the Securities and Exchange Commission, the Commodity Futures Trading Commission, or State regulatory agency, as appropriate, for a subsidiary that is a depository institution or a functionally regulated subsidiary of a bank holding company before commencing an examination of the subsidiary under this section; and

"(ii) to the fullest extent possible, avoid duplication of examination activities, reporting requirements, and requests for information."

(c) AUTHORITY TO REGULATE FUNCTIONALLY REGULATED SUBSIDIARIES OF BANK HOLDING COMPANIES

The Bank Holding Company Act of 1956 (12 U.S.C. 1841 et seq.) is amended—(1) in section 5(c)(5)(B) (12 U.S.C. 1844(c)(5)(B)), by striking clause (v) and inserting the following: "(v) an entity that is subject to regulation by, or registration with, the Commodity Futures Trading Commission, with respect to activities conducted as a futures commission merchant, commodity trading adviser, commodity pool, commodity pool operator, swap execution facility, swap data repository, swap dealer, major swap participant, and activities that are incidental to such commodities and swaps activities."; and (2) by striking section 10A (12 U.S.C. 1848a).

(d) ACQUISITIONS OF BANKS

Section 3(c) of the Bank Holding Company Act of 1956 (12 U.S.C. 1842(c)) is amended by adding at the end the following: "(7) FINANCIAL STABILITY.—In every case, the Board shall take into consideration the extent to which a proposed acquisition, merger, or consolidation would result in greater or more concentrated risks to the stability of the United States banking or financial system."

(e) ACQUISITIONS OF NONBANKS

(1) NOTICE PROCEDURES

Section 4(j)(2)(A) of the Bank Holding Company Act of 1956 (12 U.S.C. 1843(j)(2)(A)) is amended by striking "or unsound banking practices" and inserting "unsound banking practices, or risk to the stability of the United States banking or financial system".

(2) ACTIVITIES THAT ARE FINANCIAL IN NATURE

Section 4(k)(6)(B) of the Bank Holding Company Act of 1956 (12 U.S.C. 1843(k)(6)(B)) is amended to read as follows:

"(B) APPROVAL NOT REQUIRED FOR CERTAIN FINANCIAL ACTIVITIES.—

"(i) IN GENERAL

Except as provided in subsection (j) with regard to the acquisition of a savings association and clause (ii), a financial holding company may commence any activity, or acquire any company, pursuant to paragraph (4) or any regulation prescribed or order issued under paragraph (5), without prior approval of the Board.

"(ii) EXCEPTION

A financial holding company may not acquire a company, without the prior approval of the Board, in a transaction in which the total consolidated assets to be acquired by the financial holding company exceed $10,000,000,000.

"(iii) HART-SCOTT-RODINO FILING REQUIREMENT

Solely for purposes of section 7A(c)(8) of the Clayton Act (15 U.S.C. 18a(c)(8)), the transactions subject to the requirements of this paragraph shall be treated as if the approval of the Board is not required.".

(f) BANK MERGER ACT TRANSACTIONS

Section 18(c)(5) of the Federal Deposit Insurance Act (12 U.S.C. 1828(c)(5)) is amended, in the matter immediately following subparagraph (B), by striking "and the convenience and needs of the community to be served" and inserting "the convenience and needs of the community to be served, and the risk to the stability of the United States banking or financial system".

(g) REPORTS BY SAVINGS AND LOAN HOLDING COMPANIES

Section 10(b)(2) of the Home Owners' Loan Act (12 U.S.C. 1467a(b)(2)) is amended—

(1) by striking "Each savings" and inserting the following:

"(A) IN GENERAL.—Each savings"; and

(2) by adding at the end the following:

"(B) USE OF EXISTING REPORTS AND OTHER SUPERVISORY INFORMATION

The Board shall, to the fullest extent possible, use—

"(i) reports and other supervisory information that the savings and loan holding company or any subsidiary thereof has been required to provide to other Federal or State regulatory agencies;

"(ii) externally audited financial statements of the savings and loan holding company or subsidiary;

"(iii) information that is otherwise available from Federal or State regulatory agencies; and

"(iv) information that is otherwise required to be reported publicly.

"(C) AVAILABILITY

Upon the request of the Board, a savings and loan holding company or a subsidiary of a savings and loan holding company shall promptly provide to the Board any information described in clauses (i) through (iii) of subparagraph (B)."

(h) EXAMINATION OF SAVINGS AND LOAN HOLDING COMPANIES

(1) DEFINITIONS

Section 2 of the Home Owners' Loan Act (12 U.S.C. 1462) is amended by adding at the end the following:

"(10) APPROPRIATE FEDERAL BANKING AGENCY

The term 'appropriate Federal banking agency' has the same meaning as in section 3(q) of the Federal Deposit Insurance Act (12 U.S.C. 1813(q)).

"(11) FUNCTIONALLY REGULATED SUBSIDIARY

The term 'functionally regulated subsidiary' has the same meaning as in section 5(c)(5) of the Bank Holding Company Act of 1956 (12 U.S.C. 1844(c)(5))."

(2) EXAMINATION

Section 10(b) of the Home Owners' Loan Act (12 U.S.C. 1467a(b)) is amended by striking paragraph (4) and inserting the following:

"(4) EXAMINATIONS

"(A) IN GENERAL

Subject to subtitle B of the Consumer Financial Protection Act of 2010, the Board may make examinations of a savings and loan holding company and each subsidiary of a

savings and loan holding company system, in order to—

"(i) inform the Board of—

"(I) the nature of the operations and financial condition of the savings and loan holding company and the subsidiary;

"(II) the financial, operational, and other risks within the savings and loan holding company system that may pose a threat to—

"(aa) the safety and soundness of the savings and loan holding company or of any depository institution subsidiary of the savings and loan holding company; or

"(bb) the stability of the financial system of the United States; and

"(III) the systems of the savings and loan holding company for monitoring and controlling the risks described in subclause (II); and

"(ii) monitor the compliance of the savings and loan holding company and the subsidiary with—

"(I) this Act;

"(II) Federal laws that the Board has specific jurisdiction to enforce against the company or subsidiary; and

"(III) other than in the case of an insured depository institution or functionally regulated subsidiary, any other applicable provisions of Federal law.

"(B) USE OF REPORTS TO REDUCE EXAMINATIONS

For purposes of this subsection, the Board shall, to the fullest extent possible, rely on—

"(i) the examination reports made by other Federal or State regulatory agencies relating to a savings and loan holding company and any subsidiary; and

"(ii) the reports and other information required under paragraph (2).

"(C) COORDINATION WITH OTHER REGULATORS

The Board shall—

"(i) provide reasonable notice to, and consult with, the appropriate Federal banking agency, the Securities and Exchange Commission, the Commodity Futures Trading Commission, or State regulatory agency, as appropriate, for a subsidiary that is a depository institution or a functionally regulated subsidiary of a savings and loan holding company before commencing an examination of the subsidiary under this section; and

"(ii) to the fullest extent possible, avoid duplication of examination activities, reporting requirements, and requests for information."

(i) DEFINITION OF THE TERM "SAVINGS AND LOAN HOLDING COMPANY"

Section 10(a)(1)(D)(ii) of the Home Owners' Loan Act (12 U.S.C. 1467a(a)(1)(D)(ii)) is amended to read as follows:

"(ii) EXCLUSION

The term 'savings and loan holding company' does not include—

"(I) a bank holding company that is registered under, and subject to, the Bank Holding Company Act of 1956 (12 U.S.C. 1841 et seq.), or to any company directly or indirectly controlled by such company (other than a savings association);

"(II) a company that controls a savings association that functions solely in a trust or fiduciary capacity as described in section 2(c)(2)(D) of the Bank Holding Company Act of 1956 (12 U.S.C. 1841(c)(2)(D)); or

"(III) a company described in subsection (c)(9)(C) solely by virtue of such company's control of an intermediate holding company established pursuant to section 10A."

(j) EFFECTIVE DATE

The amendments made by this section shall take effect on the transfer date.

§ 605. Assuring Consistent Oversight of Permissible Activities of Depository Institution Subsidiaries of Holding Companies

(a) IN GENERAL

The Federal Deposit Insurance Act (12 U.S.C. 1811 et seq.) is amended by inserting after section 25 the following new section:

"SEC. 26. ASSURING CONSISTENT OVERSIGHT OF SUBSIDIARIES OF HOLDING COMPANIES.

"(a) DEFINITIONS

For purposes of this section:

"(1) BOARD.—The term 'Board' means the Board of Governors of the Federal Reserve System.

"(2) FUNCTIONALLY REGULATED SUBSIDIARY.—The term 'functionally regulated subsidiary' has the same meaning as in section 5(c)(5) of the Bank Holding Company Act.

"(3) LEAD INSURED DEPOSITORY INSTITUTION.—The term 'lead insured depository institution' has the same meaning as in section 2(o)(8) of the Bank Holding Company Act.

"(b) EXAMINATION REQUIREMENTS

Subject to subtitle B of the Consumer Financial Protection Act of 2010, the Board shall examine the activities of a nondepository institution subsidiary (other than a functionally regulated subsidiary or a subsidiary of a depository institution) of a depository institution holding company that are permissible for the insured depository institution subsidiaries of the depository institution holding company in the same manner, subject to the same standards, and with the same frequency as would be required if such activities were conducted in the lead insured depository institution of the depository institution holding company.

"(c) STATE COORDINATION

"(1) CONSULTATION AND COORDINATION

If a nondepository institution subsidiary is supervised by a State bank supervisor or other State regulatory authority, the Board, in conducting the examinations required in subsection (b), shall consult and coordinate with such State regulator.

"(2) ALTERNATING EXAMINATIONS PERMITTED

The examinations required under subsection (b) may be conducted in joint or alternating manner with a State regulator, if the Board determines that an examination of a nondepository institution subsidiary conducted by the State carries out the purposes of this section.

"(d) APPROPRIATE FEDERAL BANKING AGENCY BACKUP EXAMINATION AUTHORITY

"(1) IN GENERAL

In the event that the Board does not conduct examinations required under subsection (b) in the same manner, subject to the same standards, and with the same frequency as would be required if such activities were conducted by the lead insured depository institution subsidiary of the depository institution holding company, the appropriate Federal banking agency for the lead insured depository institution may recommend in writing (which shall include a written explanation of the concerns giving rise to the recommendation) that the Board perform the examination required under subsection (b).

"(2) EXAMINATION BY AN APPROPRIATE FEDERAL BANKING AGENCY

If the Board does not, before the end of the 60–day period beginning on the date on which the Board receives a recommendation under paragraph (1), begin an examination as required under subsection (b) or provide a written explanation or plan to the appropriate Federal banking agency making such recommendation responding to the concerns raised by the appropriate Federal banking agency for the lead insured depository institution, the appropriate Federal banking agency for the lead insured depository institution may, subject to the Consumer Financial Protection Act of 2010, examine the activities that are permissible for a depository institution subsidiary conducted by such nondepository institution subsidiary (other than a functionally regulated subsidiary or a subsidiary of a depository institution) of the depository institution holding company as if the nondepository institution subsidiary were an insured depository institution for which the appropriate Federal banking agency of the lead insured depository institution was the appropriate Federal banking agency, to determine whether the activities—

"(A) pose a material threat to the safety and soundness of any insured depository institution subsidiary of the depository institution holding company;

"(B) are conducted in accordance with applicable Federal law; and

"(C) are subject to appropriate systems for monitoring and controlling the financial, operating, and other material risks of the activ-

ities that may pose a material threat to the safety and soundness of the insured depository institution subsidiaries of the holding company.

"(3) AGENCY COORDINATION WITH THE BOARD

An appropriate Federal banking agency that conducts an examination pursuant to paragraph (2) shall coordinate examination of the activities of nondepository institution subsidiaries described in subsection (b) with the Board in a manner that—

"(A) avoids duplication;

"(B) shares information relevant to the supervision of the depository institution holding company;

"(C) achieves the objectives of subsection (b); and

"(D) ensures that the depository institution holding company and the subsidiaries of the depository institution holding company are not subject to conflicting supervisory demands by such agency and the Board.

"(4) FEE PERMITTED FOR EXAMINATION COSTS

An appropriate Federal banking agency that conducts an examination or enforcement action pursuant to this section may collect an assessment, fee, or such other charge from the subsidiary as the appropriate Federal banking agency determines necessary or appropriate to carry out the responsibilities of the appropriate Federal banking agency in connection with such examination.

"(e) REFERRALS FOR ENFORCEMENT BY APPROPRIATE FEDERAL BANKING AGENCY

"(1) RECOMMENDATION OF ENFORCEMENT ACTION

The appropriate Federal banking agency for the lead insured depository institution, based upon its examination of a nondepository institution subsidiary conducted pursuant to subsection (d), or other relevant information, may submit to the Board, in writing, a recommendation that the Board take enforcement action against such nondepository institution subsidiary, together with an explanation of the concerns giving rise to the recommendation, if the appropriate Federal banking agency determines (by a vote of its members, if applicable) that the activities of the nondepository institution subsidiary pose a material threat to the safety and soundness of any insured depository institution subsidiary of the depository institution holding company.

"(2) BACK–UP AUTHORITY OF THE APPROPRIATE FEDERAL BANKING AGENCY

If, within the 60–day period beginning on the date on which the Board receives a recommendation under paragraph (1), the Board does not take enforcement action against the nondepository institution subsidiary or provide a plan for supervisory or enforcement action that is acceptable to the appropriate Federal banking agency that made the recommendation pursuant to paragraph (1), such agency may take the recommended enforcement action against the nondepository institution subsidiary, in the same manner as if the nondepository institution subsidiary were an insured depository institution for which the agency was the appropriate Federal banking agency.

"(f) COORDINATION AMONG APPROPRIATE FEDERAL BANKING AGENCIES

Each Federal banking agency, prior to or when exercising authority under subsection (d) or (e) shall—

"(1) provide reasonable notice to, and consult with, the appropriate Federal banking agency or State bank supervisor (or other State regulatory agency) of the nondepository institution subsidiary of a depository institution holding company that is described in subsection (d) before commencing any examination of the subsidiary;

"(2) to the fullest extent possible—

"(A) rely on the examinations, inspections, and reports of the appropriate Federal banking agency or the State bank supervisor (or other State regulatory agency) of the subsidiary;

"(B) avoid duplication of examination activities, reporting requirements, and requests for information; and

"(C) ensure that the depository institution holding company and the subsidiaries of the depository institution holding company are

not subject to conflicting supervisory demands by the appropriate Federal banking agencies.

"(g) RULE OF CONSTRUCTION

No provision of this section shall be construed as limiting any authority of the Board, the Corporation, or the Comptroller of the Currency under any other provision of law."

(b) EFFECTIVE DATE

The amendment made by subsection (a) shall take effect on the transfer date.

§ 606. Requirements for Financial Holding Companies to Remain Well Capitalized and Well Managed

(a) AMENDMENT

Section 4(l)(1) of the Bank Holding Company Act of 1956 (12 U.S.C. 1843(l)(1)) is amended—

(1) in subparagraph (B), by striking "and" at the end;

(2) by redesignating subparagraph (C) as subparagraph (D);

(3) by inserting after subparagraph (B) the following: "(C) the bank holding company is well capitalized and well managed; and"; and

(4) in subparagraph (D)(ii), as so redesignated, by striking "subparagraphs (A) and (B)" and inserting "subparagraphs (A), (B), and (C)".

(b) HOME OWNERS' LOAN ACT AMENDMENT

Section 10(c)(2) of the Home Owners' Loan Act (12 U.S.C. 1467a(c)(2)) is amended by adding at the end the following new subparagraph: "(H) Any activity that is permissible for a financial holding company (as such term is defined under section 2(p) of the Bank Holding Company Act of 1956 (12 U.S.C. 1841(p)) to conduct under section 4(k) of the Bank Holding Company Act of 1956 if—

"(i) the savings and loan holding company meets all of the criteria to qualify as a financial holding company, and complies with all of the requirements applicable to a financial holding company, under sections 4(l) and 4(m) of the Bank Holding Company Act and section 804(c) of the Community Reinvestment Act of 1977 (12 U.S.C. 2903(c)) as if the savings and loan holding company was a bank holding company; and "(ii) the savings and loan holding company conducts the activity in accordance with the same terms, conditions, and requirements that apply to the conduct of such activity by a bank holding company under the Bank Holding Company Act of 1956 and the Board's regulations and interpretations under such Act.''

(c) EFFECTIVE DATE

The amendments made by this section shall take effect on the transfer date.

§ 607. Standards for Interstate Acquisitions

(a) ACQUISITION OF BANKS

Section 3(d)(1)(A) of the Bank Holding Company Act of 1956 (12 U.S.C. 1842(d)(1)(A)) is amended by striking "adequately capitalized and adequately managed" and inserting "well capitalized and well managed".

(b) INTERSTATE BANK MERGERS

Section 44(b)(4)(B) of the Federal Deposit Insurance Act (12 U.S.C. 1831u(b)(4)(B)) is amended by striking "will continue to be adequately capitalized and adequately managed" and inserting "will be well capitalized and well managed".

(c) EFFECTIVE DATE

The amendments made by this section shall take effect on the transfer date.

§ 608. Enhancing Existing Restrictions on Bank Transactions with Affiliates

(a) AFFILIATE TRANSACTIONS

Section 23A of the Federal Reserve Act (12 U.S.C. 371c) is amended—

(1) in subsection (b)—

(A) in paragraph (1), by striking subparagraph (D) and inserting the following: "(D) any investment fund with respect to which a member bank or affiliate thereof is an investment adviser; and"; and

(B) in paragraph (7)—

(i) in subparagraph (A), by inserting before the semicolon at the end the following: ", including a purchase of assets subject to an agreement to repurchase";

(ii) in subparagraph (C), by striking ", including assets subject to an agreement to repurchase,";

(iii) in subparagraph (D)—

(I) by inserting "or other debt obligations" after "acceptance of securities"; and

(II) by striking "or" at the end; and

(iv) by adding at the end the following: "(F) a transaction with an affiliate that involves the borrowing or lending of securities, to the extent that the transaction causes a member bank or a subsidiary to have credit exposure to the affiliate; or "(G) a derivative transaction, as defined in paragraph (3) of section 5200(b) of the Revised Statutes of the United States (12 U.S.C. 84(b)), with an affiliate, to the extent that the transaction causes a member bank or a subsidiary to have credit exposure to the affiliate;";

(2) in subsection (c)—

(A) in paragraph (1)—

(i) in the matter preceding subparagraph (A), by striking "subsidiary" and all that follows through "time of the transaction" and inserting "subsidiary, and any credit exposure of a member bank or a subsidiary to an affiliate resulting from a securities borrowing or lending transaction, or a derivative transaction, shall be secured at all times"; and

(ii) in each of subparagraphs (A) through (D), by striking "or letter of credit" and inserting "letter of credit, or credit exposure";

(B) by striking paragraph (2);

(C) by redesignating paragraphs (3) through (5) as paragraphs (2) through (4), respectively;

(D) in paragraph (2), as so redesignated, by inserting before the period at the end ", or credit exposure to an affiliate resulting from a securities borrowing or lending transaction, or derivative transaction"; and

(E) in paragraph (3), as so redesignated—

(i) by inserting "or other debt obligations" after "securities"; and

(ii) by striking "or guarantee" and all that follows through "behalf of," and inserting "guarantee, acceptance, or letter of credit issued on behalf of, or credit exposure from a securities borrowing or lending transaction, or derivative transaction to,";

(3) in subsection (d)(4), in the matter preceding subparagraph

(A), by striking "or issuing" and all that follows through "behalf of," and inserting "issuing a guarantee, acceptance, or letter of credit on behalf of, or having credit exposure resulting from a securities borrowing or lending transaction, or derivative transaction to,"; and

(4) in subsection (f)—

(A) in paragraph (2)—

(i) by striking "or order";

(ii) by striking "if it finds" and all that follows through the end of the paragraph and inserting the following: "if—

"(i) the Board finds the exemption to be in the public interest and consistent with the purposes of this section, and notifies the Federal Deposit Insurance Corporation of such finding; and

"(ii) before the end of the 60–day period beginning on the date on which the Federal Deposit Insurance Corporation receives notice of the finding under clause (i), the Federal Deposit Insurance Corporation does not object, in writing, to the finding, based on a determination that the exemption presents an unacceptable risk to the Deposit Insurance Fund.";

(iii) by striking the Board and inserting the following: "(A) IN GENERAL.—The Board"; and

(iv) by adding at the end the following:

"(B) ADDITIONAL EXEMPTIONS

"(i) NATIONAL BANKS

The Comptroller of the Currency may, by order, exempt a transaction of a national bank from the requirements of this section if—

"(I) the Board and the Office of the Comptroller of the Currency jointly find the exemption to be in the public interest and consistent with the purposes of this section and notify the Federal Deposit Insurance Corporation of such finding; and

"(II) before the end of the 60–day period beginning on the date on which the Federal Deposit Insurance Corporation receives notice of the finding under subclause (I), the

Federal Deposit Insurance Corporation does not object, in writing, to the finding, based on a determination that the exemption presents an unacceptable risk to the Deposit Insurance Fund.

"(ii) STATE BANKS

The Federal Deposit Insurance Corporation may, by order, exempt a transaction of a State nonmember bank, and the Board may, by order, exempt a transaction of a State member bank, from the requirements of this section if—

"(I) the Board and the Federal Deposit Insurance Corporation jointly find that the exemption is in the public interest and consistent with the purposes of this section; and

"(II) the Federal Deposit Insurance Corporation finds that the exemption does not present an unacceptable risk to the Deposit Insurance Fund."; and

(B) by adding at the end the following:

"(4) AMOUNTS OF COVERED TRANSACTIONS

The Board may issue such regulations or interpretations as the Board determines are necessary or appropriate with respect to the manner in which a netting agreement may be taken into account in determining the amount of a covered transaction between a member bank or a subsidiary and an affiliate, including the extent to which netting agreements between a member bank or a subsidiary and an affiliate may be taken into account in determining whether a covered transaction is fully secured for purposes of subsection (d)(4). An interpretation under this paragraph with respect to a specific member bank, subsidiary, or affiliate shall be issued jointly with the appropriate Federal banking agency for such member bank, subsidiary, or affiliate.".

(b) TRANSACTIONS WITH AFFILIATES

Section 23B(e) of the Federal Reserve Act (12 U.S.C. 371c–1(e)) is amended—

(1) by striking the undesignated matter following subparagraph (B);

(2) by redesignating subparagraphs (A) and (B) as clauses (i) and (ii), respectively, and adjusting the clause margins accordingly;

(3) by redesignating paragraphs (1) and (2) as subparagraphs (A) and (B), respectively, and adjusting the subparagraph margins accordingly;

(4) by striking "The Board" and inserting the following:

"(1) IN GENERAL

The Board"; (5) in paragraph (1)(B), as so redesignated—

(A) in the matter preceding clause (i), by inserting before "regulations" the following: "subject to paragraph (2), if the Board finds that an exemption or exclusion is in the public interest and is consistent with the purposes of this section, and notifies the Federal Deposit Insurance Corporation of such finding,"; and

(B) in clause (ii), by striking the comma at the end and inserting a period; and (6) by adding at the end the following:

"(2) EXCEPTION

The Board may grant an exemption or exclusion under this subsection only if, during the 60–day period beginning on the date of receipt of notice of the finding from Corporation does not object, in writing, to such exemption or exclusion, based on a determination that the exemption presents an unacceptable risk to the Deposit Insurance Fund."

(c) HOME OWNERS' LOAN ACT

Section 11 of the Home Owners' Loan Act (12 U.S.C. 1468) is amended by adding at the end the following:

"(d) EXEMPTIONS.—

"(1) FEDERAL SAVINGS ASSOCIATIONS

The Comptroller of the Currency may, by order, exempt a transaction of a Federal savings association from the requirements of this section if—

"(A) the Board and the Office of the Comptroller of the Currency jointly find the exemption to be in the public interest and consistent with the purposes of this section and notify the Federal Deposit Insurance Corporation of such finding; and

"(B) before the end of the 60–day period beginning on the date on which the Federal Deposit Insurance Corporation receives notice of the finding under subparagraph (A),

the Federal Deposit Insurance Corporation does not object, in writing, to the finding, based on a determination that the exemption presents an unacceptable risk to the Deposit Insurance Fund.

"(2) STATE SAVINGS ASSOCIATION

The Federal Deposit Insurance Corporation may, by order, exempt a transaction of a State savings association from the requirements of this section if the Board and the Federal Deposit Insurance Corporation jointly find that—

"(A) the exemption is in the public interest and consistent with the purposes of this section; and

"(B) the exemption does not present an unacceptable risk to the Deposit Insurance Fund.".

(d) EFFECTIVE DATE

The amendments made by this section shall take effect 1 year after the transfer date.

§ 609. Eliminating Exceptions for Transactions with Financial Subsidiaries

(a) AMENDMENT

Section 23A(e) of the Federal Reserve Act (12 U.S.C. 371c(e)) is amended—

(1) by striking paragraph (3); and

(2) by redesignating paragraph (4) as paragraph (3).

(b) PROSPECTIVE APPLICATION OF AMENDMENT

The amendments made by this section shall apply with respect to any covered transaction between a bank and a subsidiary of the bank, as those terms are defined in section 23A of the Federal Reserve Act (12 U.S.C. 371c), that is entered into on or after the date of enactment of this Act.

(c) EFFECTIVE DATE

The amendments made by this section shall take effect 1 year after the transfer date.

§ 610. Lending Limits Applicable to Credit Exposure on Derivative Transactions, Repurchase Agreements, Reverse Repurchase Agreements, and Securities Lending and Borrowing Transactions

(a) NATIONAL BANKS

Section 5200(b) of the Revised Statutes of the United States (12 U.S.C. 84(b)) is amended—

(1) in paragraph (1), by striking "shall include" and all that follows through the end of the paragraph and inserting the following: "shall include—

"(A) all direct or indirect advances of funds to a person made on the basis of any obligation of that person to repay the funds or repayable from specific property pledged by or on behalf of the person;

"(B) to the extent specified by the Comptroller of the Currency, any liability of a national banking association to advance funds to or on behalf of a person pursuant to a contractual commitment; and

"(C) any credit exposure to a person arising from a derivative transaction, repurchase agreement, reverse repurchase agreement, securities lending transaction, or securities borrowing transaction between the national banking association and the person;";

(2) in paragraph (2), by striking the period at the end and inserting "; and"; and

(3) by adding at the end the following: "(3) the term 'derivative transaction' includes any transaction that is a contract, agreement, swap, warrant, note, or option that is based, in whole or in part, on the value of, any interest in, or any quantitative measure or the occurrence of any event relating to, one or more commodities, securities, currencies, interest or other rates, indices, or other assets.".

(b) SAVINGS ASSOCIATIONS

Section 5(u)(3) of the Home Owners' Loan Act (12 U.S.C. 1464(u)(3)) is amended by striking "Director" each place that term appears and inserting "Comptroller of the Currency".

(c) EFFECTIVE DATE

The amendments made by this section shall take effect 1 year after the transfer date.

§ 611. Consistent Treatment of Derivative Transactions in Lending Limits

(a) AMENDMENT

Section 18 of the Federal Deposit Insurance Act (12 U.S.C. 1828) is amended by adding at the end the following: "(y) STATE LENDING LIMIT TREATMENT OF DERIVATIVES TRANS-ACTIONS.—An insured State bank may engage in a derivative transaction, as defined in section 5200(b)(3) of the Revised Statutes of the United States (12 U.S.C. 84(b)(3)), only if the law with respect to lending limits of the State in which the insured State bank is chartered takes into consideration credit exposure to derivative transactions.".

(b) EFFECTIVE DATE

The amendment made by this section shall take effect 18 months after the transfer date.

§ 612. Restriction on Conversions of Troubled Banks

(a) CONVERSION OF A NATIONAL BANKING ASSOCIATION

The Act entitled "An Act to provide for the conversion of national banking associations into and their merger or consolidation with State banks, and for other purposes." (12 U.S.C. 214 et seq.) is amended by adding at the end the following:

"SEC. 10. PROHIBITION ON CONVERSION.

"A national banking association may not convert to a State bank or State savings association during any period in which the national banking association is subject to a cease and desist order (or other formal enforcement order) issued by, or a memorandum of understanding entered into with, the Comptroller of the Currency with respect to a significant supervisory matter.".

(b) CONVERSION OF A STATE BANK OR SAVINGS ASSOCIATION

Section 5154 of the Revised Statutes of the United States (12 U.S.C. 35) is amended by adding at the end the following: "The Comptroller of the Currency may not approve the conversion of a State bank or State savings association to a national banking association or Federal savings association during any period in which the State bank or State savings association is subject to a cease and desist order (or other formal enforcement order) issued by, or a memorandum of understanding entered into with, a State bank supervisor or the appropriate Federal banking agency with respect to a significant supervisory matter or a final enforcement action by a State Attorney General.".

(c) CONVERSION OF A FEDERAL SAVINGS ASSOCIATION

Section 5(i) of the Home Owners' Loan Act (12 U.S.C. 1464(i)) is amended by adding at the end the following:

"(6) LIMITATION ON CERTAIN CONVERSIONS BY FEDERAL SAVINGS ASSOCIATIONS

A Federal savings association may not convert to a State bank or State savings association during any period in which the Federal savings association is subject to a cease and desist order (or other formal enforcement order) issued by, or a memorandum of understanding entered into with, the Office of Thrift Supervision or the Comptroller of the Currency with respect to a significant supervisory matter.".

(d) EXCEPTION

The prohibition on the approval of conversions under the amendments made by subsections (a), (b), and (c) shall not apply, if—

(1) the Federal banking agency that would be the appropriate Federal banking agency after the proposed conversion gives the appropriate Federal banking agency or State bank supervisor that issued the cease and desist order (or other formal enforcement order) or memorandum of understanding, as appropriate, written notice of the proposed conversion including a plan to address the significant supervisory matter in a manner that is consistent with the safe and sound operation of the institution;

(2) within 30 days of receipt of the written notice required under paragraph (1), the appropriate Federal banking agency or State bank supervisor that issued the cease and desist order (or other formal enforcement order) or memorandum of understanding, as appropriate, does not object to the conversion or the plan to address the significant supervisory matter;

(3) after conversion of the insured depository institution, the appropriate Federal banking agency after the conversion implements such plan; and

(4) in the case of a final enforcement action by a State Attorney General, approval of the conversion is conditioned on compliance by the insured depository institution with the terms of such final enforcement action.

(e) NOTIFICATION OF PENDING ENFORCEMENT ACTIONS

(1) COPY OF CONVERSION APPLICATION

At the time an insured depository institution files a conversion application, the insured depository institution shall transmit a copy of the conversion application to—

(A) the appropriate Federal banking agency for the insured depository institution; and

(B) the Federal banking agency that would be the appropriate Federal banking agency of the insured depository institution after the proposed conversion.

(2) NOTIFICATION AND ACCESS TO INFORMATION

Upon receipt of a copy of the application described in paragraph (1), the appropriate Federal banking agency for the insured depository institution proposing the conversion shall—

(A) notify the Federal banking agency that would be the appropriate Federal banking agency for the institution after the proposed conversion in writing of any ongoing supervisory or investigative proceedings that the appropriate Federal banking agency for the institution proposing to convert believes is likely to result, in the near term and absent the proposed conversion, in a cease and desist order (or other formal enforcement order) or memorandum of understanding with respect to a significant supervisory matter; and

(B) provide the Federal banking agency that would be the appropriate Federal banking agency for the institution after the proposed conversion access to all investigative and supervisory information relating to the proceedings described in subparagraph (A).

§ 613. De Novo Branching into States

(a) NATIONAL BANKS

Section 5155(g)(1)(A) of the Revised Statutes of the United States (12 U.S.C. 36(g)(1)(A)) is amended to read as follows:

"(A) the law of the State in which the branch is located, or is to be located, would permit establishment of the branch, if the national bank were a State bank chartered by such State; and".

(b) STATE INSURED BANKS

Section 18(d)(4)(A)(i) of the Federal Deposit Insurance Act (12 U.S.C. 1828(d)(4)(A)(i)) is amended to read as follows:

> "(i) the law of the State in which the branch is located, or is to be located, would permit establishment of the branch, if the bank were a State bank chartered by such State; and".

§ 614. Lending Limits to Insiders

(a) EXTENSIONS OF CREDIT

Section 22(h)(9)(D)(i) of the Federal Reserve Act (12 U.S.C. 375b(9)(D)(i)) is amended—

(1) by striking the period at the end and inserting "; or";

(2) by striking "a person" and inserting "the person";

(3) by striking "extends credit by making" and inserting the following: "extends credit to a person by—"(I) making"; and

(4) by adding at the end the following: "(II) having credit exposure to the person arising from a derivative transaction (as defined in section 5200(b) of the Revised Statutes of the United States (12 U.S.C. 84(b))), repurchase agreement, reverse repurchase agreement, securities lending transaction, or securities borrowing transaction between the member bank and the person.".

(b) EFFECTIVE DATE

The amendments made by this section shall take effect 1 year after the transfer date.

§ 615. Limitations on Purchases of Assets from Insiders

(a) AMENDMENT TO THE FEDERAL DEPOSIT INSURANCE ACT

Section 18 of the Federal Deposit Insurance Act (12 U.S.C. 1828) is amended by adding at the end the following:

> "(z) GENERAL PROHIBITION ON SALE OF ASSETS
>
> "(1) IN GENERAL
>
> An insured depository institution may not purchase an asset from, or sell an asset to, an executive officer, director, or principal shareholder of the insured depository institution, or any related interest of such person (as such terms are defined in section 22(h) of Federal Reserve Act), unless—

> "(A) the transaction is on market terms; and
>
> "(B) if the transaction represents more than 10 percent of the capital stock and surplus of the insured depository institution, the transaction has been approved in advance by a majority of the members of the board of directors of the insured depository institution who do not have an interest in the transaction.
>
> "(2) RULEMAKING
>
> The Board of Governors of the Federal Reserve System may issue such rules as may be necessary to define terms and to carry out the purposes this subsection. Before proposing or adopting a rule under this paragraph, the Board of Governors of the Federal Reserve System shall consult with the Comptroller of the Currency and the Corporation as to the terms of the rule.".

(b) AMENDMENTS TO THE FEDERAL RESERVE ACT

Section 22(d) of the Federal Reserve Act (12 U.S.C. 375) is amended to read as follows: "(d) [Reserved]".

(c) EFFECTIVE DATE

The amendments made by this section shall take effect on the transfer date.

§ 616. Regulations Regarding Capital Levels

(a) CAPITAL LEVELS OF BANK HOLDING COMPANIES

Section 5(b) of the Bank Holding Company Act of 1956 (12 U.S.C. 1844(b)) is amended—

(1) by inserting after "orders" the following: ", including regulations and orders relating to the capital requirements for bank holding companies,"; and

(2) by adding at the end the following: "In establishing capital regulations pursuant to this subsection, the Board shall seek to make such requirements countercyclical, so that the amount of capital required to be maintained by a company increases in times of economic expansion and decreases in times of economic contraction, consistent with the safety and soundness of the company.".

(b) CAPITAL LEVELS OF SAVINGS AND LOAN HOLDING COMPANIES

Section 10(g)(1) of the Home Owners' Loan Act (12 U.S.C. 1467a(g)(1)) is amended—

(1) by inserting after "orders" the following: ", including regulations and orders relating to capital requirements for savings and loan holding companies,"; and

(2) by inserting at the end the following: "In establishing capital regulations pursuant to this subsection, the appropriate Federal banking agency shall seek to make such requirements countercyclical so that the amount of capital required to be maintained by a company increases in times of economic expansion and decreases in times of economic contraction, consistent with the safety and soundness of the company.".

(c) CAPITAL LEVELS OF INSURED DEPOSITORY INSTITUTIONS

Section 908(a)(1) of the International Lending Supervision Act of 1983 (12 U.S.C. 3907(a)(1)) is amended by adding at the end the following: "Each appropriate Federal banking agency shall seek to make the capital standards required under this section or other provisions of Federal law for insured depository institutions countercyclical so that the amount of capital required to be maintained by an insured depository institution increases in times of economic expansion and decreases in times of economic contraction, consistent with the safety and soundness of the insured depository institution."

(d) SOURCE OF STRENGTH

The Federal Deposit Insurance Act (12 U.S.C. 1811 et seq.) is amended by inserting after section 38 (12 U.S.C. 1831o) the following:

"SEC. 38A. SOURCE OF STRENGTH.

"(a) HOLDING COMPANIES

The appropriate Federal banking agency for a bank holding company or savings and loan holding company shall require the bank holding company or savings and loan holding company to serve as a source of financial strength for any subsidiary of the bank holding company or savings and loan holding company that is a depository institution.

"(b) OTHER COMPANIES

If an insured depository institution is not the subsidiary of a bank holding company or savings and loan holding company, the appropriate Federal banking agency for the insured depository institution shall require any company that directly or indirectly controls the insured depository institution to serve as a source of financial strength for such institution.

"(c) REPORTS

The appropriate Federal banking agency for an insured depository institution described in subsection (b) may, from time to time, require the company, or a company that directly or indirectly controls the insured depository institution, to submit a report, under oath, for the purposes of—

"(1) assessing the ability of such company to comply with the requirement under subsection (b); and

"(2) enforcing the compliance of such company with the requirement under subsection (b).

"(d) RULES

Not later than 1 year after the transfer date, as defined in section 311 of the Enhancing Financial Institution Safety and Soundness Act of 2010, the appropriate Federal banking agencies shall jointly issue final rules to carry out this section.

"(e) DEFINITION

In this section, the term 'source of financial strength' means the ability of a company that directly or indirectly owns or controls an insured depository institution to provide financial assistance to such insured depository institution in the event of the financial distress of the insured depository institution.".

(e) EFFECTIVE DATE

The amendments made by this section shall take effect on the transfer date.

§ 617. Elimination of Elective Investment Bank Holding Company framework

(a) AMENDMENT

Section 17 of the Securities Exchange Act of 1934 (15 U.S.C. 78q) is amended—

(1) by striking subsection (i); and

(2) by redesignating subsections (j) and (k) as subsections (i) and (j), respectively.

(b) EFFECTIVE DATE

The amendments made by this section shall take effect on the transfer date.

§ 618. Securities Holding Companies

(a) DEFINITIONS

In this section—

(1) the term "associated person of a securities holding company" means a person directly or indirectly controlling, controlled by, or under common control with, a securities holding company;

(2) the term "foreign bank" has the same meaning as in section 1(b)(7) of the International Banking Act of 1978 (12 U.S.C. 3101(7));

(3) the term "insured bank" has the same meaning as in section 3 of the Federal Deposit Insurance Act (12 U.S.C. 1813);

(4) the term "securities holding company"—

(A) means—(i) a person (other than a natural person) that owns or controls 1 or more brokers or dealers registered with the Commission; and

(ii) the associated persons of a person described in clause (i); and

(B) does not include a person that is—

(i) a nonbank financial company supervised by the Board under title I;

(ii) an insured bank (other than an institution described in subparagraphs (D), (F), or (H) of section 2(c)(2) of the Bank Holding Company Act of 1956 (12 U.S.C. 1841(c)(2)) or a savings association;

(iii) an affiliate of an insured bank (other than an institution described in subparagraphs (D), (F), or (H) of section 2(c)(2) of the Bank Holding Company Act of 1956 (12 U.S.C. 1841(c)(2)) or an affiliate of a savings association;

(iv) a foreign bank, foreign company, or company that is described in section 8(a) of the International Banking Act of 1978 (12 U.S.C. 3106(a));

(v) a foreign bank that controls, directly or indirectly, a corporation chartered under section 25A of the Federal Reserve Act (12 U.S.C. 611 et seq.); or

(vi) subject to comprehensive consolidated supervision by a foreign regulator;

(5) the term "supervised securities holding company" means a securities holding company that is supervised by the Board of Governors under this section; and

(6) the terms "affiliate", "bank", "bank holding company", "company", "control", "savings association", and "subsidiary" have the same meanings as in section 2 of the Bank Holding Company Act of 1956.

(b) SUPERVISION OF A SECURITIES HOLDING COMPANY NOT HAVING A BANK OR SAVINGS ASSOCIATION AFFILIATE

(1) IN GENERAL

A securities holding company that is required by a foreign regulator or provision of foreign law to be subject to comprehensive consolidated supervision may register with the Board of Governors under paragraph (2) to become a supervised securities holding company. Any securities holding company filing such a registration shall be supervise in accordance with this section, and shall comply with the rules and orders prescribed by the Board of Governors applicable to supervised securities holding companies.

(2) REGISTRATION AS A SUPERVISED SECURITIES HOLDING COMPANY

(A) REGISTRATION

A securities holding company that elects to be subject to comprehensive consolidated supervision shall register by filing with the Board of Governors such information and documents as the Board of Governors, by regulation, may prescribe as necessary or appropriate in furtherance of the purposes of this section.

(B) EFFECTIVE DATE

A securities holding company that registers under subparagraph (A) shall be deemed to be a supervised securities holding company, effective on the date that is 45 days after the date of receipt of the registration information and documents under subparagraph(A) by the Board of Governors, or within such shorter period as the Board of Governors, by rule or order, may determine.

(c) SUPERVISION OF SECURITIES HOLDING COMPANIES

(1) RECORDKEEPING AND REPORTING

(A) RECORDKEEPING AND REPORTING REQUIRED

Each supervised securities holding company and each affiliate of a supervised securities holding company shall make and keep for periods determined by the Board of Governors such records, furnish copies of such records, and make such reports, as the Board of Governors determines to be necessary or appropriate to carry out this section, to prevent evasions thereof, and to monitor compliance by the supervised securities holding company or affiliate with applicable provisions of law.

(B) FORM AND CONTENTS.—

(i) IN GENERAL

Any record or report required to be made, furnished, or kept under this paragraph shall—

(I) be prepared in such form and according to such specifications (including certification by a registered public accounting firm), as the Board of Governors may require; and

(II) be provided promptly to the Board of Governors at any time, upon request by the Board of Governors.

(ii) CONTENTS

Records and reports required to be made, furnished, or kept under this paragraph may include—

(I) a balance sheet or income statement of the supervised securities holding company or an affiliate of a supervised securities holding company;

(II) an assessment of the consolidated capital and liquidity of the supervised securities holding company;

(III) a report by an independent auditor attesting to the compliance of the supervised securities holding company with the internal risk management and internal control objectives of the supervised securities holding company; and

(IV) a report concerning the extent to which the supervised securities holding company or affiliate has complied with the provisions of this section and any regulations prescribed and orders issued under this section.

(2) USE OF EXISTING REPORTS

(A) IN GENERAL

The Board of Governors shall, to the fullest extent possible, accept reports in fulfillment of the requirements of this paragraph that a supervised securities holding company or an affiliate of a supervised securities holding company has been required to provide to another regulatory agency or a self-regulatory organization.

(B) AVAILABILITY

A supervised securities holding company or an affiliate of a supervised securities holding company shall promptly provide to the Board of Governors, at the request of the Board of Governors, any report described in subparagraph (A), as permitted by law.

(3) EXAMINATION AUTHORITY

(A) FOCUS OF EXAMINATION AUTHORITY

The Board of Governors may make examinations of any supervised securities holding company and any affiliate of a supervised securities holding company to carry out this subsection, to prevent evasions thereof, and to monitor compliance by the supervised securities holding company or affiliate with applicable provisions of law.

(B) DEFERENCE TO OTHER EXAMINATIONS

For purposes of this subparagraph, the Board of Governors shall, to the fullest extent possible, use the reports of examination made by other appropriate Federal or State regulatory authorities with respect to any functionally regulated subsidiary or any institution described in subparagraph (D),(F), or (H) of section 2(c)(2) of the Bank Holding Company Act of 1956 (12 U.S.C. 1841(c)(2)).

(d) CAPITAL AND RISK MANAGEMENT

(1) IN GENERAL

The Board of Governors shall, by regulation or order, prescribe capital adequacy and other risk management standards for supervised securities holding companies that are appropriate to protect the safety and soundness of the supervised securities holding companies and address the risks posed to financial stability by supervised securities holding companies.

(2) DIFFERENTIATION

In imposing standards under this subsection, the Board of Governors may differentiate among supervised securities holding companies on an individual basis, or by category, taking into consideration the requirements under paragraph (3).

(3) CONTENT

Any standards imposed on a supervised securities holding company under this subsection shall take into account—

(A) the differences among types of business activities carried out by the supervised securities holding company;

(B) the amount and nature of the financial assets of the supervised securities holding company;

(C) the amount and nature of the liabilities of the supervised securities holding company, including the degree of reliance on short-term funding;

(D) the extent and nature of the off-balance sheet exposures of the supervised securities holding company;

(E) the extent and nature of the transactions and relationships of the supervised securities holding company with other financial companies;

(F) the importance of the supervised securities holding company as a source of credit for households, businesses, and State and local governments, and as a source of liquidity for the financial system; and

(G) the nature, scope, and mix of the activities of the supervised securities holding company.

(4) NOTICE

A capital requirement imposed under this subsection may not take effect earlier than 180 days after the date on which a supervised securities holding company is provided notice of the capital requirement.

(e) OTHER PROVISIONS OF LAW APPLICABLE TO SUPERVISED SECURITIES HOLDING COMPANIES

(1) FEDERAL DEPOSIT INSURANCE ACT

Subsections (b), (c) through (s), and (u) of section 8 of the Federal Deposit Insurance Act (12 U.S.C. 1818) shall apply to any supervised securities holding company, and to any subsidiary (other than a bank or an institution described in subparagraph (D), (F), or (H) of section 2(c)(2) of the Bank Holding Company Act of 1956 (12 U.S.C. 1841(c)(2))) of a super-

vised securities holding company, in the same manner as such subsections apply to a bank holding company for which the Board of Governors is the appropriate Federal banking agency. For purposes of applying such subsections to a supervised securities holding company or a subsidiary (other than a bank or an institution described in subparagraph (D), (F), or (H) of section 2(c)(2) of the Bank Holding Company Act of 1956 (12 U.S.C. 1841(c)(2))) of a supervised securities holding company, the Board of Governors shall be deemed the appropriate Federal banking agency for the supervised securities holding company or subsidiary.

(2) BANK HOLDING COMPANY ACT OF 1956

Except as the Board of Governors may otherwise provide by regulation or order, a supervised securities holding company shall be subject to the provisions of the Bank Holding Company Act of 1956 (12 U.S.C. 1841 et seq.) in the same manner and to the same extent a bank holding company is subject to such provisions, except that a supervised securities holding company may not, by reason of this paragraph, be deemed to be a bank holding company for purposes of section 4 of the Bank Holding Company Act of 1956 (12 U.S.C. 1843).

§ 619. Prohibitions on Proprietary Trading and Certain Relationships with Hedge Funds and Private Equity Funds

The Bank Holding Company Act of 1956 (12 U.S.C. 1841 et seq.) is amended by adding at the end the following:

"SEC. 13. PROHIBITIONS ON PROPRIETARY TRADING AND CERTAIN RELATIONSHIPS WITH HEDGE FUNDS AND PRIVATE EQUITY FUNDS.

"(a) IN GENERAL

"(1) PROHIBITION

Unless otherwise provided in this section, a banking entity shall not—

"(A) engage in proprietary trading; or

"(B) acquire or retain any equity, partnership, or other ownership interest in or sponsor a hedge fund or a private equity fund.

"(2) NONBANK FINANCIAL COMPANIES SUPERVISED BY THE BOARD

Any nonbank financial company supervised by the Board that engages in proprietary trading or takes or retains any equity, partnership, or other ownership interest in or sponsors a hedge fund or a private equity fund shall be subject, by rule, as provided in subsection (b)(2), to additional capital requirements for and additional quantitative limits with regards to such proprietary trading and taking or retaining any equity, partnership, or other ownership interest in or sponsorship of a hedge fund or a private equity fund, except that permitted activities as described in subsection (d) shall not be subject to the additional capital and additional quantitative limits except as provided in subsection (d)(3), as if the nonbank financial company supervised by the Board were a banking entity.

(b) STUDY AND RULEMAKING

"(1) STUDY

Not later than 6 months after the date of enactment of this section, the Financial Stability Oversight Council shall study and make recommendations on implementing the provisions of this section so as to—

"(A) promote and enhance the safety and soundness of banking entities;

"(B) protect taxpayers and consumers and enhance financial stability by minimizing the risk that insured depository institutions and the affiliates of insured depository institutions will engage in unsafe and unsound activities;

"(C) limit the inappropriate transfer of Federal subsidies from institutions that benefit from deposit insurance and liquidity facilities of the Federal Government to unregulated entities;

"(D) reduce conflicts of interest between the self-interest of banking entities and nonbank financial companies supervised by the Board, and the interests of the customers of such entities and companies;

"(E) limit activities that have caused undue risk or loss in banking entities and nonbank financial companies supervised by the Board, or that might reasonably be expected to create undue risk or loss in such banking entities and nonbank financial companies supervised by the Board;

"(F) appropriately accommodate the business of insurance within an insurance company, subject to regulation in accordance with the relevant insurance company investment laws, while protecting the safety and soundness of any banking entity with which such insurance company is affiliated and of the United States financial system; and

"(G) appropriately time the divestiture of illiquid assets that are affected by the implementation of the prohibitions under subsection (a).

"(2) RULEMAKING

"(A) IN GENERAL

Unless otherwise provided in this section, not later than 9 months after the completion of the study under paragraph (1), the appropriate Federal banking agencies, the Securities and Exchange Commission, and the Commodity Futures Trading Commission, shall consider the findings of the study under paragraph (1) and adopt rules to carry out this section, as provided in subparagraph (B).

"(B) COORDINATED RULEMAKING

"(i) REGULATORY AUTHORITY

The regulations issued under this paragraph shall be issued by—

"(I) the appropriate Federal banking agencies, jointly, with respect to insured depository institutions;

"(II) the Board, with respect to any company that controls an insured depository institution, or that is treated as a bank holding company for purposes of section 8 of the International Banking Act, any nonbank financial company supervised by the Board, and any subsidiary of any of the foregoing (other than a subsidiary for which an agency described in subclause (I), (III), or (IV) is the primary financial regulatory agency);

"(III) the Commodity Futures Trading Commission, with respect to any entity for which the Commodity Futures Trading Commission is the primary financial regulatory agency, as defined in section 2 of the Dodd–Frank Wall Street Reform and Consumer Protection Act; and

"(IV) the Securities and Exchange Commission, with respect to any entity for which the Securities and Exchange Commission is the primary financial regulatory agency, as defined in section 2 of the Dodd–Frank Wall Street Reform and Consumer Protection Act.

"(ii) COORDINATION, CONSISTENCY, AND COMPARABILITY

In developing and issuing regulations pursuant to this section, the appropriate Federal banking agencies, the Securities and Exchange Commission, and the Commodity Futures Trading Commission shall consult and coordinate with each other, as appropriate, for the purposes of assuring, to the extent possible, that such regulations are comparable and provide for consistent application and implementation of the applicable provisions of this section to avoid providing advantages or imposing disadvantages to the companies affected by this subsection and to protect the safety and soundness of banking entities and nonbank financial companies supervised by the Board.

"(iii) COUNCIL ROLE

The Chairperson of the Financial Stability Oversight Council shall be responsible for coordination of the regulations issued under this section.

"(c) EFFECTIVE DATE

"(1) IN GENERAL

Except as provided in paragraphs (2) and (3), this section shall take effect on the earlier of—

"(A) 12 months after the date of the issuance of final rules under subsection (b); or

"(B) 2 years after the date of enactment of this section.

"(2) CONFORMANCE PERIOD FOR DIVESTITURE

A banking entity or nonbank financial company supervised by the Board shall bring its activities and investments into compliance with the requirements of this section not later than 2 years after the date on which the requirements become effective pursuant to this section or 2 years after the date on which the entity or company becomes a nonbank financial company supervised by the Board. The Board may, by rule or order,

extend this two-year period for not more than one year at a time, if, in the judgment of the Board, such an extension is consistent with the purposes of this section and would not be detrimental to the public interest. The extensions made by the Board under the preceding sentence may not exceed an aggregate of 3 years.

"(3) EXTENDED TRANSITION FOR ILLIQUID FUNDS

"(A) APPLICATION

The Board may, upon the application of a banking entity, extend the period during which the banking entity, to the extent necessary to fulfill a contractual obligation that was in effect on May 1, 2010, may take or retain its equity, partnership, or other ownership interest in, or otherwise provide additional capital to, an illiquid fund.

"(B) TIME LIMIT ON APPROVAL

The Board may grant 1 extension under subparagraph (A), which may not exceed 5 years.

"(4) DIVESTITURE REQUIRED

Except as otherwise provided in subsection (d)(1)(G), a banking entity may not engage in any activity prohibited under subsection(a)(1)(B) after the earlier of—

"(A) the date on which the contractual obligation to invest in the illiquid fund terminates; and

"(B) the date on which any extensions granted by the Board under paragraph (3) expire.

"(5) ADDITIONAL CAPITAL DURING TRANSITION PERIOD

Notwithstanding paragraph (2), on the date on which the rules are issued under subsection (b)(2), the appropriate Federal banking agencies, the Securities and Exchange Commission, and the Commodity Futures Trading Commission shall issue rules, as provided in subsection (b)(2), to impose additional capital requirements, and any other restrictions, as appropriate, on any equity, partnership, or ownership interest in or sponsorship of a hedge fund or private equity fund by a banking entity.

"(6) SPECIAL RULEMAKING

Not later than 6 months after the date of enactment of this section, the Board shall issues rules to implement paragraphs (2) and (3).

"(d) PERMITTED ACTIVITIES

"(1) IN GENERAL

Notwithstanding the restrictions under subsection (a), to the extent permitted by any other provision of Federal or State law, and subject to the limitations under paragraph (2) and any restrictions or limitations that the appropriate Federal banking agencies, the Securities and Exchange Commission, and the Commodity Futures Trading Commission, may determine, the following activities (in this section referred to as 'permitted activities') are permitted:

"(A) The purchase, sale, acquisition, or disposition of obligations of the United States or any agency thereof, obligations, participations, or other instruments of or issued by the Government National Mortgage Association, the Federal National Mortgage Association, the Federal Home Loan Mortgage Corporation, a Federal Home Loan Bank, the Federal Agricultural Mortgage Corporation, or a Farm Credit System institution chartered under and subject to the provisions of the Farm Credit Act of 1971 (12 U.S.C. 2001 et seq.), and obligations of any State or of any political subdivision thereof.

"(B) The purchase, sale, acquisition, or disposition of securities and other instruments described in subsection (h)(4) in connection with underwriting or market-making-related activities, to the extent that any such activities permitted by this subparagraph are designed not to exceed the reasonably expected near term demands of clients, customers, or counterparties.

"(C) Risk-mitigating hedging activities in connection with and related to individual or aggregated positions, contracts, or other holdings of a banking entity that are designed to reduce the specific risks to the banking entity in connection with and related to such positions, contracts, or other holdings.

"(D) The purchase, sale, acquisition, or disposition of securities and other instruments described in subsection (h)(4) on behalf of customers.

"(E) Investments in one or more small business investment companies, as defined in section 102 of the Small Business Investment Act of 1958 (15 U.S.C. 662), investments designed primarily to promote the public welfare, of the type permitted under paragraph (11) of section 5136 of the Revised Statutes of the United States (12 U.S.C. 24), or investments that are qualified rehabilitation expenditures with respect to a qualified rehabilitated building or certified historic structure, as such terms are defined in section 47 of the Internal Revenue Code of 1986 or a similar State historic tax credit program.

"(F) The purchase, sale, acquisition, or disposition of securities and other instruments described in subsection (h)(4) by a regulated insurance company directly engaged in the business of insurance for the general account of the company and by any affiliate of such regulated insurance company, provided that such activities by any affiliate are solely for the general account of the regulated insurance company, if—

"(i) the purchase, sale, acquisition, or disposition is conducted in compliance with, and subject to, the insurance company investment laws, regulations, and written guidance of the State or jurisdiction in which each such insurance company is domiciled; and

"(ii) the appropriate Federal banking agencies, after consultation with the Financial Stability Oversight Council and the relevant insurance commissioners of the States and territories of the United States, have not jointly determined, after notice and comment, that a particular law, regulation, or written guidance described in clause (i) is insufficient to protect the safety and soundness of the banking entity, or of the financial stability of the United States.

"(G) Organizing and offering a private equity or hedge fund, including serving as a general partner, managing member, or trustee of the fund and in any manner selecting or controlling (or having employees, officers, directors, or agents who constitute) a majority of the directors, trustees, or management of the fund, including any necessary expenses for the foregoing, only if—

"(i) the banking entity provides bona fide trust, fiduciary, or investment advisory services;

"(ii) the fund is organized and offered only in connection with the provision of bona fide trust, fiduciary, or investment advisory services and only to persons that are customers of such services of the banking entity;

"(iii) the banking entity does not acquire or retain an equity interest, partnership interest, or other ownership interest in the funds except for a de minimis investment subject to and in compliance with paragraph (4);

"(iv) the banking entity complies with the restrictions under paragraphs (1) and (2) of subparagraph (f);

"(v) the banking entity does not, directly or indirectly, guarantee, assume, or otherwise insure the obligations or performance of the hedge fund or private equity fund or of any hedge fund or private equity fund in which such hedge fund or private equity fund invests;

"(vi) the banking entity does not share with the hedge fund or private equity fund, for corporate, marketing, promotional, or other purposes, the same name or a variation of the same name;

"(vii) no director or employee of the banking entity takes or retains an equity interest, partnership interest, or other ownership interest in the hedge fund or private equity fund, except for any director or employee of the banking entity who is directly engaged in providing investment advisory or other services to the hedge fund or private equity fund; and

"(viii) the banking entity discloses to prospective and actual investors in the fund, in writing, that any losses in such hedge fund or private equity fund are borne solely by investors in the fund and not by the banking entity, and otherwise complies with any additional rules of the appropriate Federal banking agencies, the Securities and Exchange Commission, or the Commodity Futures Trading Commission, as provided in subsection (b)(2), designed to ensure that losses in such hedge fund or private equity

fund are borne solely by investors in the fund and not by the banking entity.

"(H) Proprietary trading conducted by a banking entity pursuant to paragraph (9) or (13) of section 4(c), provided that the trading occurs solely outside of the United States and that the banking entity is not directly or indirectly controlled by a banking entity that is organized under the laws of the United States or of one or more States.

"(I) The acquisition or retention of any equity, partnership, or other ownership interest in, or the sponsorship of, a hedge fund or a private equity fund by a banking entity pursuant to paragraph (9) or (13) of section 4(c) solely outside of the United States, provided that no ownership interest in such hedge fund or private equity fund is offered for sale or sold to a resident of the United States and that the banking entity is not directly or indirectly controlled by a banking entity that is organized under the laws of the United States or of one or more States.

"(J) Such other activity as the appropriate Federal banking agencies, the Securities and Exchange Commission, and the Commodity Futures Trading Commission determine, by rule, as provided in subsection (b)(2), would promote and protect the safety and soundness of the banking entity and the financial stability of the United States.

"(2) LIMITATION ON PERMITTED ACTIVITIES

"(A) IN GENERAL

No transaction, class of transactions, or activity may be deemed a permitted activity under paragraph (1) if the transaction, class of transactions, or activity—

"(i) would involve or result in a material conflict of interest (as such term shall be defined by rule as provided in subsection (b)(2)) between the banking entity and its clients, customers, or counterparties;

"(ii) would result, directly or indirectly, in a material exposure by the banking entity to high-risk assets or high-risk trading strategies (as such terms shall be defined by rule as provided in subsection (b)(2));

"(iii) would pose a threat to the safety and soundness of such banking entity; or "(iv) would pose a threat to the financial stability of the United States.

"(B) RULEMAKING

The appropriate Federal banking agencies, the Securities and Exchange Commission, and the Commodity Futures Trading Commission shall issue regulations to implement subparagraph (A), as part of the regulations issued under subsection (b)(2).

"(3) CAPITAL AND QUANTITATIVE LIMITATIONS

The appropriate Federal banking agencies, the Securities and Exchange Commission, and the Commodity Futures Trading Commission shall, as provided in subsection (b)(2), adopt rules imposing additional capital requirements and quantitative limitations, including diversification requirements, regarding the activities permitted under this section if the appropriate Federal banking agencies, the Securities and Exchange Commission, and the Commodity Futures Trading Commission determine that additional capital and quantitative limitations are appropriate to protect the safety and soundness of banking entities engaged in such activities.

"(4) DE MINIMIS INVESTMENT

"(A) IN GENERAL

A banking entity may make and retain an investment in a hedge fund or private equity fund that the banking entity organizes and offers, subject to the limitations and restrictions in subparagraph (B) for the purposes of—

"(i) establishing the fund and providing the fund with sufficient initial equity for investment to permit the fund to attract unaffiliated investors; or

"(ii) making a de minimis investment.

"(B) LIMITATIONS AND RESTRICTIONS ON INVESTMENTS

"(i) REQUIREMENT TO SEEK OTHER INVESTORS

A banking entity shall actively seek unaffiliated investors to reduce or dilute the investment of the banking entity to the amount permitted under clause (ii).

"(ii) LIMITATIONS ON SIZE OF INVESTMENTS

Notwithstanding any other provision of law, investments by a banking entity in a hedge fund or private equity fund shall—

"(I) not later than 1 year after the date of establishment of the fund, be reduced through redemption, sale, or dilution to an amount that is not more than 3 percent of the total ownership interests of the fund;

"(II) be immaterial to the banking entity, as defined, by rule, pursuant to subsection (b)(2), but in no case may the aggregate of all of the interests of the banking entity in all such funds exceed 3 percent of the Tier 1 capital of the banking entity.

"(iii) CAPITAL

For purposes of determining compliance with applicable capital standards under paragraph (3), the aggregate amount of the outstanding investments by a banking entity under this paragraph, including retained earnings, shall be deducted from the assets and tangible equity of the banking entity, and the amount of the deduction shall increase commensurate with the leverage of the hedge fund or private equity fund.

"(C) EXTENSION

Upon an application by a banking entity, the Board may extend the period of time to meet the requirements under subparagraph (B)(ii)(I) for 2 additional years, if the Board finds that an extension would be consistent with safety and soundness and in the public interest.

"(e) ANTI–EVASION

"(1) RULEMAKING

The appropriate Federal banking agencies, the Securities and Exchange Commission, and the Commodity Futures Trading Commission shall issue regulations, as part of the rulemaking provided for in subsection (b)(2), regarding internal controls and recordkeeping, in order to insure compliance with this section.

"(2) TERMINATION OF ACTIVITIES OR INVESTMENT.—Notwithstanding any other provision of law, whenever an appropriate Federal banking agency, the Securities and Exchange Commission, or the Commodity

Futures Trading Commission, as appropriate, has reasonable cause to believe that a banking entity or nonbank financial company supervised by the Board under the respective agency's jurisdiction has made an investment or engaged in an activity in a manner that functions as an evasion of the requirements of this section (including through an abuse of any permitted activity) or otherwise violates the restrictions under this section, the appropriate Federal banking agency, the Securities and Exchange Commission, or the Commodity Futures Trading Commission, as appropriate, shall order, after due notice and opportunity for hearing, the banking entity or nonbank financial company supervised by the Board to terminate the activity and, as relevant, dispose of the investment. Nothing in this paragraph shall be construed to limit the inherent authority of any Federal agency or State regulatory authority to further restrict any investments or activities under otherwise applicable provisions of law.

"(f) LIMITATIONS ON RELATIONSHIPS WITH HEDGE FUNDS AND PRIVATE EQUITY FUNDS

"(1) IN GENERAL

No banking entity that serves, directly or indirectly, as the investment manager, investment adviser, or sponsor to a hedge fund or private equity fund, or that organizes and offers a hedge fund or private equity fund pursuant to paragraph (d)(1)(G), and no affiliate of such entity, may enter into a transaction with the fund, or with any other hedge fund or private equity fund that is controlled by such fund, that would be a covered transaction, as defined in section 23A of the Federal Reserve Act (12 U.S.C. 371c), with the hedge fund or private equity fund, as if such banking entity and the affiliate thereof were a member bank and the hedge fund or private equity fund were an affiliate thereof.

"(2) TREATMENT AS MEMBER BANK

A banking entity that serves, directly or indirectly, as the investment manager, investment adviser, or sponsor to a hedge fund or private equity fund, or that organizes and offers a hedge fund or private equity fund pursuant to paragraph (d)(1)(G), shall be subject to section 23B of the Federal Reserve Act (12 U.S.C. 371c–1), as if such banking entity were a member bank and such hedge fund or private equity fund were an affiliate thereof.

"(3) PERMITTED SERVICES

"(A) IN GENERAL

Notwithstanding paragraph (1), the Board may permit a banking entity to enter into any prime brokerage transaction with any hedge fund or private equity fund in which a hedge fund or private equity fund managed, sponsored, or advised by such banking entity has taken an equity, partnership, or other ownership interest, if—

"(i) the banking entity is in compliance with each of the limitations set forth in subsection (d)(1)(G) with regard to a hedge fund or private equity fund organized and offered by such banking entity;

"(ii) the chief executive officer (or equivalent officer) of the banking entity certifies in writing annually (with a duty to update the certification if the information in the certification materially changes) that the conditions specified in subsection (d)(1)(g)(v) are satisfied; and

"(iii) the Board has determined that such transaction is consistent with the safe and sound operation and condition of the banking entity.

"(B) TREATMENT OF PRIME BROKERAGE TRANSACTIONS

For purposes of subparagraph (A), a prime brokerage transaction described in subparagraph (A) shall be subject to section 23B of the Federal Reserve Act (12 U.S.C. 371c–1) as if the counterparty were an affiliate of the banking entity.

"(4) APPLICATION TO NONBANK FINANCIAL COMPANIES SUPERVISED BY THE BOARD

The appropriate Federal banking agencies, the Securities and Exchange Commission, and the Commodity Futures Trading Commission shall adopt rules, as provided in subsection (b)(2), imposing additional capital charges or other restrictions for nonbank financial companies supervised by the Board to address the risks to and conflicts of interest of banking entities described in paragraphs (1), (2), and (3) of this subsection.

"(g) RULES OF CONSTRUCTION

"(1) LIMITATION ON CONTRARY AUTHORITY

Except as provided in this section, notwithstanding any other provision of law, the prohibitions and restrictions under this section shall apply to activities of a banking entity or nonbank financial company supervised by the Board, even if such activities are authorized for a banking entity or nonbank financial company supervised by the Board.

"(2) SALE OR SECURITIZATION OF LOANS

Nothing in this section shall be construed to limit or restrict the ability of a banking entity or nonbank financial company supervised by the Board to sell or securitize loans in a manner otherwise permitted by law.

"(3) AUTHORITY OF FEDERAL AGENCIES AND STATE REGULATORY AUTHORITIES

Nothing in this section shall be construed to limit the inherent authority of any Federal agency or State regulatory authority under otherwise applicable provisions of law.

"(h) DEFINITIONS

In this section, the following definitions shall apply:

"(1) BANKING ENTITY

The term 'banking entity' means any insured depository institution (as defined in section 3 of the Federal Deposit Insurance Act (12 U.S.C. 1813)), any company that controls an insured depository institution, or that is treated as a bank holding company for purposes of section 8 of the International Banking Act of1978, and any affiliate or subsidiary of any such entity. For purposes of this paragraph, the term 'insured depository institution' does not include an institution that functions solely in a trust or fiduciary capacity, if—

"(A) all or substantially all of the deposits of such institution are in trust funds and are received in a bona fide fiduciary capacity;

"(B) no deposits of such institution which are insured by the Federal Deposit Insurance Corporation are offered or marketed by or through an affiliate of such institution;

"(C) such institution does not accept demand deposits or deposits that the depositor may withdraw by check or similar means for payment to third parties or others or make commercial loans; and

"(D) such institution does not—

"(i) obtain payment or payment related services from any Federal Reserve bank, including any service referred to in section 11A of the Federal Reserve Act (12 U.S.C. 248a); or

"(ii) exercise discount or borrowing privileges pursuant to section 19(b)(7) of the Federal Reserve Act (12 U.S.C. 461(b)(7)).

"(2) HEDGE FUND; PRIVATE EQUITY FUND

The terms 'hedge fund' and 'private equity fund' mean an issuer that would be an investment company, as defined in the Investment Company Act of 1940 (15 U.S.C. 80a–1 et seq.), but for section 3(c)(1) or 3(c)(7) of that Act, or such similar funds as the appropriate Federal banking agencies, the Securities and Exchange Commission, and the Commodity Futures Trading Commission may, by rule, as provided in subsection (b)(2), determine.

"(3) NONBANK FINANCIAL COMPANY SUPERVISED BY THE BOARD

The term 'nonbank financial company supervised by the Board' means a nonbank financial company supervised by the Board of Governors, as defined in section 102 of the Financial Stability Act of 2010.

"(4) PROPRIETARY TRADING

The term 'proprietary trading', when used with respect to a banking entity or nonbank financial company supervised by the Board, means engaging as a principal for the trading account of the banking entity or nonbank financial company supervised by the Board in any transaction to purchase or sell, or otherwise acquire or dispose of, any security, any derivative, any contract of sale of a commodity for future delivery, any option on any such security, derivative, or contract, or any other security or financial instrument that the appropriate Federal banking agencies, the Securities and Exchange Commission, and the Commodity Futures Trading Commission may, by rule as provided in subsection (b)(2), determine.

"(5) SPONSOR

The term to 'sponsor' a fund means—

"(A) to serve as a general partner, managing member, or trustee of a fund;

"(B) in any manner to select or to control (or to have employees, officers, or directors, or agents who constitute) a majority of the directors, trustees, or management of a fund; or

"(C) to share with a fund, for corporate, marketing, promotional, or other purposes, the same name or a variation of the same name.

"(6) TRADING ACCOUNT

The term 'trading account' means any account used for acquiring or taking positions in the securities and instruments described in paragraph (4) principally for the purpose of selling in the near term (or otherwise with the intent to resell in order to profit from short-term price movements), and any such other accounts as the appropriate Federal banking agencies, the Securities and Exchange Commission, and the Commodity Futures Trading Commission may, by rule as provided in subsection (b)(2), determine.

"(7) ILLIQUID FUND

"(A) IN GENERAL

The term 'illiquid fund' means a hedge fund or private equity fund that—

"(i) as of May 1, 2010, was principally invested in, or was invested and contractually committed to principally invest in, illiquid assets, such as portfolio companies, real estate investments, and venture capital investments; and

"(ii) makes all investments pursuant to, and consistent with, an investment strategy to principally invest in illiquid assets. In issuing rules regarding this subparagraph, the Board shall take into consideration the terms of investment for the hedge fund or private equity fund, including contractual obligations, the ability of the fund to divest of assets held by the fund, and any other factors that the Board determines are appropriate.

"(B) HEDGE FUND

For the purposes of this paragraph, the term 'hedge fund' means any fund identified under subsection (h)(2), and does not include a private equity fund, as such term is used in section 203(m) of the Investment Advisers Act of 1940 (15 U.S.C. 80b–3(m)).".

§ 620. Study of Bank Investment Activities

(a) STUDY

(1) IN GENERAL

Not later than 18 months after the date of enactment of this Act, the appropriate Federal banking agencies shall jointly review and prepare a report on the activities that a banking entity, as such term is defined in the Bank Holding Company Act of 1956 (12 U.S.C. 1841 et. seq.), may engage in under Federal and State law, including activities authorized by statute and by order, interpretation and guidance.

(2) CONTENT

In carrying out the study under paragraph

(1), the appropriate Federal banking agencies shall review and consider—

(A) the type of activities or investments;

(B) any financial, operational, managerial, or reputation risks associated with or presented as a result of the banking entity engaged in the activity or making the investment; and

(C) risk mitigation activities undertaken by the banking entity with regard to the risks.

(b) REPORT AND RECOMMENDATIONS TO THE COUNCIL AND TO CONGRESS

The appropriate Federal banking agencies shall submit to the Council, the Committee on Financial Services of the House of Representatives, and the Committee on Banking, Housing, and Urban Affairs of the Senate the study conducted pursuant to subsection (a) no later than 2 months after its completion. In addition to the information described in subsection (a), the report shall include recommendations regarding—

(1) whether each activity or investment has or could have a negative effect on the safety and

soundness of the banking entity or the United States financial system;

(2) the appropriateness of the conduct of each activity or type of investment by banking entities; and

(3) additional restrictions as may be necessary to address risks to safety and soundness arising from the activities or types of investments described in subsection (a).

§ 621.　Conflicts of Interest

(a) IN GENERAL

The Securities Act of 1933 (15 U.S.C. 77a et seq.) is amended by inserting after section 27A the following:

"SEC. 27B. CONFLICTS OF INTEREST RELATING TO CERTAIN SECURITIZATIONS.

"(a) IN GENERAL

An underwriter, placement agent, initial purchaser, or sponsor, or any affiliate or subsidiary of any such entity, of an asset-backed security (as such term is defined in section 3 of the Securities and Exchange Act of 1934 (15 U.S.C. 78c), which for the purposes of this section shall include a synthetic asset-backed security), shall not, at any time for a period ending on the date that is one year after the date of the first closing of the sale of the asset-backed security, engage in any transaction that would involve or result in any material conflict of interest with respect to any investor in a transaction arising out of such activity.

"(b) RULEMAKING

Not later than 270 days after the date of enactment of this section, the Commission shall issue rules for the purpose of implementing subsection (a).

"(c) EXCEPTION

The prohibitions of subsection (a) shall not apply to—

"(1) risk-mitigating hedging activities in connection with positions or holdings arising out of the underwriting, placement, initial purchase, or sponsorship of an asset-backed security, provided that such activities are designed to reduce the specific risks to the underwriter, placement agent, initial purchaser, or sponsor associated with positions

or holdings arising out of such underwriting, placement, initial purchase, or sponsorship; or

"(2) purchases or sales of asset-backed securities made pursuant to and consistent with—

"(A) commitments of the underwriter, placement agent, initial purchaser, or sponsor, or any affiliate or subsidiary of any such entity, to provide liquidity for the asset-backed security, or

"(B) bona fide market-making in the asset backed security.

"(d) RULE OF CONSTRUCTION

This subsection shall not otherwise limit the application of section 15G of the Securities Exchange Act of 1934.".

(b) EFFECTIVE DATE

Section 27B of the Securities Act of 1933, as added by this section, shall take effect on the effective date of final rules issued by the Commission under subsection (b) of such section 27B, except that subsections (b) and (d) of such section 27B shall take effect on the date of enactment of this Act.

§ 622.　Concentration Limits on Large Financial Firms

The Bank Holding Company Act of 1956 (12 U.S.C. 1841 et seq.) is amended by adding at the end the following:

"SEC. 14. CONCENTRATION LIMITS ON LARGE FINANCIAL FIRMS.

"(a) DEFINITIONS

In this section—

"(1) the term 'Council' means the Financial Stability Oversight Council;

"(2) the term 'financial company' means—

"(A) an insured depository institution;

"(B) a bank holding company;

"(C) a savings and loan holding company;

"(D) a company that controls an insured depository institution;

"(E) a nonbank financial company supervised by the Board under title I of the Dodd–Frank Wall Street Reform and Consumer Protection Act; and

"(F) a foreign bank or company that is treated as a bank holding company for purposes of this Act; and

"(3) the term 'liabilities' means—

"(A) with respect to a United States financial company—

"(i) the total risk-weighted assets of the financial company, as determined under the risk-based capital rules applicable to bank holding companies, as adjusted to reflect exposures that are deducted from regulatory capital; less

"(ii) the total regulatory capital of the financial company under the risk-based capital rules applicable to bank holding companies;

"(B) with respect to a foreign-based financial company—

"(i) the total risk-weighted assets of the United States operations of the financial company, as determined under the applicable risk-based capital rules, as adjusted to reflect exposures that are deducted from regulatory capital; less

"(ii) the total regulatory capital of the United States operations of the financial company, as determined under the applicable risk-based capital rules; and

"(C) with respect to an insurance company or other nonbank financial company supervised by the Board, such assets of the company as the Board shall specify by rule, in order to provide for consistent and equitable treatment of such companies.

"(b) CONCENTRATION LIMIT

Subject to the recommendations by the Council under subsection (e), a financial company may not merge or consolidate with, acquire all or substantially all of the assets of, or otherwise acquire control of, another company, if the total consolidated liabilities of the acquiring financial company upon consummation of the transaction would exceed 10 percent of the aggregate consolidated liabilities of all financial companies at the end of the calendar year preceding the transaction.

"(c) EXCEPTION TO CONCENTRATION LIMIT

With the prior written consent of the Board, the concentration limit under subsection (b) shall not apply to an acquisition—

"(1) of a bank in default or in danger of default;

"(2) with respect to which assistance is provided by the Federal Deposit Insurance Corporation under section 13(c) of the Federal Deposit Insurance Act (12 U.S.C. 1823(c)); or

"(3) that would result only in a de minimis increase in the liabilities of the financial company.

"(d) RULEMAKING AND GUIDANCE

The Board shall issue regulations implementing this section in accordance with the recommendations of the Council under subsection (e), including the definition of terms, as necessary. The Board may issue interpretations or guidance regarding the application of this section to an individual financial company or to financial companies in general.

"(e) COUNCIL STUDY AND RULEMAKING

"(1) STUDY AND RECOMMENDATIONS

Not later than 6 months after the date of enactment of this section, the Council shall—

"(A) complete a study of the extent to which the concentration limit under this section would affect financial stability, moral hazard in the financial system, the efficiency and competitiveness of United States financial firms and financial markets, and the cost and availability of credit and other financial services to households and businesses in the United States; and

"(B) make recommendations regarding any modifications to the concentration limit that the Council determines would more effectively implement this section.

"(2) RULEMAKING

Not later than 9 months after the date of completion of the study under paragraph (1), and notwithstanding subsections (b) and (d), the Board shall issue final regulations implementing this section, which shall reflect any recommendations by the Council under paragraph (1)(B).".

§ 623. Interstate Merger Transactions

(a) INTERSTATE MERGER TRANSACTIONS
Section 18(c) of the Federal Deposit Insurance Act (12 U.S.C. 1828(c)) is amended by adding at the end the following:

"(13)(A) Except as provided in subparagraph (B), the responsible agency may not approve an application for an interstate merger transaction if the resulting insured depository institution (including all insured depository institutions which are affiliates of the resulting insured depository institution), upon consummation of the transaction, would control more than 10 percent of the total amount of deposits of insured depository institutions in the United States.

"(B) Subparagraph (A) shall not apply to an interstate merger transaction that involves 1 or more insured depository institutions in default or in danger of default, or with respect to which the Corporation provides assistance under section 13.

"(C) In this paragraph

"(i) the term 'interstate merger transaction' means a merger transaction involving 2 or more insured depository institutions that have different home States and that are not affiliates; and

"(ii) the term 'home State' means—

"(I) with respect to a national bank, the State in which the main office of the bank is located;

"(II) with respect to a State bank or State savings association, the State by which the State bank or State savings association is chartered; and

"(III) with respect to a Federal savings association, the State in which the home office (as defined by the regulations of the Director of the Office of Thrift Supervision, or, on and after the transfer date, the Comptroller of the Currency) of the Federal savings association is located.".

(b) ACQUISITIONS BY BANK HOLDING COMPANIES

(1) IN GENERAL

Section 4 of the Bank Holding Company Act of 1956 (12 U.S.C. 1843) is amended—

(A) in subsection (i), by adding at the end the following:

"(8) INTERSTATE ACQUISITIONS

"(A) IN GENERAL

The Board may not approve an application by a bank holding company to acquire an insured depository institution under subsection (c)(8) or any other provision of this Act if—

"(i) the home State of such insured depository institution is a State other than the home State of the bank holding company; and

"(ii) the applicant (including all insured depository institutions which are affiliates of the applicant) controls, or upon consummation of the transaction would control, more than 10 percent of the total amount of deposits of insured depository institutions in the United States.

"(B) EXCEPTION

Subparagraph (A) shall not apply to an acquisition that involves an insured depository institution in default or in danger of default, or with respect to which the Federal Deposit Insurance Corporation provides assistance under section 13 of the Federal Deposit Insurance Act (12 U.S.C. 1823)."; and (B) in subsection (k)(6)(B), by striking "savings association" and inserting "insured depository institution".

(2) DEFINITIONS

Section 2(o)(4) of the Bank Holding Company Act of 1956 (12 U.S.C. 1841(o)(4)) is amended—

(A) in subparagraph (B), by striking "and" at the end;

(B) in subparagraph (C)(ii), by striking the period at the end and inserting a semicolon; and

(C) by adding at the end the following:

"(D) with respect to a State savings association, the State by which the savings association is chartered; and

"(E) with respect to a Federal savings association, the State in which the home office (as defined by the regulations of the Director of the Office of Thrift Supervision, or, on and after the transfer date, the Comptroller of the Currency) of the Federal savings association is located.".

(c) ACQUISITIONS BY SAVINGS AND LOAN HOLDING COMPANIES

Section 10(e)(2) of the Home Owners' Loan Act (12 U.S.C. 1467a(e)(2)) is amended—

(1) in paragraph (2)—

(A) in subparagraph (C), by striking "or" at the end;

(B) in subparagraph (D), by striking the period at the end and inserting ", or"; and

(C) by adding at the end the following:

"(E) in the case of an application by a savings and loan holding company to acquire an insured depository institution, if—

"(i) the home State of the insured depository institution is a State other than the home State of the savings and loan holding company;

"(ii) the applicant (including all insured depository institutions which are affiliates of the applicant) controls, or upon consummation of the transaction would control, more than 10 percent of the total amount of deposits of insured depository institutions in the United States; and

"(iii) the acquisition does not involve an insured depository institution in default or in danger of default, or with respect to which the Federal Deposit Insurance Corporation provides assistance under section 13 of the Federal Deposit Insurance Act (12 U.S.C. 1823)."; and

(2) by adding at the end the following:

"(7) DEFINITIONS

For purposes of paragraph (2)(E)—

"(A) the terms 'default', 'in danger of default', and 'insured depository institution' have the same meanings as in section 3 of the Federal Deposit Insurance Act (12 U.S.C. 1813); and

"(B) the term 'home State' means—

"(i) with respect to a national bank, the State in which the main office of the bank is located;

"(ii) with respect to a State bank or State savings association, the State by which the savings association is chartered;

"(iii) with respect to a Federal savings association, the State in which the home office

(as defined by the regulations of the Director of the Office of Thrift Supervision, or, on and after the transfer date, the Comptroller of the Currency) of the Federal savings association is located; and

"(iv) with respect to a savings and loan holding company, the State in which the amount of total deposits of all insured depository institution subsidiaries of such company was the greatest on the date on which the company became a savings and loan holding company.".

§ 624. Qualified Thrift Lenders

Section 10(m)(3) of the Home Owners' Loan Act (12 U.S.C. 1467a(m)(3)) is amended—

(1) by striking subparagraph (A) and inserting the following:

"(A) IN GENERAL

A savings association that fails to become or remain a qualified thrift lender shall immediately be subject to the restrictions under subparagraph (B)."; and

(2) in subparagraph (B)(i), by striking subclause (III) and inserting the following:

"(III) DIVIDENDS

The savings association may not pay dividends, except for dividends that—

"(aa) would be permissible for a national bank;

"(bb) are necessary to meet obligations of a company that controls such savings association; and

"(cc) are specifically approved by the Comptroller of the Currency and the Board after a written request submitted to the Comptroller of the Currency and the Board by the savings association not later than 30 days before the date of the proposed payment.

"(IV) REGULATORY AUTHORITY

A savings association that fails to become or remain a qualified thrift lender shall be deemed to have violated section 5 of the Home Owners' Loan Act (12 U.S.C. 1464) and subject to actions authorized by section 5(d) of the Home Owners' Loan Act (12 U.S.C. 1464(d)).".

§ 625. Treatment of Dividends by Certain Mutual Holding Companies

(a) IN GENERAL

Section 10(o) of the Home Owners' Loan Act (12 U.S.C. 1467a(o)) is amended by adding at the end the following:

"(11) DIVIDENDS

"(A) DECLARATION OF DIVIDENDS

"(i) ADVANCE NOTICE REQUIRED

Each subsidiary of a mutual holding company that is a savings association shall give the appropriate Federal banking agency and the Board notice not later than 30 days before the date of a proposed declaration by the board of directors of the savings association of any dividend on the guaranty, permanent, or other nonwithdrawable stock of the savings association.

"(ii) INVALID DIVIDENDS

Any dividend described in clause (i) that is declared without giving notice to the appropriate Federal banking agency and the Board under clause (i), or that is declared during the 30–day period preceding the date of a proposed declaration for which notice is given to the appropriate Federal banking agency and the Board under clause (i), shall be invalid and shall confer no rights or benefits upon the holder of any such stock.

"(B) WAIVER OF DIVIDENDS

A mutual holding company may waive the right to receive any dividend declared by a subsidiary of the mutual holding company, if—

"(i) no insider of the mutual holding company, associate of an insider, or tax-qualified or non-tax-qualified employee stock benefit plan of the mutual holding company holds any share of the stock in the class of stock to which the waiver would apply; or

"(ii) the mutual holding company gives written notice to the Board of the intent of the mutual holding company to waive the right to receive dividends, not later than 30 days before the date of the proposed date of payment of the dividend, and the Board does not object to the waiver.

"(C) RESOLUTION INCLUDED IN WAIVER NOTICE

A notice of a waiver under subparagraph (B) shall include a copy of the resolution of the board of directors of the mutual holding company, in such form and substance as the Board may determine, together with any supporting materials relied upon by the board of directors of the mutual holding company, concluding that the proposed dividend waiver is consistent with the fiduciary duties of the board of directors to the mutual members of the mutual holding company.

"(D) STANDARDS FOR WAIVER OF DIVIDEND

The Board may not object to a waiver of dividends under subparagraph (B) if—

"(i) the waiver would not be detrimental to the safe and sound operation of the savings association;

"(ii) the board of directors of the mutual holding company expressly determines that a waiver of the dividend by the mutual holding company is consistent with the fiduciary duties of the board of directors to the mutual members of the mutual holding company; and

"(iii) the mutual holding company has, prior to December 1, 2009—

"(I) reorganized into a mutual holding company under subsection (o);

"(II) issued minority stock either from its mid-tier stock holding company or its subsidiary stock savings association; and

"(III) waived dividends it had a right to receive from the subsidiary stock savings association.

"(E) VALUATION

"(i) IN GENERAL

The appropriate Federal banking agency shall consider waived dividends in determining an appropriate exchange ratio in the event of a full conversion to stock form.

"(ii) EXCEPTION

In the case of a savings association that has reorganized into a mutual holding company, has issued minority stock from a mid-tier stock holding company or a subsidiary stock savings association of the mutual holding company, and has waived dividends it had a right to receive from a subsidiary savings association before December 1, 2009, the appropriate Federal banking agency shall not consider waived dividends in determining an appropriate exchange ratio in the event of a full conversion to stock form.''.

(b) EFFECTIVE DATE

The amendment made by subsection (a) shall take effect on the transfer date.

§ 626. Intermediate Holding Companies

The Home Owners' Loan Act (12 U.S.C. 1461 et seq.) is amended by inserting after section 10 (12 U.S.C. 1467a) the following new section:

"SEC. 10A. INTERMEDIATE HOLDING COMPANIES.

''(a) DEFINITION

For purposes of this section:

''(1) FINANCIAL ACTIVITIES

The term 'financial activities' means activities described in clauses (i) and (ii) of section 10(c)(9)(A).

''(2) GRANDFATHERED UNITARY SAVINGS AND LOAN HOLDING COMPANY

The term 'grandfathered unitary savings and loan holding company' means a company described in section 10(c)(9)(C).

''(3) INTERNAL FINANCIAL ACTIVITIES

The term 'internal financial activities' includes—

''(A) internal financial activities conducted by a grand-fathered savings and loan holding company or any affiliate; and

''(B) internal treasury, investment, and employee benefit functions.

''(b) REQUIREMENT

''(1) IN GENERAL

''(A) ACTIVITIES OTHER THAN FINANCIAL ACTIVITIES

If a grandfathered unitary savings and loan holding company conducts activities other than financial activities, the Board may require such company to establish and conduct all or a portion of such financial activities in or through an intermediate holding company, which shall be a savings and loan holding company, established pursuant to regulations of the Board, not later than 90 days (or

such longer period as the Board may deem appropriate) after the transfer date.

''(B) OTHER ACTIVITIES

Notwithstanding subparagraph (A), the Board shall require a grandfathered unitary savings and loan holding company to establish an intermediate holding company if the Board makes a determination that the establishment of such intermediate holding company is necessary—

''(i) to appropriately supervise activities that are determined to be financial activities; or

''(ii) to ensure that supervision by the Board does not extend to the activities of such company that are not financial activities.

''(2) INTERNAL FINANCIAL ACTIVITIES

''(A) TREATMENT OF INTERNAL FINANCIAL ACTIVITIES

For purposes of this subsection, the internal financial activities of a grandfathered unitary savings and loan holding company shall not be required to be placed in an intermediate holding company.

''(B) GRANDFATHERED ACTIVITIES

A grandfathered unitary savings and loan holding company may continue to engage in an internal financial activity, subject to review by the Board to determine whether engaging in such activity presents undue risk to the grandfathered unitary savings and loan holding company or to the financial stability of the United States, if—

''(i) the grandfathered unitary savings and loan holding company engaged in the activity during the year before the date of enactment of this section; and

''(ii) at least 2/3 of the assets or 2/3 of the revenues generated from the activity are from or attributable to the grandfathered unitary savings and loan holding company.

''(3) SOURCE OF STRENGTH

A grandfathered unitary savings and loan holding company that directly or indirectly controls an intermediate holding company established under this section shall serve as a source of strength to its subsidiary intermediate holding company.

''(4) PARENT COMPANY REPORTS

The Board, may from time to time, examine and require reports under oath from a grand-fathered unitary savings and loan holding company that controls an intermediate holding company, and from the appropriate officers or directors of such company, solely for purposes of ensuring compliance with the provisions of this section, including assessing the ability of the company to serve as a source of strength to its subsidiary intermediate holding company as required under paragraph (3) and enforcing compliance with such requirement.

"(5) LIMITED PARENT COMPANY ENFORCEMENT

"(A) IN GENERAL

In addition to any other authority of the Board, the Board may enforce compliance with the provisions of this subsection that are applicable to any company described in paragraph (1)(A) that controls an intermediate holding company under section 8 of the Federal Deposit Insurance Act, and a company described in paragraph (1)(A) shall be subject to such section (solely for purposes of this subparagraph) in the same manner and to the same extent as if the company described in paragraph (1)(A) were a savings and loan holding company.

"(B) APPLICATION OF OTHER ACT

Any violation of this subsection by a grandfathered unitary savings and loan holding company that controls an intermediate holding company may also be treated as a violation of the Federal Deposit Insurance Act for purposes of subparagraph (A).

"(C) NO EFFECT ON OTHER AUTHORITY

No provision of this paragraph shall be construed as limiting any authority of the Board or any other Federal agency under any other provision of law.

"(c) REGULATIONS

The Board—

"(1) shall promulgate regulations to establish the criteria for determining whether to require a grandfathered unitary savings and loan holding company to establish an intermediate holding company under subsection (b); and

"(2) may promulgate regulations to establish any restrictions or limitations on transactions between an intermediate holding company or a parent of such company and its affiliates, as necessary to prevent unsafe and unsound practices in connection with transactions between the intermediate holding company, or any subsidiary thereof, and its parent company or affiliates that are not subsidiaries of the intermediate holding company, except that such regulations shall not restrict or limit any transaction in connection with the bona fide acquisition or lease by an unaffiliated person of assets, goods, or services.

"(d) RULES OF CONSTRUCTION

"(1) ACTIVITIES

Nothing in this section shall be construed to require a grandfathered unitary savings and loan holding company to conform its activities to permissible activities.

"(2) PERMISSIBLE CORPORATE REORGANIZATION

The formation of an intermediate holding company as required in subsection (b) shall be presumed to be a permissible corporate reorganization as described in section 10(c)(9)(D).".

§ 627. Interest–Bearing Transaction Accounts Authorized

(a) REPEAL OF PROHIBITION ON PAYMENT OF INTEREST ON DEMAND DEPOSITS

(1) FEDERAL RESERVE ACT

Section 19(i) of the Federal Reserve Act (12 U.S.C. 371a) is amended to read as follows:

"(i) [Repealed]".

(2) HOME OWNERS' LOAN ACT

The first sentence of section 5(b)(1)(B) of the Home Owners' Loan Act (12 U.S.C. 1464(b)(1)(B)) is amended by striking "savings association may not—" and all that follows through "(ii) permit any" and inserting "savings association may not permit any".

(3) FEDERAL DEPOSIT INSURANCE ACT

Section 18(g) of the Federal Deposit Insurance Act (12 U.S.C. 1828(g)) is amended to read as follows:

"(g) [Repealed]".

(b) EFFECTIVE DATE

The amendments made by subsection (a) shall take effect 1 year after the date of the enactment of this Act.

§ 628. Credit Card Bank Small Business Lending

Section 2(c)(2)(F)(v) of the Bank Holding Company Act of 1956 (12 U.S.C. 1841(c)(2)(F)(v)) is amended by inserting before the period the following: ", other than credit card loans that are made to businesses that meet the criteria for a small business concern to be eligible for business loans under regulations established by the Small Business Administration under part 121 of title 13, Code of Federal Regulations".

TITLE X—BUREAU OF CONSUMER FINANCIAL PROTECTION

Subtitle D—Preservation of State Law

§ 1041. Relation to State Law

(a) IN GENERAL

(1) RULE OF CONSTRUCTION

This title, other than sections 1044 through 1048, may not be construed as annulling, altering, or affecting, or exempting any person subject to the provisions of this title from complying with, the statutes, regulations, orders, or interpretations in effect in any State, except to the extent that any such provision of law is inconsistent with the provisions of this title, and then only to the extent of the inconsistency.

(2) GREATER PROTECTION UNDER STATE LAW

For purposes of this subsection, a statute, regulation, order, or interpretation in effect in any State is not inconsistent with the provisions of this title if the protection that such statute, regulation, order, or interpretation affords to consumers is greater than the protection provided under this title. A determination regarding whether a statute, regulation, order, or interpretation in effect in any State is inconsistent with the provisions of this title may be made by the Bureau on its own motion or in response to a nonfrivolous petition initiated by any interested person.

(b) RELATION TO OTHER PROVISIONS OF ENUMERATED CONSUMER LAWS THAT RELATE TO STATE LAW

No provision of this title, except as provided in section 1083, shall be construed as modifying, limiting, or superseding the operation of any provision of an enumerated consumer law that relates to the application of a law in effect in any State with respect to such Federal law.

(c) ADDITIONAL CONSUMER PROTECTION REGULATIONS IN RESPONSE TO STATE ACTION

(1) NOTICE OF PROPOSED RULE REQUIRED

The Bureau shall issue a notice of proposed rulemaking whenever a majority of the States has enacted a resolution in support of the establishment or modification of a consumer protection regulation by the Bureau.

(2) BUREAU CONSIDERATIONS REQUIRED FOR ISSUANCE OF FINAL REGULATION

Before prescribing a final regulation based upon a notice issued pursuant to paragraph (1), the Bureau shall take into account whether—

(A) the proposed regulation would afford greater protection to consumers than any existing regulation;

(B) the intended benefits of the proposed regulation for consumers would outweigh any increased costs or inconveniences for consumers, and would not discriminate unfairly against any category or class of consumers; and

(C) a Federal banking agency has advised that the proposed regulation is likely to present an unacceptable safety and soundness risk to insured depository institutions.

(3) EXPLANATION OF CONSIDERATIONS

The Bureau—

(A) shall include a discussion of the considerations required in paragraph (2) in the Federal Register notice of a final regulation prescribed pursuant to this subsection; and

(B) whenever the Bureau determines not to prescribe a final regulation, shall publish an explanation of such determination in the Federal Register, and provide a copy of such explanation to each State that enacted a resolution in support of the proposed regulation, the Committee on Banking, Housing, and Urban Affairs of the Senate, and the Committee on Financial Services of the House of Representatives.

(4) RESERVATION OF AUTHORITY

No provision of this subsection shall be construed as limiting or restricting the authority of the Bureau to enhance consumer protection standards established pursuant to this title in response to its own motion or in response to a request by any other interested person.

(5) RULE OF CONSTRUCTION

No provision of this subsection shall be construed as exempting the Bureau from complying with subchapter II of chapter 5 of title 5, United States Code.

(6) DEFINITION

For purposes of this subsection, the term "consumer protection regulation" means a regulation that the Bureau is authorized to prescribe under the Federal consumer financial laws.

§ 1042. Preservation of Enforcement Powers of States

(a) IN GENERAL

(1) ACTION BY STATE

Except as provided in paragraph (2), the attorney general (or the equivalent thereof) of any State may bring a civil action in the name of such State in any district court of the United States in that State or in State court that is located in that State and that has jurisdiction over the defendant, to enforce provisions of this title or regulations issued under this title, and to secure remedies under provisions of this title or remedies otherwise provided under other law. A State regulator may bring a civil action or other appropriate proceeding to enforce the provisions of this title or regulations issued under this title with respect to any entity that is State-chartered, incorporated, licensed, or otherwise authorized to do business under State law (except as provided in paragraph (2)), and to secure remedies under provisions of this title or remedies otherwise provided under other provisions of law with respect to such an entity.

(2) ACTION BY STATE AGAINST NATIONAL BANK OR FEDERAL SAVINGS ASSOCIATION TO ENFORCE RULES

(A) IN GENERAL

Except as permitted under subparagraph (B), the attorney general (or equivalent thereof) of any State may not bring a civil action in the name of such State against a national bank or Federal savings association to enforce a provision of this title.

(B) ENFORCEMENT OF RULES PERMITTED

The attorney general (or the equivalent thereof) of any State may bring a civil action in the name of such State against a national bank or Federal savings association in any district court of the United States in the State or in State court that is located in that State and that has jurisdiction over the defendant to enforce a regulation prescribed by the Bureau under a provision of this title and to secure remedies under provisions of

this title or remedies otherwise provided under other law.

(3) RULE OF CONSTRUCTION

No provision of this title shall be construed as modifying, limiting, or superseding the operation of any provision of an enumerated consumer law that relates to the authority of a State attorney general or State regulator to enforce such Federal law.

(b) CONSULTATION REQUIRED

(1) NOTICE

(A) IN GENERAL

Before initiating any action in a court or other administrative or regulatory proceeding against any covered person as authorized by subsection (a) to enforce any provision of this title, including any regulation prescribed by the Bureau under this title, a State attorney general or State regulator shall timely provide a copy of the complete complaint to be filed and written notice describing such action or proceeding to the Bureau and the prudential regulator, if any, or the designee thereof.

(B) EMERGENCY ACTION

If prior notice is not practicable, the State attorney general or State regulator shall provide a copy of the complete complaint and the notice to the Bureau and the prudential regulator, if any, immediately upon instituting the action or proceeding.

(C) CONTENTS OF NOTICE

The notification required under this paragraph shall, at a minimum, describe—

(i) the identity of the parties;

(ii) the alleged facts underlying the proceeding; and

(iii) whether there may be a need to coordinate the prosecution of the proceeding so as not to interfere with any action, including any rulemaking, undertaken by the Bureau, a prudential regulator, or another Federal agency.

(2) BUREAU RESPONSE

In any action described in paragraph

(1), the Bureau may—

(A) intervene in the action as a party;

(B) upon intervening—

(i) remove the action to the appropriate United States district court, if the action was not originally brought there; and

(ii) be heard on all matters arising in the action; and

(C) appeal any order or judgment, to the same extent as any other party in the proceeding may.

(c) REGULATIONS

The Bureau shall prescribe regulations to implement the requirements of this section and, from time to time, provide guidance in order to further coordinate actions with the State attorneys general and other regulators.

(d) PRESERVATION OF STATE AUTHORITY

(1) STATE CLAIMS

No provision of this section shall be construed as altering, limiting, or affecting the authority of a State attorney general or any other regulatory or enforcement agency or authority to bring an action or other regulatory proceeding arising solely under the law in effect in that State.

(2) STATE SECURITIES REGULATORS

No provision of this title shall be construed as altering, limiting, or affecting the authority of a State securities commission (or any agency or office performing like functions) under State law to adopt rules, initiate enforcement proceedings, or take any other action with respect to a person regulated by such commission or authority.

(3) STATE INSURANCE REGULATORS

No provision of this title shall be construed as altering, limiting, or affecting the authority of a State insurance commission or State insurance regulator under State law to adopt rules, initiate enforcement proceedings, or take any other action with respect to a person regulated by such commission or regulator.

§ 1043.　Preservation of Existing Contracts

This title, and regulations, orders, guidance, and interpretations prescribed, issued, or established by the Bureau, shall not be construed to alter or affect the applicability of any regulation, order, guidance, or interpretation prescribed, issued, and established by the Comptroller of the Currency or the Director of the Office of Thrift Supervision regarding the applicability of State law under Federal banking law to any contract entered into on or before the date of enactment of this Act, by national banks, Federal savings associations, or subsidiaries thereof that are regulated and supervised by the Comptroller of the Currency or the Director of the Office of Thrift Supervision, respectively.

§ 1044.　State Law Preemption Standards for National Banks and Subsidiaries Clarified

(a) IN GENERAL

Chapter one of title LXII of the Revised Statutes of the United States (12 U.S.C. 21 et seq.) is amended by inserting after section 5136B the following new section:

"SEC. 5136C. STATE LAW PREEMPTION STANDARDS FOR NATIONAL BANKS AND SUBSIDIARIES CLARIFIED.

"(a) DEFINITIONS

For purposes of this section, the following definitions shall apply:

"(1) NATIONAL BANK

The term 'national bank' includes—

"(A) any bank organized under the laws of the United States; and

"(B) any Federal branch established in accordance with the International Banking Act of 1978.

"(2) STATE CONSUMER FINANCIAL LAWS

The term 'State consumer financial law' means a State law that does not directly or indirectly discriminate against national banks and that directly and specifically regulates the manner, content, or terms and conditions of any financial transaction (as may be authorized for national banks to engage in), or any account related thereto, with respect to a consumer.

"(3) OTHER DEFINITIONS

The terms 'affiliate', 'subsidiary', 'includes', and 'including' have the same meanings as in section 3 of the Federal Deposit Insurance Act.

"(b) PREEMPTION STANDARD

"(1) IN GENERAL

State consumer financial laws are preempted, only if—

"(A) application of a State consumer financial law would have a discriminatory effect on national banks, in comparison with the effect of the law on a bank chartered by that State;

"(B) in accordance with the legal standard for preemption in the decision of the Supreme Court of the United States in Barnett Bank of Marion County, N. A. v. Nelson, Florida Insurance Commissioner, et al., 517 U.S. 25 (1996), the State consumer financial law prevents or significantly interferes with the exercise by the national bank of its powers; and any preemption determination under this subparagraph may be made by a court, or by regulation or order of the Comptroller of the Currency on a case-by-case basis, in accordance with applicable law; or

"(C) the State consumer financial law is preempted by a provision of Federal law other than this title.

"(2) SAVINGS CLAUSE

This title and section 24 of the Federal Reserve Act (12 U.S.C. 371) do not preempt, annul, or affect the applicability of any State law to any subsidiary or affiliate of a national bank (other than a subsidiary or affiliate that is chartered as a national bank).

"(3) CASE–BY–CASE BASIS

"(A) DEFINITION

As used in this section the term 'case-by-case basis' refers to a determination pursuant to this section made by the Comptroller concerning the impact of a particular State consumer financial law on any national bank that is subject to that law, or the law of any other State with substantively equivalent terms.

"(B) CONSULTATION

When making a determination on a case-by-case basis that a State consumer financial law of another State has substantively equivalent terms as one that the Comptroller is preempting, the Comptroller shall first consult with the Bureau of Consumer Financial Protection and shall take the views of the Bureau into account when making the determination.

"(4) RULE OF CONSTRUCTION

This title does not occupy the field in any area of State law.

"(5) STANDARDS OF REVIEW

"(A) PREEMPTION

A court reviewing any determinations made by the Comptroller regarding preemption of a State law by this title or section 24 of the Federal Reserve Act (12 U.S.C. 371) shall assess the validity of such determinations, depending upon the thoroughness evident in the consideration of the agency, the validity of the reasoning of the agency, the consistency with other valid determinations made by the agency, and other factors which the court finds persuasive and relevant to its decision.

"(B) SAVINGS CLAUSE

Except as provided in subparagraph (A), nothing in this section shall affect the deference that a court may afford to the Comptroller in making determinations regarding the meaning or interpretation of title LXII of the Revised Statutes of the United States or other Federal laws.

"(6) COMPTROLLER DETERMINATION NOT DELEGABLE

Any regulation, order, or determination made by the Comptroller of the Currency under paragraph (1)(B) shall be made by the Comptroller, and shall not be delegable to another officer or employee of the Comptroller of the Currency.

"(c) SUBSTANTIAL EVIDENCE

No regulation or order of the Comptroller of the Currency prescribed under subsection (b)(1)(B), shall be interpreted or applied so as to invalidate, or otherwise declare inapplicable to a national bank, the provision of the State consumer financial law, unless substantial evidence, made on the record of the proceeding, supports the specific finding regarding the preemption of such provision in accordance with the legal standard of the decision of the Supreme Court of the United States in Barnett Bank of Marion County, N.A. v. Nelson, Florida Insurance Commissioner, et al., 517 U.S. 25 (1996).

"(d) PERIODIC REVIEW OF PREEMPTION DETERMINATIONS

"(1) IN GENERAL

The Comptroller of the Currency shall periodically conduct a review, through notice and public comment, of each determination that a provision of Federal law preempts a State consumer financial law. The agency shall conduct such review within the 5–year period after prescribing or otherwise issuing such determination, and at least once during each 5–year period thereafter. After conducting the review of, and inspecting the comments made on, the determination, the agency shall publish a notice in the Federal Register announcing the decision to continue or rescind the determination or a proposal to amend the determination. Any such notice of a proposal to amend a determination and the subsequent resolution of such proposal shall comply with the procedures set forth in subsections (a) and (b) of section 5244 of the Revised Statutes of the United States (12 U.S.C. 43 (a), (b)).

"(2) REPORTS TO CONGRESS

At the time of issuing a review conducted under paragraph (1), the Comptroller of the Currency shall submit a report regarding such review to the Committee on Financial Services of the House of Representatives and the Committee on Banking, Housing, and Urban Affairs of the Senate. The report submitted to the respective committees shall address whether the agency intends to continue, rescind, or propose to amend any determination that a provision of Federal law preempts a State consumer financial law, and the reasons therefor.

"(e) APPLICATION OF STATE CONSUMER FINANCIAL LAW TO SUBSIDIARIES AND AFFILIATES

Notwithstanding any provision of this title or section 24 of Federal Reserve Act (12 U.S.C. 371), a State consumer financial law shall apply to a subsidiary or affiliate of a national bank (other than a subsidiary or affiliate that is chartered as a national bank) to the same extent that the State consumer financial law applies to any person, corporation, or other entity subject to such State law.

"(f) PRESERVATION OF POWERS RELATED TO CHARGING INTEREST

No provision of this title shall be construed as altering or otherwise affecting the authority conferred by section 5197 of the Revised Statutes of the United States (12 U.S.C. 85) for the charging of interest by a national bank at the rate allowed by the laws of the State, territory, or district where the bank is located, including with respect to the meaning of 'interest' under such provision.

"(g) TRANSPARENCY OF OCC PREEMPTION DETERMINATIONS

The Comptroller of the Currency shall publish and update no less frequently than quarterly, a list of preemption determinations by the Comptroller of the Currency then in effect that identifies the activities and practices covered by each determination and the requirements and constraints determined to be preempted.".

(b) CLERICAL AMENDMENT

The table of sections for chapter one of title LXII of the Revised Statutes of the United States is amended by inserting after the item relating to section 5136B the following new item:

> "Sec. 5136C. State law preemption standards for national banks and subsidiaries clarified.".

§ 1045. Clarification of Law Applicable to Nondepository Institution Subsidiaries

Section 5136C of the Revised Statutes of the United States (as added by this subtitle) is amended by adding at the end the following:

"(h) CLARIFICATION OF LAW APPLICABLE TO NONDEPOSITORY INSTITUTION SUBSIDIARIES AND AFFILIATES OF NATIONAL BANKS

"(1) DEFINITIONS

For purposes of this subsection, the terms 'depository institution', 'subsidiary', and 'affiliate' have the same meanings as in section 3 of the Federal Deposit Insurance Act.

"(2) RULE OF CONSTRUCTION

No provision of this title or section 24 of the Federal Reserve Act (12 U.S.C. 371) shall be construed as preempting, annulling, or affecting the applicability of State law to any subsidiary, affiliate, or agent of a national bank (other than a subsidiary, affiliate, or agent that is chartered as a national bank).".

§ 1046. State Law Preemption Standards for Federal Savings Associations and Subsidiaries clarified

(a) IN GENERAL

The Home Owners' Loan Act (12 U.S.C. 1461 et seq.) is amended by inserting after section 5 the following new section:

"SEC. 6. STATE LAW PREEMPTION STANDARDS FOR FEDERAL SAVINGS ASSOCIATIONS CLARIFIED.

"(a) IN GENERAL

Any determination by a court or by the Director or any successor officer or agency regarding the relation of State law to a provision of this Act or any regulation or order prescribed under this Act shall be made in accordance with the laws and legal standards applicable to national banks regarding the preemption of State law.

"(b) PRINCIPLES OF CONFLICT PRE-EMPTION APPLICABLE

Notwithstanding the authorities granted under sections 4 and 5, this Act does not occupy the field in any area of State law.".

(b) CLERICAL AMENDMENT

The table of sections for the Home Owners' Loan Act (12 U.S.C. 1461 et seq.) is amended by striking the item relating to section 6 and inserting the following new item:

"Sec. 6. State law preemption standards for Federal savings associations and subsidiaries clarified.".

§ 1047. Visitorial Standards for National Banks and Savings Associations

(a) NATIONAL BANKS

Section 5136C of the Revised Statutes of the United States (as added by this subtitle) is amended by adding at the end the following:

"(i) VISITORIAL POWERS

"(1) IN GENERAL

In accordance with the decision of the Supreme Court of the United States in Cuomo v. Clearing House Assn., L. L. C. (129 S. Ct. 2710 (2009)), no provision of this title which relates to visitorial powers or otherwise limits or restricts the visitorial authority to which any national bank is subject shall be construed as limiting or restricting the authority of any attorney general (or other chief law enforcement officer) of any State to bring an action against a national bank in a court of appropriate jurisdiction to enforce an applicable law and to seek relief as authorized by such law.

"(j) ENFORCEMENT ACTIONS

The ability of the Comptroller of the Currency to bring an enforcement action under this title or section 5 of the Federal Trade Commission Act does not preclude any private party from enforcing rights granted under Federal or State law in the courts.".

(b) SAVINGS ASSOCIATIONS

Section 6 of the Home Owners' Loan Act (as added by this title) is amended by adding at the end the following:

"(c) VISITORIAL POWERS

The provisions of sections 5136C(i) of the Revised Statutes of the United States shall apply to Federal savings associations, and any subsidiary thereof, to the same extent and in the same manner as if such savings associations, or subsidiaries thereof, were national banks or subsidiaries of national banks, respectively.".

"(d) ENFORCEMENT ACTIONS

The ability of the Comptroller of the Currency to bring an enforcement action under this Act or section 5 of the Federal Trade Commission Act does not preclude any private party from enforcing rights granted under Federal or State law in the courts.".

§ 1048. Effective Date

This subtitle shall become effective on the designated transfer date.

MCKINNEY'S CONSOLIDATED LAWS OF NEW YORK ANNOTATED

N.Y. BANKING LAW §   **Page**

§ 10. Declaration of policy

It is hereby declared to be the policy of the state of New York that the business of all banking organizations shall be supervised and regulated through the banking department in such manner as to insure the safe and sound conduct of such business, to conserve their assets, to prevent hoarding of money, to eliminate unsound and destructive competition among such banking organizations and thus to maintain public confidence in such business and protect the public interest and the interests of depositors, creditors, shareholders and stockholders.

§ 12. Superintendent of banks; acting superintendent; discretion

1. The superintendent of banks shall be the head of the banking department. He shall be appointed by the governor, by and with the advice and consent of the senate, and shall hold office until the end of the term of the governor by whom he was appointed and until his successor is appointed and has qualified. Within fifteen days from the time of notice of his appointment, the superintendent shall take and subscribe the constitutional oath of office.

2. The superintendent may, in his discretion, designate one of his deputies to act as superintendent during the superintendent's absence or inability to act. If the office of superintendent is vacant, or if the superintendent's absence or inability to act continues for a period of more than thirty successive days, the governor may designate a deputy to act as superintendent until the filling of the vacancy or the return or recovery of the superintendent.

3. Whenever in this chapter the superintendent is authorized but not required to take any action or his approval is required as a condition precedent to the doing of any act, the taking of such action and the giving of such approval shall be within his sound discretion. In taking any action with respect to any banking organization, and in approving or disapproving any application made by a banking organization, the superintendent shall give due consideration to the policy of the state of New York as declared in section ten of this chapter.

§ 13. Banking board

1. There shall be in the banking department a banking board which shall consist of seventeen members. The superintendent shall be a member of the board and its chairman and executive head. The other sixteen members shall be appointed by the governor by and with the advice and consent of the senate. Each member, other than the superintendent and the first person appointed to fill a new membership on the board, shall serve for a term of three years from the first day of March in the year in which he was appointed and until his successor has been appointed and has qualified. Any member appointed pursuant to the provisions of this section may be removed from office by the governor whenever in his judgment the public interest may require. In case of such removal the governor shall file with the department of state a statement of the cause of such removal.

2. Of the sixteen members other than the superintendent, eight shall have had banking experience, and of these eight there shall be one member whose banking experience shall have been gained in group one, one in group two, one in group three, one in group four, one in group five, one in group six, one in group seven, and one in group eight of the following groups:

Group one: banks, trust companies and private bankers located in the city of New York and having total assets of one billion dollars or more as shown by the last periodical reports of condition received by the superintendent.

Group two: banks, trust companies and private bankers located outside the city of New York and having total assets of one hundred fifty million dollars or more as shown by the last periodical reports of condition received by the superintendent.

Group three: banks, trust companies and private bankers other than those in group one and group two.

Group four: savings banks located in the city of New York and the counties of Westchester, Rockland, Nassau and Suffolk.

Group five: savings banks other than those in group four.

Group six: savings and loan associations.

Group seven: credit unions.

Group eight: foreign banking corporations licensed pursuant to this article to maintain a branch or agency in this state. Notwithstanding any inconsistent provision of this chapter or any other law of this state, the member whose banking experience shall have been gained in this group shall be a resident of this state but need not be a citizen of the United States.

Provided, however, that if the superintendent determines, in his or her sole discretion, that following the rules regulating the method of selecting candidates described in subdivision three of this section, with respect to a vacancy in the office of the member required to have banking experience gained in group six shall not result in the selection of a candidate meeting the requirements of this subdivision, candidates for consideration by the governor to fill such vacancy shall be selected from among persons whose banking experience has been gained in any one or more of the groups two, three and five. A candidate appointed by the governor to fill such vacancy shall be deemed to have gained his or her experience in group six.

3. The board shall make rules to regulate the method of selecting candidates for consideration by the governor to fill a vacancy in the office of any of the eight members herein required to have banking experience. Such rules and any amendments thereto shall be subject to the approval of the governor.

4. The members other than the superintendent shall receive no salary but their expenses incurred in attending meetings shall be paid out of the state treasury, on certificate of the superintendent, upon the audit and warrant of the comptroller. The board shall make provision for the holding of regular meetings. The board shall meet at any time on call by the superintendent upon two days' notice. The superintendent shall call a meeting upon two days' notice upon the written request of any two members. The board may by resolution provide for a shorter notice of meeting. Any action which may be taken by the board at a meeting may be taken by instrument in writing signed by all members of the board without a meeting and any action so taken shall have the same force and effect for all purposes as if taken at a meeting. Any number of copies of any such instrument each bearing one or more signatures shall be deemed a single instrument. The board shall elect a secretary and such other officers as it deems necessary. The secretary and other officers so elected need not be members. The board shall cause a record of its proceedings to be kept. For the purpose of considering questions before it, the board shall have access to all books and papers in the department including all reports and communications, and the members shall treat such reports and communications as confidential.

§ 14. Powers of the banking board

1. For the purpose of effectuating the policy declared in section ten of this article, the banking board shall have power, by a three-fifths vote of all its members, to make, alter and amend rules and regulations not inconsistent with law. Such rules and regulations shall be brought to the attention of those affected thereby in a manner to be prescribed by the board. Without limiting the foregoing power, resolutions or rules or regulations may be so adopted for the following specific purposes:

(a) To approve organization certificates, private bankers' certificates and applications of foreign corporations for licenses to do business in this state, submitted to it by the superintendent as provided in this article.

(b) To determine the purposes for which and the extent to which capital notes or debentures shall be considered and treated as capital stock of corporate banking organizations; but capital notes or debentures shall not be considered or treated as capital stock for the purposes of sections one hundred ten and one hundred eleven of this chapter.

(c) To grant permission to a trust company, including a national bank, to establish one or more common trust funds upon application and after inquiry concerning the qualifications of such trust company to maintain and manage the same, and to regulate the conduct and management of any common trust fund and for such purpose, but not by way of limitation of the foregoing power, to prescribe (1) the records and accounts to be kept of such common trust funds; (2) the procedure to be followed in adding moneys to or withdrawing moneys or investments from any such common trust fund; (3) the methods and standards to be employed in determining the value of such common trust funds and of the assets and investments thereof; (4) the maximum amount of moneys of any estate, trust or fund which may be invested in any common trust fund;

and (5) the maximum proportionate share of any such common trust fund which may be apportioned to any estate, trust or fund; and in connection with such powers to classify the corporations maintaining such common trust funds according to the population of the city, town or village in which the principal offices of such corporations are respectively located and to prescribe the minimum total of any such common trust fund and the permissible limits of investment therein in accordance with such classification.

(cc) To approve the incorporation by or on behalf of trust companies and national banks with trust powers of a mutual trust investment company to form a medium for the common investment of funds held by trust companies, including national banks, acting as executors, administrators, guardians, inter-vivos or testamentary trustees or committees or conservators either alone or with individual co-fiduciaries, and any amendments of the certificate of incorporation of such mutual trust investment company, and to regulate the conduct and management of such mutual trust investment company and for such purpose, but not by way of limitation of the foregoing power, to prescribe (1) the records and accounts to be kept by such mutual trust investment company; (2) the procedure to be followed in the sale or redemption of stocks or shares therein; (3) the methods and standards to be employed in determining the value of such shares in the mutual trust investment company and the assets and investments thereof; and (4) the maximum proportionate shares of any such mutual trust investment company which may be apportioned or sold to any one trust company or national bank.

(d) To authorize a bank or a trust company to invest in the capital stock of a corporation not included among the corporations in the capital stock of which investment is expressly authorized by this chapter.

(e) To authorize a savings bank to invest in the capital stock, capital notes and debentures of and to transfer property to, a trust company or other corporation, as provided in article six of this chapter.

(ee) To authorize a savings and loan association to invest in the capital stock, capital notes and debentures of and to transfer property to, a trust company or other corporation, as provided in article ten of this chapter.

(f) To authorize savings banks to invest in corporate interest bearing obligations not otherwise eligible for investment, provided application for such authorization shall have been made by not less than twenty savings banks or by a trust company all of the capital stock of which is owned by not less than twenty savings banks. Any authorization made pursuant to this subdivision may be revoked upon a majority vote of all the members of the board.

(g) To prescribe from time to time: (1) the rates of interest which may be paid on deposits with any banking organization and with any branch or agency of a foreign banking corporation; and (2) the rates of dividends which may be paid on shares of any savings and loan association or credit union, and to prohibit the payment of such interest or such dividends by any banking organization or by any branch of a foreign banking corporation. Interest or dividend rates so prescribed need not be uniform.

[(gg) Repealed.]

(h) To limit and regulate withdrawals of deposits or shares from any banking organization, if the board shall find that such limitation and regulation are necessary because of the existence of unusual and extraordinary circumstances. The board shall enter such finding on its records.

(i) To prescribe from time to time reserves against deposits to be maintained by banks and trust companies pursuant to article three of this chapter; provided that no reserve requirement imposed by the board against either time or demand deposits shall require any bank or trust company to maintain total reserves in an amount greater than it would be required to maintain if it were at the time a member of the federal reserve system; and provided further, however, that a bank or trust company not a member of the federal reserve system may be authorized by the board to maintain total reserves against deposits in an amount lower than the reserves required by article three of this chapter to be maintained, either in individual cases or by general regulations of the board on such basis as the board may deem reasonable or appropriate in view of the character of the business transacted by such bank or trust company.

(ii) To exempt from reserve requirements prescribed by or pursuant to this chapter deposits payable to the United States by any banking organization arising solely as a result of subscriptions made by or through any such banking organization for United States government securities issued under the authority of the second liberty bond act as amended.

(j) To grant permission to officers, directors, clerks or employees of banks, trust companies and industrial banks to engage in the issue, flotation, underwriting, public sale or distribution at wholesale or retail, or through syndicate participation of stocks, bonds or other similar securities, and to revoke such permission, both as provided in this chapter.

(k) To prescribe the methods and standards to be used (1) in making the examinations provided for in this chapter, and (2) in valuing the assets of banking organizations.

() To prescribe the form and contents of periodical reports of condition to be rendered to the superintendent by banks, trust companies, private bankers, and branches of foreign banking corporations, and the manner of publication of such reports.

(m) To postpone or omit the calling for and rendering of reports provided for by this chapter if the board shall find that such postponement or omission is necessary because of the existence of unusual and extraordinary circumstances. The board shall enter such finding on its records.

(n) To define what is an unsafe manner of conducting the business of banking organizations.

(o) To define what is a safe or unsafe condition of a banking organization.

(p) To make variations from the requirements of this chapter, provided such variations are in harmony with the spirit of the law, if the board shall find that such variations are necessary because of the existence of unusual and extraordinary circumstances. The board shall enter such finding on its records.

(q) To establish safe and sound methods of banking and safeguard the interests of depositors, creditors, shareholders and stockholders generally in times of emergency.

(qq) To permit any banking organization, national banking association, federal mutual savings bank, federal savings and loan association and federal credit union to offer graduated payment mortgages which shall conform to the provisions of section two hundred seventy-nine of the real property law.

[(r) Renumbered (t).]

(s) To permit authorized lenders, as defined by section two hundred eighty or two hundred eighty-a of the real property law, to offer reverse mortgage loans which shall conform to the provisions of section two hundred eighty or two hundred eighty-a of the real property law.

(t) To exercise any other power conferred upon the board by law.

2. The board shall consider and make recommendations upon any matter which the superintendent may submit to it for recommendations, and pass upon and determine any matter which he shall submit to it for determination.

3. The board shall submit to the superintendent proposals for any amendments to this chapter which it deems desirable.

§ 14–a. Rate of interest; banking board to adopt regulations

1. The maximum rate of interest provided for in section 5–501 of the general obligations law shall be sixteen per centum per annum.

2. The rate of interest as so prescribed under this section shall include as interest any and all amounts paid or payable, directly or indirectly, by any person, to or for the account of the lender in consideration for the making of a loan or forbearance as defined by the banking board pursuant to subdivision three of this section.

3. The banking board shall have the power, by a three-fifths vote of all its members, to adopt

such regulations as it shall deem necessary or proper to implement the provisions of this section. The banking board shall make available to the public copies of all regulations adopted pursuant to this section.

4. Such regulations as shall have been adopted pursuant to the provisions of this chapter and in effect immediately prior to the effective date of this section, shall continue in effect until such time as new regulations shall have been adopted by the banking board and shall become effective.

5. Whenever reference is made in this chapter or in any other law, contract or document to the rate of interest prescribed or to be prescribed by the banking board or the superintendent pursuant to this section or any former section fourteen-a of this chapter, such reference shall be deemed a reference to the rate of interest prescribed in subdivision one of this section.

6. Notwithstanding the provisions of subdivision five of this section, the rate of interest charged, taken or received on any loan or forbearance, which would have otherwise been subject to the provisions of former section fourteen-a of this chapter, made or entered into between the effective date of this section and the first day of February, nineteen hundred eighty-one pursuant to a commitment which was made or entered into prior to the effective date of United States Public Law 96–161 and which provides for interest at the prevailing rate at the time of closing shall not exceed the rate of eleven and one-quarter per centum per annum.

7. Nothing contained in this section nor in any other provision of this act whereunder this section is added to the banking law shall be deemed to prohibit the charging of interest at the rates provided or permitted by United States Public Laws 96–161, 96–221 and 96–399, where applicable.

§ 14–b. Power of the banking board to prescribe minimum rate of interest on mortgage escrow accounts

1. The banking board shall have the power to prescribe, from time to time but not more often than once in every three month period, by a three-fifths vote of all its members, by regulation a minimum rate of, and method or basis of computing, interest that a mortgage investing institution shall be required to pay on each es-

crow account maintained with respect to a mortgage on a one to six family residence occupied by the owner or on any property owned by a cooperative apartment corporation, as defined in subdivision twelve of section three hundred sixty of the tax law, (as such subdivision was in effect on December thirtieth, nineteen hundred sixty), and located in this state, which rate shall be greater than the rate of interest required to be paid under section 5–601 or 5–602 of the general obligations law.

2. In making such determination the banking board shall consider pertinent economic and cost factors including, but not limited to: (i) current yields on short term investments, (ii) current dividend rates paid on regular savings accounts throughout this state, (iii) currently prevailing interest rates on conventional and insured or guaranteed mortgage loans in this state, (iv) cost factors in maintaining escrow accounts and (v) such other pertinent economic or cost factors that the banking board shall deem to be appropriate. Prior to the banking board's prescription of any such minimum rate of interest, the superintendent shall make a written recommendation to the banking board as to such minimum rate of interest, reciting the economic and cost data and criteria upon which such recommendation is based. Prior to making such recommendation, the superintendent may invite presentation, by interested persons, of information and data relating to economic and cost factors relevant to such minimum rate of interest.

3. The banking board may promulgate such regulations as it deems necessary and proper to implement and define the provisions of this section. The banking board may prescribe the minimum rate of interest from time to time, but not more often than once in any three-month period, and shall provide reasonable notice to the public of any change in the rate of interest, of the effective date of such change, which shall be not less than seven days following the adoption of such change by the banking board, and of any rule or regulation adopted pursuant to this subdivision.

4. In no event shall interest be required to be paid on escrow accounts where (i) there is a contract between the mortgagor and the mortgage investing institution, entered into before the date this subdivision shall have become a law which contains an express disclaimer of an obli-

gation on the part of the mortgage investing institution to pay interest on such accounts, or (ii) the payment of such interest would violate any federal law or regulation, or (iii) such accounts are maintained with a mortgage servicing company, neither affiliated with nor owned in whole or in part by the mortgage investing institution, under a written contract, entered into before the date this subdivision shall have become a law, which contract does not permit the mortgage investing institution to earn or receive a return from the investment of such accounts.

5. "Mortgage investing institution" as used in this section and in section 5–601 or 5–602 of the general obligations law shall mean and include any bank, trust company, national bank, savings bank, savings and loan association, federal savings and loan association, private banker, credit union, investment company, insurance company, pension fund, mortgage company or other entity which makes, extends or holds a mortgage on any one to six family residence occupied by the owner or any property owned by a cooperative apartment corporation, as defined in subdivision twelve of section three hundred sixty of the tax law, (as such subdivision was in effect on December thirtieth, nineteen hundred sixty), and located in this state.

6. "Escrow account" as used in this section and in section 5–601 or 5–602 of the general obligations law shall mean any account established pursuant to an agreement between a mortgagor and a mortgage investing institution whereby the mortgagor pays to the mortgage investing institution or his designee amounts to be used for the payment of insurance premiums, water rents or any similar charges, and shall also include real property tax escrow accounts as defined in title three-A of article nine of the real property tax law.

7. "One to six family residence" as used in this section and in section 5–601 or 5–602 of the general obligations law shall mean property used primarily for residential purposes for one to six families, including property held in condominium form, and which is occupied in whole or in part by the owner.

8. If any provision of this section, or the application of such provision to any individual, company, corporation or circumstance, shall be held invalid, the remainder of this section, and the application of such section to individuals, companies, corporations, or circumstances other than those to which it is held invalid, shall not be affected thereby.

§ 14–c. Power of the banking board to prescribe criteria for disclosure of information on savings and time accounts

1. The banking board shall promulgate rules and regulations with respect to the disclosure of information on savings and time accounts by all banking organizations and out-of-state state banks authorized to operate and maintain branches pursuant to article five-C of this chapter. Such rules and regulations shall set forth guidelines for, but not be limited to the following:

(a) disclosure of the annual rate of simple interest; the effective annual yield; the formula used in calculating interest; the frequency of compounding and crediting of interest; date on which a deposit begins to earn interest; any delay in crediting a deposited instrument; grace periods for deposits and withdrawals; the minimum balance required to earn interest; the method of determining the balance on which interest is paid; the minimum length of time funds must remain on deposit to earn interest; any fees levied on inactive accounts; any charges, penalties or other conditions imposed upon withdrawals; any penalties for the closing of an account before a specific date; and any other fees, charges or penalties.

(b) form, content and distribution of information.

2. The banking board may alter or amend rules and regulations or promulgate additional rules and regulations as it deems necessary and proper to effectuate the provisions of subdivision one.

§ 14–d. Power of the banking board to prescribe a reasonable period of time permitting the drawing on items received for deposit in a customer's account

1. It is the public policy of this state to provide all banking customers with the ability to draw against items deposited for collection with any banking institution located in this state within a reasonable period of time.

2. The banking board shall promulgate regulations, which may be amended from time to time, establishing a reasonable period of time within which a banking institution must permit a banking customer to draw, as of right, on an item which has been received for deposit in the customer's account.

3. The superintendent is authorized to gather from banking institutions such information as may be required by the banking board for the promulgation of the regulations required by this section.

4. (a) Except as otherwise provided in paragraph (b) of this subdivision, a provision in any agreement between a banking institution and its banking customer which provides for a period of time longer than the period prescribed under regulations promulgated pursuant to this section is unreasonable for purposes of article four of the uniform commercial code and, in lieu thereof, the maximum period of time permitted in the regulation shall be deemed controlling. For all other purposes the provisions of this section shall not be deemed or construed to alter or impair any right or obligation under the uniform commercial code.

(b) This section does not prohibit a banking institution and a banking customer from agreeing in writing to a greater period of time than that otherwise prescribed by regulation pursuant to this section for the drawing against items because of special circumstances, provided that, such agreement is not contained in a pre-printed form and is not a usual, regular business practice of the institution.

5. Such regulations shall require every banking institution to notify each of its banking customers, in writing, of the applicable time limitations on the right to draw on items received for deposit in the customer's account and to keep posted in a conspicuous place at each branch, a notice substantially setting forth the generally applicable time limitations of the banking institution's customers' rights to draw on items deposited to their accounts.

6. The banking board is empowered, upon a determination that the uniform application of a regulation adopted pursuant to this section would result in unsafe or unsound banking practices, to issue such further regulation or order with respect thereto as it deems appropriate.

7. In this section "banking institution" has the same meaning ascribed to it by section nine-f of this chapter and "item" has the same meaning ascribed to it by the uniform commercial code.

§ 14–e. Power of the banking board to authorize the operation of savings banks and savings and loan associations in stock form

1. Notwithstanding any other provision of law to the contrary, the banking board is authorized, by a three-fifths vote of all its members, to promulgate such rules and regulations as shall facilitate:

(a) The organization and operation of stock-form savings banks and stock-form savings and loan associations,

(b) The conversion of mutual savings banks and savings and loan associations to stock form, and

(c) Mergers and acquisitions of assets or of capital stock between and among all of the foregoing banking institutions and between and among such institutions and any other banking institution.

The banking board is authorized to define and implement, by general regulation, the terms and provisions of this section. In adopting such regulations, the banking board shall take into account the declaration of policy contained in section one of a chapter of the laws of nineteen hundred eighty-four entitled "An Act to amend the banking law, in relation to the organization and incorporation of stock-form savings banks and stock-form savings and loan associations and the conversion of mutual savings banks and mutual savings and loan associations to stock form". In connection with such regulations, the banking board is empowered to apply to such stock-form organizations any provision of this chapter, in whole or in part, as shall be applicable to any other stock-form banking organization and to vary any condition, requirement or provision of article two, fifteen or sixteen of this chapter.

2. Such applications as the banking board may prescribe under paragraph (a), (b) or (c) of subdivision one of this section shall each be accompanied by an investigation fee as prescribed pursuant to section eighteen-a of this article.

3. Without limiting the foregoing, the banking board, if it shall determine that unusual and

extraordinary circumstances exist, shall be authorized, by resolution, special or general regulation, to apply or to deem inapplicable to any banking institution referred to in subdivision one of this section, such provisions of this chapter in whole or in part, as it shall find appropriate in connection with the organization, operation, conversion, merger or any other transaction involving a stock-form savings bank or stock-form savings and loan association, provided, however, that such actions are in harmony with the spirit of the law and are necessary because of the existence of such circumstances.

§ 14–f. Power of the banking board to require the provision of basic banking services

1. The legislature finds and declares that certain consumers residing in this state may be unable to afford, without undue financial hardship, the cost of maintaining a consumer transaction account at a banking institution located in this state. It is the policy of this state that, consistent with safe and sound banking practices, banking institutions make available lower cost banking services to consumers. It is further intended that no banking institution be required to offer lower cost banking services at a cost to account holders which is less than the actual cost to the banking institution to provide such services.

2. Except as otherwise provided in this section, every banking institution shall make available to consumers a consumer transaction account, to be known as a "basic banking account", with the following features to be prescribed by the banking board by regulation:

(a) the maximum amount which a banking institution may require as an initial deposit, if any;

(b) the maximum amount a banking institution may require as a minimum balance, if any, to maintain such account;

(c) eight withdrawal transactions, including those conducted at electronic facilities, during any periodic cycle at no additional charge to the account holder; and

(d) the maximum amount a banking institution may charge per periodic cycle for the use of such account.

3. With respect to any transactions in excess of the number specified in accordance with paragraph (c) of subdivision two of this section, (a) a banking institution may impose a reasonable per-transaction charge, or (b) it may impose the fees and charges normally applied to other consumer transaction accounts available at that banking institution provided that any charge per periodic cycle imposed hereunder must be reduced by the charge imposed under paragraph (d) of subdivision two of this section; provided however, that at no time shall the fees and charges on the basic banking account exceed the amount that is normally applied to other consumer transaction accounts available at that banking institution.

4. A banking institution may require as a condition for opening or maintaining a basic banking account, (a) that the holder of a basic banking account be a resident of this state; and (b) the direct deposit to the banking institution of recurring payments such as, but not limited to, social security, wage, or pension payments where direct deposit is available to both the consumer and the banking institution.

5. Except as provided in this section and any rules and regulations promulgated hereunder, a basic banking account may be offered subject to the same rules, conditions and terms normally applicable to other consumer transaction accounts offered by the banking institution; provided that the fees and charges for specific services other than those otherwise provided in this section shall not exceed those imposed by the banking institution for the same services in connection with other consumer transaction accounts offered by the banking institution.

6. No banking institution shall be required to permit any person to open or maintain a basic banking account pursuant to this section if such person maintains another consumer transaction account either at that banking institution or any other banking institution.

7. In lieu of the basic banking account required by this section, a banking institution may make available an alternative account or other banking services determined by the superintendent to be at least as advantageous to consumers as the basic banking account.

8. Where a banking institution posts in the public area of its offices notice of the availability of its other consumer transaction accounts, it shall also post equally conspicuous notice in such

public areas and in the same manner the availability of its basic banking accounts. Where a banking institution makes available in such public areas material describing the terms of its other consumer transaction accounts, it shall also make comparable descriptive material available in the same such areas and in the same manner for its basic banking account.

9. For purposes of this section:

(a) "banking institution" means any bank, trust company, savings bank, savings and loan association, or credit union, or branch of a foreign banking corporation the deposits of which are insured by the Federal Deposit Insurance Corporation, which is incorporated, chartered, organized or licensed under the laws of this state or any other state or the United States, and, in the ordinary course of its business, offers consumer transaction accounts to the general public or, in the case of a credit union, to its members;

(b) "consumer transaction account" means a demand deposit account, negotiable order of withdrawal account, share draft account or similar account used primarily for personal, family or household purposes.

10. For purposes of this section, any banking institution which offers share draft accounts shall use the term "basic share draft account" instead of "basic banking account".

11. If any provision of this section, or the application of such provision to any person or circumstance shall be held invalid, the remainder of this section, and the application of such provisions thereof to persons or circumstances other than those as to which it is held invalid, shall not be affected thereby.

§ 14–g. [Deemed repealed Sept. 10, 2007, pursuant to L. 1997, c. 3]

§ 14–h. [Expires and repealed Sept. 10, 2007]

§ 18. Fees for copies and certifications

Notwithstanding any provision of this chapter to the contrary, for every copy of any paper filed in the department and for the certification thereof, the superintendent may charge such amounts by regulation as the superintendent, in his or her discretion, determines to be fair and reasonable.

§ 19. Assessments for deficiency in reserves against deposits

If any banking organization or branch of a foreign banking corporation shall not maintain the total reserves prescribed by or pursuant to this chapter, the superintendent may levy an assessment upon it for such period as any deficiency in its total reserves amounting to one per centum or more of its deposits against which reserves are required to be maintained shall continue, at rates not in excess of the following:

(1) Six per centum per annum upon any such deficiency not exceeding two per centum of such deposits.

(2) Eight per centum per annum upon any additional deficiency in excess of two and not exceeding three per centum of such deposits.

(3) Ten per centum per annum upon any additional deficiency in excess of three and not exceeding four per centum of such deposits.

(4) Twelve per centum per annum upon any additional deficiency therein.

§ 23. Acceptance or rejection of certificate; investigation fees

Within twenty days after the receipt by the superintendent of any organization certificate of a corporation proposed to be organized under this chapter, or any private banker's certificate together with such documents as are required to be filed therewith, the superintendent shall, if such certificate and such accompanying documents comply in form and substance with the requirements of this chapter, file such certificate for examination and note thereon the date of such filing. If such certificate or such accompanying documents do not comply in all respects with the requirements of this chapter, the superintendent shall, within twenty days after receipt thereof, return them to the persons from whom they were received, calling attention to the defect or defects therein.

At the time of submission of the certificate and accompanying documents an investigation fee as prescribed pursuant to section eighteen-a of this article shall be paid to the superintendent, to be retained by him or her if the certificate and accompanying documents are filed. If the certificate and accompanying documents are not filed because of defects therein, the investigation fee is to be returned with such papers to the persons from whom they were received.

§ 24. Investigation by superintendent; refusal or approval; filing certificate

1. Within ninety days after the date when any organization certificate or private banker's certificate shall have been filed for examination, the superintendent, if he shall find after investigation and examination of what he deems to be the best sources of information at his command that the character, responsibility and general fitness of the person or persons named in such certificate are such as to command confidence and warrant belief that the business of the proposed corporation or private banker will be honestly and efficiently conducted in accordance with the intent and purpose of this chapter, and that the public convenience and advantage will be promoted by allowing such proposed corporation or private banker to engage in business, shall submit such certificate to the banking board together with all papers, correspondence and other information in his possession relating thereto, including the results of his investigation and his recommendation in the matter. Such period of ninety days may be extended, by a written consent executed by a majority of the persons from whom the superintendent received such organization certificate or private banker's certificate, for such additional reasonable period of time as may be required for applicants to comply with conditions precedent stipulated by the superintendent as being a prerequisite to his recommendation to the banking board.

2. If three-fifths of the members of the board, after consideration of all relevant information available to them, shall vote for approval, the superintendent, if he is still satisfied, upon the considerations set forth in subdivision one of this section, that such proposed corporation or private banker should be permitted to engage in business, shall approve such certificate and endorse upon each of the duplicates the date of such approval. He shall forthwith cause notice of such approval to be given to the proposed incorporators or private banker and one of the duplicate certificates to be filed in the office of the department and the other in the office of the clerk of the county in which the principal office of such proposed corporation or private banker is to be located. In a case in which a private banker certificate is submitted to the superintendent for the purpose of continuing the business in connection with a change in its partnership, the superintendent shall approve the private banker certificate without any action by the banking board upon making a determination that the private banker should be permitted to continue its business based upon the considerations set forth in subdivision one of this section.

3. If three-fifths of the members of the banking board shall not vote for approval, or if the superintendent, either prior or subsequent to the submission of such certificate to the board, is not satisfied, upon the considerations set forth in subdivision one of this section, that such proposed corporation or private banker should be permitted to engage in business, the superintendent shall refuse such certificate and shall endorse thereon the date of such refusal and return one of the duplicates to the proposed incorporators or private banker from whom such certificate was received.

4. The provisions of this section shall not apply to any organization certificate required to be filed in the office of the superintendent by section two hundred sixty-b, by section four hundred ten, by section four hundred eleven or by section four hundred eighty-six of this chapter.

§ 25. Authorization certificate; when and to whom issued; contents; filing and recording

1. If the superintendent shall find that a corporation or private banker, the certificate of which has been approved and filed as provided in section twenty-four of this article, has in good faith complied with all the requirements of law and fulfilled all the conditions precedent to commencing business imposed by this chapter, he shall, within ninety days after the date of such approval, or within such longer period thereafter as he may permit pursuant to the second sentence of this subdivision, but in no case after the expiration of that period, issue under his hand and the official seal of the department, in triplicate, an authorization certificate to the person or persons named in such organization certificate or private banker's certificate. The superintendent may extend the period within which he may issue the authorization certificate by an additional sixty days, provided, however, that he shall have determined that such extension of time is needed for raising capital, for fulfilling any other condition precedent to the commencement of business

or for satisfying any other requirement of organization, whether imposed by statute or regulation, and that such extension is consistent with the declaration of policy contained in section ten of this chapter. Such authorization certificate shall state that the corporation or private banker named therein has complied with the provisions of this chapter and that it is authorized to transact the business specified therein. Such authorization certificate shall be conclusive evidence that all conditions precedent have been fulfilled and that the corporation has been formed under this chapter, except in an action or special proceeding brought by the superintendent or the attorney general. The superintendent shall cause one of the triplicate authorization certificates to be transmitted to the corporation or private banker thereby authorized to commence business, another to be filed in the office of the department, and the third to be filed in the county clerk's office in which the organization certificate or the private banker's certificate has been filed. The copies of the authorization certificate filed in the offices of the superintendent and the county clerk shall be attached to the copies of the organization certificate or private banker's certificate previously filed and such certificates shall be recorded in the records of incorporation therein.

2. Any corporation which shall not receive an authorization certificate within the time period provided by subdivision one of this section shall forfeit its rights and privileges as a corporation and its corporate powers shall cease and determine.

3. Any corporation which shall not commence business within six months after the date on which its authorization certificate is issued by the superintendent shall forfeit its rights and privileges as a corporation and its corporate powers shall cease and determine unless the time within which such business may be commenced has been extended by the superintendent. Upon satisfactory cause being shown, the superintendent may grant an extension for a period of not more than one year. Such extension shall be granted by order executed, transmitted and filed in the manner provided for an authorization certificate in subdivision one of this section.

§ 28–b. Credit needs of local communities

1. Each banking institution as defined in subdivision four of this section to which the Community Reinvestment Act of 1977, United States P.L. 95–128, applies shall file with the superintendent a copy of each report and document which it is required to prepare for or file with one or more federal agencies pursuant to the provisions of that law and the rules and regulations promulgated thereunder. Where a banking institution has filed such reports or documents with the superintendent, an update of the reports or documents shall be required at such time as the banking institution requests the superintendent to take any action on any application to which the provisions of subdivision three of this section apply.

2. A special committee is hereby created to consist of seven members to be appointed as follows: three members shall be appointed by the governor, two members shall be appointed by the temporary president of the senate and two members shall be appointed by the speaker of the assembly. The chairman of the committee shall be appointed by the governor. The members appointed to such committee shall be chosen from consumer groups, banking institutions, business and labor organizations and other groups representative of the public-at-large. Such committee shall receive from the superintendent all reports furnished pursuant to this section and such other information as the superintendent may deem relevant. Such committee shall review such reports and the current lending and investment policies of banking institutions, and not later than February first, nineteen hundred eighty, shall make an interim report to the governor and to the legislature, and a final report to the governor and the legislature not later than November fifteenth, nineteen hundred eighty. Such reports may contain recommendations of the committee in legislative form.

3.(a) When taking any action on an application made by a banking institution under section one hundred five, two hundred twenty-four, two hundred forty, or three hundred ninety-six of this chapter for a branch office or under section one hundred ninety-one of this chapter for a public accommodation office or under section six hundred one-b of this chapter for approval or disapproval of a merger or purchase of assets, or taking any action on an application made by a banking institution under section one hundred five-a, two hundred forty-a or three hundred nine-ty-six-a of this chapter for the use or installation of an automated teller machine, point-of-sale terminal or similar electronic facility or on any other application to which the banking board shall by rule or regulation make applicable the provisions of this section, the superintendent shall take into account, among other factors, an assessment, in writing, of the record of performance of the banking institution in helping to meet the credit needs of its entire community, including low and moderate-income neighborhoods, consistent with safe and sound operation of the banking institution. Such assessment and any written communications from the banking department to a banking institution relating to such assessment shall be made available to the public upon request, provided that nothing contained in this subdivision shall be deemed to alter, amend or affect the provisions of subdivision ten of section thirty-six of this chapter. In making such assessment the superintendent shall review all reports and documents filed with him pursuant to subdivision one of this section and any signed, written comments received by him which specifically relate to the banking institution's performance in helping to meet the credit needs of its community. In addition, the superintendent shall consider the following factors in assessing a banking institution's record of performance:

(1) Activities conducted by the banking institution to ascertain credit needs of its community, including the extent of the banking institution's efforts to communicate with members of its community regarding the credit services being provided by the banking institution;

(2) The extent of the banking institution's marketing and special credit-related programs to make members of the community aware of the credit services offered by the banking institution;

(3) The extent of participation by the banking institution's board of directors or board of trustees in formulating the banking institution's policies and reviewing its performance with respect to the purposes of the Community Reinvestment Act of 1977;

(4) Any practices intended to discourage application for types of credit set forth in the banking institution's Community Reinvestment Act Statement(s);

(5) The geographic distribution of the banking institution's credit extensions, credit applications and credit denials;

(6) Evidence of prohibited discriminatory or other illegal credit practices;

(7) The banking institution's record of opening and closing offices and providing services at offices;

(8) The banking institution's participation, including investments, in local community development and redevelopment projects or programs;

(9) The banking institution's origination of residential mortgage loans, housing rehabilitation loans, home improvement loans and small business or small farm loans within its community or the purchase of such loans originated in its community;

(10) The banking institution's participation in governmentally-insured, guaranteed or subsidized loan programs for housing, small businesses or small farms;

(11) The banking institution's ability to meet various community credit needs based on its financial condition, size, legal impediments, local economic condition and other factors;

(11–a) The geographic distribution, availability and use of automatic teller machines, point-of-sale terminals, personal computer banking, debit cards or similar electronic facilities or services; and any training of customers thereon among every branch of the banking institution, if the institution offers such services to any of its customers; and

(12) Other factors that, in the judgment of the superintendent and banking board, reasonably bear upon the extent to which a banking institution is helping to meet the credit needs of its entire community, including, without limitation, the banking institution's participation in credit counseling services.

(b) In assessing the record of performance of a banking institution pursuant to the provisions of paragraph (a) of this subdivision, the superintendent may, where he deems it appropriate, provide for public hearings when an objection to the banking institution's application has been submitted.

(c) An assessment of a banking institution's record of performance under paragraph (a) of this subdivision may be the basis for denying an application under the provisions of this section.

(d) When taking any action pursuant to paragraph (a) of this subdivision, the superintendent shall request from the applicant banking institution and from the appropriate federal bank regulatory authorities any documents, other than those required to be filed with the superintendent by this section or by other applicable statutes or regulations, which are (a) filed with the federal bank regulatory authorities in connection with the application or (b) produced by the applicant banking institution or others in connection with the application.

4. Notwithstanding any other provision of this chapter or law to the contrary, the term banking institution when used in this section shall mean and include all banks, trust companies, savings banks, savings and loan associations, credit unions and foreign banking corporations incorporated, chartered, organized or licensed under the laws of this state.

5. The banking board is hereby authorized and empowered, by a three-fifths vote of all its members, to promulgate rules and regulations effectuating the provisions of this section, including any rules and regulations providing that the assessment of banking institutions referred to in subdivision three of this section shall be made on a graduated numerical basis.

6. If any clause, sentence, paragraph, subdivision or part of this section or the application thereof to any person, firm, or corporation, or circumstance shall be adjudged by any court of competent jurisdiction to be invalid or unconstitutional, such judgment shall not affect, impair or invalidate the remainder thereof, but shall be confined (i) in its operation to the clause, sentence, paragraph, subdivision, or part of this section or (ii) in its application to the person, firm or corporation, or circumstance, directly involved in the controversy in which such judgment shall have been rendered.

§ 29. Branch offices; public accommodation offices; approval or refusal; certificate; investigation fee

When a banking organization seeks to open a branch office or public accommodation office, it shall submit a written application to the superintendent. The application shall contain such information as the superintendent deems necessary. At the time of making such application, an investigation fee as prescribed pursuant to section eighteen–a of this article shall be paid to the superintendent for each branch office or public accommodation office for which leave to open is sought. If the superintendent finds that the opening of the branch office or public accommodation office is consistent with the declaration of policy set forth in section ten of this article and that the applicant is in compliance with section twenty-eight-b of this article, he or she shall issue a certificate in triplicate under his or her hand and the official seal of the department authorizing the opening and occupation of such branch office or public accommodation office and specifying the date on or after which and the conditions under which it may be opened and the place where it shall be located. The superintendent shall cause one of such triplicate certificates to be transmitted to the applicant, another to be filed in the office of the department and the third to be filed in the office of the clerk of the county in which the principal office of the applicant is located. If the superintendent shall not find that the opening of the branch or public accommodation office is consistent with the declaration of policy set forth in section ten of this article or that the applicant is in compliance with section twenty-eight-b of this article, he or she shall notify the applicant that the application has been denied.

No investigation fee for branch applications shall be collected from applicants if such branch applications are filed in conjunction with proceedings under section one hundred thirty-six, four hundred ten or subdivision eight of section six hundred five of this chapter.

§ 40. Revocation of authorization certificate or license or suspension of activities in certain cases

1. If the superintendent shall find that (i) any of the reasons for taking possession of the busi-

ness and property of a banking organization or of the business and property in this state of a foreign banking corporation enumerated in section six hundred six of this chapter, shall exist with respect to a private banker to which the superintendent has issued an authorization certificate or a foreign banking corporation to which the superintendent has issued a license or (ii) any fact or condition exists which would be grounds for denial of an application for such a license issued to a foreign banking corporation, as defined by the banking board by regulation, he may, after notice and hearing thereon, revoke such license or authorization certificate. Notice of such revocation, under the superintendent's hand and the official seal of the department, shall be executed in triplicate and one copy shall be transmitted to such private banker or foreign corporation, another shall be filed in the office of the department and the third shall be filed in the office of the clerk of the county in which the authorization certificate or license of such private banker or foreign corporation has been filed. The superintendent may, in his discretion, publish a copy of such notice, with such other facts as he may deem proper, in the state register.

2. If the superintendent finds that any of the grounds for revocation described in subdivision one of this section are present with respect to a foreign banking corporation licensed pursuant to this chapter and in addition the superintendent finds it necessary to protect the interest of depositors or the public, the superintendent may issue, without notice and hearing, an order suspending or otherwise limiting the activities of the foreign banking corporation, for a period not to exceed ninety days, pending investigation or hearing.

§ 94. Change from bank to trust company; from trust company to bank

A bank complying with the minimum capital stock requirements specified in subdivision nine of section four thousand one of this chapter may become a trust company by filing a certificate pursuant to subdivision two of section eight thousand one of this chapter to provide that it shall have the powers specified in section one hundred of this article. A trust company may become a bank by filing a certificate pursuant to subdivision two of section eight thousand one of this chapter to provide that it shall not have the powers specified in section one hundred of this article. Prior to or simultaneously with the filing

of such certificate, such trust company shall if its title contains the term "trust company" file a certificate pursuant to subdivision two of section eight thousand one of this chapter for the purpose of omitting such term from its title.

§ 96. General powers

Every bank and every trust company shall, subject to the restrictions and limitations contained in this chapter, have the following powers:

1. To discount, purchase and negotiate promissory notes, drafts, bills of exchange, other evidences of debt, and obligations in writing to pay in installments or otherwise all or part of the price of personal property or that of the performance of services; purchase accounts receivable, whether or not they are obligations in writing; lend money on real or personal security; borrow money and secure such borrowings by pledging assets; buy and sell exchange, coin and bullion; and receive deposits of moneys, securities or other personal property upon such terms as the bank or trust company shall prescribe; and exercise all such incidental powers as shall be necessary to carry on the business of banking. For purposes of this subdivision, the term "accounts receivable" shall not include the right to receive payment for property to be sold at a future date or services to be rendered at a future date.

2. To accept for payment at a future date, drafts drawn upon it by its customers and to issue letters of credit authorizing the holders thereof to draw upon it or its correspondents at sight or on time.

3. (a) To receive upon deposit for safe-keeping for hire upon terms and conditions to be prescribed by the bank or trust company, money, securities, papers of any kind and any other personal property;

(b) To engage in the safe deposit business by renting vaults, safe deposit boxes and other receptacles upon premises occupied by the bank or trust company, upon such terms and conditions as may be prescribed by the bank or trust company.

4. To issue by its board of directors capital notes or debentures, when so specifically authorized by the superintendent, and, when so specifically authorized by the superintendent, to receive in payment therefor, in whole or in part, mortgages, interests therein or other property and to

retain, unrecorded or unregistered, assignments or conveyances of such mortgages, interests therein or other property, provided that the superintendent shall not approve the retention of any assignment of mortgage or interest therein or any conveyance of other property, which may be recorded or registered, without record or registration thereof, except where such mortgage, interest therein or other property is assigned or conveyed by a corporation organized under the banking law or by a corporation wholly owned by not less than twenty savings banks of this state.

5. To become a member of a federal reserve bank, and to have and exercise all powers, not in conflict with the laws of this state, which are conferred upon any such member by the federal reserve act. Such bank or trust company and its directors, officers and stockholders shall continue to be subject, however, to all liabilities and duties imposed upon them by any law of this state and to all the provisions of this chapter relating to banks and trust companies.

6. To assume and discharge such obligations to Federal Deposit Insurance Corporation as may be necessary or required for the purpose of maintaining deposit insurance in such corporation.

7. (a) To act as financial agent of the United States Government and as depositary of public money of the United States (including, without being limited to, revenues and funds of the United States, and any funds the deposit of which is subject to the control or regulation of the United States or any of its officers, agents, or employees, and Postal Savings funds); and to perform all such reasonable duties as depositary of such public money and as financial agent of the United States Government as may be required of it; and to pledge assets or furnish other security, satisfactory in form and amount to the Secretary of the Treasury of the United States, for the safekeeping and prompt payment of such public money deposited with it and for the faithful performance of its duties as financial agent of the United States Government.

(b) To pledge assets or furnish other security, satisfactory in form and amount to judges of courts of bankruptcy, for the repayment of deposits of the money of estates under the national bankruptcy act.

(c) To pledge assets or furnish other security, satisfactory in form and amount to the depositor, for the repayment of moneys held in the name of any state (which term shall include every territory of the United States, the District of Columbia, and the Commonwealth of Puerto Rico), or of any foreign nation, or of any Indian nation or tribe, or of any political subdivision or instrumentality or authority of any of them, when required to be secured by applicable law, decree, regulation or resolution, and to pledge assets or furnish other security for the repayment of moneys held as fiduciary, or in the name of a fiduciary, of any trust created by any such state, foreign nation, Indian nation or tribe, political subdivision, instrumentality or authority as required by the terms of such trust; provided, however, that before any pledge or security is made or furnished to any depositor other than this state or a political subdivision, instrumentality or authority of this state, the bank or trust company shall obtain a certified or official copy of such law, decree, regulation, or resolution or trust requiring such pledge or other security, and an opinion of counsel that such pledge or security is required by such law, decree, regulation, or resolution or by the terms of such trust.

[8. Repealed.]

9. To execute and deliver such guaranties as may be incidental to carrying on the business of a bank or trust company.

10. To exercise, subject to such regulations as may be issued from time to time by the banking board, through any foreign branch office (other than one opened or occupied in another state of the United States, the District of Columbia, any territory of the United States, Guam, American Samoa, the United States Virgin Islands, and the Northern Mariana Islands) opened and occupied with the approval of the superintendent and the banking board as provided in section one hundred five of this chapter, such further powers as may be usual in connection with the transaction of the business of banking in the place where such foreign branch office shall transact business, provided that no such foreign branch office shall engage in the general business of producing, distributing, buying or selling goods, wares, or merchandise, nor, except with respect to securities issued by any foreign nation or any political

subdivision, agency or instrumentality thereof, engage or participate, directly or indirectly, in the business of underwriting, selling or distributing securities.

11. To designate one or more agents (except its employees) to issue or sell its travelers checks or money orders at locations other than its principal office or branch offices authorized pursuant to section one hundred five of this chapter, subject to such rules and regulations as the superintendent may make from time to time.

12. To acquire and lease personal property, or to acquire personal property subject to an existing lease together with the lessor's interest therein, subject to such limitations and conditions as the banking board may from time to time prescribe by general regulation.

13. To reserve or order transportation, travel accommodations or other travel services.

14. To arrange, purchase or sell loans secured by liens on interests in real estate, subject to such terms, conditions and limitations as may be prescribed by the superintendent by regulation.

§ 96–a. Servicing of mortgages by banks

1. Every bank shall, subject to the restrictions and limitations contained in this article, have the power to service mortgages, and the superintendent shall have the power to prescribe, by specific or general regulation, the extent to which, and the conditions upon which, mortgages may be serviced.

2. No bank shall, by virtue of the provisions contained in this section, be deemed to have the powers defined and described in subdivision two of section one hundred of this article.

3. The grant of powers to banks by or pursuant to this section shall not be deemed to limit or restrict any other banking organizations, heretofore or hereafter organized, in the exercise of their lawful powers.

§ 96–b. Payroll payment by banks or trust companies

1. Every bank and trust company shall have the power to enter into contracts with any municipal corporation, school district, district corporation, town or county improvement district, public authority, or public corporation to receive in a single payment, for each pay period, the total payroll of such corporations, districts or authori-

ties and deposit the same in accordance with the terms of such contract, which shall include provision for deposits for withholding, retirement and insurance, if any.

2. The amount due each employee shall be disbursed or credited in accordance with the directions of each employee to saving or checking accounts, or loan or mortgage accounts within such bank or trust company or to a single account in another bank or trust company or savings bank or savings and loan association or may be payable in cash or by check to such employee.

§ 96–c. Power to act as trustee under self-employed retirement trust or individual retirement trust

Every bank without fiduciary powers may, subject to any regulations and restrictions prescribed by the superintendent of banks, act as trustee under a retirement plan established pursuant to the provisions of the act of congress entitled "Self-employed Individuals Tax Retirement Act of 1962" as such provisions may be amended from time to time, and under an individual retirement account plan established pursuant to the amendments to the provisions of the Internal Revenue Code contained in the act of congress entitled "Employee Retirement Income Security Act of 1974" as such provisions may be amended from time to time, provided that the provisions of such retirement or individual retirement account plan require the funds of such trust to be invested exclusively in deposits in banks, trust companies, savings banks, savings and loan associations or federal savings and loan associations whose principal offices are located in this state. In the event that any such retirement or individual retirement account plan, which in the judgment of the bank, constituted a qualified plan under the provisions of the applicable act of congress hereinabove mentioned and the regulations promulgated thereunder at the time the trust was established and accepted by the bank is subsequently determined not to be such a qualified plan or subsequently ceases to be such a qualified plan, in whole or in part, the bank may, nevertheless, continue to act as trustee of any deposits theretofore made under such plan and to dispose of the same in accordance with the directions of the depositor and the beneficiaries thereof. No bank, in respect to deposits made under this section, shall be required to segregate such deposits from other deposits of such bank, provided, however, that the bank shall keep appropriate records showing in proper detail all transactions engaged in under the authority of this section.

§ 96–d. Banking development districts

1. [Opening par. eff. until Jan. 1, 2012, pursuant to L. 1998, c. 526, § 4. See, also, opening par. below.] There is hereby created a banking development district program, the purpose of which is to encourage the establishment of commercial bank branches in geographic locations where there is a demonstrated need for banking services. The banking board shall, in consultation with the department of economic development, promulgate rules and regulations, after public hearing and comment, which set forth the criteria for the establishment of banking development districts. Such criteria shall include, but not be limited to, the following:

[Opening par. eff. Jan. 1, 2012, pursuant to L. 1998, c. 526, § 4. See, also, opening par. above.] There is hereby created a banking development district program, the purpose of which is to encourage the establishment of bank branches in geographic locations where there is a demonstrated need for banking services. The banking board shall, in consultation with the department of economic development, promulgate rules and regulations, after public hearing and comment, which set forth the criteria for the establishment of banking development districts. Such criteria shall include, but not be limited to, the following:

(a) the location, number, and proximity of sites where banking services are available within the district;

(b) the identification of consumer needs for banking services within the district;

(c) the economic viability and local credit needs of the community within the district;

(d) the existing commercial development within the district;

(e) the impact additional banking services would have on potential economic development in the district; and

(f) such other criteria which the superintendent in his or her discretion shall identify as appropriate.

2. A local government, in conjunction with a bank, trust company or national bank, may submit an application to the superintendent for the designation of a banking development district. The superintendent shall issue a determination on such an application within sixty days of receiving such application. If an application is approved, the superintendent shall transmit notification of such approval to the local government, the bank, trust company or national bank, the state comptroller, the commissioner of taxation and finance, the commissioner of the department of economic development, the temporary president of the senate and the speaker of the assembly.

2–a. Notwithstanding any other provision of law, an application may be submitted by a local government in conjunction with a bank, trust company or national bank which has already opened a bank branch within such area, provided such branch was opened after December thirty-first, nineteen hundred ninety-six. In considering the criteria authorized pursuant to subdivision one of this section, the superintendent shall also take into account the importance and benefits of preserving the banking services offered by the existing branch.

3. [Eff. Jan. 1, 2012, pursuant to L. 1998, c. 526, § 4. See, also, subd. 3 below.] The establishment of a branch in a banking development district by a bank, trust company or national bank shall be subject to all applicable state and federal laws regarding the establishment of branch offices, including the provisions of section one hundred five of this article, provided however that the branch application fee required pursuant to section twenty-nine of this chapter shall be waived for any such branch. A bank or trust company may submit an application to open a branch office simultaneously with the submission of the application for the designation of a banking development district.

3–a. [Eff. after Jan. 1, 2012, pursuant to L. 1998, c. 526, § 4. See, also, subd. 3 above.] The establishment of a branch in a banking development district by a bank, trust company or national bank shall be subject to all applicable state and federal laws regarding the establishment of branch offices, including the provisions of section one hundred five of this article. A bank or trust company may submit an application to open a branch office simultaneously with the submission of the application for the designation of a banking development district.

4. For the purposes of this section, the term "local government" shall mean a county, town, city or village.

5. [Expires and deemed repealed Jan. 1, 2012, pursuant to L.1998, c. 526, § 4.] (a) Notwithstanding the provisions of subdivision two of section two hundred thirty-seven of this chapter; for the purposes of this section, paragraph c of subdivision two of section ten of the general municipal law, subdivision six of section one hundred five of the state finance law and section four hundred eighty-five-f of the real property tax law, any reference to a bank, trust company or national bank shall be deemed to include a savings bank, savings and loan association, federal savings and loan association or federal savings bank; provided, however, that such provisions of law do not grant a savings bank, savings and loan association, federal savings and loan association or federal savings bank eligibility to accept municipal or public funds or municipal or public moneys other than for the limited purposes of the establishment of a branch in a banking development district pursuant to this section. Any such municipal or public funds or moneys shall be deposited only at the branch established pursuant to this section, and any municipal funds or moneys may be deposited only by the sponsoring municipality in which the branch and banking development district are located; provided further that any such municipal or public funds or moneys shall be subject to the same requirements which apply to municipal or public funds or moneys deposited in a bank, trust company or national bank and shall also be subject to the provisions of section one hundred five of the state finance law or section ten of the general municipal law relating to such deposits.

(b) Notwithstanding any other provision of law, the banking board shall promulgate rules and regulations to authorize the participation of savings banks, savings and loan associations, federal savings banks and federal savings and loan associations in the program established pursuant to this section.

§ 97. Power to purchase securities and stocks

Subject to the restrictions and limitations contained in this chapter, a bank or trust company may invest in and have and exercise all rights of ownership with respect to:

1. Bonds, notes, debentures and other obligations for payment of money, which are not in default as to either principal or interest when acquired.

2. Stocks of any city, county, town or village of this state which are not in default as to either principal or interest when acquired.

3. Stock of a federal reserve bank in the amount necessary to qualify for membership in such reserve bank.

4. Stock of each of the following to an amount not in excess of ten per centum of the capital stock, surplus fund and undivided profits of such bank or trust company:

(a) Any safe deposit company which does business on premises owned or leased by the bank or trust company or the vaults of which are connected with or adjacent to an office of such bank or trust company; provided that the purchase and holding of such stock is first duly authorized by resolution of the board of directors of the bank or trust company and by written approval of the superintendent, stating the number and amount of the shares which may be so purchased and held, excepting that the bank or trust company may, without the written approval of the superintendent, acquire the stock owned by a former director of the safe deposit company at the time that he ceased to be a director. The bank or trust company may not pay, without the prior written approval of the superintendent, more for such stock than the cost thereof to the director.

(b) Any investment company qualified to exercise the powers specified in subdivision two of section five hundred eight of this chapter;

(c) The Bank for International Settlements.

[(d) Relettered (c).]

4-a. When the banking board shall have adopted such regulations as shall permit such ownership or investment, and subject to such restrictions as the banking board may prescribe, stock or other equity investments in subsidiary corporations engaged in, or to be organized to engage in the following activities:

(a) To acquire and lease personal property under the same terms and conditions as provided in subdivision twelve of section ninety-six of this article;

(b) To purchase accounts receivable as provided in subdivision one of section ninety-six of this article;

(c) To be a corporation organized pursuant to the provisions of section twenty-five (a) of an act of congress entitled the "Federal Reserve Act";

(d) To own or operate real or personal property acquired through foreclosure or in settlement or reduction of debts due it;

(e) To own or operate real or personal property for use as bank premises; or

(f) To transact any other business in which the bank or trust company may engage directly.

4–b.   Common or preferred stock of any corporation created or existing under the laws of the United States or of any state, district or territory thereof, or of the commonwealth of Puerto Rico, other than the stock of a bank, trust company, national bank, savings bank, banking corporation or a life insurance company as defined in section one hundred seven of the insurance law, provided that: (a) such common or preferred stock is registered on a national securities exchange, as provided in an act of congress of the United States entitled the "Securities Exchange Act of 1934", approved June sixth, nineteen hundred thirty-four, as amended, or such other exchange or market system as the superintendent shall approve by regulation; (b) the aggregate amount of all investments in common and preferred stock as permitted by this subdivision shall at no time exceed two percent of the assets or twenty percent of the capital, surplus and undivided profits of the bank or trust company, whichever is less; (c) the aggregate amount of all investments in the common and preferred stock of any one issuer pursuant to this subdivision, together with the aggregate amount of all investments in the bonds, debentures, notes or other obligations of such issuer made pursuant to paragraph (i) of subdivision one of section one hundred three of this chapter, shall at no time exceed one percent

of the assets or fifteen percent of the capital, surplus and undivided profits of the bank or trust company, whichever is less; and (d) no bank or trust company shall at any time hold pursuant to this subdivision more than two percent of the total issued and outstanding shares of stock of any one issuer.

4–c. Subject to such restrictions as the banking board may prescribe, stock or other equity interest in one or more small business investment companies, as authorized pursuant to the provisions of an act of congress entitled "Small Business Investment Act of 1958," as amended, or in any entity established to invest solely in such small business investment companies, except that in no event shall the total amount of such investments exceed five percent of the capital stock, surplus fund and undivided profits of such bank or trust company.

5.   So much of the capital stock of any other corporation as may be specifically authorized by the laws of this state or by resolution of the banking board upon a three-fifths vote of all its members.

The superintendent is authorized to adopt such rules and regulations as shall permit banks and trust companies to make a loan which provides for receipt of shares of stock of, or a share of the profits, income or earnings of, a borrower in consideration for making the loan.

A bank or trust company may acquire stock in settlement or reduction of a loan, or advance of credit or in exchange for an investment previously made in good faith and in the ordinary course of business, where such acquisition of stock is necessary in order to minimize or avoid loss in connection with any such loan, advance of credit or investment previously made in good faith. A trust company may acquire stock from any estate, trust or fund with respect to which such trust company is acting in a fiduciary capacity, if a claim is asserted or may be asserted against it with respect to the purchase or retention of such stock for such estate, trust or fund, (a) where such acquisition by the trust company has been authorized or directed by a court, or (b) where such trust company has been advised by its counsel in writing that it has incurred a contingent or potential liability with respect to the purchase or retention of such stock and such trust company desires to relieve itself from such liability. Stocks acquired pursuant to the provisions of this paragraph may be held for such period as the board of directors deems advisable.

A bank or trust company may continue to hold any bonds or other securities or stock which it holds in accordance with the provisions of law at the time this act takes effect.

No bank or trust company shall purchase, acquire, or hold any stock of any corporation except as provided in this section.

§ 98. Power to take and hold real estate; restrictions

1. A bank or trust company may purchase, hold, lease and convey real property as follows:

(a) A plot whereon there is or may be erected a building suitable for the convenient transaction of its business, from portions of which not required for its own use a revenue may be derived, and a plot whereon parking accommodations are, or are to be, provided, with or without charge, primarily for its customers or employees or both, and a building or a portion or portions thereof for use by the bank or trust company in its business, provided that the aggregate of all investments of any bank or trust company in such plots and buildings and in a leased building or a portion or portions thereof or in the stock, debentures or other obligations of any corporation holding such plots or buildings and of all loans to or upon the security of the stock of any such corporation shall not exceed forty per centum of the aggregate of the capital stock, surplus fund and undivided profits of such bank or trust company, except with the approval of the superintendent. Any bank or trust company having, prior to April twenty-third, nineteen hundred thirty-four, made loans and investments in excess of the limitations prescribed by this paragraph may retain any such loans and investments notwithstanding such limitations.

(b) Such as shall be conveyed to it in satisfaction of debts previously contracted in the course of its business.

(c) Such as it shall purchase at sales under judgments, decrees or mortgages held by it.

(d) Such as may be specifically authorized by resolution of the banking board upon a

three-fifths vote of all its members, provided, however, that the banking board upon a three-fifths vote of all its members may delegate to the superintendent the authority to approve the purchase, lease, conveyance or other acquisition or sale of real property which is located outside the United States, its territories and possessions, and which is used principally as the residence of one or more directors, officers, or employees of the bank or trust company.

(e) A whole or part interest in a "project", as defined in the New York state urban development corporation act, pursuant to sections six or eight of such act. An investment by a bank or trust company in a single project shall not exceed one per centum of the assets or fifteen per centum of the combined capital stock, surplus fund and undivided profits of such bank or trust company, whichever is less, and the aggregate of all investments of a bank or trust company in such projects and investments in securities of any "subsidiary" of the New York state urban development corporation, as defined in the New York state urban development corporation act, shall not exceed five per centum of the assets or seventy-five per centum of the combined capital stock, surplus fund and undivided profits of such bank or trust company, whichever is less.

2. All real estate purchased by any bank or trust company or taken by it in settlement of debts due it, shall be conveyed to it in its name or, subject to such regulations and restrictions as the banking board finds to be necessary and proper, may be taken in the name of a duly authorized nominee. All such conveyances shall be immediately recorded or registered in the office of the proper recording officer of the county in which such real estate is located.

§ 98-a. Club accounts

1. No contract under which a bank or trust company agrees to repay deposits of fixed sums made at regular intervals at a given time with all interest or dividends credited thereon, or to repay said deposits when, together with interest or dividends credited thereon, they shall equal a specified sum, may provide for any forfeiture of the sums deposited in the event of the discontinuance of the regular payments. Interest or divi-

dends on club accounts, if offered, must be credited at least quarterly and may not be forfeited once credited, in the event of the discontinuance of regular payments.

2. Any bank which provides for deposits in club accounts shall, in all advertising, announcements or brochures pertaining to such accounts, state whether or not interest or dividends are paid thereon and, if interest or dividends are paid, shall state the rate or form of interest or dividends so paid in accordance with any rules and regulations that may be prescribed by the superintendent.

§ 100. Fiduciary powers

Every trust company shall have, subject to the restrictions and limitations contained in this chapter, the following powers:

1. To act as the fiscal or transfer agent of the United States, any state, municipality, body politic or corporation; and in such capacity to receive and disburse money, to transfer, register and countersign certificates of stock, bonds or other evidences of indebtedness or other securities, and to act as attorney in fact or agent of any person or corporation, foreign or domestic, for any lawful purpose.

2. To act as trustee under any mortgage or bonds issued by any municipality, body politic or corporation, foreign or domestic, and accept and execute any other municipal or corporate trust not prohibited by the laws of this state.

3. To be appointed and to act under the order or appointment of any court of competent jurisdiction:

(a) As guardian, receiver, trustee, committee or conservator of the estate of any minor, mentally ill person, mentally retarded person, person of unsound mind, alcohol abuser or conservatee or in any other fiduciary capacity;

(b) As receiver, trustee, or committee of the property or estate of any person in insolvency or bankruptcy proceedings.

4. To be appointed and to accept the appointment of executor or of trustee under the last will and testament or administrator with or without the will annexed of the estate of any deceased person.

5. To take, accept and execute any and all such trusts, duties and powers of whatever nature or description as may be conferred upon or entrusted or committed to it by any person or persons, or any body politic, corporation, domestic or foreign, or other authority by grant, assignment, transfer, devise, bequest or otherwise, or which may be entrusted or committed or transferred to it or vested in it by order of any court of competent jurisdiction, or any surrogate, and to receive, take, manage, hold and dispose of according to the terms of such trust, duty or power, any property or estate, real or personal, which may be the subject of any such trust, duty or power.

Provided that no trust company shall have any right or power to make any contract, or to accept or execute any trust whatever, which it would not be lawful for any individual to make, accept or execute.

§ 101. Additional powers of certain trust companies

Every trust company which at the time this act takes effect lawfully possesses and exercises the power, for hire, to examine titles to real estate, to procure and furnish information in relation thereto, and to guarantee or insure the title to real estate to persons interested, in such real estate or in mortgages thereon, against loss, by reason of defective title or other encumbrances of or upon, such real estate, shall continue to possess such power, but no other trust company shall hereafter have or exercise such power.

§ 102. Powers of specially chartered trust companies

Every trust company incorporated by a special law shall possess the powers of trust companies incorporated under this chapter and shall be subject to such provisions of this chapter as are not inconsistent with the special laws relating to such specially chartered company.

§ 102–a. Limited liability trust companies

1. Trust companies which (a) do not receive deposits from the general public and (b) have been exempted by the banking board from the requirements of section thirty-two of this chapter, may be formed and operated as limited liability trust companies. Such limited liability trust companies shall be formed in accordance with, shall operate in compliance with, and shall meet

all of the requirements of the limited liability company law and this chapter, except that to the extent any provision of the limited liability company law shall be inconsistent with the provisions of this chapter, the provisions of this chapter shall govern; provided, however, that limited liability trust companies shall not have perpetual existence.

2. Notwithstanding any other provision of this chapter, a limited liability trust company shall dissolve and its affairs shall be wound up upon the occurrence of any event specified in section seven hundred one of the limited liability company law. Upon such a dissolution, the provisions of this chapter shall govern the winding up of the affairs of the limited liability trust company and the distribution of its assets. Further, upon such a dissolution, if the members of a limited liability trust company wish to continue the existence of the company and meet the requirements of section seven hundred one of the limited liability company law, they shall apply for and may receive the approval of the superintendent for new articles of organization and a new authorization certificate.

3. Trust companies which have been formed and are operating pursuant to this article and article fifteen of this chapter on the effective date of this section, and which meet the requirements of subdivision one of this section, may, with the approval of the banking board, convert into limited liability trust companies, provided that they meet all of the other requirements of this chapter as if they were newly formed companies.

4. The superintendent is hereby authorized and empowered to make such general rules and regulations as may be necessary and proper to effectuate the provisions of this chapter relating to the formation and operation of limited liability trust companies.

§ 131. Prohibitions against encroachments upon certain powers of banks and trust companies

1. No person unauthorized by law shall subscribe to or become a member of, or be in any way interested in any association, institution or company formed or to be formed for the purpose of issuing notes or other evidences of debt to be loaned or put in circulation as money; nor shall any such person subscribe to or become in any way interested in any bank or trust company or

fund created or to be created for the like purposes or either of them. No corporation, domestic or foreign, other than a national bank or a federal reserve bank, unless expressly authorized by the laws of this state, shall employ any part of its property, or be in any way interested in any fund which shall be employed for the purpose of receiving deposits, making discounts, receiving for transmission or transmitting money in any manner whatsoever, or issuing notes or other evidences of debt to be loaned or put into circulation as money, except that a small business investment company as defined in and operating pursuant to the provisions of an act of congress entitled "Small Business Investment Act of 1958," may act as depository or fiscal agent of the United States when so designated by the secretary of the treasury without violating the provisions of this section, except that a corporation duly licensed by the superintendent under article thirteen-A of this chapter or therein expressly excepted from the application of said article may engage in the business of selling or issuing checks or the business of receiving money for transmission or transmitting the same and except that services of an agent or representative may be performed in connection with the obligations of issuers including, without limitation, those mentioned in section six hundred seventy of this chapter where each such marketable obligation has a face value of not less than one hundred thousand dollars. No corporation, domestic or foreign, other than a corporation formed under or subject to this chapter or the banking laws of the United States except an express company having contracts with railroad companies for the operation of an express service upon the lines of such railroad companies, or a transatlantic steamship company, or a telegraph company, or a corporation incorporated prior to the year eighteen hundred and fifty, to promote the welfare of immigrants, shall possess the power of receiving money for transmission or of transmitting the same, by draft, traveler's check, money order or otherwise. The discounting of bills, notes or evidences of debt by a corporation organized solely for the purpose of enabling producers of farm, dairy, horticultural or other agricultural products or cooperative corporations of such producers to avail themselves of the provisions of an act of congress approved March fourth, nineteen hundred and twenty-three, known as the agricultural credits act of nineteen hundred and twenty-three, same being subchapter three of chapter seven of title twelve of the code of laws of the United States as adopted by congress January third, nineteen hundred thirty-five, and amendments thereto, where such discounting is solely in connection with the rediscount of such bills, notes or evidences of debt under the provisions of said act of congress shall not be deemed or construed to be a form of banking, nor shall the making of such discounts be deemed to violate any provisions of law pertaining to banking. Except as otherwise provided in article twelve-D of this chapter, engaging in the business of loaning money in this state on bonds, notes or other evidences of indebtedness, secured by deeds of trust or mortgages upon real property or personal property situated in, upon or appurtenant thereto, and/or purchasing of or otherwise acquiring existing bonds, notes or other evidences of indebtedness, deeds of trust or mortgages of or upon such properties, or any interest therein, and the holding of the same, or the endorsing, selling, assigning, transferring or disposing of the same to another corporation, by a domestic business corporation, or by a foreign corporation which is authorized to transact business in this state, shall not be deemed or construed to violate any of the provisions of this chapter. The purchase or other acquisition on original issue or subsequent transfer for less than the principal amount thereof or otherwise at a discount of any evidences of indebtedness or other obligations for the payment of money shall not by reason of such discount be or be deemed to be a violation of the provisions of this section.

2.   No person, association of persons or corporation, unless expressly authorized by law, shall keep any office for the purpose of issuing any evidences of debt, to be loaned or put in circulation as money; nor shall they issue any bills or promissory notes or other evidences of debt for the purpose of loaning them or putting them in circulation as money, unless thereto specially authorized by law.

3.   Except as otherwise provided in article five or article five-C of this chapter, no corporation other than a trust company shall have or exercise in this state the power of receiving deposits of money, securities or other personal property from any person or corporation in trust, or have or exercise in this state any of the powers specified in section one hundred of this article, or have or maintain an office in this state for the transaction of, or transact, directly or indirectly,

any such or similar business, except that a federal reserve bank may exercise the powers conferred by subdivision one of such section if authorized so to do by the laws of the United States and any domestic corporation legally exercising any of the powers conferred by such subdivision at the time this act takes effect may continue to exercise such powers, and a foreign banking corporation or trust company incorporated under the laws of another state, which by the law of the state of its incorporation may act as trustee, guardian, executor, administrator, or in any other fiduciary capacity under any last will and testament or codicil thereto or other testamentary writing or under any deed of trust inter vivos or other written instrument establishing a trust, or by the appointment of any court of said state, may act in this state in any such fiduciary capacity, provided similar domestic corporations which have the power under the law of this state to act herein in any such fiduciary capacity, are permitted to act in like fiduciary capacity in the state where such foreign corporation has its domicile, provided that if such foreign corporation proposes to act in any fiduciary capacity in this state and to do so is required to file its qualification in the surrogate's court of this state, it shall file in the office of the clerk of the surrogate's court of the county in which application for such appointment is pending (a) a duly executed instrument in writing, by its terms of indefinite duration and irrevocable, appointing such clerk and his successors its true and lawful attorney, upon whom all process in any action or proceeding against such fiduciary, affecting or relating to the state, trust or fund represented or held by such fiduciary or the acts of defaults of such corporation in reference to such estate, trust or fund may be served with the same force and effect as if it were a domestic corporation and had been lawfully served with process within the state, and (b) a copy of its charter certified by its secretary under its corporate seal, together with the post office address of its principal office; provided further that if such foreign corporation proposes to act in any other fiduciary capacity in the state, it shall file in the office of the superintendent (a) a duly executed instrument in writing, by its terms of indefinite duration and irrevocable, appointing the superintendent and his successors its true and lawful attorney, upon whom all process in any action or proceeding against such fiduciary affecting or relating to the estate, trust or fund held or represented by such fiduciary or the acts or defaults of such corporation in reference to such estate, trust or fund may be served with the same force and effect as if it were a domestic corporation and had been lawfully served with process within the state, (b) a written certificate of designation, which may be changed from time to time thereafter by the filing of a new certificate of designation, specifying the name and address of the officer, agent, or other person to whom such process shall be forwarded by the superintendent, and (c) a copy of its charter certified by its secretary under its corporate seal, together with the post office address of its principal office.

4.   Except as otherwise provided in article five or article five-C of this chapter, no foreign corporation, having authority to act in this state as trustee, guardian, executor, administrator, or in any other fiduciary capacity shall establish or maintain, directly or indirectly, any branch office or agency in this state. Notwithstanding any other provisions of this chapter, a bank or trust company incorporated under the laws of another state, which is authorized by its charter and by the laws of the state of its incorporation to exercise in such state any or all of the fiduciary powers that trust companies are authorized to exercise in this state pursuant to sections one hundred, one hundred-a, one hundred-b, one hundred-c and one hundred-d of this article, may establish and maintain a trust office in this state for purposes of exercising any or all of the fiduciary powers authorized by the laws of the state of its incorporation; provided, however, that such exercise does not exceed the powers authorized under sections one hundred, one hundred-a, one hundred-b, one hundred-c and one hundred-d of this article; provided further, however, an out-of-state state bank or trust company may not establish a trust office in this state, unless a bank or trust company authorized to exercise any or all fiduciary powers under sections one hundred, one hundred-a, one hundred-b, one hundred-c and one hundred-d of this article is permitted to establish a trust office and exercise substantially similar fiduciary powers on substantially the same basis as permitted an out-of-state state bank or trust company pursuant to this subdivision, in the state where such out-of-state state bank or trust company is so incorporated. A trust office established or maintained by such an out-of-state state bank or trust company pursuant to this subdivision shall not be considered to be a branch office pursuant to any other provisions of this chapter; provided, however, that any such out-of-state state bank or trust company seeking to establish and maintain a trust office or open any additional trust offices in this state shall submit a notice to the superintendent describing the proposed activities of the office and such other information as the superintendent shall request. The trust office may commence operation thirty days after the superintendent receives such notice, unless the superintendent notifies the out-of-state state bank or trust company in writing within such time period that such office may not commence operation or that additional information or time is required for the superintendent to consider such notice. Such out-of-state state bank or trust company may establish and maintain additional trust offices in this state pursuant to and consistent with the provisions of this subdivision, provided that the superintendent finds that the establishment and maintenance of any and all trust offices by such out-of-state state bank or trust company is and continues to be consistent with the goals set forth in the declaration of policy contained in section ten of this chapter. If any such foreign corporation or out-of-state state bank or trust company violates this provision, such foreign corporation or out-of-state state bank or trust company shall not thereafter be appointed or act in any such fiduciary capacity in this state. The validity of any mortgage heretofore given by a foreign corporation to a trust company doing business within a foreign domicile of such mortgagor to secure the payment of an issue of bonds shall not be affected by any of the provisions of this section and such mortgage shall be enforceable in accordance with the laws of this state against property covered thereby within the state of New York.

5.   Any out-of-state state bank or trust company subject to the provision of subdivision three or four of this section may be either in corporate form or organized as a limited liability company.

6.   Every person, and every corporation, director, agent, officer or member thereof, who shall violate any provision of this section, directly or indirectly or assent to such violation, shall forfeit an amount as determined pursuant to section forty-four of this chapter to the people of the state.

§ 136.   Change of national banking association into state bank by conversion or merger

1.   A national banking association may convert into or merge with a state bank under a

state charter, provided that the action taken complies with federal law. Each such conversion or merger shall be subject to the requirements of this chapter.

2. In the case of each conversion, a written plan of conversion shall be submitted, in duplicate, to the superintendent. Such plan shall be in form satisfactory to the superintendent, shall prescribe the terms and conditions of the conversion and the mode of carrying it into effect and shall have annexed thereto and forming a part thereof an organization certificate of the state bank which is to result from the conversion. Such organization certificate shall be in the form prescribed by section ninety of this chapter with such variations, if any, as shall be satisfactory to the superintendent. With such plan of conversion there shall be submitted, in duplicate, to the superintendent a certificate of the president, secretary or cashier of the national banking association certifying that all steps have been taken which are necessary under federal law to the consummation of the conversion. The superintendent shall approve or disapprove such plan of conversion within ninety days of such submission thereof to him. If the superintendent shall approve such plan, he shall file one duplicate thereof, together with one duplicate of such certificate submitted therewith and the original of the approval of the superintendent, in the office of the superintendent, and the other duplicate of such plan, together with a duplicate of such certificate and a duplicate of the superintendent's approval, shall be filed in the office of the clerk of the county in which the principal office of the state bank is to be located. Upon such filing in the office of the superintendent, the conversion shall become effective, unless a later date is specified in the plan, in which event the conversion shall become effective upon such later date, and the organization certificate attached to such plan shall thereafter be the organization certificate of the state bank for all purposes.

3. In the case of each merger, a written plan of merger shall be submitted, in duplicate, to the superintendent. Such plan shall be in form satisfactory to the superintendent and shall prescribe the terms and conditions of the merger and the mode of carrying it into effect. Such plan may provide the name to be borne by the state bank, as receiving corporation, if such name is to be changed. Such plan may also name the persons who shall constitute the first board of directors of the state bank after the merger shall have been accomplished, provided that the number and qualifications of such persons shall be in accordance with the provisions of this chapter relating to the number and qualifications of directors of a state bank; or such plan may provide for a meeting of the stockholders to elect a board of directors within sixty days after such merger, and may make provision for conducting the affairs of the state bank meanwhile. With such plan of merger there shall be submitted, in duplicate, to the superintendent the following: (a) by the national banking association, a certificate of the president, secretary or cashier of such association certifying that all steps have been taken which are necessary under federal law to the consummation of the merger; (b) by the state bank, a certificate of the president, secretary or cashier certifying that such plan of merger has been approved by the board of directors of the state bank by a majority vote of all the members thereof, that such plan has been submitted to the stockholders of the state bank at a meeting thereof held upon notice of at least fifteen days, specifying the time, place and object of such meeting and addressed to each stockholder at the address appearing upon the books of the state bank and published at least once a week for two successive weeks in one newspaper in the county in which the state bank has its principal place of business, and that such plan of merger has been approved at such meeting by the vote of the stockholders owning at least two-thirds in amount of the stock of the state bank, except that such certificate submitted by the state bank need not certify that such plan was submitted to or approved by vote of the stockholders of the state bank if (i) the total assets of the national banking association do not exceed ten per centum of the total assets of the state bank and (ii) the plan of merger does not change the name or the authorized shares of capital stock of the state bank or make or require any other change or amendment for which the approval or consent of stockholders of the state bank would be required under provisions of law other than this section.

4. As used in this section, the term "state bank" means a bank or trust company. For purposes of merger under this section the term "national banking association" means one or more national banking associations.

5. With the written plan of conversion submitted under subdivision two hereof, there shall

be paid to the superintendent an investigation fee as prescribed pursuant to section eighteen-a of this chapter; provided, however, that no investigation fee shall be payable under this subdivision with respect to a merger to which subdivision two of section one hundred thirty-six-b of this article is applicable, and with the written plan of merger submitted under subdivision three hereof there shall be paid to the superintendent an investigation fee as prescribed pursuant to section eighteen-a of this chapter.

§ 136–a. Purchase of assets of national banking association by bank or trust company

1. A state bank or trust company may acquire, whether by purchase or otherwise, other than by merger, all or a substantial part of the assets of a national banking association, provided that the action taken complies with federal law.

2. In the case of each such acquisition, a written plan providing for the acquisition by the bank or trust company of the assets of the national banking association shall be submitted, in duplicate, by the bank or trust company to the superintendent. Such plan shall be in form satisfactory to the superintendent, shall specify the selling and the acquiring corporation, and shall prescribe the terms and conditions of the acquisition and the mode of carrying it into effect.

At the time of submission for action by the superintendent of the written plan of acquisition of assets, an investigation fee as prescribed pursuant to section eighteen-a of this chapter shall be paid to the superintendent; provided, however, that no investigation fee shall be payable under this subdivision with respect to an acquisition to which subdivision two of section one hundred thirty-six-b of this article is applicable.

3. With such plan of acquisition of assets there shall also be submitted, in duplicate, to the superintendent the following: (a) by the national banking association, a certificate of the president, secretary or cashier of such association certifying that all steps have been taken which are necessary under federal law to the sale of its assets; (b) by the bank or trust company, if the assets of the national banking association exceed ten per centum of the assets of the bank or trust company, a certificate of the president, secretary or cashier certifying that such plan has been approved by the board of directors of his corpora-

tion by a majority vote of all the members thereof, and that such plan was thereafter submitted to the stockholders of such corporation at a meeting thereof held upon notice of at least fifteen days, specifying the time, place, and object of such meeting and addressed to each stockholder at the address appearing upon the books of the corporation and published at least once a week for two successive weeks in one newspaper in the county in which the bank or trust company has its principal place of business and that such plan has been approved at such meeting by the vote of stockholders owning at least two-thirds in amount of the stock of such corporation.

4. Nothing contained in this section one hundred thirty-six-a shall be construed to prohibit any other purchase of assets which is otherwise permitted by applicable law.

§ 136–b. Approval of superintendent

1. The superintendent shall approve or disapprove of a proposed merger as authorized by section one hundred thirty-six of this chapter or a proposed acquisition of all or a substantial part of the assets of a national banking association as authorized by section one hundred thirty-six-a of this chapter, as the case may be, within one hundred twenty days after the submission of the proposed plan thereof to him. In determining whether to so approve, the superintendent shall take into consideration (i) the declaration of policy contained in section ten of this chapter, (ii) whether the effect of such merger or acquisition shall be either to expand the size or extent of the resulting or acquiring institution beyond limits consistent with adequate and sound banking and the preservation thereof or result in a concentration of assets beyond limits consistent with effective competition, (iii) whether such merger or acquisition may result in such a lessening of competition as to be injurious to the interests of the public or tend toward monopoly and (iv) primarily, the public interest and needs and convenience thereof. If the superintendent shall approve such proposed merger or acquisition, he shall file the plan, together with such certificates and the original of the approval of the superintendent, in the office of the superintendent, and, in the case of merger, a duplicate of the plan, together with a duplicate of each of such certificates and a duplicate of the superintendent's approval, shall be filed in the office of the clerk of the county in which the principal office of the

receiving corporation is located. Upon such filing in the office of the superintendent, the merger or acquisition shall become effective, unless a later date is specified in the plan, in which event the merger or acquisition shall become effective upon such later date.

2. Notwithstanding the provisions of subdivision one of this section, the approval of the superintendent shall not be required with respect to such merger or acquisition, if any of the corporations which are to merge, or if the selling or acquiring corporation, is a banking subsidiary of a bank holding company, and the banking board pursuant to section one hundred forty-two of this chapter has granted its approval for such bank holding company, or any trustee or trustees who hold voting stock of such banking subsidiary for the benefit of the stockholders or members of such bank holding company, to vote the stock of such banking subsidiary in favor of the proposed merger or acquisition. The superintendent shall file the plan of merger or acquisition and the certificates submitted to him pursuant to section one hundred thirty-six or section one hundred thirty-six-a of this chapter, together with a certified copy of the resolution of the banking board granting such approval, in the office of the superintendent, and, in the case of a merger, a duplicate of the plan and of each of such certificates, together with a certified copy of such resolution, shall be filed in the office of the clerk of the county in which the receiving corporation is located. Upon such filing in the office of the superintendent, the merger or acquisition shall become effective, unless a later date is specified in the plan, in which event the merger or acquisition shall become effective upon such later date. For purposes of this subdivision, the terms "bank holding company" and "banking subsidiary" shall have the meanings stated in section one hundred forty-one of this chapter.

§ 136–c. Effect of merger or conversion of national banking association into state bank

1. At the time when a merger or conversion under sections one hundred thirty-six and one hundred thirty-six-b of this chapter becomes effective.

(a) the resulting state bank shall be considered the same business and corporate entity as the national banking association, although

as to rights, powers and duties, the resulting bank is a state bank;

(b) all of the property, rights, powers and franchises of the national banking association shall vest in the resulting state bank and the resulting state bank shall be subject to and be deemed to have assumed all of the debts, liabilities, obligations and duties of the national banking association and to have succeeded to all of its relationships, fiduciary or otherwise, as fully and to the same extent as if such property, rights, powers, franchises, debts, liabilities, obligations, duties and relationships had been originally acquired, incurred or entered into by the resulting state bank; provided, however, that the resulting state bank shall not, through such conversion or merger, acquire power to engage in any business or to exercise any right, privilege or franchise which is not conferred by the provisions of this chapter upon such resulting state bank;

(c) any reference to the national banking association in any contract, will or document, whether executed or taking effect before or after the conversion or merger, shall be considered a reference to the resulting state bank if not inconsistent with the other provisions of the contract, will or document;

(d) a pending action or other judicial proceeding to which the national banking association is a party, shall not be deemed to have abated or to have discontinued by reason of the conversion or merger, but may be prosecuted to final judgment, order or decree in the same manner as if the conversion or merger had not been made; or the resulting state bank may be substituted as a party to such action or proceeding, and any judgment, order or decree may be rendered for or against it that might have been rendered for or against the national banking association if the conversion or merger had not occurred.

2. As used in this section, the term "state bank" means a bank or trust company.

§ 137. Change of state bank into national banking association by conversion, merger or consolidation

1. A state bank may, by vote of the stockholders owning at least two-thirds in amount of its

stock, convert into, or merge or consolidate with, a national banking association under the charter of a national banking association in the manner provided by federal law and without approval of any state authority.

2. The franchise of a state bank as a state bank shall automatically terminate when its conversion into or its merger or consolidation with a national banking association under a federal charter is consummated and the resulting national banking association shall be considered the same business and corporate entity as the state bank, although as to rights, powers and duties the resulting bank is a national banking association.

3. At the time when such conversion, merger or consolidation becomes effective

(a) all of the property, rights, powers and franchises of the state bank shall vest in the national banking association and the national banking association shall be subject to and be deemed to have assumed all of the debts, liabilities, obligations and duties of the state bank and to have succeeded to all of its relationships, fiduciary or otherwise, as fully and to the same extent as if such property, rights, powers, franchises, debts, liabilities, obligations, duties and relationships had been originally acquired, incurred or entered into by the national banking association; provided, however, that nothing in this section shall be deemed to authorize the national banking association to maintain as its own office any office previously maintained by the state bank, and authority, if any, to maintain any such office shall be governed by applicable federal law;

(b) any reference to the state bank in any contract, will or document, whether executed or taking effect before or after the conversion, merger or consolidation, shall be considered a reference to the national banking association if not inconsistent with the other provisions of the contract, will or document;

(c) a pending action or other judicial proceeding to which the state bank is a party, shall not be deemed to have abated or to have discontinued by reason of the conversion, merger or consolidation, but may be prosecuted to final judgment, order or decree in

the same manner as if the conversion, merger or consolidation had not been made; or the national banking association may be substituted as a party to such action or proceeding, and any judgment, order or decree may be rendered for or against it that might have been rendered for or against the state bank if the conversion, merger or consolidation had not occurred.

4. As used in this section, the term "state bank" means any bank, trust company or other banking organization engaged in the business of receiving deposits other than a mutual savings bank. For purposes of merger or consolidation under this section the term "national banking association" means one or more national banking associations, and the term "state bank" means one or more state banks.

§ 195. Rules, regulations and orders

The banking board by a three-fifths vote of all the members thereof shall have power to adopt, amend and enforce such rules, regulations and orders as it may deem necessary to enable it to administer and carry out the provisions of this article and to prevent evasions thereof.

§ 208. Nondiscriminatory treatment of insured state banks and national banks

Notwithstanding any other laws of this state, a state bank, which is incorporated in another state and whose deposits are insured by Federal Deposit Insurance Corporation, shall have the same protection, privileges and immunities, including the right to sue, collect debts, realize on collateral security, enforce liens, claims and obligations, and protect its property in this state, as a national bank whose principal office is located in the same state as such state bank, and such state bank and its shares, securities and evidences of indebtedness shall enjoy the same privileges, protections and immunities as those of such a national bank and shall not be subject to any disability, incapacity, restriction, regulation, penalty, fee, fine or taxation which is not imposed by this state in the case of such a national bank, provided however that this section shall not apply with respect to any state bank and its shares, securities and evidences of indebtedness unless such state bank's state of incorporation has a statute with provisions substantially similar to this section which is applicable to a state bank incorporated in this state. As used in this section the term "state bank" shall mean any commercial bank or trust company.

Chapter I. Comptroller of the Currency, Department of the Treasury
12 C.F.R. (Selected Sections)

CODE OF FEDERAL REGULATIONS TITLE 12. BANKS AND BANKING

CHAPTER I. COMPTROLLER OF THE CURRENCY, DEPARTMENT OF THE TREASURY
PART 1. Investment Securities

Sec. 1.1 Authority, purpose, and scope.

(a) Authority. This part is issued pursuant to 12 U.S.C. 1 et seq., 12 U.S.C. 24 (Seventh), and 12 U.S.C. 93a.

(b) Purpose. This part prescribes standards under which national banks may purchase, sell, deal in, underwrite, and hold securities, consistent with the authority contained in 12 U.S.C. 24 (Seventh) and safe and sound banking practices.

(c) Scope. The standards set forth in this part apply to national banks, District of Columbia banks, and federal branches of foreign banks. Further, pursuant to 12 U.S.C. 335, State banks that are members of the Federal Reserve System are subject to the same limitations and conditions that apply to national banks in connection with purchasing, selling, dealing in, and underwriting securities and stock. In addition to activities authorized under this part, foreign branches of national banks are authorized to conduct international activities and invest in securities pursuant to 12 CFR part 211.

Sec. 1.2 Definitions.

(a) Capital and surplus means:

(1) A bank's Tier 1 and Tier 2 capital calculated under the OCC's risk-based capital standards set forth in appendix A to 12 CFR part 3 (or comparable capital guidelines of the appropriate Federal banking agency) as reported in the bank's Consolidated Report of Condition and Income filed under 12 U.S.C. 161 (or under 12 U.S.C. 1817 in the case of a state member bank); plus

(2) The balance of a bank's allowance for loan and lease losses not included in the bank's Tier 2 capital, for purposes of the calculation of risk-based capital described in paragraph (a)(1) of this section, as reported in the bank's Consolidated Report of Condition and Income filed under 12 U.S.C. 161 (or under 12 U.S.C. 1817 in the case of a state member bank).

(b) General obligation of a State or political subdivision means:

(1) An obligation supported by the full faith and credit of an obligor possessing general powers of taxation, including property taxation; or

(2) An obligation payable from a special fund or by an obligor not possessing general powers of taxation, when an obligor possessing general powers of taxation, including property taxation, has unconditionally promised to make payments into the fund or otherwise provide funds to cover all required payments on the obligation.

(c) Investment company means an investment company, including a mutual fund, registered under section 8 of the Investment Company Act of 1940, 15 U.S.C. 80a–8.

(d) Investment grade means a security that is rated in one of the four highest rating categories by:

(1) Two or more NRSROs; or

(2) One NRSRO if the security has been rated by only one NRSRO.

(e) Investment security means a marketable debt obligation that is not predominantly speculative in nature. A security is not predominantly speculative in nature if it is rated investment grade. When a security is not rated, the security must be the credit equivalent of a security rated investment grade.

(f) Marketable means that the security:

(1) Is registered under the Securities Act of 1933, 15 U.S.C. 77a et seq.;

(2) Is a municipal revenue bond exempt from registration under the Securities Act of 1933, 15 U.S.C. 77c(a)(2);

(3) Is offered and sold pursuant to Securities and Exchange Commission Rule 144A, 17 CFR 230.144A, and rated investment grade or is the credit equivalent of investment grade; or

(4) Can be sold with reasonable promptness at a price that corresponds reasonably to its fair value.

(g) Municipal bonds means obligations of a State or political subdivision other than general obligations, and includes limited obligation bonds, revenue bonds, and obligations that satisfy the requirements of section 142(b)(1) of the Internal Revenue Code of 1986 issued by or on behalf of any State or political subdivision of a State, including any municipal corporate instrumentality of 1 or more States, or any public agency or authority of any State or political subdivision of a State.

(h) NRSRO means a nationally recognized statistical rating organization.

(i) Political subdivision means a county, city, town, or other municipal corporation, a public authority, and generally any publicly-owned entity that is an instrumentality of a State or of a municipal corporation.

(j) Type I security means:

(1) Obligations of the United States;

(2) Obligations issued, insured, or guaranteed by a department or an agency of the United States Government, if the obligation, insurance, or guarantee commits the full faith and credit of the United States for the repayment of the obligation;

(3) Obligations issued by a department or agency of the United States, or an agency or political subdivision of a State of the United States, that represent an interest in a loan or a pool of loans made to third parties, if the full faith and credit of the United States has been validly pledged for the full and timely payment of interest on, and principal of, the loans in the event of non-payment by the third party obligor(s);

(4) General obligations of a State of the United States or any political subdivision thereof; and municipal bonds if the national bank is well capitalized as defined in 12 CFR 6.4(b)(1);

(5) Obligations authorized under 12 U.S.C. 24 (Seventh) as permissible for a national bank to deal in, underwrite, purchase, and sell for the bank's own account, including qualified Canadian government obligations; and

(6) Other securities the OCC determines to be eligible as Type I securities under 12 U.S.C. 24 (Seventh).

(k) Type II security means an investment security that represents:

(1) Obligations issued by a State, or a political subdivision or agency of a State, for housing, university, or dormitory purposes that would not satisfy the definition of Type I securities pursuant to paragraph (j) of Sec. 1.2;

(2) Obligations of international and multilateral development banks and organizations listed in 12 U.S.C. 24 (Seventh);

(3) Other obligations listed in 12 U.S.C. 24 (Seventh) as permissible for a bank to deal in, underwrite, purchase, and sell for the bank's own account, subject to a limitation per obligor of 10 percent of the bank's capital and surplus; and

(4) Other securities the OCC determines to be eligible as Type II securities under 12 U.S.C. 24 (Seventh).

(*l*) Type III security means an investment security that does not qualify as a Type I, II, IV, or V security. Examples of Type III securities include corporate bonds and municipal bonds that do not satisfy the definition of Type I securities pursuant to paragraph (j) of Sec. 1.2 or the definition of Type II securities pursuant to paragraph (k) of Sec. 1.2.

(m) Type IV security means:

(1) A small business-related security as defined in section 3(a)(53)(A) of the Securities Exchange Act of 1934, 15 U.S.C. 78c(a)(53)(A), that is rated investment grade or is the credit equivalent thereof, that is fully secured by interests in a pool of loans to numerous obligors.

(2) A commercial mortgage-related security that is offered or sold pursuant to section 4(5) of the Securities Act of 1933, 15 U.S.C. 77d(5), that is rated investment grade or is the credit equivalent thereof, or a commercial mortgage-related security as described in section 3(a)(41) of the Securities Exchange Act of 1934, 15 U.S.C. 78c(a)(41), that is rated investment grade in one of the two highest investment grade rating categories, and that represents ownership of a promissory note or certificate of interest or participation that is directly secured by a first lien on one or more parcels of real estate upon which one or more commercial structures are located and that is fully secured by interests in a pool of loans to numerous obligors.

(3) A residential mortgage-related security that is offered and sold pursuant to section 4(5) of the Securities Act of 1933, 15 U.S.C. 77d(5), that is rated investment grade or is the credit equivalent thereof, or a residential mortgage-related security as described in section

3(a)(41) of the Securities Exchange Act of 1934, 15 U.S.C. 78c(a)(41), that is rated investment grade in one of the two highest investment grade rating categories, and that does not otherwise qualify as a Type I security.

(n) Type V security means a security that is:

(1) Rated investment grade;

(2) Marketable;

(3) Not a Type IV security; and

(4) Fully secured by interests in a pool of loans to numerous obligors and in which a national bank could invest directly.

[61 FR 63982, Dec. 2, 1996, as amended at 66 FR 34791, July 2, 2001]

Sec. 1.3 Limitations on dealing in, underwriting, and purchase and sale of securities.

(a) Type I securities. A national bank may deal in, underwrite, purchase, and sell Type I securities for its own account. The amount of Type I securities that the bank may deal in, underwrite, purchase, and sell is not limited to a specified percentage of the bank's capital and surplus.

(b) Type II securities. A national bank may deal in, underwrite, purchase, and sell Type II securities for its own account, provided the aggregate par value of Type II securities issued by any one obligor held by the bank does not exceed 10 percent of the bank's capital and surplus. In applying this limitation, a national bank shall take account of Type II securities that the bank is legally committed to purchase or to sell in addition to the bank's existing holdings.

(c) Type III securities. A national bank may purchase and sell Type III securities for its own account, provided the aggregate par value of Type III securities issued by any one obligor held by the bank does not exceed 10 percent of the bank's capital and surplus. In applying this limitation, a national bank shall take account of Type III securities that the bank is legally committed to purchase or to sell in addition to the bank's existing holdings.

(d) Type II and III securities; other investment securities limitations. A national bank may not hold Type II and III securities issued by any one obligor with an aggregate par value exceeding 10 percent of the bank's capital and surplus. However, if the proceeds of each issue are to be used to acquire and lease real estate and related facilities to economically and legally separate industrial tenants, and if each issue is payable solely from and secured by a first lien on the revenues to be derived from rentals paid by the lessee under net noncancellable leases, the bank may apply the 10 percent investment limitation separately to each issue of a single obligor.

(e) Type IV securities—

(1) General. A national bank may purchase and sell Type IV securities for its own account. Except as described in paragraph (e)(2) of this section, the amount of the Type IV securities that a bank may purchase and sell is not limited to a specified percentage of the bank's capital and surplus.

(2) Limitation on small business-related securities rated in the third and fourth highest rating categories by an NRSRO. A national bank may hold small business-related securities, as defined in section 3(a)(53)(A) of the Securities Exchange Act of 1934, 15 U.S.C. 78c(a)(53)(A), of any one issuer with an aggregate par value not exceeding 25 percent of the bank's capital and surplus if those securities are rated investment grade in the third or fourth highest investment grade rating categories. In applying this limitation, a national bank shall take account of securities that the bank is legally committed to purchase or to sell in addition to the bank's existing holdings. No percentage of capital and surplus limit applies to small business related securities rated investment grade in the highest two investment grade rating categories.

(f) Type V securities. A national bank may purchase and sell Type V securities for its own account provided that the aggregate par value of Type V securities issued by any one issuer held by the bank does not exceed 25 percent of the bank's capital and surplus. In applying this limitation, a national bank shall take account of Type V securities that the bank is legally committed to purchase or to sell in addition to the bank's existing holdings.

(g) Securitization. A national bank may securitize and sell assets that it holds, as a part of its banking business. The amount of securitized loans and obligations that a bank may sell is not limited to a specified percentage of the bank's capital and surplus.

(h) Investment company shares–

(1) General. A national bank may purchase and sell for its own account investment company shares provided that:

(i) The portfolio of the investment company consists exclusively of assets that the national bank may purchase and sell for its own account under this part; and

(ii) The bank's holdings of investment company shares do not exceed the limitations in Sec. 1.4(e).

(2) Other issuers. The OCC may determine that a national bank may invest in an entity that is exempt from registration as an investment company under section 3(c)(1) of the Investment Company Act of 1940, provided that the portfolio of the entity consists exclusively of assets that a national bank may purchase and sell for its own account under this part.

(i) Securities held based on estimates of obligor's performance.

(1) Notwithstanding §§ 1.2(d) and (e), a national bank may treat a debt security as an investment security for purposes of this part if the bank concludes, on the basis of estimates that the bank reasonably believes are reliable, that the obligor will be able to satisfy its obligations under that security, and the bank believes that the security may be sold with reasonable promptness at a price that corresponds reasonably to its fair value.

(2) The aggregate par value of securities treated as investment securities under paragraph (i)(1) of this section may not exceed 5 percent of the bank's capital and surplus.

[61 FR 63982, Dec. 2, 1996, as amended at 64 FR 60098, Nov. 4, 1999]

PART 3. Minimum Capital Ratios; Issuances of Directives

Sec. 3.1 Authority.

This part is issued under the authority of 12 U.S.C. 1 et seq., 93a, 161, 1818, 3907 and 3909.

[59 FR 64563, Dec. 15, 1994]

Sec. 3.2 Definitions.

For the purposes of this part:

(a) Adjusted total assets means the average total assets figure required to be computed for and stated in a bank's most recent quarterly Consolidated Report of Condition and Income (Call Report) minus end-of-quarter intangible assets, deferred tax assets, and credit-enhancing interest-only strips, that are deducted from Tier 1 capital, and minus nonfinancial equity investments for which a Tier 1 capital deduction is required pursuant to section 2(c)(5) of appendix A of this part 3. The OCC reserves the right to require a bank to compute and maintain its capital ratios on the basis of actual, rather than average, total assets when necessary to carry out the purposes of this part.

(b) Bank means a national banking association or District of Columbia Bank.

(c) Tier 1 capital means Tier 1 capital as determined according to section 2 of appendix A of this part, including the deductions described therein.

(d) Tier 2 capital means Tier 2 capital as determined according to section 2 of appendix A of this part, including the limitations described therein.

(e) Total capital means Total capital as determined according to section 1(25) and section 2 of appendix A of this part, including the deductions described therein.

[55 FR 38800, Sept. 21, 1990, as amended at 60 FR 7907, Feb. 10, 1995; 67 FR 3795, Jan. 25, 2002]

Sec. 3.5 Applicability.

This subpart is applicable to all banks unless the Office determines, pursuant to the procedures set forth in subpart C, that different minimum capital ratios are appropriate for an individual bank based upon its particular circumstances, or unless different minimum capital ratios have been established or are established for an individual bank in a written agreement or a temporary or final order pursuant to 12 U.S.C. 1818 (b) or (c), or as a condition for approval of an application.

Sec. 3.6 Minimum capital ratios.

(a) Risk-based capital ratio. All national banks must have and maintain the minimum risk-based capital ratio as set forth in appendix A (and, for certain banks, in appendix B).

(b) Total assets leverage ratio. All national banks must have and maintain Tier 1 capital in an amount equal to at least 3.0 percent of adjusted total assets.

(c) *Additional leverage ratio requirement.* An institution operating at or near the level in paragraph (b) of this section should have well-diversified risks, including no undue interest rate risk exposure; excellent control systems; good earnings; high asset quality; high liquidity; and well managed on-and off-balance sheet activities; and in general be considered a strong banking organization, rated composite 1 under the Uniform Financial Institutions Rating System (CAMELS) rating system of banks. For all but the most highly-rated banks meeting the conditions set forth in this paragraph (c), the minimum Tier 1 leverage ratio is 4 percent. In all cases, banking institutions should hold capital commensurate with the level and nature of all risks.

[55 FR 38800, Sept. 21, 1990, as amended at 61 FR 47367, Sept. 6, 1996; 64 FR 10199, Mar. 2, 1999]

Appendix A to Part 3. Risk–Based Capital Guidelines

Section 2. Components of Capital.

A national bank's qualifying capital base consists of two types of capital–core (Tier 1) and supplementary (Tier 2).

(a) *Tier 1 Capital.* The following elements comprise a national bank's Tier 1 capital:

(1) Common stockholders' equity;

(2) Noncumulative perpetual preferred stock and related surplus; and[1]

(3) Minority interests in the equity accounts of consolidated subsidiaries, except that the following are not included in Tier 1 capital or total capital:

(i) Minority interests in a small business investment company or investment fund that holds nonfinancial equity investments and minority interests in a subsidiary that is engaged in nonfinancial activities and is held under one of the legal authorities listed in section 1(c)(23) of this appendix A.

(ii) Minority interests in consolidated asset-backed commercial paper programs sponsored by a bank if the consolidated assets are excluded from risk-weighted assets pursuant to section 3(a)(s)(i) of this appendix A.

(b) *Tier 2 Capital.* The following elements comprise a national bank's Tier 2 capital:

(1) Allowance for loan and lease losses, up to a maximum of 1.25% of risk-weighted assets,[2] subject to the transition rules in section 4(a)(2) of this appendix A;

(2) Cumulative perpetual preferred stock, long-term preferred stock, convertible preferred stock, and any related surplus, without limit, if the issuing national bank has the option to defer payment of dividends on these instruments. For long-term preferred stock, the amount that is eligible to be included as Tier 2 capital is reduced by 20% of the original amount of the instrument (net of redemptions) at the beginning of each of the last five years of the life of the instrument;

(3) Hybrid capital instruments, without limit. Hybrid capital instruments are those instruments that combine certain characteristics of debt and equity, such as perpetual debt. To be included as Tier 2 capital, these instruments must meet the following criteria:[3]

(i) The instrument must be unsecured, subordinated to the claims of depositors and general creditors, and fully paid-up;

1. [n.2] Preferred stock issues where the dividend is reset periodically based upon current market conditions and the bank's current credit rating, including but not limited to, auction rate, money market or remarketable preferred stock, are assigned to Tier 2 capital, regardless of whether the dividends are cumulative or noncumulative.

2. [n.3] The amount of the allowance for loan and lease losses that may be included in capital is based on a percentage of risk-weighted assets. The gross sum of risk-weighted assets used in this calculation includes all risk-weighted assets, with the exception of the assets required to be deducted under section 3 in establishing risk-weight-

ed assets (i.e., the assets required to be deducted from capital under section 2(c)) of this appendix. A banking organization may deduct reserves for loan and lease losses in excess of the amount permitted to be included as capital, as well as allocated transfer risk reserves and reserves held against other real estate owned, from the gross sum of risk-weighted assets in computing the denominator of the risk-based capital ratio.

3. [n.4] Mandatory convertible debt instruments that meet the requirements of 12 CFR 3.100(e)(5), or that have been previously approved as capital by the OCC, are treated as qualifying hybrid capital instruments.

(ii) The instrument must not be redeemable at the option of the holder prior to maturity, except with the prior approval of the OCC;

(iii) The instrument must be available to participate in losses while the issuer is operating as a going concern (in this regard, the instrument must automatically convert to common stock or perpetual preferred stock, if the sum of the retained earnings and capital surplus accounts of the issuer shows a negative balance); and

(iv) The instrument must provide the option for the issuer to defer principal and interest payments, if

(A) The issuer does not report a net profit for the most recent combined four quarters, and

(B) The issuer eliminates cash dividends on its common and preferred stock.

(4) Term subordinated debt instruments, and intermediate-term preferred stock and related surplus are included in Tier 2 capital, but only to a maximum of 50% of Tier 1 capital as calculated after deductions pursuant to section 2(c) of this appendix. To be considered capital, term subordinated debt instruments shall meet the requirements of Sec. 3.100(f)(1). However, pursuant to 12 CFR 5.47, the OCC may, in some cases, require that the subordinated debt be approved by the OCC before the subordinated debt may qualify as Tier 2 capital or may require prior approval for any prepayment (including payment pursuant to an acceleration clause or redemption prior to maturity) of the subordinated debt. Also, at the beginning of each of the last five years for the life of either type of instrument, the amount that is eligible to be included as Tier 2 capital is reduced by 20% of the original amount of that instrument (net of redemptions).

(5) Up to 45 percent of the pretax net unrealized holding gains (that is, the excess, if any, of the fair value over historical cost) on available-for-sale equity securities with readily determinable fair values.[4] Unrealized gains (losses) on other types of assets, such as bank premises and available-for-sale debt securities, are not included in Tier 2 capital, but the OCC may take these unrealized gains (losses) into account as additional factors when assessing a bank's overall capital adequacy.

(c) Deductions from Capital. The following items are deducted from the appropriate portion of a national bank's capital base when calculating its risk-based capital ratio:

(1) Deductions from Tier 1 Capital. The following items are deducted from Tier 1 capital before the Tier 2 portion of the calculation is made:

(i) Goodwill;

(ii) Other intangible assets, except as provided in section 2(c)(2) of this appendix A;

(iii) Deferred tax assets, except as provided in section 2(c)(3) of this appendix A, that are dependent upon future taxable income, which exceed the lesser of either:

(A) The amount of deferred tax assets that the bank could reasonably expect to realize within one year of the quarter-end Call Report, based on its estimate of future taxable income for that year; or

(B) 10% of Tier 1 capital, net of goodwill and all intangible assets other than purchased credit card relationships, mortgage servicing assets and non-mortgage servicing assets; and

(iv) Credit-enhancing interest-only strips (as defined in section 4(a)(3) of this appendix A), as provided in section 2(c)(4).

(v) Nonfinancial equity investments as provided by section 2(c)(5) of this appendix A.

(2) Qualifying intangible assets. Subject to the following conditions, mortgage servicing assets, nonmortgage servicing assets[5] and purchased credit card relationships need not be deducted from Tier 1 capital:

---

4. [n.5] The OCC reserves the authority to exclude all or a portion of unrealized gains from Tier 2 capital if the OCC determines that the equity securities are not prudently valued.

5. [n.6] Intangible assets are defined to exclude IO strips receivable related to these mortgage and non-mortgage servicing assets. See section 1(c)(14) of this appendix A. Consequently, IO strips receivable related to mortgage and non-mortgage servicing assets are not required to be deducted under section 2(c)(2) of this appendix A. However, credit-enhancing interest-only strips as defined in section 4(a)(3) are deducted from Tier 1 capital in accordance with section 2(c)(4) of this appendix A. Any non credit-enhancing IO strips receivable are subject to a 100% risk weight under section 3(a)(4) of this appendix A.

(i) The total of all intangible assets that are included in Tier 1 capital is limited to 100 percent of Tier 1 capital, of which no more than 25 percent of Tier 1 capital can consist of purchased credit card relationships and non-mortgage servicing assets in the aggregate. Calculation of these limitations must be based on Tier 1 capital net of goodwill and all other identifiable intangibles, other than purchased credit card relationships, mortgage servicing assets and non-mortgage servicing assets.

(ii) Banks must value each intangible asset included in Tier 1 capital at least quarterly at the lesser of:

(A) 90 percent of the fair value of each intangible asset, determined in accordance with section 2(c)(2)(iii) of this appendix A; or

(B) 100 percent of the remaining unamortized book value.

(iii) The quarterly determination of the current fair value of the intangible asset must include adjustments for any significant changes in original valuation assumptions, including changes in prepayment estimates.

(iv) Banks may elect to deduct disallowed servicing assets on a basis that is net of any associated deferred tax liability. Deferred tax liabilities netted in this manner cannot also be netted against deferred tax assets when determining the amount of deferred tax assets that are dependent upon future taxable income.

(3) Deferred tax assets—

(i) Net unrealized gains and losses on available-for-sale securities. Before calculating the amount of deferred tax assets subject to the limit in section 2(c)(1)(iii) of this appendix A, a bank may eliminate the deferred tax effects of any net unrealized holding gains and losses on available-for-sale debt securities. Banks report these net unrealized holding gains and losses in their Call Reports as a separate component of equity capital, but exclude them from the definition of common stockholders' equity for regulatory capital purposes. A bank that adopts a policy to deduct these amounts must apply that approach consistently in all future calculations of the amount of disallowed deferred tax

assets under section 2(c)(1)(iii) of this appendix A.

(ii) Consolidated groups. The amount of deferred tax assets that a bank can realize from taxes paid in prior carryback years and from reversals of existing taxable temporary differences generally would not be deducted from capital. However, for a bank that is a member of a consolidated group (for tax purposes), the amount of carryback potential a bank may consider in calculating the limit on deferred tax assets under section 2(c)(1)(iii) of this appendix A, may not exceed the amount that the bank could reasonably expect to have refunded by its parent holding company.

(iii) Nontaxable Purchase Business Combination. In calculating the amount of net deferred tax assets under section 2(c)(1)(iii) of this appendix A, a deferred tax liability that is specifically associated with an intangible asset (other than purchased mortgage servicing rights and purchased credit card relationships) due to a nontaxable purchase business combination may be netted against that intangible asset. Only the net amount of the intangible asset must be deducted from Tier 1 capital. Deferred tax liabilities netted in this manner cannot also be netted against deferred tax assets when determining the amount of net deferred tax assets that are dependent upon future taxable income.

(iv) Estimated future taxable income. Estimated future taxable income does not include net operating loss carryforwards to be used during that year or the amount of existing temporary differences expected to reverse within the year. A bank may use future taxable income projections for their closest fiscal year, provided it adjusts the projections for any significant changes that occur or that it expects to occur. Such projections must include the estimated effect of tax planning strategies that the bank expects to implement to realize net operating losses or tax credit carryforwards that will otherwise expire during the year.

(4) Credit-enhancing interest-only strips. Credit-enhancing interest-only strips, whether purchased or retained, that exceed 25% of Tier 1 capital must be deducted from Tier 1 capital. Purchased and retained credit-enhancing inter-

est-only strips, on a non-tax adjusted basis, are included in the total amount that is used for purposes of determining whether a bank exceeds its Tier 1 capital.

(i) The 25% limitation on credit-enhancing interest-only strips will be based on Tier 1 capital net of goodwill and all identifiable intangibles, other than purchased credit card relationships, mortgage servicing assets and non-mortgage servicing assets.

(ii) Banks must value each credit-enhancing interest-only strip included in Tier 1 capital at least quarterly. The quarterly determination of the current fair value of the credit-enhancing interest-only strip must include adjustments for any significant changes in original valuation assumptions, including changes in prepayment estimates.

(iii) Banks may elect to deduct disallowed credit-enhancing interest-only strips on a basis that is net of any associated deferred tax liability. Deferred tax liabilities netted in this manner cannot also be netted against deferred tax assets when determining the amount of deferred tax assets that are dependent upon future taxable income.

(5) Nonfinancial equity investments–

(i) General.

(A) A bank must deduct from its Tier 1 capital the appropriate percentage, as determined in accordance with Table A, of the adjusted carrying value of all nonfinancial equity investments held by the bank and its subsidiaries.

Table A—Deduction for Nonfinancial Equity Investments

Aggregate adjusted carrying value of all nonfinancial equity investments held directly or indirectly by banks (as a percentage of the Tier 1 capital of the bank)[6]	Deduction from Tier 1 Capital (as a percentage of the adjusted carrying value of the investment)
Less than 15 percent	8.0 percent.
Greater than or equal to 15 percent but less than 25 percent.	12.0 percent.
Greater than or equal to 25 percent	25.0 percent.

(B) Deductions for nonfinancial equity investments must be applied on a marginal basis to the portions of the adjusted carrying value of nonfinancial equity investments that fall within the specified ranges of the bank's Tier 1 capital. For example, if the adjusted carrying value of all nonfinancial equity investments held by a bank equals 20 percent of the Tier 1 capital of the bank, then the amount of the deduction would be 8 percent of the adjusted carrying value of all investments up to 15 percent of the bank's Tier 1 capital, and 12 percent of the adjusted carrying value of all investments equal to, or in excess of, 15 percent of the bank's Tier 1 capital.

(C) The total adjusted carrying value of any nonfinancial equity investment that is subject to deduction under section 2(c)(5) of this appendix A is excluded from the bank's weighted risk assets for purposes of computing the denominator of the bank's risk-based capital ratio. For example, if 8 percent of the adjusted carrying value of a nonfinancial equity investment is deducted from Tier 1 capital, the entire adjusted carrying value of the investment will be excluded from risk-weighted assets in calculating the denominator of the risk-based capital ratio.

(D) Banks engaged in equity investment activities, including those banks with a high concentration in nonfinancial equity investments (e.g., in excess of 50 percent of Tier 1 capital), will be monitored and may be subject to heightened supervision, as appropriate, by the OCC to ensure that such banks maintain capital levels that are appropriate in light of their equity investment activities,

---

6. [n.1] For purposes of calculating the adjusted carrying value of nonfinancial equity investments as a percentage of Tier 1 capital, Tier 1 capital is defined as the sum of the Tier 1 capital elements net of goodwill and net of all identifiable intangible assets other than mortgage servicing assets, nonmortgage servicing assets and purchased credit card relationships, but prior to the deduction for disallowed mortgage servicing assets, disallowed non-mortgage servicing assets, disallowed purchased credit card relationships, disallowed credit-enhancing interest only strips (both purchased and retained), disallowed deferred tax assets, and nonfinancial equity investments.

and the OCC may impose a higher capital charge in any case where the circumstances, such as the level of risk of the particular investment or portfolio of investments, the risk management systems of the bank, or other information, indicate that a higher minimum capital requirement is appropriate.

(ii) Small business investment company investments.

(A) Notwithstanding section 2(c)(5)(i) of this appendix A, no deduction is required for nonfinancial equity investments that are made by a bank or its subsidiary through a SBIC that is consolidated with the bank, or in a SBIC that is not consolidated with the bank, to the extent that such investments, in the aggregate, do not exceed 15 percent of the Tier 1 capital of the bank. Except as provided in paragraph (c)(5)(ii)(B) of this section, any nonfinancial equity investment that is held through or in a SBIC and not deducted from Tier 1 capital will be assigned to the 100 percent risk-weight category and included in the bank's consolidated risk-weighted assets.

(B) If a bank has an investment in a SBIC that is consolidated for accounting purposes but the SBIC is not wholly owned by the bank, the adjusted carrying value of the bank's nonfinancial equity investments held through the SBIC is equal to the bank's proportionate share of the SBIC's adjusted carrying value of its equity investments in nonfinancial companies. The remainder of the SBIC's adjusted carrying value (i.e., the minority interest holders' proportionate share) is excluded from the risk-weighted assets of the bank.

(C) If a bank has an investment in a SBIC that is not consolidated for accounting purposes and has current information that identifies the percentage of the SBIC's assets that are equity investments in nonfinancial companies, the bank may reduce the adjusted carrying value of its investment in the SBIC proportionately to reflect the percentage of the adjusted carrying value of the SBIC's assets that are not equity investments in nonfinancial companies. The amount by which the adjusted carrying value of the bank's investment in the SBIC is reduced under this paragraph will be risk-

weighted at 100 percent and included in the bank's risk-weighted assets.

(D) To the extent the adjusted carrying value of all nonfinancial equity investments that the bank holds through a consolidated SBIC or in a nonconsolidated SBIC equals or exceeds, in the aggregate, 15 percent of the Tier 1 capital of the bank, the appropriate percentage of such amounts, as set forth in Table A, must be deducted from the bank's Tier 1 capital. In addition, the aggregate adjusted carrying value of all nonfinancial equity investments held through a consolidated SBIC and in a nonconsolidated SBIC (including any nonfinancial equity investments for which no deduction is required) must be included in determining, for purposes of Table A the total amount of nonfinancial equity investments held by the bank in relation to its Tier 1 capital.

(iii) Nonfinancial equity investments excluded.

(A) Notwithstanding section 2(c)(5)(i) and (ii) of this appendix A, no deduction from Tier 1 capital is required for the following:

(1) Nonfinancial equity investments (or portion of such investments) made by the bank prior to March 13, 2000, and continuously held by the bank since March 13, 2000.

(2) Nonfinancial equity investments made on or after March 13, 2000, pursuant to a legally binding written commitment that was entered into by the bank prior to March 13, 2000, and that required the bank to make the investment, if the bank has continuously held the investment since the date the investment was acquired.

(3) Nonfinancial equity investments received by the bank through a stock split or stock dividend on a nonfinancial equity investment made prior to March 13, 2000, provided that the bank provides no consideration for the shares or interests received, and the transaction does not materially increase the bank's proportional interest in the nonfinancial company.

(4) Nonfinancial equity investments received by the bank through the exercise on or after March 13, 2000, of an option, warrant, or other agreement that provides the bank with the right, but not the obligation, to acquire

equity or make an investment in a nonfinancial company, if the option, warrant, or other agreement was acquired by the bank prior to March 13, 2000, and the bank provides no consideration for the nonfinancial equity investments.

(B) Any excluded nonfinancial equity investments described in section 2(c)(5)(iii)(A) of this appendix A must be included in determining the total amount of nonfinancial equity investments held by the bank in relation to its Tier 1 capital for purposes of Table A. In addition, any excluded nonfinancial equity investments will be risk weighted at 100 percent and included in the bank's risk-weighted assets.

(6) Deductions from total capital. The following items are deducted from total capital:

(i) Investments, both equity and debt, in unconsolidated banking and finance subsidiaries that are deemed to be capital of the subsidiary;[7] and

(ii) Reciprocal holdings of bank capital instruments.

PART 5. Rules, Policies, and Procedures for Corporate Activities

Sec. 5.20 Organizing a bank.

(a) Authority. 12 U.S.C. 21, 22, 24(Seventh), 26, 27, 92a, 93a, 1814(b), 1816, and 2903.

(b) Licensing requirements. Any person desiring to establish a national bank shall submit an application and obtain prior OCC approval.

(c) Scope. This section describes the procedures and requirements governing OCC review and approval of an application to establish a national bank, including a national bank with a special purpose. Information regarding an application to establish an interim national bank solely to facilitate a business combination is set forth in Sec. 5.33.

(d) Definitions. For purposes of this section:

(1) Bankers' bank means a bank owned exclusively (except to the extent directors' qualifying shares are required by law) by other depository institutions or depository institution

holding companies (as that term is defined in section 3 of the Federal Deposit Insurance Act, 12 U.S.C. 1813), the activities of which are limited by its articles of association exclusively to providing services to or for other depository institutions, their holding companies, and the officers, directors, and employees of such institutions and companies, and to providing correspondent banking services at the request of other depository institutions or their holding companies.

(2) Control means control as used in section 2 of the Bank Holding Company Act, 12 U.S.C. 1841(a)(2).

(3) Final approval means the OCC action issuing a charter certificate and authorizing a national bank to open for business.

(4) Holding company means any company that controls or proposes to control a national bank whether or not the company is a bank holding company under section 2 of the Bank Holding Company Act, 12 U.S.C. 1841(a)(1).

(5) Lead depository institution means the largest depository institution controlled by a bank holding company based on a comparison of the average total assets controlled by each depository institution as reported in its Consolidated Report of Condition and Income required to be filed for the immediately preceding four calendar quarters.

(6) Organizing group means five or more persons acting on their own behalf, or serving as representatives of a sponsoring holding company, who apply to the OCC for a national bank charter.

(7) Preliminary approval means a decision by the OCC permitting an organizing group to go forward with the organization of the proposed national bank. A preliminary approval generally is subject to certain conditions that an applicant must satisfy before the OCC will grant final approval.

(e) Statutory requirements—

(1) General. The OCC charters a national bank under the authority of the National Bank Act of 1864, as amended, 12 U.S.C. 1 et seq. The bank may be a special purpose bank that

---

7. [n.7] The OCC may require deduction of investments in other subsidiaries and associated companies, on a case-by-case basis.

limits its activities to fiduciary activities or to any other activities within the business of banking. A special purpose bank that conducts activities other than fiduciary activities must conduct at least one of the following three core banking functions: receiving deposits; paying checks; or lending money. The name of a proposed bank must include the word "national." In determining whether to approve an application to establish a national bank, the OCC verifies that the proposed national bank has complied with the following requirements of the National Bank Act. A national bank shall:

(i) Draft and file articles of association with the OCC;

(ii) Draft and file an organization certificate containing specified information with the OCC;

(iii) Ensure that all capital stock is paid in; and

(iv) Have at least five elected directors.

(2) Community Reinvestment Act. Twelve CFR part 25 requires the OCC to take into account a proposed insured national bank's description of how it will meet its CRA objectives.

(f) Policy—

(1) General. The marketplace is normally the best regulator of economic activity, and competition within the marketplace promotes efficiency and better customer service. Accordingly, it is the OCC's policy to approve proposals to establish national banks, including minority-owned institutions, that have a reasonable chance of success and that will be operated in a safe and sound manner. It is not the OCC's policy to ensure that a proposal to establish a national bank is without risk to the organizers or to protect existing institutions from healthy competition from a new national bank.

(2) Policy considerations.

(i) In evaluating an application to establish a national bank, the OCC considers whether the proposed bank:

(A) Has organizers who are familiar with national banking laws and regulations;

(B) Has competent management, including a board of directors, with ability and experience relevant to the types of services to be provided;

(C) Has capital that is sufficient to support the projected volume and type of business;

(D) Can reasonably be expected to achieve and maintain profitability; and

(E) Will be operated in a safe and sound manner.

(ii) The OCC may also consider additional factors listed in section 6 of the Federal Deposit Insurance Act, 12 U.S.C. 1816, including the risk to the Federal deposit insurance fund, and whether the proposed bank's corporate powers are consistent with the purposes of the Federal Deposit Insurance Act and the National Bank Act.

(3) OCC evaluation. The OCC evaluates a proposed national bank's organizing group and its operating plan together. The OCC's judgment concerning one may affect the evaluation of the other. An organizing group and its operating plan must be stronger in markets where economic conditions are marginal or competition is intense.

(g) Organizing group—

(1) General. Strong organizing groups generally include diverse business and financial interests and community involvement. An organizing group must have the experience, competence, willingness, and ability to be active in directing the proposed national bank's affairs in a safe and sound manner. The bank's initial board of directors generally is comprised of many, if not all, of the organizers. The business plan or operating plan and other information supplied in the application must demonstrate an organizing group's collective ability to establish and operate a successful bank in the economic and competitive conditions of the market to be served. Each organizer should be knowledgeable about the operating plan. A poor business plan or operating plan reflects adversely on the organizing group's ability, and the OCC generally denies applications with poor operating plans.

(2) Management selection. The initial board of directors must select competent senior executive officers before the OCC grants final approval. Early selection of executive officers, especially the chief executive officer, contributes favorably to the preparation and review of a business plan or operating plan that is accu-

rate, complete, and appropriate for the type of bank proposed and its market, and reflects favorably upon an application. As a condition of the charter approval, the OCC retains the right to object to and preclude the hiring of any officer, or the appointment or election of any director, for a two-year period from the date the bank commences business.

(3) *Financial resources.*

(i) Each organizer must have a history of responsibility, personal honesty, and integrity. Personal wealth is not a prerequisite to become an organizer or director of a national bank. However, directors' stock purchases, individually and in the aggregate, should reflect a financial commitment to the success of the national bank that is reasonable in relation to their individual and collective financial strength. A director should not have to depend on bank dividends, fees, or other compensation to satisfy financial obligations.

(ii) Because directors are often the primary source of additional capital for a bank not affiliated with a holding company, it is desirable that an organizer who is also proposed as a director of the national bank be able to supply or have a realistic plan to enable the bank to obtain capital when needed.

(iii) Any financial or other business arrangement, direct or indirect, between the organizing group or other insider and the proposed national bank must be on nonpreferential terms.

(4) *Organizational expenses.*

(i) Organizers are expected to contribute time and expertise to the organization of the bank. Organizers should not bill excessive charges to the bank for professional and consulting services or unduly rely upon these fees as a source of income.

(ii) A proposed national bank shall not pay any fee that is contingent upon an OCC decision. Such action generally is grounds for denial of the application or withdrawal of preliminary approval. Organizational expenses for denied applications are the sole responsibility of the organizing group.

(5) *Sponsor's experience and support.* A sponsor must be financially able to support the new bank's operations and to provide or locate capital when needed. The OCC primarily considers the financial and managerial resources of the sponsor and the sponsor's record of performance, rather than the financial and managerial resources of the organizing group, if an organizing group is sponsored by:

(i) An existing holding company;

(ii) Individuals currently affiliated with other depository institutions; or

(iii) Individuals who, in the OCC's view, are otherwise collectively experienced in banking and have demonstrated the ability to work together effectively.

(h) *Business plan or Operating plan*—

(1) *General.*

(i) Organizers of a proposed national bank shall submit a business plan or operating plan that adequately addresses the statutory and policy considerations set forth in paragraphs (e) and (f)(2) of this section. The plan must reflect sound banking principles and demonstrate realistic assessments of risk in light of economic and competitive conditions in the market to be served.

(ii) The OCC may offset deficiencies in one factor by strengths in one or more other factors. However, deficiencies in some factors, such as unrealistic earnings prospects, may have a negative influence on the evaluation of other factors, such as capital adequacy, or may be serious enough by themselves to result in denial. The OCC considers inadequacies in an operating plan to reflect negatively on the organizing group's ability to operate a successful bank.

(2) *Earnings prospects.* The organizing group shall submit pro forma balance sheets and income statements as part of the operating plan. The OCC reviews all projections for reasonableness of assumptions and consistency with the business plan or operating plan.

(3) *Management.*

(i) The organizing group shall include in the business plan or operating plan information sufficient to permit the OCC to evaluate the overall management ability of the organizing group. If the organizing group has limited banking experience or community involvement, the senior executive officers must be able to compensate for such deficiencies.

(ii) The organizing group may not hire an officer or elect or appoint a director if the OCC objects to that person at any time prior to the date the bank commences business.

(4) Capital. A proposed bank must have sufficient initial capital, net of any organizational expenses that will be charged to the bank's capital after it begins operations, to support the bank's projected volume and type of business.

(5) Community service.

(i) The business plan or operating plan must indicate the organizing group's knowledge of and plans for serving the community. The organizing group shall evaluate the banking needs of the community, including its consumer, business, nonprofit, and government sectors. The business plan or operating plan must demonstrate how the proposed bank responds to those needs consistent with the safe and sound operation of the bank. The provisions of this paragraph may not apply to an application to organize a bank for a special purpose.

(ii) As part of its business plan or operating plan, the organizing group shall submit a statement that demonstrates its plans to achieve CRA objectives.

(iii) Because community support is important to the long-term success of a bank, the organizing group shall include plans for attracting and maintaining community support.

(6) Safety and soundness. The business plan or operating plan must demonstrate that the organizing group (and the sponsoring company, if any), is aware of, and understands, national banking laws and regulations, and safe and sound banking operations and practices. The OCC will deny an application that does not meet these safety and soundness requirements.

(7) Fiduciary services. The business plan or operating plan must indicate if the proposed bank intends to offer fiduciary services. The information required by Sec. 5.26 shall be filed with the charter application. A separate application is not required.

(i) Procedures–

(1) Prefiling meeting. The OCC normally requires a prefiling meeting with the organizers of a proposed national bank before the organizers file an application. Organizers should be familiar with the OCC's chartering policy and procedural requirements in the Manual before the prefiling meeting. The prefiling meeting normally is held in the district office where the application will be filed but may be held at another location at the request of the applicant.

(2) Business plan or operating plan. An organizing group shall file a business plan or operating plan that addresses the subjects discussed in paragraph (h) of this section.

(3) Spokesperson. The organizing group shall designate a spokesperson to represent the organizing group in all contacts with the OCC. The spokesperson shall be an organizer and proposed director of the new bank, except a representative of the sponsor or sponsors may serve as spokesperson if an application is sponsored by an existing holding company, individuals currently affiliated with other depository institutions, or individuals who, in the OCC's view, are otherwise collectively experienced in banking and have demonstrated the ability to work together effectively.

(4) Decision notification. The OCC notifies the spokesperson and other interested persons in writing of its decision on an application.

(5) Post-decision activities.

(i) Before the OCC grants final approval, a proposed national bank must be established as a legal entity. A national bank becomes a legal entity after it has filed its organization certificate and articles of association with the OCC as required by law. In addition, the organizing group shall elect a board of directors. The proposed bank may not conduct the business of banking until the OCC grants final approval.

(ii) For all capital obtained through a public offering a proposed national bank shall use an offering circular that complies with the OCC's securities offering regulations, 12 CFR part 16.

(iii) A national bank in organization shall raise its capital before it commences business. Preliminary approval expires if a national bank in organization does not raise the required capital within 12 months from the date the OCC grants preliminary approval. Approval expires if the national bank does not commence business within 18 months from the date the OCC grants preliminary approval.

(j) Expedited review. An application to establish a full-service national bank that is sponsored by a bank holding company whose lead depository institution is an eligible bank or eligible depository institution is deemed preliminarily approved by the OCC as of the 15th day after the close of the public comment period or the 45th day after the filing is received by the OCC, whichever is later, unless the OCC:

(1) Notifies the applicant prior to that date that the filing is not eligible for expedited review, or the expedited review process is extended, under Sec. 5.13(a)(2); or

(2) Notifies the applicant prior to that date that the OCC has determined that the proposed bank will offer banking services that are materially different than those offered by the lead depository institution.

(k) National bankers' banks–

(1) Activities and customers. In addition to the other requirements of this section, when an organizing group seeks to organize a national bankers' bank, the organizing group shall list in the application the anticipated activities and customers or clients of the proposed national bankers' bank.

(2) Waiver of requirements. At the organizing group's request, the OCC may waive requirements that are applicable to national banks in general if those requirements are inappropriate for a national bankers' bank and would impede its ability to provide desired services to its market. An applicant must submit a request for a waiver with the application and must support the request with adequate justification and legal analysis. A national bankers' bank that is already in operation may also request a waiver. The OCC cannot waive statutory provisions that specifically apply to national bankers' banks pursuant to 12 U.S.C. 27(b)(1).

(3) Investments. A national bank may invest up to ten percent of its capital and surplus in a bankers' bank and may own five percent or less of any class of a bankers' bank's voting securities.

(*l*) Special purpose banks. An applicant for a national bank charter that will limit its activities to fiduciary activities, credit card operations, or another special purpose shall adhere to established charter procedures with modifications appropriate for the circumstances as determined by the OCC. An applicant for a national bank charter that will have a community development focus shall also adhere to established charter procedures with modifications appropriate for the circumstances as determined by the OCC. In addition to the other requirements in this section, a bank limited to fiduciary activities, credit card operations, or another special purpose may not conduct that business until the OCC grants final approval for the bank to commence operations. A national bank that seeks to invest in a bank with a community development focus must comply with applicable requirements of 12 CFR part 24.

[[eds.] as amended by 68 FR 70129, Dec. 17, 2003, (effective Aug. 16, 2004)]

Sec. 5.24 Conversion.

(a) Authority. 12 U.S.C. 35, 93a, 214a, 214b, 214c, and 2903.

(b) Licensing requirements. A state bank (including a "state bank" as defined in 12 U.S.C. 214(a)) or a Federal savings association shall submit an application and obtain prior OCC approval to convert to a national bank charter. A national bank shall give notice to the OCC before converting to a state bank (including a "state bank" as defined in 12 U.S.C. 214(a)) or Federal savings association.

(c) Scope. This section describes procedures and standards governing OCC review and approval of an application by a state bank or Federal savings association to convert to a national bank charter. This section also describes notice procedures for a national bank seeking to convert to a state bank or Federal savings association.

(d) Conversion of a state bank or Federal savings association to a national bank—

(1) Policy. Consistent with the OCC's chartering policy, it is OCC policy to allow conversion to a national bank charter by another financial institution that can operate safely and soundly as a national bank in compliance with applicable laws, regulations, and policies. The OCC may deny an application by any state bank (including a "state bank" as defined in 12 U.S.C. 214(a)) and any Federal savings associa-

tion to convert to a national bank charter on the basis of the standards for denial set forth in Sec. 5.13(b), or when conversion would permit the applicant to escape supervisory action by its current regulator.

(2) Procedures.

(i) Prefiling communications. The applicant should consult with the appropriate district office prior to filing if it anticipates that its application will raise unusual or complex issues. If a prefiling meeting is appropriate, it will normally be held in the district office where the application will be filed, but may be held at another location at the request of the applicant.

(ii) A state bank (including a state bank as defined in 12 U.S.C. 214(a)) or Federal savings association shall submit its application to convert to a national bank to the appropriate district office. The application must:

(A) Be signed by the president or other duly authorized officer;

(B) Identify each branch that the resulting bank expects to operate after conversion;

(C) Include the institution's most recent audited financial statements (if any);

(D) Include the latest report of condition and report of income (the most recent daily statement of condition will suffice if the institution does not file these reports);

(E) Unless otherwise advised by the OCC in a prefiling communication, include an opinion of counsel that, in the case of a state bank, the conversion is not in contravention of applicable state law, or in the case of a Federal savings association, the conversion is not in contravention of applicable Federal law;

(F) State whether the institution wishes to exercise fiduciary powers after the conversion;

(G) Identify all subsidiaries that will be retained following the conversion, and provide the information and analysis of the subsidiaries' activities that would be required if the converting bank or savings association were a national bank establishing each subsidiary pursuant to Sec. Sec. 5.34 or 5.39; and

(H) Identify any nonconforming assets (including nonconforming subsidiaries) and nonconforming activities that the institution engages in, and describe the plans to retain or divest those assets.

(iii) The OCC may permit a national bank to retain such nonconforming assets of a state bank, subject to conditions and an OCC determination of the carrying value of the retained assets, pursuant to 12 U.S.C. 35.

(iv) Approval for an institution to convert to a national bank expires if the conversion has not occurred within six months of the OCC's preliminary approval of the application.

(v) When the OCC determines that the applicant has satisfied all statutory and regulatory requirements, including those set forth in 12 U.S.C. 35, and any other conditions, the OCC issues a charter certificate. The certificate provides that the institution is authorized to begin conducting business as a national bank as of a specified date.

(3) Exceptions to rules of general applicability. Sections 5.8, 5.10, and 5.11 do not apply to this section. However, if the OCC concludes that an application presents significant and novel policy, supervisory, or legal issues, the OCC may determine that any or all parts of Sec. Sec. 5.8, 5.10, and 5.11 apply.

(4) Expedited review. An application by an eligible depository institution to convert to a national bank charter is deemed approved by the OCC as of the 30th day after the filing is received by the OCC, unless the OCC notifies the applicant prior to that date that the filing is not eligible for expedited review under Sec. 5.13(a)(2).

(e) Conversion of a national bank to a state bank–

(1) Procedure. A national bank may convert to a state bank, in accordance with 12 U.S.C. 214c, without prior OCC approval. Termination of the national bank's status as a national bank occurs upon the bank's completion of the requirements of 12 U.S.C. 214a, and upon the appropriate district office's receipt of the bank's national bank charter (or copy) in connection with the consummation of the transaction.

(2) Notice of intent. A national bank that desires to convert to a state bank shall submit to the appropriate district office a notice of its intent to convert. The national bank shall file

this notice when it first submits a request to convert to the appropriate state authorities. The appropriate district office then provides instructions to the national bank for terminating its status as a national bank.

(3) *Exceptions to the rules of general applicability.* Sections 5.5 through 5.8, and 5.10 through 5.13, do not apply to the conversion of a national bank to a state bank.

(f) *Conversion of a national bank to a Federal savings association.* A national bank may convert to a Federal savings association without prior OCC approval. The requirements and procedures set forth in paragraph (e) of this section and 12 U.S.C. 214a and 12 U.S.C. 214c apply to a conversion to a Federal savings association, except as follows:

(1) In paragraph (e) of this section references to "appropriate state authorities" mean "appropriate Federal authorities"; and

(2) References in 12 U.S.C. 214c to the "law of the State in which the national banking association is located" and "any State authority" mean "laws and regulations governing Federal savings associations" and "Office of Thrift Supervision," respectively.

[61 FR 60363, Nov. 27, 1996, as amended at 65 FR 12910, Mar. 10, 2000]

Sec. 5.34 Operating subsidiaries.

(a) *Authority.* 12 U.S.C. 24 (Seventh), 24a, 93a, 3101 et seq.

(b) *Licensing requirements.* A national bank must file a notice or application as prescribed in this section to acquire or establish an operating subsidiary, or to commence a new activity in an existing operating subsidiary.

(c) *Scope.* This section sets forth authorized activities and application or notice procedures for national banks engaging in activities through an operating subsidiary. The procedures in this section do not apply to financial subsidiaries authorized under Sec. 5.39. Unless provided otherwise, this section applies to a Federal branch or agency that acquires, establishes, or maintains any subsidiary that a national bank is authorized to acquire or establish under this section in the same manner and to the same extent as if the Federal branch or agency were a national bank, except that the ownership interest required in paragraphs (e)(2) and (e)(5)(i)(B) of this section

shall apply to the parent foreign bank of the Federal branch or agency and not to the Federal branch or agency.

(d) *Definitions.* For purposes of this Sec. 5.34:

(1) *Authorized product* means a product that would be defined as insurance under section 302(c) of the Gramm–Leach–Bliley Act (Public Law 106–102, 113 Stat. 1338, 1407) (GLBA) (15 U.S.C. 6712) that, as of January 1, 1999, the OCC had determined in writing that national banks may provide as principal or national banks were in fact lawfully providing the product as principal, and as of that date no court of relevant jurisdiction had, by final judgment, overturned a determination by the OCC that national banks may provide the product as principal. An authorized product does not include title insurance, or an annuity contract the income of which is subject to treatment under section 72 of the Internal Revenue Code of 1986 (26 U.S.C. 72).

(2) *Well capitalized* means the capital level described in 12 CFR 6.4(b)(1) or, in the case of a Federal branch or agency, the capital level described in 12 CFR 4.7(b)(1)(iii).

(3) *Well managed* means, unless otherwise determined in writing by the OCC:

(i) In the case of a national bank:

(A) The national bank has received a composite rating of 1 or 2 under the Uniform Financial Institutions Rating System in connection with its most recent examination; or

(B) In the case of any national bank that has not been examined, the existence and use of managerial resources that the OCC determines are satisfactory.

(ii) In the case of a Federal branch or agency:

(A) The Federal branch or agency has received a composite ROCA supervisory rating (which rates risk management, operational controls, compliance, and asset quality) of 1 or 2 at its most recent examination; or

(B) In the case of a Federal branch or agency that has not been examined, the existence and use of managerial resources that the OCC determines are satisfactory.

(e) *Standards and requirements*—

(1) Authorized activities. A national bank may conduct in an operating subsidiary activities that are permissible for a national bank to engage in directly either as part of, or incidental to, the business of banking, as determined by the OCC, or otherwise under other statutory authority, including:

(i) Providing authorized products as principal; and

(ii) Providing title insurance as principal if the national bank or subsidiary thereof was actively and lawfully underwriting title insurance before November 12, 1999, and no affiliate of the national bank (other than a subsidiary) provides insurance as principal. A subsidiary may not provide title insurance as principal if the state had in effect before November 12, 1999, a law which prohibits any person from underwriting title insurance with respect to real property in that state.

(2) Qualifying subsidiaries. An operating subsidiary in which a national bank may invest includes a corporation, limited liability company, or similar entity if the parent bank owns more than 50 percent of the voting (or similar type of controlling) interest of the operating subsidiary; or the parent bank otherwise controls the operating subsidiary and no other party controls more than 50 percent of the voting (or similar type of controlling) interest of the operating subsidiary. However, the following subsidiaries are not operating subsidiaries subject to this section:

(i) A subsidiary in which the bank's investment is made pursuant to specific authorization in a statute or OCC regulation (e.g., a bank service company under 12 U.S.C. 1861 et seq. or a financial subsidiary under section 5136A of the Revised Statutes (12 U.S.C. 24a)); and

(ii) A subsidiary in which the bank has acquired, in good faith, shares through foreclosure on collateral, by way of compromise of a doubtful claim, or to avoid a loss in connection with a debt previously contracted.

(3) Examination and supervision. An operating subsidiary conducts activities authorized under this section pursuant to the same authorization, terms and conditions that apply to the conduct of such activities by its parent national bank. If, upon examination, the OCC determines that the operating subsidiary is operating in violation of law, regulation, or written condition, or in an unsafe or unsound manner or otherwise threatens the safety or soundness of the bank, the OCC will direct the bank or operating subsidiary to take appropriate remedial action, which may include requiring the bank to divest or liquidate the operating subsidiary, or discontinue specified activities. OCC authority under this paragraph is subject to the limitations and requirements of section 45 of the Federal Deposit Insurance Act (12 U.S.C. 1831v) and section 115 of the Gramm-Leach-Bliley Act (12 U.S.C. 1820a).

(4) Consolidation of figures—

(i) National banks. Pertinent book figures of the parent national bank and its operating subsidiary shall be combined for the purpose of applying statutory or regulatory limitations when combination is needed to effect the intent of the statute or regulation, e.g., for purposes of 12 U.S.C. 56, 60, 84, and 371d.

(ii) Federal branch or agencies. Transactions conducted by all of a foreign bank's Federal branches and agencies and State branches and agencies, and their operating subsidiaries, shall be combined for the purpose of applying any limitation or restriction as provided in 12 CFR 28.14.

(5) Procedures—

(i) Application required.

(A) Except as provided in paragraph (e)(5)(iv) or (e)(5)(vi) of this section, a national bank that intends to acquire or establish an operating subsidiary, or to perform a new activity in an existing operating subsidiary, must first submit an application to, and receive approval from, the OCC. The application must include a complete description of the bank's investment in the subsidiary, the proposed activities of the subsidiary, the organizational structure and management of the subsidiary, the relations between the bank and the subsidiary, and other information necessary to adequately describe the proposal. To the extent the application relates to the initial affiliation of the bank with a company engaged in insurance activities, the bank should describe the type of insurance activity that the company is engaged in and has present plans to conduct. The bank must also list for each state the lines of business for which the company holds, or will hold, an insurance license, indicating the state where the company holds a resident license or charter, as applicable. The application must state whether the operating subsidiary will conduct any activity at a location other than the main office or a previously approved branch of the bank. The OCC may require the applicant to submit a legal analysis if the proposal is novel, unusually complex, or raises substantial unresolved legal issues. In these cases, the OCC encourages applicants to have a pre-filing meeting with the OCC.

(B) A national bank must file an application and obtain prior approval before acquiring or establishing an operating subsidiary, or performing a new activity in an existing operating subsidiary, if the bank controls the subsidiary but owns 50 percent or less of the voting (or similar type of controlling) interest of the subsidiary. These applications are not subject to the filing exemption in paragraph (e)(5)(vi) of this section and are not eligible for the notice procedures in paragraph (e)(5)(iv) of this section.

(ii) Exceptions to rules of general applicability. Sections 5.8, 5.10, and 5.11 do not apply to this section. However, if the OCC concludes that an application presents significant and novel policy, supervisory, or legal issues, the OCC may determine that some or all provisions in Sec. Sec. 5.8, 5.10, and 5.11 apply.

(iii) OCC review and approval. The OCC reviews a national bank's application to determine whether the proposed activities are legally permissible and to ensure that the proposal is consistent with safe and sound banking practices and OCC policy and does not endanger the safety or soundness of the parent national bank. As part of this process, the OCC may request additional information and analysis from the applicant.

(iv) Notice process for certain activities. A national bank that is "well capitalized" and "well managed" may acquire or establish an operating subsidiary, or perform a new activity in an existing operating subsidiary, by providing the appropriate district office written notice within 10 days after acquiring or establishing the subsidiary, or commencing the activity, if the activity is listed in paragraph (e)(5)(v) of this section. The written notice must include a complete description of the bank's investment in the subsidiary and of the activity conducted and a representation and undertaking that the activity will be conducted in accordance with OCC policies contained in guidance issued by the OCC regarding the activity. To the extent the notice relates to the initial affiliation of the bank with a company engaged in insurance activities, the bank should describe the type of insurance activity that the company is engaged in and has present plans to conduct. The bank must also list for each state the lines of business for which the company holds, or will hold, an insurance license, indicating the state where the company holds a resident license or charter, as applicable. Any bank receiving approval under this paragraph is deemed to have agreed that the subsidiary will conduct the activity in a manner consistent with published OCC guidance.

(v) Activities eligible for notice. The following activities qualify for the notice procedures, provided the activity is conducted pursuant to the same terms and conditions as would be applicable if the activity were conducted directly by a national bank:

(A) Holding and managing assets acquired by the parent bank, including investment assets and property acquired by the bank through foreclosure or otherwise in good faith to compromise a doubtful claim, or in the ordinary course of collecting a debt previously contracted;

(B) Providing services to or for the bank or its affiliates, including accounting, auditing, appraising, advertising and public relations, and financial advice and consulting;

(C) Making loans or other extensions of credit, and selling money orders, savings bonds, and travelers checks;

(D) Purchasing, selling, servicing, or warehousing loans or other extensions of credit, or interests therein;

(E) Providing courier services between financial institutions;

(F) Providing management consulting, operational advice, and services for other financial institutions;

(G) Providing check guaranty, verification and payment services;

(H) Providing data processing, data warehousing and data transmission products, services, and related activities and facilities, including associated equipment and technology, for the bank or its affiliates;

(I) Acting as investment adviser (including an adviser with investment discretion) or financial adviser or counselor to governmental entities or instrumentalities, businesses, or individuals, including advising registered investment companies and mortgage or real estate investment trusts, furnishing economic forecasts or other economic information, providing investment advice related to futures and options on futures, and providing consumer financial counseling;

(J) Providing tax planning and preparation services;

(K) Providing financial and transactional advice and assistance, including advice and assistance for customers in structuring, arranging, and executing mergers and acquisitions, divestitures, joint ventures, leveraged buyouts, swaps, foreign exchange, derivative transactions, coin and bullion, and capital restructurings;

(L) Underwriting and reinsuring credit related insurance to the extent permitted under section 302 of the GLBA (15 U.S.C. 6712);

(M) Leasing of personal property and acting as an agent or adviser in leases for others;

(N) Providing securities brokerage or acting as a futures commission merchant, and providing related credit and other related services;

(O) Underwriting and dealing, including making a market, in bank permissible securities and purchasing and selling as principal, asset backed obligations;

(P) Acting as an insurance agent or broker, including title insurance to the extent per-

mitted under section 303 of the GLBA (15 U.S.C. 6713);

(Q) Reinsuring mortgage insurance on loans originated, purchased, or serviced by the bank, its subsidiaries, or its affiliates, provided that if the subsidiary enters into a quota share agreement, the subsidiary assumes less than 50 percent of the aggregate insured risk covered by the quota share agreement. A "quota share agreement" is an agreement under which the reinsurer is liable to the primary insurance underwriter for an agreed upon percentage of every claim arising out of the covered book of business ceded by the primary insurance underwriter to the reinsurer;

(R) Acting as a finder pursuant to 12 CFR 7.1002 to the extent permitted by published OCC precedent;[15]

(S) Offering correspondent services to the extent permitted by published OCC precedent;

(T) Acting as agent or broker in the sale of fixed or variable annuities;

(U) Offering debt cancellation or debt suspension agreements;

(V) Providing real estate settlement, closing, escrow, and related services; and real estate appraisal services for the subsidiary, parent bank, or other financial institutions;

(W) Acting as a transfer or fiscal agent;

(X) Acting as a digital certification authority to the extent permitted by published OCC precedent, subject to the terms and conditions contained in that precedent; and

(Y) Providing or selling public transportation tickets, event and attraction tickets, gift certificates, prepaid phone cards, promotional and advertising material, postage stamps, and Electronic Benefits Transfer (EBT) script, and similar media, to the extent permitted by published OCC precedent, subject to the terms and conditions contained in that precedent.

(vi) No application or notice required. A national bank may acquire or establish an op-

---

15. [n.1] See, e.g., the OCC's monthly publication "Interpretations and Actions." Beginning with the May 1996 issue, the OCC's Web site provides access to electron-ic versions of "Interpretations and Actions" (www.occ. treas.gov).

erating subsidiary without filing an application or providing notice to the OCC, if the bank is adequately capitalized or well capitalized and the:

(A) Activities of the new subsidiary are limited to those activities previously reported by the bank in connection with the establishment or acquisition of a prior operating subsidiary;

(B) Activities in which the new subsidiary will engage continue to be legally permissible for the subsidiary; and

(C) Activities of the new subsidiary will be conducted in accordance with any conditions imposed by the OCC in approving the conduct of these activities for any prior operating subsidiary of the bank.

(vii) Fiduciary powers. If an operating subsidiary proposes to exercise investment discretion on behalf of customers or provide investment advice for a fee, the national bank must have prior OCC approval to exercise fiduciary powers pursuant to Sec. 5.26.

(6) Annual Report on Operating Subsidiaries—

(i) Filing requirement. Each national bank shall prepare and file with the OCC an Annual Report on Operating Subsidiaries containing the information set forth in paragraph (e)(6)(ii) of this section for each of its operating subsidiaries that:

(A) Is not functionally regulated within the meaning of section 5(c)(5) of the Bank Holding Company Act of 1956, as amended (12 U.S.C. 1844(c)(5)); and

(B) Does business directly with consumers in the United States. For purposes of paragraph (e)(6) of this section, an operating subsidiary, or any subsidiary thereof, does business directly with consumers if, in the ordinary course of its business, it provides products or services to individuals to be used primarily for personal, family, or household purposes.

(ii) Information required. The Annual Report on Operating Subsidiaries must contain the following information for each covered operating subsidiary listed:

(A) The name and charter number of the parent national bank;

(B) The name (include any "dba" (doing business as), abbreviated names, or trade names used to identify the operating subsidiary when it does business directly with consumers), mailing address (include the street address or post office box, city, state, and zip code), e-mail address (if any), and telephone number of the operating subsidiary;

(C) The principal place of business of the operating subsidiary, if different from the address provided pursuant to paragraph (e)(6)(ii)(B) of this section; and

(D) The lines of business in which the operating subsidiary is doing business directly with consumers by designating the appropriate code contained in appendix B (NAICS Activity Codes for Commonly Reported Activities) to the Instructions for Preparation of Report of Changes in Organizational Structure, Form FR Y–10, a copy of which is set forth on the OCC's Web site at http://www.occ.gov. If the operating subsidiary is engaged in an activity not set forth in this list, a national bank shall report the code 0000 and provide a brief description of the activity.

(iii) Filing time frames and availability of information. Each national bank's Annual Report on Operating Subsidiaries shall contain information current as of December 31st for the year prior to the year the report is filed. The national bank shall submit its first Annual Report on Operating Subsidiaries (for information as of December 31, 2004) to the OCC on or before January 31, 2005, and on or before January 31st each year thereafter. The national bank may submit the Annual Report on Operating Subsidiaries electronically or in another format prescribed by the OCC. The OCC will make available to the public the information contained in the Annual Report on Operating Subsidiaries on its Web site at http://www.occ.gov.

[65 FR 12911, Mar. 10, 2000; 66 FR 49097, Sept. 26, 2001; 66 FR 62914, Dec. 4, 2001; 68 FR 70131, Dec. 17, 2003; 69 FR 64481, Nov. 5, 2004]

Sec. 5.39 Financial subsidiaries.

(a) Authority. 12 U.S.C. 93a and section 121 of Public Law 106–102, 113 Stat. 1338, 1373.

(b) Approval requirements. A national bank must file a notice as prescribed in this section prior to acquiring a financial subsidiary or engaging in activities authorized pursuant to section 5136A(a)(2)(A)(i) of the Revised Statutes (12 U.S.C. 24a) through a financial subsidiary. When a financial subsidiary proposes to conduct a new activity permitted under Sec. 5.34, the bank shall follow the procedures in Sec. 5.34(e)(5) instead of paragraph (i) of this section.

(c) Scope. This section sets forth authorized activities, approval procedures, and, where applicable, conditions for national banks engaging in activities through a financial subsidiary.

(d) Definitions. For purposes of this Sec. 5.39:

(1) Affiliate has the meaning set forth in section 2 of the Bank Holding Company Act of 1956 (12 U.S.C. 1841), except that the term "affiliate" for purposes of paragraph (h)(5) of this section shall have the meaning set forth in sections 23A or 23B of the Federal Reserve Act (12 U.S.C. 371c and 371c–1), as applicable.

(2) Appropriate Federal banking agency has the meaning set forth in section 3 of the Federal Deposit Insurance Act (12 U.S.C. 1813).

(3) Company has the meaning set forth in section 2 of the Bank Holding Company Act of 1956 (12 U.S.C. 1841), and includes a limited liability company (LLC).

(4) Control has the meaning set forth in section 2 of the Bank Holding Company Act of 1956 (12 U.S.C. 1841).

(5) Eligible debt means unsecured long-term debt that is:

(i) Not supported by any form of credit enhancement, including a guaranty or standby letter of credit; and

(ii) Not held in whole or in any significant part by any affiliate, officer, director, principal shareholder, or employee of the bank or any other person acting on behalf of or with funds from the bank or an affiliate of the bank.

(6) Financial subsidiary means any company that is controlled by one or more insured depository institutions, other than a subsidiary that:

(i) Engages solely in activities that national banks may engage in directly and that are conducted subject to the same terms and conditions that govern the conduct of these activities by national banks; or

(ii) A national bank is specifically authorized to control by the express terms of a Federal statute (other than section 5136A of the Revised Statutes), and not by implication or interpretation, such as by section 25 of the Federal Reserve Act (12 U.S.C. 601–604a), section 25A of the Federal Reserve Act (12 U.S.C. 611–631), or the Bank Service Company Act (12 U.S.C. 1861 et seq.)

(7) Insured depository institution has the meaning set forth in section 3 of the Federal Deposit Insurance Act (12 U.S.C. 1813).

(8) Long term debt means any debt obligation with an initial maturity of 360 days or more.

(9) Subsidiary has the meaning set forth in section 2 of the Bank Holding Company Act of 1956 (12 U.S.C. 1841).

(10) Tangible equity has the meaning set forth in 12 CFR 6.2(g).

(11) Well capitalized with respect to a depository institution means the capital level designated as "well capitalized" by the institution's appropriate Federal banking agency pursuant to section 38 of the Federal Deposit Insurance Act (12 U.S.C. 1831o).

(12) Well managed means:

(i) Unless otherwise determined in writing by the appropriate Federal banking agency, the institution has received a composite rating of 1 or 2 under the Uniform Financial Institutions Rating System (or an equivalent rating under an equivalent rating system) in connection with the most recent examination or subsequent review of the depository institution and, at least a rating of 2 for management, if such a rating is given; or

(ii) In the case of any depository institution that has not been examined by its appropriate Federal banking agency, the existence and use of managerial resources that the appropriate Federal banking agency determines are satisfactory.

(e) Authorized activities. A financial subsidiary may engage only in the following activities:

(1) Activities that are financial in nature and activities incidental to a financial activity, authorized pursuant to 5136A(a)(2)(A)(i) of the Revised Statutes (12 U.S.C. 24a) (to the extent

not otherwise permitted under paragraph (e)(2) of this section), including:

(i) Lending, exchanging, transferring, investing for others, or safeguarding money or securities;

(ii) Engaging as agent or broker in any state for purposes of insuring, guaranteeing, or indemnifying against loss, harm, damage, illness, disability, death, defects in title, or providing annuities as agent or broker;

(iii) Providing financial, investment, or economic advisory services, including advising an investment company as defined in section 3 of the Investment Company Act (15 U.S.C. 80a–3);

(iv) Issuing or selling instruments representing interests in pools of assets permissible for a bank to hold directly;

(v) Underwriting, dealing in, or making a market in securities;

(vi) Engaging in any activity that the Board of Governors of the Federal Reserve System has determined, by order or regulation in effect on November 12, 1999, to be so closely related to banking or managing or controlling banks as to be a proper incident thereto (subject to the same terms and conditions contained in the order or regulation, unless the order or regulation is modified by the Board of Governors of the Federal Reserve System);

(vii) Engaging, in the United States, in any activity that a bank holding company may engage in outside the United States and the Board of Governors of the Federal Reserve System has determined, under regulations prescribed or interpretations issued pursuant to section 4(c)(13) of the Bank Holding Company Act of 1956 (12 U.S.C. 1843(c)(13)) as in effect on November 11, 1999, to be usual in connection with the transaction of banking or other financial operations abroad; and

(viii) Activities that the Secretary of the Treasury in consultation with the Board of Governors of the Federal Reserve System, as provided in section 5136A of the Revised Statutes, determines to be financial in nature or incidental to a financial activity; and

(2) Activities that may be conducted by an operating subsidiary pursuant to Sec. 5.34.

(f) Impermissible activities. A financial subsidiary may not engage as principal in the following activities:

(1) Insuring, guaranteeing, or indemnifying against loss, harm, damage, illness, disability or death, or defects in title (except to the extent permitted under sections 302 or 303(c) of the Gramm–Leach–Bliley Act (GLBA)), 113 Stat. 1407–1409, (15 U.S.C. 6712 or 15 U.S.C. 6713) or providing or issuing annuities the income of which is subject to tax treatment under section 72 of the Internal Revenue Code (26 U.S.C. 72);

(2) Real estate development or real estate investment, unless otherwise expressly authorized by law; and

(3) Activities authorized for bank holding companies by section 4(k)(4)(H) or (I) (12 U.S.C. 1843) of the Bank Holding Company Act, except activities authorized under section 4(k)(4)(H) that may be permitted in accordance with section 122 of the GLBA, 113 Stat. 1381.

(g) Qualifications. A national bank may, directly or indirectly, control a financial subsidiary or hold an interest in a financial subsidiary only if:

(1) The national bank and each depository institution affiliate of the national bank are well capitalized and well managed;

(2) The aggregate consolidated total assets of all financial subsidiaries of the national bank do not exceed the lesser of 45 percent of the consolidated total assets of the parent bank or $50 billion (or such greater amount as is determined according to an indexing mechanism jointly established by regulation by the Secretary of the Treasury and the Board of Governors of the Federal Reserve System); and

(3) If the national bank is one of the 100 largest insured banks, determined on the basis of the bank's consolidated total assets at the end of the calendar year, the bank has at least one issue of outstanding eligible debt that is currently rated in one of the three highest investment grade rating categories by a nationally recognized statistical rating organization. If the national bank is one of the second 50 largest insured banks, it may either satisfy this requirement or satisfy alternative criteria the Secretary of the Treasury and the Board of Governors of the Federal Reserve System es-

tablish jointly by regulation. This paragraph (g)(3) does not apply if the financial subsidiary is engaged solely in activities in an agency capacity.

(h) *Safeguards.* The following safeguards apply to a national bank that establishes or maintains a financial subsidiary:

(1) For purposes of determining regulatory capital:

(i) The national bank must deduct the aggregate amount of its outstanding equity investment, including retained earnings, in its financial subsidiaries from its total assets and tangible equity and deduct such investment from its total risk-based capital (this deduction shall be made equally from Tier 1 and Tier 2 capital); and

(ii) The national bank may not consolidate the assets and liabilities of a financial subsidiary with those of the bank;

(2) Any published financial statement of the national bank shall, in addition to providing information prepared in accordance with generally accepted accounting principles, separately present financial information for the bank in the manner provided in paragraph (h)(1) of this section;

(3) The national bank must have reasonable policies and procedures to preserve the separate corporate identity and limited liability of the bank and the financial subsidiaries of the bank;

(4) The national bank must have procedures for identifying and managing financial and operational risks within the bank and the financial subsidiary that adequately protect the national bank from such risks;

(5) Sections 23A and 23B of the Federal Reserve Act (12 U.S.C. 371c and 371c–1) apply to transactions involving a financial subsidiary in the following manner:

(i) A financial subsidiary shall be deemed to be an affiliate of the bank and shall not be deemed to be a subsidiary of the bank;

(ii) The restrictions contained in section 23A(a)(1)(A) of the Federal Reserve Act shall not apply with respect to covered transactions between a bank and any individual financial subsidiary of the bank;

(iii) The bank's investment in the financial subsidiary shall not include retained earnings of the financial subsidiary;

(iv) Any purchase of, or investment in, the securities of a financial subsidiary of a bank by an affiliate of the bank will be considered to be a purchase of or investment in such securities by the bank; and

(v) Any extension of credit by an affiliate of a bank to a financial subsidiary of the bank may be considered an extension of credit by the bank to the financial subsidiary if the Board of Governors of the Federal Reserve System determines that such treatment is necessary or appropriate to prevent evasions of the Federal Reserve Act and the GLBA.

(6) A financial subsidiary shall be deemed a subsidiary of a bank holding company and not a subsidiary of the bank for purposes of the anti-tying prohibitions set forth in 12 U.S.C. 1971 et seq.

(i) *Procedures to engage in activities through a financial subsidiary.* A national bank that intends, directly or indirectly, to acquire control of, or hold an interest in, a financial subsidiary, or to commence a new activity in an existing financial subsidiary, must obtain OCC approval through the procedures set forth in paragraph (i)(1) or (i)(2) of this section.

(1) *Certification with subsequent notice.*

(i) At any time, a national bank may file a "Financial Subsidiary Certification" with the appropriate district office listing the bank's depository institution affiliates and certifying that the bank and each of those affiliates is well capitalized and well managed.

(ii) Thereafter, at such time as the bank seeks OCC approval to acquire control of, or hold an interest in, a new financial subsidiary, or commence a new activity authorized under section 5136A(a)(2)(A)(i) of the Revised Statutes (12 U.S.C. 24a) in an existing subsidiary, the bank may file a written notice with the appropriate district office at the time of acquiring control of, or holding an interest in, a financial subsidiary, or commencing such activity in an existing subsidiary. The written notice must be labeled "Financial Subsidiary Notice" and must:

(A) State that the bank's Certification remains valid;

(B) Describe the activity or activities conducted by the financial subsidiary. To the extent the notice relates to the initial affiliation of the bank with a company engaged in insurance activities, the bank should describe the type of insurance activity that the company is engaged in and has present plans to conduct. The bank must also list for each state the lines of business for which the company holds, or will hold, an insurance license, indicating the state where the company holds a resident license or charter, as applicable;

(C) Cite the specific authority permitting the activity to be conducted by the financial subsidiary. (Where the authority relied on is an agency order or interpretation under section 4(c)(8) or 4(c)(13), respectively, of the Bank Holding Company Act of 1956, a copy of the order or interpretation should be attached);

(D) Certify that the bank will be well capitalized after making adjustments required by paragraph (h)(1) of this section;

(E) Demonstrate the aggregate consolidated total assets of all financial subsidiaries of the national bank do not exceed the lesser of 45 percent of the bank's consolidated total assets or $50 billion (or the increased level established by the indexing mechanism); and

(F) If applicable, certify that the bank meets the eligible debt requirement in paragraph (g)(3) of this section.

(2) *Combined certification and notice.* A national bank may file a combined certification and notice with the appropriate district office at least five business days prior to acquiring control of, or holding an interest in, a financial subsidiary, or commencing a new activity authorized pursuant to section 5136A(a)(2)(A)(i) of the Revised Statutes in an existing subsidiary. The written notice must be labeled "Financial Subsidiary Certification and Notice" and must:

(i) List the bank's depository institution affiliates and certify that the bank and each depository institution affiliate of the bank is well capitalized and well managed;

(ii) Describe the activity or activities to be conducted in the financial subsidiary. To the extent the notice relates to the initial affiliation of the bank with a company engaged in insurance activities, the bank should describe the type of insurance activity that the company is engaged in and has present plans to conduct. The bank must also list for each state the lines of business for which the company holds, or will hold, an insurance license, indicating the state where the company holds a resident license or charter, as applicable;

(iii) Cite the specific authority permitting the activity to be conducted by the financial subsidiary. (Where the authority relied on is an agency order or interpretation under section 4(c)(8) or 4(c)(13), respectively, of the Bank Holding Company Act of 1956, a copy of the order or interpretation should be attached);

(iv) Certify that the bank will remain well capitalized after making the adjustments required by paragraph (h)(1) of this section;

(v) Demonstrate the aggregate consolidated total assets of all financial subsidiaries of the national bank do not exceed the lesser of 45% of the bank's consolidated total assets or $50 billion (or the increased level established by the indexing mechanism); and

(vi) If applicable, certify that the bank meets the eligible debt requirement in paragraph (g)(3) of this section.

(3) *Exceptions to rules of general applicability.* Sections 5.8, 5.10, 5.11, and 5.13 do not apply to activities authorized under this section.

(4) *Community Reinvestment Act (CRA).* A national bank may not apply under this paragraph (i) to commence a new activity authorized under section 5136A(a)(2)(A)(i) of the Revised Statutes (12 U.S.C. 24a), or directly or indirectly acquire control of a company engaged in any such activity, if the bank or any of its insured depository institution affiliates received a CRA rating of less than "satisfactory record of meeting community credit needs" on its most recent CRA examination prior to when the bank would file a notice under this section.

(j) *Failure to continue to meet certain qualification requirements—*

(1) *Qualifications and safeguards.* A national bank, or, as applicable, its affiliated depository

institutions, must continue to satisfy the qualification requirements set forth in paragraphs (g)(1) and (2) of this section and the safeguards in paragraphs (h)(1), (2), (3) and (4) of this section following its acquisition of control of, or an interest in, a financial subsidiary. A national bank that fails to continue to satisfy these requirements will be subject to the following procedures and requirements:

(i) The OCC shall give notice to the national bank and, in the case of an affiliated depository institution to that depository institution's appropriate Federal banking agency, promptly upon determining that the national bank, or, as applicable, its affiliated depository institution, does not continue to meet the requirements in paragraph (g)(1) or (2) of this section or the safeguards in paragraph (h)(1), (2), (3), or (4) of this section. The bank shall be deemed to have received such notice three business days after mailing of the letter by the OCC;

(ii) Not later than 45 days after receipt of the notice under paragraph (j)(1)(i) of this section, or any additional time as the OCC may permit, the national bank shall execute an agreement with the OCC to comply with the requirements in paragraphs (g)(1) and (2) and (h)(1), (2), (3), and (4) of this section;

(iii) The OCC may impose limitations on the conduct or activities of the national bank or any subsidiary of the national bank as the OCC determines appropriate under the circumstances and consistent with the purposes of section 5136A of the Revised Statutes; and

(iv) The OCC may require a national bank to divest control of a financial subsidiary if the national bank does not correct the conditions giving rise to the notice within 180 days after receipt of the notice provided under paragraph (j)(1)(i) of this section.

(2) Eligible debt rating requirement. A national bank that does not continue to meet the qualification requirement set forth in paragraph (g)(3) of this section, applicable where the bank's financial subsidiary is engaged in activities other than solely in an agency capacity, may not directly or through a subsidiary, purchase or acquire any additional equity capital of any such financial subsidiary until the bank meets the requirement in paragraph (g)(3) of this section. For purposes of this paragraph (j)(2), the term "equity capital" includes, in addition to any equity investment, any debt instrument issued by the financial subsidiary if the instrument qualifies as capital of the subsidiary under federal or state law, regulation, or interpretation applicable to the subsidiary.

(k) Examination and supervision. A financial subsidiary is subject to examination and supervision by the OCC, subject to the limitations and requirements of section 45 of the Federal Deposit Insurance Act (12 U.S.C. 1831v) and section 115 of the GLBA (12 U.S.C. 1820a).

[65 FR 12914, Mar. 10, 2000]

PART 7. Bank Activities And Operations

Sec. 7.1000 National bank ownership of property.

(a) Investment in real estate necessary for the transaction of business–

(1) General. Under 12 U.S.C. 29(First), a national bank may invest in real estate that is necessary for the transaction of its business.

(2) Type of real estate. For purposes of 12 U.S.C. 29(First), this real estate includes:

(i) Premises that are owned and occupied (or to be occupied, if under construction) by the bank, its branches, or its consolidated subsidiaries;

(ii) Real estate acquired and intended, in good faith, for use in future expansion;

(iii) Parking facilities that are used by customers or employees of the bank, its branches, and its consolidated subsidiaries;

(iv) Residential property for the use of bank officers or employees who are:

(A) Located in remote areas where suitable housing at a reasonable price is not readily available; or

(B) Temporarily assigned to a foreign country, including foreign nationals temporarily assigned to the United States; and

(v) Property for the use of bank officers, employees, or customers, or for the temporary lodging of such persons in areas where suitable commercial lodging is not readily available, provided that the purchase and operation of the property qualifies as a deductible business expense for Federal tax purposes.

(3) *Permissible means of holding.* A national bank may acquire and hold real estate under this paragraph (a) by any reasonable and prudent means, including ownership in fee, a leasehold estate, or in an interest in a cooperative. The bank may hold this real estate directly or through one or more subsidiaries. The bank may organize a bank premises subsidiary as a corporation, partnership, or similar entity (e.g., a limited liability company).

(b) *Fixed assets.* A national bank may own fixed assets necessary for the transaction of its business, such as fixtures, furniture, and data processing equipment.

(c) *Investment in bank premises—*

(1) *Investment limitation; approval.* 12 U.S.C. 371d governs when OCC approval is required for national bank investment in bank premises. A bank may seek approval from the OCC in accordance with the procedures set forth in 12 CFR 5.37.

(2) *Option to purchase.* An unexercised option to purchase bank premises or stock in a corporation holding bank premises is not an investment in bank premises. A national bank must receive OCC approval to exercise the option if the price of the option and the bank's other investments in bank premises exceed the amount of the bank's capital stock.

(d) *Other real property—*

(1) *Lease financing of public facilities.* A national bank may purchase or construct a municipal building, school building, or other similar public facility and, as holder of legal title, lease the facility to a municipality or other public authority having resources sufficient to make all rental payments as they become due. The lease agreement must provide that the lessee will become the owner of the building or facility upon the expiration of the lease.

(2) *Purchase of employee's residence.* To facilitate the efficient use of bank personnel, a national bank may purchase the residence of an employee who has been transferred to another area in order to spare the employee a loss in the prevailing real estate market. The bank must arrange for early divestment of title to such property.

[61 FR 4862, Feb. 9, 1996, as amended at 61 FR 60387, Nov. 27, 1996]

Sec. 7.1001 National bank acting as general insurance agent.

Pursuant to 12 U.S.C. 92, a national bank may act as an agent for any fire, life, or other insurance company in any place the population of which does not exceed 5,000 inhabitants. This provision is applicable to any office of a national bank when the office is located in a community having a population of less than 5,000, even though the principal office of such bank is located in a community whose population exceeds 5,000.

Sec. 7.1002 National bank acting as finder.

(a) *General.* It is part of the business of banking under 12 U.S.C. 24(Seventh) for a national bank to act as a finder, bringing together interested parties to a transaction.

(b) *Permissible finder activities.* A national bank that acts as a finder may identify potential parties, make inquiries as to interest, introduce or arrange contacts or meetings of interested parties, act as an intermediary between interested parties, and otherwise bring parties together for a transaction that the parties themselves negotiate and consummate. The following list provides examples of permissible finder activities. This list is illustrative and not exclusive; the OCC may determine that other activities are permissible pursuant to a national bank's authority to act as a finder.

(1) Communicating information about providers of products and services, and proposed offering prices and terms to potential markets for these products and services;

(2) Communicating to the seller an offer to purchase or a request for information, including forwarding completed applications, application fees, and requests for information to third-party providers;

(3) Arranging for third-party providers to offer reduced rates to those customers referred by the bank;

(4) Providing administrative, clerical, and record keeping functions related to the bank's finder activity, including retaining copies of

documents, instructing and assisting individuals in the completion of documents, scheduling sales calls on behalf of sellers, and conducting market research to identify potential new customers for retailers;

(5) Conveying between interested parties expressions of interest, bids, offers, orders, and confirmations relating to a transaction;

(6) Conveying other types of information between potential buyers, sellers, and other interested parties; and

(7) Establishing rules of general applicability governing the use and operation of the finder service, including rules that:

(i) Govern the submission of bids and offers by buyers, sellers, and other interested parties that use the finder service and the circumstances under which the finder service will pair bids and offers submitted by buyers, sellers, and other interested parties; and

(ii) Govern the manner in which buyers, sellers, and other interested parties may bind themselves to the terms of a specific transaction.

(c) Limitation. The authority to act as a finder does not enable a national bank to engage in brokerage activities that have not been found to be permissible for national banks.

(d) Advertisement and fee. Unless otherwise prohibited by Federal law, a national bank may advertise the availability of, and accept a fee for, the services provided pursuant to this section.

[67 FR 35004, May 17, 2002]

Sec. 7.4000 Visitorial powers.

(a) General rule.

(1) Only the OCC or an authorized representative of the OCC may exercise visitorial powers with respect to national banks, except as provided in paragraph (b) of this section. State officials may not exercise visitorial powers with respect to national banks, such as conducting examinations, inspecting or requiring the production of books or records of national banks, or prosecuting enforcement actions, except in limited circumstances authorized by federal law. However, production of a bank's records (other than non-public OCC information under 12 CFR part 4, subpart C) may be required under normal judicial procedures.

(2) For purposes of this section, visitorial powers include:

(i) Examination of a bank;

(ii) Inspection of a bank's books and records;

(iii) Regulation and supervision of activities authorized or permitted pursuant to federal banking law; and

(iv) Enforcing compliance with any applicable federal or state laws concerning those activities.

(3) Unless otherwise provided by Federal law, the OCC has exclusive visitorial authority with respect to the content and conduct of activities authorized for national banks under Federal law.

(b) Exceptions to the general rule. Under 12 U.S.C. 484, the OCC's exclusive visitorial powers are subject to the following exceptions:

(1) Exceptions authorized by Federal law. National banks are subject to such visitorial powers as are provided by Federal law. Examples of laws vesting visitorial power in other governmental entities include laws authorizing state or other Federal officials to:

(i) Inspect the list of shareholders, provided that the official is authorized to assess taxes under state authority (12 U.S.C. 62; this section also authorizes inspection of the shareholder list by shareholders and creditors of a national bank);

(ii) Review, at reasonable times and upon reasonable notice to a bank, the bank's records solely to ensure compliance with applicable state unclaimed property or escheat laws upon reasonable cause to believe that the bank has failed to comply with those laws (12 U.S.C. 484(b));

(iii) Verify payroll records for unemployment compensation purposes (26 U.S.C. 3305(c));

(iv) Ascertain the correctness of Federal tax returns (26 U.S.C. 7602);

(v) Enforce the Fair Labor Standards Act (29 U.S.C. 211); and

(vi) Functionally regulate certain activities, as provided under the Gramm–Leach–Bliley Act, Pub. L. 106–102, 113 Stat. 1338 (Nov. 12, 1999).

(2) *Exception for courts of justice.* National banks are subject to such visitorial powers as are vested in the courts of justice. This exception pertains to the powers inherent in the judiciary and does not grant state or other governmental authorities any right to inspect, superintend, direct, regulate or compel compliance by a national bank with respect to any law, regarding the content or conduct of activities authorized for national banks under Federal law.

(3) *Exception for Congress.* National banks are subject to such visitorial powers as shall be, or have been, exercised or directed by Congress or by either House thereof or by any committee of Congress or of either House duly authorized.

(c) *Report of examination.* The report of examination made by an OCC examiner is designated solely for use in the supervision of the bank. The bank's copy of the report is the property of the OCC and is loaned to the bank and any holding company thereof solely for its confidential use. The bank's directors, in keeping with their responsibilities both to depositors and to shareholders, should thoroughly review the report. The report may be made available to other persons only in accordance with the rules on disclosure in 12 CFR part 4.

[64 FR 60100, Nov. 4, 1999; 69 FR 1904, Jan. 13, 2004]

Sec. 7.4006 Applicability of State law to national bank operating subsidiaries.

Unless otherwise provided by Federal law or OCC regulation, State laws apply to national bank operating subsidiaries to the same extent that those laws apply to the parent national bank.

Sec. 7.4007 Deposit-taking.

(a) *Authority of national banks.* A national bank may receive deposits and engage in any activity incidental to receiving deposits, including issuing evidence of accounts, subject to such terms, conditions, and limitations prescribed by the Comptroller of the Currency and any other applicable Federal law.

(b) *Applicability of state law.*

(1) Except where made applicable by Federal law, state laws that obstruct, impair, or condition a national bank's ability to fully exercise its Federally authorized deposit-taking powers are not applicable to national banks.

(2) A national bank may exercise its deposit-taking powers without regard to state law limitations concerning:

(i) Abandoned and dormant accounts;[16]

(ii) Checking accounts;

(iii) Disclosure requirements;

(iv) Funds availability;

(v) Savings account orders of withdrawal;

(vi) State licensing or registration requirements (except for purposes of service of process); and

(vii) Special purpose savings services;[17]

(c) *State laws that are not preempted.* State laws on the following subjects are not inconsistent with the deposit-taking powers of national banks and apply to national banks to the extent that they only incidentally affect the exercise of national banks' deposit-taking powers:

(1) Contracts;

(2) Torts;

(3) Criminal law;[18]

(4) Rights to collect debts;

(5) Acquisition and transfer of property;

(6) Taxation;

(7) Zoning; and

---

16. [n.3] This does not apply to state laws of the type upheld by the United States Supreme Court in *Anderson Nat'l Bank v. Luckett,* 321 U.S. 233 (1944), which obligate a national bank to "pay [deposits] to the persons entitled to demand payment according to the law of the state where it does business." Id. at 248–249.

17. [n.4] State laws purporting to regulate national bank fees and charges are addressed in 12 CFR 7.4002.

18. [n.5] But see the distinction drawn by the Supreme Court in *Easton v. Iowa,* 188 U.S. 220, 238 (1903) between "crimes defined and punishable at common law or by the general statutes of a state and crimes and offences cognizable under the authority of the United States." The Court stated that "[u]ndoubtedly a state has the legitimate power to define and punish crimes by general laws applicable to all persons within its jurisdiction * * *. But it is without lawful power to make such special laws applicable to banks organized and operating under the laws of the United States." Id. at 239 (holding that Federal law governing the operations of national banks preempted a state criminal law prohibiting insolvent banks from accepting deposits).

(8) Any other law the effect of which the OCC determines to be incidental to the deposit-taking operations of national banks or otherwise consistent with the powers set out in paragraph (a) of this section.

[[eds.] 69 Fed. Reg. 1904, Jan. 13, 2004 (effective Feb. 12, 2004)]

Sec. 7.4008 Lending.

(a) Authority of national banks. A national bank may make, sell, purchase, participate in, or otherwise deal in loans and interests in loans that are not secured by liens on, or interests in, real estate, subject to such terms, conditions, and limitations prescribed by the Comptroller of the Currency and any other applicable Federal law.

(b) Standards for loans. A national bank shall not make a consumer loan subject to this Sec. 7.4008 based predominantly on the bank's realization of the foreclosure or liquidation value of the borrower's collateral, without regard to the borrower's ability to repay the loan according to its terms. A bank may use any reasonable method to determine a borrower's ability to repay, including, for example, the borrower's current and expected income, current and expected cash flows, net worth, other relevant financial resources, current financial obligations, employment status, credit history, or other relevant factors.

(c) Unfair and deceptive practices. A national bank shall not engage in unfair or deceptive practices within the meaning of section 5 of the Federal Trade Commission Act, 15 U.S.C. 45(a)(1), and regulations promulgated thereunder in connection with loans made under this Sec. 7.4008.

(d) Applicability of state law.

(1) Except where made applicable by Federal law, state laws that obstruct, impair, or condition a national bank's ability to fully exercise its Federally authorized non-real estate lending powers are not applicable to national banks.

(2) A national bank may make non-real estate loans without regard to state law limitations concerning:

(i) Licensing, registration (except for purposes of service of process), filings, or reports by creditors;

(ii) The ability of a creditor to require or obtain insurance for collateral or other credit enhancements or risk mitigants, in furtherance of safe and sound banking practices;

(iii) Loan-to-value ratios;

(iv) The terms of credit, including the schedule for repayment of principal and interest, amortization of loans, balance, payments due, minimum payments, or term to maturity of the loan, including the circumstances under which a loan may be called due and payable upon the passage of time or a specified event external to the loan;

(v) Escrow accounts, impound accounts, and similar accounts;

(vi) Security property, including leaseholds;

(vii) Access to, and use of, credit reports;

(viii) Disclosure and advertising, including laws requiring specific statements, information, or other content to be included in credit application forms, credit solicitations, billing statements, credit contracts, or other credit-related documents;

(ix) Disbursements and repayments; and

(x) Rates of interest on loans.[19]

(e) State laws that are not preempted. State laws on the following subjects are not inconsistent with the non-real estate lending powers of national banks and apply to national banks to the extent that they only incidentally affect the exercise of national banks' non-real estate lending powers:

(1) Contracts;

(2) Torts;

(3) Criminal law;[20]

(4) Rights to collect debts;

---

19. [n.6] The limitations on charges that comprise rates of interest on loans by national banks are determined under Federal law. See 12 U.S.C. 85; 12 CFR 7.4001. State laws purporting to regulate national bank fees and charges that do not constitute interest are addressed in 12 CFR 7.4002.

20. [n.7] See supra note 5 regarding the distinction drawn by the Supreme Court in Easton v. Iowa, 188 U.S. 220, 238 (1903) between "crimes defined and punishable at common law or by the general statutes of a state and crimes and offences cognizable under the authority of the United States."

(5) Acquisition and transfer of property;

(6) Taxation;

(7) Zoning; and

(8) Any other law the effect of which the OCC determines to be incidental to the non-real estate lending operations of national banks or otherwise consistent with the powers set out in paragraph (a) of this section.

[[eds.] 69 Fed. Reg. 1904, Jan. 13, 2004 (effective Feb. 12, 2004)]

Sec. 7.4009 Applicability of state law to national bank operations.

(a) Authority of national banks. A national bank may exercise all powers authorized to it under Federal law, including conducting any activity that is part of, or incidental to, the business of banking, subject to such terms, conditions, and limitations prescribed by the Comptroller of the Currency and any applicable Federal law.

(b) Applicability of state law. Except where made applicable by Federal law, state laws that obstruct, impair, or condition a national bank's ability to fully exercise its powers to conduct activities authorized under Federal law do not apply to national banks.

(c) Applicability of state law to particular national bank activities.

(1) The provisions of this section govern with respect to any national bank power or aspect of a national bank's operations that is not covered by another OCC regulation specifically addressing the applicability of state law.

(2) State laws on the following subjects are not inconsistent with the powers of national banks and apply to national banks to the extent that they only incidentally affect the exercise of national bank powers:

(i) Contracts;

(ii) Torts;

(iii) Criminal law;[21]

(iv) Rights to collect debts;

(v) Acquisition and transfer of property;

(vi) Taxation;

(vii) Zoning; and

(viii) Any other law the effect of which the OCC determines to be incidental to the exercise of national bank powers or otherwise consistent with the powers set out in paragraph (a) of this section.

[[eds.] 69 Fed. Reg. 1904, Jan. 13, 2004 (effective Feb. 12, 2004)]

PART 32. Lending Limits

Sec. 32.1 Authority, purpose and scope.

(a) Authority. This part is issued pursuant to 12 U.S.C. 1 et seq., 12 U.S.C. 84, and 12 U.S.C. 93a.

(b) Purpose. The purpose of this part is to protect the safety and soundness of national banks by preventing excessive loans to one person, or to related persons that are financially dependent, and to promote diversification of loans and equitable access to banking services.

(c) Scope.

(1) This part applies to all loans and extensions of credit made by national banks and their domestic operating subsidiaries. This part does not apply to loans made by a national bank and its domestic operating subsidiaries to the bank's "affiliates," as that term is defined in 12 U.S.C. 371c(b)(1), to the bank's operating subsidiaries, or to Edge Act or Agreement Corporation subsidiaries.

(2) The lending limits in this part are separate and independent from the investment limits prescribed by 12 U.S.C. 24 (Seventh), and a national bank may make loans or extensions of credit to one borrower up to the full amount permitted by this part and also hold eligible securities of the same obligor up to the full amount permitted under 12 U.S.C. 24 (Seventh) and 12 CFR part 1.

(3) Extensions of credit to executive officers, directors and principal shareholders of national banks, and their related interests are subject to limits prescribed by 12 U.S.C. 375a and 375b in addition to the lending limits established by 12 U.S.C. 84 and this part.

(4) In addition to the foregoing, loans and extensions of credit made by national banks and their domestic operating subsidiaries must be consistent with safe and sound banking practices.

---

21.   [n.8] Id.

Sec. 32.2 Definitions.

(a) Borrower means a person who is named as a borrower or debtor in a loan or extension of credit, or any other person, including a drawer, endorser, or guarantor, who is deemed to be a borrower under the "direct benefit" or the "common enterprise" tests set forth in Sec. 32.5.

(b) Capital and surplus means—

(1) A bank's Tier 1 and Tier 2 capital calculated under the OCC's risk-based capital standards set forth in Appendix A to 12 CFR part 3 as reported in the bank's Consolidated Report of Condition and Income filed under 12 U.S.C. 161; plus

(2) The balance of a bank's allowance for loan and lease losses not included in the bank's Tier 2 capital, for purposes of the calculation of risk-based capital described in paragraph (b)(1) of this section, as reported in the bank's Call Report filed under 12 U.S.C. 161.

(c) Close of business means the time at which a bank closes its accounting records for the business day.

(d) Consumer means the user of any products, commodities, goods, or services, whether leased or purchased, but does not include any person who purchases products or commodities for resale or fabrication into goods for sale.

(e) Consumer paper means paper relating to automobiles, mobile homes, residences, office equipment, household items, tuition fees, insurance premium fees, and similar consumer items. Consumer paper also includes paper covering the lease (where the bank is not the owner or lessor) or purchase of equipment for use in manufacturing, farming, construction, or excavation.

(f) Contractual commitment to advance funds.

(1) The term includes a bank's obligation to–

(i) Make payment (directly or indirectly) to a third person contingent upon default by a customer of the bank in performing an obligation and to make such payment in keeping with the agreed upon terms of the customer's contract with the third person, or to make payments upon some other stated condition;

(ii) Guarantee or act as surety for the benefit of a person;

(iii) Advance funds under a qualifying commitment to lend, as defined in paragraph (m) of this section, and

(iv) Advance funds under a standby letter of credit as defined in paragraph (s) of this section, a put, or other similar arrangement.

(2) The term does not include commercial letters of credit and similar instruments where the issuing bank expects the beneficiary to draw on the issuer, that do not guarantee payment, and that do not provide for payment in the event of a default by a third party.

(g) Control is presumed to exist when a person directly or indirectly, or acting through or together with one or more persons–

(1) Owns, controls, or has the power to vote 25 percent or more of any class of voting securities of another person;

(2) Controls, in any manner, the election of a majority of the directors, trustees, or other persons exercising similar functions of another person; or

(3) Has the power to exercise a controlling influence over the management or policies of another person.

(h) Current market value means the bid or closing price listed for an item in a regularly published listing or an electronic reporting service.

(i) Eligible bank means a national bank that:

(1) Is well capitalized as defined in 12 CFR 6.4(b)(1); and

(2) Has a composite rating of 1 or 2 under the Uniform Financial Institutions Rating System in connection with the bank's most recent examination or subsequent review, with at least a rating of 2 for asset quality and for management.

(j) Financial instrument means stocks, notes, bonds, and debentures traded on a national securities exchange, OTC margin stocks as defined in Regulation U, 12 CFR part 221, commercial paper, negotiable certificates of deposit, bankers' acceptances, and shares in money market and mutual funds of the type that issue shares in which banks may perfect a security interest. Financial instruments may be denominated in foreign currencies that are freely convertible to U.S. dollars. The term "financial instrument" does not include mortgages.

(k) Loans and extensions of credit means a bank's direct or indirect advance of funds to or on behalf of a borrower based on an obligation of the borrower to repay the funds or repayable from specific property pledged by or on behalf of the borrower.

(1) Loans or extensions of credit for purposes of 12 U.S.C. 84 and this part include—

(i) A contractual commitment to advance funds, as defined in paragraph (f) of this section;

(ii) A maker or endorser's obligation arising from a bank's discount of commercial paper;

(iii) A bank's purchase of securities subject to an agreement that the seller will repurchase the securities at the end of a stated period, but not including a bank's purchase of Type I securities, as defined in part 1 of this chapter, subject to a repurchase agreement, where the purchasing bank has assured control over or has established its rights to the Type I securities as collateral;

(iv) A bank's purchase of third-party paper subject to an agreement that the seller will repurchase the paper upon default or at the end of a stated period. The amount of the bank's loan is the total unpaid balance of the paper owned by the bank less any applicable dealer reserves retained by the bank and held by the bank as collateral security. Where the seller's obligation to repurchase is limited, the bank's loan is measured by the total amount of the paper the seller may ultimately be obligated to repurchase. A bank's purchase of third party paper without direct or indirect recourse to the seller is not a loan or extension of credit to the seller;

(v) An overdraft, whether or not prearranged, but not an intra-day overdraft for which payment is received before the close of business of the bank that makes the funds available;

(vi) The sale of Federal funds with a maturity of more than one business day, but not Federal funds with a maturity of one day or less or Federal funds sold under a continuing contract; and

(vii) Loans or extensions of credit that have been charged off on the books of the bank in whole or in part, unless the loan or extension of credit—

(A) Is unenforceable by reason of discharge in bankruptcy;

(B) Is no longer legally enforceable because of expiration of the statute of limitations or a judicial decision; or

(C) Is no longer legally enforceable for other reasons, provided that the bank maintains sufficient records to demonstrate that the loan is unenforceable.

(2) The following items do not constitute loans or extensions of credit for purposes of 12 U.S.C. 84 and this part—

(i) Additional funds advanced for the benefit of a borrower by a bank for payment of taxes, insurance, utilities, security, and maintenance and operating expenses necessary to preserve the value of real property securing the loan, consistent with safe and sound banking practices, but only if the advance is for the protection of the bank's interest in the collateral, and provided that such amounts must be treated as an extension of credit if a new loan or extension of credit is made to the borrower;

(ii) Accrued and discounted interest on an existing loan or extension of credit, including interest that has been capitalized from prior notes and interest that has been advanced under terms and conditions of a loan agreement;

(iii) Financed sales of a bank's own assets, including Other Real Estate Owned, if the financing does not put the bank in a worse position than when the bank held title to the assets;

(iv) A renewal or restructuring of a loan as a new "loan or extension of credit," following the exercise by a bank of reasonable efforts, consistent with safe and sound banking practices, to bring the loan into conformance with the lending limit, unless new funds are advanced by the bank to the borrower (except as permitted by Sec. 32.3(b)(5)), or a new borrower replaces the original borrower, or unless the OCC determines that a renewal or restructuring was undertaken as a means to evade the bank's lending limit;

(v) Amounts paid against uncollected funds in the normal process of collection; and

(vi) (A) That portion of a loan or extension of credit sold as a participation by a bank on a nonrecourse basis, provided that the participation results in a pro rata sharing of credit risk proportionate to the respective interests of the originating and participating lenders. Where a participation agreement provides that repayment must be applied first to the portions sold, a pro rata sharing will be deemed to exist only if the agreement also provides that, in the event of a default or comparable event defined in the agreement, participants must share in all subsequent repayments and collections in proportion to their percentage participation at the time of the occurrence of the event.

(B) When an originating bank funds the entire loan, it must receive funding from the participants before the close of business of its next business day. If the participating portions are not received within that period, then the portions funded will be treated as a loan by the originating bank to the borrower. If the portions so attributed to the borrower exceed the originating bank's lending limit, the loan may be treated as nonconforming subject to Sec. 32.6, rather than a violation, if:

(1) The originating bank had a valid and unconditional participation agreement with a participating bank or banks that was sufficient to reduce the loan to within the originating bank's lending limit;

(2) The participating bank reconfirmed its participation and the originating bank had no knowledge of any information that would permit the participant to withhold its participation; and

(3) The participation was to be funded by close of business of the originating bank's next business day.

(*l*) Person means an individual; sole proprietorship; partnership; joint venture; association; trust; estate; business trust; corporation; limited liability company; not-for-profit corporation; sovereign government or agency, instrumentality, or political subdivision thereof; or any similar entity or organization.

(m) Qualifying commitment to lend means a legally binding written commitment to lend that, when combined with all other outstanding loans and qualifying commitments to a borrower, was

within the bank's lending limit when entered into, and has not been disqualified.

(1) In determining whether a commitment is within the bank's lending limit when made, the bank may deduct from the amount of the commitment the amount of any legally binding loan participation commitments that are issued concurrent with the bank's commitment and that would be excluded from the definition of "loan or extension of credit" under paragraph (k)(2)(vi) of this section.

(2) If the bank subsequently chooses to make an additional loan and that subsequent loan, together with all outstanding loans and qualifying commitments to a borrower, exceeds the bank's applicable lending limit at that time, the bank's qualifying commitments to the borrower that exceed the bank's lending limit at that time are deemed to be permanently disqualified, beginning with the most recent qualifying commitment and proceeding in reverse chronological order. When a commitment is disqualified, the entire commitment is disqualified and the disqualified commitment is no longer considered a "loan or extension of credit." Advances of funds under a disqualified or non-qualifying commitment may only be made to the extent that the advance, together with all other outstanding loans to the borrower, do not exceed the bank's lending limit at the time of the advance, calculated pursuant to Sec. 32.4.

(n) Readily marketable collateral means financial instruments and bullion that are salable under ordinary market conditions with reasonable promptness at a fair market value determined by quotations based upon actual transactions on an auction or similarly available daily bid and ask price market.

(o) Readily marketable staple means an article of commerce, agriculture, or industry, such as wheat and other grains, cotton, wool, and basic metals such as tin, copper and lead, in the form of standardized interchangeable units, that is easy to sell in a market with sufficiently frequent price quotations.

(1) An article comes within this definition if–

(i) The exact price is easy to determine; and

(ii) The staple itself is easy to sell at any time at a price that would not be considerably less than the amount at which it is valued as collateral.

(2) Whether an article qualifies as a readily marketable staple is determined on the basis of the conditions existing at the time the loan or extension of credit that is secured by the staples is made.

(p) Residential real estate loan means a loan or extension of credit that is secured by 1–4 family residential real estate.

(q) Sale of Federal funds means any transaction between depository institutions involving the transfer of immediately available funds resulting from credits to deposit balances at Federal Reserve Banks, or from credits to new or existing deposit balances due from a correspondent depository institution.

(r) Small business loan means a loan or extension of credit "secured by nonfarm nonresidential properties" or "a commercial or industrial loan" as defined in the instructions for preparation of the Consolidated Report of Condition and Income.

(s) Standby letter of credit means any letter of credit, or similar arrangement, that represents an obligation to the beneficiary on the part of the issuer:

(1) To repay money borrowed by or advanced to or for the account of the account party;

(2) To make payment on account of any indebtedness undertaken by the account party; or

(3) To make payment on account of any default by the account party in the performance of an obligation.

[63 FR 15746, Apr. 1, 1998; 66 FR 31120, June 11, 2001; 66 FR 55072, Nov. 1, 2001; 69 FR 51357, Aug. 19, 2004]

Sec. 32.3 Lending limits.

(a) Combined general limit. A national bank's total outstanding loans and extensions of credit to one borrower may not exceed 15 percent of the bank's capital and surplus, plus an additional 10 percent of the bank's capital and surplus, if the amount that exceeds the bank's 15 percent general limit is fully secured by readily marketable collateral, as defined in Sec. 32.2(n). To qualify for the additional 10 percent limit, the bank must perfect a security interest in the collateral

under applicable law and the collateral must have a current market value at all times of at least 100 percent of the amount of the loan or extension of credit that exceeds the bank's 15 percent general limit.

(b) Loans subject to special lending limits. The following loans or extensions of credit are subject to the lending limits set forth below. When loans and extensions of credit qualify for more than one special lending limit, the special limits are cumulative.

(1) Loans secured by bills of lading or warehouse receipts covering readily marketable staples.

(i) A national bank's loans or extensions of credit to one borrower secured by bills of lading, warehouse receipts, or similar documents transferring or securing title to readily marketable staples, as defined in Sec. 32.2(o), may not exceed 35 percent of the bank's capital and surplus in addition to the amount allowed under the bank's combined general limit. The market value of the staples securing the loan must at all times equal at least 115 percent of the amount of the outstanding loan that exceeds the bank's combined general limit.

(ii) Staples that qualify for this special limit must be nonperishable, may be refrigerated or frozen, and must be fully covered by insurance if such insurance is customary. Whether a staple is non-perishable must be determined on a case-by-case basis because of differences in handling and storing commodities.

(iii) This special limit applies to a loan or extension of credit arising from a single transaction or secured by the same staples, provided that the duration of the loan or extension of credit is:

(A) Not more than ten months if secured by nonperishable staples; or

(B) Not more than six months if secured by refrigerated or frozen staples.

(iv) The holder of the warehouse receipts, order bills of lading, documents qualifying as documents of title under the Uniform Commercial Code, or other similar documents, must have control and be able to obtain immediate possession of the staple so that the bank is able to sell the underlying staples and promptly transfer title and possession to a purchaser if default should occur on a loan secured by such documents. The existence of a brief notice period, or similar procedural requirements under applicable law, for the disposal of the collateral will not affect the eligibility of the instruments for this special limit.

(A) Field warehouse receipts are an acceptable form of collateral when issued by a duly bonded and licensed grain elevator or warehouse having exclusive possession and control of the staples even though the grain elevator or warehouse is maintained on the premises of the owner of the staples.

(B) Warehouse receipts issued by the borrower-owner that is a grain elevator or warehouse company, duly-bonded and licensed and regularly inspected by state or Federal authorities, may be considered eligible collateral under this provision only when the receipts are registered with an independent registrar whose consent is required before the staples may be withdrawn from the warehouse.

(2) Discount of installment consumer paper.

(i) A national bank's loans and extensions of credit to one borrower that arise from the discount of negotiable or nonnegotiable installment consumer paper, as defined at Sec. 32.2(e), that carries a full recourse endorsement or unconditional guarantee by the person selling the paper, may not exceed 10 percent of the bank's capital and surplus in addition to the amount allowed under the bank's combined general limit. An unconditional guarantee may be in the form of a repurchase agreement or separate guarantee agreement. A condition reasonably within the power of the bank to perform, such as the repossession of collateral, will not make conditional an otherwise unconditional guarantee.

(ii) Where the seller of the paper offers only partial recourse to the bank, the lending limits of this section apply to the obligation of the seller to the bank, which is measured by the total amount of paper the seller may be obligated to repurchase or has guaranteed.

(iii) Where the bank is relying primarily upon the maker of the paper for payment of the loans or extensions of credit and not upon any full or partial recourse endorsement or guarantee by the seller of the paper, the lending limits of this section apply only to the maker. The bank must substantiate its reliance on the maker with–

(A) Records supporting the bank's independent credit analysis of the maker's ability to repay the loan or extension of credit, maintained by the bank or by a third party that is contractually obligated to make those records available for examination purposes; and

(B) A written certification by an officer of the bank authorized by the bank's board of directors or any designee of that officer, that the bank is relying primarily upon the maker to repay the loan or extension of credit.

(iv) Where paper is purchased in substantial quantities, the records, evaluation, and certification must be in a form appropriate for the class and quantity of paper involved. The bank may use sampling techniques, or other appropriate methods, to independently verify the reliability of the credit information supplied by the seller.

(3) Loans secured by documents covering livestock.

(i) A national bank's loans or extensions of credit to one borrower secured by shipping documents or instruments that transfer or secure title to or give a first lien on livestock may not exceed 10 percent of the bank's capital and surplus in addition to the amount allowed under the bank's combined general limit. The market value of the livestock securing the loan must at all times equal at least 115 percent of the amount of the outstanding loan that exceeds the bank's combined general limit. For purposes of this subsection, the term "livestock" includes dairy and beef cattle, hogs, sheep, goats, horses, mules, poultry and fish, whether or not held for resale.

(ii) The bank must maintain in its files an inspection and valuation for the livestock pledged that is reasonably current, taking into account the nature and frequency of turnover of the livestock to which the documents relate, but in any case not more than 12 months old.

(iii) Under the laws of certain states, persons furnishing pasturage under a grazing contract may have a lien on the livestock for the amount due for pasturage. If a lien that is based on pasturage furnished by the lienor prior to the bank's loan or extension of credit is assigned to the bank by a recordable instrument and protected against being defeated by some other lien or claim, by payment to a person other than the bank, or otherwise, it will qualify under this exception provided the amount of the perfected lien is at least equal to the amount of the loan and the value of the livestock is at no time less than 115 percent of the portion of the loan or extension of credit that exceeds the bank's combined general limit. When the amount due under the grazing contract is dependent upon future performance, the resulting lien does not meet the requirements of the exception.

(4) *Loans secured by dairy cattle.* A national bank's loans and extensions of credit to one borrower that arise from the discount by dealers in dairy cattle of paper given in payment for the cattle may not exceed 10 percent of the bank's capital and surplus in addition to the amount allowed under the bank's combined general limit. To qualify, the paper–

(i) Must carry the full recourse endorsement or unconditional guarantee of the seller; and

(ii) Must be secured by the cattle being sold, pursuant to liens that allow the bank to maintain a perfected security interest in the cattle under applicable law.

(5) Additional advances to complete project financing pursuant to renewal of a qualifying commitment to lend. A national bank may renew a qualifying commitment to lend, as defined by Sec. 32.2(m), and complete funding under that commitment if all of the following criteria are met—

(i) The completion of funding is consistent with safe and sound banking practices and is made to protect the position of the bank;

(ii) The completion of funding will enable the borrower to complete the project for which the qualifying commitment to lend was made; and

(iii) The amount of the additional funding does not exceed the unfunded portion of the bank's qualifying commitment to lend.

(c) *Loans not subject to the lending limits.* The following loans or extensions of credit are not subject to the lending limits of 12 U.S.C. 84 or this part.

(1) *Loans arising from the discount of commercial or business paper.*

(i) Loans or extensions of credit arising from the discount of negotiable commercial or business paper that evidences an obligation to the person negotiating the paper. The paper—

(A) Must be given in payment of the purchase price of commodities purchased for resale, fabrication of a product, or any other business purpose that may reasonably be expected to provide funds for payment of the paper; and

(B) Must bear the full recourse endorsement of the owner of the paper, except that paper discounted in connection with export transactions, that is transferred without recourse, or with limited recourse, must be supported by an assignment of appropriate insurance covering the political, credit, and transfer risks applicable to the paper, such as insurance provided by the Export–Import Bank.

(ii) A failure to pay principal or interest on commercial or business paper when due does not result in a loan or extension of credit to the maker or endorser of the paper; however, the amount of such paper thereafter must be counted in determining whether additional loans or extensions of credit to the same borrower may be made within the limits of 12 U.S.C. 84 and this part.

(2) *Bankers' acceptances.* A bank's acceptance of drafts eligible for rediscount under 12 U.S.C. 372 and 373, or a bank's purchase of acceptances created by other banks that are eligible for rediscount under those sections; but not including—

(i) A bank's acceptance of drafts ineligible for rediscount (which constitutes a loan by the bank to the customer for whom the acceptance was made, in the amount of the draft);

(ii) A bank's purchase of ineligible acceptances created by other banks (which constitutes a loan from the purchasing bank to the accepting bank, in the amount of the purchase price); and

(iii) A bank's purchase of its own acceptances (which constitutes a loan to the bank's customer for whom the acceptance was made, in the amount of the purchase price).

(3) (i) Loans secured by U.S. obligations. Loans or extensions of credit, or portions thereof, to the extent fully secured by the current market value of:

(A) Bonds, notes, certificates of indebtedness, or Treasury bills of the United States or by similar obligations fully guaranteed as to principal and interest by the United States;

(B) Loans to the extent guaranteed as to repayment of principal by the full faith and credit of the U.S. government, as set forth in paragraph (c)(4)(ii) of this section.

(ii) To qualify under this paragraph, the bank must perfect a security interest in the collateral under applicable law.

(4) Loans to or guaranteed by a Federal agency.

(i) Loans or extensions of credit to any department, agency, bureau, board, commission, or establishment of the United States or any corporation wholly owned directly or indirectly by the United States.

(ii) Loans or extensions of credit, including portions thereof, to the extent secured by unconditional takeout commitments or guarantees of any of the foregoing governmental entities. The commitment or guarantee–

(A) Must be payable in cash or its equivalent within 60 days after demand for payment is made;

(B) Is considered unconditional if the protection afforded the bank is not substantially diminished or impaired if loss should result from factors beyond the bank's control. Protection against loss is not materially diminished or impaired by procedural requirements, such as an agreement to pay on the obligation only in the event of default, including default over a specific period of time, a requirement that notification of default be given within a specific period after its occur-

rence, or a requirement of good faith on the part of the bank.

(5) Loans to or guaranteed by general obligations of a State or political subdivision.

(i) A loan or extension of credit to a State or political subdivision that constitutes a general obligation of the State or political subdivision, as defined in part 1 of this chapter, and for which the lending bank has an opinion of counsel or the opinion of that State Attorney General, or other State legal official with authority to opine on the obligation in question, that the loan or extension of credit is a valid and enforceable general obligation of the borrower; and

(ii) A loan or extension of credit, including portions thereof, to the extent guaranteed or secured by a general obligation of a State or political subdivision and for which the lending bank has an opinion of counsel or the opinion of that State Attorney General, or other State legal official with authority to opine on the guarantee or collateral in question, that the guarantee or collateral is a valid and enforceable general obligation of that public body.

(6) Loans secured by segregated deposit accounts. Loans or extensions of credit, including portions thereof, to the extent secured by a segregated deposit account in the lending bank, provided a security interest in the deposit has been perfected under applicable law.

(i) Where the deposit is eligible for withdrawal before the secured loan matures, the bank must establish internal procedures to prevent release of the security without the lending bank's prior consent.

(ii) A deposit that is denominated and payable in a currency other than that of the loan or extension of credit that it secures may be eligible for this exception if the currency is freely convertible to U.S. dollars.

(A) This exception applies to only that portion of the loan or extension of credit that is covered by the U.S. dollar value of the deposit.

(B) The lending bank must establish procedures to periodically revalue foreign currency deposits to ensure that the loan or extension of credit remains fully secured at all times.

(7) Loans to financial institutions with the approval of the Comptroller. Loans or extensions of credit to any financial institution or to any receiver, conservator, superintendent of banks, or other agent in charge of the business and property of a financial institution when an emergency situation exists and a national bank is asked to provide assistance to another financial institution, and the loan is approved by the Comptroller. For purposes of this paragraph, financial institution means a commercial bank, savings bank, trust company, savings association, or credit union.

(8) Loans to the Student Loan Marketing Association. Loans or extensions of credit to the Student Loan Marketing Association.

(9) Loans to industrial development authorities. A loan or extension of credit to an industrial development authority or similar public entity created to construct and lease a plant facility, including a health care facility, to an industrial occupant will be deemed a loan to the lessee, provided that–

(i) The bank evaluates the creditworthiness of the industrial occupant before the loan is extended to the authority;

(ii) The authority's liability on the loan is limited solely to whatever interest it has in the particular facility;

(iii) The authority's interest is assigned to the bank as security for the loan or the industrial occupant issues a promissory note to the bank that provides a higher order of security than the assignment of a lease; and

(iv) The industrial occupant's lease rentals are assigned and paid directly to the bank.

(10) Loans to leasing companies. A loan or extension of credit to a leasing company for the purpose of purchasing equipment for lease will be deemed a loan to the lessee, provided that–

(i) The bank evaluates the creditworthiness of the lessee before the loan is extended to the leasing corporation;

(ii) The loan is without recourse to the leasing corporation;

(iii) The bank is given a security interest in the equipment and in the event of default, may proceed directly against the equipment and the lessee for any deficiency resulting from the sale of the equipment;

(iv) The leasing corporation assigns all of its rights under the lease to the bank;

(v) The lessee's lease payments are assigned and paid to the bank; and

(vi) The lease terms are subject to the same limitations that would apply to a national bank acting as a lessor.

[60 FR 8532, Feb. 15, 1995, as amended at 63 FR 15746, Apr. 1, 1998; 66 FR 31120, June 11, 2001; 66 FR 35072, Nov. 1, 2001]

Sec. 32.4 Calculation of lending limits.

(a) Calculation date. For purposes of determining compliance with 12 U.S.C. 84 and this part, a bank shall determine its lending limit as of the most recent of the following dates:

(1) The last day of the preceding calendar quarter; or

(2) The date on which there is a change in the bank's capital category for purposes of 12 U.S.C. 1831o and 12 CFR 6.3.

(b) Effective date.

(1) A bank's lending limit calculated in accordance with paragraph (a)(1) of this section will be effective as of the earlier of the following dates:

(i) The date on which the bank's Call Report is submitted; or

(ii) The date on which the bank's Call Report is required to be submitted.

(2) A bank's lending limit calculated in accordance with paragraph (a)(2) of this section will be effective on the date that the limit is to be calculated.

(c) More frequent calculations. If the OCC determines for safety and soundness reasons that a bank should calculate its lending limit more frequently than required by paragraph (a) of this section, the OCC may provide written notice to the bank directing the bank to calculate its lending limit at a more frequent interval, and the bank shall thereafter calculate its lending limit at that interval until further notice.

[63 FR 15746, Apr. 1, 1998]

Sec. 32.5 Combination rules.

(a) General rule. Loans or extensions of credit to one borrower will be attributed to another person and each person will be deemed a borrower—

(1) When proceeds of a loan or extension of credit are to be used for the direct benefit of the other person, to the extent of the proceeds so used; or

(2) When a common enterprise is deemed to exist between the persons.

(b) *Direct benefit.* The proceeds of a loan or extension of credit to a borrower will be deemed to be used for the direct benefit of another person and will be attributed to the other person when the proceeds, or assets purchased with the proceeds, are transferred to another person, other than in a bona fide arm's length transaction where the proceeds are used to acquire property, goods, or services.

(c) *Common enterprise.* A common enterprise will be deemed to exist and loans to separate borrowers will be aggregated:

(1) When the expected source of repayment for each loan or extension of credit is the same for each borrower and neither borrower has another source of income from which the loan (together with the borrower's other obligations) may be fully repaid. An employer will not be treated as a source of repayment under this paragraph because of wages and salaries paid to an employee, unless the standards of paragraph (c)(2) of this section are met;

(2) When loans or extensions of credit are made—

(i) To borrowers who are related directly or indirectly through common control, including where one borrower is directly or indirectly controlled by another borrower; and

(ii) Substantial financial interdependence exists between or among the borrowers. Substantial financial interdependence is deemed to exist when 50 percent or more of one borrower's gross receipts or gross expenditures (on an annual basis) are derived from transactions with the other borrower. Gross receipts and expenditures include gross revenues/expenses, intercompany loans, dividends, capital contributions, and similar receipts or payments;

(3) When separate persons borrow from a bank to acquire a business enterprise of which those borrowers will own more than 50 percent of the voting securities or voting interests, in which case a common enterprise is deemed to

exist between the borrowers for purposes of combining the acquisition loans; or

(4) When the OCC determines, based upon an evaluation of the facts and circumstances of particular transactions, that a common enterprise exists.

(d) *Special rule for loans to a corporate group.*

(1) Loans or extensions of credit by a bank to a corporate group may not exceed 50 percent of the bank's capital and surplus. This limitation applies only to loans subject to the combined general limit. A corporate group includes a person and all of its subsidiaries. For purposes of this paragraph, a corporation or a limited liability company is a subsidiary of a person if the person owns or beneficially owns directly or indirectly more than 50 percent of the voting securities or voting interests of the corporation or company.

(2) Except as provided in paragraph (d)(1) of this section, loans or extensions of credit to a person and its subsidiary, or to different subsidiaries of a person, are not combined unless either the direct benefit or the common enterprise test is met.

(e) *Special rules for loans to partnerships, joint ventures, and associations—*

(1) *Partnership loans.* Loans or extensions of credit to a partnership, joint venture, or association are deemed to be loans or extensions of credit to each member of the partnership, joint venture, or association. This rule does not apply to limited partners in limited partnerships or to members of joint ventures or associations if the partners or members, by the terms of the partnership or membership agreement, are not held generally liable for the debts or actions of the partnership, joint venture, or association, and those provisions are valid under applicable law.

(2) *Loans to partners.*

(i) Loans or extensions of credit to members of a partnership, joint venture, or association are not attributed to the partnership, joint venture, or association unless either the direct benefit or the common enterprise tests are met. Both the direct benefit and common enterprise tests are met between a member of a partnership, joint venture or association and such partnership, joint venture or association, when loans or extensions of credit are made to the member to purchase an interest in the partnership, joint venture or association.

(ii) Loans or extensions of credit to members of a partnership, joint venture, or association are not attributed to other members of the partnership, joint venture, or association unless either the direct benefit or common enterprise test is met.

(f) Loans to foreign governments, their agencies, and instrumentalities—

(1) Aggregation. Loans and extensions of credit to foreign governments, their agencies, and instrumentalities will be aggregated with one another only if the loans or extensions of credit fail to meet either the means test or the purpose test at the time the loan or extension of credit is made.

(i) The means test is satisfied if the borrower has resources or revenue of its own sufficient to service its debt obligations. If the government's support (excluding guarantees by a central government of the borrower's debt) exceeds the borrower's annual revenues from other sources, it will be presumed that the means test has not been satisfied.

(ii) The purpose test is satisfied if the purpose of the loan or extension of credit is consistent with the purposes of the borrower's general business.

(2) Documentation. In order to show that the means and purpose tests have been satisfied, a bank must, at a minimum, retain in its files the following items:

(i) A statement (accompanied by supporting documentation) describing the legal status and the degree of financial and operational autonomy of the borrowing entity;

(ii) Financial statements for the borrowing entity for a minimum of three years prior to the date the loan or extension of credit was made or for each year that the borrowing entity has been in existence, if less than three;

(iii) Financial statements for each year the loan or extension of credit is outstanding;

(iv) The bank's assessment of the borrower's means of servicing the loan or extension of credit, including specific reasons in support of that assessment. The assessment shall

include an analysis of the borrower's financial history, its present and projected economic and financial performance, and the significance of any financial support provided to the borrower by third parties, including the borrower's central government; and

(v) A loan agreement or other written statement from the borrower which clearly describes the purpose of the loan or extension of credit. The written representation will ordinarily constitute sufficient evidence that the purpose test has been satisfied. However, when, at the time the funds are disbursed, the bank knows or has reason to know of other information suggesting that the borrower will use the proceeds in a manner inconsistent with the written representation, it may not, without further inquiry, accept the representation.

(3) Restructured loans–

(i) Non-combination rule. Notwithstanding paragraphs (a) through (e) of this section, when previously outstanding loans and other extensions of credit to a foreign government, its agencies, and instrumentalities (i.e., public-sector obligors) that qualified for a separate lending limit under paragraph (f)(1) of this section are consolidated under a central obligor in a qualifying restructuring, such loans will not be aggregated and attributed to the central obligor. This includes any substitution in named obligors, solely because of the restructuring. Such loans (other than loans originally attributed to the central obligor in their own right) will not be considered obligations of the central obligor and will continue to be attributed to the original public-sector obligor for purposes of the lending limit.

(ii) Qualifying restructuring. Loans and other extensions of credit to a foreign government, its agencies, and instrumentalities will qualify for the non-combination process under paragraph (f)(3)(i) of this section only if they are restructured in a sovereign debt restructuring approved by the OCC, upon request by a bank for application of the non combination rule. The factors that the OCC will use in making this determination include, but are not limited to, the following:

(A) Whether the restructuring involves a substantial portion of the total commercial bank loans outstanding to the foreign government, its agencies, and instrumentalities;

(B) Whether the restructuring involves a substantial number of the foreign country's external commercial bank creditors;

(C) Whether the restructuring and consolidation under a central obligor is being done primarily to facilitate external debt management; and

(D) Whether the restructuring includes features of debt or debt-service reduction.

(iii) 50 percent aggregate limit. With respect to any case in which the non-combination process under paragraph (f)(3)(i) of this section applies, a national bank's loans and other extensions of credit to a foreign government, its agencies and instrumentalities, (including restructured debt) shall not exceed, in the aggregate, 50 percent of the bank's capital and surplus.

PART 34. Real Estate Lending and Appraisals

Sec. 34.3 General rule.

(a) A national bank may make, arrange, purchase, or sell loans or extensions of credit, or interests therein, that are secured by liens on, or interests in, real estate (real estate loans), subject to 12 U.S.C. 1828(*o*) and such restrictions and requirements as the Comptroller of the Currency may prescribe by regulation or order.

(b) A national bank shall not make a consumer loan subject to this subpart based predominantly on the bank's realization of the foreclosure or liquidation value of the borrower's collateral, without regard to the borrower's ability to repay the loan according to its terms. A bank may use any reasonable method to determine a borrower's ability to repay, including, for example, the borrower's current and expected income, current and expected cash flows, net worth, other relevant financial resources, current financial obligations, employment status, credit history, or other relevant factors.

(c) A national bank shall not engage in unfair or deceptive practices within the meaning of section 5 of the Federal Trade Commission Act, 15 U.S.C. 45(a)(1), and regulations promulgated

thereunder in connection with loans made under this part.

[[eds.] as amended 69 FR 1904, Jan. 13, 2004 (effective Feb. 12, 2004)]

Sec. 34.4 Applicability of state law.

(a) Except where made applicable by Federal law, state laws that obstruct, impair, or condition a national bank's ability to fully exercise its Federally authorized real estate lending powers do not apply to national banks. Specifically, a national bank may make real estate loans under 12 U.S.C. 371 and Sec. 34.3, without regard to state law limitations concerning:

(1) Licensing, registration (except for purposes of service of process), filings, or reports by creditors;

(2) The ability of a creditor to require or obtain private mortgage insurance, insurance for other collateral, or other credit enhancements or risk mitigants, in furtherance of safe and sound banking practices;

(3) Loan-to-value ratios;

(4) The terms of credit, including schedule for repayment of principal and interest, amortization of loans, balance, payments due, minimum payments, or term to maturity of the loan, including the circumstances under which a loan may be called due and payable upon the passage of time or a specified event external to the loan;

(5) The aggregate amount of funds that may be loaned upon the security of real estate;

(6) Escrow accounts, impound accounts, and similar accounts;

(7) Security property, including leaseholds;

(8) Access to, and use of, credit reports;

(9) Disclosure and advertising, including laws requiring specific statements, information, or other content to be included in credit application forms, credit solicitations, billing statements, credit contracts, or other credit-related documents;

(10) Processing, origination, servicing, sale or purchase of, or investment or participation in, mortgages;

(11) Disbursements and repayments;

(12) Rates of interest on loans;[22]

(13) Due-on-sale clauses except to the extent provided in 12 U.S.C. 1701j–3 and 12 CFR part 591; and

(14) Covenants and restrictions that must be contained in a lease to qualify the leasehold as acceptable security for a real estate loan.

(b) State laws on the following subjects are not inconsistent with the real estate lending powers of national banks and apply to national banks to the extent that they only incidentally affect the exercise of national banks' real estate lending powers:

(1) Contracts;

(2) Torts;

(3) Criminal law;[23]

(4) Homestead laws specified in 12 U.S.C. 1462a(f);

(5) Rights to collect debts;

(6) Acquisition and transfer of real property;

(7) Taxation;

(8) Zoning; and

(9) Any other law the effect of which the OCC determines to be incidental to the real estate lending operations of national banks or otherwise consistent with the powers and purposes set out in Sec. 34.3(a).

[[eds.] as amended 69 FR 1904, Jan. 13, 2004 (effective Feb. 12, 2004)]

---

22. [n.1] The limitations on charges that comprise rates of interest on loans by national banks are determined under Federal law. See 12 U.S.C. 85 and 1735f–7a; 12 CFR 7.4001. State laws purporting to regulate national bank fees and charges that do not constitute interest are addressed in 12 CFR 7.4002.

23. [n.2] But see the distinction drawn by the Supreme Court in Easton v. Iowa, 188 U.S. 220, 238 (1903) between "crimes defined and punishable at common law or by the general statutes of a state and crimes and offences cognizable under the authority of the United States." The Court stated that "[u]ndoubtedly a state has the legitimate power to define and punish crimes by general laws applicable to all persons within its jurisdiction * * *. But it is without lawful power to make such special laws applicable to banks organized and operating under the laws of the United States." Id. at 239 (holding that Federal law governing the operations of national banks preempted a state criminal law prohibiting insolvent banks from accepting deposits).

CHAPTER II.   FEDERAL RESERVE SYSTEM
12 C.F.R. (Selected Sections)

CODE OF FEDERAL REGULATIONS TITLE 12. BANKS AND BANKING

CHAPTER II. FEDERAL RESERVE SYSTEM
PART 223. Transaction Between Member Banks And Their Affiliates (Regulation W)

Sec. 223.1 Authority, purpose, and scope.

(a) Authority. The Board of Governors of the Federal Reserve System (Board) has issued this part (Regulation W) under the authority of sections 23A(f) and 23B(e) of the Federal Reserve Act (12 U.S.C. 371c(f), 371c–1(e)).

(b) Purpose. Sections 23A and 23B of the Federal Reserve Act (12 U.S.C. 371c, 371c–1) establish certain quantitative limits and other prudential requirements for loans, purchases of assets, and certain other transactions between a member bank and its affiliates. This regulation implements sections 23A and 23B by defining terms used in the statute, explaining the statute's requirements, and exempting certain transactions.

(c) Scope. Sections 23A and 23B and this regulation apply by their terms to "member banks"— that is, any national bank, State bank, trust company, or other institution that is a member of the Federal Reserve System. In addition, the Federal Deposit Insurance Act (12 U.S.C. 1828(j)) applies sections 23A and 23B to insured State nonmember banks in the same manner and to the same extent as if they were member banks. The Home Owners' Loan Act (12 U.S.C. 1468(a)) also applies sections 23A and 23B to insured savings associations in the same manner and to the same extent as if they were member banks (and imposes two additional restrictions).

Sec. 223.2 What is an "affiliate" for purposes of sections 23A and 23B and this part?

(a) For purposes of this part and except as provided in paragraphs (b) and (c) of this section, "affiliate" with respect to a member bank means:

(1) Parent companies. Any company that controls the member bank;

(2) Companies under common control by a parent company. Any company, including any subsidiary of the member bank, that is con-

trolled by a company that controls the member bank;

(3) Companies under other common control. Any company, including any subsidiary of the member bank, that is controlled, directly or indirectly, by trust or otherwise, by or for the benefit of shareholders who beneficially or otherwise control, directly or indirectly, by trust or otherwise, the member bank or any company that controls the member bank;

(4) Companies with interlocking directorates. Any company in which a majority of its directors, trustees, or general partners (or individuals exercising similar functions) constitute a majority of the persons holding any such office with the member bank or any company that controls the member bank;

(5) Sponsored and advised companies. Any company, including a real estate investment trust, that is sponsored and advised on a contractual basis by the member bank or an affiliate of the member bank;

(6) Investment companies.

(i) Any investment company for which the member bank or any affiliate of the member bank serves as an investment adviser, as defined in section 2(a)(20) of the Investment Company Act of 1940 (15 U.S.C. 80a–2(a)(20)); and

(ii) Any other investment fund for which the member bank or any affiliate of the member bank serves as an investment advisor, if the member bank and its affiliates own or control in the aggregate more than 5 percent of any class of voting securities or of the equity capital of the fund;

(7) Depository institution subsidiaries. A depository institution that is a subsidiary of the member bank;

(8) Financial subsidiaries. A financial subsidiary of the member bank;

(9) Companies held under merchant banking or insurance company investment authority–

(i) In general. Any company in which a holding company of the member bank owns or controls, directly or indirectly, or acting through one or more other persons, 15 percent or more of the equity capital pursuant to section 4(k)(4)(H) or (I) of the Bank Holding Company Act (12 U.S.C. 1843(k)(4)(H) or (I)).

(ii) *General exemption.* A company will not be an affiliate under paragraph (a)(9)(i) of this section if the holding company presents information to the Board that demonstrates, to the Board's satisfaction, that the holding company does not control the company.

(iii) *Specific exemptions.* A company also will not be an affiliate under paragraph (a)(9)(i) of this section if:

(A) No director, officer, or employee of the holding company serves as a director, trustee, or general partner (or individual exercising similar functions) of the company;

(B) A person that is not affiliated or associated with the holding company owns or controls a greater percentage of the equity capital of the company than is owned or controlled by the holding company, and no more than one officer or employee of the holding company serves as a director or trustee (or individual exercising similar functions) of the company; or

(C) A person that is not affiliated or associated with the holding company owns or controls more than 50 percent of the voting shares of the company, and officers and employees of the holding company do not constitute a majority of the directors or trustees (or individuals exercising similar functions) of the company.

(iv) *Application of rule to private equity funds.* A holding company will not be deemed to own or control the equity capital of a company for purposes of paragraph (a)(9)(i) of this section solely by virtue of an investment made by the holding company in a private equity fund (as defined in the merchant banking subpart of the Board's Regulation Y (12 CFR 225.173(a))) that owns or controls the equity capital of the company unless the holding company controls the private equity fund under 12 CFR 225.173(d)(4).

(v) *Definition.* For purposes of this paragraph (a)(9), "holding company" with respect to a member bank means a company that controls the member bank, or a company that is controlled by shareholders that control the member bank, and all subsidiar-

ies of the company (including any depository institution that is a subsidiary of the company).

(10) *Partnerships associated with the member bank or an affiliate.* Any partnership for which the member bank or any affiliate of the member bank serves as a general partner or for which the member bank or any affiliate of the member bank causes any director, officer, or employee of the member bank or affiliate to serve as a general partner;

(11) *Subsidiaries of affiliates.* Any subsidiary of a company described in paragraphs (a)(1) through (10) of this section; and

(12) *Other companies.* Any company that the Board determines by regulation or order, or that the appropriate Federal banking agency for the member bank determines by order, to have a relationship with the member bank, or any affiliate of the member bank, such that covered transactions by the member bank with that company may be affected by the relationship to the detriment of the member bank.

(b) "*Affiliate*" with respect to a member bank does not include:

(1) *Subsidiaries.* Any company that is a subsidiary of the member bank, unless the company is:

(i) A depository institution;

(ii) A financial subsidiary;

(iii) Directly controlled by:

(A) One or more affiliates (other than depository institution affiliates) of the member bank; or

(B) A shareholder that controls the member bank or a group of shareholders that together control the member bank;

(iv) An employee stock option plan, trust, or similar organization that exists for the benefit of the shareholders, partners, members, or employees of the member bank or any of its affiliates; or

(v) Any other company determined to be an affiliate under paragraph (a)(12) of this section;

(2) *Bank premises.* Any company engaged solely in holding the premises of the member bank;

(3) *Safe deposit.* Any company engaged solely in conducting a safe deposit business;

(4) *Government securities.* Any company engaged solely in holding obligations of the United States or its agencies or obligations fully guaranteed by the United States or its agencies as to principal and interest; and

(5) *Companies held DPC.* Any company where control results from the exercise of rights arising out of a bona fide debt previously contracted. This exclusion from the definition of "affiliate" applies only for the period of time specifically authorized under applicable State or Federal law or regulation or, in the absence of such law or regulation, for a period of two years from the date of the exercise of such rights. The Board may authorize, upon application and for good cause shown, extensions of time for not more than one year at a time, but such extensions in the aggregate will not exceed three years.

(c) For purposes of subpart F (implementing section 23B), "affiliate" with respect to a member bank also does not include any depository institution.

Sec. 223.3 What are the meanings of the other terms used in sections 23A and 23B and this part?

For purposes of this part:

(a) *Aggregate amount of covered transactions* means the amount of the covered transaction about to be engaged in added to the current amount of all outstanding covered transactions.

(b) *Appropriate Federal banking agency* with respect to a member bank or other depository institution has the same meaning as in section 3 of the Federal Deposit Insurance Act (12 U.S.C. 1813).

(c) "Bank holding company" has the same meaning as in 12 CFR 225.2.

(d) "Capital stock and surplus" means the sum of:

(1) A member bank's tier 1 and tier 2 capital under the risk-based capital guidelines of the appropriate Federal banking agency, based on the member bank's most recent consolidated Report of Condition and Income filed under 12 U.S.C. 1817(a)(3);

(2) The balance of a member bank's allowance for loan and lease losses not included in its tier 2 capital under the risk-based capital guidelines of the appropriate Federal banking agen-

cy, based on the member bank's most recent consolidated Report of Condition and Income filed under 12 U.S.C. 1817(a)(3); and

(3) The amount of any investment by a member bank in a financial subsidiary that counts as a covered transaction and is required to be deducted from the member bank's capital for regulatory capital purposes.

(e) *Carrying value* with respect to a security means (unless otherwise provided) the value of the security on the financial statements of the member bank, determined in accordance with GAAP.

(f) *Company* means a corporation, partnership, limited liability company, business trust, association, or similar organization and, unless specifically excluded, includes a member bank and a depository institution.

(g) *Control.*

(1) *In general.* "Control" by a company or shareholder over another company means that:

(i) The company or shareholder, directly or indirectly, or acting through one or more other persons, owns, controls, or has power to vote 25 percent or more of any class of voting securities of the other company;

(ii) The company or shareholder controls in any manner the election of a majority of the directors, trustees, or general partners (or individuals exercising similar functions) of the other company; or

(iii) The Board determines, after notice and opportunity for hearing, that the company or shareholder, directly or indirectly, exercises a controlling influence over the management or policies of the other company.

(2) *Ownership or control of shares as fiduciary.* Notwithstanding any other provision of this regulation, no company will be deemed to control another company by virtue of its ownership or control of shares in a fiduciary capacity, except as provided in paragraph (a)(3) of Sec. 223.2 or if the company owning or controlling the shares is a business trust.

(3) *Ownership or control of securities by subsidiary.* A company controls securities, assets, or other ownership interests owned or controlled, directly or indirectly, by any subsidiary

(including a subsidiary depository institution) of the company.

(4) *Ownership or control of convertible instruments.* A company or shareholder that owns or controls instruments (including options or warrants) that are convertible or exercisable, at the option of the holder or owner, into securities, controls the securities, unless the company or shareholder presents information to the Board that demonstrates, to the Board's satisfaction, that the company or shareholder should not be deemed to control the securities.

(5) *Ownership or control of nonvoting securities.* A company or shareholder that owns or controls 25 percent or more of the equity capital of another company controls the other company, unless the company or shareholder presents information to the Board that demonstrates, to the Board's satisfaction, that the company or shareholder does not control the other company.

(h) *Covered transaction with respect to an affiliate* means:

(1) An extension of credit to the affiliate;

(2) A purchase of, or an investment in, a security issued by the affiliate;

(3) A purchase of an asset from the affiliate, including an asset subject to recourse or an agreement to repurchase, except such purchases of real and personal property as may be specifically exempted by the Board by order or regulation;

(4) The acceptance of a security issued by the affiliate as collateral for an extension of credit to any person or company; and

(5) The issuance of a guarantee, acceptance, or letter of credit, including an endorsement or standby letter of credit, on behalf of the affiliate, a confirmation of a letter of credit issued by the affiliate, and a cross-affiliate netting arrangement.

(i) *Credit transaction with an affiliate* means:

(1) An extension of credit to the affiliate;

(2) An issuance of a guarantee, acceptance, or letter of credit, including an endorsement or standby letter of credit, on behalf of the affiliate and a confirmation of a letter of credit issued by the affiliate; and

(3) A cross-affiliate netting arrangement.

(j) *Cross-affiliate netting arrangement* means an arrangement among a member bank, one or more affiliates of the member bank, and one or more nonaffiliates of the member bank in which:

(1) A nonaffiliate is permitted to deduct any obligations of an affiliate of the member bank to the nonaffiliate when settling the nonaffiliate's obligations to the member bank; or

(2) The member bank is permitted or required to add any obligations of its affiliate to a nonaffiliate when determining the member bank's obligations to the nonaffiliate.

(k) "*Depository institution*" means, unless otherwise noted, an insured depository institution (as defined in section 3 of the Federal Deposit Insurance Act (12 U.S.C. 1813)), but does not include any branch of a foreign bank. For purposes of this definition, an operating subsidiary of a depository institution is treated as part of the depository institution.

(*l*) "*Derivative transaction*" means any derivative contract listed in sections III.E.1.a. through d. of Appendix A to 12 CFR part 225 and any similar derivative contract, including a credit derivative contract.

(m) "*Eligible affiliated mutual fund securities*" has the meaning specified in paragraph (c)(2) of Sec. 223.24.

(n) "*Equity capital*" means:

(1) With respect to a corporation, preferred stock, common stock, capital surplus, retained earnings, and accumulated other comprehensive income, less treasury stock, plus any other account that constitutes equity of the corporation; and

(2) With respect to a partnership, limited liability company, or other company, equity accounts similar to those described in paragraph (n)(1) of this section.

(*o*) "*Extension of credit*" to an affiliate means the making or renewal of a loan, the granting of a line of credit, or the extending of credit in any manner whatsoever, including on an intraday basis, to an affiliate. An extension of credit to an affiliate includes, without limitation:

(1) An advance to an affiliate by means of an overdraft, cash item, or otherwise;

(2) A sale of Federal funds to an affiliate;

(3) A lease that is the functional equivalent of an extension of credit to an affiliate;

(4) An acquisition by purchase, discount, exchange, or otherwise of a note or other obligation, including commercial paper or other debt securities, of an affiliate;

(5) Any increase in the amount of, extension of the maturity of, or adjustment to the interest rate term or other material term of, an extension of credit to an affiliate; and

(6) Any other similar transaction as a result of which an affiliate becomes obligated to pay money (or its equivalent).

(p) "Financial subsidiary"

(1) In general. Except as provided in paragraph (p)(2) of this section, the term "financial subsidiary" means any subsidiary of a member bank that:

(i) Engages, directly or indirectly, in any activity that national banks are not permitted to engage in directly or that is conducted under terms and conditions that differ from those that govern the conduct of such activity by national banks; and

(ii) Is not a subsidiary that a national bank is specifically authorized to own or control by the express terms of a Federal statute (other than 12 U.S.C. 24a), and not by implication or interpretation.

(2) Exceptions. "Financial subsidiary" does not include:

(i) A subsidiary of a member bank that is considered a financial subsidiary under paragraph (p)(1) of this section solely because the subsidiary engages in the sale of insurance as agent or broker in a manner that is not permitted for national banks; and

(ii) A subsidiary of a State bank (other than a subsidiary described in section 46(a) of the Federal Deposit Insurance Act (12 U.S.C. 1831w(a))) that is considered a financial subsidiary under paragraph (p)(1) of this section solely because the subsidiary engages in one or more of the following activities:

(A) An activity that the State bank may engage in directly under applicable Federal and State law and that is conducted under the same terms and conditions that govern the conduct of the activity by the State bank; and

(B) An activity that the subsidiary was authorized by applicable Federal and State law

to engage in prior to December 12, 2002, and that was lawfully engaged in by the subsidiary on that date.

(3) Subsidiaries of financial subsidiaries. If a company is a financial subsidiary under paragraphs (p)(1) and (p)(2) of this section, any subsidiary of such a company is also a financial subsidiary.

(q) "Foreign bank" and an "agency," "branch," or "commercial lending company" of a foreign bank have the same meanings as in section 1(b) of the International Banking Act of 1978 (12 U.S.C. 3101).

(r) "GAAP" means U.S. generally accepted accounting principles.

(s) "General purpose credit card" has the meaning specified in paragraph (c)(4)(ii) of Sec. 223.16.

(t) In contemplation. A transaction between a member bank and a nonaffiliate is presumed to be "in contemplation" of the nonaffiliate becoming an affiliate of the member bank if the member bank enters into the transaction with the nonaffiliate after the execution of, or commencement of negotiations designed to result in, an agreement under the terms of which the nonaffiliate would become an affiliate.

(u) "Intraday extension of credit" has the meaning specified in paragraph (l)(2) of Sec. 223.42.

(v) "Low-quality asset" means:

(1) An asset (including a security) classified as "substandard," "doubtful," or "loss," or treated as "special mention" or "other transfer risk problems," either in the most recent report of examination or inspection of an affiliate prepared by either a Federal or State supervisory agency or in any internal classification system used by the member bank or the affiliate (including an asset that receives a rating that is substantially equivalent to "classified" or "special mention" in the internal system of the member bank or affiliate);

(2) An asset in a nonaccrual status;

(3) An asset on which principal or interest payments are more than thirty days past due;

(4) An asset whose terms have been renegotiated or compromised due to the deteriorating financial condition of the obligor; and

(5) An asset acquired through foreclosure, repossession, or otherwise in satisfaction of a

debt previously contracted, if the asset has not yet been reviewed in an examination or inspection.

(w) "Member bank" means any national bank, State bank, banking association, or trust company that is a member of the Federal Reserve System. For purposes of this definition, an operating subsidiary of a member bank is treated as part of the member bank.

(x) "Municipal securities" has the same meaning as in section 3(a)(29) of the Securities Exchange Act of 1934 (17 U.S.C. 78c(a)(29)).

(y) "Nonaffiliate" with respect to a member bank means any person that is not an affiliate of the member bank.

(z) "Obligations of, or fully guaranteed as to principal and interest by, the United States or its agencies" includes those obligations listed in 12 CFR 201.108(b) and any additional obligations as determined by the Board. The term does not include Federal Housing Administration or Veterans Administration loans.

(aa) "Operating subsidiary" with respect to a member bank or other depository institution means any subsidiary of the member bank or depository institution other than a subsidiary described in paragraphs (b)(1)(i) through (v) of Sec. 223.2.

(bb) "Person" means an individual, company, trust, joint venture, pool, syndicate, sole proprietorship, unincorporated organization, or any other form of entity.

(cc) "Principal underwriter" has the meaning specified in paragraph (c)(1) of Sec. 223.53.

(dd) "Purchase of an asset" by a member bank from an affiliate means the acquisition by a member bank of an asset from an affiliate in exchange for cash or any other consideration, including an assumption of liabilities. The merger of an affiliate into a member bank is a purchase of assets by the member bank from an affiliate if the member bank assumes any liabilities of the affiliate or pays any other form of consideration in the transaction.

(ee) Riskless principal. A company is "acting exclusively as a riskless principal" if, after receiving an order to buy (or sell) a security from a customer, the company purchases (or sells) the security in the secondary market for its own account to offset a contemporaneous sale to (or purchase from) the customer.

(ff) "Securities" means stocks, bonds, debentures, notes, or similar obligations (including commercial paper).

(gg) "Securities affiliate" with respect to a member bank means:

(1) An affiliate of the member bank that is registered with the Securities and Exchange Commission as a broker or dealer; or

(2) Any other securities broker or dealer affiliate of a member bank that is approved by the Board.

(hh) "State bank" has the same meaning as in section 3 of the Federal Deposit Insurance Act (12 U.S.C. 1813).

(ii) "Subsidiary" with respect to a specified company means a company that is controlled by the specified company.

(jj) "Voting securities" has the same meaning as in 12 CFR 225.2.

(kk) "Well capitalized" has the same meaning as in 12 CFR 225.2 and, in the case of any holding company that is not a bank holding company, "well capitalized" means that the holding company has and maintains at least the capital levels required for a bank holding company to be well capitalized under 12 CFR 225.2.

(ll) "Well managed" has the same meaning as in 12 CFR 225.2.

Sec. 223.11 What is the maximum amount of covered transactions that a member bank may enter into with any single affiliate?

A member bank may not engage in a covered transaction with an affiliate (other than a financial subsidiary of the member bank) if the aggregate amount of the member bank's covered transactions with such affiliate would exceed 10 percent of the capital stock and surplus of the member bank.

Sec. 223.12 What is the maximum amount of covered transactions that a member bank may enter into with all affiliates?

A member bank may not engage in a covered transaction with any affiliate if the aggregate amount of the member bank's covered transactions with all affiliates would exceed 20 percent of the capital stock and surplus of the member bank.

Sec. 223.13 What safety and soundness requirement applies to covered transactions?

A member bank may not engage in any covered transaction, including any transaction exempt under this regulation, unless the transaction is on terms and conditions that are consistent with safe and sound banking practices.

Sec. 223.14 What are the collateral requirements for a credit transaction with an affiliate?

(a) Collateral required for extensions of credit and certain other covered transactions. A member bank must ensure that each of its credit transactions with an affiliate is secured by the amount of collateral required by paragraph (b) of this section at the time of the transaction.

(b) Amount of collateral required.

(1) The rule. A credit transaction described in paragraph (a) of this section must be secured by collateral having a market value equal to at least:

(i) 100 percent of the amount of the transaction, if the collateral is:

(A) Obligations of the United States or its agencies;

(B) Obligations fully guaranteed by the United States or its agencies as to principal and interest;

(C) Notes, drafts, bills of exchange, or bankers' acceptances that are eligible for rediscount or purchase by a Federal Reserve Bank; or

(D) A segregated, earmarked deposit account with the member bank that is for the sole purpose of securing credit transactions between the member bank and its affiliates and is identified as such;

(ii) 110 percent of the amount of the transaction, if the collateral is obligations of any State or political subdivision of any State;

(iii) 120 percent of the amount of the transaction, if the collateral is other debt instruments, including loans and other receivables; or

(iv) 130 percent of the amount of the transaction, if the collateral is stock, leases, or other real or personal property.

(2) Example. A member bank makes a $1,000 loan to an affiliate. The affiliate posts as collateral for the loan $500 in U.S. Treasury securities, $480 in corporate debt securities, and $130 in real estate. The loan satisfies the collateral requirements of this section because $500 of the loan is 100 percent secured by obligations of the United States, $400 of the loan is 120 percent secured by debt instruments, and $100 of the loan is 130 percent secured by real estate.

(c) Ineligible collateral. The following items are not eligible collateral for purposes of this section:

(1) Low-quality assets;

(2) Securities issued by any affiliate;

(3) Equity securities issued by the member bank, and debt securities issued by the member bank that represent regulatory capital of the member bank;

(4) Intangible assets (including servicing assets), unless specifically approved by the Board; and

(5) Guarantees, letters of credit, and other similar instruments.

(d) Perfection and priority requirements for collateral.

(1) Perfection. A member bank must maintain a security interest in collateral required by this section that is perfected and enforceable under applicable law, including in the event of default resulting from bankruptcy, insolvency, liquidation, or similar circumstances.

(2) Priority. A member bank either must obtain a first priority security interest in collateral required by this section or must deduct from the value of collateral obtained by the member bank the lesser of:

(i) The amount of any security interest in the collateral that is senior to that of the member bank; or

(ii) The amount of any credit secured by the collateral that is senior to that of the member bank.

(3) Example. A member bank makes a $2,000 loan to an affiliate. The affiliate grants the member bank a second priority security inter-

est in a piece of real estate valued at $3,000. Another institution that previously lent $1,000 to the affiliate has a first priority security interest in the entire parcel of real estate. This transaction is not in compliance with the collateral requirements of this section. Due to the existence of the prior third-party lien on the real estate, the effective value of the real estate collateral for the member bank for purposes of this section is only $2,000—$600 less than the amount of real estate collateral required by this section for the transaction ($2,000 x 130 percent = $2,600).

(e) *Replacement requirement for retired or amortized collateral.* A member bank must ensure that any required collateral that subsequently is retired or amortized is replaced with additional eligible collateral as needed to keep the percentage of the collateral value relative to the amount of the outstanding credit transaction equal to the minimum percentage required at the inception of the transaction.

(f) *Inapplicability of the collateral requirements to certain transactions.* The collateral requirements of this section do not apply to the following transactions.

(1) *Acceptances.* An acceptance that already is fully secured either by attached documents or by other property that is involved in the transaction and has an ascertainable market value.

(2) *The unused portion of certain extensions of credit.* The unused portion of an extension of credit to an affiliate as long as the member bank does not have any legal obligation to advance additional funds under the extension of credit until the affiliate provides the amount of collateral required by paragraph (b) of this section with respect to the entire used portion (including the amount of the requested advance) of the extension of credit.

(3) *Purchases of affiliate debt securities in the secondary market.* The purchase of a debt security issued by an affiliate as long as the member bank purchases the debt security from a nonaffiliate in a bona fide secondary market transaction.

Sec. 223.15 May a member bank purchase a low-quality asset from an affiliate?

(a) *In general.* A member bank may not purchase a low-quality asset from an affiliate unless, pursuant to an independent credit evaluation,

the member bank had committed itself to purchase the asset before the time the asset was acquired by the affiliate.

(b) *Exemption for renewals of loan participations involving problem loans.* The prohibition contained in paragraph (a) of this section does not apply to the renewal of, or extension of additional credit with respect to, a member bank's participation in a loan to a nonaffiliate that was originated by an affiliate if:

(1) The loan was not a low-quality asset at the time the member bank purchased its participation;

(2) The renewal or extension of additional credit is approved, as necessary to protect the participating member bank's investment by enhancing the ultimate collection of the original indebtedness, by the board of directors of the participating member bank or, if the originating affiliate is a depository institution, by:

(i) An executive committee of the board of directors of the participating member bank; or

(ii) One or more senior management officials of the participating member bank, if:

(A) The board of directors of the member bank approves standards for the member bank's renewals or extensions of additional credit described in this paragraph (b), based on the determination set forth in paragraph (b)(2) of this section;

(B) Each renewal or extension of additional credit described in this paragraph (b) meets the standards; and

(C) The board of directors of the member bank periodically reviews renewals and extensions of additional credit described in this paragraph (b) to ensure that they meet the standards and periodically reviews the standards to ensure that they continue to meet the criterion set forth in paragraph (b)(2) of this section;

(3) The participating member bank's share of the renewal or extension of additional credit does not exceed its proportional share of the original transaction by more than 5 percent, unless the member bank obtains the prior written approval of its appropriate Federal banking agency; and

(4) The participating member bank provides its appropriate Federal banking agency with written notice of the renewal or extension of additional credit not later than 20 days after consummation.

Sec. 223.16 What transactions by a member bank with any person are treated as transactions with an affiliate?

(a) *In general.* A member bank must treat any of its transactions with any person as a transaction with an affiliate to the extent that the proceeds of the transaction are used for the benefit of, or transferred to, an affiliate.

(b) *Certain agency transactions.*

(1) Except to the extent described in paragraph (b)(2) of this section, an extension of credit by a member bank to a nonaffiliate is not treated as an extension of credit to an affiliate under paragraph (a) of this section if:

(i) The proceeds of the extension of credit are used to purchase an asset through an affiliate of the member bank, and the affiliate is acting exclusively as an agent or broker in the transaction; and

(ii) The asset purchased by the nonaffiliate is not issued, underwritten, or sold as principal by any affiliate of the member bank.

(2) The interpretation set forth in paragraph (b)(1) of this section does not apply to the extent of any agency fee, brokerage commission, or other compensation received by an affiliate from the proceeds of the extension of credit. The receipt of such compensation may qualify, however, for the exemption contained in paragraph (c)(2) of this section.

(c) *Exemptions.* Notwithstanding paragraph (a) of this section, the following transactions are not subject to the quantitative limits of Sec. Sec. 223.11 and 223.12 or the collateral requirements of Sec. 223.14. The transactions are, however, subject to the safety and soundness requirement of Sec. 223.13 and the market terms requirement and other provisions of subpart F (implementing section 23B).

(1) *Certain riskless principal transactions.* An extension of credit by a member bank to a nonaffiliate, if:

(i) The proceeds of the extension of credit are used to purchase a security through a securities affiliate of the member bank, and

the securities affiliate is acting exclusively as a riskless principal in the transaction;

(ii) The security purchased by the nonaffiliate is not issued, underwritten, or sold as principal (other than as riskless principal) by any affiliate of the member bank; and

(iii) Any riskless principal mark-up or other compensation received by the securities affiliate from the proceeds of the extension of credit meets the market terms standard set forth in paragraph (c)(2) of this section.

(2) *Brokerage commissions, agency fees, and riskless principal mark-ups.* An affiliate's retention of a portion of the proceeds of an extension of credit described in paragraph (b) or (c)(1) of this section as a brokerage commission, agency fee, or riskless principal mark-up, if that commission, fee, or mark-up is substantially the same as, or lower than, those prevailing at the same time for comparable transactions with or involving other nonaffiliates, in accordance with the market terms requirement of Sec. 223.51.

(3) *Preexisting lines of credit.* An extension of credit by a member bank to a nonaffiliate, if:

(i) The proceeds of the extension of credit are used to purchase a security from or through a securities affiliate of the member bank; and

(ii) The extension of credit is made pursuant to, and consistent with any conditions imposed in, a preexisting line of credit that was not established in contemplation of the purchase of securities from or through an affiliate of the member bank.

(4) *General purpose credit card transactions.*

(i) *In general.* An extension of credit by a member bank to a nonaffiliate, if:

(A) The proceeds of the extension of credit are used by the nonaffiliate to purchase a product or service from an affiliate of the member bank; and

(B) The extension of credit is made pursuant to, and consistent with any conditions imposed in, a general purpose credit card issued by the member bank to the nonaffiliate.

(ii) *Definition.* "General purpose credit card" means a credit card issued by a member bank that is widely accepted by merchants that are not affiliates of the member bank for the purchase of products or services, if:

(A) Less than 25 percent of the total value of products and services purchased with the card by all cardholders are purchases of products and services from one or more affiliates of the member bank;

(B) All affiliates of the member bank would be permissible for a financial holding company (as defined in 12 U.S.C. 1841) under section 4 of the Bank Holding Company Act (12 U.S.C. 1843), and the member bank has no reason to believe that 25 percent or more of the total value of products and services purchased with the card by all cardholders are or would be purchases of products and services from one or more affiliates of the member bank; or

(C) The member bank presents information to the Board that demonstrates, to the Board's satisfaction, that less than 25 percent of the total value of products and services purchased with the card by all cardholders are and would be purchases of products and services from one or more affiliates of the member bank.

(iii) *Calculating compliance.* To determine whether a credit card qualifies as a general purpose credit card under the standard set forth in paragraph (c)(4)(ii)(A) of this section, a member bank must compute compliance on a monthly basis, based on cardholder purchases that were financed by the credit card during the preceding 12 calendar months. If a credit card has qualified as a general purpose credit card for 3 consecutive months but then ceases to qualify in the following month, the member bank may continue to treat the credit card as a general purpose credit card for such month and three additional months (or such longer period as may be permitted by the Board).

(iv) *Example of calculating compliance with the 25 percent test.* A member bank seeks to qualify a credit card as a general purpose credit card under paragraph (c)(4)(ii)(A) of this section. The member bank assesses its compliance under paragraph (c)(4)(iii) of this section on the 15th day of every month (for the preceding 12 calendar months). The credit card qualifies as a general purpose

credit card for at least three consecutive months. On June 15, 2005, however, the member bank determines that, for the 12–calendar-month period from June 1, 2004, through May 31, 2005, 27 percent of the total value of products and services purchased with the card by all cardholders were purchases of products and services from an affiliate of the member bank. Unless the credit card returns to compliance with the 25 percent limit by the 12–calendar-month period ending August 31, 2005, the card will cease to qualify as a general purpose credit card as of September 1, 2005. Any outstanding extensions of credit under the credit card that were used to purchase products or services from an affiliate of the member bank would become covered transactions at such time.

Sec. 223.41 What covered transactions are exempt from the quantitative limits and collateral requirements?

The following transactions are not subject to the quantitative limits of Sec. Sec. 223.11 and 223.12 or the collateral requirements of Sec. 223.14. The transactions are, however, subject to the safety and soundness requirement of Sec. 223.13 and the prohibition on the purchase of a low-quality asset of Sec. 223.15.

(a) *Parent institution/subsidiary institution transactions.* Transactions with a depository institution if the member bank controls 80 percent or more of the voting securities of the depository institution or the depository institution controls 80 percent or more of the voting securities of the member

(b) *Transactions between a member bank and a depository institution owned by the same holding company.* Transactions with a depository institution if the same company controls 80 percent or more of the voting securities of the member bank and the depository institution.

(c) *Certain loan purchases from an affiliated depository institution.* Purchasing a loan on a non-recourse basis from an affiliated depository institution.

(d) *Internal corporate reorganization transactions.* Purchasing assets from an affiliate (including in connection with a transfer of securities issued by an affiliate to a member bank described in paragraph (a) of Sec. 223.31), if:

(1) The asset purchase is part of an internal corporate reorganization of a holding company and involves the transfer of all or substantially all of the shares or assets of an affiliate or of a division or department of an affiliate;

(2) The member bank provides its appropriate Federal banking agency and the Board with written notice of the transaction before consummation, including a description of the primary business activities of the affiliate and an indication of the proposed date of the asset purchase;

(3) The member bank's top-tier holding company commits to its appropriate Federal banking agency and the Board before consummation either:

(i) To make quarterly cash contributions to the member bank, for a two-year period following the member bank's purchase, equal to the book value plus any write-downs taken by the member bank, of any transferred assets that have become low-quality assets during the quarter; or

(ii) To repurchase, on a quarterly basis for a two-year period following the member bank's purchase, at a price equal to the book value plus any write-downs taken by the member bank, any transferred assets that have become low-quality assets during the quarter;

(4) The member bank's top-tier holding company complies with the commitment made under paragraph (d)(3) of this section;

(5) A majority of the member bank's directors reviews and approves the transaction before consummation;

(6) The value of the covered transaction (as computed under this part), when aggregated with the value of any other covered transactions (as computed under this part) engaged in by the member bank under this exemption during the preceding 12 calendar months, represents less than 10 percent of the member bank's capital stock and surplus (or such higher amount, up to 25 percent of the member bank's capital stock and surplus, as may be permitted by the member bank's appropriate Federal banking agency after conducting a review of the member bank's financial condition and the quality of the assets transferred to the member bank); and

(7) The holding company and all its subsidiary member banks and other subsidiary depository institutions are well capitalized and well managed and would remain well capitalized upon consummation of the transaction.

Sec. 223.42 What covered transactions are exempt from the quantitative limits, collateral requirements, and low-quality asset prohibition?

The following transactions are not subject to the quantitative limits of Sec. Sec. 223.11 and 223.12, the collateral requirements of Sec. 223.14, or the prohibition on the purchase of a low-quality asset of Sec. 223.15. The transactions are, however, subject to the safety and soundness requirement of Sec. 223.13.

(a) Making correspondent banking deposits. Making a deposit in an affiliated depository institution (as defined in section 3 of the Federal Deposit Insurance Act (12 U.S.C. 1813)) or affiliated foreign bank that represents an ongoing, working balance maintained in the ordinary course of correspondent business.

(b) Giving credit for uncollected items. Giving immediate credit to an affiliate for uncollected items received in the ordinary course of business.

(c) Transactions secured by cash or U.S. government securities.

(1) In general. Engaging in a credit transaction with an affiliate to the extent that the transaction is and remains secured by:

(i) Obligations of the United States or its agencies;

(ii) Obligations fully guaranteed by the United States or its agencies as to principal and interest; or

(iii) A segregated, earmarked deposit account with the member bank that is for the sole purpose of securing credit transactions between the member bank and its affiliates and is identified as such.

(2) Example. A member bank makes a $100 non-amortizing term loan to an affiliate secured by U.S. Treasury securities with a market value of $50 and real estate with a market value of $75. The value of the covered transaction is $50. If the market value of the U.S. Treasury securities falls to $45 during the life of the loan, the value of the covered transaction would increase to $55.

(d) *Purchasing securities of a servicing affiliate.* Purchasing a security issued by any company engaged solely in providing services described in section 4(c)(1) of the Bank Holding Company Act (12 U.S.C. 1843(c)(1)).

(e) *Purchasing certain liquid assets.* Purchasing an asset having a readily identifiable and publicly available market quotation and purchased at or below the asset's current market quotation. An asset has a readily identifiable and publicly available market quotation if the asset's price is quoted routinely in a widely disseminated publication that is readily available to the general public.

(f) *Purchasing certain marketable securities.* Purchasing a security from a securities affiliate, if:

(1) The security has a "ready market," as defined in 17 CFR 240.15c3–1(c)(11)(i);

(2) The security is eligible for a State member bank to purchase directly, subject to the same terms and conditions that govern the investment activities of a State member bank, and the member bank records the transaction as a purchase of a security for purposes of its Call Report, consistent with the requirements for a State member bank;

(3) The security is not a low-quality asset;

(4) The member bank does not purchase the security during an underwriting, or within 30 days of an underwriting, if an affiliate is an underwriter of the security, unless the security is purchased as part of an issue of obligations of, or obligations fully guaranteed as to principal and interest by, the United States or its agencies;

(5) The security's price is quoted routinely on an unaffiliated electronic service that provides indicative data from real-time financial networks, provided that:

(i) The price paid by the member bank is at or below the current market quotation for the security; and

(ii) The size of the transaction executed by the member bank does not cast material doubt on the appropriateness of relying on the current market quotation for the security; and

(6) The member bank maintains, for a period of two years, records and supporting information that are sufficient to enable the appropri-ate Federal banking agency to ensure the member bank's compliance with the terms of this exemption.

(g) *Purchasing municipal securities.* Purchasing a municipal security from a securities affiliate if:

(1) The security is rated by a nationally recognized statistical rating organization or is part of an issue of securities that does not exceed $25 million;

(2) The security is eligible for purchase by a State member bank, subject to the same terms and conditions that govern the investment activities of a State member bank, and the member bank records the transaction as a purchase of a security for purposes of its Call Report, consistent with the requirements for a State member bank; and

(3) (i) The security's price is quoted routinely on an unaffiliated electronic service that provides indicative data from real-time financial networks, provided that:

(A) The price paid by the member bank is at or below the current market quotation for the security; and

(B) The size of the transaction executed by the member bank does not cast material doubt on the appropriateness of relying on the current market quotation for the security; or

(ii) The price paid for the security can be verified by reference to two or more actual, current price quotes from unaffiliated broker-dealers on the exact security to be purchased or a security comparable to the security to be purchased, where:

(A) The price quotes obtained from the unaffiliated broker-dealers are based on a transaction similar in size to the transaction that is actually executed; and

(B) The price paid is no higher than the average of the price quotes; or

(iii) The price paid for the security can be verified by reference to the written summary provided by the syndicate manager to syndicate members that discloses the aggregate par values and prices of all bonds sold from the syndicate account, if the member bank:

(A) Purchases the municipal security during the underwriting period at a price that is at or below that indicated in the summary; and

(B) Obtains a copy of the summary from its securities affiliate and retains the summary for three years.

(h) Purchasing an extension of credit subject to a repurchase agreement. Purchasing from an affiliate an extension of credit that was originated by the member bank and sold to the affiliate subject to a repurchase agreement or with recourse.

(i) Asset purchases by a newly formed member bank. The purchase of an asset from an affiliate by a newly formed member bank, if the appropriate Federal banking agency for the member bank has approved the asset purchase in writing in connection with its review of the formation of the member bank.

(j) Transactions approved under the Bank Merger Act. Any merger or consolidation between a member bank and an affiliated depository institution or U.S. branch or agency of a foreign bank, or any acquisition of assets or assumption of deposit liabilities by a member bank from an affiliated depository institution or U.S. branch or agency of a foreign bank, if the transaction has been approved by the responsible Federal banking agency pursuant to the Bank Merger Act (12 U.S.C. 1828(c)).

(k) Purchasing an extension of credit from an affiliate. Purchasing from an affiliate, on a nonrecourse basis, an extension of credit, if:

(1) The extension of credit was originated by the affiliate;

(2) The member bank makes an independent evaluation of the creditworthiness of the borrower before the affiliate makes or commits to make the extension of credit;

(3) The member bank commits to purchase the extension of credit before the affiliate makes or commits to make the extension of credit;

(4) The member bank does not make a blanket advance commitment to purchase extensions of credit from the affiliate; and

(5) The dollar amount of the extension of credit, when aggregated with the dollar amount of all other extensions of credit purchased from the affiliate during the preceding 12 calendar months by the member bank and its depository institution affiliates, does not represent more than 50 percent (or such lower percent as is imposed by the member bank's appropriate Federal banking agency) of the dollar amount of extensions of credit originated by the affiliate during the preceding 12 calendar months.

(l) Intraday extensions of credit.

(1) In general. An intraday extension of credit to an affiliate, if the member bank:

(i) Has established and maintains policies and procedures reasonably designed to manage the credit exposure arising from the member bank's intraday extensions of credit to affiliates in a safe and sound manner, including policies and procedures for:

(A) Monitoring and controlling the credit exposure arising at any one time from the member bank's intraday extensions of credit to each affiliate and all affiliates in the aggregate; and

(B) Ensuring that any intraday extension of credit by the member bank to an affiliate complies with the market terms requirement of Sec. 223.51;

(ii) Has no reason to believe that the affiliate will have difficulty repaying the extension of credit in accordance with its terms; and

(iii) Ceases to treat any such extension of credit (regardless of jurisdiction) as an intraday extension of credit at the end of the member bank's business day in the United States.

(2) Definition. Intraday extension of credit by a member bank to an affiliate means an extension of credit by a member bank to an affiliate that the member bank expects to be repaid, sold, or terminated, or to qualify for a complete exemption under this regulation, by the end of its business day in the United States.

(m) Riskless principal transactions. Purchasing a security from a securities affiliate of the member bank if:

(1) The member bank or the securities affiliate is acting exclusively as a riskless principal in the transaction; and

(2) The security purchased is not issued, underwritten, or sold as principal (other than as riskless principal) by any affiliate of the member bank.

Sec. 223.43 What are the standards under which the Board may grant additional exemptions from the requirements of section 23A?

(a) The standards. The Board may, at its discretion, by regulation or order, exempt transactions or relationships from the requirements of section 23A and subparts B, C, and D of this part if it finds such exemptions to be in the public interest and consistent with the purposes of section 23A.

(b) Procedure. A member bank may request an exemption from the requirements of section 23A and subparts B, C, and D of this part by submitting a written request to the General Counsel of the Board. Such a request must:

(1) Describe in detail the transaction or relationship for which the member bank seeks exemption;

(2) Explain why the Board should exempt the transaction or relationship; and

(3) Explain how the exemption would be in the public interest and consistent with the purposes of section 23A.

Sec. 223.51 What is the market terms requirement of section 23B?

A member bank may not engage in a transaction described in Sec. 223.52 unless the transaction is:

(a) On terms and under circumstances, including credit standards, that are substantially the same, or at least as favorable to the member bank, as those prevailing at the time for comparable transactions with or involving nonaffiliates; or

(b) In the absence of comparable transactions, on terms and under circumstances, including credit standards, that in good faith would be offered to, or would apply to, nonaffiliates.

Sec. 223.52 What transactions with affiliates or others must comply with section 23B's market terms requirement?

(a) The market terms requirement of Sec. 223.51 applies to the following transactions:

(1) Any covered transaction with an affiliate, unless the transaction is exempt under paragraphs (a) through (c) of Sec. 223.41 or paragraphs (a) through (e) or (h) through (j) of Sec. 223.42;

(2) The sale of a security or other asset to an affiliate, including an asset subject to an agreement to repurchase;

(3) The payment of money or the furnishing of a service to an affiliate under contract, lease, or otherwise;

(4) Any transaction in which an affiliate acts as an agent or broker or receives a fee for its services to the member bank or to any other person; and

(5) Any transaction or series of transactions with a nonaffiliate, if an affiliate:

(i) Has a financial interest in the nonaffiliate; or

(ii) Is a participant in the transaction or series of transactions.

(b) For the purpose of this section, any transaction by a member bank with any person will be deemed to be a transaction with an affiliate of the member bank if any of the proceeds of the transaction are used for the benefit of, or transferred to, the affiliate.

Sec. 223.53 What asset purchases are prohibited by section 23B?

(a) Fiduciary purchases of assets from an affiliate. A member bank may not purchase as fiduciary any security or other asset from any affiliate unless the purchase is permitted:

(1) Under the instrument creating the fiduciary relationship;

(2) By court order; or

(3) By law of the jurisdiction governing the fiduciary relationship.

(b) Purchase of a security underwritten by an affiliate.

(1) A member bank, whether acting as principal or fiduciary, may not knowingly purchase or otherwise acquire, during the existence of any underwriting or selling syndicate, any security if a principal underwriter of that security is an affiliate of the member bank.

(2) Paragraph (b)(1) of this section does not apply if the purchase or acquisition of the security has been approved, before the security is initially offered for sale to the public, by a majority of the directors of the member bank based on a determination that the purchase is a sound investment for the member bank, or

for the person on whose behalf the member bank is acting as fiduciary, as the case may be, irrespective of the fact that an affiliate of the member bank is a principal underwriter of the security.

(3) The approval requirement of paragraph (b)(2) of this section may be met if:

(i) A majority of the directors of the member bank approves standards for the member bank's acquisitions of securities described in paragraph (b)(1) of this section, based on the determination set forth in paragraph (b)(2) of this section;

(ii) Each acquisition described in paragraph (b)(1) of this section meets the standards; and

(iii) A majority of the directors of the member bank periodically reviews acquisitions described in paragraph (b)(1) of this section to ensure that they meet the standards and periodically reviews the standards to ensure that they continue to meet the criterion set forth in paragraph (b)(2) of this section.

(4) A U.S. branch, agency, or commercial lending company of a foreign bank may comply with paragraphs (b)(2) and (b)(3) of this section by obtaining the approvals and reviews required by paragraphs (b)(2) and (b)(3) from either:

(i) A majority of the directors of the foreign bank; or

(ii) A majority of the senior executive officers of the foreign bank.

(c) Special definitions. For purposes of this section:

(1) "Principal underwriter" means any underwriter who, in connection with a primary distribution of securities:

(i) Is in privity of contract with the issuer or an affiliated person of the issuer;

(ii) Acting alone or in concert with one or more other persons, initiates or directs the formation of an underwriting syndicate; or

(iii) Is allowed a rate of gross commission, spread, or other profit greater than the rate allowed another underwriter participating in the distribution.

(2) "Security" has the same meaning as in section 3(a)(10) of the Securities Exchange Act of 1934 (15 U.S.C. 78c(a)(10)).

PART 225. Bank Holding Companies And Change In Bank Control (Regulation Y)

Sec. 225.21 Prohibited nonbanking activities and acquisitions; exempt bank holding companies.

[Source: Reg. Y, 62 FR 9329, Feb. 28, 1997, unless otherwise noted.]

(a) Prohibited nonbanking activities and acquisitions. Except as provided in Sec. 225.22 of this subpart, a bank holding company or a subsidiary may not engage in, or acquire or control, directly or indirectly, voting securities or assets of a company engaged in, any activity other than:

(1) Banking or managing or controlling banks and other subsidiaries authorized under the BHC Act; and

(2) An activity that the Board determines to be so closely related to banking, or managing or controlling banks as to be a proper incident thereto, including any incidental activities that are necessary to carry on such an activity, if the bank holding company has obtained the prior approval of the Board for that activity in accordance with the requirements of this regulation.

(b) Exempt bank holding companies. The following bank holding companies are exempt from the provisions of this subpart:

(1) Family-owned companies. Any company that is a "company covered in 1970" (as defined in section 2(b) of the BHC Act), more than 85 percent of the voting securities of which was collectively owned on June 30, 1968, and continuously thereafter, by members of the same family (or their spouses) who are lineal descendants of common ancestors.

(2) Labor, agricultural, and horticultural organizations. Any company that was on January 4, 1977, both a bank holding company and a labor, agricultural, or horticultural organization exempt from taxation under section 501 of the Internal Revenue Code (26 U.S.C. 501(c)).

(3) Companies granted hardship exemption. Any bank holding company that has controlled only one bank since before July 1, 1968, and

that has been granted an exemption by the Board under section 4(d) of the BHC Act, subject to any conditions imposed by the Board.

(4) Companies granted exemption on other grounds. Any company that acquired control of a bank before December 10, 1982, without the Board's prior approval under section 3 of the BHC Act, on the basis of a narrow interpretation of the term demand deposit or commercial loan, if the Board has determined that:

(i) Coverage of the company as a bank holding company under this subpart would be unfair or represent an unreasonable hardship; and

(ii) Exclusion of the company from coverage under this part is consistent with the purposes of the BHC Act and section 106 of the Bank Holding Company Act Amendments of 1970 (12 U.S.C. 1971, 1972(1)). The provisions of Sec. 225.4 of subpart A of this part do not apply to a company exempt under this paragraph.

Sec. 225.22 Exempt nonbanking activities and acquisitions.

(a) Certain de novo activities. A bank holding company may, either directly or indirectly, engage de novo in any nonbanking activity listed in Sec. 225.28(b) (other than operation of an insured depository institution) without obtaining the Board's prior approval if the bank holding company:

(1) Meets the requirements of paragraphs (c) (1), (2), and (6) of Sec. 225.23;

(2) Conducts the activity in compliance with all Board orders and regulations governing the activity; and

(3) Within 10 business days after commencing the activity, provides written notice to the appropriate Reserve Bank describing the activity, identifying the company or companies engaged in the activity, and certifying that the activity will be conducted in accordance with the Board's orders and regulations and that the bank holding company meets the requirements of paragraphs (c) (1), (2), and (6) of Sec. 225.23.

(b) Servicing activities. A bank holding company may, without the Board's prior approval under this subpart, furnish services to or perform services for, or establish or acquire a company that engages solely in servicing activities for:

(1) The bank holding company or its subsidiaries in connection with their activities as authorized by law, including services that are necessary to fulfill commitments entered into by the subsidiaries with third parties, if the bank holding company or servicing company complies with the Board's published interpretations and does not act as principal in dealing with third parties; and

(2) The internal operations of the bank holding company or its subsidiaries. Services for the internal operations of the bank holding company or its subsidiaries include, but are not limited to:

(i) Accounting, auditing, and appraising;

(ii) Advertising and public relations;

(iii) Data processing and data transmission services, data bases, or facilities;

(iv) Personnel services;

(v) Courier services;

(vi) Holding or operating property used wholly or substantially by a subsidiary in its operations or for its future use;

(vii) Liquidating property acquired from a subsidiary;

(viii) Liquidating property acquired from any sources either prior to May 9, 1956, or the date on which the company became a bank holding company, whichever is later; and

(ix) Selling, purchasing, or underwriting insurance, such as blanket bond insurance, group insurance for employees, and property and casualty insurance.

(c) Safe deposit business. A bank holding company or nonbank subsidiary may, without the Board's prior approval, conduct a safe deposit business, or acquire voting securities of a company that conducts such a business.

(d) Nonbanking acquisitions not requiring prior Board approval. The Board's prior approval is not required under this subpart for the following acquisitions:

(1) DPC acquisitions.

(i) Voting securities or assets, acquired by foreclosure or otherwise, in the ordinary course of collecting a debt previously contracted (DPC property) in good faith, if the DPC property is divested within two years of acquisition.

(ii) The Board may, upon request, extend this two-year period for up to three additional years. The Board may permit additional extensions for up to 5 years (for a total of 10 years), for shares, real estate or other assets where the holding company demonstrates that each extension would not be detrimental to the public interest and either the bank holding company has made good faith attempts to dispose of such shares, real estate or other assets or disposal of the shares, real estate or other assets during the initial period would have been detrimental to the company.

(iii) Transfers of DPC property within the bank holding company system do not extend any period for divestiture of the property.

(2) Securities or assets required to be divested by subsidiary. Voting securities or assets required to be divested by a subsidiary at the request of an examining federal or state authority (except by the Board under the BHC Act or this regulation), if the bank holding company divests the securities or assets within two years from the date acquired from the subsidiary.

(3) Fiduciary investments. Voting securities or assets acquired by a bank or other company (other than a trust that is a company) in good faith in a fiduciary capacity, if the voting securities or assets are:

(i) Held in the ordinary course of business; and

(ii) Not acquired for the benefit of the company or its shareholders, employees, or subsidiaries.

(4) Securities eligible for investment by national bank. Voting securities of the kinds and amounts explicitly eligible by federal statute (other than section 4 of the Bank Service Corporation Act, 12 U.S.C. 1864) for investment by a national bank, and voting securities acquired prior to June 30, 1971, in reliance on section 4(c)(5) of the BHC Act and interpretations of the Comptroller of the Currency under section 5136 of the Revised Statutes (12 U.S.C. 24(7)).

(5) Securities or property representing 5 percent or less of a company. Voting securities of a company or property that, in the aggregate, represent 5 percent or less of the outstanding shares of any class of voting securities of a company, or that represent a 5 percent interest or less in the property, subject to the provisions of 12 CFR 225.137.

(6) Securities of investment company. Voting securities of an investment company that is solely engaged in investing in securities and that does not own or control more than 5 percent of the outstanding shares of any class of voting securities of any company.

(7) Assets acquired in ordinary course of business. Assets of a company acquired in the ordinary course of business, subject to the provisions of 12 CFR 225.132, if the assets relate to activities in which the acquiring company has previously received Board approval under this regulation to engage.

(8) Asset acquisitions by lending company or industrial bank. Assets of an office(s) of a company, all or substantially all of which relate to making, acquiring, or servicing loans if:

(i) The acquiring company has previously received Board approval under this regulation or is not required to obtain prior Board approval under this regulation to engage in lending activities or industrial banking activities;

(ii) The assets acquired during any 12-month period do not represent more than 50 percent of the risk-weighted assets (on a consolidated basis) of the acquiring lending company or industrial bank, or more than $100 million, whichever amount is less;

(iii) The assets acquired do not represent more than 50 percent of the selling company's consolidated assets that are devoted to lending activities or industrial banking business;

(iv) The acquiring company notifies the Reserve Bank of the acquisition within 30 days after the acquisition; and

(v) The acquiring company, after giving effect to the transaction, meets the Board's Capital Adequacy Guidelines (Appendix A of this part), and the Board has not previously notified the acquiring company that it may not acquire assets under the exemption in this paragraph.

(e) Acquisition of securities by subsidiary banks—

(1) National bank. A national bank or its subsidiary may, without the Board's approval under this subpart, acquire or retain securities on the basis of section 4(c)(5) of the BHC Act in accordance with the regulations of the Comptroller of the Currency.

(2) State bank. A state-chartered bank or its subsidiary may, insofar as federal law is concerned, and without the Board's prior approval under this subpart:

(i) Acquire or retain securities, on the basis of section 4(c)(5) of the BHC Act, of the kinds and amounts explicitly eligible by federal statute for investment by a national bank; or

(ii) Acquire or retain all (but, except for directors' qualifying shares, not less than all) of the securities of a company that engages solely in activities in which the parent bank may engage, at locations at which the bank may engage in the activity, and subject to the same limitations as if the bank were engaging in the activity directly.

(f) Activities and securities of new bank holding companies. A company that becomes a bank holding company may, for a period of two years, engage in nonbanking activities and control voting securities or assets of a nonbank subsidiary, if the bank holding company engaged in such activities or controlled such voting securities or assets on the date it became a bank holding company. The Board may grant requests for up to three one-year extensions of the two-year period.

(g) Grandfathered activities and securities. Unless the Board orders divestiture or termination under section 4(a)(2) of the BHC Act, a "company covered in 1970," as defined in section 2(b) of the BHC Act, may:

(1) Retain voting securities or assets and engage in activities that it has lawfully held or engaged in continuously since June 30, 1968; and

(2) Acquire voting securities of any newly formed company to engage in such activities.

(h) Securities or activities exempt under Regulation K. A bank holding company may acquire voting securities or assets and engage in activities as authorized in Regulation K (12 CFR part 211).

Sec. 225.28 List of permissible nonbanking activities.

(a) Closely related nonbanking activities. The activities listed in paragraph (b) of this section are so closely related to banking or managing or controlling banks as to be a proper incident thereto, and may be engaged in by a bank holding company or its subsidiary in accordance with the requirements of this regulation.

(b) Activities determined by regulation to be permissible

(1) Extending credit and servicing loans. Making, acquiring, brokering, or servicing loans or other extensions of credit (including factoring, issuing letters of credit and accepting drafts) for the company's account or for the account of others.

(2) Activities related to extending credit. Any activity usual in connection with making, acquiring, brokering or servicing loans or other extensions of credit, as determined by the Board. The Board has determined that the following activities are usual in connection with making, acquiring, brokering or servicing loans or other extensions of credit:

(i) Real estate and personal property appraising. Performing appraisals of real estate and tangible and intangible personal property, including securities.

(ii) Arranging commercial real estate equity financing. Acting as intermediary for the financing of commercial or industrial income-producing real estate by arranging for the transfer of the title, control, and risk of such a real estate project to one or more investors, if the bank holding company and its affiliates do not have an interest in, or participate in managing or developing, a real estate project for which it arranges equity financing, and do not promote or sponsor the development of the property.

(iii) Check-guaranty services. Authorizing a subscribing merchant to accept personal checks tendered by the merchant's customers in payment for goods and services, and purchasing from the merchant validly authorized checks that are subsequently dishonored.

(iv) *Collection agency services.* Collecting overdue accounts receivable, either retail or commercial.

(v) *Credit bureau services.* Maintaining information related to the credit history of consumers and providing the information to a credit grantor who is considering a borrower's application for credit or who has extended credit to the borrower.

(vi) *Asset management, servicing, and collection activities.* Engaging under contract with a third party in asset management, servicing, and collection[1] of assets of a type that an insured depository institution may originate and own, if the company does not engage in real property management or real estate brokerage services as part of these services.

(vii) *Acquiring debt in default.* Acquiring debt that is in default at the time of acquisition, if the company:

(A) Divests shares or assets securing debt in default that are not permissible investments for bank holding companies, within the time period required for divestiture of property acquired in satisfaction of a debt previously contracted under Sec. 225.12(b);[2]

(B) Stands only in the position of a creditor and does not purchase equity of obligors of debt in default (other than equity that may be collateral for such debt); and

(C) Does not acquire debt in default secured by shares of a bank or bank holding company.

(viii) *Real estate settlement servicing.* Providing real estate settlement services.[3]

(3) *Leasing personal or real property.* Leasing personal or real property or acting as agent, broker, or adviser in leasing such property if:

(i) The lease is on a nonoperating basis;[4]

(ii) The initial term of the lease is at least 90 days;

(iii) In the case of leases involving real property:

(A) At the inception of the initial lease, the effect of the transaction will yield a return that will compensate the lessor for not less than the lessor's full investment in the property plus the estimated total cost of financing the property over the term of the lease from rental payments, estimated tax benefits, and the estimated residual value of the property at the expiration of the initial lease; and

(B) The estimated residual value of property for purposes of paragraph (b)(3)(iii)(A) of this section shall not exceed 25 percent of the acquisition cost of the property to the lessor.

(4) *Operating nonbank depository institutions—*

(i) *Industrial banking.* Owning, controlling, or operating an industrial bank, Morris Plan bank, or industrial loan company, so long as the institution is not a bank.

(ii) *Operating savings association.* Owning, controlling, or operating a savings association, if the savings association engages only in deposit-taking activities, lending, and other activities that are permissible for bank holding companies under this subpart C.

---

1. [n.2] Asset management services include acting as agent in the liquidation or sale of loans and collateral for loans, including real estate and other assets acquired through foreclosure or in satisfaction of debts previously contracted.

2. [n.3] For this purpose, the divestiture period for property begins on the date that the debt is acquired, regardless of when legal title to the property is acquired.

3. [n.4] For purposes of this section, real estate settlement services do not include providing title insurance as principal, agent, or broker.

4. [n.5] The requirement that the lease be on a nonoperating basis means that the bank holding company may not, directly or indirectly, engage in operating, servicing, maintaining, or repairing leased property during the lease term. For purposes of the leasing of automobiles, the requirement that the lease be on a nonoperating basis means that the bank holding company may not, directly or indirectly: (1) Provide servicing, repair, or maintenance of the leased vehicle during the lease term; (2) purchase parts and accessories in bulk or for an individual vehicle after the lessee has taken delivery of the vehicle; (3) provide the loan of an automobile during servicing of the leased vehicle; (4) purchase insurance for the lessee; or (5) provide for the renewal of the vehicle's license merely as a service to the lessee where the lessee could renew the license without authorization from the lessor. The bank holding company may arrange for a third party to provide these services or products.

(5) *Trust company functions.* Performing functions or activities that may be performed by a trust company (including activities of a fiduciary, agency, or custodial nature), in the manner authorized by federal or state law, so long as the company is not a bank for purposes of section 2(c) of the Bank Holding Company Act.

(6) *Financial and investment advisory activities.* Acting as investment or financial advisor to any person, including (without, in any way, limiting the foregoing):

(i) Serving as investment adviser (as defined in section 2(a)(20) of the Investment Company Act of 1940, 15 U.S.C. 80a–2(a)(20)), to an investment company registered under that act, including sponsoring, organizing, and managing a closed-end investment company;

(ii) Furnishing general economic information and advice, general economic statistical forecasting services, and industry studies;

(iii) Providing advice in connection with mergers, acquisitions, divestitures, investments, joint ventures, leveraged buyouts, recapitalizations, capital structurings, financing transactions and similar transactions, and conducting financial feasibility studies;[5]

(iv) Providing information, statistical forecasting, and advice with respect to any transaction in foreign exchange, swaps, and similar transactions, commodities, and any forward contract, option, future, option on a future, and similar instruments;

(v) Providing educational courses, and instructional materials to consumers on individual financial management matters; and

(vi) Providing tax-planning and tax-preparation services to any person.

(7) *Agency transactional services for customer investments—*

(i) *Securities brokerage.* Providing securities brokerage services (including securities clearing and/or securities execution services on an exchange), whether alone or in combination with investment advisory services, and incidental activities (including related securities credit activities and custodial services), if the securities brokerage services are restricted to buying and selling securities solely as agent for the account of customers and do not include securities underwriting or dealing.

(ii) *Riskless principal transactions.* Buying and selling in the secondary market all types of securities on the order of customers as a "riskless principal" to the extent of engaging in a transaction in which the company, after receiving an order to buy (or sell) a security from a customer, purchases (or sells) the security for its own account to offset a contemporaneous sale to (or purchase from) the customer.

This does not include:

(A) Selling bank-ineligible securities[6] at the order of a customer that is the issuer of the securities, or selling bank-ineligible securities in any transaction where the company has a contractual agreement to place the securities as agent of the issuer; or

(B) Acting as a riskless principal in any transaction involving a bank-ineligible security for which the company or any of its affiliates acts as underwriter (during the period of the underwriting or for 30 days thereafter) or dealer.[7]

(iii) *Private placement services.* Acting as agent for the private placement of securities in accordance with the requirements of the Securities Act of 1933 (1933 Act) and the rules of the Securities and Exchange Commission, if the company engaged in the activity does not purchase or repurchase for its own account the securities being placed, or hold in inventory unsold portions of issues of these securities.

---

5. [n.6] Feasibility studies do not include assisting management with the planning or marketing for a given project or providing general operational or management advice.

6. [n.7] A bank-ineligible security is any security that a State member bank is not permitted to underwrite or deal in under 12 U.S.C. 24 and 335.

7. [n.8] A company or its affiliates may not enter quotes for specific bank-ineligible securities in any dealer quotation system in connection with the company's riskless principal transactions; except that the company or its affiliates may enter "bid" or "ask" quotations, or publish "offering wanted" or "bid wanted" notices on trading systems other than NASDAQ or an exchange, if the company or its affiliate does not enter price quotations on different sides of the market for a particular security during any two-day period.

(iv) Futures commission merchant. Acting as a futures commission merchant (FCM) for unaffiliated persons in the execution, clearance, or execution and clearance of any futures contract and option on a futures contract traded on an exchange in the United States or abroad if:

(A) The activity is conducted through a separately incorporated subsidiary of the bank holding company, which may engage in activities other than FCM activities (including, but not limited to, permissible advisory and trading activities); and

(B) The parent bank holding company does not provide a guarantee or otherwise become liable to the exchange or clearing association other than for those trades conducted by the subsidiary for its own account or for the account of any affiliate.

(v) Other transactional services. Providing to customers as agent transactional services with respect to swaps and similar transactions, any transaction described in paragraph (b)(8) of this section, any transaction that is permissible for a state member bank, and any other transaction involving a forward contract, option, futures, option on a futures or similar contract (whether traded on an exchange or not) relating to a commodity that is traded on an exchange.

(8) Investment transactions as principal–

(i) Underwriting and dealing in government obligations and money market instruments. Underwriting and dealing in obligations of the United States, general obligations of states and their political subdivisions, and other obligations that state member banks of the Federal Reserve System may be authorized to underwrite and deal in under 12 U.S.C. 24 and 335, including banker's acceptances and certificates of deposit, under the same limitations as would be applicable if the activity were performed by the bank holding company's subsidiary member banks or its subsidiary nonmember banks as if they were member banks.

(ii) Investing and trading activities. Engaging as principal in:

(A) Foreign exchange;

(B) Forward contracts, options, futures, options on futures, swaps, and similar contracts, whether traded on exchanges or not, based on any rate, price, financial asset (including gold, silver, platinum, palladium, copper, or any other metal approved by the Board), nonfinancial asset, or group of assets, other than a bank-ineligible security,[8] if:

(1) A state member bank is authorized to invest in the asset underlying the contract;

(2) The contract requires cash settlement;

(3) The contract allows for assignment, termination, or offset prior to delivery or expiration, and the company—

(i) Makes every reasonable effort to avoid taking or making delivery of the asset underlying the contract; or

(ii) Receives and instantaneously transfers title to the underlying asset, by operation of contract and without taking or making physical delivery of the asset; or

(4) The contract does not allow for assignment, termination, or offset prior to delivery or expiration and is based on an asset for which futures contracts or options on futures contracts have been approved for trading on a U.S. contract market by the Commodity Futures Trading Commission, and the company—

(i) Makes every reasonable effort to avoid taking or making delivery of the asset underlying the contract; or

(ii) Receives and instantaneously transfers title to the underlying asset, by operation of contract and without taking or making physical delivery of the asset.

(C) Forward contracts, options,[9] futures, options on futures, swaps, and similar con-

---

8. [n.9] A bank-ineligible security is any security that a state member bank is not permitted to underwrite or deal in under 12 U.S.C. 24 and 335.

9. [n.10] This reference does not include acting as a dealer in options based on indices of bank-ineligible securities when the options are traded on securities exchanges.

These options are securities for purposes of the federal securities laws and bank-ineligible securities for purposes of section 20 of the Glass–Steagall Act, 12 U.S.C. 337. Similarly, this reference does not include acting as a dealer in any other instrument that is a bank-ineligible security for purposes of section 20. A bank holding compa-

tracts, whether traded on exchanges or not, based on an index of a rate, a price, or the value of any financial asset, nonfinancial asset, or group of assets, if the contract requires cash settlement.

(iii) Buying and selling bullion, and related activities. Buying, selling and storing bars, rounds, bullion, and coins of gold, silver, platinum, palladium, copper, and any other metal approved by the Board, for the company's own account and the account of others, and providing incidental services such as arranging for storage, safe custody, assaying, and shipment.

(9) Management consulting and counseling activities–

(i) Management consulting.

(A) Providing management consulting advice:[10]

(1) On any matter to unaffiliated depository institutions, including commercial banks, savings and loan associations, savings banks, credit unions, industrial banks, Morris Plan banks, cooperative banks, industrial loan companies, trust companies, and branches or agencies of foreign banks;

(2) On any financial, economic, accounting, or audit matter to any other company.

(B) A company conducting management consulting activities under this subparagraph and any affiliate of such company may not:

(1) Own or control, directly or indirectly, more than 5 percent of the voting securities of the client institution; and

(2) Allow a management official, as defined in 12 CFR 212.2(h), of the company or any of its affiliates to serve as a management official of the client institution, except where such interlocking relationship is permitted pursuant to an exemption granted under 12 CFR 212.4(b) or otherwise permitted by the Board.

(C) A company conducting management consulting activities may provide management consulting services to customers not described in paragraph (b)(9)(i)(A)(1) of this section or regarding matters not described in paragraph (b)(9)(i)(A)(2) of this section, if the total annual revenue derived from those management consulting services does not exceed 30 percent of the company's total annual revenue derived from management consulting activities.

(ii) Employee benefits consulting services. Providing consulting services to employee benefit, compensation and insurance plans, including designing plans, assisting in the implementation of plans, providing administrative services to plans, and developing employee communication programs for plans.

(iii) Career counseling services. Providing career counseling services to:

(A) A financial organization[11] and individuals currently employed by, or recently displaced from, a financial organization;

(B) Individuals who are seeking employment at a financial organization; and

(C) Individuals who are currently employed in or who seek positions in the finance, accounting, and audit departments of any company.

(10) Support services–

(i) Courier services. Providing courier services for:

(A) Checks, commercial papers, documents, and written instruments (excluding currency or bearer-type negotiable instruments) that are exchanged among banks and financial institutions; and

(B) Audit and accounting media of a banking or financial nature and other business records and documents used in processing

ny may deal in these instruments in accordance with the Board's orders on dealing in bank-ineligible securities.

10. [n.11] In performing this activity, bank holding companies are not authorized to perform tasks or operations or provide services to client institutions either on a daily or continuing basis, except as necessary to instruct the client institution on how to perform such services for itself. See also the Board's interpretation of bank management consulting advice (12 CFR 225.131).

11. [n.12] Financial organization refers to insured depository institution holding companies and their subsidiaries, other than nonbanking affiliates of diversified savings and loan holding companies that engage in activities not permissible under section 4(c)(8) of the Bank Holding Company Act (12 U.S.C. 1842(c)(8)).

such media.[12]

(ii) Printing and selling MICR-encoded items. Printing and selling checks and related documents, including corporate image checks, cash tickets, voucher checks, deposit slips, savings withdrawal packages, and other forms that require Magnetic Ink Character Recognition (MICR) encoding.

(11) Insurance agency and underwriting–

(i) Credit insurance. Acting as principal, agent, or broker for insurance (including home mortgage redemption insurance) that is:

(A) Directly related to an extension of credit by the bank holding company or any of its subsidiaries; and

(B) Limited to ensuring the repayment of the outstanding balance due on the extension of credit[13] in the event of the death, disability, or involuntary unemployment of the debtor.

(ii) Finance company subsidiary. Acting as agent or broker for insurance directly related to an extension of credit by a finance company[14] that is a subsidiary of a bank holding company, if:

(A) The insurance is limited to ensuring repayment of the outstanding balance on such extension of credit in the event of loss or damage to any property used as collateral for the extension of credit; and

(B) The extension of credit is not more than $10,000, or $25,000 if it is to finance the purchase of a residential manufactured

home[15] and the credit is secured by the home; and

(C) The applicant commits to notify borrowers in writing that:

(1) They are not required to purchase such insurance from the applicant;

(2) Such insurance does not insure any interest of the borrower in the collateral; and

(3) The applicant will accept more comprehensive property insurance in place of such single-interest insurance.

(iii) Insurance in small towns. Engaging in any insurance agency activity in a place where the bank holding company or a subsidiary of the bank holding company has a lending office and that:

(A) Has a population not exceeding 5,000 (as shown in the preceding decennial census); or

(B) Has inadequate insurance agency facilities, as determined by the Board, after notice and opportunity for hearing.

(iv) Insurance-agency activities conducted on May 1, 1982. Engaging in any specific insurance-agency activity[16] if the bank holding company, or subsidiary conducting the specific activity, conducted such activity on May 1, 1982, or received Board approval to conduct such activity on or before May 1, 1982.[17] A bank holding company or subsidiary engaging in a specific insurance agency activity under this clause may:

(A) Engage in such specific insurance agency activity only at locations:

---

12. [n.13] See also the Board's interpretation on courier activities (12 CFR 225.129), which sets forth conditions for bank holding company entry into the activity.

13. [n.14] Extension of credit includes direct loans to borrowers, loans purchased from other lenders, and leases of real or personal property so long as the leases are nonoperating and full-payout leases that meet the requirements of paragraph (b)(3) of this section.

14. [n.15] Finance company includes all non-deposit-taking financial institutions that engage in a significant degree of consumer lending (excluding lending secured by first mortgages) and all financial institutions specifically defined by individual states as finance companies and that engage in a significant degree of consumer lending.

15. [n.16] These limitations increase at the end of each calendar year, beginning with 1982, by the percentage increase in the Consumer Price Index for Urban Wage Earners and Clerical Workers published by the Bureau of Labor Statistics.

16. [n.17] Nothing contained in this provision shall preclude a bank holding company subsidiary that is authorized to engage in a specific insurance-agency activity under this clause from continuing to engage in the particular activity after merger with an affiliate, if the merger is for legitimate business purposes and prior notice has been provided to the Board.

17. [n.18] For the purposes of this paragraph, activities engaged in on May 1, 1982, include activities carried on subsequently as the result of an application to engage in such activities pending before the Board on May 1, 1982, and approved subsequently by the Board or as the result of the acquisition by such company pursuant to a binding written contract entered into on or before May 1, 1982, of another company engaged in such activities at the time of the acquisition.

(1) In the state in which the bank holding company has its principal place of business (as defined in 12 U.S.C. 1842(d));

(2) In any state or states immediately adjacent to such state; and

(3) In any state in which the specific insurance-agency activity was conducted (or was approved to be conducted) by such bank holding company or subsidiary thereof or by any other subsidiary of such bank holding company on May 1, 1982; and

(B) Provide other insurance coverages that may become available after May 1, 1982, so long as those coverages insure against the types of risks as (or are otherwise functionally equivalent to) coverages sold or approved to be sold on May 1, 1982, by the bank holding company or subsidiary.

(v) Supervision of retail insurance agents. Supervising on behalf of insurance underwriters the activities of retail insurance agents who sell:

(A) Fidelity insurance and property and casualty insurance on the real and personal property used in the operations of the bank holding company or its subsidiaries; and

(B) Group insurance that protects the employees of the bank holding company or its subsidiaries.

(vi) Small bank holding companies. Engaging in any insurance-agency activity if the bank holding company has total consolidated assets of $50 million or less. A bank holding company performing insurance-agency activities under this paragraph may not engage in the sale of life insurance or annuities except as provided in paragraphs (b)(11) (i) and (iii) of this section, and it may not continue to engage in insurance-agency activities pursuant to this provision more than 90 days after the end of the quarterly reporting period in which total assets of the holding company and its subsidiaries exceed $50 million.

(vii) Insurance-agency activities conducted before 1971. Engaging in any insurance-agency activity performed at any location in the United States directly or indirectly by a bank holding company that was engaged in insurance-agency activities prior to January 1, 1971, as a consequence of approval by the Board prior to January 1, 1971.

(12) Community development activities–

(i) Financing and investment activities. Making equity and debt investments in corporations or projects designed primarily to promote community welfare, such as the economic rehabilitation and development of low-income areas by providing housing, services, or jobs for residents.

(ii) Advisory activities. Providing advisory and related services for programs designed primarily to promote community welfare.

(13) Money orders, savings bonds, and traveler's checks. The issuance and sale at retail of money orders and similar consumer-type payment instruments; the sale of U.S. savings bonds; and the issuance and sale of traveler's checks.

(14) Data processing.

(i) Providing data processing, data storage and data transmission services, facilities (including data processing, data storage and data transmission hardware, software, documentation, or operating personnel), databases, advice, and access to such services, facilities, or data-bases by any technological means, if:

(A) The data to be processed, stored or furnished are financial, banking or economic; and

(B) The hardware provided in connection therewith is offered only in conjunction with software designed and marketed for the processing, storage and transmission of financial, banking, or economic data, and where the general purpose hardware does not constitute more than 30 percent of the cost of any packaged offering.

(ii) A company conducting data processing, data storage, and data transmission activities may conduct data processing, data storage, and data transmission activities not described in paragraph (b)(14)(i) of this section if the total annual revenue derived from those activities does not exceed 49 percent of the company's total annual revenues derived from data processing, data storage and data transmission activities.

[68 FR 39810, July 3, 2003; 68 FR 41901, July 16, 2003; 68 FR 68499, Dec. 9, 2003]

Sec. 225.86 What activities are permissible for any financial holding company?

The following activities are financial in nature or incidental to a financial activity:

(a) Activities determined to be closely related to banking.

(1) Any activity that the Board had determined by regulation prior to November 12, 1999, to be so closely related to banking as to be a proper incident thereto, subject to the terms and conditions contained in this part, unless modified by the Board. These activities are listed in Sec. 225.28.

(2) Any activity that the Board had determined by an order that was in effect on November 12, 1999, to be so closely related to banking as to be a proper incident thereto, subject to the terms and conditions contained in this part and those in the authorizing orders. These activities are:

(i) Providing administrative and other services to mutual funds (Societe Generale, 84 Federal Reserve Bulletin 680 (1998));

(ii) Owning shares of a securities exchange (J.P. Morgan & Co, Inc., and UBS AG, 86 Federal Reserve Bulletin 61 (2000));

(iii) Acting as a certification authority for digital signatures and authenticating the identity of persons conducting financial and nonfinancial transactions (Bayerische Hypound Vereinsbank AG, et al., 86 Federal Reserve Bulletin 56 (2000));

(iv) Providing employment histories to third parties for use in making credit decisions and to depository institutions and their affiliates for use in the ordinary course of business (Norwest Corporation, 81 Federal Reserve Bulletin 732 (1995));

(v) Check cashing and wire transmission services (Midland Bank, PLC, 76 Federal Reserve Bulletin 860 (1990) (check cashing); Norwest Corporation, 81 Federal Reserve Bulletin 1130 (1995) (money transmission));

(vi) In connection with offering banking services, providing notary public services, selling postage stamps and postage-paid envelopes, providing vehicle registration services, and selling public transportation tickets and tokens (Popular, Inc., 84 Federal Reserve Bulletin 481 (1998)); and

(vii) Real estate title abstracting (The First National Company, 81 Federal Reserve Bulletin 805 (1995)).

(b) Activities determined to be usual in connection with the transaction of banking abroad. Any activity that the Board had determined by regulation in effect on November 11, 1999, to be usual in connection with the transaction of banking or other financial operations abroad (see Sec. 211.5(d) of this chapter), subject to the terms and conditions in part 211 and Board interpretations in effect on that date regarding the scope and conduct of the activity. In addition to the activities listed in paragraphs (a) and (c) of this section, these activities are:

(1) Providing management consulting services, including to any person with respect to nonfinancial matters, so long as the management consulting services are advisory and do not allow the financial holding company to control the person to which the services are provided;

(2) Operating a travel agency in connection with financial services offered by the financial holding company or others; and

(3) Organizing, sponsoring, and managing a mutual fund, so long as:

(i) The fund does not exercise managerial control over the entities in which the fund invests; and

(ii) The financial holding company reduces its ownership in the fund, if any, to less than 25 percent of the equity of the fund within one year of sponsoring the fund or such additional period as the Board permits.

(c) Activities permitted under section 4(k)(4) of the BHC Act (12 U.S.C. 1843(k)(4)). Any activity defined to be financial in nature under sections 4(k)(4)(A) through (E), (H) and (I) of the BHC Act (12 U.S.C. 1843(k)(4)(A) through (E), (H) and (I)).

(d) Activities determined to be financial in nature or incidental to financial activities by the Board—

(1) Acting as a finder—Acting as a finder in bringing together one or more buyers and sellers of any product or service for transactions that the parties themselves negotiate and consummate.

(i) What is the scope of finder activities? Acting as a finder includes providing any or all of the following services through any means–

(A) Identifying potential parties, making inquiries as to interest, introducing and referring potential parties to each other, and arranging contacts between and meetings of interested parties;

(B) Conveying between interested parties expressions of interest, bids, offers, orders and confirmations relating to a transaction; and

(C) Transmitting information concerning products and services to potential parties in connection with the activities described in paragraphs (d)(1)(i)(A) and (B) of this section.

(ii) What are some examples of finder services? The following are examples of the services that may be provided by a finder when done in accordance with paragraphs (d)(1)(iii) and (iv) of this section. These examples are not exclusive.

(A) Hosting an electronic marketplace on the financial holding company's Internet web site by providing hypertext or similar links to the web sites of third party buyers or sellers.

(B) Hosting on the financial holding company's servers the Internet web site of—

(1) A buyer (or seller) that provides information concerning the buyer (or seller) and the products or services it seeks to buy (or sell) and allows sellers (or buyers) to submit expressions of interest, bids, offers, orders and confirmations relating to such products or services; or

(2) A government or government agency that provides information concerning the services or benefits made available by the government or government agency, assists persons in completing applications to receive such services or benefits from the government or agency, and allows persons to transmit their applications for services or benefits to the government or agency.

(C) Operating an Internet web site that allows multiple buyers and sellers to exchange information concerning the products and services that they are willing to purchase or sell, locate potential counterparties for transactions, aggregate orders for goods or services with those made by other parties, and enter into transactions between themselves.

(D) Operating a telephone call center that provides permissible finder services.

(iii) What limitations are applicable to a financial holding company acting as a finder?

(A) A finder may act only as an intermediary between a buyer and a seller.

(B) A finder may not bind any buyer or seller to the terms of a specific transaction or negotiate the terms of a specific transaction on behalf of a buyer or seller, except that a finder may–

(1) Arrange for buyers to receive preferred terms from sellers so long as the terms are not negotiated as part of any individual transaction, are provided generally to customers or broad categories of customers, and are made available by the seller (and not by the financial holding company); and

(2) Establish rules of general applicability governing the use and operation of the finder service, including rules that–

(i) Govern the submission of bids and offers by buyers and sellers that use the finder service and the circumstances under which the finder service will match bids and offers submitted by buyers and sellers; and

(ii) Govern the manner in which buyers and sellers may bind themselves to the terms of a specific transaction.

(C) A finder may not–

(1) Take title to or acquire or hold an ownership interest in any product or service offered or sold through the finder service;

(2) Provide distribution services for physical products or services offered or sold through the finder service;

(3) Own or operate any real or personal property that is used for the purpose of manufacturing, storing, transporting, or assembling physical products offered or sold by third parties; or

(4) Own or operate any real or personal property that serves as a physical location for the physical purchase, sale or distribution of products or services offered or sold by third parties.

(D) A finder may not engage in any activity that would require the company to register or obtain a license as a real estate agent or broker under applicable law.

(iv) What disclosures are required? A finder must distinguish the products and services offered by the financial holding company from those offered by a third party through the finder service.

(2) [Reserved]

(e) Activities permitted under section 4(k)(5) of the Bank Holding Company Act (12 U.S.C. 1843(k)(5)).

(1) The following types of activities are financial in nature or incidental to a financial activity when conducted pursuant to a determination by the Board under paragraph (e)(2) of this section:

(i) Lending, exchanging, transferring, investing for others, or safeguarding financial assets other than money or securities;

(ii) Providing any device or other instrumentality for transferring money or other financial assets; and

(iii) Arranging, effecting, or facilitating financial transactions for the account of third parties.

(2) Review of specific activities.

(i) Is a specific request required? A financial holding company that wishes to engage on the basis of paragraph (e)(1) of this section in an activity that is not otherwise permissible for a financial holding company must obtain a determination from the Board that the activity is permitted under paragraph (e)(1).

(ii) Consultation with the Secretary of the Treasury. After receiving a request under this section, the Board will provide the Secretary of the Treasury with a copy of the request and consult with the Secretary in accordance with section 4(k)(2)(A) of the Bank Holding Company Act (12 U.S.C. 1843(k)(2)(A)).

(iii) Board action on requests. After consultation with the Secretary, the Board will promptly make a written determination regarding whether the specific activity described in the request is included in an activity category listed in paragraph (e)(1) of this section and is therefore either financial in nature or incidental to a financial activity.

(3) What factors will the Board consider? In evaluating a request made under this section, the Board will take into account the factors listed in section 4(k)(3) of the BHC Act (12 U.S.C. 1843(k)(3)) that it must consider when determining whether an activity is financial in nature or incidental to a financial activity.

(4) What information must the request contain? Any request by a financial holding company under this section must be in writing and must:

(i) Identify and define the activity for which the determination is sought, specifically describing what the activity would involve and how the activity would be conducted; and

(ii) Provide information supporting the requested determination, including information regarding how the proposed activity falls into one of the categories listed in paragraph (e)(1) of this section, and any other information required by the Board concerning the proposed activity.

[Reg. Y, 66 FR 415, Jan. 3, 2001, as amended at 66 FR 19081, Apr. 13, 2001]

Chapter III.   Federal Deposit Insurance Corporation
12 C.F.R. (Selected Sections)

Chapter IV.   Export–Import Bank of the United States

CODE OF FEDERAL REGULATIONS TITLE 12. BANKS AND BANKING

CHAPTER III. FEDERAL DEPOSIT INSURANCE CORPORATION
PART 330. Deposit Insurance Coverage

Sec. 330.1 Definitions.

For the purposes of this part:

(a) Act means the Federal Deposit Insurance Act (12 U.S.C. 1811 et seq.).

(b) Corporation means the Federal Deposit Insurance Corporation.

(c) Default has the same meaning as provided under section 3(x) of the Act (12 U.S.C. 1813(x)).

(d) Deposit has the same meaning as provided under section 3(*l*) of the Act (12 U.S.C. 1813(*l*)).

(e) Deposit account records means account ledgers, signature cards, certificates of deposit, passbooks, corporate resolutions authorizing accounts in the possession of the insured depository institution and other books and records of the insured depository institution, including records maintained by computer, which relate to the insured depository institution's deposit taking function, but does not mean account statements, deposit slips, items deposited or cancelled checks.

(f) FDIC means the Federal Deposit Insurance Corporation.

(g) Independent activity. A corporation, partnership or unincorporated association shall be deemed to be engaged in an "independent activity" if the entity is operated primarily for some purpose other than to increase deposit insurance.

(h) Insured branch means a branch of a foreign bank any deposits in which are insured in accordance with the provisions of the Act.

(i) Insured deposit has the same meaning as that provided under section 3(m)(1) of the Act (12 U.S.C. 1813(m)(1)).

(j) Insured depository institution is any depository institution whose deposits are insured pursuant to the Act, including a foreign bank having an insured branch.

(k) Natural person means a human being.

(*l*) Non-contingent trust interest means a trust interest capable of determination without evaluation of contingencies except for those covered by the present worth tables and rules of calculation for their use set forth in Sec. 20.2031–7 of the Federal Estate Tax Regulations (26 CFR 20.2031–7) or any similar present worth or life expectancy tables which may be adopted by the Internal Revenue Service.

(m) Sole proprietorship means a form of business in which one person owns all the assets of the business, in contrast to a partnership or corporation.

(n) Standard maximum deposit insurance amount, referred to as "the SMDIA" hereafter, means $100,000 adjusted pursuant to subparagraph (F) of section 11(a)(1) of the FDI Act (12 U.S.C. 1821(a)(1)(F)). The current SMDIA is $100,000. All the examples in this regulation use the current SMDIA of $100,000.

(o) Trust estate means the determinable and beneficial interest of a beneficiary or principal in trust funds but does not include the beneficial interest of an heir or devisee in a decedent's estate.

(p) Trust funds means funds held by an insured depository institution as trustee pursuant to any irrevocable trust established pursuant to any statute or written trust agreement.

(q) Trust interest means the interest of a beneficiary in an irrevocable express trust (other than an employee benefit plan) created either by written trust instrument or by statute, but does not include any interest retained by the settlor.

[71 FR 14631, March 23, 2006; 71 FR 53549, Sept. 12, 2006]

Sec. 330.2 Purpose.

The purpose of this part is to clarify the rules and define the terms necessary to afford deposit insurance coverage under the Act and provide rules for the recognition of deposit ownership in various circumstances.

Sec. 330.3 General principles.

(a) Ownership rights and capacities. The insurance coverage provided by the Act and this part is based upon the ownership rights and capacities in which deposit accounts are maintained at insured depository institutions. All deposits in an insured depository institution which are maintained in the same right and capacity (by or for the benefit of a particular depositor or depositors) shall be added together and insured in accordance with this part. Deposits maintained in different rights and capacities, as recognized under this part, shall be insured separately from each other. (Example: Single ownership accounts and joint ownership accounts are insured separately from each other.)

(b) Deposits maintained in separate insured depository institutions or in separate branches of the same insured depository institution. Any deposit accounts maintained by a depositor at one insured depository institution are insured separately from, and without regard to, any deposit accounts that the same depositor maintains at any other separately chartered and insured depository institution, even if two or more separately chartered and insured depository institutions are affiliated through common ownership. (Example: Deposits held by the same individual at two different banks owned by the same bank holding company would be insured separately, per bank.)

The deposit accounts of a depositor maintained in the same right and capacity at different branches or offices of the same insured depository institution are not separately insured; rather they shall be added together and insured in accordance with this part.

(c) Deposits maintained by foreigners and deposits denominated in foreign currency. The availability of deposit insurance is not limited to citizens and residents of the United States. Any person or entity that maintains deposits in an insured depository institution is entitled to the deposit insurance provided by the Act and this part. In addition, deposits denominated in a foreign currency shall be insured in accordance with this part. Deposit insurance for such deposits shall be determined and paid in the amount of United States dollars that is equivalent in value to the amount of the deposit denominated in the foreign currency as of close of business on the date of default of the insured depository institution. The exchange rates to be used for such conversions are the 12 PM rates (the "noon buying rates for cable transfers") quoted for major currencies by the Federal Reserve Bank of New York on the date of default of the insured depository institution, unless the deposit agreement specifies that some other widely recognized exchange rates are to be used for all purposes under that agreement, in which case, the rates so specified shall be used for such conversions.

(d) Deposits in insured branches of foreign banks. Deposits in an insured branch of a foreign bank which are payable by contract in the United States shall be insured in accordance with this part, except that any deposits to the credit of the foreign bank, or any office, branch, agency or any wholly owned subsidiary of the foreign bank, shall not be insured. All deposits held by a depositor in the same right and capacity in more than one insured branch of the same foreign bank shall be added together for the purpose of determining the amount of deposit insurance.

(e) Deposits payable solely outside of the United States and certain other locations. Any obligation of an insured depository institution which is payable solely at an office of such institution located outside the States of the United States, the District of Columbia, Puerto Rico, Guam, the Commonwealth of the Northern Mariana Islands, American Samoa, the Trust Territory of the Pacific Islands, and the Virgin Islands, is not a deposit for the purposes of this part.

(f) International banking facility deposits. An "international banking facility time deposit," as defined by the Board of Governors of the Federal Reserve System in Regulation D (12 CFR 204.8(a)(2)), or in any successor regulation, is not a deposit for the purposes of this part.

(g) Bank investment contracts. As required by section 11(a)(8) of the Act (12 U.S.C. 1821(a)(8)), any liability arising under any investment contract between any insured depository institution and any employee benefit plan which expressly permits "benefit responsive withdrawals or transfers" (as defined in section 11(a)(8) of the Act) are not insured deposits for purposes of this part. The term "substantial penalty or adjustment" used in section 11(a)(8) of the Act means, in the case of a deposit having an original term which exceeds one year, all interest earned on the amount withdrawn from the date of deposit or for six months, whichever is less; or, in the case of a deposit having an original term of one year or less, all interest earned on the amount withdrawn from the date of deposit or three months, whichever is less.

(h) Application of state or local law to deposit insurance determinations. In general, deposit insurance is for the benefit of the owner or owners of funds on deposit. However, while ownership under state law of deposited funds is a necessary condition for deposit insurance, ownership under state law is not sufficient for, or decisive in, determining deposit insurance coverage. Deposit insurance coverage is also a function of the deposit account records of the insured depository institution and of the provisions of this part, which, in the interest of uniform national rules for deposit insurance coverage, are controlling for purposes of determining deposit insurance coverage.

(i) Determination of the amount of a deposit–

(1) General rule. The amount of a deposit is the balance of principal and interest unconditionally credited to the deposit account as of the date of default of the insured depository institution, plus the ascertainable amount of interest to that date, accrued at the contract rate (or the anticipated or announced interest or dividend rate), which the insured depository institution in default would have paid if the deposit had matured on that date and the insured depository institution had not failed. In the absence of any such announced or anticipated interest or dividend rate, the rate for this purpose shall be whatever rate was paid in the immediately preceding payment period.

(2) Discounted certificates of deposit. The amount of a certificate of deposit sold by an insured depository institution at a discount from its face value is its original purchase price plus the amount of accrued earnings calculated by compounding interest annually at the rate necessary to increase the original purchase price to the maturity value over the life of the certificate.

(3) Waiver of minimum requirements. In the case of a deposit with a fixed payment date, fixed or minimum term, or a qualifying or notice period that has not expired as of such date, interest thereon to the date of closing shall be computed according to the terms of the deposit contract as if interest had been credited and as if the deposit could have been withdrawn on such date without any penalty or reduction in the rate of earnings.

(j) Continuation of insurance coverage following the death of a deposit owner. The death of a deposit owner shall not affect the insurance coverage of the deposit for a period of six months following the owner's death unless the deposit account is restructured. The operation of this grace period, however, shall not result in a reduc-

tion of coverage. If an account is not restructured within six months after the owner's death, the insurance shall be provided on the basis of actual ownership in accordance with the provisions of Sec. 330.5(a)(1).

[63 FR 25756, May 11, 1998, as amended at 64 FR 15656, Apr. 1, 1999]

Sec. 330.6 Single ownership accounts.

(a) Individual accounts. Funds owned by a natural person and deposited in one or more deposit accounts in his or her own name shall be added together and insured up to the SMDIA in the aggregate. Exception: Despite the general requirement in this paragraph (a), if more than one natural person has the right to withdraw funds from an individual account (excluding persons who have the right to withdraw by virtue of a Power of Attorney), the account shall be treated as a joint ownership account (although not necessarily a qualifying joint account) and shall be insured in accordance with the provisions of Sec. 330.9, unless the deposit account records clearly indicate, to the satisfaction of the FDIC, that the funds are owned by one individual and that other signatories on the account are merely authorized to withdraw funds on behalf of the owner.

(b) Sole proprietorship accounts. Funds owned by a business which is a "sole proprietorship" (as defined in Sec. 330.1(m)) and deposited in one or more deposit accounts in the name of the business shall be treated as the individual account(s) of the person who is the sole proprietor, added to any other individual accounts of that person, and insured up to the SMDIA in the aggregate.

(c) Single-name accounts containing community property funds. Community property funds deposited into one or more deposit accounts in the name of one member of a husband-wife community shall be treated as the individual account(s) of the named member, added to any other individual accounts of that person, and insured up to the SMDIA in the aggregate.

(d) Accounts of a decedent and accounts held by executors or administrators of a decedent's estate. Funds held in the name of a decedent or in the name of the executor, administrator, or other personal representative of his or her estate and deposited into one or more deposit accounts shall be added together and insured up to the SMDIA in the aggregate; provided, however, that nothing in this paragraph (d) shall affect the operation of

Sec. 330.3(j). The deposit insurance provided by this paragraph (d) shall be separate from any insurance coverage provided for the individual deposit accounts of the executor, administrator, other personal representative or the beneficiaries of the estate.

[71 FR 14631, March 23, 2006; 71 FR 53549, Sept. 12, 2006]

Sec. 330.9 Joint ownership accounts.

(a) *Separate insurance coverage.* Qualifying joint accounts, whether owned as joint tenants with the right of survivorship, as tenants in common or as tenants by the entirety, shall be insured separately from any individually owned (single ownership) deposit accounts maintained by the co-owners. (Example: If A has a single ownership account and also is a joint owner of a qualifying joint account, A's interest in the joint account would be insured separately from his or her interest in the individual account.) Qualifying joint accounts in the names of both husband and wife which are comprised of community property funds shall be added together and insured up to twice the SMDIA separately from any funds deposited into accounts bearing their individual names.

(b) *Determination of insurance coverage.* The interests of each co-owner in all qualifying joint accounts shall be added together and the total shall be insured up to the SMDIA. (Example: "A & B" have a qualifying joint account with a balance of $60,000; "A & C" have a qualifying joint account with a balance of $80,000; and "A & B & C" have a qualifying joint account with a balance of $150,000. A's combined ownership interest in all qualifying joint accounts would be $120,000 ($30,000 plus $40,000 plus $50,000); therefore, A's interest would be insured in the amount of $100,000 and uninsured in the amount of $20,000. B's combined ownership interest in all qualifying joint accounts would be $80,000 ($30,000 plus $50,000); therefore, B's interest would be fully insured. C's combined ownership interest in all qualifying joint accounts would be $90,000 ($40,000 plus $50,000); therefore, C's interest would be fully insured.)

(c) *Qualifying joint accounts.*

(1) A joint deposit account shall be deemed to be a qualifying joint account, for purposes of this section, only if:

(i) All co-owners of the funds in the account are "natural persons" (as defined in Sec. 330.1(k)); and

(ii) Each co-owner has personally signed a deposit account signature card; and

(iii) Each co-owner possesses withdrawal rights on the same basis.

(2) The signature-card requirement of paragraph (c)(1)(ii) of this section shall not apply to certificates of deposit, to any deposit obligation evidenced by a negotiable instrument, or to any account maintained by an agent, nominee, guardian, custodian or conservator on behalf of two or more persons.

(3) All deposit accounts that satisfy the criteria in paragraph (c)(1) of this section, and those accounts that come within the exception provided for in paragraph (c)(2) of this section, shall be deemed to be jointly owned provided that, in accordance with the provisions of Sec. 330.5(a), the FDIC determines that the deposit account records of the insured depository institution are clear and unambiguous as to the ownership of the accounts. If the deposit account records are ambiguous or unclear as to the manner in which the deposit accounts are owned, then the FDIC may, in its sole discretion, consider evidence other than the deposit account records of the insured depository institution for the purpose of establishing the manner in which the funds are owned. The signatures of two or more persons on the deposit account signature card or the names of two or more persons on a certificate of deposit or other deposit instrument shall be conclusive evidence that the account is a joint account (although not necessarily a qualifying joint account) unless the deposit records as a whole are ambiguous and some other evidence indicates, to the satisfaction of the FDIC, that there is a contrary ownership capacity.

(d) *Nonqualifying joint accounts.* A deposit account held in two or more names which is not a qualifying joint account, for purposes of this section, shall be treated as being owned by each named owner, as an individual, corporation, partnership, or unincorporated association, as the case may be, and the actual ownership interest of each individual or entity in such account shall be added to any other single ownership accounts of such individual or other accounts of such entity, and shall be insured in accordance with the provisions of this part governing the insurance of such accounts.

(e) *Determination of interests.* The interests of the co-owners of qualifying joint accounts, held as tenants in common, shall be deemed equal, unless otherwise stated in the depository institution's deposit account records. This section applies regardless of whether the conjunction "and" or "or" is used in the title of a joint deposit account, even when both terms are used, such as in the case of a joint deposit account with three or more co-owners.

[64 FR 15656, April 1, 1999; 64 FR 62102, Nov. 16, 1999; 71 FR 14631, March 23, 2006; 71 FR 53549, Sept. 12, 2006]

PART 337. Unsafe And Unsound Banking Practices

Sec. 337.1 Scope.

The provisions of this part apply to certain banking practices which are likely to have adverse effects on the safety and soundness of insured State nonmember banks or which are likely to result in violations of law, rule, or regulation.

Sec. 337.2 Standby letters of credit.

(a) *Definition.* As used in this section, the term standby letter of credit means any letter of credit, or similar arrangement however named or described, which represents an obligation to the beneficiary on the part of the issuer: (1) To repay money borrowed by or advanced to or for the account of the account party, or (2) to make payment on account of any indebtedness undertaken by the account party, or (3) to make payment on account of any default (including any statement of default) by the account party in the performance of an obligation.[1] The term similar arrangement includes the creation of an acceptance or similar undertaking.

(b) *Restriction.* A standby letter of credit issued by an insured State nonmember bank shall be combined with all other standby letters of credit and all loans for purposes of applying any legal limitation on loans of the bank (including limitations on loans to any one borrower, on loans to affiliates of the bank, or on aggregate loans); *Provided, however,* That if such standby letter of credit is subject to separate limitation under applicable State or federal law, then the separate limitation shall apply in lieu of the loan limitation.[2]

(c) *Exceptions.* All standby letters of credit shall be subject to the provisions of paragraph (b) of this section except where:

(1) Prior to or at the time of issuance, the issuing bank is paid an amount equal to the bank's maximum liability under the standby letter of credit; or,

(2) Prior to or at the time of issuance, the issuing bank has set aside sufficient funds in a segregated deposit account, clearly earmarked for that purpose, to cover the bank's maximum liability under the standby letter of credit.

(d) *Disclosure.* Each insured State nonmember bank must maintain adequate control and subsidiary records of its standby letters of credit comparable to the records maintained in connection with the bank's direct loans so that at all times the bank's potential liability thereunder and the bank's compliance with this section may be readily determined. In addition, all such standby letters of credit must be adequately reflected on the bank's published financial statements.

Sec. 337.3 Limits on extensions of credit to executive officers, directors, and principal shareholders of insured nonmember banks.

(a) With the exception of 12 CFR 215.5(b), 215.5(c)(3), 215.5(c)(4), and 215.11, insured nonmember banks are subject to the restrictions contained in subpart A of Federal Reserve Board Regulation O (12 CFR Part 215, subpart A) to the same extent and to the same manner as though they were member banks.

---

1. As defined in this paragraph (a), the term standby letter of credit would not include commercial letters of credit and similar instruments where the issuing bank expects the beneficiary to draw upon the issuer, which do not "guaranty" payment of a money obligation of the account party and which do not provide that payment is occasioned by default on the part of the account party.

2. Where the standby letter of credit is subject to a non-recourse participation agreement with another bank or other banks, this section shall apply to the issuer and each participant in the same manner as in the case of a participated loan.

(b) For the purposes of compliance with Sec. 215.4(b) of Federal Reserve Board Regulation O, no insured nonmember bank may extend credit or grant a line of credit to any of its executive officers, directors, or principal shareholders or to any related interest of any such person in an amount that, when aggregated with the amount of all other extensions of credit and lines of credit by the bank to that person and to all related interests of that person, exceeds the greater of $25,000 or five percent of the bank's capital and unimpaired surplus,[3] or $500,000 unless (1) the extension of credit or line of credit has been approved in advance by a majority of the entire board of directors of that bank and (2) the interested party has abstained from participating directly or indirectly in the voting.

(c) (1) No insured nonmember bank may extend credit in an aggregate amount greater than the amount permitted in paragraph (c)(2) of this section to a partnership in which one or more of the bank's executive officers are partners and, either individually or together, hold a majority interest. For the purposes of paragraph (c)(2) of this section, the total amount of credit extended by an insured nonmember bank to such partnership is considered to be extended to each executive officer of the insured nonmember bank who is a member of the partnership.

(2) An insured nonmember bank is authorized to extend credit to any executive officer of the bank for any other purpose not specified in Sec. 215.5(c)(1) and (2) of Federal Reserve Board Regulation O (12 CFR 215.5(c)(1) and (2)) if the aggregate amount of such other extensions of credit does not exceed at any one time the higher of 2.5 percent of the bank's capital and unimpaired surplus or $25,000 but in no event more than $100,000, provided, however, that no such extension of credit shall be subject to this limit if the extension of credit is secured by:

(i) A perfected security interest in bonds, notes, certificates of indebtedness, or Treasury bills of the United States or in other such obligations fully guaranteed as to principal and interest by the United States;

(ii) Unconditional takeout commitments or guarantees of any department, agency, bu-

reau, board, commission or establishment of the United States or any corporation wholly owned directly or indirectly by the United States; or

(iii) A perfected security interest in a segregated deposit account in the lending bank.

(3) Any extension of credit that was outstanding on May 28, 1992 and that would if made on or after that date violate paragraph (c)(1) or paragraph (c)(2) of this Sec. 337.3 shall be reduced in amount by May 28, 1993 so that the extension of credit is in compliance with the lending limit set forth in paragraphs (c)(1) and (c)(2) of this section. Any renewal or extension of such an extension of credit on or after May 28, 1992 shall be made only on terms that will bring the extension of credit into compliance with the lending limit of paragraphs (c)(1) and (c)(2) of this section by May 28, 1993, however, any extension of credit made before May 28, 1992 that bears a specific maturity date of May 28, 1993 or later shall be repaid in accordance with its repayment schedule in existence on or before May 28, 1992.

(4) If an insured nonmember bank is unable to bring all extensions of credit outstanding as of May 28, 1992 into compliance as required by paragraph (c)(3) of this Sec. 337.3, the bank may at the discretion of the appropriate FDIC regional director (Division of Supervision and Consumer Protection (DSC)) obtain, for good cause shown, not more than two additional one-year periods to come into compliance.

(5) For the purposes of paragraph (c) of this section, the definitions of the terms used in Federal Reserve Board Regulation O shall apply including the exclusion of executive officers of a bank's parent bank holding company and executive officers of any other subsidiary of that bank holding company from the definition of executive officer for the purposes of complying with the loan restrictions contained in section 22(g) of the Federal Reserve Act. For the purposes of complying with Sec. 215.5(d) of Federal Reserve Board Regulation O, the reference to "the amount specified for a category of credit in paragraph (c) of this section" shall be understood to refer to the amount specified in paragraph (c)(2) of this Sec. 337.3.

---

3. For the purposes of Sec. 337.3, an insured nonmember bank's capital and unimpaired surplus shall have the same meaning as found in Sec. 215.2(f) of Federal Reserve Board Regulation O (12 CFR 215.2(f)).

[47 FR 47003, Oct. 22, 1982, as amended at 48 FR 42971, Sept. 21, 1983; 57 FR 7649, Mar. 4, 1992; 57 FR 17850, Apr. 28, 1992; 57 FR 28457, June 25, 1992; 59 FR 66668, Dec. 28, 1994]

Sec. 337.6 Brokered deposits.

(a) Definitions. For the purposes of this Sec. 337.6, the following definitions apply:

(1) Appropriate Federal banking agency has the same meaning as provided under section 3(q) of the Federal Deposit Insurance Act (12 U.S.C. 1813(q)).

(2) Brokered deposit means any deposit that is obtained, directly or indirectly, from or through the mediation or assistance of a deposit broker.

(3) Capital categories.

(i) For purposes of section 29 of the Federal Deposit Insurance Act and this Sec. 337.6, the terms well capitalized, adequately capitalized, and undercapitalized,[4] shall have the same meaning as to each insured depository institution as provided under regulations implementing section 38 of the Federal Deposit Insurance Act issued by the appropriate federal banking agency for that institution.[5]

(ii) If the appropriate federal banking agency reclassifies a well capitalized insured depository institution as adequately capitalized pursuant to section 38 of the Federal Deposit Insurance Act, the institution so reclassified shall be subject to the provisions applicable to such lower capital category under this Sec. 337.6.

(iii) An insured depository institution shall be deemed to be within a given capital category for purposes of this Sec. 337.6 as of the date the institution is notified of, or is deemed to have notice of, its capital category, under regulations implementing section 38 of the Federal Deposit Insurance Act issued by the appropriate federal banking agency for that institution.[6]

(4) Deposit has the same meaning as provided under section 3(l) of the Federal Deposit Insurance Act (12 U.S.C. 1813(1)).

(5) Deposit broker.

(i) The term deposit broker means:

(A) Any person engaged in the business of placing deposits, or facilitating the placement of deposits, of third parties with insured depository institutions, or the business of placing deposits with insured depository institutions for the purpose of selling interests in those deposits to third parties; and

(B) An agent or trustee who establishes a deposit account to facilitate a business arrangement with an insured depository institution to use the proceeds of the account to fund a prearranged loan.

(ii) The term deposit broker does not include:

(A) An insured depository institution, with respect to funds placed with that depository institution;

(B) An employee of an insured depository institution, with respect to funds placed with the employing depository institution;

(C) A trust department of an insured depository institution, if the trust or other fiduciary relationship in question has not been established for the primary purpose of placing funds with insured depository institutions;

---

4. [n.11] The term undercapitalized includes any institution that is significantly undercapitalized or critically undercapitalized under regulations implementing section 38 of the Federal Deposit Insurance Act and issued by the appropriate federal banking agency for that institution.

5. [n.12] For the most part, the capital measure terms are defined in the following regulations: FDIC—12 CFR part 325, subpart B; Board of Governors of the Federal Reserve System—12 CFR part 208; Office of the Comptroller of the Currency—12 CFR part 6; Office of Thrift Supervision—12 CFR part 565.

6. [n.13] The regulations implementing section 38 of the Federal Deposit Insurance Act and issued by the federal banking agencies generally provide that an insured depository institution is deemed to have been notified of

its capital levels and its capital category as of the most recent date: (1) A Consolidated Report of Condition and Income or Thrift Financial Report is required to be filed with the appropriate federal banking agency; (2) A final report of examination is delivered to the institution; or (3) Written notice is provided by the appropriate federal banking agency to the institution of its capital category for purposes of section 38 of the Federal Deposit Insurance Act and implementing regulations or that the institution's capital category has changed. Provisions specifying the effective date of determination of capital category are generally published in the following regulations: FDIC—12 CFR 325.102. Board of Governors of the Federal Reserve System—12 CFR 208.32. Office of the Comptroller of the Currency—12 CFR 6.3. Office of Thrift Supervision—12 CFR 565.3.

(D) The trustee of a pension or other employee benefit plan, with respect to funds of the plan;

(E) A person acting as a plan administrator or an investment adviser in connection with a pension plan or other employee benefit plan provided that person is performing managerial functions with respect to the plan;

(F) The trustee of a testamentary account;

(G) The trustee of an irrevocable trust (other than one described in paragraph (a)(5)(i)(B) of this section), as long as the trust in question has not been established for the primary purpose of placing funds with insured depository institutions;

(H) A trustee or custodian of a pension or profit-sharing plan qualified under section 401(d) or 403(a) of the Internal Revenue Code of 1986 (26 U.S.C. 401(d) or 403(a));

(I) An agent or nominee whose primary purpose is not the placement of funds with depository institutions; or

(J) An insured depository institution acting as an intermediary or agent of a U.S. government department or agency for a government sponsored minority or women-owned depository institution deposit program.

(iii) Notwithstanding paragraph (a)(5)(ii) of this section, the term deposit broker includes any insured depository institution that is not well-capitalized, and any employee of any such insured depository institution, which engages, directly or indirectly, in the solicitation of deposits by offering rates of interest (with respect to such deposits) which are significantly higher than the prevailing rates of interest on deposits offered by other insured depository institutions in such depository institution's normal market area.

(6) Employee means any employee:

(i) Who is employed exclusively by the insured depository institution;

(ii) Whose compensation is primarily in the form of a salary;

(iii) Who does not share such employee's compensation with a deposit broker; and

(iv) Whose office space or place of business is used exclusively for the benefit of the insured depository institution which employs such individual.

(7) FDIC means the Federal Deposit Insurance Corporation.

(8) Insured depository institution means any bank, savings association, or branch of a foreign bank insured under the provisions of the Federal Deposit Insurance Act (12 U.S.C. 1811 et seq.).

(b) Solicitation and acceptance of brokered deposits by insured depository institutions.

(1) A well capitalized insured depository institution may solicit and accept, renew or roll over any brokered deposit without restriction by this section.

(2) (i) An adequately capitalized insured depository institution may not accept, renew or roll over any brokered deposit unless it has applied for and been granted a waiver of this prohibition by the FDIC in accordance with the provisions of this section.

(ii) Any adequately capitalized insured depository institution that has been granted a waiver to accept, renew or roll over a brokered deposit may not pay an effective yield on any such deposit which, at the time that such deposit is accepted, renewed or rolled over, exceeds by more than 75 basis points:

(A) The effective yield paid on deposits of comparable size and maturity in such institution's normal market area for deposits accepted from within its normal market area; or

(B) The national rate paid on deposits of comparable size and maturity for deposits accepted outside the institution's normal market area. For purposes of this paragraph (b)(2)(ii)(B), the national rate shall be:

(1) 120 percent of the current yield on similar maturity U.S. Treasury obligations; or

(2) In the case of any deposit at least half of which is uninsured, 130 percent of such applicable yield.

(3) (i) An undercapitalized insured depository institution may not accept, renew or roll over any brokered deposit.

(ii) An undercapitalized insured depository institution may not solicit deposits by offering an effective yield that exceeds by more than 75 basis points the prevailing effective yields on insured deposits of comparable maturity in such institution's normal market area or in the market area in which such deposits are being solicited.

(4) For purposes of the restriction contained in paragraphs (b)(2)(ii)(A) and (b)(3)(ii) of this section, the effective yields in the relevant markets are the average of effective yields offered by other insured depository institutions in the market area in which deposits are being solicited. An effective yield on a deposit with an odd maturity violates paragraphs (b)(2)(ii)(A) and (b)(3)(ii) of this section if it is more than 75 basis points higher than the yield calculated by interpolating between the yields offered by other insured depository institutions on deposits of the next longer and shorter maturities offered in the market. A market area is any readily defined geographical area in which the rates offered by any one insured depository institution soliciting deposits in that area may affect the rates offered by other insured depository institutions operating in the same area.

(c) Waiver. The FDIC may, on a case-by-case basis and upon application by an adequately capitalized insured depository institution, waive the prohibition on the acceptance, renewal or rollover of brokered deposits upon a finding that such acceptance, renewal or rollover does not constitute an unsafe or unsound practice with respect to such institution. The FDIC may conclude that it is not unsafe or unsound and may grant a waiver when the acceptance, renewal or rollover of brokered deposits is determined to pose no undue risk to the institution. Any waiver granted may be revoked at any time by written notice to the institution. For filing requirements, consult 12 CFR 303.243.

(d) Exclusion for institutions in FDIC conservatorship. No insured depository institution for which the FDIC has been appointed conservator shall be subject to the prohibition on the acceptance, renewal or rollover of brokered deposits contained in this Sec. 337.6 or section 29 of the Federal Deposit Insurance Act for 90 days after the date on which the institution was placed in conservatorship. During this 90-day period, the institution shall, nevertheless, be subject to the restriction on the payment of interest contained in paragraph (b)(2)(ii) of the section. After such 90-day period, the institution may not accept, renew or roll over any brokered deposit.

(e) [Reserved]

[57 FR 23941, June 5, 1992, as amended at 58 FR 54935, Oct. 25, 1993; 60 FR 31384, June 15, 1995; 63 FR 44750, Aug. 20, 1998; 66 FR 17622, Apr. 3, 2001]

PART 362. Activities Of Insured State Banks And Insured Savings Associations

Sec. 362.1 Purpose and scope.

(a) This subpart, along with the notice and application procedures in subpart G of part 303 of this chapter, implements the provisions of section 24 of the Federal Deposit Insurance Act (12 U.S.C. 1831a) that restrict and prohibit insured State banks and their subsidiaries from engaging in activities and investments that are not permissible for national banks and their subsidiaries. The phrase "activity permissible for a national bank" means any activity authorized for national banks under any statute including the National Bank Act (12 U.S.C. 21 et seq.), as well as activities recognized as permissible for a national bank in regulations, official circulars, bulletins, orders or written interpretations issued by the Office of the Comptroller of the Currency (OCC).

(b) This subpart does not cover the following activities:

(1) Activities conducted other than "as principal," defined for purposes of this subpart as activities conducted as agent for a customer, conducted in a brokerage, custodial, advisory, or administrative capacity, or conducted as trustee, or in any substantially similar capacity. For example, this subpart does not cover acting solely as agent for the sale of insurance, securities, real estate, or travel services; nor does it cover acting as trustee, providing personal financial planning advice, or safekeeping services;

(2) Interests in real estate in which the real property is used or intended in good faith to be used within a reasonable time by an insured State bank or its subsidiaries as offices or related facilities for the conduct of its business or future expansion of its business or used as public welfare investments of a type permissible for national banks; and

(3) Equity investments acquired in connection with debts previously contracted (DPC) if the insured State bank does not hold the property for speculation and takes only such actions as would be permissible for a national bank's DPC. The bank must dispose of the property within the shorter of the period set by Federal law for national banks or the period allowed under State law. For real estate, national banks may not hold DPC for more than 10 years. For equity securities, national banks must generally divest DPC as soon as possible consistent with obtaining a reasonable return.

(c) A subsidiary of an insured state bank may not engage in real estate investment activities that are not permissible for a subsidiary of a national bank unless the bank does so through a subsidiary of which the bank is a majority owner, is in compliance with applicable capital standards, and the FDIC has determined that the activity poses no significant risk to the appropriate deposit insurance fund. This subpart provides standards for majority-owned subsidiaries of insured state banks engaging in real estate investment activities that are not permissible for a subsidiary of a national bank.

(d) The FDIC intends to allow insured State banks and their subsidiaries to undertake only safe and sound activities and investments that do not present significant risks to the deposit insurance funds and that are consistent with the purposes of Federal deposit insurance and other applicable law. This subpart does not authorize any insured State bank to make investments or to conduct activities that are not authorized or that are prohibited by either State or Federal law.

[66 FR 1028, Jan. 5, 2001; 71 FR 20527, April 21, 2006]

Sec. 362.2 Definitions.

For the purposes of this subpart, the following definitions will apply:

(a) Bank, State bank, savings association, State savings association, depository institution, insured depository institution, insured State bank, Federal savings association, and insured State nonmember bank shall each have the same respective meaning contained in section 3 of the Federal Deposit Insurance Act (12 U.S.C. 1813).

(b) Activity means the conduct of business by a state-chartered depository institution, including acquiring or retaining an equity investment or other investment.

(c) Change in control means any transaction:

(1) By a State bank or its holding company for which a notice is required to be filed with the FDIC, or the Board of Governors of the Federal Reserve System (FRB), pursuant to section 7(j) of the Federal Deposit Insurance Act (12 U.S.C. 1817(j)) except a transaction that is presumed to be an acquisition of control under the FDIC's or FRB's regulations implementing section 7(j);

(2) As a result of which a State bank eligible for the exception described in Sec. 362.3(a)(2)(iii) is acquired by or merged into a depository institution that is not eligible for the exception, or as a result of which its holding company is acquired by or merged into a holding company which controls one or more bank subsidiaries not eligible for the exception; or

(3) In which control of the State bank is acquired by a bank holding company in a transaction requiring FRB approval under section 3 of the Bank Holding Company Act (12 U.S.C. 1842), other than a one bank holding company formation in which all or substantially all of the shares of the holding company will be owned by persons who were shareholders of the bank.

(d) Company means any corporation, partnership, limited liability company, business trust, association, joint venture, pool, syndicate or other similar business organization.

(e) Control means the power to vote, directly or indirectly, 25 percent or more of any class of the voting securities of a company, the ability to control in any manner the election of a majority of a company's directors or trustees, or the ability to exercise a controlling influence over the management and policies of a company.

(f) Convert its charter means an insured State bank undergoes any transaction that causes the bank to operate under a different form of charter than it had as of December 19, 1991, except a change from mutual to stock form shall not be considered a charter conversion.

(g) Equity investment means an ownership interest in any company; any membership interest that includes a voting right in any company; any interest in real estate; any transaction which in substance falls into any of these categories even though it may be structured as some other form of business transaction; and includes an equity security. The term "equity investment" does not include any of the foregoing if the interest is taken as security for a loan.

(h) Equity security means any stock (other than adjustable rate preferred stock, money market (auction rate) preferred stock, or other newly developed instrument determined by the FDIC to have the character of debt securities), certificate of interest or participation in any profit-sharing agreement, collateral-trust certificate, preorganization certificate or subscription, transferable share, investment contract, or voting-trust certificate; any security immediately convertible at the option of the holder without payment of substantial additional consideration into such a security; any security carrying any warrant or right to subscribe to or purchase any such security; and any certificate of interest or participation in, temporary or interim certificate for, or receipt for any of the foregoing.

(i) Extension of credit, executive officer, director, principal shareholder, and related interest each has the same respective meaning as is applicable for the purposes of section 22(h) of the Federal Reserve Act (12 U.S.C. 375b) and Sec. 337.3 of this chapter.

(j) Institution shall have the same meaning as "state-chartered depository institution."

(k) Majority-owned subsidiary means any corporation in which the parent insured State bank owns a majority of the outstanding voting stock.

(*l*) National securities exchange means a securities exchange that is registered as a national securities exchange by the Securities and Exchange Commission pursuant to section 6 of the Securities Exchange Act of 1934 (15 U.S.C. 78f) and the National Market System, i.e., the top tier of the National Association of Securities Dealers Automated Quotation System.

(m) Real estate investment activity means any interest in real estate (other than as security for a loan) held directly or indirectly that is not permissible for a national bank.

(n) Residents of the state includes individuals living in the State, individuals employed in the State, any person to whom the company provided insurance as principal without interruption since such person resided in or was employed in the State, and companies or partnerships incorporated in, organized under the laws of, licensed to do business in, or having an office in the State.

(*o*) Security has the same meaning as it has in part 344 of this chapter.

(p) Significant risk to the deposit insurance fund shall be understood to be present whenever the FDIC determines there is a high probability that any insurance fund administered by the FDIC may suffer a loss. Such risk may be present either when an activity contributes or may contribute to the decline in condition of a particular state-chartered depository institution or when a type of activity is found by the FDIC to contribute or potentially contribute to the deterioration of the overall condition of the banking system.

(q) State-chartered depository institution means any State bank or State savings association insured by the FDIC.

(r) Subsidiary means any company that is owned or controlled directly or indirectly by one or more insured depository institutions.

(s) Tier one capital has the same meaning as set forth in part 325 of this chapter for an insured State nonmember bank. For other state-chartered depository institutions, the term "tier one capital" has the same meaning as set forth in the capital regulations adopted by the appropriate Federal banking agency.

(t) Well-capitalized has the same meaning set forth in part 325 of this chapter for an insured State nonmember bank. For other state-chartered depository institutions, the term "well-capitalized" has the same meaning as set forth in the capital regulations adopted by the appropriate Federal banking agency.

[66 FR 1028, Jan. 5, 2001; 71 FR 20527, April 21, 2006]

Sec. 362.3 Activities of insured State banks.

(a) Equity investments.

(1) Prohibited equity investments. No insured State bank may directly or indirectly acquire or retain as principal any equity investment of a type that is not permissible for a national bank unless one of the exceptions in paragraph (a)(2) of this section applies.

(2) Exceptions.

(i) Equity investment in majority-owned subsidiaries. An insured State bank may acquire or retain an equity investment in a subsidiary of which the bank is a majority owner, provided that the subsidiary is engaging in activities that are allowed pursuant to the provisions of or by application under Sec. 362.4(b).

(ii) Investments in qualified housing projects. An insured State bank may invest as a limited partner in a partnership, or as a noncontrolling interest holder of a limited liability company, the sole purpose of which is to invest in the acquisition, rehabilitation, or new construction of a qualified housing project, provided that the bank's aggregate investment (including legally binding commitments) does not exceed, when made, 2 percent of total assets as of the date of the bank's most recent consolidated report of condition prior to making the investment. For the purposes of this paragraph (a)(2)(ii), Aggregate investment means the total book value of the bank's investment in the real estate calculated in accordance with the instructions for the preparation of the consolidated report of condition. Qualified housing project means residential real estate intended to primarily benefit lower income persons throughout the period of the bank's investment including any project that has received an award of low income housing tax credits under section 42 of the Internal Revenue Code (26 U.S.C. 42) (such as a reservation or allocation of credits) from a State or local housing credit agency. A residential real estate project that does not qualify for the tax credit under section 42 of the Internal Revenue Code will qualify under this exception if 50 percent or more of the housing units are to be occupied by lower income persons. A project will be considered residential despite the fact that some portion of the total square footage of the project is utilized for commercial purposes, provided that such commercial use is not the primary purpose of the project. Lower income has the same meaning as "low income" and "moderate income" as defined for the purposes of Sec. 345.12(n) (1) and (2) of this chapter.

(iii) Grandfathered investments in common or preferred stock; shares of investment companies.

(A) General. An insured State bank that is located in a State which as of September 30, 1991, authorized investment in:

(1)(i) Common or preferred stock listed on a national securities exchange (listed stock); or

(ii) Shares of an investment company registered under the Investment Company Act of 1940 (15 U.S.C. 80a–1 et seq.) (registered shares); and

(2) Which during the period beginning on September 30, 1990, and ending on November 26, 1991, made or maintained an investment in listed stock or registered shares, may retain whatever lawfully acquired listed stock or registered shares it held and may continue to acquire listed stock and/or registered shares, provided that the bank files a notice in accordance with section 24(f)(6) of the Federal Deposit Insurance Act in compliance with Sec. 303.121 of this chapter and the FDIC processes the notice without objection under Sec. 303.122 of this chapter. Approval will be granted only if the FDIC determines that acquiring or retaining the stock or shares does not pose a significant risk to the appropriate deposit insurance fund. Approval may be subject to whatever conditions or restrictions the FDIC determines are necessary or appropriate.

(B) Loss of grandfather exception. The exception for grandfathered investments under paragraph (a)(2)(iii)(A) of this section shall no longer apply if the bank converts its charter or the bank or its parent holding company undergoes a change in control. If any of these events occur, the bank may retain its existing investments unless directed by the FDIC or other applicable authority to divest the listed stock or registered shares.

(C) Maximum permissible investment. A bank's aggregate investment in listed stock and registered shares under paragraph (a)(2)(iii)(A) of this section shall in no event exceed, when made, 100 percent of the bank's tier one capital as measured on the bank's most recent consolidated report of condition (call report) prior to making any such investment. The lower of the bank's cost as determined in accordance with call report instructions or the market value of the listed stock and shares shall be used to determine compliance. The FDIC may determine when acting upon a notice filed in accordance with paragraph (a)(2)(iii)(A)(2) of this section that the permissible limit for any particular insured State bank is something less than 100 percent of tier one capital.

(iv) Stock investment in insured depository institutions owned exclusively by other banks and savings associations. An insured State bank may acquire or retain the stock of an insured depository institution if the insured depository institution engages only in activities permissible for national banks; the insured depository institution is subject to examination and regulation by a State bank supervisor; the voting stock is owned by 20 or more insured depository institutions, but no one institution owns more than 15 percent of the voting stock; and the insured depository institution's stock (other than directors' qualifying shares or shares held under or acquired through a plan established for the benefit of the officers and employees) is owned only by insured depository institutions.

(v) Stock investment in insurance companies—

(A) Stock of director and officer liability insurance company. An insured State bank may acquire and retain up to 10 percent of the outstanding stock of a corporation that solely provides or reinsures directors', trustees', and officers' liability insurance coverage or bankers' blanket bond group insurance coverage for insured depository institutions.

(B) Stock of savings bank life insurance company. An insured State bank located in Massachusetts, New York, or Connecticut may own stock in a savings bank life insurance company, provided that the savings bank life insurance company provides written disclosures to purchasers or potential purchasers of life insurance policies, other insurance products, and annuities that are consistent with the disclosures described in the Interagency Statement on the Retail Sale of Nondeposit Investment Products (FIL–9–

94,[7] February 17, 1994) or any successor requirement which indicates that the policies, products, and annuities are not FDIC insured deposits, are not guaranteed by the bank and are subject to investment risks, including possible loss of the principal amount invested.

(b) Activities other than equity investments—

(1) Prohibited activities. An insured State bank may not directly or indirectly engage as principal in any activity, that is not an equity investment, and is of a type not permissible for a national bank unless one of the exceptions in paragraph (b)(2) of this section applies.

(2) Exceptions—

(i) Consent obtained through application. An insured State bank that meets and continues to meet the applicable capital standards set by the appropriate Federal banking agency may conduct activities prohibited by paragraph (b)(1) of this section if the bank obtains the FDIC's prior written consent. Consent will be given only if the FDIC determines that the activity poses no significant risk to the affected deposit insurance fund. Applications for consent should be filed in accordance with Sec. 303.121 of this chapter and will be processed under Sec. 303.122(b) of this chapter. Approvals granted under Sec. 303.122(b) of this chapter may be made subject to any conditions or restrictions found by the FDIC to be necessary to protect the deposit insurance funds from risk, to prevent unsafe or unsound banking practices, and/or to ensure that the activity is consistent with the purposes of Federal deposit insurance and other applicable law.

(ii) Insurance underwriting—

(A) Savings bank life insurance. An insured State bank that is located in Massachusetts, New York or Connecticut may provide as principal savings bank life insurance through a department of the bank, provided that the department meets the core standards of paragraph (c) of this section or submits an application in compliance with Sec. 303.121 of this chapter and the FDIC

---

7. [n.1] Financial institution letters (FILs) are available in the FDIC Public Information Center, room 100, 801 17th Street, N.W., Washington, D.C. 20429.

grants its consent under the procedures in Sec. 303.122(b) of this chapter, and the department provides purchasers or potential purchasers of life insurance policies, other insurance products and annuities written disclosures that are consistent with the disclosures described in the Interagency Statement on the Retail Sale of Nondeposit Investment Products (FIL–9–94, February 17, 1994) and any successor requirement which indicates that the policies, products and annuities are not FDIC insured deposits, are not guaranteed by the bank, and are subject to investment risks, including the possible loss of the principal amount invested.

(B) Federal crop insurance. Any insured State bank that was providing insurance as principal on or before September 30, 1991, which was reinsured in whole or in part by the Federal Crop Insurance Corporation, may continue to do so.

(C) Grandfathered insurance underwriting. A well-capitalized insured State bank that on November 21, 1991, was lawfully providing insurance as principal through a department of the bank may continue to provide the same types of insurance as principal to the residents of the State or States in which the bank did so on such date provided that the bank's department meets the core standards of paragraph (c) of this section, or submits an application in compliance with Sec. 303.121 of this chapter and the FDIC grants its consent under the procedures in Sec. 303.122(b) of this chapter.

(iii) Acquiring and retaining adjustable rate and money market preferred stock.

(A) An insured State bank's investment of up to 15 percent of the bank's tier one capital in adjustable rate preferred stock or money market (auction rate) preferred stock does not represent a significant risk to the deposit insurance funds. An insured State bank may conduct this activity without first obtaining the FDIC's consent, provided that the bank meets and continues to meet the applicable capital standards as prescribed by the appropriate Federal banking agency. The fact that prior consent is not required by this subpart does not preclude the FDIC from taking any appropriate action with respect to

the activities if the facts and circumstances warrant such action.

(B) An insured State bank may acquire or retain other instruments of a type determined by the FDIC to have the character of debt securities and not to represent a significant risk to the deposit insurance funds. Such instruments shall be included in the 15 percent of tier one capital limit imposed in paragraph (b)(2)(iii)(A) of this section. An insured State bank may conduct this activity without first obtaining the FDIC's consent, provided that the bank meets and continues to meet the applicable capital standards as prescribed by the appropriate Federal banking agency. The fact that prior consent is not required by this subpart does not preclude the FDIC from taking any appropriate action with respect to the activities if the facts and circumstances warrant such action.

(c) Core standards. For any insured State bank to be eligible to conduct insurance activities listed in paragraph (b)(2)(ii)(A) or (C) of this section, the bank must conduct the activities in a department that meets the following core separation and operating standards:

(1) The department is physically distinct from the remainder of the bank;

(2) The department maintains separate accounting and other records;

(3) The department has assets, liabilities, obligations and expenses that are separate and distinct from those of the remainder of the bank;

(4) The department is subject to State statute that requires its obligations, liabilities and expenses be satisfied only with the assets of the department; and

(5) The department informs its customers that only the assets of the department may be used to satisfy the obligations of the department.

[71 FR 20527, April 21, 2006]

Sec. 362.4 Subsidiaries of insured State banks.

(a) Prohibition. A subsidiary of an insured State bank may not engage as principal in any activity that is not of a type permissible for a subsidiary of a national bank, unless it meets one of the exceptions in paragraph (b) of this section.

(b) Exceptions—

(1) Consent obtained through application. A subsidiary of an insured State bank may conduct otherwise prohibited activities if the bank obtains the FDIC's prior written consent and the insured State bank meets and continues to meet the applicable capital standards set by the appropriate Federal banking agency. Consent will be given only if the FDIC determines that the activity poses no significant risk to the affected deposit insurance fund. Applications for consent should be filed in accordance with Sec. 303.121 of this chapter and will be processed under Sec. 303.122(b) of this chapter. Approvals granted under Sec. 303.122(b) of this chapter may be made subject to any conditions or restrictions found by the FDIC to be necessary to protect the deposit insurance funds from risk, to prevent unsafe or unsound banking practices, and/or to ensure that the activity is consistent with the purposes of Federal deposit insurance and other applicable law.

(2) Grandfathered insurance underwriting subsidiaries. A subsidiary of an insured State bank may:

(i) Engage in grandfathered insurance underwriting if the insured State bank or its subsidiary on November 21, 1991, was lawfully providing insurance as principal. The subsidiary may continue to provide the same types of insurance as principal to the residents of the State or states in which the bank or subsidiary did so on such date provided that:

(A)(1) The bank meets the capital requirements of paragraph (e) of this section; and

(2) The subsidiary is an "eligible subsidiary" as described in paragraph (c)(2) of this section; or

(B) The bank submits an application in compliance with Sec. 303.121 of this chapter and the FDIC grants its consent under the procedures in Sec. 303.122(b) of this chapter.

(ii) Continue to provide as principal title insurance, provided the bank was required before June 1, 1991, to provide title insurance as a condition of the bank's initial chartering under State law and neither the bank nor its parent holding company undergoes a change in control.

(iii) May continue to provide as principal insurance which is reinsured in whole or in part by the Federal Crop Insurance Corporation if the subsidiary was engaged in the activity on or before September 30, 1991.

(3) Majority-owned subsidiaries' ownership of equity investments that represent a control interest in a company. The FDIC has determined that investment in the following by a majority-owned subsidiary of an insured State bank does not represent a significant risk to the deposit insurance funds:

(i) Equity investment in a company engaged in real estate or securities activities authorized in paragraph (b)(5) of this section if the bank complies with the following restrictions and files a notice in compliance with Sec. 303.121 of this chapter and the FDIC processes the notice without objection under Sec. 303.122(a) of this chapter. The FDIC is not precluded from taking any appropriate action or imposing additional requirements with respect to the activity if the facts and circumstances warrant such action. If changes to the management or business plan of the company at any time result in material changes to the nature of the company's business or the manner in which its business is conducted, the insured State bank shall advise the appropriate regional director (DSC) in writing within 10 business days after such change. Investment under this paragraph is authorized if:

(A) The majority-owned subsidiary controls the company;

(B) The bank meets the core eligibility criteria of paragraph (c)(1) of this section;

(C) The majority-owned subsidiary meets the core eligibility criteria of paragraph (c)(2) of this section (including any modifications thereof applicable under paragraph (b)(5)(i) of this section), or the company is a corporation meeting such criteria;

(D) The bank's transactions with the majority-owned subsidiary, and the bank's transactions with the company, comply with the investment and transaction limits of paragraph (d) of this section;

(E) The bank complies with the capital requirements of paragraph (e) of this section with respect to the majority-owned subsidiary and the company; and

(F) To the extent the company is engaged in securities activities authorized by paragraph (b)(5)(ii) of this section, the bank and the company comply with the additional requirements therein as if the company were a majority-owned subsidiary.

(ii) Equity securities of a company engaged in the following activities, if the majority-owned subsidiary controls the company or the company is controlled by insured depository institutions, and the bank meets and continues to meet the applicable capital standards as prescribed by the appropriate Federal banking agency. The FDIC consents that a majority-owned subsidiary may conduct such activity without first obtaining the FDIC's consent. The fact that prior consent is not required by this subpart does not preclude the FDIC from taking any appropriate action with respect to the activity if the facts and circumstances warrant such action:

(A) Any activity that is permissible for a national bank, including such permissible activities that may require the company to register as a securities broker;

(B) Acting as an insurance agency;

(C) Engaging in any activity permissible for an insured State bank under Sec. 362.3(b)(2)(iii) to the same extent permissible for the insured bank thereunder, so long as instruments held under this paragraph (b)(3)(ii)(C), paragraph (b)(7) of this section, and Sec. 362.3(b)(2)(iii) in the aggregate do not exceed the limit set by Sec. 362.3(b)(2)(iii);

(D) Engaging in any activity permissible for a majority-owned subsidiary of an insured State bank under paragraph (b)(6) of this section to the same extent and manner permissible for the majority-owned subsidiary thereunder; and

(4) Majority-owned subsidiary's ownership of certain securities that do not represent a control interest–

(i) Grandfathered investments in common or preferred stock and shares of investment companies. Any insured State bank that has received approval to invest in common or preferred stock or shares of an investment

company pursuant to Sec. 362.3(a)(2)(iii) may conduct the approved investment activities through a majority-owned subsidiary of the bank without any additional approval from the FDIC provided that any conditions or restrictions imposed with regard to the approval granted under Sec. 362.3(a)(2)(iii) are met.

(ii) Bank stock. An insured State bank may indirectly through a majority-owned subsidiary organized for such purpose invest in up to ten percent of the outstanding stock of another insured bank.

(5) Majority-owned subsidiaries conducting real estate investment activities and securities underwriting. The FDIC has determined that the following activities do not represent a significant risk to the deposit insurance funds, provided that the activities are conducted by a majority-owned subsidiary of an insured State bank in compliance with the core eligibility requirements listed in paragraph (c) of this section; any additional requirements listed in paragraph (b)(5) (i) or (ii) of this section; the bank complies with the investment and transaction limitations of paragraph (d) of this section; and the bank meets the capital requirements of paragraph (e) of this section. The FDIC consents that these listed activities may be conducted by a majority-owned subsidiary of an insured State bank if the bank files a notice in compliance with Sec. 303.121 of this chapter and the FDIC processes the notice without objection under Sec. 303.122(a) of this chapter. The FDIC is not precluded from taking any appropriate action or imposing additional requirements with respect to the activities if the facts and circumstances warrant such action. If changes to the management or business plan of the majority-owned subsidiary at any time result in material changes to the nature of the majority-owned subsidiary's business or the manner in which its business is conducted, the insured State bank shall advise the appropriate regional director (DSC) in writing within 10 business days after such change. Such a majority-owned subsidiary may:

(i) Real estate investment activities. Engage in real estate investment activities. However, the requirements of paragraph (c)(2) (ii), (v), (vi), and (xi) of this section need not be met if the bank's investment in the equity securities of the subsidiary does not exceed 2 percent of the bank's tier one capital; the bank has only one subsidiary engaging in real estate investment activities; and the bank's total investment in the subsidiary does not include any extensions of credit from the bank to the subsidiary, any debt instruments issued by the subsidiary, or any other transaction originated by the bank that is used to benefit the subsidiary.

(ii) *Securities activities.* Engage in the public sale, distribution or underwriting of securities that are not permissible for a national bank under section 16 of the Banking Act of 1933 (12 U.S.C. 24 Seventh), provided that the insured state nonmember bank lawfully controlled or acquired the subsidiary and had an approved notice or order from the FDIC prior to November 12, 1999 and provided that the following additional conditions are, and continue to be, met:

(A) The state-chartered depository institution adopts policies and procedures, including appropriate limits on exposure, to govern the institution's participation in financing transactions underwritten or arranged by an underwriting majority-owned subsidiary;

(B) The state-chartered depository institution may not express an opinion on the value or the advisability of the purchase or sale of securities underwritten or dealt in by a majority-owned subsidiary unless the state-chartered depository institution notifies the customer that the majority-owned subsidiary is underwriting or distributing the security;

(C) The majority-owned subsidiary is registered with the Securities and Exchange Commission, is a member in good standing with the appropriate self-regulatory organization, and promptly informs the appropriate regional director (DSC) in writing of any material actions taken against the majority-owned subsidiary or any of its employees by the State, the appropriate self-regulatory organizations or the Securities and Exchange Commission; and

(D) The state-chartered depository institution does not knowingly purchase as principal or fiduciary during the existence of any underwriting or selling syndicate any securities underwritten by the majority-owned subsidiary unless the purchase is approved by the state-chartered depository institution's board of directors before the securities are initially offered for sale to the public.

(6) *Real estate leasing.* A majority-owned subsidiary of an insured State bank acting as lessor under a real property lease which is the equivalent of a financing transaction, meeting the lease criteria of paragraph (b)(6)(i) of this section and the underlying real estate requirements of paragraph (b)(6)(ii) of this section, does not represent a significant risk to the deposit insurance funds. A majority-owned subsidiary may conduct this activity without first obtaining the FDIC's consent, provided that the bank meets and continues to meet the applicable capital standards as prescribed by the appropriate Federal banking agency. The fact that prior consent is not required by this subpart does not preclude the FDIC from taking any appropriate action with respect to the activity if the facts and circumstances warrant such action.

(i) *Lease criteria*—

(A) *Capital lease.* The lease must qualify as a capital lease as to the lessor under generally accepted accounting principles.

(B) *Nonoperating basis.* The bank and the majority-owned subsidiary shall not, directly or indirectly, provide or be obligated to provide servicing, repair, or maintenance to the property, except that the lease may include provisions permitting the subsidiary to protect the value of the leased property in the event of a change in circumstances that increases the subsidiary's exposure to loss, or the subsidiary may take reasonable and appropriate action to salvage or protect the value of the leased property in such circumstances.

(ii) *Underlying real property requirements*—

(A) *Acquisition.* The majority-owned subsidiary may acquire specific real estate to be leased only after the subsidiary has entered into:

(1) A lease meeting the requirements of paragraph (b)(6)(i) of this section;

(2) A legally binding written commitment to enter into such a lease; or

(3) A legally binding written agreement that indemnifies the subsidiary against loss in

connection with its acquisition of the property.

(B) *Improvements.* Any expenditures by the majority-owned subsidiary to make reasonable repairs, renovations, and improvements necessary to render the property suitable to the lessee shall not exceed 25 percent of the majority-owned subsidiary's full investment in the real estate.

(C) *Divestiture.* At the expiration of the initial lease (including any renewals or extensions thereof), the majority-owned subsidiary shall, as soon as practicable but in any event no less than two years, either:

(1) Re-lease the property under a lease meeting the requirement of paragraph (b)(6)(i)(B) of this section; or

(2) Divest itself of all interest in the property.

(7) *Acquiring and retaining adjustable rate and money market preferred stock and similar instruments.* The FDIC has determined it does not present a significant risk to the deposit insurance funds for a majority-owned subsidiary of an insured State bank to engage in any activity permissible for an insured State bank under Sec. 362.3(b)(2)(iii), so long as instruments held under this paragraph, paragraph (b)(3)(ii)(C) of this section, and Sec. 362.3(b)(2)(iii) in the aggregate do not exceed the limit set by Sec. 362.3(b)(2)(iii). A majority-owned subsidiary may conduct this activity without first obtaining the FDIC's consent, provided that the bank meets and continues to meet the applicable capital standards as prescribed by the appropriate Federal banking agency. The fact that prior consent is not required by this subpart does not preclude the FDIC from taking any appropriate action with respect to the activity if the facts and circumstances warrant such action.

(c) *Core eligibility requirements.* If specifically required by this part or by FDIC order, any state-chartered depository institution that wishes to be eligible and continue to be eligible to conduct as principal activities through a subsidiary that are not permissible for a subsidiary of a national bank must be an "eligible depository institution" and the subsidiary must be an "eligible subsidiary".

(1) A state-chartered depository institution is an "eligible depository institution" if it:

(i) Has been chartered and operating for three or more years, unless the appropriate regional director (DSC) finds that the state-chartered depository institution is owned by an established, well-capitalized, well-managed holding company or is managed by seasoned management;

(ii) Has an FDIC-assigned composite rating of 1 or 2 assigned under the Uniform Financial Institutions Rating System (UFIRS) (or such other comparable rating system as may be adopted in the future) as a result of its most recent Federal or State examination for which the FDIC assigned a rating;

(iii) Received a rating of 1 or 2 under the "management" component of the UFIRS as assigned by the institution's appropriate Federal banking agency;

(iv) Has a satisfactory or better Community Reinvestment Act rating at its most recent examination conducted by the institution's appropriate Federal banking agency;

(v) Has a compliance rating of 1 or 2 at its most recent examination conducted by the institution's appropriate Federal banking agency; and

(vi) Is not subject to a cease and desist order, consent order, prompt corrective action directive, formal or informal written agreement, or other administrative agreement with its appropriate Federal banking agency or chartering authority.

(2) A subsidiary of a state-chartered depository institution is an "eligible subsidiary" if it:

(i) Meets applicable statutory or regulatory capital requirements and has sufficient operating capital in light of the normal obligations that are reasonably foreseeable for a business of its size and character within the industry;

(ii) Is physically separate and distinct in its operations from the operations of the state-chartered depository institution, provided that this requirement shall not be construed to prohibit the state-chartered depository institution and its subsidiary from sharing the same facility if the area where the subsidiary conducts business with the public is clearly distinct from the area where customers of the state-chartered depository institution conduct business with the institution. The extent of the separation will vary according to the type and frequency of customer contact;

(iii) Maintains separate accounting and other business records;

(iv) Observes separate business entity formalities such as separate board of directors' meetings;

(v) Has a chief executive officer of the subsidiary who is not an employee of the institution;

(vi) Has a majority of its board of directors who are neither directors nor executive officers of the state-chartered depository institution;

(vii) Conducts business pursuant to independent policies and procedures designed to inform customers and prospective customers of the subsidiary that the subsidiary is a separate organization from the state-chartered depository institution and that the state-chartered depository institution is not responsible for and does not guarantee the obligations of the subsidiary;

(viii) Has only one business purpose within the types described in paragraphs (b)(2) and (b)(5) of this section;

(ix) Has a current written business plan that is appropriate to the type and scope of business conducted by the subsidiary;

(x) Has qualified management and employees for the type of activity contemplated, including all required licenses and memberships, and complies with industry standards; and

(xi) Establishes policies and procedures to ensure adequate computer, audit and accounting systems, internal risk management controls, and has necessary operational and managerial infrastructure to implement the business plan.

(d) Investment and transaction limits–

(1) General. If specifically required by this part or FDIC order, the following conditions and restrictions apply to an insured State bank and its subsidiaries that engage in and wish to continue to engage in activities which are not permissible for a national bank subsidiary.

(2) Investment limits–

(i) Aggregate investment in subsidiaries. An insured state bank's aggregate investment in all subsidiaries conducting activities subject to this paragraph (d) shall not exceed 20 percent of the insured State bank's tier one capital.

(ii) Definition of investment.

(A) For purposes of this paragraph (d), the term "investment" means:

(1) Any extension of credit to the subsidiary by the insured State bank;

(2) Any debt securities, as such term is defined in part 344 of this chapter, issued by the subsidiary held by the insured State bank;

(3) The acceptance by the insured State bank of securities issued by the subsidiary as collateral for an extension of credit to any person or company; and

(4) Any extensions of credit by the insured State bank to any third party for the purpose of making a direct investment in the subsidiary, making any investment in which the subsidiary has an interest, or which is used for the benefit of, or transferred to, the subsidiary.

(B) For the purposes of this paragraph (d), the term "investment" does not include:

(1) Extensions of credit by the insured State bank to finance sales of assets by the subsidiary which do not involve more than the normal degree of risk of repayment and are extended on terms that are substantially similar to those prevailing at the time for comparable transactions with or involving unaffiliated persons or companies;

(2) An extension of credit by the insured State bank to the subsidiary that is fully collateralized by government securities, as such term is defined in Sec. 344.3 of this chapter; or

(3) An extension of credit by the insured State bank to the subsidiary that is fully collateralized by a segregated deposit in the insured State bank.

(3) Transaction requirements—

(i) Arm's length transaction requirement. With the exception of giving the subsidiary immediate credit for uncollected items received in the ordinary course of business, an insured State bank may not carry out any of the following transactions with a subsidiary subject to this paragraph (d) unless the transaction is on terms and conditions that are substantially the same as those prevailing at the time for comparable transactions with unaffiliated parties:

(A) Make an investment in the subsidiary;

(B) Purchase from or sell to the subsidiary any assets (including securities);

(C) Enter into a contract, lease, or other type of agreement with the subsidiary;

(D) Pay compensation to a majority-owned subsidiary or any person or company who has an interest in the subsidiary; or

(E) Engage in any such transaction in which the proceeds thereof are used for the benefit of, or are transferred to, the subsidiary.

(ii) Prohibition on purchase of low quality assets. An insured State bank is prohibited from purchasing a low quality asset from a subsidiary subject to this paragraph (d). For purposes of this subsection, "low quality asset" means:

(A) An asset classified as "substandard", "doubtful", or "loss" or treated as "other assets especially mentioned" in the most recent report of examination of the bank;

(B) An asset in a nonaccrual status;

(C) An asset on which principal or interest payments are more than 30 days past due; or

(D) An asset whose terms have been renegotiated or compromised due to the deteriorating financial condition of the obligor.

(iii) Insider transaction restriction. Neither the insured State bank nor the subsidiary subject to this paragraph (d) may enter into any transaction (exclusive of those covered by Sec. 337.3 of this chapter) with the bank's executive officers, directors, principal shareholders or related interests of such persons which relate to the subsidiary's activities unless:

(A) The transactions are on terms and conditions that are substantially the same as those prevailing at the time for comparable transactions with persons not affiliated with the insured State bank; or

(B) The transactions are pursuant to a benefit or compensation program that is widely available to employees of the bank, and that does not give preference to the bank's executive officers, directors, principal shareholders or related interests of such persons over other bank employees.

(iv) Anti-tying restriction. Neither the insured State bank nor the majority-owned subsidiary may require a customer to either buy any product or use any service from the other as a condition of entering into a transaction.

(4) Collateralization requirements.

(i) An insured State bank is prohibited from making an investment in a subsidiary subject to this paragraph (d) unless such transaction is fully-collateralized at the time the transaction is entered into. No insured State bank may accept a low quality asset as collateral. An extension of credit is fully collateralized if it is secured at the time of the transaction by collateral having a market value equal to at least:

(A) 100 percent of the amount of the transaction if the collateral is composed of:

(1) Obligations of the United States or its agencies;

(2) Obligations fully guaranteed by the United States or its agencies as to principal and interest;

(3) Notes, drafts, bills of exchange or bankers acceptances that are eligible for rediscount or purchase by the Federal Reserve Bank; or

(4) A segregated, earmarked deposit account with the insured State bank;

(B) 110 percent of the amount of the transaction if the collateral is composed of obligations of any State or political subdivision of any State;

(C) 120 percent of the amount of the transaction if the collateral is composed of other debt instruments, including receivables; or

(D) 130 percent of the amount of the transaction if the collateral is composed of stock, leases, or other real or personal property.

(ii) An insured State bank may not release collateral prior to proportional payment of the extension of credit; however, collateral may be substituted if there is no diminution of collateral coverage.

(5) Investment and transaction limits extended to insured State bank subsidiaries. For purposes of applying paragraphs (d)(2) through (d)(4) of this section, any reference to "insured State bank" means the insured State bank and any subsidiaries of the insured State bank which are not themselves subject under this part or FDIC order to the restrictions of this paragraph (d).

(e) Capital requirements. If specifically required by this part or by FDIC order, any insured State bank that wishes to conduct or continue to conduct as principal activities through a subsidiary that are not permissible for a subsidiary of a national bank must:

(1) Be well-capitalized after deducting from its tier one capital the investment in equity securities of the subsidiary as well as the bank's pro rata share of any retained earnings of the subsidiary;

(2) Reflect this deduction on the appropriate schedule of the bank's consolidated report of income and condition; and

(3) Use such regulatory capital amount for the purposes of the bank's assessment risk classification under part 327 of this chapter and its categorization as a "well-capitalized", an "adequately capitalized", an "undercapitalized", or a "significantly undercapitalized" institution as defined in Sec. 325.103(b) of this chapter, provided that the capital deduction shall not be used for purposes of determining whether the bank is "critically undercapitalized" under part 325 of this chapter.

[66 FR 1028, Jan. 5, 2001; 71 FR 20527, April 21, 2006]

Sec. 362.5 Approvals previously granted.

(a) FDIC consent by order or notice. An insured State bank that previously filed an application or notice under part 362 in effect prior to January 1, 1999 (see 12 CFR part 362 revised as of January 1, 1998), and obtained the FDIC's consent to engage in an activity or to acquire or retain a majority-owned subsidiary engaging as principal in an activity or acquiring and retaining any investment that is prohibited under this subpart may continue that activity or retain that

investment without seeking the FDIC's consent, provided that the insured State bank and its subsidiary, if applicable, continue to meet the conditions and restrictions of the approval. An insured State bank which was granted approval based on conditions which differ from the requirements of Sec. 362.4(c)(2), (d) and (e) will be considered to meet the conditions and restrictions of the approval relating to being an eligible subsidiary, meeting investment and transactions limits, and meeting capital requirements if the insured State bank and subsidiary meet the requirements of Sec. 362.4(c)(2), (d) and (e). If the majority-owned subsidiary is engaged in real estate investment activities not exceeding 2 percent of the tier one capital of a bank and meeting the other conditions of Sec. 362.4(b)(5)(i), the majority-owned subsidiary's compliance with Sec. 362.4(c)(2) under the preceding sentence may be pursuant to the modifications authorized by Sec. 362.4(b)(5)(i). Once an insured State bank elects to comply with Sec. 362.4 (c)(2), (d), and (e), it may not revert to the corresponding provisions of the approval order.

(b) Approvals by regulation—

(1)-(5) [Reserved]

(6) Adjustable rate or money market preferred stock. An insured State bank owning adjustable rate or money market (auction rate) preferred stock pursuant to Sec. 362.4(c)(3)(v) in effect prior to January 1, 1999 (see 12 CFR part 362 revised as of January 1, 1998), in excess of the amount limit in Sec. 362.3(b)(2)(iii) may continue to hold any overlimit shares of such stock acquired before January 1, 1999, until redeemed or repurchased by the issuer, but such stock shall be included as part of the amount limit in Sec. 362.3(b)(2)(iii) when determining whether the bank may acquire new stock thereunder.

(c) Charter conversions.

(1) An insured State bank that has converted its charter from an insured state savings association may continue activities through a majority-owned subsidiary that were permissible prior to the time it converted its charter only if the insured State bank receives the FDIC's consent. Except as provided in paragraph (c)(2) of this section, the insured State bank should apply under Sec. 362.4(b)(1), submit any notice required under Sec. 362.4(b) (4) or (5), or com-

ply with the provisions of Sec. 362.4(b) (3), (6), or (7) if applicable, to continue the activity.

(2) *Exception for prior consent.* If the FDIC had granted consent to the savings association under section 28 of the Federal Deposit Insurance Act (12 U.S.C. 1831(e)) prior to the time the savings association converted its charter, the insured State bank may continue the activities without providing notice or making application to the FDIC, provided that the bank and its subsidiary as applicable are in compliance with:

(i) The terms of the FDIC approval order; and

(ii) The provisions of Sec. 362.4(c)(2), (d), and (e) regarding operating as an "eligible subsidiary", "investment and transaction limits", and "capital requirements".

(3) *Divestiture.* An insured State bank that does not receive FDIC consent shall divest of the nonconforming investment as soon as practical but in no event later than two years from the date of charter conversion.

[63 FR 66326, Dec. 1, 1998, as amended at 66 FR 1028, Jan. 5, 2001]

Sec. 362.16 Purpose and scope.

[Source: 66 FR 1029, Jan. 5, 2001, unless otherwise noted.]

(a) This subpart, along with the notice and application procedures in subpart G of part 303 of this chapter, implements section 46 of the Federal Deposit Insurance Act (12 U.S.C. 1831w) and requires that an insured state nonmember bank certify certain facts and file a notice with the FDIC before the insured state nonmember bank may control or hold an interest in a financial subsidiary under section 46(a) of the Federal Deposit Insurance Act. This subpart also implements the statutory Community Reinvestment Act (CRA) (12 U.S.C. 2901 et seq.) requirement set forth in subsection (4)(*l*)(2) of the Bank Holding Company Act (12 U.S.C. 1843(*l*)(2)), which is applicable to state nonmember banks that commence new activities through a financial subsidiary or directly or indirectly acquire control of a company engaged in an activity under section 46(a).

(b) This subpart does not cover activities conducted other than "as principal". For purposes of this subpart, activities conducted other than "as principal" are defined as activities conducted as agent for a customer, conducted in a brokerage, custodial, advisory, or administrative capacity, or conducted as trustee, or in any substantially similar capacity. For example, this subpart does not cover acting solely as agent for the sale of insurance, securities, real estate, or travel services; nor does it cover acting as trustee, providing personal financial planning advice, or safekeeping services.

Sec. 362.17 Definitions.

For the purposes of this subpart, the following definitions will apply:

(a) *Activity, company, control, insured depository institution, insured state bank, insured state nonmember bank* and *subsidiary* have the same meaning as provided in subpart A of this part.

(b) *Affiliate* has the same meaning provided in subpart B of this part.

(c) *Financial subsidiary* means any company that is controlled by one or more insured depository institutions other than:

(1) A subsidiary that only engages in activities that the state nonmember bank is permitted to engage in directly and that are conducted on the same terms and conditions that govern the conduct of the activities by the state nonmember bank; or

(2) A subsidiary that the state nonmember bank is specifically authorized to control by the express terms of a federal statute (other than section 46(a) of the Federal Deposit Insurance Act (12 U.S.C. 1831w)), and not by implication or interpretation, such as the Bank Service Company Act (12 U.S.C. 1861 et seq.).

(d) *Tangible equity* and *Tier 2 capital* have the same meaning as set forth in part 325 of this chapter.

(e) *Well-managed* means:

(1) Unless otherwise determined in writing by the appropriate federal banking agency, the institution has received a composite rating of 1 or 2 under the Uniform Financial Institutions Rating System (or an equivalent rating under an equivalent rating system) in connection with the most recent state or federal examination or subsequent review of the depository institution and at least a rating of 2 for management, if such a rating is given; or

(2) In the case of any depository institution that has not been examined by its appropriate federal banking agency, the existence and use of managerial resources that the appropriate federal banking agency determines are satisfactory.

Sec. 362.18 Financial subsidiaries of insured state nonmember banks.

(a) "As principal" activities. An insured state nonmember bank may not obtain control of or hold an interest in a financial subsidiary that engages in activities as principal or commence any such new activity pursuant to section 46(a) of the Federal Deposit Insurance Act (12 U.S.C. 1831w) unless the insured state nonmember bank files a notice containing the information required in Sec. 303.121(b) of this chapter and certifies that:

(1) The insured state nonmember bank is well-managed;

(2) The insured state nonmember bank and all of its insured depository institution affiliates are well-capitalized as defined in the appropriate capital regulation and guidance of each institution's primary federal regulator; and

(3) The insured state nonmember bank will deduct the aggregate amount of its outstanding equity investment, including retained earnings, in all financial subsidiaries that engage in activities as principal pursuant to section 46(a) of the Federal Deposit Insurance Act (12 U.S.C. 1831w), from the bank's total assets and tangible equity and deduct such investment from its total risk-based capital (this deduction shall be made equally from Tier 1 and Tier 2 capital).

(b) Community Reinvestment Act (CRA). An insured state nonmember bank may not commence any new activity subject to section 46(a) of the Federal Deposit Insurance Act (12 U.S.C. 1831w) or directly or indirectly acquire control of a company engaged in any such activity pursuant to Sec. 362.18(a)(1), if the bank or any of its insured depository institution affiliates received a CRA rating of less than "satisfactory record of meeting community credit needs" in its most recent CRA examination.

(c) Other requirements. An insured state nonmember bank controlling or holding an interest in a financial subsidiary under section 46(a) of the Federal Deposit Insurance Act (12 U.S.C. 1831w) must meet and continue to meet the requirements set forth in paragraph (a) of this section as long as the insured state nonmember bank holds the financial subsidiary and:

(1) Disclose and continue to disclose the capital separation required in paragraph (a)(3) in any published financial statements;

(2) Comply and continue to comply with sections 23A and 23B of the Federal Reserve Act (12 U.S.C. 371c and 371c–1) as if the subsidiary were a financial subsidiary of a national bank; and

(3) Comply and continue to comply with the financial and operational standards provided by section 5136A(d) of the Revised Statutes of the United States (12 U.S.C. 24A(d)), unless otherwise determined by the FDIC.

(d) Securities underwriting. If the financial subsidiary of the insured state nonmember bank will engage in the public sale, distribution or underwriting of stocks, bonds, debentures, notes, or other securities activity of a type permissible for a national bank only through a financial subsidiary, then the state nonmember bank and the financial subsidiary also must comply and continue to comply with the following additional requirements:

(1) The securities business of the financial subsidiary must be physically separate and distinct in its operations from the operations of the bank, provided that this requirement shall not be construed to prohibit the bank and its financial subsidiary from sharing the same facility if the area where the financial subsidiary conducts securities business with the public is physically distinct from the routine deposit taking area of the bank;

(2) The financial subsidiary must conduct its securities business pursuant to independent policies and procedures designed to inform customers and prospective customers of the financial subsidiary that the financial subsidiary is a separate organization from the insured state nonmember bank and that the insured state nonmember bank is not responsible for and does not guarantee the obligations of the financial subsidiary;

(3) The bank must adopt policies and procedures, including appropriate limits on exposure, to govern its participation in financing transactions underwritten by its financial subsidiary; and

(4) The bank must not express an opinion on the value or the advisability of the purchase or sale of securities underwritten or dealt in by its financial subsidiary unless the bank notifies the customer that the entity underwriting, making a market, distributing or dealing in the securities is a financial subsidiary of the bank.

(e) *Applications for exceptions to certain requirements.* Any insured state nonmember bank that is unable to comply with the well-managed requirement of Sec. 362.18(a)(1) and (c)(1), any state nonmember bank that has appropriate reasons for not meeting the financial and operational standards applicable to a financial subsidiary of a national bank conducting the same activities as provided in Sec. 362.18(c)(3) or any state nonmember bank and its financial subsidiary subject to the securities underwriting activities requirements in Sec. 362.18(d) that is unable to meet such requirements may submit an application in compliance with Sec. 303.121 of this chapter to seek a waiver or modification of such requirements under the procedure in Sec. 303.122(b) of this chapter. The FDIC may impose additional prudential safeguards as are necessary as a condition of its consent.

(f) *Failure to meet requirements.*

(1) *Notification by FDIC.* The FDIC will notify the insured state nonmember bank in writing and identify the areas of noncompliance, if:

(i) The FDIC finds that an insured state nonmember bank or any of its insured depository institution affiliates is not in compliance with the CRA requirement of Sec. 362.18(b) at the time any new activity is commenced or control of the financial subsidiary is acquired;

(ii) The FDIC finds that the facts to which an insured state nonmember bank certified under Sec. 362.18(a) are not accurate in whole or in part; or

(iii) The FDIC finds that the insured state nonmember bank or any of its insured depository institution affiliates or the financial subsidiary fails to meet or continue to comply with the requirements of Sec. 362.18(c) and (d), if applicable, and the FDIC has not granted an exception under the procedures set forth in Sec. 362.18(e) and in Sec. 303.122(b) of this chapter.

(2) *Notification by state nonmember bank.* An insured state nonmember bank that controls or holds an interest in a financial subsidiary must promptly notify the FDIC if the bank becomes aware that any depository institution affiliate of the bank has ceased to be well-capitalized.

(3) *Subsequent action by FDIC.* The FDIC may take any appropriate action or impose any limitations, including requiring that the insured state nonmember bank to divest control of any such financial subsidiary, on the conduct or activities of the insured state nonmember bank or any financial subsidiary of the insured state bank that fails to:

(i) Meet the requirements listed in Sec. 362.18(a) and (b) at the time that any new section 46 activity is commenced or control of a financial subsidiary is acquired by an insured state nonmember bank; or

(ii) Meet and continue to meet the requirements listed in Sec. 362.18(c) and (d), as applicable.

(g) *Coordination with section 24 of the Federal Deposit Insurance Act.*

(1) *Continuing authority under section 24.* Notwithstanding Sec. 362.18(a) through (f), an insured state bank may retain its interest in any subsidiary:

(i) That was conducting a financial activity with authorization in accordance with section 24 of the Federal Deposit Insurance Act (12 U.S.C. 1831a) and the applicable implementing regulation found in subpart A of this part 362 before the date on which any such activity became for the first time permissible for a financial subsidiary of a national bank; and

(ii) Which insured state nonmember bank and its subsidiary continue to meet the conditions and restrictions of the section 24 order or regulation approving the activity as well as other applicable law.

(2) *Continuing authority under section 24(f) of the Federal Deposit Insurance Act.* Notwithstanding Sec. 362.18(a) through (f), an insured state bank with authority under section 24(f) of the Federal Deposit Insurance Act (12 U.S.C. 1831a(f)) to hold equity securities may continue to establish new subsidiaries to engage in that investment activity.

(3) Relief from conditions. Any state nonmember bank that meets the requirements of paragraph (g)(1) of this section or that is subject to section 46(b) of the Federal Deposit Insurance Act (12 U.S.C. 1831w(b)) may submit an application in compliance with Sec. 303.121 of this chapter and seek the consent of the FDIC under the procedure in Sec. 303.122(b) of this chapter for modification of any conditions or restrictions the FDIC previously imposed in connection with a section 24 order or regulation approving the activity.

(4) New financial subsidiaries. Notwithstanding subpart A of this part 362, an insured state bank may not, on or after November 12, 1999, acquire control of, or acquire an interest in, a financial subsidiary that engages in activities as principal or commences any new activity under section 46(a) of the Federal Deposit Insurance Act (12 U.S.C. 1831w) other than as provided in this section.

†